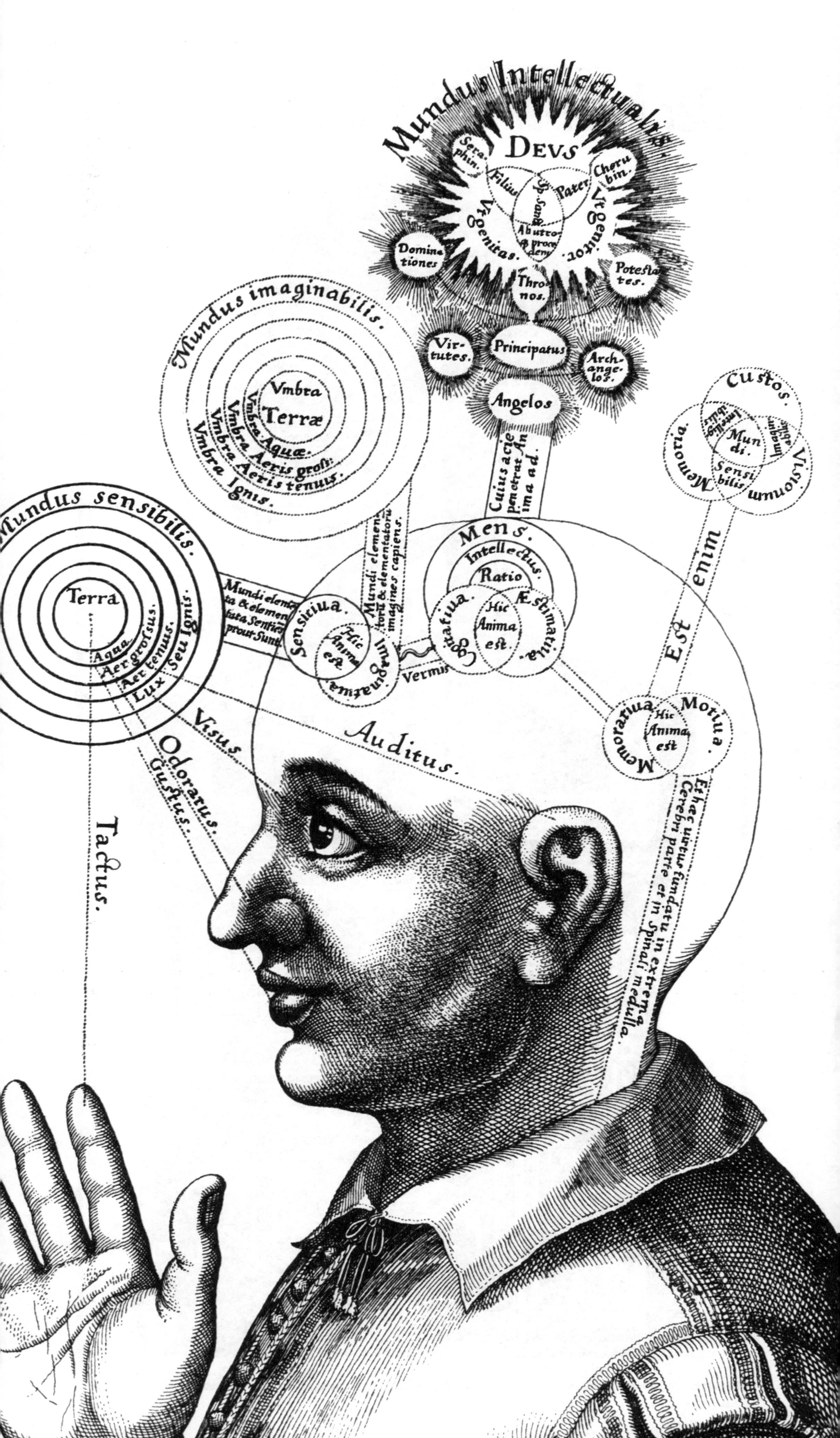

Mundus Intellectualis.
Devs
Sera phin.
Cheru bin.
Filius
Pater
Abutro & procedens
Domina tiones
Potesta tes.
Thro nos.
Vir tutes.
Principatus
Arch ange los.
Angelos
Cuius acie penetrat Anima ad.
Mundus imaginabilis.
Vmbra Terræ
Vmbra Aquæ.
Vmbra Aeris grossi.
Vmbra Aeris tenuis.
Vmbra Ignis.
Mundus sensibilis.
Terra
Aqua
Aer grossus.
Aer tenuis.
Lux Seu Ignis.
Mundi elementorum & elementatorum imagines capiens.
Sensitiua.
Hic Anima est
Imaginatiua.
Vermis
Mens.
Intellectus.
Ratio
Cogitatiua.
Hic Anima est
Æstimatiua.
Custos.
Mundi.
Sensibilis
Memoria
Visionum
Est enim
Memoratiua
Hic Anima est
Motiua.
Et hæc virtus fundatur in extrema Cerebri parte et in Spinali medulla.
Visus
Auditus.
Odoratus.
Gustus.
Tactus.

Der Mensch als Industriepalast

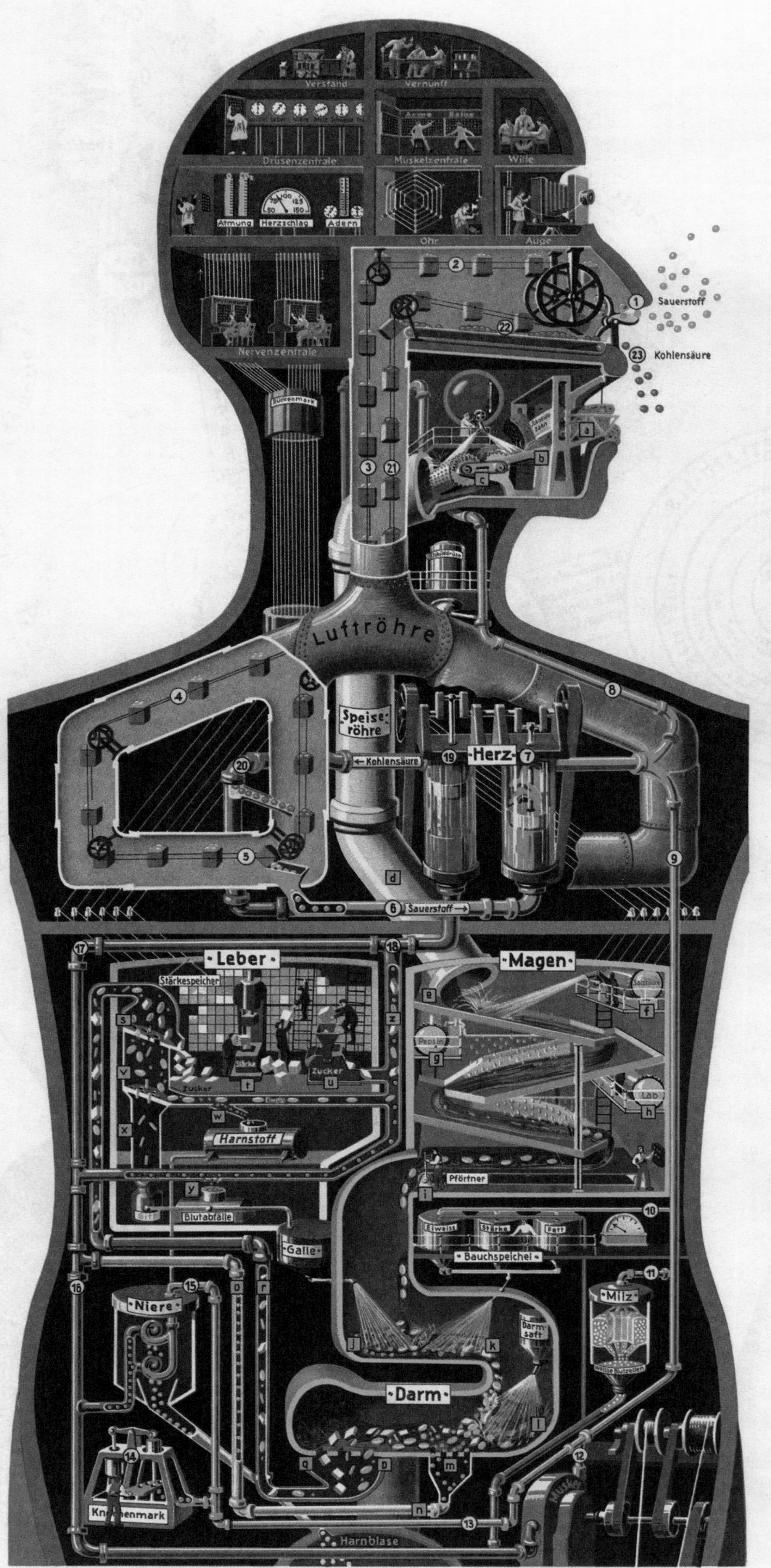

Beilage zu Kahn, DAS LEBEN DES MENSCHEN / Franckh'sche Verlagshandlung, Stuttgart /

Sandra Rendgen
Ed. Julius Wiedemann

Information Graphics

TASCHEN

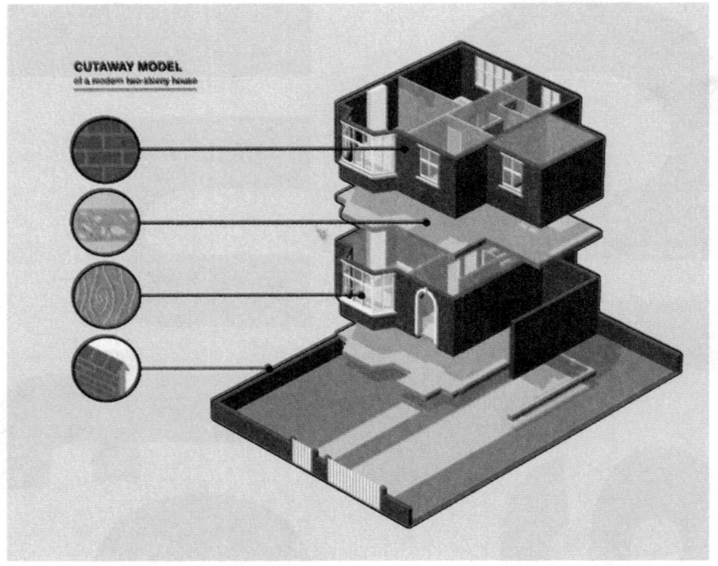
CUTAWAY MODEL
of a modern two-storey house

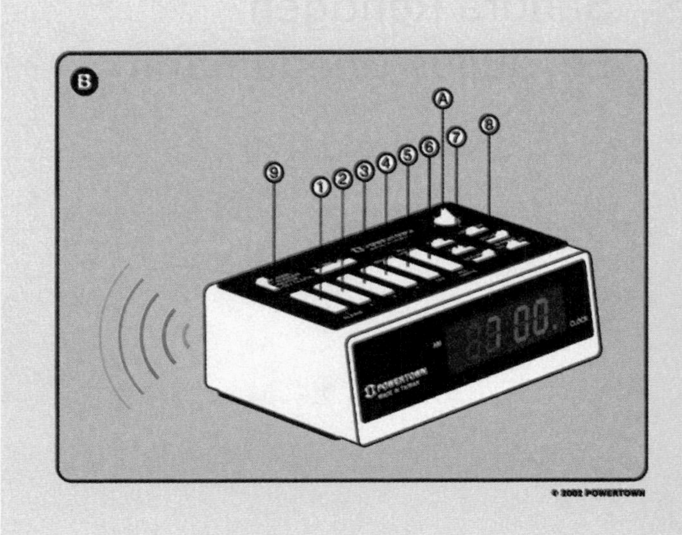
B
POWERTOWN
© 2002 POWERTOWN

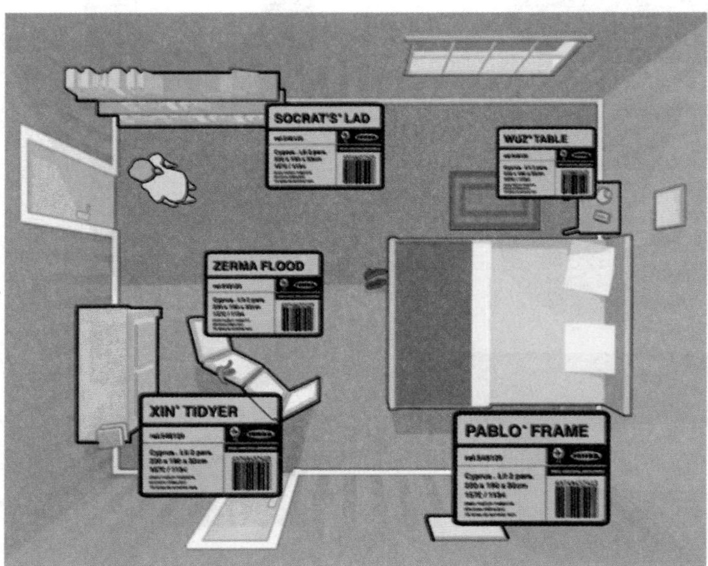
SOCRAT'S' LAD
WUZ' TABLE
ZERMA FLOOD
XIN' TIDYER
PABLO' FRAME

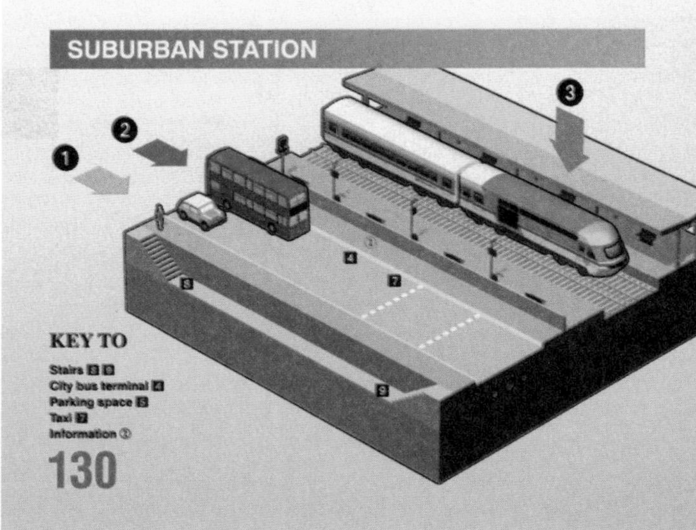
SUBURBAN STATION
KEY TO
Stairs
City bus terminal
Parking space
Taxi
Information
130

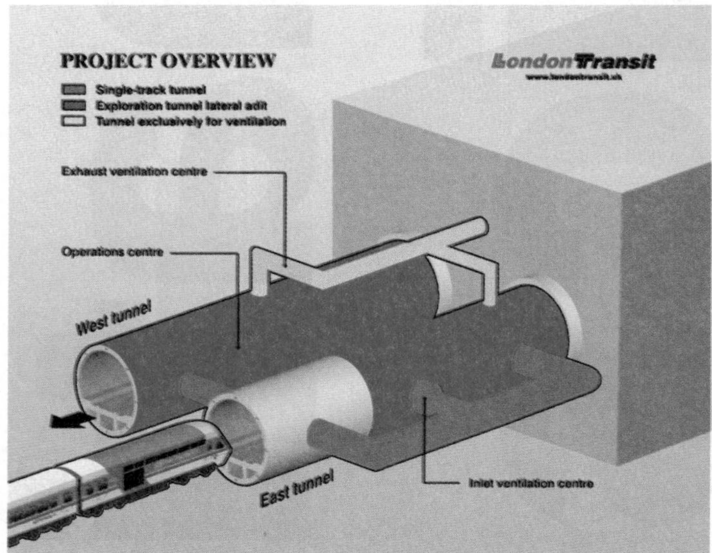
PROJECT OVERVIEW
London Transit
www.londontransit.uk
Single-track tunnel
Exploration tunnel lateral adit
Tunnel exclusively for ventilation
Exhaust ventilation centre
Operations centre
West tunnel
East tunnel
Inlet ventilation centre

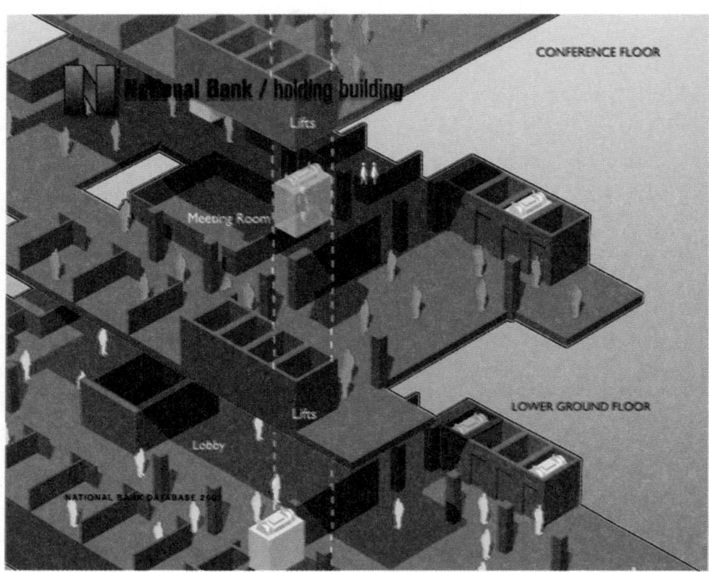
National Bank / holding building
CONFERENCE FLOOR
Lifts
Meeting Room
Lifts
Lobby
LOWER GROUND FLOOR

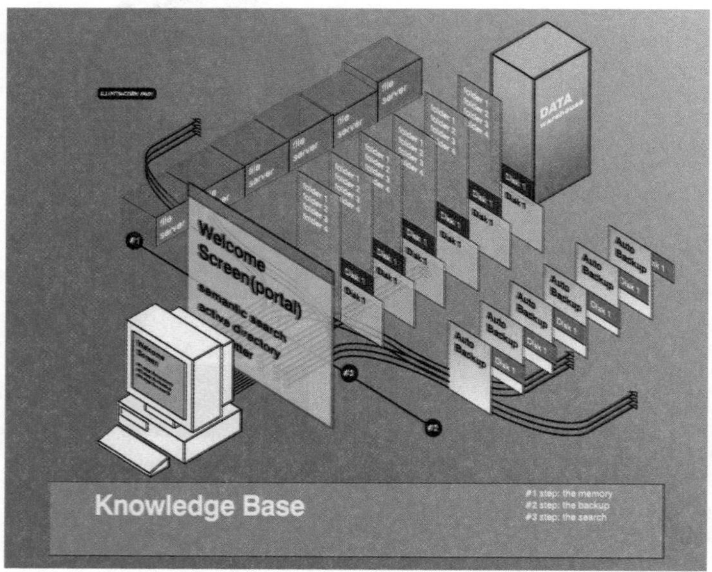
DATA
Welcome Screen(portal)
semantic search
active directory
Knowledge Base
#1 step: the memory
#2 step: the backup
#3 step: the search

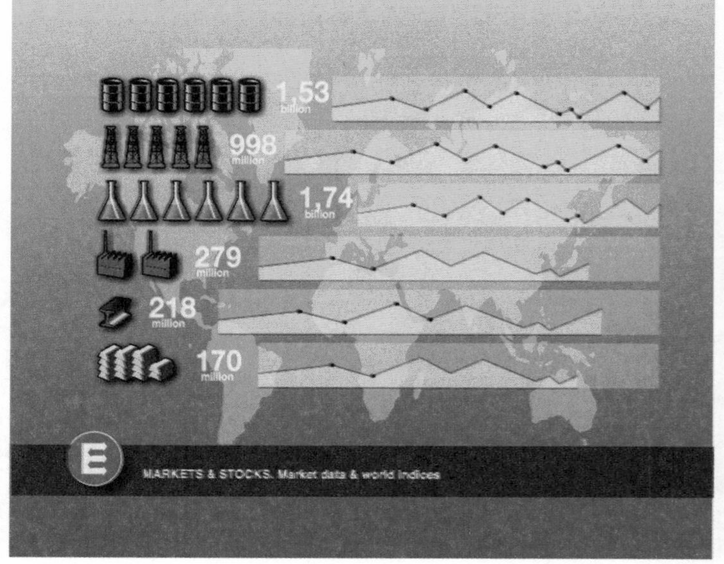
1,53 billion
998 million
1,74 billion
279 million
218 million
170 million
E
MARKETS & STOCKS. Market data & world indices

Essays

Projects

ca. 17,000 BC

ca. 17,000 BC

The cave paintings of Lascaux consist of approximately 2,000 images of men, animals and abstract signs. Although the exact interpretation is still being disputed, it seems certain that the creators of the paintings included extensive information in their images.

Die Höhlenmalereien von Lascaux bestehen aus etwa 2000 Bildern von Menschen, Tieren und abstrakten Zeichen. Obwohl die genaue Deutung umstritten bleibt, scheint sicher, dass die Schöpfer der Malereien umfangreiche Informationen in die Bildfolge einschrieben.

Les peintures des grottes de Lascaux se composent d'environ 2000 images d'hommes, d'animaux et de signes abstraits. Leur interprétation exacte est encore débattue, mais il semble certain que les auteurs y aient inclus une grande quantité d'informations.

Sandra Rendgen

7—36

1144 BC

1144 BC

In Ancient Egyptian tombs, walls were completely covered with symbols and hieroglyphs in order to record information on the life of the deceased. This was supplemented with images of deities (here from the tomb of Ramses VI).

In den altägyptischen Grabkammern wurden die Wände vollflächig mit Bildzeichen und Hieroglyphen bedeckt, um Informationen über das Leben der Verstorbenen festzuhalten. Ergänzt werden diese durch Darstellungen von Göttern (hier die Grabkammer von Ramses VI).

Dans les tombes de l'Ancienne Égypte, les murs étaient entièrement recouverts de symboles et de hiéroglyphes qui consignaient des informations sur la vie du défunt. Ils étaient complétés par des images de divinités (ici, la tombe de Ramsès VI).

Introduction

Sandra Rendgen

Data are the new raw material. Today, infinite amounts of new information can be accessed in seconds and across large distances. However, raw data in themselves are of negligible value – they need to be filtered and evaluated. That's why professional data and information management will be a central cultural tool in the decades to come.

The graphic representation of data and information has been around for a long time, and not just in the world of science. Newspapers regularly publish statistics in chart form; magazines make use of infographics to explain anything from natural phenomena to the latest technology. In business, economic data are communicated in the form of diagrams. User manuals and safety instructions frequently make use of schematic drawings.

For a long time the genre tended to attract little attention, even though infographics have been almost omnipresent for decades. Of the innumerable examples, only a few had much thought and work put into their design. In contrast to other areas of graphic design, infographics had few style-defining precursors. Added to this, there is always a certain amount of tension between graphic design and the accurate depiction of data. On the one hand, infographics are supposed to convert complex problems into images that are easy to understand, but on the other, there is traditionally a suspicion that "beautiful" graphics may tell lies.

Since the turn of the millennium there has been a renewed interest in the visualisation of data and information in many different areas, including journalism, science, art and design. The new trend has even penetrated pop culture: the Norwegian music duo Röyksopp released a music video in 2002 which consisted solely of animated infographics (p.4). The video depicts the life of a young woman in London and segments an entire day into infographics.

There are a number of reasons for this renewed interest. More and more statistical data are freely available and there is more demand for them to be processed. Visual interactive user interfaces are required to access digital archives, whilst the introduction of digital devices in general is changing our reading habits. Communication is shifting towards generally shorter texts in combination with charts and images; hence information graphics are taking centre stage.

This book documents the recent upswing of information graphics and data visualisation. Key issues are discussed by the authors of the essays, such as the aims of data visualisation or the professional handling of information. The historical images accompanying the introduction and essays, on the other hand, demonstrate that there is an old tradition of depicting knowledge in diagrams and charts.

Information graphics are hybrids and hence difficult to define. Text, image and geometric shapes are indissolubly interlaced to produce single entities. This does not follow automatically from the data, but has to be developed. The French cartographer and theoretician Jacques Bertin commented that, "A graphic representation is not merely a drawing, but often entails a heavy responsibility when deciding on how to proceed. One does not 'draw' a graphic representation in a solid form; instead one constructs it and rearranges it until every relationship between the data has been revealed."[1]

In 1967 Bertin wrote a standard work on the graphic means available for depicting data. In addition to the two dimensions of the (paper's) surface on which points, lines and planes can be drawn there are six other options for visually representing data: size, value, texture, colour, orientation and form. Every possible visual construction is composed out of this basic vocabulary combined with text labels.[2]

Various tendencies can be discerned within the hybrid field of information graphics and data visualisation, even though it may not be possible to subject it to a strict division into groups. On the one hand,

visualisation is the process of visual conversion. On the other hand, the term *visualisation* separates interactive dynamic representations from static *charts*. A distinction is also made between *qualitative information* and *quantitative data*. Data are numerical, and their traditional representation is the abstract diagram devoid of figurative images. By contrast, information graphics present qualitative relationships – for example, how an oil rig works. Schematic drawings are often used in this context.

A major difference between individual works also consists in their specific purpose. Many are aimed at a broad audience and seek to provide clear explanations. Conversely there are other depictions that serve above all as scientific tools to aid analysis. In these cases, the main concern is to recognise patterns in data or to arrange information in a clear way. For a long time, diagrams, sketches and maps have been used for such functions, as can be seen from the following historical examples.

The Legible World

Maps, for instance, afford an overall view. They allow us to recognise and order the world. In the cartography of the Middle Ages, as opposed to its later developments, there was no separation between the geographic features of the Earth's surface and the landscape's historic and religious character. Hence the Ebstorf Map, which was made in ca. 1300 in northern Germany, shows all of the then known world on an area 3.5 metres in diameter (p.15). Aligned towards the east, this map is centred on Jerusalem and based on the medieval tripartite division of the world into Europe (below left), Africa (below right) and Asia (top), with India in the upper central area.

The world is overlaid upon the figure of Christ (head, hands and feet), and there is a depiction of the Garden of Eden to the left of his head. In the bottom right, the Mediterranean Sea is shown in a vertical direction. Innumerable animals, people, buildings and narrative scenes enrich the geographic arrangement with strategically placed information about the world's religions and cultures. The map is a visual display, an arrangement of knowledge into a single image.

Anatomical atlases also create an overview of things that cannot be captured by the eye (p.16). Early anatomical works had already availed themselves of schematic drawings of the human body in order to record medical knowledge. Abstract figures show the position and function of various organs. Several Renaissance artists in turn revisited these schematic drawings; Leonardo da Vinci (p.18) and Albrecht Dürer, for instance, investigated human proportions in order to achieve realistic representations of the body.

The role of the structure of the cosmos was as central in late Renaissance thought as that of the properties of the body. Many scientists used diagrams to explain their cosmological theories. The English philosopher and physician Robert Fludd, for instance, designed a diagram in 1618 in which he presented the universe as the stretched chord of a monochord – tuned by the hand of God (p.32). The musical notes A, B, C, D, E, F and G are inscribed on the neck of the instrument, as are, from the bottom up, the four elements and the seven celestial bodies: the Moon, Mercury, Venus, the Sun, Mars, Jupiter and Saturn.

At this level cosmic reality ends, and above it are the supernatural regions. The dotted circles represent the harmonic proportions that rule the cosmos. This scheme reflects the belief that the universe was organised in line with numerical proportions, and that music mirrored this cosmic order. Diagrams were suitable for illustrating such theories because the scientists could use them to show the complex reference systems they could see in the cosmos.

In parallel with the development of cartography, which from the early modern period was experiencing a golden age, there had been since the 17th century attempts at expanding geographic maps by adding extra information. As an example, in 1741 the German

ca. 1090

linguist Gottfried Hensel designed four maps showing the then known continents along with the languages spoken in them (p.47). The individual areas are annotated with characters from their respective alphabets, and there are also tables of all the characters. The maps are designed to provide a full tableau of all the linguistic signs of the world, and thereby substantiate a universal theory of human language. Hensel's designs are among the first examples in which colour was deployed to demarcate geographic areas by theme.[3]

Statistical Patterns

Politicians need aids to help them make decisions. With the development of the modern state in the late 18th century came an increased need to base political decisions on reliable data. For this reason, statistics – the science of the systematic treatment of demographic and economic data – was developed. Unlike today, such numbers were initially accessible only to a small circle of officials and politicians. However, even these experts found that statistics were abstract and not highly descriptive. It is therefore no coincidence that graphic representations were soon developed.

The simplest way of noting data was by means of tables, but by 1786 the Scottish engineer and economist William Playfair had developed diagrams to depict economic figures (p.52). He represented imports and exports to and from England in a time-series chart, and showed England's foreign trade balance in bar charts. In 1820 August Crome developed a comprehensive graphic overview of statistical data for the King of Prussia (p.54). The large tableau compares all the German states on the basis of a series of data, which includes area, state income, military budget and number of army troops.

Another graphic innovation, the flow map, was developed by the French engineer Charles Joseph Minard. Flow maps are a cross between maps and flow charts, and visualise the movement of objects. Minard produced dozens of such maps during the course of his professional life. In 1869 he applied the principle to a historic subject and created one of the most famous of all infographics: a map of Napoleon's catastrophic Russian campaign (p.67). Napoleon had set out for Russia with 422,000 soldiers and returned with only 10,000. The map links numerous variables including the army's direction, declining size, dates and a temperature diagram.

Another format was developed by the English nurse and statistician Florence Nightingale. After her harrowing experiences in the Crimean War, where many soldiers fell victim to the abysmal health care provided, she described the mortality of soldiers over a period of two years in a polar area diagram (p.66). The vast majority of soldiers, shown in blue, died from avoidable infections. Despite scattered criticism of its partly disproportional representation, this diagram is a famous example of the visual expressiveness of statistical graphics.

The Well-Informed Public

The widespread availability of newspapers and magazines is an innovation of the last century. New printing techniques permitted the mass distribution of printed products and made it easier to include images in

ca. 1090

The embroidered Bayeux Tapestry from the Middle Ages shows the Norman conquest of England over a length of 68 metres. The historic events are narrated in 58 individual scenes which include additional text explanations.

Der gestickte Teppich von Bayeux aus dem Mittelalter zeigt auf 68 Meter Länge die Eroberung Englands durch die Normannen. Das historische Geschehen wird in einer Abfolge von 58 Szenen erzählt, die durch Beschriftungen zusätzlich erläutert werden.

Les broderies de la tapisserie de Bayeux, qui date du Moyen Âge, illustrent la conquête de l'Angleterre par les Normands sur une longueur de 68 mètres. Les événements historiques sont narrés en 58 scènes qui comprennent des explications écrites.

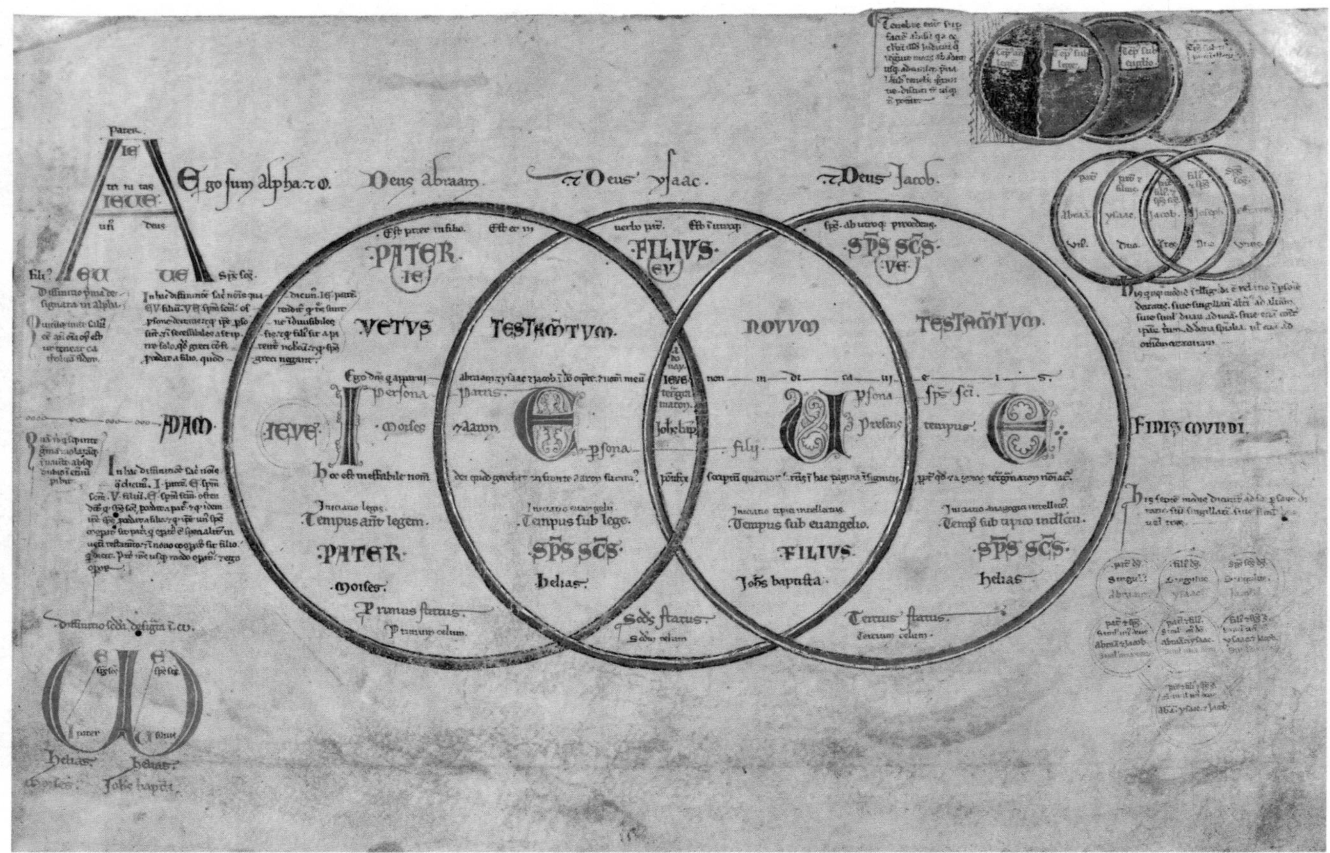

ca. 1190

texts. As this was happening, the popularisation of information and data graphics became unstoppable. At the same time graphic design became generally more professional, not just in the print media but also in public spaces for which guidance systems and aids to orientation were invented.

In 1920s Vienna, the philosopher and economist Otto Neurath sought ways of providing workers and employees with information about societal conditions. To do this he conceived posters that depicted statistical relationships (p.80–81). His posters used standardised pictographs and were designed to be understood by anyone, anywhere in the world. Proportions are denoted by varying the number of particular pictographs. One of the people who worked with Neurath on the design of the posters and pictographs was the graphic designer Gerd Arntz. Thanks to the modern style and progressive attitude of Otto Neurath's pictorial statistics, they continue to serve as a major reference for designers who are concerned with the representation of information and data.

A famous example of the spread of infographics in everyday life is the London Underground map devised by Harry Beck. The starting point was provided by the realisation that the map's primary function was to help people find their way around the Underground network and it therefore did not need to be geographically accurate. Earlier versions had depicted the actual course of the Underground lines within the city and were therefore visually unclear. Beck significantly modified the map by designing a diagrammatic version (p.82). All lines run parallel to the page edges or at a 45-degree angle. Distances between stations are always of equal length, while the stylised course of the Thames is the sole visual reference to the city. To this day the design provides a model on which many of the world's public transport maps are based.

A further example of the spread of information graphics is its increasing use in newspapers and magazines. While statistics in newspapers were often enough represented just with numbers, some magazines like *McCall's* or *Fortune* introduced a lively graphic language for statistical charts (p.87). The popularisation of information and data graphics also spread to business communication. Business reports and presentations often require numbers to be represented graphically. Equally, over the course of the 20th century we have come to take for granted all kinds of pictorial instructions, such as how to assemble furniture, use electrical appliances, and how to behave in the event of emergencies.

Suspicious Data

Information graphics are intended to explain how things really are. Thanks to their scientific aura they found acceptance in the mass media and advertising, and they continue to stand for objectivity and accuracy of information. Whereas in earlier centuries only scientists worked with data and information graphics, they were joined in the 20th century by editors and advertising professionals. However, general popularisation brings with it a level of degeneration, and content-related weaknesses are frequently found in graphic representations.

Since the 1950s several authors, including John Tukey, Jacques Bertin and Edward Tufte, have grappled with the accuracy of graphic representation. In 1954 Darrell Huff published the entertaining book, *How to Lie with Statistics*. He noted numerous cases from advertising and the media in which distorted statistical information was used to emphasise particular statements. His criticism of graphic representations included charts that lacked labelling, and insufficient comparative data to allow a proper evaluation of figures.

The political scientist and statistician Edward Tufte systematically developed these observations and published a series of standard works in which he criticised distortions in graphic representations, for instance, his book *The Visual Display of Quantitative*

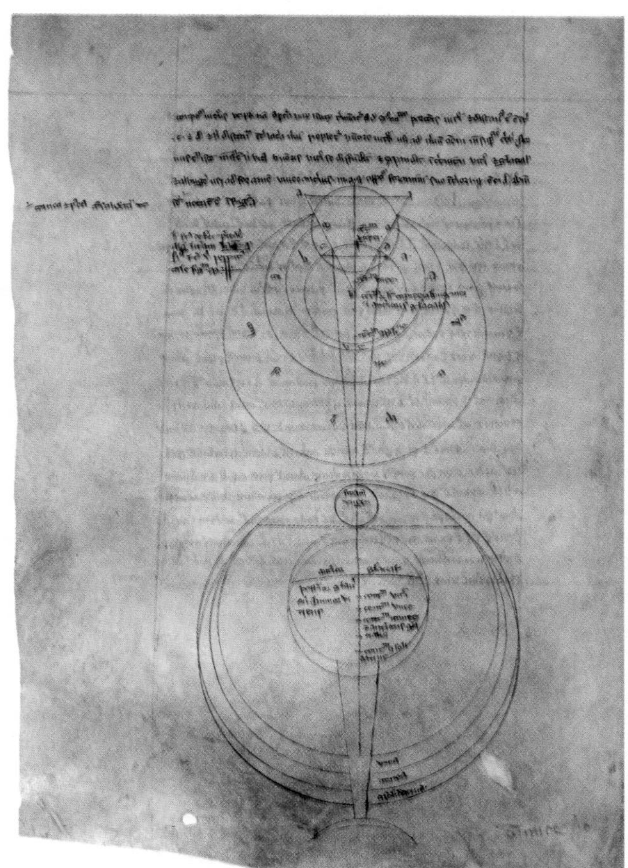

1280

Information, first published in 1982. Tufte analysed graphics published in major daily newspapers and criticised the tendency to enrich statistical diagrams with pictorial metaphors. Although graphic designers were trying to make abstract numbers easier to understand, they also frequently let themselves get carried away by the pictorial metaphor and so created a visual distortion of the data.

As a reaction to this negligence, Tufte developed his own, strictly minimalist design code for data visualisation. He made a plea for labelling to be complete, for restraint in design and a reduction of superfluous "ink". Every dot and line should contain information. Anything more he considered superfluous adornment. He gave excessively decorated graphics the term *chartjunk*.

These analyses have been a significant factor in leading major Western newspapers to practise a certain level of restraint in their infographics design in order to avoid jeopardising the seriousness of their statements. By way of contrast, magazines tend to be more open to pictorial representations. Nigel Holmes, Peter Grundy and John Grimwade are among the designers who have shaped a new and unconventional style (compare their works in this volume). Furthermore, studies have shown that the use of images helps readers remember infographics for longer.[4]

The architect and designer Richard Saul Wurman has been studying the effective transmission of information since the 1960s. Starting with the "data explosion" that came with the development of computer technology, he coined the term "information architecture". In numerous publications he developed ways of clarifying complex relationships by means of structured design. In an essay in this book he introduces his LATCH information-structuring system.

In Wurman's dictum "Understanding is Power" we discern an idea which also resonates in the information pyramid made up of *data*, *information*, *knowledge* and *wisdom*. This concept comes from information science and describes the hierarchical relationships between the individual levels: *data* are the unprocessed symbols; *information* is the processed data, which in turn produces *knowledge* in the reader. The last level of *wisdom* implies not only a deeper understanding, but also the possibility of *acting* in line with this understanding. Therefore, whoever has processed the data and has achieved wisdom via information and knowledge knows what needs to be done. In this model, which is still seen as a point of reference in information visualisation, there resonates the progressive idea that information can motivate action.

ca. 1190

The monk Joachim of Fiore used diagrams to represent his theory of the three ages which correlate to the Holy Trinity. The age of the Father (recounted in the Old Testament of the Bible) was followed by that of the Son (as told in the New Testament). According to Fiore's prediction, this was in turn to be followed by the celestial age of the Holy Spirit.

Der Mönch Joachim von Fiore nutzte Diagramme für die Darstellung seiner Lehre von den drei Zeitaltern, die mit der Heiligen Dreifaltigkeit korrelieren. Auf das Zeitalter des Vaters (dargestellt im Alten Testament der Bibel) folgte das Zeitalter des Sohnes (das dem Neuen Testament entspricht). Nach Fiores Voraussage sollte darauf wiederum das himmlische Zeitalter des Heiligen Geistes folgen.

Le moine Joachim de Fiore a utilisé des diagrammes pour représenter sa théorie des trois âges, en corrélation avec la Sainte Trinité. L'âge du Père (raconté dans l'Ancien Testament de la Bible) était suivi de l'âge du Fils (raconté dans le Nouveau Testament). Selon la prédiction de Fiore, cela devait être suivi de l'âge céleste du Saint-Esprit.

1280

The English scholar Roger Bacon tried to establish exact mathematics and empirical natural research as the foundation of all science. He is also known for his research in the field of optics: this plate shows a study on the nature of light.

Der englische Gelehrte Roger Bacon versuchte, die exakte Mathematik und empirische Naturforschungen als Grundlage aller Wissenschaften zu etablieren. Berühmt sind auch seine Forschungen zur Optik – dieses Blatt zeigt eine Studie zur Beschaffenheit des Lichts.

Le savant anglais Roger Bacon voulait faire des mathématiques exactes et de la recherche naturelle empirique les fondations de toute science. Il est aussi connu pour ses recherches dans le domaine de l'optique: cette planche montre une étude sur la nature de la lumière.

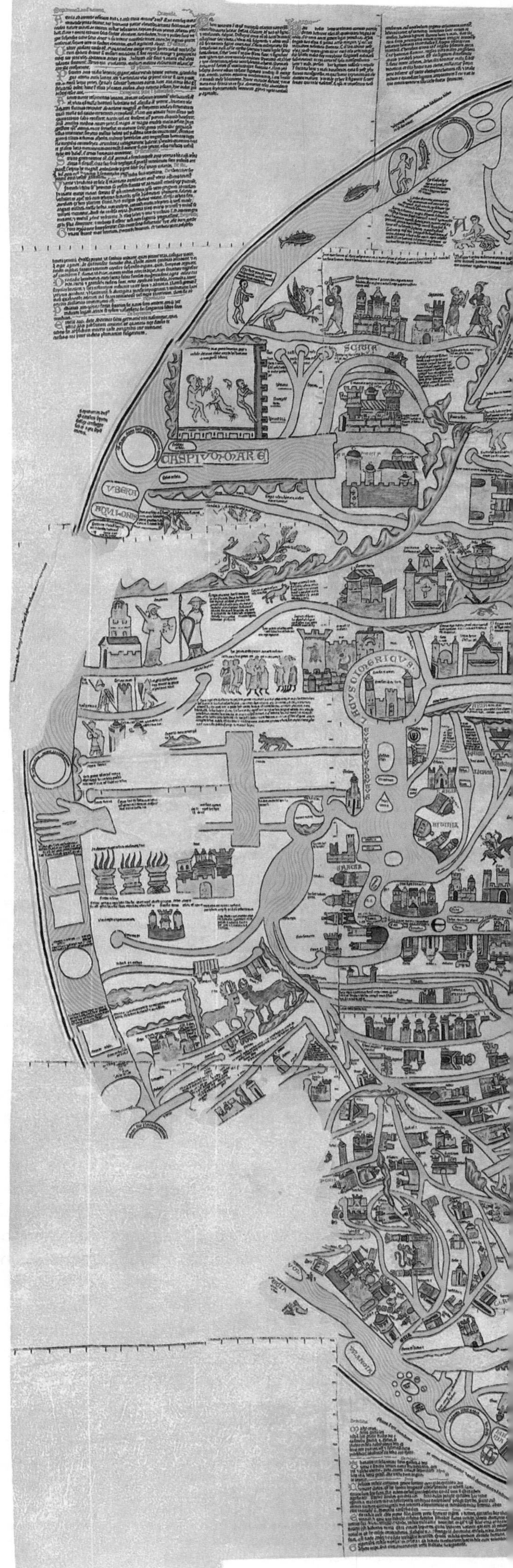

Data Future
Today the users themselves have become the authors. With the spread of personal computers, almost everyone has the tools needed to produce graphics. The best-known example of this is Microsoft's PowerPoint presentation software which has been distributed on a huge scale and which any office worker can use to visualise his own statistics. The enormous number of badly prepared charts with which we have since been inundated has no doubt contributed to the bad reputation of pie charts and bar charts. In 2003, Colin Powell achieved dubious fame with his evidence to the UN regarding Iraq's weapons of mass destruction – which significantly contributed to the start of the Iraq war. Among other things he gave a poorly prepared presentation, which included information graphics and labelled satellite photographs.

The plethora of badly designed visualisations coincides with a growing need to deal with the flood of information with a certain degree of professionalism. No longer is data secret knowledge. With a general freedom of information, which has now become legally anchored in many countries, comes a public culture of information. At a time when everyone is swamped by information it is necessary firstly to subject data to precise analysis and secondly to prepare it in an intelligent and appealing way. This requires a general *visual literacy*.

Graphic designers are reacting to this and are increasingly interested in developing a visual language for information and data. They do not want graphic representations merely to be factually accurate; they must also reflect good design. Theoreticians are looking at the way in which visual design impacts on the cognitive comprehension of graphic representations. For instance, Paolo Ciuccarelli of the DensityDesign Research Lab in Milan argues in his essay in this book for improving the way in which scientific research is communicated to the public. He pleads for a stronger integration of

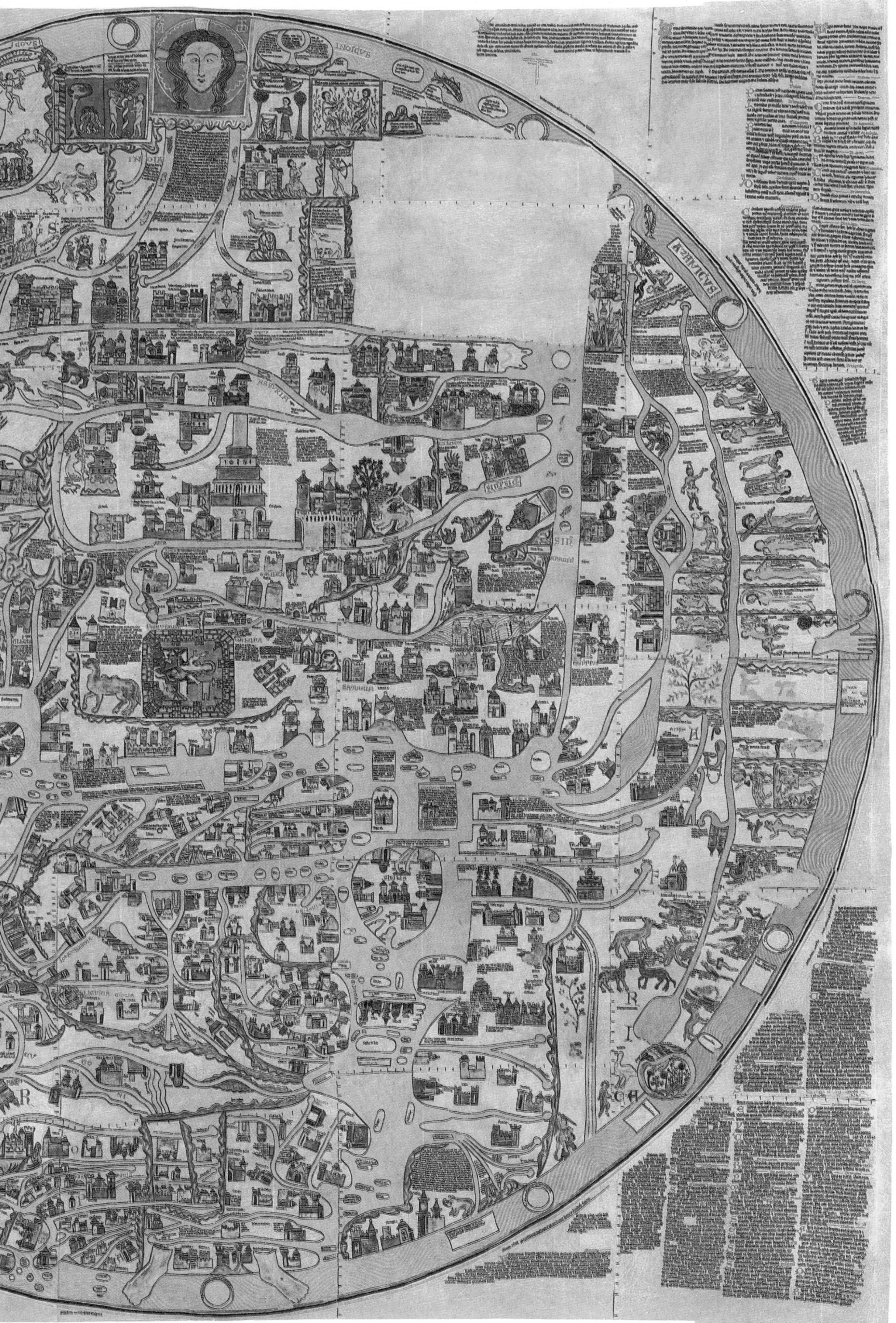

1300

1300

This medieval world map from around 1300 shows the then known continents Africa (right), Europe (left) and Asia (centre top). The geographical rendering is supplemented by mythological stories and creatures as well as historical facts.

Diese mittelalterliche Weltkarte, die um 1300 entstand, zeigt die damals bekannten Kontinente Afrika (rechts), Europa (links) und Asien (Mitte oben). Die geografische Darstellung wird ergänzt um Mythen, Fabeltiere und historische Angaben.

Cette carte du monde des années 1300 montre l'Afrique (à droite), l'Europe (à gauche) et l'Asie (au centre, en haut) telles qu'elles étaient connues alors. La géographie est complétée d'histoires, de créatures mythologiques et de faits historiques.

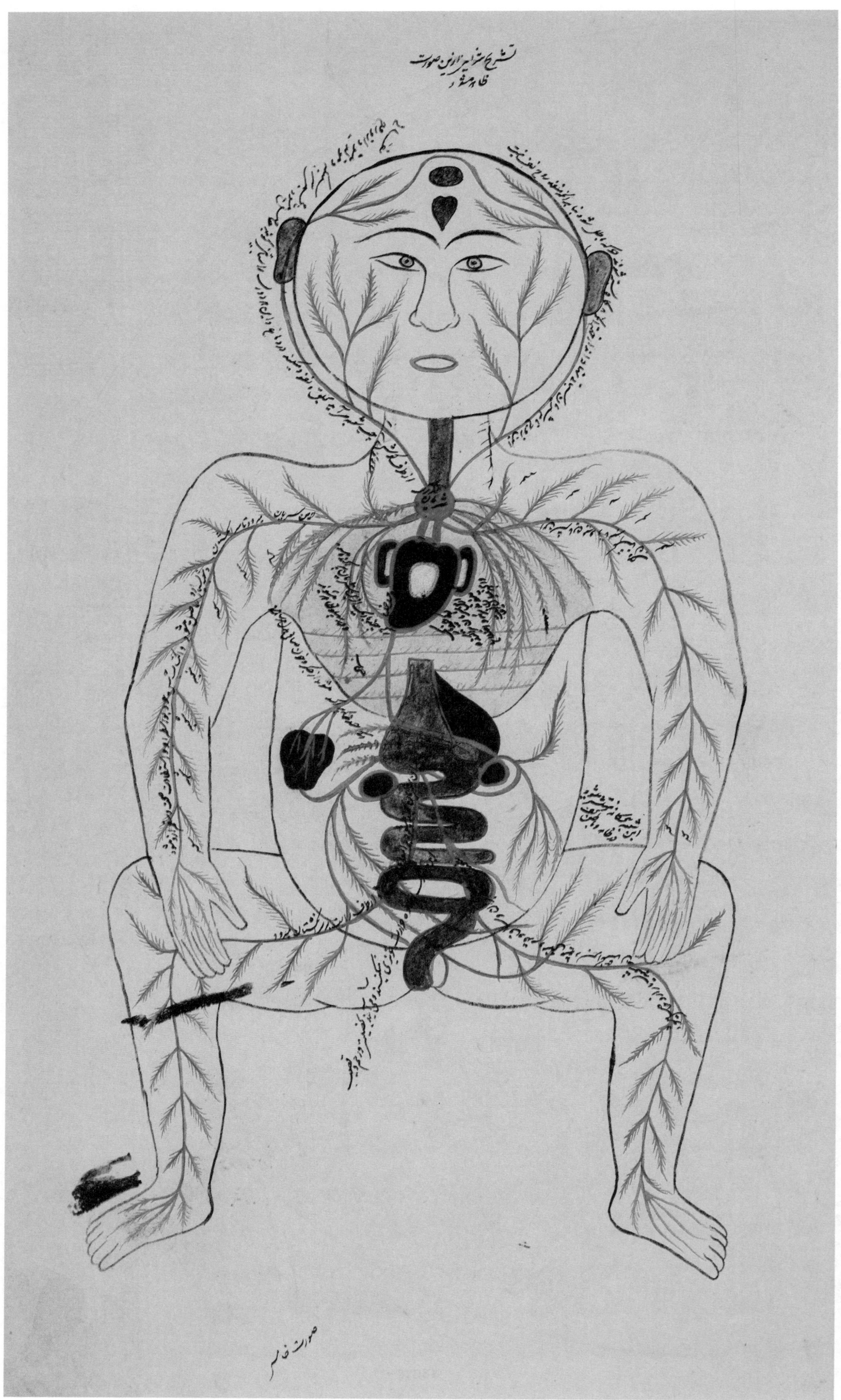

1390

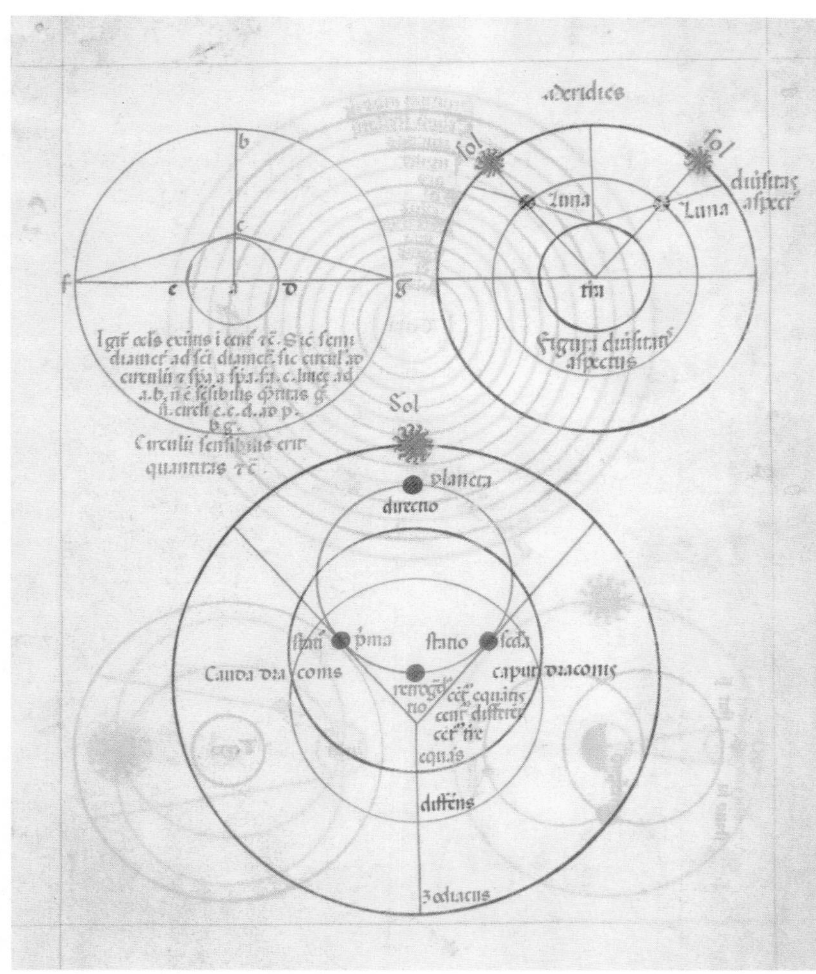

1460

narrative elements into abstract graphics in order to increase understanding.

However, interaction designers develop interactive data visualisations so that users can independently discover, compare and comment on data. Platforms like Many Eyes, for example, provide an opportunity for visualising and publishing data in a variety of basic patterns. Online comment functions allow users to discuss and hence control the different visualisations. The interpretation of statistical data becomes a cooperative process.

Journalists in turn consider the wealth of data as a new source for balanced reporting. Simon Rogers from the London-based *Guardian* describes under the heading of *data journalism* the way in which the availability of statistics on the Internet has massively expanded journalistic practice in the last ten years. In his essay, a moment of democratisation can be heard; journalists can evaluate political events with greater nuance when alternative sources of information are available to them.

This book portrays the changes in information graphics over the last ten years on the basis of 200 projects from a variety of different fields. Scientists, journalists and designers are represented, as are freelance artists who have their own ways of interpreting the genre. The culture of information visualisation that was created in this period will continue to grow and differentiate. We keenly await future developments.

1 Bertin, Jacques: *La graphique et le traitement graphique de l'information*. Paris: Flammarion, 1977. Translation 1981, *Graphics and graphic information-processing* by William J. Berg and Paul Scott.
2 Bertin, Jacques: *Sémiologie Graphique. Les diagrammes, les réseaux, les cartes*. Paris: Gauthier-Villars, 1967. Translation 1983, *Semiology of Graphics* by William William J. Berg.
3 Robinson, Arthur H.: *Early Thematic Mapping in the History of Cartography*. Chicago and London: Chicago University Press, 1982, p.54.
4 Bateman, Scott et al.: *Useful Junk? The Effects of Visual Embellishment on Comprehension and Memorability of Charts*. University of Saskatchewan, Department of Computer Science. Paper Presented on CHI, April 2010.

1390

Illustrations have always played a cardinal role in the passing-on of medical knowledge. This schematic drawing of the circulation of the blood originates from the so-called *Anatomy of Mansur*, assembled in the late 14th century in Iran.

Illustrationen spielten von jeher eine zentrale Rolle bei der Weitergabe von medizinischen Kenntnissen. Diese schematische Zeichnung des Blutkreislaufs stammt aus der sogenannten *Anatomie von Mansur* und entstand im späten 14. Jahrhundert im Iran.

Les illustrations ont toujours joué un rôle fondamental dans la transmission des connaissances médicales. Ce dessin schématique de la circulation du sang est tiré de *L'Anatomie de Mansur*, datant de la fin du XIVe siècle et originaire d'Iran.

1460

The Italian manuscript *De sphaera* is a lavishly illustrated volume on astrology. Aside from many detailed illustrations, the codex comprises several diagrams showing the structure of the universe and the system of the planets.

Die italienische Handschrift *De sphaera* ist ein reich illustrierter Band über Astrologie. Neben zahlreichen detaillierten Abbildungen enthält der Kodex mehrere Diagramme, die den Aufbau des Universums und die Anordnung der Planeten zeigen.

Le manuscrit italien *De sphaera* est un ouvrage magnifiquement illustré sur l'astrologie. Outre de nombreuses illustrations détaillées, ce codex comprend plusieurs diagrammes qui montrent la structure de l'univers et le système des planètes.

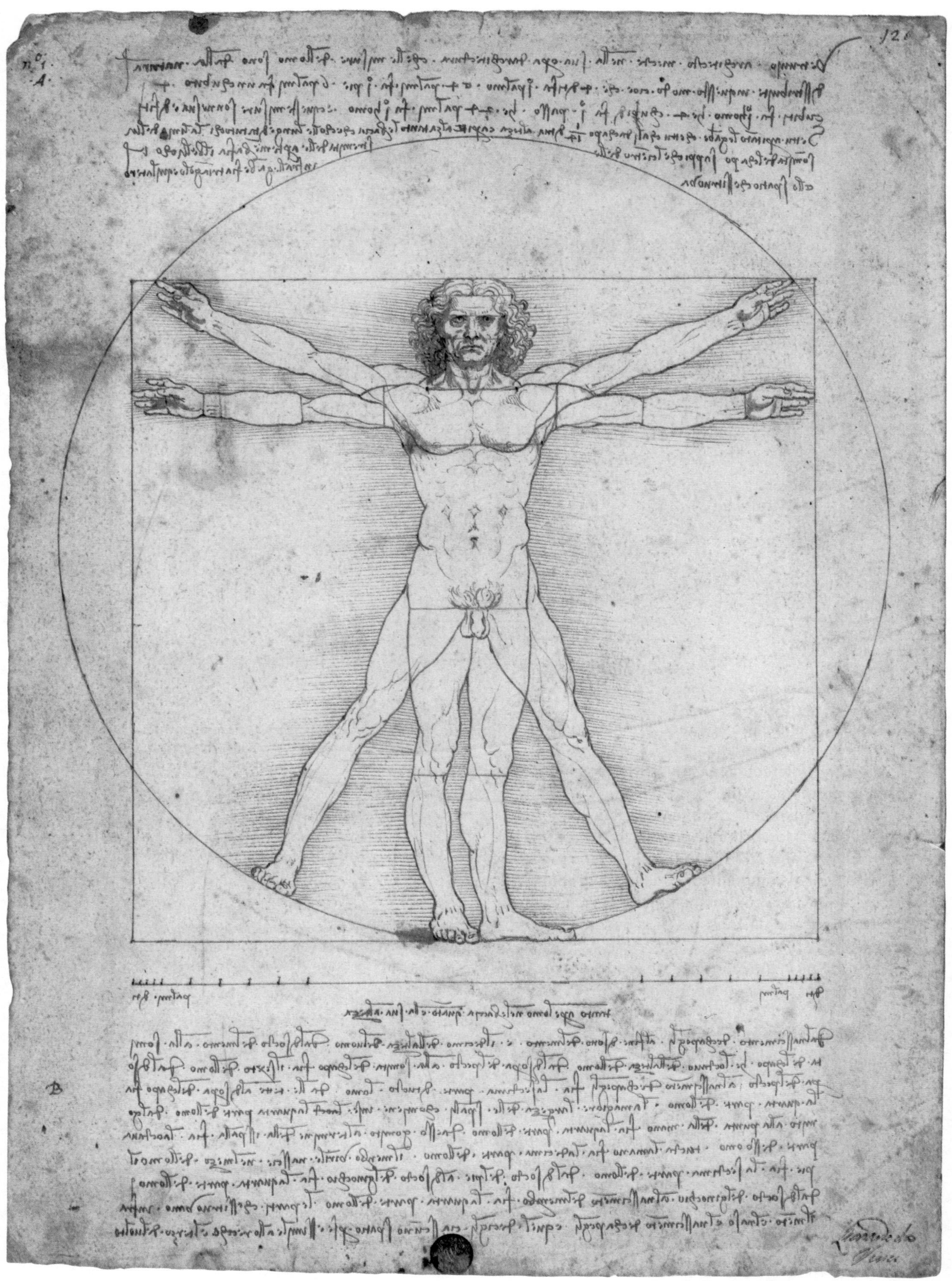

1487

1487

Leonardo da Vinci visualises the ideal human proportions as described by the Roman architect Vitruvius in this famous drawing from the late 15th century. The ideal male body is inscribed in the forms of a square and a circle.

In dieser berühmten Zeichnung visualisiert Leonardo da Vinci Ende des 15. Jahrhunderts die idealen menschlichen Proportionen, wie sie der römische Architekt Vitruv beschrieb. Der ideale männliche Körper ist in ein Quadrat und einen Kreis eingeschrieben.

Dans ce célèbre dessin de la fin du XVe siècle, Léonard de Vinci représente les proportions humaines idéales telles qu'elles sont décrites par l'architecte romain Vitruvius. Le corps masculin idéal s'inscrit dans un carré et dans un cercle.

Einleitung

Sandra Rendgen

Daten sind der neue Rohstoff. Unendliche Mengen an Informationen sind heute sekundenschnell und über große Entfernungen hinweg abrufbar. Doch Rohdaten an sich sind kaum von Wert – sie müssen gefiltert und ausgewertet werden. Der professionelle Umgang mit Daten und Informationen wird eine zentrale Kulturtechnik der kommenden Jahrzehnte sein.

Schon lange gibt es grafische Darstellungen von Daten und Informationen, nicht nur in der Wissenschaft. Tageszeitungen veröffentlichen regelmäßig statistische Grafiken, Zeitschriften nutzen Infografiken, um Naturphänomene oder neueste Technologien zu erklären. Im Geschäftsleben werden wirtschaftliche Daten in Diagrammen kommuniziert. Bedienungsanleitungen oder Sicherheitshinweise verwenden häufig schematische Zeichnungen.

Obwohl Infografiken seit Jahrzehnten fast überall benutzt werden, blieb das Genre lange Zeit eher unauffällig. Nur ein kleiner Teil der zahllosen Beispiele war gut und aufwendig gestaltet. Im Unterschied zu anderen Bereichen im Grafikdesign gab es für Infografiken nur wenige stilprägende Vorbilder. Zudem besteht immer eine gewisse Spannung zwischen der grafischen Gestaltung und der korrekten Darstellung der Daten. Einerseits sollen Infografiken komplexe Probleme in leicht verständliche Bilder übersetzen. Andererseits existiert ein althergebrachtes Misstrauen, dass „schöne“ Grafiken lügen könnten.

Seit der Jahrtausendwende gibt es ein neues Interesse an der Visualisierung von Daten und Informationen. Viele Bereiche sind daran beteiligt: Journalisten und Wissenschaftler, Designer und Künstler. Bis in die Pop-Kultur ist der neue Trend vorgedrungen: Das norwegische Duo Röyksopp veröffentlichte 2002 ein Musikvideo, das ausschließlich aus animierten Grafiken besteht (S. 4). Es zeigt das Leben einer jungen Londonerin – ein ganzer Tag, zerlegt in Infografiken.

Die Gründe für das neue Interesse sind vielfältig: Statistische Daten sind zunehmend frei verfügbar und verlangen nach Aufbereitung. Digitale Archive brauchen eine visuelle interaktive Nutzeroberfläche, um erschlossen zu werden. Die Einführung digitaler Endgeräte ändert die Lesegewohnheiten. Die Kommunikation verlagert sich auf zumeist kürzere Texte in Verbindung mit Grafiken und Bildern, und damit rücken auch Informationsgrafiken ins Zentrum der Aufmerksamkeit.

Das vorliegende Buch dokumentiert den jüngsten Aufschwung von Informationsgrafiken und Datenvisualisierungen. Die Autoren der Essays diskutieren zentrale Fragen, wie die Ziele von Visualisierungen oder den professionellen Umgang mit Informationen. Die begleitenden historischen Beispiele im Essayteil hingegen zeigen, dass die Darstellung von Wissen in Diagrammen und Grafiken eine alte Tradition hat.

Informationsgrafiken sind schwer bestimmbare Zwitter. Unauflösbar verschränken sich Text, Bild und geometrische Formen zu einer Einheit. Diese ergibt sich nicht von selbst aus den Daten, sie muss entwickelt werden. Der französische Kartograf und Theoretiker Jacques Bertin schrieb dazu: „Eine grafische Darstellung bedeutet nicht nur eine Zeichnung, sondern oft eine schwere Verantwortung bei der Entscheidung, wie vorzugehen ist. Man ‚zeichnet‘ nicht eine grafische Darstellung in einer festen Form, sondern man konstruiert sie und ordnet sie um, bis alle Beziehungen aufgedeckt sind, die zwischen den Daten bestehen.“[1]

Bertin verfasste 1967 ein Standardwerk über die grafischen Mittel zur Darstellung von Datenwerten. Neben den zwei Dimensionen der (Papier)-Fläche, auf denen Punkt, Linie und Fläche erstellt werden können, gibt es sechs weitere Möglichkeiten, um Datenwerte visuell zu zeigen: Größe, Helligkeitswert, Muster, Farbe, Richtung und Form. Aus diesem grundlegenden Vokabular, verbunden mit Textlabels, setzen sich alle möglichen visuellen Konstruktionen zusammen.[2]

Im hybriden Feld von Informationsgrafiken und Datenvisualisierung lassen sich verschiedene Tendenzen ausmachen, wenn auch eine strenge Unterteilung

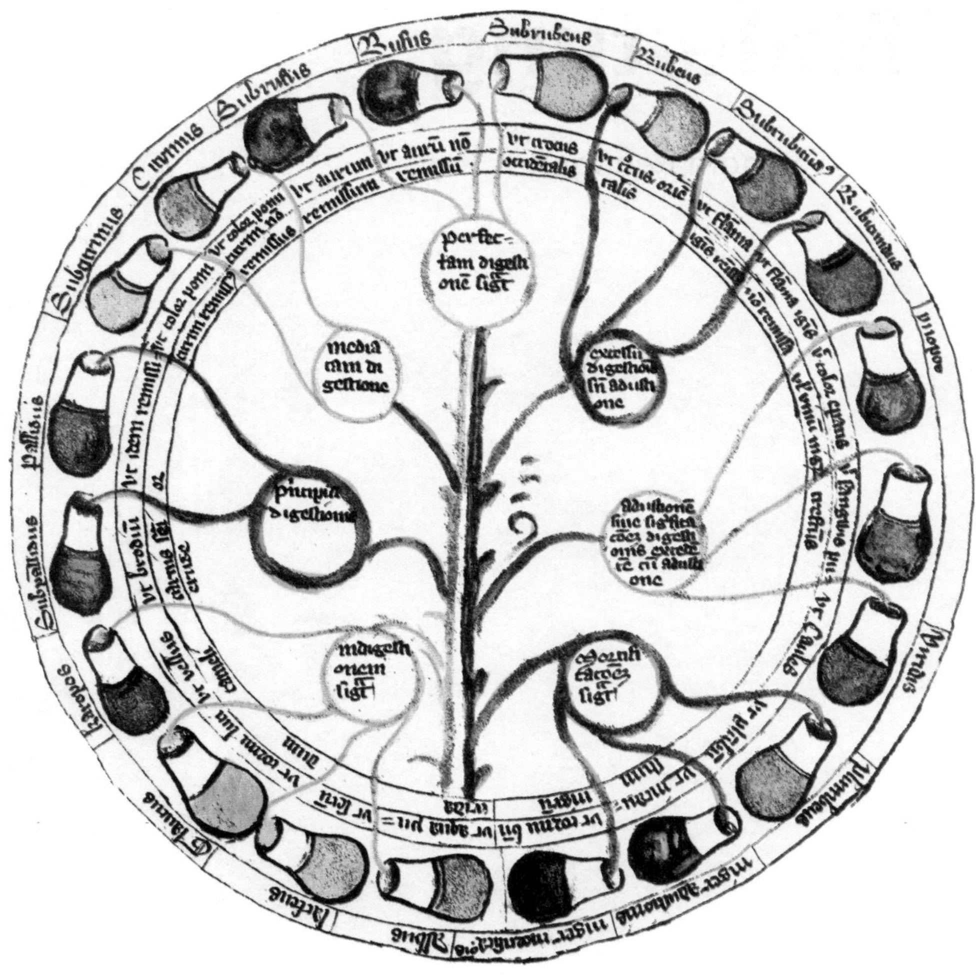

1491

in Gruppen nicht möglich ist. *Visualisierung* ist einerseits der Prozess der visuellen Umsetzung. Andererseits trennt der Begriff *Visualisierung* eine interaktive dynamische Darstellung von einer statischen *Grafik*. Überdies wird zwischen *qualitativer Information* und *quantitativen Daten* unterschieden. Daten sind numerisch, die traditionelle Form dafür ist das abstrakte Diagramm ohne figürliche Darstellungen. Informationsgrafiken dagegen stellen qualitative Zusammenhänge vor: beispielsweise wie eine Bohrinsel funktioniert. Hier kommen häufig schematische Zeichnungen zum Einsatz.

Ein zentraler Unterschied zwischen den einzelnen Arbeiten besteht auch in ihrer jeweiligen Zielsetzung. Viele richten sich an ein breites Publikum und sollen einen Sachverhalt leicht verständlich erklären. Demgegenüber gibt es andere Darstellungen, die in der Wissenschaft vor allem als Denkwerkzeug dienen. Hier geht es vorrangig darum, Muster in Daten zu erkennen oder Informationen übersichtlich anzuordnen. Eine solche Funktion von Diagrammen, Skizzen und Karten ist schon lange bekannt, wie die folgenden historischen Beispiele zeigen.

Die lesbare Welt

Karten beispielsweise gewähren Übersicht. Sie ermöglichen es, die Welt zu erkennen und zu ordnen. Anders als die spätere Kartografie trennte man im Mittelalter nicht zwischen geografischen Merkmalen der Erdoberfläche und den historischen und religiösen Prägungen einer Landschaft. So zeigt die Ebstorfer Weltkarte, entstanden um 1300 in Norddeutschland, die gesamte damals bekannte Welt auf einer Fläche von dreieinhalb Meter Durchmesser (S.15). Ausgerichtet nach Osten und mit dem ummauerten Jerusalem im Zentrum, orientiert sich die Karte an der mittelalterlichen Dreiteilung der Welt in Europa (unten links), Afrika (unten rechts) und Asien (oben) mit Indien in der oberen Mitte.

Die Welt ist eingebettet in die Figur Christi (Kopf, Hände und Füße), links des Hauptes findet sich die Darstellung des Paradieses. Das Mittelmeer verläuft im rechten unteren Teil von unten nach oben. Unzählige Tiere, Menschen, Gebäude und narrative Szenen reichern die geografische Anordnung mit strukturiertem Wissen über Religionen und Kulturen der Welt an. Die Karte ist eine Schautafel, eine visuelle Anordnung von Wissen in einem einzigen Bild.

Übersicht schaffen über Dinge, die das Auge nicht erfassen kann – das ist auch die Leistung von anatomischen Atlanten (S.16). Bereits frühe Anatomiewerke bedienen sich der schematischen Zeichnung des menschlichen Körpers, um medizinische Kenntnisse festzuhalten. Abstrahierte Figuren zeigen die Lage und Funktionsweise verschiedener Organe. Verschiedene Künstler der Renaissance wiederum griffen die schematischen Zeichnungen auf. Leonardo da Vinci (S.18) und Albrecht Dürer etwa untersuchten die menschlichen Proportionen, um eine möglichst naturgetreue Körperdarstellung zu erreichen.

Ebenso wie die Beschaffenheit des Körpers spielte der Aufbau des Kosmos eine zentrale Rolle im Denken der (ausgehenden) Renaissance. Zahlreiche Forscher nutzten Diagramme, um ihre kosmologischen Theorien zu erklären. Der englische Philosoph und Mediziner Robert Fludd etwa entwarf 1618 ein Diagramm, in dem er das Universum als gespannte Saite auf einem Monochord vorstellte – gestimmt von der Hand Gottes (S.32). Auf dem Hals des Instruments sind die musikalischen Töne A.B.C.D.E.F.G eingeschrieben, sowie von unten nach oben die vier Elemente und die sieben Himmelskörper Mond, Merkur, Venus, Sonne, Mars, Jupiter und Saturn.

Auf dieser Höhe endet die kosmische Wirklichkeit, darüber befinden sich die übernatürlichen Bereiche. Die gestrichelten Kreise zeigen die harmonischen Proportionen, die den Kosmos beherrschen. Dieser Entwurf spiegelt die Auffassung wider, dass das Universum nach Zahlenverhältnissen geordnet und die Musik Abbild dieser kosmischen Ordnung sei. Diagramme waren für solche Theorien geeignet, weil

Already in Antiquity and the Middle Ages the colour of urine served as an important piece of evidence for the diagnosis of various ailments. This so-called uroscopy wheel shows urine flasks in different colours, indicating various diseases.

Bereits in der Antike und im Mittelalter war die Farbe des Urins für Ärzte ein wichtiges Indiz zur Diagnose verschiedener Krankheiten. Dieses sogenannte Uroskopie-Rad zeigt Uringläser in verschiedenen Farben, die auf unterschiedliche Krankheiten hindeuten.

Dans l'Antiquité et au Moyen Âge, la couleur de l'urine était déjà une indication importante pour diagnostiquer différentes affections. Cette « roue d'uroscopie » montre des flacons d'urine de différentes couleurs pour différentes maladies.

die Forscher in ihnen die komplizierten Bezugssysteme zeigen konnten, die sie im Kosmos sahen.

Parallel zur Entwicklung der Kartografie, die seit der frühen Neuzeit eine Blüte erlebte, gab es seit dem 17. Jahrhundert Ansätze, geografische Karten um zusätzliche Themen zu erweitern. So entwarf der deutsche Sprachwissenschaftler Gottfried Hensel 1741 vier thematische Karten der damals bekannten Kontinente, auf denen er die Sprachen der Völker zeigte (S. 47). Die einzelnen Gebiete sind mit den Zeichen ihres jeweiligen Alphabets beschriftet, zusätzlich gibt es Tabellen aller Schriftzeichen. Die Karten dienten dazu, ein vollständiges Tableau aller sprachlichen Zeichen der Welt aufzustellen und damit eine universale Theorie der menschlichen Sprache zu begründen. Hensels Entwürfe sind unter den frühesten Beispielen, in denen Farben verwendet werden, um geografische Flächen thematisch voneinander abzugrenzen.[3]

Statistische Muster

Politiker brauchen Entscheidungshilfen. Mit der Herausbildung moderner Staaten im späten 18. Jahrhundert wurde es zunehmend notwendig, politische Entschlüsse auf verlässliche Daten zu gründen. So entstand die Statistik: die Wissenschaft vom systematischen Umgang mit demografischen und wirtschaftlichen Daten. Anders als heute waren solche Zahlen zunächst nur einem kleinen Kreis von Beamten und Politikern zugänglich. Selbst für diese Experten jedoch waren Statistiken abstrakt und wenig anschaulich. Daher ist es kein Zufall, dass schon bald grafische Darstellungen entwickelt wurden.

Die einfachste Art, Daten zu notieren, war die Tabelle, doch bereits 1786 entwickelte der schottische Ingenieur und Ökonom William Playfair Diagramme zur Darstellung ökonomischer Kennzahlen (S. 52). In Zeitreihen stellte er Importe und Exporte von und nach England dar, in Balkendiagrammen zeigte er die Außenhandelsbilanz Englands. Eine umfassende grafische Übersicht statistischer Daten entwickelte auch August Crome 1820 für den preußischen König (S. 54). Das großformatige Tableau vergleicht alle deutschen Bundesstaaten mit einer ganzen Serie von Daten: Fläche, Staatseinkommen, Militäretat, Mannschaftsstärke der Armee etc.

Eine weitere grafische Innovation entwickelte der französische Ingenieur Charles Joseph Minard: die Flowmap. Flowmaps sind eine Kreuzung aus Karten und Flussdiagrammen, die die Bewegung von Objekten visualisieren. Im Laufe seines Berufslebens fertigte Minard Dutzende solcher Karten an. 1869 wandte er das Prinzip auf ein historisches Thema an und erstellte eine der berühmtesten Infografiken überhaupt: eine Karte über den katastrophalen Verlauf von Napoleons Russlandfeldzug (S. 67). Mit 422 000 Soldaten war Napoleon nach Russland aufgebrochen, mit nur 10 000 kehrte er zurück. Die Karte verbindet zahlreiche Variablen wie die Marschrichtung und abnehmende Mannschaftsstärke der Armee, Zeitangaben und ein Temperaturdiagramm.

Ein anderes Format entwickelte die englische Krankenpflegerin und Statistikerin Florence Nightingale. Nach erschütternden Erfahrungen im Krimkrieg, wo zahlreiche verwundete Soldaten der katastrophalen Gesundheitsversorgung zum Opfer fielen, stellte sie in einem Polar-Area-Diagramm die Sterblichkeit von Soldaten über den Verlauf von zwei Jahren dar (S. 66). Der blau gezeigte, übermäßig große Teil von Soldaten verstarb an vermeidbaren Infektionskrankheiten. Trotz vereinzelter Kritik an der teils unproportionalen Darstellung ist dieses Diagramm ein berühmtes Beispiel für die visuelle Aussagekraft von statistischen Grafiken.

Die informierte Öffentlichkeit

Zeitungen und Zeitschriften für alle – das war eine große Neuerung des letzten Jahrhunderts. Neue Drucktechniken erlaubten die massenhafte Verbreitung von Druck-Erzeugnissen und erleichterten die Einbindung von Grafiken in Texte. Im Zuge dessen erlebten Informations- und Datengrafiken eine unaufhaltsame

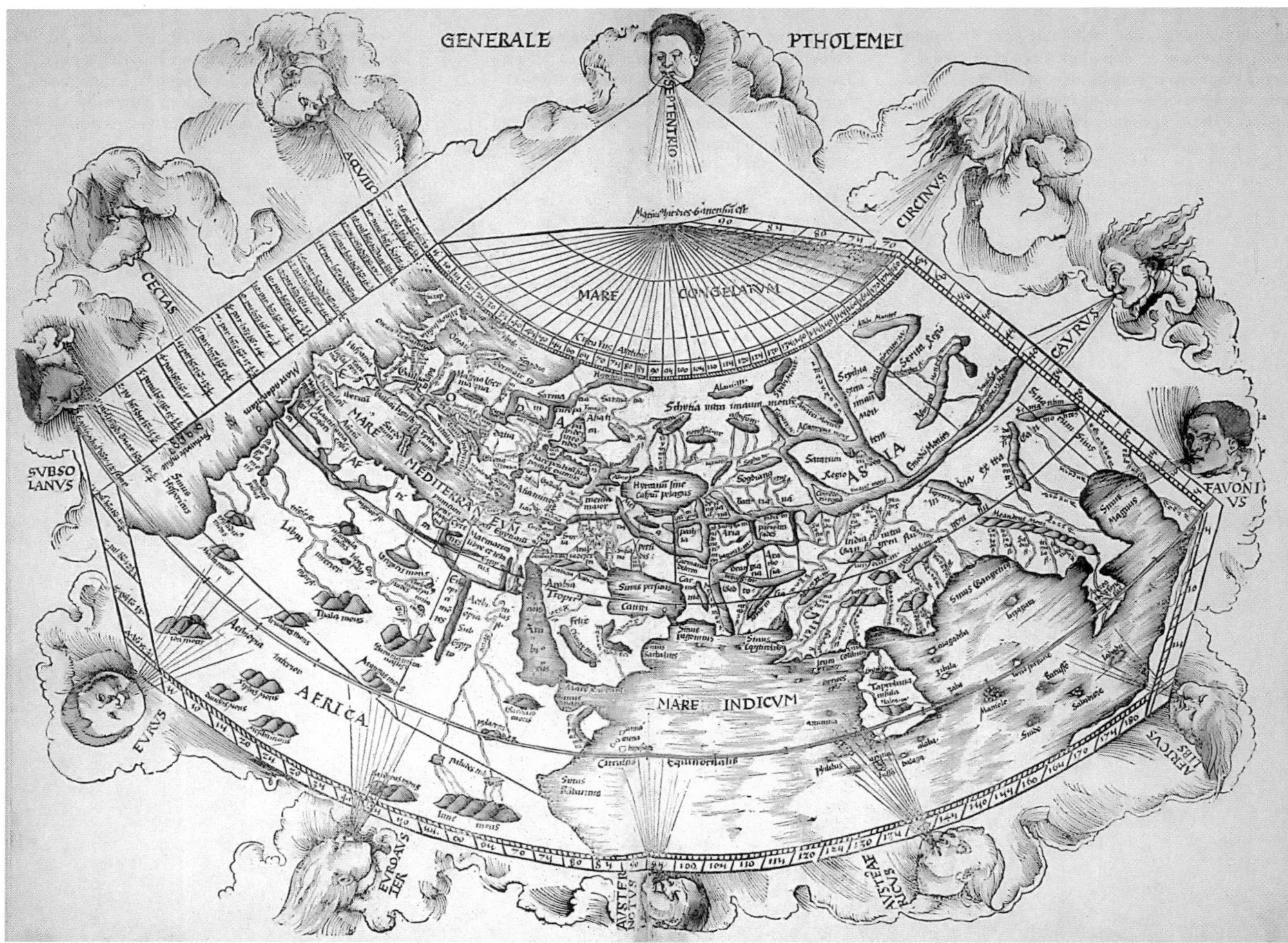

1520

Popularisierung. Gleichzeitig wurde auch das Grafikdesign insgesamt professioneller, nicht nur in den Printmedien, sondern auch im öffentlichen Raum, für den beispielsweise Leitsysteme und Orientierungshilfen entworfen wurden.

Im Wien der 1920er-Jahre verfolgte der Philosoph und Ökonom Otto Neurath den aufklärerischen Anspruch, Arbeiter und Angestellte über gesellschaftliche Zustände zu informieren. Er konzipierte dazu Schautafeln, die statistische Verhältnisse darstellen (S. 80–81). Seine Tafeln benutzen typisierte Bildzeichen und sollten voraussetzungslos und international verständlich sein. Mengenverhältnisse werden durch die variable Anzahl von Bildzeichen angezeigt. Das Design der Tafeln und Bildzeichen erarbeitete Neurath unter anderem mit dem Grafikdesigner Gerd Arntz. Sowohl in ihrer modernen Gestaltung als auch in ihrem aufklärerischen Gestus ist die Bildstatistik von Otto Neurath bis heute eine wichtige Referenz für Designer, die sich mit der Darstellung von Informationen und Daten befassen.

Ein berühmtes Beispiel für die Verbreitung von Infografiken im Alltag ist der Plan der Londoner U-Bahn von Harry Beck. Ausgangspunkt war die Beobachtung, dass der Plan in erster Linie zur Orientierung innerhalb des U-Bahn-Netzes dienen muss und geografische Genauigkeit nicht nötig ist. Frühere Versionen zeigten den realen Linienverlauf in der Stadt und waren daher unübersichtlich. Beck modifizierte den Plan signifikant, als er eine diagrammatische Version entwarf (S. 82). Alle Linien verlaufen gerade oder in einem Winkel von 45 Grad. Der Abstand zwischen allen Stationen ist gleich groß. Der stilisierte Verlauf der Themse ist der einzige visuelle Bezug zur Stadt. Dieser Entwurf bildet bis heute die Vorlage für zahlreiche Verkehrspläne in aller Welt.

Ein weiteres Beispiel für die Verbreitung von Informationsgrafiken ist die zunehmende Verwendung in Zeitungen und Zeitschriften. Während dort Statistiken bisher vor allem in nackten Zahlen dargestellt wurden, entwickelten einige Magazine wie *McCall's* oder *Fortune* eine lebendige Bildsprache für statistische Grafiken (S. 87). Die Popularisierung von Informations- und Datengrafiken griff auch auf die geschäftliche Kommunikation über. Geschäftsberichte und Präsentationen erfordern häufig die grafische Darstellung von Zahlen. Ebenso selbstverständlich wurden im Laufe des 20. Jahrhunderts bildliche Erklärungen für jedwede Art von Instruktionen, wie beispielsweise den Aufbau eines Möbelstücks, die Funktionsweise von Elektrogeräten oder Sicherheitshinweise für das Verhalten in Notfällen.

Verdächtige Daten

Informationsgrafiken sollen erklären, wie die Dinge wirklich sind. Mit dieser wissenschaftlichen Aura fanden sie Eingang in die Massenmedien und die Werbung, und nach wie vor transportieren sie diesen Anspruch von sachlich richtiger Information. Während in früheren Jahrhunderten ausschließlich Wissenschaftler mit Daten- und Informationsgrafiken arbeiteten, sind es im 20. Jahrhundert auch Redakteure und Werbefachleute. Die allgemeine Popularisierung bringt auch eine gewisse Verflachung mit sich, denn häufig lassen sich inhaltliche Schwächen bei der grafischen Umsetzung konstatieren.

Seit den 1950er-Jahren setzten sich mehrere Autoren mit der Frage nach der Korrektheit grafischer Darstellung auseinander, wie etwa John Tukey, Jacques Bertin oder Edward Tufte. 1954 veröffentlichte Darrell Huff das unterhaltsame Buch *How to Lie With Statistics.* Er notierte zahlreiche Fälle aus der Werbung und den Medien, in denen verzerrte statistische Angaben bestimmte Aussagen unterstreichen sollten. An Grafiken kritisierte er Manipulationen wie die mangelnde Auszeichnung von Graphen oder fehlende Vergleichsgrößen, um die dargestellten Zahlen angemessen beurteilen zu können.

Der Politologe und Statistiker Edward Tufte führte diese Beobachtungen systematisch weiter und

ca. 1600

1520

The teachings of the ancient geographer Ptolemy were widely accepted during the Renaissance. He had invented perspective for projection and plotted longitudes and latitudes. This map also includes additional information on major winds.

Die Lehren des antiken Geografen Ptolemäus fanden während der Renaissance eine enorme Verbreitung. Er führte die perspektivische Projektion ein und zeichnete Längen- und Breitengrade ein. Die Karte enthält auch Informationen zu den wichtigsten Winden.

Les enseignements du géographe antique Ptolémée ont joui d'une large reconnaissance pendant la Renaissance. Il a inventé la perspective pour la projection, et a tracé les longitudes et latitudes. Cette carte comprend également des informations sur les principaux vents.

ca. 1600

This Mexican city view comes from the atlas *Cities of the World*, which was published between 1572 and 1617 in Cologne. The atlas collects numerous city views from four continents. Many maps additionally feature figures in local costumes.

Diese mexikanische Stadtansicht stammt aus dem Atlas *Städte der Welt*, erschienen zwischen 1572 und 1617 in Köln. Der Atlas versammelte zahlreiche Stadtansichten von vier Kontinenten. Viele Karten zeigen zudem Figuren in lokaler Tracht.

Cette ville mexicaine est tirée de l'atlas *Villes du Monde*, publié entre 1572 et 1617 à Cologne. Cet atlas rassemble de nombreuses vues de villes des quatre continents. La plupart montrent des personnages vêtus des costumes locaux.

1533

Petrus Apianus was a German mathematician and astronomer. This book title-page features a solar quadrant for measuring the sun's angle of elevation and thus the time of day. The scale is a mesh of intersecting date lines (vertical) and hour lines (horizontal).

Petrus Apianus war ein deutscher Mathematiker und Astronom. Diese Buchtitelseite zeigt einen Sonnenquadranten zur Höhenbestimmung der Sonne und damit der Tageszeit. Die Skala zeigt ein Netz sich schneidender Datumslinien (vertikal) und Stundenlinien (horizontal).

Petrus Apianus était un mathématicien et astronome allemand. Cette page de titre montre un quadrant solaire pour mesurer l'angle d'élévation du soleil, et donc l'heure. Les lignes des dates (à la verticale) et des heures (à l'horizontale) forment une grille.

veröffentlichte eine Reihe von Standardwerken, in denen er Verzerrungen in grafischen Darstellungen kritisierte, so zum Beispiel in seinem zuerst 1982 erschienenen Buch *The Visual Display of Quantitative Information*. Tufte analysierte Grafiken aus großen Tageszeitungen und kritisierte die Tendenz, statistische Diagramme mit Bildmetaphern anzureichern. Während die Grafiker beabsichtigten, die abstrakten Zahlen verständlicher zu gestalten, ließen sie sich häufig von der Bildmetapher mitreißen und kreierten eine visuelle Verzerrung der Daten.

Als Reaktion auf diese Nachlässigkeit entwickelte Tufte einen eigenen, streng minimalistischen Designkodex zur Datenvisualisierung. Er plädierte für vollständige Beschriftungen, zurückhaltendes Design und die Reduktion von überflüssiger „Tinte": Möglichst jeder Punkt und jeder Strich sollte Information enthalten. Alles, was darüber hinausgeht, sei unnötige Dekoration. Für Grafiken, die sich in exzessiver Weise der Verzierung hingeben, prägte er den Begriff *Chartjunk* („Diagrammschrott").

Nicht zuletzt in Reaktion auf diese Analysen wird von den großen westlichen Tageszeitungen eine gewisse Zurückhaltung in der Gestaltung von Infografiken geübt, um die Seriosität der Aussagen nicht zu gefährden. Demgegenüber sind Zeitschriften eher für bildhafte Darstellungen offen. Nigel Holmes, Peter Grundy und John Grimwade gehören zu den Designern, die einen neuen unkonventionellen Stil geprägt haben (*vergleiche ihre Arbeiten in diesem Band*). Untersuchungen haben zudem gezeigt, dass die Verwendung von Bildern dazu beiträgt, dass Leser sich Infografiken länger merken können.[4]

Der Architekt und Designer Richard Saul Wurman beschäftigt sich seit den 1960er-Jahren mit der Frage, wie sich Informationen effektiv vermitteln lassen. Ausgehend von der „Datenexplosion", die die Entwicklung der Computertechnologie mit sich brachte, prägte er den Begriff der Informationsarchitektur. In zahlreichen Publikationen entwickelte er Ansätze, um komplexe Zusammenhänge durch ein strukturiertes Design verständlich zu machen. In seinem Essay erläutert er unter anderem sein System „LATCH" zur Strukturierung von Informationen, das auch in diesem Buch Anwendung findet.

In Wurmans Diktum „Understanding is Power" klingt eine Vorstellung an, die sich auch in der sogenannten Informationspyramide aus *Daten*, *Information*, *Wissen* und *Weisheit* wiederfindet. Dieses Konzept aus der Informationswissenschaft beschreibt die hierarchischen Beziehungen zwischen den einzelnen Ebenen: *Daten* sind die unbearbeiteten Zeichen; *Informationen* sind aufbereitete Angaben, die wiederum beim Leser *Wissen* erzeugen. Die letzte Stufe der *Weisheit* impliziert nicht nur ein vertieftes Verständnis von Zusammenhängen, sondern auch die Möglichkeit, diesem Verständnis entsprechend *zu handeln*. Wer also die Daten verarbeitet hat und von der Information über das Wissen bis zur Weisheit gelangt ist – der weiß, was zu tun ist. Auch in diesem Modell, das bis heute als Bezugspunkt in der Informationsvisualisierung gilt, schwingt die aufklärerische Vorstellung mit, dass Informationen zum Handeln motivieren können.

Data Future

Heute werden die Nutzer selbst zu Autoren. Mit der Verbreitung von Personalcomputern verfügt fast jeder selbst über Werkzeuge zur Erstellung von Grafiken. Bekanntestes Beispiel ist die Präsentationssoftware PowerPoint von Microsoft, die seit den 1990er-Jahren massenhaft verbreitet ist und mit der jeder Büroangestellte seine eigenen Statistiken visualisieren kann. Die Unmenge von schlecht aufbereiteten Charts, die seitdem die Welt überschwemmt hat, hat zweifellos zum allgemein schlechten Ruf von Torten- und Balkendiagrammen beigetragen. Zweifelhafte Berühmtheit erlangte 2003 auch Colin Powells Beweisführung vor der UNO, dass der Irak über Massenvernichtungswaffen verfüge – mit der er entscheidend zum Beginn des Irakkriegs beitrug. Er zeigte unter anderem eine

HOROSCOPION APIANI

GENERALE DIGNOSCENDIS HORIS CVIVSCVMQVE generis aptissimum, neq; id ex Sole tantum interdiu, sed & noctu ex Luna, aliisq; Planetis & Stellis quibusdam fixis, quo per vniuersum Rhomanum imperium atq; adeò vbiuis gentium vti queas, adiuncta ratione, qua vtaris, expeditissima, nunc ab illo primum & inuentum & æditum.

His accedit distantiarum, altitudinum, & profunditatum per idem hoc instrumentum dimetiendarum ratio longè accuratissima & ingeniosa. Similiter in quam altitudinem aqua naturaliter citrà omne artis beneficium, Deinde quanto sublimius scaturigine sua adminiculo artis per cannales deduci posit.

Nocturna quoq; adnexa est obseruatio horaria ex digitis manuum, priori illa quæ superiori anno vnà cũ Quadrante ædita est, tũ promptior tũ expeditior.

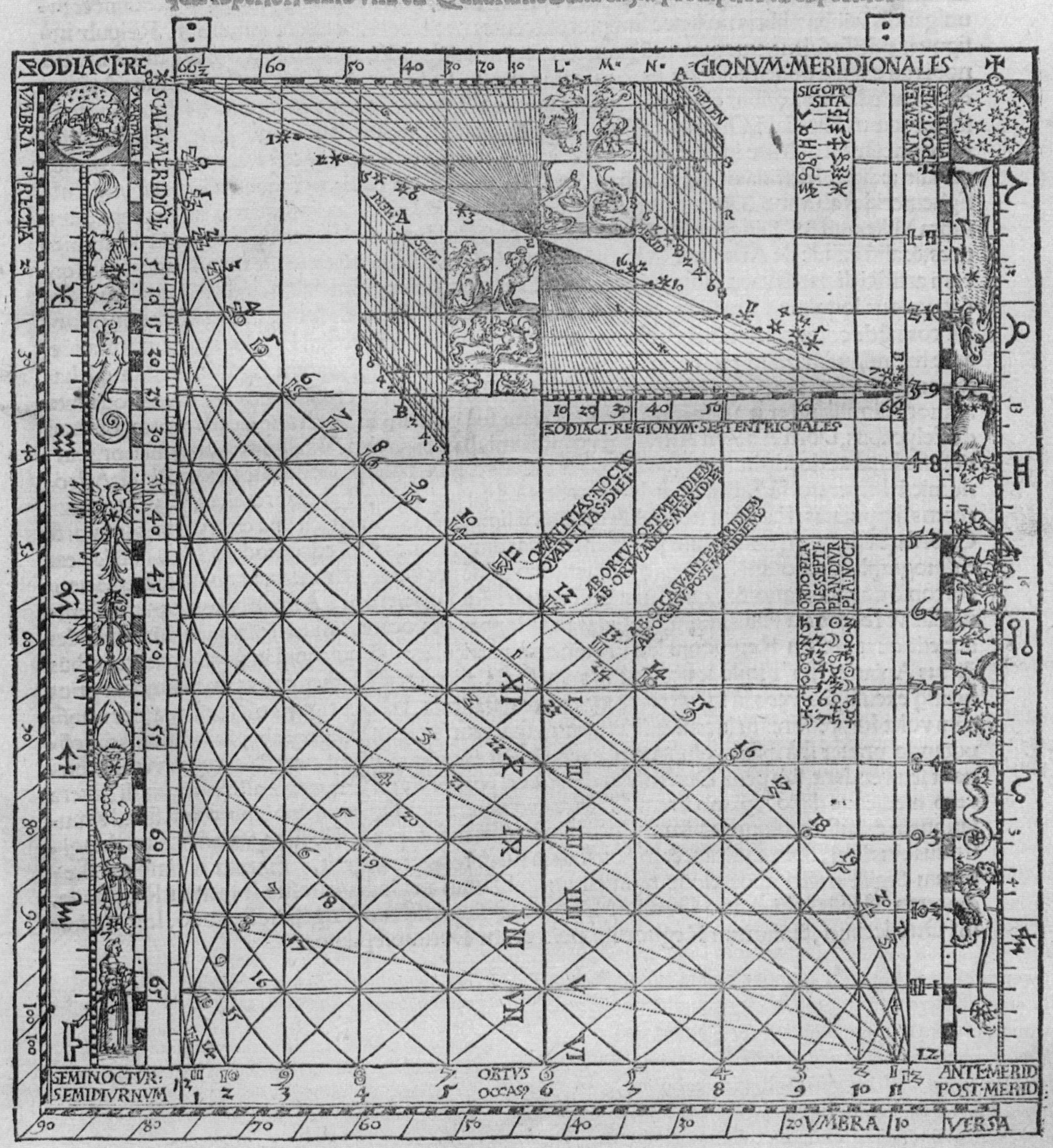

1533

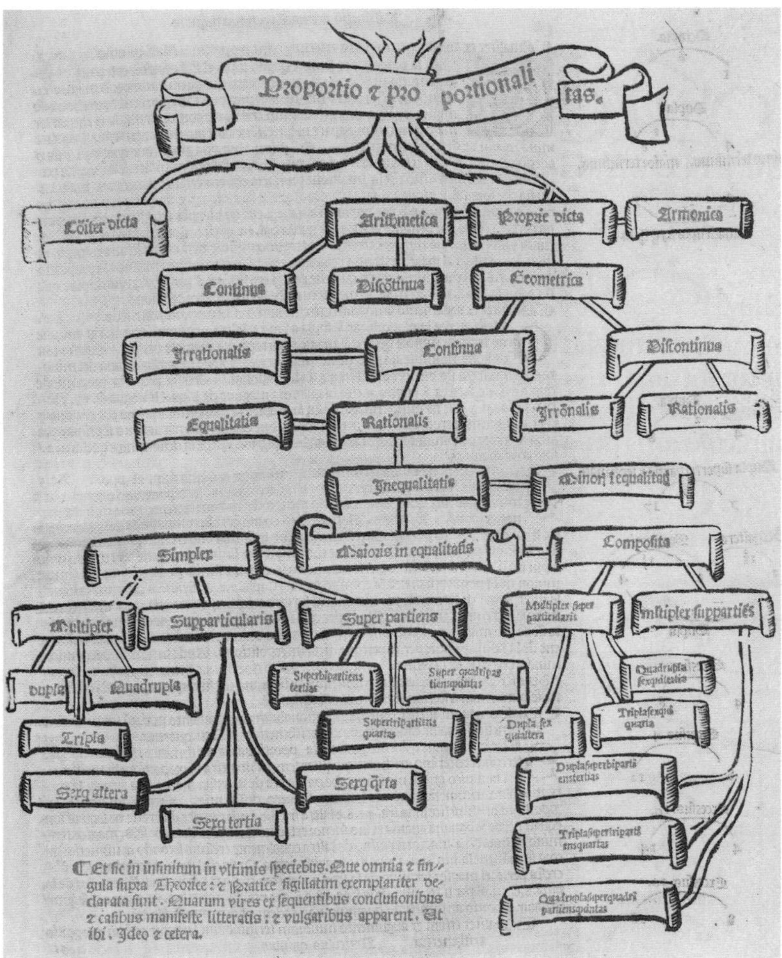

1523

durchschnittlich aufbereitete Präsentation, die Informationsgrafiken und beschriftete Satellitenfotos enthielt.

Gleichzeitig mit der Vielzahl schlecht gestalteter Visualisierungen wächst der Anspruch, der Informationsflut mit einer gewissen Professionalität zu begegnen. Daten sind kein Geheimwissen mehr. Mit der allgemeinen Informationsfreiheit, die inzwischen in vielen Ländern gesetzlich verankert ist, entsteht eine öffentliche Informationskultur. In einer Zeit, in der jedermann von Informationen überrollt wird, ist es nötig, die Daten erstens präzise zu analysieren und zweitens intelligent und ansprechend aufzubereiten. Dafür braucht es eine allgemeine *visual literacy*.

Grafikdesigner reagieren darauf und sind vermehrt daran interessiert, eine visuelle Sprache für Informationen und Daten zu entwickeln. Sie wollen nicht nur sachlich korrekte Grafiken, sondern auch ein gutes Design. Theoretiker untersuchen, wie sich die visuelle Gestaltung auf die kognitive Erfassung von Grafiken auswirkt. Paolo Ciuccarelli etwa vom DensityDesign Research Lab in Mailand spricht sich in seinem Essay für eine bessere Vermittlung wissenschaftlicher Forschung in der Öffentlichkeit aus. Er plädiert dafür, verstärkt narrative Elemente in die abstrakten Grafiken zu integrieren, um das Verständnis zu erhöhen.

Interaktionsdesigner dagegen entwickeln interaktive Datenvisualisierungen, mit denen die Nutzer selbstständig Daten entdecken, vergleichen und kommentieren können. Plattformen wie Many Eyes beispielsweise bieten die Möglichkeit, Daten in verschiedenen Grundmustern zu visualisieren und zu veröffentlichen. Online-Kommentarfunktionen führen dazu, dass die Nutzer die unterschiedlichen Visualisierungen diskutieren und damit auch kontrollieren. Die Interpretation von statistischen Daten wird zu einem gemeinsamen Prozess.

Journalisten wiederum begreifen den Datenreichtum als neue Quelle für eine ausgewogene Berichterstattung. Simon Rogers vom Londoner *Guardian* beschreibt unter dem Stichwort *data journalism*, wie die Verfügbarkeit von Statistiken im Internet die journalistische Praxis in den vergangenen zehn Jahren massiv erweitert hat. In seinem Essay klingt ein Moment von Demokratisierung an – Journalisten können politische Ereignisse differenzierter beurteilen, wenn ihnen alternative Informationsquellen zur Verfügung stehen.

Dieses Buch zeichnet den Aufbruch der vergangenen zehn Jahre anhand von zweihundert Projekten aus verschiedenen Bereichen nach. Wissenschaftler, Journalisten und Designer sind ebenso vertreten wie freie Künstler, die das Genre auf eigene Art interpretieren. Die in dieser Zeit entstandene Kultur der Informationsvisualisierung wird weiter wachsen und sich ausdifferenzieren. Wir erwarten gespannt die nächsten Entwicklungen.

1 Bertin, Jacques: *Graphische Darstellung und die graphische Weiterverarbeitung der Information.* Berlin / New York: Walter de Gruyter, 1982, S. 16.

2 Bertin, Jacques: *Graphische Semiologie. Diagramme, Netze, Karten.* Berlin / New York: Walter de Gruyter, 1974.

3 Robinson, Arthur H.: *Early Thematic Mapping in the History of Cartography.* Chicago and London: Chicago University Press, 1982, S. 54.

4 Bateman, Scott et al.: *Useful Junk? The Effects of Visual Embellishment on Comprehension and Memorability of Charts.* University of Saskatchewan, Department of Computer Science. Paper Presented on CHI, April 2010.

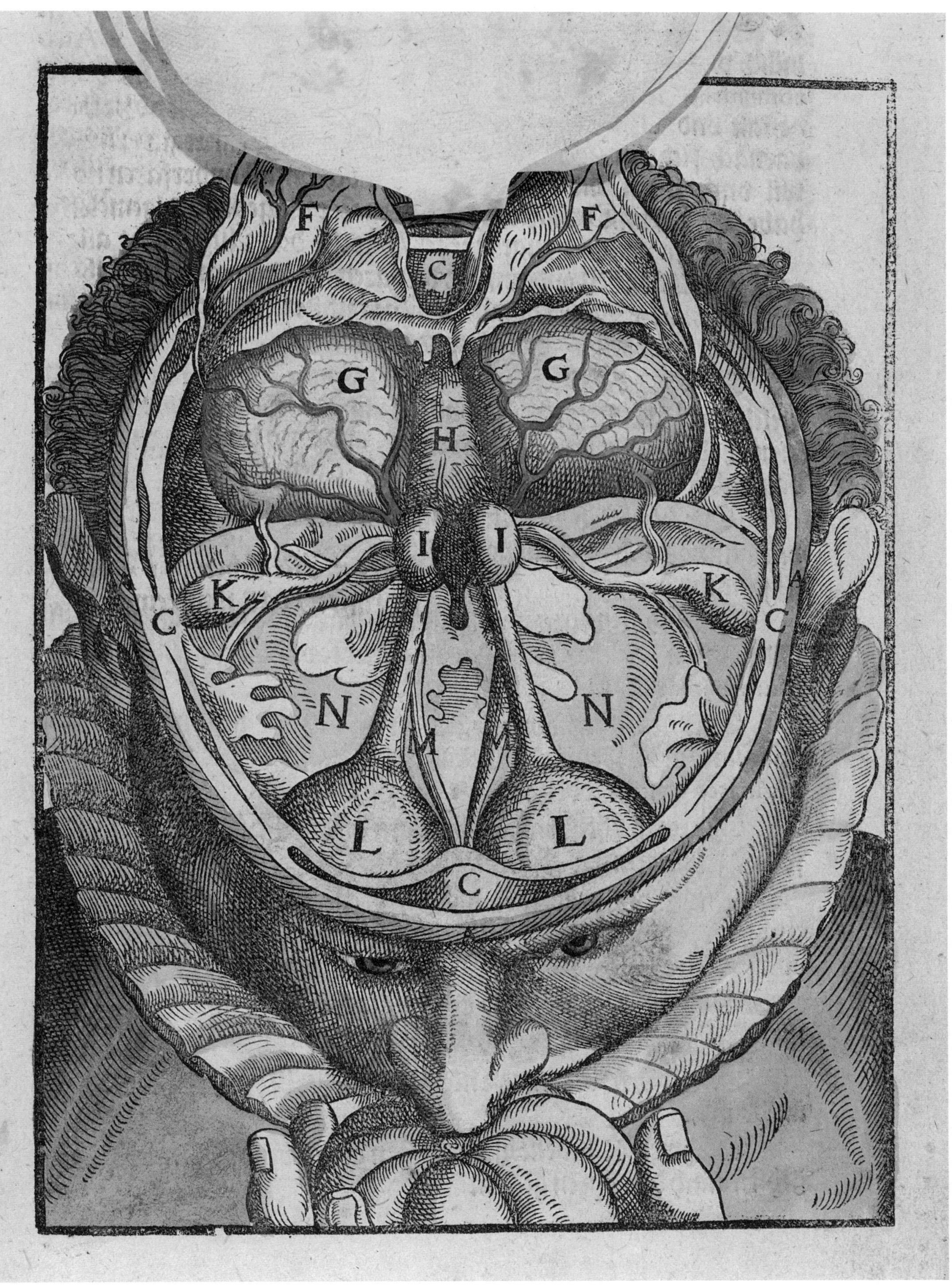

1583

1523

In his book *Summa de Arithmetica*, Franciscan friar Luca Pacioli collected the mathematical knowledge of his time. This table displays his doctrine of proportions and shows different types of proportional relations, particularly in geometry.

In seinem Buch *Summa de Arithmetica* versammelte der Franziskanermönch Luca Pacioli das mathematische Fachwissen seiner Zeit. Diese Tafel zeigt seine Proportionslehre. Aufgeschlüsselt sind verschiedene Arten proportionaler Verhältnisse, vor allem in der Geometrie.

Dans son livre *Summa de Arithmetica*, le moine franciscain Luca Pacioli a rassemblé toutes les connaissances mathématiques de son époque. Ce tableau présente sa doctrine des proportions et montre différents types de relations proportionnelles, particulièrement dans le domaine de la géométrie.

1583

The German physician Georg Bartisch published a book on ophthalmology containing 92 full-page woodcuts. Here, the inner brain is shown. The woodcut contains several overlays to reveal the layers of the brain's anatomy.

Der deutsche Arzt Georg Bartisch veröffentlichte ein Lehrbuch zur Augenheilkunde mit 92 ganzseitigen Holzschnitten. Hier wird das Innere des Gehirns gezeigt. Der Holzschnitt enthält mehrere Papierlagen, um die Anatomie schichtenweise zu enthüllen.

Le médecin allemand Georg Bartish a publié un livre sur l'ophtalmologie qui contient 92 gravures pleine page. Ici, c'est l'intérieur du cerveau qui est montré. La gravure est faite de plusieurs couches superposées pour représenter l'anatomie du cerveau.

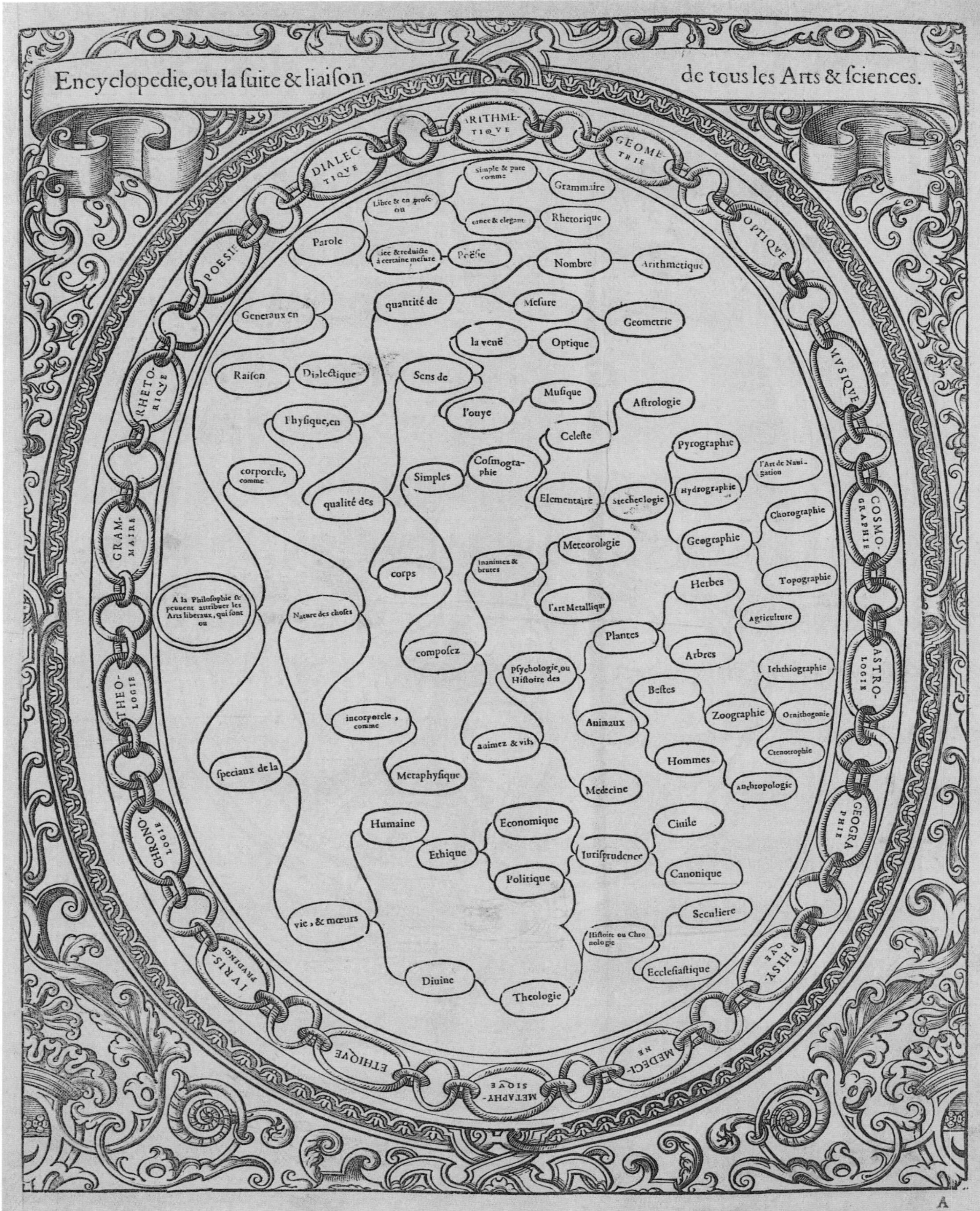

1587

1587

In his book *Tableaux accomplis de tous les arts libéraux*, the French humanist Christophe de Savigny created an encyclopaedic overview of all the sciences of his time. It contains many "organigrams" which show the break-down of all the individual scientific disciplines.

Der französische Humanist Christophe de Savigny schuf in seinem Buch *Tableaux accomplis de tous les arts libéraux* eine enzyklopädische Übersicht aller Wissenschaften seiner Zeit. Das Buch enthält zahlreiche „Organigramme", in denen die wissenschaftlichen Disziplinen einzeln aufgeschlüsselt werden.

Dans son ouvrage *Tableaux accomplis de tous les arts libéraux*, l'humaniste français Christophe de Savigny a créé un aperçu encyclopédique de toutes les sciences de son époque. Il contient de nombreux « organigrammes » qui décomposent toutes les disciplines scientifiques dans le détail.

Introduction

Sandra Rendgen

Les données sont la matière première du moment. Des quantités infinies d'informations inédites sont aujourd'hui accessibles en quelques secondes, quelle que soit la distance. Toutefois, les données brutes ont en soi une valeur négligeable, car elles doivent être filtrées et évaluées. C'est pourquoi la gestion professionnelle des données et des informations s'annonce comme un outil culturel clé pour les prochaines décennies.

La représentation graphique des données et des informations existe depuis longtemps. Les journaux publient régulièrement des statistiques sous forme de graphiques, les magazines ont recours à des infographies pour tout expliquer, des phénomènes naturels aux technologies de pointe. Dans le monde des affaires, les données économiques sont communiquées sous forme de diagrammes. Les manuels d'utilisation et les instructions de sécurité aussi s'appuient souvent sur des schémas.

Pendant longtemps, le genre est passé pratiquement inaperçu, même si les infographies ont été quasiment omniprésentes pendant des décennies. Mais peu étaient le résultat d'une vraie réflexion. Contrairement à d'autres branches du graphisme, dans l'infographie peu de précurseurs ont marqué des styles particuliers. En outre, il existe toujours des tensions entre le design graphique et la représentation précise des données. Les infographies sont censées convertir des problèmes complexes en images faciles à comprendre, mais le doute plane toujours: les graphismes «esthétiques» peuvent cacher des mensonges.

Depuis le début du millénaire, la visualisation des données et des informations connaît un regain d'intérêt dans divers domaines, dont le journalisme, la science, l'art et le design. La nouvelle tendance s'est même fait une place dans la culture pop: le duo norvégien Röyksopp a lancé en 2002 un clip vidéo uniquement composé d'infographies animées (p.4). La vidéo présente la vie d'une jeune femme à Londres et des moments de la journée sous forme d'infographies.

Cet intérêt accru tient à plusieurs raisons. De plus en plus de données statistiques sont disponibles gratuitement, et leur traitement est en demande croissante. Il faut des interfaces interactives et visuelles pour accéder aux archives numériques, et l'arrivée des appareils numériques change nos habitudes de lecture. La communication se fait à l'aide de textes généralement plus courts et assortis de graphiques et d'images, ce qui laisse une place de choix aux infographies.

Cet ouvrage aborde la récente évolution des infographies et de la visualisation des données. Les auteurs des essais analysent des thèmes qui revêtent une importance particulière, comme le but de la visualisation des données ou le traitement professionnel de l'information. Les images historiques qui accompagnent l'introduction et les essais montrent quant à eux qu'il existe une longue tradition dans la représentation des connaissances à l'aide de diagrammes et de graphiques.

Les infographies sont des hybrides et sont donc difficiles à définir. Le texte, les images et les formes géométriques s'entrecroisent inextricablement pour donner des entités. Les données ne dictent pas automatiquement le résultat, un développement est nécessaire. Le cartographe et théoricien français Jacques Bertin l'explique: «Une représentation graphique n'est pas un simple dessin, elle implique souvent une grande responsabilité au moment de décider comment procéder. Il ne suffit pas de ‹dessiner› une représentation graphique dans une forme solide. Il faut la construire et l'organiser jusqu'à ce que toutes les relations entre les données soient révélées.»[1]

En 1967, Bertin a écrit un essai sur les moyens graphiques disponibles pour représenter des données. En plus des deux dimensions de la surface (du papier) sur laquelle peuvent être dessinés des points, des lignes et des plans, six autres éléments permettent de représenter visuellement des données: la taille, la valeur, la texture, la couleur, l'orientation et la forme. Chaque construction visuelle reprend ce vocabulaire de base, que des intitulés viennent compléter[2].

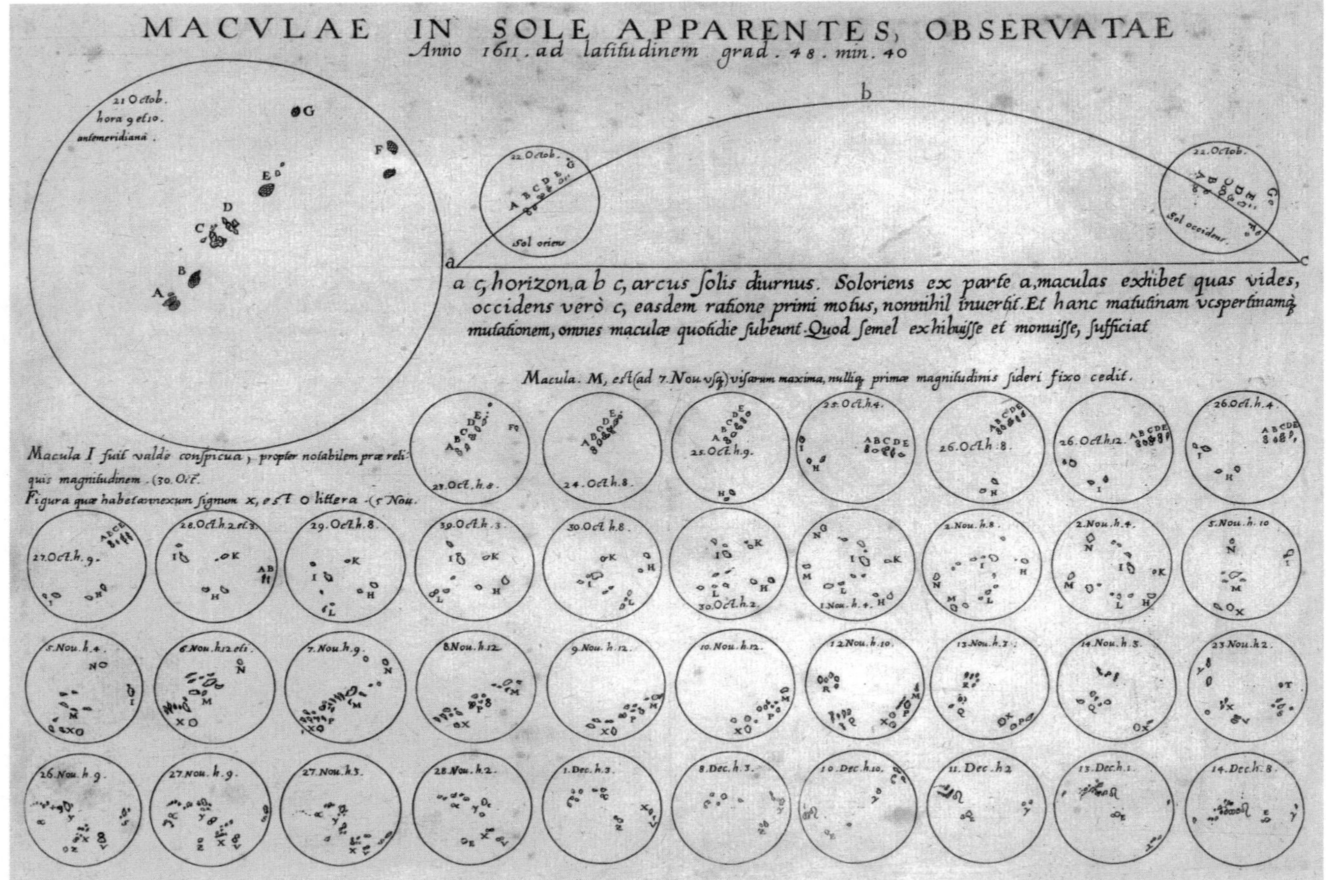

1613

Diverses tendances s'apprécient dans le domaine hybride des infographies et de la visualisation de données, mais elles ne peuvent pas être organisées en groupes bien distincts. D'une part, la *visualisation* est le processus de conversion visuelle. D'autre part, le terme *visualisation* distingue les représentations dynamiques et interactives des *graphiques* statiques. Distinction est aussi faite entre *informations qualitatives* et *données quantitatives*. Les données sont numériques et leur représentation habituelle est un diagramme abstrait dépourvu d'images figuratives. À l'inverse, les infographies affichent des relations qualitatives: par exemple, comment fonctionne une plate-forme pétrolière. Les schémas sont dans ce contexte souvent utilisés.

La grande différence entre les travaux tient aussi à l'objectif de chacun. Beaucoup s'adressent au grand public et visent à fournir des explications claires. D'autres représentations servent pour leur part d'outils scientifiques pour aider l'analyse. Dans ce cas, la difficulté principale est de reconnaître des schémas au sein des données et d'organiser les informations de façon claire. Les diagrammes, croquis et cartes remplissent ces fonctions depuis longtemps, comme le montrent les exemples historiques suivants.

Le monde lisible

Les cartes, par exemple, offrent une vue d'ensemble. Elles permettent de reconnaître et d'organiser le monde. Au Moyen-Âge, la cartographie ne faisait pas la distinction entre les éléments géographiques à la surface de la Terre et les aspects historiques et religieux du paysage, comme c'est maintenant le cas. La mappemonde d'Ebstorf, établie autour de 1300 dans le nord de l'Allemagne, montre ainsi l'ensemble du monde connu sur une surface de 3,5 mètres de diamètre (p. 15). Alignée à l'est, cette carte est centrée sur Jérusalem et repose sur la division tripartite médiévale du monde entre l'Europe (en bas à gauche), l'Afrique (en bas à droite) et l'Asie (en haut), l'Inde se trouvant dans la partie supérieure, au milieu.

Le monde est superposé à la figure du Christ (visage, mains et pieds) et le Jardin d'Éden est représenté à gauche de sa tête. En bas à droite, la mer Méditerranée est placée à la verticale. De nombreux animaux, bâtiments et scènes enrichissent l'organisation géographique avec des informations sur les religions et les cultures, placées stratégiquement. La carte est une présentation visuelle, une organisation de connaissances dans une même image.

Les atlas anatomiques donnent aussi une vue d'ensemble que l'œil ne peut pas capter (p. 16). Les premières œuvres sur l'anatomie avaient déjà eu recours à des schémas du corps humain pour illustrer des connaissances médicales. Les figures abstraites montrent la position et la fonction de différents organes. Plusieurs artistes de la Renaissance ont revisité le croquis: Léonard de Vinci (p. 18) et Albrecht Dürer ont par exemple étudié les proportions humaines pour offrir des représentations réalistes du corps.

Le rôle de la structure du cosmos a occupé une place aussi centrale que les propriétés anatomiques dans la pensée de la fin de la Renaissance. De nombreux scientifiques se sont servis de diagrammes pour expliquer les théories cosmologiques. Le philosophe et physicien anglais Robert Fludd a par exemple élaboré en 1618 un diagramme représentant l'univers comme la corde tendue (par la main de Dieu) d'un instrument à une seule corde (p. 32). Les notes de musique A, B, C, D, E, F et G sont inscrites sur le manche de l'instrument, tout comme, de bas en haut, les quatre éléments et les sept corps célestes: la Lune, Mercure, Vénus, le Soleil, Mars, Jupiter et Saturne.

La réalité cosmique s'arrête à ce niveau, surmontée par les régions surnaturelles. Les cercles en pointillés représentent les proportions harmoniques du cosmos. Ce schéma reflète la croyance d'un univers organisé de façon linéaire avec des proportions numériques, et une conception de la musique comme image de l'ordre cosmique. Les diagrammes convenaient à l'illustration de telles théories, car les scientifiques pouvaient les

In the course of his research, the Italian scientist Galileo Galilei found various proofs for heliocentrism. One of them was the discovery and description of sun spots which he documented in a series of drawings.

Im Laufe seiner Forschungen fand der italienische Wissenschaftler Galileo Galilei viele Belege für das heliozentrische Weltbild. Dazu gehörte auch seine Entdeckung und Beschreibung der Sonnenflecken, die er in einer Serie von Zeichnungen dokumentierte.

Au cours de ses recherches, le scientifique italien Galileo Galilei a trouvé plusieurs preuves de l'héliocentrisme. L'une d'elles vient de la découverte et de la description des taches solaires, documentées dans une série de dessins.

utiliser pour montrer les systèmes de références complexes détectés dans le cosmos.

Parallèlement au développement de la cartographie, qui depuis le début de l'ère moderne était en plein âge d'or, le XVIIe siècle a connu plusieurs tentatives de sophistication des cartes géographiques en leur ajoutant d'autres informations. En 1741 par exemple, le linguiste allemand Gottfried Hensel a conçu quatre cartes montrant les continents connus à l'époque et les langues qui y étaient parlées (p. 47). Les différentes zones sont annotées dans les caractères de l'alphabet correspondant et complétées de tableaux avec l'ensemble des caractères. Les cartes sont conçues pour offrir le tableau complet de tous les signes linguistiques dans le monde, et donc établir une théorie universelle sur le langage humain. Les œuvres d'Hensel font partie des premiers exemples d'utilisation de la couleur pour distinguer des zones géographiques par thème[3].

Schémas statistiques

Les hommes politiques ont besoin d'aide pour prendre des décisions. Le développement de la société moderne à la fin du XVIIIe siècle s'est accompagné d'un besoin croissant de fonder les décisions politiques sur des données fiables. Les statistiques, la science du traitement systématique des données démographiques et économiques, ont vu le jour pour cette raison. Contrairement à aujourd'hui, ces chiffres n'étaient alors accessibles que pour un cercle réduit de fonctionnaires et de politiciens. Pourtant, même ces experts trouvaient les statistiques abstraites et guère descriptives. Il n'est pas étonnant que les représentations graphiques aient rapidement gagné du terrain.

La façon la plus simple de présenter des données était de recourir à des tableaux; en 1786 toutefois, l'ingénieur et économiste écossais William Playfair a mis au point des diagrammes pour illustrer des données économiques (p. 52). Il a représenté les importations et les exportations de l'Angleterre dans un graphique chronologique et montré la balance du commerce extérieur du pays sous forme de diagrammes à barres. En 1820, August Crome a élaboré une présentation graphique complète des données statistiques pour le roi de Prusse (p. 54). Le grand tableau comparait tous les états allemands à partir d'une série de données, dont la zone, les revenus, le budget et les effectifs militaires.

Autre innovation graphique, la carte figurative a été conçue par l'ingénieur français Charles Joseph Minard. Les cartes figuratives sont un mélange de carte et d'organigramme, et permettent de visualiser le mouvement d'objets. Minard a créé des dizaines de cartes du genre au cours de sa vie professionnelle. En 1869, il a appliqué ce principe à un sujet historique et créé l'une des infographies les plus célèbres: une carte de la catastrophique campagne de Russie de Napoléon (p. 67). Napoléon est en effet parti pour la Russie avec 422 000 soldats et en est revenu avec seulement 10 000. La carte met en rapport de nombreuses variables, y compris la direction de l'armée, sa taille décroissante, des dates et un diagramme des températures.

Un autre format a été mis au point par l'infirmière et statisticienne anglaise Florence Nightingale. Après ses expériences déchirantes lors de la guerre de Crimée, au cours de laquelle de nombreux soldats ont perdu la vie à cause de la qualité déplorable des soins, elle a décrit la mortalité des combattants sur une période de deux ans dans un diagramme polaire (p. 66). La grande majorité des soldats, en bleu, sont morts à la suite d'infections qui auraient pu être évitées. Malgré des critiques sur sa représentation en partie disproportionnée, ce diagramme offre un bon exemple de l'expressivité visuelle des graphiques statistiques.

Le public bien informé

La large diffusion des journaux et des magazines date du siècle dernier. Les nouvelles techniques d'impression ont permis la distribution massive de produits imprimés et facilité l'insertion d'images dans les textes. En parallèle, la représentation visuelle des

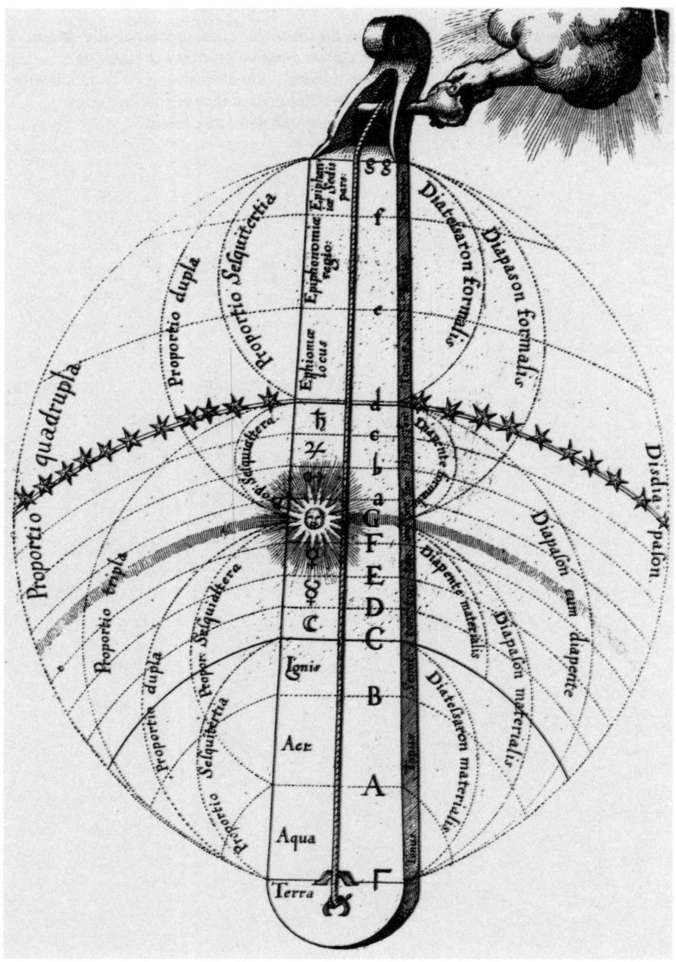

1618

informations et données s'est irrépressiblement popularisée. Le design graphique a alors pris une tournure en général plus professionnelle, non seulement dans la presse écrite, mais aussi dans les espaces publics pour lesquels ont été inventés des systèmes de guidage et des aides à l'orientation.

Dans la Vienne des années 1920, le philosophe et économiste Otto Neurath a créé des affiches décrivant des relations statistiques (p. 80–81) pour informer les travailleurs sur les conditions sociales. Ses affiches utilisaient des pictogrammes standardisés et étaient conçues pour être comprises de tous, n'importe où dans le monde. Les proportions sont indiquées en changeant le nombre de pictogrammes. Le graphiste Gerd Arntz a été l'un des collaborateurs de Neurath sur la conception des affiches et des pictogrammes. Grâce à leur style moderne et à leur aspect évolutif, les statistiques picturales d'Otto Neurath sont restées une référence importante pour les designers intéressés par la représentation des informations et des données.

Le plan du métro de Londres conçu par Harry Beck est un exemple célèbre de la prolifération des infographies dans la vie quotidienne. Le point de départ a été une prise de conscience: la fonction première du plan étant d'aider les gens à s'orienter dans le réseau de métro, il n'avait pas à être précis en termes géographiques. Les versions antérieures représentaient le parcours réel des lignes dans la ville, ce qui les rendait visuellement confuses. Beck a complètement modifié le plan en créant une version schématique (p. 82). Toutes les lignes sont parallèles aux bords de la page ou à un angle de 45 degrés. La distance séparant les stations est toujours la même, et la Tamise stylisée est l'unique référence visuelle de la ville. À ce jour, cette conception est toujours un modèle dont s'inspirent de nombreux plans de transports publics dans le monde.

Autre exemple de cette propagation des infographies: leur présence croissante dans les journaux et les magazines. Les revues économiques étaient par le passé surtout noircies de numéros et de statistiques en noir et blanc, mais certains magazines comme *McCall's* ou *Fortune* ont introduit un langage visuel vivant pour les graphiques (p. 87). La popularisation des représentations graphiques des informations et données a également gagné le terrain de la communication commerciale. Les rapports d'activité et les présentations doivent souvent montrer des chiffres sous forme graphique. De la même façon, au cours du XXe siècle, nous nous sommes habitués à toutes sortes d'instructions picturales: modes d'emploi pour assembler un meuble, pour utiliser des appareils électroménagers, pour agir en cas de danger, etc.

Données suspectes

Les infographies visent à expliquer la vraie nature des choses. Grâce à leur aura scientifique, les médias et la publicité les ont adoptées pour présenter des informations de façon précise et objective. Alors qu'aux siècles précédents seuls les scientifiques manipulaient des graphiques de données, ils ont été rejoints au XXe siècle par les éditeurs et les professionnels de la publicité. La popularisation de masse s'est cependant accompagnée d'une certaine détérioration, et le contenu des représentations graphiques est souvent pauvre.

Depuis les années 1950, plusieurs auteurs, dont John Tukey, Jacques Bertin et Edward Tufte, s'intéressent à la précision des représentations graphiques. En 1954, Darrell Huff a publié le réjouissant *How to Lie with Statistics*. Il a relevé dans la publicité et la presse plusieurs cas montrant que des informations statistiques faussées avaient servi à étayer certaines affirmations. Sa critique des représentations graphiques portait notamment sur des graphiques mal expliqués et sur des données comparatives insuffisantes pour permettre d'évaluer correctement les chiffres.

Le scientifique et statisticien politique Edward Tufte a développé ces observations méthodiquement et publié une série de travaux dans lesquels il critiquait les déformations des représentations gra-

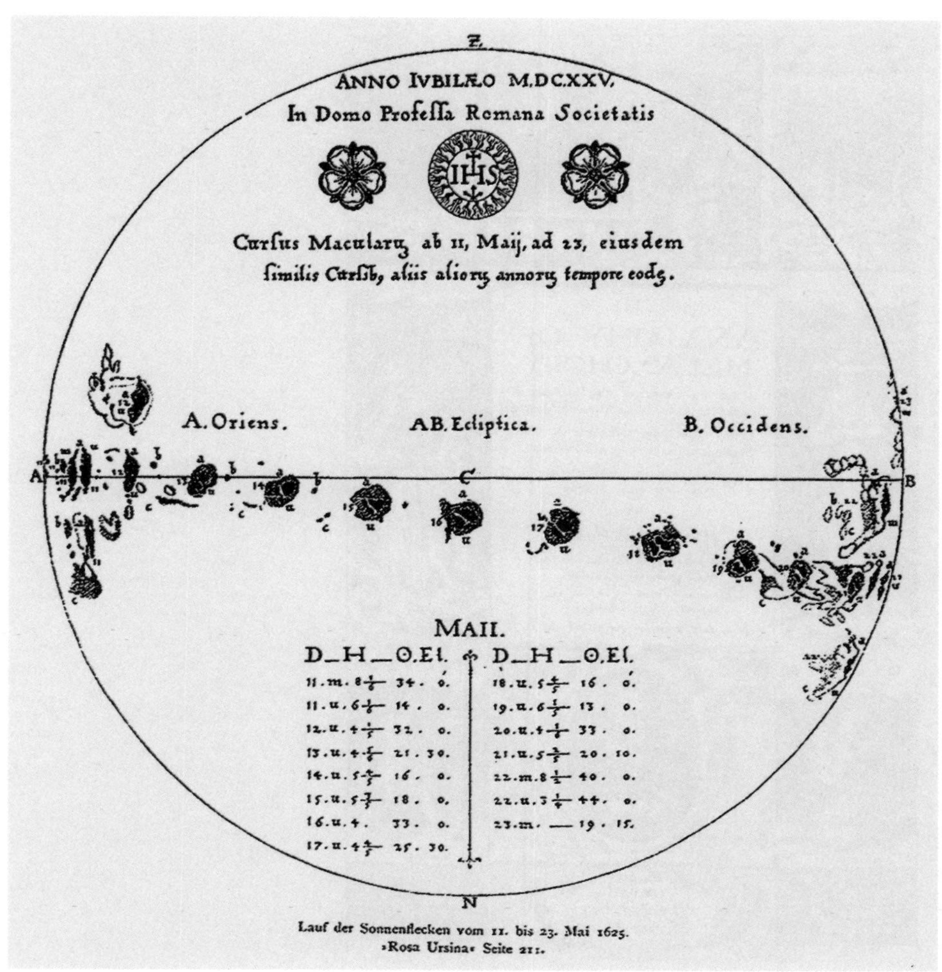

1626

phiques, par exemple dans son ouvrage *The Visual Display of Quantitative Information*, publié pour la première fois en 1982. Tufte a analysé les graphiques publiés dans les principaux quotidiens et critiqué la tendance à assortir les diagrammes statistiques de métaphores imagées. Même si les graphistes tentaient de simplifier la lecture de chiffres abstraits, ils se laissaient souvent emporter par la métaphore et créaient des distorsions visuelles des données.

Tufte a élaboré son propre code très minimaliste pour la visualisation des données. Il exhorte les graphistes à définir correctement tous les éléments graphiques, à faire preuve de sobriété, et à limiter « l'encre » superflue. Chaque point et chaque ligne doivent être significatifs. Le reste n'était à ses yeux que fioritures, au point de qualifier les graphiques trop chargés de *déchets graphiques*.

Ces analyses ont été décisives pour encourager les principaux journaux occidentaux à limiter dans une certaine mesure le design de leurs infographies et ne pas compromettre le sérieux de leurs déclarations. À l'inverse, les magazines ont tendance à laisser plus de marge aux représentations picturales. Nigel Holmes, Peter Grundy et John Grimwade font partie des concepteurs qui ont créé un nouveau style non conventionnel (comparez leurs travaux dans cet ouvrage). Par ailleurs, des études ont montré que le recours aux images aide les lecteurs à mémoriser plus longtemps les infographies[4].

L'architecte et designer Richard Saul Wurman étudie la transmission efficace des informations depuis les années 1960. Partant de « l'explosion de données » survenue avec le développement des technologies informatiques, il a inventé le terme « architecture de l'information ». Dans de nombreuses publications, il a expliqué les moyens de présenter clairement des relations complexes à l'aide d'un design structuré. Dans un essai publié dans cet ouvrage, il expose son système de structuration de l'information, qu'il a baptisé LATCH.

La maxime de Wurman « Comprendre, c'est pouvoir » exprime une idée déjà présente dans la pyramide de l'information, composée de *données*, *informations*, *savoir* et *sagesse*. Ce concept vient des sciences de l'information : les *données* sont les symboles non traités, les *informations* les données traitées, apportant du *savoir* au lecteur. Le dernier niveau de *sagesse* implique une compréhension poussée, ainsi que la possibilité d'*agir* conformément à cette compréhension. Aussi, la personne ayant traité les données et étant parvenue à la sagesse par le biais d'informations et de savoir sait ce qu'elle doit faire. Ce modèle, toujours considéré comme une référence en matière de visualisation des informations, suggère que l'information peut être moteur d'action.

1618

In his book *De musica mundana*, the English scientist Robert Fludd described the ordering principle of the universe based on musical harmonies. Musical notes as well as the four elements and seven celestial bodies are inscribed on the neck of the instrument.

In seinem Buch *De musica mundana* beschreibt der englische Wissenschaftler Robert Fludd die Ordnung des Universums anhand musikalischer Harmonien. Auf dem Hals des Instruments sind die musikalischen Töne eingeschrieben sowie die vier Elemente und sieben Himmelskörper.

Dans son ouvrage *De Musica Mundana*, le scientifique anglais Robert Fludd a décrit le principe d'ordonnancement de l'univers à partir des harmonies musicales. Les notes de musique, les quatre éléments et sept corps célestes sont inscrits sur le manche de l'instrument.

1626

Parallel to his contemporary Galileo, the German Christoph Scheiner also worked on exploring the nature of sun spots. In his book *Rosa Ursina sive Sol* he described his observations and drew the course of the sun spots over the period of one year.

Wie sein Zeitgenosse Galileo befasste sich auch der Deutsche Christoph Scheiner mit der Erforschung der Sonnenflecken. In dem Buch *Rosa Ursina sive Sol* beschrieb er seine Beobachtungen und zeichnete die Bahn der Sonnenflecken über den Verlauf eines Jahres.

Parallèlement à son contemporain Galilée, l'Allemand Christoph Scheiner a également exploré la nature des taches solaires. Dans son livre *Rosa Ursina sive Sol*, il décrit ses observations et dessine le parcours des taches solaire sur une période d'un an.

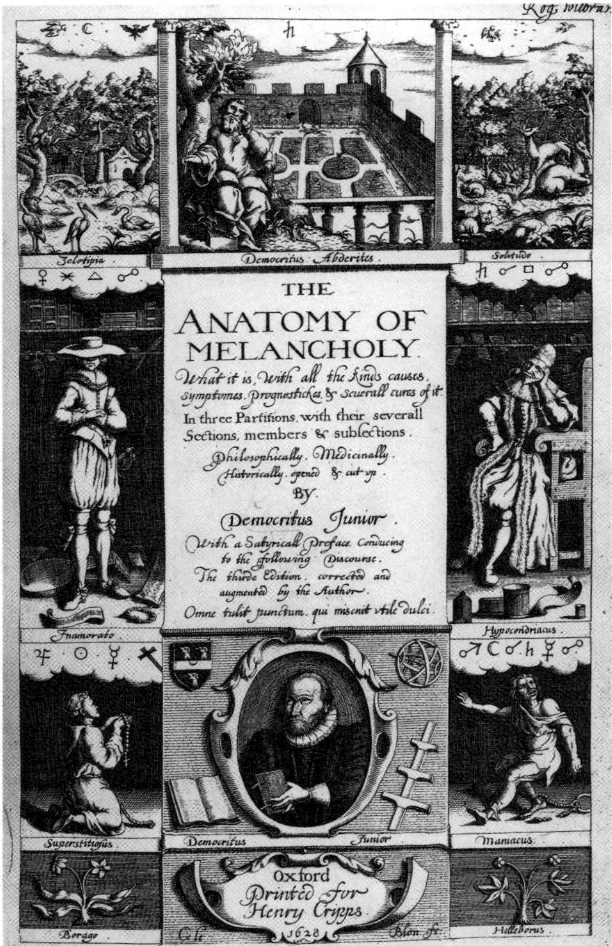
THE
ANATOMY OF
MELANCHOLY.
What it is, With all the Kinds causes, Symptomes, Prognostickes, & Severall cures of it.
In three Partitions, with their severall
Sections, members & subsections.
Philosophically, Medicinally,
Historically, opened & cut up.
BY
Democritus Junior.
With a Satyricall Preface, Conducing
to the following Discourse.
The thirde Edition, corrected and
augmented by the Author.
Omne tulit punctum, qui miscuit utile dulci.

1628

Le futur des données

Aujourd'hui, les utilisateurs sont eux-mêmes auteurs. La propagation des PC a fourni à tout le monde les outils graphiques nécessaires. Le meilleur exemple est le cas du logiciel PowerPoint de Microsoft, distribué à grande échelle et que n'importe quel employé de bureau peut utiliser pour visualiser ses propres statistiques. Le nombre considérable de graphiques mal conçus qui se sont depuis répandus n'a fait qu'alimenter la mauvaise réputation des diagrammes à secteurs et à barres. En 2003, Colin Powell a remporté à l'ONU une notoriété douteuse avec ses preuves d'existence d'armes de destruction massive, facteur déterminant dans le déclenchement de la guerre en Irak. Il a entre autres offert une présentation mal préparée, à base de graphiques et de photos satellite annotées.

La pléthore de visualisations mal conçues coïncide avec le besoin croissant de gérer le flux d'informations avec un certain degré de professionnalisme. Les données ne sont plus confidentielles. La liberté d'information, désormais légalement ancrée dans la plupart des pays, apporte une culture publique de l'information. Abreuvés d'informations, nous devons soumettre les données à une analyse précise, avant de les préparer de façon intelligente et attrayante, ce qui demande des *compétences visuelles*.

À cela, les graphistes répondent par un intérêt accru à élaborer un langage visuel pour les informations et les données. Ils ne veulent pas que les représentations graphiques se bornent à être simplement exactes, elles doivent aussi afficher un design de qualité. Les théoriciens réfléchissent à l'influence du design visuel sur la compréhension cognitive des représentations graphiques. Par exemple, Paolo Ciuccarelli, du DensityDesign Research Lab à Milan, encourage dans son essai publié dans ces pages à améliorer la communication de la recherche scientifique. Il prône l'intégration d'éléments narratifs aux graphiques abstraits pour faciliter la compréhension.

Les concepteurs d'interaction créent toutefois des visualisations interactives de données pour que les utilisateurs puissent découvrir, comparer et commenter ces données. Des plateformes comme Many Eyes, par exemple, permettent de visualiser et de publier des données dans différents modèles de base. Grâce aux fonctions de commentaires en ligne, les utilisateurs discutent et donc contrôlent les différentes visualisations. L'interprétation des données statistiques devient un processus coopératif.

Les journalistes voient quant à eux la richesse des données comme une nouvelle source pour équilibrer leurs recherches. Simon Rogers, du *Guardian* à Londres, qualifie de *journalisme de données* cette pratique journalistique qui a connu une forte croissance au cours des 10 dernières années grâce à la disponibilité de statistiques sur Internet. Son essai évoque un moment de démocratisation: les journalistes peuvent évaluer des événements politiques de façon plus nuancée quand ils disposent de plusieurs sources d'informations.

Cet ouvrage présente l'évolution des infographies au cours de la dernière décennie, à partir de 200 projets issus de domaines très variés. Scientifiques, journalistes et concepteurs y sont représentés, ainsi que des artistes freelance qui ont leur vision personnelle du genre. La culture de la visualisation des informations qui est née ne cessera de grandir et de se différencier. Nous attendons avec impatience les développements à venir.

1 Bertin, Jacques: *La graphique et le traitement graphique de l'information*. Paris: Flammarion, 1977.
2 Bertin, Jacques: *Sémiologie Graphique. Les diagrammes, les réseaux, les cartes*. Paris: La Haye, Mouton, Gauthier-Villars, 1967.
3 Robinson, Arthur H.: *Early Thematic Mapping in the History of Cartography*. Chicago and London: Chicago University Press, 1982, p. 54.
4 Bateman, Scott et al.: *Useful Junk? The Effects of Visual Embellishment on Comprehension and Memorability of Charts*. Université de Saskatchewan, avril 2010.

1636

1628

In *The Anatomy of Melancholy*, Robert Burton collected all the knowledge of his time on the subject of depression. The emblems in the frontispiece symbolise various aspects of melancholy, like hypochondria, superstition or madness.

In *The Anatomy of Melancholy* trug der Wissenschaftler Robert Burton alles zusammen, was seinerzeit über Depressionen bekannt war. Die Embleme des Frontispizes symbolisieren verschiedene Aspekte der Melancholie, wie etwa Hypochondrie, Aberglauben oder Wahnsinn.

Dans *The Anatomy of Melancholy*, Robert Burton a rassemblé toutes les connaissances de son époque sur la dépression. Les emblèmes du frontispice symbolisent différents aspects de la mélancolie, comme l'hypocondrie, la superstition ou la folie.

1636

Musical theory was one of the research fields of the French monk Marin Mersenne. In his book *Harmonicorum Libri XII*, he analysed the nature of sound. The work contains numerous diagrams, amongst others about the tuning of various instruments.

Der französische Mönch Marin Mersenne beschäftigte sich unter anderem mit Musiktheorie. In seinem Buch *Harmonicorum Libri XII* untersuchte er die Natur des Klangs. Das Werk enthält zahlreiche Diagramme, unter anderem zur Stimmung verschiedener Instrumente.

La théorie musicale était l'un des domaines de recherche du moine français Marin Mersenne. Dans son livre *Harmonicorum Libri XII*, il a analysé la nature du son. Cet ouvrage contient de nombreux diagrammes, entre autres sur l'accordage de différents instruments.

1644

1644

The English physician John Bulwer published a treatise on gestures, which he considered a universal expression of human reason. The graphics each show one example and label it with what it expresses, like remorse, shame or confidence.

Der englische Arzt John Bulwer veröffentlichte eine Untersuchung zur Gestik, die er als universellen Ausdruck des Verstandes betrachtete. Die Grafiken zeigen jeweils eine Geste und eine Beschreibung dessen, was sie ausdrückt, wie etwa Reue, Scham oder Vertrauen.

Le médecin anglais John Bulwer a publié un traité sur les gestes, qu'il considérait comme une expression universelle de la raison humaine. Les images montrent chacune un exemple, et indiquent ce que le geste exprime, comme le remords, la honte ou la confiance.

Richard Saul Wurman 37—56

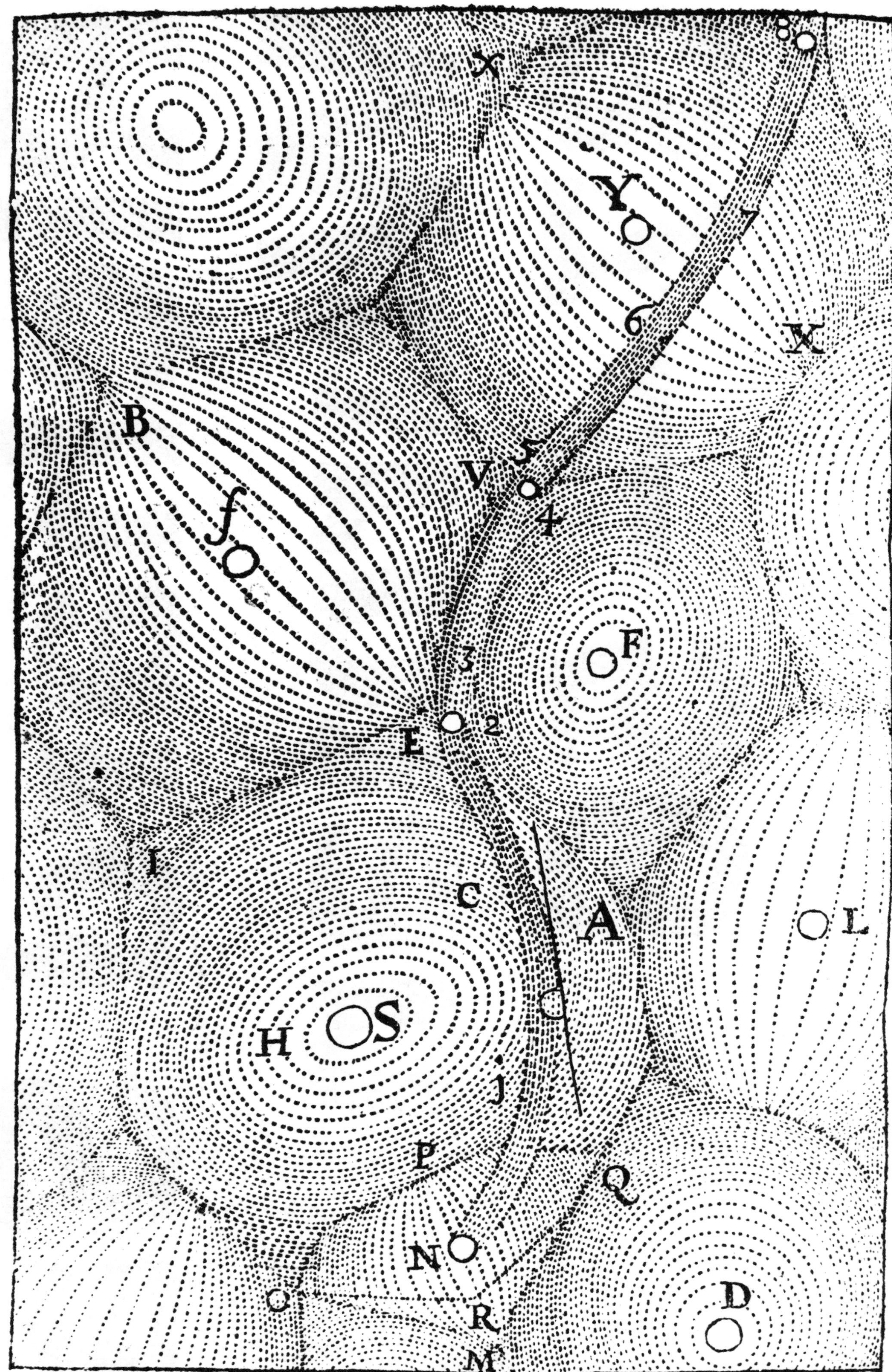

1668

1668

The philosopher René Descartes was convinced that there is no empty space and that the universe is filled with matter. This graphic illustrates how elementary particles gather around the fixed stars. The thick line shows the course of a comet.

Der Philosoph René Descartes nahm an, dass es keinen leeren Raum gebe und dass das Universum mit Materie gefüllt sei. Diese Grafik verdeutlicht, wie sich die Elementarteilchen in Wirbeln um die Fixsterne herum versammeln. Die breite Linie zeigt die Bahn eines Kometen.

Le philosophe René Descartes était convaincu que le vide n'existait pas, et que l'espace était rempli de matière. Cette image montre comment les particules élémentaires se rassemblent autour des étoiles fixes. La ligne plus épaisse montre le trajet d'une comète.

How I strive to understand what it is like not to understand

Richard Saul Wurman

There is a tsunami of data that is crashing on to the beaches of the civilized world. This is a tidal wave of unrelated, growing data formed in bits and bytes, coming in an unorganized, uncontrolled, incoherent cacophony of foam. It's filled with flotsam and jetsam. It's filled with the sticks and bones and shells of inanimate and animate life. None of it is easily related; none of it comes with any organizational methodology.

As it washes up on our beaches, we see people in suits and ties skipping along the shoreline, men and women in fine shirts and blouses dressed for business. We see academics, designers and government officials, all getting their shoes wet and slowly submerging in the dense trough of stuff. Their trousers and slacks soaked, they walk stupidly into the water, smiling – a false smile of confidence and control. The tsunami is a wall of data – data produced at greater and greater speed, greater and greater amounts to store in memory, amounts that double, it seems, with each sunset. On tape, on disks, on paper, sent by streams of light bouncing off the cloud, careening through the ether of Wi-Fi, 3G, 4G, G squared. Faster, more and more and more Twitters, texts and Facebooking. They nod their heads and say, "Yes, this is important, this is good stuff. The person sitting next to me, sitting in the next office down the aisle, they understand it, so I will smile, making believe I understand it too."

These same people read their newspapers, their iPhone, iPad, their smart-this or smart-that, thinking they understand the issues of the day, whether it's the recession, depression, windfall or downfall, the healthcare debacle, national debt or international debt, taxes, the balance or the imbalance, trade, the dollar more valuable-good? Less valuable-good? They nod their heads, knee-jerking to key words in headlines, but unable to tell anybody else, including themselves, the essence of any issue.

All day, from morning at home, to workday lunches to dinner at night, out loud or to themselves, they "uh-huh, uh-huh, uh-huh", making believe they understand a reference to a name, a reference to a fact, the references to knowledge that supposedly makes the world coherent. They "uh-huh" some friend, some teacher, a boss, a peer when a book or movie or magazine article, or piece of machinery, or software, or hardware is discussed. They "uh-huh" everybody because they were taught when they were young that it is not good to look stupid, that it is not good to say "I don't know", it is not good to ask questions, not good to focus on failure. Instead, the rewards come from acknowledging or answering everything with "I know". So they ask each other "keepin' busy"?

You're supposed to look smart in our society. You are supposed to gain expertise and to sell it as the means of moving ahead in your career. You are supposed to focus on what you know how to do, and then do it better and better. You're supposed to revel in some niche of ability. That is where the rewards are supposed to come from.

Of course, when you sell your expertise – and what I mean by sell is to move ahead in a corporation, or sell an idea to a publisher, or a script to a producer, or sell an ability to a client – when you sell your expertise, by definition, you're selling from a limited repertoire. However, when you sell your ignorance, when you sell your desire to learn about something, when you sell your desire to create and explore and navigate paths to knowledge and understanding, when you sell your *curiosity* – you sell from a bucket with an infinitely deep bottom that represents an unlimited repertoire. And, you sell in a way that's not intimidating, in a way that joins the explanation to the fascination that comes with that understanding.

How opposite is our life from what we have been taught. Our educational system is based on the memorization of things we're not interested in, bulimicly spewed out on a paper called a test, and then forgotten. We learn to use our short-term memory rather than long-term memory. Many of our interests are shunted aside. The teenagers' interest in music,

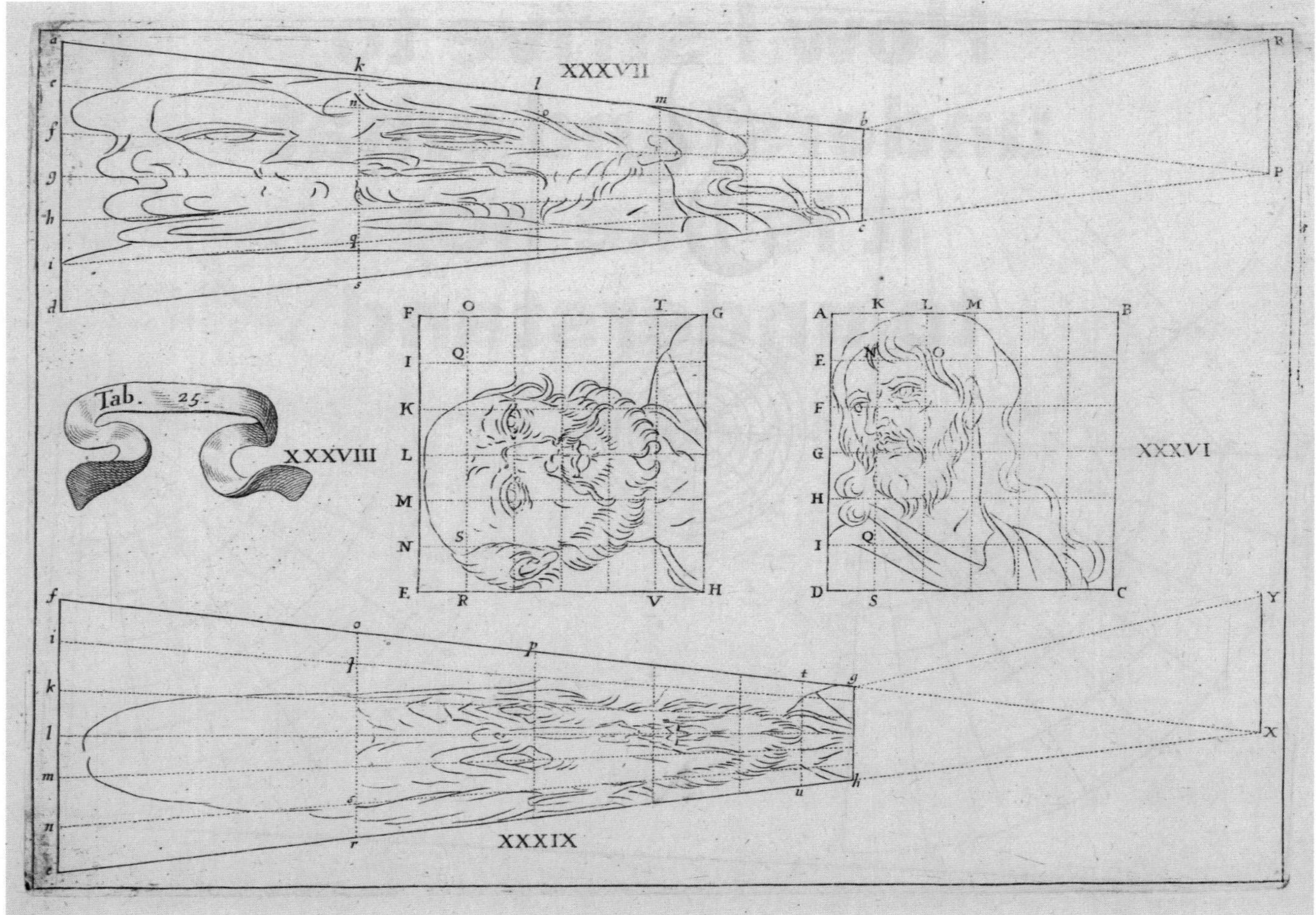

1638

movies, games, cars and sports are looked on as second-rate themes for their lives instead of embraced as connections to all knowledge and wisdom. The car connects to the history of transportation, to our road systems, to our cities and our highways. It connects to the balance of payments and economics around the world. To steel and iron, and steel construction, and plastics and design. It connects to physics and mathematics and chemistry. It connects to foreign languages and culture. To medicine and governmental policy. And, all the things the car connects to connect to everything else. So do sports. And so does entertainment, which connects to technologies of all sorts, to design and hardware and software and information. Information is validated by understanding. We are what we understand.

We remember what we are interested in. That is the definition of learning.

If I throw 140,000 words randomly on the floor, I wouldn't call it a dictionary. However, if I attach a phrase of meaning to each word, and organize them alphabetically, I could. In addition, if I group those words by meanings on the same subject, it is the beginning of an encyclopedia: a book organized both by alphabet and category. The ability to find something goes hand-in-hand with how well it's organized and the way by which it is organized. We choose to organize the dictionary alphabetically, and for most of us, most of the time, that's a useful organizing principle.

In fact, the alphabet is the only organizing principle that we actually have to learn. Because the alphabet was not given to us by God. Alphabets change with languages: the Russian alphabet is different from English, in Japan it is different again. For us, the alphabet is a learned order of 26 letters. The 26 letters have no functional sequence, but have proved useful in the evolution of our literate society. It really works quite well and it is one of our acceptable ways of organizing information. Now we could organize dictionary words by groups. All words that have to do with climate or weather could be together, all words that have to do with automobiles or speed or traffic could be together, all words about health and well-being could be lumped in a group. Therefore, great groups of these words could have one or another category as their organizing principle. In turn, the categories could be organized alphabetically, with words about automobiles in that category in the beginning under the "A's", and words about animals and zoology under "A" and "Z".

Some things are best organized by where they are. The thousands of roads and sites and towns and bodies of water are best organized by location on a map. We want to be able to find those places that are immediately around us as we look on a map. We certainly don't want to drive across France alphabetically. We don't want the United States in an atlas organized with Alabama first, and Alaska next, and Washington last, because we don't drive that way. That's not how we find where we're going, or how we find something.

As I looked into the organization of information, I realized that there were only five ways to do it. They can be remembered by the acronym LATCH: (L) by location, (A) by alphabet, (T) by time (many museum shows are organized by timeline; the famous timeline by Charlie Eames, created for his film *The World of Franklin and Jefferson*, was probably one of the best ever devised), (C) by category (the way department stores are organized), and (H) by hierarchy, from the largest to the smallest of something, from the reddest to the lightest red, from the densest to the least dense, and so on.

These are all examples of information architecture: the building of information structures that allow others to understand. But the structures of information go well beyond basic organization. Many principles of clarity can be employed. For example, you only understand something new relative to something you already understand, whether visually, verbally, or numerically. Something will have an understandable size if it is

C.

Inſtrumenta Muſica. Klangſpiele.

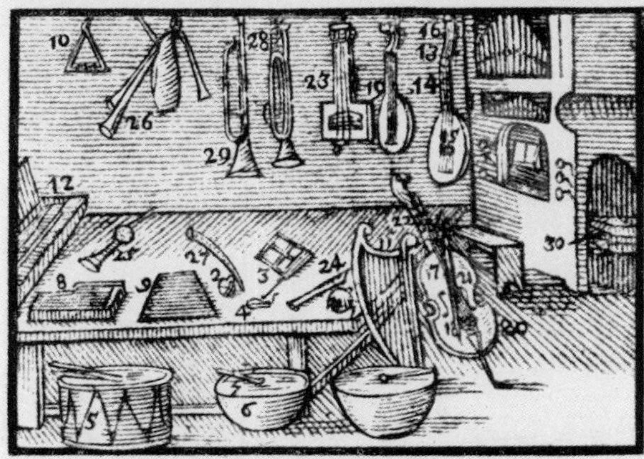

Muſicalnſtrumenta ſunt,	Klangſpiele ſind /
quæ edunt Vocem:	die eine Stimme von ſich gebe:
Primò,	Erſtlich /
cùm pulſantur,	wann ſie geſchlagen werden /
ut *Cymbalum* 1	als / die Cymbel 1
piſtillo,	mit dem Schwengel;
Tintinnabulum 2	die Schelle / 2 (Knöpflein;
intus globulo ferreo;	inwendig mit einem eiſernen
Crepitaculum, 3	das Klepperlein / 3
circumverſando;	durch umdrehen;
Crembalum, 4	die Maultrommel/ 4
ori admotum,	an den Mund gehalten /
digito;	mit dem Finger;
Tympanum 5	die Trummel 5
& *Ahenum*, 6	und Pauke/ 6
Claviculâ, 7	mit dem Schlegel/ 7

1658

related to the size of something you know. This is easy to see when viewing a photograph of a building that seems to have no human scale. Or visiting a painting and being surprised by its size, because all the reproductions of it are not relative to a human being. Scale always relates to us.

Well, why am I going into the organization of information in such detail? Just to show that thoughtful structuring of information is an essential skill that a graphic designer, information architect, or information designer needs to have in his or her repertoire. There is not a single school with a degree program called *Understanding* or *The Question*.

In 1962, nearly 50 years ago, I produced my first book with plans of 50 of the world's cities, all drawn to the same scale. Nobody had done that before. Five years later I created an urban atlas, again with all maps and legends and statistical analysis in the same scale, the same weighing of information. Now in 2011, I am revisiting the comparative information that affects the 51% of the world's population that live in urbanized areas (according to the United Nations), which is predicted to increase to 70% in the next few decades. This move to urbanization is undoubtedly the greatest mega-trend of the 21st century, which makes the inability of city-to-city conversation even more inexplicable.

It is understandably counterintuitive to believe any of the following:

- No two cities in the world draw their maps to the same scale.
- No two cities in the world use the same map legends.
- There is no standardized method for collecting information or what is collected.
- The names of land use on legends vary widely. Actually there are hundreds of different names relative to residential, commercial, light commercial, recreational and cemetery uses.
- There are no standard ways to display information which break it down according to category or by incidence of occurrence. In verbal language (if this information were being described in text) category would correspond to a noun and incidence would be represented by a verb.
- And now to cap it all off, as every major city spills over its political borders, there exists no standard method for establishing these new edges.
- If you don't have a border or defined area, you can't collect data and describe density, you can't compare. Cities can't talk to each other, learn or understand each other.
- Understanding precedes action.

1638

In his book about the applications of perspective, the French mathematician Jean François Niceron described the construction of distorted images. The illustration shows the perspectival transformation of two portraits into an anamorphosis.

In seinem Buch über die Anwendung der Perspektive beschrieb der französische Mathematiker Jean François Niceron die Konstruktion von verzerrten Abbildungen. Die Tafel zeigt die perspektivische Umwandlung zweier Porträts in eine Anamorphose.

Dans son livre sur les applications de la perspective, le mathématicien français Jean-François Niceron a décrit la construction d'images déformées. L'illustration montre l'anamorphose de la perspective de deux portraits.

1658

The Bohemian philosopher Comenius developed a pictorial system of education. His book *Orbis sensualium pictus* was the first illustrated children's encyclopaedia. Individual elements in the images are labelled and explained, e.g. musical instruments in this example.

Der böhmische Philosoph Comenius entwickelte eine bildbezogene Pädagogik. Sein Buch *Orbis sensualium pictus* war die erste illustrierte Enzyklopädie für Kinder. Einzelne Elemente in den Bildern, wie hier etwa Musikinstrumente, werden mit Zahlen bezeichnet und erklärt.

Le philosophe bohémien Comenius a créé un système éducatif basé sur les images. Son livre *Orbis sensualium pictus* a été la première encyclopédie illustrée pour les enfants. Le nom et la définition de chaque élément sont indiqués, par ex. ici des instruments de musique.

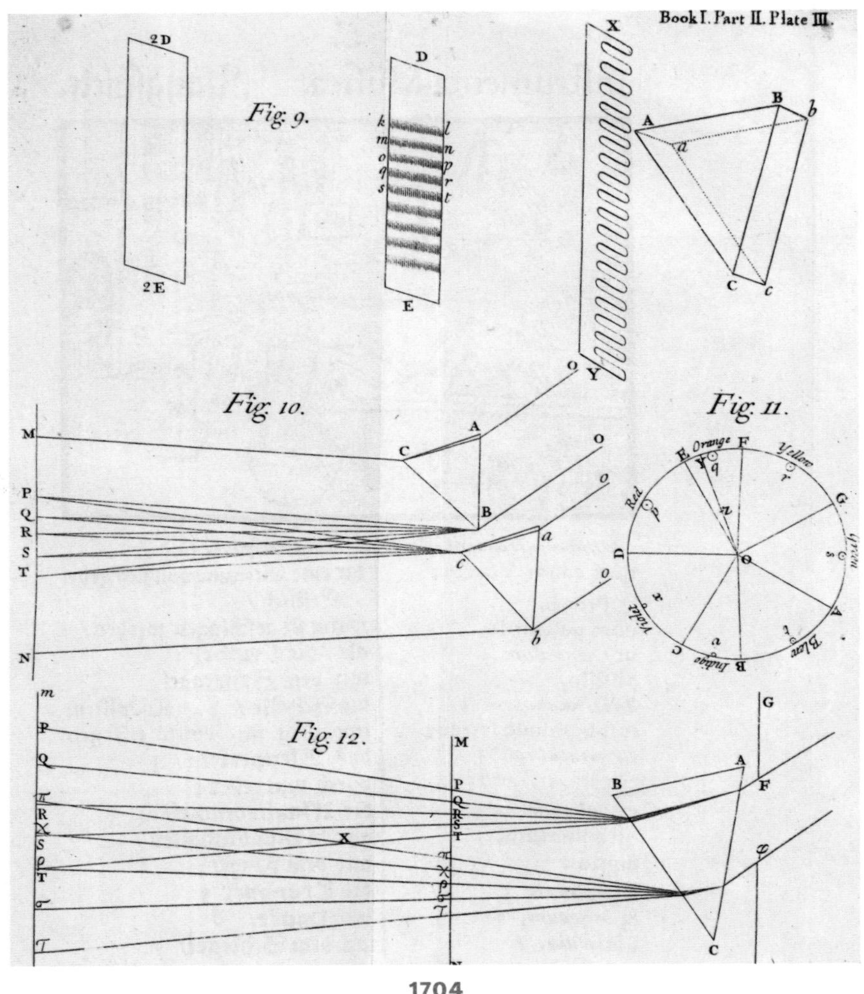

1704

My last point is a somewhat apocryphal look at movies, which in their earliest form archived stage shows. My iPad archives books and magazines and occasionally shows me a trumped-up version of a page turning. I am still waiting for the new modality – an iPad that can nod, that I can talk to, that upon my request automatically changes its degree of difficulty or intensity of content, that has nuance, that talks back and suggests links and connections that help me in my waking dream: my journey to understanding.

My waking dream is to have a network of 20, 50, 100 urban observatories around the world. They would show live, real-time exhibitions of understandable information from city to city.

Imagine walking into such a place, and the first experience is to be immersed in whatever great festival or parade or light show that is occurring someplace else in the world. Then to the room of complete information about land use, economics, growth, displayed on a globe which shows the changes of our blue planet: its urbanization, interaction, weather patterns, earthquakes, floods, pestilence, war, but also the migration of people to the largest cities around the world. And this globe would also be animated by changes in borders and explorations. An aquarium, a planet earth focused on people as opposed to frogs in the wilderness. Of course as urbanization grows, wilderness diminishes, so that yang will not be forgotten.

I believe we are at this cusp.

A first toe in the warm bath of this new modality.

Richard Saul Wurman is an architect, information architect, author of 83 books and founder of the TED, TEDMED and eg conferences.

1704

In his treatise *Opticks*, Isaac Newton demonstrated among other things that sunlight consists of coloured components. The diagrams above show the refraction of beams of white light in prisms and the succession of the spectral colours.

In seinem Traktat *Opticks* wies Isaac Newton unter anderem nach, dass Sonnenlicht aus farbigen Bestandteilen zusammengesetzt ist. Die Diagramme zeigen die Zerlegung von weißen Lichtstrahlen mithilfe von Prismen und die Folge der Spektralfarben.

Dans son traité *Opticks*, Isaac Newton a démontré entre autres que la lumière du soleil est constituée d'éléments colorés. Les diagrammes du haut montrent la réfraction des rayons de lumière blanche dans les prismes, et la succession des couleurs du spectre.

ca. 1724

In 1715, Edmond Halley succeeded in precisely predicting a solar eclipse. He produced a map with the expected path of the moon's shadow over England. Later, this map was augmented with data about a second eclipse which took place in 1724.

1715 gelang es Edmond Halley, eine Sonnenfinsternis präzise vorherzusagen. Er erstellte eine Karte mit dem erwarteten Verlauf des Mondschattens über England. Später ergänzte er die Karte mit Angaben zu einer zweiten Finsternis des Jahres 1724.

En 1715, Edmond Halley a réussi à prévoir une éclipse solaire avec une grande précision. Cette carte indique le parcours de l'ombre de la Lune à travers l'Angleterre. Plus tard, elle s'est vu ajouter des données sur une deuxième éclipse en 1724.

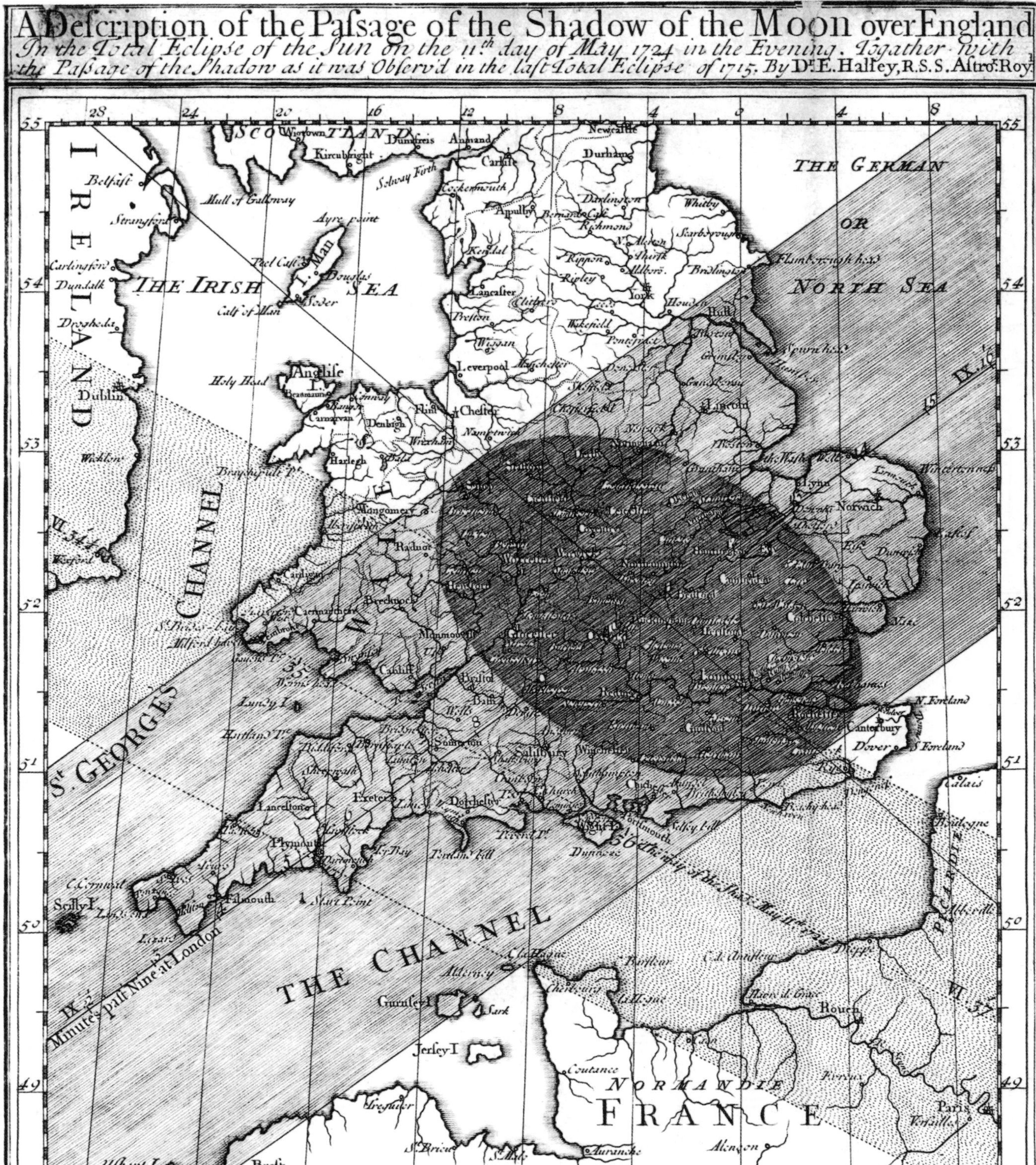

Since the Publication of our Predictions of this Eclipse has had the desired effect, and many curious Persons have been excited thereby to communicate their Observations from most parts of the Kingdom, we thought it might not be unacceptable to represent after the same manner the passage of the Shade, as it really happened; whereby it will appear that tho' our Numbers pretend not to be altogether perfect, yet the correction they need is very small.

At London the Eclipse was carefully Observed to begin at 8h. 6′ mane, and to become Total at 9h. 9′. It continued Total 3′. 23″, and ended at 10h. 20′. And by the Accounts we have received from Abroad, the Center of the Shade past nearly over Plymouth, Exeter, Buckingham and Huntingdon, leaving Bath and Lynn a little on the left, and Oxford and Ely on the right. The Southern limit past over Cranbrook in Kent, leaving Newhaven and Canterbury a very little without: And the Northern limit entered on the Coast of Wales in St. Bride's-bay, & left England near Flamborough-head, all which the Map more particularly describes. The greater diameter of ye Shade having been 170 Geog: Miles or Minutes, and ye lesser 110.

The Numbers on the middle parallel line, as in our former, denote ye place of ye Center of ye Shade at so many minutes past Nine at London. By help of this and of ye other diameter of ye shaded Oval (conjugate to ye on wch ye Center moved) passing over ye places where the greatest Obscurity was at ye same instant as at London, we may very nearly find ye time of ye greatest darkness at any other place in ye Map. For drawing a line parallel to this conjugate diameter thro' ye proposed place, it will cross ye way of ye Shade at ye minute of ye greatest Obscurity reckon'd as at London, and by allowing ye difference of Meridians, at ye place itself. Thus for example, the greatest Eclipse will be found at York at 9h. 10′, at Dublin 8h. 42½′, at Brest 8h. 43½′. After ye same manner may ye time of Total Darkness be had, by drawing a line parallel to ye way of ye Shade by ye Place propos'd: For as much of that line as falls within ye shadowed Oval, measur'd on the Scale of minutes, will shew how long that place continued within the true Shade quam proxime.

We give you likewise ye Transit of ye Shade, as it will pass over ye West of England in ye Eclipse yt will be Anno 1724 May 11. P.M. in wch ye Northern limit passes very near Dublin & Oxford. But it will scarce reach London where it begins at 5h. 39′, is greatest at 6h. 35½′, & ends at 7h. 27½′ in ye Evening.

ca. 1724

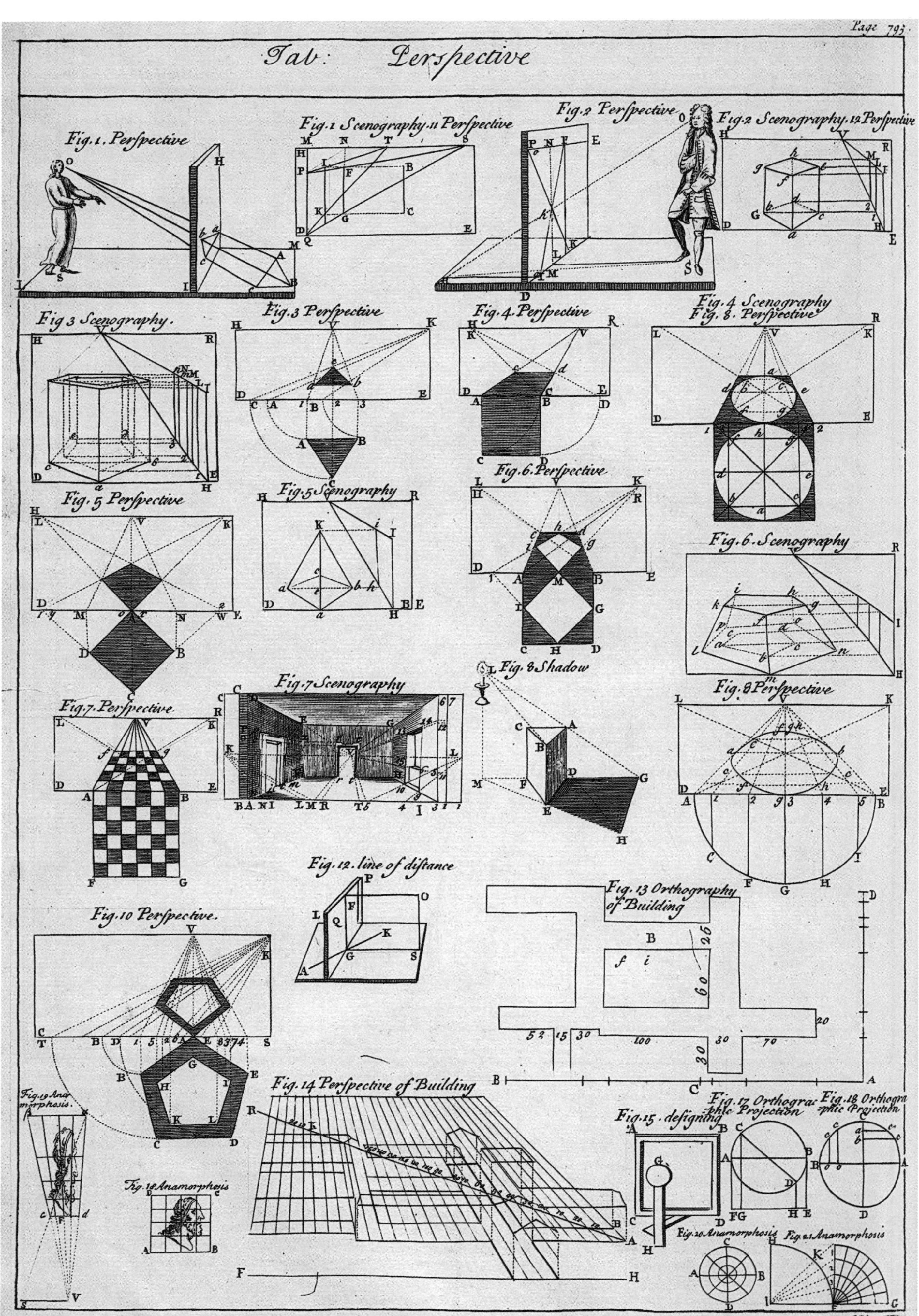

1728

1728

The *Cyclopedia*, published by Ephraim Chambers from 1728, was the first comprehensive dictionary written in English. It contained several tables with graphics and diagrams. This example demonstrates the mathematical construction of perspectival depictions.

Die *Cyclopedia*, veröffentlicht ab 1728 von Ephraim Chambers, war das erste umfassende Lexikon in englischer Sprache. Es enthielt etliche Tafeln mit Grafiken und Diagrammen. Das Beispiel zeigt die mathematische Konstruktion perspektivischer Darstellungen.

Edward Chambers a publié *Cyclopedia* à partir de 1728. C'était le premier dictionnaire complet écrit en anglais. Il contenait plusieurs illustrations avec des schémas et des diagrammes. Cet exemple explique la construction mathématique des représentations en perspective.

Wie ich zu verstehen versuche, was es bedeutet, nicht zu verstehen

Richard Saul Wurman

Eine wahre Datenflut brandet an die Küsten der zivilisierten Welt. Es ist eine Welle beziehungsloser, stetig wachsender Daten aus Bits und Bytes, die mit einer unstrukturierten, unkontrollierten, unverständlichen Kakofonie der Gischt heranrollt. Und was dieser Schaum mitspült, ist fast nur Ballast und Treibgut: Hölzer, Stöcke, Knochen und Gehäuse der belebten und der unbelebten Natur. Nichts von all dem lässt sich einander mühelos zuordnen, nichts unterliegt einer ordnenden Methodik.

Während all das an unsere Strände gespült wird, sehen wir Menschen in Anzügen und mit Krawatten die Küste entlanggehen, Männer und Frauen, die elegante Hemden und Blusen tragen, Geschäftskleidung. Wir sehen Akademiker, Designer und Beamte. Ihre Schuhe werden feucht, und sie versinken allmählich in der kompakten Substanz. Mit klatschnassen Hosenbeinen laufen sie töricht ins Wasser und lächeln – ein falsches Lächeln, das Selbstvertrauen und Kontrolle ausstrahlt. Es sind Massen von Daten – Daten, die mit immer größerer Geschwindigkeit und in immer größerem Umfang erzeugt werden, die im Gedächtnis gespeichert werden müssen und deren Ausmaß sich scheinbar mit jedem Sonnenuntergang verdoppelt. Sie befinden sich auf Band, auf Scheiben, auf Papier, werden über Lichtströme gesendet, die sich an Rechnerwolken brechen, oder schlingern durch den Äther von Wi-Fi, 3G, 4G und G hoch zwei. Twittern, simsen, facebooken – immer schneller, immer mehr. Jeder nickt und sagt: „Ja, das ist wichtig, das ist sehr gut. Mein Platznachbar und der Kollege aus dem Büro nebenan – sie verstehen das, also lächele ich und tue so, als verstünde ich es auch."

Dieselben Leute lesen ihre Zeitung, ihr iPhone, ihr iPad, ihr Smart-Dieses und -Jenes und denken, sie verstünden die Themen des Tages, seien es Rezession, Depression, Aufschwung oder Konjunkturrückgang, das Debakel des Gesundheitswesens, die staatliche oder die globale Verschuldung, Steuern, der ausgeglichene oder unausgeglichene Haushalt, Handel, Dollar mit hohem Wert? Niedrigem Wert? Bei den entsprechenden Schlüsselwörtern in den Schlagzeilen nicken sie reflexartig, können aber niemandem – einschließlich ihrer selbst – erklären, was es mit diesen Themen tatsächlich auf sich hat.

Den ganzen Tag über, ob morgens zu Hause, mittags in der Kantine oder abends beim Essen, murmeln sie, mal laut, mal leise, ihr zustimmendes „Mhm, mhm" und geben vor, den Verweis auf einen Namen, die Referenz auf eine Tatsache oder die Anspielung auf eine Erkenntnis zu verstehen, durch die die Welt angeblich einheitlicher würde. Sie vermitteln einem Freund, einem Lehrer, einem Vorgesetzten oder einem Bekannten murmelnd ihre Zustimmung, wenn ein Buch, ein Film oder ein Zeitungsartikel, ein Maschinenteil, Soft- oder Hardware diskutiert wird. Sie murmeln ständig zustimmend, weil ihnen in ihrer Kindheit und Jugend beigebracht wurde, dass es nicht gut ist, dumm zu wirken; dass es nicht gut ist, „Das weiß ich nicht" zu sagen; dass es nicht gut ist, Fragen zu stellen, nicht gut, das Augenmerk auf das eigene Unvermögen zu richten. Belohnt wird, wer bestätigt, wer alles mit „Ich weiß" beantworten kann. Also fragt man sich gegenseitig: „Alles im grünen Bereich?"

In unserer Gesellschaft muss man gescheit wirken. Man soll sich Fachwissen aneignen und es verkaufen, um im Beruf voranzukommen. Man soll sich auf das konzentrieren, von dem man weiß, dass man es kann, und es dann immer besser machen. Man soll sich in einer Fähigkeitsnische einrichten. Dort soll einen dann die Belohnung erwarten.

Natürlich greift man, wenn man sein Fachwissen verkauft – und mit „verkaufen" meine ich, dass man in einem Unternehmen aufsteigt, dass man einem Verleger eine Idee, einem Produzenten ein Drehbuch oder einem Kunden eine Fähigkeit verkauft –, per definitionem auf ein begrenztes Angebot zurück. Wenn man jedoch seine Unwissenheit verkauft, seinen Wunsch, etwas zu lernen, wenn man sein Begehren verkauft, Wege zu Wissen und zu Verständnis zu suchen, sie zu

These early thematic maps show the geographical distribution of various languages, together with the characters of their alphabet. European countries are labelled with the Lord's Prayer written in their respective languages.

Diese frühen thematischen Karten zeigen die geografische Verteilung verschiedener Sprachen zusammen mit den Zeichen ihres Alphabets. Die europäischen Länder sind mit dem Vaterunser in der Landessprache bezeichnet.

Ces premières cartes thématiques montrent la distribution géographique de différentes langues, ainsi que les caractères de leur alphabet. Les pays européens sont accompagnés du Notre Père dans leur langue respective.

erschließen und an ihnen entlangzusteuern, wenn man also seine „Neugier" verkauft – dann schöpft man aus einem Fass mit sehr tiefem Boden, dessen Angebot schier unbegrenzt ist. Außerdem ist das eine Verkaufsmethode, die nicht einschüchtert, eine Verkaufsmethode, die neben der Erklärung auch noch die Begeisterung bereithält, die es mit sich bringt, wenn man etwas versteht.

Wie sehr unterscheidet sich unser Leben doch von dem, was man uns beigebracht hat. Unser Bildungssystem beruht darauf, dass wir uns Dinge einprägen, die uns nicht interessieren, die wir auf ein Blatt Papier speien, man nennt das Prüfung, und dann vergessen. Wir lernen eher, unser Kurzzeit- als unser Langzeitgedächtnis zu nutzen. Viele unserer Interessen werden beiseitegewischt. Das Interesse von Teenagern an Musik, Filmen, Spielen, Autos und Sport wird als zweitrangig für ihr Leben abgetan und nicht als Verbindung zu Wissen und Weisheit betrachtet. Das Auto hat mit der Geschichte des Transportwesens zu tun, mit dem Straßensystem, mit unseren Städten und Autobahnen. Es hat mit der Zahlungsbilanz und der Weltwirtschaft zu tun, mit Stahl, Eisen, Stahlbau, Kunststoff und Gestaltung. Es hat mit Physik, Mathematik und Chemie zu tun, mit Fremdsprachen und anderen Kulturen. Mit Medizin und Politik. Und alles, was mit dem Auto zu tun hat, hat mit allem anderen zu tun. Das Gleiche gilt für Sport. Und für den Unterhaltungssektor, der mit jeder Form von Technik zu tun hat, mit Gestaltung, mit Hard- und Software sowie mit Information. Information wird erst durch Verständnis wertvoll. Wir sind, was wir verstehen.

Wir merken uns das, wofür wir uns interessieren. Das ist die Definition von Lernen.

Wenn ich 140.000 Wörter ungeordnet auf den Boden werfe, würde ich das nicht als Wörterbuch bezeichnen. Wenn ich jedoch jedes Wort um einen Bedeutungskontext ergänze und alle Wörter alphabetisch anordne, entsteht eines. Stelle ich die Wörter überdies ihrer Bedeutung nach zu Themenkreisen zusammen, habe ich den Anfang einer Enzyklopädie: ein Buch, das sowohl alphabetisch als auch inhaltlich geordnet ist. Die Fähigkeit, etwas zu finden, hängt davon ab, wie gut und auf welche Weise etwas geordnet ist. Wir haben in unserem Kulturkreis beschlossen, Wörterbücher alphabetisch anzuordnen, und für die meisten von uns ist das auch meistens ein sinnvolles Organisationsprinzip.

Das Alphabet ist übrigens das einzige Organisationsprinzip, das wir eigens lernen müssen. Weil es uns nicht von Gott gegeben ist. Das Alphabet unterscheidet sich je nach Sprache: Das russische Alphabet ist anders als das deutsche, und beide unterscheiden sich wiederum vom japanischen. Für uns ist es eine erlernte Anordnung von 26 Buchstaben. Diese 26 Buchstaben haben keine sinnvolle Abfolge, haben sich aber bei der Entwicklung unserer Bildungsgesellschaft als nützlich erwiesen. Das Alphabet funktioniert recht gut und ist eine der besseren Arten, Information zu ordnen. Wir könnten Wörterbucheinträge natürlich auch nach Gruppen gliedern. Alle Wörter, die mit dem Klima und dem Wetter zu tun haben, könnten in eine Gruppe kommen, alle Wörter, die mit Autos, Geschwindigkeit und Verkehr zu tun haben, in eine zweite, und alle Wörter, die sich um Gesundheit und Wohlbefinden drehen, könnten in eine dritte Gruppe gesteckt werden. Das heißt, große Gruppen dieser Wörter könnten die eine oder die andere Kategorie als Organisationsprinzip haben. Diese Kategorien wiederum könnten alphabetisch angeordnet werden, Auto-Wörter kämen also in die Kategorie am Anfang unter den Buchstaben „A", und Tier- und Zoologie-Wörter stünden unter „T" bzw. „Z".

Anderes wird am besten nach dem Ort sortiert, an dem es sich befindet. Die Tausenden von Straßen, Stätten, Ortschaften und Gewässer lassen sich am besten durch die Verortung auf einer Landkarte organisieren. Wenn wir auf eine Landkarte schauen, möchten wir die Orte finden können, die sich in unserer näheren Umgebung befinden. Wir möchten gewiss

EVROPA Poly-Glotta
Linguarum Genealogiam exhibens, una cum Literis, scribendique modis, Omnium Gentium.
MARE GERMANICVM
MARE MEDITERRANEVM
RVSSICA
POLONICA
GALLICA
HISPANICA
ITALICA
GERMANICA
HVNGARICA
PONTVS EVXINVS
Cyprus
Creta
Sardinia
Opera Godofr. Hensel delineata
Excusa prostat in Officina Homanniana

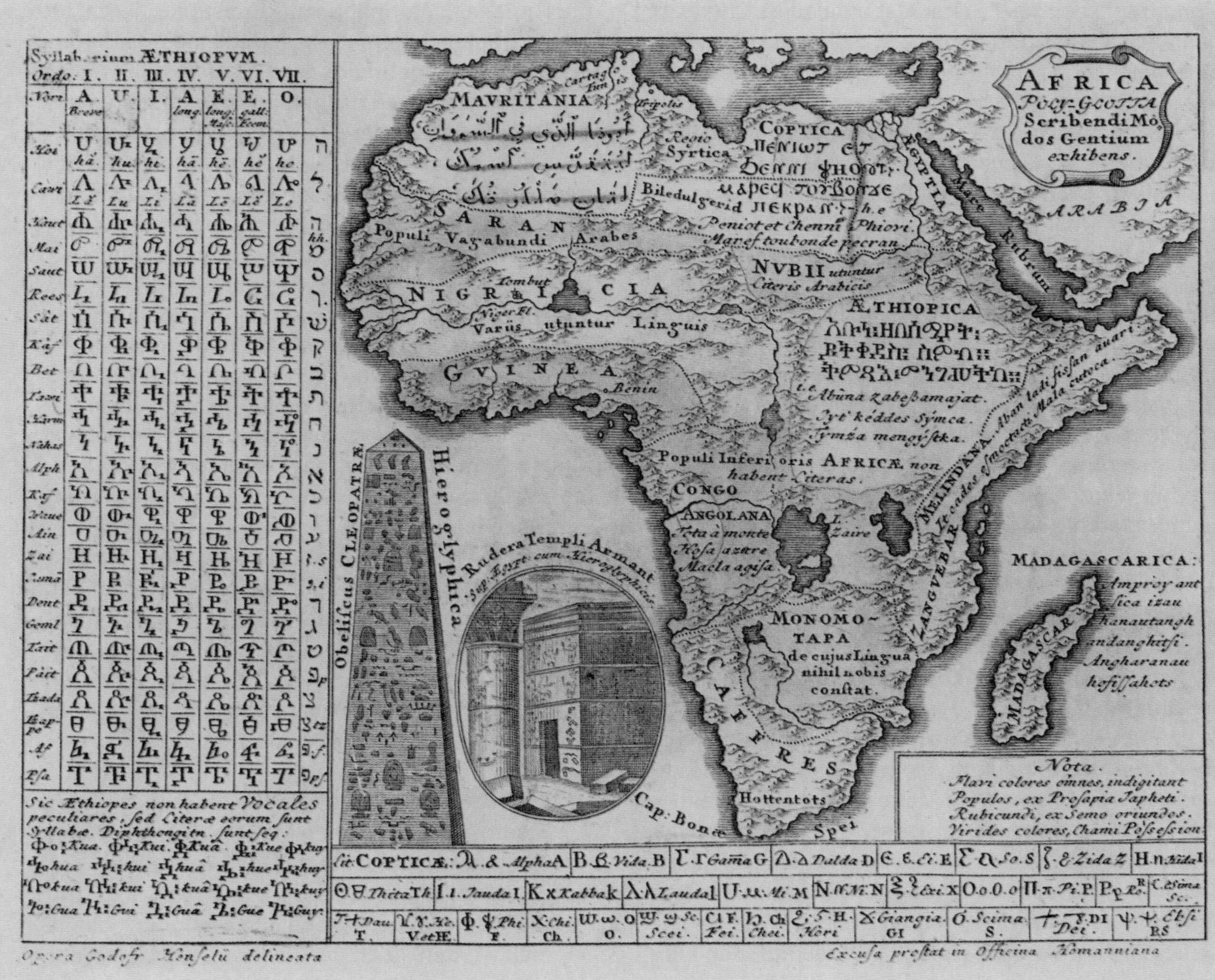
AFRICA
Poly-Glotta
Scribendi Modos Gentium exhibens.
Syllabarium ÆTHIOPVM.
MAVRITANIA
COPTICA
SARAN
Populi Vagabundi Arabes
NIGRICIA
GVINEA
NVBII utuntur Literis Arabicis
ÆTHIOPICA
ARABIA
Mare Rubrum
Populi Inferioris AFRICÆ non habent Literas.
CONGO
ANGOLANA
MONOMOTAPA de cujus Lingua nihil nobis constat.
CAFFRES
Hottentots
Cap. Bonæ Spei
ZANGVEBAR
MADAGASCARICA:
Obeliscus CLEOPATRÆ
Hieroglyphica
Rudera Templi Armant
Nota.
Flavi colores omnes, indigitant Populos, ex Prosapia Japheti.
Rubicundi, ex Semo oriundos.
Virides colores, Chami Possession.
Opera Godofr. Hensel delineata
Excusa prostat in Officina Homanniana

1741

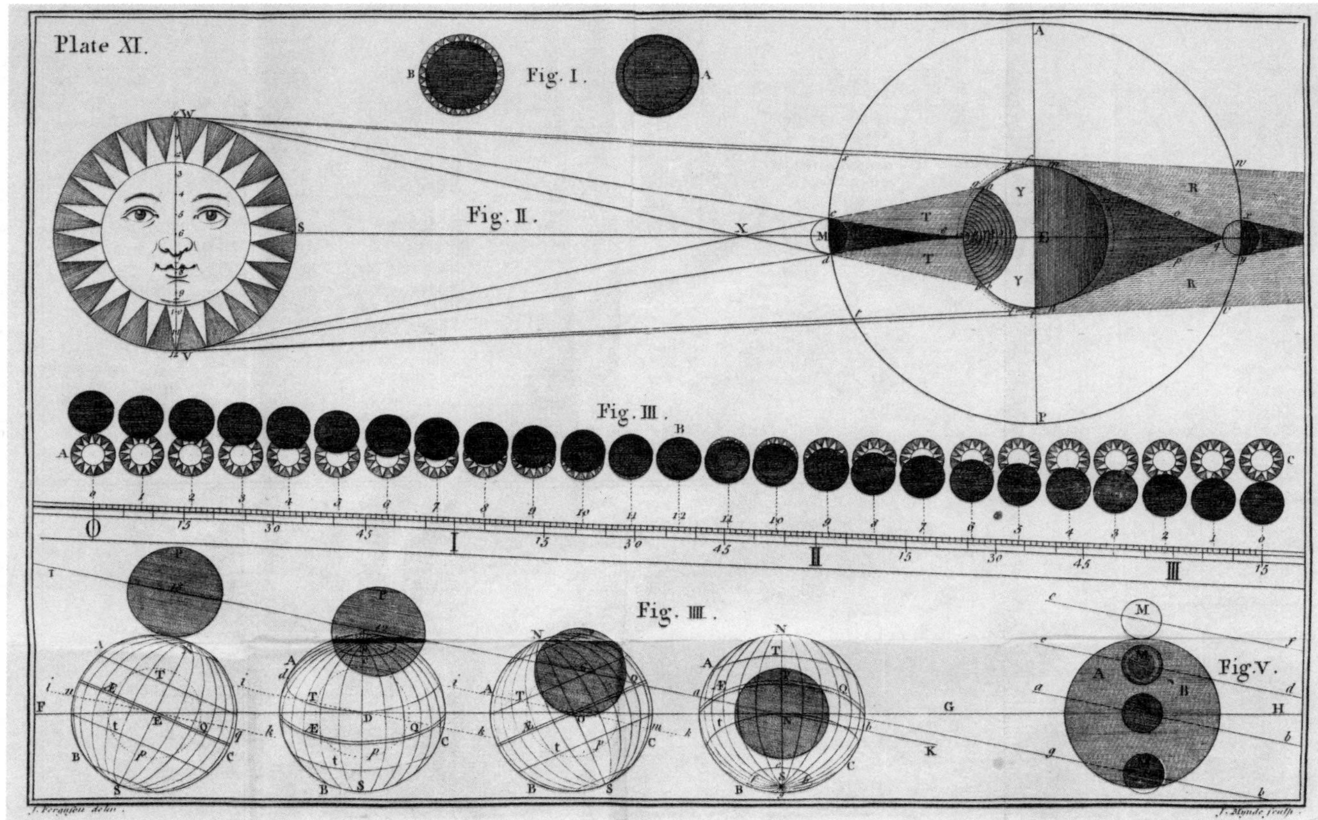

1756

nicht in alphabetischer Reihenfolge durch Frankreich reisen. Der Atlas der Vereinigten Staaten sollte nicht so strukturiert sein, dass zuerst Alabama aufgeführt wird, dann Alaska und zum Schluss Washington, denn so bewegen wir uns nicht fort. Das ist nicht unsere Art festzustellen, wohin wir gehen oder etwas zu finden.

Als ich mich mit der Organisation von Information auseinandersetzte, wurde mir klar, dass es dafür nur fünf Möglichkeiten gibt. Diese fünf Arten kann man sich mithilfe des Akronyms LATCH[1] merken. L – Organisation aufgrund von Lokalisierung, A – Organisation nach dem Alphabet, T – Organisation nach Zeit („T" von engl. „time"; viele Museumsausstellungen orientieren sich an einer Zeitachse; die berühmte Timeline, die Charlie Eames für seinen Film *The World of Franklin and Jefferson* entwarf, ist vermutlich die beste, die je erdacht wurde), C – Organisation nach Kategorie („C" von engl. „category"; auf diese Art werden Warenhäuser angelegt) und H – Organisation nach Hierarchie, vom Größten zum Kleinsten, vom leuchtendsten zum blassesten Rot, vom Dichtesten zum Durchlässigsten und so weiter.

Das alles sind Beispiele für Informationsarchitektur: für das Errichten von Informationsstrukturen, die Verständnis ermöglichen. Allerdings gehen Informationsstrukturen weit über das bloße Ordnen hinaus. Es können zahlreiche Prinzipien eingesetzt werden, die Klarheit vermitteln. So kann man etwas Neues beispielsweise nur in dem Maße verstehen, in dem es – visuell, verbal oder numerisch – Bezug auf etwas nimmt, das man bereits verstanden hat. Ein Objekt hat nur dann eine nachvollziehbare Größe, wenn es im Verhältnis zu etwas steht, dessen Größe bereits bekannt ist. Das kann man ganz einfach feststellen, wenn man die Fotografie eines Gebäudes betrachtet, auf der kein Mensch zu sehen ist, der zum Vergleich herangezogen werden kann. Oder wenn man vor einem Gemälde steht und von seiner Größe überrascht ist, weil keine Reproduktion es je relativ zur Größe eines Menschen gezeigt hat. Der Maßstab bezieht sich stets auf uns selbst.

Weshalb ich derart ausführlich über die Organisation von Information spreche? Nur um zu zeigen, dass die Fähigkeit, Information klug zu strukturieren, für einen Grafiker, Informationsarchitekten oder Informationsdesigner unabdingbar ist. Es gibt keine einzige Ausbildungsstätte, die einen Studiengang anbietet, der „Verständnis" oder „Die Fragestellung" heißt.

1962, vor fast fünfzig Jahren, veröffentlichte ich mein erstes Buch mit Plänen von weltweit fünfzig Großstädten, die allesamt in demselben Maßstab gezeichnet waren. Das hatte es zuvor noch nie gegeben. Fünf Jahre später folgte ein urbaner Atlas, in dem alle Landkarten, Stadtpläne, Legenden und statistischen Analysen ebenfalls in demselben Maßstab gehalten waren; die Information war also gleich gewichtet. Jetzt, anno 2011, kehre ich zu der vergleichenden Information zurück, die jene einundfünfzig Prozent der Weltbevölkerung betrifft, die (den Vereinten Nationen zufolge) in urbanisierten Regionen leben; in den kommenden Jahrzehnten soll die Zahl auf siebzig Prozent steigen. Diese Tendenz zur Urbanisierung ist zweifelsohne der größte Megatrend des 21. Jahrhunderts, was das Unvermögen, Städte direkt miteinander in Beziehung zu setzen, noch unerklärbarer macht.

Es widerstrebt einem verständlicherweise, auch nur einen der folgenden Punkte zu glauben:

- Keine zwei Städte auf der Welt zeichnen ihre Stadtpläne im gleichen Maßstab.
- Keine zwei Städte auf der Welt verwenden dieselbe Zeichenlegende.
- Weder die Frage, welche Informationen gesammelt werden, noch die Methode, wie sie erhoben werden, unterliegen Normen.
- Die Ausdrücke für Landnutzungsarten weichen je nach Legende stark voneinander ab. Es gibt Hunderte unterschiedliche Bezeichnungen für Wohn-, Industrie-, Gewerbe- und Erholungsgebiete oder Friedhöfe.

1756

This etching was published in the popular book *Astronomy Explained upon Newton's Principles* by the Scot James Ferguson. The diagrams show the alignments responsible for solar and lunar eclipses on Earth.

Dieser Stich stammt aus einem populären Buch des Schotten James Ferguson: *Astronomy Explained upon Newton's Principles*. Die Diagramme zeigen die Konstellationen, die auf der Erde eine Sonnen- oder Mondfinsternis hervorrufen.

Cette gravure a été publiée dans le livre populaire *Astronomy explained upon Newton's Principles* de l'Écossais James Ferguson. Les schémas montrent les alignements responsables des éclipses solaires et lunaires sur la Terre.

- Es gibt keine Standards zur Darstellung von Information, die diese nach Kategorie oder nach Häufigkeit aufschlüsselt. In Worten (sollte diese Information in einem Text beschrieben werden) entspräche „Kategorie" einem Substantiv, „Häufigkeit" würde als Verb ausgedrückt.
- Der Gipfel all dessen: Während jede Großstadt über ihre politischen Grenzen hinauswuchert, gibt es keine standardisierte Methode, um diese neuen Stadtränder zu ermitteln.
- Ohne Grenzen oder ein klar umrissenes Gebiet kann man keine Daten erheben, kann man die Dichte nicht beschreiben, kann man nicht vergleichen. So können Städte nicht miteinander reden, voneinander lernen oder sich gegenseitig verstehen.
- Handeln setzt Verstehen voraus.

Als Letztes ein vielleicht unorthodoxer Seitenblick auf Filme: In ihrer frühesten Form boten sie vor allem kopierte Bühnenshows. Genauso archiviert mein iPad heute Bücher und Zeitschriften und zeigt mir bisweilen eine fiktive Version des Umblätterns. Ich warte noch auf die neue Modalität – ein iPad, das nicken kann, mit dem ich sprechen kann, das auf meine Nachfrage hin automatisch den Schwierigkeitsgrad oder die Intensität der Inhalte verändert, das Zwischentöne kennt, das mir widerspricht und mir Verbindungen und Links vorschlägt, die mir bei meinem Wachtraum weiterhelfen: bei meiner Reise zum Verstehen.

Mein Wachtraum handelt von einem Netzwerk, das aus zwanzig, fünfzig, hundert urbanen Observatorien in aller Welt besteht. Sie würden direkt, von Stadt zu Stadt, live und in Echtzeit verständlich aufbereitete Informationen ausstellen.

Stellen Sie sich vor, Sie würden einen solchen Ort betreten. Als Erstes würden Sie in das große Festival, in die Parade oder in die Lichtshow eintauchen, die gerade irgendwo auf der Welt stattfindet. Dann gehen Sie in den Raum der vollständigen Information zu den Themen Landnutzung, Ökonomie und Wachstum. Sie werden auf einem Globus dargestellt, der die Veränderungen auf unserem Planeten veranschaulicht: Urbanisierung, Interaktion, Wettermuster, Erdbeben, Überschwemmungen, Seuchen, Kriege, aber auch die Abwanderung von Menschen in die größten Städte der Welt. Auf diesem Globus würden auch Änderungen in Grenzverläufen sowie Forschungen animiert wiedergegeben. Ein Aquarium, ein Planet Erde, dessen Fokus auf die Menschen gerichtet ist anstatt auf die Frösche in der Wildnis. Selbstverständlich wird mit der voranschreitenden Urbanisierung die Wildnis zurückgedrängt, sodass auch die Kehrseite nicht vergessen wird.

Ich glaube, wir haben diesen Scheitelpunkt erreicht. Der große Zeh steckt schon im warmen Bad dieser neuen Modalität.

Richard Saul Wurman ist Architekt und Informationsarchitekt sowie Autor von 83 Büchern. Er gründete die TED, TEDMED und die eg Konferenzen.

1 A.d.Ü.: Englisch für „Schnappschloss".

Pl. I. *A Magic Square of Squares.*

200	217	232	249	8	25	40	57	72	89	104	121	136	153	168	185
58	39	26	7	250	231	218	199	186	167	154	135	122	103	90	71
198	219	230	251	6	27	38	59	70	91	102	123	134	155	166	187
60	37	28	5	252	229	220	197	188	165	156	133	124	101	92	69
201	216	233	248	9	24	41	56	73	88	105	120	137	152	169	184
55	42	23	10	247	234	215	202	183	170	151	138	119	106	87	74
203	214	235	246	11	22	43	54	75	86	107	118	139	150	171	182
53	44	21	12	245	236	213	204	181	172	149	140	117	108	85	76
205	212	237	244	13	20	45	52	77	84	109	116	141	148	173	180
51	46	19	14	243	238	211	206	179	174	147	142	115	110	83	78
207	210	239	242	15	18	47	50	79	82	111	114	143	146	175	178
49	48	17	16	241	240	209	208	177	176	145	144	113	112	81	80
196	221	228	253	4	29	36	61	68	93	100	125	132	157	164	189
62	35	30	3	254	227	222	195	190	163	158	131	126	99	94	67
194	223	226	255	2	31	34	63	66	95	98	127	130	159	162	191
64	33	32	1	256	225	224	193	192	161	160	129	128	97	96	65

B. Franklin inv. I. Ferguson delin. *J. Mynde sc.*

The great Square is divided into 256 small squares; in which, all the Numbers from 1 to 256 are so placed, as to have the following Properties.

1. The sum of all the 16 Numbers, in any column, horizontal or vertical, is 2056.
2. The sum of half a column, either horizontal or Vertical, is 1028, the half of 2056.
3. The sum in any oblique Line ascending, added to that in the oblique Line descending from it, is 2056.
4. The sum of all the numbers added together, in the 4 little squares next the 4 corners, is 2056.
5. If a square hole (as below) be cut in a piece of paper, of such a size as to take in just 16 of the small squares, and be laid upon any part of the great Square; the sum of all the 16 Numbers seen through the hole will be 2056, the same as in any column.

The Hole

244	13	20	45
14	243	238	211
242	15	18	47
16	241	240	209

2056

1760

1760

In a magic square the sums of all rows, columns and diagonals are equal. It is constructed by systematically writing down ordered numerical sequences. This example by Benjamin Franklin dates from around 1760.

In einem magischen Quadrat ist die Summe aller Zeilen, Spalten und Diagonalen gleich. Man konstruiert es durch die systematische Aufzeichnung von geordneten Zahlenfolgen. Benjamin Franklin schuf diese Version um 1760.

Dans un carré magique, les sommes de toutes les lignes, colonnes et diagonales sont égales. On le construit en écrivant des séquences numériques dans un ordre systématique. Cet exemple de Benjamin Franklin date des années 1760.

Mes efforts pour comprendre ce que représente le fait de ne pas comprendre

Richard Saul Wurman

Un tsunami de données s'écrase sur les plages du monde civilisé. Ce raz-de-marée d'informations chaque fois plus nombreuses et hétérogènes, sous forme de bits et d'octets, s'approche dans une cacophonie confuse, incontrôlée et incohérente d'écume. Il vient chargé d'épaves. Il compte d'innombrables bâtons, os et fossiles de formes de vie animées et inanimées. Tous ces éléments sont difficiles à mettre en relation et aucun ne vient avec une méthodologie organisationnelle.

Quand il inonde nos plages, nous voyons des gens en costume cravate se promener le long du bord de mer, des hommes et des femmes en chemises et blouses élégantes pour aller travailler. Nous voyons des professeurs, des designers et des fonctionnaires, tous ont leurs chaussures mouillées et sont lentement submergés dans ce gouffre de choses. Leurs pantalons trempés, ils marchent bêtement dans l'eau, souriants (un faux sourire de confiance et de contrôle). Le tsunami est un mur de données générées toujours plus vite, dans des quantités toujours croissantes à stocker en mémoire, quantités qui semblent doubler à chaque coucher de soleil. Sur des bandes, des disques, du papier, dans des flots de lumière renvoyée par les nuages, passant par l'éther du Wi-Fi, 3G, 4G, G squared. Plus vite, plus de données, de tweets, de SMS, d'entrées dans Facebook. Ils acquiescent et disent « oui, c'est important, c'est bien. La personne assise à côté de moi, celle assise dans le bureau au bout du couloir, tous comprennent; je vais donc sourire et faire croire que je comprends aussi ».

Ces mêmes personnes lisent les journaux, leur iPhone, leur iPad ou autre accessoire intelligent pensant qu'elles comprennent les problèmes actuels, s'il est question de récession, de dépression, de croissance ou de recul, de débâcle du système de santé, de la dette nationale ou internationale, des impôts, d'équilibre ou de déséquilibre, de commerce, du dollar plus ou moins coté. Elles hochent la tête, réagissent par réflexe aux mots clés des gros titres, mais sont incapables de dire quelle est l'essence du problème.

Toute la journée, le matin à la maison, au déjeuner au travail et jusqu'au dîner le soir, à voix haute ou pour elles-mêmes, elles disent « oui, oui » pour faire croire qu'elles comprennent une référence à un nom, à un fait, aux connaissances qui sont censées rendre le monde cohérent. Elles disent « oui, oui » à un ami, un professeur, un patron, un collègue quand la discussion porte sur un livre, un film, un article dans un magazine, une machine, un logiciel ou un appareil. Elles disent « oui, oui » à tout le monde car on leur a appris dans leur enfance qu'il ne faut pas avoir l'air stupide, qu'il n'est pas bien de dire « je ne sais pas », de poser des questions, de rester sur un échec. La récompense s'obtient en répondant par « je sais » à tout. Se posent-elles donc mutuellement des questions pour s'occuper?

Vous êtes censé avoir l'air intelligent en société. Vous êtes supposé acquérir des compétences et les vendre pour prospérer dans votre carrière. Vous êtes censé vous en tenir à ce que vous savez faire et le faire chaque fois mieux. Vous êtes supposé vous complaire dans un créneau de capacités. C'est de là que sont censées venir les récompenses.

Évidemment, quand vous vendez votre savoir (vendre dans le sens de progresser dans une entreprise ou vendre une idée à un éditeur, un script à un producteur, un service à un client), vous le faites par définition à partir d'un répertoire limité. Toutefois, quand vous vendez votre ignorance, quand vous vendez votre volonté d'apprendre quelque chose, quand vous vendez votre souhait de créer, d'explorer et de parcourir les chemins menant au savoir et à la compréhension, quand vous vendez votre *curiosité*, vous le faites à partir d'un puits quasiment sans fond représentant un répertoire illimité. De plus, cette vente n'est pas intimidante, elle allie l'explication à la fascination liée à cette compréhension.

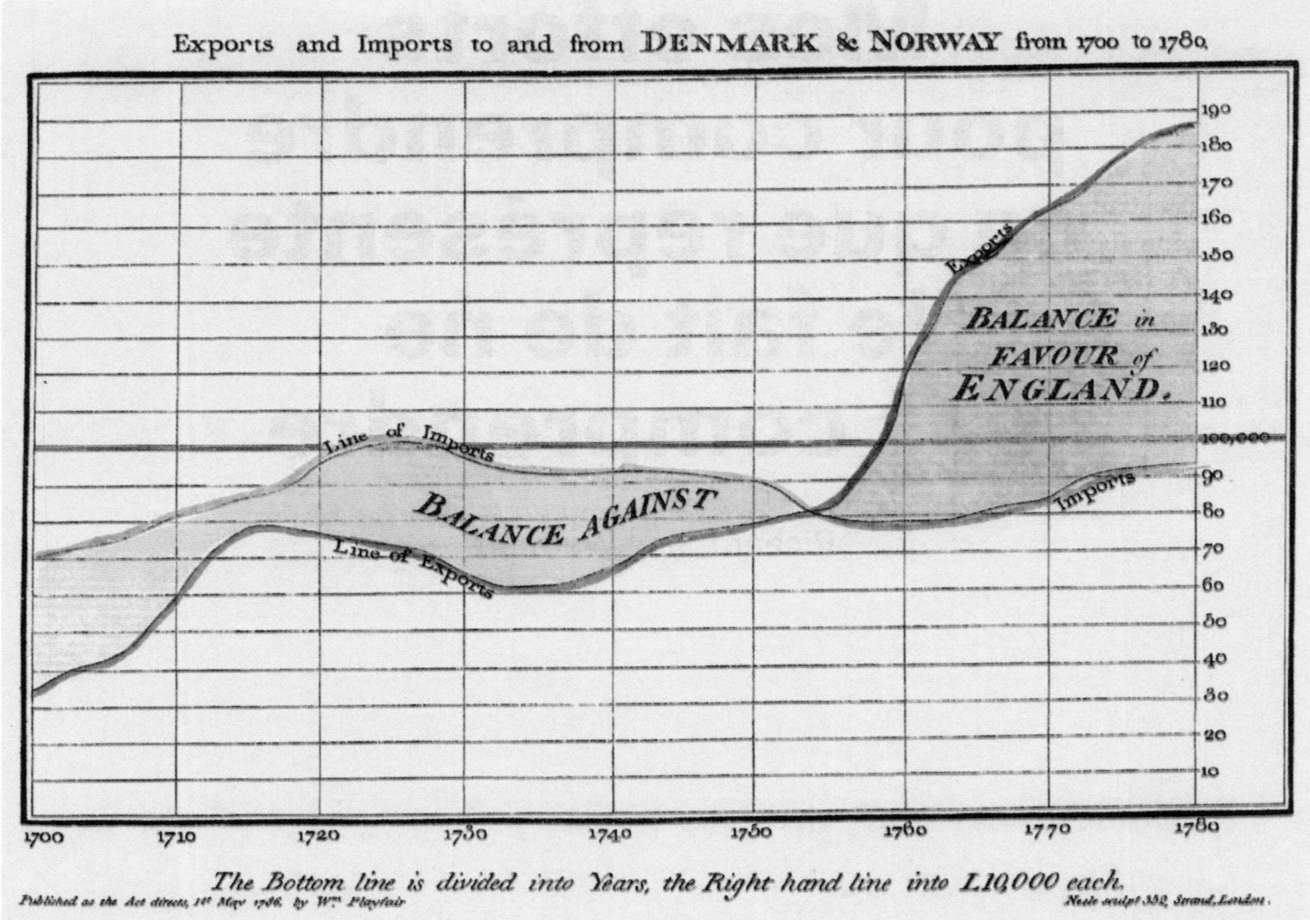

1786

Notre vie est bien contraire à ce que l'on nous a appris. Notre système éducatif repose sur la mémorisation de sujets inintéressants, débités de façon boulimique sur un papier appelé examen, puis oubliés. Nous apprenons à utiliser notre mémoire à court terme et négligeons la mémoire à long terme. La plupart de nos intérêts sont mis de côté. L'intérêt des adolescents pour la musique, les films, les jeux, les voitures et les sports sont abordés comme des sujets au rabais au lieu d'être compris comme des connexions au savoir et la sagesse. La voiture renvoie à l'histoire des transports, à notre système routier, à nos villes et à nos autoroutes. Elle renvoie à la balance des paiements et à l'économie mondiale. À la sidérurgie, à la construction en acier, aux plastiques et au design. Elle renvoie à la physique, aux mathématiques et à la chimie. Elle renvoie aux langues et à la culture. À la médecine et à la politique. Et tout ce à quoi la voiture renvoie est lié à tout le reste. Il en va de même pour les sports, ainsi que pour les loisirs, qui renvoient aux technologies de toutes sortes, au design, au matériel informatique, aux logiciels et aux informations. Les informations sont validées par la compréhension. Nous sommes ce que nous comprenons.

Nous nous souvenons de ce qui nous intéresse. Telle est la définition de l'apprentissage.

Si je jette par terre 140 000 mots, je n'aurai pas un dictionnaire. En revanche, si j'associe une signification à chaque mot et les classe dans l'ordre alphabétique, le résultat s'en approcherait fort. En outre, si je regroupe ces mots par significations sur le même sujet, j'ai le début d'une encyclopédie : un ouvrage organisé par ordre alphabétique et par catégorie. La possibilité d'y faire des recherches dépend de la qualité et du fondement de l'organisation. Nous choisissons d'organiser le dictionnaire par ordre alphabétique et pour la plupart des gens, dans la plupart des cas, ce principe fonctionne.

En fait, l'alphabet est le seul principe d'organisation que nous devions apprendre, car il n'est pas une création divine. Les alphabets changent selon la langue : l'alphabet russe est différent de l'anglais, mais aussi du japonais. Pour nous, l'alphabet est une série de 26 lettres dont l'ordre séquentiel n'a aucune fonction, mais qui se sont avérées utiles dans l'évolution de notre société lettrée. Elles fonctionnent plutôt bien et correspondent à l'une des façons acceptables d'organiser l'information. Nous pourrions organiser les entrées du dictionnaire par groupes. Tous les mots concernant le climat ou la météo pourraient être ensemble, tous ceux relatifs aux automobiles, à la vitesse ou au trafic également, tous ceux liés à la santé et au bien-être formeraient un autre groupe. Ainsi, les grands groupes de mots pourraient avoir une catégorie comme principe d'organisation. À leur tour, les catégories pourraient être classées par ordre alphabétique, avec les mots sur les automobiles sous « A », et les mots sur les animaux et la zoologie sous « A » et « Z ».

Certaines choses s'organisent mieux selon leur emplacement. Les milliers de routes, sites, villes et plans d'eau se comprennent mieux sur une carte. Nous voulons pouvoir trouver immédiatement les endroits qui se trouvent à proximité de nous en observant la carte. Évidemment, nous ne voulons pas traverser la France dans l'ordre alphabétique, pas plus que nous souhaitons que les États-Unis soient organisés dans un atlas avec l'Alabama en premier, puis l'Alaska, et Washington en dernier, car nos déplacements ne suivent pas cette logique. Ce n'est pas notre façon de savoir où aller ou comment trouver ce que nous cherchons.

En me penchant sur l'organisation des informations, j'ai réalisé qu'il n'y avait que cinq manières de procéder et qu'elles pouvaient être mémorisées sous l'acronyme LATCH : (L) pour lieu, (A) pour alphabet, (T) pour temps (de nombreuses expositions dans les musées sont montées de façon chronologique ; la célèbre chronologie de Charlie Eames, réalisée pour son film *The World of Franklin and Jefferson*,

The Scottish economist and engineer William Playfair is considered to be one of the inventors of statistical bar and pie charts. This example from his 1786 *Commercial and Political Atlas* shows the English foreign trade balance with Norway and Denmark.

Der schottische Ökonom und Ingenieur William Playfair gilt als Erfinder von statistischen Balken- und Tortendiagrammen. Dieses Beispiel aus seinem *Commercial and Political Atlas* von 1786 zeigt die Außenhandelsbilanz Englands gegenüber Norwegen und Dänemark.

L'économiste et ingénieur écossais William Playfair est l'un des inventeurs des graphiques à barres et à secteurs. Cet exemple tiré de son *Commercial and Political Atlas* de 1786 montre la balance du commerce extérieur de l'Angleterre avec la Norvège et le Danemark.

est sans doute l'une des meilleures qui existent), (C) pour catégorie (comme dans les grands magasins) et (H) pour hiérarchie, du plus grand au plus petit d'une chose, du plus rouge au moins rouge, du plus dense au moins dense, etc.

Tous ces exemples illustrent l'architecture des informations, la construction de structures qui permettent à autrui de comprendre. Mais les structures de données vont bien au-delà de l'organisation de base et nombre de principes peuvent s'appliquer à des fins de clarté. Par exemple, on ne comprend quelque chose de nouveau que par rapport à autre chose que l'on comprend déjà, que ce soit visuellement, verbalement ou numériquement. Pour comprendre la taille d'une chose il faut la comparer à autre chose, dont on connaît déjà la taille. Cette logique est facile à vérifier si vous observez une photo de bâtiment dénuée de repères à échelle humaine. Ou si vous voyez un tableau dans un musée et êtes surpris par sa taille, parce que les reproductions que vous aviez vues jusqu'alors n'étaient pas à la même échelle. L'échelle s'en réfère toujours à nous.

Pourquoi entrer autant dans le détail sur l'organisation des informations ? Juste pour montrer que la structuration bien pensée des informations est une compétence essentielle qu'un graphiste, un architecte de l'information ou un designer de l'information doivent posséder comme corde à leur arc. Il n'existe pas une seule école qui propose un programme intitulé *Comprendre* ou *La question*.

En 1962, il y a donc près de 50 ans, j'ai réalisé mon premier ouvrage avec les plans de 50 villes du monde, tous tracés à la même échelle. Personne n'avait encore jamais fait ça. Cinq ans après, j'ai créé un atlas urbain, là encore avec toutes les cartes, les légendes et l'analyse statistique à la même échelle, avec le même poids d'informations. Aujourd'hui, en 2011, je travaille sur l'information comparative qui concerne les 51 % de la population mondiale vivant dans des zones urbanisées (selon les Nations Unies), censés passer la barre des 70 % dans les prochaines décennies. Ce passage à l'urbanisation est sans conteste la tendance la plus en vogue du XXIe siècle, ce qui rend encore plus inexplicable l'impossible communication entre les villes.

Il est parfaitement contraire à l'intuition de croire ce qui suit :

- Il n'y a pas deux villes dans le monde qui tracent leurs plans à la même échelle.
- Il n'y a pas deux villes dans le monde qui utilisent les mêmes légendes pour les cartes.
- Il n'existe pas de méthode standardisée pour collecter des informations.
- Les noms employés pour l'utilisation du sol dans les légendes varient énormément. Il existe en fait des centaines d'appellations différentes pour les zones résidentielles, commerciales, commerciales non intensives, de loisirs et les cimetières.
- Il n'existe pas de façon standard de présenter les informations selon la catégorie ou par incidence d'occurrence. En langage verbal (si ces informations ont été décrites dans un texte), la catégorie correspondrait à un nom et l'incidence à un verbe.
- Et pour compléter le tout, comme toutes les grandes villes débordent sur leurs frontières politiques, il n'existe pas de méthode standard pour établir de nouvelles limites.
- Sans frontière ou zone définie, vous ne pouvez pas collecter des données, décrire la densité et faire des comparaisons. Les villes ne peuvent pas se parler entre elles, apprendre ou se comprendre mutuellement.
- La compréhension précède l'action.

Le dernier point est une observation quelque peu apocryphe des films, qui au tout début servaient à stocker des spectacles. Mon iPad stocke des livres et des magazines et simule parfois le fait de tourner des pages. J'attends toujours une nouvelle modalité : un iPad qui peut acquiescer, à qui je peux parler,

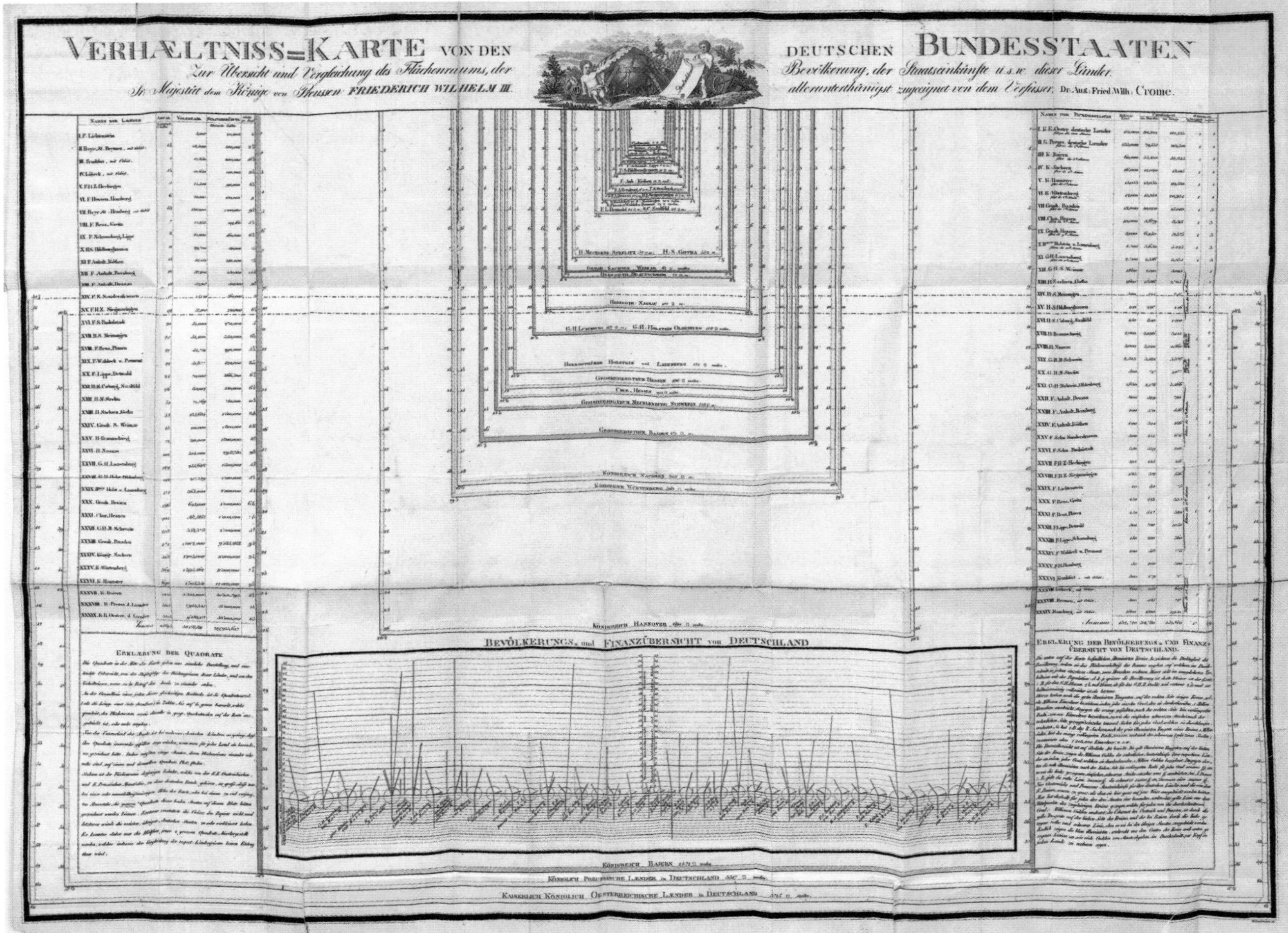

ca. 1820

qui change automatiquement son degré de difficulté ou l'intensité de son contenu à la demande, qui a le sens de la nuance, qui répond et suggère des liens et des connexions pour m'aider dans mon rêve éveillé: mon voyage vers la compréhension.

Mon rêve éveillé est d'avoir un réseau de 20, 50, 100 observatoires urbains à travers la planète, présentant en temps réel des informations intelligibles d'une ville à une autre.

Imaginez-vous en train de vous promener dans ce genre d'endroit: comme première expérience, vous êtes plongé dans un festival, défilé ou spectacle de lumières quelque part dans le monde. Puis vous passez à une pièce remplie d'informations complètes sur l'exploitation du sol, l'économie, la croissance, le tout sur un globe montrant les changements de notre planète, son urbanisation, son interaction, les phénomènes climatiques, les tremblements de terre, les crues, la peste, les guerres, mais aussi la migration des hommes vers les plus grandes villes de la planète. Ce globe est aussi animé par des changements concernant les frontières et les explorations. Un aquarium, une planète Terre centrée sur les personnes plutôt que sur la nature. Il va de soi que l'urbanisation se fait aux dépens du monde sauvage, qui rapetisse à vue d'œil: ce yang ne sera donc pas oublié.

Je pense que nous nous trouvons à ce seuil de basculement.

Un premier orteil dans le bain chaud de cette nouvelle modalité.

Richard Saul Wurman est architecte, architecte de l'information, auteur de 83 livres et fondateur des conférences TED, TEDMED et eg.

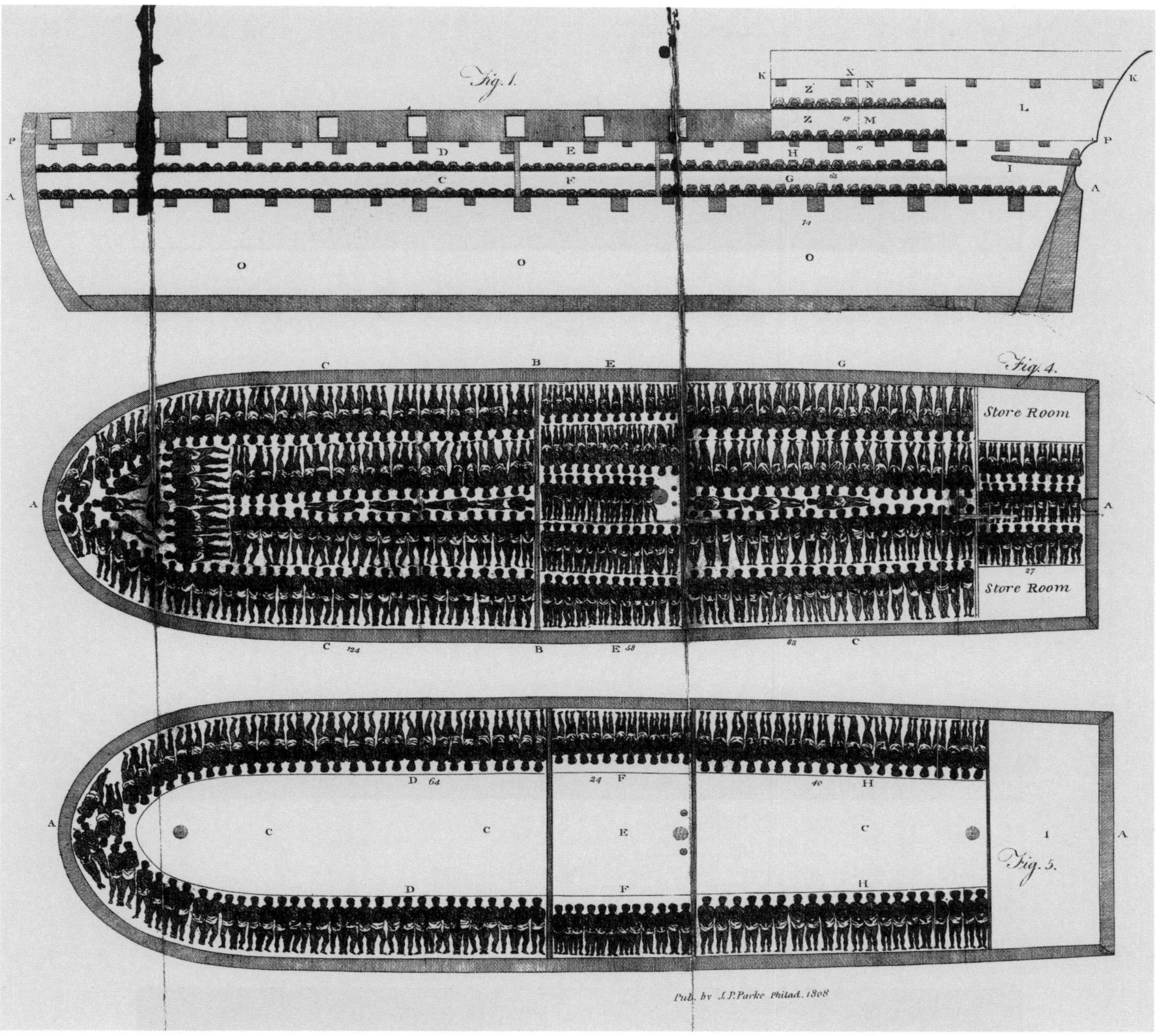

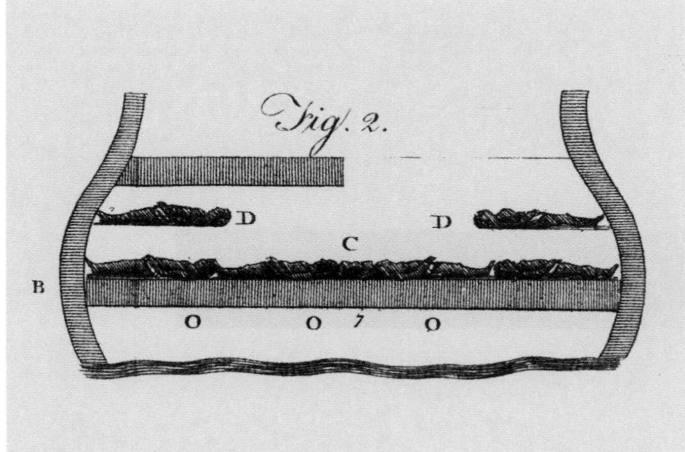

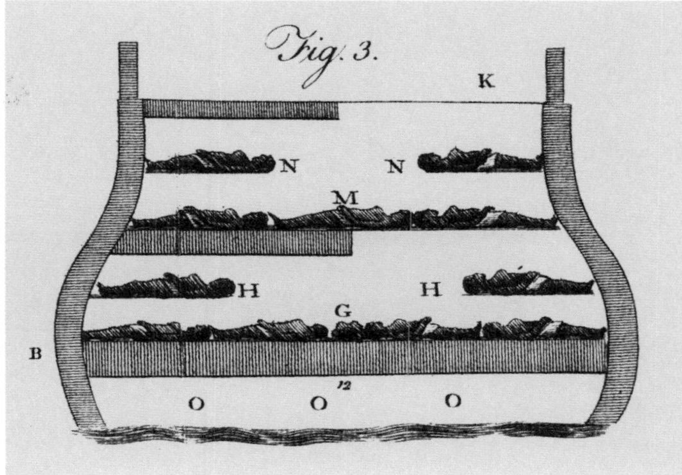

1808

ca. 1820

With this "relational map" from ca. 1820, the statistician Friedrich August Crome developed a display format to compare the very different German federal countries in regard to their size, economical and military power.

Mit dieser „Verhältniskarte" der deutschen Bundesstaaten entwickelte der Statistiker Friedrich August Crome um 1820 eine Darstellungsform, um die sehr unterschiedlichen deutschen Länder in Bezug auf ihre Größe, Wirtschaftskraft und militärische Stärke zu vergleichen.

Dans cette « carte relationnelle » des années 1820, le statisticien Friedrich August Crome organise les données de façon à comparer les États fédéraux allemands en fonction de leur taille et de leur puissance économique et militaire.

1808

English politician Thomas Clarkson was active in the fight against the slave trade and collected evidence for the inhumane treatment of slaves. In this diagram he illustrates how they were penned up for transportation.

Der englische Politiker Thomas Clarkson engagierte sich gegen den Sklavenhandel und sammelte Belege für die unmenschliche Behandlung der Sklaven. In diesem Diagramm zeigte er, wie die Gefangenen für den Transport zusammengepfercht wurden.

Le politicien anglais Thomas Clarkson était engagé dans la lutte contre le commerce des esclaves et a rassemblé des preuves de leur traitement inhumain. Dans ce diagramme, il montre comment ils étaient parqués lors de leur transport.

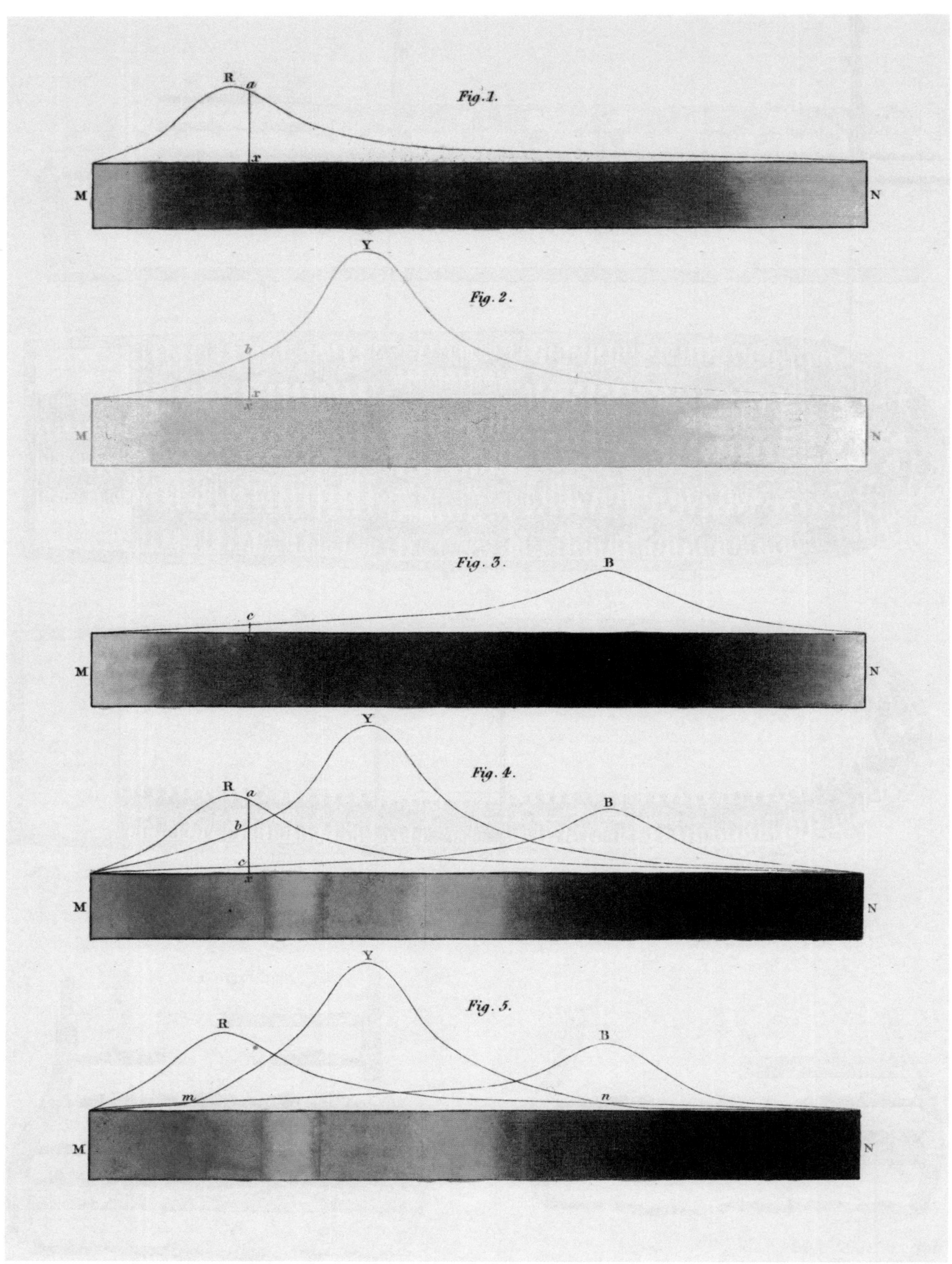

1834

1834

This drawing by David Brewster shows the then known spectrum of solar radiation, including infrared light, visible light and UV radiation (from top). The bottom bars show the complete radiation spectrum including the colours of the visible light.

Diese Zeichnung von David Brewster zeigt die damals bekannte Sonnenstrahlung. Dazu gehören Infrarotstrahlen, das sichtbare Licht und die UV-Strahlung (von oben). Die unteren Balken zeigen das gesamte Strahlenspektrum einschließlich der Farben des sichtbaren Lichts.

Ce dessin de David Brewster montre le spectre des rayons solaires tel qu'il était connu alors, avec la lumière infrarouge, la lumière visible et les rayons ultraviolets (de haut en bas). Les barres du bas montrent tout le spectre, avec les couleurs de la lumière visible.

Simon Rogers 57—76

METHODS OF ASCERTAINING

THE LONGITUDE.

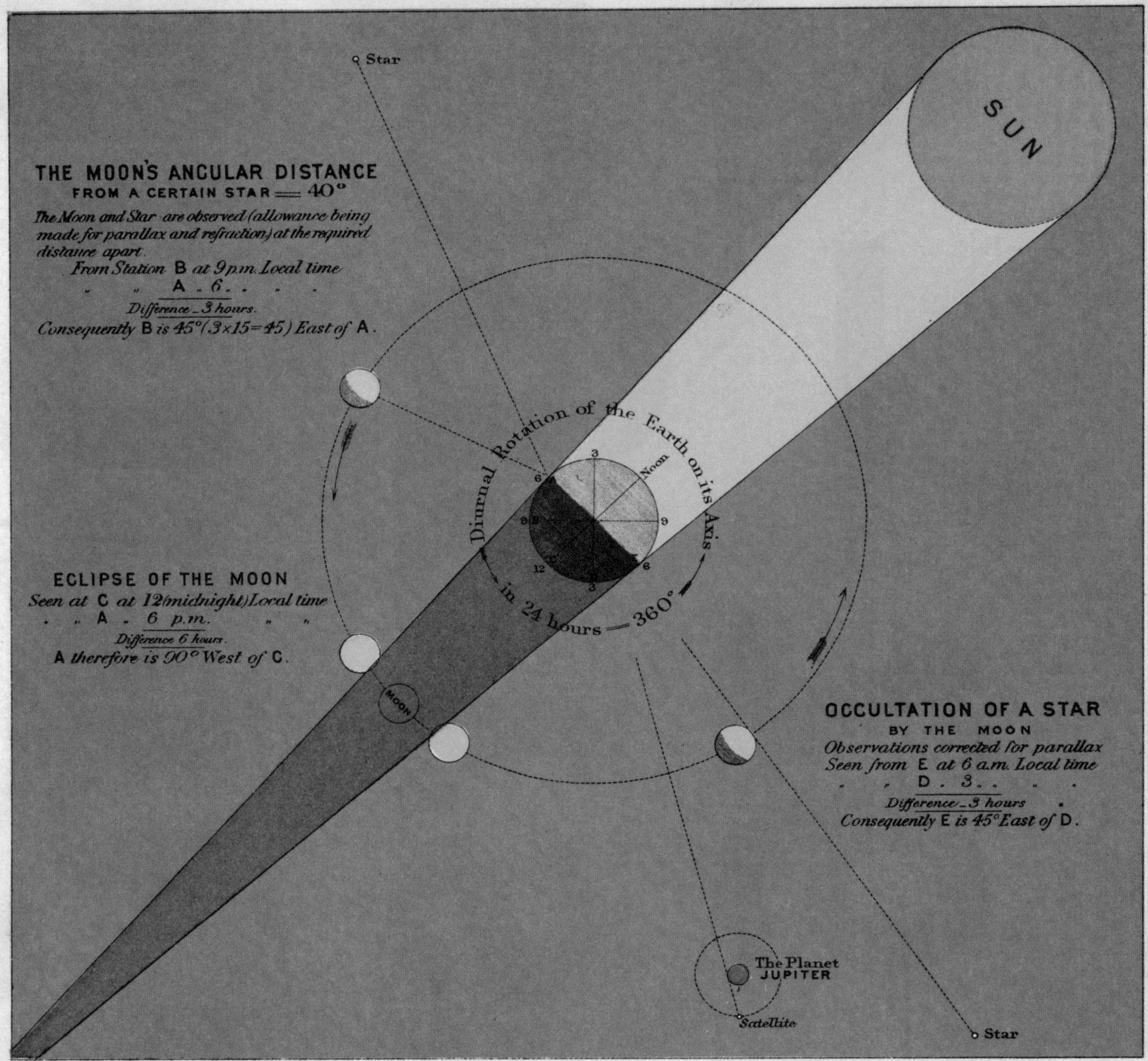
Star
SUN
THE MOON'S ANCULAR DISTANCE
FROM A CERTAIN STAR = 40°
The Moon and Star are observed (allowance being made for parallax and refraction) at the required distance apart.
From Station B at 9 p.m. Local time
" " A . 6 . . . .
Difference _ 3 hours.
Consequently B is 45° (3×15=45) East of A.
Diurnal Rotation of the Earth on its Axis in 24 hours = 360°
Noon
ECLIPSE OF THE MOON
Seen at C at 12 (midnight) Local time
. " A . 6 p.m. " "
Difference 6 hours.
A therefore is 90° West of C.
MOON
OCCULTATION OF A STAR
BY THE MOON
Observations corrected for parallax
Seen from E at 6 a.m. Local time
" " D . 3 . . . .
Difference _ 3 hours
Consequently E is 45° East of D.
The Planet
JUPITER
Satellite
Star

The Longitude of a place is determined by comparing relative times under two different meridians. In consequence of the Earth's rotation upon its axis the Sun appears to move round the Earth from East to West in 24 hours. Places, therefore, to the Eastward of a given meridian have noon sooner, and those to the Westward later, by so much time as the Sun requires to pass over the interval between their meridians.

Each of the phenomena shown upon the diagram is seen *at the same instant* from all parts of the Earth at which it may be visible. The exact moment of the occurrence can be calculated in advance, and is stated in the Nautical Almanac in the local time of the meridian of Greenwich. So, then the difference between the observer's local time when any of these appearances happen and that stated in the Almanac will be the time required by the Sun to pass between his meridan and that of Greenwich; and being turned into degrees at the rate of 15° for 1 hour, will give his longitude East or West according as the local time may be the greater or the less. For example, suppose an eclipse of the Moon to begin according to the Almanac at 10 p.m., and that at the place of observation when the phenomenon happens, the *local* time is 6 p.m., the difference is 4 hours, or 60 degrees of longitude, and Westward of Greenwich. Again, an eclipse of one of Jupiter's Satellites is observed at 4 a.m., local time, when it occurs the time at Greenwich, as stated in the Almanac, is 2 a.m. The difference turned into degrees gives the observer's longitude thirty degrees East of Greenwich.

The longitude is also found by comparing *local* time with that of an accurate chronometer set to, and keeping, Greenwich time.

LONDON: JAMES REYNOLDS & SONS, 174, STRAND.

1850

1850

This educational chart drawn by John Emslie shows three different methods for determining longitude on the Earth. In contrast to latitudes, the determination of longitudes proved very complicated up until the eighteenth century.

Diese Schautafel zu Lehrzwecken, gezeichnet von John Emslie, zeigt drei unterschiedliche Methoden, den Längengrad auf der Erde zu bestimmen. Anders als für die Breitengrade war die Bestimmung der geografischen Länge bis in das 18. Jahrhundert sehr schwierig.

Ce schéma pédagogique dessiné par John Emslie montre trois méthodes pour déterminer la longitude sur la Terre. Contrairement aux latitudes, le calcul des longitudes est resté très compliqué jusqu'au XVIIIe siècle.

How data changed journalism

Simon Rogers

"Data journalism" or "computer-assisted reporting"? What is it? How do you describe it? Is it even real journalism? These are just two terms for the latest trend in journalism, a field combining spreadsheets, graphics, data analysis and the biggest news stories to dominate reporting in the last two years.

The WikiLeaks releases on Afghanistan, Iraq and the US embassy cables; the UK MPs' expenses scandal; the global recession; even the swine flu panic... reporting on all of those events was arguably only possible because of (and irrevocably changed by) the existence of reporters who are not afraid of maths, know how to use a spreadsheet, work with the latest web visualisation tools and – crucially – know what questions to ask.

What is data journalism? It reflects the new transparency movement spreading across the globe, from Washington DC to Sydney, via California, London, Paris and Spain. It's hard to know what came first: the data or the demand for it. Or maybe the two have grown symbiotically. But it seems there was a tipping point where a number of factors combined to form an unstoppable movement. I would argue they were:

- the widespread availability of data via the Internet
- easy-to-use spreadsheet packages on every home computer
- a growing interest in visualising data, to make it easier to understand
- some huge news stories we might never have heard of without data-based reporting

A crucial early step was taken when President Barack Obama, as one of his first legislative acts, announced the US government would launch a new site: data.gov. This was not a million years ago – only 2009.

Data.gov would be a single portal for government datasets, the spreadsheets hitherto published to deafening silence by individual government departments. Go to data.gov today and you will find 1,500 datasets covering everything from crime rates through agricultural planning to the latest population estimates. Some of the stuff is esoterically weird – you can get live data for US river levels, for instance; and some of it is dramatically interesting – the FBI's homicide data gives a breakdown of firearm murders by each US state, with details of which kind of gun was responsible.

The US was followed by countries across the world: Australia, New Zealand and in the UK data.gov.uk, launched by inventor of the worldwide web Sir Tim Berners-Lee. At a more local level, cities and state governments joined the race too: London, Toronto, Vancouver, New York, San Francisco, as well as a good number of US states. More recently, non-English language sites have been launched: from Catalonia in Spain and Paris in France, for instance. If you want to see more sites, you can check out our search engine of open data sites around the world: www.guardian.co.uk/world-government-data.

But you'd be wrong to think this process was entirely led by governments. There's the pioneering work of enthusiasts like Hans Rosling with his Gapminder project. Or the huge impression made by Al Gore's use of charts in his lectures on climate change.

Then there are transparency campaigners like the *Guardian*'s Free our Data movement, which has long called for governments to release the data they charge for. We have, after all, paid for it – why can't we have access to massive datasets such as post-code data and Ordnance Survey geography. Thanks to those campaigns, the UK's official mapmaker Ordnance Survey has been forced to release its data.

Locally, those big campaigns have translated to thousands of ultra-local journalists, reporters who might write about an area only a few miles wide. These reporters either hunt down the data they need or demand their local governments give it to them

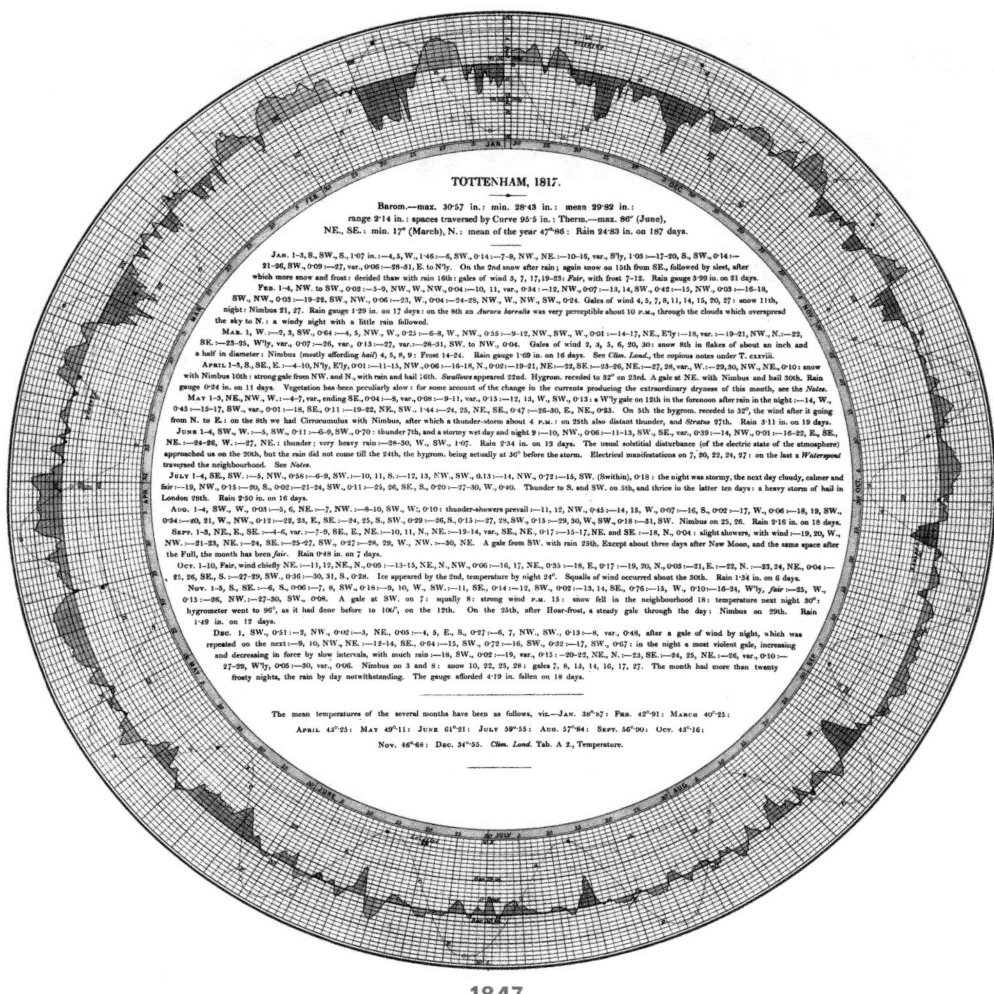

1847

through Freedom of Information legislation. This is the Open Data movement in action.

There are still some rules, of course: crucially, the data has to be available in a form you can manipulate – as an Excel spreadsheet or a CSV file. Why does that matter? Well, traditionally, statistics were published in the least accessible format possible: books, and then later as Adobe PDF files. PDF files look like books, read like books and may as well be books; they're of absolutely no use to anyone wanting to analyse the data for themselves or to visualise that data. In the past, when we all relied on official bodies to tell us what we needed to know, it didn't matter if the data was aggregated and analysed for us. But now we trust governments very little, and traditional media outlets even less. We want to know the numbers behind the story for ourselves – to see if we're being told the truth and discover our own stories.

If a dataset is published as a spreadsheet it's suddenly easier to use. If that data is properly formatted, i.e. country names have codes on them so you can tell the difference between "Burma" and "Myanmar", or "Congo" and "Congo, Dem Rep" – well, suddenly you can start mashing data together, combining poverty rates with carbon emissions or crime figures with economic growth, for instance. Then you can start to create journalism which either works in words or even graphics – or both. Sometimes just reproducing a table tells you a story.

A lot of this isn't new – it's just easier now for us to all find. In fact what governments have offered have been, for the most part, portals to collections of data they all offered anyway. But there is new information out there too. In the UK, the coalition government elected in 2010 has committed itself to releasing a "tsunami of data" as part of its transparency agenda. And, only a few months in, we have seen huge datasets released: every government item of spending over £25,000; salaries of senior civil servants; detailed Treasury spending records; street-by-street crime data and individual hospitals' performance on fighting superbugs like MRSA.

Very soon, every local authority in England will have published every individual item of spending over £500. Some commentators worry about the end of local journalism with the closure of newspapers around the country. But here is an endless source of stories just waiting to reward reporters hungry enough to find them.

In the new industry, all of that data has combined with a feeling, maybe even a hunch, that no one trusts or likes their news source very much any more. At a time when established news organisations have to fight with bloggers and citizen journalists for their very existence, there has been a move towards explaining the news, to being open about the sources of our stories. One of the hits has been the independent website Where Does My Money Go? Its main purpose is simply to explain how the British government spends its money.

At the *Guardian*, we launched our first official foray into data journalism at the same time as we launched our Open Platform API. The Datablog (guardian.co.uk/datablog) – which I edit – was to be a small blog offering the full datasets behind our news stories. In just two years it has become a portal to world data and data visualisation bringing in around a million page impressions a month. Now it consists of a front page (guardian.co.uk/data); searches of world government and global development data; data visualisations by *Guardian* graphic artists and others (including Information is Beautiful's David McCandless) and tools for exploring public-spending data.

As a news editor and journalist working with graphics, for me it was a logical extension of work I was already doing. Every day I was accumulating new datasets and wrangling with them to try to make sense of the news stories of the day. In turn, my professional life has been bookended by war. My first day on the paper's newsdesk was September 10, 2001. After the events of

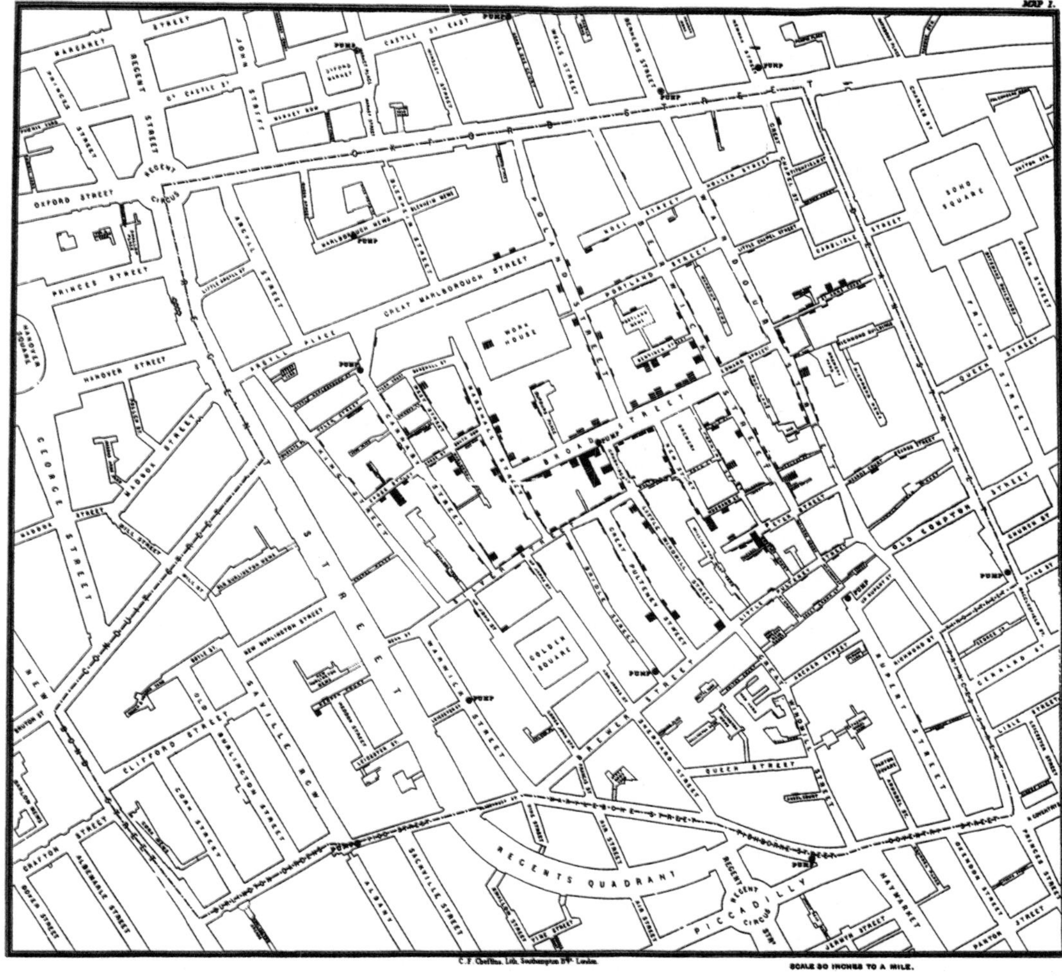

1854

the following day, the results have been reverberating through the newspaper's pages ever since.

Gradually, the Datablog's work reflected and added to the stories we faced. We crowdsourced 458,000 documents relating to MPs' expenses and we analysed the detailed data of which MPs had claimed what. We helped our users explore detailed Treasury spending databases and published the data behind the news.

But the game-changer for data journalism happened in spring 2010. It began with a spreadsheet: 92,201 rows of data, each one containing a detailed breakdown of a military event in Afghanistan. This was the WikiLeaks war logs. Part one, that is. There were to be two more episodes to follow: Iraq and the cables. The official term for the first two parts was SIGACTS: the US military Significant Actions Database. A recent article in the *New York Times* explained how US soldiers were drowning under the weight of detailed datasets. SIGACTS was one of these. Recorded by soldiers in the field, this was war as it was fought, complete with military jargon and incredible detail.

With the WikiLeaks files we had two criteria for success: help our journalists access the information, break down and analyse the data – and make it available for our users. The Afghanistan and Iraq data came to us as huge spreadsheet files, over 92,000 rows of data in the first, nearly 400,000 rows in the second. Iraq and Afghanistan are now the most-documented wars in history. By contrast, the Vietnam war revealed in 1972 by the Pentagon papers was only 7,000 pages.

The data was well structured: each event had the following key data: time, date, a description, casualty figures and – crucially – detailed latitude and longitude. The cables, by contrast, were a mess – a huge text file, with fields running into one another and merging together. The work to clean up that database of 251,000 records was immense.

In the data team we started filtering the numbers to help us tell the key stories of the war: in Afghanistan it was the rise in IED (improvised explosive device) attacks. This data allowed us to see that the south, where the British and Canadian troops are, was the worst-hit area – which backed up what our reporters who had covered the war knew. In Iraq it was breaking down the huge casualty numbers – over 109,000 people's deaths were detailed in the dataset.

The casualties data brought its own challenges, repeated again when we dealt with the Iraq data. It was often inaccurately compiled and incomplete – we compared Nato-recorded casualties too, to test the veracity of the data, and the results varied.

1847

Luke Howard played an important role in establishing meteorology as a science. This plate from his work *Barometrographia* visualises weather data collected in Tottenham, London, in 1817. The circular graph shows barometric pressure and lunar phases over the course of the year.

Luke Howard trug zur Durchsetzung der Meteorologie als Wissenschaft bei. Diese Tafel aus seinem Buch *Barometrographia* visualisiert Wetterdaten, die in Tottenham in London im Jahr 1817 gemessen wurden. Der kreisförmige Graph zeigt Luftdruck und Mondphasen über den Verlauf eines Jahres.

Luke Howard a joué un grand rôle dans l'ascension de la météorologie au statut de science. Cette planche de son ouvrage *Barometrographia* représente des données collectées à Tottenham, Londres, en 1817. Le graphique circulaire montre la pression barométrique et les phases de la Lune.

1854

The London physician John Snow held the novel view that cholera was caused by polluted drinking water. In this map he proved that the accumulation of cases was centred around a contaminated well during a cholera epidemic in 1854.

Der Londoner Arzt John Snow vertrat die neuartige These, dass Cholera durch kontaminiertes Trinkwasser ausgelöst wird. Während einer Cholera-Epidemie im Jahr 1854 bewies er mit dieser Karte die Häufung von Krankheitsfällen rund um einen verseuchten Brunnen.

Le médecin londonien John Snow a été l'un des premiers à penser que le choléra était causé par de l'eau potable polluée. Avec cette carte, il a prouvé que les cas d'une épidémie de 1854 étaient concentrés autour d'un puits contaminé.

1858

This *Table of Universal History* was published in Paris. It visualises the complete history of humankind, top down, from the creation of Adam and Eve to the then present day. Individual cultures are depicted as rivers.

Dieses *Tableau der Universalgeschichte* wurde in Paris veröffentlicht. Es visualisiert von oben nach unten die gesamte Menschheitsgeschichte von der Schöpfung Adams und Evas bis in die damalige Gegenwart. Verschiedene Kulturen sind als einzelne Flüsse dargestellt.

Ce *Tableau de l'histoire universelle* a été publié à Paris. C'est une représentation de toute l'histoire de l'humanité, de haut en bas, depuis la création d'Adam et Ève. Les différentes cultures sont représentées sous la forme de rivières.

Using developers to help map the data, we created a map of every IED explosion in Afghanistan, the data team working with graphic artists to work out what needed to be displayed and the best way of doing it. Online, this translated into an interactive graphic where users could play out the attacks over time. With the Iraq table we opted to use a free tool – Google Fusion Tables – to map out each one of the 66,000 incidents where someone died. It was not perfect, but a start in trying to map the patterns of destruction which had ravaged Iraq.

Guardian developers including Alastair Dant created online interactives, showing attacks over time, or a single day's worth of events. We allowed users to download selected sets of the data to see for themselves how the story unfolded. And we provided interactive guides and data breakdowns for key documents.

That is just one set of stories, a single high-point in data journalism's road to acceptance. There are still reporters out there who don't get what all the fuss is about, who really don't want to know about maths or spreadsheets. But for others, this new wave represents a way to save journalism. A new role for journalists as a bridge and guide between those in power who have the data (and are rubbish at explaining it) and the public who desperately want to understand the data and access it but need help. We can be that bridge.

In future our role may even be in supplying data as trusted sources, as a "safe" location of quality information. Sometimes people talk about the Internet killing journalism. The WikiLeaks story was a combination of the two: traditional journalistic skills and the power of the technology, harnessed to tell an amazing story. In future, data journalism may not seem amazing and new; for now it is. The world has changed and it is data that has changed it.

Simon Rogers is a journalist. He edits the *Guardian* Datastore and is engaged with the professional journalistic use of statistical data.

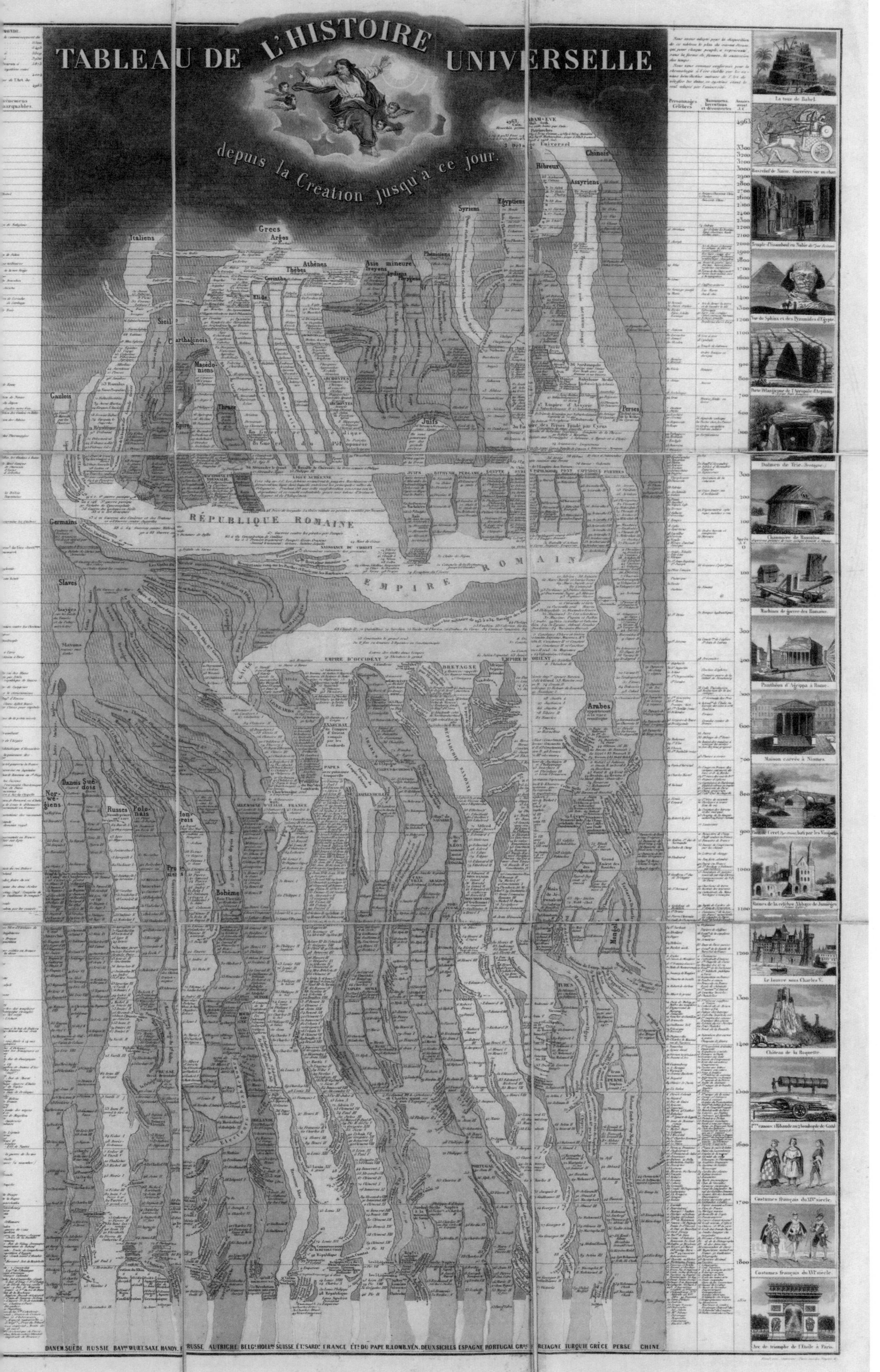
TABLEAU DE L'HISTOIRE UNIVERSELLE
depuis la Création jusqu'à ce jour.
RÉPUBLIQUE ROMAINE
EMPIRE ROMAIN
DANEM SUÈDE RUSSIE BAVre WURT SAXE HANOV. PRUSSE AUTRICHE BELG HOLLde SUISSE ÉTs SARDs FRANCE ÉTs DU PAPE R.LOMB.VÉN. DEUX SICILES ESPAGNE PORTUGAL GRde BRETAGNE TURQUIE GRÈCE PERSE CHINE
La tour de Babel.
Dolmen de Trie.
Chaumière de Romulus.
Machines de guerre des Romains.
Panthéon d'Agrippa à Rome.
Maison carrée à Nismes.
Le Louvre sous Charles V.
Château de la Roquette.
Costumes français du XIVe siècle.
Costumes français du XVIe siècle.
Arc de triomphe de l'Etoile à Paris.

1858

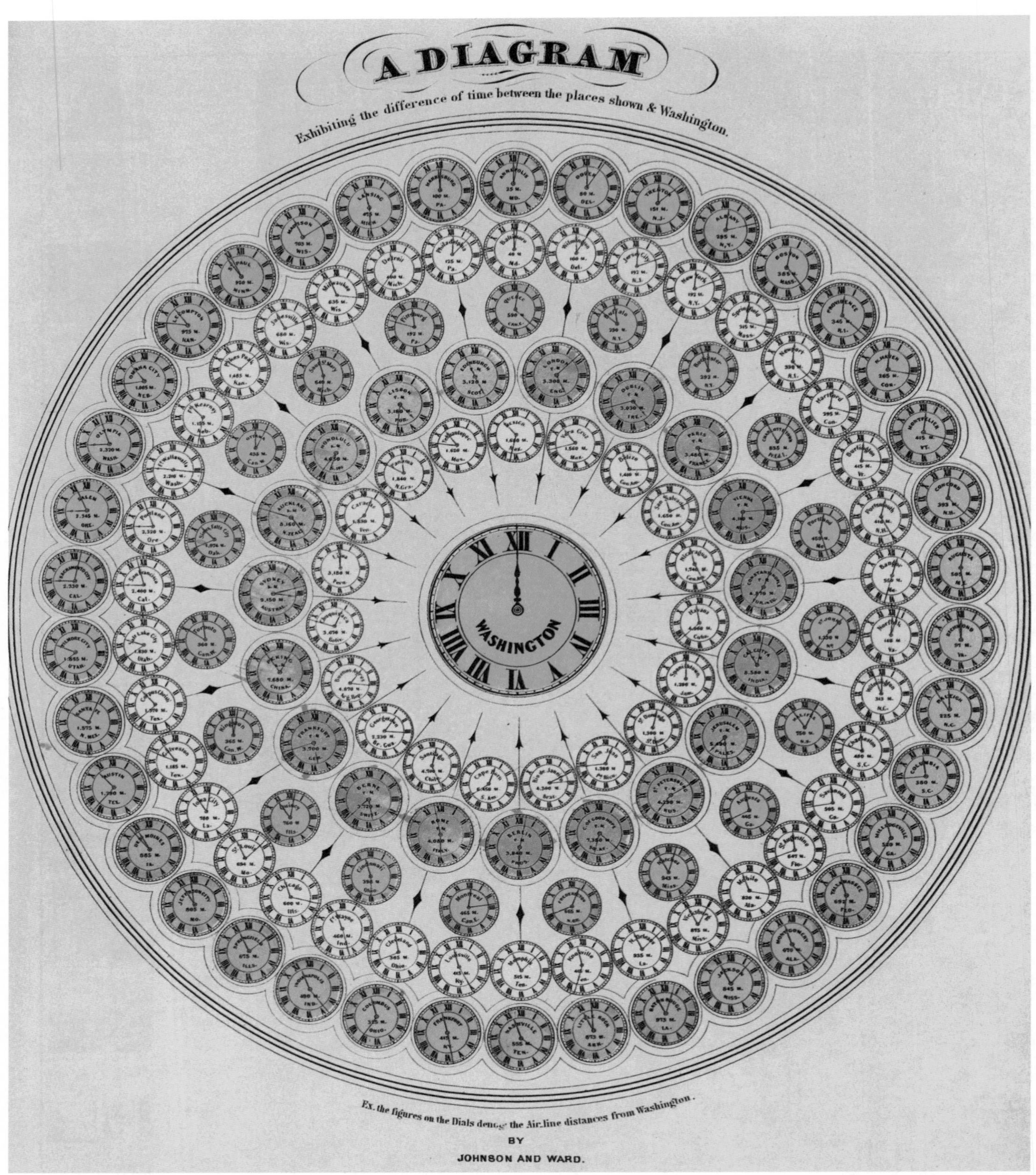

A DIAGRAM
Exhibiting the difference of time between the places shown & Washington.
WASHINGTON
Ex. the figures on the Dials denote the Air-line distances from Washington.
BY
JOHNSON AND WARD.

1862

1862

This diagram visualises time differences seen from Washington, D.C. (centre). Numerous smaller clocks symbolise places around the globe. Each clock face shows the local time and names place, country and the distance to Washington in miles.

Dieses Diagramm visualisiert Zeitverschiebungen aus der Perspektive von Washington, D.C. (Mitte). Zahlreiche kleinere Uhren stehen für Orte rings um den Globus. Das Zifferblatt zeigt die lokale Zeit und nennt Ort, Land und die Entfernung nach Washington in Meilen.

Ce diagramme représente les différences horaires par rapport à Washington (au centre). Les petites horloges symbolisent des villes du monde entier. Chacune indique l'heure locale, le nom de l'endroit, le pays, et la distance par rapport à Washington en miles.

Wie Daten den Journalismus veränderten

Simon Rogers

„Datenjournalismus" oder „computergestützte Recherche"? Was ist das? Wie beschreibt man es? Ist das überhaupt Journalismus? Diese beiden Begriffe sind nur zwei von vielen für den neuesten Trend im Journalismus, einen Trend, der Tabellenkalkulationen, Grafiken und Datenanalysen mit nachrichtenwürdigen Storys verbindet und die Berichterstattung der letzten beiden Jahre zunehmend geprägt hat.

Die WikiLeaks-Enthüllungen zu Afghanistan, dem Irak und den Depeschen der US-amerikanischen Botschaften, der Spesenskandal britischer Abgeordneter, die globale Rezession, selbst die Panik wegen der Schweinegrippe – Berichte über diese Themen verdanken wir Journalisten, die keine Angst vor Mathematik haben, Tabellenkalkulationen zu benutzen verstehen, mit den neuesten Visualisierungs-Tools für das Internet vertraut sind und – das ist ganz wesentlich – wissen, welche Fragen sie stellen müssen. (Natürlich wurde die Berichterstattung dadurch auch unwiderruflich verändert.)

Was ist Datenjournalismus? Auf jeden Fall spiegelt sich in ihm die neue Transparenzbewegung, die sich über den ganzen Globus ausbreitet, von Washington D.C. über Kalifornien, London, Paris und Spanien bis nach Sydney. Es ist schwer zu sagen, was zuerst da war: die Information oder die Nachfrage danach. Vielleicht entwickelten sich beide auch symbiotisch. Scheinbar jedoch gab es einen kritischen Punkt, an dem mehrere Faktoren sich zu einer unaufhaltsamen Bewegung ausformten. Meiner Ansicht nach waren das folgende Umstände:

- die weitverbreitete Verfügbarkeit von Daten über das Internet,
- die vorinstallierten Softwarepakete mit einfach zu handhabenden Tabellenkalkulationen auf jedem PC,
- das wachsende Interesse an der Visualisierung von Daten, um Information verständlicher aufzubereiten,
- einige Enthüllungsberichte, von denen wir ohne datengestützten Journalismus nie erfahren hätten.

Ein entscheidender früher Schritt in diese Richtung wurde unternommen, als der amerikanische Präsident Barack Obama als eines seiner ersten Gesetzesvorhaben ankündigte, die US-Regierung werde die neue Website data.gov einrichten. Das geschah nicht vor Ewigkeiten, sondern im Jahr 2009, liegt also noch gar nicht so lange zurück.

Data.gov war als Portal für staatliche Datensammlungen gedacht; diese bestanden aus Listen, bei deren Veröffentlichung die jeweiligen Behörden bis dato auf völliges Desinteresse gestoßen waren. Wer heute data.gov besucht, findet dort 1500 Datensammlungen zu Themen, die von Verbrechensraten über landwirtschaftliche Planung bis hin zu den neuesten Schätzungen zur Bevölkerungsentwicklung reichen. Einige Informationen sind vielleicht von untergeordnetem Interesse, etwa die aktuellsten Angaben zum Wasserstand der Flüsse in Amerika, andere sind ungeheuer aufschlussreich: In den Mordstatistiken des FBI werden für jeden Bundesstaat die Anzahl der Tötungsdelikte durch Schusswaffen aufgeführt sowie Einzelheiten zu der jeweiligen Tatwaffe.

Zahlreiche Länder in aller Welt folgten diesem Beispiel, etwa Australien und Neuseeland. In Großbritannien wurde data.gov.uk von Sir Tim Berners-Lee ins Leben gerufen, dem Erfinder des World Wide Web. Auch auf lokaler und regionaler Ebene fanden sich viele Nachahmer, neben London, Toronto, Vancouver, New York und San Francisco auch eine ganze Reihe US-amerikanischer Bundesstaaten. In jüngster Zeit wurden auch Websites gegründet, die nicht auf der englischen Sprache basieren, etwa die von Katalonien oder Paris. Weitere Internetseiten dieser Art lassen sich mithilfe unserer Suchmaschine für Open-Data-Websites auf der ganzen Welt finden: www.guardian.co.uk/world-government-data.

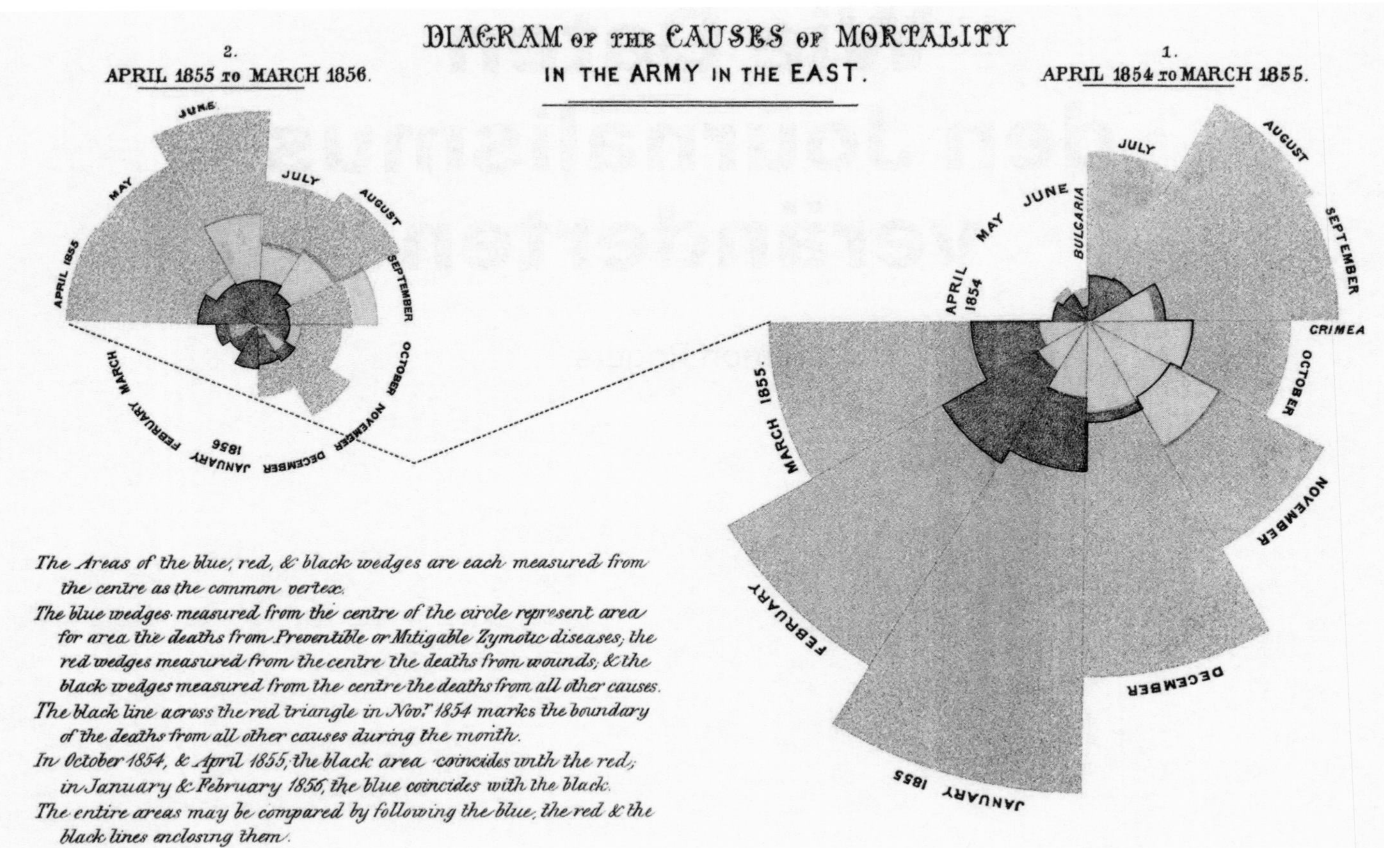

1858

Es wäre allerdings falsch anzunehmen, dass dieser Prozess ausschließlich von staatlichen Behörden in Gang gesetzt worden wäre. Man vergesse die Pionierarbeit von Enthusiasten wie Hans Rosling mit seinem Gapminder-Projekt nicht oder denke an den überwältigenden Eindruck, den die Statistiken hinterließen, mit denen Al Gore seine Vorträge zum Klimawandel untermauerte.

Überdies gibt es Transparenzaktivisten wie die „Free our Data"-Bewegung der englischen Tageszeitung *The Guardian*, die Regierungen seit Langem dazu drängt, ihre mit Steuergeldern erhobenen Daten zu veröffentlichen. Schließlich haben wir dafür bezahlt – warum also sollten wir die gewaltigen Sammlungen etwa von Postleitzahlen und von Vermessungsämtern erhobener Daten nicht einsehen können? Dank derartiger Kampagnen etwa wurde Ordnance Survey, der offizielle Kartenhersteller Großbritanniens, gezwungen, seine Daten zugänglich zu machen.

In England sind diese großen Kampagnen Tausenden lokal arbeitender Journalisten zugutegekommen, die oft über ein Gebiet von nur wenigen Quadratkilometern berichten. Diese Reporter stöbern entweder die benötigten Daten auf, oder sie fordern die zuständige Lokalbehörde mit Verweis auf die Informationsfreiheit auf, ihnen die Information zur Verfügung zu stellen. Das ist gelebte Open-Data-Bewegung.

Natürlich gibt es nach wie vor gewisse Regeln. Allen voran müssen die Daten in einer Form vorliegen, die es erlaubt, sie zu bearbeiten, als Excel-Spreadsheet oder als CSV-Datei. Weshalb das wichtig ist? Früher wurden Statistiken in Formaten veröffentlicht, die sich denkbar schlecht zur Bearbeitung eigneten: zuerst als Bücher, später als Adobe-PDF-Dateien. PDF-Dateien sehen aus wie Bücher, lesen sich wie Bücher und könnten ebenso gut Bücher sein – für jemanden, der die Information selbst analysieren oder sie visualisieren möchte, sind PDF-Dateien absolut nutzlos. Früher verließen wir uns darauf, dass staatliche Behörden uns mitteilten, was wir wissen mussten; folglich war es unerheblich, dass die Daten zusammengefasst und für uns analysiert wurden. Heute jedoch vertrauen wir den Regierungen nur noch sehr bedingt und den herkömmlichen Medien noch weniger. Wir möchten selbst die Zahlen hinter den Storys kennen – um herauszufinden, ob man uns die Wahrheit sagt, und um unsere eigenen Geschichten zu entdecken.

Wird eine Datensammlung als Tabellenkalkulation veröffentlicht, ist sie ungleich einfacher zu benutzen. Wenn die Daten zudem richtig formatiert sind, das heißt, dass Ländernamen Codes haben, sodass man zwischen „Burma" und „Myanmar" oder „Kongo" und „Kongo, Dem. Rep." unterscheiden kann – dann kann man plötzlich Daten zueinander in Beziehung setzen, kann Armutsquoten mit dem Ausstoß von Kohlendioxid korrelieren und Verbrechenszahlen mit Wirtschaftswachstum, um nur zwei Beispiele zu nennen. Das ist die Basis für eine Berichterstattung, die entweder mit Worten arbeitet oder mit Grafiken – oder mit beidem. Manchmal genügt ja eine Tabelle, um eine Geschichte zu erzählen.

Vieles von all dem ist nicht neu – heute ist es lediglich einfacher, alles zu finden. Regierungen stellen in der Regel nur Portale zu Datensammlungen zur Verfügung, die sie ohnehin schon bekannt gemacht haben. Aber es gibt auch neu erstellte Informationen. In Großbritannien verpflichtete sich die 2010 gewählte liberalkonservative Koalitionsregierung, im Rahmen ihres Transparenzversprechens eine Flut von Daten zu publizieren. Und heute, nur wenige Monate später, sind tatsächlich bereits gewaltige Datenmengen veröffentlicht worden: jeder Etatposten der Regierung über GBP 25.000, die Gehälter leitender Beamter, Aufzeichnungen über Staatsausgaben, nach Straßen aufgeschlüsselte Verbrechensdaten und die Erfolge einzelner Krankenhäuser bei der Bekämpfung von potenziell tödlichen Erregern wie MRSA-Bakterien.

Schon sehr bald wird jede Lokalbehörde in England Ausgaben über GBP 500 uneingeschränkt veröffentlicht haben. Einige Pressevertreter äußern sich

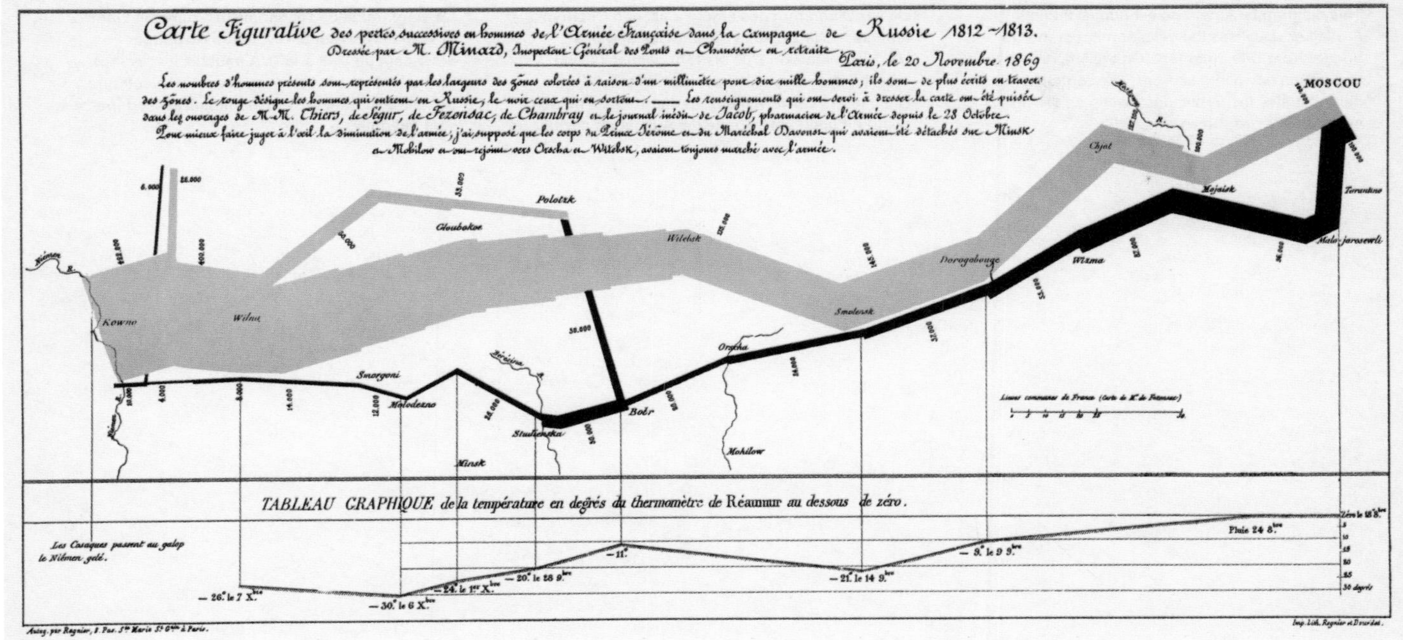

1869

angesichts des landesweiten Zeitungssterbens besorgt über das drohende Ende des Lokaljournalismus. Hier jedoch wartet ein schier endloser Fundus von Geschichten nur darauf, von investigativen Reportern ans Licht gebracht zu werden.

In der sich neu entwickelnden Journalismusbranche wurden diese Daten aus dem Gefühl, vielleicht auch der Ahnung heraus zusammengeführt, dass niemand mehr seinen Nachrichtenquellen vertraut oder sie wirklich mag. In einer Zeit, in der etablierte Nachrichtenorganisationen mit Bloggern und Bürgerjournalisten um ihre blanke Existenz kämpfen, muss man versuchen, die Nachrichten zu erklären und die Quellen seiner Geschichten aufzudecken. Einer der großen Erfolge in dieser Hinsicht ist die unabhängige Website *Where Does My Money Go?* („Wohin fließt mein Geld?"). Ihr Hauptziel besteht einfach darin zu erklären, wie der britische Staat sein Geld ausgibt.

Beim *Guardian* unternahmen wir unseren ersten Ausflug in den Datenjournalismus genau zu der Zeit, als wir die Programmierschnittstelle für unsere Open-Platform in Betrieb nahmen. Der Datenblog (guardian.co.uk/datablog), den ich betreue, war als kleiner Blog geplant, der lediglich die gesamten Informationen darlegen sollte, die unseren Nachrichten zugrunde liegen. Innerhalb von nur zwei Jahren hat er sich zu einem Portal für Daten aus aller Welt und für Datenvisualisierung entwickelt, der auf monatlich rund eine Million Seitenabrufe kommt. Jetzt umfasst er eine Startseite (guardian.co.uk/data), Suchmaschinen für weltweit von Regierungen erfasste Daten und Daten zur globalen Entwicklung, für Datenvisualisierungen von Grafikern des *Guardian* und anderen (wie etwa David McCandless von Information is Beautiful) sowie Tools zum Durchsuchen von Daten über Ausgaben der öffentlichen Hand.

Für mich als Nachrichtenredakteur und -journalist, der mit Grafiken arbeitet, war das eine logische Fortsetzung meiner bisherigen Tätigkeit. Jeden Tag häufte ich neue Daten an und mühte mich mit ihnen ab, um daraus möglichst sinnvolle Nachrichtenstorys des Tages zu gestalten. Mein Berufsleben begann mit dem Krieg. Mein erster Tag am Newsdesk des *Guardian* war der 10. September 2001. Die Auswirkungen, die die Ereignisse des darauffolgenden Tages hatten, schlagen sich seitdem auf den Zeitungsseiten nieder.

Allmählich reflektierte die Arbeit des Datenblogs nicht nur die Geschichten, an denen wir arbeiteten, sie ergänzte sie auch. Durch Crowdsourcing erfassten wir 458.000 Dokumente, die die Ausgaben der britischen Parlamentsabgeordneten belegten, und analysierten genau, welcher Abgeordnete was in Rechnung gestellt hatte. Wir halfen unseren Usern, detaillierte Datensammlungen zu den Ausgaben

1858

The English nurse Florence Nightingale conceived of this polar area diagram to display the high mortality rate in British military hospitals during the Crimean War. Shown in blue is the large majority of soldiers who died of infectious diseases.

Die englische Krankenpflegerin Florence Nightingale entwickelte dieses Polar-Area-Diagramm, um die hohe Sterblichkeitsrate in britischen Lazaretten während des Krimkriegs zu zeigen. Der übergroße, blau dargestellte Teil der Soldaten verstarb an Infektionskrankheiten.

L'infirmière anglaise Florence Nightingale a conçu ce diagramme polaire à secteurs pour montrer le taux de mortalité élevé dans les hôpitaux militaires britanniques lors de la guerre de Crimée. La grande majorité de soldats décédés de maladies infectieuses est indiquée en bleu.

1869

The development of the so-called flow map is based on the work of the French engineer Charles Joseph Minard. This famous example visualises the casualties during Napoleon's invasion of Russia as a narrowing flow of soldiers.

Die Entwicklung der sogenannten Flow Maps geht auf den französischen Ingenieur Charles Joseph Minard zurück. Dieses berühmte Beispiel von 1869 visualisiert die Verluste während Napoleons Russlandfeldzug durch einen immer schmaler werdenden Strom von Soldaten.

Le développement des cartes de flux est basé sur le travail de l'ingénieur français Charles Joseph Minard. Cet exemple célèbre représente les pertes humaines lors de l'invasion de la Russie par Napoléon sous la forme d'un flux de soldats de plus en plus étroit.

This diagram by American economist Francis A. Walker visualises the development of the US budget from 1789 up to 1870. On the left, revenues are broken down into sources. The central column demonstrates the public debt, while on the right, expenditures are shown.

Dieses Diagramm des amerikanischen Ökonoms Francis A. Walker stellt die Entwicklung des US-Haushalts von 1789 bis 1870 dar. Links sind verschiedene Einnahmequellen aufgeschlüsselt. Die mittlere Leiste visualisiert die Staatsschulden, während die rechte Spalte die Ausgaben anzeigt.

Ce diagramme de l'économiste américain Francis A. Walker représente l'évolution du budget américain de 1789 à 1870. À gauche, les revenus sont décomposés selon les sources. La colonne du milieu montre la dette publique, et les dépenses sont indiquées à droite.

des Finanzministeriums zu sichten, und veröffentlichten die Daten hinter den Nachrichten.

Der eigentliche Wendepunkt für den Datenjournalismus kam jedoch im Frühjahr 2010. Es begann mit einem Spreadsheet: 92.201 Datenreihen, die jeweils detailliert ein militärisches Ereignis in Afghanistan schilderten. Das waren die WikiLeaks-Kriegstagebücher. Deren erster Teil, um exakt zu sein. Zwei weitere Teile sollten folgen: zum Irak und zu den Depeschen. Die offizielle Bezeichnung für die ersten beiden Teile war SIGACTS: *Significant Actions Database* (etwa: „Datenbank wichtiger Aktionen") des US-Militärs. Kürzlich wurde in einem Artikel der *New York Times* berichtet, dass die amerikanischen Soldaten von der Masse der detaillierten Daten erdrückt würden. SIGACTS war Teil davon. Die Dokumente wurden von Soldaten im Feld aufgezeichnet und erfassten den Krieg so, wie er ablief, in militärischer Sprache und mit unglaublicher Detailfülle.

Bei den WikiLeaks-Dateien ging es für uns um zweierlei: Wir wollten unseren Journalisten behilflich sein, die Informationen abzurufen, die Daten aufzuschlüsseln und sie zu analysieren – und wir wollten sie unseren Lesern zugänglich machen. Die Daten über Afghanistan und den Irak gelangten als gigantische Spreadsheet-Dateien zu uns, mehr als 92.000 Datenreihen im ersten Fall, fast 400.000 Reihen im zweiten. Die Kriege in Afghanistan und dem Irak sind mittlerweile die am umfangreichsten dokumentierten Kriege der Geschichte. Zum Vergleich: Die Pentagon-Papiere, mit denen 1972 die Hintergründe des Vietnamkriegs aufgedeckt wurden, umfassten ganze 7.000 Seiten.

Die Daten waren gut gegliedert, zu jedem Eintrag wurden folgende Schlüsseldaten mitgeliefert: Uhrzeit, Datum, eine Beschreibung, Verluste und – das Wichtigste – genaue geografische Angaben. Die Depeschen hingegen erreichten uns als Informationschaos – eine gigantische Textdatei, in der Felder ineinander übergingen und miteinander verschmolzen. Es war eine Herausforderung, diese Datenbank mit 251.000 Dokumenten zu ordnen.

Im Datenteam begannen wir damit, die Zahlen zu filtern, um die wesentlichen Geschichten der beiden Kriege herauszuarbeiten. In Afghanistan war das der Anstieg der Angriffe mit USBV (Unkonventionelle Spreng- oder Brandvorrichtungen). Anhand dieser Daten erkannten wir, dass der Süden, wo die britischen und kanadischen Soldaten stationiert sind, am meisten betroffen war – was die Einschätzung unserer Kriegsberichterstatter dort bestätigte. Beim Irak ging es uns darum, die gewaltige Zahl der Todesopfer – die Datei enthielt Angaben zu mehr als 109.000 Todesfällen – aufzuschlüsseln.

Die Daten über die Verluste stellten uns vor große Herausforderungen, die sich wiederholten, als wir uns mit den Irak-Daten beschäftigten. Sie waren häufig inkorrekt zusammengestellt und unvollständig – um sie zu überprüfen, verglichen wir sie mit den von der Nato dokumentierten Todesfällen; die Ergebnisse waren zum Teil abweichend.

Mithilfe von Entwicklern, die die Daten kartierten, entstand eine Landkarte, auf der jede in Afghanistan stattgefundene USBV-Explosion verzeichnet ist. Das Datenteam arbeitete eng mit Grafikern zusammen, um zu entscheiden, welche Inhalte angeführt werden mussten und wie sie sich am besten darstellen ließen. Online zeigte sich das als interaktive Grafik, in der die User die Angriffe chronologisch nachvollziehen konnten. Bei der Irak-Tabelle entschieden wir uns für ein Open-Source-Tool – Google Fusion Tables –, um jeden einzelnen der 66.000 Zwischenfälle mit Todesopfern zu dokumentieren. Es war nicht perfekt, aber immerhin ein Anfang, um die Muster der Zerstörung im Irak nachzuzeichnen.

Guardian-Entwickler, unter anderem Alastair Dant, gestalteten online interaktive Elemente, die die Angriffe über einen Zeitablauf hinweg oder im Verlauf eines einzelnen Tages dokumentierten. Wir ermöglichten den Usern, ausgewählte Daten herunterzuladen, damit

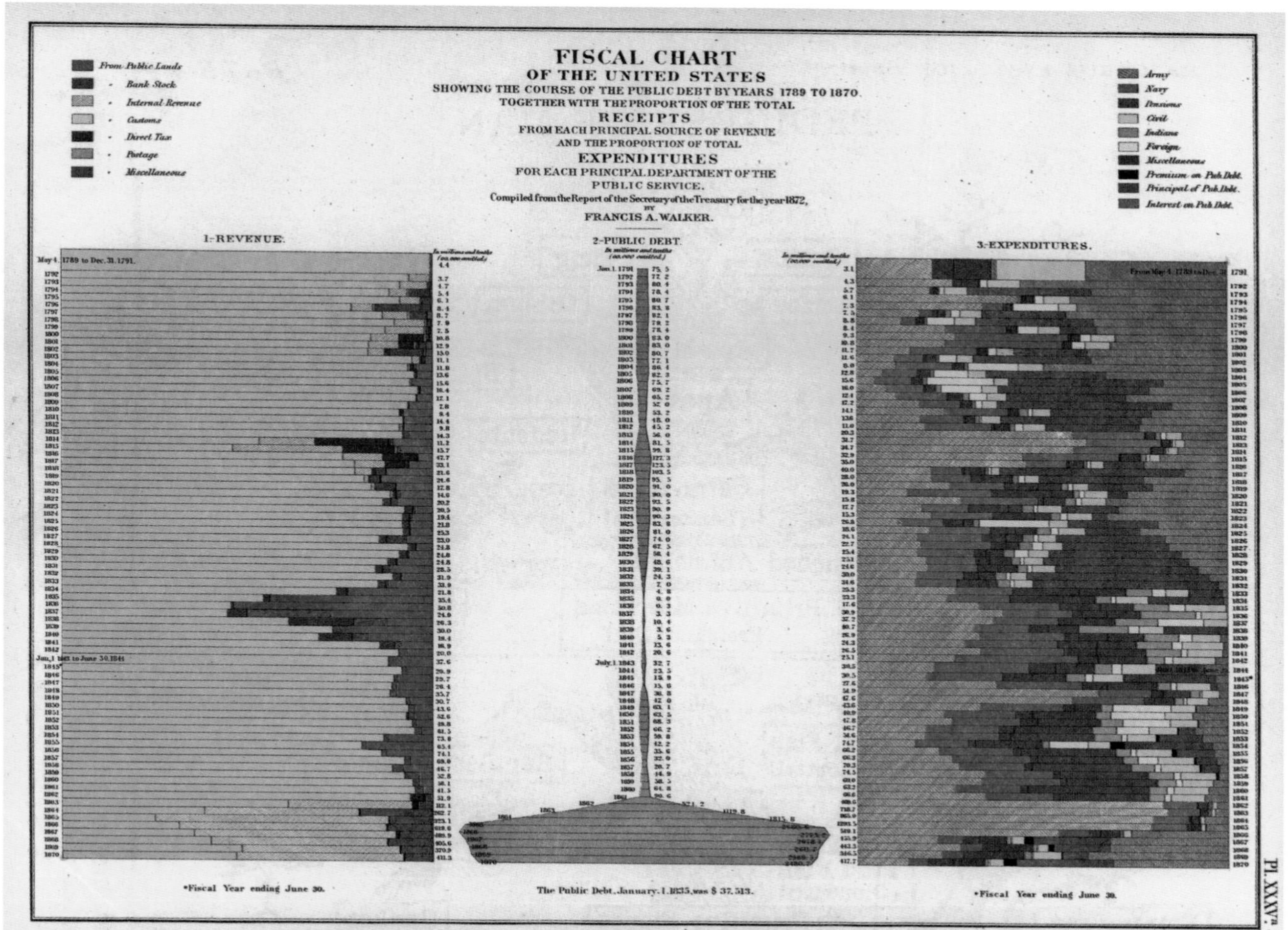

1872

sie den Ablauf der Ereignisse selbst nachvollziehen konnten. Für die wichtigsten Dokumente stellten wir interaktive Guides und Datenaufschlüsselungen zur Verfügung.

Das ist nur eine von sehr vielen Geschichten, ein einzelnes Highlight auf dem Weg des Datenjournalismus zur Akzeptanz. Es gibt immer noch viele Reporter, die nichts von Mathematik und Tabellenkalkulationen wissen wollen und nicht verstehen, worum manche ihrer Kollegen so viel Aufhebens machen. Andere hingegen betrachten diesen neuen Trend als mögliche Rettung für den Journalismus. Eine neue Rolle für Journalisten – als Brücke und Wegweiser zwischen den Mächtigen, die die Informationen haben (und überfordert sind, sie zu erklären), und der Öffentlichkeit, die diese Informationen unbedingt sehen und verstehen möchte, dabei jedoch Hilfe benötigt. Diese Brücke könnten wir sein.

In Zukunft könnte unsere Rolle sogar darin bestehen, als vertrauenswürdige Quelle Daten zu liefern und als „sicherer" Provider hochwertiger Informationen zu dienen. Manchmal heißt es, das Internet sei der Tod des Journalismus. Im Falle von WikiLeaks haben sich diese beiden Medien jedoch die Hand gereicht: Herkömmliche journalistische Arbeit paarte sich mit den Fähigkeiten der Technik, um eine verblüffende Story zu erzählen. In näherer oder fernerer Zukunft wird uns der Datenjournalismus wohl nicht mehr verblüffend erscheinen, momentan ist er es aber durchaus noch. Die Welt hat sich verändert, und bewirkt haben das Daten.

Simon Rogers ist Journalist. Er betreut den *Guardian* Datastore und engagiert sich für den professionellen journalistischen Gebrauch von Statistiken.

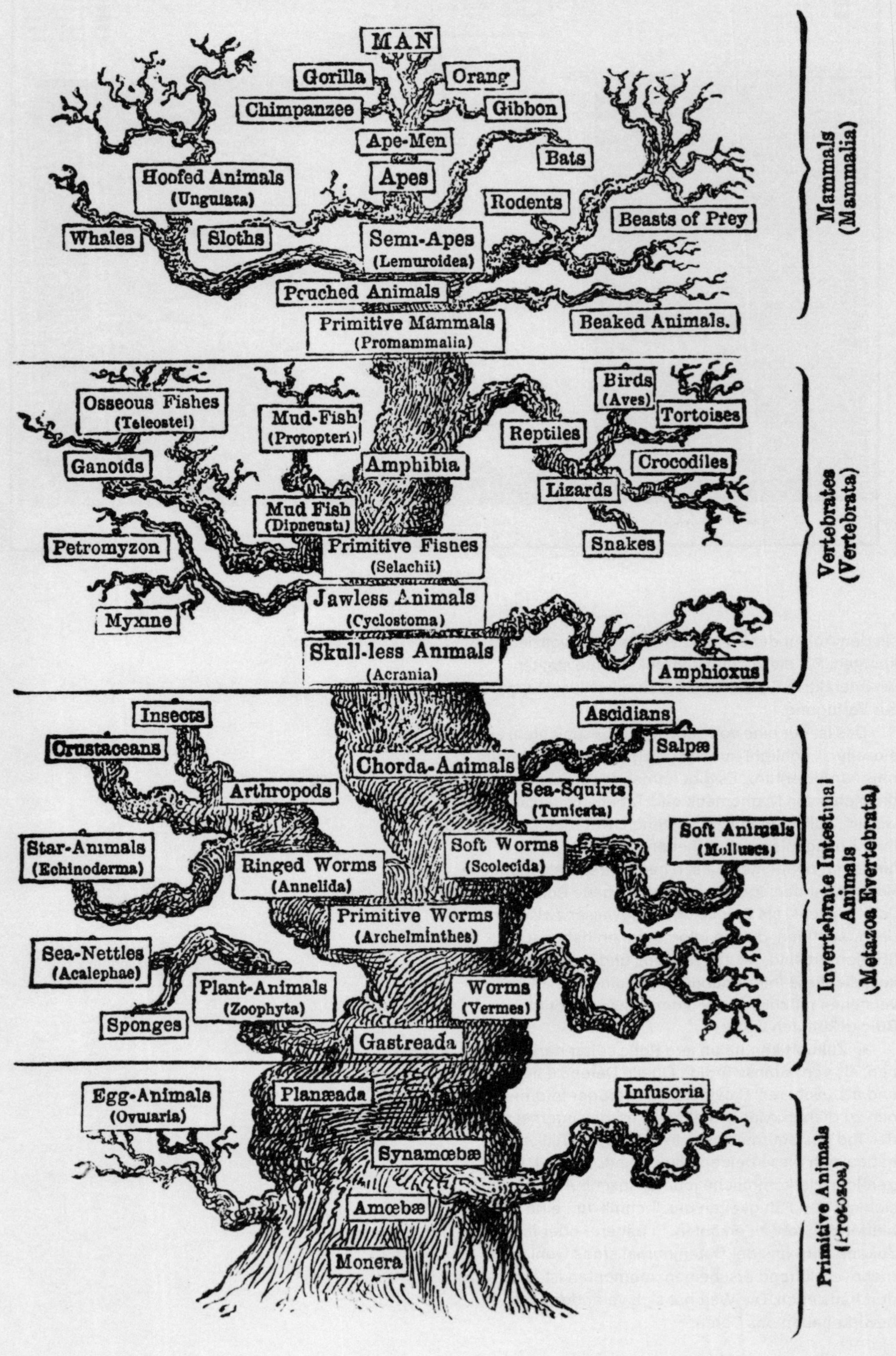

1879

1879

The German biologist Ernst Haeckel advocated Charles Darwin's theory of evolution and expanded it to his own theory of origin. He used a tree to visualise his idea of the evolution of man starting with the most primitive organisms.

Der deutsche Biologe Ernst Haeckel propagierte Charles Darwins Abstammungslehre und baute sie zu einer eigenen Theorie aus. Anhand des Baumes visualisierte er seine Vorstellung von der Evolution des Menschen, ausgehend von den primitivsten Organismen.

Le biologiste allemand Ernst Haeckel a défendu la théorie de l'évolution de Charles Darwin, et l'a étendue à sa propre théorie des origines. Il a utilisé un arbre pour représenter son idée de l'évolution de l'Homme à partir des organismes les plus primitifs.

Comment l'information a changé le journalisme

Simon Rogers

« Journalisme de données » ou « reportage assisté par ordinateur » ? De quoi s'agit-il ? Comment le décrire ? Est-il même vraiment question de journalisme ? Ce ne sont que deux des expressions désignant la dernière tendance en journalisme, une combinaison de tableaux, de graphiques, d'analyses de données et des nouvelles les plus importantes qui dominent les reportages depuis deux ans.

Les publications de WikiLeaks sur l'Afghanistan, l'Iraq et les câbles diplomatiques américains, le scandale des notes de frais des parlementaires au Royaume-Uni, la récession mondiale, la panique de la grippe A H1N1 ... Les reportages sur tous ces événements n'ont sans doute été possibles (et changés de façon irrévocable) que grâce à l'existence de journalistes qui ne craignent pas les mathématiques, savent comment interpréter un tableau, travaillent avec les derniers outils de visualisation web et, avant tout, savent quelles questions poser.

Qu'est-ce que le journalisme de données ? Il reflète le nouveau mouvement de transparence qui se répand à travers la planète, de Washington DC à Sydney en passant par la Californie, Londres, Paris et l'Espagne. Il est difficile de savoir ce qui est venu en premier : les données elles-mêmes, ou la demande de ces données. Peut-être que les deux ont évolué en symbiose. Un point critique a toutefois été atteint, un seuil auquel plusieurs facteurs se sont combinés pour former un mouvement imparable. Il s'agit selon moi :

- de la disponibilité à grande échelle des données via Internet,
- des applications de tableurs simples d'emploi sur tous les PC,
- d'un intérêt croissant pour la représentation graphique des données afin de les rendre plus intelligibles,
- d'un certain nombre de nouvelles de poids dont nous n'aurions peut-être jamais eu vent sans les reportages fondés sur les données.

Avec l'un de ses premiers actes législatifs, le président Barack Obama a pris une décision cruciale en annonçant que le gouvernement américain allait lancer un nouveau site web nommé data.gov. Et cette annonce ne date pas d'il y a un million d'années, seulement de 2009.

Le site data.gov se veut un portail pour les fichiers de données du gouvernement, des tableaux jusqu'ici passés sous un silence assourdissant par les ministères. Si vous consultez aujourd'hui le site data.gov, vous aurez accès à 1500 fichiers sur toutes sortes de sujets, comme le taux de criminalité, la planification agricole ou le dernier recensement de la population. Certains renseignements sont plutôt curieux (vous pouvez par exemple obtenir des données en temps réel sur le niveau des rivières du pays), d'autres extrêmement intéressants (les données du FBI sur les homicides détaillent les assassinats par arme à feu pour chaque État, en précisant le type de pistolet employé).

L'initiative des États-Unis a été copiée par d'autres pays : Australie, Nouvelle-Zélande et Royaume-Uni (data.gov.uk, lancé par l'inventeur du Web Sir Tim Berners-Lee). À une échelle plus locale, des villes et des États individuels ont rejoint le mouvement : Londres, Toronto, Vancouver, New York, San Francisco, ainsi qu'un bon nombre d'États américains. Plus récemment, des sites dans d'autres langues que l'anglais ont vu le jour : la Catalogne en Espagne ou Paris en France, par exemple. Pour consulter d'autres sites, utilisez notre moteur de recherche de sites de données ouvertes : www.guardian.co.uk/world-government-data.

Ne pensez toutefois pas que ce processus a été entièrement mené par les gouvernements. Ce serait oublier le travail pionnier de passionnés comme Hans Rosling et son projet *Gapminder*, ou encore l'impact suscité par la façon dont Al Gore a utilisé les graphiques lors de ses conférences sur le changement climatique.

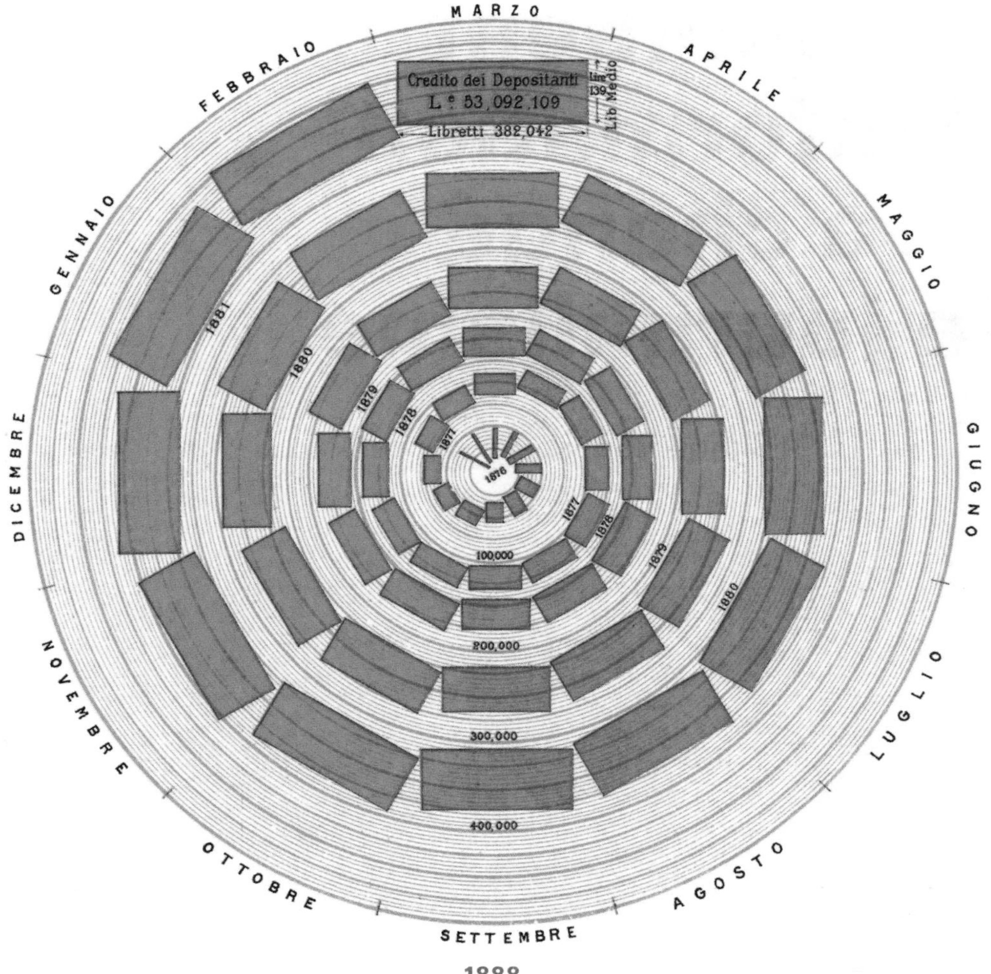

1888

Il existe aussi des militants de la transparence, comme le mouvement Free our Data du *Guardian*, qui appelle depuis longtemps les gouvernements à publier les données qu'ils font payer. Après tout, nous avons déjà payé pour leur constitution, alors pourquoi ne pas pouvoir accéder à ces énormes ensembles de données, comme les codes postaux et la cartographie de l'Ordnance Survey. Grâce à ce type de campagne, l'agence officielle de cartographie du Royaume-Uni a été obligée de publier ses informations.

Au niveau local, ces grandes campagnes se sont traduites par l'apparition de milliers de journalistes ultralocaux, des reporters qui peuvent écrire sur des sujets d'une portée de quelques kilomètres. Ces reporters traquent les informations dont ils ont besoin ou demandent aux autorités locales de les leur fournir en alléguant le droit à la liberté d'information. Tel est le mouvement *Open Data* en pleine action.

Il existe évidemment encore des règles: avant toute chose, les données doivent être disponibles sous une forme exploitable, comme une feuille de calcul Excel ou un fichier CSV. Pourquoi est-ce si important? Au départ, les statistiques étaient publiées dans le format le moins accessible possible: des livres, puis des fichiers Adobe PDF. Les fichiers PDF ressemblent à des livres, se lisent comme des livres et peuvent d'ailleurs être aussi des livres. Ils sont totalement inutilisables pour les personnes qui veulent analyser les données ou les visualiser. Dans le passé, quand nous avions tous recours aux institutions pour qu'elles nous disent ce que nous devions faire, peu importait si les données étaient collectées et analysées pour nous. Mais aujourd'hui, nous ne nous fions guère des gouvernements, et encore moins des médias traditionnels. Nous voulons connaître les chiffres derrière les faits, pour savoir si l'on nous dit la vérité et pour découvrir nos propres histoires.

Si un ensemble de données est publié sous forme de feuille de calcul, il est immédiatement plus simple à utiliser. Si ces données sont dans un format correct (par ex. les noms de pays ont des codes pour distinguer «Burma» et «Myanmar», ou «Congo» et «Rép. dém. du Congo»), vous pouvez croiser ces informations, en combinant par exemple les taux de pauvreté et les émissions de CO_2, ou les statistiques de criminalité et la croissance économique. Ensuite vous pouvez exercer un journalisme qui fonctionne avec des mots et/ou des graphiques. Parfois, le simple fait de reproduire un tableau dévoile une histoire.

Dans tout cela, peu de choses sont nouvelles, mais elles sont désormais plus faciles à trouver. En fait, les gouvernements ont surtout fourni des portails vers des collections de données qui étaient de toute façon déjà disponibles. Vous pouvez toutefois trouver aussi des informations inédites. Au Royaume-Uni, le gouvernement de coalition élu en 2010 s'est engagé à publier un «tsunami de données» dans le cadre de ses efforts de transparence. Après quelques mois seulement au pouvoir, de nombreux fichiers ont en effet été publiés: toutes les dépenses du gouvernement pour un montant supérieur à 25 000 livres, les salaires des hauts fonctionnaires, les dépenses détaillées du Trésor, les données sur la criminalité rue par rue et les résultats des hôpitaux en matière de lutte contre des infections comme le SARM.

Bientôt, toutes les autorités locales d'Angleterre auront publié la moindre dépense dépassant 500 livres. Certains commentateurs s'inquiètent de la fin du journalisme local en voyant des journaux disparaître dans tout le pays. Pourtant, il y a là une source d'articles inépuisable qui n'attend que d'apaiser la soif des reporters.

Dans ce nouveau secteur, toutes ces données sont accompagnées du sentiment, peut-être de l'intuition, que personne ne croit plus et n'aime plus vraiment sa source d'informations. À l'heure où les organismes de presse doivent rivaliser avec les bloggers et les journalistes citoyens pour survivre, on assiste à une volonté d'expliquer les nouvelles, de donner accès aux sources des histoires. L'un des grands succès de

1888

This chart by the Italian statistician Antonio Gabaglio provides both a historical and a quantitative display. It shows the monthly savings deposits at the Italian Post in the period from 1876 to 1881.

Diese Grafik des italienischen Statistikers Antonio Gabaglio liefert sowohl eine historische als auch quantitative Darstellung. Sie zeigt anschaulich die monatlichen Spareinlagen bei der italienischen Post zwischen 1876 und 1881.

Ce graphique du statisticien italien Antonio Gabaglio donne une représentation historique et quantitative à la fois. Il montre les dépôts effectués chaque mois sur des comptes d'épargne de la Poste italienne entre 1876 et 1881.

ce type a été enregistré par le site web indépendant *Where Does My Money Go?*, dont l'objectif est ni plus ni moins d'expliquer comment le gouvernement britannique dépense son argent.

Au *Guardian*, nous avons lancé notre première incursion officielle dans le journalisme de données, en même temps que notre API Open Platform. Datablog (guardian.co.uk/datablog), dont je suis l'éditeur, devait être un petit blog mettant à disposition l'ensemble des données qui étaient à la base de nos articles. En deux ans à peine, c'est devenu un portail de données mondiales et de visualisation des informations, avec environ un million d'impressions par mois. Il compte désormais une première page (guardian.co.uk/data), la possibilité de faire des recherches sur les données fournies par les gouvernements et sur le développement mondial, des présentations graphiques réalisées par les graphistes du *Guardian* et d'autres (dont David McCandless d'Information is Beautiful) et des outils pour explorer les données sur les dépenses publiques.

En tant que rédacteur et journaliste travaillant avec des graphismes, il s'agissait pour moi du prolongement logique du travail que je faisais déjà. J'accumulais chaque jour de nouvelles données et me débattais pour donner un sens aux nouvelles du jour. Ma vie professionnelle a été marquée par la guerre. J'ai commencé à la rédaction du journal le 10 septembre 2001. Après les événements du jour suivant, les pages du journal se sont fait écho des résultats depuis lors.

Peu à peu, le travail du blog a reflété et complété les faits auxquels nous avons été confrontés. Nous avons obtenu auprès des internautes 458 000 documents concernant les notes de frais des parlementaires britanniques et analysé le détail de ce que chacun d'eux avait réclamé. Nous avons aidé nos utilisateurs à consulter les bases de données des dépenses du Trésor et publié les renseignements derrière ces nouvelles.

L'événement qui a changé les règles du jeu en matière de journalisme de données s'est produit au printemps 2010. Tout a commencé avec une feuille de calcul: 92 201 lignes de données, chacune détaillant un fait militaire en Afghanistan. C'était les journaux de guerre de WikiLeaks. Du moins le premier chapitre, car deux autres épisodes ont suivi: l'Iraq et les câbles diplomatiques. Le terme officiel pour qualifier les deux premières parties est SIGACTS, acronyme désignant la base de données des actions clés de l'armée américaine. Un article récent paru dans le *New York Times* expliquait comment les soldats américains étaient submergés par les données. SIGACTS en faisait partie. Enregistrée par les soldats sur le terrain, il s'agissait de la guerre telle qu'elle était vécue, assortie du jargon militaire et d'un niveau de détail incroyable.

Avec les fichiers WikiLeaks, nous avions deux impératifs: aider les journalistes à accéder aux informations, à organiser et à analyser les données, puis les mettre à disposition de nos utilisateurs. Les données sur l'Afghanistan et l'Iraq nous sont parvenues sous la forme d'énormes feuilles de calcul, avec plus de 92 000 lignes dans la première et près de 400 000 dans la seconde. L'Iraq et l'Afghanistan sont désormais les guerres les plus documentées de l'histoire. Pour comparaison, la guerre du Vietnam révélée en 1972 par les documents du Pentagone ne cumulait que 7 000 pages.

Les données étaient bien structurées et chaque événement incluait les renseignements clés suivants: heure, date, description, nombre de victimes et, essentiel, la latitude et la longitude. Les câbles étaient en revanche très confus, dans un gigantesque fichier de texte, avec des parties qui se chevauchaient et se mélangeaient. Le travail de nettoyage de cette base de données de 251 000 entrées a été colossal.

L'équipe chargée des données a commencé à filtrer les chiffres pour nous aider à extraire les principales histoires de la guerre comme, en Afghanistan, la recrudescence des attaques à la bombe artisanale. Ces données nous ont permis de voir que le sud, où se trouvaient les troupes britanniques et canadiennes, était la zone la plus touchée, ce qui est venu corroborer

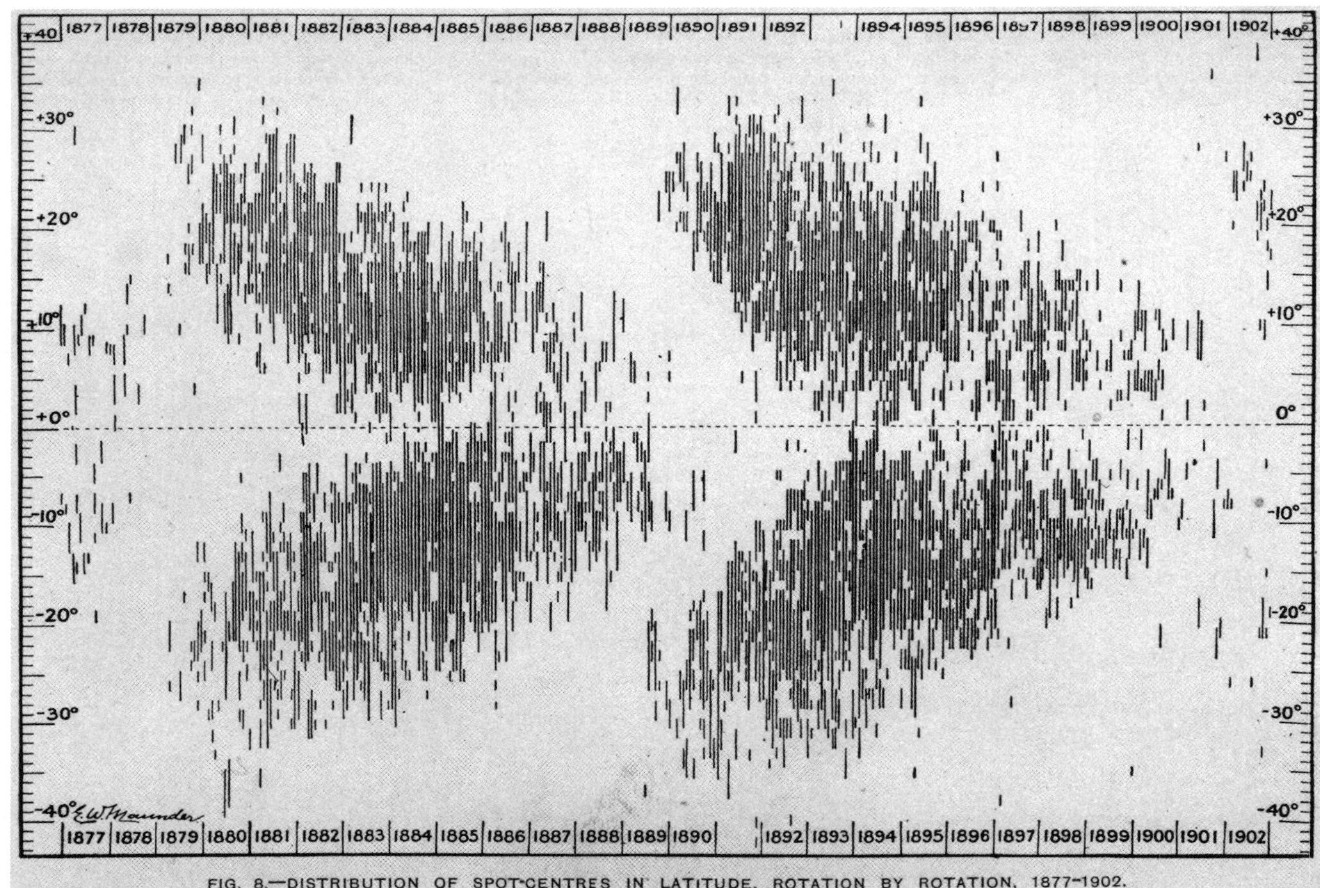

1904

ce que nos reporters couvrant la guerre savaient déjà. Pour l'Iraq, nous disposions du détail des nombreuses victimes, avec plus de 109 000 morts recensées.

Les données sur les victimes ont posé des difficultés qui leur étaient propres, situation qui s'est reproduite au moment de traiter les renseignements sur l'Iraq. Elles étaient souvent mal compilées et incomplètes; nous avons fait la comparaison avec les statistiques de l'OTAN pour vérifier la véracité des données et les résultats étaient très variables.

Avec l'aide de développeurs pour organiser ces informations, nous avons créé une matrice de toutes les explosions de bombe artisanale en Afghanistan. L'équipe chargée des données a travaillé avec des graphistes pour identifier ce qui devait être présenté et la meilleure façon de le faire. Le résultat en ligne a donné une illustration interactive où les utilisateurs pouvaient voir le déroulement des attaques dans le temps. Dans le cas de l'Iraq, nous avons employé l'outil gratuit Google Fusion Tables afin d'organiser les 66 000 incidents lors desquels des personnes ont perdu la vie. Le résultat n'était pas parfait, mais permettait de commencer à identifier les schémas de destruction qui ont ravagé l'Iraq.

Les développeurs du *Guardian*, dont Alastair Dant, ont créé des outils interactifs en ligne montrant le déroulement complet des attaques ou les événements au cours d'une journée. Nous avons permis aux utilisateurs de télécharger certains fichiers pour qu'ils découvrent l'histoire par eux-mêmes. Nous avons aussi fourni des guides interactifs et une ventilation des données pour les principaux documents.

Il ne s'agit que d'un lot d'histoires, d'un pic isolé dans le chemin du journalisme de données vers l'acceptation. Certains reporters ne comprennent pas toute cette agitation et ne veulent rien savoir des mathématiques et des feuilles de calcul. Pour d'autres cependant, cette nouvelle vague est l'occasion de sauver le journalisme. Un nouveau rôle pour les journalistes comme pont et guide entre les gens de pouvoir qui détiennent l'information (et ne savent pas comment l'expliquer) et le public qui veut à tout prix comprendre de quoi il retourne et y accéder, mais qui a besoin d'aide pour le faire. Nous pouvons être ce pont.

Notre rôle sera peut-être de fournir des données sous forme de sources fiables, de créer un lieu « sûr » pour des informations de qualité. Les gens disent parfois qu'Internet est la mort du journalisme. L'histoire de WikiLeaks a été une combinaison des deux: des compétences journalistiques traditionnelles et la puissance de la technologie, exploitées pour raconter une histoire incroyable. Un jour, le journalisme de données n'aura peut-être plus rien de surprenant ou d'inédit, mais pour l'heure, il l'est. Le monde a changé et ce sont les données qui sont à l'origine de ce changement.

Simon Rogers est journaliste. Il dirige le Datastore du *Guardian* et s'intéresse à l'utilisation des données statistiques dans le journalisme.

May 4, 1912] *THE SPHERE* 103

THE LOSS of the "TITANIC."

The Results Analysed and Shown in a Special "Sphere" Diagram

Drawn from the Official Figures Given in the House of Commons

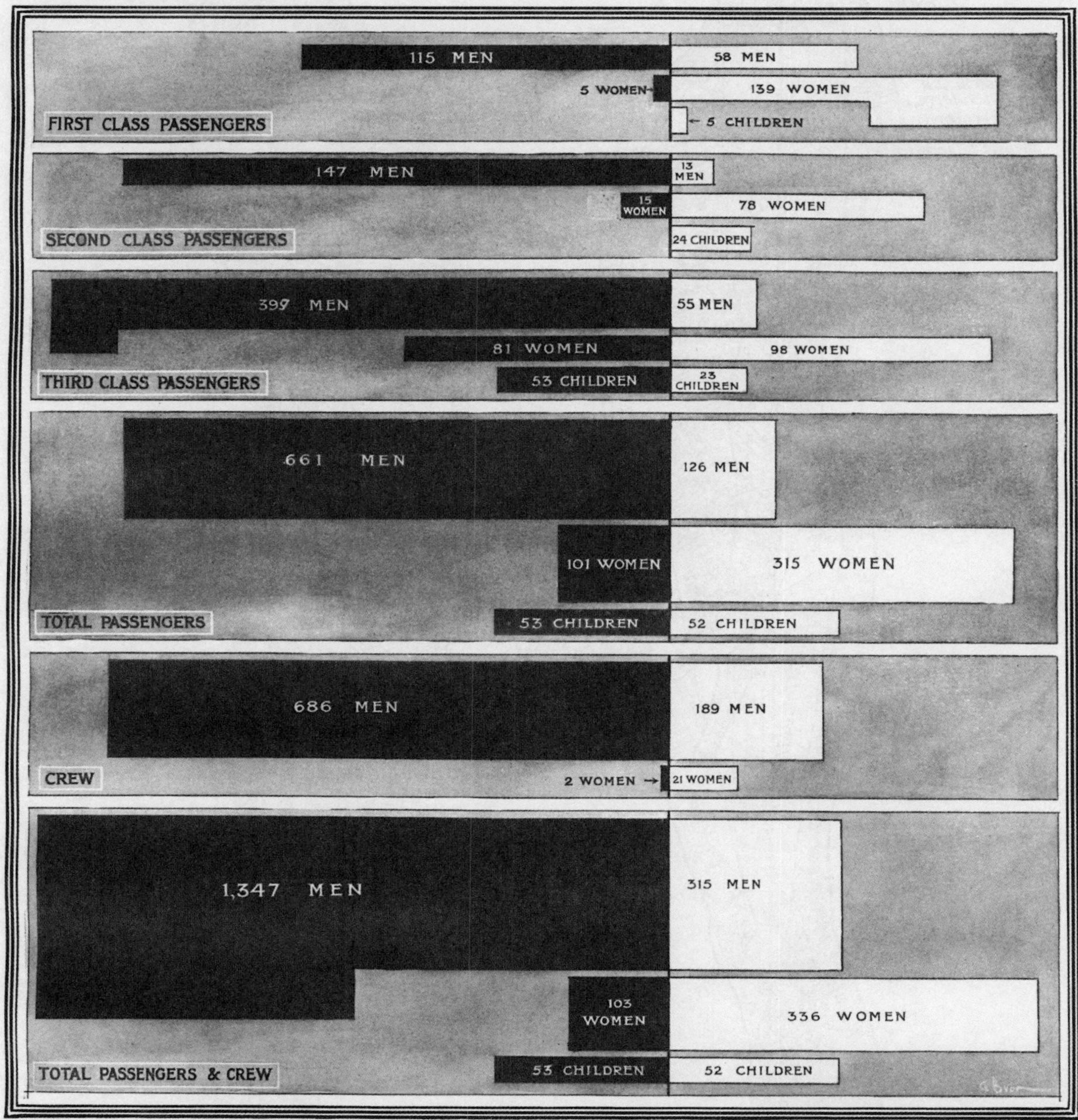

SPECIALLY DRAWN FOR "THE SPHERE" BY G. BRON

The Black Indicates Passengers and Crew NOT SAVED, the White Indicates the SAVED

The official figures given last week show that the first figures (as given in "The Sphere" of last week) were in excess of the real numbers on board by about 132. The actual figures are as above. The actual numbers of the saved and lost are given above; the percentage is shown below

NUMBERS OF SAVED

	Per cent.
First class	63
Second class	42
Third class	25
Crew	23

FIRST CLASS

	Carried	Saved	Per cent.
Men	173	58	34
Women	144	139	97
Children	5	5	100
	322	202	63

SECOND CLASS

	Carried	Saved	Per cent.
Men	160	13	8
Women	93	78	84
Children	24	24	100
	277	115	42

THIRD CLASS

	Carried	Saved	Per cent.
Men	454	55	12
Women	179	98	55
Children	76	23	30
	709	176	25

THE CREW

	Carried	Saved	Per cent.
Men	875	189	22
Women	23	21	91
	898	210	23

PASSENGERS AND CREW

	Carried	Saved	Per cent.
Men	1,662	315	19
Women	439	336	77
Children	105	52	49
Totals	2,206	703	32

c

1912

1904

The English astronomer Edward Maunder discovered that sun spots reappear at certain latitudes of the Sun in a regular cycle of eleven years. Because of their shape, his records are popularly known as "butterfly diagrams".

Edward Maunder, ein englischer Astronom, entdeckte, dass die Sonnenflecken in einem regelmäßigen Zyklus von elf Jahren immer wieder auf bestimmten Breitengraden der Sonne auftreten. Seine Aufzeichnungen wurden ihrer Form wegen als „Schmetterlingsdiagramme" bekannt.

L'astronome anglais Edward Maunder a découvert que les taches solaires réapparaissent à certaines latitudes du Soleil selon un cycle régulier de onze ans. À cause de leur forme, ses graphiques sont connus sous le nom de « diagrammes en papillon ».

1912

This diagram visualises the official statistics on casualties and people saved during the sinking of the *Titanic*, broken down into different categories. It was published in the British magazine *The Sphere*.

Dieses Diagramm visualisiert die offizielle Statistik über Tote und Gerettete beim Untergang der *Titanic*, unterteilt nach verschiedenen Kategorien. Es erschien in der britischen Illustrierten *The Sphere*.

Ce diagramme représente les statistiques officielles des morts et des rescapés du naufrage du Titanic, décomposées en plusieurs catégories. Il a été publié dans le magazine britannique *The Sphere*.

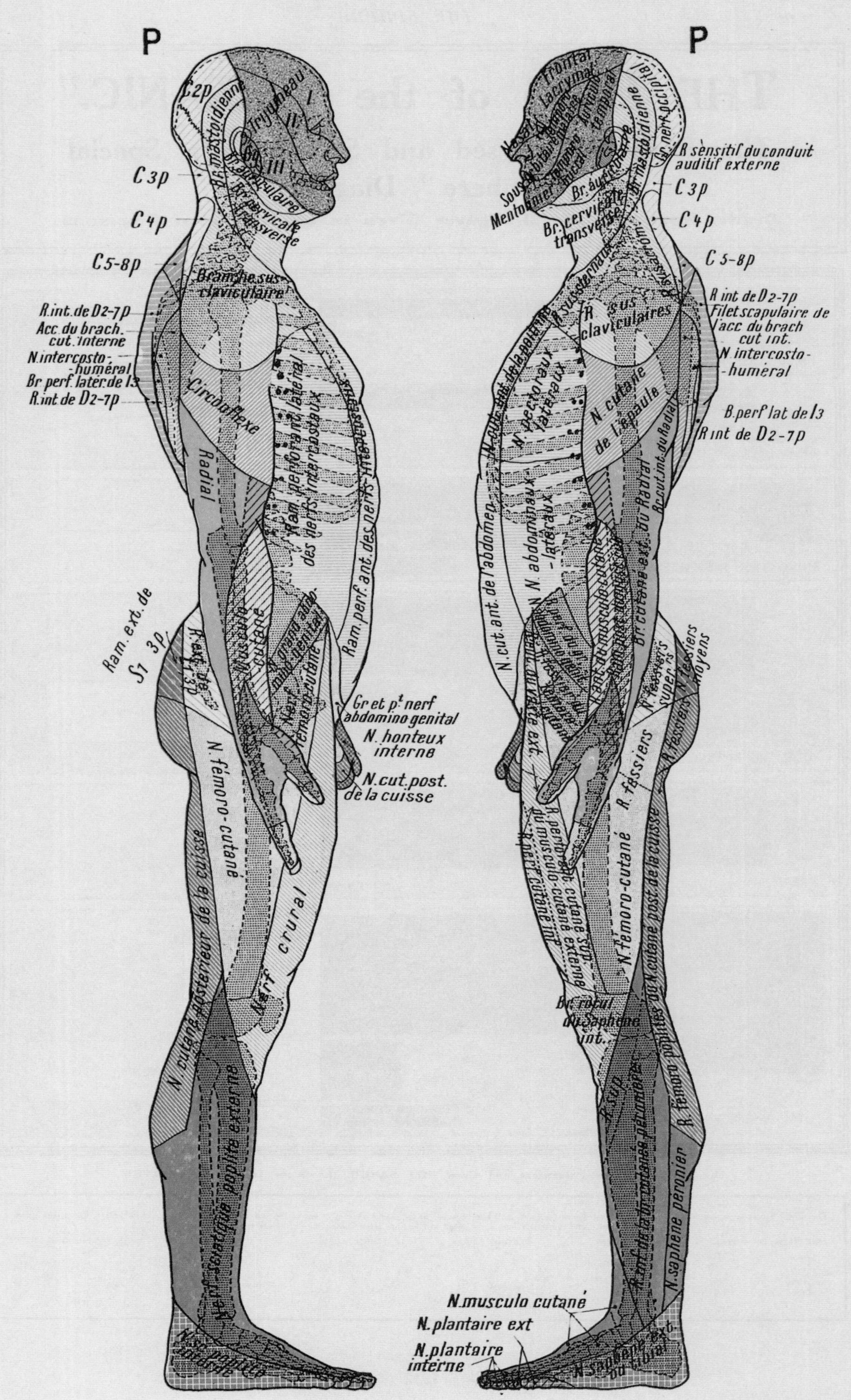

Fig. 381 et 382. — Topographie sensitive périphérique de la peau de la face latérale du corps. Le profil droit représente la distribution cutanée des gros troncs nerveux périphériques; le profil gauche les territoires de chacun de leurs rameaux cutanés.

1914

1914

Joseph Jules Dejerine was a French neurologist whose book *Sémiologie des affections du système nerveux* is considered a classic of his discipline. Amongst other things, he described in it the anatomy of the nervous system, using coloured graphics.

Joseph Jules Dejerine war ein französischer Neurologe, dessen Buch *Sémiologie des affections du système nerveux* als Klassiker seines Faches gilt. Darin beschrieb er unter anderem die Anatomie des Nervensystems mithilfe von kolorierten Grafiken.

Joseph Jules Dejerine était un neurologue français, dont le livre *Sémiologie des affections du système nerveux* est considéré comme un classique de la discipline. Il y décrit, entre autres, l'anatomie du système nerveux à l'aide d'illustrations en couleur.

Paolo Ciuccarelli 77—95

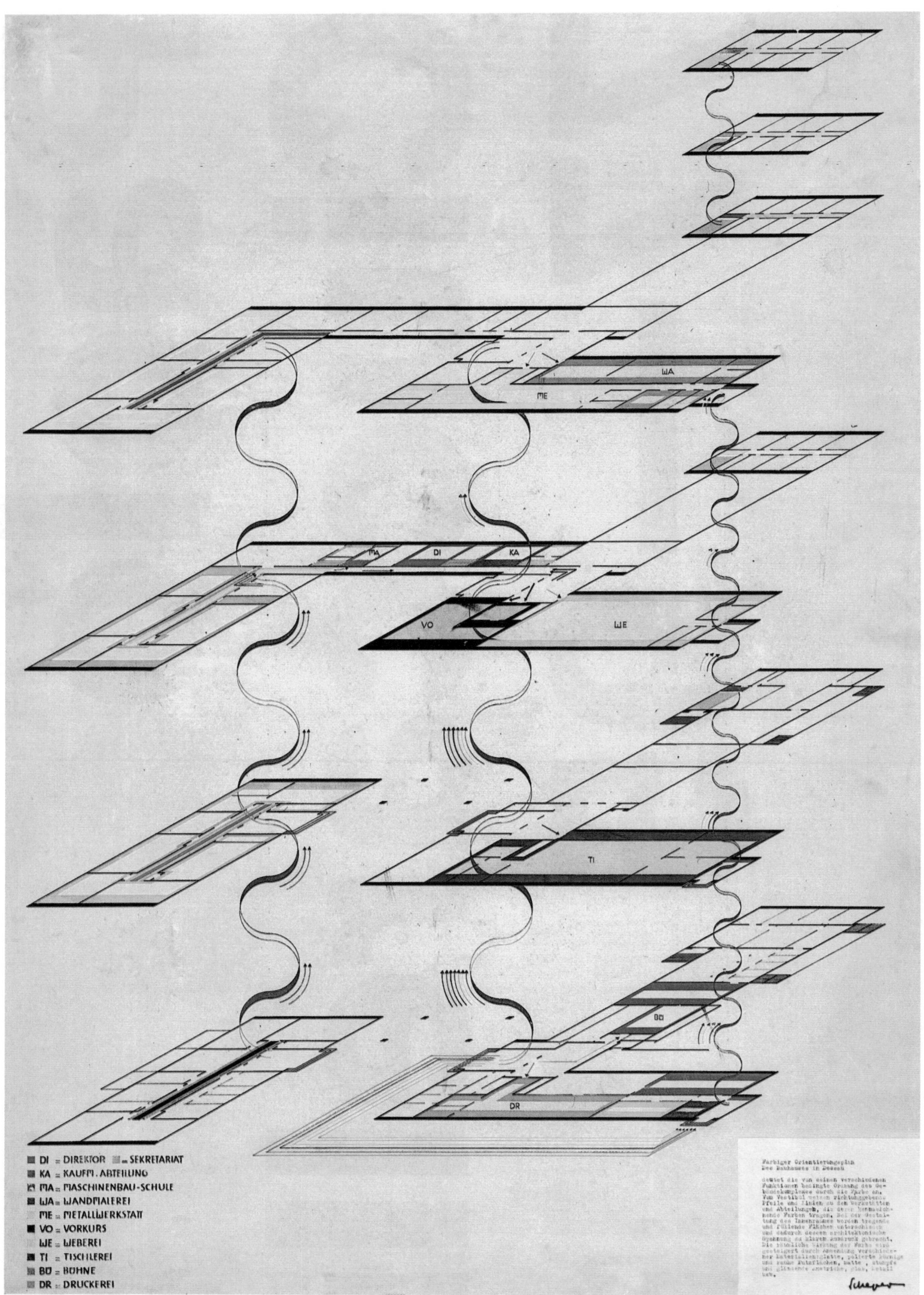

1926

1926

This orientation map was created by Bauhaus teacher Hinnerk Scheper and visualises the room layout in the Bauhaus building in Dessau, Germany. Single floors are shown one upon the other. Colours signify the functions of individual parts of the building.

Dieser Orientierungsplan stammt von dem Bauhausmeister Hinnerk Scheper und zeigt die Raumaufteilung im Bauhausgebäude in Dessau. Die einzelnen Geschosse werden übereinander dargestellt, Farben signalisieren die unterschiedlichen Funktionen von Gebäudeteilen.

Cette carte d'orientation de Hinnerk Scheper, professeur au Bauhaus, représente la disposition des salles dans le bâtiment de Dessau, en Allemagne. Les étages sont montrés les uns sur les autres. Les couleurs indiquent les fonctions des différentes parties.

Turning visualisations into stories and "big pictures"

Paolo Ciuccarelli

The amount of socially relevant data that reaches the public through various media is increasing: epidemics, wars, technological innovations, natural disasters, financial crises and genomic discoveries are all examples of information being released in our ever-expanding cycle of news reporting. Social and economic issues are more often narrated nowadays with numbers complementing text, frequently also accompanied by visual representations of data. This is a major step forward in the human quest for knowledge, but does it really contribute to public understanding of socio-economic phenomena?

It is clear that there is room for improvement, especially in the visual communication of data and information generated by research organisations. These institutions are experiencing an unprecedented opportunity to fill the critical historical debt they have toward society. While scientists have earned recognition and a measure of autonomy, they are still generally considered distant and elitist. They must cope with a public sense of distance and scepticism, and a lack of interest and appreciation. Sometimes they are faced with fierce opposition, despite the relevance of their research for both human and societal development. This gap between sciences and the public has widened over the years, partly because scientists tend to use a specific and often impenetrable language, even on the rare occasions where a clear comment to the public was necessary.

Now, to be granted the resources (money and personnel) and freedom (political independence) necessary to carry on their research, scientific organisations need, more than ever, a close relationship with society; political support, based on broad public consensus, is of utmost importance. Moreover, decisions that affect the activity of research bodies are taken outside of the scientific community more often. Non-experts have the means and the will to participate in decision-making processes in place of experts. The very method of even defining the *expert* is a challenge.

Scientists must nurture a constructive relationship with society. The need for trust is particularly evident when controversial issues are discussed, especially when not even the researchers have a universal consensus. Nuclear energy, global warming, electromagnetic pollution and Genetically Modified Organisms (GMOs) are just a few examples of the many ongoing debates which include strong irrational components.

For these reasons, the marriage between the scientific community and society may be uneasy, but it is certainly necessary. It has not yet been openly celebrated because of a basic communication problem: the sciences and the public do not speak the same language. As the European Commission states in its document "Communicating Science":[1] "The same data that for scientists are another piece to add to a well-known picture of knowledge (and emotions), for the public are only an isolated fragment of information, with almost no meaning."

When the aim is to let the public *see* social or economic problems, simple data visualisations are not enough. People need visual orientation tools. The most important condition for effective participation is to know and understand the context: who are the participants, what are their points of view, which feelings and interests are involved, and which positive and negative forces influence the evolution of the phenomena.

Scientists should try to humanise, if not popularise their communication. If they want to be trusted and gain public legitimacy, they must also be authentic and honest about their limits, insecurities and weaknesses. It is not only a matter of economic survival, it is their ethical duty towards society. Socio-economic issues are by nature complex; one cannot understand them if considering only one aspect. They are ambiguous and blurred; they cannot be measured, and can only be represented in qualitative terms. They are observed using methods having inherent errors and approximations. Data never exactly correspond to the phenomena they are supposed to synthesise.

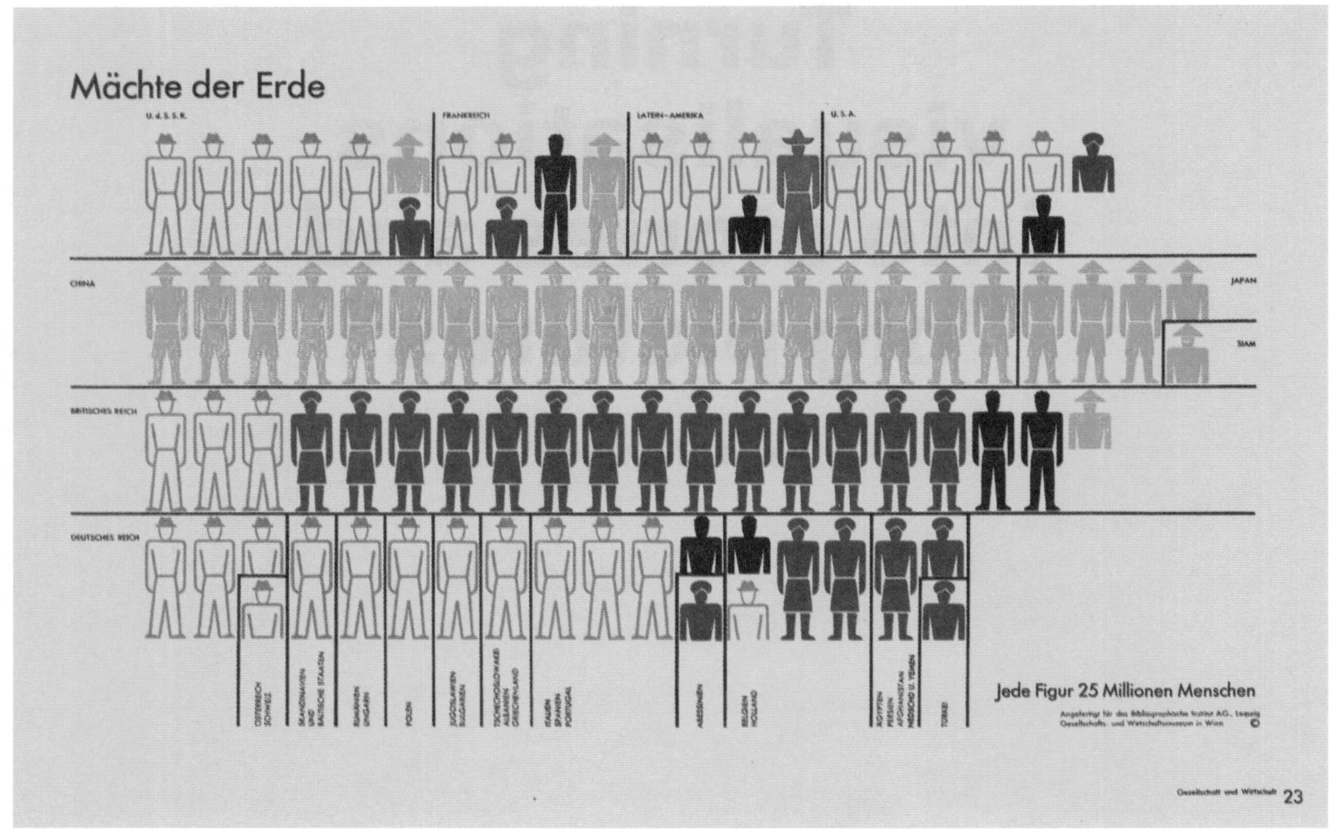

1930

Information design and, more specifically, narrative visualisations, can play an important role. Narrative visualisation uses communicative elements that are not limited to the purpose of conveying facts. These elements go beyond the mere visualisation of data, they draw the bigger context of the phenomena. At the visualisation research lab DensityDesign in Milan (which I direct), complex works of data visualisation are therefore called *visual macroscopes*. This term describes visualisations as tools that allow people to see not the infinitely small or the infinitely distant, as *microscopes* and *telescopes* do, but the infinitely complex.[2] Agreeing with John Thackara, visualisations are understood as "Tools and aesthetic notions, that help us understand – and act mindfully – in the big picture."

In close cooperation with statistics researchers, we recently worked on the visualisation of poverty as a complex socio-economic problem. The project was guided by a common belief: in order to really make people understand what poverty is about, a nuanced or *fuzzy* perspective is needed. The general aim was to go beyond the conventional, non-exhaustive, *0-1*, *yes-no*, *included-excluded* pattern of communication. This approach led to visualisations in which multiple dimensions and uncertainties were taken into account. The visualisation of uncertainty in the field of Digital Humanities is also the core topic of a collaboration with the Stanford Humanities Center. This joint project is to map the written exchanges between the greatest thinkers of the Enlightenment. One of the very first subjects of conversation was discussing the traditional visualisation modes for such flows and exchanges: does the visualisation of the path of a letter sent from Sender A to Recipient B with a simple, straight line really convey the meaning of dispatching that letter at that time, within the social and cultural context? The awareness of the story behind the data is fundamental to having a real understanding of the phenomena. Moreover, there is also a degree of uncertainty and incompleteness in the database that must be reflected in the visualisation.

The approach presented here (i.e. to amend data visualisation by using a narrative dimension) does not only affect the communication between researchers and society. It also offers opportunities to foster relationships between different disciplines and research groups. Scientists must deal with increasingly complex issues which cannot be tackled by just one discipline. Experts from a wide range of scientific domains, each with different knowledge backgrounds, collaborate on joint projects. It is crucial to build a shared body of information, together with the possibility of sharing hypotheses and ideas: that's exactly where information design and narrative visualisation can play their role.

Just like sciences, governmental institutions often face the same risks – distance, distrust, scepticism and unmotivated opposition; their quest for accountability and trust is very similar. Many projects that go under the label of *open data* publish a growing source of information on socio-economic phenomena, without any explanation. So, is *open data* really *open*? How much can people really understand when they just collect, from a gigantic data warehouse, small slices of a pie whose size they are totally unaware of? Can you get an idea of a phenomenon's big picture just by playing with chunks of data? What can you learn if the story behind the data is hidden?

Governments that dare to face the sea of open data explore how they can go beyond understanding and *encourage* their citizens to become involved. The same goes for sciences and research organisations. The use of narrative elements in data visualisation can fuel commitment. Narrative elements cannot be considered as mere embellishments, they have a specific function in that they build the story – the narration – that is necessary to re-create the context and make sense of the data. To do so, one must leave the protected realm of research domains, and play with issues like *beauty* and *pleasure*. In other fields of design research it is quite established that *emotion* is a cognitive force which contributes to sense-making, facilitates interaction and

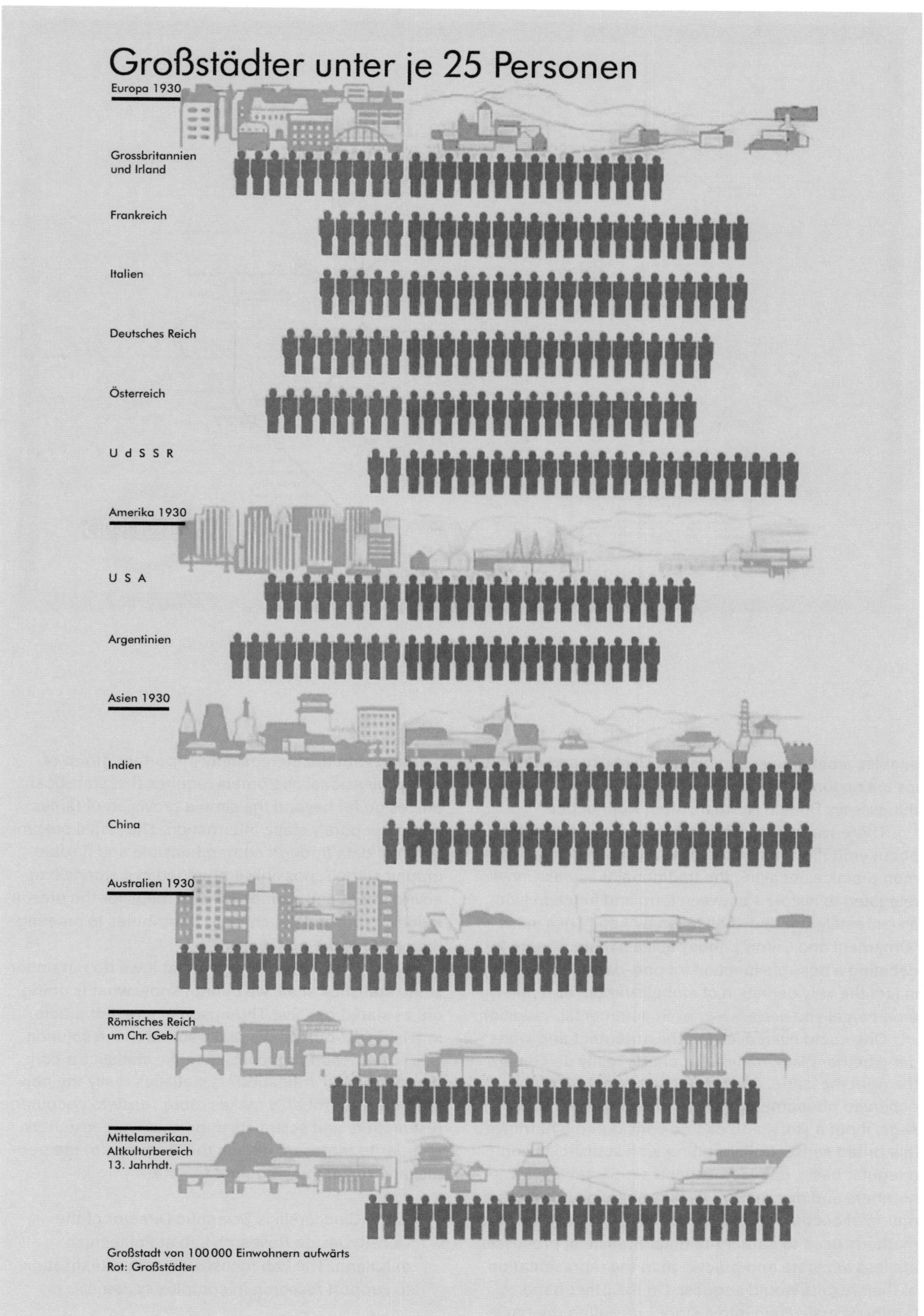

1930

1930

With the objective of promoting national education, Austrian economist Otto Neurath created many display boards in which social and economic issues were explained in a simple way. Quantities are displayed through a varying number of icons.

Der österreichische Ökonom Otto Neurath schuf Bildtafeln für die Volksbildung, in denen er soziale und wirtschaftliche Zusammenhänge auf einfache Weise zu vermitteln suchte. Mengenverhältnisse wurden dargestellt durch eine wechselnde Anzahl von Bildzeichen.

L'économiste autrichien Otto Neurath a créé de nombreuses affiches qui expliquent simplement des thèmes sociaux et économiques en vue de promouvoir l'éducation du pays. Les quantités sont indiquées grâce au nombre de pictogrammes.

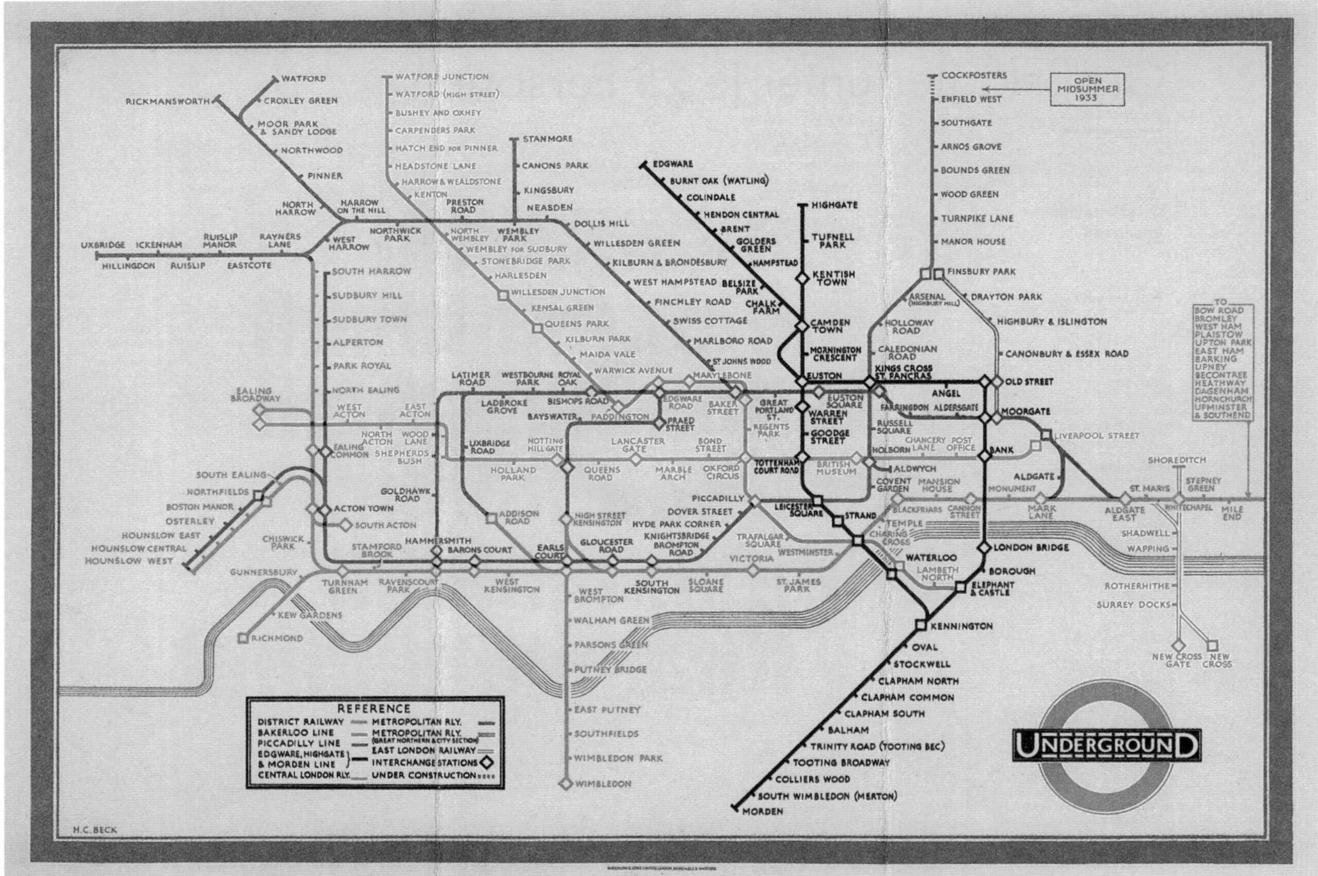

1933

enables a better user experience. Usability and aesthetics are no longer in opposition to each other: attractive things, says Donald Norman, often work better![3]

There was a time when complaints were made about embellishment in data visualisation being a common practice, recalling the traditional tensions – now relegated to history – between form and function (with an extremely strict position taken by Adolf Loos in his "Ornament and Crime"). Today at least there is room for debating a possible function for non-data ink,[4] denying in fact the very definition of embellishment as a purely ornamental and useless – or even detrimental – addition.

One could even overturn the argument and wonder whether plain, minimalist charts really do convey the right message, appropriate to the nature of the observed phenomena. Any picture conveys a message, if not a story, and can be considered a narrative in a broad sense. Collaborating with statisticians on a regular basis, one learns that a simple table with numbers and decimals in its very simplicity conveys a notion of accuracy that may not be consistent with the methods used to gather the data. Statistical processes are less accurate and precise than the representation of their results would suggest. On the other hand, turning visualisation into a story – revealing the background, building up a context – asks for a designer's point of view. It goes far from neutrality and demands responsibility. Any visualisation is an interpretation, and it is the designer's responsibility to be fully aware of the intentionality of any communication artefact.

If storytelling is "the world's second-oldest profession,"[5] it is because it reflects a fundamental need of every human being. It is related to the human desire for knowledge, the need to understand and make sense of the phenomena we face. We want to know what the story is, and possibly be able to tell others what we have discovered and learned. These days, this fundamental need seems to become more apparent to institutions dealing with collecting and communicating social data: "It is indisputable that successful communication with the increasingly important group of non-professional customers requires that statistical offices go far beyond the simple provision of tables and other purely static information. The visual presentation of data through comprehensible and flexible graphical tools, possibly embedded in a storytelling environment and connected with maps for the presentation of spatial data, crucially contributes to meeting the needs of the non-expert."[6]

We can probably all agree that if we do not understand statistics at all, we cannot know what is going on, as stated by Clive Thompson in a recent article in *Wired US*,[7] but are we really sure that the solution is, as Thompson proposes, to make statistics a core part of general education? Is statistics really the new grammar? It probably makes more sense to encourage researchers and scientists to partner with designers, in order to represent data in the language of the people, and not in the language of data.

Paolo Ciuccarelli is Scientific Director of the DensityDesign Research Lab at Politecnico di Milano. The Lab focuses on data visualisation to support research in complex systems.

1 Carrada, G.: *Communicating Science*. European Commission. Directorate-General for Research, 2006.
2 De Rosnay, J.: *The Macroscope*. New York: Harper & Row, 1979.
3 Norman, D.: "Emotion and design: Attractive things work better", *Interactions* magazine, ix (4), 2002, 36–42.
4 Bateman, Scott et al.: *Useful Junk? The Effects of Visual Embellishment on Comprehension and Memorability of Charts*. University of Saskatchewan, Department of Computer Science. Paper Presented on CHI, April 2010.
5 Gershon, N. and Page, W.: "What storytelling can do for information visualization". *Communications of the ACM*, 44 (8), 2001, 31–37.
6 Mittag, H.: "Educating the Public, The Role of E-Learning and Visual Communication of Official Data". Invited paper at the Statistical Commission and Economic Commission for Europe, Conference of European Statisticians, Paris, 12–15 June 2006. United Nations, Economic and Social Council, ECE/CES/2006.
7 Thompson, C.: "Why We Should Learn the Language of Data", *Wired US*, April 2010.

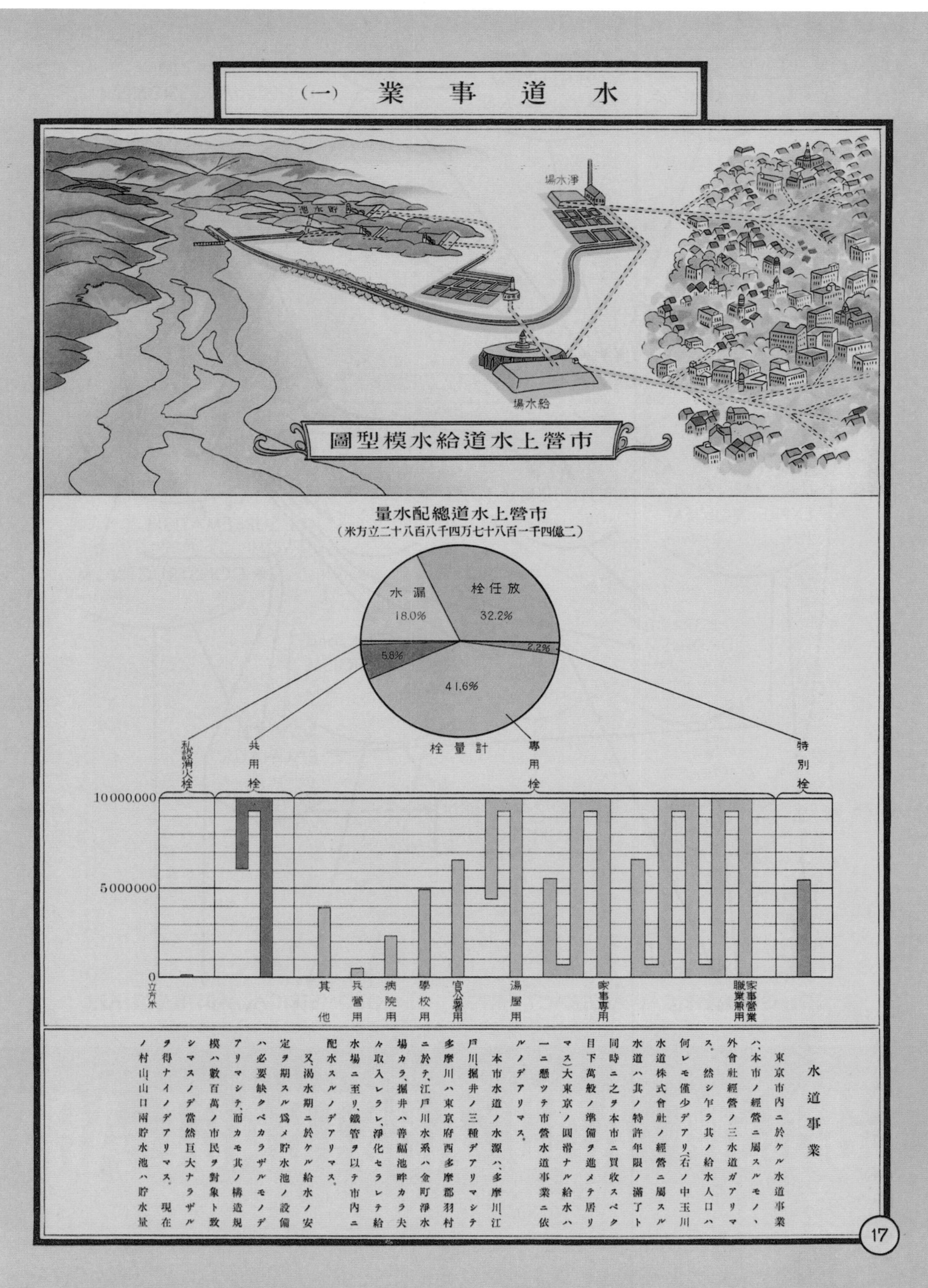

1935

1933

Harry Beck was the first to draw a diagrammatical map of London's Underground system. His version served as a model for many other maps worldwide. The individual lines are simplified in order to render junction points more clearly.

Harry Beck entwarf 1933 als Erster eine diagrammatische Darstellung des Londoner U-Bahn-Netzes, die als Vorbild für viele weitere Karten weltweit diente. Die einzelnen Linien sind vereinfacht dargestellt, um die Knotenpunkte besser visualisieren zu können.

Harry Beck a été le premier à dessiner une carte schématique du métro londonien. Sa version a servi de modèle pour de nombreuses autres cartes dans le monde. Les lignes sont simplifiées pour représenter les correspondances plus clairement.

1935

The diagrams in this print break down the water consumption in Tokyo by various users. In the lower diagram, some bars are bent in order to provide correct representations of the very different consumption rates (given in cubic metres of water) within the limited scale.

Die Diagramme auf diesem Blatt schlüsseln den Wasserverbrauch in Tokio nach verschiedenen Nutzern auf. Im unteren Diagramm sind einige Balken gebogen, um die stark unterschiedlichen Verbrauchsmengen (angegeben in Kubikmeter Wasser) auf der engen Skala korrekt darzustellen.

Les diagrammes de cette estampe analysent la consommation d'eau à Tokyo selon les utilisateurs. En bas, certaines barres sont repliées pour donner une représentation correcte des quantités très différentes (en mètres cubes d'eau) sur une échelle limitée.

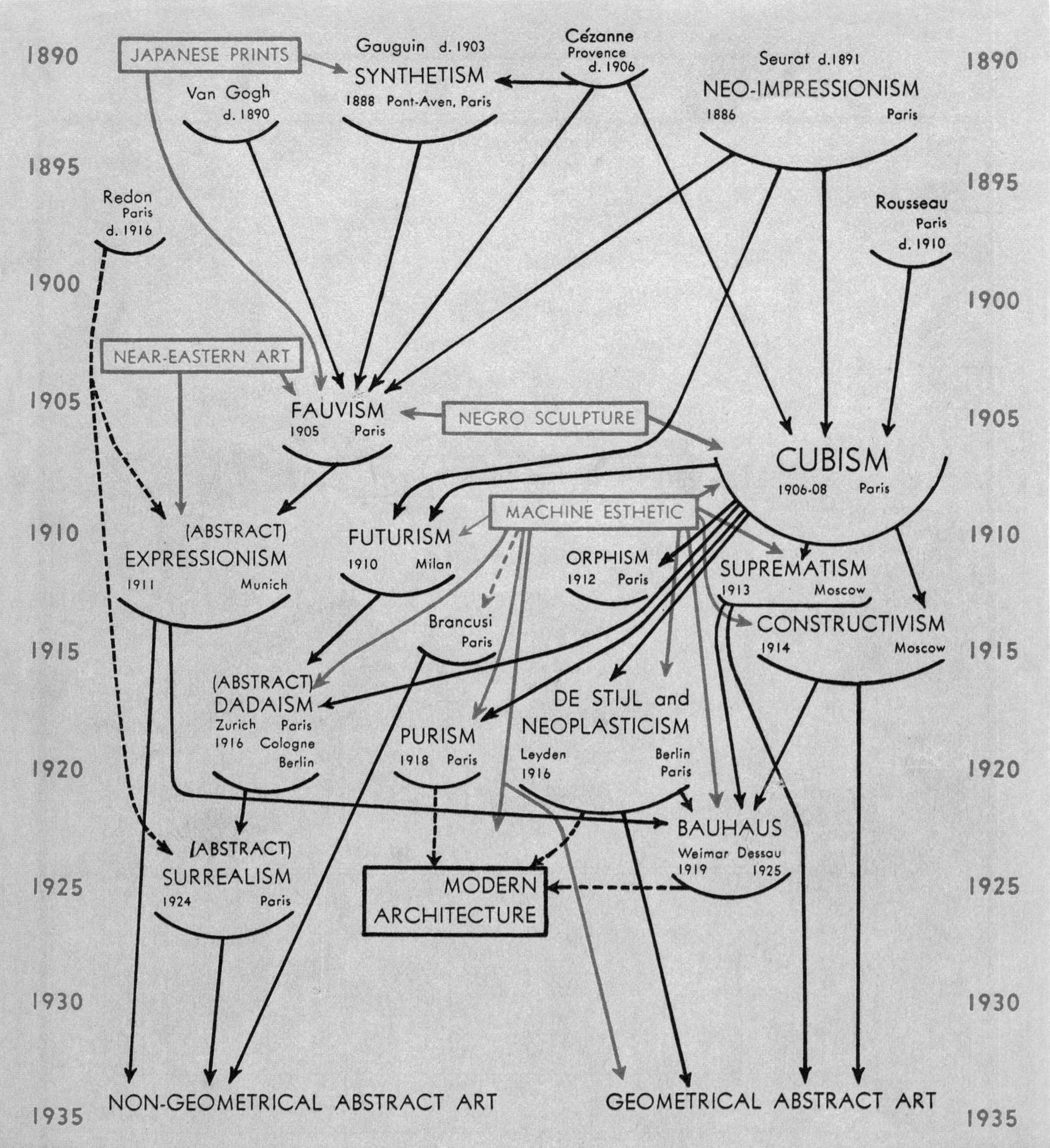

1936

1936

MoMA's director Alfred H. Barr sketched the history of modern art on this famous cover of an exhibition catalogue. He conceived of a sort of family tree of styles. External influences like *Machine Esthetic* or *Japanese Prints* are marked in red.

Auf diesem berühmten Cover eines Ausstellungskatalogs skizzierte MoMA-Direktor Alfred H. Barr die Entwicklung der modernen Kunst. Er entwarf eine Art Stammbaum der Stilrichtungen. Rot markiert sind äußere Einflüsse wie *Maschinenästhetik* oder *Japanische Drucke*.

Alfred H. Barr, directeur du MoMA, a schématisé l'histoire de l'art moderne sur cette célèbre couverture de catalogue à l'aide d'une généalogie des styles. Les influences externes telles que l'*Esthétique de la machine* ou les *Estampes japonaises* sont indiquées en rouge.

Wie aus Visualisierungen Geschichten und „das große Ganze“ werden

Paolo Ciuccarelli

Die Menge gesellschaftlich relevanter Daten, die mittels verschiedener Medien an die Öffentlichkeit gelangt, nimmt ständig zu: Epidemien, Kriege, technische Neuerungen, Naturkatastrophen, Finanzkrisen und genomische Entdeckungen sind nur einige Beispiele für die Informationen, die in unseren stetig wachsenden Nachrichtenkreislauf einfließen. Soziale und ökonomische Themen werden heute zunehmend anhand von Zahlen erläutert, die einen Text begleiten, und häufig geht damit auch eine visuelle Aufbereitung der Daten einher. Das ist zwar ein großer Fortschritt für den schier unstillbaren Wissensdurst der Menschheit, aber trägt es wirklich dazu bei, sozioökonomische Phänomene einer breiten Allgemeinheit verständlich zu machen?

Dass es Spielraum für Verbesserungen gibt, ist nicht von der Hand zu weisen, insbesondere bei der visuellen Vermittlung von Daten und Informationen, die von Forschungseinrichtungen zusammengestellt werden. Diese Institutionen haben nun die einmalige Chance, ihrer kritischen historischen Verpflichtung gegenüber der Gesellschaft gerecht zu werden. Obwohl Naturwissenschaftler ein hohes Maß an Ansehen und auch ein gewisses Maß an Autonomie genießen, gelten sie im Allgemeinen noch immer als elitär und realitätsfremd. Sie haben mit einer distanzierten und skeptischen Öffentlichkeit ebenso zu kämpfen wie mit einem Mangel an Interesse und Anerkennung. Trotz der Bedeutung, die ihre Forschung für die Entwicklung der Menschheit und der Gesellschaft zweifelsohne hat, sehen sie sich bisweilen mit heftigen Angriffen konfrontiert. Die Kluft zwischen den Naturwissenschaften und der Öffentlichkeit ist im Lauf der Jahre immer größer geworden, zum Teil deshalb, weil Wissenschaftler selbst in den wenigen Fällen, in denen eine verständliche öffentliche Stellungnahme gefragt ist, zu einem spezifischen, häufig unzugänglichen Fachjargon tendieren.

Mehr denn je müssen Forschungseinrichtungen heute den Schulterschluss mit der Gesellschaft suchen, um die notwendigen Ressourcen (Geld und Mitarbeiter) und die Freiheit (politische Unabhängigkeit) gewährt zu bekommen, ohne die sie ihre Arbeit nicht fortsetzen können: Politische Unterstützung, die auf breitem öffentlichen Konsens beruht, ist das Gebot der Stunde. Zudem werden Entscheidungen, die die Arbeit von Forschungseinrichtungen beeinflussen, immer häufiger außerhalb der Wissenschaftsgemeinde getroffen. Anstelle von Experten haben Fachfremde die Mittel und den Willen, sich an Entscheidungsprozessen zu beteiligen. Allein schon eine Methode zu finden, die einen „Experten“ definiert, ist eine anspruchsvolle Aufgabe.

Naturwissenschaftler müssen eine konstruktive Beziehung zur Gesellschaft aufbauen. Wie notwendig Vertrauen ist, zeigt sich vor allem dann, wenn umstrittene Themen diskutiert werden, und insbesondere, wenn die Forscher selbst keine übereinstimmende Meinung dazu vertreten. Atomenergie, Klimawandel, Elektrosmog und gentechnisch veränderte Organismen (GVO) sind nur einige Beispiele für die zurzeit zahlreich geführten Diskussionen, bei denen auch viele irrationale Komponenten eine Rolle spielen.

Aus diesen Gründen mag die Partnerschaft zwischen Wissenschaftsgemeinde und Gesellschaft zwar schwierig sein, notwendig ist sie allemal. Dass diese Partnerschaft noch nicht allgemein wahrgenommen wird, liegt an einem grundlegenden Kommunikationsproblem: Wissenschaft und Öffentlichkeit sprechen unterschiedliche Sprachen. Wie die Europäische Kommission in der Broschüre *Communicating Science*[1] feststellt: „Dieselben Daten, die für Forscher lediglich ein weiteres Puzzleteil darstellen, das sie in ein ihnen vertrautes Wissens- (und Gefühls-) Bild einfügen können, sind für die Öffentlichkeit isolierte, nahezu bedeutungslose Informationsbröckchen.“

Wenn es darum geht, der Öffentlichkeit soziale oder ökonomische Probleme vor Augen zu führen, genügt eine einfache Visualisierung der Daten nicht. Um sich zu orientieren, benötigen die Menschen

visuelle Instrumente. Die wichtigste Voraussetzung für eine erfolgreiche Teilhabe ist es, den Kontext einer Problemstellung zu kennen und zu verstehen: Wer ist beteiligt? Welche Meinung vertreten die Einzelnen? Welche Gefühle und Interessen sind im Spiel? Welche positiven und negativen Kräfte beeinflussen die Entwicklung eines Phänomens?

Naturwissenschaftler sollten versuchen, ihre Kommunikation menschlicher zu gestalten, wenn nicht gar populärer. Um Vertrauen und öffentliche Legitimation zu gewinnen, müssen auch sie selbst glaubwürdig sein und eigene Grenzen, Schwächen oder Unsicherheiten ehrlich eingestehen. Das ist nicht nur eine Frage ihres ökonomischen Überlebens, es ist ihre ethische Verpflichtung gegenüber der Gesellschaft. Sozioökonomische Fragestellungen sind von Natur aus komplex; man kann sie nicht verstehen, wenn man lediglich einen Aspekt betrachtet. Sie sind mehrdeutig und unklar, quantitativ nicht messbar und nur qualitativ darzustellen. Sie werden mithilfe von Methoden betrachtet, denen Fehlerquoten und Annäherungswerte zu eigen sind. Die Daten korrespondieren nie eins zu eins mit dem Phänomen, das sie abbilden sollen.

Informationsdesign und insbesondere narrative Visualisierung können hier eine wichtige Rolle spielen. Die narrative Visualisierung setzt Kommunikationselemente ein, die sich nicht auf das Vermitteln bloßer Fakten beschränken; sie gehen über die reine Veranschaulichung der Daten hinaus und zeigen den gesamten Kontext eines Phänomens. Bei DensityDesign in Mailand, einem Forschungslabor für Visualisierung (das ich leite), werden komplexe Werke der Datenvisualisierung daher „visuelle Makroskope" (engl. „visual macroscopes") genannt. Hinter diesem Ausdruck steht der Gedanke, Visualisierung als Hilfsmittel zu betrachten, welches es den Menschen ermöglicht, das unendlich Komplexe zu sehen und nicht, wie bei einem „Mikroskop" oder einem „Teleskop", das unendlich Kleine oder das unendlich Ferne.[2] In Übereinstimmung mit John Thackara werden Visualisierungen als „Werkzeuge und ästhetische Denkbilder" verstanden, „die uns helfen, Dinge in einem größeren Zusammenhang zu begreifen und entsprechend zu handeln".

In enger Zusammenarbeit mit Statistikern beschäftigten wir uns unlängst mit der Visualisierung von Armut als komplexem sozioökonomischen Problem. Das Projekt wurde von einem grundlegenden Gedanken geleitet: Um den Menschen wirklich verständlich nahezubringen, worum es beim Thema Armut geht, bedarf es einer nuancierten, „unscharfen" Betrachtung. Das Hauptziel bestand darin, über das übliche, unzulängliche Kommunikationsmuster von „0 – 1", „ja – nein", „einschließlich – ausschließlich" hinauszugehen. Dieser Ansatz führte zu Visualisierungen, die vielfältige Dimensionen und Unwägbarkeiten berücksichtigten. Die Visualisierung von Unwägbarkeiten im Bereich der Digital Humanities ist auch ein Kernthema unseres Gemeinschaftsprojekts mit dem Stanford Humanities Center. Dabei geht es darum, den schriftlichen Austausch zwischen den größten Denkern der Aufklärung zu veranschaulichen. Einer der ersten Punkte, die wir diskutierten, waren die herkömmlichen Visualisierungsmethoden für einen derartigen Austausch und Informationsfluss: Vermittelt die Visualisierung des Postweges, den ein Brief von Absender A an Empfänger B nahm, durch eine einfache gerade Linie tatsächlich die Bedeutung dessen, was es innerhalb des damaligen sozialen und kulturellen Kontexts bedeutete, einen Brief zu versenden? Die Kenntnis der Geschichte hinter den Daten ist Voraussetzung für ein wirkliches Verständnis des Phänomens. Zudem enthält der Datenbestand auch ein gewisses Maß an Unsicherheit und Unvollständigkeit, das in der Visualisierung zum Ausdruck kommen muss.

Die hier vorgestellte Herangehensweise (nämlich die Datenvisualisierung, um eine narrative Dimension zu ergänzen) beeinflusst nicht nur die Kommunikation zwischen Forschern und Gesellschaft, sie bietet auch die Möglichkeit, Beziehungen zwischen unterschiedlichen Disziplinen und Forschungsgruppen auszubauen.

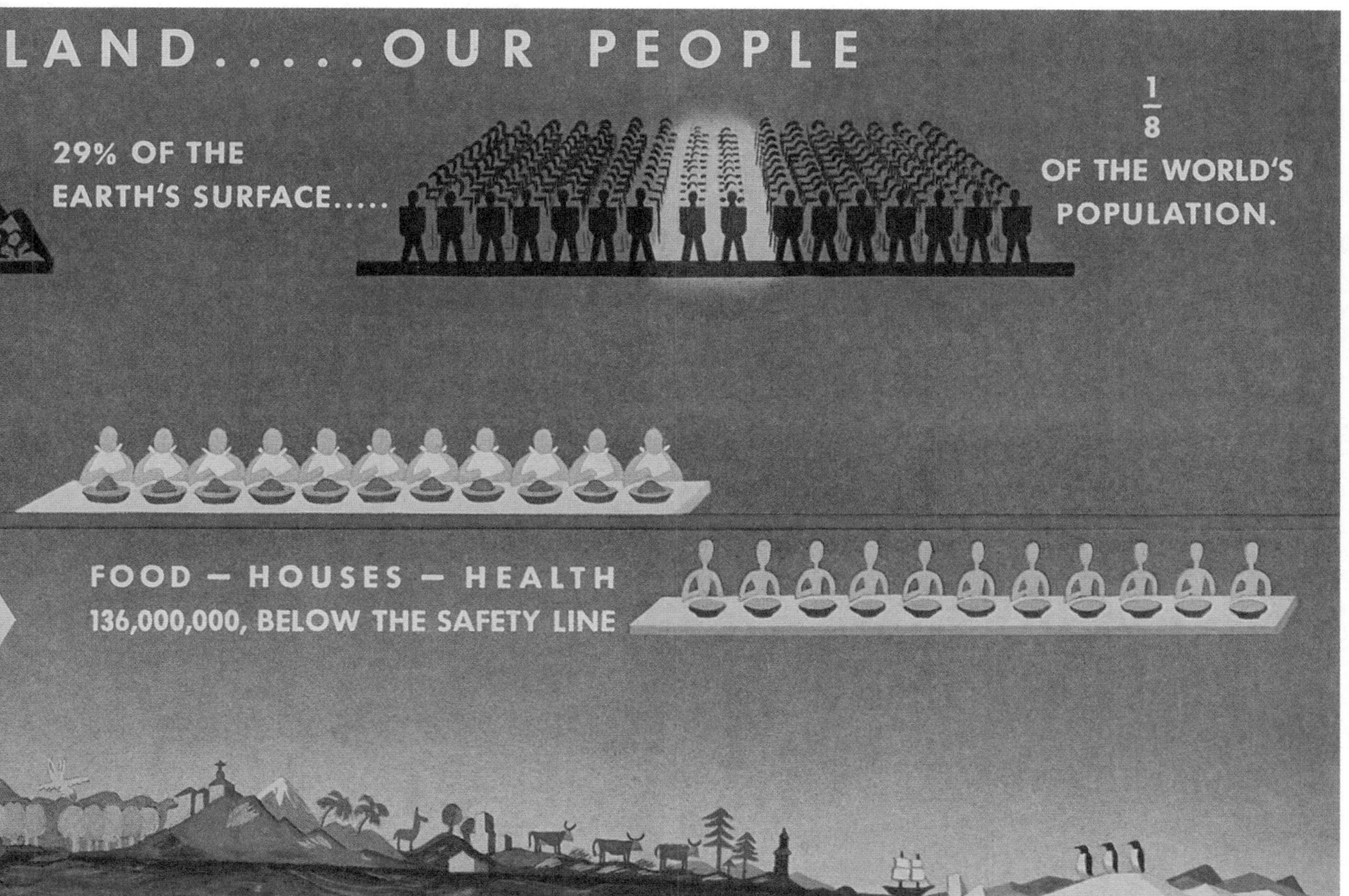
LAND.....OUR PEOPLE
29% OF THE
EARTH'S SURFACE.....
1/8
OF THE WORLD'S
POPULATION.
FOOD – HOUSES – HEALTH
136,000,000, BELOW THE SAFETY LINE

ca. 1940

Forscher beschäftigen sich mit zunehmend komplexen Themen, denen eine Disziplin alleine nicht mehr gerecht werden kann. Fachleute vieler verschiedener Wissenschaftsbereiche mit unterschiedlichem Wissenshintergrund arbeiten in Gemeinschaftsprojekten zusammen. Es ist wichtig geworden, einen gemeinsam genutzten Informationspool zu bilden, nicht minder wichtig ist die Möglichkeit, sich hinsichtlich Hypothesen und Ideen auszutauschen. Genau das ist der Punkt, an dem Informationsdesign und narrative Visualisierung ins Spiel kommen.

Staatliche Institutionen haben häufig mit denselben Problemen zu kämpfen wie die Naturwissenschaften: Distanz, Misstrauen, Skepsis, unmotivierte Ablehnung. Ähnlich ist deshalb auch ihr Streben nach Verantwortlichkeit und Vertrauen. Viele Projekte, die unter dem Label „Open Data" laufen, veröffentlichen eine wachsende Menge von Informationen über sozioökonomische Phänomene, allerdings ohne jede Erklärung. So stellt sich die Frage: Sind Open Data, „offene Daten", wirklich offen? Wie können Menschen etwas wirklich verstehen, wenn sie aus einem gigantischen Datensupermarkt kleine Stücke eines Kuchens, dessen Größe sie gar nicht kennen, zusammenklauben? Kann man eine Vorstellung vom Gesamtbild eines Phänomens bekommen, indem man mit Bruchstücken von Daten spielt? Was kann man überhaupt lernen, wenn die Geschichte hinter den Daten verborgen bleibt?

Regierungen, die sich dem Meer offener Daten zu stellen wagen, untersuchen, wie sie über das reine Verstehen hinausgehen und ihre Bürger „ermutigen" können, sich einzubringen. Dasselbe gilt für die Wissenschaft und für Forschungsinstitute. Der Einsatz narrativer Elemente in der Datenvisualisierung kann Engagement befördern. Narrative Elemente dürfen nicht als bloßes Beiwerk betrachtet werden, sie spielen eine ganz spezifische Rolle: Sie liefern die Geschichte, die notwendig ist, um den Kontext nachzuvollziehen und die Daten zu verstehen. Dazu muss man den geschützten Bereich der Forschung verlassen und sich mit Fragen wie „Schönheit" und „Vergnügen" auseinandersetzen. In anderen Bereichen der Designforschung gilt „Emotion" als anerkannte kognitive Kraft, die zum Vermitteln von Sinngehalt beiträgt, Interaktion erleichtert und eine bessere Nutzererfahrung ermöglicht. Bedienerfreundlichkeit und Ästhetik sind keine Gegensätze: Attraktiv Gestaltetes, behauptet Donald Norman, funktioniert oft besser![3]

Es gab eine Zeit, als Klagen laut wurden, wonach Ausschmückungen in der Datenvisualisierung eine fast schon vulgäre Praxis seien. Das erinnert an die traditionelle – mittlerweile in die Geschichte eingegangene – Auseinandersetzung über Form versus Funktionalität (eine extrem strenge Position vertrat Adolf Loos in seiner Streitschrift *Ornament und Verbrechen*). Heute ist es zumindest möglich, eine Diskussion über den möglichen Zweck von Non-Data-Ink zu führen,[4] was allein die Definition von Ausschmückung als rein ornamentales und nutzloses – wenn nicht gar abträgliches – Beiwerk ad absurdum führt.

Man könnte das Argument sogar umkehren und fragen, ob schlichte, minimalistische Diagramme überhaupt die richtige, dem Wesen des beobachteten Phänomens entsprechende Botschaft vermitteln. Jedes Bild vermittelt eine Botschaft, wenn nicht sogar eine Geschichte, und kann im weitesten Sinn als eine

ca. 1940

In the 1930s, magazines like *Fortune* or *McCall's* developed a vivid visual language for statistical data. In this graphic for *McCall's*, Irving Geis visualised data concerning the population of the Americas, e.g. an ethnic breakdown and the number of poor people.

Zeitschriften wie *Fortune* oder *McCall's* entwickelten in den 1930er-Jahren eine lebendige Bildsprache für statistische Angaben. In dieser Grafik für *McCall's* visualisierte Irving Geis Bevölkerungsdaten für den amerikanischen Kontinent wie ethnische Zusammensetzung und Anzahl der Armen.

Dans les années 1930, des magazines tels que *Fortune* ou *McCall's* ont créé un langage visuel vivant pour les données statistiques. Ici, dans *McCall's*, Irving Geis analyse la population des Amériques avec entre autres la composition ethnique et le nombre de pauvres.

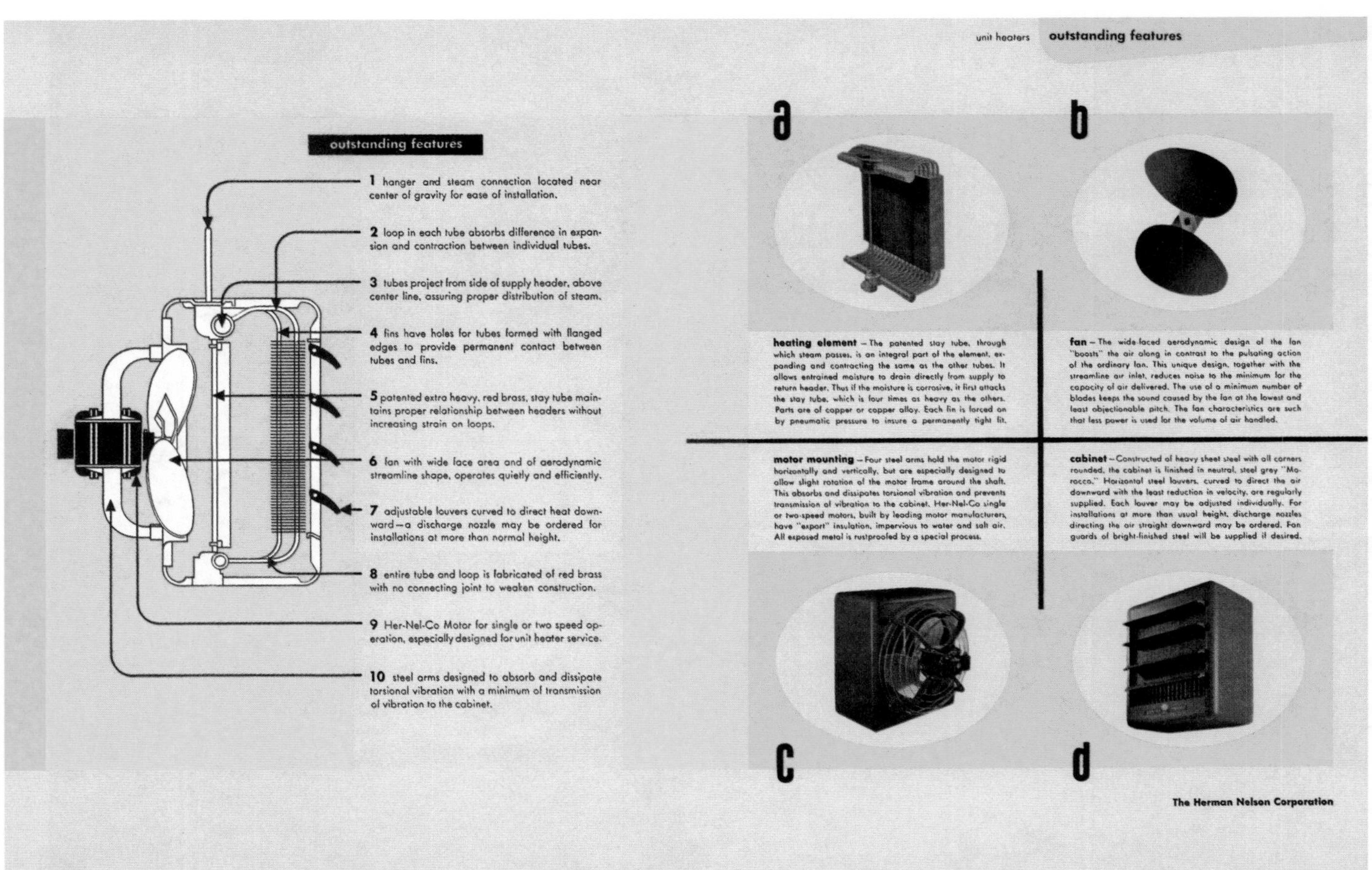

ca. 1950

Erzählung verstanden werden. Wer regelmäßig mit Statistikern zusammenarbeitet, weiß, dass eine schlichte Tabelle mit Zahlen und Dezimalen allein aufgrund ihrer Schlichtheit den Eindruck von Genauigkeit vermittelt, was nicht unbedingt den Methoden entspricht, mit denen die Daten erhoben wurden. Statistische Prozesse sind weniger präzise, als die Darstellung ihrer Ergebnisse vermuten lässt. Wer andererseits eine Visualisierung in eine Geschichte umwandeln will – die Hintergründe aufzeigt und einen Kontext aufbaut –, benötigt den Blickwinkel eines Grafikers. Der verlässt unweigerlich das Feld der Neutralität, sein Verantwortungsgefühl ist gefragt. Jede Visualisierung ist eine Interpretation, und es liegt in der Verantwortung des Grafikers, die Absicht hinter dem zu vermittelnden Sachverhalt genau zu kennen.

Wenn Geschichtenerzählen „der zweitälteste Beruf der Welt"[5] ist, dann deshalb, weil Geschichten zu den Grundbedürfnissen der Menschheit gehören. Sie sind eng mit dem menschlichen Wissensdurst verbunden, mit dem Bedürfnis, die Phänomene, denen wir begegnen, zu verstehen und ihren Sinn zu begreifen. Wir wollen erfahren, wie die Geschichte weitergeht, und, wenn möglich, anderen mitteilen, was wir entdeckt und gelernt haben. Offenbar wird dieses grundlegende Bedürfnis den Institutionen, die soziale Daten sammeln und kommunizieren, langsam bewusst: „Es ist unbestritten, dass eine erfolgreiche Kommunikation mit der zunehmend einflussreichen Gruppe nicht-professioneller Kunden weit mehr von den Statistikbehörden erfordert als die bloße Bereitstellung von Tabellen und anderer rein statistischer Informationen. Die visuelle Präsentation von Daten mittels verständlicher und flexibler grafischer Werkzeuge, die, womöglich in eine narrative Umgebung eingebettet, durch Illustrationen zur Präsentation räumlicher Daten ergänzt werden, leistet einen wesentlichen Beitrag, um den Ansprüchen Fachfremder zu genügen."[6]

Wie Clive Thompson kürzlich in einem Artikel in *Wired US* schrieb,[7] sind wir uns wahrscheinlich alle darin einig, dass wir nicht wissen können, was vor sich geht, wenn wir keine Ahnung von Statistik haben. Aber kann die Lösung wirklich darin bestehen, Statistik zum festen Bestandteil des Lehrplans zu machen, wie Thompson es vorschlägt? Ist Statistik tatsächlich die neue Grammatik? Vermutlich ist es sinnvoller, Forscher und Wissenschaftler zur Zusammenarbeit mit Grafikern zu bewegen, damit Daten in der Sprache der Menschen dargestellt werden und nicht in der Sprache der Daten.

Paolo Ciuccarelli ist Wissenschaftlicher Direktor des DensityDesign Research Lab am Politecnico di Milano. Das Forschungsprojekt befasst sich mit der Datenvisualisierung von komplexen Systemen.

1 Carrada, G.: *Communicating Science*, Europäische Kommission, Generaldirektion Forschung, 2006.
2 De Rosnay, J.: *Das Makroskop* (aus dem Franz. von Hans Dieter Heck), Stuttgart 1977.
3 Norman, D.: „Emotion and design: Attractive things work better", in: *Interactions* ix (4), 2002, S. 36–42.
4 Bateman, S. et al.: „Useful Junk? The Effects of Visual Embellishment on Comprehension and Memorability of Charts", in: *ACM Conference on Human Factors in Computing Systems* (CHI 2010), 2010.
5 Gershon, N. und Page, W.: „What storytelling can do for information visualization", in: *Communications of the ACM* 44 (8), 2001, S. 31–37.
6 Mittag, H.: „Educating the Public, The Role of E-Learning and Visual Communication of Official Data". Invited Paper bei der Statistical Commission and Economic Commission for Europe, Konferenz Europäischer Statistiker, Paris, 12–15. Juni 2006. Vereinte Nationen, Wirtschafts- und Sozialrat, ECE/CES/2006.
7 Thompson, C.: „Why We Should Learn the Language of Data", in: *Wired US*, April 2010.

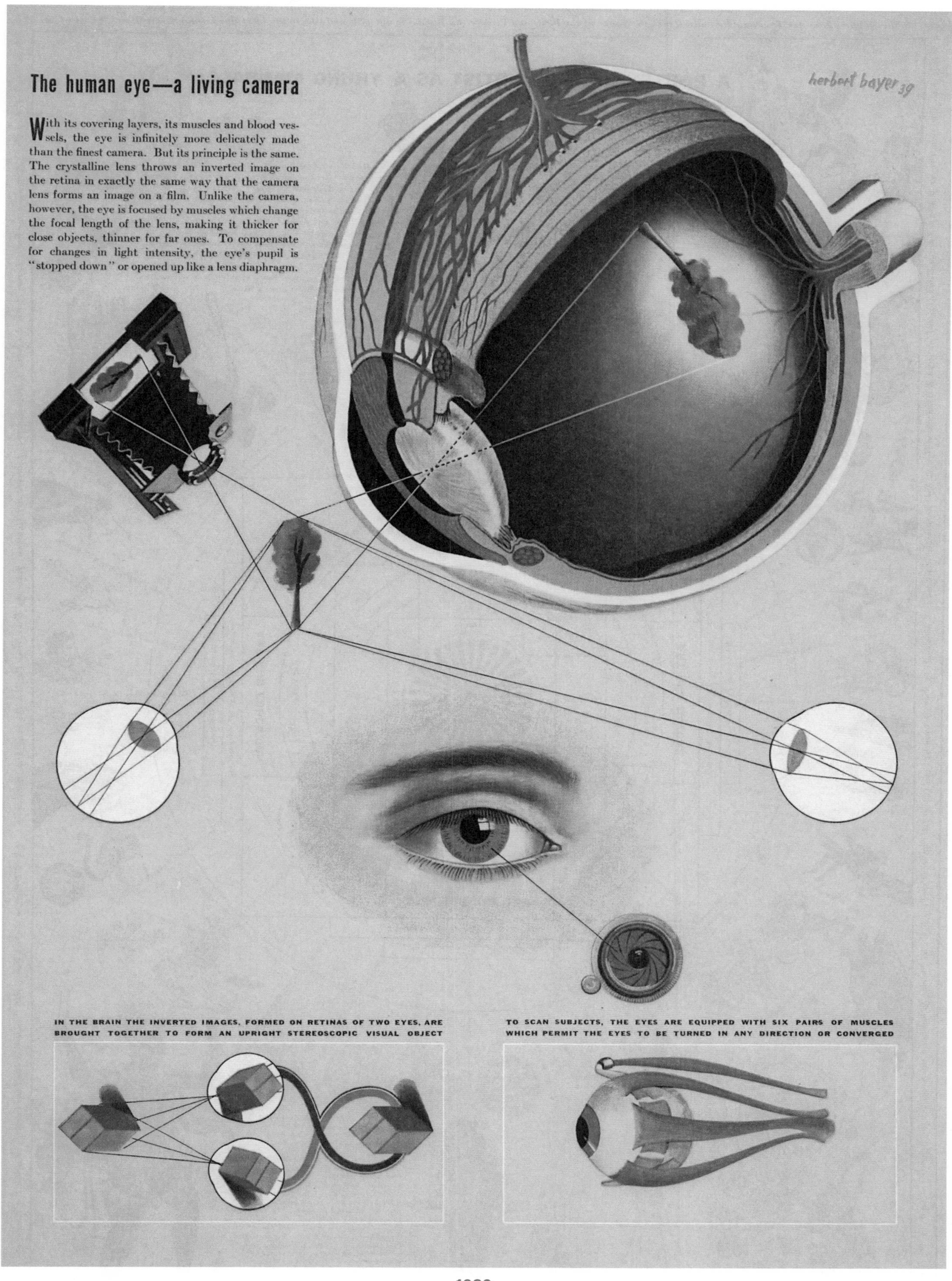

1939

ca. 1950

Czech designer Ladislav Sutnar focused on the clear structuring of information, both in the creation of exhibits as well as in his graphic designs. Exemplary are the industrial catalogues he designed for various clients.

Der tschechische Designer Ladislav Sutnar befasste sich eingehend mit der Strukturierung von Informationen, sowohl in der Ausstellungsgestaltung als auch im Grafikdesign. Beispielgebend sind etwa die Industriekataloge, die er für verschiedene Kunden gestaltete.

Le designer tchèque Ladislav Sutnar s'intéressait à la clarté de la structure des informations, dans ses expositions comme dans ses graphismes. Les catalogues industriels qu'il a réalisés pour plusieurs clients en sont un bel exemple.

1939

Herbert Bayer was an influential designer, architect and typographer, who studied and taught at Bauhaus Dessau in Germany. His work is considered an inspiring example in the field of information design to this day. This piece was created after his emigration to the US.

Herbert Bayer war ein einflussreicher Designer, Architekt und Typograf, der am Bauhaus Dessau studierte und lehrte. Sein Werk gilt bis heute als prägendes Vorbild im Bereich Informationsgestaltung. Diese Grafik schuf er nach seiner Emigration in die USA.

Herbert Bayer était un designer, architecte et typographe qui a étudié et enseigné au Bauhaus à Dessau, en Allemagne. Son œuvre est aujourd'hui encore exemplaire dans le domaine du design de l'information. Ce schéma est postérieur à son émigration aux États-Unis.

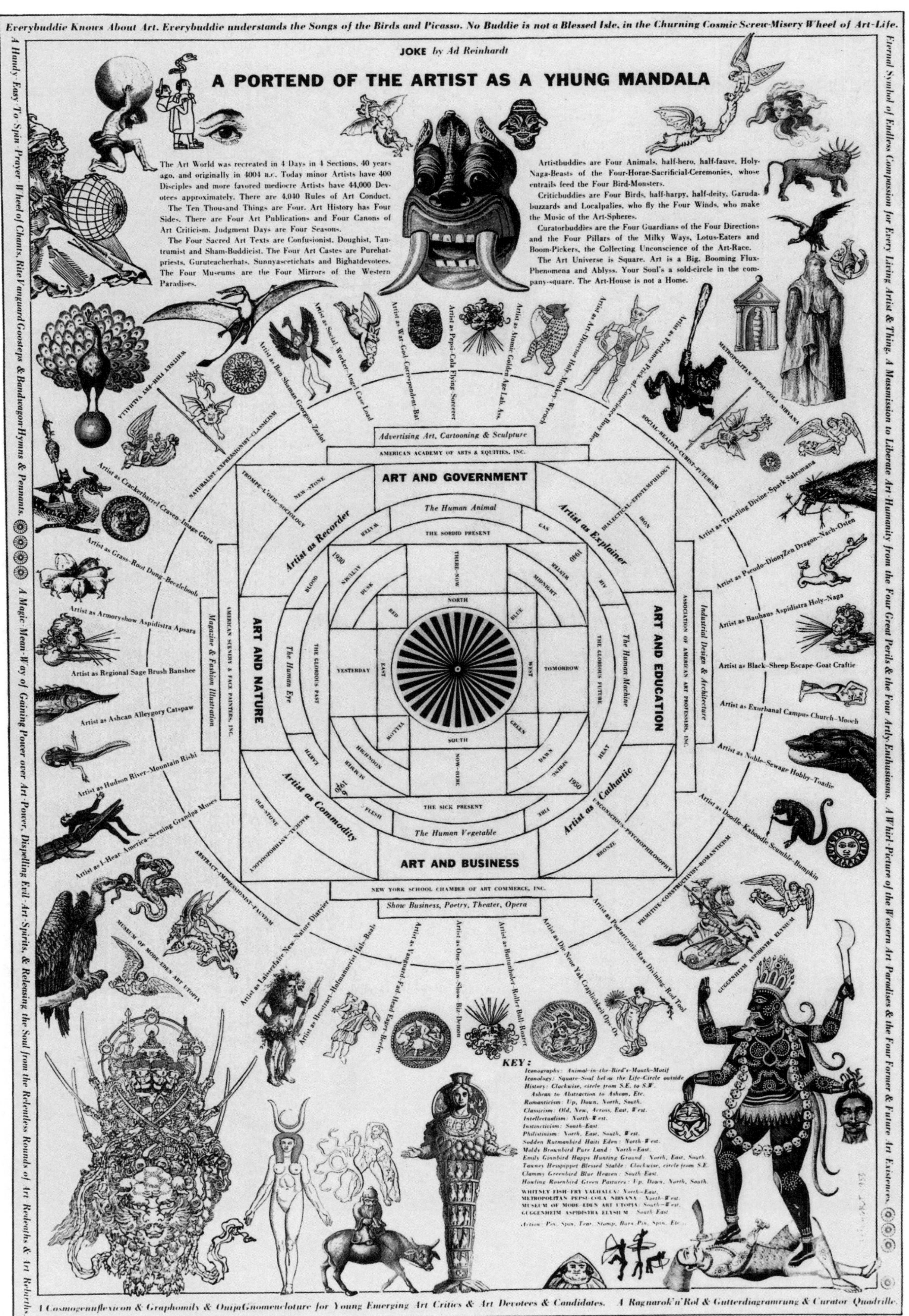

1955

1955

Starting in the 1940s, artist Ad Reinhardt created a series of "art comics". This "art mandala" ironically shows the relationships between art, nature, economy and politics. Many "godly incarnations" of the artist surround the central diagram.

Seit den 1940er-Jahren schuf der Künstler Ad Reinhardt zahlreiche „art comics". Dieses „Kunst-Mandala" zeigt ironisch die Beziehungen zwischen Kunst, Natur, Wirtschaft und Politik. Das Diagramm ist umrahmt von „göttlichen Verkörperungen" des Künstlers.

Ad Reinhardt a créé des « bandes dessinées artistiques » à partir des années 1940. Ce « mandala artistique » ironise sur les relations entre l'art, la nature, l'économie et la politique. Des « incarnations divines » de l'artiste entourent le diagramme central.

Transformer les visualisations en histoires et « vues d'ensemble »

Paolo Ciuccarelli

Le public reçoit à travers différents médias une quantité croissante de données socialement pertinentes: épidémies, guerres, innovations technologiques, catastrophes naturelles, crises financières et découvertes génomiques sont autant d'exemples d'informations diffusées dans le cycle toujours plus vaste de l'actualité. Aujourd'hui, les problèmes de caractère social et économique sont plus souvent présentés par un texte assorti de chiffres et de représentations visuelles des données. Il s'agit d'un grand pas en avant dans la quête de savoir de l'homme; favorise-t-il pour autant la compréhension des phénomènes socioéconomiques par le grand public?

Les choses sont sans conteste améliorables, notamment en matière de communication visuelle des données et des informations émises par les organismes de recherche. Ces institutions se voient offrir une chance sans précédent de payer l'énorme dette historique accumulée envers la société. Les scientifiques ont certes gagné en reconnaissance et en autonomie, mais ils restent considérés comme des personnages distants et élitistes. Ils doivent donc combattre ce sentiment général de distance et de scepticisme, accompagné d'un manque d'intérêt et d'appréciation. Ils sont parfois confrontés à une opposition féroce, en dépit de la pertinence de leurs recherches pour les progrès de l'homme et de la société. Cet écart entre la science et le public s'est creusé au fil des ans, en partie parce que les scientifiques ont tendance à employer un jargon souvent impénétrable, même dans les rares cas où un commentaire simple est attendu.

Aujourd'hui, afin d'obtenir les ressources (en financement et en personnel) et la liberté (l'indépendance politique) nécessaires pour mener à bien leurs recherches, les organisations scientifiques doivent plus que jamais entretenir une relation étroite avec la société et bénéficier à tout prix d'un soutien politique s'appuyant sur un large consensus public. Par ailleurs, les décisions concernant l'activité des organismes de recherche sont plus souvent prises en dehors de la communauté scientifique. Les non-experts ont les moyens et la volonté de prendre part aux processus de prise de décision à la place des experts. Même la façon de définir ce qu'est un *expert* s'avère complexe.

Les scientifiques doivent donc entretenir une relation constructive avec la société. Le besoin de confiance se fait notamment sentir pour les sujets qui prêtent à controverse, en particulier en l'absence d'un consensus universel au sein de la communauté des chercheurs. L'énergie nucléaire, le réchauffement de la planète, la pollution électromagnétique et les organismes génétiquement modifiés (OGM) ne sont que quelques-uns des nombreux débats actuels, alimentés de forts composants irrationnels.

C'est pourquoi le mariage de la communauté scientifique et de la société, bien que délicat, est assurément nécessaire. Il n'a pas encore été célébré ouvertement à cause d'un problème de communication de base: les scientifiques et le public ne parlent pas le même langage. Comme l'indique la Commission européenne dans le document « Communiquer la science »[1]: « Les mêmes données qui, pour les scientifiques, sont un élément de plus à ajouter à une représentation claire du savoir (et des émotions), ne sont pour le public qu'un fragment isolé d'informations, quasiment dénué de sens ».

Lorsque l'objectif est de permettre au public de *voir* des problèmes sociaux ou économiques, des visualisations simples des données ne suffisent pas; les gens ont besoin d'outils d'orientation visuelle. La condition d'une participation efficace est de connaître et de comprendre le contexte: qui sont les participants, quels sont leurs points de vue, quels sentiments et intérêts entrent en jeu, et quelles forces positives et négatives influencent l'évolution du phénomène.

Les scientifiques doivent tenter d'humaniser, sinon de vulgariser, leur communication. S'ils veulent être écoutés et gagner une légitimité publique, ils doivent être authentiques et honnêtes à propos de

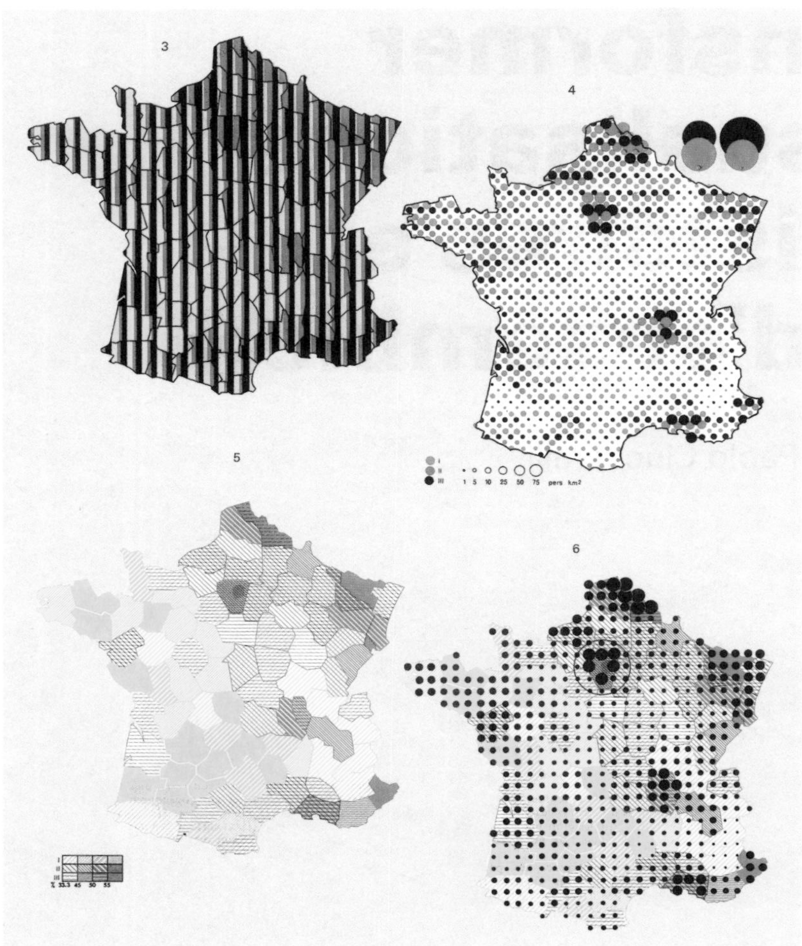

1967

leurs limites, leurs insécurités et leurs faiblesses. Il ne s'agit pas uniquement d'une question de survie économique, mais d'un devoir éthique envers la société. Les sujets socioéconomiques sont par nature complexes et ne peuvent être compris si l'on ne considère qu'un seul de leurs aspects. Ils sont ambigus et flous, impossibles à mesurer, et leur représentation ne peut se faire qu'en termes qualitatifs. Leur observation se fait à l'aide de méthodes qui portent en elles-mêmes des erreurs et des approximations. Les données ne correspondent jamais exactement au phénomène qu'elles sont censées résumer.

Le traitement graphique de l'information, et en particulier la visualisation narrative, peut jouer un rôle important. La visualisation narrative s'appuie sur des éléments de communication qui ne se limitent pas à véhiculer des faits. Ces éléments vont au-delà de la simple visualisation de données car ils plantent le décor plus large du phénomène. Au laboratoire de recherche en visualisation DensityDesign à Milan (que je dirige), les travaux complexes de visualisation des données sont qualifiés de *macroscopes visuels*. Ce terme décrit les visualisations comme des outils permettant aux gens de voir non pas l'infiniment petit ou loin, comme le font les *microscopes* et les *télescopes*, mais l'infiniment complexe[2]. Je suis d'accord avec John Thackara, les visualisations sont « des outils et des notions esthétiques qui nous aident à comprendre (et à agir en connaissance de cause) au niveau global ».

En collaboration étroite avec des chercheurs en statistiques, nous avons récemment travaillé sur la visualisation de la pauvreté en tant que problème socioéconomique complexe. Le projet a été motivé par une conviction commune: pour que les gens comprennent vraiment en quoi consiste la pauvreté, une perspective nuancée ou *floue* est nécessaire. L'objectif général était de dépasser le modèle de communication conventionnel et non exhaustif de type *0-1*, *oui-non*, *inclus-exclus*. Cette approche a donné des visualisations comprenant plusieurs dimensions et incertitudes. La visualisation de l'incertitude dans le domaine des sciences humaines numériques est également le sujet principal d'une collaboration avec le Stanford Humanities Center. Ce projet commun vise à établir une carte de la correspondance écrite entre les grands penseurs des Lumières. L'un des tout premiers sujets de conversation a porté sur les modes traditionnels de visualisation pour ce genre de flux et d'échanges: la visualisation du parcours d'une lettre envoyée de l'expéditeur A au destinataire B par une simple ligne droite transmet-elle vraiment ce que représentait l'envoi d'une lettre à cette époque, dans le contexte social et culturel ? Il est fondamental d'avoir conscience de l'histoire derrière les données pour bien comprendre le phénomène. En outre, le degré d'incertitude et d'inachèvement de la base de données doit se voir reflété dans la visualisation.

L'approche présentée ici (à savoir modifier la visualisation des données grâce à une dimension narrative) n'affecte pas la communication entre les chercheurs et la société. Elle permet de favoriser les relations entre plusieurs disciplines et groupes de recherche. Les scientifiques doivent faire face à des problèmes toujours plus complexes auxquels une seule discipline ne peut s'affronter. Les experts d'un large éventail de domaines scientifiques, chacun fort d'un bagage de connaissances propres, collaborent sur des projets communs. Il est essentiel de mettre en place un tronc commun d'informations et de permettre le partage d'hypothèses et d'idées: c'est précisément sur ce point que le traitement graphique de l'information et la visualisation narrative peuvent intervenir.

Les institutions gouvernementales courent souvent les mêmes risques que la science: distance, méfiance, scepticisme et opposition démotivée. Leur quête de responsabilité et de confiance est alors fort similaire. De nombreux projets de *données ouvertes* génèrent, sans la moindre explication, une source

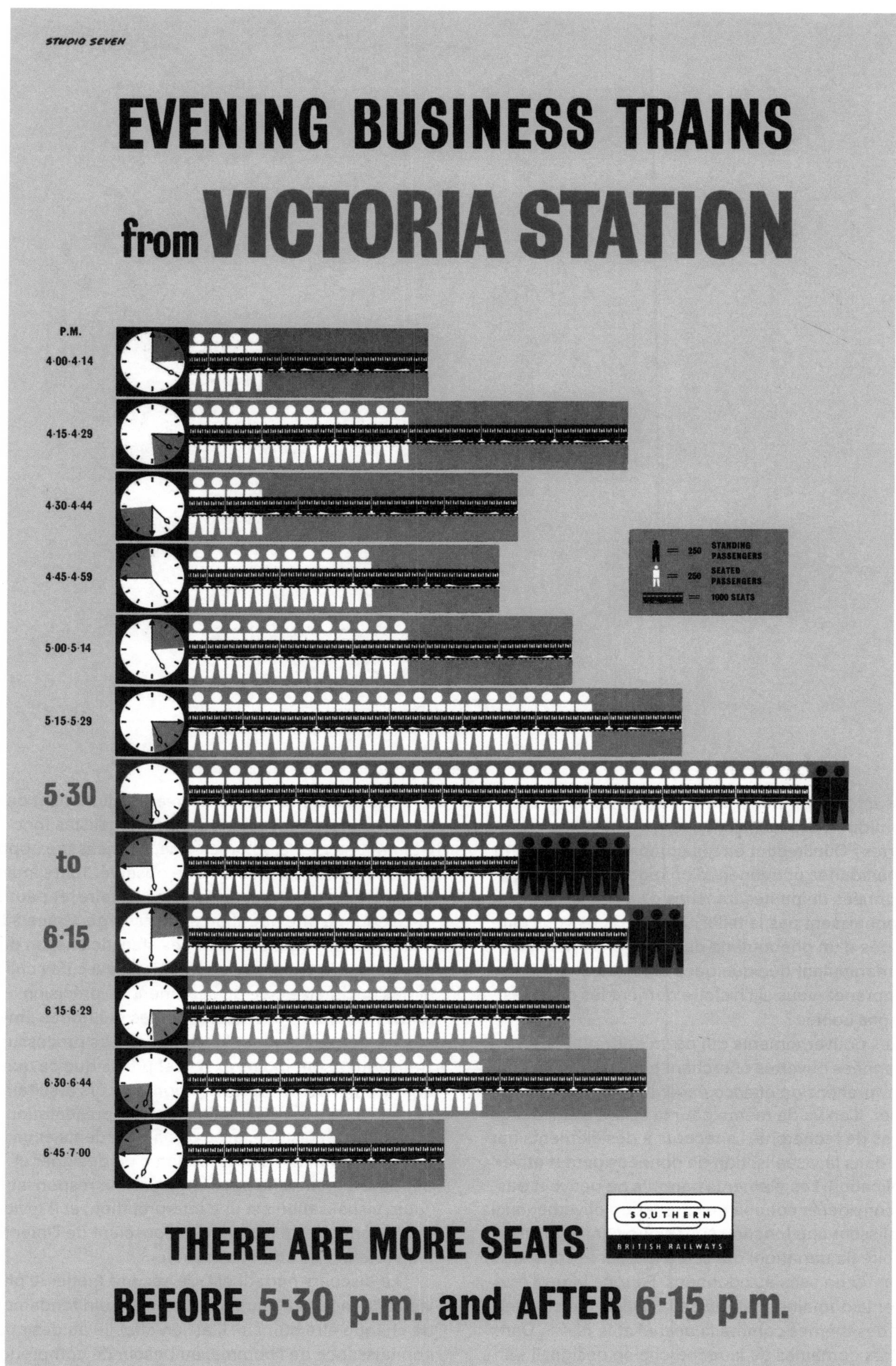

1960

1967

In 1967 the French cartographer Jacques Bertin wrote a standard reference on the graphic depiction of quantitative data. These maps of France for example show how multi-dimensional quantitative data can be mapped on a geographical area.

Der französische Kartograf Jacques Bertin verfasste 1967 ein Standardwerk über die grafische Darstellung von quantitativen Daten. Diese Frankreichkarten etwa zeigen, wie mehrdimensionale quantitative Daten auf einer geografischen Fläche kartiert werden können.

En 1967, le cartographe français Jacques Bertin a écrit un ouvrage de référence sur la représentation graphique des données quantitatives. Ces cartes de France montrent comment représenter des données quantitatives multidimensionnelles sur une aire géographique.

1960

This poster by British Railways shows the congestion of trains during rush hour and suggests passengers take earlier or later trains instead.
The timeline runs top down, the bars showing the proportion of passengers and available seats.

Auf diesem Poster zeigt British Railways die Überfüllung der Züge während der Hauptverkehrszeit und rät, frühere oder spätere Züge zu benutzen. Die Zeitleiste verläuft von oben nach unten, in den Balken ist das Verhältnis von Passagieren und Platzanzahl dargestellt.

Cette affiche de British Railways montre la fréquentation des trains à l'heure de pointe et conseille aux passagers de voyager plus tôt ou plus tard. La ligne temporelle va de haut en bas, et les barres montrent la proportion de passagers et de sièges disponibles.

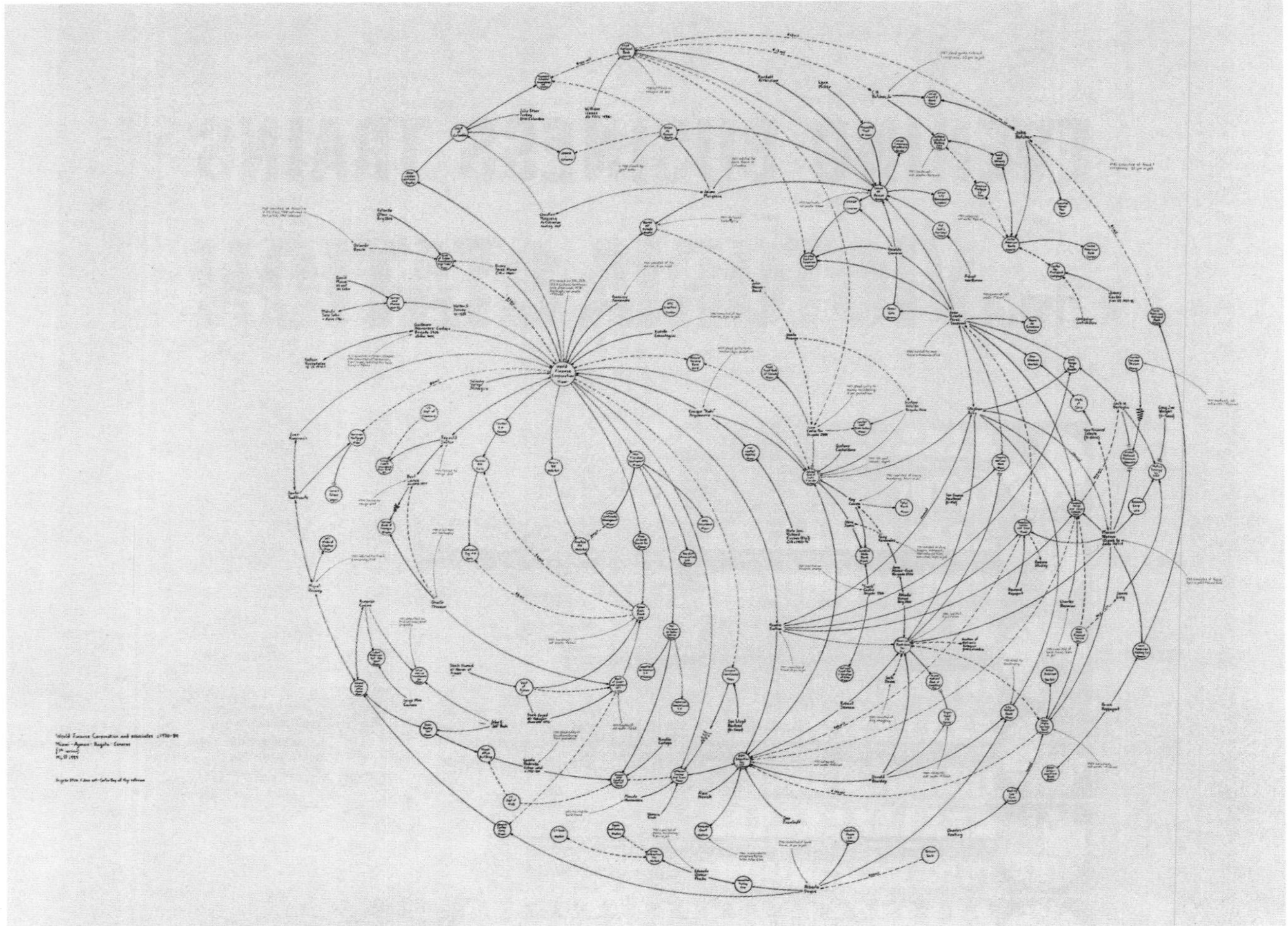

1999

croissante d'informations sur les phénomènes socioéconomiques. Les *données ouvertes* sont-elles vraiment *ouvertes*? Quelle peut être la compréhension quand des personnes obtiennent d'un gigantesque entrepôt de données de petites tranches d'un gâteau dont elles ne connaissent pas la taille? Pouvez-vous vous faire une idée d'un phénomène dans son ensemble en n'en manipulant que quelques blocs de données? Qu'apprenez-vous si l'histoire derrière les données n'est pas contée?

Les gouvernements qui osent s'affronter à l'océan de données ouvertes cherchent comment dépasser la compréhension et *encourager* leurs citoyens à s'impliquer. Il en va de même pour la science et les organismes de recherche. Le recours à des éléments narratifs dans la visualisation de données peut motiver l'implication. Les éléments narratifs ne peuvent pas être considérés comme de simples enjolivements: ils remplissent une fonction spécifique car ils racontent l'histoire (la narration) qui sert à recréer le contexte et donner un sens aux données. Pour ce faire, il faut quitter le domaine protégé de la recherche et jouer avec des thèmes comme la *beauté* et le *plaisir*. Dans d'autres domaines de la recherche en design, il s'entend que l'*émotion* est une force cognitive qui contribue à donner un sens, facilite l'interaction et permet une meilleure expérience de l'utilisateur. Utilité et esthétique ne s'opposent plus mutuellement: les choses attirantes, comme dit Donald Norman, fonctionnent souvent mieux[3]!

Il fut un temps où l'enjolivement systématique de la représentation visuelle des données était critiqué, ce qui rappelait les tensions coutumières (aujourd'hui dépassées) entre la forme et la fonction (avec une position radicale adoptée par Adolf Loos dans son œuvre «Ornement et crime»). Aujourd'hui au moins il y a une marge pour parler d'une possible fonction des éléments graphiques hors données[4], en réfutant la définition même de l'enjolivement comme simple ajout décoratif et inutile, voire nuisible.

Il est aussi possible d'inverser l'argument et de se demander si des graphiques minimalistes font vraiment passer le bon message, un message approprié à la nature du phénomène observé. Toute image transmet un message, parfois une histoire, et peut être prise comme une narration au sens large. Grâce à la collaboration régulière avec des statisticiens, on découvre que la simplicité d'un tableau avec des chiffres et des décimales crée un sentiment de précision pouvant s'avérer inadéquat pour les méthodes employées pour regrouper les données. Les processus statistiques sont moins exacts et précis que ce que donne à penser la représentation de leurs résultats. Par ailleurs, la transformation d'une représentation graphique en histoire, avec des antécédents et un contexte, demande l'intervention d'un designer et dépasse la neutralité pour engager une responsabilité. Toute visualisation est une interprétation, et il revient au designer d'être pleinement conscient de l'intention d'un artefact de communication.

Le discours narratif est «le second métier le plus vieux du monde»[5] car il reflète un besoin fondamental de chaque être humain. Il est en effet lié au désir de connaissance de l'homme, au besoin de comprendre les phénomènes et de leur donner un sens. Nous voulons connaître l'histoire et pouvoir éventuellement raconter à autrui ce que nous avons découvert et appris. Dernièrement, ce besoin fondamental semble plus présent pour les institutions chargées de regrouper et de communiquer des données sociales: «Il est indéniable qu'une communication réussie avec le groupe toujours plus important des clients non professionnels passe par l'effort des instituts de statistiques à fournir plus que des tableaux et autres informations statiques. La présentation visuelle des données par le biais d'outils graphiques intelligibles et flexibles, éventuellement intégrés à un environnement narratif et assorti de cartes pour montrer des données spatiales, favorise grandement la réponse aux besoins des non experts»[6].

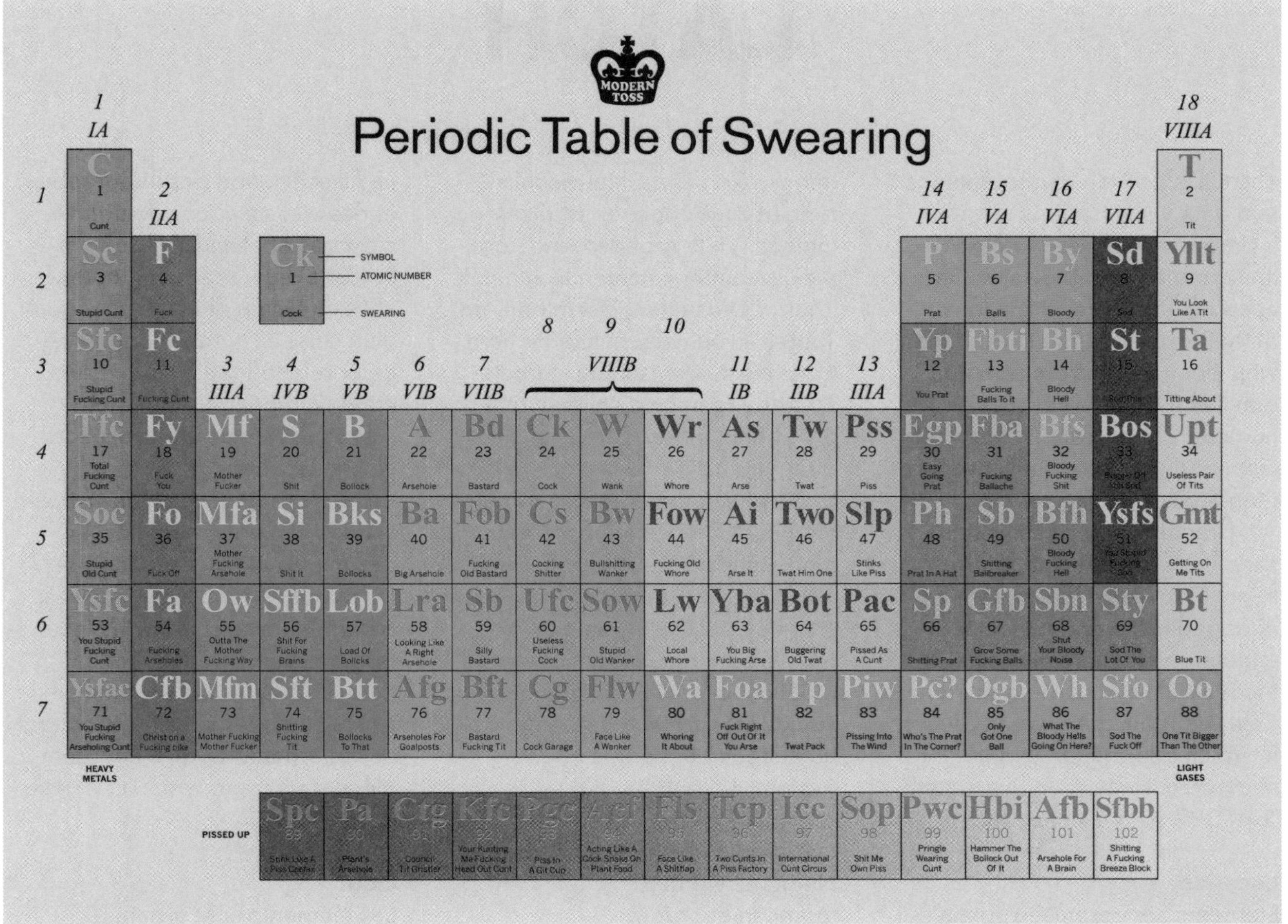

2010

Sans rien comprendre des statistiques, nous ne pouvons logiquement pas savoir ce qu'il se passe, comme l'explique Clive Thompson dans un récent article paru dans *Wired US* [7], mais sommes-nous vraiment certains que la solution soit, comme le suggère Thompson, de faire des statistiques un élément essentiel de l'éducation générale? Les statistiques sont-elles la nouvelle grammaire? Il est probablement plus logique d'encourager les chercheurs et les scientifiques à s'associer aux designers pour représenter les données dans la langue des hommes, et non dans la langue des données.

Paolo Ciuccarelli est directeur scientifique du laboratoire expérimental DensityDesign de l'Université polytechnique de Milan, un projet qui s'intéresse à la représentation des données dans la recherche sur les systèmes complexes.

1 Carrada, G.: *Communiquer la science*. Commission européenne. Direction-Générale de la Recherche et de l'Innovation, 2006.
2 De Rosnay, J.: *The Macroscope*. New York: Harper & Row, 1979.
3 Norman, D.: « Emotion and design: Attractive things work better ». *Interactions* magazine, IX, (4) 2002, 36–42.
4 Bateman, S. et al.: « Useful Junk? The Effects of Visual Embellishment on Comprehension and Memorability of Charts ». Dans *ACM Conference on Human Factors in Computing Systems* (CHI 2010).
5 Gershon, N. and Page, W.: « What storytelling can do for information visualization ». *Communications of the ACM*, 44 (8) 2001, 31–37.
6 Mittag, H.: « Educating the Public, The Role of E-Learning and Visual Communication of Official Data ». Communication sollicitée à la Commission de statistique et la Commission économique pour l'Europe, Conférence des statisticiens européens, Paris, 12–15 juin 2006. Nations Unies, Conseil économique et social, ECE/CES/2006.
7 Thompson, C.: « Why We Should Learn the Language of Data », *Wired US*, avril 2010.

1999

The artist Mark Lombardi became known for his "sociograms" describing scandalous ties between economy and politics. This example focuses on the World Finance Corp. that laundered money for the Colombian drug mafia in the 1970s.

Der Künstler Mark Lombardi wurde mit „Soziogrammen" bekannt, in denen er skandalöse Verflechtungen zwischen Wirtschaft und Politik aufzeichnete. Hier steht die World Finance Corp. im Fokus, die in den 1970er-Jahren Geldwäsche für die kolumbianische Drogenmafia betrieb.

L'artiste Mark Lombardi est devenu célèbre pour ses « sociogrammes » qui décrivent des liens scandaleux entre l'économie et la politique. Cet exemple analyse la World Finance Corp., qui a blanchi de l'argent pour les narcotrafiquants colombiens dans les années 1970.

2010

The Periodic Table combines several classifications, dividing the elements by nuclear charge (ordering number), periodically recurring attributes (rows) and groups (columns). Modern Toss ironically adapted this system for swear-words.

Das Periodensystem kombiniert mehrere Klassifikationen – es unterscheidet die Elemente sowohl nach Kernladung (Ordnungszahl), periodisch wiederkehrenden Eigenschaften (Zeilen) und nach Gruppen (Spalten). Modern Toss wandte dieses System ironisch auf Flüche an.

Le tableau périodique des éléments combine plusieurs classifications, et divise les éléments selon leur charge nucléaire (numéro), attributs périodiques (lignes) et groupes (colonnes). Modern Toss a réalisé une adaptation ironique de ce système pour les jurons.

LATCH

The classification of infographics and data visualisations is not a simple matter. Many works are complex, and they all differ according to topic, in the form of their expression or in their tone, which can range from scientific gravitas to tongue-in-cheek humour. Classifications are rarely clear and there are many overlapping areas.

Graphics and visualisations serve to communicate information. The way in which data are arranged is the critical factor in enabling readers to understand them quickly. According to Richard Saul Wurman, there are five ways in which information can be structured. He termed this system "LATCH", which stands for:

Location
Elements are organised spatially

Alphabet
Elements are organised alphabetically

Time
Elements are organised against a timeline

Category
Elements are divided into classes

Hierarchy
Elements are ranked in order of priority

Since infographics make less use of text there are fewer alphabetical examples, which is why this book does not include a section entitled "Alphabet". In many works, however, data is organised by combining several criteria. This is the case, for example, when timelines and weather data are added to maps.

This kind of combined representation is particularly found in animated and interactive visualisations. Nowadays, digital records can be organised flexibly by location, time or other criteria. The projects in this book have been allocated to individual chapters according to their dominant structural feature.

Infografiken und Datenvisualisierungen zu gruppieren ist nicht einfach. Viele Arbeiten sind komplex, sie unterscheiden sich nach Thema, Darstellungsform oder im Tonfall – von wissenschaftlichem Ernst bis zu ironischem Humor. Zuordnungen sind selten eindeutig, überall treten Überschneidungen auf.

Grafiken und Visualisierungen dienen der Informationsvermittlung. Entscheidend ist, wie Daten geordnet sind, damit sie vom Leser schnell erfasst werden. Richard Saul Wurman zufolge gibt es fünf Möglichkeiten, Informationen zu strukturieren. Nach den Anfangsbuchstaben benannte er das System „LATCH“:

Location
Elemente werden räumlich geordnet

Alphabet
Elemente werden alphabetisch geordnet

Time
Elemente werden in einer Zeitabfolge präsentiert

Category
Elemente werden nach Typ unterschieden

Hierarchy
Elemente werden in eine Rangfolge gebracht

Da Infografiken kaum mit Text arbeiten, gibt es nur vereinzelt alphabetische Beispiele. Dieses Buch enthält daher kein Kapitel zum Alphabet. Viele Arbeiten verbinden mehrere Kriterien, um Daten zu ordnen – etwa wenn eine Karte um eine Zeitreihe und Wetterdaten ergänzt wird.

Animierte und interaktive Visualisierungen fördern solche kombinierten Darstellungen besonders – digitale Datensätze können heute flexibel nach Ort, Zeit oder anderen Kategorien sortiert werden. Die Zuordnung von Projekten in die einzelnen Kapitel orientiert sich am jeweils dominanten Ordnungsprinzip.

La classification des infographies et des visualisations de données n'est pas chose aisée. De nombreuses œuvres sont complexes, et l'expression et le ton changent d'un sujet à l'autre, allant du sérieux scientifique à l'ironie. Les classifications sont rarement claires et de nombreux aspects se chevauchent.

Les graphiques et les visualisations servent à faire passer des informations. La façon dont les données sont organisées est déterminante pour que les lecteurs les comprennent rapidement. Selon Richard Saul Wurman, il existe cinq manières de structurer des informations, qu'il a rassemblées sous l'acronyme « LATCH », à savoir :

Lieu
Les éléments sont organisés de façon spatiale

Alphabet
Les éléments sont organisés de façon alphabétique

Temps
Les éléments sont organisés de façon chronologique

Catégorie
Les éléments sont divisés en classes

Hiérarchie
Les éléments sont classés selon leur priorité

Les infographies ayant peu recours au texte, il existe moins d'exemples alphabétiques, ce qui explique pourquoi l'ouvrage ne compte pas de section « Alphabet ». Dans de nombreuses créations toutefois, les données sont organisées en combinant plusieurs critères. Tel est le cas, par exemple, si des chronologies et des données météorologiques sont ajoutées à des plans.

Ce type de représentation combinée se retrouve notamment dans les visualisations animées et interactives. Les données numériques peuvent actuellement être organisées avec flexibilité en fonction du lieu, du temps ou d'autres critères. Les projets de cet ouvrage ont été répartis dans les chapitres selon leur principal aspect structurel.

Location 97—208

“If you can’t explain it simply, you don’t understand it well enough.”

„Wenn man etwas nicht einfach erklären kann, hat man es nicht richtig verstanden.“

« Si vous ne pouvez pas expliquer un concept à un enfant de six ans, c’est que vous ne le maîtrisez pas vraiment. »

Attributed to Albert Einstein

Location

Elements are organised spatially

Location

Elemente werden räumlich geordnet

Lieu

Les éléments sont organisés de façon chronologique

Everything that happens occurs somewhere. To find one's bearings in the world one must first orient oneself spatially: where do things happen? By organising objects spatially, one obtains an overview and can place side by side the items that occur concurrently within a space. Cartography is the science of depicting geographical information. For centuries it revolved around the question of how to project the curvature of the Earth on to paper. Topographical maps deal with the correct depiction of the Earth's surface, whereas thematic maps supplement spatial information with additional data (*The Geotaggers' World Atlas*, p.185).

Unlike photographically precise satellite images, maps use graphic means to make generalisations about the world. Maps are selective and standardise characteristic features, and therein lies their strength. Although they are a medium of simultaneity, some maps introduce a time element: for instance, in the context of a journey, the traversing of space can be depicted within a certain time-frame (*Flight AF447*, p.129).

Until recently maps were the main medium for storing geographical data, but a fundamental change is on the horizon thanks to the digital revolution. Space-related data can now be stored in databases, which in turn provide the starting point for complex visualisations. In addition, there are some works that do not place spatially sorted data on maps, but list them by name of country. These relate to the mental map of the world that we all hold in our heads (*A_B_ peace & terror etc.*, p.101).

Visualising information in maps goes beyond real spaces; imagined spaces can also be mapped. Mental maps show how relationships are arranged spatially in the imagination. For instance, Hugleikur Dagsson's map of Iceland uses the island's contours as the template for a mental image of his homeland (*The Land of Ice*, p.188). Esther Aarts arranges violent street names so that together they form the shape of a skull (*Map to Ghost Town*, p.154).

The organisation of information by place does not end with maps. Spatial arrangements can also be found in schematic drawings, which depict technical facilities or natural phenomena such as underground volcanoes (cf. *Sleeping Giant*, p.177). The human body, too, has repeatedly been considered as a spatial arrangement. Medicine is subdivided into specialisations based on different areas of the body, and each different body-part has its own monetary value (*Body Parts*, p.112). Geometry as a branch of mathematics is also concerned with spatial arrangements; its subject is the projection of multi-dimensional structures on to a two-dimensional surface (*Real Magick in Theory and Practise*, p.169).

Alles, was geschieht, hat einen Ort. Will man sich in der Welt zurechtfinden, muss man sich zuerst räumlich orientieren – wo geschieht etwas? Dinge räumlich zu ordnen heißt, sich eine Übersicht zu verschaffen – nebeneinanderzustellen, was gleichzeitig im Raum passiert. Die Kartografie ist die Wissenschaft von der Darstellung geografischer Informationen. Jahrhundertelang drehte sie sich um die Frage, wie man die gekrümmte Erdoberfläche auf Papier projiziert. Topografische Karten befassen sich mit der korrekten Abbildung der Erdoberfläche, thematische Karten dagegen reichern die räumlichen Informationen mit zusätzlichen Daten an (*The Geotaggers' World Atlas*, S. 185).

Anders als fotografisch genaue Satellitenbilder verallgemeinern Karten die Welt mit grafischen Mitteln. Sie treffen eine Auswahl und typisieren charakteristische Merkmale – darin liegt ihre Stärke. Obwohl Karten ein Medium der Gleichzeitigkeit sind, wird in manchen Karten eine Zeitdimension eingeführt, etwa wenn im Zusammenhang einer Reise die Überwindung des Raumes in einer bestimmten Zeitspanne dargestellt wird (*Flight AF447*, S. 129).

Während bis vor Kurzem Karten die zentrale Speicherform für geografische Daten waren, deutet sich mit der digitalen Revolution ein fundamentaler Wandel an. Raumbezogene Daten lassen sich nun in Datenbanken speichern, die wiederum den Ausgangspunkt für komplexe Visualisierungen bieten. Außerdem gibt es einige Arbeiten, die räumlich sortierte Daten nicht auf einer Karte platzieren, sondern nach Ländernamen auflisten. Sie beziehen sich dann auf die memorierte Karte der Welt, die jeder im Kopf hat (*A_B_ peace & terror etc.*, S. 101).

Die Visualisierung von Informationen in Karten geht über reale Räume hinaus: Imaginierte Räume lassen sich ebenfalls kartieren. Mentale Karten zeigen, wie Zusammenhänge in der Vorstellung räumlich angeordnet werden. Hugleikur Dagssons Karte von Island beispielsweise nutzt die Umrisse der Insel, um ein mentales Bild seiner Heimat zu zeichnen (*The Land of Ice*, S. 188). Esther Aarts erfundene Anordnung von Horrorvokabeln formt einen Totenkopf (*Map to Ghost Town*, S. 154).

Die Sortierung von Informationen nach Orten erschöpft sich nicht in Karten. Räumliche Anordnungen finden sich auch in schematischen Zeichnungen – sie zeigen technische Anlagen oder Naturphänomene wie etwa unterirdische Vulkane (vgl. *Sleeping Giant*, S. 177). Auch der menschliche Körper ist immer wieder als räumliche Anordnung gedacht worden. Die Medizin unterteilt sich nach Körperregionen, und heute wie früher haben verschiedene Körperteile einen eigenen finanziellen Wert (*Body Parts*, S. 112). Die Geometrie als Teilgebiet der Mathematik befasst sich ebenfalls mit räumlichen Anordnungen – ihr Gegenstandsbereich ist die Projektion von mehrdimensionalen Strukturen auf die zweidimensionale Fläche (*Real Magick in Theory and Practise*, S. 169).

Tous les événements se déroulent à un certain endroit. Pour trouver son chemin, il faut s'orienter dans l'espace : où ont lieu les choses ? Le fait d'organiser les objets de façon spatiale permet d'avoir une vue d'ensemble et de placer des événements simultanés dans un espace. La cartographie est la science qui représente les informations géographiques. Pendant des siècles, elle a cherché à savoir comment représenter la courbe de la Terre sur papier. Les cartes topographiques s'attachent à la représentation correcte de la surface de la Terre, alors que les cartes thématiques viennent compléter les informations spatiales avec d'autres données (*The Geotaggers' World Atlas*, p.185).

Contrairement aux images satellite qui offrent une photographie exacte, les cartes ont recours à des moyens graphiques pour présenter des généralisations sur le monde. Les cartes sont sélectives et standardisent des éléments types, c'est là toute leur force. Même si elles apportent des informations simultanées, certaines introduisent un élément temporel : par exemple, dans le contexte d'un voyage, la traversée d'un espace peut être décrite selon une chronologie (*Flight AF447*, p.129).

Il y a encore peu, les cartes étaient le principal support de stockage de données géographiques ; un changement fondamental s'opère cependant grâce à l'ère numérique. Les données d'ordre spatial peuvent désormais être stockées dans des bases de données, lesquelles sont le point de départ pour des visualisations complexes. Par ailleurs, au lieu de placer des données sur des cartes, certains travaux les répertorient par nom de pays, ce qui renvoie à la carte mentale du monde que nous avons tous en tête (*A_B_ peace & terror etc.*, p.101).

La visualisation des informations figurant dans les cartes va au-delà des espaces réels, car il est possible d'illustrer aussi des espaces imaginés. Les cartes heuristiques montrent l'organisation spatiale des relations dans l'imagination. Par exemple, dans sa carte de l'Islande, Hugleikur Dagsson prend les contours de l'île comme modèle d'image mentale pour sa terre natale (*The Land of Ice*, p.188). Esther Aarts assemble des noms de rues à connotation violente pour obtenir la forme d'un crâne (*Map to Ghost Town*, p.154).

L'organisation des informations par lieu ne se cantonne pas aux cartes. Les organisations spatiales se rencontrent aussi dans des dessins schématiques représentant des installations techniques ou des phénomènes naturels comme des volcans souterrains (cf. *Sleeping Giant*, p.177). Le corps humain sert aussi souvent de schéma d'organisation spatiale. La médecine est divisée en spécialisations par rapport aux parties du corps, lesquelles possèdent leur propre valeur monétaire (*Body Parts*, p.112). La géométrie, en tant que discipline mathématique, est également concernée par les organisations spatiales, car elle repose sur la projection de structures multidimensionnelles sur une surface en deux dimensions (*Real Magick in Theory and Practise*, p.169).

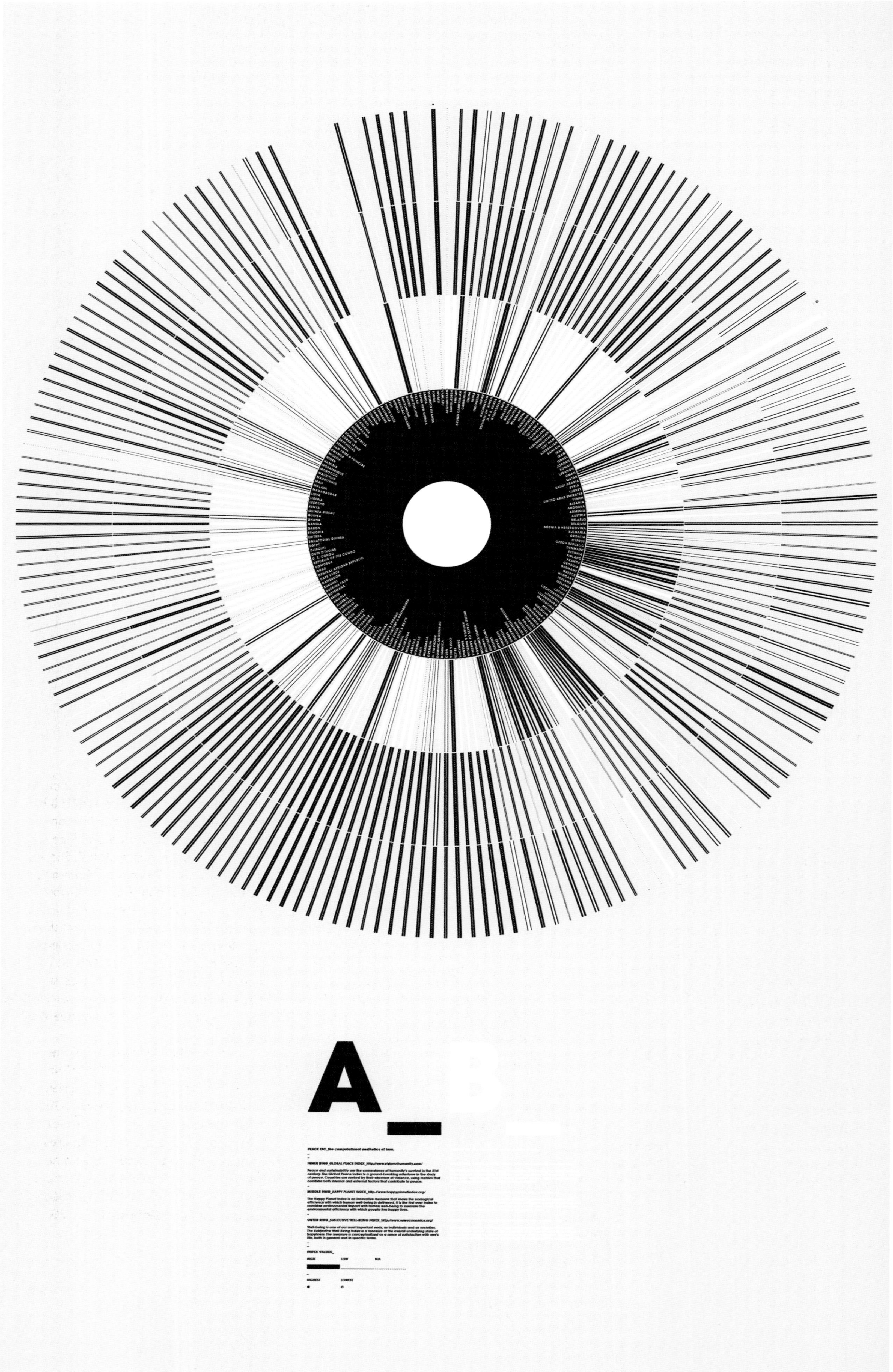

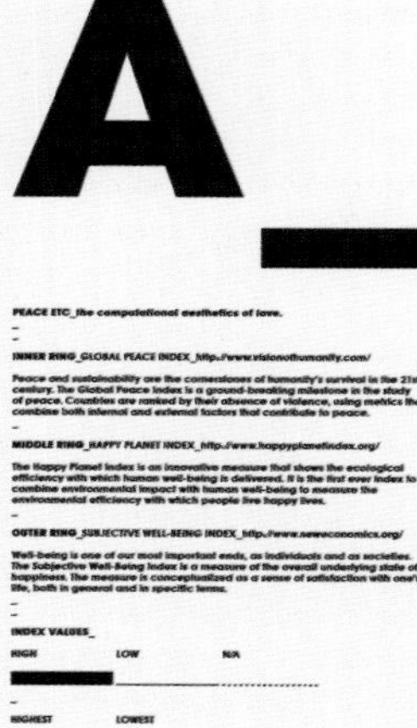
A_
PEACE ETC_the computational aesthetics of love.
INNER RING_GLOBAL PEACE INDEX_http://www.visionofhumanity.com/
Peace and sustainability are the cornerstones of humanity's survival in the 21st century. The Global Peace Index is a ground-breaking milestone in the study of peace. Countries are ranked by their absence of violence, using metrics that combine both internal and external factors that contribute to peace.
MIDDLE RING_HAPPY PLANET INDEX_http://www.happyplanetindex.org/
The Happy Planet Index is an innovative measure that shows the ecological efficiency with which human well-being is delivered. It is the first ever index to combine environmental impact with human well-being to measure the environmental efficiency with which people live happy lives.
OUTER RING_SUBJECTIVE WELL-BEING INDEX_http://www.neweconomics.org/
Well-being is one of our most important ends, as individuals and as societies. The Subjective Well-Being Index is a measure of the overall underlying state of happiness. The measure is conceptualized as a sense of satisfaction with one's life, both in general and in specific terms.
INDEX VALUES_
HIGH
LOW
N/A
HIGHEST
LOWEST

Project Info: Dual-sided screen print, 2008, UK
Data Source: Global Peace Index; SIPRI; Happy Planet Index; Subjective Well-Being Index; Political Terror Scale
Design: Peter Crnokrak (The Luxury of Protest)
Awards: AIGA 365, 2009

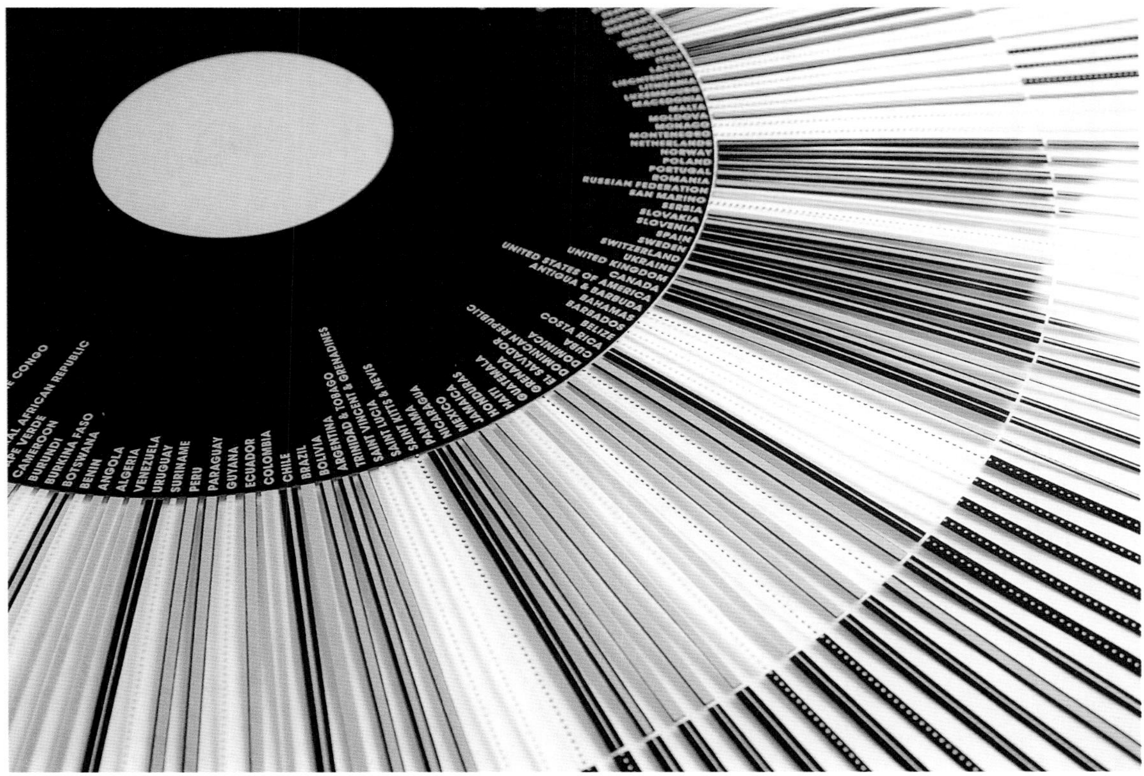

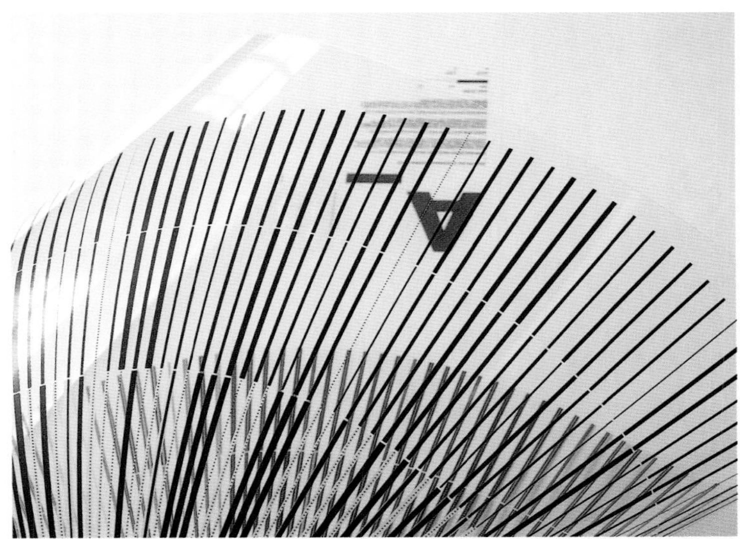

A_B_ peace & terror etc.

This diagram surveys how the 192 member states of the UN contribute to global peace or terror. The inner circle lists all states in alphabetical order. The outer circles visualise various indices for contributions to peace or terror. Peace is shown in black and is derived from the Global Peace Index, the Happy Planet Index and the Subjective Well-Being Index (from the centre outwards).

The terror contributions of each country are shown in white and are derived from the Political Terror Scale, Weapon Holdings per Capita and Military Expenditure per Capita (from the centre outwards). Originally this diagram was issued as a double-sided transparent poster, with peace printed on the A-side and war on the B-side.

Dieses Diagramm untersucht, welchen Beitrag jeder der 192 Mitgliedsstaaten der Vereinten Nationen zu Frieden oder Terror auf der Welt leistet. Im innersten Kreis stehen alle Länder in alphabetischer Reihenfolge. Die äußeren Kreise visualisieren die Daten mehrerer globaler Untersuchungen zu Frieden oder Krieg. Frieden ist schwarz gezeichnet. Die abgebildeten Werte beruhen auf dem Global Peace Index, dem Happy Planet Index und dem Subjective Well-Being Index (von innen nach außen).

Die kriegerischen Aktivitäten jedes Landes sind weiß dargestellt und fußen auf dem Political Terror Scale, dem Waffenbesitz pro Kopf und den Militärausgaben pro Kopf (von innen nach außen). Ursprünglich wurde das Diagramm als zweiseitig bedrucktes transparentes Plakat veröffentlicht, das die Angaben zum Frieden auf der A-Seite und die Terrordaten auf der B-Seite zeigte.

Ce diagramme examine la contribution des 192 États membres de l'ONU à la paix ou au terrorisme dans le monde. Le cercle intérieur donne une liste de tous les États par ordre alphabétique. Les cercles extérieurs représentent plusieurs indices mesurant la contribution à la paix ou au terrorisme. La paix est représentée en noir et les informations sont tirées, du centre vers l'extérieur, de l'indice de paix global (Global Peace Index), de l'indice de bonheur de la planète (Happy Planet Index) et de l'indice du bien-être subjectif (Subjective Well-Being Index).

Les contributions au terrorisme sont représentées en blanc, et les informations sont tirées, du centre vers l'extérieur, de l'échelle du terrorisme politique (Political Terror Scale), du nombre d'armes par habitant et des dépenses militaires par habitant. À l'origine, ce diagramme a été imprimé sous forme d'affiche transparente double face, avec la paix imprimée sur la face A, et la guerre sur la face B.

The Car of the Future

"The Car of the Future" highlights recent innovations for making cars safer and smarter. It is centred around an abstract illustration of a car showing some of its inner components. Inserts explain each of these innovations. Most of the insert graphics show specific traffic situations, in which the new devices and auto-responding systems would be activated.

The happy globe graphic at the bottom is a symbol which refers to the abandoning of a main engine, and instead the use of indivdual motors for each wheel. At the top right, one of the inserts explains the enhanced functionality of shock absorbers. The night-blue colour is reminiscent of the colour scheme of silver grey and blue often employed to advertise innovative automobile technology.

„Das Auto der Zukunft" zeigt technische Innovationen, durch die Autos sicherer und intelligenter werden. Das abstrahierte Bild eines Autos, das hier im Mittelpunkt steht, hebt auch einige Innenbauteile hervor. In Text-Bildkästen wird deren jeweilige Technologie erläutert. Die meisten der kleinen Grafiken zeigen bestimmte Situationen im Straßenverkehr, bei denen die neuen Entwicklungen und automatischen Reaktionssysteme zum Einsatz kommen.

Die Zeichnung des glücklichen Planeten unten auf der Seite symbolisiert den Verzicht auf einen zentralen Motor; hier verfügt jedes Rad über einen eigenen Motor. In einem Kasten oben rechts wird die verbesserte Funktionsweise von Stoßdämpfern erklärt. Die dunkelblaue Farbe lehnt sich an das Farbschema von Silbergrau und Blau an, das häufig bei der Vorstellung innovativer Automobiltechnik verwendet wird.

« La voiture du futur » met en lumière les récentes innovations en matière de sécurité et d'intelligence automobile. Au centre, l'illustration abstraite d'une voiture laisse voir certains de ses composants. Des cadres expliquent chacune de ces innovations. La plupart des illustrations des cadres montrent des situations spécifiques sur la route dans lesquelles les nouveaux équipements et systèmes automatiques s'activeraient.

L'image de planète heureuse dans le bas est un symbole qui fait allusion à l'abandon du moteur principal au profit de moteurs individuels pour chaque roue. En haut à droite, l'un des cadres explique l'amélioration des amortisseurs. La couleur bleu nuit évoque la palette de gris argent et bleu souvent employée dans les publicités pour les innovations technologiques dans l'automobile.

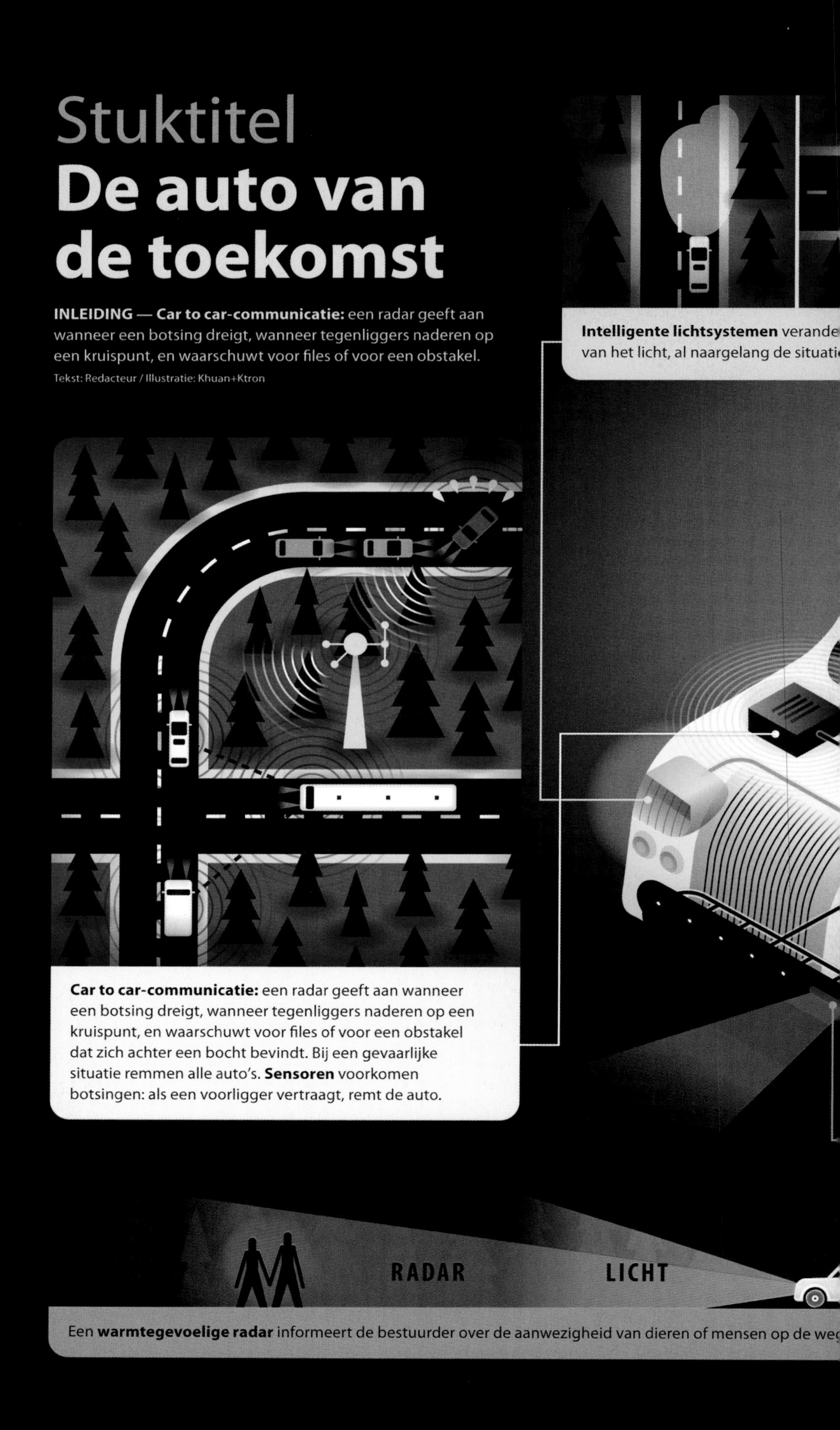

Stuktitel
De auto van de toekomst
INLEIDING — Car to car-communicatie: een radar geeft aan wanneer een botsing dreigt, wanneer tegenliggers naderen op een kruispunt, en waarschuwt voor files of voor een obstakel.
Tekst: Redacteur / Illustratie: Khuan+Ktron
Intelligente lichtsystemen verande
van het licht, al naargelang de situati
Car to car-communicatie: een radar geeft aan wanneer een botsing dreigt, wanneer tegenliggers naderen op een kruispunt, en waarschuwt voor files of voor een obstakel dat zich achter een bocht bevindt. Bij een gevaarlijke situatie remmen alle auto's. Sensoren voorkomen botsingen: als een voorligger vertraagt, remt de auto.
RADAR
LICHT
Een warmtegevoelige radar informeert de bestuurder over de aanwezigheid van dieren of mensen op de we

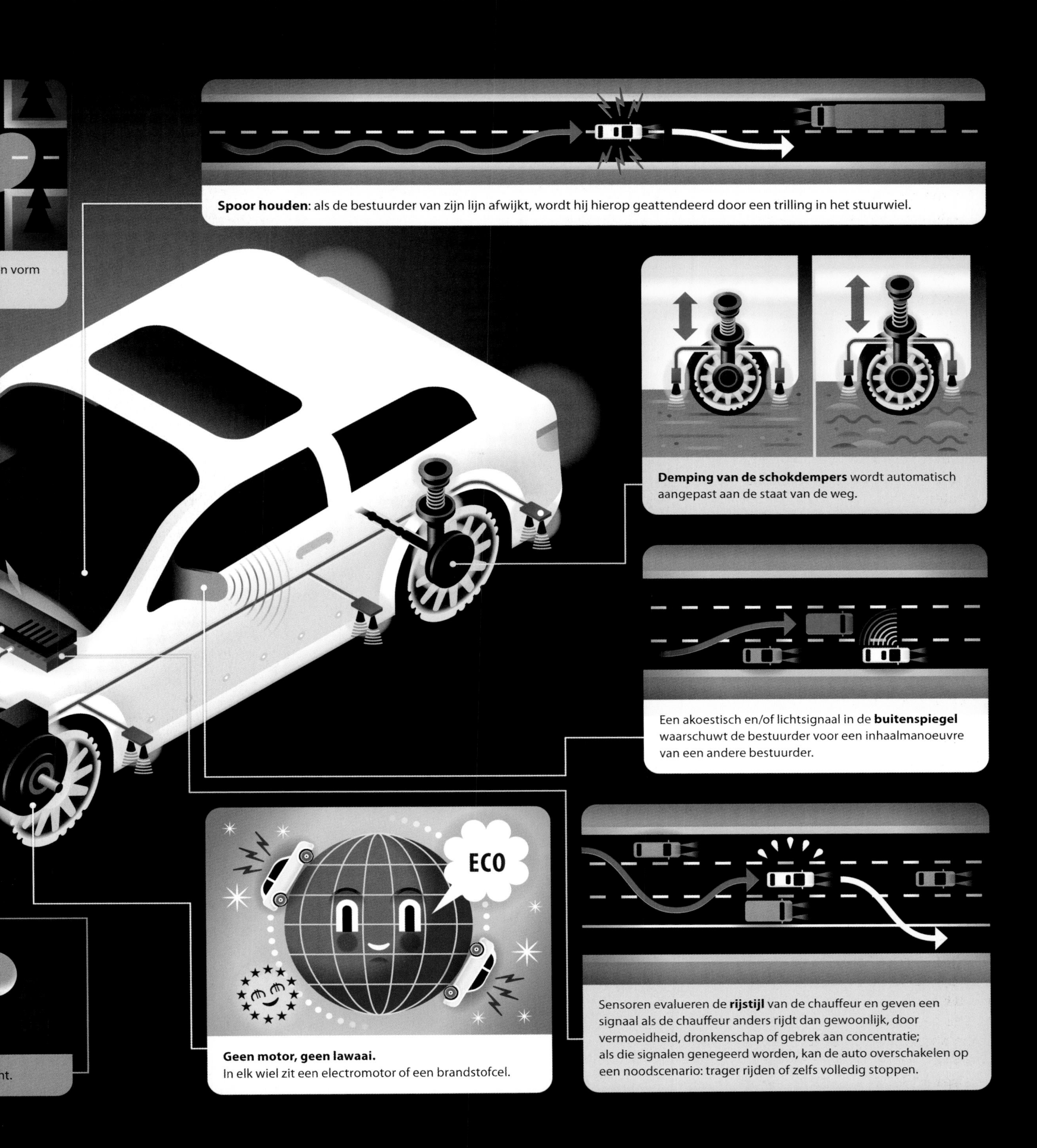

Spoor houden: als de bestuurder van zijn lijn afwijkt, wordt hij hierop geattendeerd door een trilling in het stuurwiel.
en vorm
Demping van de schokdempers wordt automatisch aangepast aan de staat van de weg.
Een akoestisch en/of lichtsignaal in de **buitenspiegel** waarschuwt de bestuurder voor een inhaalmanoeuvre van een andere bestuurder.
ECO
Geen motor, geen lawaai.
In elk wiel zit een electromotor of een brandstofcel.
Sensoren evalueren de **rijstijl** van de chauffeur en geven een signaal als de chauffeur anders rijdt dan gewoonlijk, door vermoeidheid, dronkenschap of gebrek aan concentratie; als die signalen genegeerd worden, kan de auto overschakelen op een noodscenario: trager rijden of zelfs volledig stoppen.
cht.

Project Info: *Knack*, magazine article, 2009, Belgium
Design: Steebz (Khuan + Ktron)

An American Watershe

Five decades after authorizing the building of canals and levee control flooding, Congress has acted to restore the flow of fr that sustains the United States' only subtropical preserve.

Gulf Coast Visitors Center

Everglades City

TEN THOUSAND ISLANDS
Mangroves stand on oyster beds in this system of barrier islands and estuarine inner bays and islands.

BIG CYPRESS NATIONAL PRESERVE

Miccosukee Cultural Center

Shark Valley Visitors Center

Tram tour

Observation tower

SHARK RIVER SLOUGH

TAMIAMI TRAIL

EVERGLADES NATIONAL PARK

Park boundary

GULF OF MEXICO

THE SLOUGHS
The main source of freshwater, sloughs are the swift centers of broad, shallow (less than three feet deep), marshy rivers that flow south from Lake Okeechobee.

Homestea

PINELANDS

Long Pine Key

Royal Palm Visitors Center

Anhinga Trail

WILDERNESS WATERWAY
Numbered markers guide canoes, kayaks, and small outboards through 99 miles of Gulf Coast wetlands between Everglades City and Flamingo.

TAYLOR SLOUGH

Nine Mile Pond

CAPE SABLE

Coot Bay Pond

Flamingo

Flamingo Visitors Center

KEY

Freshwater areas

Saltwater areas

0 5 10
MILES

FLORIDA BAY
Interconnected basins of fresh and salt water mix in this 850-square-mile ecosystem that has an average depth of less than 3½ feet.

Ecosystems under threat

Cape Sable seaside sparrow

Roseate spoonbill

Brown pelican

Great blue heron

Schaus swallowtail butterfly

Green turtle

West Indian manatee

American crocodile

Largemouth bass

Sawgrass

MARINE/ESTUARY | MANGROVES | SLOUGH | HAMMOCK

SALTWATER HABITAT

FRESHWATER HABI

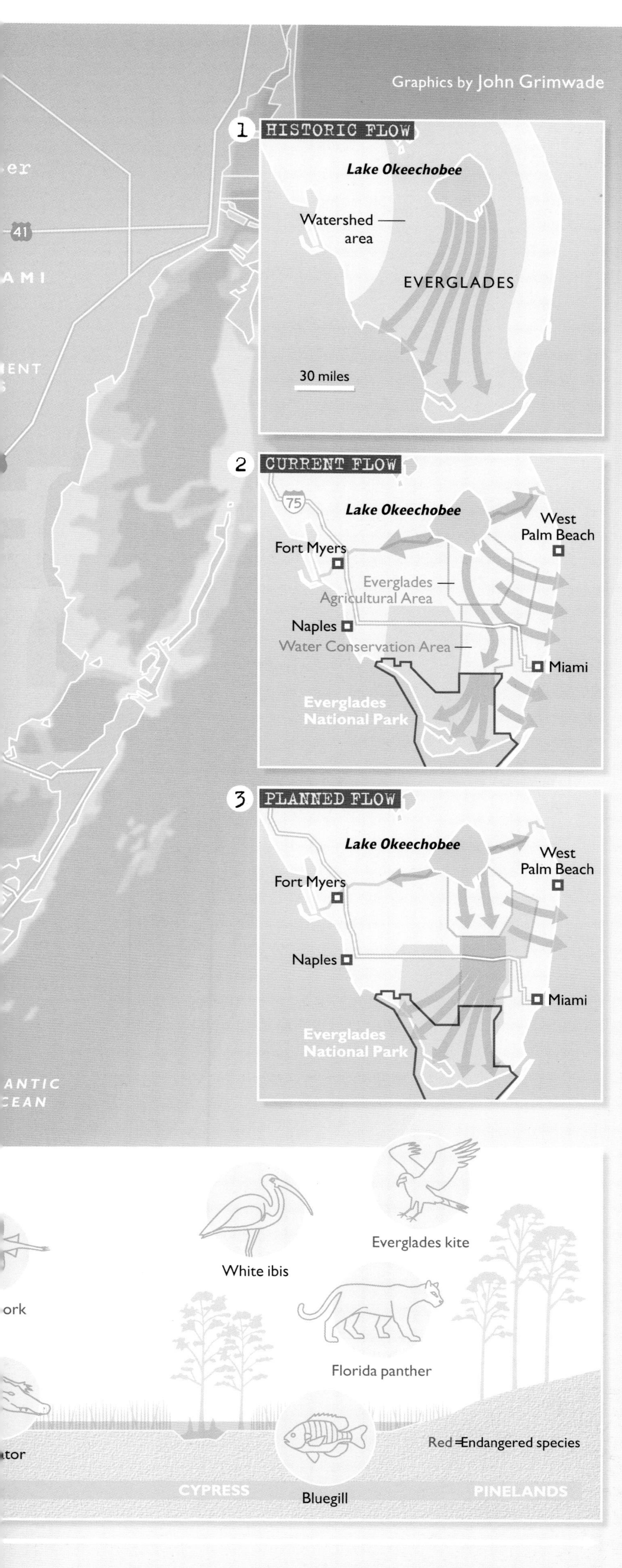

An American Watershed

The Everglades in Florida are a system of sub-tropical wetlands, fed by fresh waters from Lake Okeechobee in the north which form a very wide slow-moving river. After decades of draining, a major restoration plan for the Everglades was agreed by US Congress in 2000. This map shows the Everglades National Park, which safeguards the southern part of the wetlands.

The sequence of historical maps on the right demonstrate how the water-flows had been modified in the past for the fresh-water supplies of cities in the area, and how the plans were to restore much of the natural water-flow to preserve the Everglades. The panorama at the bottom lists endangered species living in the area.

Die Everglades in Florida sind ein System subtropischer Feuchtgebiete. Der Wasserzufluss stammt aus dem Okeechobee-See im Norden, der einen sehr breiten, trägen Fluss bildet. Nachdem das Gebiet jahrzehntelang systematisch trockengelegt wurde, verabschiedete der US-Kongress im Jahr 2000 umfas-sende Pläne zur Wiederherstellung der Wetlands. Diese Karte zeigt den Everglades National Park, der den südlichen Teil des Marschlands schützt.

Die Abfolge historischer Karten rechts verdeutlicht, wie der Wasserzufluss in der Vergangenheit durch die Trinkwasserversorgung der umliegenden Städte beeinträchtigt wurde, und zeigt die Pläne zur Wiederherstellung der natürlichen Strömungsverhältnisse, durch die die Everglades bewahrt werden sollen. Der Kasten unten führt die gefährdeten Arten der Region auf.

Les Everglades, en Floride, sont un système de zones humides alimentées en eau douce par le lac Okeechobee, au nord, qui forme une large rivière au cours tranquille. Après un drainage qui a duré des dizaines d'années, le Congrès américain a convenu d'un grand plan de restauration des Everglades en 2000. Cette carte montre le Parc national des Everglades, qui protège la partie sud des zones humides.

À droite, une série de cartes chronologiques montre comment les cours d'eau ont été modifiés par le passé pour alimenter les villes de la région en eau douce, et révèle que les plans étaient de restaurer la plupart des cours naturels afin de préserver les Everglades. En bas, le panorama dresse une liste des espèces en voie d'extinction qui vivent dans la région.

Project Info: *Condé Nast Traveler*, magazine article, 2003, USA
Design: Robert Best
Illustration: John Grimwade

QUAL É A MAIOR ARTÉRIA?

aorta
safena magna

É a aorta, uma superartéria com 3 centímetros de diâmetro e 50 de comprimento. Começando no coração e terminando perto da região genital, ela leva o sangue oxigenado a todas as partes do corpo. Em comprimento, porém, a aorta perde para uma superveia que fica na perna. Com cerca de 70 centímetros num homem de altura mediana, a veia safena magna é o maior vaso sanguíneo do corpo.

POR QUE A ARÉOLA DO SEIO TEM COR E PELE DIFERENTES?

Esta região tem a córnea – subcamada mais superficial da epiderme – muito fina, o que torna a pele da aréola do seio bem mais lisa do que a do resto do corpo. Já a cor é mais forte porque nesta região há maior atividade dos melanócitos, células produtoras de melanina, um pigmento de cor marrom-escura.

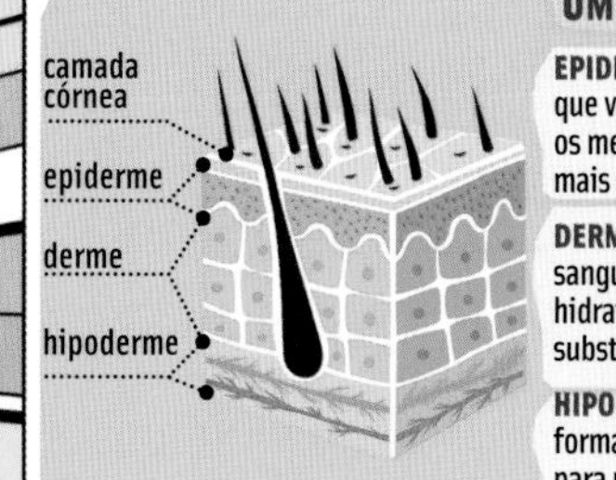

UM CORTE NA PELE

EPIDERME É a camada mais externa, que vive "descascando". Aqui ficam os melanócitos e a córnea, subcamada mais superficial da epiderme

DERME Camada rica em vasos sanguíneos e nervos. Mantém a pele hidratada e flexível, produzindo substâncias como colágeno e elastina

HIPODERME Camada mais profunda, formada principalmente de gordura para proteger o corpo contra o frio

QUANTAS VEZES TROCAMOS DE PELE?

As células da pele se renovam a cada 20 ou 30 dias. Isso significa que ao longo da vida "trocamos" de pele umas mil vezes! Mas a troca só envolve a camada mais externa, a epiderme.

Apesar de quase imperceptível, essa renovação dá um trabalho danado, afinal, a pele é o maior órgão do corpo humano, com cerca de 2 m². Com exceção dos olhos, mucosas, unhas e orifícios alimentares e genitais, toda nossa superfície corporal é coberta por esse super-revestimento.

QUANTOS MÚSCULOS A GENTE TEM?

O corpo humano tem mais de 600 músculos. Apesar de ser sinônimo de força, o bíceps, músculo da parte da frente do braço, não leva o título de mais forte do corpo. O grande campeão é o masseter, músculo responsável pela mastigação. Graças a ele, uma mordida de dois segundos é capaz de exercer uma pressão equivalente a 124 quilos.

As centenas de músculos que temos fazem desse tipo de tecido o item mais pesado na composição do corpo humano. Veja como o nosso peso é distribuído:

MÚSCULOS
40% do peso

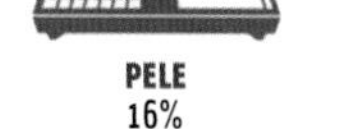

PELE
16%

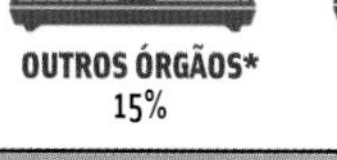

OUTROS ÓRGÃOS*
15%

OSSOS
14%

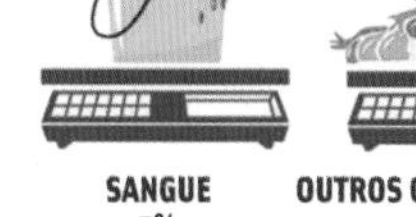

SANGUE
7%

OUTROS COMPONENTES**
8%

*CÉREBRO, CORAÇÃO, PULMÕES, RINS, FÍGADO, ESTÔMAGO, INTESTINOS, BAÇO, PÂNCREAS E BEXIGA
**TENDÕES, LIGAMENTOS, CARTILAGENS, GLÂNDULAS, NERVOS, DENTES E OUTROS TECIDOS
OBS: VALORES ESTIMADOS PARA UM ADULTO

cartilagem tireóide (gogó)
glândula tireóide
pulmão
aorta
pulmão
coração
aréola

POR QUE SÓ OS HOMENS TÊM GOGÓ?

Por causa da maior quantidade do hormônio testosterona. É ele que faz crescer o gogó, o nome popular da cartilagem tireóide e região que nos homens é cheia de receptores de testosterona. Essa cartilagem fica um pouco acima da glândula tireóide, que produz hormônios que regulam boa parte do organismo.

O outro nome popular do gogó, pomo-de-adão, tem origem bíblica e faz alusão ao fato de Adão ter comido o fruto proibido no paraíso e um pedaço dele ter ficado entalado na sua garganta.

QUANTO AR CABE NOS PULMÕES?

Os pulmões comportam uns 5 litros de ar, mas apenas meio litro é renovado a cada respiração. Como nossa freqüência respiratória é de cerca de 15 movimentos por minuto, respiramos 7,5 litros de ar nesse intervalo de tempo. Fazendo as contas, respiramos 450 litros de ar em uma hora; 10 800 litros em um dia; 3,9 milhões de litros em um ano; e por volta de 276 milhões de litros de ar ao longo de 70 anos!

O CORAÇÃO É DO TAMANHO DO PUNHO?

Sim. O coração de um adulto tem cerca de 12 centímetros de comprimento por 8 ou 9 centímetros de largura, o que corresponde ao tamanho aproximado de um punho fechado. Mas as proporções mais exatas no corpo humano estão nos ossos da mão e são vitais para que ela possa exercer a função de pegar as coisas. Veja como essas proporções funcionam:

A falanges distais
B falanges médias
C falanges proximais
D metacarpos (na palma das mãos)
E carpos (ossos do punho)

1ª PROPORÇÃO: a soma do comprimento da falange distal com a falange média é igual ao tamanho da falange proximal do dedo (A + B = C)

2ª PROPORÇÃO: a soma da falange média com a proximal é igual ao tamanho do metacarpo (B + C = D)

QUANTO SANGUE CIRCULA NO CORPO?

Cinco litros, em média. Para distribuir o sangue pelo organismo, o coração bate cerca de 70 vezes por minuto. A cada batida, ele bombeia 90 mililitros de sangue, que percorrem o corpo em apenas um minuto. No caso de um acidente que provoque hemorragia grave, o máximo de sangue que o corpo pode perder antes que a pessoa morra é 2 litros. >>

The Greatest Curiosities of the Human Body

This series of four double-spreads presents the human body and its countless little secrets. In the middle of each spread, a part of the human figure is laid out as one of four sequential sections, like a map representing an unknown territory. The bubbles show a tiny figure in a funny little spacecraft – he explores the unknown territory, gliding through blood vessels, falling into the intestines, exiting through the penis.

Other bubbles at key points on the body work like magnifying glasses, facilitating an X-ray view into the body. Text boxes along both sides add interesting details: how you could fill an ordinary swimming-pool with the saliva produced during an average human life-span, or how fingernails grow faster than toenails.

Thema dieser vier Doppelseiten umfassenden Serie sind der menschliche Körper und seine unzähligen kleinen Geheimnisse. Im Zentrum jeder Doppelseite ist ein Teil des menschlichen Körpers zu sehen, wie eine Landkarte, die unbekanntes Territorium darstellt. Die Blasen zeigen eine winzige Figur in einer lustigen kleinen Raumfähre – sie erforscht das unbekannte Territorium, fährt durch Blutgefäße, stürzt in Organe und gelangt durch den Penis wieder ins Freie.

Zusätzliche Kreise an wichtigen Körperteilen funktionieren wie eine Lupe und ermöglichen einen Röntgenblick in den Körper. Textkästen zu beiden Seiten erläutern interessante Details: etwa dass man ein ganzes Schwimmbecken mit dem Speichel füllen könnte, den ein Mensch im Laufe seines Lebens durchschnittlich erzeugt, oder dass Fingernägel schneller wachsen als Zehennägel.

Cette série de quatre doubles pages examine le corps humain et ses innombrables petits secrets. Chaque double page présente en son centre une section du corps, comme la carte d'un territoire inconnu. Les bulles montrent un personnage dans un drôle de petit vaisseau spatial – il explore ce territoire inconnu, glisse le long des vaisseaux sanguins, tombe dans les intestins, et sort par le pénis.

D'autres bulles placées à des endroits stratégiques fonctionnent comme des loupes et donnent une vision de l'intérieur du corps. Les cadres de texte situés sur les deux côtés ajoutent des détails intéressants: par exemple, que la salive produite au cours d'une vie moyenne peut remplir une piscine, ou que les ongles des mains poussent plus vite que les ongles des pieds.

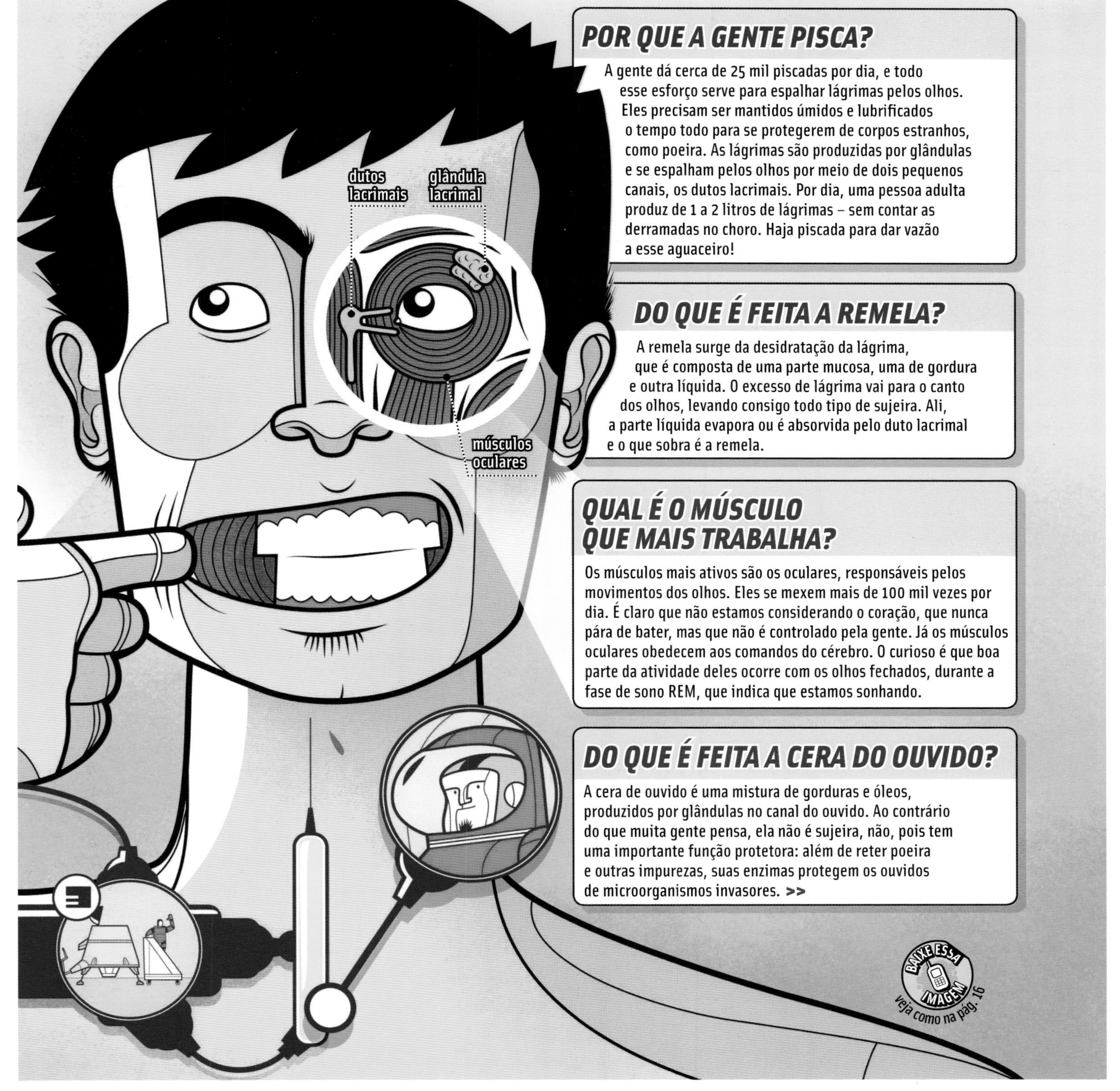

POR QUE A GENTE PISCA?
A gente dá cerca de 25 mil piscadas por dia, e todo esse esforço serve para espalhar lágrimas pelos olhos. Eles precisam ser mantidos úmidos e lubrificados o tempo todo para se protegerem de corpos estranhos, como poeira. As lágrimas são produzidas por glândulas e se espalham pelos olhos por meio de dois pequenos canais, os dutos lacrimais. Por dia, uma pessoa adulta produz de 1 a 2 litros de lágrimas – sem contar as derramadas no choro. Haja piscada para dar vazão a esse aguaceiro!
dutos lacrimais
glândula lacrimal
músculos oculares
DO QUE É FEITA A REMELA?
A remela surge da desidratação da lágrima, que é composta de uma parte mucosa, uma de gordura e outra líquida. O excesso de lágrima vai para o canto dos olhos, levando consigo todo tipo de sujeira. Ali, a parte líquida evapora ou é absorvida pelo duto lacrimal e o que sobra é a remela.
QUAL É O MÚSCULO QUE MAIS TRABALHA?
Os músculos mais ativos são os oculares, responsáveis pelos movimentos dos olhos. Eles se mexem mais de 100 mil vezes por dia. É claro que não estamos considerando o coração, que nunca pára de bater, mas que não é controlado pela gente. Já os músculos oculares obedecem aos comandos do cérebro. O curioso é que boa parte da atividade deles ocorre com os olhos fechados, durante a fase de sono REM, que indica que estamos sonhando.
DO QUE É FEITA A CERA DO OUVIDO?
A cera de ouvido é uma mistura de gorduras e óleos, produzidos por glândulas no canal do ouvido. Ao contrário do que muita gente pensa, ela não é sujeira, não, pois tem uma importante função protetora: além de reter poeira e outras impurezas, suas enzimas protegem os ouvidos de microorganismos invasores. >>
BAIXE ESSA IMAGEM
veja como na pág. 16

AS MAIORES CURIOSIDADES DO CORPO HUMANO

Você sabia que a pele é mais pesada que os ossos?
Que o sangue passa por algumas artérias a mais de 100 km/h?
Pois é, não faltam fatos intrigantes sobre nossa anatomia.
Fique por dentro deles entrando numa superconsulta médica,
capaz de curar qualquer curioso!

YURI VASCONCELOS / GABRIEL SILVEIRA / ALESSANDRA KALKO / FABIO VOLPE

QUANTA SALIVA A GENTE PRODUZ NA VIDA?

É uma quantidade de babar! Uma pessoa saudável produz entre 1 e 2 litros de saliva por dia. Fazendo as contas para alguém que viva até uns 70 anos, dá algo como 30 mil litros de pura baba, o suficiente para encher uma piscina média. A saliva tem como principal função ajudar na mastigação e na digestão da comida.

QUAL É O MENOR OSSO DO CORPO?

É o estribo, um ossinho dentro do ouvido que mede entre 2,5 e 3,4 milímetros. Ele tem esse nome por parecer um estribo usado em cavalos. Apesar de minúsculo, tem um papel essencial na audição: ele capta as vibrações do tímpano, junto com o martelo e a bigorna, amplificando a onda sonora.

O DENTE DE SISO SERVE PRA QUÊ?

Pra nada. Nos nossos antepassados das cavernas, os dentes de siso ajudavam na mastigação de raízes, carnes e outros alimentos mais duros. Com o passar do tempo, nossa dieta mudou, passamos a ingerir alimentos mais macios e os sisos perderam sua importância. Também chamados de terceiros molares, os sisos são programados para nascer entre os 17 e os 20 anos. Confira ao lado quando surgem todos os dentes da boca humana.

DENTE POR DENTE

1 ANO A boca tem, no máximo, seis dentes. Mastigar alimentos duros ainda é difícil

2 ANOS E MEIO A dentição de leite está completa, contando com 20 dentes

12 ANOS A criança não tem mais nenhum dente de leite; todos os 28 são definitivos

17 ANOS Com o nascimento dos sisos, a dentadura com 32 dentes fica completa

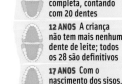

O HOMEM É O ANIMAL COM MAIS NEURÔNIOS?

Definir o número de neurônios não é tarefa fácil. Estima-se que cada ser humano tenha cerca de 100 bilhões dessas células nervosas. Perto de animais pesquisados em laboratórios, como macacos e ratos, de fato somos os campeões. Mas o problema é que não existem estudos sobre a quantidade de neurônios em animais de grande porte, como ursos, elefantes ou baleias.

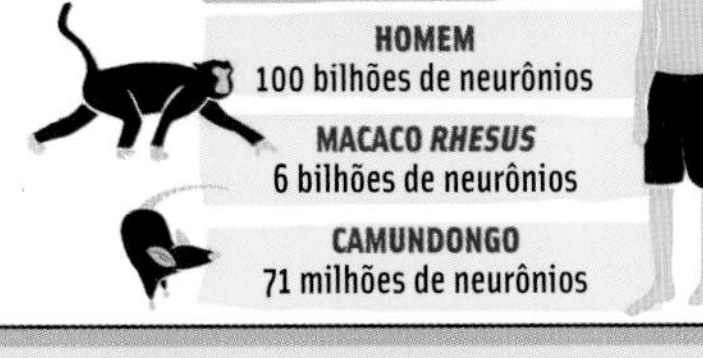

REI DOS MACACOS (E DOS RATOS)

HOMEM 100 bilhões de neurônios

MACACO *RHESUS* 6 bilhões de neurônios

CAMUNDONGO 71 milhões de neurônios

POR QUE A GENTE PISCA?

A gente dá cerca de 25 mil piscadas por dia, e todo esse esforço serve para espalhar lágrimas pelos olhos. Eles precisam ser mantidos úmidos e lubrificados o tempo todo para se protegerem de corpos estranhos, como poeira. As lágrimas são produzidas por glândulas e se espalham pelos olhos por meio de dois pequenos canais, os dutos lacrimais. Por dia, uma pessoa adulta produz de 1 a 2 litros de lágrimas – sem contar as derramadas no choro. Haja piscada para dar vazão a esse aguaceiro!

DO QUE É FEITA A REMELA?

A remela surge da desidratação da lágrima, que é composta de uma parte mucosa, uma de gordura e outra líquida. O excesso de lágrima vai para o canto dos olhos, levando consigo todo tipo de sujeira. Ali, a parte líquida evapora ou é absorvida pelo duto lacrimal e o que sobra é a remela.

QUAL É O MÚSCULO QUE MAIS TRABALHA?

Os músculos mais ativos são os oculares, responsáveis pelos movimentos dos olhos. Eles se mexem mais de 100 mil vezes por dia. É claro que não estamos considerando o coração, que nunca pára de bater, mas que não é controlado pela gente. Já os músculos oculares obedecem aos comandos do cérebro. O curioso é que boa parte da atividade deles ocorre com os olhos fechados, durante a fase de sono REM, que indica que estamos sonhando.

DO QUE É FEITA A CERA DO OUVIDO?

A cera de ouvido é uma mistura de gorduras e óleos, produzidos por glândulas no canal do ouvido. Ao contrário do que muita gente pensa, ela não é sujeira, não, pois tem uma importante função protetora: além de reter poeira e outras impurezas, suas enzimas protegem os ouvidos de microorganismos invasores. >>

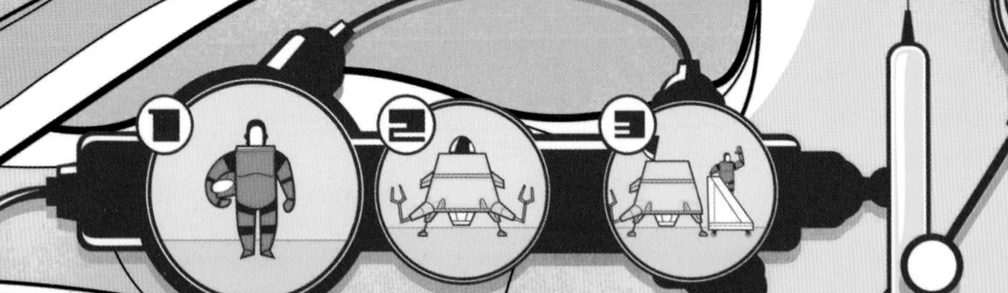

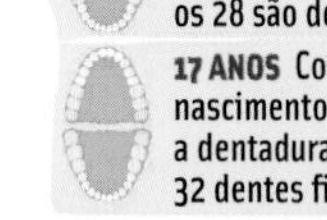

BAIXE ESSA IMAGEM veja como na pág. 16

Project Info: *Mundo Estranho*, magazine article, 2008, Brazil
Research: Fabio Volpe, Yuri Vasconscelos
Design: Alessandra Kalko
Illustration: Gabriel Silveira

Project Info: Screen print, 2006, USA
Data Source: Captain John Phillips: "Pirate Code of Conduct", 1724
Design: Michael Spitz

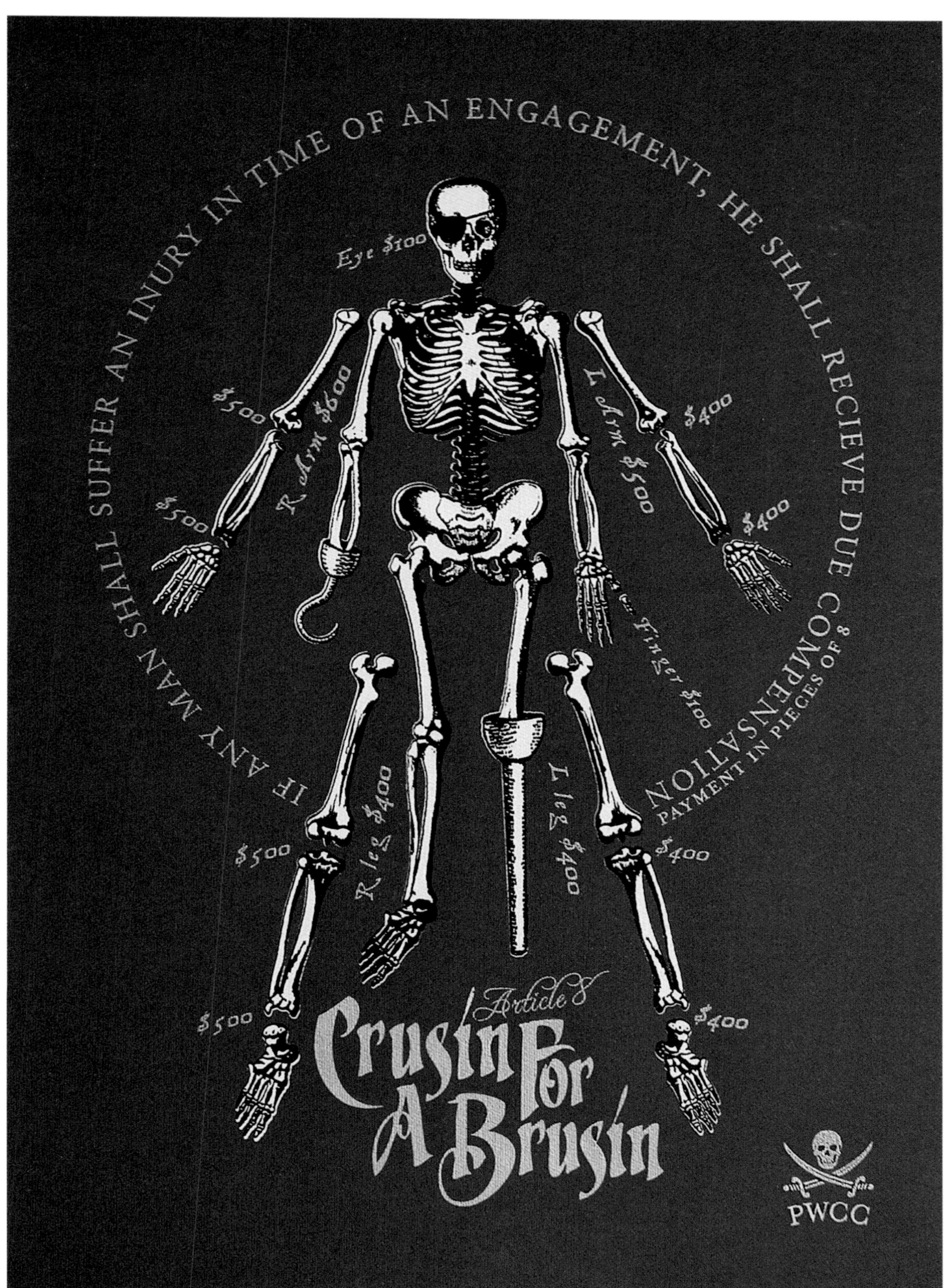

Crusin for a Brusin

With piracy having become a modern phenomenon around Somalia, this piece gains a slightly ghoulish relevance. It refers to the pirate codes that captains set for their crew members in earlier times. Besides setting up rules of conduct, these codes governed the distribution of stolen goods and the compensation a pirate would receive in the event of injury.

In this graphic, Michael Spitz quotes Article 8 of Captain John Phillips' code from 1724. Around the skeleton, price tags show how much compensation was due to a pirate should he lose a body part in the course of battle. Prices are given in Spanish dollars, a historical currency widely used in the 18th century.

Die Tatsache, dass die Piraterie vor der Küste von Somalia auch für die moderne Welt zum Problem geworden ist, verleiht dieser Grafik eine durchaus makabere Bedeutung. Sie bezieht sich auf den Piratenkodex, den die Kapitäne ihrer Besatzung in früheren Zeiten vorschrieben. Neben dem sozialen Umgang miteinander wurde darin die Verteilung gekaperter Güter ebenso geregelt wie die Kompensation, die ein Pirat im Fall einer Verletzung erhielt.

In dieser Grafik zitiert Michael Spitz den Artikel 8 aus dem Kodex von Captain John Phillips aus dem Jahr 1724. „Preisschilder" entlang des Skeletts zeigen die Höhe der Entschädigung, die einem Piraten bei Verlust des betreffenden Körperteils im Kampf zustand. Die Summen sind in spanischen Real angegeben, einer im 18. Jahrhundert weithin gebräuchlichen Währung.

La piraterie étant devenue un phénomène moderne dans la région de la Somalie, cette illustration acquiert une signification quelque peu morbide. Elle fait référence aux codes que les capitaines de pirates établissaient autrefois pour leurs équipes. Ces codes définissaient des normes de conduite, mais gouvernaient également la répartition des marchandises volées et la compensation que les pirates recevaient en cas de blessure.

Dans cette illustration, Michael Spitz cite l'article 8 du code du capitaine John Phillips, qui date de 1724. Autour du squelette, des étiquettes de prix indiquent la compensation qui était due à un pirate s'il perdait un membre au cours de la bataille. Les prix sont donnés en réaux espagnols, une monnaie dont l'utilisation était très répandue au XVIIIe siècle.

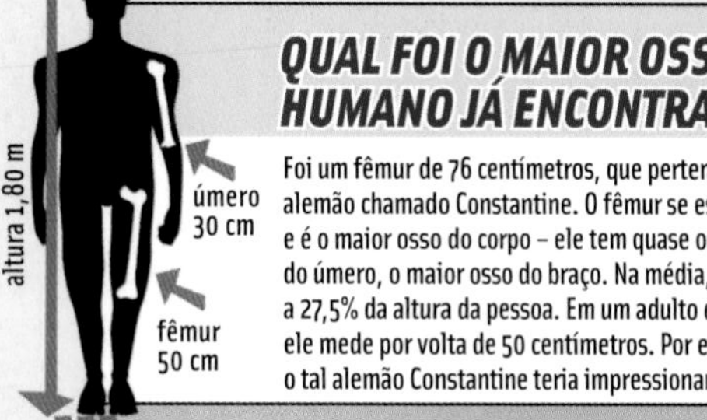

QUAL FOI O MAIOR OSSO HUMANO JÁ ENCONTRADO?

Foi um fêmur de 76 centímetros, que pertenceu a um "gigante" alemão chamado Constantine. O fêmur se estende da bacia ao joelho e é o maior osso do corpo – ele tem quase o dobro do tamanho do úmero, o maior osso do braço. Na média, o fêmur corresponde a 27,5% da altura da pessoa. Em um adulto de 1,80 m, portanto, ele mede por volta de 50 centímetros. Por essa proporção, o tal alemão Constantine teria impressionantes 2,76 metros de altura!

É VERDADE QUE O NÚMERO DE OSSOS DIMINUI AO LONGO DA VIDA?

É verdade, sim! Quando nascemos, nosso esqueleto tem cerca de 300 ossos, mas, na idade adulta, são apenas 206. Mas pode ficar tranqüilo, você não vai perder nenhum osso... O que acontece é que alguns deles se fundem à medida que crescemos. O melhor exemplo é na bacia. Em bebês, cada lado dela é formado por três ossos: ísquio, ílio e púbis. Com o passar do tempo, eles se juntam, dando origem a um só grande osso, chamado ilíaco.

BEBÊ — ílio, púbis, ísquio
ADULTO — ilíaco

AS UNHAS DOS PÉS CRESCEM NA MESMA VELOCIDADE QUE AS UNHAS DAS MÃOS?

Não, as unhas das mãos crescem quatro vezes mais rápido do que as dos pés. No dia-a-dia, nem dá para perceber tanto, mas, se você desencanasse de cortá-las durante um ano, ia ver uma diferença e tanto! O curioso é que as unhas da mão dominante – a direita dos destros e a esquerda dos canhotos – também crescem mais rapidamente do que as da outra mão.

QUANTOS QUILÔMETROS DE "VEIAS" HÁ NO CORPO?

Se a gente pudesse uni-los em linha reta, conseguiríamos algo como 100 mil quilômetros de vasos sangüíneos! Isso é o suficiente para dar mais de duas voltas e meia em torno da Terra. Existem cinco tipos de vasos sangüíneos, como mostra o infográfico abaixo:

ARTÉRIAS Levam o sangue rico em oxigênio do coração para o resto do corpo

ARTERÍOLAS Artérias pequenas, que cumprem a mesma função que suas "irmãs" maiores

VEIAS Carregam o sangue até o coração e os pulmões, onde ele recebe oxigênio

VÊNULAS São veias pequenas, que cumprem a mesma função que suas "irmãs" maiores

CAPILARES Unem vênulas e arteríolas; neles ocorrem as trocas gasosas com as células

POR QUE TEMOS REFLEXO NO JOELHO?

Quando o médico dá uma "martelada" no nosso joelho, ele aciona um intricado mecanismo que faz com que a perna se mova para a frente. Esse movimento, conhecido como reflexo patelar – de patela, o osso do joelho –, é uma resposta involuntária a um estímulo sensorial. Veja como ele ocorre:

medula espinhal
nervo motor
nervo sensorial
musculatura da coxa

1. A "martelada" no joelho estimula receptores sensitivos, gerando um sinal nervoso. Esse sinal não chega até o cérebro. Por isso a reação é automática, não depende da nossa vontade
2. O sinal segue por um nervo sensorial – que transmite sensações captadas pelo corpo – até chegar à medula espinhal
3. Na medula, o sinal passa do nervo sensorial para um nervo motor – que transmite estímulos de movimento
4. O nervo motor leva o sinal de movimento até a musculatura da coxa. O sinal manda os músculos contrair, o que faz a perna se deslocar para a frente

COMO O SANGUE QUE CHEGA AOS PÉS SOBE DE VOLTA AO CORAÇÃO?

válvulas
sangue subindo
sangue bloqueado

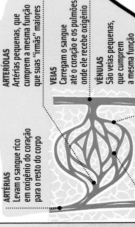

1. A grande velocidade com que o sangue desce até os pés já dá o primeiro embalo para a subida. Além disso, cada pisada no chão bombeia um pouco o sangue pra cima
2. Os músculos da panturrilha também ajudam a bombear o sangue. Suas contrações comprimem as veias e empurram a circulação
3. Mas o grande segredo da subida é o sistema de válvulas dentro das veias. Elas abrem quando o sangue bombeado passa e fecham em seguida, impedindo que ele volte pra baixo

POR QUE O PÊLO DA PERNA CRESCE MENOS QUE O FIO DE CABELO?

A única explicação que os especialistas têm é evolutiva. Os pêlos que cobriam nossos antepassados primatas tinham várias funções, entre elas a proteção tanto contra o frio como contra os raios solares. Quando os primeiros hominídeos passaram a caminhar sob duas pernas, o sol passou a incidir mais fortemente sobre a cabeça e menos sobre o resto do corpo. Assim, o pêlo do corpo perdeu sua função e rareou. Já os pêlos da cabeça passaram a ser mais necessários para a proteção e cresceram com mais vigor, dando origem ao cabelo. :-P

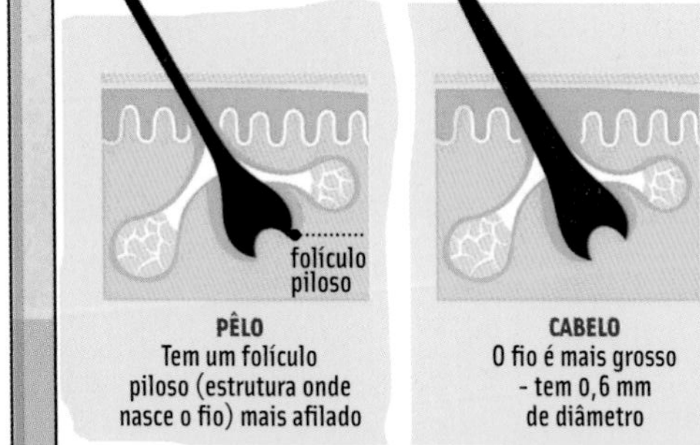

PÊLO Tem um folículo piloso (estrutura onde nasce o fio) mais afilado

CABELO O fio é mais grosso - tem 0,6 mm de diâmetro

CONSULTORIA: ANDRÉ NERSISSIAN, PROFESSOR DE EDUCAÇÃO FÍSICA; DANIEL BALBACHEVSKY, ORTOPEDISTA; FERNANDO SPAGNUOLO, ENDOCRINOLOGISTA; FLÁVIO DANTAS, CLÍNICO GERAL; LUCIANO BARSANTI, MÉDICO TRICOLOGISTA – ESPECIALISTA EM CABELO; MARCELO MACHADO, ODONTOLOGISTA; MÁRCIA MAHANA, ODONTOLOGISTA; MARCOS MAIA, DERMATOLOGISTA; NADIM ZIHRAN HONAIN, GASTROENTEROLOGISTA; NEWTON DE BARROS JÚNIOR, CIRURGIÃO VASCULAR; RENATO NEVES, OFTALMOLOGISTA; ROBERTO ONISHI, PNEUMOLOGISTA; SÉRGIO FORTIER, HEMATOLOGISTA; SUZANA HERCULANO-HOUZEL, NEUROCIENTISTA; VANDERLI MARCHIORI, NUTRICIONISTA

Body Parts

With the option of replacing dysfunctional body-parts through surgery, replacement human organs have become a somewhat creepy commodity. This piece does the maths and shows the market value of all body parts and organs.

As this is more of a financial issue, designer Peter Grundy didn't opt for a medical type of illustration, but located each organ on an abstract body map and tagged it with its open-market price. The funny graphical body conception serves as an effective antidote to the uncomfortable idea of us being worth roundabout as much as a small car.

Seitdem es möglich ist, Körperteile, die nicht mehr funktionstüchtig sind, chirurgisch zu ersetzen, sind menschliche Organe zu einer etwas unheimlichen Ware geworden. Diese Grafik zeigt den Marktwert sämtlicher Körperteile und Organe und rechnet alles zusammen.

Da es hier um finanzielle Aspekte geht, entschied sich der Grafiker Peter Grundy gegen eine medizinische Illustration und positionierte jedes Organ stattdessen auf einer abstrakten Karte des Körpers; auf dem Etikett steht jeweils der Preis, der auf dem offenen Markt dafür bezahlt wird. Die ironische grafische Darstellung des Körpers lenkt von der unbehaglichen Vorstellung ab, dass unser materieller Wert in etwa dem eines Kleinwagens entspricht.

Avec la possibilité de remplacer les parties du corps humain qui ne fonctionnent plus, les organes de rechange sont devenus une marchandise quelque peu sinistre. Cette illustration fait les calculs et montre la valeur marchande de toutes les parties du corps.

Comme il s'agit plutôt d'une question financière, le graphiste Peter Grundy s'est éloigné de l'illustration médicale, et a décidé de situer chaque organe sur une carte abstraite du corps humain, étiqueté de son prix sur le marché libre. Le style graphique ludique est un antidote efficace contre l'idée assez désagréable qui se dégage de l'ensemble : nous valons à peu près autant qu'une petite voiture.

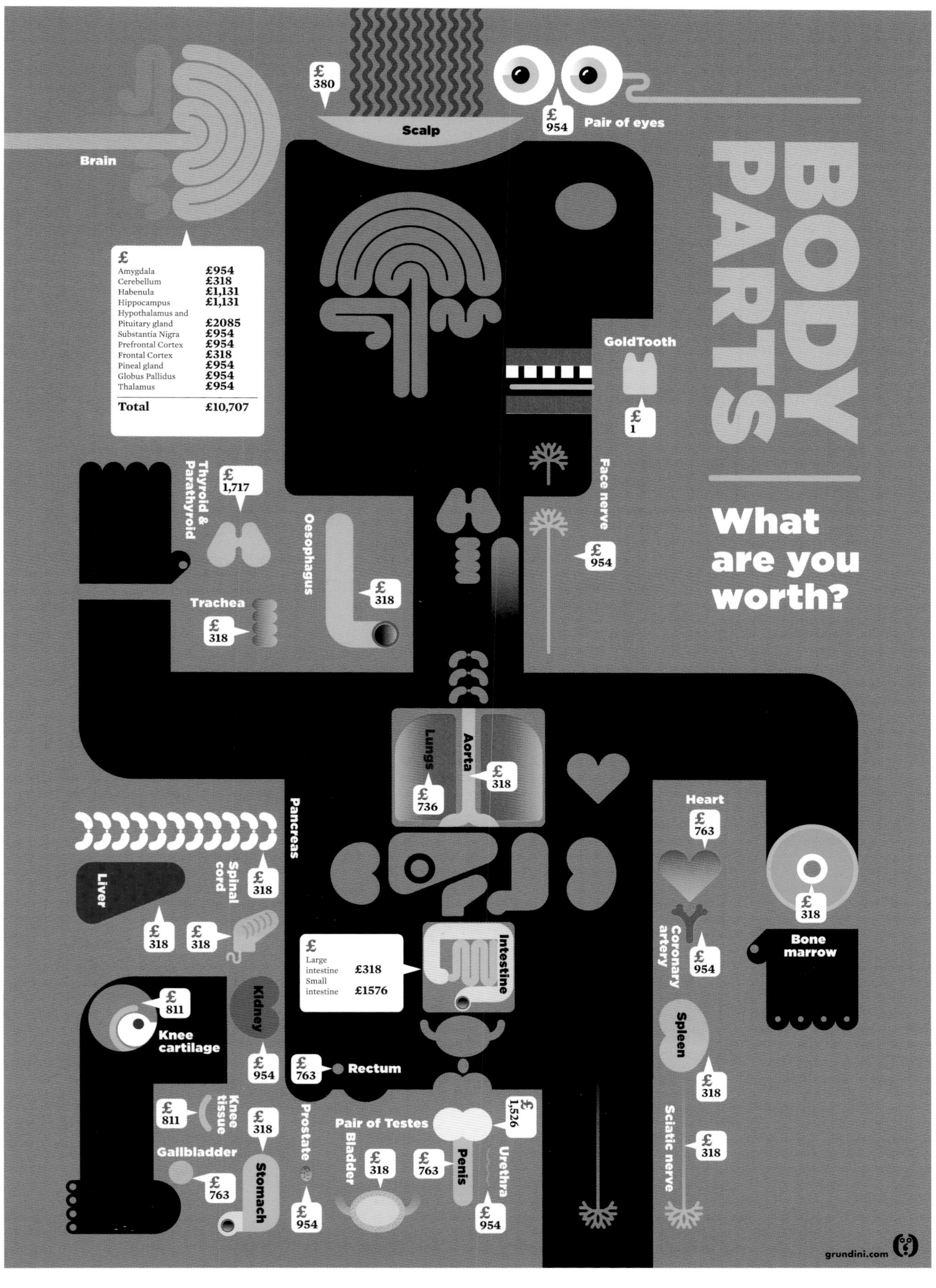

Project Info: *Esquire*, magazine article, 2006, UK
Design: Peter Grundy (Grundini)
Art Direction: Alex Breuer
Awards: AOI Images 2007

QUAL É O MÁXIMO DE COMIDA QUE CABE NO ESTÔMAGO?

Com um formato parecido ao da letra J, o estômago é um órgão elástico. Quando vazio, tem um volume de apenas 50 mililitros. Mas, se você comer sem parar, ele pode aumentar em 80 vezes sua capacidade, o equivalente a entuchar 3 ou 4 litros de comida.
Se a pessoa insistir em continuar ingerindo rango além desse volume, pode acabar vomitando. Ao lado você confere a "tradução" dessa capacidade em lanches do tipo fast food:

2 Big Mac

2 refrigerantes de 500 ml

2 porções grandes de batata frita

2 milk shakes de 500 ml

= 4 litros

QUAIS SÃO OS MAIORES ÓRGÃOS INTERNOS?

Nas páginas anteriores você já viu que a pele é o maior e o mais pesado órgão do corpo. Mas, se a gente for considerar apenas os órgãos internos, temos outros dois campeões. Em peso, ninguém bate o fígado, que tem entre 1,3 e 1,5 quilo. Agora, se o critério for comprimento, o título fica com o intestino, que, somando o grosso e o delgado, tem uns 7,5 metros de extensão. O delgado, que começa no estômago, mede cerca de 6 metros e tem 2 ou 3 centímetros de diâmetro. O grosso tem 1,5 metro e diâmetro de até 8 centímetros. Enquanto o intestino delgado continua a digestão iniciada no estômago, o grosso é responsável pela produção do cocô.

PRA QUE SERVE O CÓCCIX?

Esse ossinho, que fica na base da nossa coluna, parece não ter nenhuma utilidade hoje em dia. Mas, num passado remoto, ele devia fazer parte da cauda de nossos ancestrais, que sumiu com a evolução. Basta ver ao lado, no esqueleto de um babuíno, como a cauda é uma simples continuação da coluna dos macacos.

O cóccix humano é na verdade uma fusão de quatro pequenas vértebras. Veja como se dividem os ossos da nossa coluna vertebral:

COLUNA HUMANA
7 vértebras cervicais (região do pescoço)
12 vértebras torácicas (na altura do tórax)
5 vértebras lombares (na área da cintura)
osso sacro
cóccix

BABUÍNO
coluna
cauda

QUEM É MAIS RÁPIDO: OS ESPERMATOZÓIDES OU O SANGUE?

Movendo-se a cerca de 45 km/h, um espermatozóide deixaria pra trás os melhores atletas do mundo nos 100 metros rasos – que atingem no máximo 37 km/h. Mas numa "corrida orgânica" ele perderia feio para a circulação sanguínea e outros velocistas do corpo. Confira como seria esse racha:

CORRIDA MALUCA
IMPULSO NERVOSO 360 km/h
ESPIRRO 150 km/h
SANGUE 108 km/h*
ESPERMATOZÓIDE 45 km/h*

*NA AORTA, AO SAIR DO CORAÇÃO

fígado
estômago
baço
intestino grosso
intestino delgado
cocô
reto
esfíncter

QUANTO COCÔ UMA PESSOA PRODUZ POR DIA?

São 150 gramas, em média. As fezes produzidas se acumulam na porção final do intestino grosso, onde fica o reto. Quando o "estoque" atinge uns 30 gramas, automaticamente se abre o esfíncter interno, uma musculatura que libera o cocô para sair. Ao mesmo tempo, o cérebro manda um sinal dizendo que é hora de sentar no trono. Ainda bem que uma outra parte da musculatura do reto, o esfíncter externo, é controlada pela gente. É ele que nos dá tempo suficiente para ir até uma privada antes de soltar a porqueira toda.

QUAL É A PRODUÇÃO DIÁRIA DE PUM?

Entre 1 litro e 1,5 litro! A maior parte da matéria-prima para os puns são gases que engolimos enquanto falamos ou comemos. O ar ingerido vai até o estômago. Parte dele pode voltar pela boca, na forma de arroto. O resto ou é absorvido pelo organismo ou segue para o intestino, onde se junta com gases malcheirosos produzidos pela ação das bactérias sobre a comida. O pum produzido se acumula no reto até ser liberado. Quando prendemos um "rojão", o gás fedorento volta para o intestino até ter uma oportunidade mais discreta para escapar...

QUAL É O ÓRGÃO MAIS DISPENSÁVEL DO CORPO?

Se você der o azar de lesionar um órgão, torça para ser o baço. Ele tem lá suas funções, como remover os glóbulos vermelhos velhos demais e produzir parte dos anticorpos que nos protegem de vírus e bactérias. Mas dá para viver sem ele, o que não rola sem coração, pulmões, fígado, estômago, pâncreas ou intestino – sem os dois rins também não dá.

Quando alguém sofre uma pancada forte na barriga e danifica o baço, a ponto de ele precisar ser removido, o fígado se encarrega da "limpeza" dos glóbulos vermelhos. Já a imunidade da pessoa fica debilitada com a menor produção de anticorpos. >>

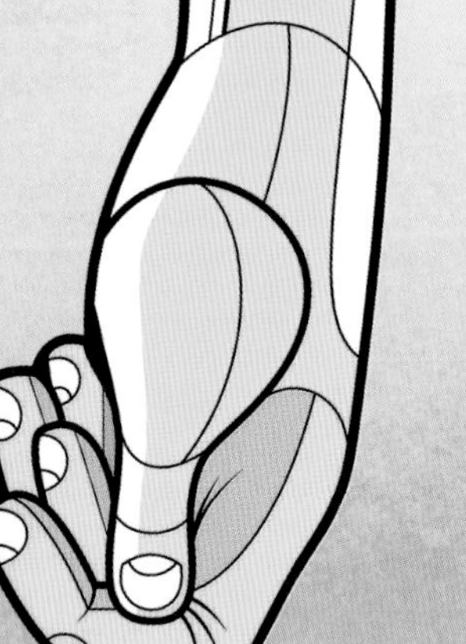

Circos

The sequencing of the dog genome, completed in 2005, revealed large overlaps between the dog and human genomes – a similarity arising from shared ancestry. This diagram charts some of these similarities in genes by arranging chromosomes – organised structures of DNA containing many genes – around a circle.

Selected human chromosomes are shown – each marked by its own colour – along the top (blue outer band), dog chromosomes are shown along the bottom (orange outer band). Where DNA in a dog chromosome matches human DNA, colour-coded stripes on the inner ring indicate the corresponding human chromosomes. Some of the patterns in dog-human homology are indicated by bands connecting similar regions. This visualisation was created using Circos, software which allows the showing of multidimensional relations between objects in a circular layout.

Die Entzifferung des Erbguts von Hunden wurde 2005 abgeschlossen. Sie offenbarte überraschende genetische Ähnlichkeiten zwischen Hunden und Menschen, die auf unsere gemeinsame Abstammung zurückzuführen sind. Anhand dieses Diagramms, in dem die Chromosomen kreisförmig angeordnet sind, lassen sich einige solcher genetischen Überlappungen nachvollziehen.

Innerhalb des blauen äußeren Halbkreises oben sind ausgewählte menschliche Chromosomen dargestellt, innerhalb des orangefarbenen Halbkreises unten ausgewählte Chromosomen eines Hundes. Die Chromosomen enthalten jeweils eine große Anzahl von Genen und sind hier als Farbfelder dargestellt. Ausgehend vom Hundechromosom Nr. 15 machen farbige Verbindungslinien sichtbar, wo es genetische Übereinstimmungen mit menschlichen Chromosomen gibt. Die Visualisierung wurde mit der Software Circos erstellt, mit der sich mehrdimensionale Beziehungen zwischen Objekten in einem Kreislayout darstellen lassen.

Le séquençage du génome du chien, achevé en 2005, a révélé que de grandes parties des génomes du chien et de l'humain coïncident – une similarité qui vient de nos ancêtres communs. Ce diagramme représente certaines de ces similarités en disposant les chromosomes – des structures d'ADN organisées qui contiennent de nombreux gènes – autour d'un cercle.

Une sélection de chromosomes humains est montrée – chacun identifié par sa propre couleur – en haut (bande extérieure bleue), et les chromosomes du chien sont montrés en bas (bande extérieure orange). Lorsque l'ADN d'un chromosome de chien correspond à l'ADN humain, les bandes de couleur à l'intérieur du cercle indiquent les chromosomes humains correspondants. Certains des schémas de l'homologie chien-humain sont indiqués par des bandes qui relient des régions similaires. Cette visualisation a été réalisée à l'aide de Circos, un logiciel qui permet de présenter des relations multidimensionnelles dans un format circulaire.

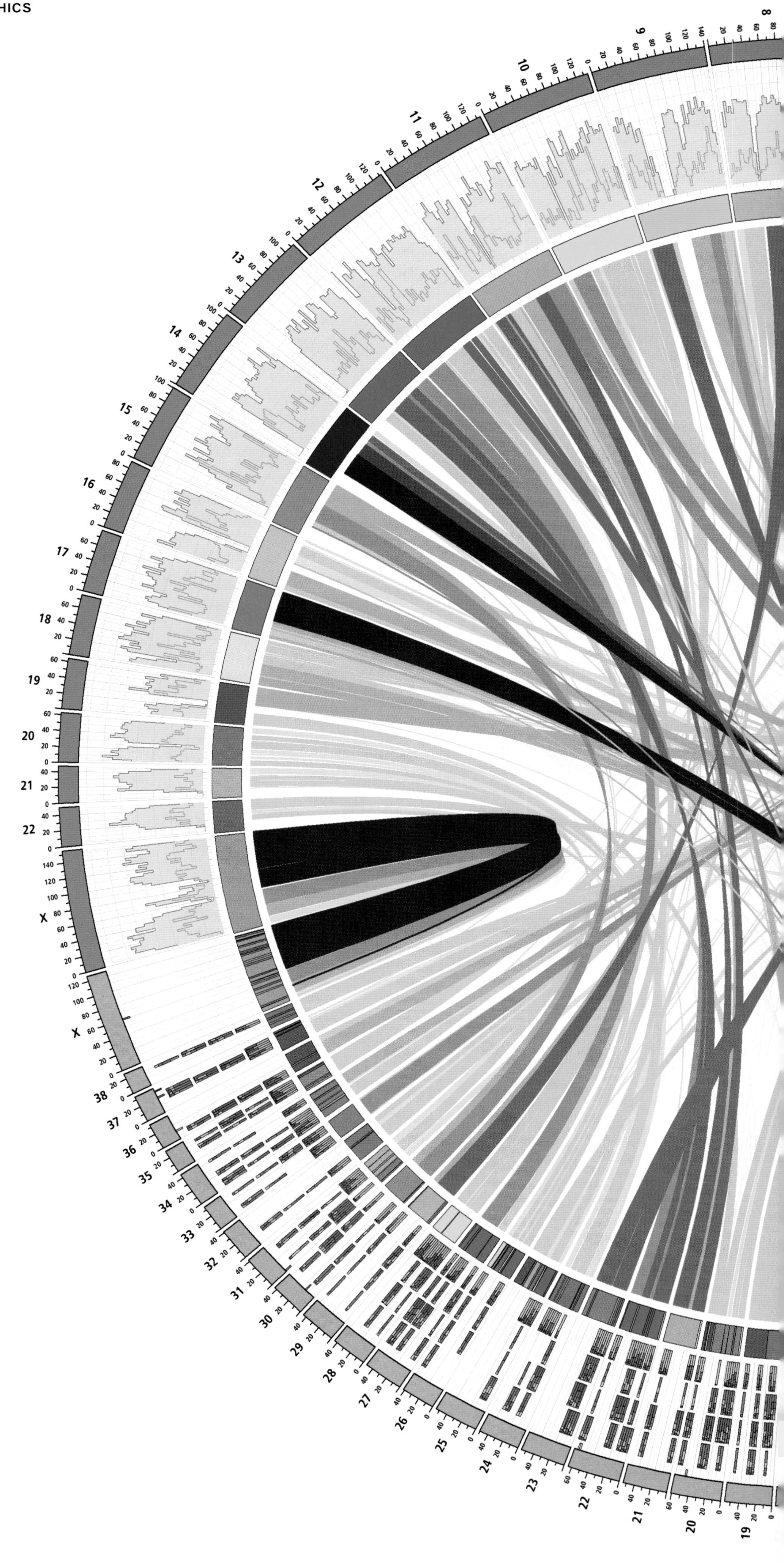
8
9
10
11
12
13
14
15
16
17
18
19
20
21
22
X
X
38
37
36
35
34
33
32
31
30
29
28
27
26
25
24
23
22
21
20
19

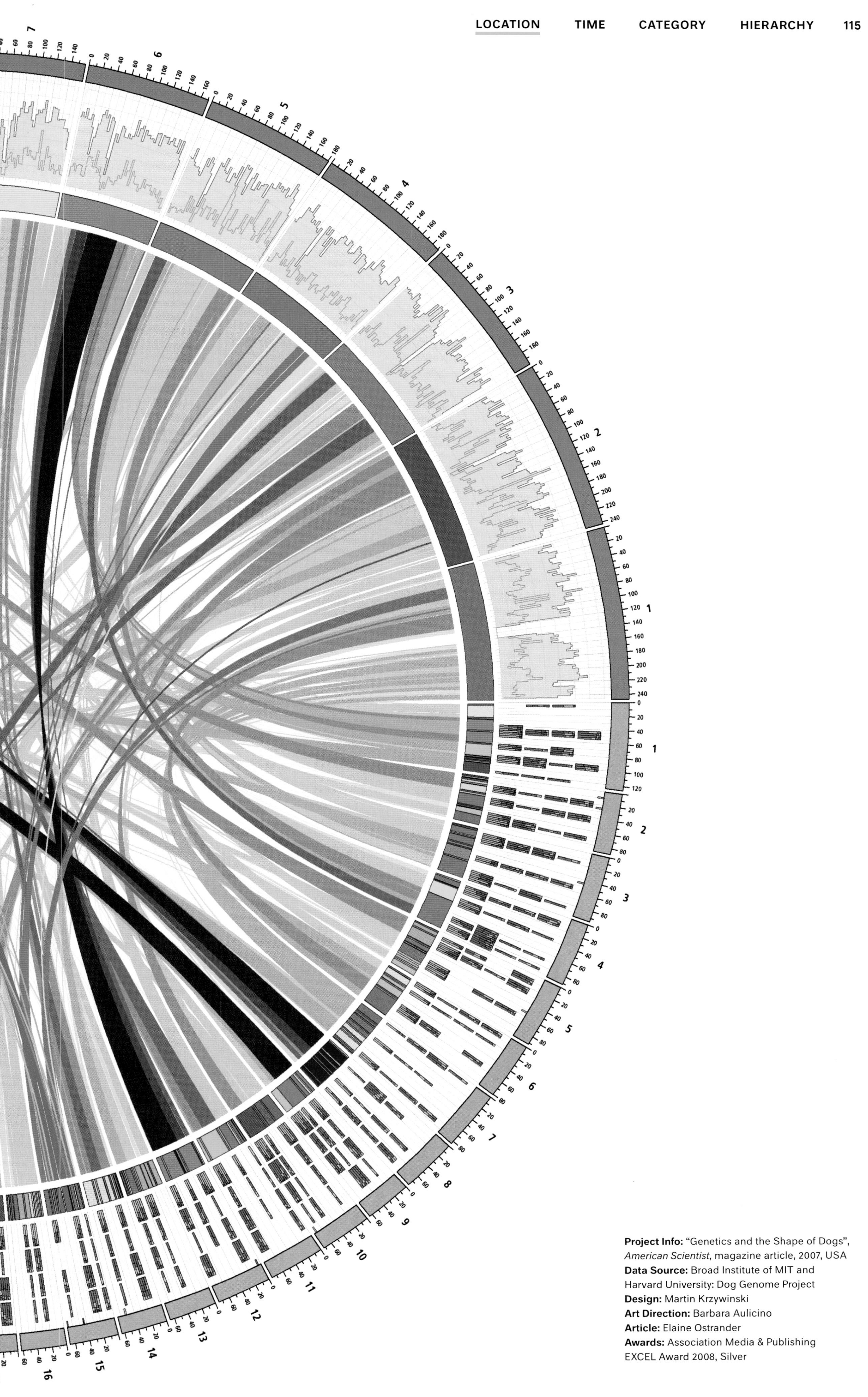

Project Info: "Genetics and the Shape of Dogs", *American Scientist*, magazine article, 2007, USA
Data Source: Broad Institute of MIT and Harvard University: Dog Genome Project
Design: Martin Krzywinski
Art Direction: Barbara Aulicino
Article: Elaine Ostrander
Awards: Association Media & Publishing EXCEL Award 2008, Silver

City Railway System

Subway maps are not intended to express correct geographical relations. In their abstract language they also do not reveal any cultural features concerning the city they correspond to. Seoul-based design studio Zero Per Zero developed a series of subway maps using cultural symbols in order to reveal cultural identity even in diagrammatic maps.

The London map is a combination of the British flag and the six London Underground zones, shown in rectangular shape. The Union Jack is continued in pale patterns throughout the map. In the Seoul map the centre is occupied by the Han River whose meandering course has been shaped to mimic the curve of the Tae Guk mark which forms the centre of the South Korean flag.

U-Bahn-Pläne dienen nicht dazu, geografische Gegebenheiten korrekt wiederzugeben. Ihre abstrakte Gestaltung verweist auch nicht auf die kulturellen Besonderheiten der betreffenden Stadt. Das in Seoul ansässige Designstudio Zero Per Zero entwarf eine Reihe von U-Bahn-Plänen mit kulturellen Symbolen, um die Identität einer Stadt auch im abstrakten U-Bahn-Plan zu vermitteln.

Der Plan von London unterlegt die sechs rechteckigen Zonen der Londoner U-Bahn mit der britischen Fahne. Der Union Jack setzt sich in blassen Mustern über den ganzen Plan fort. Der U-Bahn-Plan von Seoul wird in seiner Mitte vom Han-Fluss durchzogen. Sein schlängelnder Verlauf wurde so gestaltet, dass er die Linie nachahmt, die das Taeguk-Zeichen auf der südkoreanischen Flagge durchzieht.

Les plans du métro ne sont pas censés exprimer des relations géographiques exactes. Leur langage abstrait ne dit rien non plus des éléments culturels de la ville qu'ils décrivent. Le studio de design séoulien Zero Per Zero a conçu une série de plans du métro qui exploite des symboles culturels pour faire transparaître l'identité culturelle même dans des plans schématiques.

Le plan du métro de Londres est une combinaison du drapeau britannique et des six zones du métro londonien représentées par des formes rectangulaires. Le motif du drapeau se poursuit dans toute la carte en couleurs claires. Sur la carte du métro de Séoul, le centre est occupé par le fleuve Han dont les méandres imitent la forme du Tae Guk, le motif central du drapeau sud-coréen.

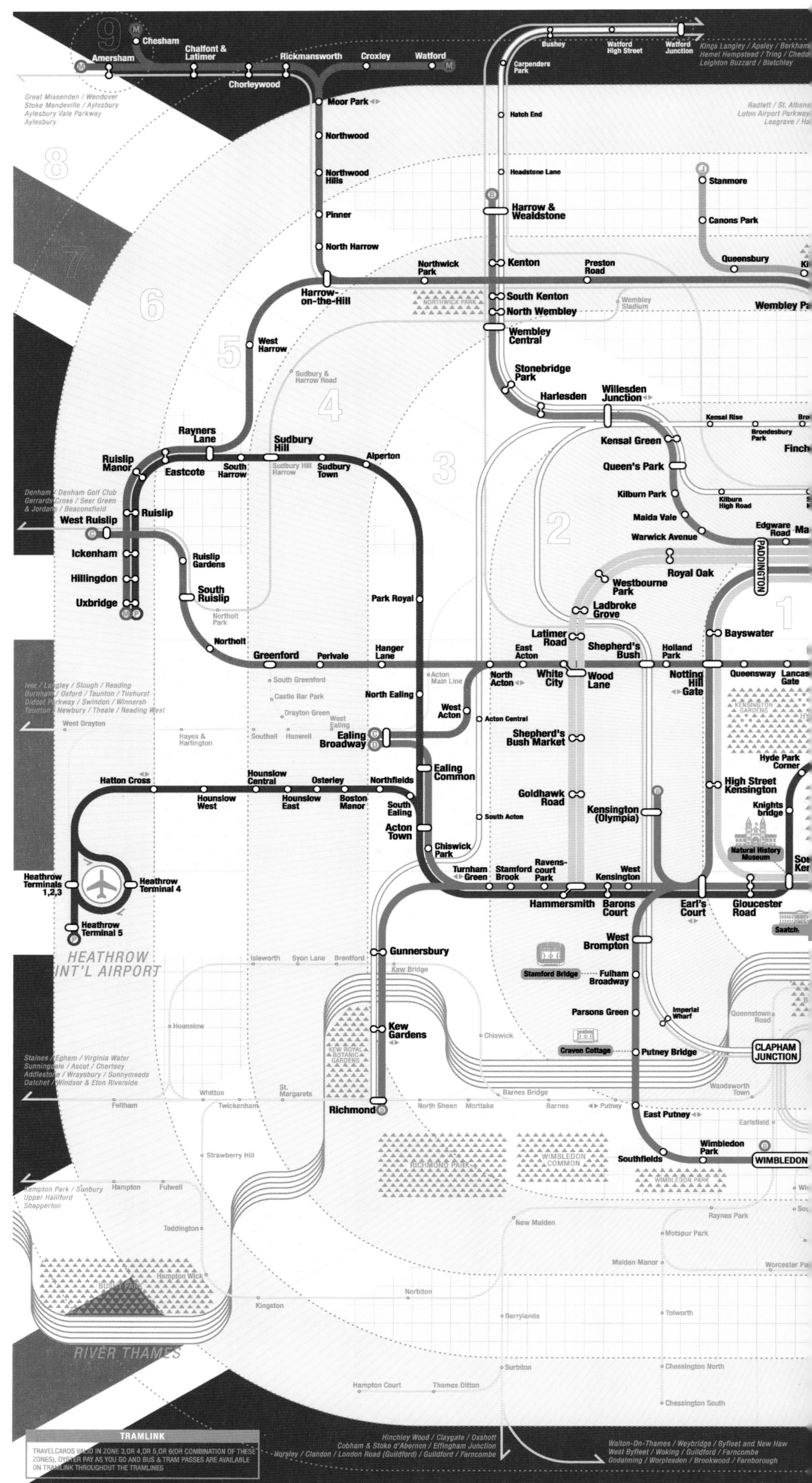

Project Info: Series of folded maps, 2010, South Korea
Design: Sol Jin, Ji-hwan Kim (Zero Per Zero)

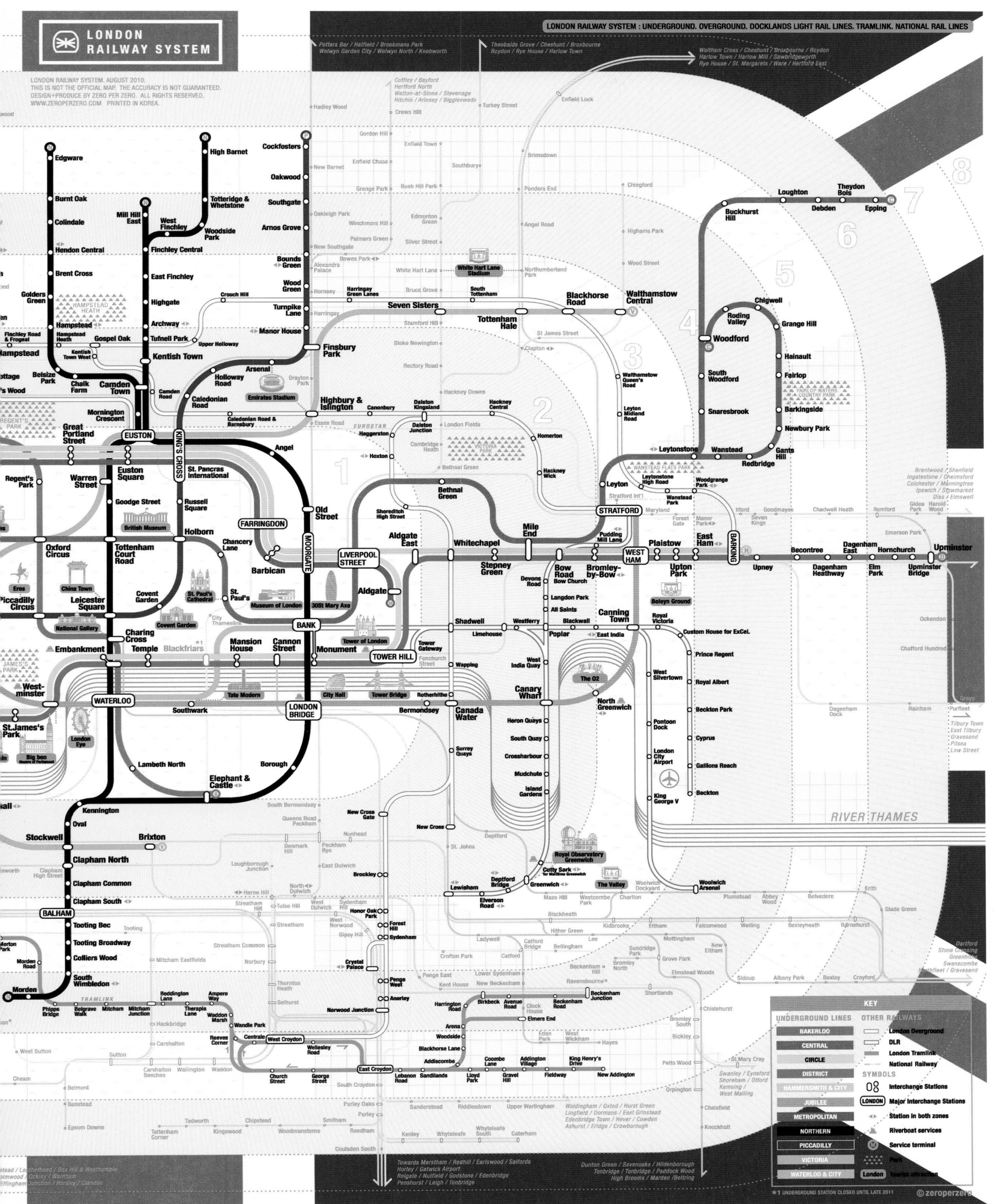
LONDON
RAILWAY SYSTEM
LONDON RAILWAY SYSTEM. AUGUST 2010.
THIS IS NOT THE OFFICIAL MAP. THE ACCURACY IS NOT GUARANTEED.
DESIGN+PRODUCE BY ZERO PER ZERO. ALL RIGHTS RESERVED.
WWW.ZEROPERZERO.COM PRINTED IN KOREA.
LONDON RAILWAY SYSTEM : UNDERGROUND. OVERGROUND. DOCKLANDS LIGHT RAIL LINES. TRAMLINK. NATIONAL RAIL LINES
Edgware
Burnt Oak
Colindale
Hendon Central
Brent Cross
Golders Green
Hampstead
High Barnet
Totteridge & Whetstone
Woodside Park
West Finchley
Mill Hill East
Finchley Central
East Finchley
Highgate
Archway
Tufnell Park
Kentish Town
Camden Town
Chalk Farm
Belsize Park
Cockfosters
Oakwood
Southgate
Arnos Grove
Bounds Green
Wood Green
Turnpike Lane
Manor House
Finsbury Park
Arsenal
Holloway Road
Caledonian Road
Emirates Stadium
Highbury & Islington
Seven Sisters
Tottenham Hale
Blackhorse Road
Walthamstow Central
White Hart Lane Stadium
Mornington Crescent
Great Portland Street
EUSTON
KING'S CROSS
St. Pancras International
Angel
Euston Square
Warren Street
Regent's Park
Goodge Street
Russell Square
British Museum
FARRINGDON
Old Street
Holborn
Chancery Lane
Barbican
MOORGATE
LIVERPOOL STREET
Oxford Circus
Tottenham Court Road
Piccadilly Circus
Leicester Square
Covent Garden
St. Paul's
Museum of London
30St Mary Axe
Aldgate
Aldgate East
BANK
National Gallery
Charing Cross
Embankment
Temple
Blackfriars
Mansion House
Cannon Street
Monument
TOWER HILL
Tower of London
Tower Gateway
Fenchurch Street
Westminster
St.James's Park
WATERLOO
Southwark
Tate Modern
City Hall
Tower Bridge
LONDON BRIDGE
London Eye
Big ben
Lambeth North
Borough
Elephant & Castle
Kennington
Oval
Stockwell
Brixton
Clapham North
Clapham Common
Clapham South
BALHAM
Tooting Bec
Tooting Broadway
Colliers Wood
South Wimbledon
Morden
Whitechapel
Bethnal Green
Mile End
Stepney Green
Bow Road
Bromley-by-Bow
WEST HAM
Plaistow
Upton Park
Boleyn Ground
East Ham
BARKING
Upney
Becontree
Dagenham Heathway
Dagenham East
Elm Park
Hornchurch
Upminster Bridge
Upminster
STRATFORD
Leyton
Leytonstone
Wanstead
Redbridge
Gants Hill
Newbury Park
Barkingside
Fairlop
Hainault
Grange Hill
Chigwell
Roding Valley
Woodford
South Woodford
Snaresbrook
Buckhurst Hill
Loughton
Debden
Theydon Bois
Epping
Shadwell
Limehouse
Westferry
Poplar
Blackwall
East India
Canning Town
Royal Victoria
Custom House for ExCeL
Prince Regent
Royal Albert
Beckton Park
Cyprus
Gallions Reach
Beckton
West Silvertown
Pontoon Dock
London City Airport
King George V
Woolwich Arsenal
West India Quay
Canary Wharf
North Greenwich
The O2
Heron Quays
South Quay
Crossharbour
Mudchute
Island Gardens
Cutty Sark
Greenwich
Deptford Bridge
Elverson Road
Lewisham
Royal Observatory Greenwich
The Valley
Canada Water
Rotherhithe
Wapping
Bermondsey
Surrey Quays
New Cross Gate
New Cross
Brockley
Honor Oak Park
Forest Hill
Sydenham
Crystal Palace
Penge West
Anerley
Norwood Junction
West Croydon
East Croydon
Wimbledon
RIVER THAMES
KEY
UNDERGROUND LINES
BAKERLOO
CENTRAL
CIRCLE
DISTRICT
HAMMERSMITH & CITY
JUBILEE
METROPOLITAN
NORTHERN
PICCADILLY
VICTORIA
WATERLOO & CITY
OTHER RAILWAYS
London Overground
DLR
London Tramlink
National Railway
SYMBOLS
Interchange Stations
Major Interchange Stations
Station in both zones
Riverboat services
Service terminal
Park
Tourist attraction
*1 UNDERGROUND STATION CLOSED UNTIL LATE 2011
©zeroperzero

SEOUL METROPOLITAN
RAILWAY SYSTEM
SEOUL RAILWAY SYSTEM. DECEMBER 2010.
THIS IS NOT THE OFFICIAL MAP. THE ACCURACY IS NOT GUARANTEED.
DESIGN+PRODUCE BY ZERO PER ZERO. ALL RIGHTS RESERVED.
WWW.ZEROPERZERO.COM PRINTED IN KOREA.
* STATION NAMES AND OPENING DATE OF THE UNBUILT SUBWAY LINES ARE SUBJECT TO CHANGE.
Incheon Int'l Airport
인천국제공항
Incheon Int'l Airport Cargo Terminal
Unseo
Geomam
Gyeyang
AREX AIRPORT LINE
Banghwa
Gaehwasan
Gaehwa
Gimpo Int'l Airport
Airport Market
Sinbanghwa
Songjeong
Magongnaru
Magok
Balsan
Ujangsan
Hwagok
Kkachisan
Yangcheon Hyanggyo
Gayang
Jeungmi
Deungchon
Yeomchang
Sinmok-Dong
Seonyudo
HAN RIVER
World Cup Stadium
Mapo-Gu Office
Mangwon
Hapjeong
Hongik Univ.
Sangsang Madang
Sinchon
Ewha Womans Univ.
Ahyeon
Aeogae
Chungjeongno
City Hall
Seoul Station
Sookmyung Women's Univ.
Namyeong
Samgakji
Sinyongsan
Yongsan
Hyochang Park
Gongdeok
Mapo
Yeouinaru
63 City
YEOUIDO AREA
Sangsu
Gwangheungchang
Daeheung
Dangsan
Nat'l Assembly
Yeouido
Saetgang
Noryangjin
Nodeul
Fish Market
Yeongdeungpo Market
Singil
Yeongdeungpo
Yeongdeungpo-Gu Office
Mullae
Daebang
Sindaebang Samgeori
Jangseung-baegi
Sinjeong
Mok-Dong
Omokgyo
Yangpyeong
Sinjeong Negeori
Yangcheon-Gu Office
Dorimcheon
Sindorim
Sinpung
Boramae
Daerim
Guro
Guro Digital Complex
Sindaebang
Sillim
Bongcheon
Namguro
Gasan Digital Complex
Onsu
Oryu-Dong
Gaebong
Guil
Cheonwang
Gwangmyeong Sageori
Cheolsan
Doksan
Geumcheon-Gu Office
Gwangmyeong
Seoksu
Gwanak
Anyang
Myeonghak
Geumjeong
Beomgye
Pyeongchon
Gunpo
Dangjeong
Uiwang
Sungkyunkwan Univ.
Digital Media City
Gajwa
Sinchon(Gyeongui)
Seodaemun
Gwanghwamun
Gyeongbok-Gung
Gyeonghui-Gung
Jonggak
Euljiro-Ilga
Deoksu-Gung
Myeong-Dong
Hoehyeon
Jeungsan
Saejeol
Eungam
Yeokchon
Gusan
Yeonsinnae
Bulgwang
Dokbawi
Nokbeon
Hongje
Muakjae
Ilsan
Tanhyeon
Unjeong
Geumneung
Geumchon
Wollong
Paju
Pungsan
Baekma
Goksan
Jichuk
Gupabal
Samsong
Wondang
Hwajeong
Daegok
Baekseok
Madu
Neunggok
Hangsin
Jeongbalsan
Juyeop
Daehwa
Hwajeon
Susaek
Gyulhyeon
Bakchon
Imhak
Gyesan
Gyeong-in National Univ. of Education
Jakjeon
Galsan
Bupyeong-Gu Office
Bupyeong Market
Bupyeong
Baegun
Dongam
Ganseok
Juan
Dohwa
Jemulpo
Dowon
Dongincheon
Incheon
WOLMI EUNHA RAIL 2011~
Dongsu
Bupyeong Samgeori
Ganseogogeori
Incheon City Hall
Arts Center
Incheon Bus Terminal
Munhak Sports Complex
Seonhak
Sinyeonsu
Woninjae
Dongchun
Dongmak
Campus Town
Technopark
BIT Zone
Univ. of Incheon
INCHEON SUBWAY LINE 1
Bucheon
Sosa
Yeokgok
Jung-Dong
Songnae
Bugae
Oido
Jeongwang
Singil-Oncheon
Ansan
Gongdan
Gojan
Jungang
Hanyang Univ. at Ansan
Sangnoksu
Banwol
Daeyami
Surisan
Sanbon
Seoul Grand Park
Sinchang
Onyang Oncheon
Baebang
Asan
Ssangyong
Bongmyeong
Cheonan

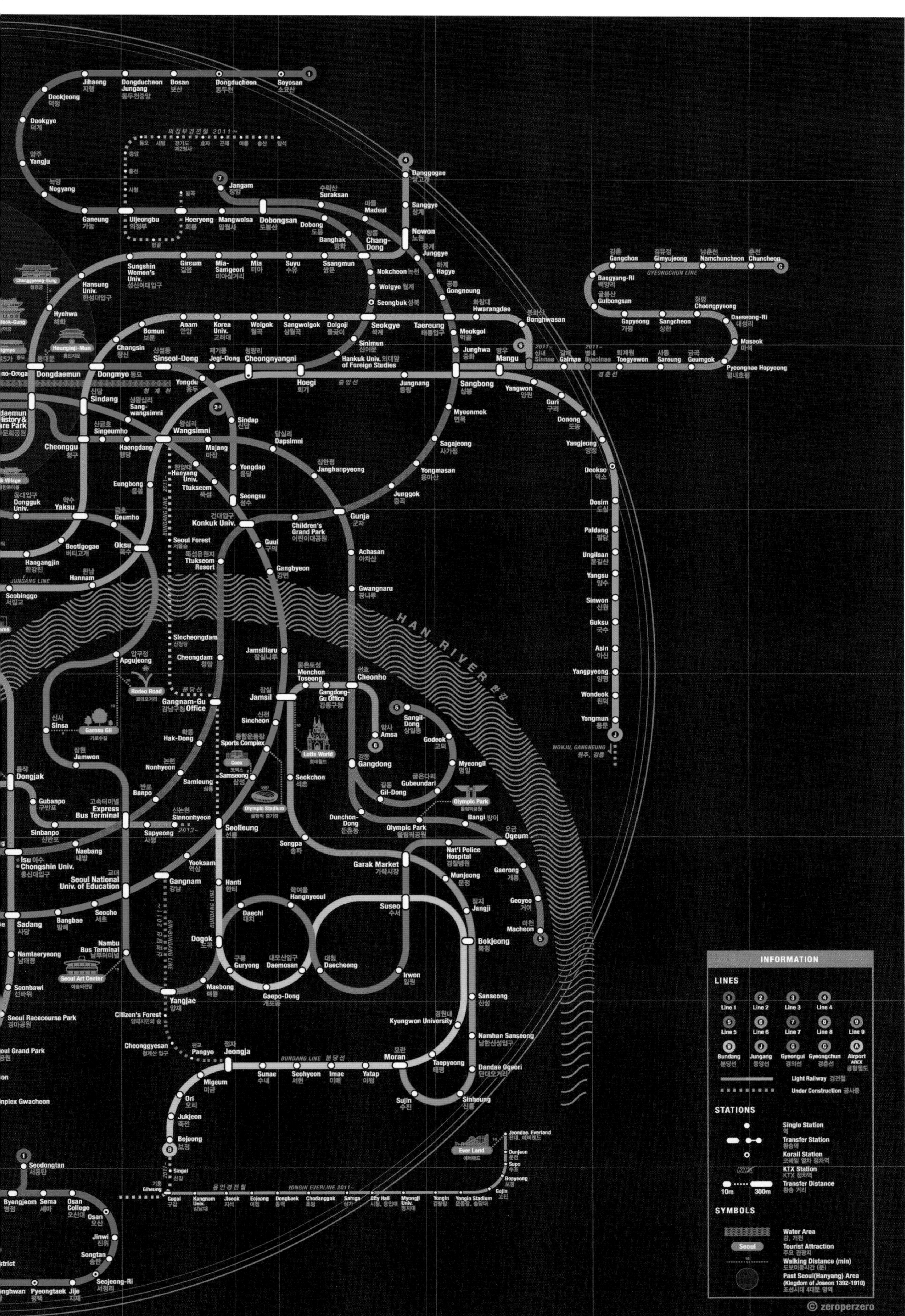
HAN RIVER 한강
INFORMATION
LINES
Line 1
Line 2
Line 3
Line 4
Line 5
Line 6
Line 7
Line 8
Line 9
Bundang 분당선
Jungang 중앙선
Gyeongui 경의선
Gyeongchun 경춘선
Airport AREX 공항철도
Light Railway 경전철
Under Construction 공사중
STATIONS
Single Station 역
Transfer Station 환승역
Korail Station 코레일 열차 정차역
KTX Station KTX 정차역
10m 300m
Transfer Distance 환승 거리
SYMBOLS
Water Area 강, 개천
Seoul
Tourist Attraction 주요 관광지
Walking Distance (min) 도보이동시간 (분)
Past Seoul(Hanyang) Area (Kingdom of Joseon 1392-1910) 조선시대 4대문 영역
© zeroperzero
Soyosan 소요산
Dongducheon 동두천
Bosan 보산
Dongducheon Jungang 동두천중앙
Jihaeng 지행
Deokjeong 덕정
Dookgye 덕계
Yangju 양주
Nogyang 녹양
Ganeung 가능
Uijeongbu 의정부
Hoeryong 회룡
Mangwolsa 망월사
Dobongsan 도봉산
Dobong 도봉
Banghak 방학
Chang-Dong 창동
Nowon 노원
Madeul 마들
Suraksan 수락산
Jangam 장암
Banggogae 당고개
Sanggye 상계
Junggye 중계
Hagye 하계
Gongneung 공릉
Hwarangdae 화랑대
Bonghwasan 봉화산
Taereung 태릉입구
Meokgol 먹골
Junghwa 중화
Mangu 망우
Sangbong 상봉
Myeonmok 면목
Sagajeong 사가정
Yongmasan 용마산
Junggok 중곡
Gunja 군자
Achasan 아차산
Gwangnaru 광나루
Cheonho 천호
Gangdong 강동
Gil-Dong 길동
Gubeundari 굽은다리
Myeongil 명일
Godeok 고덕
Sangil-Dong 상일동
Dunchon-Dong 둔촌동
Olympic Park 올림픽공원
Bangi 방이
Ogeum 오금
Gaerong 개롱
Geoyeo 거여
Macheon 마천
Hoegi 회기
Cheongnyangni 청량리
Jegi-Dong 제기동
Sinseol-Dong 신설동
Dongmyo 동묘
Dongdaemun 동대문
Sindang 신당
Wangsimni 왕십리
Haengdang 행당
Cheonggu 청구
Yaksu 약수
Geumho 금호
Oksu 옥수
Hannam 한남
Apgujeong 압구정
Sinsa 신사
Jamwon 잠원
Konkuk Univ. 건대입구
Seongsu 성수
Jamsil 잠실
Samseong 삼성
Seolleung 선릉
Gangnam 강남
Yangjae 양재
Sadang 사당
Dongjak 동작
Garak Market 가락시장
Suseo 수서
Bokjeong 복정
Moran 모란
Jeongja 정자
Pangyo 판교
Seodongtan 서동탄
Gangchon 강촌
Gimyujeong 김유정
Namchuncheon 남춘천
Chuncheon 춘천
Gapyeong 가평
Cheongpyeong 청평
Yangpyeong 양평
Yongmun 용문
Ever Land 에버랜드
Lotte World 롯데월드
Coex 코엑스
Olympic Stadium 올림픽 경기장
Rodeo Road 로데오거리
Garosu Gil 가로수길
Seoul Art Center 예술의전당
BUNDANG LINE 분당선
JUNGANG LINE
YONGIN EVERLINE 2011~

Death Row

Last week, Michael Rosales, who murdered 67-year-old Mary Felder in 1997, became the thirteenth person executed this year—in Texas. Whether or not you believe in the death penalty, it's important to know that the United States is one of 59 countries that still executes its citizens on a regular basis (we currently have more than 3,000 inmates on death row). This is a look at where, around the world, the death penalty is still used and where it has been abolished.

MAP KEY

- **DEATH PENALTY ABOLISHED** (92)
- **UNOFFICIALLY ANTI-DEATH PENALTY** (36)
  NO EXECUTIONS IN THE LAST 10 YEARS
- **DEATH PENALTY ONLY IN EXCEPTIONAL CASES** (10)
  LIKE TREASON OR WAR CRIMES
- **DEATH PENALTY STILL IN USE (59)**

✖ Albania, Andorra, Angola, Argentina, Armenia, Australia, Austria, Azerbaijan, Belgium, Bhutan, Bosnia-Herzegovina, Bulgaria, Cambodia, Canada, Cape Verde, Colombia, Co
Estonia, Finland, France, Georgia, Germany, Greece, Guinea-Bissau, Haiti, Holy See, Honduras, Hungary, Iceland, Ireland, Italy, Kiribati, Liechtenstein, Lithuania, Luxembourg
Nepal, Netherlands, New Zealand, Nicaragua, Niue, Norway, Palau, Panama, Paraguay, Philippines, Poland, Portugal, Romania, Rwanda, Samoa, San Marino, Sao Tome And P
Switzerland, Timor-Leste, Turkey, Turkmenistan, Tuvalu, Ukraine, United Kingdom, Uruguay, Uzbekistan, Vanuatu, Venezuela ✖ Algeria, Benin, Brunei, Burkina Faso, Cameroo
Malawi, Maldives, Mali, Mauritania, Morocco, Burma, Nauru, Niger, Papua New Guinea, Russia, South Korea, Sri Lanka, Suriname, Swaziland, Tajikistan, Tanzania, Togo, Tong

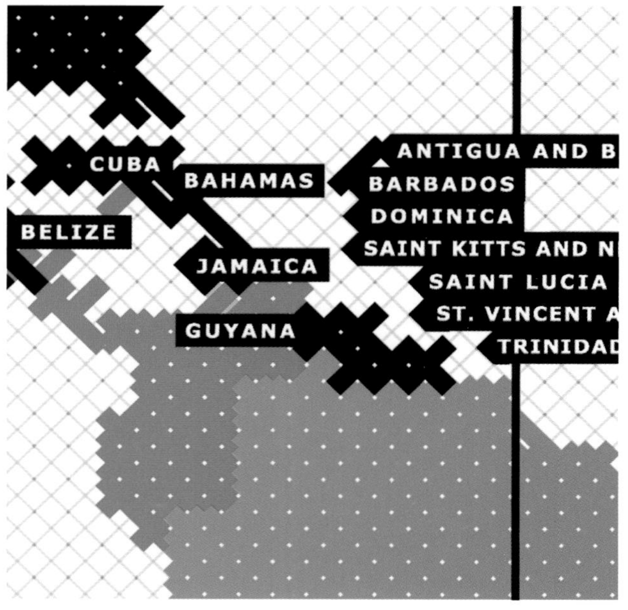

a Rica, Cote D'Ivoire, Croatia, Cyprus, Czech Republic, Denmark, Djibouti, Dominican Republic, Ecuador,
alta, Marshall Islands, Mauritius, Mexico, Micronesia, Moldova, Monaco, Montenegro, Mozambique, Namibia,
l, Serbia (including Kosovo), Seychelles, Slovakia, Slovenia, Solomon Islands, South Africa, Spain, Sweden,
an Republic, Republic of Congo, Eritrea, Gabon, Gambia, Ghana, Grenada, Kenya, Laos, Liberia, Madagascar,
oia, ✖ Bolivia, Brazil, Chile, El Salvador, Fiji, Israel, Kazakstan, Kyrgyzstan, Latvia, Peru

Death Row

In this thematic world map, countries are coloured according to whether they still use the death penalty or not. 92 countries have officially abolished it, and these are shown in blue; orange and green haven't formally abolished executions, but don't carry them out on a regular basis.

All these countries are listed below the map in their respective colours. The 59 countries which do execute citizens on a regular basis are shown in black and are named on the map. As a symbolic layer, the world map is shown behind a high fence topped with barbed wire.

Auf dieser thematischen Weltkarte sind die Länder farbig codiert, je nachdem, ob sie noch die Todesstrafe anwenden oder nicht. 92 Länder haben sie offiziell abgeschafft, diese sind blau gehalten. Orangefarbene und grüne Länder haben die Todesstrafe zwar nicht offiziell abgeschafft, vollstrecken sie aber üblicherweise nicht.

Unterhalb der Karte sind all diese Länder in ihren jeweiligen Farben aufgeführt. Die 59 Länder, in denen regelmäßig Menschen hingerichtet werden, sind schwarz gefärbt, ihr Name ist auf der Karte verzeichnet. Als symbolischer Verweis liegt die Weltkarte hinter einem hohen Maschendrahtzaun, der oben mit Stacheldraht gesichert ist.

Dans cette carte thématique du monde, les couleurs des pays indiquent s'ils utilisent encore la peine de mort. Les 92 pays qui l'ont officiellement abolie sont indiqués en bleu ; les pays en orange ou en vert ne l'ont pas officiellement abolie, mais ne l'appliquent pas systématiquement.

Tous ces pays sont énumérés sous la carte, dans leurs couleurs respectives. Les 59 pays qui exécutent leurs citoyens régulièrement sont montrés en noir et sont nommés sur la carte. La carte du monde se trouve derrière une haute clôture symbolique surmontée de barbelés.

Project Info: "The Death Penalty Around the World", *GOOD*, online article, 2009, USA
Data Source: Amnesty International
Research: Morgan Clendaniel
Design: Joshua Covarrubias (Kiss Me I'm Polish)
Art Direction: Agnieszka Gasparska (Kiss Me I'm Polish)

Dry Well-bores

Since oil was discovered in Norwegian waters in the late 1960s, the quest for gas and oil sources has driven the Norwegian economy. This series of maps reports all the futile test-drillings, showing every "dry" well-bore from the start of Norwegian oil exploitation in 1966 to 1984. By then, the exploitation of North Sea sources had peaked and a major new gas field further north was discovered.

The 150 bores are numbered and connected by lines, thus showing the chronology of testing various sites and the push to look further north. Using a number of maps, Torgeir Husevaag provides an alternative historical record. He doesn't focus on the successes of Norwegian oil exploitation, but describes how much effort these have taken.

Seitdem Ende der 1960er-Jahre vor der norwegischen Küste Öl entdeckt wurde, trieb die Suche nach Gas- und Ölvorkommen die heimische Wirtschaft an. Diese Landkarten dokumentieren alle vergeblichen Testbohrungen und zeigen jedes „trockene" Bohrloch seit Beginn der norwegischen Ölförderung 1966 bis zum Jahr 1984. Zu dieser Zeit hatte die Ölförderung in der Nordsee ihren Höhepunkt bereits überschritten, und weiter nördlich wurde ein neues Gasfeld gefunden.

Die 150 Bohrlöcher sind nummeriert und durch Linien verbunden, sodass die Chronologie der Probebohrungen und die Ausweitung der Suche nach Norden sichtbar werden. Mit seiner Landkartenserie bietet Torgeir Husevaag eine alternative historische Perspektive – er konzentriert sich nicht auf die Erfolge der norwegischen Ölförderung, sondern zeigt, welchen Einsatz sie erforderten.

Depuis que du pétrole a été découvert dans les eaux norvégiennes à la fin des années 1960, la quête de sources de gaz et de pétrole a été le moteur de l'économie de la Norvège. Cette série de cartes montre tous les puits « secs » produits par les forages de test effectués en vain depuis le début de l'exploitation pétrolière norvégienne en 1966, jusqu'en 1984. À cette date, l'exploitation des sources de la Mer du Nord avait atteint son point culminant et un nouveau champ pétrolifère important avait été découvert plus au nord.

Les 150 forages sont numérotés et reliés par des lignes, pour montrer la chronologie des tests des différents sites et l'effort d'exploration vers le nord. Torgeir Husevaag utilise plusieurs cartes pour créer un document historique alternatif. Il ne met pas l'accent sur les réussites de l'exploitation pétrolière norvégienne, mais sur les efforts entrepris.

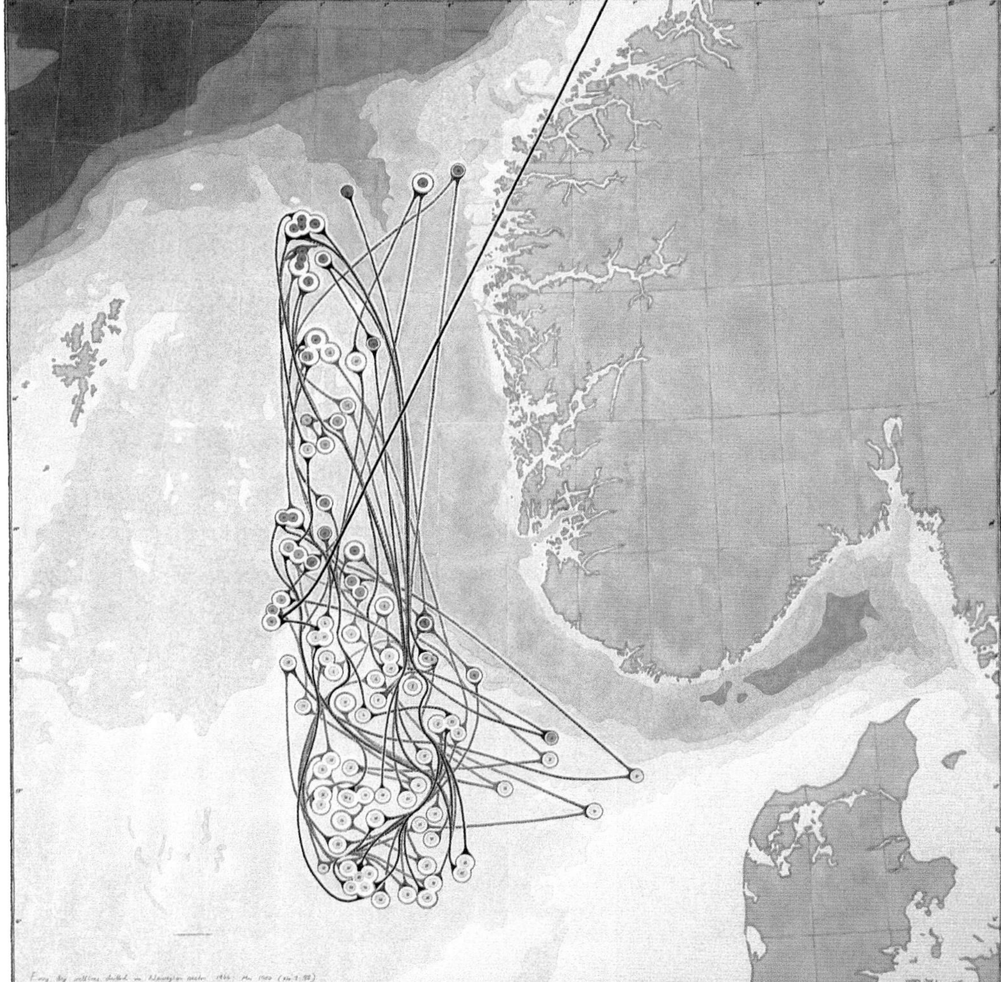

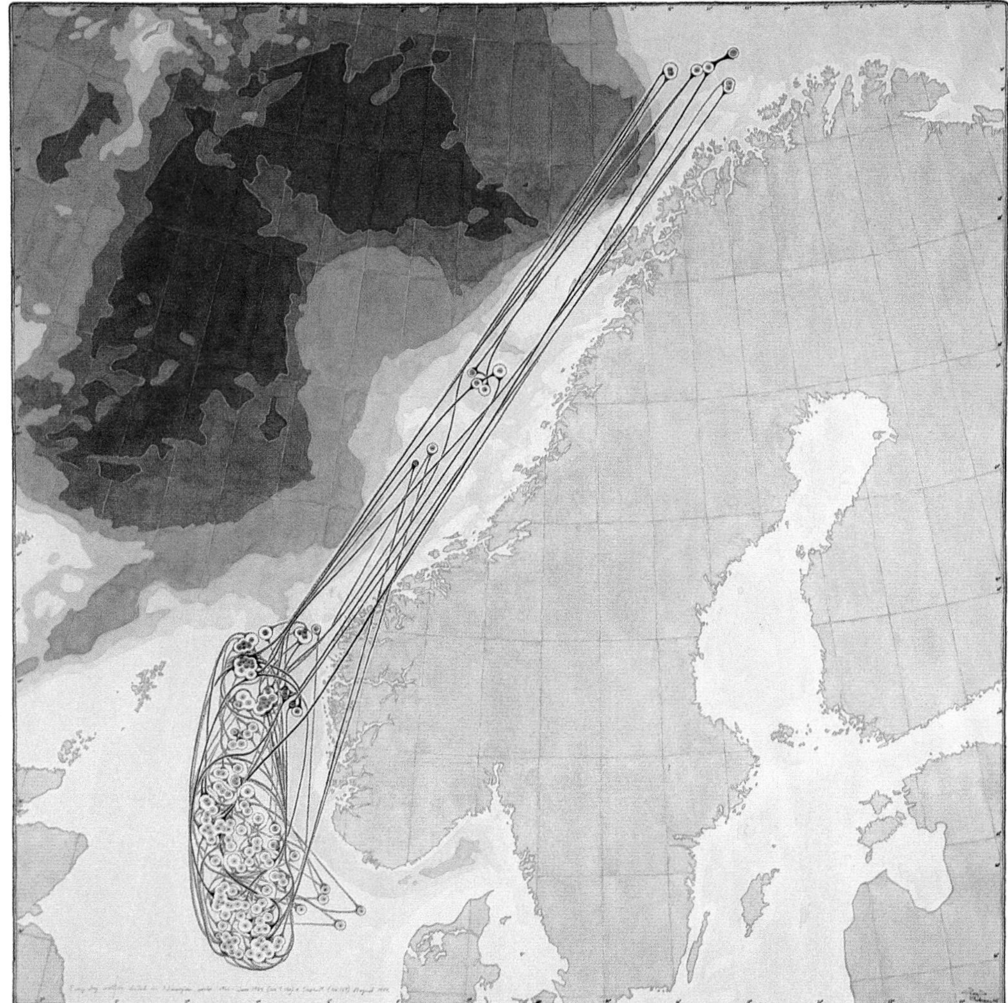

Project Info: Series of drawings, Arctic Princess/ Höegh LNG, 2005, Norway
Data Source: Norwegian Petroleum Directorate
Design: Torgeir Husevaag

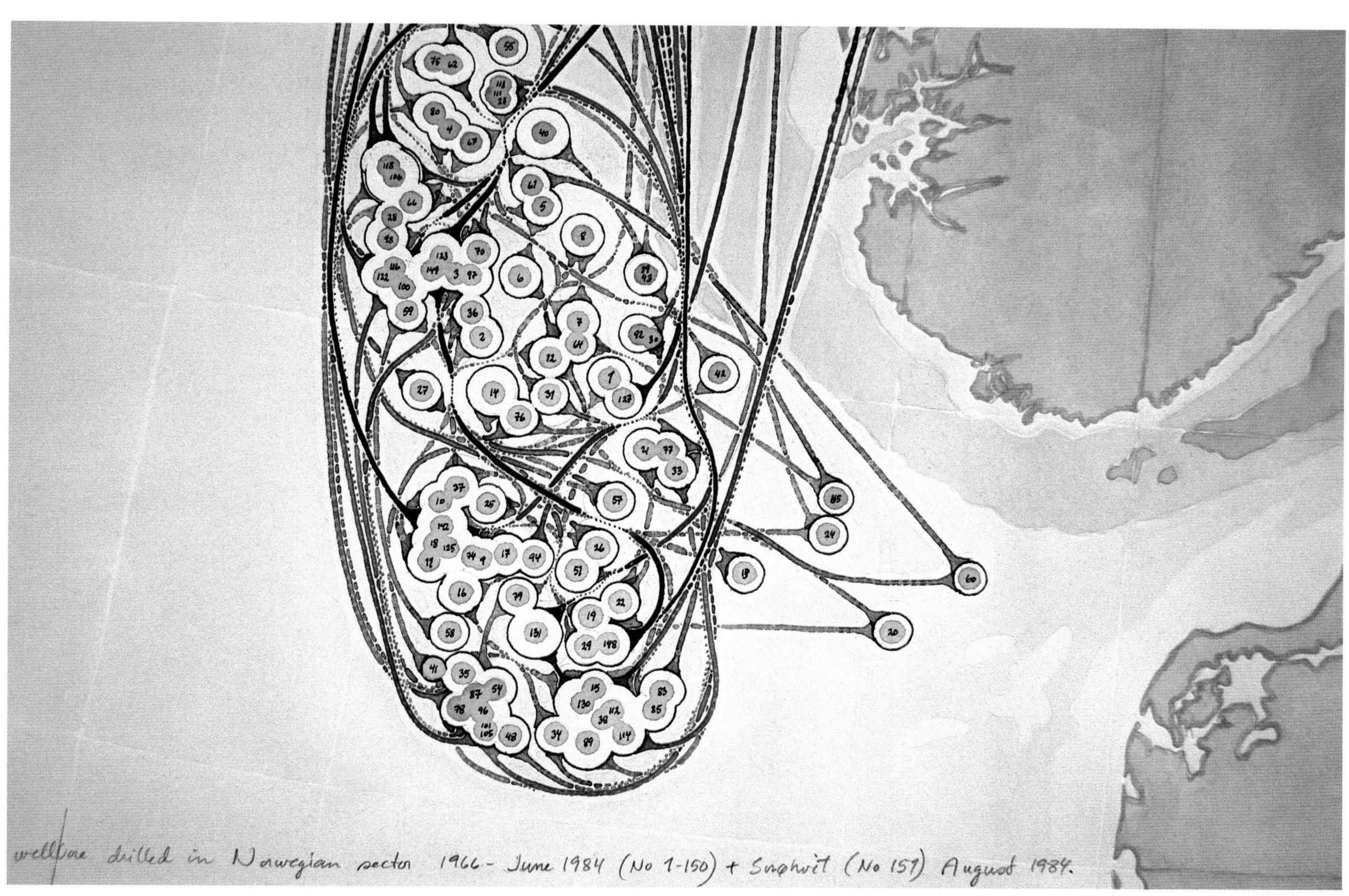
wells/are drilled in Norwegian sector 1966 - June 1984 (No 1-150) + Snøhvit (No 151) August 1984.

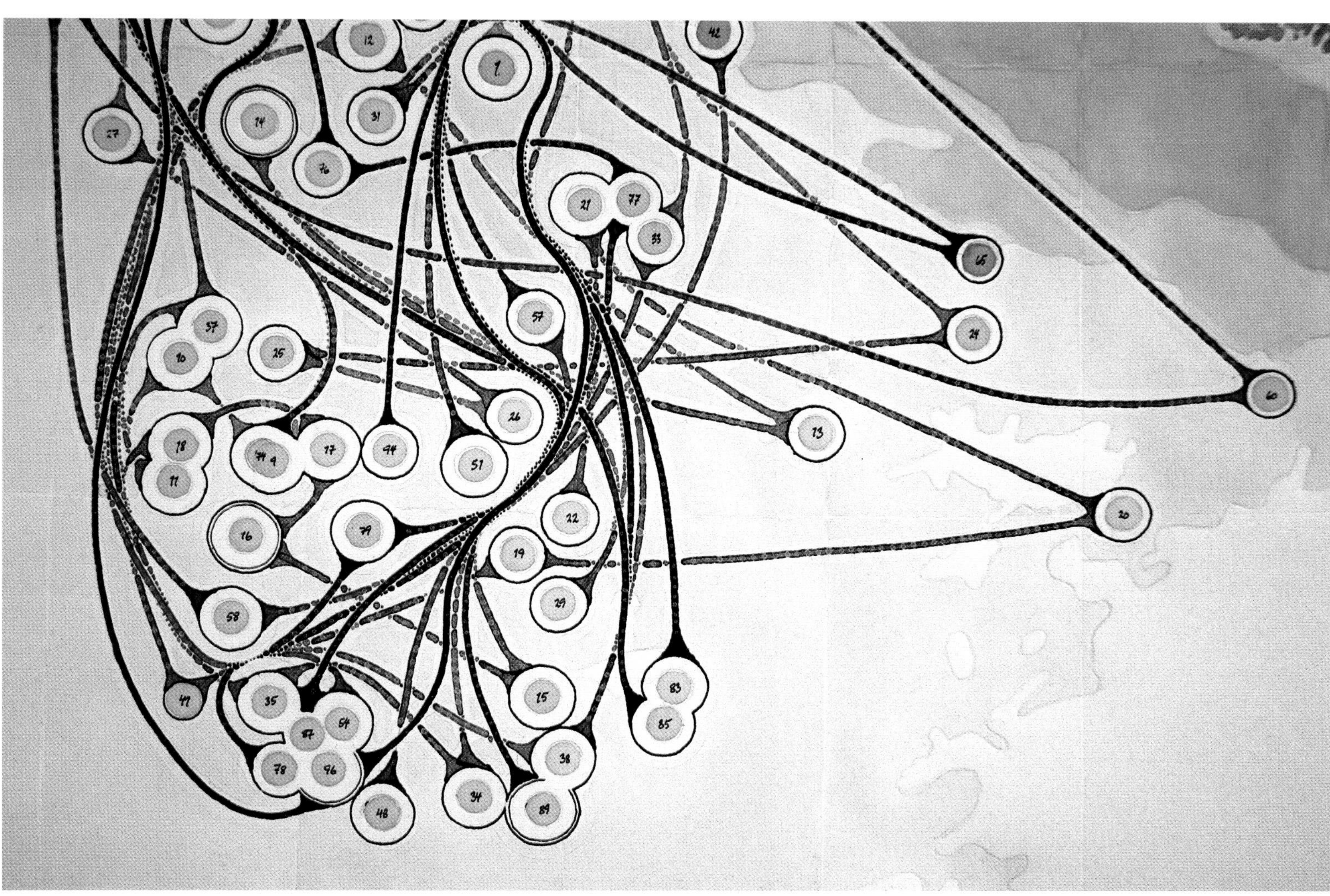

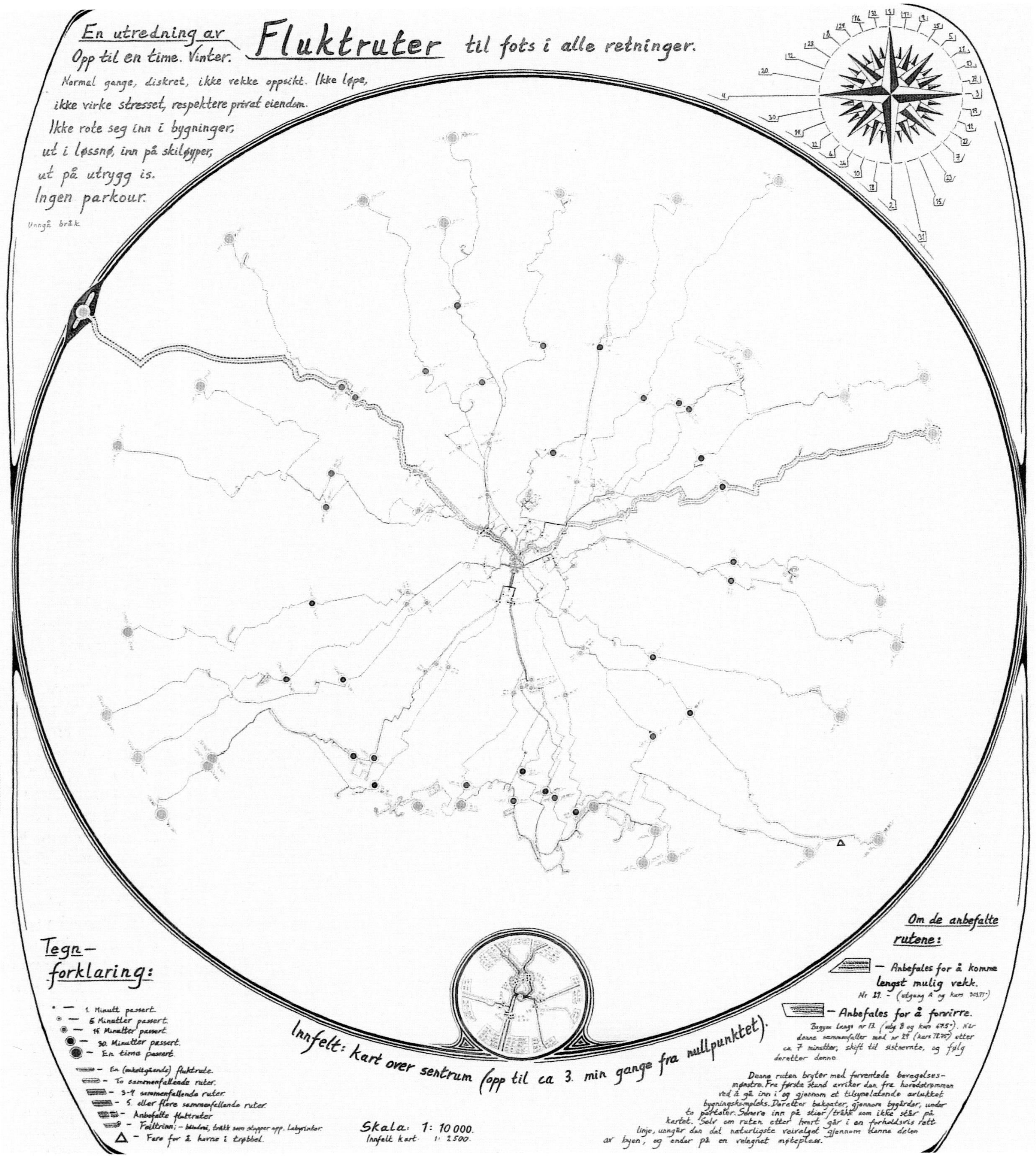

En utredning av
Opp til en time. Vinter.

Fluktruter til fots i alle retninger.

Normal gange, diskret, ikke vekke oppsikt. Ikke løpe,
ikke virke stresset, respektere privat eiendom.
Ikke rote seg inn i bygninger,
ut i løssnø, inn på skiløyper,
ut på utrygg is.
Ingen parkour.

Unngå bråk

Innfelt: kart over sentrum (opp til ca 3. min gange fra nullpunktet).

Tegnforklaring:

- 1 Minutt passert.
- 5 Minutter passert.
- 15 Minutter passert.
- 30. Minutter passert.
- En time passert.
- En (enkeltgående) fluktrute.
- To sammenfallende ruter.
- 3-4 sammenfallende ruter.
- 5. eller flere sammenfallende ruter.
- Anbefalte fluktruter
- Feiltrinn; – blindvei, tråkk som stopper opp. Labyrinter.
- △ – Fare for å havne i trøbbel.

Skala: 1: 10 000.
Innfelt kart: 1: 2500.

Om de anbefalte rutene:

– Anbefales for å komme lengst mulig vekk.
Nr 29. – (utgang A og kurs 303.75°)

– Anbefales for å forvirre.
Begynn langs nr 13. (utg. B og kurs 67.5°). Når denne sammenfaller med nr 29 (kurs 78.75) etter ca. 7 minutter, skift til sistnevnte, og følg deretter denne.

Denne ruten bryter med forventede bevegelsesmønstre. Fra første stund avviker den fra hovedstrømmen ved å gå inn i og gjennom et tilsynelatende avlukket bygningskompleks. Deretter bakgater, gjennom bygårder, under to portaler. Senere inn på stier/tråkk som ikke står på kartet. Selv om ruten etter hvert går i en forholdsvis rett linje, unngår den det naturligste veivalget gjennom denne delen av byen, og ender på en velegnet møteplass.

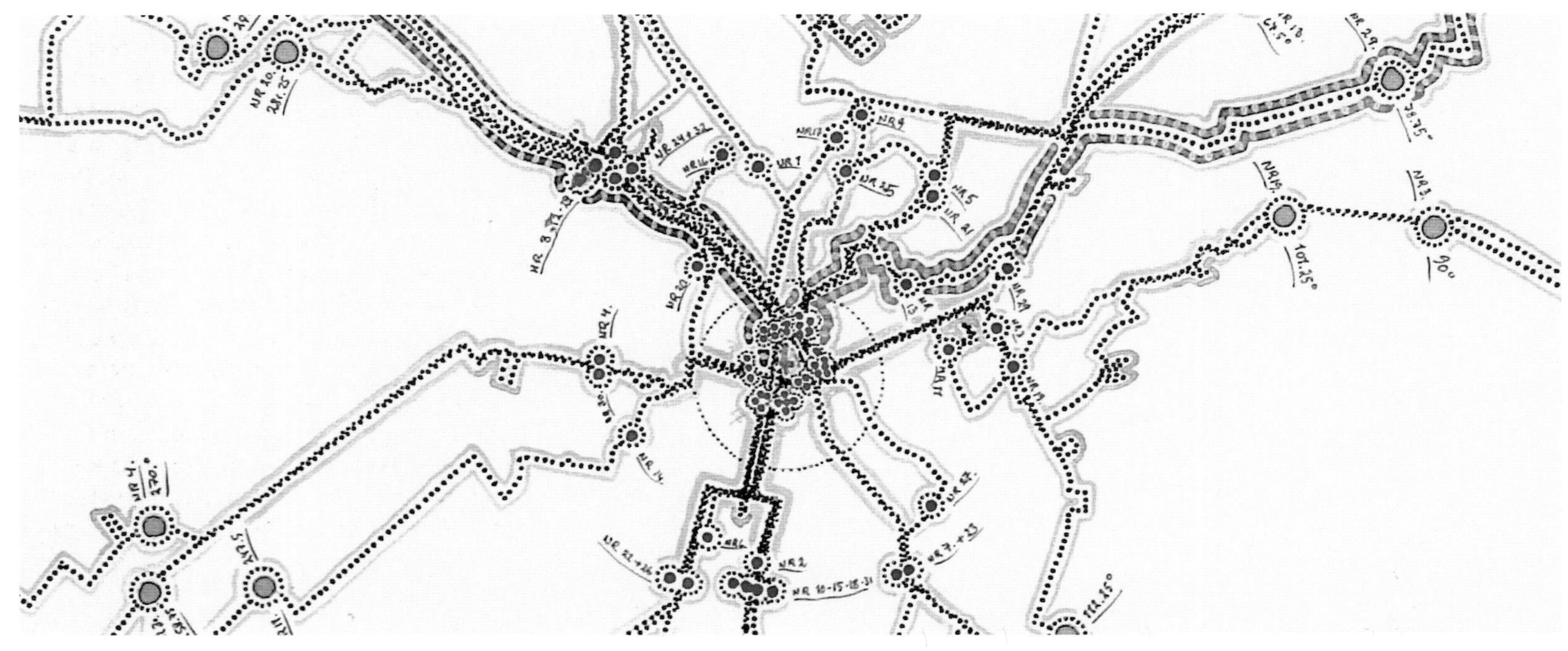

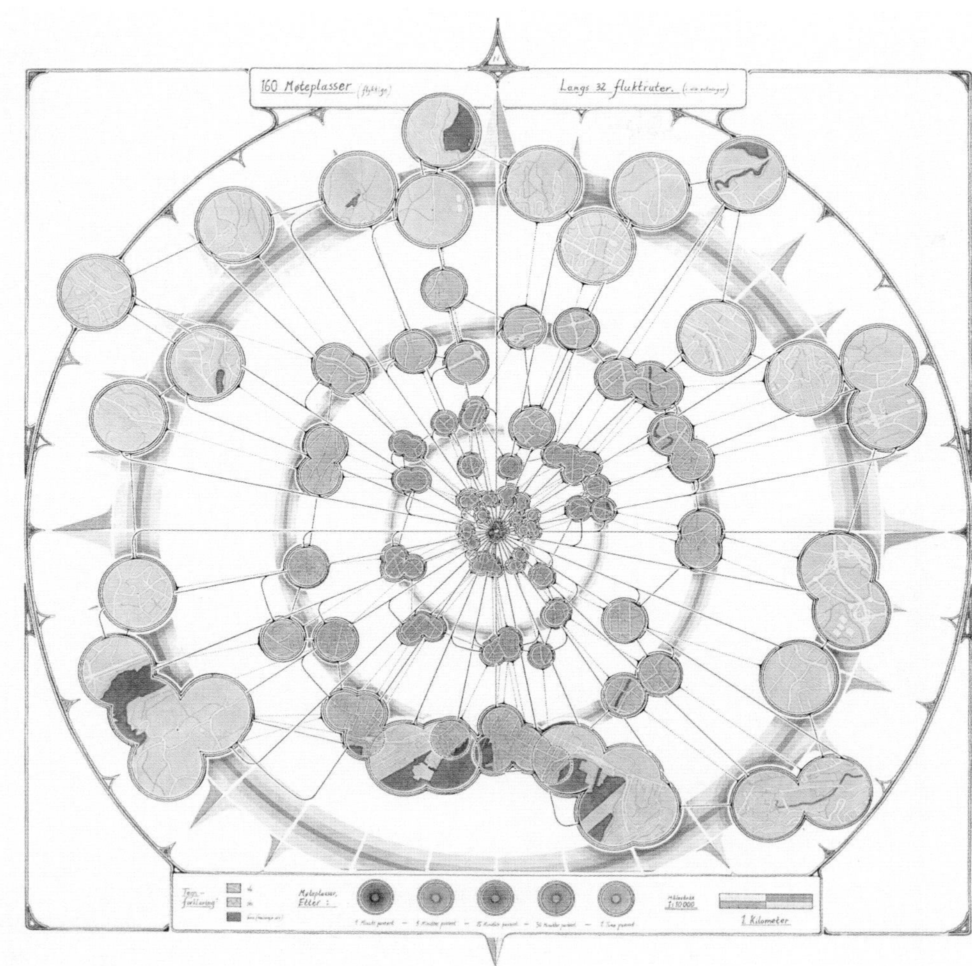

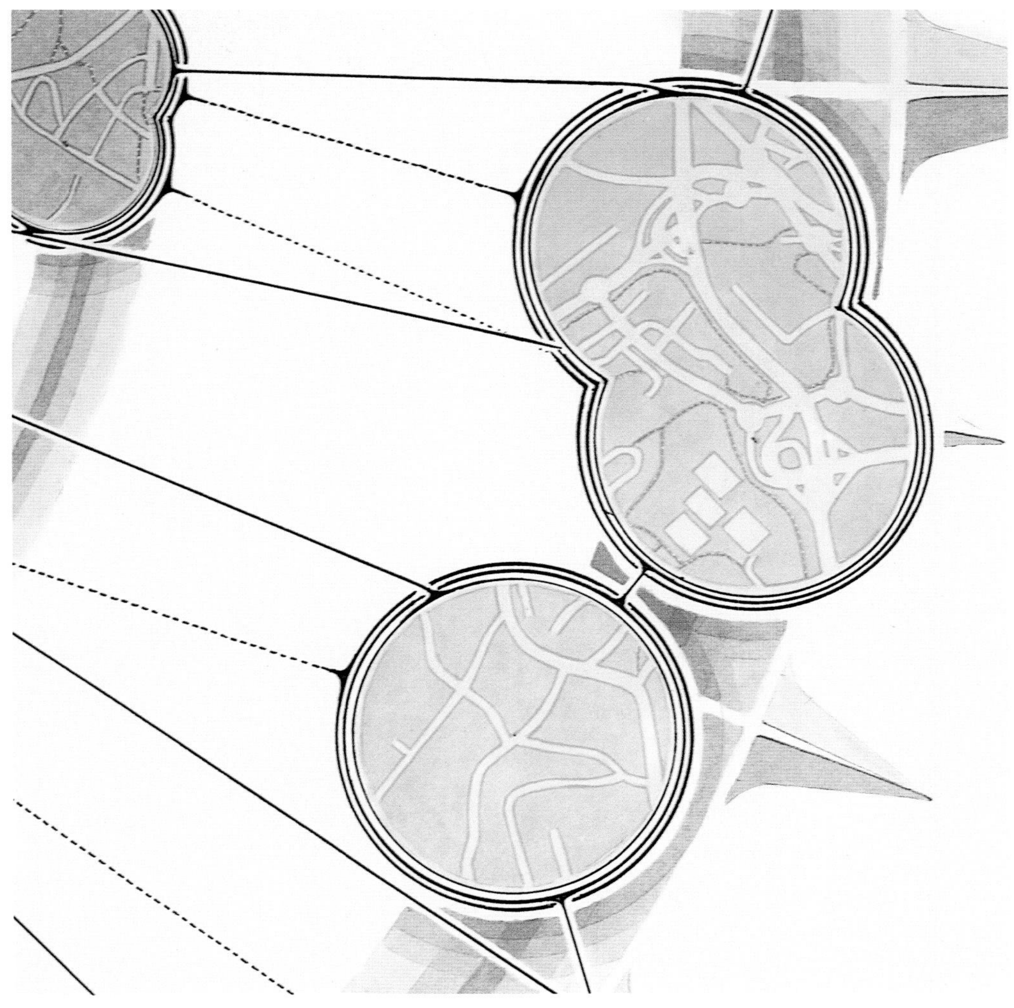

Project Info: Series of drawings, 2010–2011, Norway
Design: Torgeir Husevaag

Escape Routes

Torgeir Husevaag plotted escape routes from a given point by following these rules: "A study of escape routes by foot, in all directions. Up to an hour. Wintertime. Moving discreetly, not getting noticed, not running, staying cool. No trespassing. Keeping outdoors, avoiding ski tracks, deep snow, thin ice..." One drawing shows all 32 resulting routes, without any clue to specific location.

Two tracks are marked as the most suitable. The second drawing maps points which are reached within specific time intervals (one minute / five minutes etc.) from point zero. The circles are coloured and sized according to how long it takes to get there. Within the circles, details of the underlying map are shown. In the event that someone really was fleeing along these routes, he could easily be spotted in these areas.

Torgeir Husevaag suchte nach Fluchtwegen von einem bestimmten Punkt und folgte dabei folgenden Vorgaben: „Eine Studie von Fluchtwegen zu Fuß, in alle Richtungen. Bis zu einer Stunde. Winter. Vorsichtige Bewegungen, nicht auffallen, nicht laufen, cool bleiben. Kein unbefugtes Betreten von Grundstücken. Im Freien bleiben. Skipisten, tiefen Schnee und dünnes Eis meiden ..." Eine Zeichnung zeigt alle 32 daraus resultierenden Fluchtwege ohne Hinweis auf einen realen Ausgangspunkt.

Zwei Routen sind als die geeignetsten gekennzeichnet. Die zweite Zeichnung zeigt die Punkte, die vom Ausgangspunkt aus innerhalb eines bestimmten Zeitintervalls (eine Minute, fünf Minuten etc.) erreicht werden. Die Kreise sind farbig, ihre Größe entspricht der Zeit, in der sie zu erreichen sind. Innerhalb der Kreise sind Details der darunter liegenden Landkarte zu sehen. Wäre jemand tatsächlich auf diesen Routen geflohen, wäre er an diesen Punkten gut sichtbar gewesen.

Torgeir Husevaag a fait un relevé des voies d'issue à partir d'un endroit donné en suivant ces règles: « Une étude des voies d'issue à pied, dans toutes les directions. Jusqu'à une heure. En hiver. Par déplacements discrets, sans se faire remarquer, sans courir, calmement. Sans empiéter sur les propriétés privées. En restant à l'air libre, en évitant les pistes de ski, la neige profonde, la glace fine... » Un dessin montre les 32 itinéraires obtenus, sans aucune indication sur l'endroit spécifique.

Deux itinéraires sont identifiés comme les plus appropriés. Le deuxième dessin situe les points que l'on atteint au bout de certains intervalles de temps (une minute / cinq minutes, etc.) à partir du point zéro. La couleur et la taille des cercles sont fonction du temps qu'il faut pour y arriver. L'intérieur des cercles montre le détail de la carte sous-jacente. Si quelqu'un s'échappait vraiment en suivant ces chemins, il serait facilement repérable à ces endroits.

Feltron Annual Report

Project Info: Booklet and poster, 2008, USA
Design: Nicholas Felton

THE MAP OF A YEAR
THE FELTRON 2008 ATLAS
ISLANDERS HOCKEY GAME
LONG ISLAND
COSTA BRAVA, SPAIN
PALAFRUGELL
TAMARIU
JELLYFISH STING
CALELLA DE PALAFRUGELL
BEST BEACH BEER
BOHAN
TURISMO SHOWROOM
DUKES
ALGONQUIN
MOST SPECTACULAR CRASH
STAR JUNCTION
BROKER
LIBERTY CITY, GRAND THEFT AUTO IV
BARCELONA
MUSEU FREDERIC MARES
PORTLAND
NEWPORT
BEST FRIED OYSTERS
GOLD BEACH
RIVERVIEW RESTAURANT
AVENUE OF THE GIANTS
EUREKA
BEST HIKE
SHASTA LAKE
GARBERVILLE
POINT ARENA
START DRIVING
FINISH DRIVING
MILL VALLEY
BROOKLYN
BACK FORTY
MCMINNVILLE
AEROSPACE HIGH POINT
VISIT THE SPRUCE GOOSE
HEATHER & MARK'S WEDDING
MOUNT ANGEL
FAVORITE BOOKSTORE
POWELL'S
PORTLAND
FIRST ICE CREAM OF SUMMER
LYCHEE FLAVOR
SECRET SERVICE VISITS OFFICE
OBAMA ELECTED
AMADOR'S APPENDIX REMOVED
JULY MILES
AUGUST MILES
SEPTEMBER MILES
OCTOBER MILES
NOVEMBER MILES
DECEMBER MILES

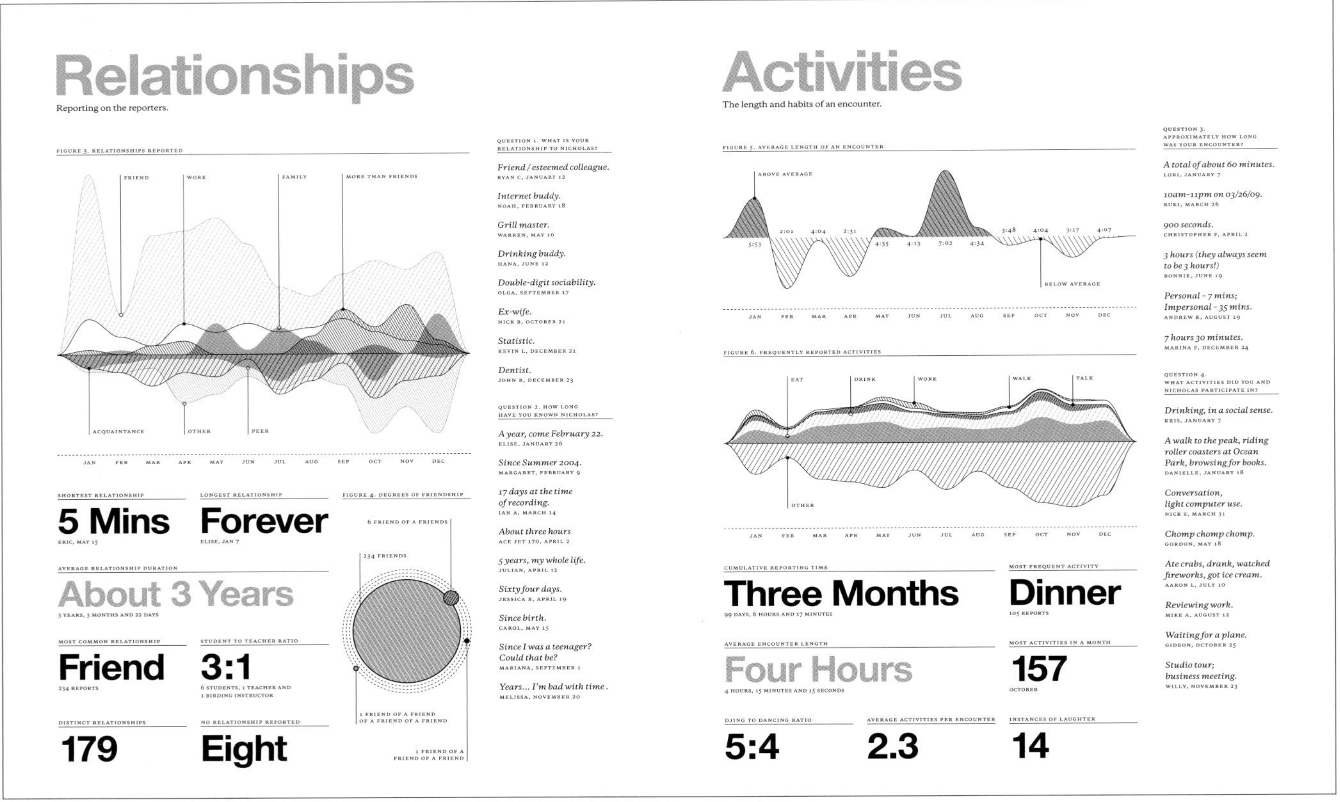

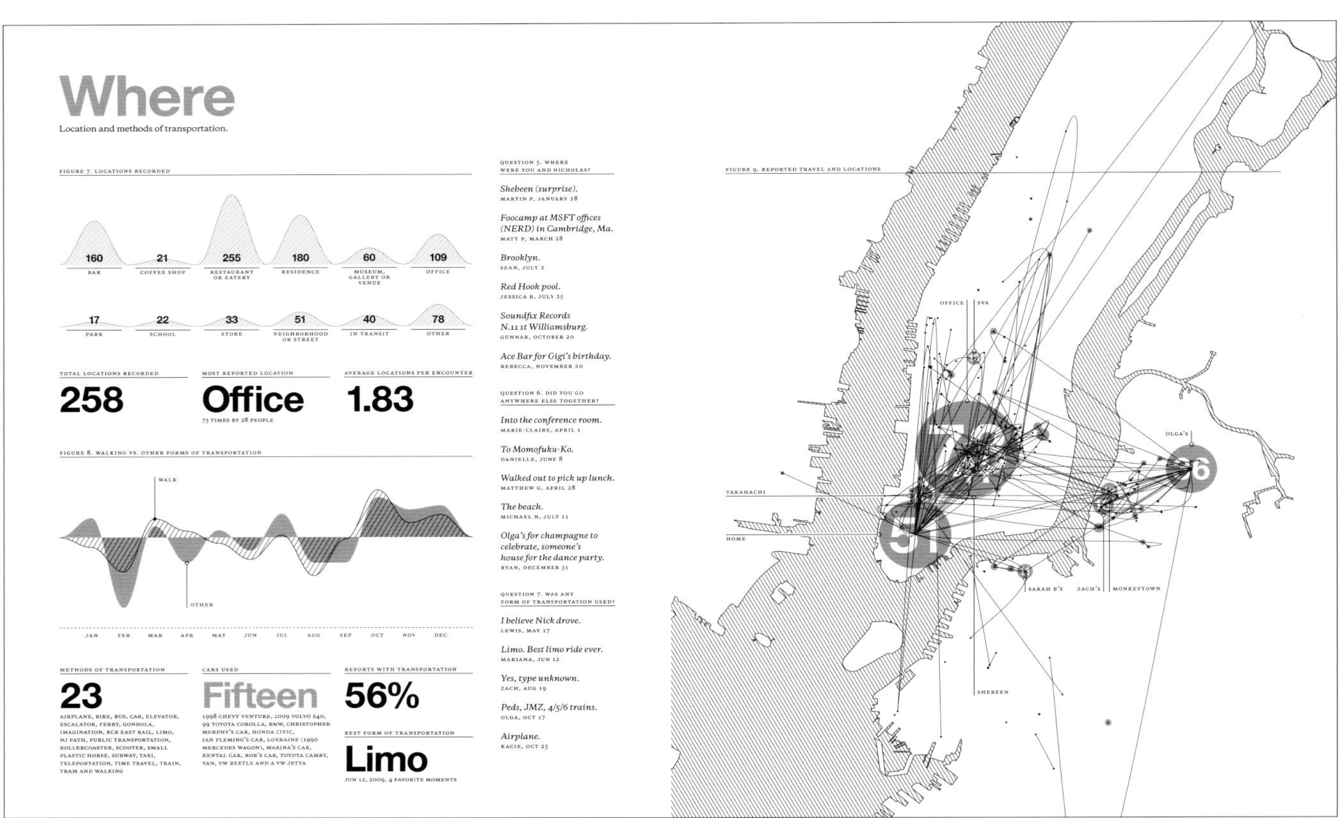

While data visualisation is mostly considered as a tool for coping with inscrutable problems, Nicholas Felton has employed it in a very personal way: to keep track of his life. Since 2005, he has published an annual report of his life, visualising meticulously logged facts relating to his travel, dining, drinking and personal experiences.

The image (previous page) shows the 2008 poster with various maps, featuring details from Felton's travels from that year. The piece is a collage of 13 maps in 20 equilateral triangles, reminiscent of Buckminster Fuller's Dymaxion world maps. Put together, the polyhedron forms the "cosmos" of Felton's life in 2008. The timeline beneath demonstrates how many miles were travelled during the year and is complemented by personal highlights.

Datenvisualisierung dient üblicherweise dazu, unübersichtliche Probleme zu erhellen. Nicholas Felton jedoch verwendet sie auf eine sehr persönliche Art, nämlich um sein Leben im Blick zu behalten. Seit 2005 veröffentlicht er jedes Jahr einen Bericht, in dem er detaillierte Fakten aus seinen Aufzeichnungen visualisiert, etwa über seine Reisen, Essen, Trinken oder persönliche Erfahrungen.

Das Bild (vorige Seite) zeigt das Plakat des Jahres 2008 mit mehreren Landkarten, auf denen Details von Feltons Reisen in diesem Jahr verzeichnet sind. Es ist eine Collage von 13 Landkarten aus 20 gleichseitigen Dreiecken, die an Buckminster Fullers Dymaxion-Weltkarten erinnert. Zusammengesetzt bildet das Polyeder den „Kosmos" von Feltons Leben 2008. Der Zeitleiste am unteren Rand des Posters ist zu entnehmen, wie viele Meilen er im Verlauf des Jahres zurückgelegt hat. Sie wird von persönlichen Erlebnissen ergänzt.

La visualisation des données est souvent considérée comme un outil pour aborder les problèmes impénétrables, mais Nicholas Feltron l'a utilisée pour un projet très personnel : suivre le déroulement de sa vie. Depuis 2005, il publie un rapport annuel sur sa vie, qui donne une visualisation de faits méticuleusement consignés concernant ses voyages, ses repas, ses boissons et ses expériences personnelles.

L'image montre l'affiche de 2008 avec plusieurs cartes exposant des détails tirés des voyages que Feltron a effectués cette année-là. C'est un collage de 13 cartes en 20 triangles équilatéraux, qui évoque les cartes du monde Dymaxion de Buckminster Fuller. Ce polyèdre constitue le « cosmos » de la vie de Feltron en 2008. En dessous, la chronologie montre le nombre de miles qu'il a parcourus pendant l'année, et est ponctuée d'événements personnels.

Flight AF447

This graphic combines data about location and time, with the globe providing the overall map motif. It depicts the journey of Air France flight AF447, which crashed into the Atlantic on the night of June 1st, 2009 on its way from Rio de Janeiro to Paris.

The names along the flight route include real places on the ground, such as Natal in Brazil, as well as names of abstract aviation waypoints which have artificial five-letter names. Orange clouds across the Atlantic mark an area with heavy thunderstorms at the time of the disaster. White lines show civilian flight-paths, dark lines mark sectors of controlled air space.

Diese Grafik verbindet Daten zur Lokalisierung und zum Zeitablauf eines Geschehens, der Globus dient dabei als Karte. Dargestellt ist die Route des Air-France-Flugs AF447, bei dem die Maschine in der Nacht des 1. Juni 2009 auf dem Weg von Rio de Janeiro nach Paris in den Atlantik stürzte.

Die Namen entlang der Flugroute umfassen zum Teil reale Orte, wie etwa Natal in Brasilien, aber auch Luftfahrt-Wegpunkte, die aus fünf Buchstaben bestehende Kunstnamen tragen. Orangefarbene Wolken über dem Atlantik zeigen das Gebiet, in dem zur Zeit des Absturzes schwere Gewitter niedergingen. Weiße Linien markieren die Luftstraßen der zivilen Luftfahrt, dunkle Linien zeigen Sektoren eines kontrollierten Luftraums an.

Cette carte combine des données géographiques et temporelles présentées sur l'image du globe. Elle représente le parcours du vol Air France AF447, qui s'est écrasé dans l'Atlantique dans la nuit du 1er juin 2009 entre Rio de Janeiro et Paris.

Les noms mentionnés le long de l'itinéraire de vol comprennent des lieux réels, comme la ville de Natal au Brésil, ainsi que des points de repère abstraits utilisés dans l'aviation, avec des noms de cinq lettres artificiels. Les nuages orange sur l'Atlantique indiquent la position de violents orages au moment de la catastrophe. Les lignes blanches montrent les itinéraires de vols civils, et les lignes foncées marquent les secteurs d'espace aérien contrôlé.

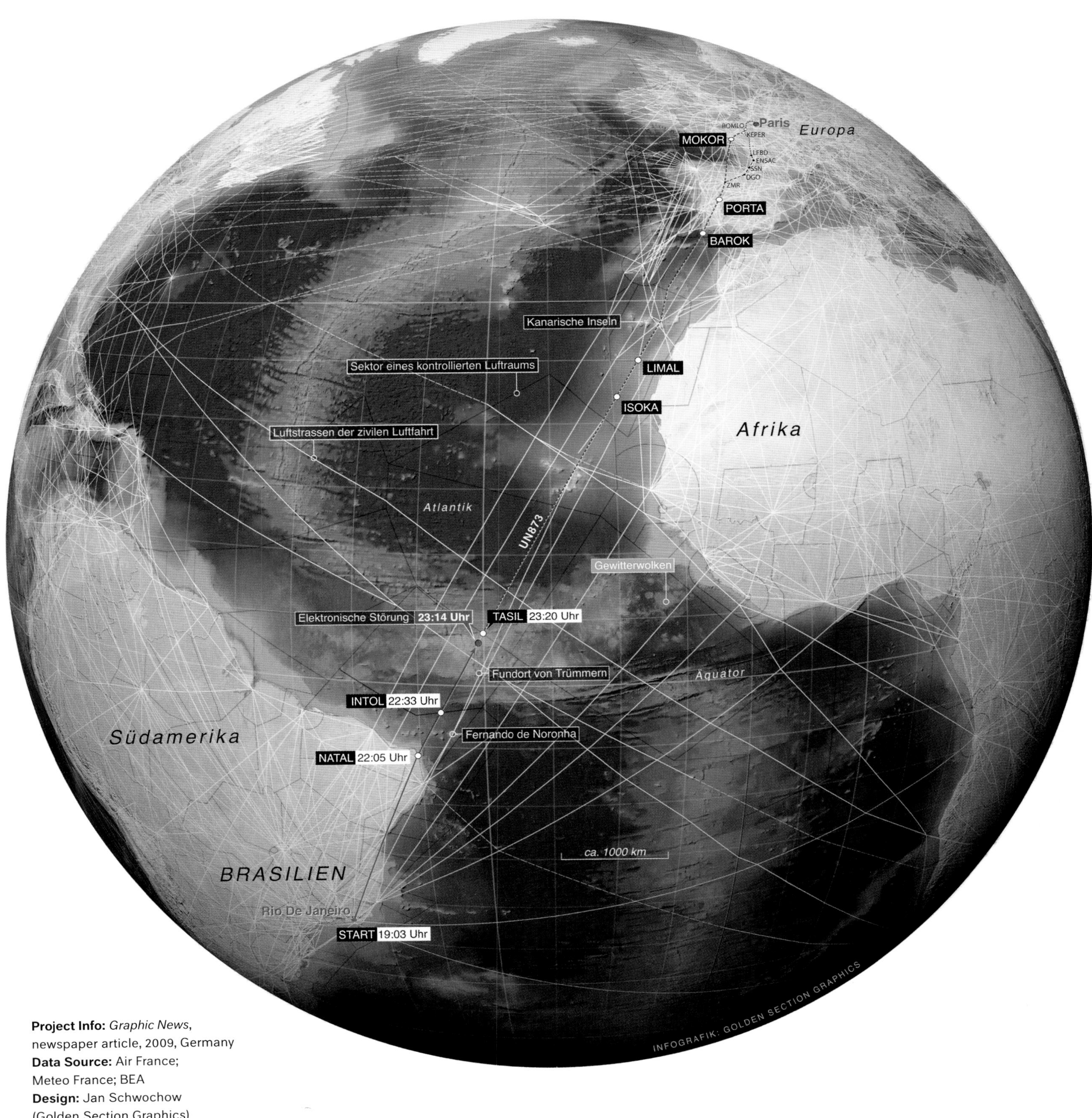

Project Info: *Graphic News*, newspaper article, 2009, Germany
Data Source: Air France; Meteo France; BEA
Design: Jan Schwochow (Golden Section Graphics)

Flight Patterns

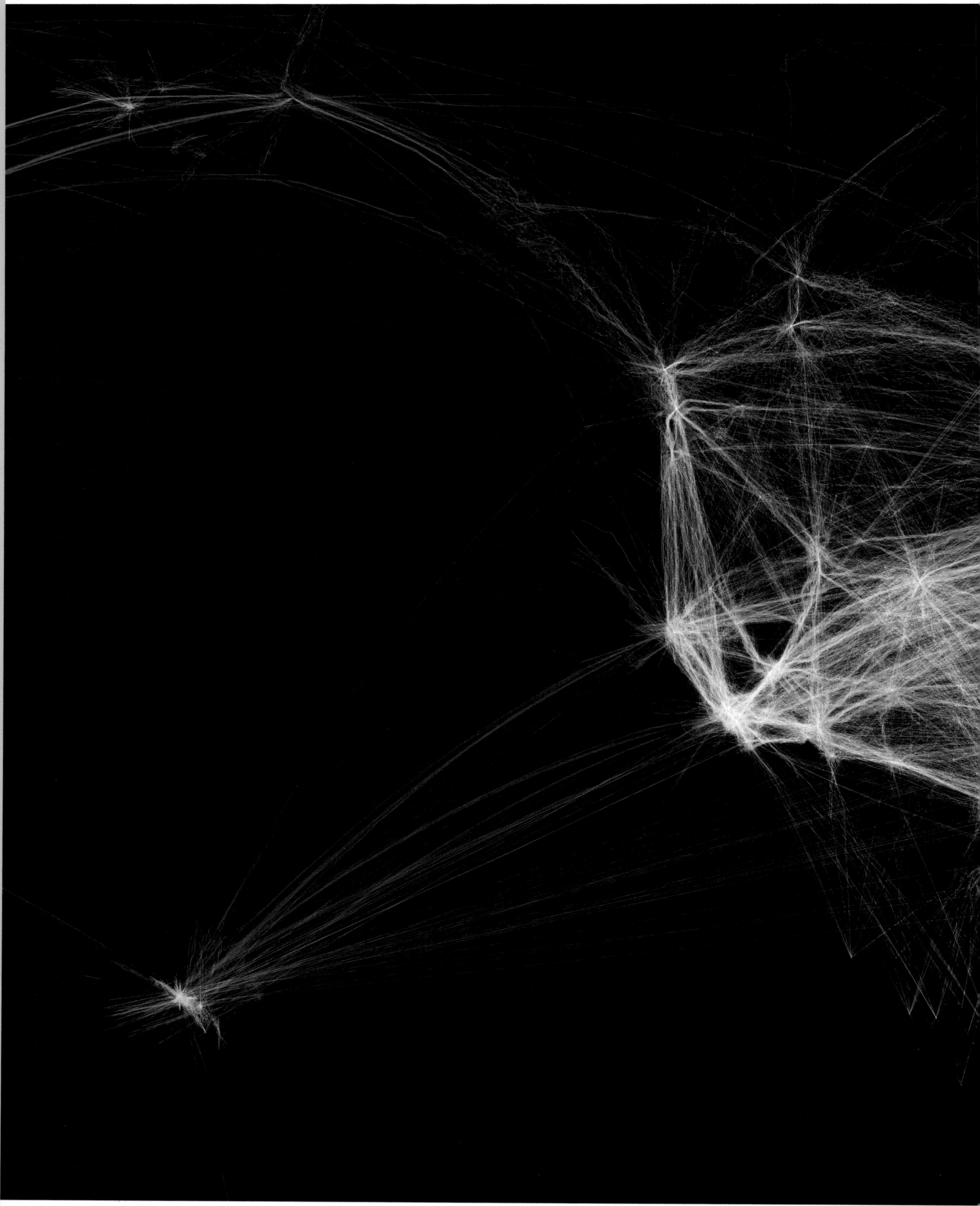

Project Info: Website and poster, 2008, USA
Data Source: Federal Aviation Administration
Design: Aaron Koblin
Awards: NSF Science Visualisation

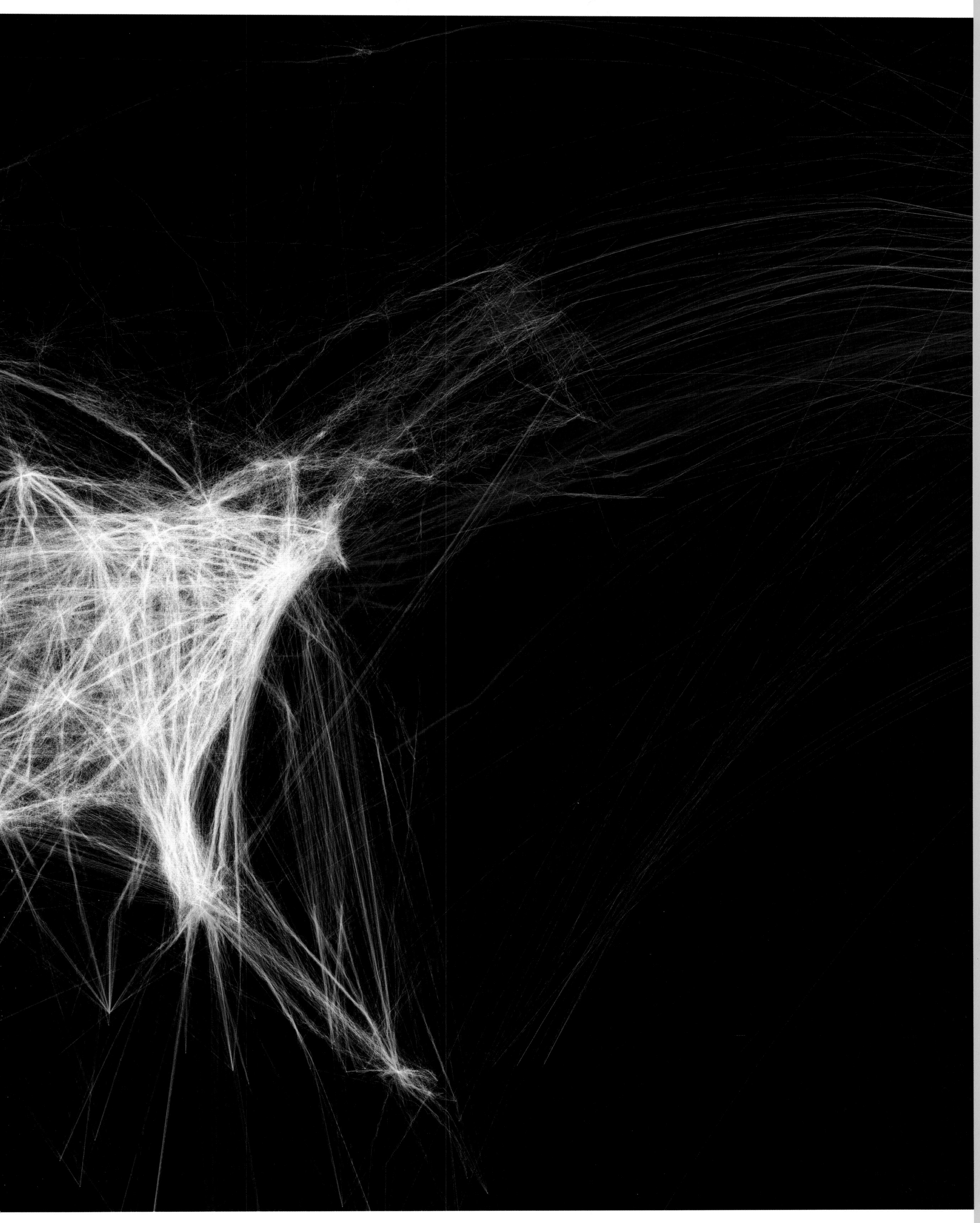

This series of visualisations developed by Aaron Koblin shows air-traffic paths over North America in coloured linear networks. The Federal Aviation Administration, the US government agency for monitoring civil air traffic, provided flight data for a 24-hour period. These were analysed and plotted using the Processing programming environment.

Without seeing the underlying US map, patterns and paths nevertheless appear. Intersections at major airports are easily visible. In continuative studies, Koblin researched into altitude, aircraft type and manufacturer. Colour coding was used to distinguish flights according to this enriched information.

Diese von Aaron Koblin entwickelte Visualisierungsreihe zeigt die Luftstraßen über Nordamerika in farbigen Liniennetzen. Die amerikanische Bundesluftfahrtbehörde Federal Aviation Administration, die den zivilen Luftverkehr überwacht, stellte dafür Daten zur Verfügung, die einen Zeitraum von 24 Stunden abdecken. Sie wurden analysiert und mithilfe der Programmiersprache „Processing" grafisch dargestellt.

Ohne die zugrunde liegende Landkarte der USA zu sehen, werden Muster und „Straßen" sichtbar. In weiterführenden Studien untersuchte Koblin Höhe, Flugzeugtypen und Hersteller. Er codierte die Flüge farbig, um diese zusätzlichen Informationen darzustellen.

Cette série de représentations mises au point par Aaron Koblin montre les couloirs aériens au-dessus de l'Amérique du Nord sous forme de réseaux linéaires colorés. L'Administration fédérale de l'aviation, l'agence gouvernementale responsable du contrôle du trafic aérien civil, a fourni les données relatives aux vols effectués sur une période de 24 heures. Ces données ont été analysées et tracées grâce à l'environnement de programmation Processing.

Sans voir la carte sous-jacente des États-Unis, on peut tout de même discerner des formes et des itinéraires. Les intersections des grands aéroports sont bien nettes. Koblin a réalisé d'autres études pour examiner les données relatives à l'altitude, au type d'avion et aux fabricants des appareils. Un code couleur a été employé pour distinguer les vols en fonction de cette information enrichie.

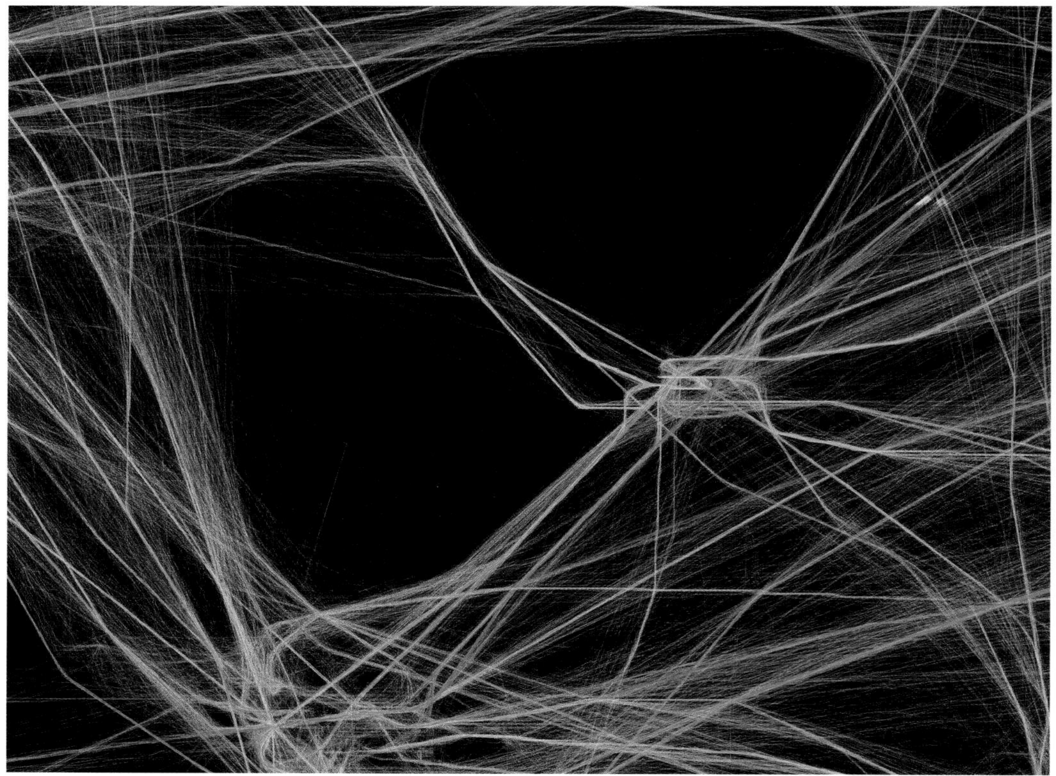

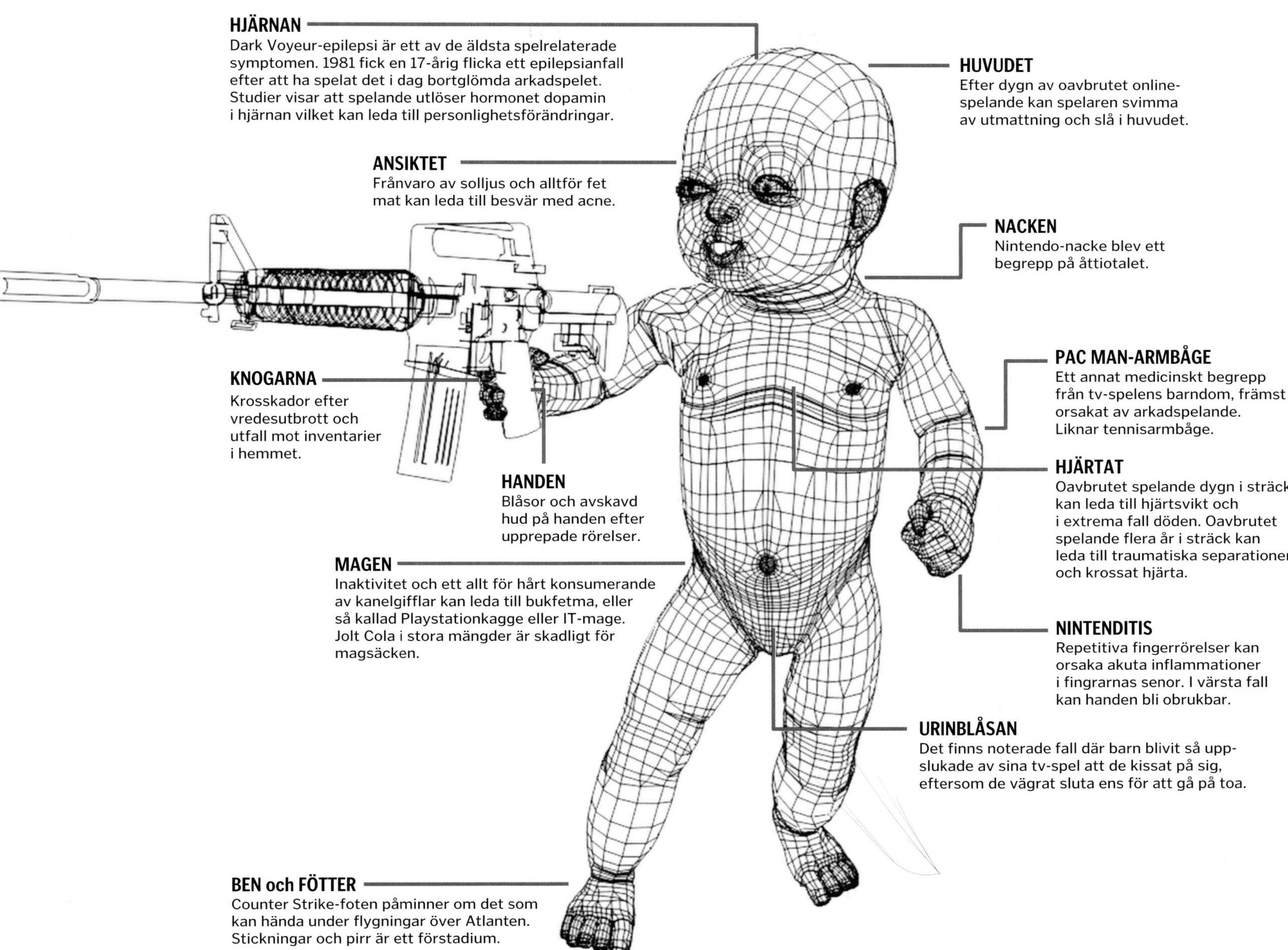

HJÄRNAN
Dark Voyeur-epilepsi är ett av de äldsta spelrelaterade symptomen. 1981 fick en 17-årig flicka ett epilepsianfall efter att ha spelat det i dag bortglömda arkadspelet. Studier visar att spelande utlöser hormonet dopamin i hjärnan vilket kan leda till personlighetsförändringar.
HUVUDET
Efter dygn av oavbrutet online-spelande kan spelaren svimma av utmattning och slå i huvudet.
ANSIKTET
Frånvaro av solljus och alltför fet mat kan leda till besvär med acne.
NACKEN
Nintendo-nacke blev ett begrepp på åttiotalet.
PAC MAN-ARMBÅGE
Ett annat medicinskt begrepp från tv-spelens barndom, främst orsakat av arkadspelande. Liknar tennisarmbåge.
KNOGARNA
Krosskador efter vredesutbrott och utfall mot inventarier i hemmet.
HJÄRTAT
Oavbrutet spelande dygn i sträck kan leda till hjärtsvikt och i extrema fall döden. Oavbrutet spelande flera år i sträck kan leda till traumatiska separationer och krossat hjärta.
HANDEN
Blåsor och avskavd hud på handen efter upprepade rörelser.
MAGEN
Inaktivitet och ett allt för hårt konsumerande av kanelgifflar kan leda till bukfetma, eller så kallad Playstationkagge eller IT-mage. Jolt Cola i stora mängder är skadligt för magsäcken.
NINTENDITIS
Repetitiva fingerrörelser kan orsaka akuta inflammationer i fingrarnas senor. I värsta fall kan handen bli obrukbar.
URINBLÅSAN
Det finns noterade fall där barn blivit så uppslukade av sina tv-spel att de kissat på sig, eftersom de vägrat sluta ens för att gå på toa.
BEN och FÖTTER
Counter Strike-foten påminner om det som kan hända under flygningar över Atlanten. Stickningar och pirr är ett förstadium.

Gaming Injuries

This piece, developed for Swedish newspaper *Svenska Dagbladet* in 2003, humorously focuses on the physical impacts of the excessive playing of computer games. It is structured around body features, using as its centre a somewhat creepy wire-frame graphic of a toddler holding a gun.

Linked to individual body-parts, possible injuries are listed and described, mimicking the language of the now omnipresent tobacco warnings: uninterrupted gaming for years on end can lead to traumatic separations and a broken heart.

Diese 2003 für die schwedische Tageszeitung *Svenska Dagbladet* gestaltete Grafik befasst sich scherzhaft mit den körperlichen Folgen exzessiven Computerspielens. Die Grafik zeigt das gruselig anmutende Drahtgittermodell eines Kleinkindes mit Schusswaffe und ist nach Körperteilen geordnet.

An den einzelnen Körperteilen werden mögliche Schäden beschrieben, ähnlich den heutzutage allgegenwärtigen Warnungen auf Tabakwaren: Jahrelanges ununterbrochenes Spielen kann zu traumatischen Trennungen und gebrochenen Herzen führen.

Cette illustration, réalisée pour le journal suédois *Svenska Dagbladet* en 2003, est une représentation humoristique des effets physiques de l'abus des jeux vidéo. Elle est structurée autour du modèle « fil de fer » assez sinistre d'un jeune enfant tenant une arme.

Les blessures potentielles sont reliées aux différentes parties du corps du modèle, et sont décrites dans un langage qui imite les avertissements antitabac aujourd'hui omniprésents : « la pratique ininterrompue des jeux vidéo pendant des années peut causer des ruptures traumatisantes et briser le cœur. »

Project Info: *Svenska Dagbladet*, newspaper article, 2003, Sweden
Research: Lars Berge
Design: Thomas Molén

Global Healthcare

In this typographic world map, Michael Spitz looks at healthcare resources around the world. Countries are represented by their ISO code, which is scaled in size according to how many doctors are available to the general population. The scaling thus distorts the geographical relations. Cuba tops the list with a ratio of one doctor per 170 inhabitants.

Countries with more than 5,000 people per doctor have a fixed scale to account for extreme variations in developing countries. The map is completed by the line along the bottom which shows the number of hospital beds per 1,000 people. The country codes are listed alphabetically, and again are scaled according to the availability of hospital care.

Auf dieser typografischen Weltkarte untersucht Michael Spitz die Gesundheitsfürsorge auf der ganzen Welt. Die einzelnen Länder sind mit ihrer ISO-Code-Kurzbezeichnung dargestellt. Ihre Größe zeigt, wieviele Ärzte der Bevölkerung in einem Land zur Verfügung stehen. Die Skalierung verzerrt damit die geografischen Abmessungen: Kuba steht mit einem Verhältnis von einem Arzt je 170 Einwohner an der Spitze.

Länder, in denen auf einen Arzt mehr als 5000 Menschen kommen, wurden alle gleich skaliert, um den extremen Unterschieden in den Entwicklungsländern Rechnung zu tragen. Ergänzt wird die Weltkarte durch eine Skala am unteren Bildrand, die die Anzahl von Krankenhausbetten pro 1000 Menschen angibt. Die Ländercodes sind alphabetisch angeordnet und entsprechend der Verfügbarkeit von Krankenhauspflege ebenfalls skaliert.

Dans cette carte typographique du monde, Michael Spitz analyse les ressources en matière de santé dans le monde. Les pays sont représentés par leur code ISO, dont la taille est fonction du nombre de médecins disponibles pour le public général. Ce rapport de taille altère les relations géographiques. Cuba prend la tête de liste avec un ratio d'un médecin pour 170 habitants.

Les pays où il y a plus de 5 000 habitants par médecin ont une échelle fixe, car dans les pays en voie de développement les variations sont énormes. Au bas de la carte, une ligne montre le nombre de lits d'hôpital pour 1 000 habitants. Les codes pays sont triés par ordre alphabétique, et leur taille est là encore un reflet de la disponibilité des soins hospitaliers.

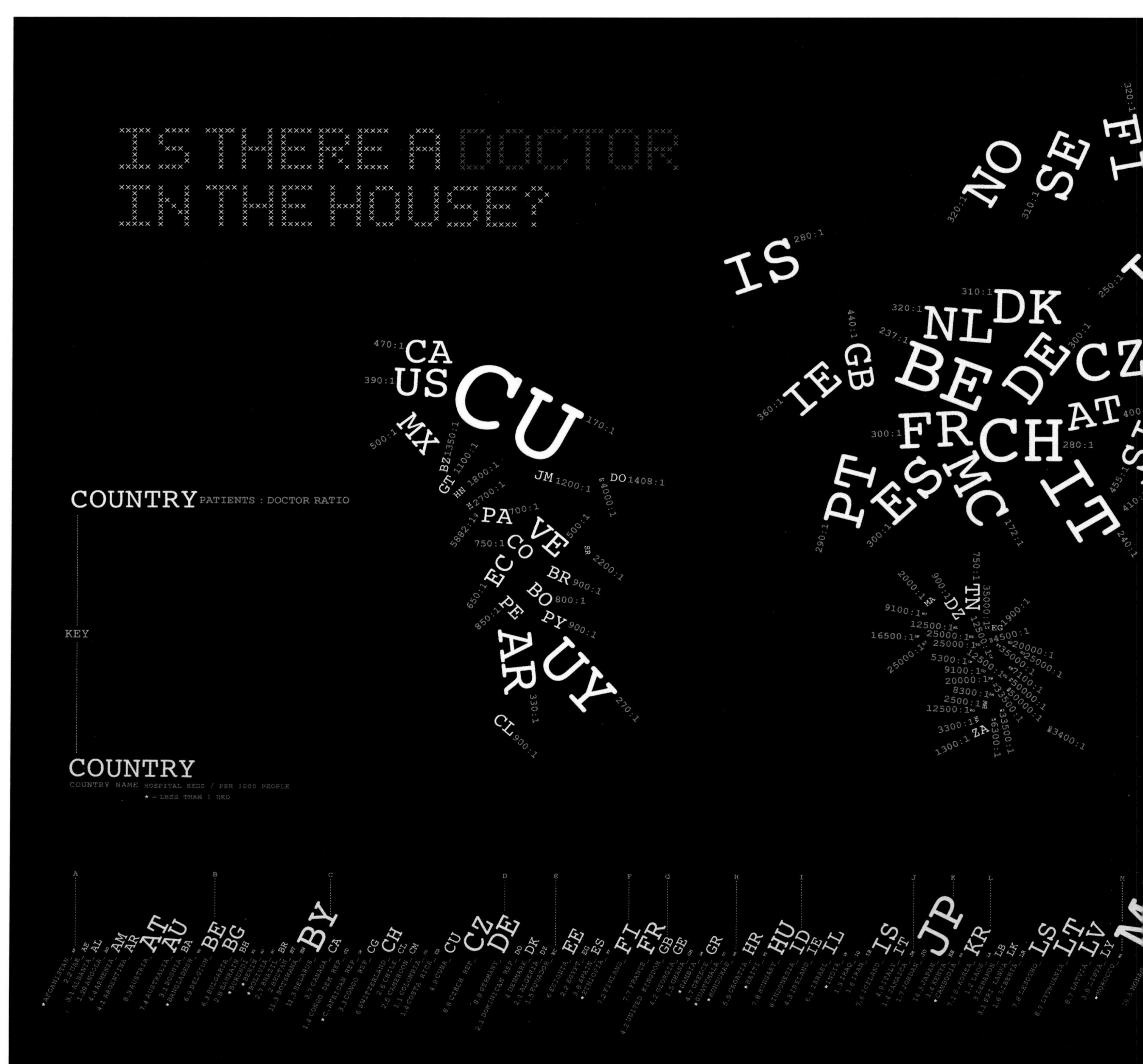

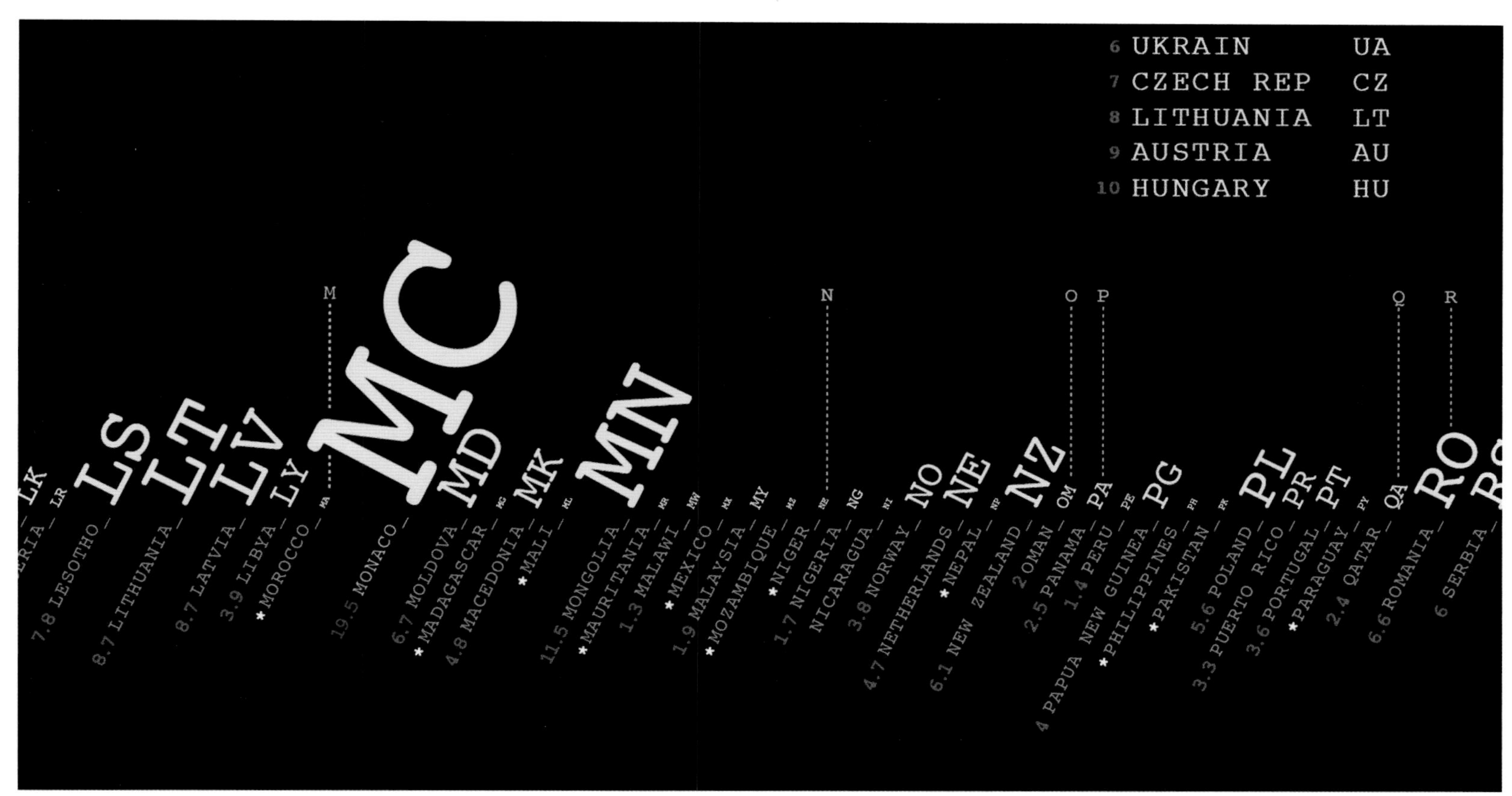

Project Info: Poster, 2008, Croatia
Data Source: The World Bank
Design: Michael Spitz

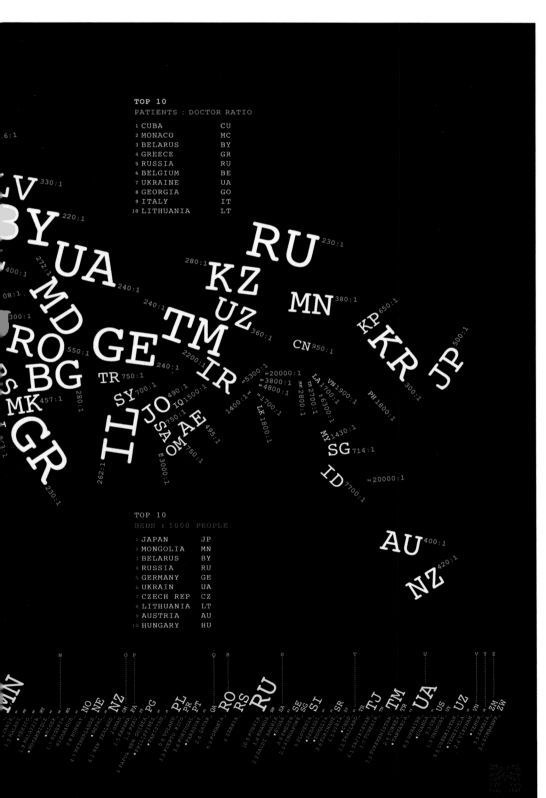

IL | **GREEN REPORT** – ANALISI GRAFICA

TUTTE LE CAUSE DI ESTINZIONE
Sono indicate anche nelle schede di queste pagine in riferimento ai 15 animali di cui parliamo

URBANIZZAZIONE
– La crescita delle aree cittadine danneggia e frammenta molti habitat.

INQUINAMENTO
– Un serio problema per specie marine, anfibi e insetti, sensibili agli agenti chimici.

SPECIE ALIENE
– L'introduzione artificiale di una specie in un ecosistema può distruggerne gli equilibri.

CAMBIAMENTO CLIMATICO
– Investe specie marine sensibili alla temperatura e gli uccelli migratori.

MEDICINA ALTER
– La medicina tradizionale cin usa ancora par animali: soprat ossa e corna.

Aiuto, chiamate Noè

Il 2010 è l'anno mondiale della biodiversità. Ricordiamoci che se scompare una specie, l'intero ecosistema può subire danni irrimediabili: senza api non avremmo frutta, caffè, cotone. La "lista rossa" degli animali a rischio è lunga. Ecco una mappa sintetica e alcuni casi-simbolo... Ma ve lo immaginate un mondo senza elefanti?

– *di* **Francesco Franchi** *e* **Daniele Lorenzetti** | *illustrazioni di* **Laura Cattaneo**

CHE RICCA LA BARRIERA
Nella mappa, i luoghi dove la ricchezza di specie viventi (marine e terrestri) è maggiore. Alti livelli di biodiversità si registrano soprattutto nelle foreste equatoriali e lungo la Grande barriera corallina

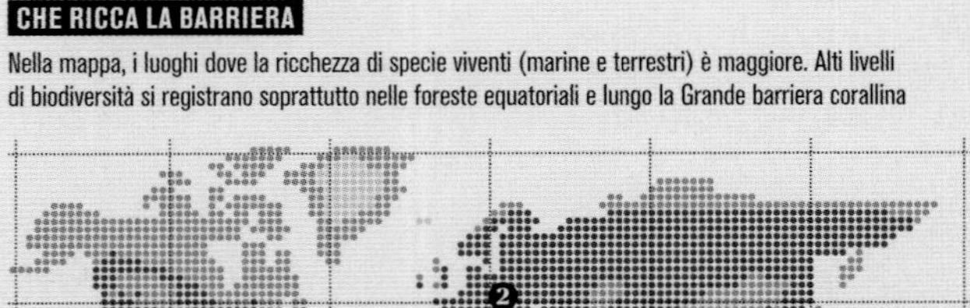

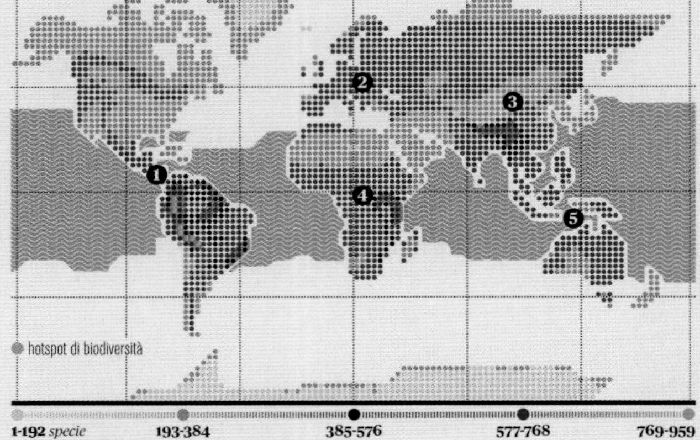

ATTENZIONE, INSETTI VULNERABILI
L'Iucn (Unione mondiale per la conservazione della natura) valuta periodicamente le specie potenzialmente a rischio. Ecco le percentuali di quelle minacciate secondo la Red List del 2008

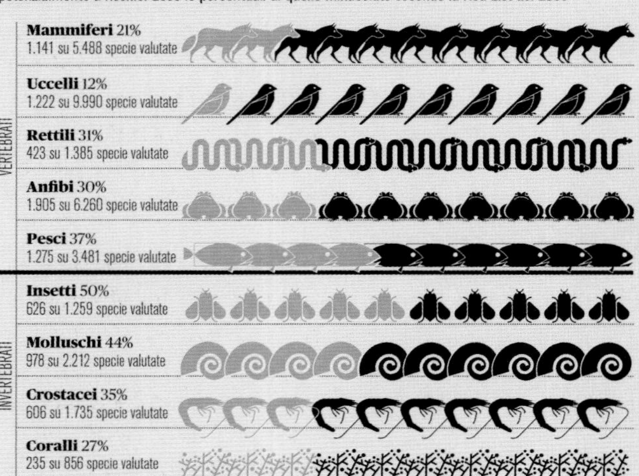

COSA SUCCEDERÀ SE CONSERVIAMO...
gli hotspot protetti · tutte le foreste tropicali · tutti gli hotspot

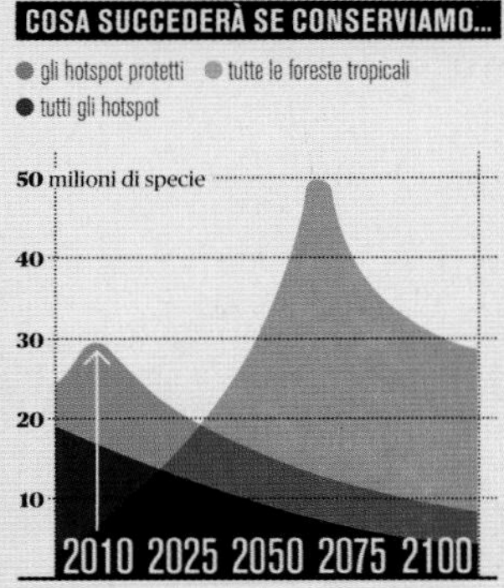

FAMIGLIE CHE NASCONO E MUIONO
600 milioni di anni di evoluzione
origine · estinzione

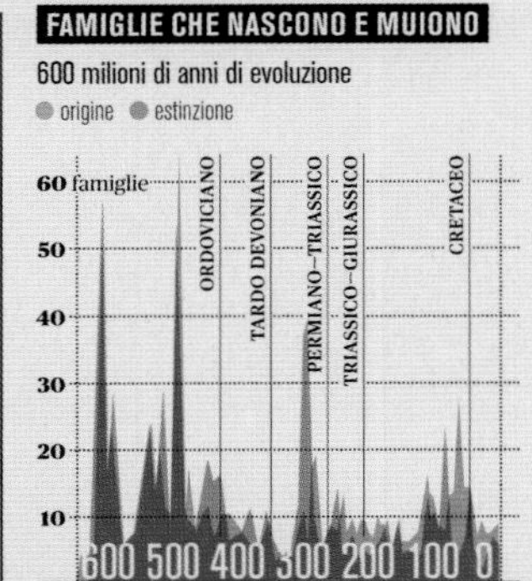

1 Americhe – *Epidemia silenziosa dal polo ai tropici*

A LONTRA DI MARE
Enhydra lutris
La riduzione delle popolazioni di lontra marina causa il proliferare dei ricci, una delle loro prede principali. Troppi ricci depauperano le riserve di kelp e macroalghe.

B ARMADILLO GIGANTE
Priodontes maximus
Un mammifero simbolo dell'ecosistema amazzonico, classificato come *endangered* nella lista rossa Iucn. La caccia indiscriminata e la riduzione degli habitat lo minacciano.

C ORSO GRIZZLY
Ursus arctos horribilis
Negli ecosistemi sub-polari come l'Alaska l'orso grizzly è al vertice della catena alimentare. È una "specie ombrello": dalla sua sopravvivenza dipende quella di molte altre.

2 Europa –

A APE
Apis mellifera
Non ancora a rischio, declino: tra le cause l' i pesticidi e le epidem La loro scomparsa sa disastro per l'impollina dipende la vita di fiori

4 Africa – Il

A RINOCERO
Diceros bicornis
Fino a metà del XX sec nelle savane africane, mammifero è arrivato dell'estinzione. Il comc nella medicina tradizio

34% *degli europei non ha mai sentito nominare la parola "biodiversità"* – *sondaggio Gallup 2007*

Project Info: *Intelligence in Lifestyle*, magazine article, 2010, Italy
Data Source: IUCN Red List 2008; Global Biodiversity Outlook; WWF; *Nature*: "Biodiversity: Extinction by Numbers"
Research: Daniele Lorenzetti
Design / Art Direction: Francesco Franchi
Illustration: Laura Cattaneo

IL
PERDITA HABITAT
– La deforestazione e la riduzione di habitat strangolano la biodiversità.
SVILUPPO AGRICOLO
– L'espansione di aree agricole causa la perdita di foreste e specie indigene.
CACCIA E PESCA
– Bracconaggio e traffico illegale di parti di animale sono una piaga globale.
ffrono le rane
LUPO ITALICO
is lupus italicus
esemplare di successo delle
egie di tutela, il lupo è tornato a
lare gli Appennini e vaste aree
pee. Il bracconaggio è stata
ma minaccia per la specie.
C PELOBATE FOSCO
Pelobates fuscus insubricus
La sottospecie del pelobate italico, tipica della Pianura padana, soffre come molti altri anfibi la distruzione di habitat umidi e viene predata da specie introdotte artificialmente quali tartarughe e rane toro.
3 Asia – Là dove regnavano le tigri
A TIGRE
Panthera tigris
È la specie simbolo della lotta per la biodiversità: ne restano 3mila esemplari adulti. Estinte tre delle nove sottospecie. Una curiosità: il 2010, secondo il calendario cinese, è proprio il suo anno.
B PANDA GIGANTE
Ailuropoda melanoleuca
La popolazione totale si attesta tra i mille e i duemila individui. È giudicato "in pericolo di estinzione". Le minacce: distruzione dell'habitat e caccia per la preziosa pelle.
C ANTILOPE TIBETANA
Pantholops hodgsonii
La popolazione di questa specie che vive sugli altopiani del Tibet si attesta sui 100mila capi. Viene cacciata per la fine lana, lo shatoosh. Le corna sono utilizzate nella medicina cinese.
rismatiche"
LEONE
hera leo
areale, un tempo esteso
ra Eurasia, si è ridotto all'Africa
hariana. L'Iucn lo considera
rabile": la sua riduzione
cia l'equilibrio dell'ecosistema.
C ELEFANTE AFRICANO
Loxodonta africana
Gli esperti ne stimano in natura circa 400mila esemplari rispetto agli 1,3 milioni degli anni Settanta. Il bracconaggio per commercio di avorio mostra una recrudescenza.
5 Oceania – Se cambia la geografia degli atolli
A CORALLI
Scleractinia
L'ordine comprende 26 famiglie. Il degrado della Grande barriera minaccia un intero ecosistema: pesci, molluschi, cavallucci marini. Effetti anche sulla geografia degli atolli.
B CASUARIO
Casuarius casuarius
Non solo i predatori, ma anche gli erbivori possono essere in pericolo: il casuario è fondamentale perché disperde, attraverso le feci, i semi delle piante di cui si nutre.
C DIAVOLO DELLA TASMANIA
Sarcophilus harrisii
Questo marsupiale, un tempo diffuso anche in Australia, vive oggi solo in Tasmania. In pericolo per la caccia e la diffusione del tumore facciale infettivo, è a rischio estinzione.
FONTI: Iucn Red List 2008; Global Biodiversity Outlook; WWF; Nature, Biodiversity: extinction by numbers | HA COLLABORATO – Prof. Maurizio Casiraghi (Università Milano Bicocca)
35

Help! Cries Noah

On the occasion of the 2010 International Year of Biodiversity, this double-spread surveyed the subject around the globe. Maps and diagrams on the left chart general facts concerning the richness of species – with a distribution world map, numbers of endangered species, an outlook to the future as well as in a historical chart covering 600 million years of evolution.

For five of the continents, more detailed information is set out. For each region, three examples of endangered animals are described. Icons indicate the reasons for their vulnerability, with all reasons explained at the top of the spread. The green line of text to the lower left reports that as of 2007, 34 % of Europeans had not even heard the term "biodiversity".

Aus Anlass des Internationalen Jahres der Artenvielfalt 2010 untersuchte diese doppelseitige Grafik das Thema Biodiversität auf der Erde. Auf der linken Seite zeigt eine Weltkarte die globale Verteilung der Arten, das Diagramm darunter repräsentiert die Anzahl gefährdeter Arten. Zwei weitere Diagramme zeigen einen Ausblick auf die Zukunft sowie eine Übersicht über 600 Millionen Jahre Evolutionsgeschichte.

Zu den fünf Kontinenten gibt es zusätzliche Informationen. Aus jeder Region werden drei Beispiele für gefährdete Arten beschrieben. Symbole erläutern den jeweiligen Grund für ihre Gefährdung, alle Gründe sind in einer Leiste oben auf der Doppelseite erklärt. In der grünen Textzeile unten links heißt es, dass 2007 insgesamt 34 % der Europäer den Begriff „Biodiversität" noch nicht kannten.

À l'occasion de l'Année internationale de la biodiversité 2010, cette double page analyse le sujet dans le monde entier. Les cartes et diagrammes de gauche présentent des informations générales sur la richesse des espèces – avec une carte de leur distribution dans le monde, les nombres d'espèces en voie d'extinction, une estimation de l'évolution de la situation, ainsi qu'un graphique chronologique qui couvre 600 millions d'années d'évolution.

Des informations plus détaillées sont présentées pour cinq continents. Trois exemples d'animaux en voie d'extinction sont décrits pour chaque région. Les icônes indiquent les raisons de leur vulnérabilité, qui sont expliquées en haut de la double page. La ligne de texte en vert en bas à gauche explique que, en 2007, 34 % des Européens n'avaient jamais entendu le terme « biodiversité ».

Historic Shift

Developed in the wake of the 2010 US mid-term elections, this map indicates the shift in votes for each individual district in the US, compared with the results of the 2008 elections. Shifts towards Republican votes are shown by red arrows pointing right, blue arrows to the left represent shifts towards Democrat votes.

The length of the vectors corresponds to the percentage points in voting results (cf. the legend to the right of the map). The motion visually implied in the arrows is a symbol for the political changes brought about by these shifts in voting results. The piece ran both in the printed edition of the *New York Times* as well as an interactive feature online.

Diese Karte entstand im Anschluss an die US-amerikanischen Wahlen 2010 und veranschaulicht die Veränderungen bei den Wählerstimmen im Vergleich zu den Wahlergebnissen von 2008. Gewinne der Republikaner sind durch rote, nach rechts weisende Pfeile dargestellt, die blauen, nach links weisenden Pfeile stellen Gewinne der Demokraten dar.

Die Länge der Pfeile entspricht der Prozentzahl der Stimmen (vgl. die Legende rechts der Karte). Die in den Vektoren visuell angedeutete Bewegung symbolisiert die politischen Veränderungen, die die Wahlergebnisse nach sich zogen. Die Grafik erschien sowohl in der gedruckten Ausgabe der *New York Times* als auch online als interaktives Feature.

Réalisée après les élections de milieu de mandat aux États-Unis en 2010, cette carte indique l'évolution des votes dans chaque district du pays par rapport aux résultats des élections de 2008. Les passages à un vote républicain sont représentés par des flèches rouges vers la droite, et les flèches bleues vers la gauche représentent les passages à un vote démocratique.

La longueur des vecteurs correspond aux points de pourcentage dans les résultats du vote (voir la légende à droite de la carte). Le mouvement visuel des flèches est un symbole des changements politiques causés par cette évolution des votes. Cette infographie a été publiée dans l'édition imprimée du *New York Times*, ainsi que sous forme de carte interactive sur le site web du journal.

Project Info: *The New York Times*, newspaper and online article, 2010, USA
Data Source: Associated Press; Dave Leip's Atlas of US Presidential Elections; Edison / Mitofsky Exit Polls
Design: Amanda Cox, Kevin Quealy, Amy Schoenfeld, Archie Tse
Graphics Director: Steve Duenes
Deputy Graphics Director: Matt Ericson

Districts Acro

In a sign of discontent with th

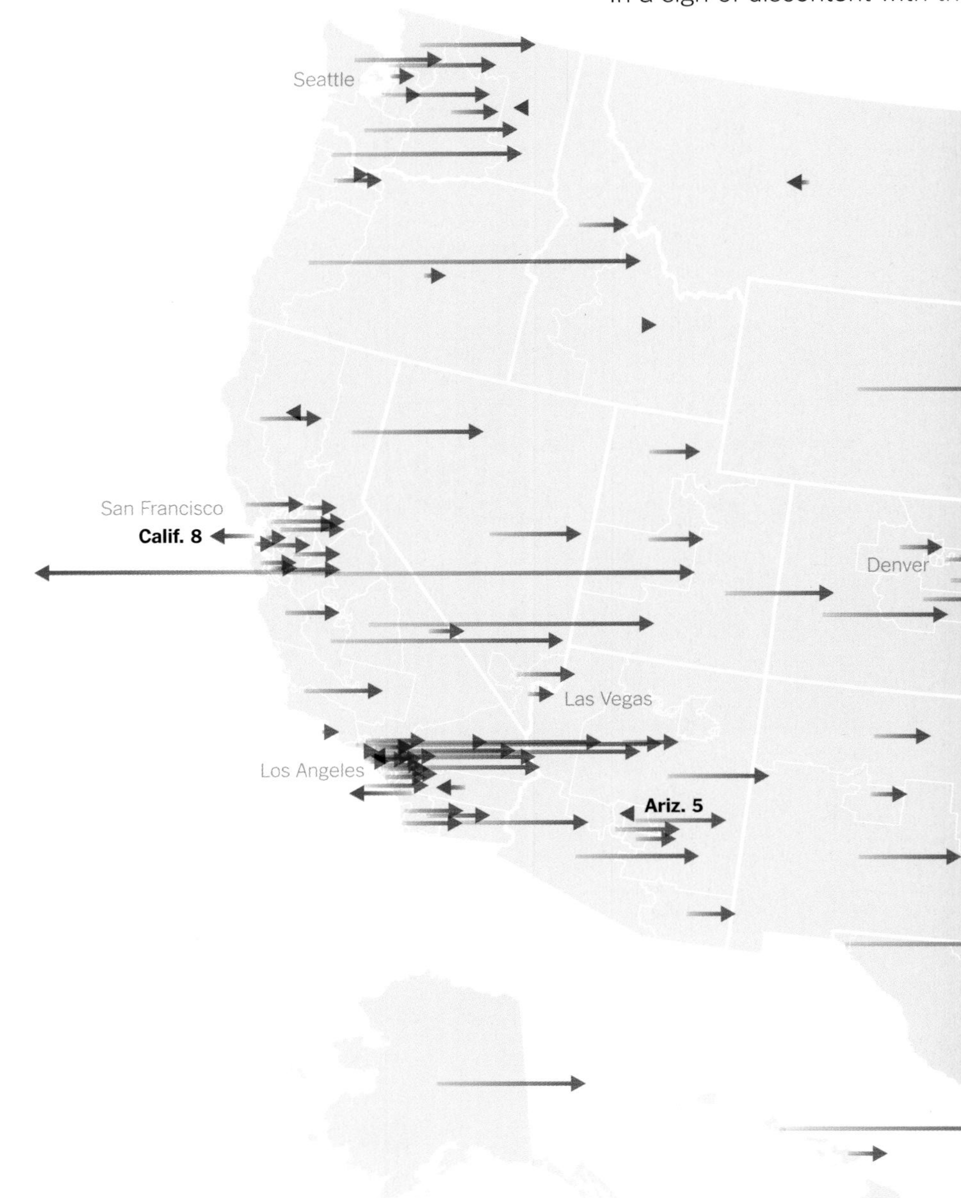

While Republicans increased their share of the vote in **California 8**, Nancy Pelosi's lead still increased in the absence of a strong third-party candidate.

Arizona 5 shifted right about 20 points — enough to switch the seat to Republicans. David Schweikert defeated the Democrat he lost to in 2008.

The
abou
Here
distr
perc

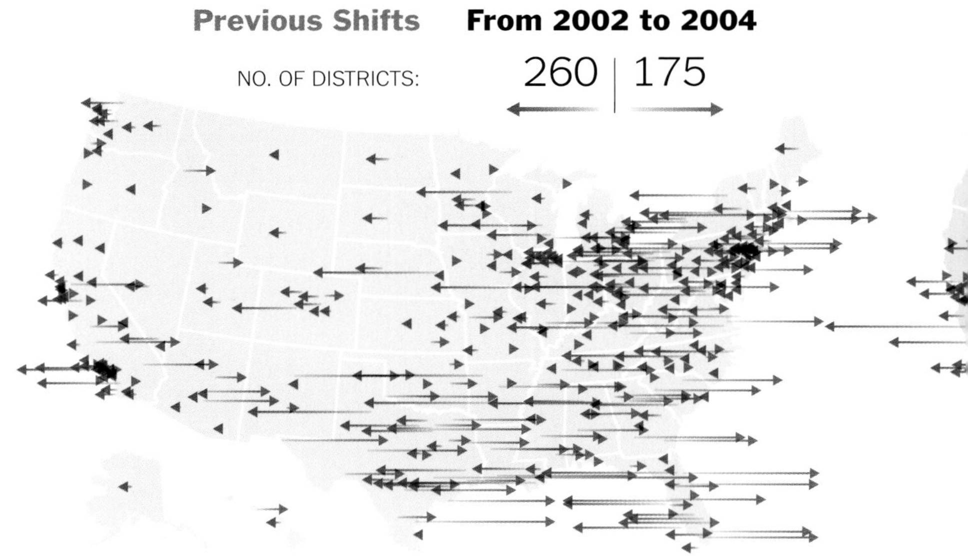

With President George W. Bush up for his second term in a close race against John Kerry, most districts voted more Democratic.

he Country Shift to the Right

ɔwer, 9 of every 10 House districts voted more Republican than they did in 2008.

The length of each arrow represents how much the vote in that House district shifted from 2008 to 2010.

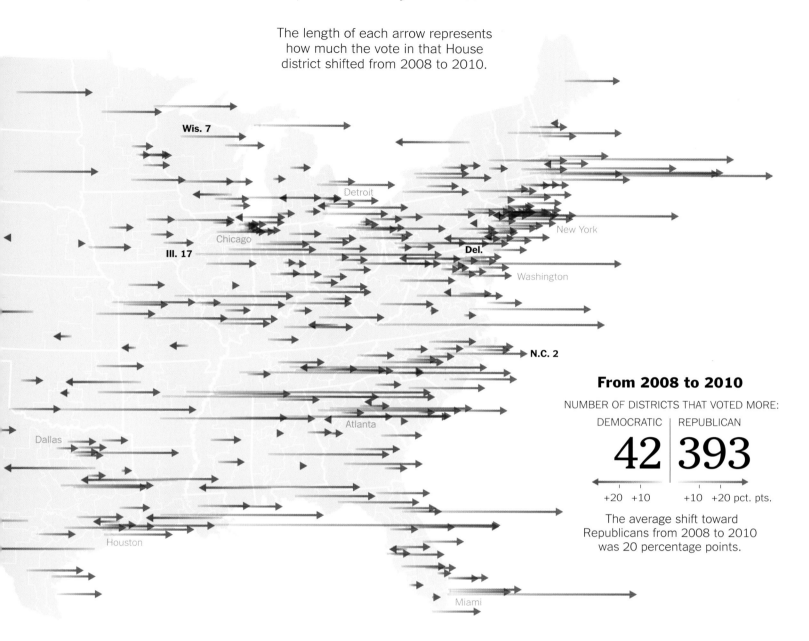

Wis. 7

Detroit

New York

Chicago

Ill. 17

Del.

Washington

N.C. 2

Atlanta

Dallas

Houston

Miami

From 2008 to 2010

NUMBER OF DISTRICTS THAT VOTED MORE:

DEMOCRATIC	REPUBLICAN
42	393
+20 +10	+10 +20 pct. pts.

The average shift toward Republicans from 2008 to 2010 was 20 percentage points.

:onsin 7 was
ɔr an open race.
ıffy, a Republican
won by 8
ts.

One of the largest shifts was in **Illinois 17**, where Republican Bobby Schilling, a pizza business owner, beat Phil Hare, a two-term Democratic incumbent.

Only a few districts voted more Democratic. In **Delaware**, the shift helped John Carney defeat Glen Urquhart for the seat held by Michael N. Castle since 1993.

Renee Ellmers delivered one of the Republican Party's narrowest gains in **North Carolina 2**, a district that Democrats won by 36 percentage points in 2008.

From 2004 to 2006

353 | 82

From 2006 to 2008

245 | 190

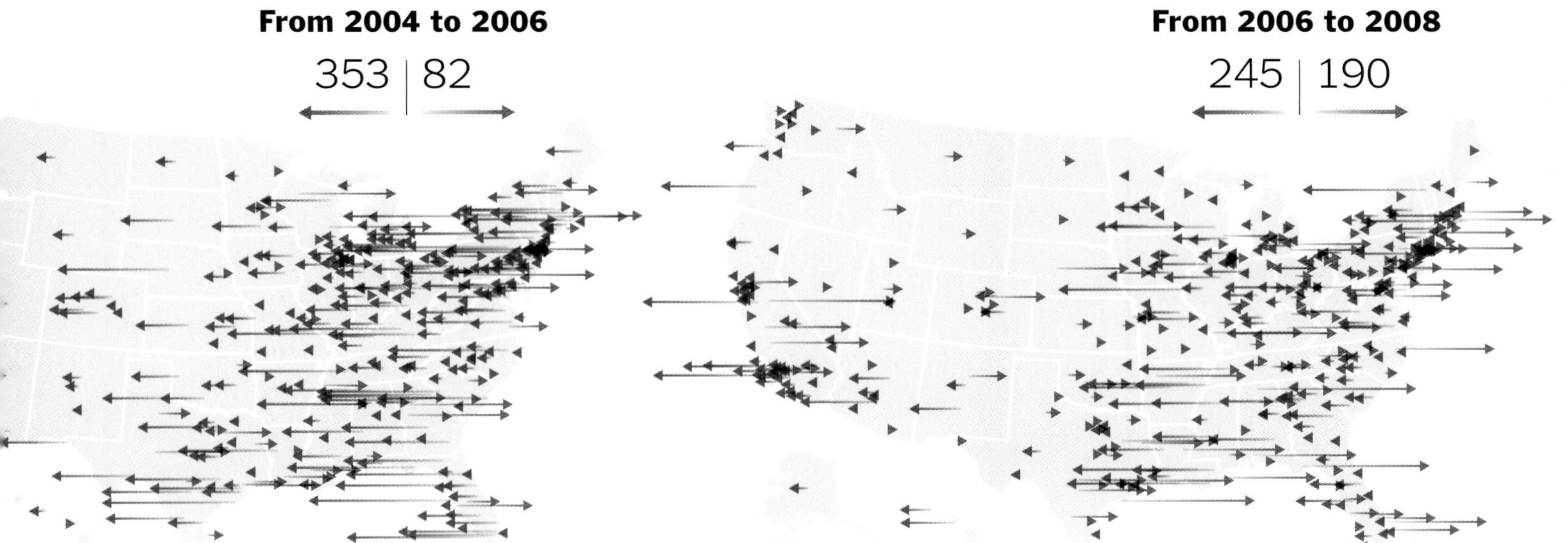

ɜnt with President Bush, the war in Iraq and the
ng of Hurricane Katrina helped the Democrats
take control of the House and Senate.

A majority of districts, riding the wave of Barack Obama's campaign, moved toward the Democrats, but the shift was less widespread than in 2006.

26 • • The Guardian | Saturday December 15 2007 The Guardian | Saturday

Climate change

Hot spots – the carbon atlas

This week's Bali meeting highlighted just how difficult it will be to secure an international agreement to reduce greenhouse gas levels by enough to save the earth from catastrophic temperature rises. This map, showing countries according to their emissions, shows why an international deal is needed – and why only one binding the big polluters can succeed

1 United States
5,957
million tonnes of carbon dioxide

7 Canada 631.26

16 Mexico 398.25

These latest UN figures for climate change emissions are from 2005, but are already dated. Reliable, but provisional estimates for 2006 by Dutch government researchers suggest China's CO2 emissions increased by 9% in 2006 and have now overtaken the US emissions, which declined by 1.4% in 2006. US emissions per person are nearly three times as great as Chinese

29 Venezuela

18 Brazil 360.57

30 Argentina

Europe

4.67bn tonnes of CO2

9% growth in carbon emissions, 1995-2005

For the first time, there is hard scientific evidence of climate change affecting Europe, said the Intergovernmental Panel on Climate Change recently. Freak weather events, such as the heatwaves of 2003, will become ever more common

6 Germany 844.17

23 Netherlands

21 Poland

8 United Kingdom 577.17

13 France 415.27

10 Italy 466.64

17 Spain 387.11

25 Turkey

20 Ukra[ine] 342.5[7]

North America

6.99bn tonnes of CO2

14% growth in carbon emissions, 1995-2005

The US as a major producer of greenhouse gases has been reluctant to accept that man-made climate change even existed – and refused to accept the Kyoto protocol. But freak weather events and an avalanche of scientific evidence have forced it to rethink its position

Central & South America

1.10bn tonnes of CO2

29% growth in carbon emissions, 1995-2005

Increased freak weather events mean the IPCC is concerned South America will be hard-hit by climate change. Agriculture, water supplies and the unique natural habitat could be affected by a temperature increase of up to 4C by the end of the century

27 Egypt

12 South Africa 423.81

Africa

1.04bn tonnes of CO2

28% growth in carbon emissions, 1995-2005

Its carbon emissions may be small but this is the continent most vulnerable to the effects of climate change, hitting food and water supplies, causing coastal flooding and an increase in tropical diseases such as malaria – as well as destroying parts of the ecosystem

14 Saudi Arabia 412.35

Middle Ea[st]

1.45bn tonnes of CO2

62% growth in carbon er[missions]

The region is a major cont[ributor to] global greenhouse gas em[issions] through an oil and gas ind[ustry that] produces over 30 percent [of] supply and over 10 percen[t]

CO2 emission growth of the highest 20 emitters, 1995 to 2005

China	87%
Saudi Arabia	76%
Iran	73%
Indonesia	69%
Spain	56%
Australia	43%
India	35%
South Korea	32%
Brazil	26%
Mexico	25%
Canada	25%
South Africa	23%
Japan	14%
US	13%
France	12%
Italy	9%
Russia	5%
UK	4%
Germany	-4%
Ukraine	-18%

Highest per person C[O2]

Top twenty plus UK, 20[05]

Qatar	61.94
Bahrain	36.58
Trinid[ad] & Toba[go]	35.5

The carbon list

Rank	Country	Tonnes per person	Million tonnes CO_2
North America			
1	United States	20.14	5,956.98
7	Canada	19.24	631.26
16	Mexico	3.75	398.25
176	Bermuda	9.53	0.62
207	St Pierre & Miquelon	11.85	0.08
Central & South America			
18	Brazil	1.94	360.57
29	Venezuela	5.99	151.29
30	Argentina	3.71	146.64
48	Chile	4.14	66.19
53	Colombia	1.36	58.80
67	Puerto Rico	9.97	39.02
69	Trinidad & Tobago	35.51	38.18
73	Cuba	2.91	32.98
74	Peru	1.12	31.31
77	Ecuador	1.79	23.90
83	Dominican Republic	1.95	17.77
88	Virgin Islands, U.S.	147.68	16.05
89	Panama	4.56	14.33
94	Bolivia	1.35	11.96
96	Jamaica	4.22	11.55
97	Netherlands Antilles	50.20	11.05
98	Guatemala	0.90	10.96
108	Honduras	0.99	7.13
113	El Salvador	0.92	6.16
114	Uruguay	1.75	6.01
115	Costa Rica	1.42	5.69
126	Nicaragua	0.79	4.30
127	The Bahamas	13.46	4.06
131	Paraguay	0.61	3.85
145	Martinique	NA	2.29
148	Guadeloupe	NA	2.02
150	Suriname	4.04	1.86
151	Haiti	0.21	1.75
153	Guyana	2.07	1.58
154	Barbados	5.16	1.44
163	French Guiana	NA	1.04
164	Aruba	10.46	1.01
166	Belize	3.32	0.93
179	Antigua and Barbuda	8.53	0.59
183	Cayman Islands	8.68	0.38
185	St Lucia	2.22	0.37
192	Grenada	2.71	0.24
193	Antarctica	NA	0.24
195	St Vincent/Grenadines	1.70	0.20
200	Saint Kitts & Nevis	3.42	0.13
202	Dominica	1.54	0.11
206	Virgin Islands, UK	3.87	0.09
208	Montserrat	7.42	0.07
210	Falkland Islands	NA	0.04
212	Turks & Caicos Is	0.60	0.01
Europe			
6	Germany	10.24	844.17
8	United Kingdom	9.55	577.17
10	Italy	8.03	466.64
13	France	6.59	415.27
17	Spain	9.60	387.11
21	Poland	7.38	284.64
23	Netherlands	16.44	269.66
25	Turkey	3.30	230.04
32	Belgium	13.10	135.81
36	Czech Republic	11.02	112.83
38	Greece	9.67	103.16
39	Romania	4.45	99.34
43	Austria	9.55	78.17
50	Portugal	6.15	64.97
52	Hungary	5.98	59.84
54	Sweden	6.53	58.77
57	Serbia & Montenegro	4.85	52.56
58	Norway	11.40	52.35
59	Finland	10.00	52.25
60	Denmark	9.38	50.96
61	Bulgaria	6.78	50.54
64	Switzerland	6.13	45.92
65	Ireland	10.98	44.10
71	Slovakia	6.99	37.81
79	Croatia	4.77	21.46
84	Bosnia & Herzegovina	3.94	17.45
86	Slovenia	8.34	16.77
92	Luxembourg	26.79	12.55
102	Cyprus	11.30	8.81
104	Macedonia	3.94	8.05
124	Albania	1.22	4.35
125	Gibraltar	155.76	4.34
132	Iceland	10.74	3.19
133	Malta	7.59	3.02
174	Faroe Islands	14.54	0.68
178	Greenland	10.47	0.59
Eurasia			
3	Russia	11.88	1,696.00
20	Ukraine	7.30	342.57
26	Kazakhstan	13.04	198.01
35	Uzbekistan	4.39	117.97
51	Belarus	6.26	61.41
63	Turkmenistan	10.06	49.64
72	Azerbaijan	4.62	37.03
81	Estonia	14.17	18.89
90	Lithuania	3.87	13.94
101	Armenia	3.27	9.61
103	Latvia	3.66	8.39
106	Tajikistan	1.06	7.20
107	Moldova	1.95	7.16
118	Kyrgyzstan	1.03	5.28
121	Georgia	1.01	4.72
Middle East			
11	Iran	6.96	450.68
14	Saudi Arabia		
31	United ArabEmirates		
40	Iraq		
45	Kuwait		
49	Israel		
56	Qatar		
62	Syria		
75	Oman		
76	Bahrain		
82	Jordan		
85	Yemen		
87	Lebanon		
Africa			
12	South Africa		
27	Egypt		
37	Nigeria		
41	Algeria		
55	Libya		
68	Morocco		
78	Tunisia		
80	Angola		
95	Zimbabwe		

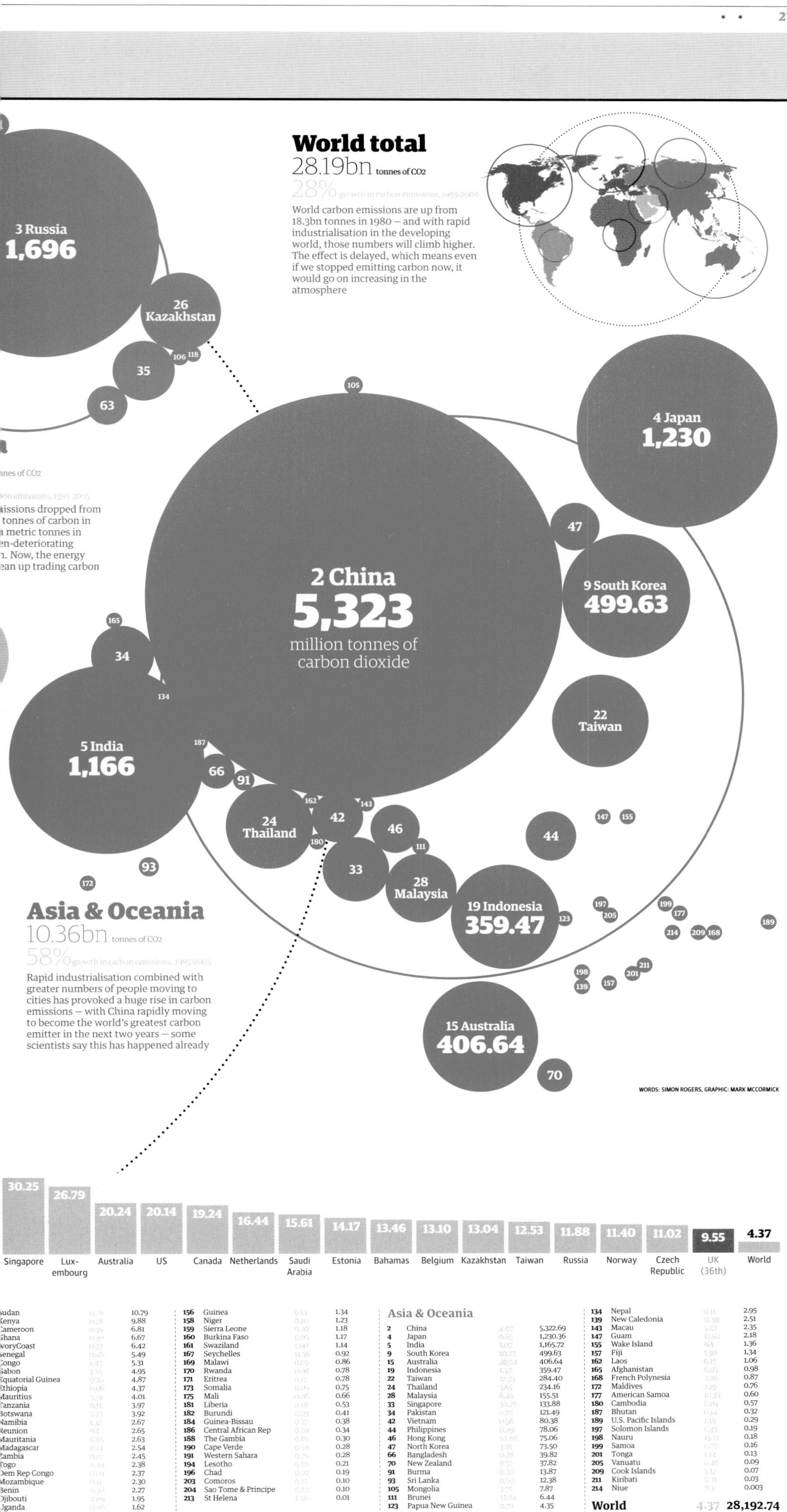
27
World total
28.19bn tonnes of CO2
28%
World carbon emissions are up from 18.3bn tonnes in 1980 – and with rapid industrialisation in the developing world, those numbers will climb higher. The effect is delayed, which means even if we stopped emitting carbon now, it would go on increasing in the atmosphere
3 Russia 1,696
26 Kazakhstan
2 China 5,323 million tonnes of carbon dioxide
4 Japan 1,230
9 South Korea 499.63
22 Taiwan
5 India 1,166
24 Thailand
28 Malaysia
19 Indonesia 359.47
15 Australia 406.64
Asia & Oceania
10.36bn tonnes of CO2
58%
Rapid industrialisation combined with greater numbers of people moving to cities has provoked a huge rise in carbon emissions – with China rapidly moving to become the world's greatest carbon emitter in the next two years – some scientists say this has happened already
WORDS: SIMON ROGERS, GRAPHIC: MARK MCCORMICK
30.25 Singapore
26.79 Luxembourg
20.24 Australia
20.14 US
19.24 Canada
16.44 Netherlands
15.61 Saudi Arabia
14.17 Estonia
13.46 Bahamas
13.10 Belgium
13.04 Kazakhstan
12.53 Taiwan
11.88 Russia
11.40 Norway
11.02 Czech Republic
9.55 UK (36th)
4.37 World
World 28,192.74

Hot Spots – the Carbon Atlas

In a cross between a hierarchy and a world map, this piece visualises how much each country produces in carbon dioxide emissions from the consumption of energy. Countries are represented by a circle, scaled according to how many tons of CO_2 they emit. All the circles are placed on the map according to their location in the world.

Bar charts along the bottom indicate for selected countries how much emissions have grown since 1995 (left) and how much CO_2 is emitted per capita (right). Since this graphic appeared in 2007, new figures from the US Energy Information Administration show that China has become the biggest emitter.

In ihrer Mischung aus Hierarchie und Weltkarte veranschaulicht diese Grafik, wie viel Kohlenstoffdioxid jedes Land durch seinen Energieverbrauch erzeugt. Kreise symbolisieren die Länder, ihre Größe entspricht der Menge des CO_2-Ausstoßes in Tonnen. Die Kreise sind entsprechend der Lage der Länder auf der Weltkarte angeordnet.

Balkendiagramme am unteren Bildrand zeigen für ausgewählte Länder den Anstieg des CO_2-Ausstoßes seit 1995 (links) sowie den CO_2-Ausstoß pro Kopf (rechts). Die Grafik entstand 2007, neuere Zahlen der US Energy Information Administration ergaben, dass mittlerweile China der größte CO_2-Erzeuger ist.

Ce croisement entre carte hiérarchique et du monde représente les émissions de dioxyde de carbone de chaque pays à partir de sa consommation d'énergie. Les pays sont représentés par un cercle, dont la taille correspond au nombre de tonnes de CO_2 émises. Tous les cercles sont situés sur la carte en fonction de leur emplacement dans le monde.

Les graphiques à barres du bas indiquent la croissance des émissions depuis 1995 (à gauche) et la quantité de CO_2 émise par habitant (à droite) pour certains pays. Depuis que cette illustration a été publiée en 2007, de nouveaux chiffres de l'Administration américaine de l'information sur l'énergie montrent que la Chine est devenue le plus grand émetteur de CO_2.

Project Info: *The Guardian*, newspaper article, 2007, UK
Research: Simon Rogers
Design: Mark McCormick
Art Direction: Michael Robinson

How the World Feels about Green Brands

Many consumers today are keen to support companies that show social and ecological responsibility. This diagram was developed by Column Five as part of *GOOD* magazine's Transparency series. It highlights how people in several leading countries feel about the economy and environment. The data visualised are based upon responses to a series of survey questions.

The heights of the bars correspond to the percentage of respondents, and thus shows the very high concern Brazilians have for the environment, whereas the majority of people in the US are more worried about the economy. The tiny rockets indicate how positively people estimate the state of the environment, with China clearly leading there.

Heute unterstützen viele Käufer bevorzugt Unternehmen, die sich ihrer gesellschaftlichen und ökologischen Verantwortung bewusst sind. Dieses Diagramm, das Column Five als Teil der „Transparency"-Serie in der Zeitschrift *GOOD* gestaltete, veranschaulicht die Haltung der Bewohner mehrerer führender Nationen zu Wirtschaft und Umwelt. Die visualisierten Daten beruhen auf Umfrageergebnissen.

Die Balkenhöhe gibt die Prozentzahl der Befragten wieder. Man erkennt das große Umweltbewusstsein der Brasilianer, während sich in den USA die Mehrzahl eher Sorgen um die Wirtschaft macht. Die kleinen Raketen zeigen an, wie positiv die Befragten den Zustand ihrer Umwelt einschätzen; hier ist eindeutig China führend.

Aujourd'hui, de nombreux consommateurs soutiennent volontiers les entreprises qui font preuve de responsabilité sociale et écologique. Ce diagramme a été mis au point par Column Five dans le cadre de la série Transparency du magazine *GOOD*. Il révèle les sentiments du public envers l'économie et l'environnement dans plusieurs grands pays. Les données représentées se basent sur les réponses à un questionnaire.

La hauteur des barres correspond au pourcentage de répondants, et montre donc que les Brésiliens sont très intéressés par l'environnement, alors qu'aux États-Unis la plupart des gens sont plus préoccupés par l'économie. Les petites fusées indiquent dans quelle mesure les gens ont une évaluation positive de l'état de l'environnement. Ici, la Chine est clairement en tête.

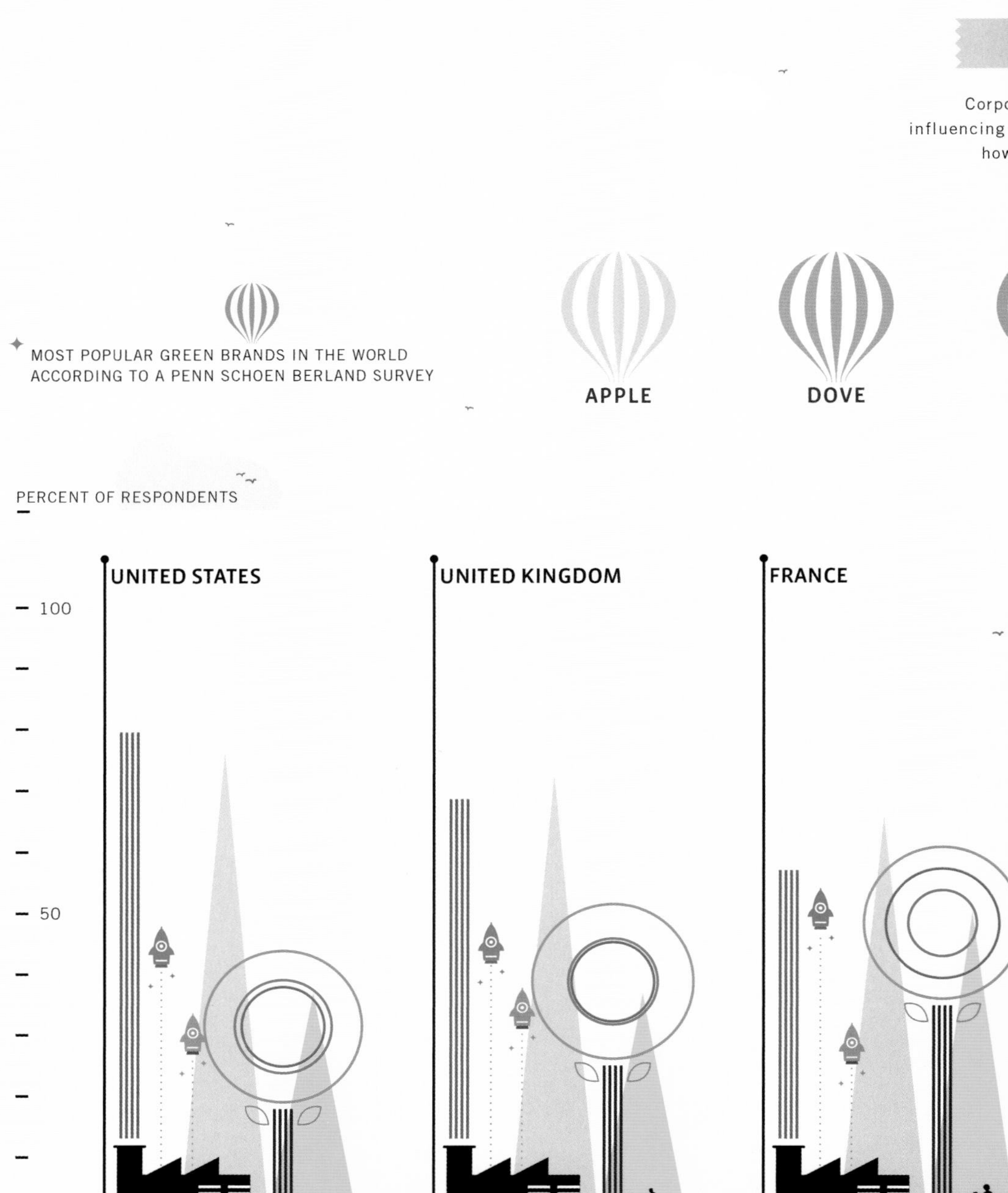

Data based on survey responses of consumers from the eight countries

Project Info: *GOOD*, website, 2010, USA
Data Source: Cohn & Wolfe; Esty Environmental Partners; Landor; Penn Schoen Berland
Research: Colin Dobrin
Design: Andrew Effendy (Column Five Media)
Art Direction: Ross Crooks

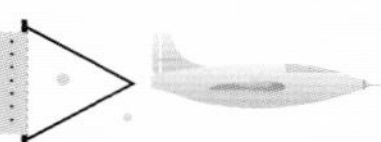

WORLD FEELS ABOUT GREEN BRANDS

consciousness has become an issue of increasing concern in our society, rception of a company, but also consumers' buying habits. Here we take stock of loping around the world, and which popular brands are on the forefront.

SOURCE:

Cohn & Wolfe
Esty Environmental Partners
Landor
Penn Schoen Berland

IKEA

MICROSOFT

NIVEA

NOKIA

TOYOTA

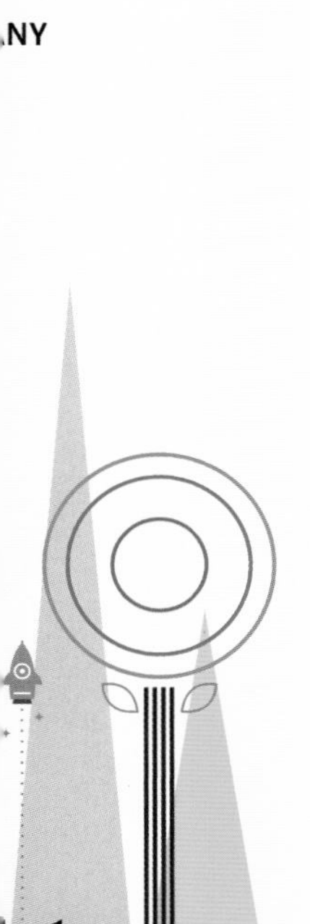

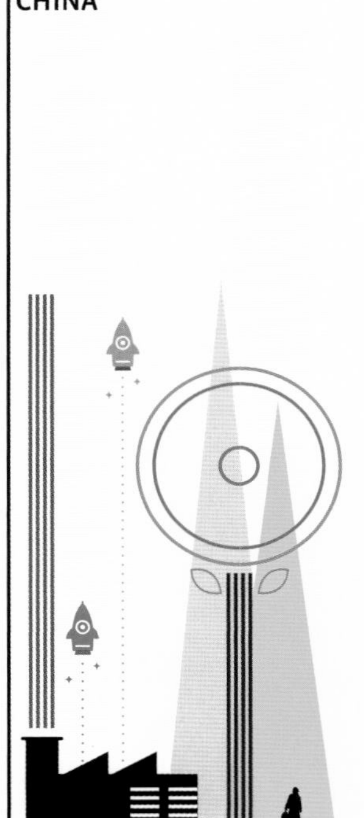

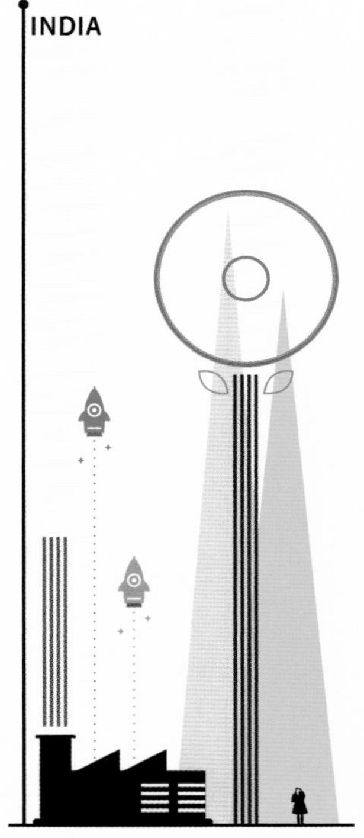

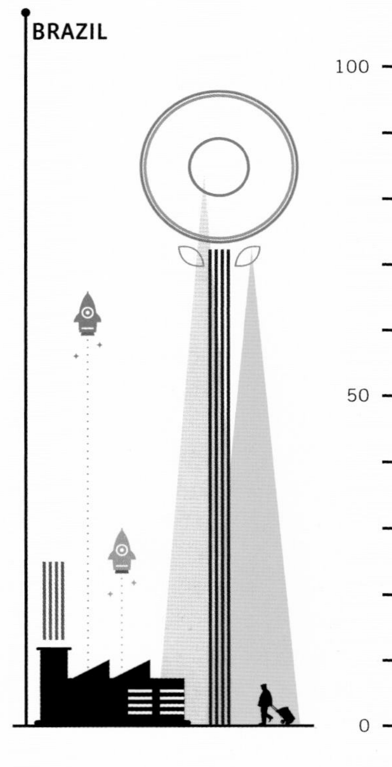

OMPANIES

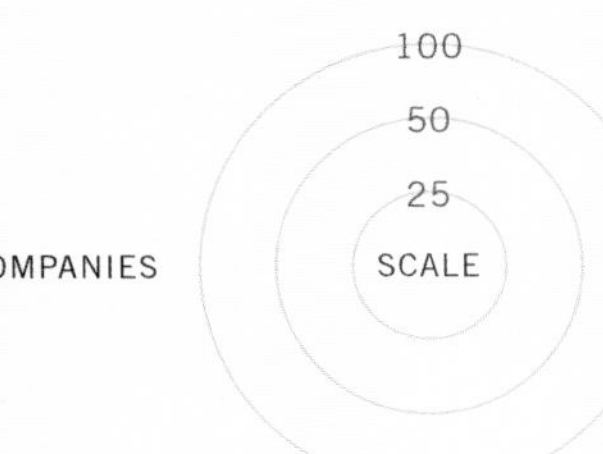

SENTIMENTS ABOUT THE DIRECTION OF THE ENVIRONMENT

MOST IMPORTANT THINGS FOR A COMPANY TO OFFER

GOOD VALUE
TRUSTWORTHINESS
ENVIRONMENTAL CONSCIOUSNESS

a collaboration between GOOD and COLUMN FIVE

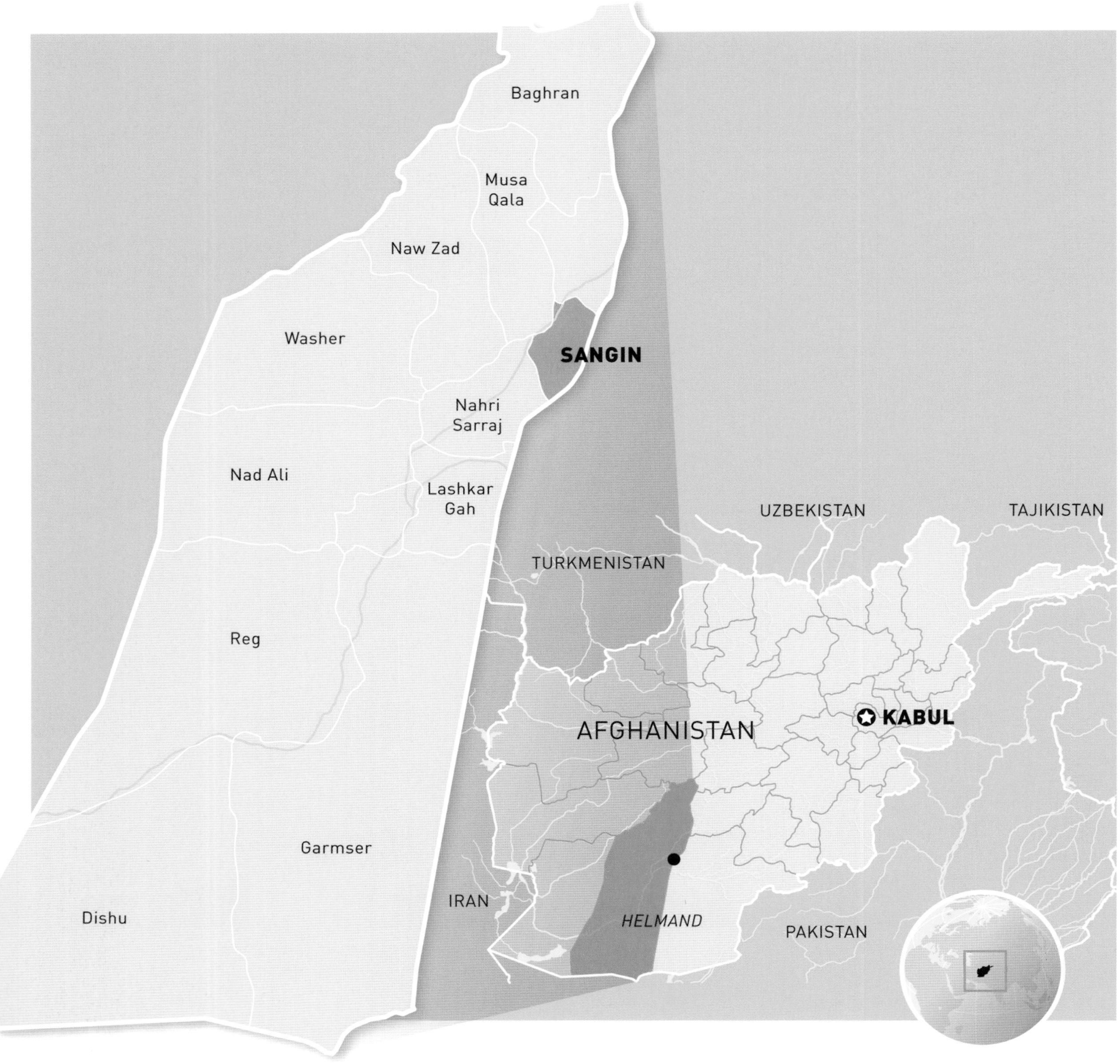

Improvised Explosive Devices

Sangin in the province of Helmand has been one of the most hard-fought areas in the Afghanistan war. British troops who have been stationed in the region from 2006–2010 experienced the fighting as the most brutal they have been involved in since the Korean War. This series of graphics explains roadside bombs, a weapon frequently used against the coalition troops in the area.

One graphic shows the device, while another explains the setting: how bombs are placed and detonated in the road. A schematic shows the Dragon Runner, a small robot deployed for the reconnaissance of unsecured territory. The motion sequence along the bottom elucidates how it removes explosive devices. The soldier silhouette in the background points up the small size of the robot.

Sangin in der Provinz Helmand gehört im Afghanistankrieg zu den heftig umkämpften Gebieten. Britische Truppen, die zwischen 2006 und 2010 in der Region stationiert waren, erlebten die Kämpfe als die brutalsten seit dem Koreakrieg. Diese Grafiken erläutern die Funktionsweise von unkonventionellen Spreng- oder Brandvorrichtungen, wie sie vielfach gegen die dort stationierten ISAF-Soldaten eingesetzt werden.

Eine Grafik zeigt die Sprengvorrichtung, eine andere erläutert den Ablauf: wie die Bomben auf die Strasse gelegt und gezündet werden. Auf einer schematischen Zeichnung ist der sogenannte Dragon Runner zu sehen, ein kleiner Roboter zur Erkundung ungesicherten Terrains. Die Bilderfolge am unteren Bildrand veranschaulicht, wie er Sprengvorrichtungen entfernt. Die Silhouette des Soldaten unterstreicht, wie klein der Roboter ist.

Sangin, dans la province de Helmand, a été l'une des régions où les combats ont été les plus violents lors de la guerre d'Afghanistan. Les troupes britanniques postées dans la région de 2006 à 2010 y ont vécu les affrontements les plus terribles depuis la guerre de Corée. Cette série d'illustrations explique le fonctionnement des bombes artisanales, une arme fréquemment utilisée contre les troupes de la coalition dans la région.

L'une des illustrations montre l'engin, et une autre explique la mise en place : comment les bombes sont positionnées et comment on les fait exploser sur la route. Un schéma montre le Dragon Runner, un petit robot déployé pour la reconnaissance des terrains non sécurisés. Dans le bas, la séquence d'animation explique comment ce robot ramasse les engins explosifs. La silhouette de soldat au deuxième plan souligne la petite taille du robot.

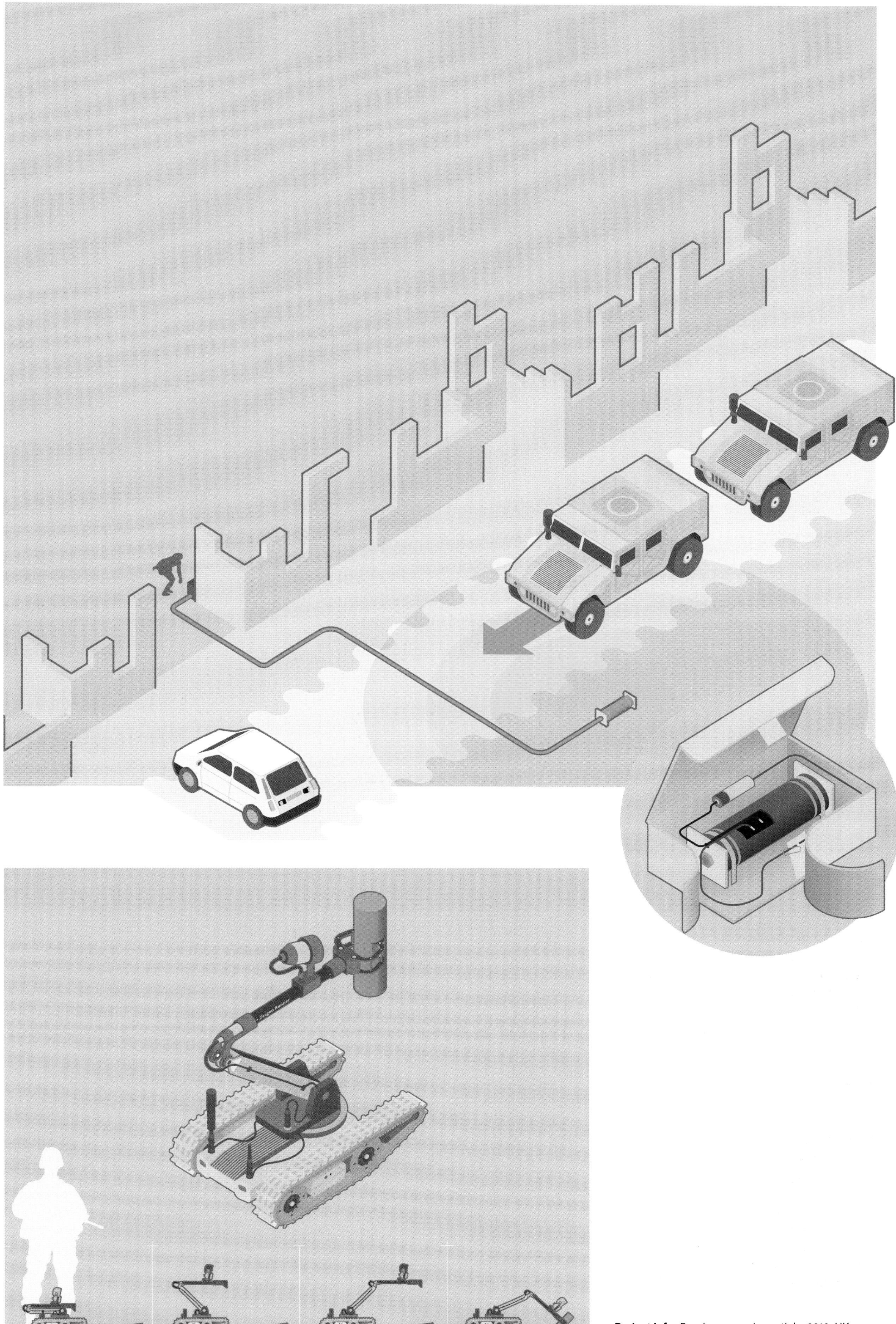

Project Info: *Esquire*, magazine article, 2010, UK
Design: Infomen

It's the Bike that Makes the World Go Round

This circle diagram looks at the use and production of bicycles around the world. The centre is occupied by a map of the northern hemisphere, with three wings swung outwards. Selected countries are marked on this map with circles, figures indicating the number of bicycles produced in each one. Dark-green stripes show the number of bicycles exported.

Imports of bicycles are shown with light-green stripes. The map is surrounded by small notes explaining local policy towards upgrading the bicycle traffic infrastructure in various countries. The chart on the left compares global production figures for cars and bikes, while the charts on the right give further key data for the Italian market.

Das Kreisdiagramm beschäftigt sich mit der weltweiten Benutzung und Produktion von Fahrrädern. Im Zentrum steht eine Karte der nördlichen Halbkugel, die zu drei Seiten hin ausgeklappt ist. Auf dieser Karte sind ausgewählte Länder durch Kreise hervorgehoben, in denen Zahlen auf die Anzahl der dort produzierten Fahrräder verweisen. Dunkelgrüne Kreisbalken repräsentieren die Zahl exportierter Räder.

Die Zahl der importierten Räder wird in hellgrünen Balken angegeben. Kleine Notizen rund um die Karte erläutern die politischen Bestrebungen in verschiedenen Ländern, um die Fahrradinfrastruktur zu verbessern. Das Diagramm links vergleicht die weltweiten Produktionszahlen von Autos und Fahrrädern, die Diagramme rechts zeigen Schlüsseldaten des italienischen Markts.

Ce diagramme circulaire analyse l'utilisation et la production de vélos dans le monde. Le centre est occupé par une carte de l'hémisphère nord, avec trois segments projetés sur les côtés. Certains pays comportent des cercles et des chiffres qui indiquent le nombre de vélos produits dans chaque pays. Les barres vert foncé représentent le nombre de vélos exportés.

Les importations de vélos sont illustrées par les barres vert clair. La carte est entourée de petites notes qui expliquent la politique locale concernant la mise à niveau de l'infrastructure pour la circulation des vélos dans différents pays. Le graphique de gauche compare les chiffres de la production mondiale de voitures et de vélos, et le graphique de droite détaille les données du marché italien.

Project Info: *Intelligence in Lifestyle*, magazine article, 2009, Italy
Data Source: Worldwatch Institute; Bike Europe; Global Insight; Bicycle Retailer & Industry News; Associazione Nazionale Ciclo Motociclo Accessori
Design: Francesco Franchi

Literary Madrid

This graphic shows a collection of literary quotes about the city of Madrid, taken from the works of famous Spanish and international writers. The circle represents an abstract map of the inner city, with Puerta del Sol in the centre, the Calle Gran Via floating as a grey streak up towards the top left and Parque del Retiro taking up most of the lower right side.

The quotes are allocated either to the place where the writer lived or to where the story took place, thus creating a net of literary references across the city.

Diese Grafik zeigt eine Sammlung literarischer Zitate über Madrid, die aus den Werken berühmter spanischer und internationaler Schriftsteller stammen. Der Kreis stellt einen abstrakten Stadtplan der Innenstadt dar, mit der Puerta del Sol in der Mitte. Die Calle Gran Via windet sich als grauer Streifen nach links oben, der Parque del Retiro nimmt den Großteil der rechten unteren Ecke ein.

Die Zitate stehen entweder dort, wo der Schriftsteller lebte, oder dort, wo die Handlung der jeweiligen Geschichte spielte; auf diese Weise entsteht ein Netz literarischer Verweise, das sich über die ganze Stadt zieht.

Cette image montre une collection de citations littéraires sur la ville de Madrid, tirées des œuvres d'écrivains célèbres espagnols et du monde entier. Le cercle représente une carte abstraite du centre-ville, avec la Puerta del Sol au milieu, la Calle Gran Via formant une veine grise qui remonte vers la gauche, et le Parque del Retiro qui occupe le côté inférieur droit.

Les citations sont affectées soit à l'endroit où l'écrivain a vécu, soit à l'endroit où l'histoire était située, ce qui crée un réseau de références littéraires sur toute la ville.

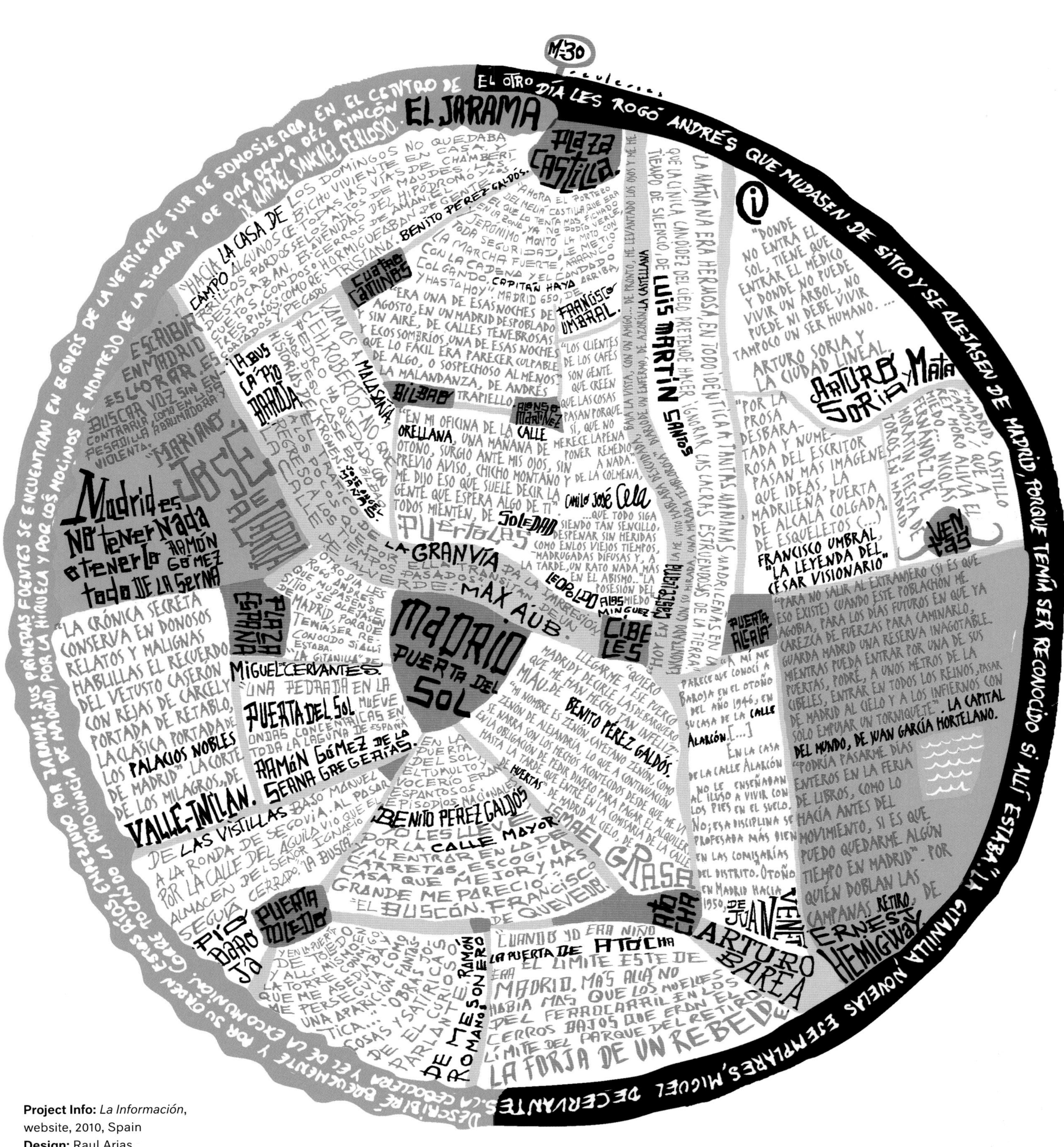

Project Info: *La Información*, website, 2010, Spain
Design: Raul Arias
Art Direction: Mario Tascon, Antonio Pasagali

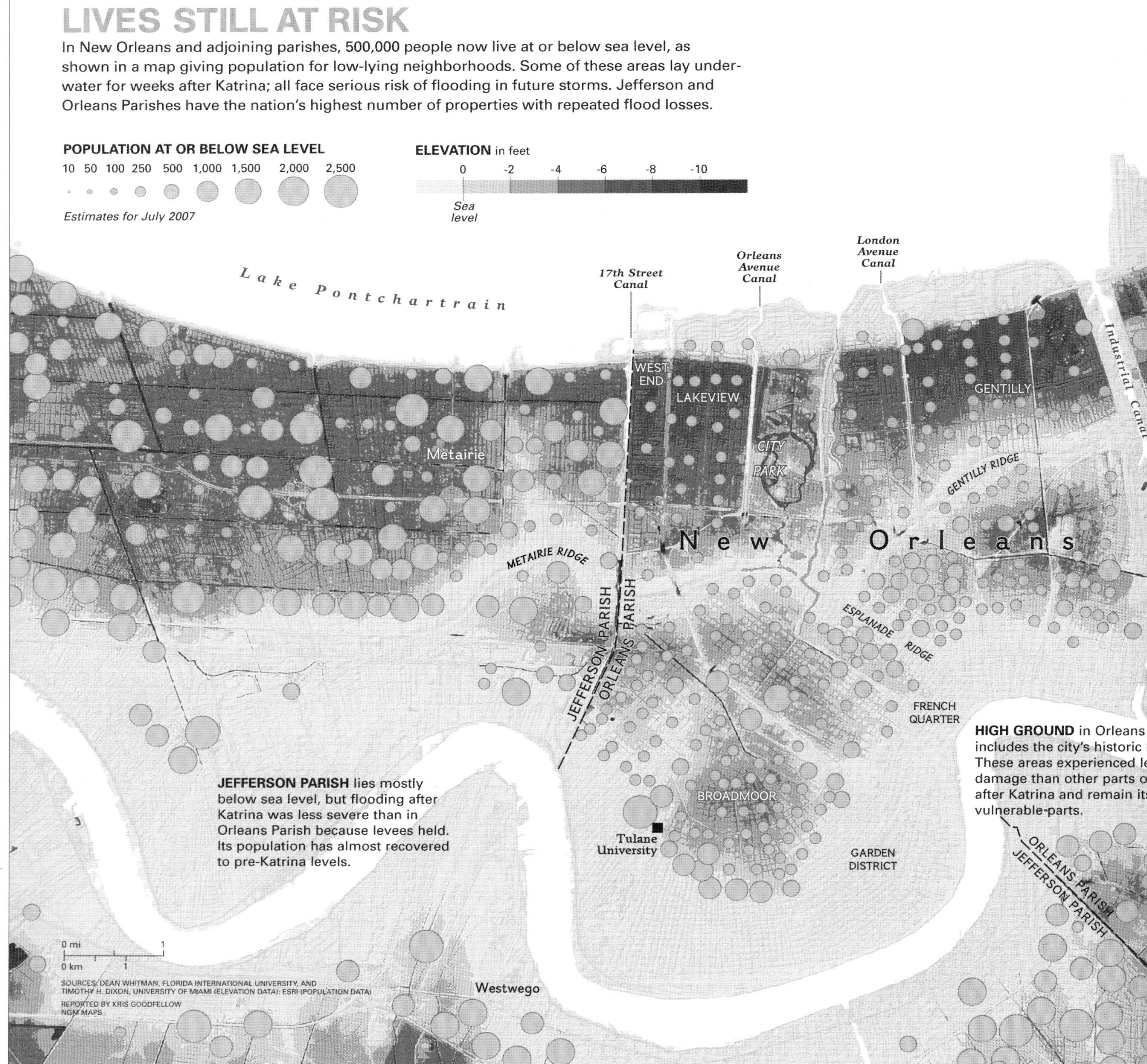
LIVES STILL AT RISK
In New Orleans and adjoining parishes, 500,000 people now live at or below sea level, as shown in a map giving population for low-lying neighborhoods. Some of these areas lay underwater for weeks after Katrina; all face serious risk of flooding in future storms. Jefferson and Orleans Parishes have the nation's highest number of properties with repeated flood losses.
POPULATION AT OR BELOW SEA LEVEL
10 50 100 250 500 1,000 1,500 2,000 2,500
Estimates for July 2007
ELEVATION in feet
0 -2 -4 -6 -8 -10
Sea level
Lake Pontchartrain
17th Street Canal
Orleans Avenue Canal
London Avenue Canal
Industrial Canal
WEST END
LAKEVIEW
GENTILLY
Metairie
CITY PARK
GENTILLY RIDGE
New Orleans
METAIRIE RIDGE
JEFFERSON PARISH
ORLEANS PARISH
ESPLANADE RIDGE
FRENCH QUARTER
HIGH GROUND in Orleans includes the city's historic These areas experienced le damage than other parts o after Katrina and remain its vulnerable parts.
JEFFERSON PARISH lies mostly below sea level, but flooding after Katrina was less severe than in Orleans Parish because levees held. Its population has almost recovered to pre-Katrina levels.
BROADMOOR
Tulane University
GARDEN DISTRICT
ORLEANS PARISH
JEFFERSON PARISH
0 mi 1
0 km 1
SOURCES: DEAN WHITMAN, FLORIDA INTERNATIONAL UNIVERSITY, AND TIMOTHY H. DIXON, UNIVERSITY OF MIAMI (ELEVATION DATA); ESRI (POPULATION DATA)
REPORTED BY KRIS GOODFELLOW
NGM MAPS
Westwego

Lives Still at Risk

This thematic map from 2007 looks at how many people living in New Orleans are exposed to the danger of flooding. After Hurricane Katrina devastated New Orleans in 2005, large parts of the city stood under water for weeks. The key part of the geographical data featured in this map is elevation – areas that are at or below sea level are marked in blue.

This geographical information is enriched with population data – yellow dots show where and how many people live below sea level and are thus greatly exposed to the danger of flooding in future storms.

Diese thematische Karte aus dem Jahr 2007 betrachtet, wie viele Einwohner von New Orleans der Gefahr einer Überschwemmung ausgesetzt sind. Nachdem der Wirbelsturm Katrina New Orleans 2005 zerstört hatte, waren große Teile der Stadt wochenlang überschwemmt. Die wichtigsten geografischen Daten dieser Karte sind die Höhenangaben; Regionen, die gleichauf mit oder unter dem Meeresspiegel liegen, sind blau gefärbt.

Diese geografische Information wird durch Bevölkerungsdaten ergänzt – gelbe Punkte zeigen an, wo und wie viele Menschen unter dem Meeresspiegel wohnen. Ihre Häuser sind bei künftigen Stürmen besonders von Überschwemmungen bedroht.

Cette carte thématique de 2007 révèle le nombre de personnes vivant à la Nouvelle-Orléans qui sont en situation de risque face au danger d'une inondation. Lorsque l'ouragan Katrina a dévasté la ville en 2005, de grandes parties de la ville sont restées sous l'eau pendant des semaines. Le principal élément des données géographiques de cette carte est l'altitude – les zones qui se trouvent au niveau de la mer ou en dessous sont identifiées en bleu.

Ces informations géographiques sont enrichies de données sur la population – les points jaunes montrent le nombre de personnes qui vivent sous le niveau de la mer, et courent donc un danger élevé dans l'éventualité d'une inondation.

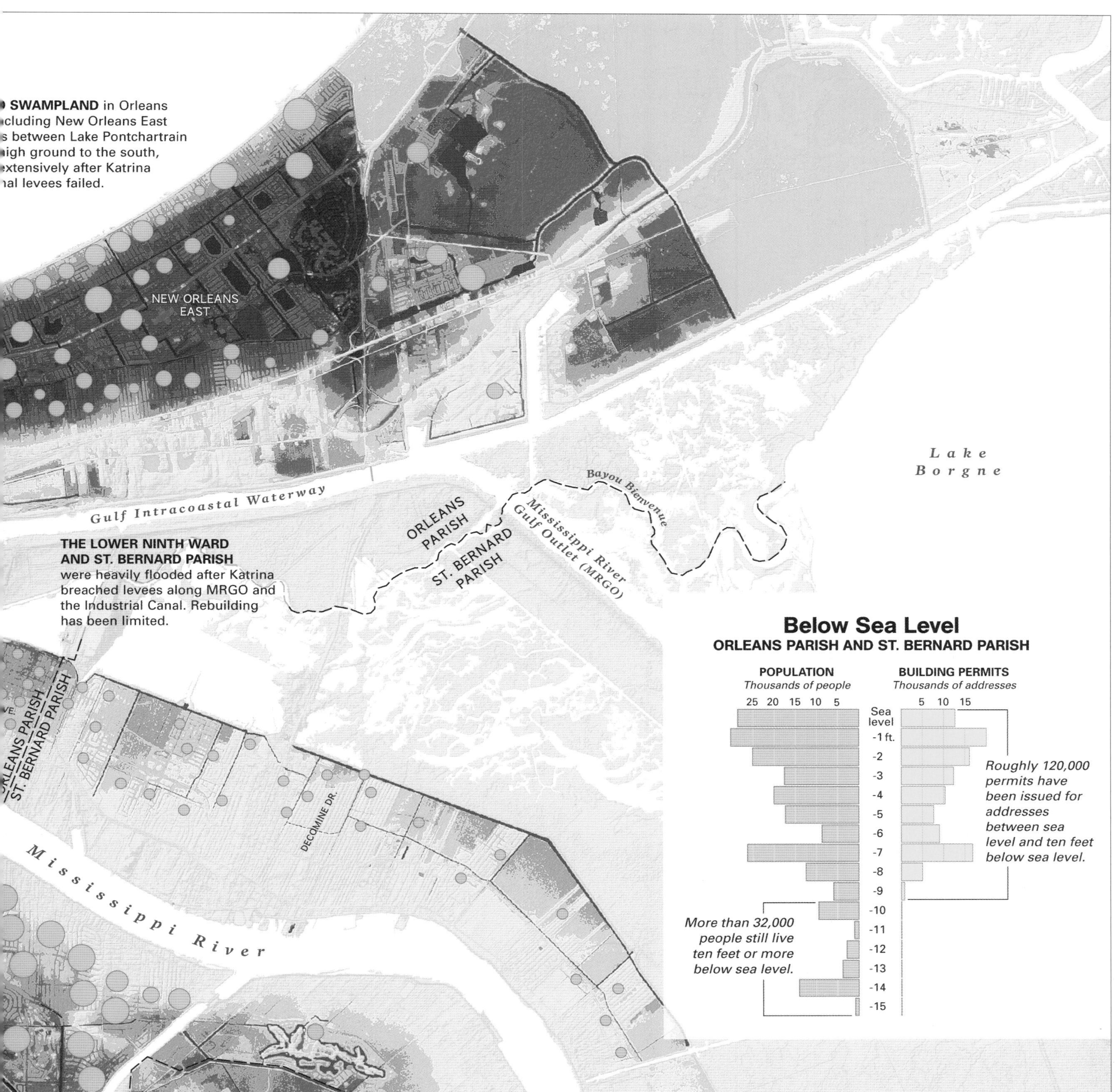

Project Info: *National Geographic*, magazine article, 2007, USA
Data Source: Dean Whitman (Florida International University); Timothy H. Dixon (University of Miami); ESRI
Research: Kris Goodfellow
Design: William McNulty
Art Direction: Charles M. Blow

Living Cartography

This interactive map enriches the bird's-eye view of a glacier landscape with various thematic layers. Created for a visitor centre in the Icelandic Vatnajökull National Park, it shows the area surrounding the Snæfell volcano. A topographical map of the region is projected on to a three-dimensional model of the landscape.

Visitors looking down on the map from above can examine further information layers relating to the flora, fauna or geology of the area. Reindeer paths or the distribution of rare plants become visible, changing with the seasons. As layers can be selected simultaneously, the visualised data become ever more qualified, showing for instance that the whooper swan nests only in areas where specific grass grows.

Diese interaktive Landkarte verbindet die Ansicht einer Gletscherlandschaft mit zusätzlichen thematischen Ebenen. Die Karte entstand für das Besucherzentrum im isländischen Nationalpark Vatnajökull und zeigt das Gebiet um den Vulkan Snæfell. Eine topografische Karte der Region wird auf ein dreidimensionales Landschaftsmodell projiziert.

Besucher, die die Landkarte aus der Vogelperspektive betrachten, können weitere Informationen zur regionalen Flora, Fauna und Geologie abrufen. So werden etwa die Wege der Rentiere oder die Verbreitung seltener Pflanzen sichtbar, sie verändern sich außerdem je nach Jahreszeit. Da mehrere Informationsebenen gleichzeitig angezeigt werden können, werden die angezeigten Daten immer spezifischer: So lässt sich etwa erkennen, dass der Singschwan nur in Gegenden nistet, in denen auch eine bestimmte Grasart vorkommt.

Cette carte interactive enrichit la vue d'avion du paysage entourant un glacier en lui superposant des cartes thématiques. Créée pour un centre d'accueil des visiteurs du Parc national islandais Vatnajökull, elle montre les environs du volcan Snæfell. Une carte topographique de la région est projetée sur une maquette tridimensionnelle du paysage.

Les visiteurs qui regardent la carte du dessus peuvent consulter d'autres types d'informations sur la flore, la faune ou la géologie de la région. Les chemins empruntés par les rennes ou la distribution des plantes rares deviennent visibles, et changent avec les saisons. Comme on peut superposer plusieurs types d'informations, les données visualisées acquièrent une signification plus précise. On voit par exemple que le cygne chanteur ne niche que là où certaines herbes poussent.

Project Info: Vatnajökull National Park, interactive installation, 2010, Iceland
Agency: ART+COM
Design: Paul Heyer, Irene Kriechbaum
Art Direction: Felix Beck
Creative Direction: Joachim Sauter

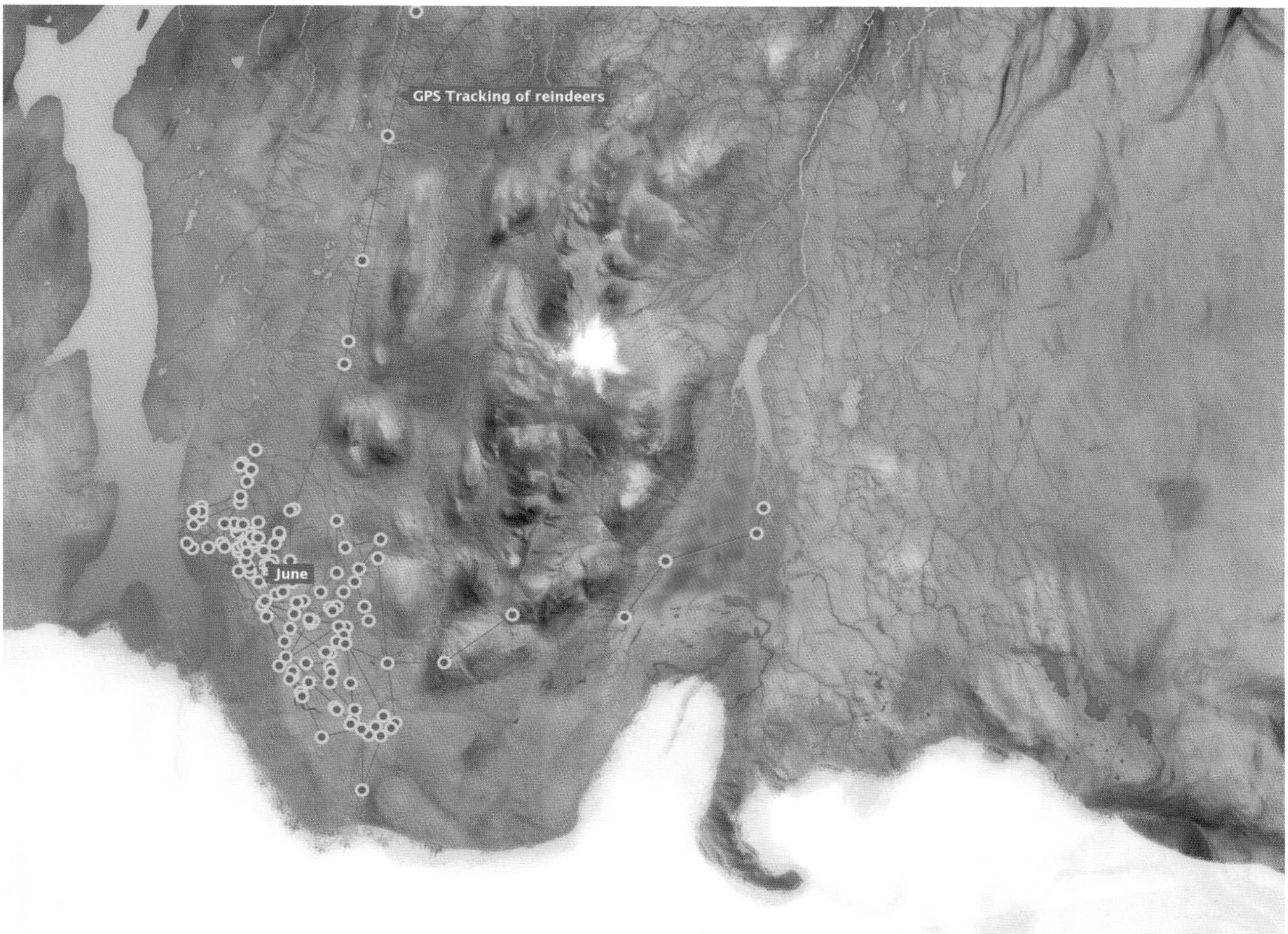

GPS Tracking of reindeers
June

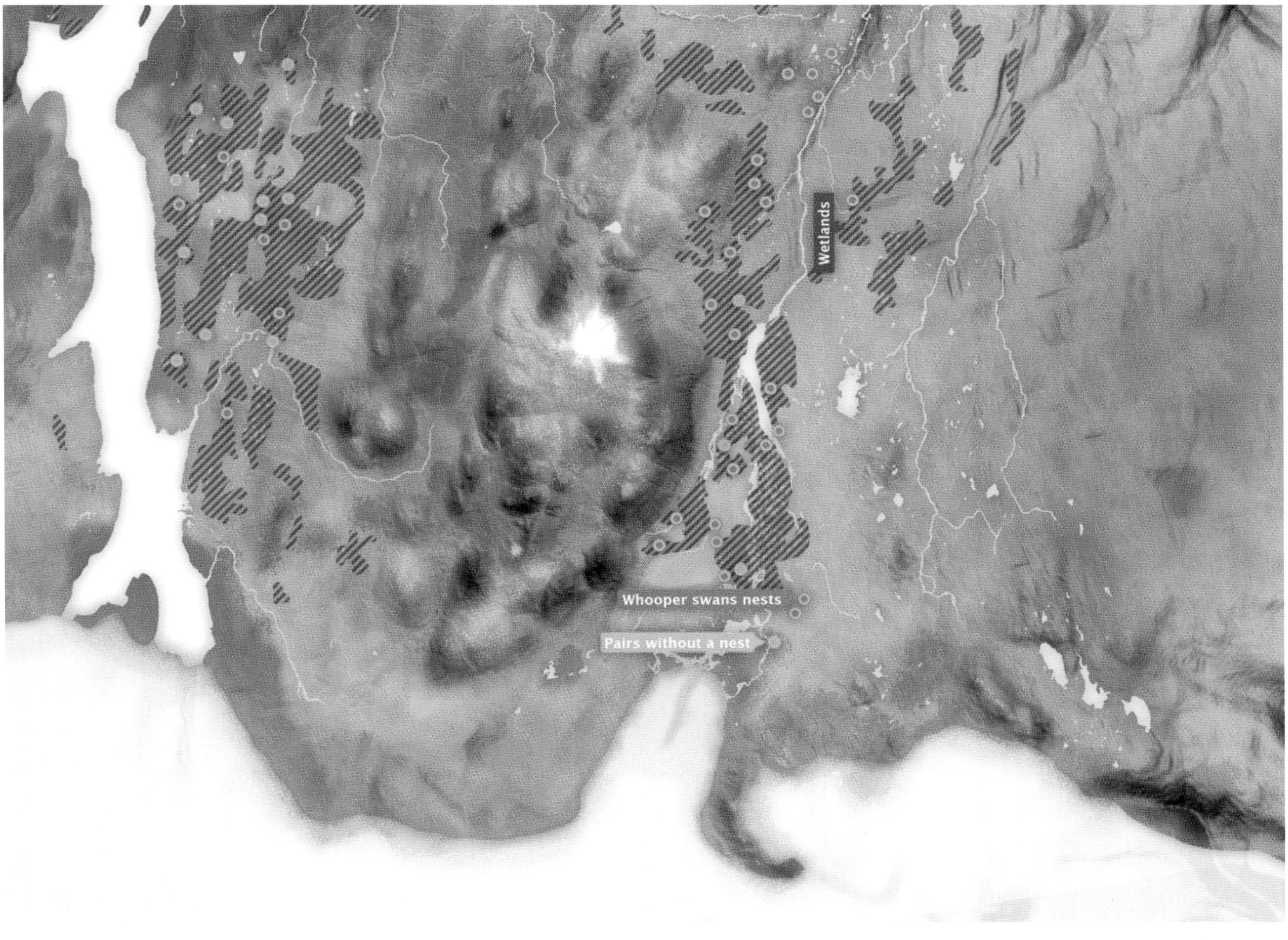

Wetlands
Whooper swans nests
Pairs without a nest

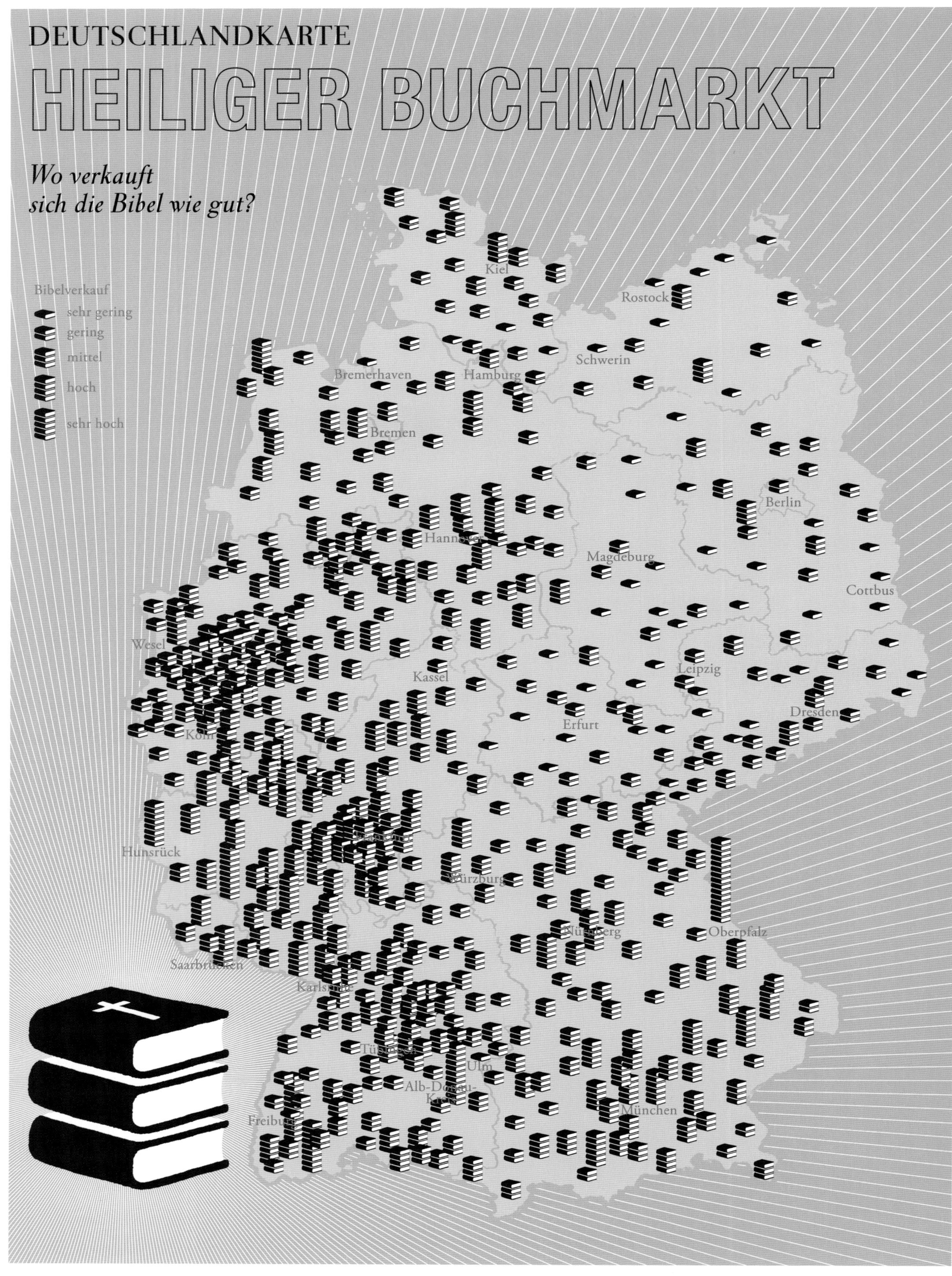

Project Info: *ZEITmagazin*, magazine article, 2008, Germany
Data Source: Initiative Neue Soziale Marktwirtschaft; Amazon; Nationale Verzehrstudie (2008); Greenpeace
Research: Matthias Stolz, Nele Heinevetter (*Die Zeit*)
Design: Ole Häntzschel
Additional Info: Series also published in a book by Knaur
Awards: Malofiej 2009

Map of Germany

This series of thematic maps of Germany is a continuous single-spread feature in the weekly magazine supplement of German newspaper *Die Zeit*. Created by various designers, they cover all kinds of everyday topics: from top hairdressers' names, the distribution of lidos across the country, down to which regions have the highest divorce rates. The visual design always makes a reference to the map's theme.

The examples shown here were designed by Ole Häntzschel. "Holy book market" records sales figures for the Bible. "Exonyms" lists German cities with their names in other languages. "Fish or Meat" shows in separate maps how much fish and meat is eaten according to gender (men shown left). "Genetically modified corn" maps the regions in which GM corn is cultivated.

Diese Serie von thematischen Deutschlandkarten entstammt einer regelmäßigen Rubrik im Magazin der Wochenzeitung *Die Zeit*. Sie werden von wechselnden Grafikern gestaltet und befassen sich mit verschiedenen Alltagsthemen: von den beliebtesten Friseurnamen über die Verteilung von Schwimmbädern bis hin zu der Frage, in welchen Regionen die Scheidungsrate am höchsten ist. Die visuelle Gestaltung bezieht sich jeweils auf das Kartenthema.

Die hier vorgestellten Beispiele stammen von Ole Häntzschel. „Heiliger Buchmarkt" verdeutlicht die Verkaufszahlen der Bibel, „Exonyme" nennt die Namen von Städten in anderen Sprachen. „Fisch oder Fleisch" zeigt auf gesonderten Karten, wie sich der Fisch- bzw. Fleischkonsum nach Geschlecht darstellt (Männer links, Frauen rechts). „Genmais" verzeichnet die Regionen, in denen das modifizierte Getreide angebaut wird.

Ces cartes thématiques de l'Allemagne appartiennent à une série d'articles publiés dans le supplément hebdomadaire du journal allemand *Die Zeit*. Créées par différents graphistes, elles couvrent toutes sortes de sujets liés à la vie quotidienne : des noms des grands coiffeurs à la distribution des piscines dans le pays, en passant par les taux de divorce au sein des différentes religions. Le graphisme fait toujours référence au thème de la carte.

Les exemples montrés ici ont été réalisés par Ole Häntzschel. « Marché du Livre saint » reprend les chiffres des ventes de la Bible. « Exonymes » donne le nom des villes allemandes dans d'autres langues. « Poisson ou viande » montre sur plusieurs cartes la consommation de poisson et de viande en fonction du sexe (les hommes sont à gauche). « Maïs génétiquement modifié » indique les régions où l'on cultive du maïs OGM.

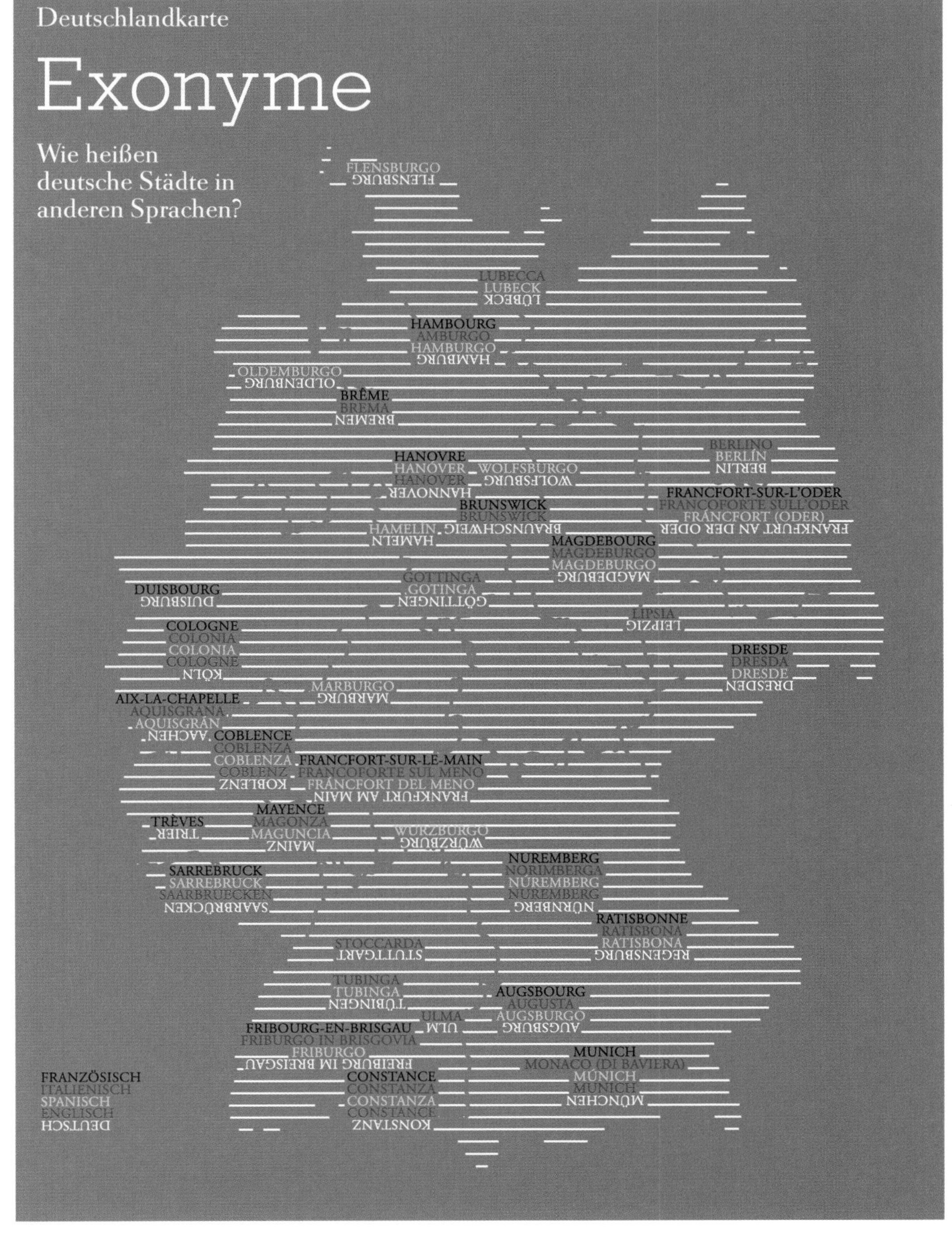

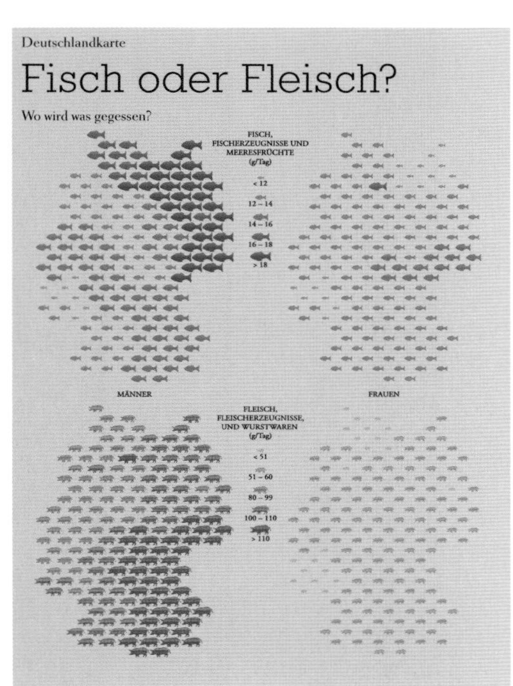

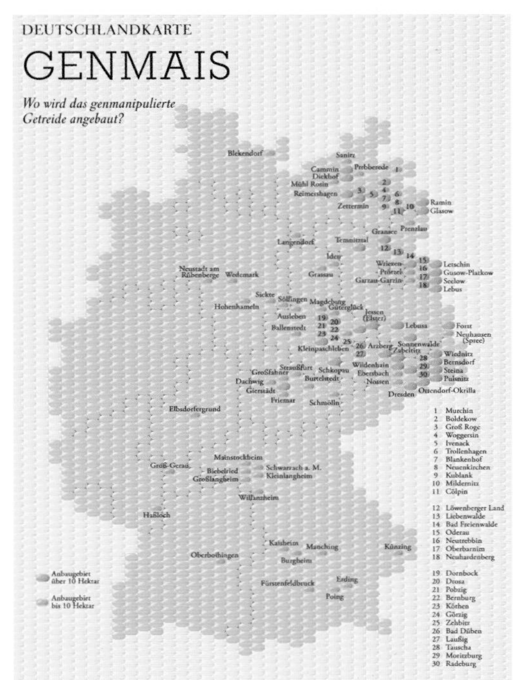

Map to Ghost Town

This map was developed as a T-shirt design and shows the fictional place of "Ghost Town", laid out in the shape of a skull. Like a traditional tourist map, it features street names and prominent attractions, using cute little pictorial elements typical for this sort of map.

All names and places were made up as horror-themed wordplay, drawing on famous references to crime and murder. The graphic mimics the format of thematic maps.

Dieser Stadtplan wurde als T-Shirt-Motiv entworfen und zeigt die fiktive Gespensterstadt „Ghost Town“, die wie ein Schädel angelegt ist. Wie auf einer herkömmlichen Touristenkarte sind Straßennamen verzeichnet und markante Orte durch ironische kleine Icons kenntlich gemacht.

Alle Namen und Ortsbezeichnungen spielen mit Wörtern aus dem Horror-Genre und verweisen auf berühmte Kriminal- und Mordgeschichten. Die Grafik nimmt damit scherzhaft Bezug auf thematische Karten.

Cette carte a été conçue pour décorer un t-shirt, et montre un lieu fictionnel, « Ghost Town », dont le plan dessine la forme d'un crâne. Comme toute carte touristique traditionnelle, elle porte des noms de rues et d'attractions qui sont indiquées à l'aide de jolies petites icônes.

Tous les noms et les lieux sont des jeux de mots sur un thème horrifique, et s'inspirent de références célèbres au crime et au meurtre. Le graphisme imite le format des cartes thématiques.

Project Info: Threadless.com, T-shirt design, 2010, USA
Design: Esther Aarts

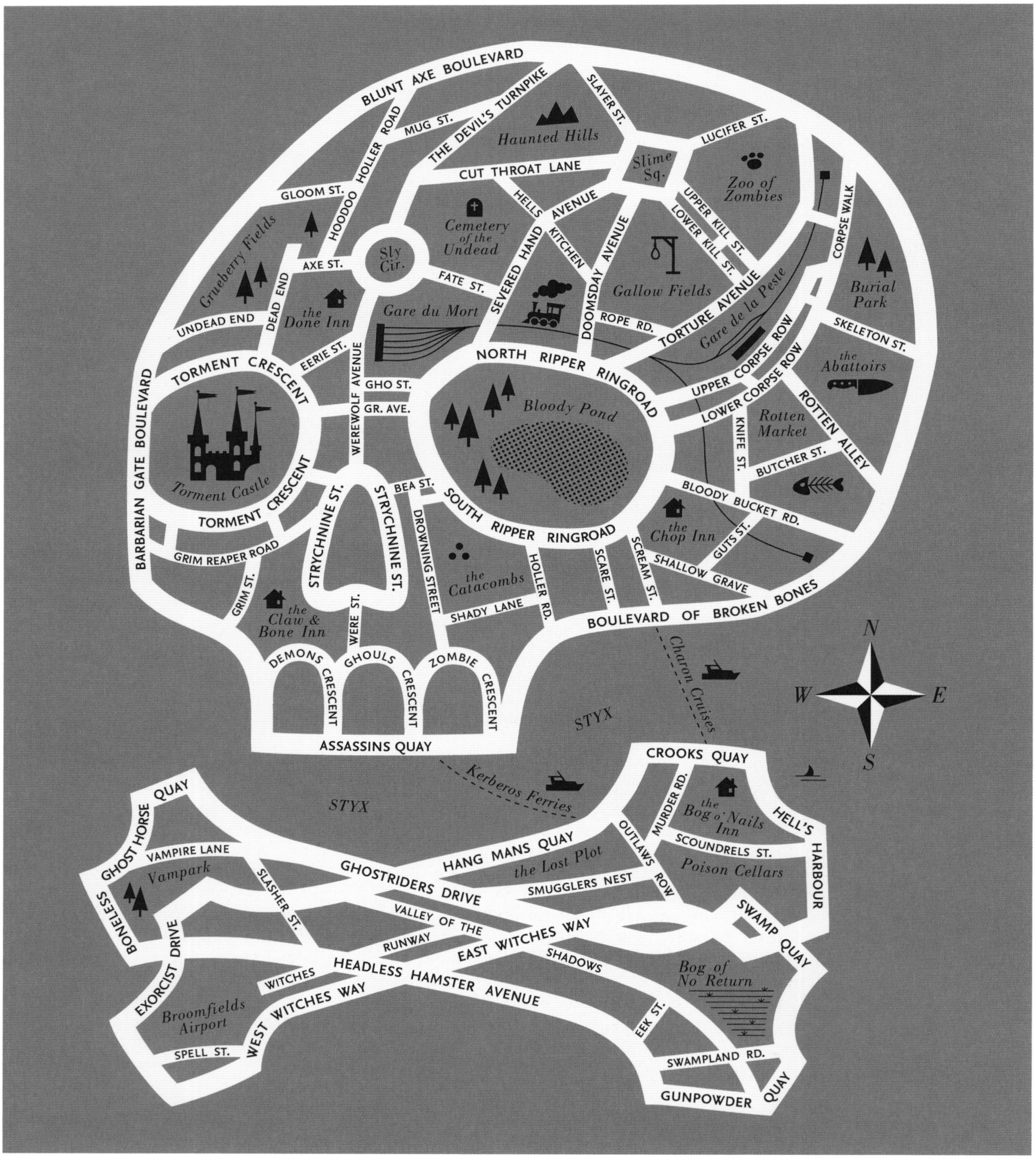

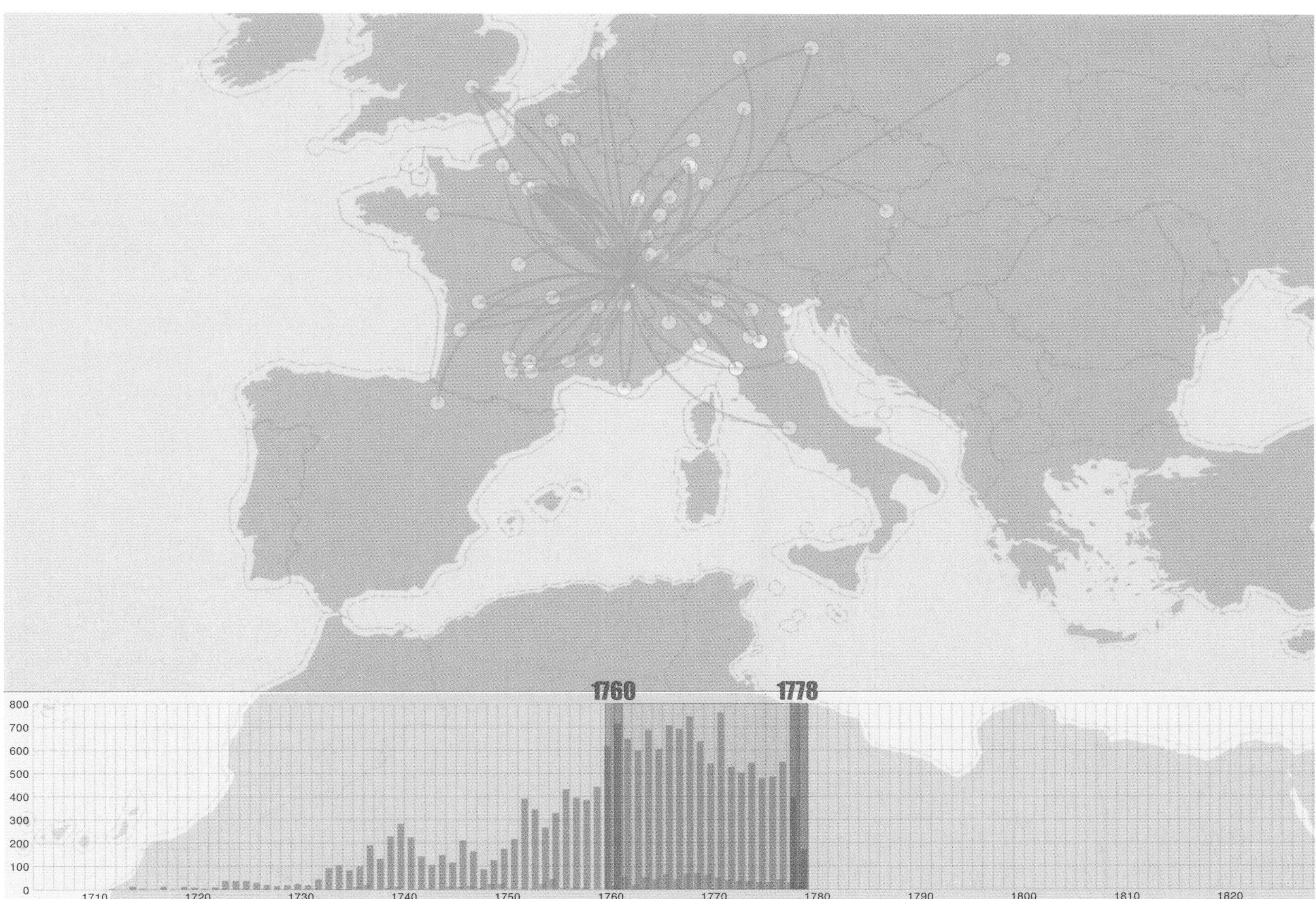

Mapping the Republic of Letters

The term "Republic of Letters" refers to the intellectual network across Europe and the Americas during the Enlightenment, which relied primarily on the exchange of handwritten letters. Drawing on digital archives of such letters, this project visualises the correspondence of some leading historical figures. Each letter is plotted according to its author, date and where it was sent from and received.

Data can be filtered via a menu. The clockwise bending of a line from A to B indicates the letter was sent in that direction. The combination of map and timeline also allows the plotting of those letters for which information on either date or location is missing. The project is a work in progress, and aims to facilitate the use of digital archives of the letters for scholars.

The image above visualises Voltaire's correspondence during the years he spent near Geneva. Grey bars in the timeline indicate that most of his communication is not mapped, as many letters contain no indication of where they were written. In the correspondence of Benjamin Franklin (following spread), many letters contain no date. These are mapped with grey lines. Franklin spent some years as US ambassador in France, which is why many of the letters were sent from Paris.

Mit dem Ausdruck der „Republik der Gelehrten" bezeichnet man ein Netzwerk von Intellektuellen und Wissenschaftlern, das sich im Zeitalter der Aufklärung über Europa und Amerika erstreckte und das vorwiegend über handschriftliche Briefe gepflegt wurde. Auf Grundlage der digitalen Archive ihrer Briefe visualisiert dieses Projekt die Korrespondenz einiger seiner führenden Köpfe. Jeder Brief wird verzeichnet entsprechend seinem Autor, dem Datum und dem Ort, an dem er abgeschickt und empfangen wurde.

Die Daten können mithilfe eines Menüs gefiltert werden. Krümmt sich eine Linie von A nach B im Uhrzeigersinn, wurde der Brief in diese Richtung geschickt. Die Kombination von Landkarte und Zeitleiste ermöglicht auch die Visualisierung von Briefen, bei denen Angaben zu Datum oder Ort fehlen. Das Projekt wird noch weiterentwickelt. Es soll Wissenschaftlern die Benutzung der digitalen Briefarchive erleichtern.

Das Bild oben zeigt Voltaires Korrespondenz aus der Zeit, als er in der Nähe von Genf lebte. Graue Balken in der Zeitleiste verweisen darauf, dass ein Großteil seiner Briefe nicht auf der Karte verzeichnet ist, weil darin jegliche Ortsangaben fehlen. In dem Schriftwechsel von Benjamin Franklin hingegen (folgende Seite) gibt es viele Briefe ohne Datum – sie sind auf der Karte in Grau eingezeichnet. Franklin lebte einige Zeit als US-Botschafter in Frankreich, weshalb er viele Briefe aus Paris verschickte.

Le terme « République des lettres » fait référence au réseau intellectuel qui existait en Europe et aux Amériques pendant les Lumières, et qui s'appuyait surtout sur l'échange de lettres écrites à la main. Ce projet exploite les archives numériques qui existent sur ces lettres pour donner une représentation de la correspondance de quelques personnages historiques. Pour chaque lettre portée sur la carte, l'auteur, la date, le lieu d'envoi et le lieu de réception sont enregistrés.

Un menu permet de filtrer les données. Le sens de l'envoi est indiqué par la courbure des lignes dans le sens des aiguilles d'une montre de A vers B. La combinaison de la carte et de la chronologie permet également de tenir compte des lettres pour lesquelles la date ou le lieu sont inconnus. Ce projet est en cours de réalisation, et vise à faciliter l'utilisation des archives numériques sur ces lettres pour les chercheurs.

L'image ci-dessus illustre la correspondance de Voltaire pendant les années qu'il a passées près de Genève. Les barres grises dans la chronologie montrent que la majeure partie de sa communication n'est pas représentée, sachant que de nombreuses lettres n'incluent pas une mention prouvant où elles ont été écrites. Dans la correspondance de Benjamin Franklin (page suivante), un grand nombre de lettres ne sont pas datées. Elles sont représentées par des lignes grises. Franklin a exercé quelques années comme ambassadeur des États-Unis en France, ce qui explique pourquoi de nombreuses lettres ont été envoyées depuis Paris.

Project Info: Interactive visualisation, since 2008, USA
Data Source: Electronic Enlightenment Project; Packard Humanities Institute; Edizione nazionale delle opere di Antonio Vallisneri; The Athanasius Kircher Project (Stanford University)
Design: Nicole Coleman, Dan Edelstein, Paula Findlen, Kofi Ohene-Adu (Stanford Humanities Center)
Tools: Protovis (Mike Bostock, Jeff Heer); Polymaps (SimpleGeo, Stamen); CloudMade; OpenStreetMap
180
160
140
120
100
80
60
40
20
0
1730
1740
1750

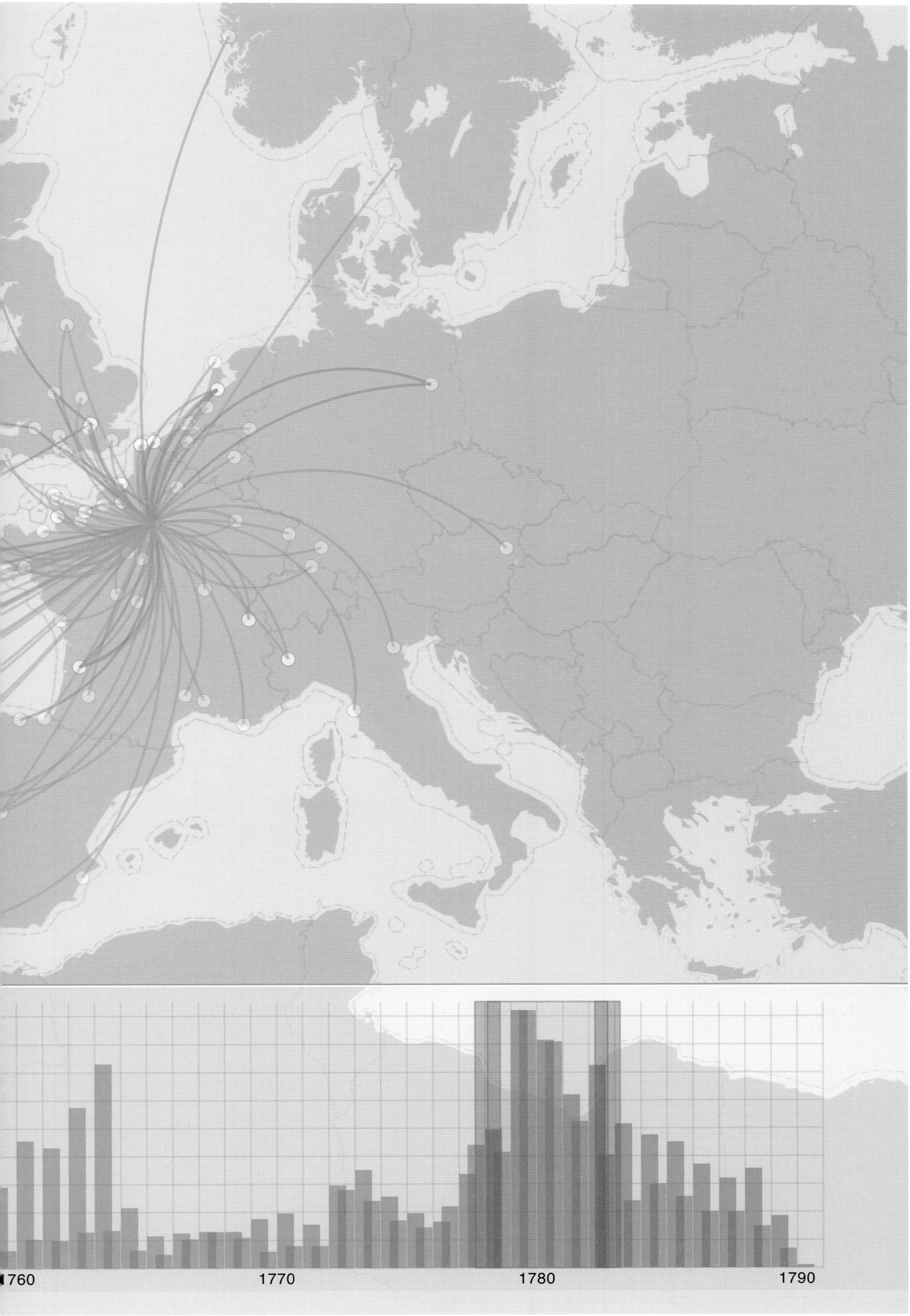

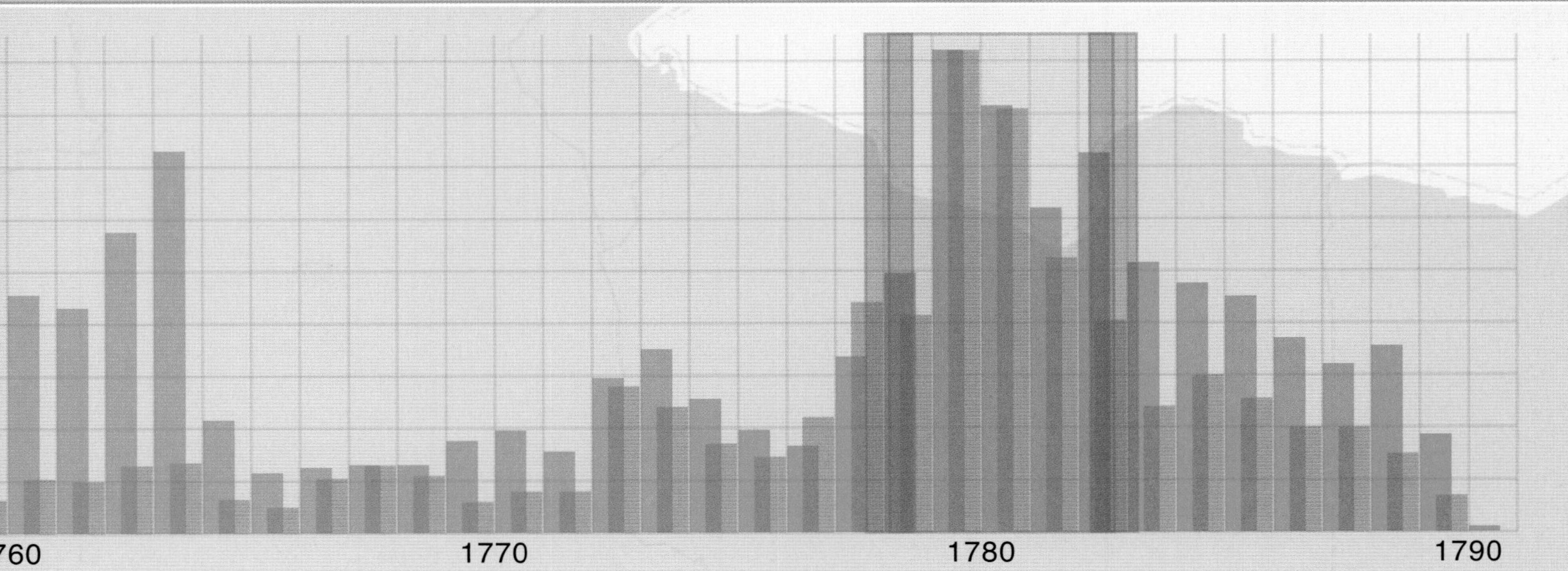
1760
1770
1780
1790

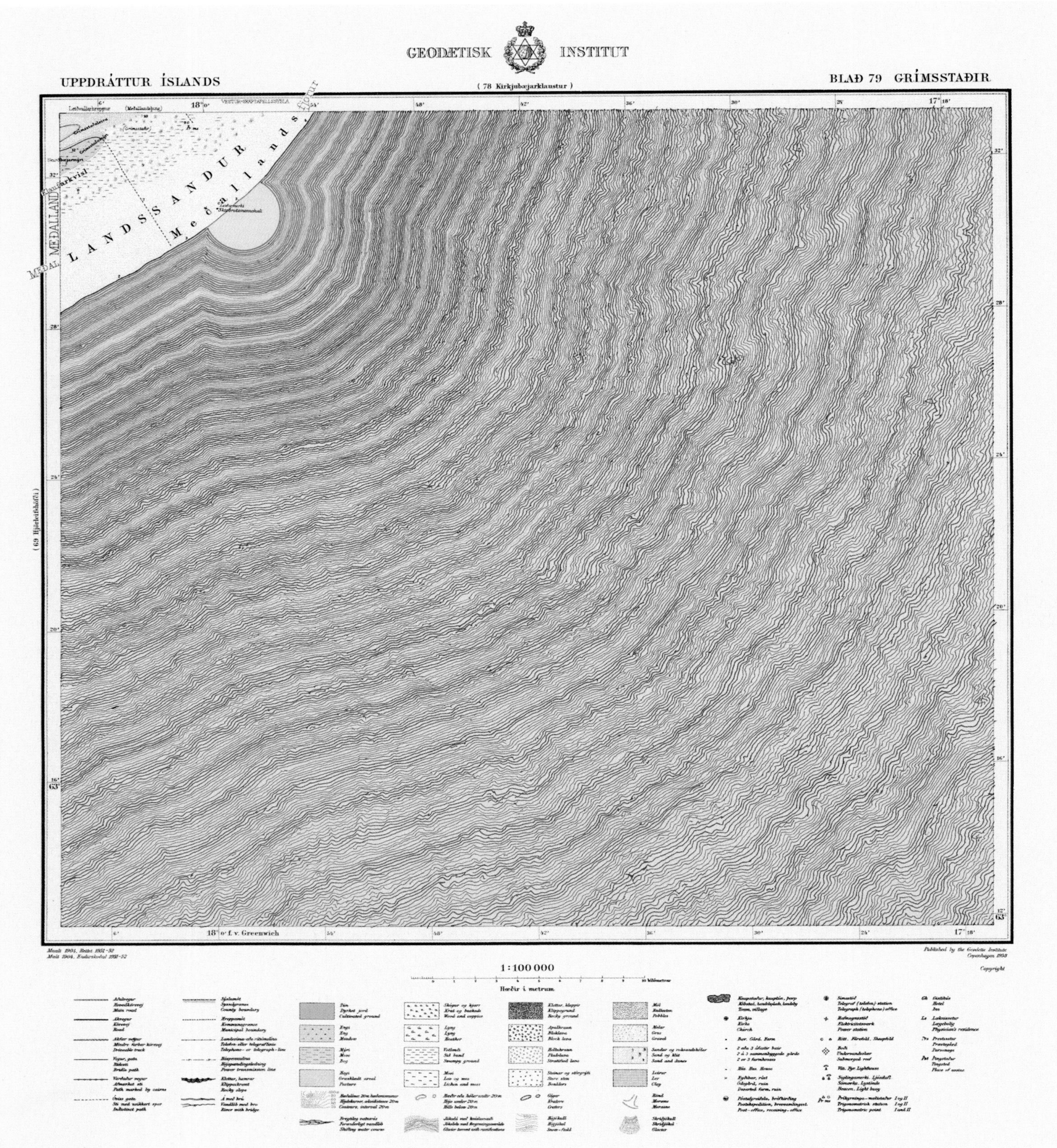

Medallandssandur

During a stay in Iceland, Norwegian artist Torgeir Husevaag stumbled upon a series of old maps. One piece struck his imagination – the sheet showed a tiny little strip of land along the south coast of Iceland. The larger part of the map, on the other hand, shows the great blue void of the sea.

Thrilled by the apparent lack of information conveyed in the map, Husevaag decided to enhance the sheets by hand-drawn visuals of invented phenomena. Referring to an old cartographic habit to fill the blank areas of unknown territory with imaginative decorations, he added pseudo-information pertaining to what happens in this large blue area which is supposed to represent the sea.

Während eines Besuchs in Island stieß der norwegische Künstler Torgeir Husevaag zufällig auf eine Reihe alter Landkarten. Ein Blatt sprach ihn besonders an – darauf war ein kleiner Streifen Land an der Südküste Islands abgebildet. Den Großteil der Karte jedoch nahm das blaue weite Meer ein.

Fasziniert vom offensichtlichen Mangel an Informationen auf dieser Landkarte, beschloss Husevaag, die Blätter mit handgezeichneten Darstellungen erfundener Phänomene auszuschmücken. Entsprechend dem alten Kartografen-Brauch, die leeren Flächen unbekannter Regionen mit fantasievollem Beiwerk zu füllen, fügte er Pseudoinformationen ein, die zeigten, was angeblich alles auf dieser großen blauen Meeresfläche passiert.

Lors d'un séjour en Islande, l'artiste norvégien Torgeir Husevaag est tombé par hasard sur une série de cartes anciennes. L'une d'elles a frappé son imagination – la feuille montrait une minuscule bande de terre le long de la côte sud de l'Islande. Mais la majeure partie de la carte ne montrait que le grand vide bleu de l'océan.

Aiguillonné par le manque d'informations mentionnées sur la carte, Husevaag a décidé de compléter ces feuilles en y dessinant à la main un phénomène imaginaire. En référence à une vieille habitude de cartographe consistant à remplir les zones vides des terres inconnues par des décorations créatives, il a ajouté des pseudo-informations sur ce qui se passe dans cette grande zone bleue censée représenter l'océan.

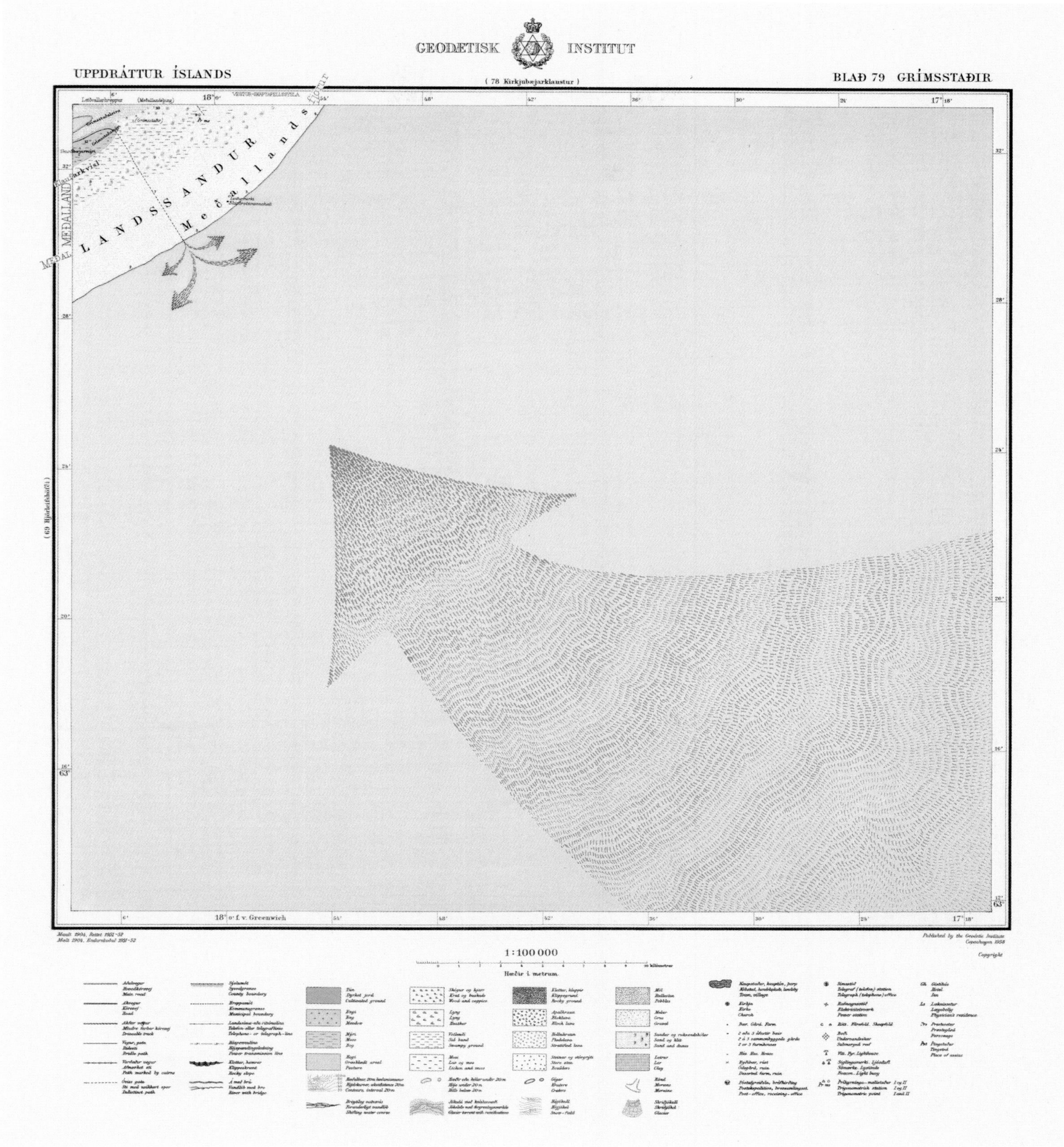

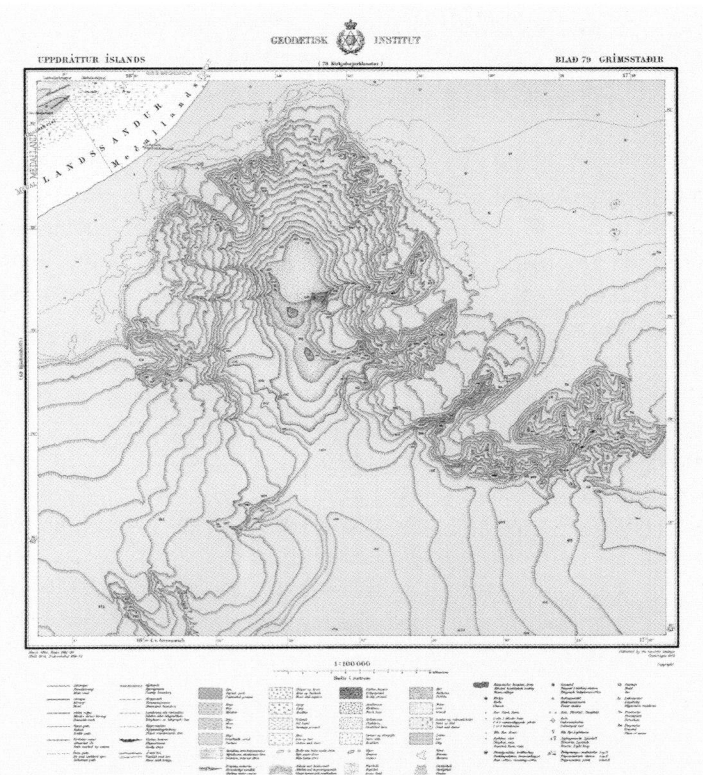

Project Info: Series of drawings, 2010, Norway / Iceland
Design: Torgeir Husevaag
Additional Info: original size each 58 x 54 cm

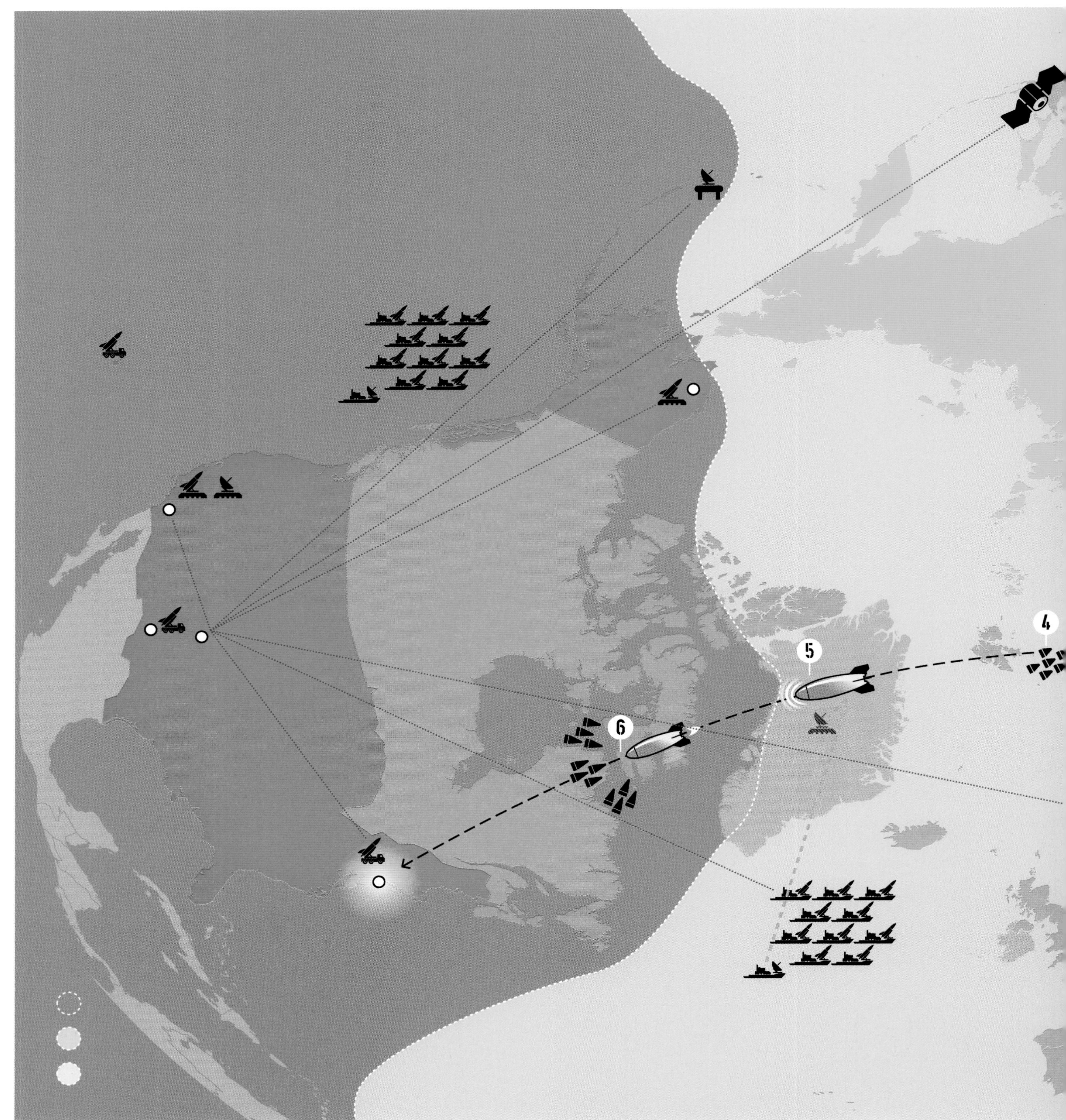

Project Info: *Süddeutsche Zeitung Wissen*, magazine article, 2008, Germany
Design: Jens Uwe Meyer (United States of the Art)

Missile Defence Shield

The US National Missile Defense Program, supported by President George W. Bush, was intended to destroy attacking missiles before they actually hit American soil. The map shows the northern hemisphere, with the US in red on the left, and Iran and North Korea as assumed aggressors in green. NATO member states are orange, whilst Russia is shown in yellow.

The ballistic trajectory of the missile is sketched out like a process in a number of steps. Black symbols mark the main projected components, such as ship-based defence systems in the oceans, as well as ground bases in Poland and the US. Various radar stations worldwide were to support the identification of an attacking missile.

Der von US-Präsident George W. Bush angestrebte Raketenabwehrschild sah vor, angreifende Raketen zu zerstören, noch ehe sie amerikanischen Boden erreichten. Die Karte zeigt die Nordhalbkugel, mit den USA links in Rot, Iran und Nordkorea als mutmaßliche Angreifer in Grün. NATO-Mitgliedsstaaten sind orange gehalten, Russland gelb.

Die Flugbahn der Rakete ist in einer Abfolge von Schritten dargestellt. Schwarze Symbole markieren die wichtigsten Komponenten der geplanten Raketenabwehr, etwa Verteidigungsschiffe auf den Ozeanen, aber auch Bodenstützpunkte in Polen und den USA. Mehrere über die Welt verteilte Radarstationen sollten die Identifizierung einer angreifenden Rakete unterstützen.

Le Programme national américain de défense antimissile, soutenu par le Président George W. Bush, a été conçu pour détruire les missiles attaquants avant même qu'ils ne touchent le sol américain. Cette carte montre l'hémisphère nord, avec les États-Unis en rouge à gauche, et les agresseurs supposés, l'Iran et la Corée du Nord, en vert. Les États membres de l'OTAN sont en orange, tandis que la Russie est en jaune.

La trajectoire balistique du missile est représentée sous forme d'un processus en plusieurs étapes. Des symboles noirs indiquent les principales composantes du projet, comme des systèmes de défense au large sur des bateaux, ainsi que des bases au sol en Pologne et aux États-Unis. Plusieurs stations de radar dans le monde entier devaient aider à identifier les missiles attaquants.

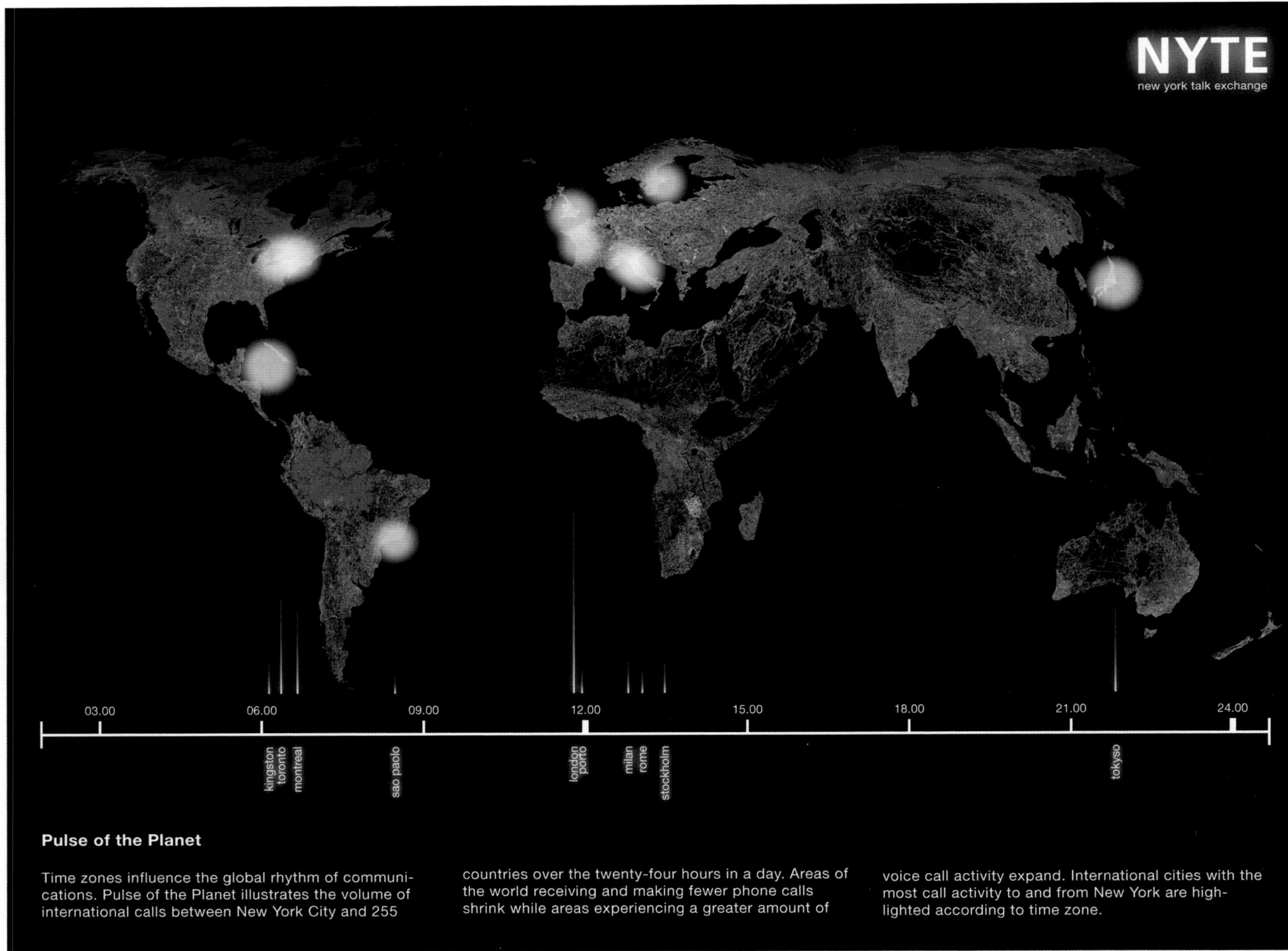

Pulse of the Planet

Time zones influence the global rhythm of communications. Pulse of the Planet illustrates the volume of international calls between New York City and 255 countries over the twenty-four hours in a day. Areas of the world receiving and making fewer phone calls shrink while areas experiencing a greater amount of voice call activity expand. International cities with the most call activity to and from New York are highlighted according to time zone.

New York Talk Exchange

NYTE was developed by the MIT SENSEable City Laboratory for the "Design and the Elastic Mind" exhibition at MoMA. The project illustrates global telephone communication in and out of New York City. Data provided by the AT&T network were used to measure the volume of Internet protocol (IP) and voice traffic at a given time. This data was plotted in three different modes.

"Globe Encounters" locates on a globe the places New Yorkers are talking to. "Pulse of the Planet" includes time as a dimension of the map: it shows how phone calls shift through the day as time zones sweep over the planet. The third visualisation zooms inside New York City's five boroughs: colour coding reveals the destinations called from particular neighbourhoods.

NYTE wurde vom MIT SENSEable City Laboratory für die Ausstellung „Design and the Elastic Mind" im MoMA entwickelt. Das Projekt illustriert die globale Telefonkommunikation von und nach New York City. Um das Gesprächsaufkommen über Telefonleitungen und via Internet zu einer vorgegebenen Zeit ermessen zu können, wurden die Daten des Telefonnetzbetreibers AT&T genutzt. Sie wurden auf drei unterschiedliche Arten aufbereitet.

Auf einem Globus zeigt „Globe Encounters" die Orte, mit denen New Yorker häufig telefonieren. „Pulse of the Planet" bezieht die Zeit als Dimension der Landkarte mit ein; sie zeigt, wie sich die Anrufe aufgrund der Zeitzonen über den Tagesverlauf verteilen. Die dritte Visualisierung konzentriert sich auf die fünf Stadtbezirke von New York: Der Farbcode zeigt die Orte, die in den einzelnen Vierteln am häufigsten angerufen werden.

NYTE est l'œuvre du laboratoire SENSEable City du MIT pour l'exposition « Design and the Elastic Mind » du MoMA. Ce projet illustre les communications téléphoniques internationales en provenance de et vers New York. Les données fournies par AT&T ont été utilisées pour mesurer le volume de trafic par protocole internet (IP) ou vocal à un moment donné. Ces informations ont été reportées sur la carte suivant trois méthodes différentes.

« Rencontres sur le globe » situe les endroits de la planète avec lesquels les New-yorkais parlent. « Pouls de la planète » ajoute à la carte une dimension temporelle : elle montre comment les appels téléphoniques changent au cours de la journée en fonction du glissement des fuseaux horaires. La troisième représentation zoome sur les cinq quartiers de New York : le code couleur indique les destinations que chaque quartier appelle.

Project Info: Museum of Modern Art, interactive installation, 2008, USA
Data Source: AT&T
Research: Assaf Biderman, Francesco Calabrese, Francisca Rojas, Andrea Vaccari, Margaret Ellen Haller (MIT SENSEable City Lab)
Design: Kristian Kloeckl, Aaron Koblin (MIT SENSEable City Lab)

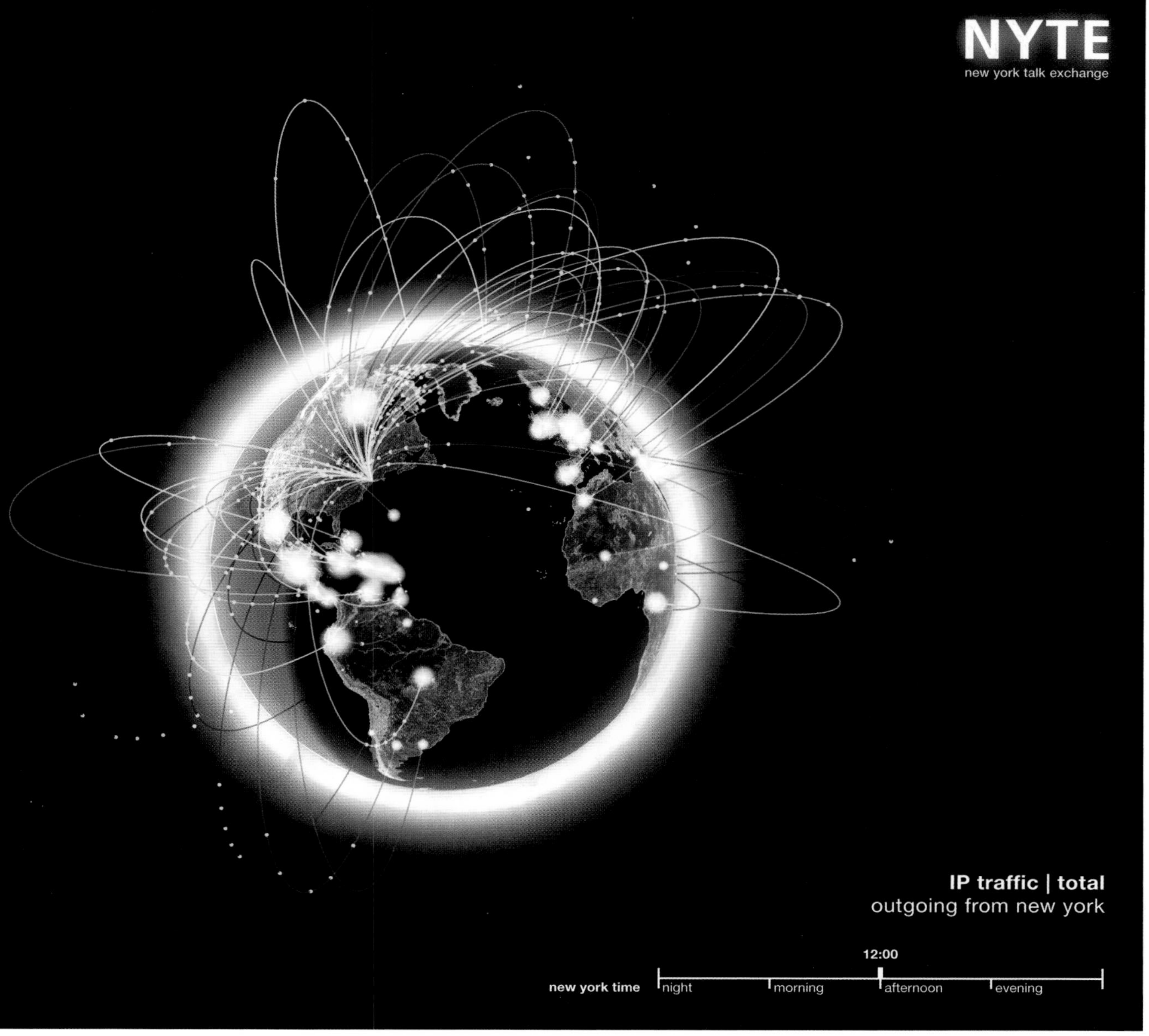

NYTE
new york talk exchange

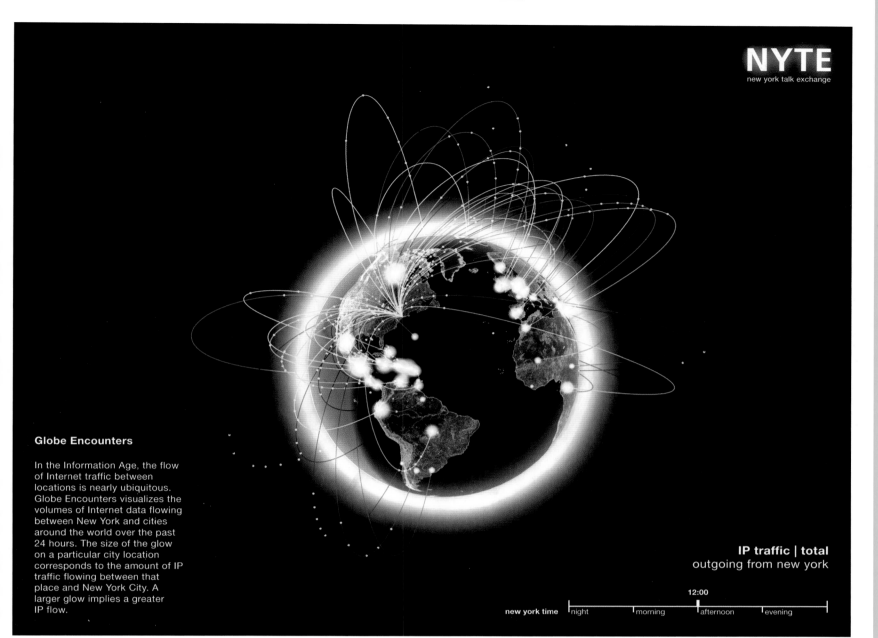

Globe Encounters

In the Information Age, the flow of Internet traffic between locations is nearly ubiquitous. Globe Encounters visualizes the volumes of Internet data flowing between New York and cities around the world over the past 24 hours. The size of the glow on a particular city location corresponds to the amount of IP traffic flowing between that place and New York City. A larger glow implies a greater IP flow.

IP traffic | total
outgoing from new york

12:00
new york time night morning afternoon evening

NYTE
new york talk exchange

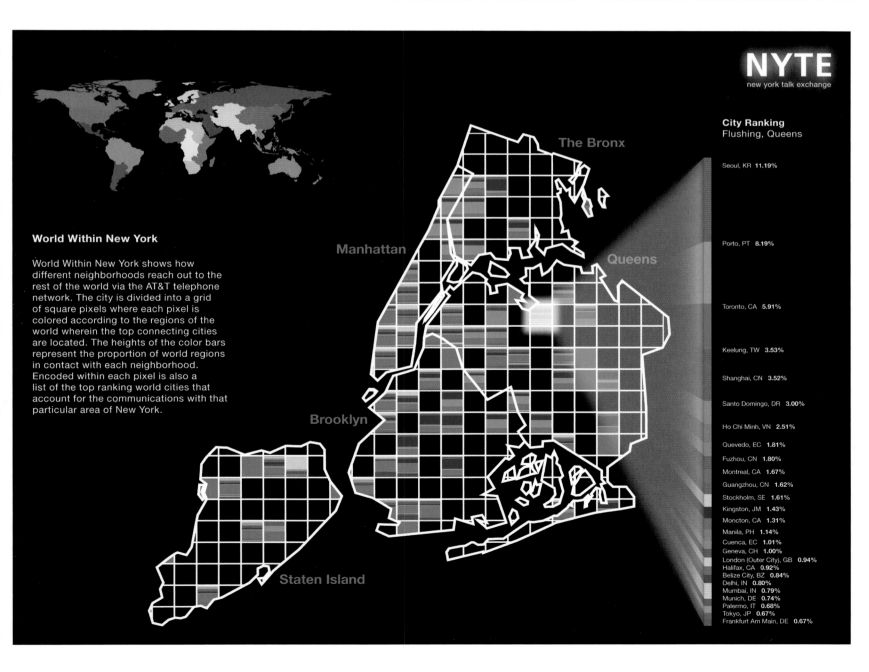

World Within New York

World Within New York shows how different neighborhoods reach out to the rest of the world via the AT&T telephone network. The city is divided into a grid of square pixels where each pixel is colored according to the regions of the world wherein the top connecting cities are located. The heights of the color bars represent the proportion of world regions in contact with each neighborhood. Encoded within each pixel is also a list of the top ranking world cities that account for the communications with that particular area of New York.

The Bronx
Manhattan
Queens
Brooklyn
Staten Island

City Ranking
Flushing, Queens

Seoul, KR **11.19%**
Porto, PT **8.19%**
Toronto, CA **5.91%**
Keelung, TW **3.53%**
Shanghai, CN **3.52%**
Santo Domingo, DR **3.00%**
Ho Chi Minh, VN **2.51%**
Quevedo, EC **1.81%**
Fuzhou, CN **1.80%**
Montreal, CA **1.67%**
Guangzhou, CN **1.62%**
Stockholm, SE **1.61%**
Kingston, JM **1.43%**
Moncton, CA **1.31%**
Manila, PH **1.14%**
Cuenca, EC **1.01%**
Geneva, CH **1.00%**
London (Outer City), GB **0.94%**
Halifax, CA **0.92%**
Belize City, BZ **0.84%**
Delhi, IN **0.80%**
Mumbai, IN **0.79%**
Munich, DE **0.74%**
Palermo, IT **0.68%**
Tokyo, JP **0.67%**
Frankfurt Am Main, DE **0.67%**

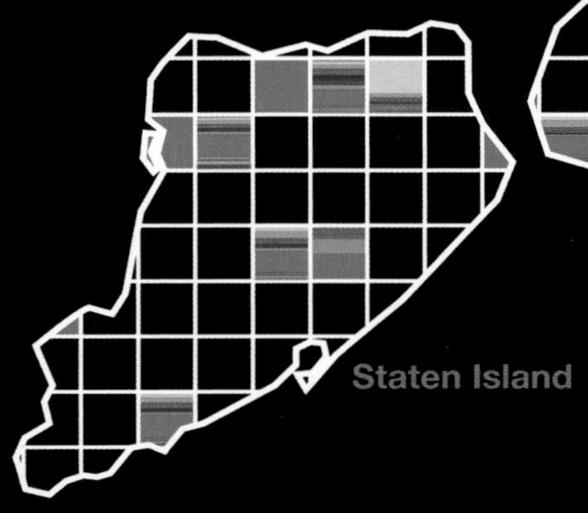

Nuclear Energy Worldwide

This thematic map for German *Greenpeace* magazine shows nuclear reactors worldwide. Colour coding denotes then current policy towards nuclear power in each country, with yellow indicating that it is to be expanded, whereas green countries had developed exit strategies which have been postponed. Striped countries were planning to re-adopt the nuclear generation of electricity.

Icons show the geographical distribution and status of all 437 reactors worldwide, as of 2010. Pie charts show the percentage of nuclear power out of the total national energy production. The bar chart to the lower right breaks down the age of all reactors, showing that the majority were built at least 25 years ago.

Diese thematische Weltkarte, entworfen für das deutsche Greenpeace-Magazin, führt alle Atomkraftwerke der Erde auf. Die Farbcodierung zeigt die damals aktuelle Atompolitik des jeweiligen Landes: Gelb bedeutet, dass die Atomkraft ausgebaut werden sollte, grüne Länder hingegen hatten Ausstiegsstrategien entwickelt, die verschoben wurden. Gestreifte Länder planten, die atomare Stromgewinnung wieder aufzunehmen.

Symbole verdeutlichen die geografische Verteilung und den Status der weltweit 437 Reaktoren (Stand 2010). Tortendiagramme geben den Prozentsatz der Atomenergie an der gesamten erzeugten Energiemenge an. Das Balkendiagramm unten rechts schlüsselt das Alter aller Reaktoren auf; daraus wird ersichtlich, dass der Großteil bereits vor mindestens 25 Jahren gebaut wurde.

Cette carte thématique pour le magazine allemand *Greenpeace* montre les réacteurs nucléaires dans le monde. Le code couleur indique la politique en vigueur dans chaque pays en matière d'énergie nucléaire au moment de la réalisation de la carte. Le jaune indique une politique d'expansion, alors que le vert indique que ces pays ont adopté des stratégies de sortie du nucléaire qui ont été reportées. Les pays hachurés comptaient reprendre la production nucléaire d'électricité.

Les icônes montrent la répartition géographique et l'état des 437 réacteurs existant au monde en 2010. Les diagrammes circulaires montrent le pourcentage d'énergie nucléaire par rapport à la production totale d'énergie dans le pays. Le graphique à barres en bas à droite décompose l'âge des réacteurs, et montre que la majorité d'entre eux ont été construits il y a au moins 25 ans.

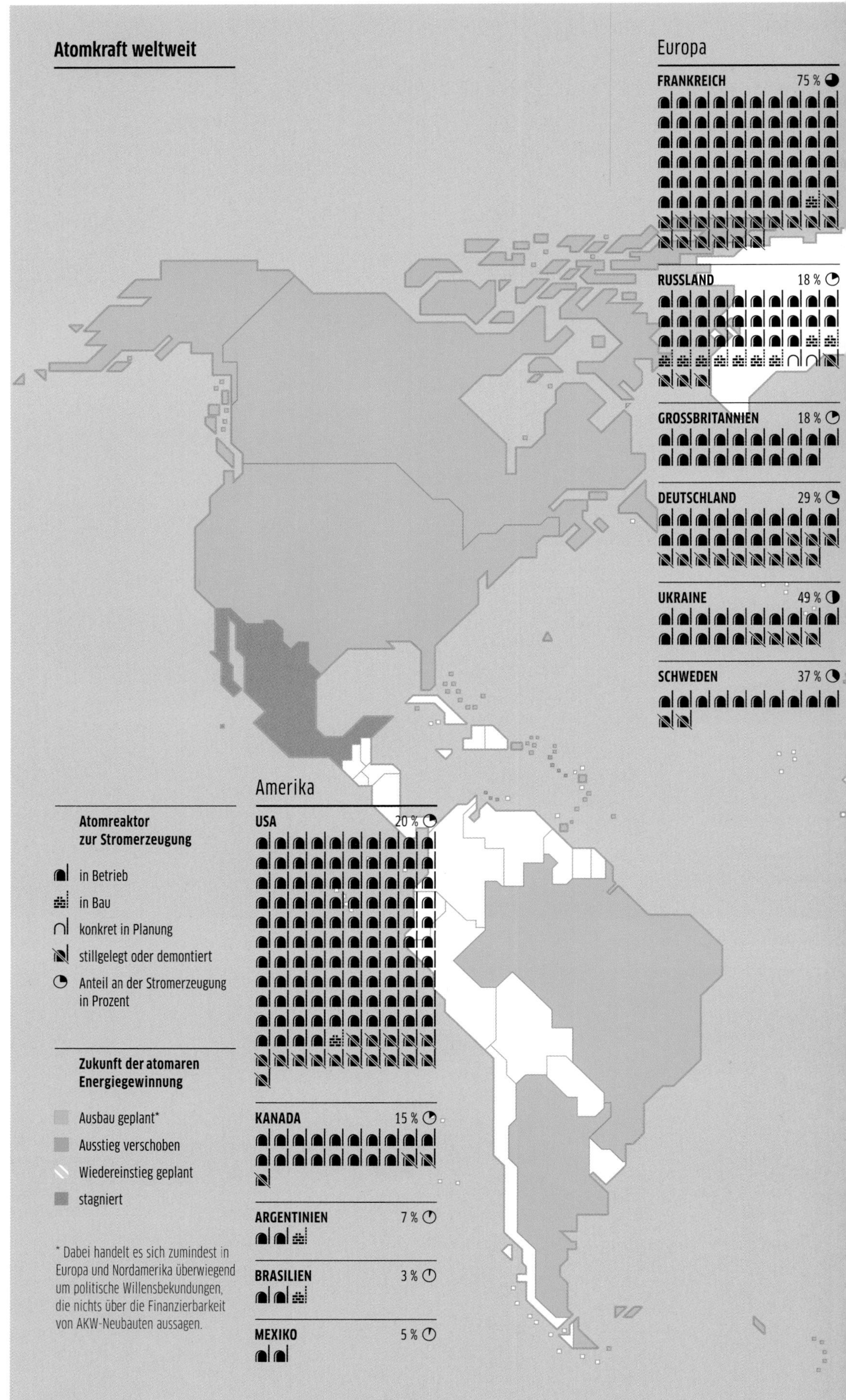

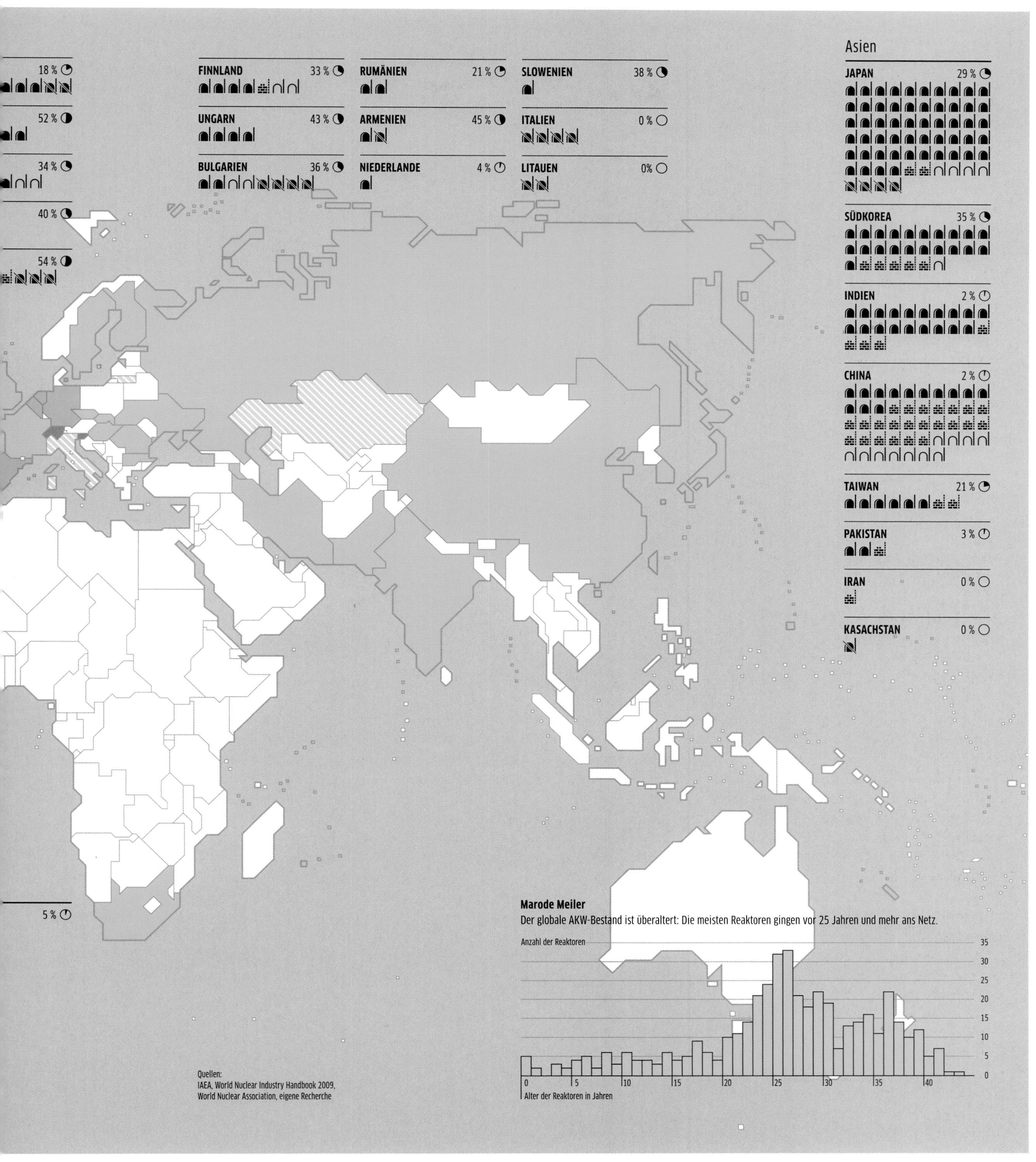

Project Info: *Greenpeace*, magazine article, 2010, Germany
Data Source: IAEA; *World Nuclear Industry Handbook* 2009; World Nuclear Association; Greenpeace Media
Design: Carsten Raffel (United States of the Art)

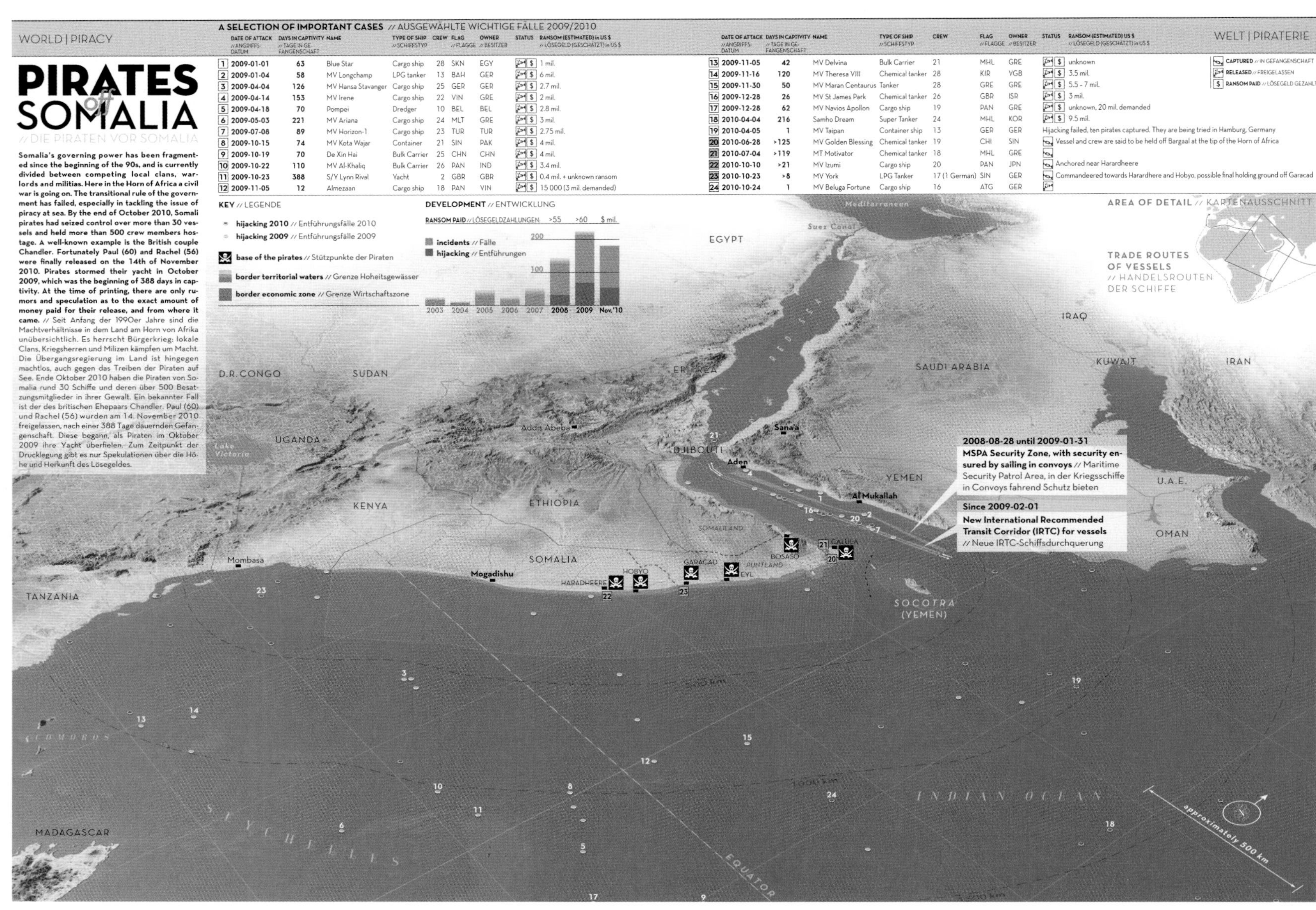

Pirates off Somalia

With the massive rise in pirate attacks, the waters off the coast of Somalia have been the most dangerous area for shipping worldwide in recent years. This graphic lists some of the major pirate attacks over the course of two years and charts these incidents on a map of the region.

The large-scale relief map is completed by a detailed list of the incidents, providing additional information regarding the type of ship, ransom paid or number of crew members.

Wegen der dramatischen Zunahme von Piratenüberfällen gelten die Gewässer vor der Küste von Somalia seit mehreren Jahren für die Schifffahrt als sehr gefährlich. Diese Grafik führt einige der schwersten Piratenangriffe der Jahre 2009/10 auf und verzeichnet sie auf einer Karte der Region.

Die großformatige Reliefkarte ist um eine detaillierte Auflistung der Angriffe ergänzt, die Informationen zu Schiffstypen, Lösegeldzahlungen oder der Anzahl der Besatzungsmitglieder enthält.

Avec l'augmentation spectaculaire des attaques de pirates, les eaux de la côte de la Somalie sont devenues la zone de navigation la plus dangereuse de ces dernières années. Cette image répertorie quelques-unes des principales attaques de pirates sur deux ans et les situe sur une carte de la région.

Cette carte en relief à grande échelle est complétée par une liste détaillée des incidents, et donne des informations supplémentaires sur le type de bateau, la rançon payée ou le nombre de membres de l'équipe.

Project Info: *In Graphics*, magazine article, 2010, Germany
Data Source: IMB Piracy Reporting Centre; UNOSAT; Ecoterra Report on Piracy in Somalia
Design: Jan Schwochow (Golden Section Graphics)

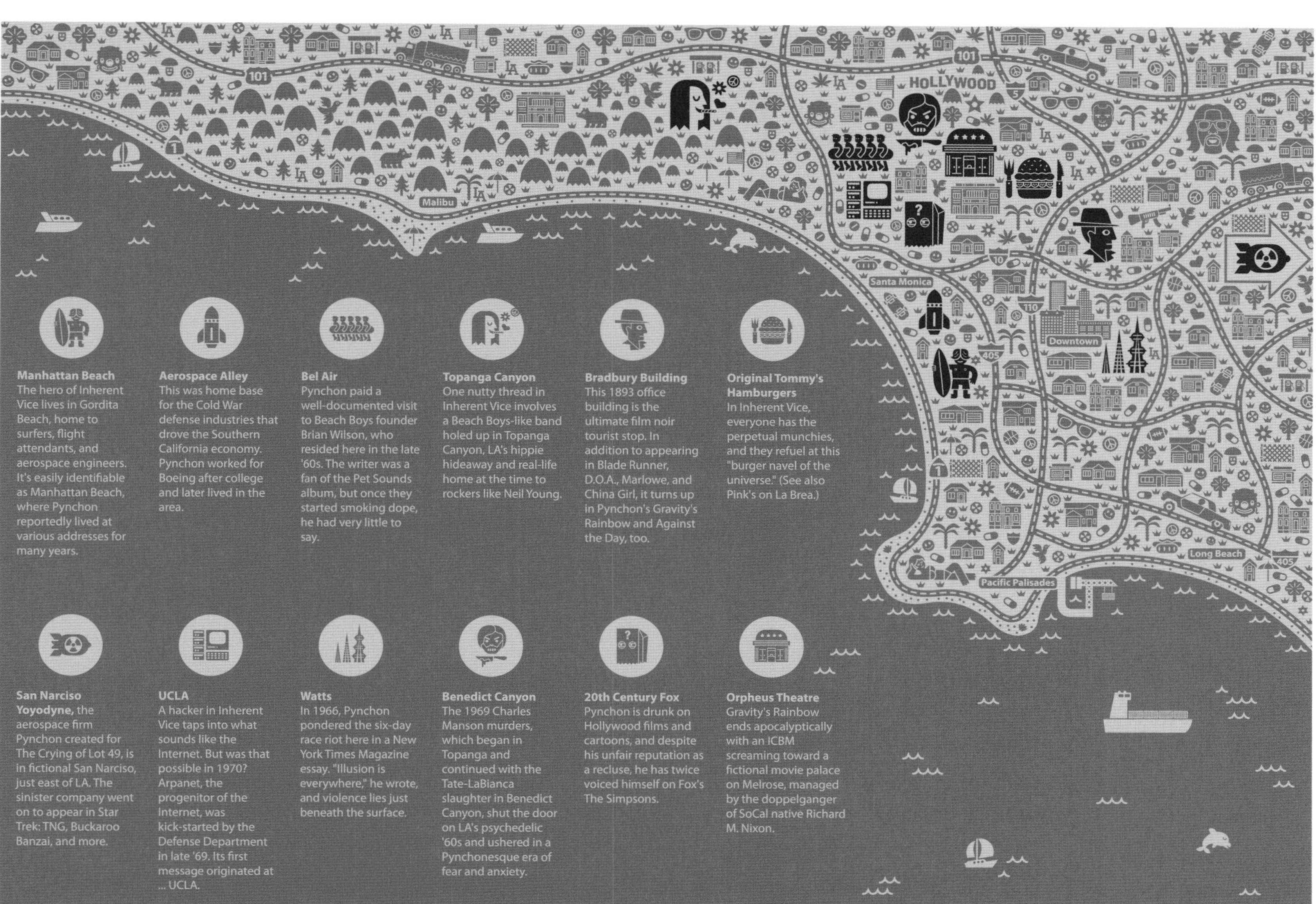

101
HOLLYWOOD
Malibu
Santa Monica
Downtown
Long Beach
Pacific Palisades
Manhattan Beach
The hero of Inherent Vice lives in Gordita Beach, home to surfers, flight attendants, and aerospace engineers. It's easily identifiable as Manhattan Beach, where Pynchon reportedly lived at various addresses for many years.
Aerospace Alley
This was home base for the Cold War defense industries that drove the Southern California economy. Pynchon worked for Boeing after college and later lived in the area.
Bel Air
Pynchon paid a well-documented visit to Beach Boys founder Brian Wilson, who resided here in the late '60s. The writer was a fan of the Pet Sounds album, but once they started smoking dope, he had very little to say.
Topanga Canyon
One nutty thread in Inherent Vice involves a Beach Boys-like band holed up in Topanga Canyon, LA's hippie hideaway and real-life home at the time to rockers like Neil Young.
Bradbury Building
This 1893 office building is the ultimate film noir tourist stop. In addition to appearing in Blade Runner, D.O.A., Marlowe, and China Girl, it turns up in Pynchon's Gravity's Rainbow and Against the Day, too.
Original Tommy's Hamburgers
In Inherent Vice, everyone has the perpetual munchies, and they refuel at this "burger navel of the universe." (See also Pink's on La Brea.)
San Narciso Yoyodyne, the aerospace firm Pynchon created for The Crying of Lot 49, is in fictional San Narciso, just east of LA. The sinister company went on to appear in Star Trek: TNG, Buckaroo Banzai, and more.
UCLA
A hacker in Inherent Vice taps into what sounds like the Internet. But was that possible in 1970? Arpanet, the progenitor of the Internet, was kick-started by the Defense Department in late '69. Its first message originated at ... UCLA.
Watts
In 1966, Pynchon pondered the six-day race riot here in a New York Times Magazine essay. "Illusion is everywhere," he wrote, and violence lies just beneath the surface.
Benedict Canyon
The 1969 Charles Manson murders, which began in Topanga and continued with the Tate-LaBianca slaughter in Benedict Canyon, shut the door on LA's psychedelic '60s and ushered in a Pynchonesque era of fear and anxiety.
20th Century Fox
Pynchon is drunk on Hollywood films and cartoons, and despite his unfair reputation as a recluse, he has twice voiced himself on Fox's The Simpsons.
Orpheus Theatre
Gravity's Rainbow ends apocalyptically with an ICBM screaming toward a fictional movie palace on Melrose, managed by the doppelganger of SoCal native Richard M. Nixon.

Pynchon's L.A.

Jan Kallwejt created this fresh take on a thematic map for American magazine *Wired*. It shows an abstract version of Los Angeles, with various references to the American writer Thomas Pynchon. Born in 1937, he lives the life of a recluse; he was reported to have lived in Los Angeles for many years, from the 1960s onwards.

Some parts of the map are marked in dark blue – these refer to places Pynchon has reportedly visited or which are described in his novels and stories. They are explained by text boxes placed over the ocean. The two-colour map itself is flat, with symbols marking natural and man-made features. Covering the whole map, the little icons form a carpet of landscape features.

Jan Kallwejt gestaltete diese frische Variante einer thematischen Karte für die amerikanische Zeitschrift *Wired*. Sie zeigt eine abstrakte Version von Los Angeles mit Verweisen auf den amerikanischen Schriftsteller Thomas Pynchon. Er wurde 1937 geboren und führt ein äußerst zurückgezogenes Leben. Angeblich verbrachte er seit den 1960er-Jahren viele Jahre in Los Angeles.

Einige Elemente sind im Stadtplan dunkelblau gefärbt – das sind Orte, die Pynchon angeblich besuchte oder die er in seinen Romanen und Kurzgeschichten beschreibt. Sie werden in den Textpassagen auf dem Meer erläutert. Die zweifarbige Karte ist völlig plan, die Symbole zeigen natürliche und vom Menschen geschaffene Attraktionen. Die kleinen Icons überziehen den Plan wie ein dichtgewebter Teppich von Landschaftsmerkmalen.

Jan Kallwejt est le créateur de cette interprétation originale de la carte thématique pour le magazine américain *Wired*. Elle montre une version abstraite de Los Angeles, avec plusieurs références à l'écrivain américain Thomas Pynchon. Né en 1937, il vit en reclus. On dit qu'il a vécu à Los Angeles de nombreuses années, à partir des années 1960.

Certaines parties de la carte sont colorées en bleu foncé. Elles indiquent les endroits que Pynchon aurait visités, ou qui sont décrits dans ses romans et nouvelles. Ces lieux sont expliqués par des cadres de texte placés sur l'océan. Cette carte bicolore est plate, avec des symboles marquant le paysage naturel et les structures humaines. Ces petites icônes recouvrent toute la carte et forment un tapis d'éléments de paysage.

Project Info: *Wired*, magazine article, 2010, USA
Design: Jan Kallwejt

24

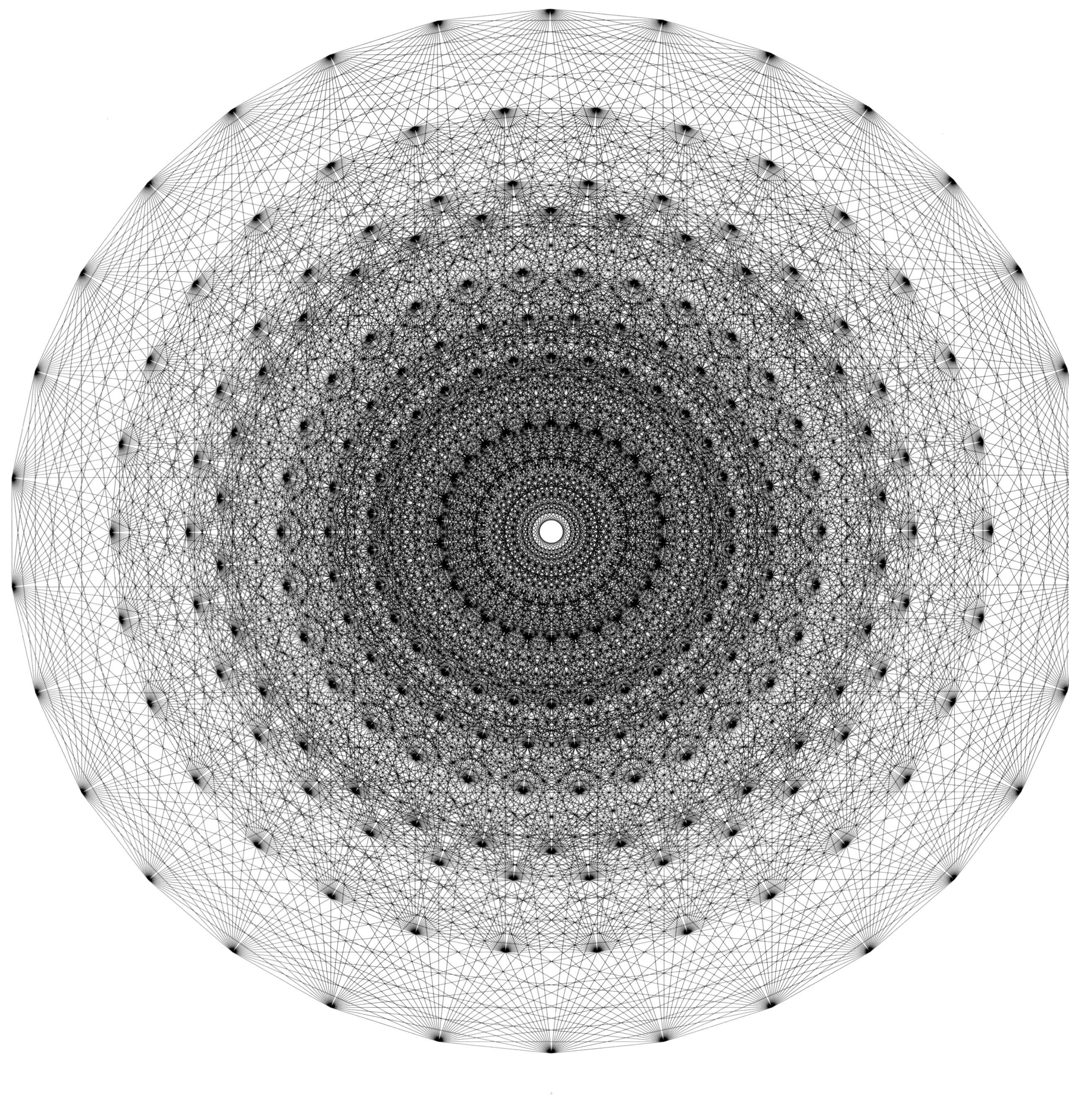

Real Magick

in

Theory and Practise

The Luxury of Protest

Real Magick in Theory and Practise

The 4_21 polytope is the algebraic form at the centre of a universal theory of everything. The theory attempts to unify quantum physics and gravitation in hopes of ultimately explaining the universe. 4_21 models particle transformations through geometry. Visualisation is a key measure for understanding the polytope – it must be drawn to see how it works. Its dimension-within-dimension structure creates a lattice that predicts all known and postulated particles and forces in the universe as it folds in space-time.

Each intersection represents an element. This visualisation by Peter Crnokrak is the most accurate to date and was hand-drawn in Illustrator to an accuracy of 1/10,000 mm. Previous attempts were limited by the inability of graphics engines to construct perfect circles.

Das Polytop 4_21 ist die algebraische Formel zu einer universalen Theorie der Materie. Es handelt sich um einen Versuch, die Quantenphysik und die Gravitation zu verbinden, um auf diese Weise das Universum zu erklären. 4_21 ist ein geometrisches Modell für die Transformation von Teilchen. Die Visualisierung der Formel ist ein wichtiges mathematisches Werkzeug – man muss sie zeichnen, um zu verstehen, wie sie funktioniert.

Ihr mehrdimensionaler Aufbau erzeugt ein Gitter, das das Verhalten aller bekannten und angenommenen Teilchen und Kräfte vorhersagt, während sich das Universum in der Raumzeit entfaltet. Jeder Schnittpunkt stellt ein Teilchen dar. Die hier gezeigte Visualisierung von Peter Crnokrak ist die bis dato genaueste und wurde in Illustrator mit einer Genauigkeit von 1/10.000 mm von Hand gezeichnet. Frühere Versuche scheiterten an der Ungenauigkeit, mit der selbst Computerprogramme Kreise zeichnen.

Le polytope 4_21 est la forme algébrique qui se trouve au centre d'une possible théorie universelle du tout. Cette théorie tente d'unifier la physique quantique et la gravitation dans l'espoir d'expliquer l'univers. 4_21 représente les transformations des particules grâce à la géométrie. La visualisation est essentielle pour comprendre ce polytope – il faut le dessiner pour voir comment il fonctionne. Sa structure à dimensions imbriquées prédit toutes les forces et particules connues et postulées dans l'univers qui se plie dans l'espace-temps.

Chaque intersection représente un élément. Cette représentation de Peter Crnokrak est la plus précise à ce jour, et a été dessinée à la main dans Illustrator avec une précision de 1/10 000e de millimètre. Les tentatives précédentes avaient été limitées par l'incapacité des moteurs graphiques à construire des cercles parfaits.

Project Info: Print, 2010, UK
Design: Peter Crnokrak (The Luxury of Protest)
Additional Info: Silk screen print on clear plastic, hand-applied 23 carat rouge gold foil, gold powder gilding

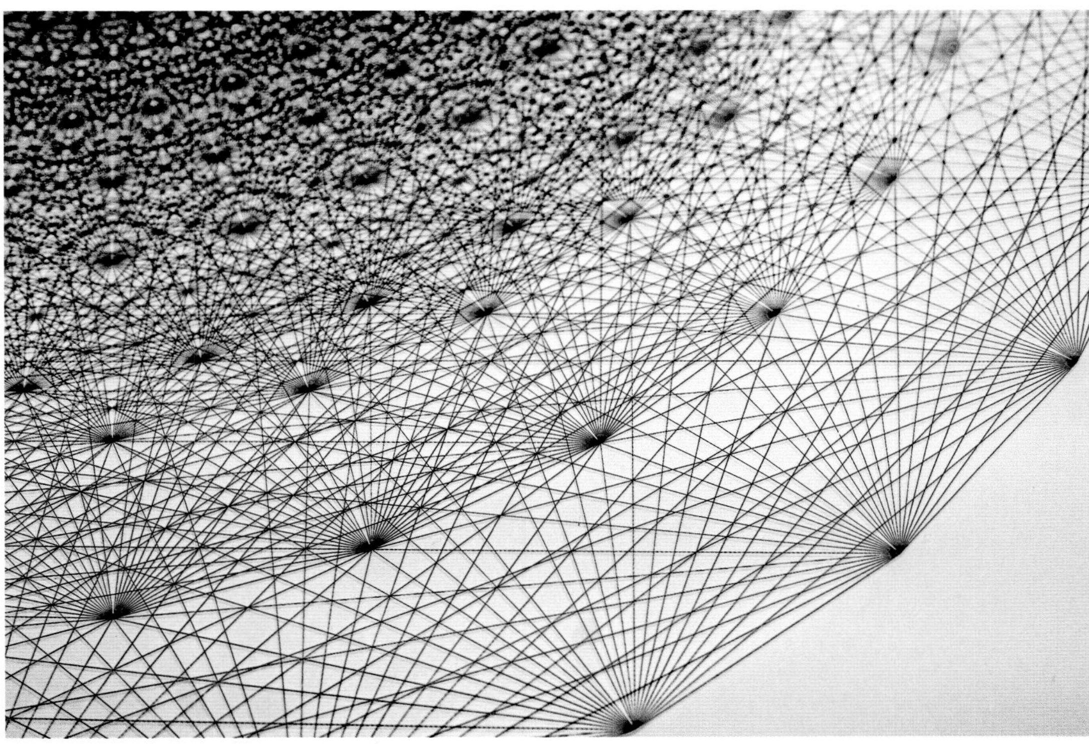

Roadtrip 2009

With this poster, Ole Østring collected together a visual report of his road-trip through Europe, from summer 2009. In the central image he presents a particular mixture of map and timeline. The route of his journey is shown on the map, with individual stop-points linked to a thick timeline, which bends around outside the actual itinerary.

This facilitates two ways of reconstructing the journey: by following it on the map, or by reading the continuous timeline. The latter provides further data as to the time of day and the type of transport used. Additional statistics on the poster provide detailed information regarding the equipment, team members and money spent on this trip.

Mit diesem Plakat liefert Ole Østring einen visuellen Bericht seiner Reise durch Europa im Sommer 2009. Für das zentrale Motiv entwarf er eine Mischung aus Landkarte und Zeitleiste. Seine Reiseroute ist auf der Karte eingezeichnet, die einzelnen Stationen sind mit einem dicken Zeitstrahl verbunden, der sich spiralförmig um die Route legt.

Dadurch kann man die Reise auf zweierlei Arten nachvollziehen – indem man ihr auf der Karte folgt oder indem man den Zeitstrahl liest. Dieser enthält weiter reichende Informationen zu Tageszeiten und genutzten Verkehrsmitteln. Zudem geben statistische Daten auf dem Poster Aufschluss über Ausrüstung, Mitreisende sowie Reiseausgaben.

Avec cette affiche, Ole Østring a réalisé un rapport visuel de son *road trip* à travers l'Europe durant l'été 2009. L'image centrale est un mélange original de carte et de chronologie. L'itinéraire de son voyage est tracé sur la carte, et les différentes étapes sont reliées à une épaisse bande chronologique qui s'enroule autour d'elles.

Cela donne deux façons de reconstruire le voyage : en le suivant sur la carte, ou en lisant la chronologie. Cette dernière méthode fournit de plus des informations sur le moment de la journée et le type de transport utilisé. Des statistiques complémentaires donnent des informations détaillées sur l'équipement, les membres de l'équipe et les sommes dépensées pour ce voyage.

Project Info: Poster, 2009, Norway
Design: Ole Østring

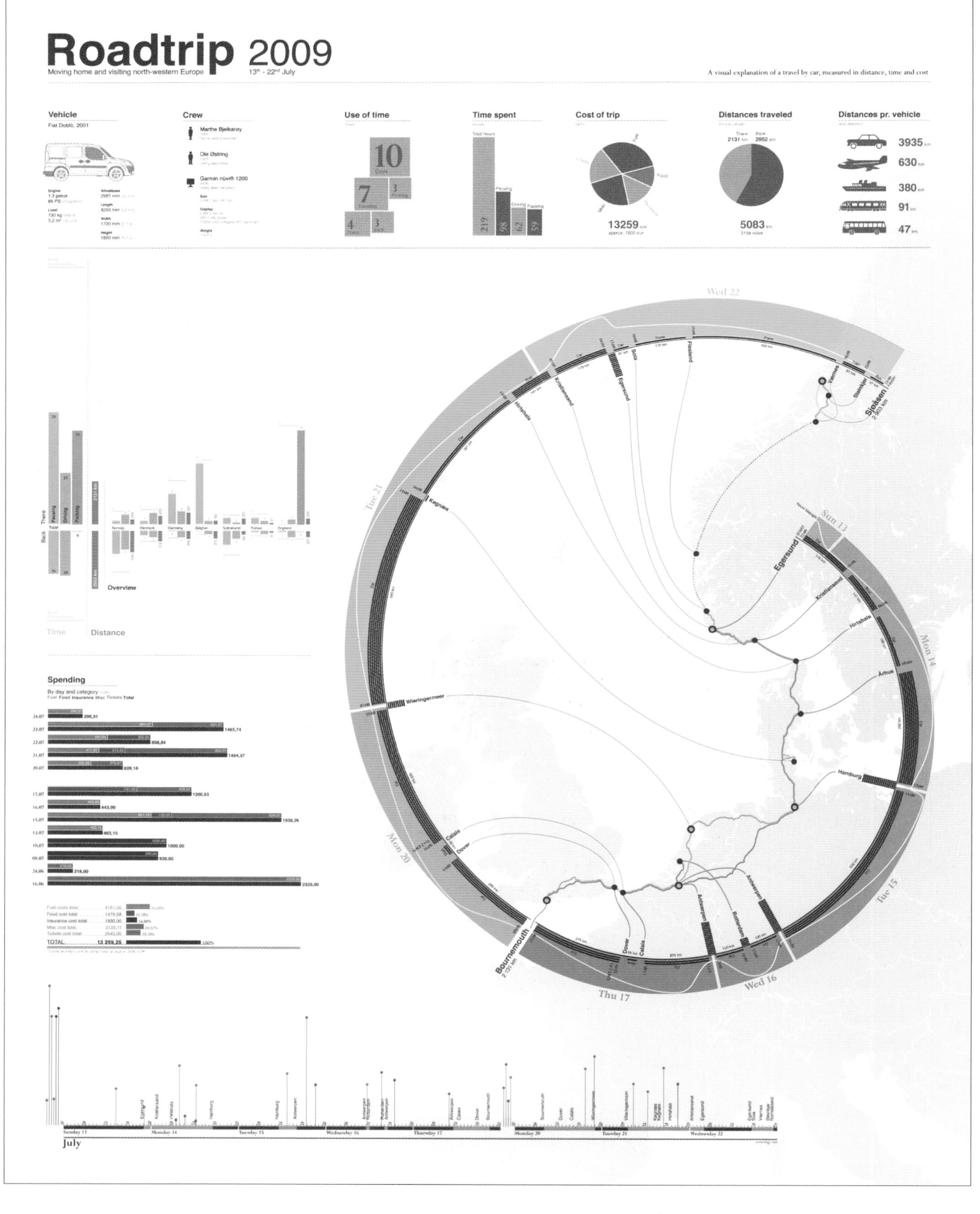

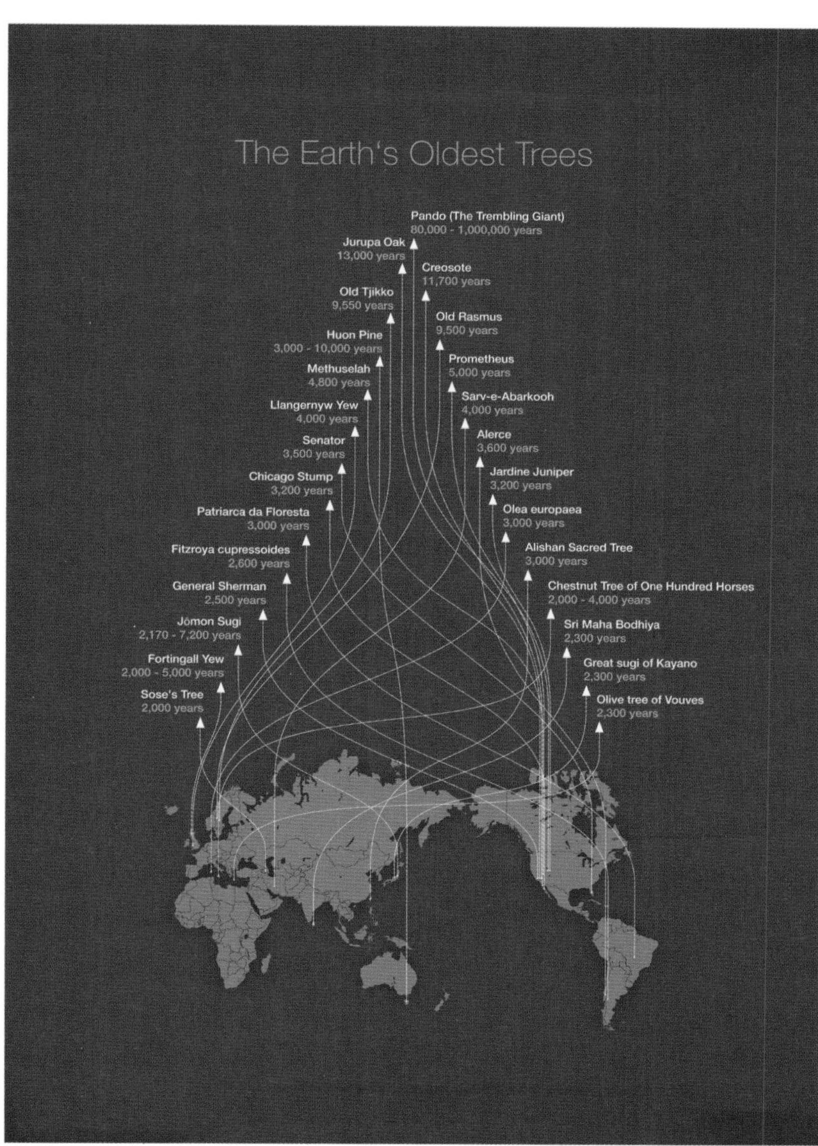

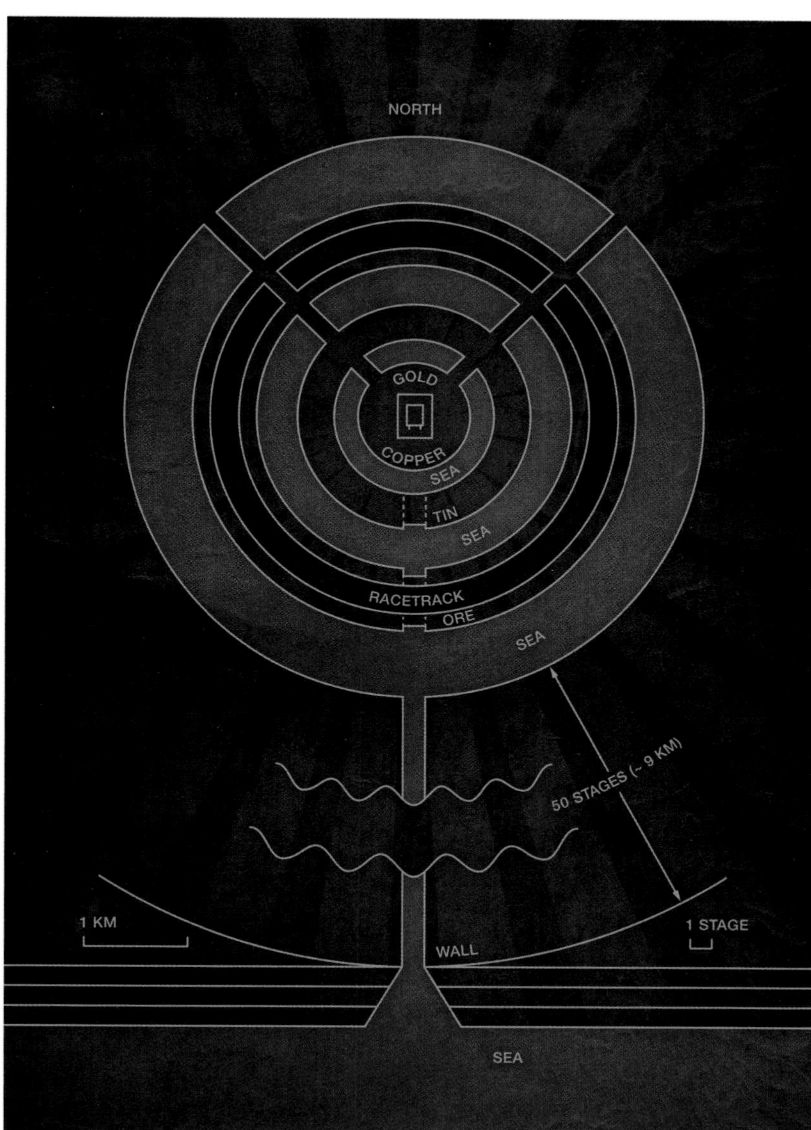

See the Bigger Picture

In his series "See the Bigger Picture", Austrian designer Michael Paukner explores the aesthetic side of visualising theory. The range of thinking he draws upon is vast and varies from ancient Inca or Celtic knowledge to scientific as well as pseudo-scientific thinking, conspiracy theories and hard mathematical or physical facts.

For each theory, he tries to discern the appropriate visual structure, employing a clean and minimal style. The series presents a whole array of world knowledge, exploring how it is possible to communicate something about the mysteries of the cosmos by finding beautiful ways to visualise how people reflect on them.

Trembling Giants (top left) interlaces a world map with a hierarchy of the world's oldest trees. *Capital of Atlantis* (top right) is a map of the main city of the mythical Atlantis, with its circular islands and canal system. Tags show Atlantis' wealth in metals. *Solar Eclipse* (following page left) shows the celestial alignment which causes a solar eclipse on Earth. *Hollow Earth* (following page right) visualises the old hypothesis that the Earth is a hollow sphere.

In seiner Serie „See the Bigger Picture“ beschäftigt sich der österreichische Grafiker Michael Paukner mit der ästhetischen Dimension bei der Visualisierung von Theorien. Seine Quellen findet er in allen möglichen Wissensgebieten, vom alten Wissen der Inka und der Kelten bis hin zu wissenschaftlichen und pseudowissenschaftlichen Überlegungen, Verschwörungstheorien und mathematischen und physikalischen Fakten.

Dabei versucht er, für jede Theorie die angemessene visuelle Struktur zu finden und sie in einem klaren, minimalistischen Stil darzustellen. Die Serie zeigt eine ganze Bandbreite von Weltwissen. Paukner untersucht, inwieweit sich die Mysterien des Universums vermitteln lassen, indem man die entsprechenden Theorien ästhetisch visualisiert.

Trembling Giants (oben links) verbindet eine Weltkarte mit einer Hierarchie der ältesten Bäume der Welt. *Capital of Atlantis* (oben rechts) zeigt die mythische Hauptstadt von Atlantis mit ihren kreisrunden Inseln und dem Kanalsystem. Die Beschriftungen verweisen auf den Edelmetallreichtum von Atlantis. *Solar Eclipse* (folgende Seite links) zeigt die Konstellation von Himmelskörpern, die eine Sonnenfinsternis auf der Erde verursacht. *Hollow Earth* (folgende Seite rechts) visualisiert die alte Theorie, dass die Erde eine hohle Sphäre sei.

Dans sa série « See the Bigger Picture », le graphiste autrichien Michael Paukner explore le côté esthétique de la représentation des théories. Il s'inspire d'un vaste éventail de pensées : le savoir ancien des Incas ou des Celtes, la pensée scientifique, mais également pseudoscientifique, les théories de la conspiration et les faits mathématiques et physiques purs et durs.

Pour chaque théorie, il essaie de trouver la structure visuelle appropriée et y applique un style épuré et minimaliste. Cette série présente tout un éventail de savoir mondial, et explore la possibilité de véhiculer les mystères du cosmos dans l'élégance de la visualisation du concept.

Trembling Giants (en haut à gauche) mêle une carte du monde et une hiérarchie des arbres les plus vieux de la planète. *Capital of Atlantis* (en haut à droite) offre une carte de la cité principale de la mythique Atlantide, avec ses îles circulaires et son système de canaux. Les intitulés montrent les ressources en métaux de l'Atlantide. *Solar Eclipse* (à gauche, page suivante) montre l'alignement céleste à l'origine d'une éclipse du Soleil sur Terre. *Hollow Earth* (à droite, page suivante) illustre l'ancienne hypothèse d'une Terre creuse.

Project Info: Series of posters, 2009–2011, Austria
Design: Michael Paukner

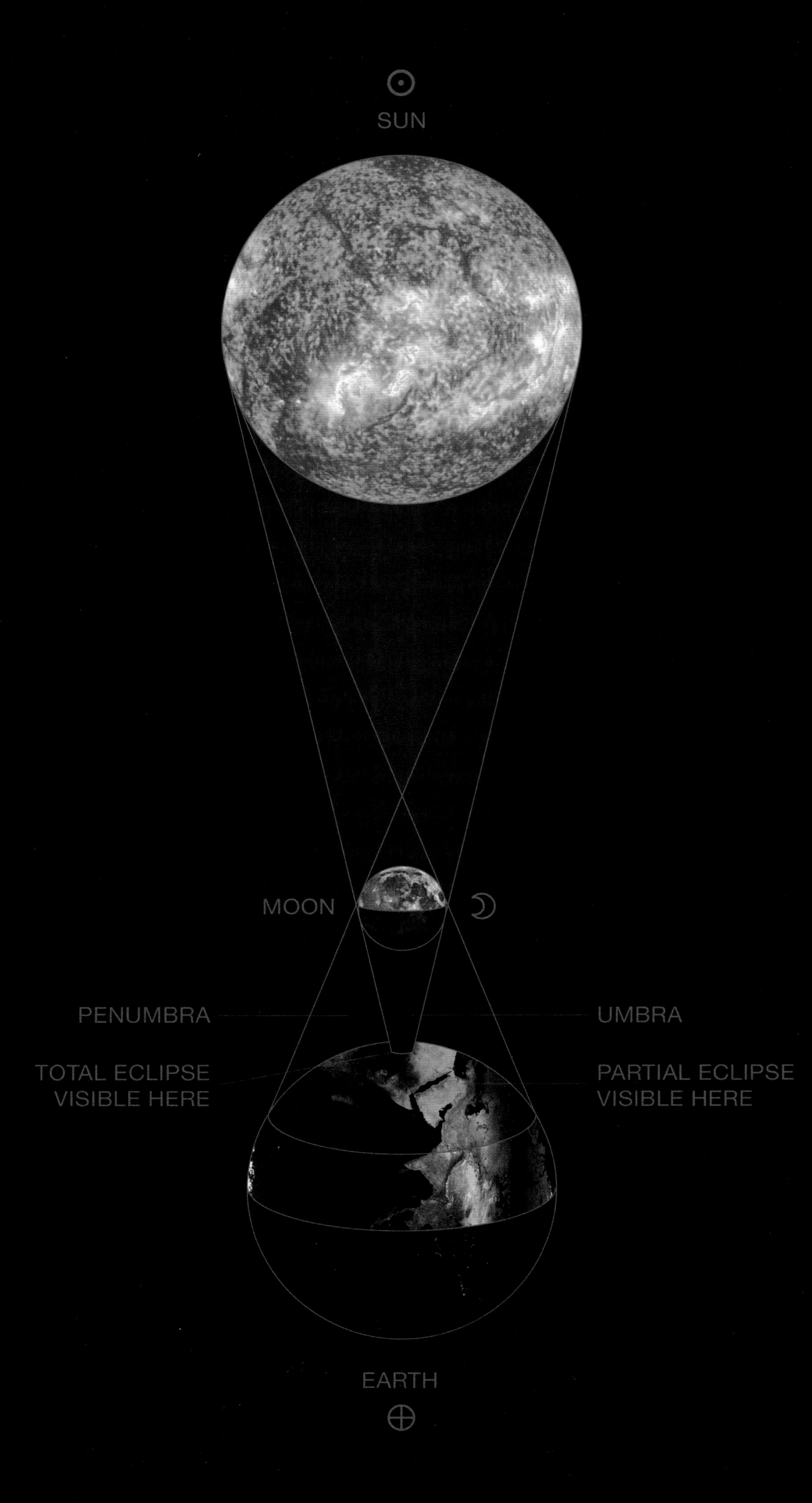
SUN
MOON
PENUMBRA
UMBRA
TOTAL ECLIPSE
VISIBLE HERE
PARTIAL ECLIPSE
VISIBLE HERE
EARTH

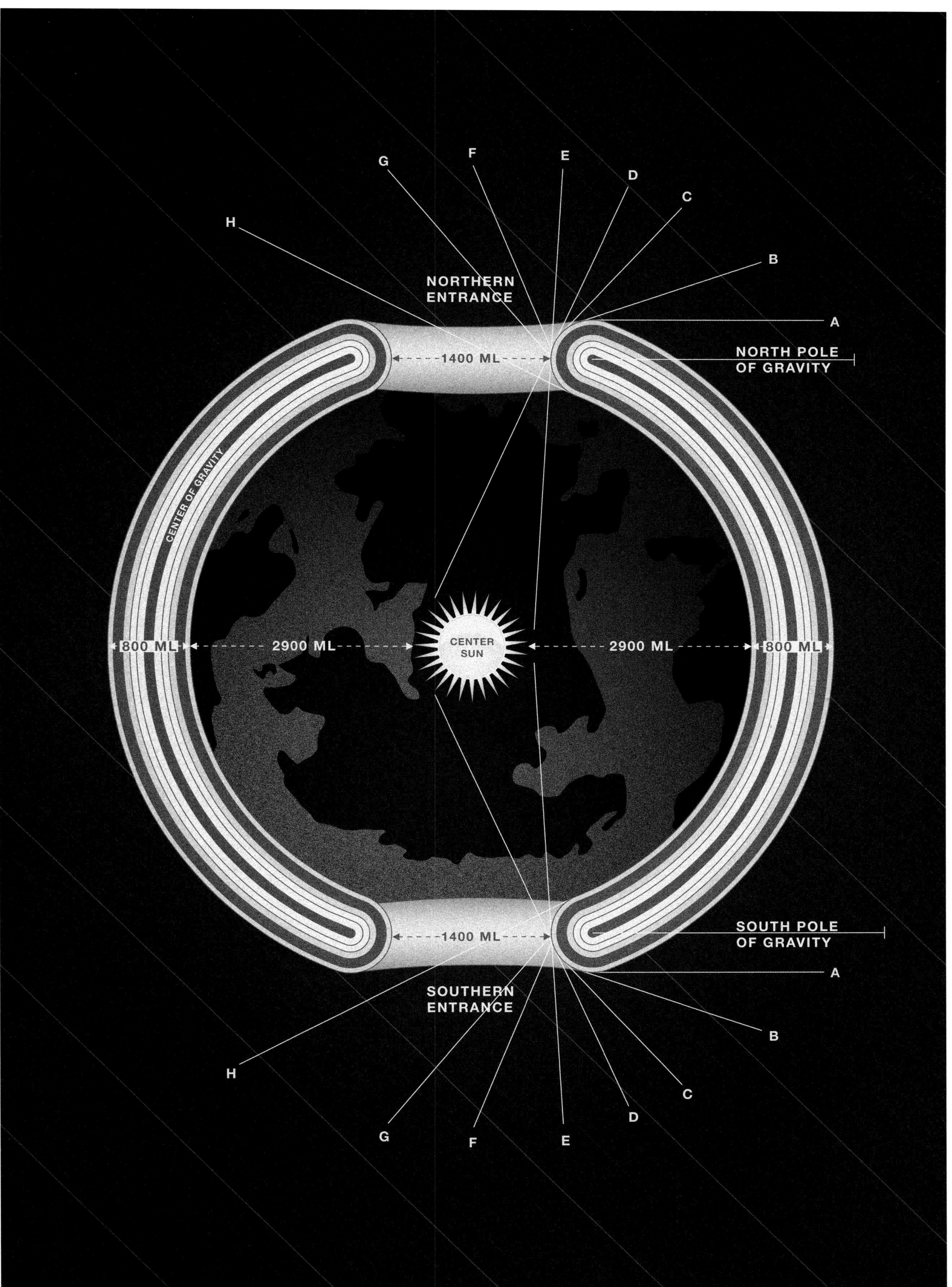
G
F
E
D
C
H
B
NORTHERN
ENTRANCE
A
1400 ML
NORTH POLE
OF GRAVITY
CENTER OF GRAVITY
800 ML
2900 ML
CENTER
SUN
2900 ML
800 ML
1400 ML
SOUTH POLE
OF GRAVITY
A
SOUTHERN
ENTRANCE
B
H
C
D
G
F
E

Setouchi Perfect Guide Casa BRUTUS September 2010

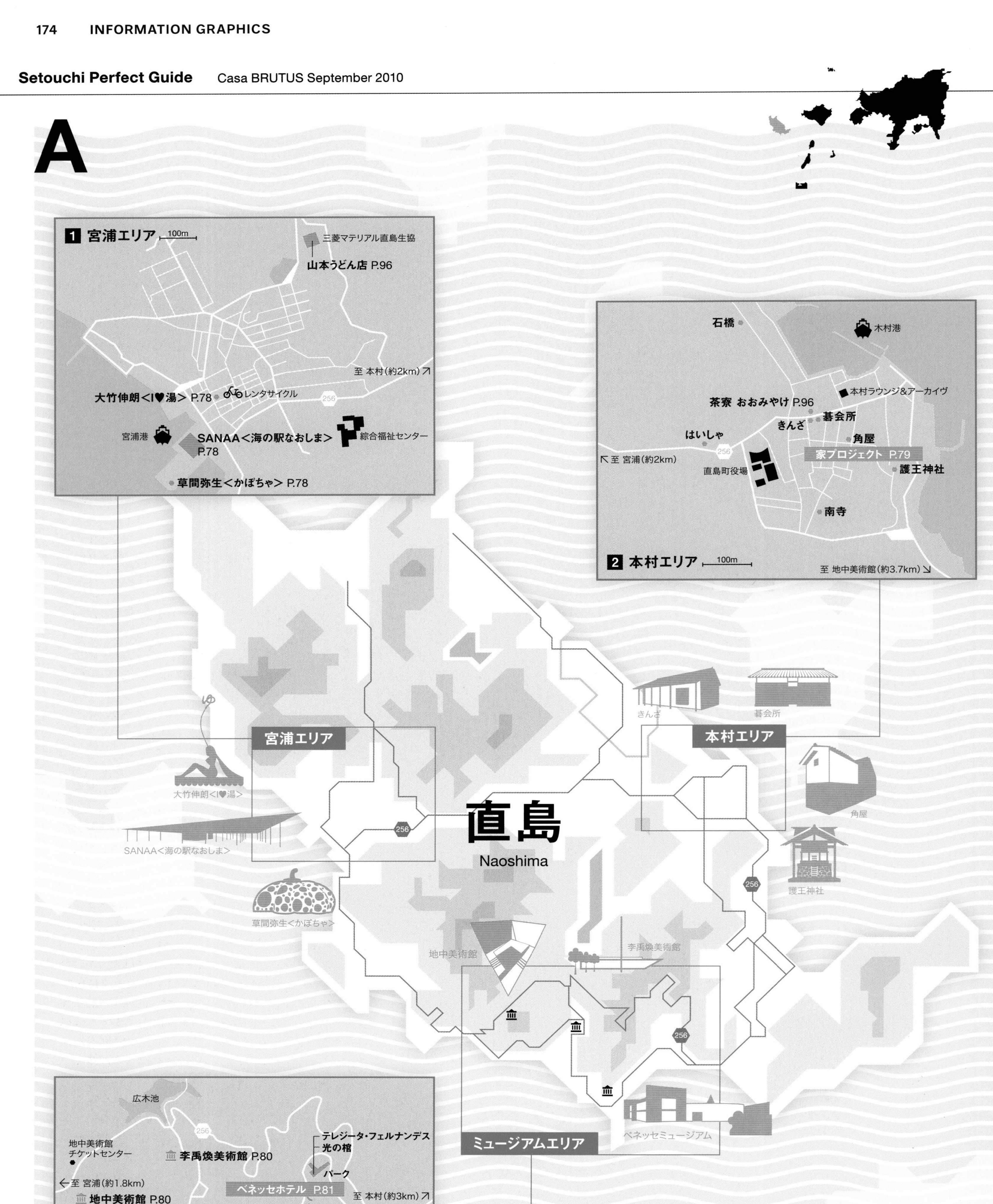

Project Info: Setouchi International Art Festival 2010, *Casa Brutus*, magazine article, 2010, Japan
Design: Tokuma, Noriyuki Tatemori (Bowlgraphics)

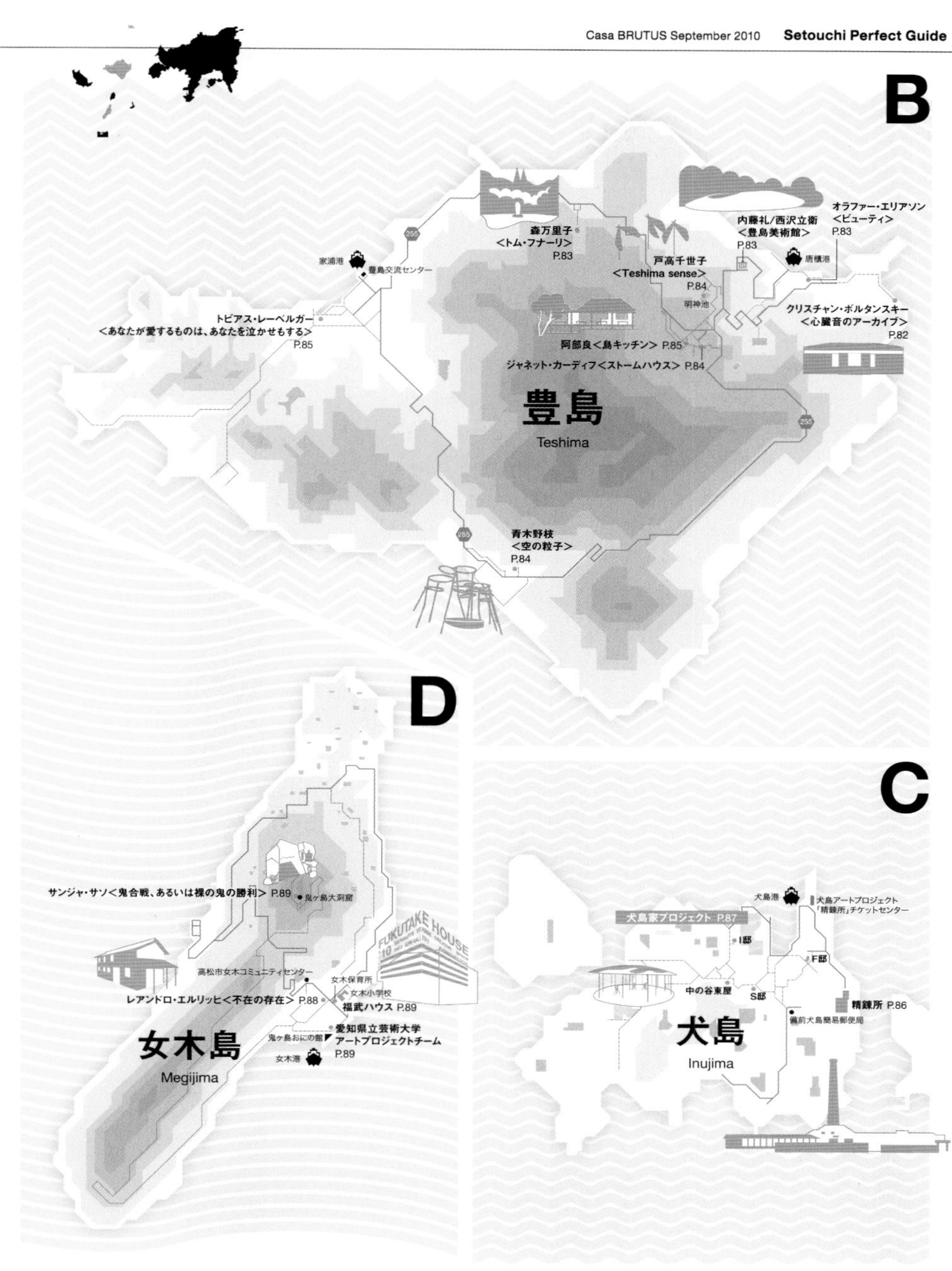

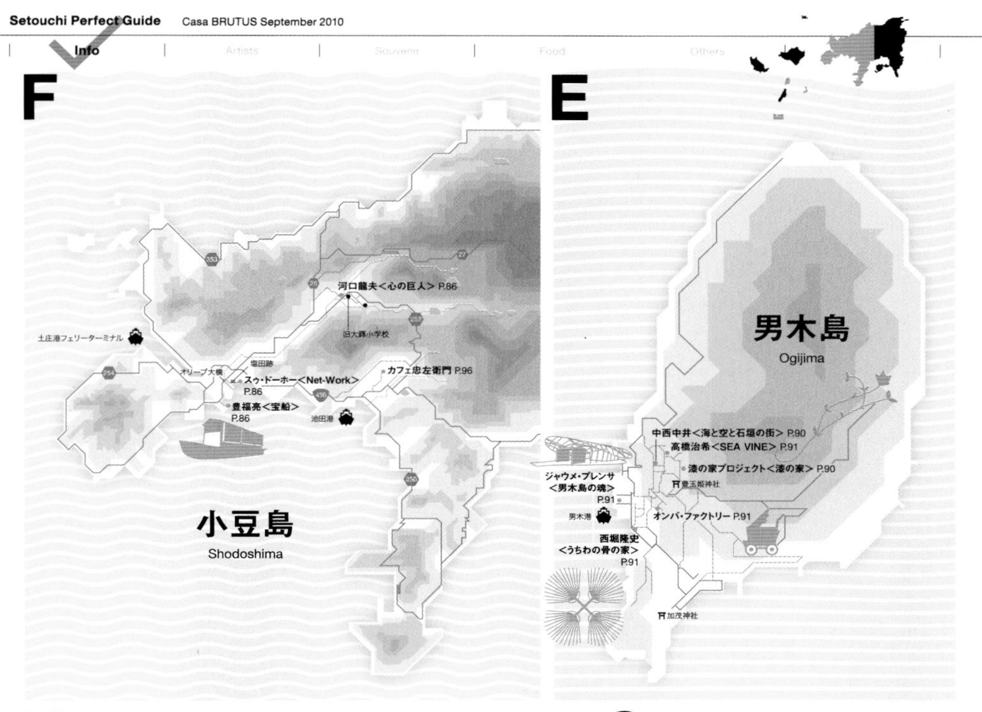

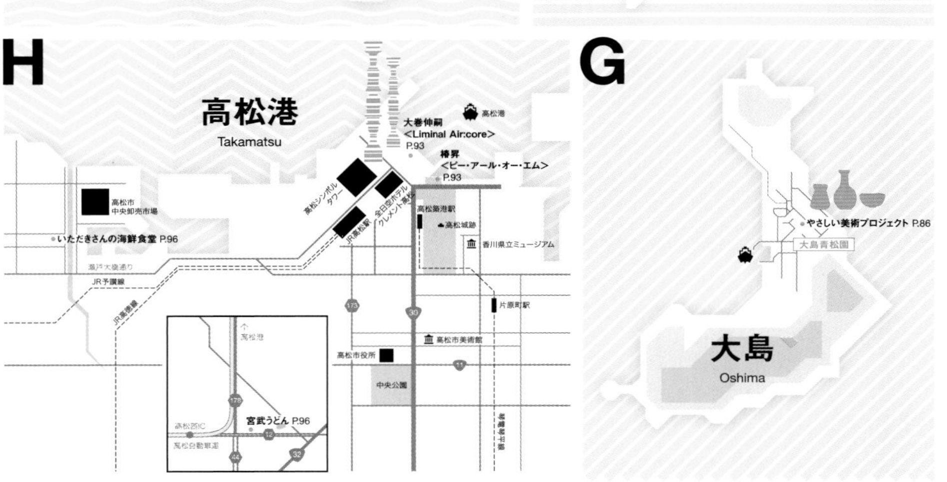

Setouchi Perfect Guide

The Seto Inland Sea is Japan's largest body of water, separating the three main islands and spotted with lots of tiny islands. In 2010, the Setouchi Art Festival was held on seven neighbouring islands. This series of maps shows the individual venues of the festival. A little icon at the top of each spread works as a guide as to which of the islands is depicted on each page.

The islands are shown as stylised shapes, with grey shades giving an impression of geographical elevation on each one. Pink icons refer to venues or artworks in the festival. Additional inserts show detailed maps. For each island, the designer Tokuma developed a varying water pattern to depict the ocean.

Die Seto-Inlandsee, Japans größtes Gewässer, trennt die drei Hauptinseln und ist von zahlreichen kleinen Inseln durchsetzt. 2010 wurde auf sieben benachbarten Inseln das Setouchi Art Festival abgehalten. Die Kartenserie zeigt die einzelnen Veranstaltungsorte. Eine kleine Grafik am oberen Bildrand zeigt jeweils, welche der sieben Inseln auf der Seite dargestellt ist.

Die Inseln sind stilisiert gezeichnet, graue Schattierungen deuten geografische Höhenunterschiede an. Pinkfarbene Symbole verweisen auf Veranstaltungsorte und Kunstwerke des Festivals, in gesonderten Kästen sind Detailkarten zu sehen. Der Grafiker Tokuma entwickelte für jede Insel ein anderes Muster zur Darstellung des Meeres.

La mer intérieure de Seto est la plus grande étendue d'eau du Japon. Elle sépare les trois îles principales et est parsemée d'une multitude d'îlots minuscules. En 2010, le festival d'art de Setouchi a été organisé sur sept îles voisines. Cette série de cartes montre les différents sites du festival. Une petite icône en haut de chaque page indique laquelle des îles est représentée.

Les contours des îles sont stylisés, et des niveaux de gris donnent une impression de relief géographique. Les icônes roses font référence aux sites ou œuvres du festival. Des cadres montrent des cartes détaillées. Le graphiste Tokuma a assigné à chaque île un motif différent pour représenter l'océan.

Shell's Big Dig

Extracting oil from fields in deep seas is one of the most technically advanced and often dangerous undertakings. In this piece, John Grimwade and Bryan Christie explain Perdido, the floating platform atop the deepest offshore production well to date, run by Shell. The main 3D illustration provides a look into the construction of the platform, indicating relative size by the addition of a ship and a helicopter.

The map to the left shows the location in the Gulf of Mexico, while a small inset strip to the right gives an impression of the actual depth at which the platform is drilling for oil, indicating that the oil-fields themselves lie very deep beneath the ocean floor.

Erdöl aus der Tiefsee zu fördern ist ein technisch höchst anspruchsvolles und oft gefährliches Unternehmen. Auf dieser Grafik erläutern John Grimwade und Bryan Christie die von Shell betriebene Bohrinsel Perdido, eine schwimmende Plattform über dem bislang tiefsten Bohrloch der Welt. Die große 3D-Illustration zeigt den Aufbau der Bohrinsel. Das Schiff und der Hubschrauber dienen dem Größenvergleich.

Auf der Karte links ist die Lage im Golf von Mexiko verzeichnet, während die schmale Grafik rechts die tatsächliche Tiefe veranschaulicht, in der von der Plattform aus nach Öl gebohrt wird; daraus wird ersichtlich, wie tief die Ölfelder unter dem Meeresboden liegen.

L'exploitation des puits de pétrole en haute mer est l'une des entreprises les plus avancées sur le plan technologique, et souvent l'une des plus dangereuses. Ici, John Grimwade et Bryan Christie expliquent Perdido, une plateforme qui flotte au-dessus du puits offshore le plus profond à ce jour, exploité par Shell. L'illustration principale en 3D donne un aperçu de la structure de la plateforme, et une idée de sa taille en la comparant avec un bateau et un hélicoptère.

La carte de gauche montre sa situation géographique dans le Golfe du Mexique, et une petite bande insérée à droite donne une idée de la profondeur à laquelle la plateforme fore pour atteindre le pétrole, indiquant ainsi que les champs pétrolifères sont profondément enfouis sous les fonds sous-marins.

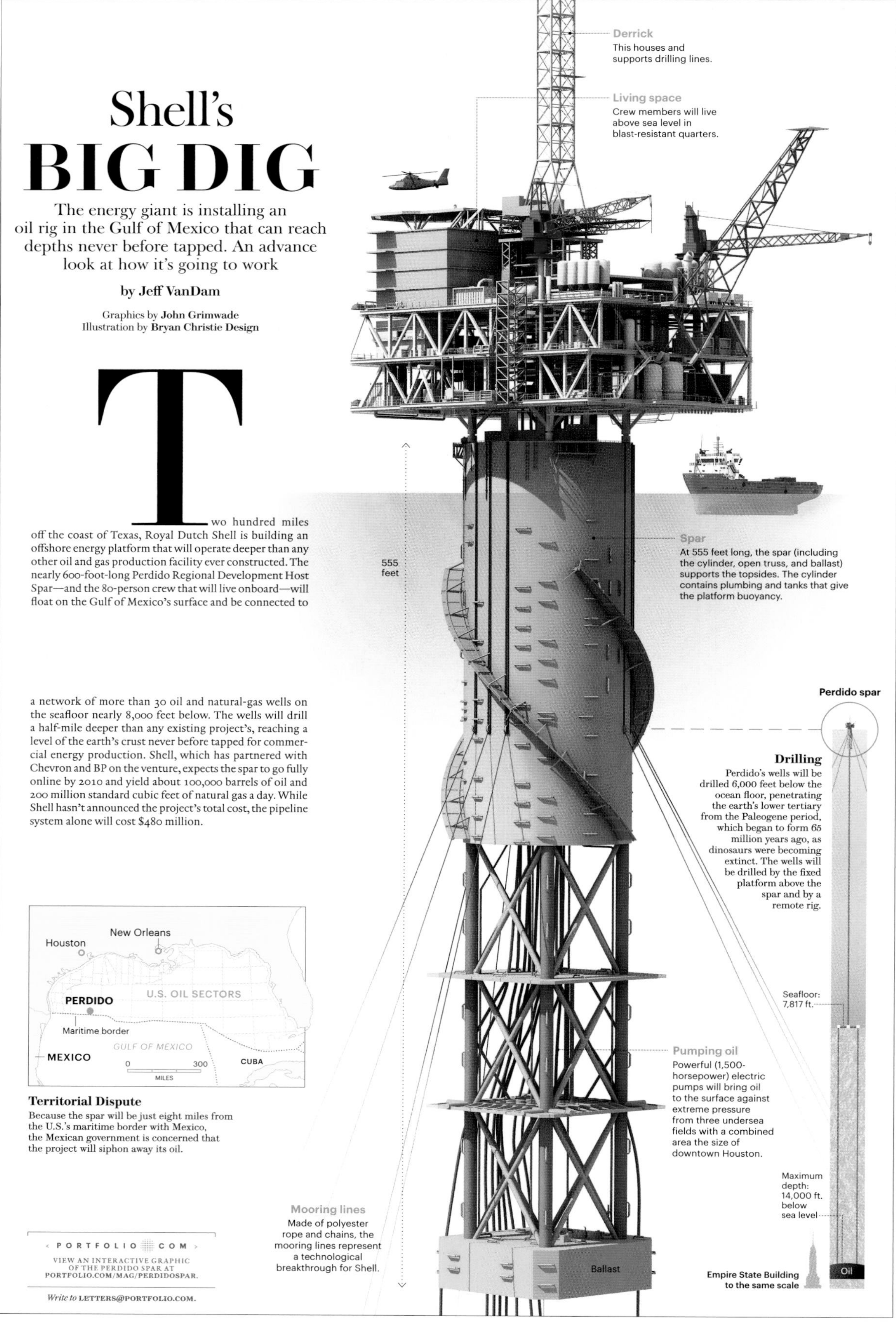

Shell's BIG DIG

The energy giant is installing an oil rig in the Gulf of Mexico that can reach depths never before tapped. An advance look at how it's going to work

by Jeff VanDam

Graphics by John Grimwade
Illustration by Bryan Christie Design

Two hundred miles off the coast of Texas, Royal Dutch Shell is building an offshore energy platform that will operate deeper than any other oil and gas production facility ever constructed. The nearly 600-foot-long Perdido Regional Development Host Spar—and the 80-person crew that will live onboard—will float on the Gulf of Mexico's surface and be connected to a network of more than 30 oil and natural-gas wells on the seafloor nearly 8,000 feet below. The wells will drill a half-mile deeper than any existing project's, reaching a level of the earth's crust never before tapped for commercial energy production. Shell, which has partnered with Chevron and BP on the venture, expects the spar to go fully online by 2010 and yield about 100,000 barrels of oil and 200 million standard cubic feet of natural gas a day. While Shell hasn't announced the project's total cost, the pipeline system alone will cost $480 million.

Derrick
This houses and supports drilling lines.
Living space
Crew members will live above sea level in blast-resistant quarters.
555 feet
Spar
At 555 feet long, the spar (including the cylinder, open truss, and ballast) supports the topsides. The cylinder contains plumbing and tanks that give the platform buoyancy.
Perdido spar
Drilling
Perdido's wells will be drilled 6,000 feet below the ocean floor, penetrating the earth's lower tertiary from the Paleogene period, which began to form 65 million years ago, as dinosaurs were becoming extinct. The wells will be drilled by the fixed platform above the spar and by a remote rig.
Seafloor: 7,817 ft.
Pumping oil
Powerful (1,500-horsepower) electric pumps will bring oil to the surface against extreme pressure from three undersea fields with a combined area the size of downtown Houston.
Maximum depth: 14,000 ft. below sea level
Oil
Empire State Building to the same scale
Mooring lines
Made of polyester rope and chains, the mooring lines represent a technological breakthrough for Shell.
Ballast
Houston
New Orleans
U.S. OIL SECTORS
PERDIDO
Maritime border
GULF OF MEXICO
MEXICO
0 300
MILES
CUBA

Territorial Dispute
Because the spar will be just eight miles from the U.S.'s maritime border with Mexico, the Mexican government is concerned that the project will siphon away its oil.

PORTFOLIO COM
VIEW AN INTERACTIVE GRAPHIC OF THE PERDIDO SPAR AT PORTFOLIO.COM/MAG/PERDIDOSPAR.

Write to LETTERS@PORTFOLIO.COM.

Project Info: *Condé Nast Portfolio*, magazine article, 2009, USA
Research: Jeff VanDam
Design: John Grimwade, Grace Lee
Art Direction: Robert Priest
Illustration: Bryan Christie

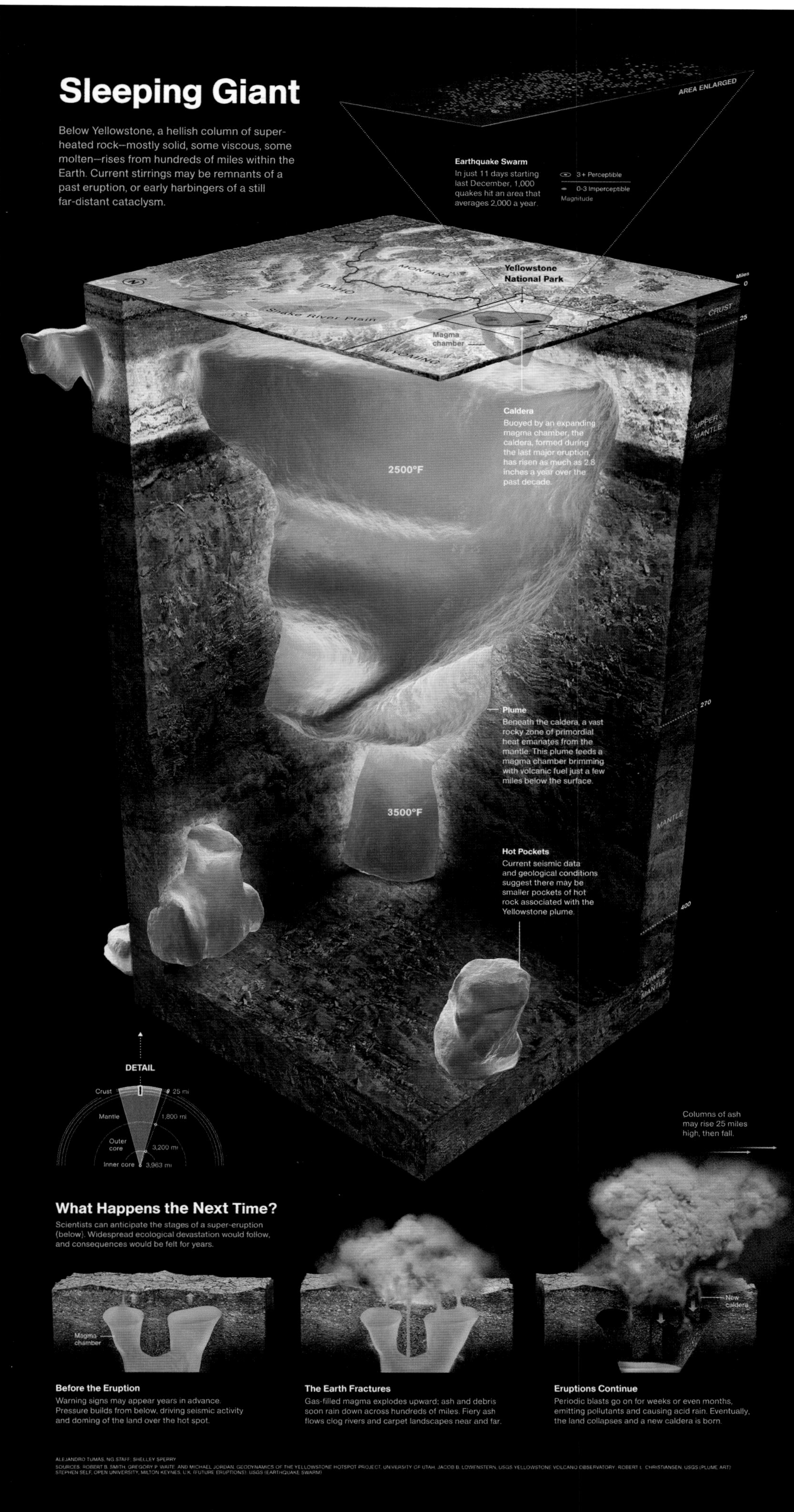

Sleeping Giant
Below Yellowstone, a hellish column of super-heated rock–mostly solid, some viscous, some molten–rises from hundreds of miles within the Earth. Current stirrings may be remnants of a past eruption, or early harbingers of a still far-distant cataclysm.
AREA ENLARGED
Earthquake Swarm
In just 11 days starting last December, 1,000 quakes hit an area that averages 2,000 a year.
3+ Perceptible
0-3 Imperceptible
Magnitude
MONTANA
IDAHO
Snake River Plain
WYOMING
Yellowstone National Park
Magma chamber
Miles
0
CRUST
25
UPPER MANTLE
270
MANTLE
400
LOWER MANTLE
Caldera
Buoyed by an expanding magma chamber, the caldera, formed during the last major eruption, has risen as much as 2.8 inches a year over the past decade.
2500°F
Plume
Beneath the caldera, a vast rocky zone of primordial heat emanates from the mantle. This plume feeds a magma chamber brimming with volcanic fuel just a few miles below the surface.
3500°F
Hot Pockets
Current seismic data and geological conditions suggest there may be smaller pockets of hot rock associated with the Yellowstone plume.
DETAIL
Crust
25 mi
Mantle
1,800 mi
Outer core
3,200 mi
Inner core
3,963 mi
Columns of ash may rise 25 miles high, then fall.
What Happens the Next Time?
Scientists can anticipate the stages of a super-eruption (below). Widespread ecological devastation would follow, and consequences would be felt for years.
Magma chamber
New caldera
Before the Eruption
Warning signs may appear years in advance. Pressure builds from below, driving seismic activity and doming of the land over the hot spot.
The Earth Fractures
Gas-filled magma explodes upward; ash and debris soon rain down across hundreds of miles. Fiery ash flows clog rivers and carpet landscapes near and far.
Eruptions Continue
Periodic blasts go on for weeks or even months, emitting pollutants and causing acid rain. Eventually, the land collapses and a new caldera is born.
ALEJANDRO TUMAS, NG STAFF; SHELLEY SPERRY
SOURCES: ROBERT B. SMITH, GREGORY P. WAITE, AND MICHAEL JORDAN, GEODYNAMICS OF THE YELLOWSTONE HOTSPOT PROJECT, UNIVERSITY OF UTAH; JACOB B. LOWENSTERN, USGS YELLOWSTONE VOLCANO OBSERVATORY; ROBERT L. CHRISTIANSEN, USGS (PLUME ART); STEPHEN SELF, OPEN UNIVERSITY, MILTON KEYNES, U.K. (FUTURE ERUPTIONS); USGS (EARTHQUAKE SWARM)

Project Info: "When Yellowstone Explodes", *National Geographic*, magazine article, 2009, USA
Data Source: Geodynamics of the Yellowstone Hotspot Project (University of Utah); USGS Yellowstone Volcano Observatory; Open University
Research: Shelley Sperry
Design: Alejandro Tumas, John Baxter
Art Direction: Juan Velasco
Illustration: Hernán Cañellas
Awards: Malofiej 2010; Society for News Design 2010

Sleeping Giant

In this piece, *National Geographic* cuts open the Earth beneath Yellowstone National Park, showing the giant column of magma resting there, about 400 miles deep. The upper square shows the Earth's surface with the National Park marked in red. A surface detail is cut out and elevated to show the seismic activity recently increasing in the area, by way of dots on a map.

Seismic activity data were drawn from USGS and GIS mapping. Below, the magma column is shown in detail. If the super-volcano erupts again, widespread devastation would follow. The 3D modelling of the column was created by specialists at the University of Ohio. Along the bottom, a series of schematic drawings shows scenarios for the near future.

In dieser Grafik schneidet *National Geographic* die Erde unter dem Yellowstone National Park auf und zeigt die gewaltige Magmasäule, die dort in rund 600 km Tiefe ruht. Das obere Quadrat präsentiert die Erdoberfläche, der Nationalpark ist darin rot eingezeichnet. Ein Detail wurde ausgeschnitten und vergrößert. Darin zeigen Punkte die steigende seismische Aktivität, die neuerdings in der Gegend gemessen wurde.

Die Angaben zur seismischen Aktivität basieren auf Daten des US Geological Survey und von Geoinformationssystemen. Unten wird die Magmasäule im Detail dargestellt. Sollte der Supervulkan erneut ausbrechen, wäre eine weiträumige Zerstörung die Folge. Das 3D-Modell der Säule wurde von Fachleuten der University of Ohio entworfen. Am unteren Bildrand zeigen schematische Zeichnungen mögliche Szenarien der näheren Zukunft.

Dans cette illustration, *National Geographic* ouvre la Terre sous le Parc national de Yellowstone pour montrer la colonne géante de magma qui repose à 400 miles de profondeur. Le carré du haut montre la surface de la Terre, et le Parc national est indiqué en rouge. Un détail de la surface est agrandi au-dessus pour montrer l'activité sismique qui a récemment augmenté dans la région au moyen de points sur une carte.

Les données relatives à l'activité sismique sont tirées de cartes de l'USGS et GIS. En dessous, la colonne de magma est montrée en détail. Si ce super-volcan entrait en éruption, il causerait des destructions à grande échelle. La modélisation en 3D de la colonne a été réalisée par des spécialistes de l'Université de l'Ohio. Dans le bas, une série de schémas montre des scénarios pour l'avenir à court terme.

Spatio-Temporal Analysis of Mega-City Growth

Based on research from the German Aerospace Center, this project uses remote sensing data to measure and analyse the effects of urbanisation throughout the world. Satellite data are transformed into a series of maps, in which urban areas and water are marked in colour.

The series shown here demonstrates the urban sprawl in the city of Manila, Philippines in three time-steps from 1975 to 2010. The exceptional spatial expansion is caused by the specific one-family-per-house architecture employed in large parts of the city. The project exemplifies how satellite data are transferred to enhanced maps in order to analyse large-scale geographical phenomena.

Ausgehend von Daten des Deutschen Zentrums für Luft- und Raumfahrt misst und analysiert dieses Projekt mithilfe von Fernerkundungsdaten die Auswirkungen der weltweiten Urbanisierung. Von Satelliten erhobene Daten werden in eine Serie von Landkarten umgewandelt, wobei urbane Bereiche und Gewässer farbig markiert werden.

Die hier abgebildete Serie zeigt den Einzugsbereich von Manila (Philippinen) in drei Zeitschritten zwischen 1975 und 2010. Das außerordentliche Wachstum der Stadt ist darauf zurückzuführen, dass weite Teile des Stadtgebietes von Einfamilienhäusern eingenommen werden. Das Projekt veranschaulicht, wie Satellitendaten in thematische Landkarten transformiert werden, um großräumige geografische Phänomene zu analysieren.

Ce projet se base sur les données télédétectées d'une étude du Centre aérospatial allemand pour mesurer et analyser les effets de l'urbanisation dans le monde. Les données satellitaires sont transformées en une série de cartes dans lesquelles les zones urbaines et les étendues d'eau sont colorées.

La série présentée ici montre l'avancée de la ville de Manille, aux Philippines, en trois étapes de 1975 à 2010. Cette expansion spatiale exceptionnelle est causée par l'architecture spécifique utilisée dans de grandes parties de la ville, constituée de maisons unifamiliales. Ce projet montre comment les données satellitaires peuvent être traduites en cartes pour analyser les phénomènes géographiques à grande échelle.

Project Info: Series of maps, 2010, Germany
Data Source: German Remote Sensing Data Center; Earth Observation Center; German Aerospace Center
Research / Design: Prof. Dr. Stefan Dech, Dr. Hannes Taubenböck, Dr. Thomas Esch (German Aerospace Center)

The Babel of Beers

Beer is a drink available in many countries. Like a display board, this double-spread presents an international status report on beer consumption and how it is regulated around the world. Each bottle represents one country, with the crown cap showing the national flag. On the bottle neck the price per half litre is given in $.

All bottles are labelled "beer" in the respective national languages, while the percentage figure beneath indicates the tax rate on alcohol in each country. Shaded bars behind each bottle show how much beer is consumed in each country, with a record per capita consumption in the Czech Republic. Symbols beneath each bottle illustrate in which public places alcohol is banned by law.

Bier ist ein universales Getränk – es gibt eine verblüffende Vielfalt von Biersorten auf der ganzen Welt. Wie auf einer Schautafel präsentiert diese Doppelseite einen internationalen Statusbericht zum Bierkonsum und den staatlichen Auflagen, denen er unterliegt. Jede Flasche repräsentiert ein Land, der Kronkorken zeigt die Nationalflagge. Auf dem Flaschenhals steht der Preis für einen halben Liter in US-Dollar.

Alle Flaschen tragen die Aufschrift „Bier" in der jeweiligen Landessprache, die darunter stehende Prozentzahl gibt die Alkoholsteuer im betreffenden Land an. Graue Balken hinter jeder Flasche zeigen den Bierkonsum pro Kopf, Spitzenreiter ist die Tschechische Republik. Symbole unter den Flaschen illustrieren, an welchen öffentlichen Orten der Alkoholkonsum gesetzlich untersagt ist.

La bière est une boisson que l'on trouve dans de nombreux pays. À la manière d'un panneau d'affichage, cette double page présente un rapport sur l'état de la consommation de bière dans le monde, ainsi que de la réglementation qui s'applique à cette boisson. Chaque bouteille représente un pays, avec la capsule portant le drapeau national. Sur le col de la bouteille, le prix du demi-litre est indiqué en dollars.

Toutes les bouteilles sont étiquetées « bière » dans la langue locale, et le pourcentage indique la taxe prélevée sur l'alcool dans chaque pays. Les barres grisées montrent la quantité de bière consommée. C'est la République tchèque qui détient le record de consommation par habitant. Sous chaque bouteille, les symboles représentent les lieux publics où la consommation d'alcool est interdite par la loi.

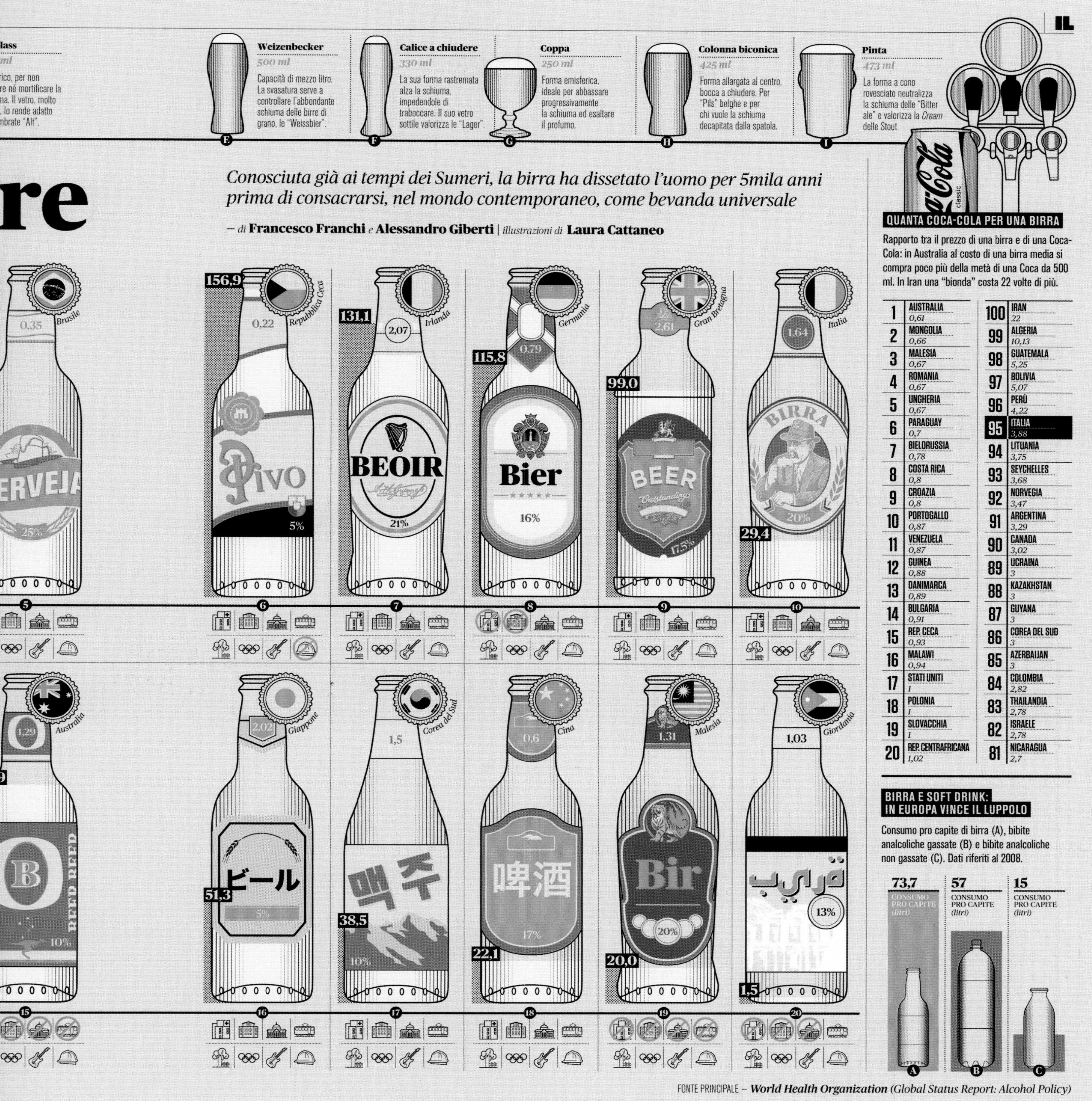

...lass
... ml
...rico, per non ...re né mortificare la ...ma. Il vetro, molto ..., lo rende adatto ...mbrate "Alt".

Weizenbecker
500 ml
Capacità di mezzo litro. La svasatura serve a controllare l'abbondante schiuma delle birre di grano, le "Weissbier".

Calice a chiudere
330 ml
La sua forma rastremata alza la schiuma, impedendole di traboccare. Il suo vetro sottile valorizza le "Lager".

Coppa
250 ml
Forma emisferica, ideale per abbassare progressivamente la schiuma ed esaltare il profumo.

Colonna biconica
425 ml
Forma allargata al centro, bocca a chiudere. Per "Pils" belghe e per chi vuole la schiuma decapitata dalla spatola.

Pinta
473 ml
La forma a cono rovesciato neutralizza la schiuma delle "Bitter ale" e valorizza la *Cream* delle Stout.

...re

Conosciuta già ai tempi dei Sumeri, la birra ha dissetato l'uomo per 5mila anni prima di consacrarsi, nel mondo contemporaneo, come bevanda universale

– *di* **Francesco Franchi** *e* **Alessandro Giberti** | *illustrazioni di* **Laura Cattaneo**

QUANTA COCA-COLA PER UNA BIRRA

Rapporto tra il prezzo di una birra e di una Coca-Cola: in Australia al costo di una birra media si compra poco più della metà di una Coca da 500 ml. In Iran una "bionda" costa 22 volte di più.

1	AUSTRALIA *0,61*	100	IRAN *22*
2	MONGOLIA *0,66*	99	ALGERIA *10,13*
3	MALESIA *0,67*	98	GUATEMALA *5,25*
4	ROMANIA *0,67*	97	BOLIVIA *5,07*
5	UNGHERIA *0,67*	96	PERÙ *4,22*
6	PARAGUAY *0,7*	95	ITALIA *3,88*
7	BIELORUSSIA *0,78*	94	LITUANIA *3,75*
8	COSTA RICA *0,8*	93	SEYCHELLES *3,68*
9	CROAZIA *0,8*	92	NORVEGIA *3,47*
10	PORTOGALLO *0,87*	91	ARGENTINA *3,29*
11	VENEZUELA *0,87*	90	CANADA *3,02*
12	GUINEA *0,88*	89	UCRAINA *3*
13	DANIMARCA *0,89*	88	KAZAKHSTAN *3*
14	BULGARIA *0,91*	87	GUYANA *3*
15	REP. CECA *0,93*	86	COREA DEL SUD *3*
16	MALAWI *0,94*	85	AZERBAIJAN *3*
17	STATI UNITI *1*	84	COLOMBIA *2,82*
18	POLONIA *1*	83	THAILANDIA *2,78*
19	SLOVACCHIA *1*	82	ISRAELE *2,78*
20	REP. CENTRAFRICANA *1,02*	81	NICARAGUA *2,7*

BIRRA E SOFT DRINK: IN EUROPA VINCE IL LUPPOLO

Consumo pro capite di birra (A), bibite analcoliche gassate (B) e bibite analcoliche non gassate (C). Dati riferiti al 2008.

FONTE PRINCIPALE – ***World Health Organization*** *(Global Status Report: Alcohol Policy)*

49

Project Info: *Intelligence in Lifestyle*, magazine article, 2010, Italy
Data Source: World Health Organization
Research: Alessandro Giberti
Design / Art Direction: Francesco Franchi
Illustration: Laura Cattaneo

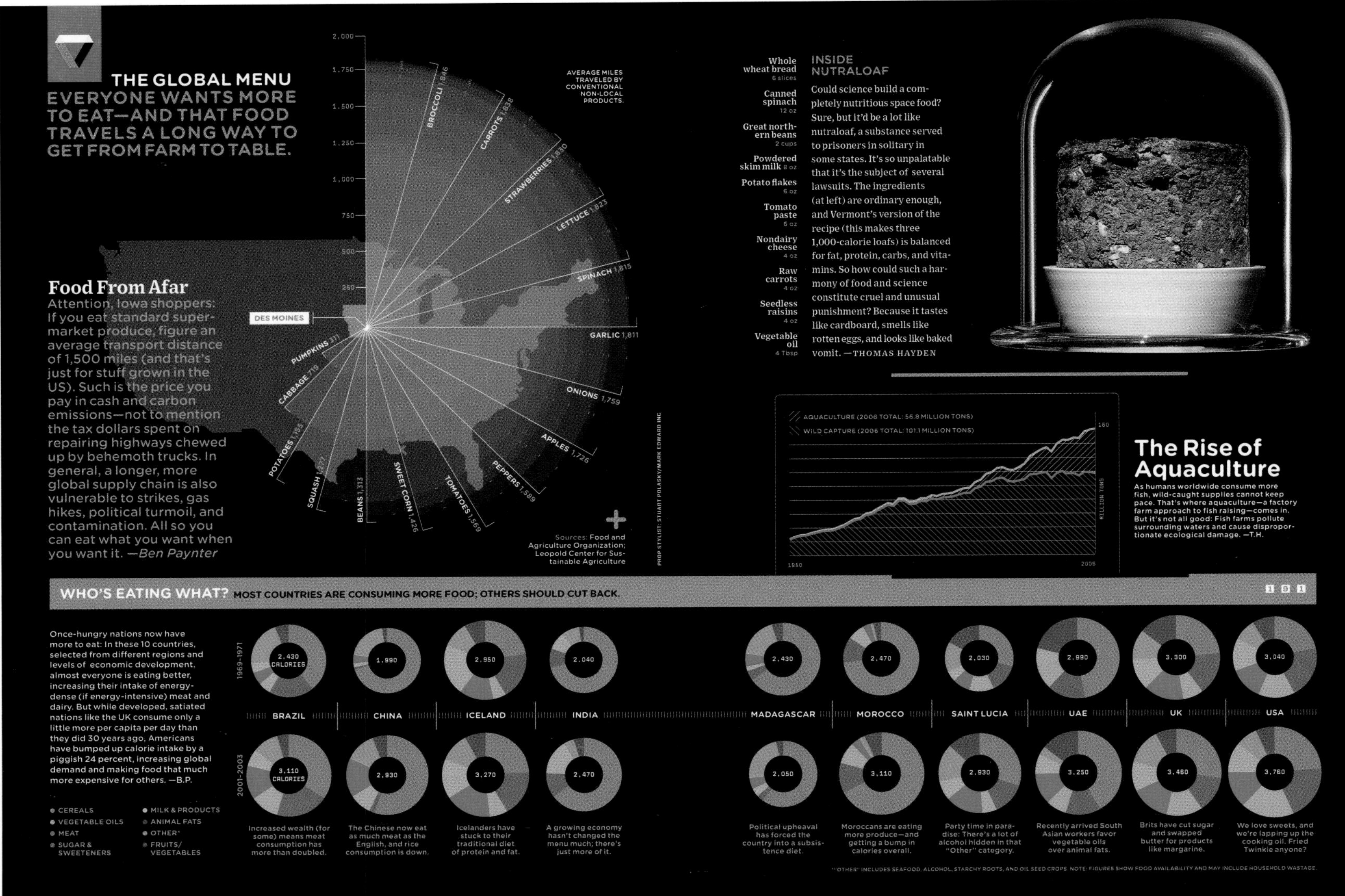

The Future of Food

This series of three double-spreads addresses trends in global food-supply. One focuses on current eating habits, with pie charts showing what and how much people eat in various countries. The map top left indicates how far supermarket produce in the US has travelled on average, based on the example of Des Moines, Iowa.

One world map locates political and social events which affect the global food-supply. The bar diagram beneath it shows food imports and exports in selected regions, demonstrating that Africa depends heavily on importing food. The other world map (bottom right) looks at states that develop genetically modified food. They are marked in green, with their height projection indicating the total area of farmland used.

Diese drei Doppelseiten umfassende Reihe wendet sich globalen Trends in der Nahrungsmittelversorgung zu. Eine Seite ist den heutigen Ernährungsgewohnheiten gewidmet, Tortendiagramme zeigen, was und wie viel Menschen in bestimmten Ländern essen. Auf der Karte oben links ist am Beispiel der Stadt Des Moines, Iowa, zu sehen, welchen Transportweg ein Supermarktprodukt in den USA durchschnittlich zurücklegt.

Eine Weltkarte zeigt politische und soziale Ereignisse mit ihren Auswirkungen auf die globale Nahrungsmittelversorgung. Das Balkendiagramm darunter veranschaulicht die Nahrungsmittelimporte und -exporte in ausgewählten Regionen; daraus wird ersichtlich, dass Afrika stark auf Importe angewiesen ist. Die zweite Weltkarte (rechts unten) beschäftigt sich mit Ländern, die genetisch veränderte Nahrungsmittel herstellen. Diese sind in Grün dargestellt, die Höhe zeigt den Umfang der landwirtschaftlichen Flächen, auf denen genma-nipulierte Pflanzen angebaut werden.

Cette série de trois doubles pages analyse les tendances dans le domaine de l'approvisionnement en nourriture dans le monde. L'une d'elles s'intéresse plus particulièrement aux habitudes alimentaires actuelles, avec des graphiques circulaires qui montrent ce que les gens mangent dans différents pays, et en quelles quantités. La première carte indique la distance que les produits des supermarchés parcourent en moyenne, en se basant sur l'exemple de la ville de Des Moines, dans l'Iowa.

Une carte du monde situe les événements politiques et sociaux qui affectent l'approvisionnement en nourriture dans le monde. Les graphiques à barres d'en dessous montrent les importations et exportations de nourriture dans certaines régions, et l'on peut voir que l'Afrique dépend fortement de l'importation de nourriture. L'autre carte du monde (à droite en bas) examine les États qui produisent de la nourriture génétiquement modifiée. Ils sont identifiés en vert, et la hauteur de leur projection indique la superficie totale de terres cultivées consacrées à cette utilisation.

Project Info: "How Science Will Solve the Next Global Crisis", *Wired*, magazine article, 2008, USA
Data Source: UN FAO; Leopold Center for Sustainable Agriculture; Jamais Cascio; Stockholm University; ETH Zurich; US EIA; US EPA; African Rice Center; ISAAA; US NCBI; *Science*
Design: Carl De Torres
Art Direction: Maili Holiman
Creative Direction: Scott Dadich
Design Director: Wyatt Mitchell
Awards: Society of Publication Designers, Gold

ATLAS
WHAT GOES WRONG

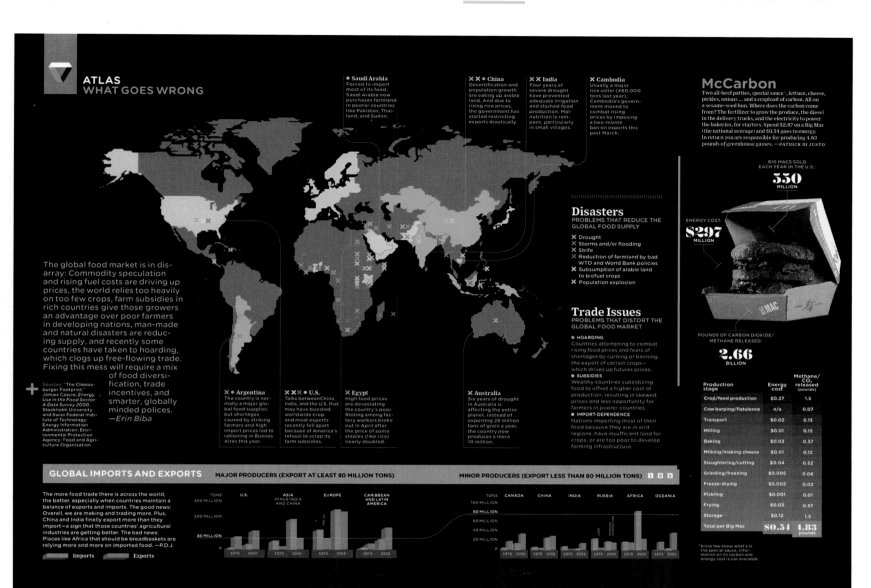

● **Saudi Arabia** Forced to import most of its food, Saudi Arabia now purchases farmland in poorer countries like Pakistan, Thailand, and Sudan.

✕ ✕ ● **China** Desertification and population growth are eating up arable land. And due to rising rice prices, the government has started restricting exports drastically.

✕ ✕ **India** Four years of severe drought have prevented adequate irrigation and slashed food production. Malnutrition is rampant, particularly in small villages.

✕ **Cambodia** Usually a major rice seller (460,000 tons last year), Cambodia's government moved to combat rising prices by imposing a two-month ban on exports this past March.

✕ ● **Argentina** The country is normally a major global food supplier, but shortages caused by striking farmers and high import prices led to rationing in Buenos Aires this year.

✕ ✕ ✕ ● **U.S.** Talks between China, India, and the U.S. that may have boosted worldwide crop and meat exports recently fell apart because of America's refusal to scrap its farm subsidies.

✕ **Egypt** High food prices are devastating the country's poor. Rioting among factory workers broke out in April after the price of some staples (like rice) nearly doubled.

✕ **Australia** Six years of drought in Australia is affecting the entire planet. Instead of exporting 28 million tons of grain a year, the country now produces a mere 10 million.

The global food market is in disarray: Commodity speculation and rising fuel costs are driving up prices, the world relies too heavily on too few crops, farm subsidies in rich countries give those growers an advantage over poor farmers in developing nations, man-made and natural disasters are reducing supply, and recently some countries have taken to hoarding, which clogs up free-flowing trade. Fixing this mess will require a mix of food diversification, trade incentives, and smarter, globally minded polices. *—Erin Biba*

Sources: "The Cheeseburger Footprint," Jamais Cascio; *Energy Use in the Food Sector: A Data Survey 2000*, Stockholm University and Swiss Federal Institute of Technology; Energy Information Administration; Environmental Protection Agency; Food and Agriculture Organization

Disasters
PROBLEMS THAT REDUCE THE GLOBAL FOOD SUPPLY

- ✕ Drought
- ✕ Storms and/or flooding
- ✕ Strife
- ✕ Reduction of farmland by bad WTO and World Bank policies
- ✕ Subsumption of arable land to biofuel crops
- ✕ Population explosion

Trade Issues
PROBLEMS THAT DISTORT THE GLOBAL FOOD MARKET

- ● **HOARDING** Countries attempting to combat rising food prices and fears of shortages by curbing or banning the export of certain crops—which drives up futures prices.
- ● **SUBSIDIES** Wealthy countries subsidizing food to offset a higher cost of production, resulting in skewed prices and less opportunity for farmers in poorer countries.
- ● **IMPORT-DEPENDENCE** Nations importing most of their food because they are in arid regions, have insufficient land for crops, or are too poor to develop farming infrastructure.

McCarbon

Two all-beef patties, special sauce*, lettuce, cheese, pickles, onions ... and a crapload of carbon. All on a sesame-seed bun. Where does the carbon come from? The fertilizer to grow the produce, the diesel in the delivery trucks, and the electricity to power the bakeries, for starters. Spend $2.87 on a Big Mac (the national average) and $0.54 goes to energy. In return you are responsible for producing 4.83 pounds of greenhouse gasses. —PATRICK DI JUSTO

BIG MACS SOLD EACH YEAR IN THE U.S.: **550** MILLION

ENERGY COST: **$297** MILLION

POUNDS OF CARBON DIOXIDE/METHANE RELEASED: **2.66** BILLION

Production stage	Energy cost	Methane/ CO_2 released (pounds)
Crop/feed production	$0.27	1.5
Cow burping/flatulence	n/a	0.07
Transport	$0.02	0.13
Milling	$0.01	0.15
Baking	$0.03	0.37
Milking/making cheese	$0.01	0.12
Slaughtering/cutting	$0.04	0.52
Grinding/freezing	$0.005	0.06
Freeze-drying	$0.002	0.03
Pickling	$0.001	0.01
Frying	$0.03	0.37
Storage	$0.12	1.5
Total per Big Mac	$0.54	4.83 pounds

*Since few know what's in the special sauce, information on its carbon and energy cost is not available.

GLOBAL IMPORTS AND EXPORTS

The more food trade there is across the world, the better, especially when countries maintain a balance of exports and imports. The good news: Overall, we are making and trading more. Plus, China and India finally export more than they import—a sign that those countries' agricultural industries are getting better. The bad news: Places like Africa that should be breadbaskets are relying more and more on imported food. —P.D.J.

Imports Exports

MAJOR PRODUCERS (EXPORT AT LEAST 80 MILLION TONS)

TONS: 300 MILLION, 200 MILLION, 80 MILLION, 0
U.S. · ASIA MINUS INDIA AND CHINA · EUROPE · CARIBBEAN AND LATIN AMERICA
1975 2005

MINOR PRODUCERS (EXPORT LESS THAN 80 MILLION TONS)

TONS: 100 MILLION, 80 MILLION, 60 MILLION, 40 MILLION, 20 MILLION, 0
CANADA · CHINA · INDIA · RUSSIA · AFRICA · OCEANIA
1975 2005

ATLAS
WHAT'S NEXT

The farmscape is changing. In the Americas, insect- and herbicide-resistant corn, soy, and canola—all genetically modified—are taking root. Even GM-phobic Europe is letting down its guard. In Africa, where crop yields are among the lowest anywhere, GM crops have yet to make an impact. But conventionally bred New Rice for Africa (Nerica) is helping boost yields south of the Sahara; and other new strains, including genetically enhanced Golden Rice, are in the works in Asia. *—Thomas Hayden*

Sources: Africa Rice Center; International Service for the Acquisition of Agri-Biotech Applications; National Center for Biotechnology Information; *Science*

GENOME PROJECTS AROUND THE WORLD, RESEARCHERS ARE SEQUENCING THE GENOMES OF HUNDREDS OF AGRICULTURALLY SIGNIFICANT PLANTS AND ANIMALS TO LEARN HOW THEY WORK.

Cassava (*Manihot esculenta*) **Department of Energy Joint Genome Institute, Walnut Creek, California** A root crop that, like bananas, grows from cuttings—not seeds—making it hard to breed. Highly tolerant of drought and poor soils.

Red flour beetle (*Tribolium castaneum*) **Human Genome Sequencing Center, Baylor College of Medicine, Houston** A thief, feeding on grains and flour. Insights into its insecticide resistance may help combat other pests.

Bovine (*Bos taurus*) **Human Genome Sequencing Center, Baylor College of Medicine, Houston** Understanding milk and beef production as well as diseases like mad cow could lead to higher productivity and smarter breeding practices.

Chicken (*Gallus gallus*) **Genome Sequencing Center, School of Medicine, Washington University in St. Louis, St. Louis, Missouri** The first bird to be sequenced was the ancestral Red Jungle Fowl breed.

Sclerotinia sclerotiorum **Broad Institute, Cambridge, Massachusetts** This fungal plant pathogen has a broad range of targets, causing everything from sunflower head rot and white mold on canola to soybean stem rot.

Coffee (*Coffea arabica*) **São Paulo (Brazil) Research Foundation; Brazilian Agricultural Research Corporation, Brasília, Brazil** This cash crop could benefit from increased yield and resistance to disease and bad weather.

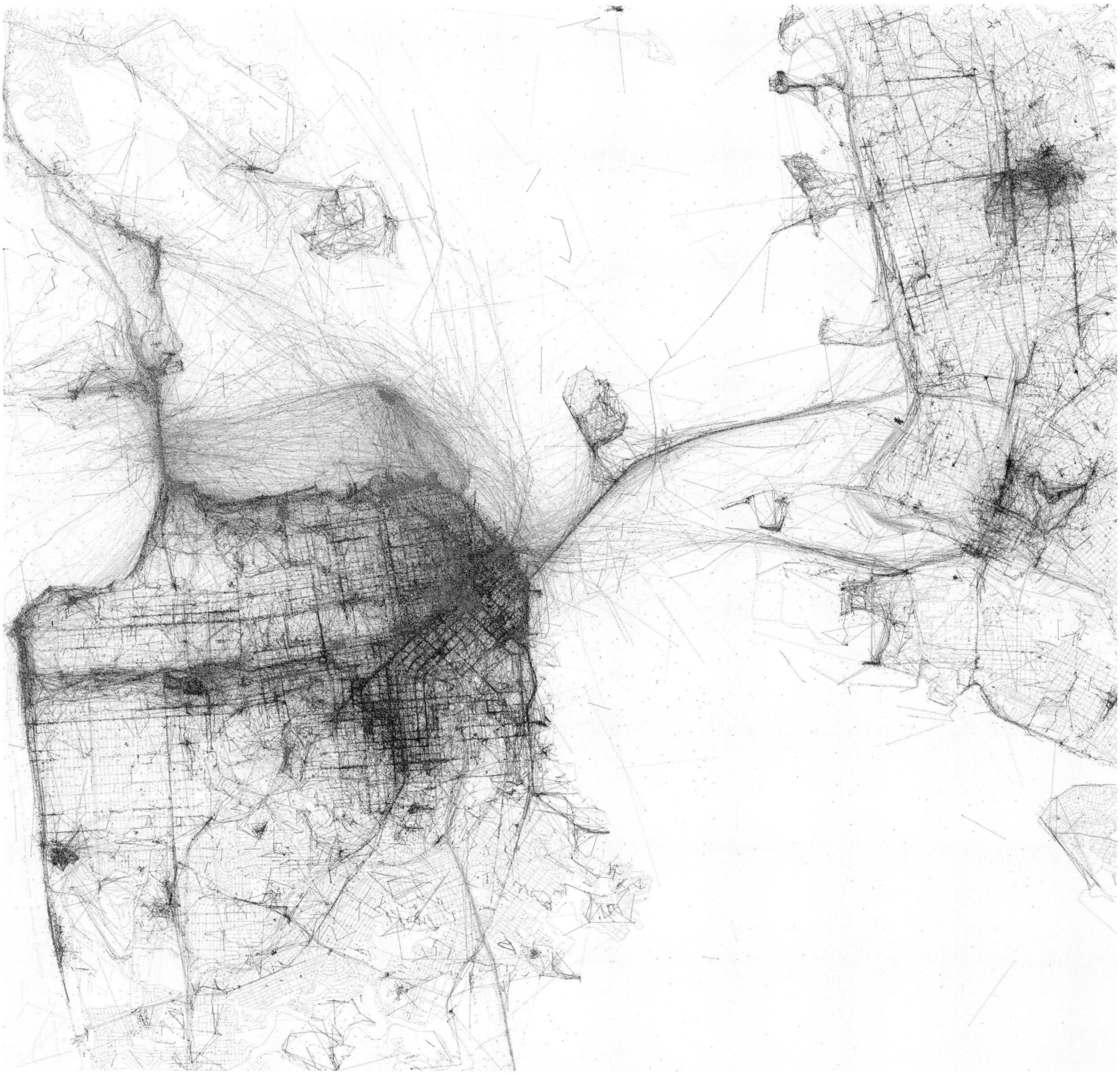

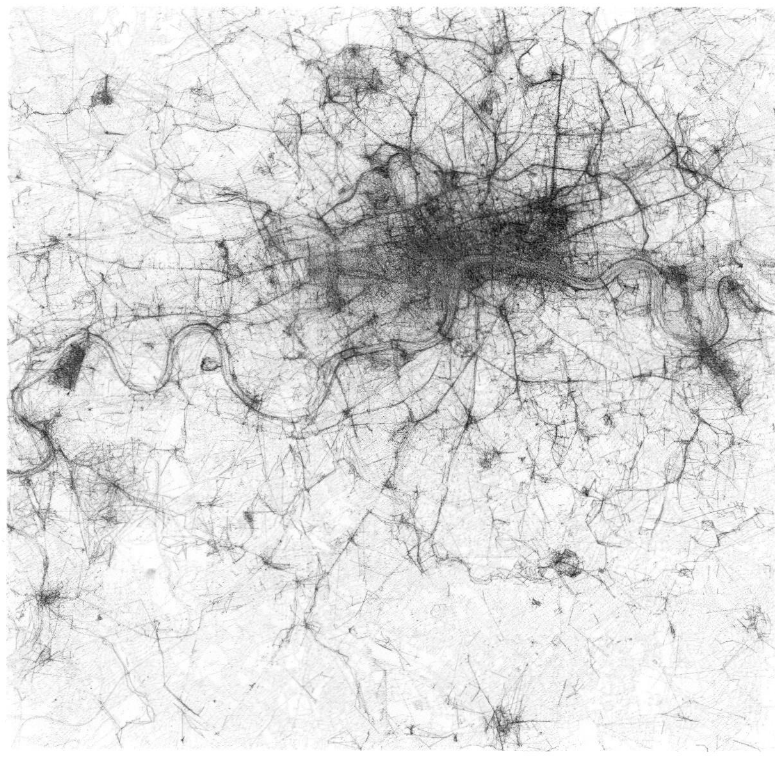

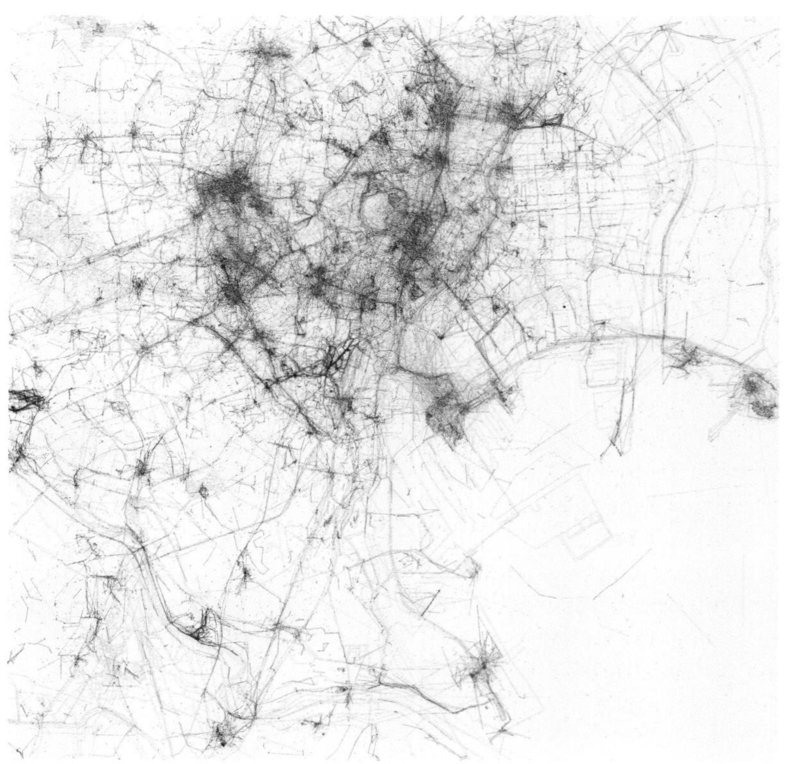

Project Info: Series of maps, 2010, USA
Data Source: Flickr and Picasa search APIs; OpenStreetMap
Design: Eric Fisher

The Geotaggers' World Atlas

This is a large series of maps showing major cities of the world. Eric Fisher collected geographical data from geotagged images that were posted on Flickr and Picasa and placed them on maps. For various cities, the maps show the distribution of the spots where these images were taken. All are scaled to the same size, oriented on the central New York cluster to fit in.

In this enhanced version, "Locals and Tourists", Fisher tried to discern which pictures were taken by tourists (red) and which by locals (blue). Yellow indicates when this distinction was unknown. The maps in this series are compelling examples of thematic maps, highlighting the most favourite places in each city. Clockwise from above right: New York, Tokyo, London and San Francisco.

Diese umfangreiche Landkartenserie zeigt Großstädte in der ganzen Welt. Eric Fisher sammelte geografische Daten von Bildern, die, mit Geo-Tags versehen, auf Flickr und Picasa eingestellt wurden, und legte sie über Landkarten. Die Karten verzeichnen für mehrere Städte die Orte, an denen die Fotos entstanden. Alle Städte sind auf dieselbe Größe skaliert und orientieren sich am Maßstab Manhattans.

In der erweiterten Version „Locals and Tourists" filterte Fisher die Einträge danach, welche Bilder von Touristen (rot) und welche von Einheimischen (blau) gemacht wurden. Wo das nicht bekannt war, wurden gelbe Punkte eingetragen. Die Grafiken dieser Serie sind ein interessantes Beispiel für thematische Karten – sie zeigen auf einen Blick die beliebtesten Orte einer Großstadt. Im Uhrzeigersinn von oben rechts: New York, Tokio, London und San Francisco.

Ceci est une grande série de cartes des grandes villes de la planète. Eric Fisher a collecté les données géographiques de photographies géolocalisées publiées sur Flickr et Picasa et les a placées sur des cartes. Les cartes montrent la distribution des endroits où les photos ont été prises. Elles sont toutes à la même échelle, et orientées sur le centre de New York.

Dans cette version améliorée, « Locaux et touristes », Fisher a essayé de faire la distinction entre les photos prises par les touristes (en rouge) et les locaux (en bleu). Le jaune indique que la provenance est inconnue. Les cartes de cette série sont d'excellents exemples de carte thématique, et mettent en valeur les endroits que les gens préfèrent dans chaque ville. Dans le sens des aiguilles d'une montre, à partir d'en haut à droite : New York, Tokyo, Londres et San Francisco.

Atlas of the New Dutch Water Defence Line

The New Dutch Water Defence Line is a military line of defence near Utrecht. Built starting in 1815, it consists of a string of forts, shelters and polders, which could be flooded in the event of attack. This atlas depicts various aspects of the system, from the strategic spatial planning to specific landscape features. Maps indicate geomorphology and locations for each component.

Diagrams visualise the inundation strategy, detail maps and elevations explain the defensive architecture of the forts. The use of five Pantone colours keeps the maps in a traditional, detail-oriented design while lending them a contemporary look. In its elaborate design, the book celebrates the tradition of the "atlas" as a collection of geographical and thematic maps.

Die Nieuwe Hollandse Waterlinie ist eine militärische Verteidigungslinie bei Utrecht, die ab 1815 errichtet wurde. Sie besteht aus einer Reihe von Festungsanlagen, Unterständen und Poldern, die bei einem Angriff geflutet werden konnten. Der Atlas stellt verschiedene Aspekte des Systems vor, von der strategischen Raumplanung bis zu landschaftlichen Besonderheiten. Auf Landkarten sind für jede Komponente Ortsangaben und geomorphologische Daten vermerkt.

Diagramme visualisieren die Flutungsstrategie, detaillierte Pläne und Höhenreliefs erläutern die Verteidigungsarchitektur der Forts. Der Atlas wurde mit fünf zusätzlichen Sonderfarben gedruckt. Obwohl die Karten sich an einem traditionellen detailreichen Design orientieren, wirken sie höchst zeitgemäß. Mit seiner aufwendigen Gestaltung ist das Buch ein wunder-bares Beispiel für die Tradition der Atlanten als Sammlung geografischer und thematischer Landkarten.

La Nouvelle Ligne de défense aquatique est une ligne de défense militaire située près d'Utrecht. Sa construction a commencé en 1815, et elle est constituée d'une série de forts, abris et polders qui pouvaient être inondés en cas d'attaque. Cet atlas illustre plusieurs aspects de ce système, de la planification spatiale stratégique aux caractéristiques spécifiques du paysage. Les cartes indiquent la géomorphologie et la situation de chaque élément.

Des diagrammes illustrent la stratégie d'inondation, et des cartes et élévations détaillées expliquent l'architecture défensive des forts. L'utilisation de cinq couleurs Pantone donne aux cartes un style traditionnel et attentif aux détails, mais moderne. Cet ouvrage élaboré avec un soin minutieux est un hommage à la tradition de l'atlas en tant que collection de cartes géographiques et thématiques.

Project Info: The Netherlands Architecture Fund, book, 2009, Netherlands
Research: Rita Brons, Bernard Colenbrander, Clemens Steenbergen, Johan van der Zwart
Design: Joost Grootens, Tine van Wel, Adam Farlie

POLDER DRAINAGE SYSTEM 78

IJsselmeer

Lek

Merwede

Waal

Benedendamse Maas

Bovendamse Maas

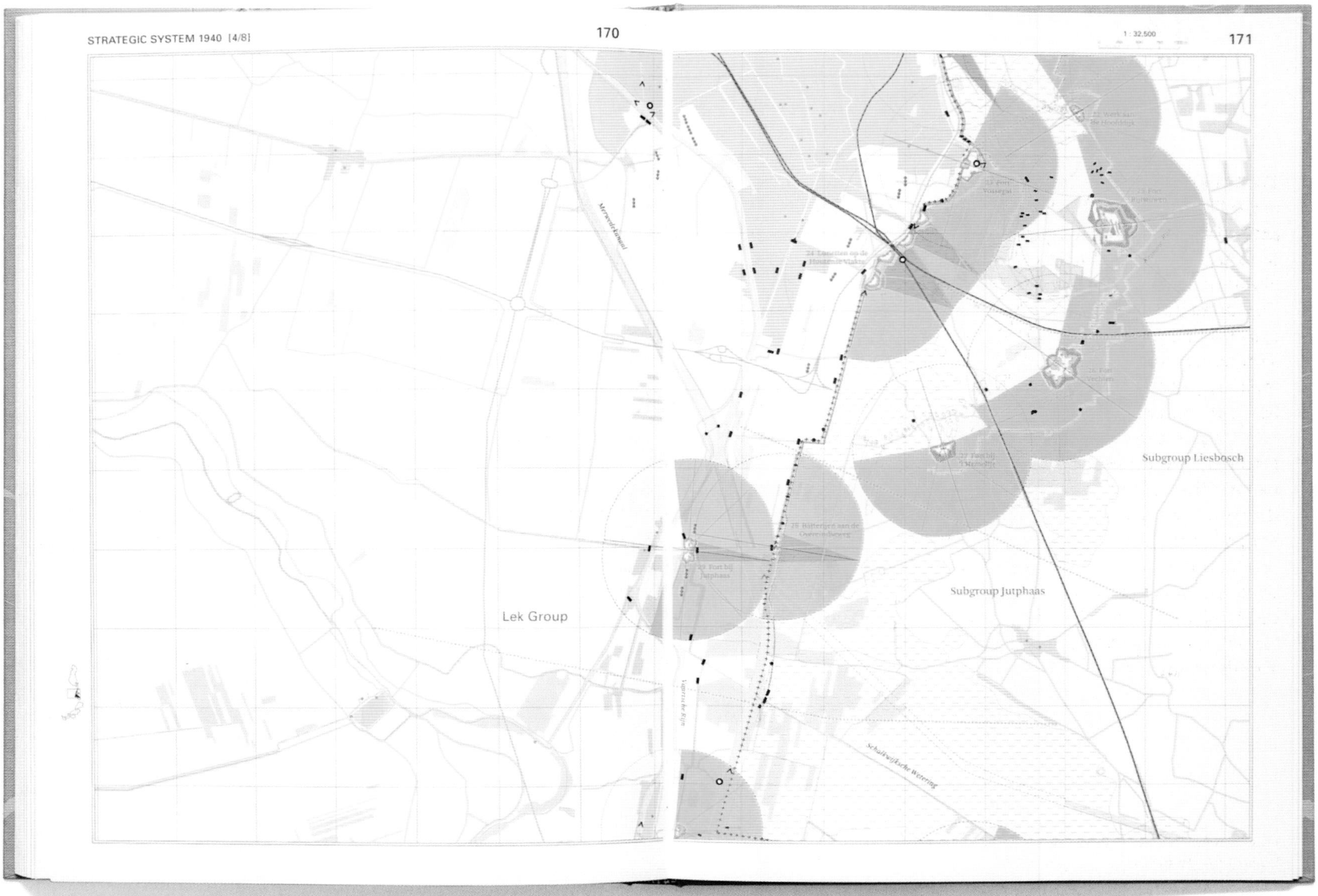

STRATEGIC SYSTEM 1940 [4/8] 170

1 : 32.500 171

Lek Group

Subgroup Jutphaas

Subgroup Liesbosch

The Land of Ice

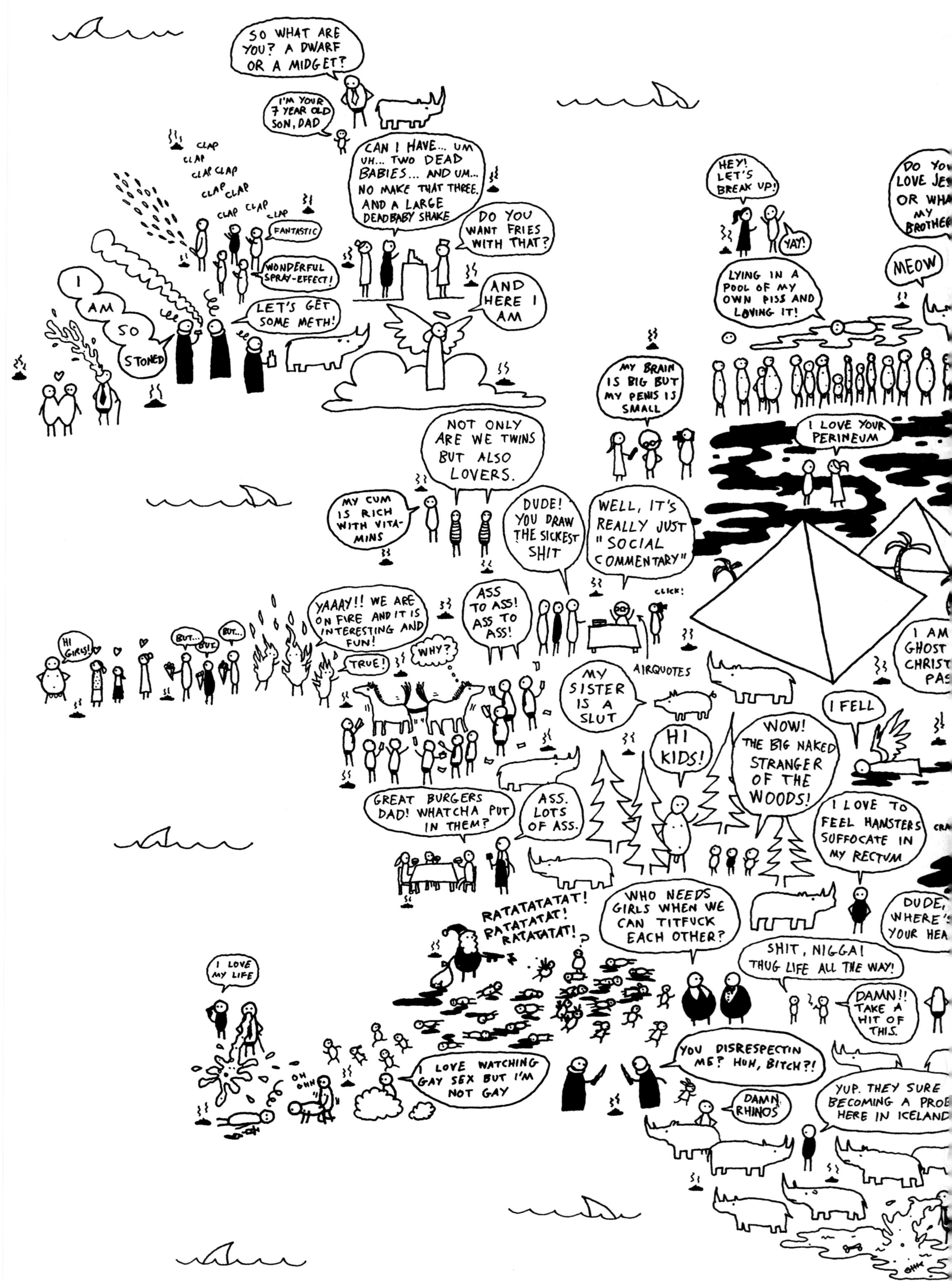

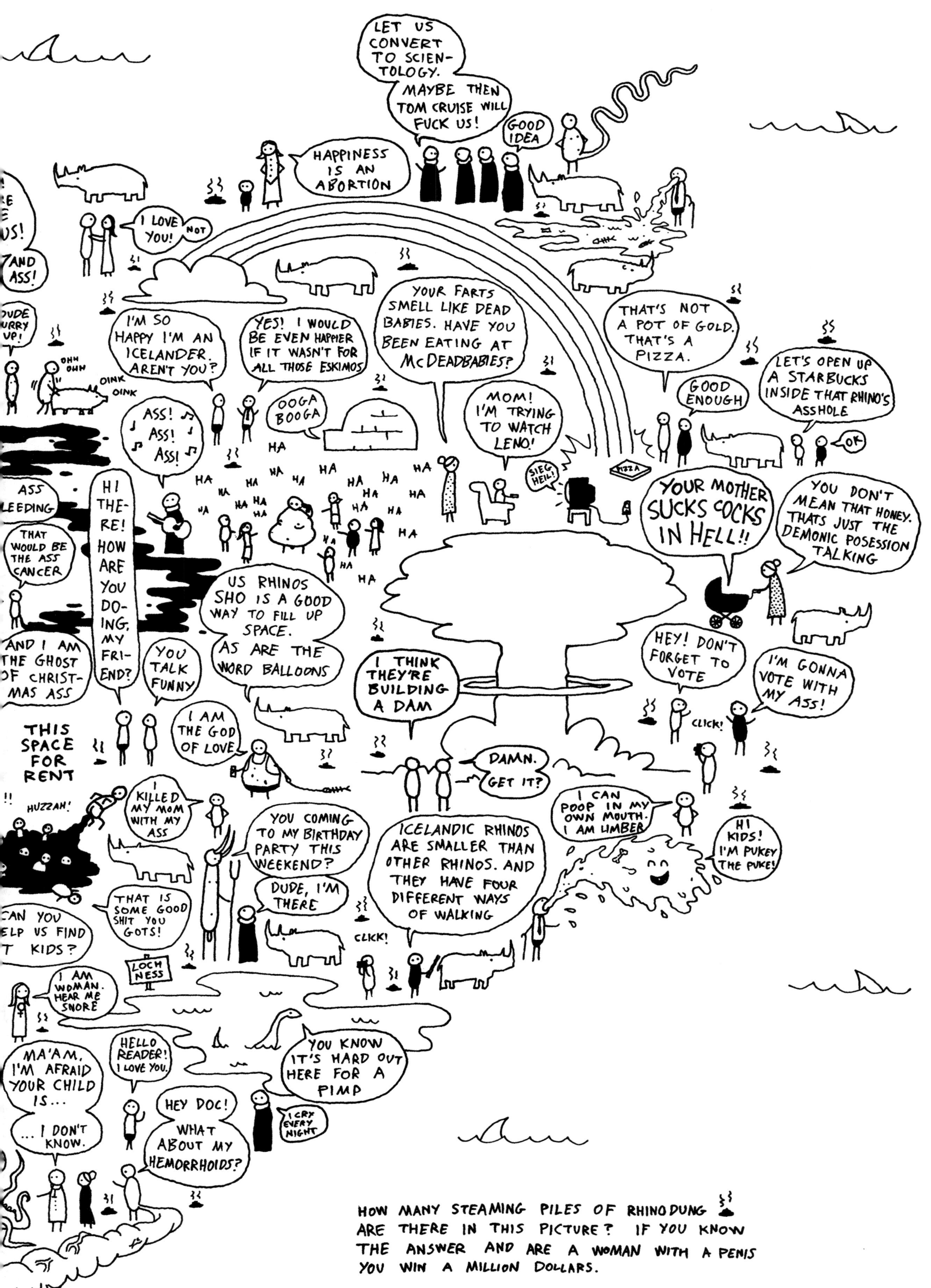

HUGLEIKUR 06

Until the financial crisis of 2009, Iceland had the reputation of being one of the world's happiest nations. According to the UN, it belongs amongst the most developed countries in the world. When asked for a contribution to an issue of the *Reykjavik Grapevine* magazine with the theme: "Iceland, happiest nation in the world", Hugleikur Dagsson drew this narrative map.

Locating information on a map is not the key issue in this piece, instead, Dagsson used the island's outlines and stuffed it brimful with micro-stories. He turned it into a mental map of his home country.

Bis zur Finanzkrise 2009 galt Island als eine der glücklichsten Nationen der Welt und gehört laut UN zu den am höchsten entwickelten Ländern. Als Hugleikur Dagsson um einen Beitrag für die Zeitschrift *Reykjavik Grapevine* zum Thema „Island, das glücklichste Land der Welt" gebeten wurde, entwarf er diese thematische Karte.

Bei der Grafik geht es weniger darum, Informationen an realen Orten zu lokalisieren. Vielmehr zeichnete Dagsson die Umrisse der Insel und füllte sie mit Miniaturgeschichten. So entstand eine kognitive Karte seiner Heimat.

Jusqu'à la crise financière de 2009, l'Islande avait la réputation d'être l'un des pays les plus heureux du monde. Selon l'ONU, elle fait partie des pays les plus développés du monde. Lorsque le magazine *Reykjavik Grapevine* a demandé à Hugleikur Dagsson de participer à un article sur le thème « L'Islande, le pays le plus heureux du monde », il a dessiné cette carte narrative.

Cette carte ne sert pas à trouver des informations. Dagsson s'est basé sur la forme de l'île et l'a remplie à craquer de microhistoires. Il l'a transformée en une carte mentale de son pays natal.

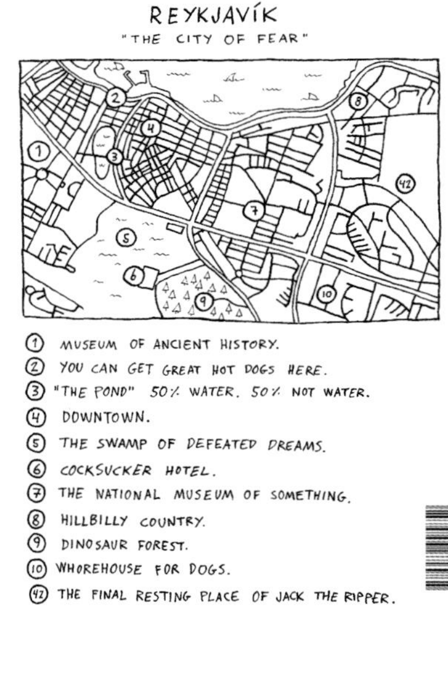

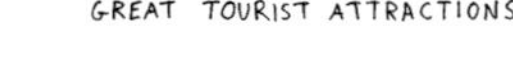

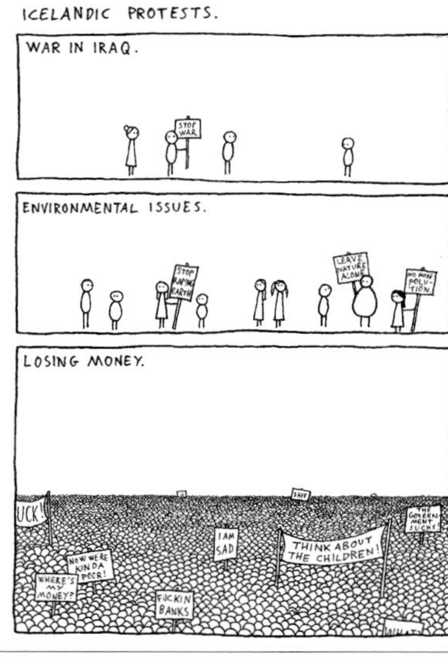

Project Info: "Iceland, Happiest Nation in the World", *The Reykjavik Grapevine*, magazine article, 2006/2010, Iceland
Design: Hugleikur Dagsson

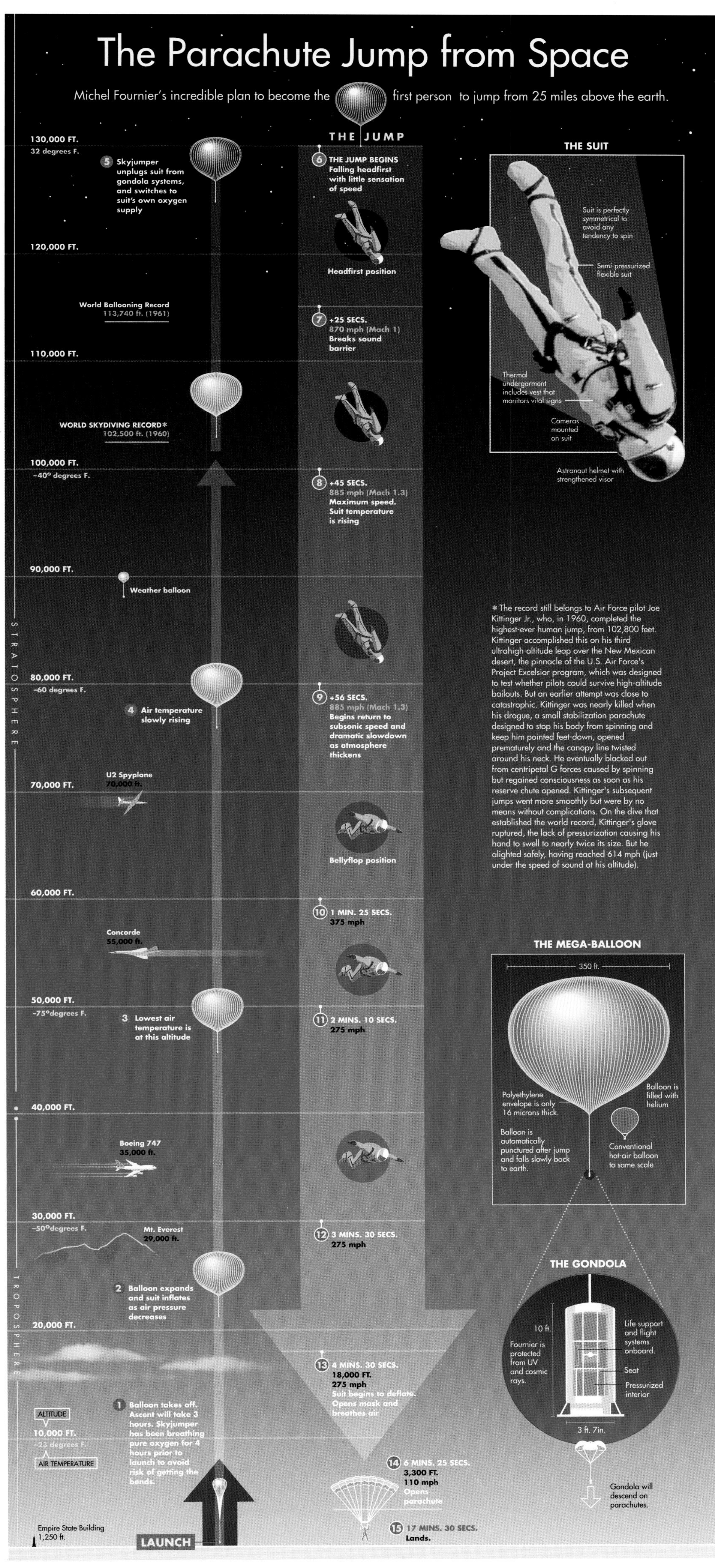

Project Info: *Popular Science*, magazine article, 2002, USA
Art Direction: Dirk Barnett
Illustration: John Grimwade

The Parachute Jump from Space

Michel Fournier is a French pilot and parachutist. After a long career in the French air force, he decided to try and break the record for the highest parachute jump ever attempted. His plan was to ascend in a helium-filled balloon to the incredible height of 40 km above ground and jump to earth with only a parachute.

The graphic is organised as an elevation chart, with height indicated on the far left. The balloon ascent and the jump are shown as steps up and down the elevation. Additional information on speed and time elapsed are provided as the reader follows the jump downwards. Detailed graphics on the right explain the necessary equipment.

Michel Fournier ist ein französischer Pilot und Fallschirmspringer. Nach einer langjährigen Laufbahn bei der französischen Luftwaffe wollte er den Versuch unternehmen, den Rekord für den höchsten je vorgenommenen Fallschirmabsprung zu brechen. Sein Plan war es, in einem mit Helium gefüllten Ballon auf die unglaubliche Höhe von 40 km aufzusteigen und mit nichts als einem Fallschirm auf die Erde zurückzuspringen.

Die Grafik ist als Höhendiagramm angelegt, die Höhe wird ganz links angegeben. Der Aufstieg des Ballons und der Sprung sind wie Schritte leiterauf und -ab dargestellt. Dem Betrachter werden zusätzliche Informationen wie Geschwindigkeits- und Zeitangaben zur Verfügung gestellt, während er dem Sprung abwärts folgt. Die Grafiken rechts erläutern die Ausrüstung.

Michel Fournier est un pilote et parachutiste français. Après une longue carrière dans l'armée de l'air française, il a décidé de tenter de battre le record d'altitude de saut en parachute. Son plan était de s'élever dans un ballon gonflé d'hélium jusqu'à l'incroyable altitude de 40 km au-dessus du sol, et de sauter avec un seul parachute.

Cette image est organisée autour d'un diagramme d'altitude, et la hauteur est indiquée sur le bord gauche. La montée du ballon et le saut sont représentés en plusieurs étapes le long de cette ligne d'altitude. Au fur et à mesure que le lecteur suit le déroulement du saut, il peut lire des informations complémentaires sur la vitesse et le temps écoulé. À droite, des illustrations détaillent l'équipement nécessaire.

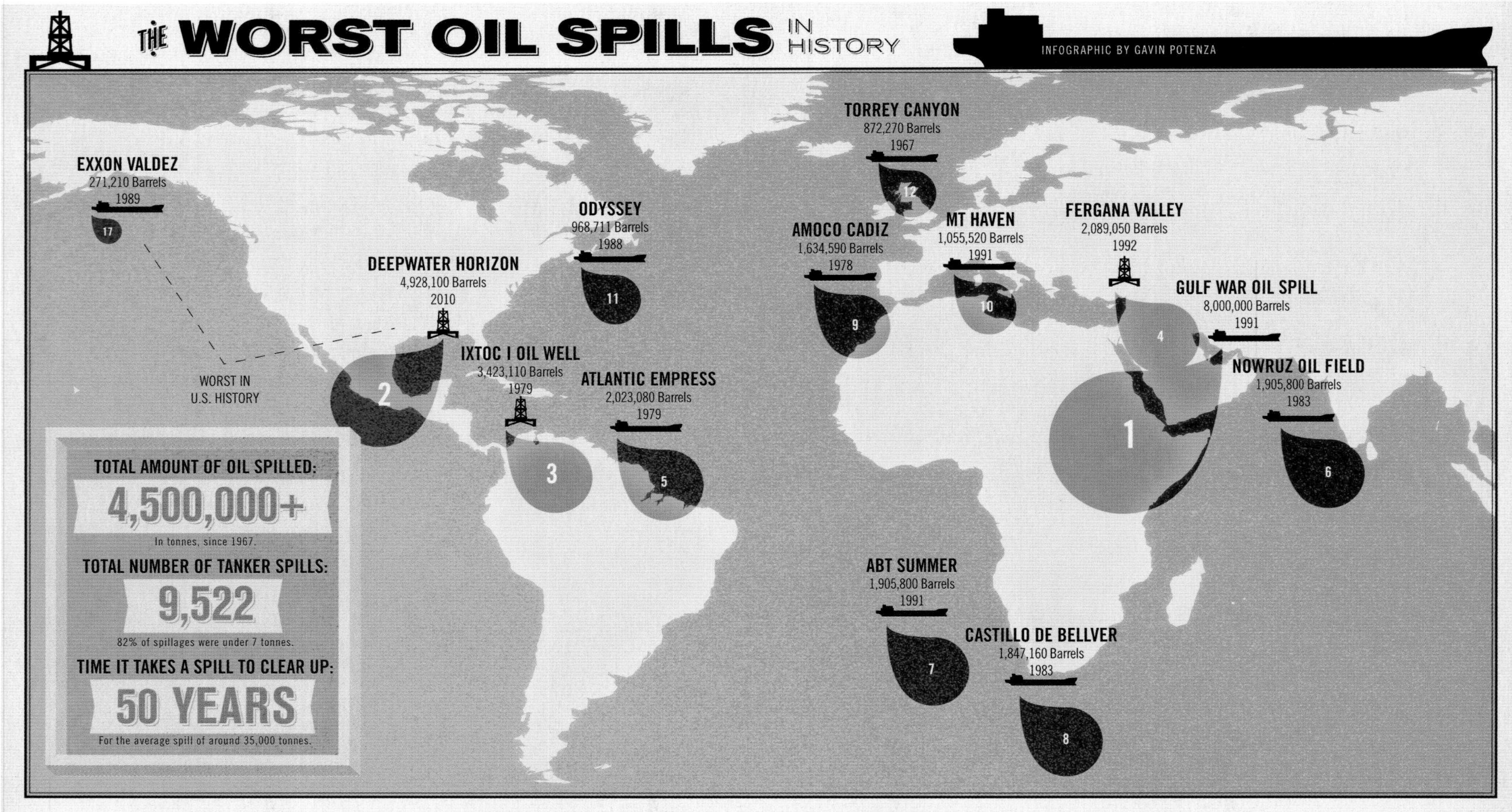

The Worst Oil Spills in History

The extraction and transportation of crude oil has repeatedly led to major accidents, which contaminate coastlines and oceans with sometimes unimaginable quantities of oil. This piece locates and ranks some of the biggest incidents on a thematic world map, indicating as well the year and how much oil was spilled.

In comparison with other previous spills, the Deepwater Horizon disaster in April 2010 ranks second behind the total oil spills that occurred during the Gulf War. One tonne of oil equals about 7.3 barrels.

Durch die Förderung und den Transport von Rohöl ist es immer wieder zu schweren Unfällen gekommen, die die Küsten und Meere mit bisweilen unvorstellbaren Mengen von Öl verseuchen. Diese thematische Karte zeigt die Orte, an denen sich einige der größten Unfälle ereignet haben, und nennt neben dem Jahr auch die Menge des ausgelaufenen Öls.

Gemessen an der Gesamtmenge freigesetzten Öls steht der Golfkrieg an erster Stelle, gefolgt von der Katastrophe auf der Deepwater Horizon im April 2010. Eine Tonne Öl entspricht etwa 7,3 Barrel.

L'extraction et le transport du pétrole brut ont fréquemment causé de graves accidents qui ont pollué le littoral et l'océan avec des quantités de pétrole parfois inimaginables. Cette carte thématique montre la position et le rang d'importance de certains des accidents les plus graves, en indiquant également l'année de l'accident et la quantité de pétrole déversé.

Comparée à d'autres marées noires précédentes, la catastrophe de la plateforme Deepwater Horizon d'avril 2010 occupe le deuxième rang, derrière l'ensemble des déversements qui ont eu lieu pendant la guerre du Golfe. Une tonne de pétrole équivaut à environ 7,3 barils.

Project Info: Website, 2010, USA
Data Source: International Tanker Owners Pollution Federation
Design: Gavin Potenza

Tour de France 2010

Held annually since 1903, the Tour de France sets a course with a huge total distance for riders to complete in the quickest possible time. The illustrated map shows the outline of France, filled with all kinds of symbols related to the individual regions or to the race in general.

Starting up north in the Netherlands the sequence of stages is marked for 2010, with tagged stops in between, up to the final destination in Paris. Whilst using the motif of a map, the piece isn't meant to locate actual specific places. Rather, it celebrates the popular event and the incredible efforts cyclists from around the world put into this road-trip.

Seit 1903 wird jedes Jahr die Tour de France abgehalten. Sie führt über eine enorme Gesamtstrecke, die die Radfahrer in kürzestmöglicher Zeit zurücklegen müssen. Die illustrierte Landkarte zeigt die Grenzen Frankreichs und enthält vielfältige Symbole, die in Zusammenhang mit bestimmten Regionen oder dem Rennen allgemein stehen.

Vom Ausgangspunkt in Holland folgt die Route den Stationen der Tour 2010 bis zum Ziel in Paris. Es wird zwar das Motiv der Landkarte verwendet, doch sollen durch die Grafik keine spezifischen Orte lokalisiert werden. Vielmehr wird die Tour als populäres Ereignis gefeiert und die unglaublichen Mühen bewundert, die Radfahrer aus aller Welt in diesem Rennen auf sich nehmen.

Le Tour de France a lieu tous les ans depuis 1903. Cette course couvre une énorme distance que les coureurs doivent parcourir le plus vite possible. La carte illustrée montre le contour de la France, rempli de toutes sortes de symboles liés aux différentes régions ou à la course en général.

La série d'étapes pour l'édition de 2010 commence dans le nord, aux Pays-Bas, et se termine à Paris. Cette illustration ressemble à une carte, mais ne sert pas à situer des lieux spécifiques. Sa mission est plutôt de rendre hommage à cet événement populaire et aux incroyables efforts que des cyclistes du monde entier investissent dans ce parcours.

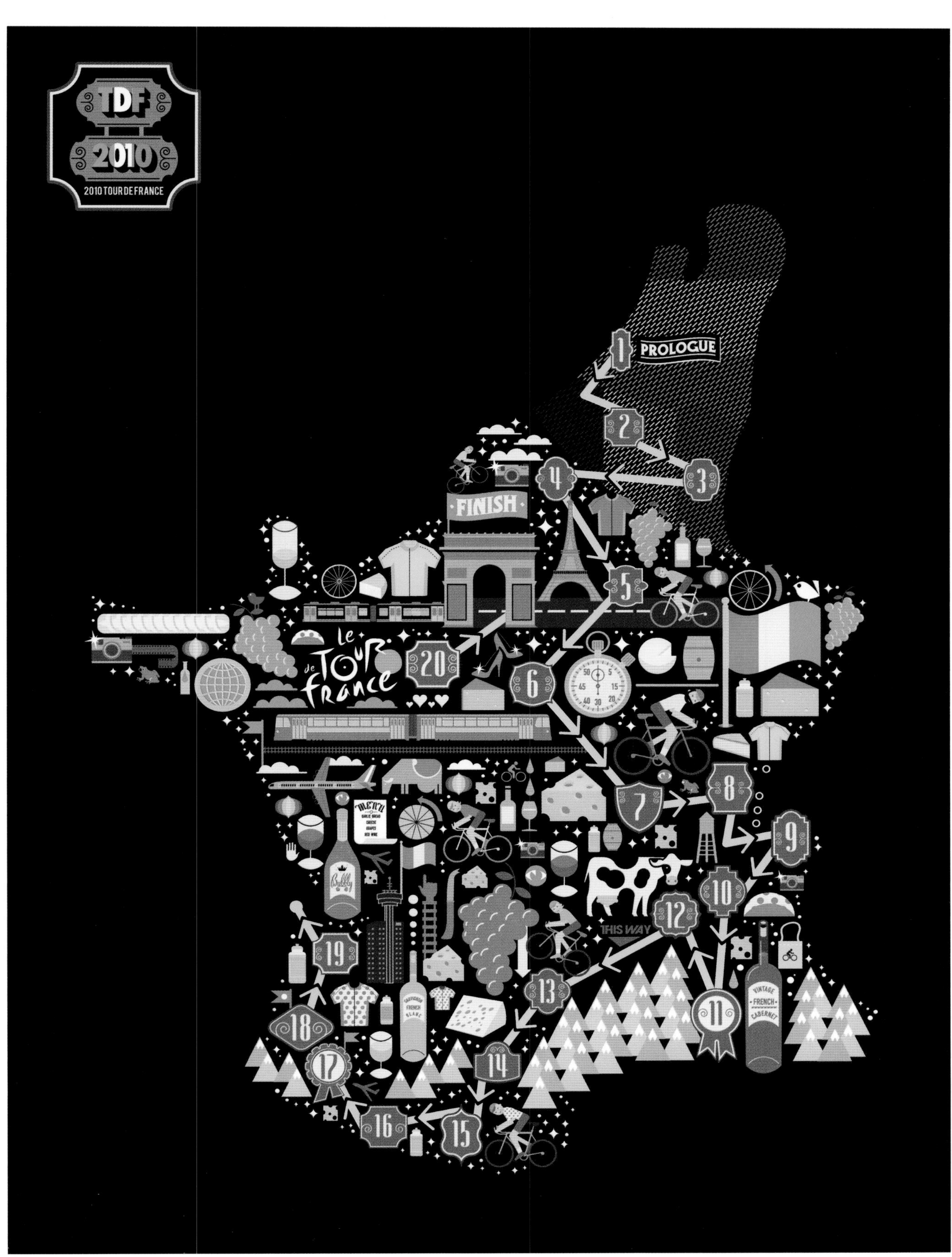

Project Info: *Bicycling*, magazine article, 2010, USA
Design: I Love Dust

Transatlantic Superhighway

This piece, developed for *Condé Nast Traveler*, visualises the air-traffic system for the North Atlantic. Based on a strip from an abstract map oriented from North America towards Europe, the graphic shows scheduled transatlantic flight-paths, in which aircraft travel at safe distances from each other while keeping constant speed and altitude.

The "safety envelope" at the top left is a detail taken from the scheduled track-system beneath and shows the minimum distances which must be kept between two aircraft. The overall layout, with the map aligned towards the top right into the dark blue, supports the association of eastward bound night-flights across the Atlantic.

Diese für *Condé Nast Traveler* entwickelte Grafik visualisiert das Luftverkehrssystem über dem Nordatlantik. Auf dem Ausschnitt einer abstrakten Landkarte, die von Nordamerika nach Europa gerichtet ist, zeigt die Grafik die transatlantischen Luftstraßen, auf denen Flugzeuge mit sicherem Abstand voneinander reisen und dabei ihre Geschwindigkeit und Höhe beibehalten.

Der „Safety Envelope" oben links ist ein Detail aus dem Luftstraßensystem und zeigt den Mindestabstand, den zwei Flugzeuge zueinander einhalten müssen. Das Design, bei dem die Landkarte nach oben rechts ins dunkle Blau ausgerichtet ist, unterstreicht die Assoziation der Nachtflüge über den Atlantik in Richtung Osten.

Cette illustration réalisée pour *Condé Nast Traveler* représente le système de trafic aérien de l'Atlantique nord. Elle est basée sur une bande tirée d'une carte abstraite orientée de l'Amérique du Nord vers l'Europe, et montre les itinéraires de vol transatlantiques. Les avions gardent une distance de sécurité entre eux tout en maintenant une vitesse et une altitude constantes.

« L'enveloppe de sécurité » en haut à gauche est un détail du système de couloirs situé en dessous, et montre les distances minimum qui doivent être respectées entre deux avions. La mise en page globale, avec la carte alignée vers le coin supérieur droit en bleu foncé, est cohérente avec l'idée de vols de nuit traversant l'Atlantique vers l'est.

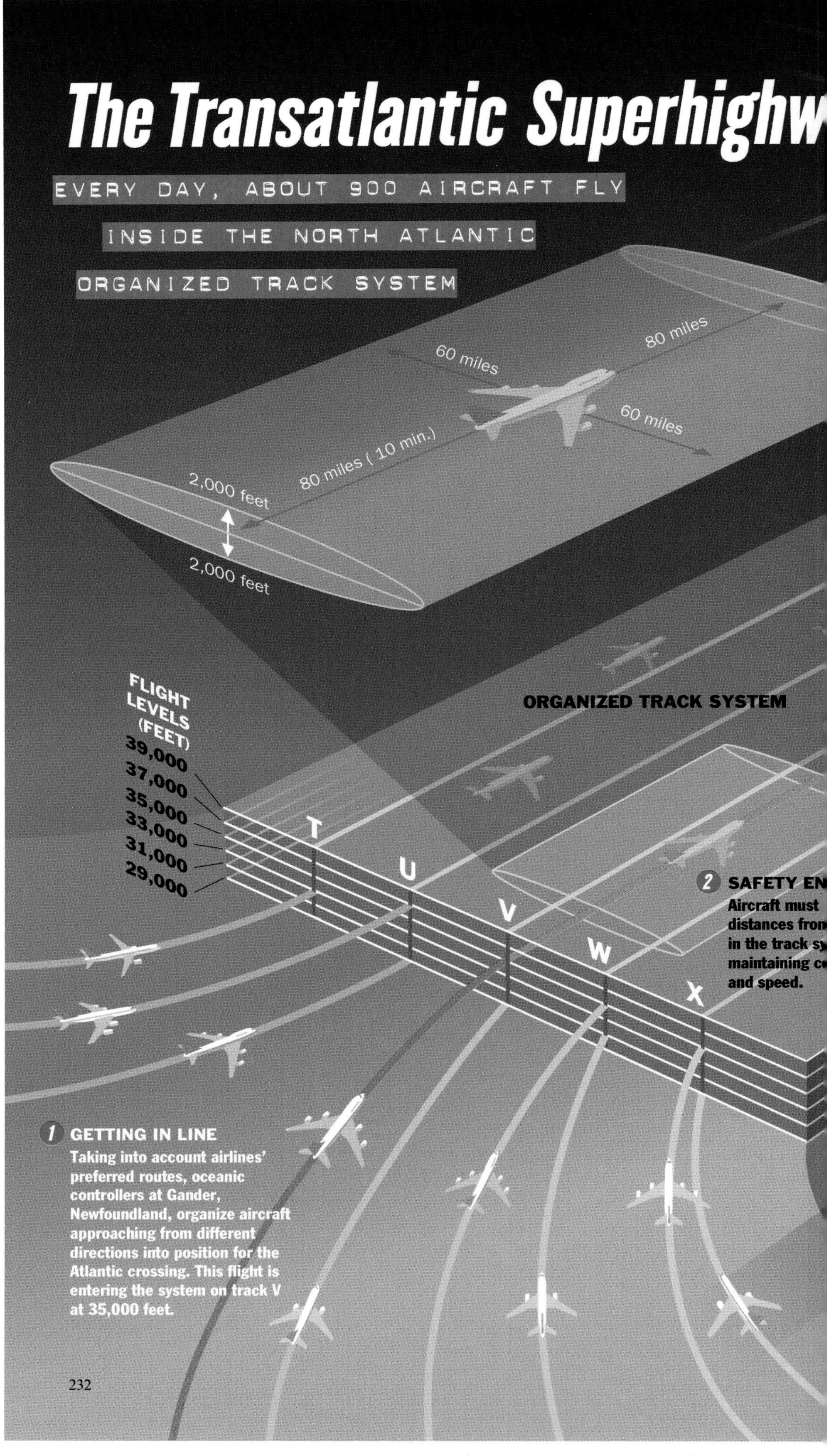

Project Info: *Condé Nast Traveler*, magazine article, 1996, USA
Design: Robert Best
Illustration: John Grimwade

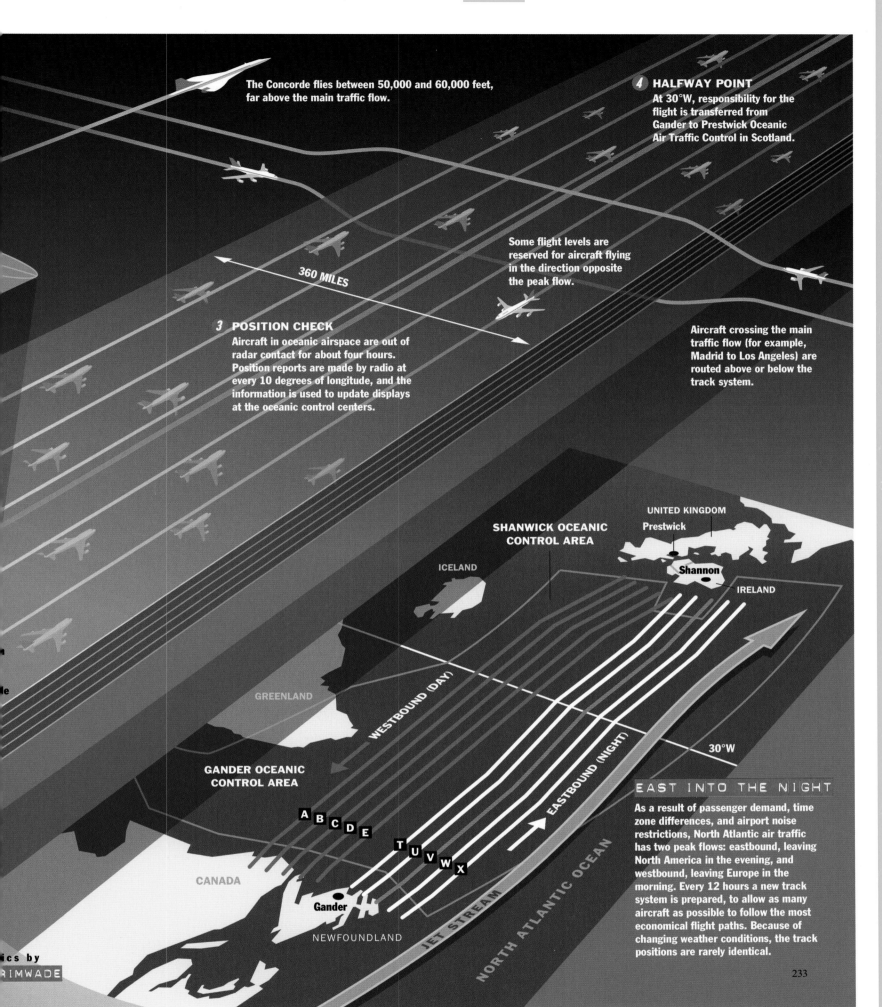

The Concorde flies between 50,000 and 60,000 feet, far above the main traffic flow.

4 HALFWAY POINT
At 30°W, responsibility for the flight is transferred from Gander to Prestwick Oceanic Air Traffic Control in Scotland.

Some flight levels are reserved for aircraft flying in the direction opposite the peak flow.

360 MILES

3 POSITION CHECK
Aircraft in oceanic airspace are out of radar contact for about four hours. Position reports are made by radio at every 10 degrees of longitude, and the information is used to update displays at the oceanic control centers.

Aircraft crossing the main traffic flow (for example, Madrid to Los Angeles) are routed above or below the track system.

UNITED KINGDOM
Prestwick
SHANWICK OCEANIC CONTROL AREA
ICELAND
Shannon
IRELAND
GREENLAND
WESTBOUND (DAY)
30°W
GANDER OCEANIC CONTROL AREA
EASTBOUND (NIGHT)
A B C D E
T U V W X
CANADA
Gander
NEWFOUNDLAND
JET STREAM
NORTH ATLANTIC OCEAN

EAST INTO THE NIGHT

As a result of passenger demand, time zone differences, and airport noise restrictions, North Atlantic air traffic has two peak flows: eastbound, leaving North America in the evening, and westbound, leaving Europe in the morning. Every 12 hours a new track system is prepared, to allow as many aircraft as possible to follow the most economical flight paths. Because of changing weather conditions, the track positions are rarely identical.

ics by
RIMWADE

233

Twilight of the Arctic Ice

The empire of ice at the top of the world is shrinking. The Arctic Ocean's summer ice pack covers little more than half its former reach, as a sweeping satellite image from September 2008 documents. Atop Greenland's formidable ice sheet, melting has also quickened. Sea ice, naturally expanding and contracting with the seasons, has covered this ocean year-round for most of the past three million years. But the Arctic is uniquely sensitive to climate change (right). Ten years ago global-warming models predicted the Arctic Ocean could be ice free in summer by 2100. Then the date dropped to 2050, and now to 2030—or sooner. As climate scientist Mark Serreze puts it, "Reality is exceeding expectations."

Ice Sustains Ice

The brilliant white of ice and snow reflects more than 80 percent of incoming sunlight. This reflective quality is called albedo. The high albedo of an ice-covered Arctic helps keep its temperatures low and preserves its ice.

A Balance of Warmth

Some of the solar energy reflected by ice or reradiated as heat returns to space. Some is absorbed into the atmosphere by greenhouse gases like carbon dioxide and water vapor, whose heat-trapping qualities make life on Earth possible.

Heating Up

Temperature rise caused by excess greenhouse gases from fossil fuels accelerates summer ice melt. Warm air holds more water vapor, creating more clouds and keeping more heat in the Arctic atmosphere.

Chain

Open wat
than 90 p
increased
the Arctic
melt and

North and South

The Northern Hemisphere has experienced a greater temperature rise than the Southern, in part because it has more land, which warms faster than open ocean. Yet troubling signs of warming in Antarctica—where the vast continental ice sheet holds 85 percent of Earth's freshwater ice—make clear that the bottom of the world is also vulnerable.

Arctic Retreat

Measured at the end of summer, the sea-ice minimum in September 1980 spanned an area slightly smaller than the contiguous United States. The September 2008 minimum was just over half that size. Regional weather patterns contributed to the even greater decline in 2007.

Project Info: *National Geographic*, poster, 2009, USA
Data Source: National Snow and Ice Data Center; National Oceanic and Atmospheric Administration; Cooperative Institute for Research in Environmental Sciences
Research: Kaitlin Yarnall
Design: Alejandro Tumas
Art Direction: Juan Velasco
Illustration: Pablo Loscri, Hernán Cañellas
Awards: Malofiej; Society for News Design

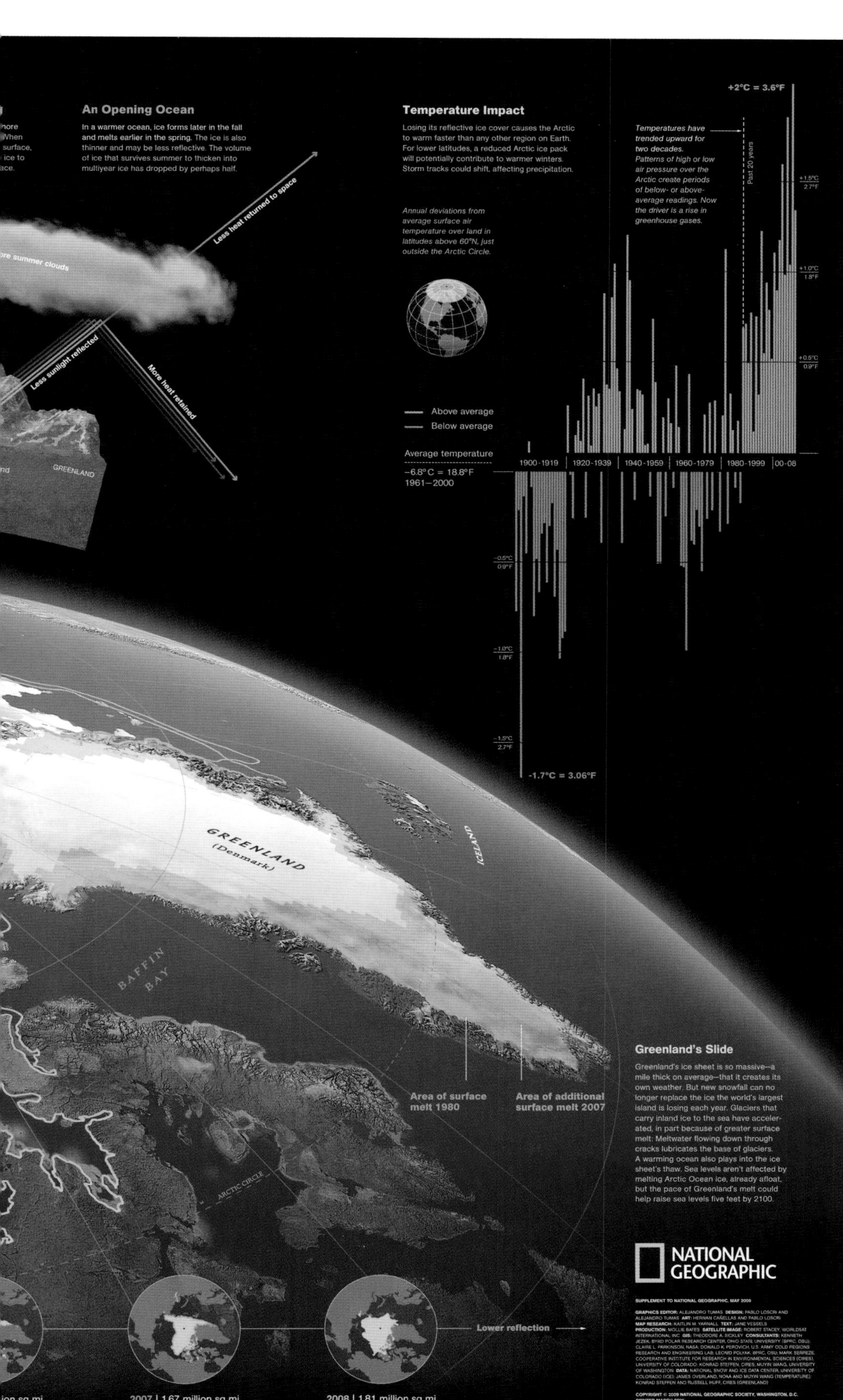

Twilight of the Arctic Ice

With this look at the North polar region, *National Geographic* tackles the melting of the polar ice caps. The centrepiece maps the current ice sheet, with coloured lines showing its extension in 2007 and in 1980. The series of maps along the bottom form a timeline, showing the shrinking in several time steps.

The schema atop the central map explains the chain reaction caused by the melting – while the ice used to reflect the sunlight, the latter is now absorbed by land-masses or the ocean and causes a further warming. The bar chart top right adds to the piece with average temperature deviations for latitudes above 60 degrees, for the time period 1900–2008.

National Geographic behandelt mit dieser Ansicht der Arktis das Thema der schmelzenden Polkappen. Die große Karte zeigt die Eiskappe heute, Farblinien markieren deren Ausdehnung 2007 bzw. 1980. Die Kartenfolge am unteren Bildrand verdeutlicht das Schrumpfen der Eismassen in mehreren Zeitschritten.

Die Grafik über dem Globus erläutert Kettenreaktionen infolge des Abschmelzens – während das Eis früher das Sonnenlicht reflektierte, wird es jetzt von den Erdmassen oder dem Meer absorbiert und führt zu weiterer Erwärmung. Das Balkendiagramm oben rechts zeigt die durchschnittlichen Temperaturabweichungen im Zeitraum von 1900–2008 für Breiten oberhalb des 60. Breitengrades.

National Geographic aborde la fonte des pôles avec cette vue de la région du pôle Nord. L'élément central est une carte de la calotte de glace actuelle, et les lignes de couleur montrent sa surface en 2007 et en 1980. La série de cartes du bas constitue une chronologie du retrait des glaces en plusieurs étapes dans le temps.

Le schéma qui couronne la carte centrale explique la réaction en chaîne causée par la fonte – la glace reflétait la lumière du soleil, qui est maintenant absorbée par les terres ou l'océan, ce qui accélère le réchauffement. Le graphique à barres en haut à droite complète l'ensemble avec les déviations de la température moyenne pour les latitudes supérieures à 60 degrés entre 1900 et 2008.

Typographic Maps

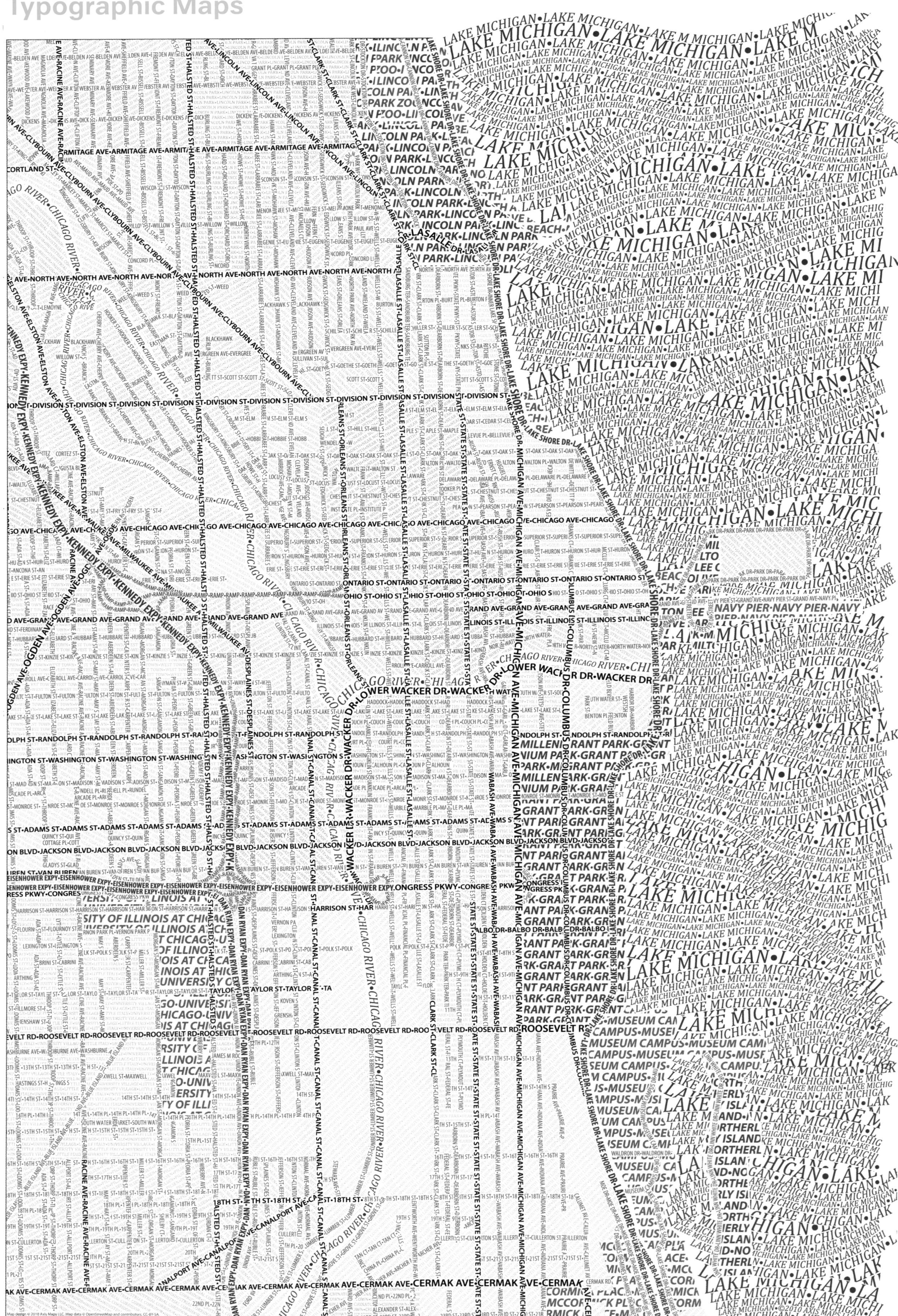

CHICAGO

DOWNTOWN, INCLUDING THE NEIGHBORHOODS OF
CABRINI GREEN • CHINATOWN • DEARBORN PARK • EAST PILSEN • FULTON RIVER DISTRICT • GOLD COAST • GOOSE ISLAND • GREEKTOWN • LINCOLN PARK • THE LOOP • NEAR EAST SIDE • NEAR NORTH • NEAR WEST SIDE • NOBLE SQUARE • OLD TOWN • OLD TOWN TRIANGLE • PILSEN • PRINTER'S ROW • RANCH TRIANGLE • RIVER NORTH • RIVER WEST • SHEFFIELD NEIGHBORS • SOUTH LOOP • STREETERVILLE • UNIVERSITY VILLAGE / LITTLE ITALY • WEST LOOP GATE • WEST TOWN

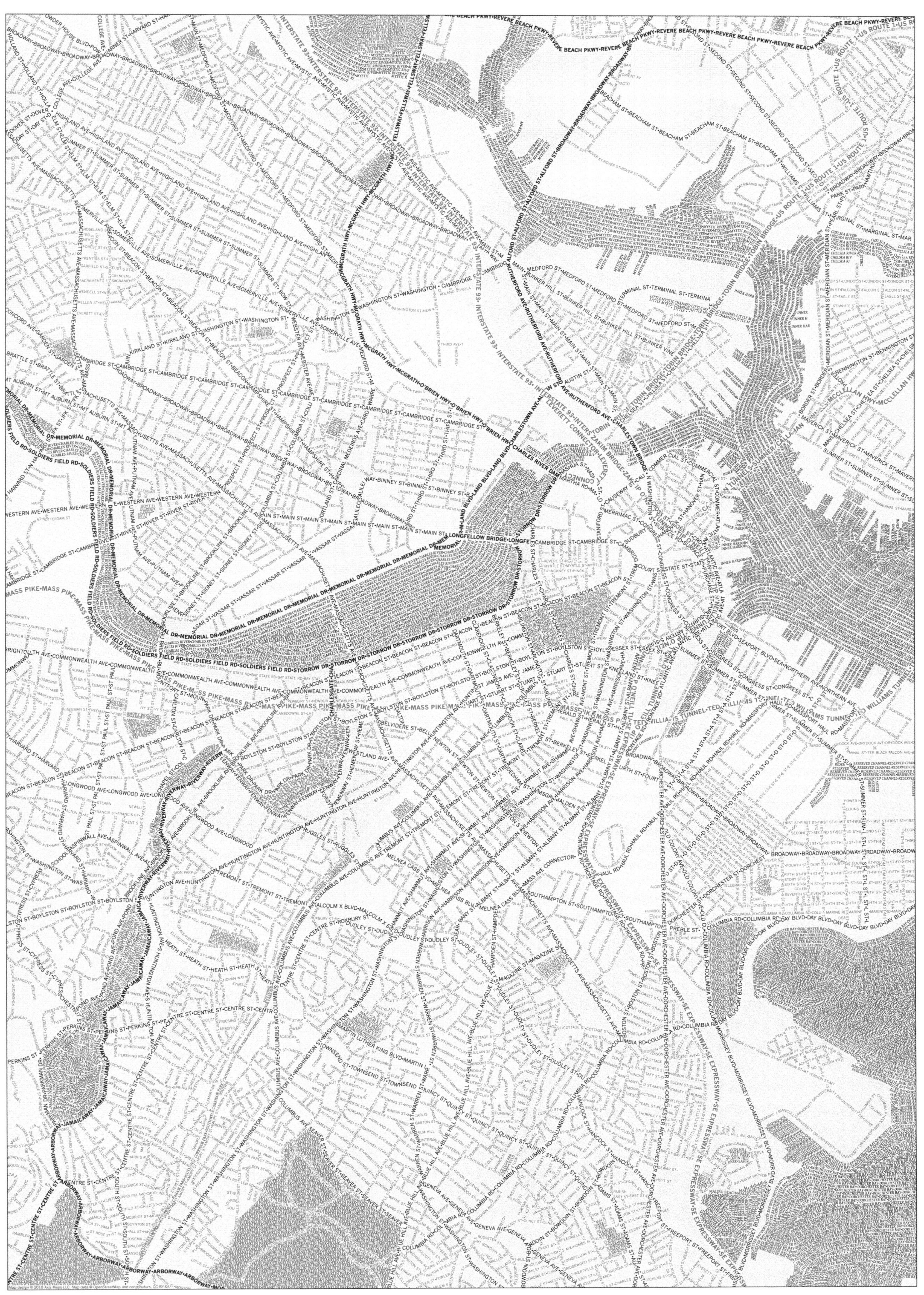

BOSTON

THE CITY CENTER, INCLUDING THE NEIGHBORHOODS OF ALLSTON • BACK BAY • BAY VILLAGE • BEACON HILL • CHARLESTOWN • CHINATOWN • DORCHESTER • DOWNTOWN • EAST BOSTON • FENWAY-KENMORE • JAMAICA PLAIN • LEATHER DISTRICT • MISSION HILL • NORTH END • ROXBURY • SOUTH BOSTON • SOUTH END • WEST END **AND PARTS OF** BROOKLINE • CAMBRIDGE • CHELSEA • EVERETT • MEDFORD • SOMERVILLE

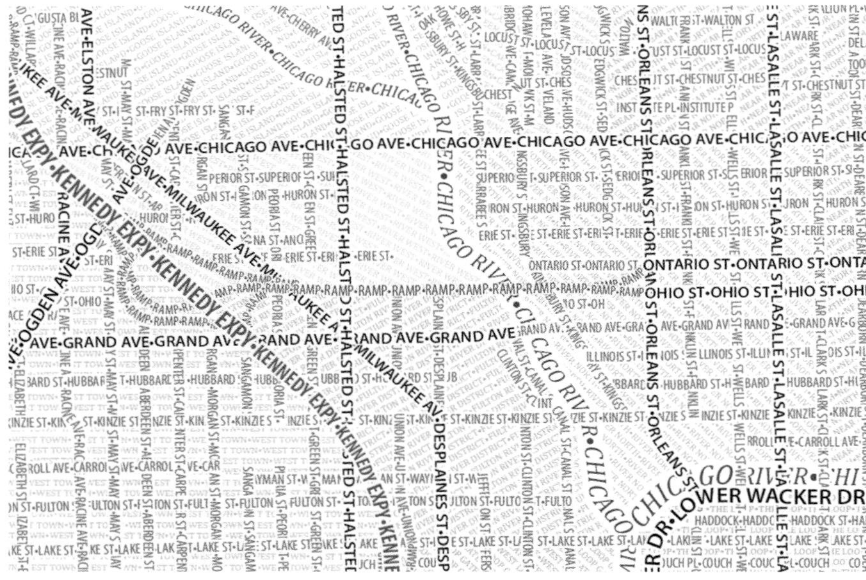

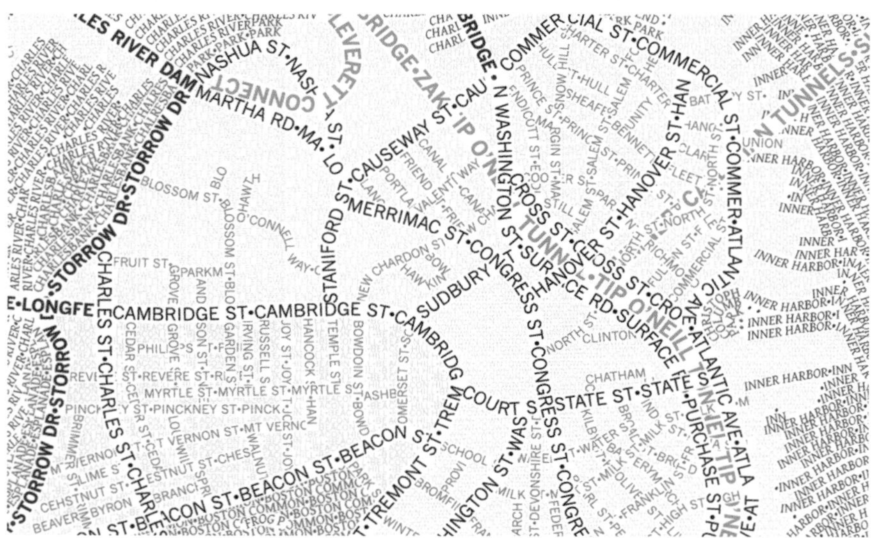

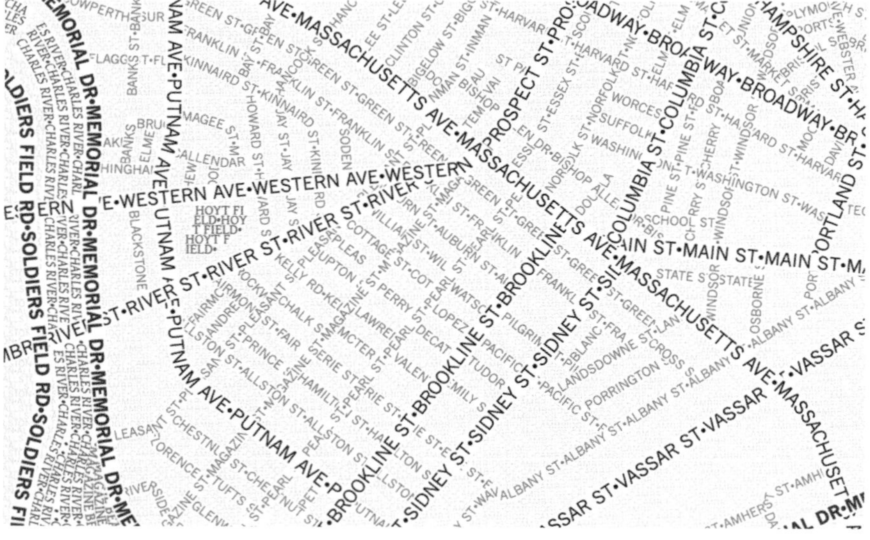

Project Info: Series of posters, 2010, USA
Data Source: OpenStreetMap
Design: Andy Woodruff, Ben Sheesley, Mark Harrower (Axis Maps)

This series of posters developed by Axis Maps accurately depicts the streets and highways, parks, neighbourhoods, coastlines and physical features of several major cities in the US, using nothing but typographic characters. They omit all the pictorial elements maps usually consist of. The full picture of the city emerges only by weaving together thousands upon thousands of carefully placed words.

Every single character was manually placed, making the design of each map an extremely time-consuming process. The city is transformed into a complex series of interwoven letters and words.

Diese Plakatserie von Axis Maps stellt die Straßen, Highways, Parks, Küstenlinien und natürlichen Gegebenheiten mehrerer amerikanischer Großstädte allein mittels typografischer Zeichen dar; auf die Bildelemente, die üblicherweise in Karten verwendet werden, wird völlig verzichtet. Das Gesamtbild der Stadt ergibt sich allein durch das Zusammenfügen Abertausender, sorgfältig positionierter Wörter.

Jeder einzelne Buchstabe wurde von Hand gesetzt, entsprechend zeitaufwendig war der Entwurf jedes Motivs. Die Stadt verwandelt sich damit in eine komplexe Serie verschlungener Buchstaben und Wörter.

Cette série d'affiches conçues par Axis Maps donne une représentation exacte des rues et routes, parcs, quartiers, côtes et caractéristiques géographiques de plusieurs grandes villes américaines, et ce, uniquement à l'aide de caractères typographiques. Elles sont dépourvues de tous les éléments d'illustration que l'on trouve habituellement dans les cartes classiques. L'image de la ville n'apparaît que dans l'entrelacement de milliers et de milliers de mots soigneusement positionnés.

Chaque caractère a été positionné manuellement, et chaque carte est le fruit d'un processus extrêmement long. La ville est transformée en une série complexe de lettres et de mots entrelacés.

VAR500 Map (2005)

VAR500 is a ranking of the 500 highest-valued technology companies in the US and Canada, started by *VAR Business* magazine. In the manner of a classical thematic map, this graphic shows the geographical distribution of the top businesses across North America. The height of each building indicates the value of each company.

Placing the map on the globe with the sunlight casting long shadows adds a dramatic visual effect – the graphic doesn't even really look like a map in the first place.

VAR500 ist ein Ranking der 500 höchstbewerteten Technologieunternehmen in den USA und Kanada, begründet von der Zeitschrift *VAR Business*. In der Art klassischer thematischer Karten zeigt die Grafik die geografische Lage der führenden Unternehmen Nordamerikas. Die Höhe der Gebäude spiegelt den Wert der jeweiligen Firma wider.

Die Platzierung auf einem Globus und die überlangen Schatten durch die Sonne erzielen einen überaus dramatischen Effekt – die Grafik wirkt auf den ersten Blick nicht wie eine Landkarte.

Le VAR500 est un classement des 500 entreprises technologiques les mieux cotées aux États-Unis et au Canada, lancé par le magazine *VAR Business*. À la manière d'une carte thématique classique, cette image montre la distribution géographique de ces entreprises en Amérique du Nord. La hauteur de chaque bâtiment indique la valeur de chaque entreprise.

En plaçant la carte sur le globe, avec le soleil projetant des ombres allongées, on obtient un effet visuel spectaculaire – cette image ne ressemble même pas vraiment à une carte.

Project Info: *VAR Business*, magazine article, 2005, USA
Design: Bryan Christie
Art Direction: Scott Gormley

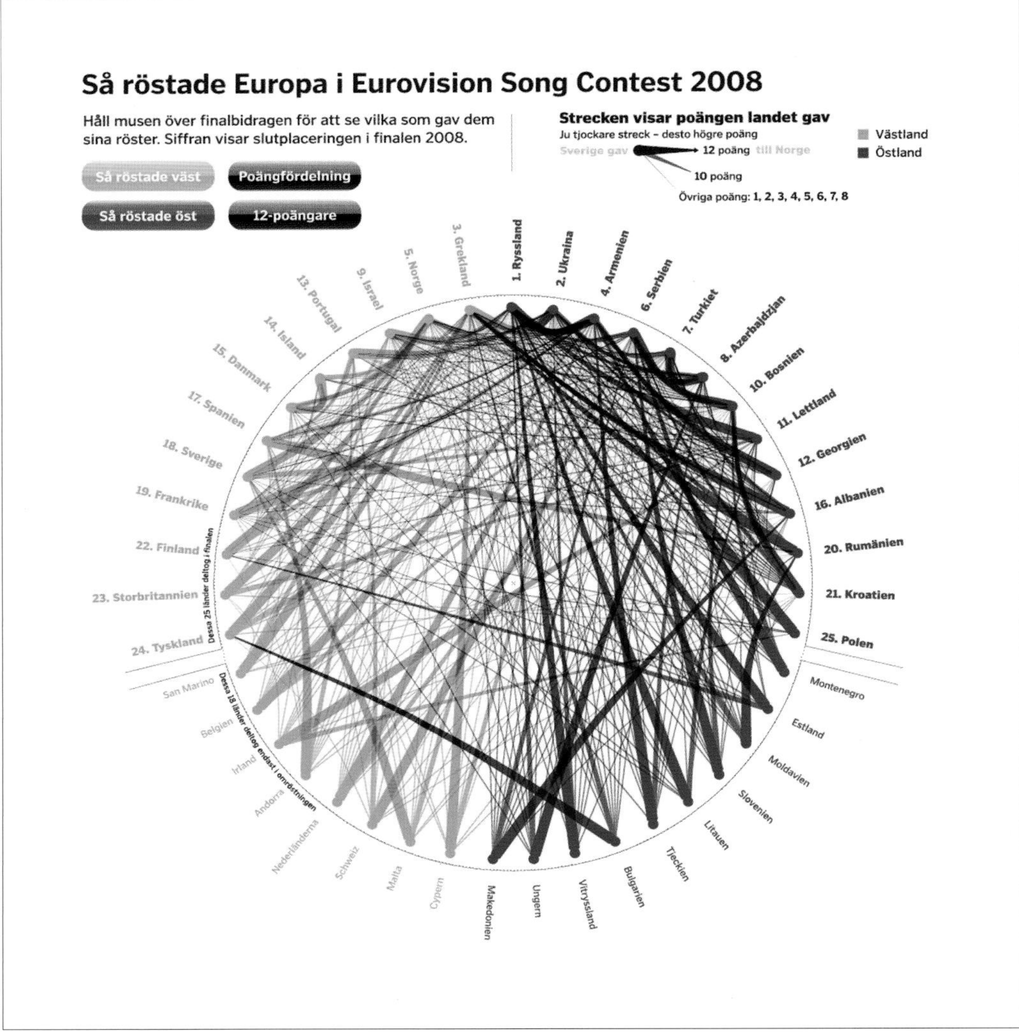

Project Info: *Svenska Dagbladet*, interactive visualisation, 2008, Sweden
Data Source: Eurovision Song Contest
Design: Thomas Molén
Awards: Malofiej 2009

Voting Patterns in the Eurovision Song Contest

The Eurovision Song Contest is an international competition held annually in Europe. Each country presents one song. The winner is determined through a voting system in which every country rates the other participants, while they are not allowed to rate themselves. Following the rumour that Eastern European countries were only voting for each other, this graphic looks into the voting patterns.

The circular diagram visualises all connections between countries. Eastern Europe is shown in blue, Western Europe is marked orange. Line thickness indicates exactly how many points were granted. And it shows: Eastern European countries mostly voted for each other, but so did the Western countries. The online interactive version allowed people to look up the voting separately for each country.

Beim jährlich stattfindenden Eurovision Song Contest ist jeweils ein Land mit einem Lied vertreten. Der Gewinner wird anhand eines Wahlsystems ermittelt, bei dem jedes Land die anderen Teilnehmer bewertet, nicht aber den eigenen Beitrag. Aufgrund der Gerüchte, dass osteuropäische Länder ausschließlich füreinander stimmen würden, untersucht diese Grafik das Wahlverhalten.

Das Kreisdiagramm zeigt sämtliche Verbindungen zwischen den einzelnen Ländern. Osteuropa ist blau gehalten, Westeuropa orange. Die Dicke der Linien verdeutlicht, wie viele Punkte gegeben wurden. Daraus ergibt sich: Osteuropäische Länder stimmten vorwiegend füreinander, die westeuropäischen allerdings auch. Die interaktive Online-Version bot zudem die Möglichkeit, das Wahlverhalten einzelner Länder zu betrachten.

Le concours Eurovision de la chanson est une compétition internationale qui a lieu tous les ans en Europe. Chaque pays présente une chanson. Le gagnant est choisi grâce à un système de votes : chaque pays note les autres participants, mais ne peut pas se noter lui-même. Suite à la rumeur selon laquelle les pays de l'Est votaient seulement pour d'autres pays de l'Est, ce graphisme explore la structure des votes.

Le diagramme circulaire représente toutes les connexions entre les pays. L'Europe de l'Est est en bleu, et l'Europe de l'Ouest en orange. L'épaisseur des lignes indique le nombre de points accordés. Et cela montre que les pays d'Europe de l'Est ont majoritairement voté entre eux, mais que les pays d'Europe de l'Ouest ont fait la même chose. La version interactive mise en ligne permettait de consulter les votes séparément pour chaque pays.

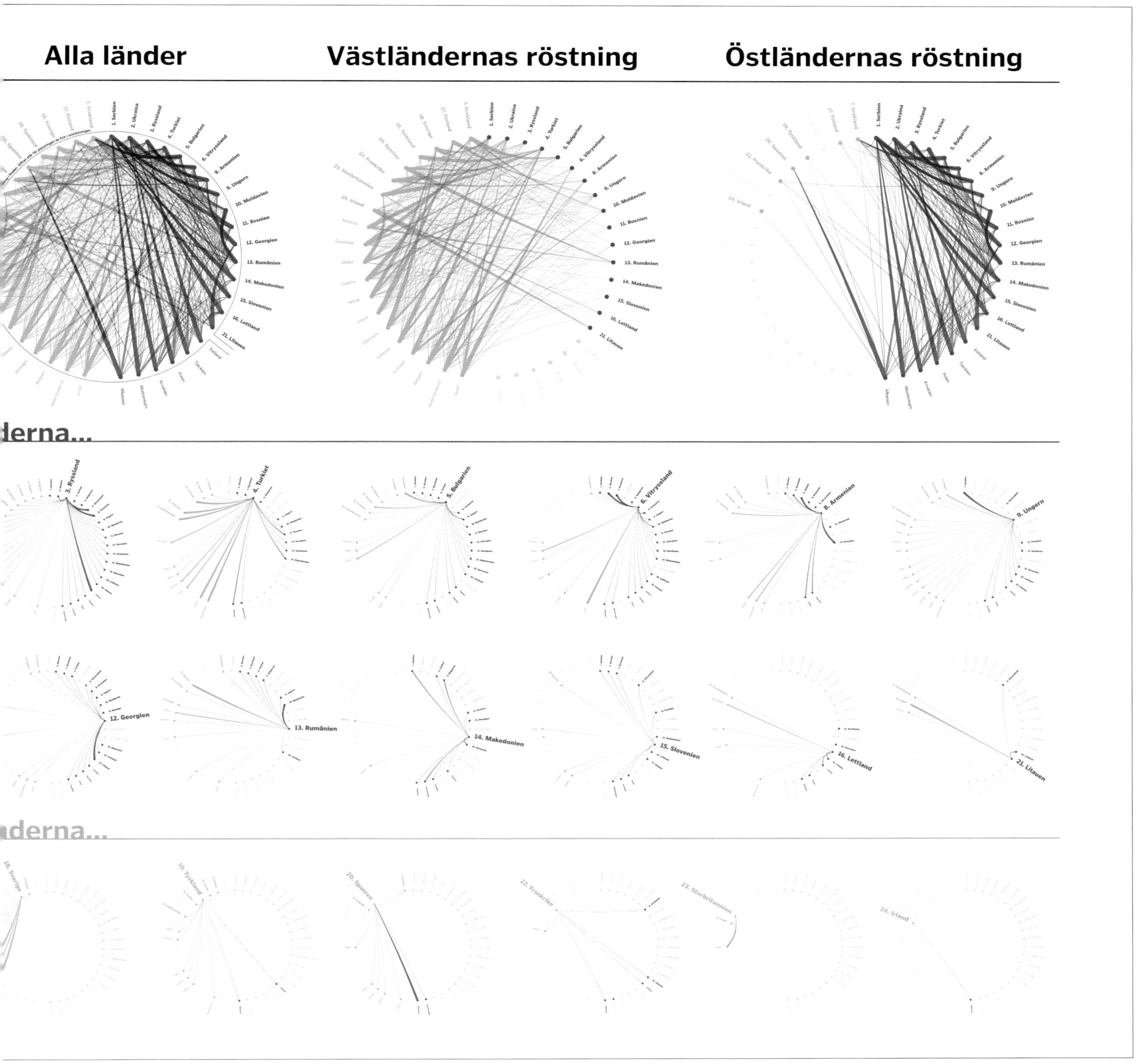

Alla länder

Västländernas röstning

Östländernas röstning

...derna...

1. Serbien, 2. Ukraina, 3. Ryssland, 4. Turkiet, 5. Bulgarien, 6. Vitryssland, 8. Armenien, 9. Ungern, 10. Moldavien, 11. Bosnien, 12. Georgien, 13. Rumänien, 14. Makedonien, 15. Slovenien, 16. Lettland, 21. Litauen

...derna...

18. Sverige, 19. Tyskland, 20. Spanien, 22. Frankrike, 23. Storbritannien, 24. Irland

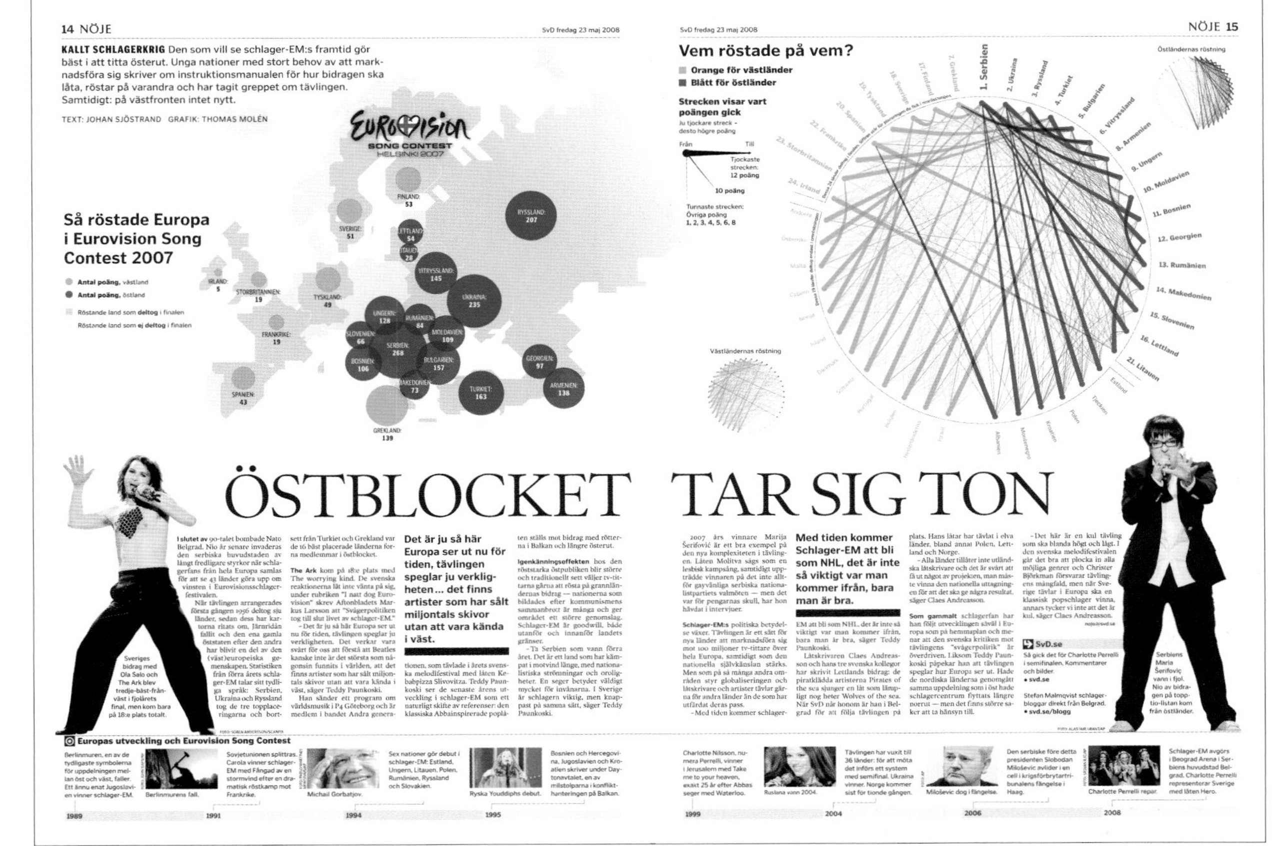

Wired Start Atlases

The well-known American technology magazine *Wired* has created an established format with its "Start" atlases. At the beginning of each issue, a double-spread tackles current topics in a thematic map.

The design varies in each case and is aligned with the problem the map discusses. The maps in this selection were created by Carl De Torres between 2007 and 2008.

Die bekannte amerikanische Technologie-Zeitschrift *Wired* schuf mit seinen „Start"-Karten ein etabliertes Format. Zu Beginn jeder Ausgabe wird auf einer doppelseitigen Karte ein aktuelles Thema behandelt.

Das Design variiert und richtet sich jeweils nach dem Thema der Karte. Die hier ausgewählten Karten wurden zwischen 2007 und 2008 von Carl De Torres entworfen.

Le célèbre magazine américain de technologie *Wired* a créé un format reconnaissable avec ses atlas « Start ». Au début de chaque numéro, une double page présente des sujets d'actualité à l'aide d'une carte thématique.

Le graphisme varie à chaque fois en fonction du problème que la carte analyse. Les cartes de cette sélection ont été créées par Carl De Torres entre 2007 et 2008.

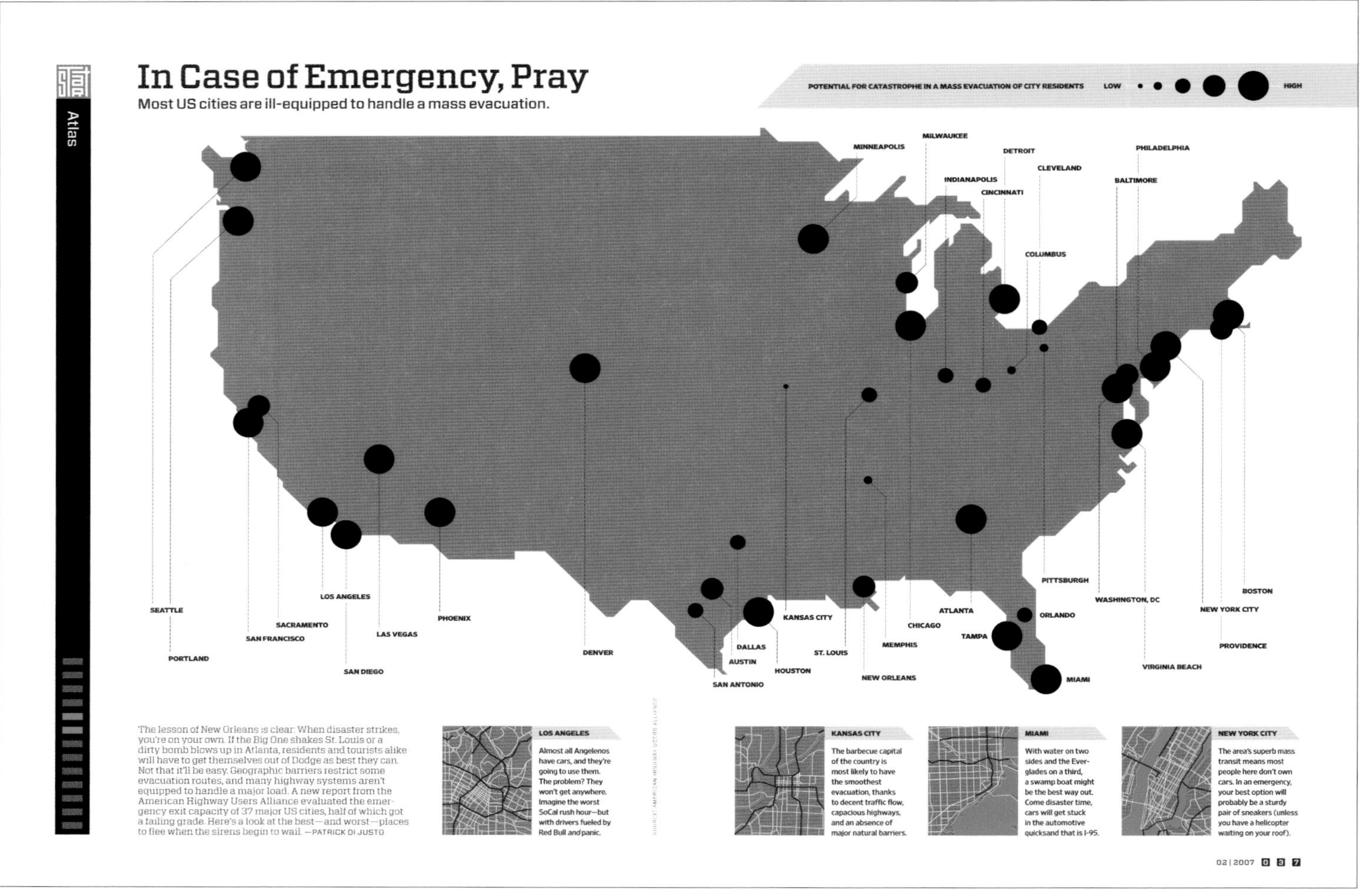

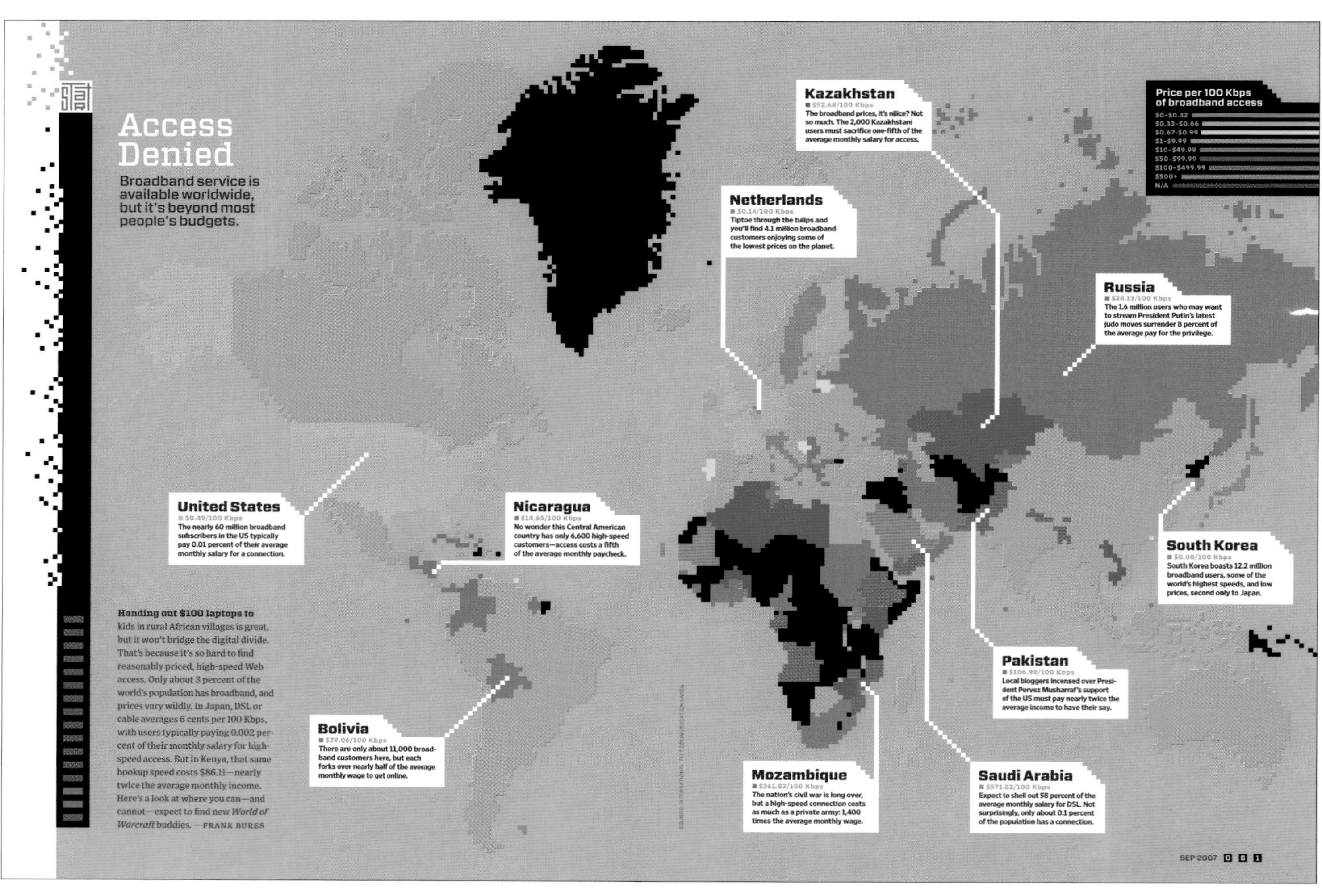

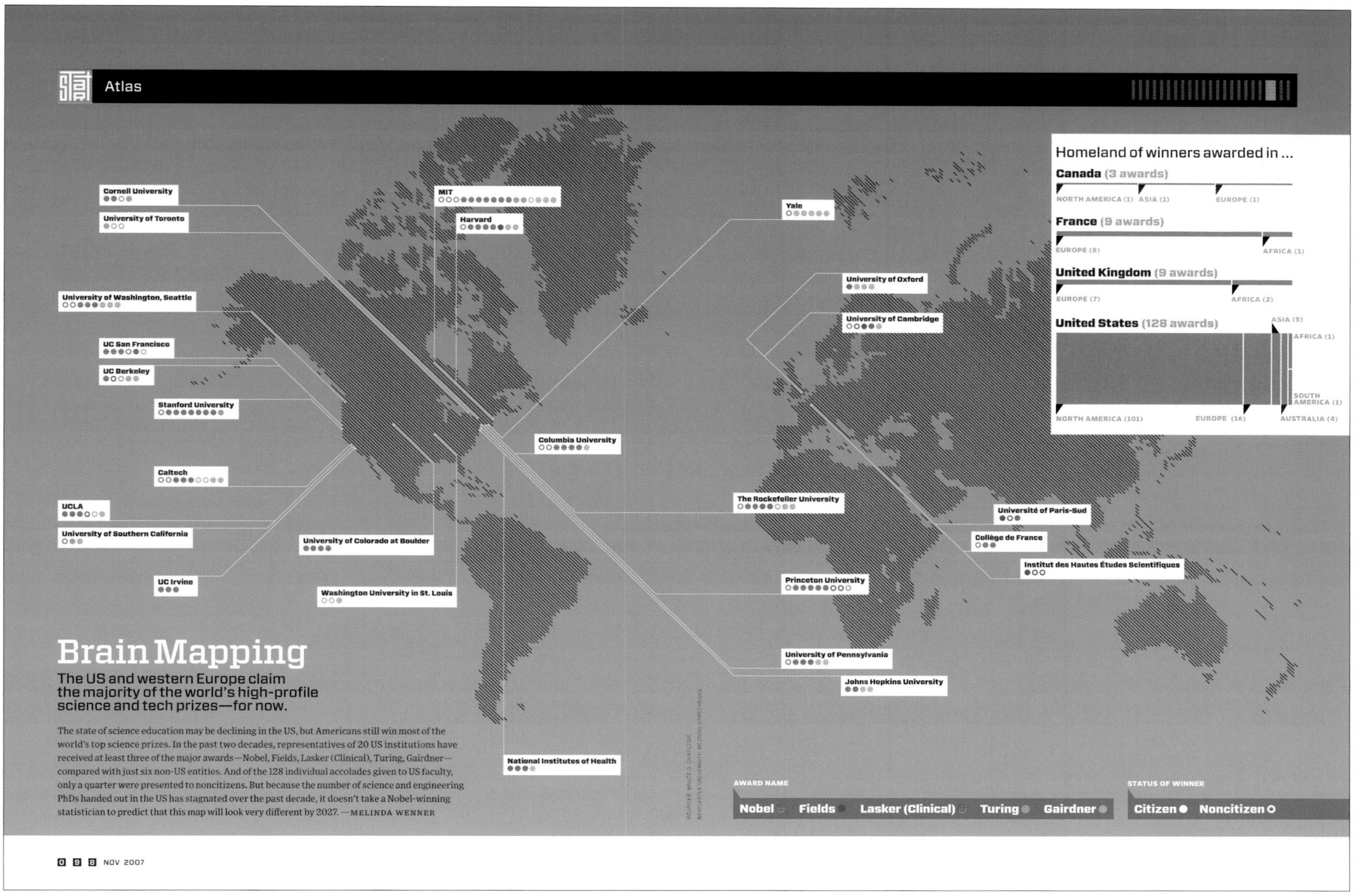

Atlas

Brain Mapping

The US and western Europe claim the majority of the world's high-profile science and tech prizes—for now.

The state of science education may be declining in the US, but Americans still win most of the world's top science prizes. In the past two decades, representatives of 20 US institutions have received at least three of the major awards—Nobel, Fields, Lasker (Clinical), Turing, Gairdner—compared with just six non-US entities. And of the 128 individual accolades given to US faculty, only a quarter were presented to noncitizens. But because the number of science and engineering PhDs handed out in the US has stagnated over the past decade, it doesn't take a Nobel-winning statistician to predict that this map will look very different by 2027. —MELINDA WENNER

Atlas

Are We Airborne Yet?

Airport delays are getting worse. Don't forget to pack your patience.

It's not your imagination: Air travel has never sucked more. The year 2007 was the worst for flight delays since the government began keeping stats more than a decade ago. In 2002, 17 percent of flights arrived late (defined by the FAA as delayed 15 minutes or more). Last summer it was nearly a third, and travel in 2008 won't be much better. Blame congestion, in part: More passengers on more planes means that a minor hitch at JFK can ripple across the entire northeast. But most of the trouble can be traced to antiquated air-traffic control technology. Until a new $22 billion satellite-based system comes online—look for it in 2025 at the earliest—try to fly out of Oakland. —MATHEW HONAN

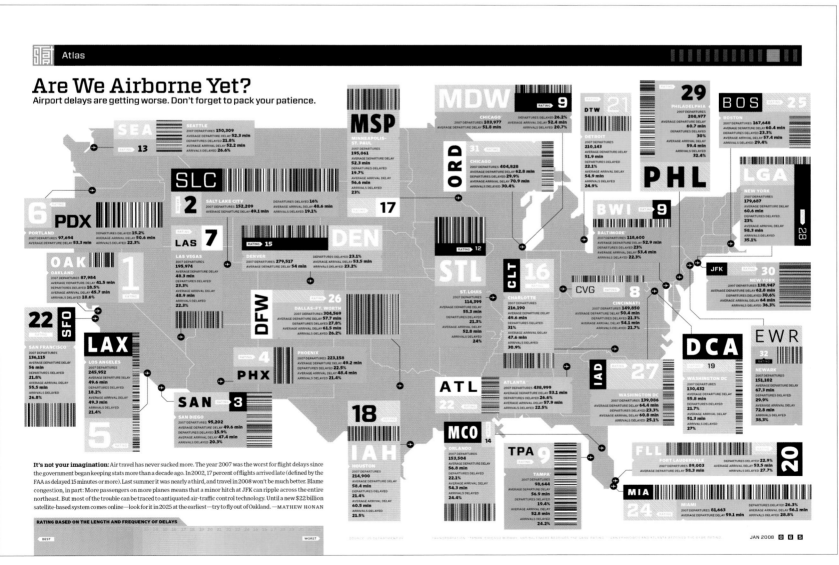

Project Info: *Wired*, magazine article, 2007–2008, USA
Data Source: American Highway Users Alliance; International Communication Union; Bruce G. Charlton (New Castle University); *Medical Hypoteses*; US Department of Transportation
Design: Carl De Torres
Creative Direction: Scott Dadich
Design Director: Wyatt Mitchell

World of Rivers

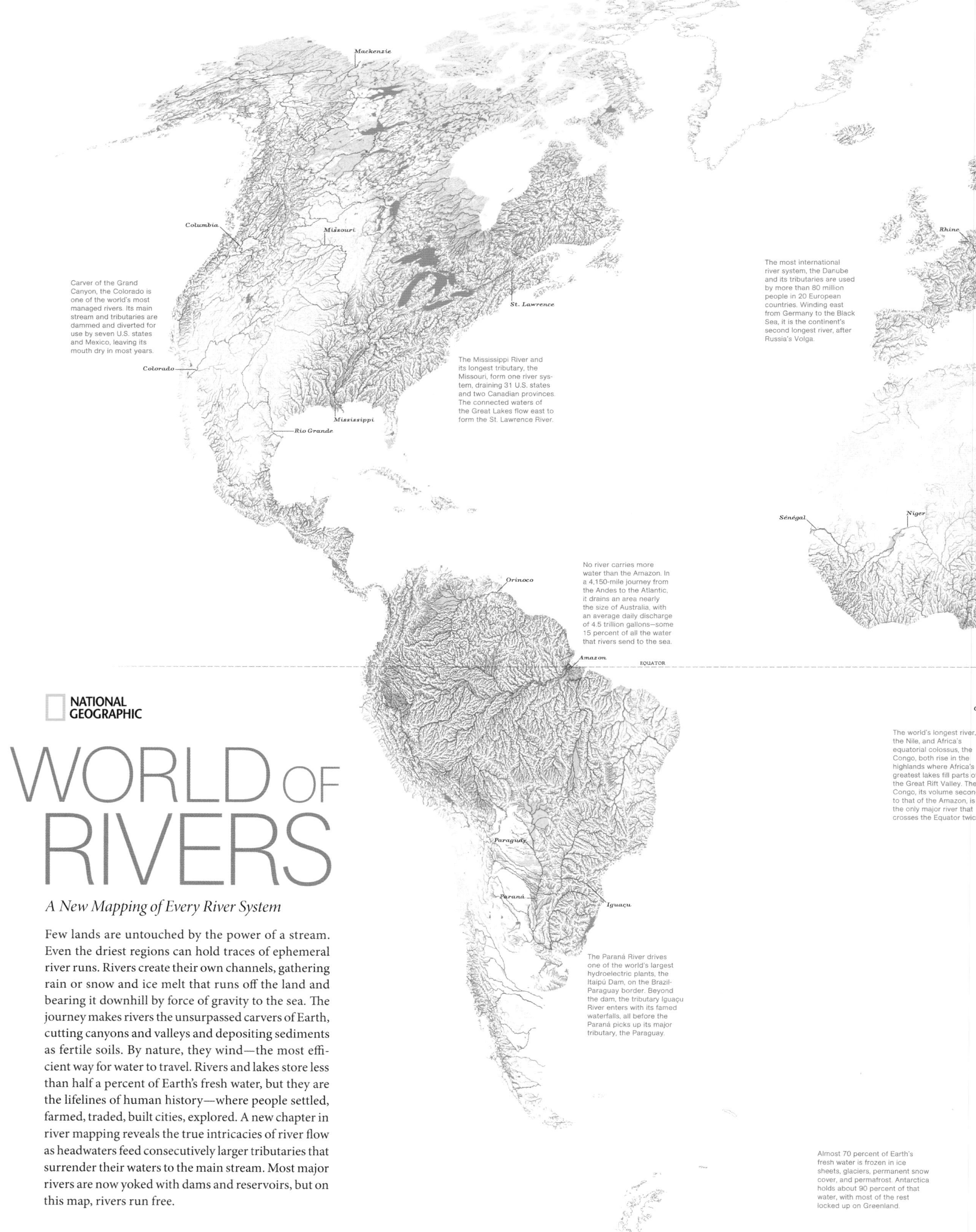

Mackenzie
Columbia
Missouri
St. Lawrence
Colorado
Mississippi
Rio Grande
Rhine
Sénégal
Niger
Orinoco
Amazon
EQUATOR
Congo
Paraguay
Paraná
Iguaçu
Carver of the Grand Canyon, the Colorado is one of the world's most managed rivers. Its main stream and tributaries are dammed and diverted for use by seven U.S. states and Mexico, leaving its mouth dry in most years.
The Mississippi River and its longest tributary, the Missouri, form one river system, draining 31 U.S. states and two Canadian provinces. The connected waters of the Great Lakes flow east to form the St. Lawrence River.
The most international river system, the Danube and its tributaries are used by more than 80 million people in 20 European countries. Winding east from Germany to the Black Sea, it is the continent's second longest river, after Russia's Volga.
No river carries more water than the Amazon. In a 4,150-mile journey from the Andes to the Atlantic, it drains an area nearly the size of Australia, with an average daily discharge of 4.5 trillion gallons—some 15 percent of all the water that rivers send to the sea.
The world's longest river, the Nile, and Africa's equatorial colossus, the Congo, both rise in the highlands where Africa's greatest lakes fill parts of the Great Rift Valley. The Congo, its volume second to that of the Amazon, is the only major river that crosses the Equator twice.
The Paraná River drives one of the world's largest hydroelectric plants, the Itaipú Dam, on the Brazil-Paraguay border. Beyond the dam, the tributary Iguaçu River enters with its famed waterfalls, all before the Paraná picks up its major tributary, the Paraguay.
Almost 70 percent of Earth's fresh water is frozen in ice sheets, glaciers, permanent snow cover, and permafrost. Antarctica holds about 90 percent of that water, with most of the rest locked up on Greenland.
NATIONAL GEOGRAPHIC
WORLD OF RIVERS
A New Mapping of Every River System
Few lands are untouched by the power of a stream. Even the driest regions can hold traces of ephemeral river runs. Rivers create their own channels, gathering rain or snow and ice melt that runs off the land and bearing it downhill by force of gravity to the sea. The journey makes rivers the unsurpassed carvers of Earth, cutting canyons and valleys and depositing sediments as fertile soils. By nature, they wind—the most efficient way for water to travel. Rivers and lakes store less than half a percent of Earth's fresh water, but they are the lifelines of human history—where people settled, farmed, traded, built cities, explored. A new chapter in river mapping reveals the true intricacies of river flow as headwaters feed consecutively larger tributaries that surrender their waters to the main stream. Most major rivers are now yoked with dams and reservoirs, but on this map, rivers run free.

Lena
Yenisey
Angara
Ob
Amur
Irtysh
Volga
Danube
Yellow
Yangtze
Tigris
Euphrates
Brahmaputra
Nile
Indus
Ganges
Salween
Mekong
Zambezi
EQUATOR
Darling
Murray
China's Yangtze River powers the Three Gorges Dam, unequaled in hydro-electric generating capacity. Another monumental project is now under way to divert water from the Yangtze to China's dry, populous north. There, the Yellow River, drawn down for irrigation and industry, often fails to reach the sea.
Sediment carried from the Himalaya and the Tibetan Plateau creates some of the world's largest river deltas, including the Indus, the Mekong, and the great delta where the Ganges meets the Brahmaputra River system. Worldwide, deltas are home to an estimated 500 million people.
Ten Longest Rivers
1. Nile (Africa) 4,400 miles
2. Amazon (South America) 4,150 miles
3. Yangtze (Asia) 3,880 miles
4. Mississippi-Missouri (North America) 3,780 miles
5. Yenisey-Angara (Asia) 3,610 miles
6. Yellow (Asia) 3,590 miles
7. Ob-Irtysh (Asia) 3,430 miles
8. Amur (Asia) 3,420 miles
9. Lena (Asia) 3,200 miles
10. Congo (Africa) 3,180 miles
The Murray-Darling is Australia's only major river system, rising in the mountain ranges of the southeast. Heavily tapped for irrigation, its flow has declined during a decade of drought. The continent's intermittent rivers and lakes can fill if water flows south after heavy seasonal rains in the tropical north.
Greenland
NORTH AMERICA
EUROPE
ASIA
ATLANTIC OCEAN
PACIFIC OCEAN
AFRICA
SOUTH AMERICA
PACIFIC OCEAN
INDIAN OCEAN
AUSTRALIA
ANTARCTICA
The Water Below
Most of the planet's liquid fresh water is groundwater, precipitation that seeps down to fill the spaces in layers of sand, gravel, and permeable rock called aquifers. Groundwater exists almost everywhere, at varying depths. Since the mid-20th century, its extraction for human use has accelerated, often at unsustainable rates. How readily groundwater recharges depends on precipitation, geology, and topography. Groundwater can emerge as a spring, the start of many rivers and for some a major contributor. Up to 40 percent of the volume of the Mississippi River is estimated to come from groundwater.
Groundwater recharge
Very high
Moderate
Very low
National Geographic Society
Gilbert M. Grosvenor, Chairman
John M. Fahey, Jr., President and CEO
Chris Johns, Editor in Chief
William E. McNulty, Director of Maps, National Geographic Magazine
SUPPLEMENT TO NATIONAL GEOGRAPHIC, APRIL 2010
PRODUCED BY NATIONAL GEOGRAPHIC MAPS FOR NATIONAL GEOGRAPHIC MAGAZINE
DESIGN: MOLLIE BATES AND ELAINE BRADLEY
TEXT: JANE VESSELS RESEARCH: CHRISTY ULLRICH
SCIENTIFIC ADVISERS: BERNHARD LEHNER, McGILL UNIVERSITY; BART WICKEL, WORLD WILDLIFE FUND GIS: TED SICKLEY
MAP PRODUCTION: DEBBIE GIBBONS AND DIANNE HUNT
MAP EDIT: MAUREEN FLYNN-STELMAN MAP DATA: WORLD WILDLIFE FUND, HYDROSHEDS; AND USGS (RIVERS); THE NATURE CONSERVANCY AND UNIVERSITY OF KASSEL CENTER FOR ENVIRONMENTAL SYSTEMS RESEARCH, WATERGAP2 (RIVER DISCHARGE); GLOBAL LAKES AND WETLANDS DATABASE, WORLD WILDLIFE FUND; NATIONAL SNOW AND ICE DATA CENTER, UNIVERSITY OF COLORADO GROUNDWATER MAP: KAITLIN YARNALL (RESEARCH); BGR/UNESCO (DATA) RIVER LENGTHS: SHAOCHUANG LIU, CHINESE ACADEMY OF SCIENCES, ET AL. (2009) AND HYDROSHEDS DATA BY BERNHARD LEHNER
FOR INFORMATION REGARDING AVAILABLE MAPS CALL 1-800-962-1643 OR WRITE TO NATIONAL GEOGRAPHIC MAPS, PO BOX 4357, EVERGREEN, CO 80437-4357. YOU CAN FIND US ON THE INTERNET AT NATIONALGEOGRAPHIC.COM/MAPS.
COPYRIGHT © 2010 NATIONAL GEOGRAPHIC SOCIETY, WASHINGTON, D.C. PRINTED FEBRUARY 2010
This map uses a modified version of a database called HydroSHEDS, a digital compilation of the world's river channels and basins mapped with unprecedented precision. HydroSHEDS is based on high-resolution elevation data gathered by NASA's space shuttle during the 2000 Shuttle Radar Topography Mission. It was developed by the World Wildlife Fund Conservation Science Program (Bernhard Lehner, Kris Verdin, Andrew Jarvis, 2008); worldwildlife.org/hydrosheds. A global hydrological model was integrated to estimate where and how much water flows.
WINKEL TRIPEL PROJECTION
0 mi 1000
0 km 1000
Map Legend
Perennial river
(Average discharge 1961-1990, gallons per second)
More than 130,000
7,500–130,000
1,250–7,499
250–1,249
Fewer than 250
Intermittent river
(Average discharge 1961-1990, gallons per second)
More than 7,500
1,250–7,500
250–1,249
Fewer than 250
Glaciated area or ice sheet
Lake
Permafrost
(More than 90 percent of the ground continuously frozen)
Major wetland

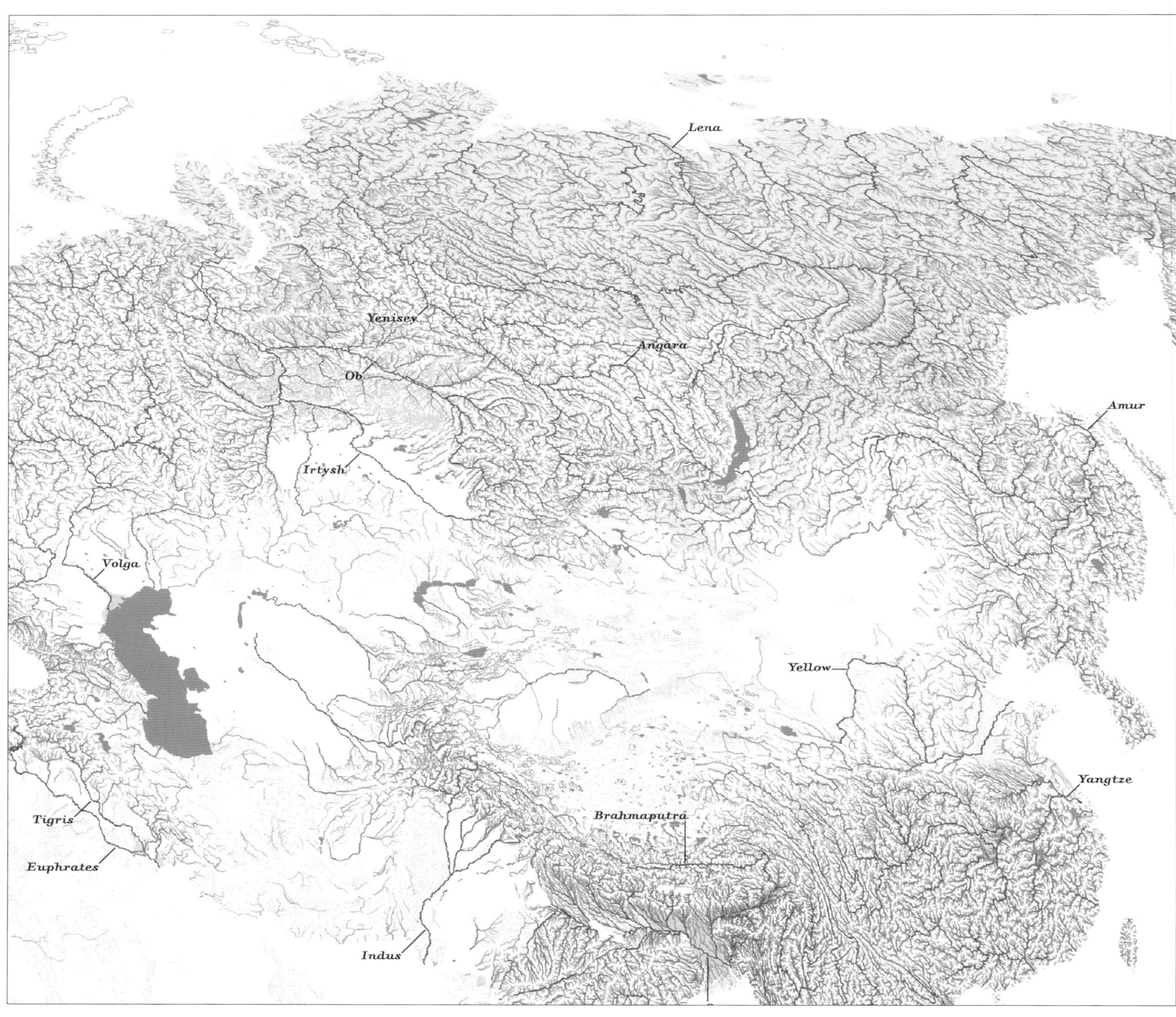

This poster by *National Geographic* shows a digital compilation of the world's river channels and basins. It is based on a large geo-referenced dataset, HydroSHEDS, which was developed by the WWF and in turn draws on high-resolution elevation data gathered by NASA from space.

With this global hydrological model, rivers and basins can be shown with unparalleled precision and estimates can be made as to how much water flows. Green shades on the map mark major wetlands, while red shades refer to arid areas.

Dieses Plakat von *National Geographic* zeigt eine digital zusammengesetzte Karte mit den Flüssen und Flussläufen der Erde. Sie beruht auf den umfangreichen Geodaten von HydroSHEDS, einer Datenbank, die vom WWF entwickelt wurde und ihrerseits auf hochaufgelöste Satellitendaten der NASA zurückgreift.

Mit diesem globalen hydrologischen Modell können Flüsse und Flussläufe mit bislang ungekannter Genauigkeit dargestellt werden. Zudem lässt sich die Wassermenge schätzen, die in ihnen fließt. Grüntöne auf der Karte markieren große Feuchtgebiete, während Rottöne auf Trockengebiete verweisen.

Cette affiche du *National Geographic* montre une compilation numérique des cours et plans d'eau du monde. Elle se base sur une vaste banque de données géoréférencées, HydroSHEDS, que le WWF a mise au point en s'appuyant sur des données d'altitude haute résolution que la NASA a collectées depuis l'espace.

Cette maquette hydrologique mondiale permet de représenter les cours et plans d'eau avec une précision sans précédent, et d'estimer le volume d'eau en circulation. La couleur verte indique les grandes zones humides, tandis que le rouge indique des zones arides.

Project Info: *National Geographic*, poster, 2007, USA
Data Source: WWF; USGS; The Nature Conservancy; Center for Environmental Systems Research (University of Kassel); NSIDC; BGR/UNESCO; Shaochuang Liu (Chinese Academy of Sciences), WaterGAP2
Research: William McNulty, Kaitlin Yarnall, Jane Vessels, Christy Ullrich
Design: Mollie Bates, Elaine Bradley
Art Direction: William McNulty, Juan Velasco
Illustration: William McNulty

Time

“One significant difficulty is knowing, given a set of data, how to glean meaningful information from it.”

„Eine große Schwierigkeit angesichts eines Datensatzes besteht darin zu wissen, wie man sinnvolle Informationen daraus zieht.“

« L’une des grandes difficultés est de savoir comment extraire des informations utiles à partir d’un certain ensemble de données. »

Ben Fry

Time

Elements are organised against a timeline

Time

Elemente werden in einer Zeitabfolge präsentiert

Temps

Les éléments sont organisés de façon spatiale

The passage of time creates a fixed sequence. Time offers a simple organisational framework, because everyone knows how events unfold over the course of time. Timelines are the classic guides for the writing of history; they show how things have developed. Also, the arrangement of events in timelines permits one to create one's own version of history (*Andy Warhol – Chelsea Girls*, p.217) or even to predict the future (*The Afghan Conflict*, p.304).

Time series are pivotal tools for scientific or sociological analyses. Specific measurements are collected periodically for complex phenomena such as the weather or stock-market fluctuations. The graphic depiction of measurement series is the most intuitive method of analysis for this kind of data (*CNN.com Traffic Analysis*, p.291). Timelines serve to describe phenomena and make trends visible, but they do not explain their causes.

In Western cultures time is generally envisioned as being linear and moving towards the future. However, in its graphic representation a timeline is not necessarily a straight line; it can also be curved (*Motown's 191 Number One Hits*, p.276) or circular (*Cosmic 140 – Art for Geeks*, p.223).

Works that follow a strict sequence also belong in this chapter. The order of text in a novel is sequential and not randomly reversible, just as a play follows a set dramatic composition. This section also considers the kinds of data analyses that provide a graphic illustration of this type of predefined sequence (*TextArc*, p.299). In addition, time can be used to structure entirely different issues: *Daily Waterfall* (p.226) focuses on a typical day to demonstrate how much water is routinely consumed.

Flow charts are a different kind of time-based infographic. They describe the course of processes (*How Books are Made*, p.244), and in informatics they can also show the sequence of operations required to solve a problem. Unlike continuous timelines, flow charts can branch off in time and show sequences with several open outcomes. They can also be used to work through a difficult decision from start to finish (*So You Need a Typeface?*, p.288 and *Guess Who? Character Identification Chart*, p.248).

Visualising processes as a circle has its origins in biology and the life-cycle of living organisms (*Swine Flu Life Cycle*, p.294). Lately this concept has also been applied to commercial products, especially in connection with aspects of sustainability. The entire life of a product from manufacture to disposal can be considered as a cycle (*Biofuel*, p.220).

Der Ablauf der Zeit stellt eine strenge Abfolge her. Zeit ist ein einfaches Organisationsschema – jedermann weiß, wie sich Ereignisse im Laufe der Zeit entfalten. Die Zeitleiste ist der klassische Leitfaden der Geschichtsschreibung – sie zeigt, wie sich etwas entwickelt hat. Die Einsortierung von Ereignissen in eine Zeitleiste bietet immer auch die Möglichkeit, eine eigene Version der Geschichte zu erschaffen (*Andy Warhol – Chelsea Girls*, S. 217) oder gar Optionen für die Zukunft zu ergründen (*The Afghan Conflict*, S. 304).

Zeitreihen sind ein zentrales Instrument in naturwissenschaftlichen oder soziologischen Analysen. Für komplexe Phänomene wie das Wetter oder die Entwicklung von Börsenkursen werden in regelmäßigen Zeitabständen bestimmte Messwerte erhoben. Die grafische Darstellung von Messreihen ist die intuitivste Analysemethode für diese Daten (*CNN.com Traffic Analysis*, S. 291). Zeitreihen dienen dazu, Erscheinungen zu beschreiben und Tendenzen sichtbar zu machen, sie erklären aber noch nicht deren Ursachen.

Westliche Kulturen stellen sich die Zeit überwiegend als linear in die Zukunft gerichtet vor. In der grafischen Umsetzung jedoch ist eine Zeitleiste nicht notwendigerweise eine gerade Linie, sie kann auch gebogen (*Motown's 191 Number One Hits*, S. 276) oder zirkulär angelegt sein (*Cosmic 140 – Art for Geeks*, S. 223).

In dieses Kapitel gehören auch alle Arbeiten, die nach einer strengen Sequenz vorgehen. Die Abfolge von Text in einem Roman ist sequenziell und nicht beliebig umkehrbar, ebenso folgt ein Theaterstück einer festgelegten Dramaturgie. Hier sind auch diejenigen Datenanalysen berücksichtigt, die eine solche vorgegebene Abfolge grafisch umsetzen (*TextArc*, S. 299). Zeit kann außerdem auch benutzt werden, um ganz andere Themen zu gliedern: *Daily Waterfall* stellt einen typischen Tagesablauf ins Zentrum, um zu zeigen, wie viel Wasser im Alltag verbraucht wird (S. 226).

Ein weiterer Typus von zeitbasierten Infografiken sind Flussdiagramme. Sie beschreiben den Ablauf von Prozessen (*How Books are Made*, S. 244), in der Informatik auch die Abfolge von Operationen zur Lösung einer Aufgabe. Anders als kontinuierliche Zeitreihen können sich Flussdiagramme in der Zeit verzweigen und Abläufe mit mehreren offenen Ausgängen zeigen. Sie lassen sich auch nutzen, um eine schwierige Entscheidung von Anfang bis Ende durchzuspielen (*So You Need a Typeface?*, S. 288, und *Guess Who? Character Identification Chart*, S. 248).

Eine zirkuläre Vorstellung von Prozessen stammt aus der Biologie – der Lebenszyklus von Lebewesen (*Swine Flu Life Cycle*, S. 294). Dieses Konzept wird in jüngerer Zeit häufig auch auf kommerzielle Produkte angewandt, insbesondere im Zusammenhang mit Nachhaltigkeitsüberlegungen. Der gesamte Lebenskreislauf eines Produktes wird in einem Zyklus von der Herstellung bis zur Entsorgung gesehen (*Biofuel*, S. 220).

Le temps qui passe crée une séquence fixe. Le temps offre un cadre organisationnel simple car tout le monde sait comment se déroulent des événements sur la durée. Les chronologies sont des supports classiques pour écrire l'histoire et montrer l'évolution de faits. Aussi, l'organisation des événements dans des chronologies permet à chacun de créer sa propre version de l'histoire (*Andy Warhol – Chelsea Girls*, p.217), voire de prédire l'avenir (*The Afghan Conflict*, p.304).

Les chronologies sont des outils essentiels pour les analyses scientifiques et sociologiques. Des mesures spécifiques sont relevées régulièrement pour des phénomènes complexes comme la météorologie ou les fluctuations de la Bourse. La représentation graphique d'une série de mesures est la méthode la plus intuitive pour analyser ce type de données (*CNN.com Traffic Analysis*, p.291). Les chronologies servent à décrire des phénomènes et à révéler des tendances, sans pour autant en expliquer les causes.

Dans les cultures occidentales, le temps est généralement considéré comme linéaire et pointant vers l'avenir. Dans sa représentation graphique cependant, une chronologie n'est pas forcément une ligne droite, elle peut aussi être courbe (*Motown's 191 Number One Hits*, p.276) ou circulaire (*Cosmic 140 – Art for Geeks*, p.223).

Les travaux qui suivent une séquence stricte appartiennent aussi à ce chapitre. L'ordre du texte dans un roman est séquentiel et non réversible de façon aléatoire, tout comme une pièce de théâtre obéit à une composition dramatique. Cette section prend également en compte les types d'analyse de données apportant une illustration graphique de ce type de séquence prédéfinie (*TextArc*, p.299). En outre, le temps peut servir à structurer des sujets complètement différents : *Daily Waterfall* (p.226) prend une journée type pour montrer la consommation habituelle d'eau.

Les diagrammes organisationnels sont un autre type d'infographie basée sur le temps. Ils décrivent le déroulement de processus (*How Books are Made*, p.244) et en informatique, ils peuvent aussi montrer la séquence d'opérations nécessaires pour résoudre un problème. Contrairement aux chronologies continues, ils peuvent bifurquer et montrer des séquences avec plusieurs résultats ouverts. Ils peuvent aussi aider à prendre une décision complexe (*So You Need a Typeface?*, p.288 et *Guess Who? Character Identification Chart*, p.248).

La visualisation circulaire de processus tire son origine de la biologie et du cycle de vie des organismes vivants (*Swine Flu Life Cycle*, p.294). Plus tard, ce concept a également été appliqué aux produits commerciaux, notamment pour les aspects relatifs au développement durable. La vie entière d'un produit, de la fabrication à la mise au rebut, peut être considérée comme un cycle (*Biofuel*, p.220).

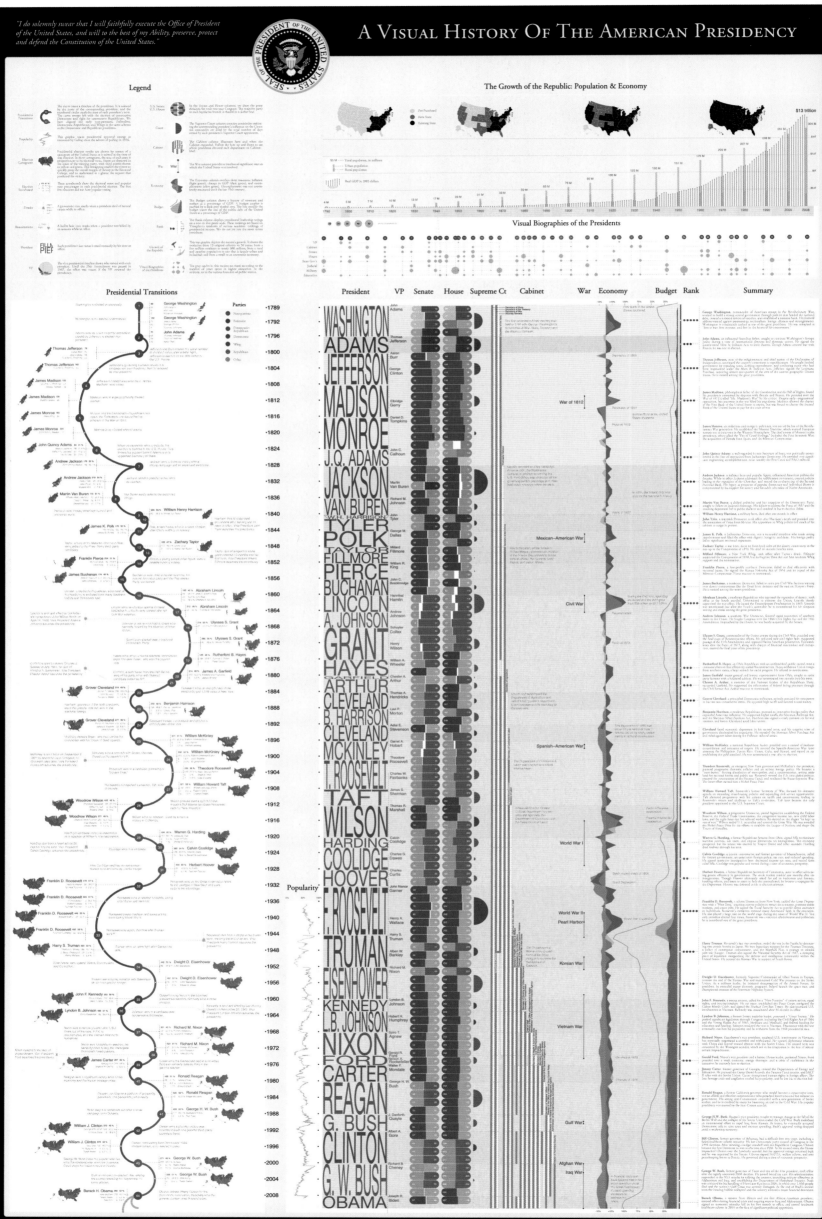

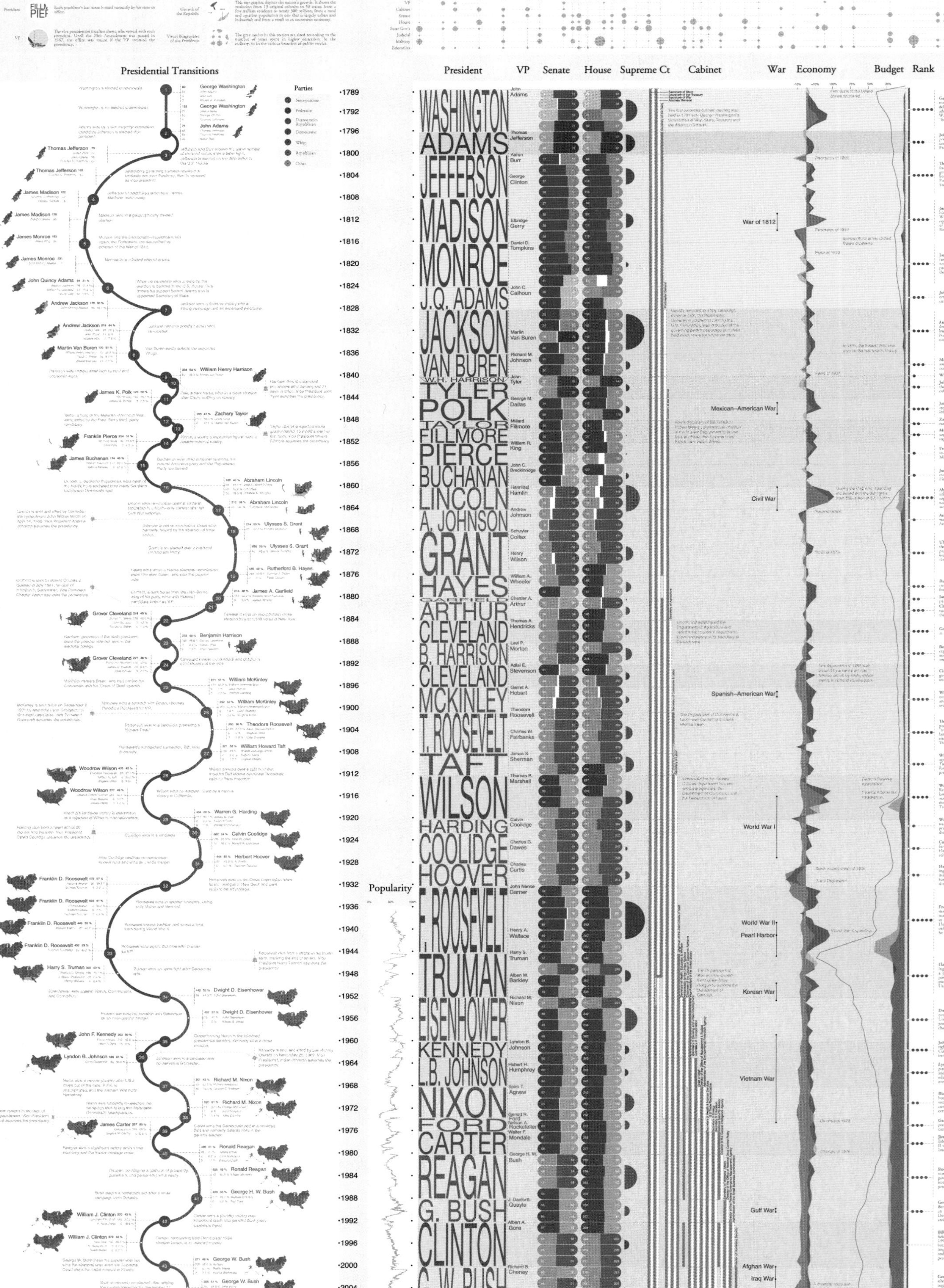
"I do solemnly swear that I will faithfully execute the Office of President of the United States, and will to the best of my Ability, preserve, protect and defend the Constitution of the United States."
A Visual History Of The American Presidency
Legend
The Growth of the Republic: Population & Economy
Visual Biographies of the Presidents
Presidential Transitions
President
VP
Senate
House
Supreme Ct
Cabinet
War
Economy
Budget
Rank
Summary
Popularity
WASHINGTON
ADAMS
JEFFERSON
MADISON
MONROE
J.Q. ADAMS
JACKSON
VAN BUREN
W.H. HARRISON
TYLER
POLK
TAYLOR
FILLMORE
PIERCE
BUCHANAN
LINCOLN
A. JOHNSON
GRANT
HAYES
GARFIELD
ARTHUR
CLEVELAND
B. HARRISON
CLEVELAND
MCKINLEY
T. ROOSEVELT
TAFT
WILSON
HARDING
COOLIDGE
HOOVER
F. ROOSEVELT
TRUMAN
EISENHOWER
KENNEDY
L.B. JOHNSON
NIXON
FORD
CARTER
REAGAN
G. BUSH
CLINTON
G. W. BUSH
OBAMA
War of 1812
Mexican-American War
Civil War
Spanish-American War
World War I
World War II
Pearl Harbor
Korean War
Vietnam War
Gulf War
Afghan War
Iraq War
$13 trillion
1789
1792
1796
1800
1804
1808
1812
1816
1820
1824
1828
1832
1836
1840
1844
1848
1852
1856
1860
1864
1868
1872
1876
1880
1884
1888
1892
1896
1900
1904
1908
1912
1916
1920
1924
1928
1932
1936
1940
1944
1948
1952
1956
1960
1964
1968
1972
1976
1980
1984
1988
1992
1996
2000
2004
2008

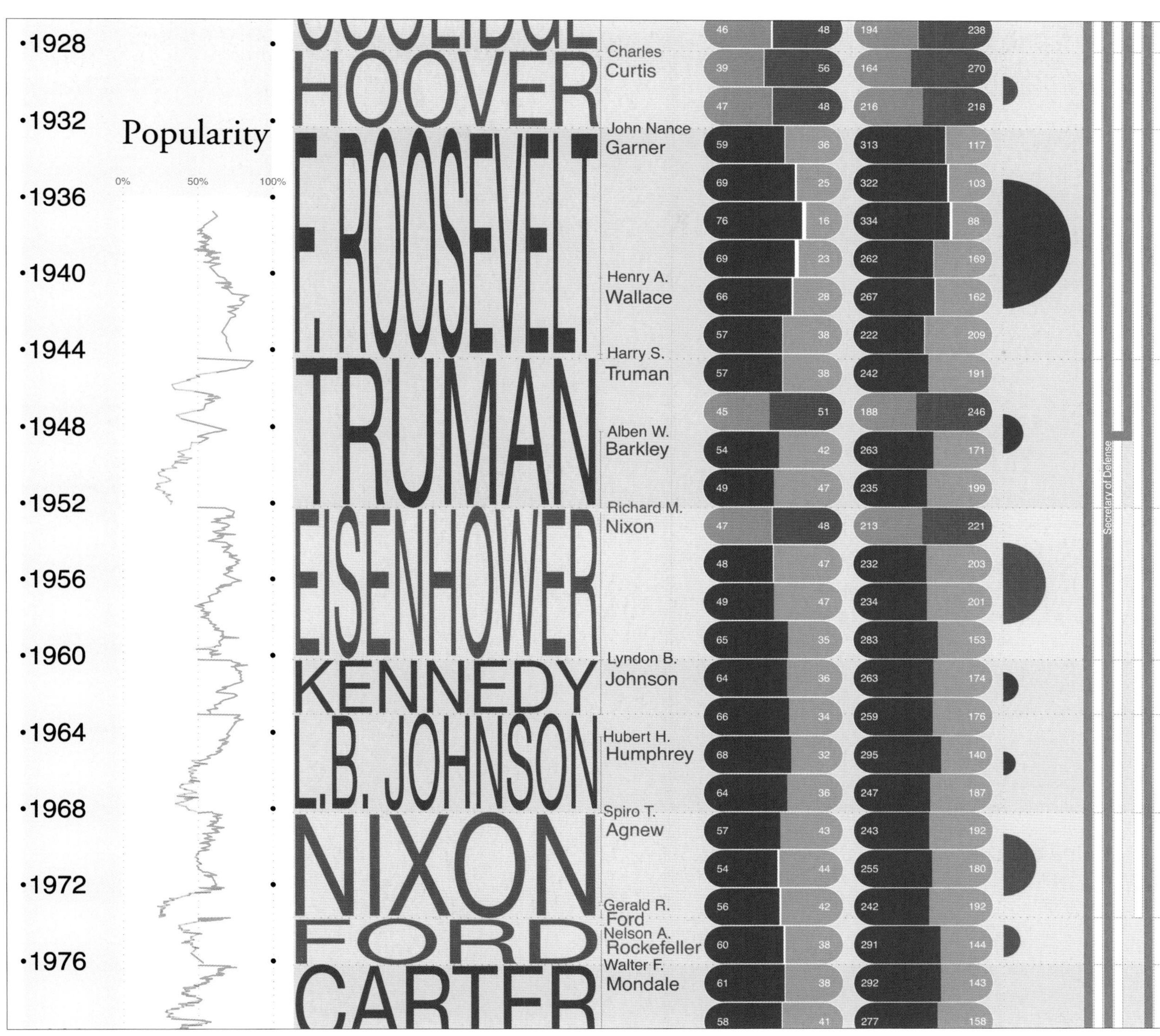

A Visual History of the American Presidency

This timeline covers 219 years of American presidency with a striking level of detail. In the centre, all the presidents since 1789 are named, with colour referring to the political party to which they were affiliated. Scaling indicates how long they were in office. The list is further enriched with data concerning majorities in Senate and Congress, the economy or the federal budget.

The Presidential Transitions timeline on the left adds a narrative of larger political trends. The horizontal timeline in the top right gives contexts for how the United States grew over this period, geographically, economically (in terms of GDP) as well as in population numbers. Below, the "visual biographies" show what career experience each president brought to office when they began their term.

Diese Zeitleiste dokumentiert 219 Regierungsjahre amerikanischer Präsidenten mit erstaunlich vielen Details. Auf der Mittelachse stehen alle Präsidenten seit 1789, die Farbe verweist auf die politische Partei, zu der sie jeweils gehörten. Die Skalierung des Namens zeigt, wie lange sie im Amt waren. Die Liste wird ergänzt durch Informationen zu den Mehrheitsverhältnissen in Senat und Kongress sowie zu Wirtschaft und Staatshaushalt.

„Presidential Transitions", die Zeitleiste links, spiegelt die größeren politischen Tendenzen. Die horizontale Zeitschiene oben rechts liefert weitere Kontextdaten zum Wachstum der USA während dieser Zeit: geografische, ökonomische (gemessen am Bruttoinlandsprodukt) sowie Bevölkerungsdaten. Die „visuellen Biografien" darunter zeigen, über welche beruflichen Erfahrungen jeder Präsident bei seinem Amtsantritt verfügte.

Cette chronologie couvre 219 ans de l'histoire des présidents américains avec un niveau de détail remarquable. Tous les présidents depuis 1789 sont mentionnés au centre, et la couleur de leur nom fait référence au parti politique auquel ils appartiennent. La taille des lettres indique la longueur de leur mandat. Cette liste est complétée par des données sur les majorités en place au Sénat et au Congrès, sur l'économie ou sur le budget fédéral.

À gauche, la chronologie des transitions présidentielles ajoute une perspective sur les tendances politiques à une échelle plus large. La chronologie horizontale en haut à droite donne le contexte de la croissance des États-Unis pendant cette période, des points de vue géographique, économique (en termes de PIB) et démographique. En dessous, les « biographies visuelles » montrent l'expérience politique de chaque président en début de mandat.

Project Info: Poster, 2010, USA
Research: Joe Williams, Eliza Keller, Abram Conrad
Design: Nathaniel Pearlman, Frank Hamilton (Timeplots)

A Visual History of the United States Supreme Court

Finding new ways to communicate history: this large-scale time-plot covers the history of the United States Supreme Court over the more than 200 years of its history. The central time series features one line for each judicial seat, with the Chief Justice represented by the top line. The lines float up and down indicating how many justices have been appointed by each political force.

Democrats are coded in blue towards the lower end, while Republican influence is coded in red towards the top. The central time-plot includes details of landmark cases, which are explained and classified along the bottom. Along the sides of the graphic, all justices are named along with biographical details as well as the appointing president and his vote results in the Senate.

Neue Ansätze der Geschichtsschreibung: Dieses großformatige Zeitschema erfasst die über 200-jährige Geschichte des US Supreme Court. Jeder Richtersitz wird im mittleren Diagramm durch eine Linie repräsentiert, der Präsident des Obersten Gerichtshofes wird durch die oberste Linie dargestellt. Das Auf und Ab der Linien zeigt, wie viele Richter durch jede Partei ernannt wurden.

Demokratische Richter sind blau markiert und weisen nach unten, während die republikanischen Richter im oberen Bereich angesiedelt und rot markiert sind. Dieses zentrale Diagramm wird ergänzt um prägnante Fälle, die am unteren Bildrand erläutert und klassifiziert werden. Rechts und links sind alle Richter namentlich aufgelistet, mit biografischen Daten, dem Präsidenten, der sie ernannt hat, sowie ihrem Wahlergebnis im Senat.

La façon de transmettre l'histoire se renouvelle : ce graphique temporel à grande échelle couvre les deux siècles d'histoire de la Cour suprême des États-Unis. La série temporelle centrale comporte une ligne pour chaque siège, la première représentant le président. Les lignes montent ou descendent pour indiquer le nombre de juges nommés pour chaque force politique.

Les démocrates sont indiqués en bleu et vers le bas, tandis que l'influence républicaine est codée en rouge et vers le haut. La grille temporelle comprend des détails sur les cas marquants, qui sont expliqués et classés dans le bas. Tous les juges sont mentionnés sur les côtés du graphique, avec des détails biographiques ainsi que le président qui les a nommés et le résultat du vote au Sénat.

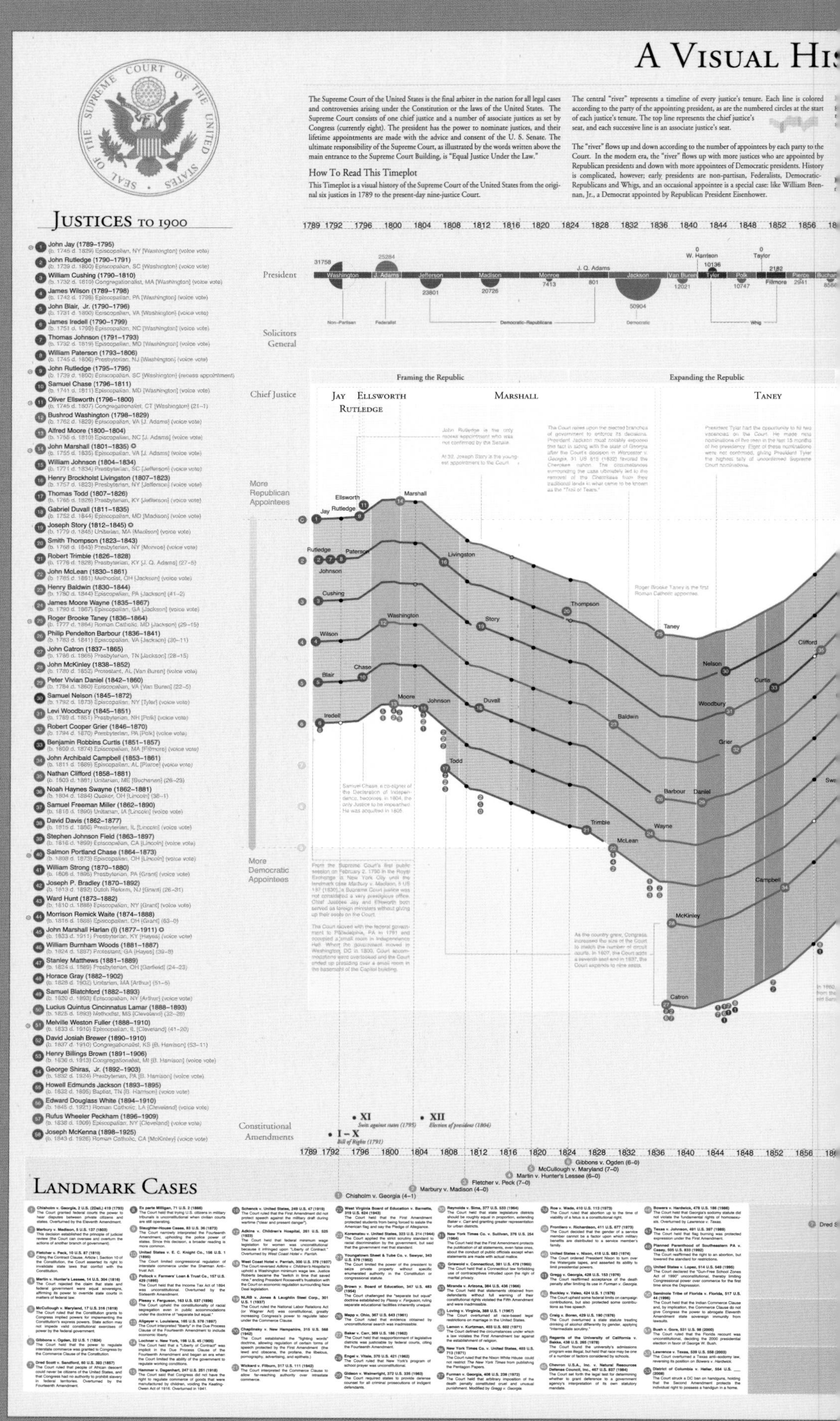

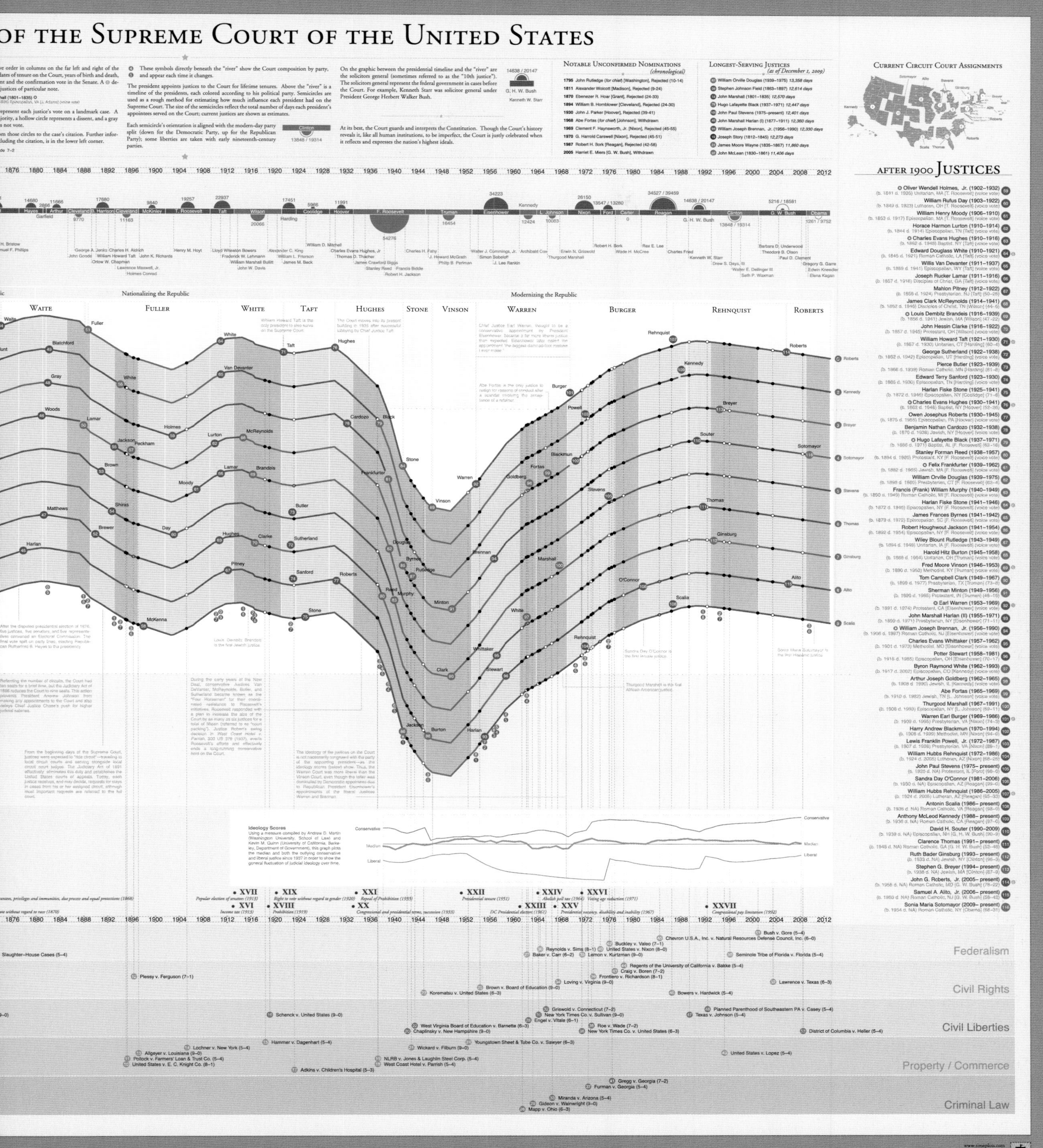

Project Info: Poster, 2009, USA
Design: Nathaniel Pearlman, Frank Hamilton, Joe Williams (Timeplots)

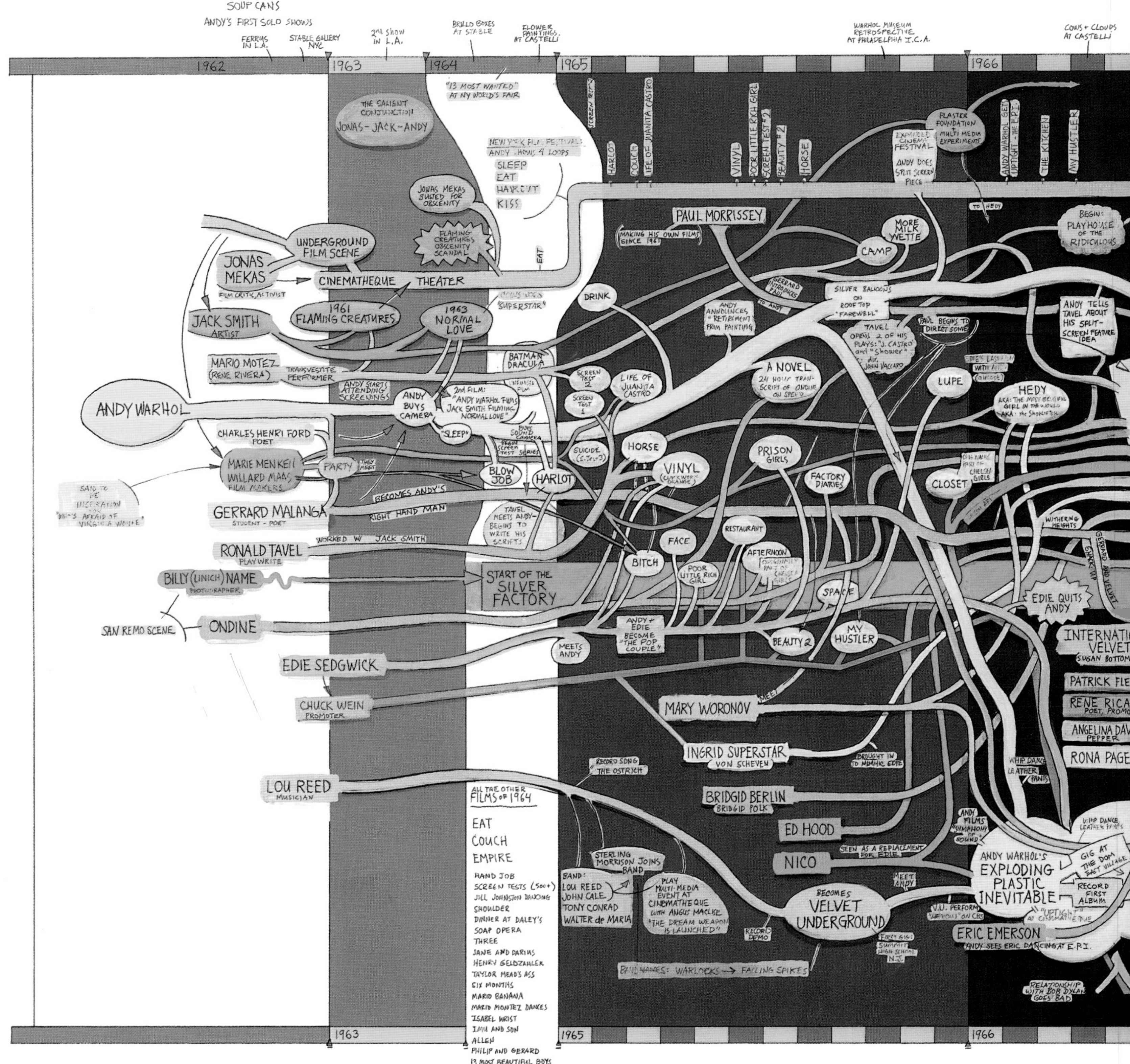

Project Info: Painting, 2008, USA
Artist: Ward Shelley
Additional Info: Original size 147 cm x 77 cm; collection of Wendy and Peter Trevisani; Ward Shelley is represented by Pierogi Gallery

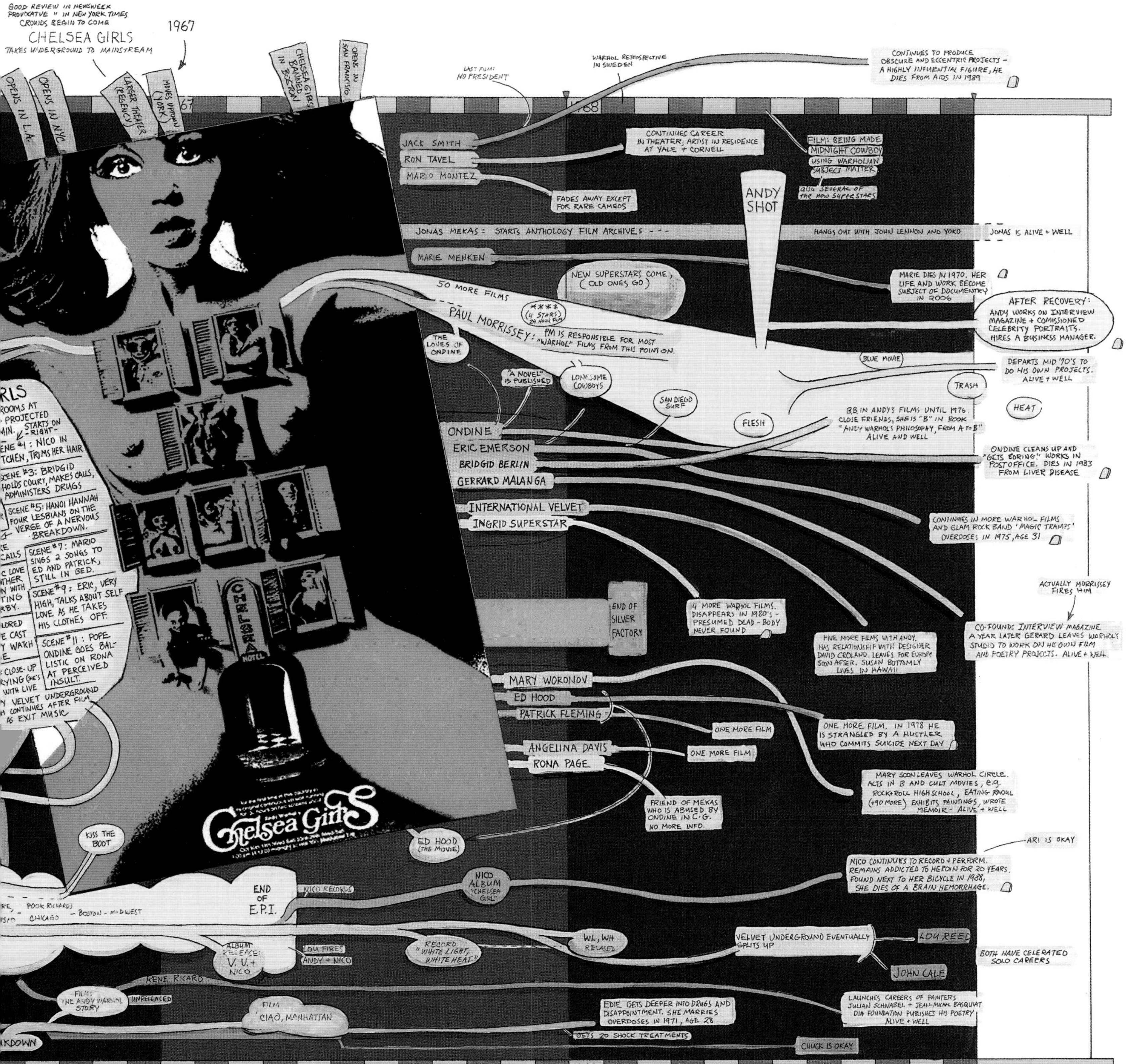

Andy Warhol – Chelsea Girls

Ward Shelley created this timeline about Andy Warhol and his work in film, and in particular about *Chelsea Girls*, with the film's poster making the centrepiece. The film is a collection of 12 scenes of ca. 30 minutes each, showed on a split screen. The yellow panel on the left of the poster lists all scenes in their order.

The chart covers the 1960s and includes biographical facts about Warhol as well as some of the people who influenced him. All those involved with *Chelsea Girls* are named in coloured tags. Apart from this particular film nearly all the films produced in the Factory are mentioned, as well as the work of the band Velvet Underground and other related artists.

Ward Shelley entwarf diese Zeitleiste zu Andy Warhol und seinem filmischen Schaffen, insbesondere zum Film *Chelsea Girls*, dessen Filmplakat auch das zentrale Motiv darstellt. Der Film ist eine Zusammenstellung von zwölf rund dreißigminütigen Szenen, die auf einem Split Screen gezeigt wurden. Auf der gelben Tafel links des Filmposters sind alle Szenen des Films chronologisch aufgeführt.

Das Bild umfasst die 1960er-Jahre und vermittelt biografische Angaben zu Warhol sowie zu einigen Menschen, die ihn beeinflussten. Alle, die an *Chelsea Girls* mitgearbeitet haben, sind auf den bunten Schildchen benannt. Abgesehen von diesem Film werden auch fast alle anderen von der Factory produzierten Filme erwähnt, wie auch die Arbeiten und Aufnahmen der Band Velvet Underground und anderer befreundeter Künstler.

Ward Shelley a créé cette chronologie sur Andy Warhol et son travail dans le cinéma, et plus particulièrement sur *Chelsea Girls*, avec l'affiche du film comme pièce centrale. Ce film est constitué de 12 scènes d'environ 30 minutes chacune, projetées en écran divisé. Le panneau jaune sur la gauche de l'affiche dresse une liste de toutes les scènes dans leur ordre d'apparition.

La chronologie couvre les années 1960, et comprend des informations sur la vie de Warhol ainsi que sur certaines des personnes qui l'ont influencé. Toutes celles qui ont un rapport avec *Chelsea Girls* sont identifiées par des bulles de couleur. Presque tous les autres films produits par la Factory sont également mentionnés, ainsi que l'œuvre du groupe Velvet Underground et d'autres artistes proches.

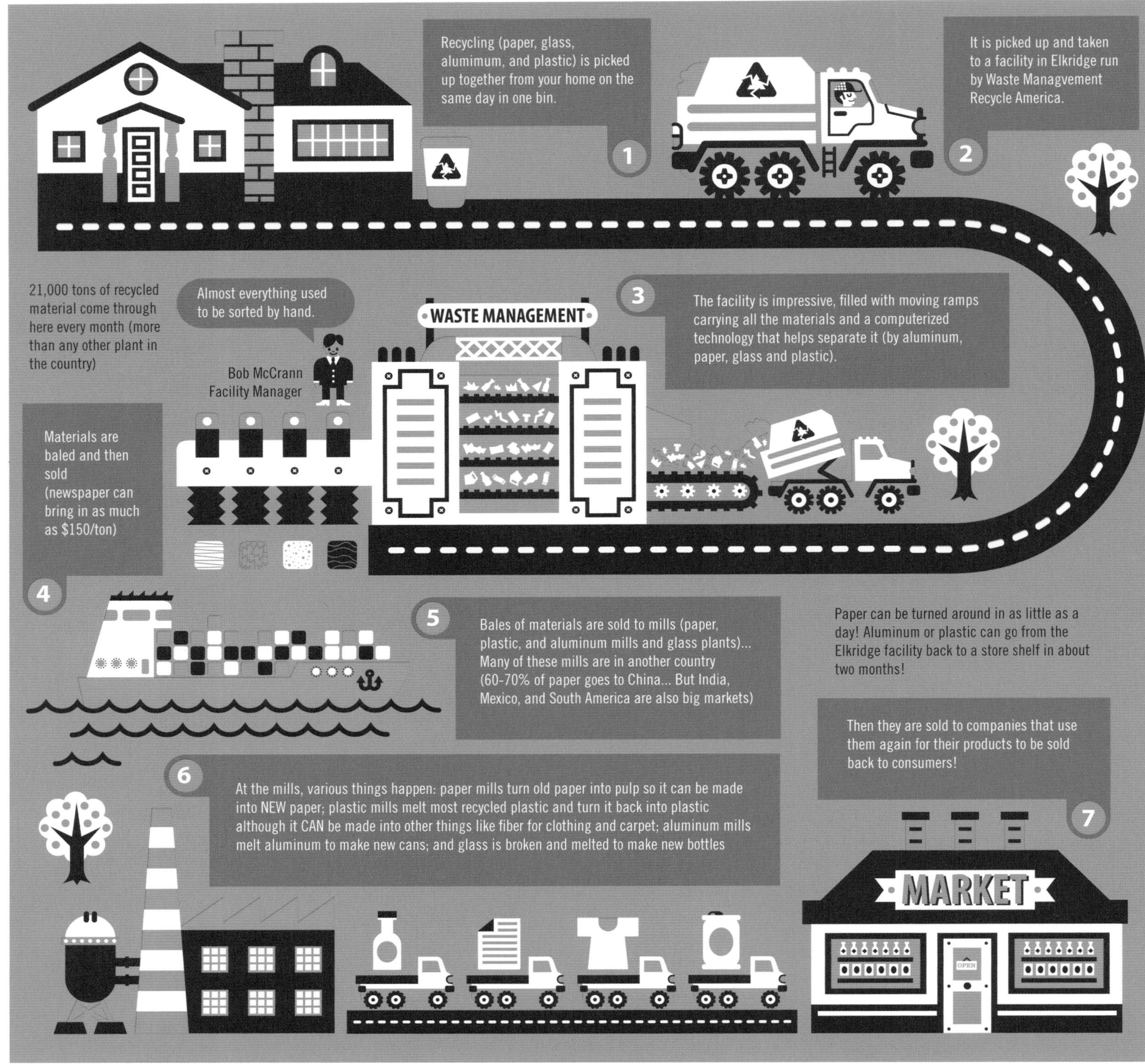

Recycling (paper, glass, alumimum, and plastic) is picked up together from your home on the same day in one bin.
1
It is picked up and taken to a facility in Elkridge run by Waste Managvement Recycle America.
2
21,000 tons of recycled material come through here every month (more than any other plant in the country)
Almost everything used to be sorted by hand.
Bob McCrann Facility Manager
WASTE MANAGEMENT
3
The facility is impressive, filled with moving ramps carrying all the materials and a computerized technology that helps separate it (by aluminum, paper, glass and plastic).
Materials are baled and then sold (newspaper can bring in as much as $150/ton)
4
5
Bales of materials are sold to mills (paper, plastic, and aluminum mills and glass plants)... Many of these mills are in another country (60-70% of paper goes to China... But India, Mexico, and South America are also big markets)
Paper can be turned around in as little as a day! Aluminum or plastic can go from the Elkridge facility back to a store shelf in about two months!
Then they are sold to companies that use them again for their products to be sold back to consumers!
6
At the mills, various things happen: paper mills turn old paper into pulp so it can be made into NEW paper; plastic mills melt most recycled plastic and turn it back into plastic although it CAN be made into other things like fiber for clothing and carpet; aluminum mills melt aluminum to make new cans; and glass is broken and melted to make new bottles
7
MARKET

Baltimore Waste Management

This graphic explains the process of recycling waste using the example of a waste-management facility near Baltimore. Starting with the average household at the top left, the process is presented as single steps on a journey.

The household's waste is picked up and delivered to the facility, then sorted and processed further by various companies. Each step is explained in little numbered boxes. As in certain children's illustrations, the picture space is flat, with no perspective.

Diese Grafik erläutert das Recycling von Müll anhand einer Entsorgungsanlage in der Nähe von Baltimore. Ausgehend von einem durchschnittlichen Haushalt oben links, wird der Ablauf in einzelnen Stationen auf einer Route dargestellt.

Der Haushaltsmüll wird abgeholt, zur Anlage geliefert und anschließend von verschiedenen Unternehmen sortiert und weiterverarbeitet. Jeder Schritt wird in nummerierten Kästen erklärt. Wie in manchen Illustrationen für Kinderbücher ist der Bildraum vollständig plan, d.h. ohne jede Perspektive gezeichnet.

Cette image explique le processus de recyclage des déchets à l'aide de l'exemple d'une usine de traitement des déchets proche de Baltimore. Le processus commence en haut à gauche dans un foyer type, et passe par différentes étapes avant de terminer son itinéraire.

Les déchets du foyer sont ramassés et livrés à l'usine, puis triés et traités par différentes entreprises. Chaque étape est expliquée dans de petits cadres numérotés. Comme dans certaines illustrations pour les enfants, l'espace est plat, sans perspective.

Project Info: *Baltimore*, magazine article, 2010, USA
Design: Jan Kallwejt

Best-Selling Books

Developed for Barcelona-based newspaper *La Vanguardia*, this piece is an unusual cross between a time series and a ranking, showing best-selling fiction books in Catalan between October 2007 and April 2008. Time runs from left to right and covers the period in 26 weekly steps. Within these, the graphic presents a succession of best-seller lists, showing evolutions and developments within the list.

Catalan authors are shown with red dots, all others with blue. For certain titles, additional information is provided, like the number of pages (yellow circle attached) or a specially low price (tagged with a black circle). The continued presence of titles on the list is indicated using solid lines, while dotted lines show connections to ranks below the top ten.

Diese Grafik für die in Barcelona erscheinende Zeitung *La Vanguardia* ist eine ungewöhnliche Mischung aus einer Zeitreihe und einer Rangliste. Sie zeigt die katalanischen Literaturbestseller zwischen Oktober 2007 und April 2008. Die Zeit verläuft in 26 Wochenschritten von links nach rechts. Dargestellt ist eine Abfolge von Bestseller-Listen sowie der wöchentlichen Veränderungen, denen sie unterliegen.

Katalanische Autoren sind durch rote Punkte dargestellt, alle anderen durch blaue. Manche Titel werden um zusätzliche Informationen ergänzt, wie etwa die Seitenzahl (in den gelben Kreisen) oder den Hinweis auf einen günstigen Preis (schwarzer Kreis). Die durchgängige Präsenz eines Titels auf der Liste wird mittels durchgezogener Linien kenntlich gemacht, punktierte Linien zeigen Verbindungen zu Plätzen außerhalb der Top Ten.

Réalisé pour le journal barcelonais *La Vanguardia*, ce diagramme est un croisement inhabituel entre une série temporelle et un classement: il montre les livres de fiction en catalan les plus vendus entre octobre 2007 et avril 2008. Le temps s'écoule de gauche à droite en 26 semaines. Pour chaque semaine, le graphique présente une succession de listes de best-sellers, et montre les évolutions.

Les auteurs catalans sont indiqués par des points rouges, et tous les autres sont en bleu. Des informations supplémentaires sont fournies pour certains titres, comme le nombre de pages (dans les cercles jaunes) ou un prix particulièrement bas (cercles noirs). Les lignes continues indiquent que les titres restent dans la liste des 10 premiers, et les lignes en pointillés correspondent au passage à un rang inférieur.

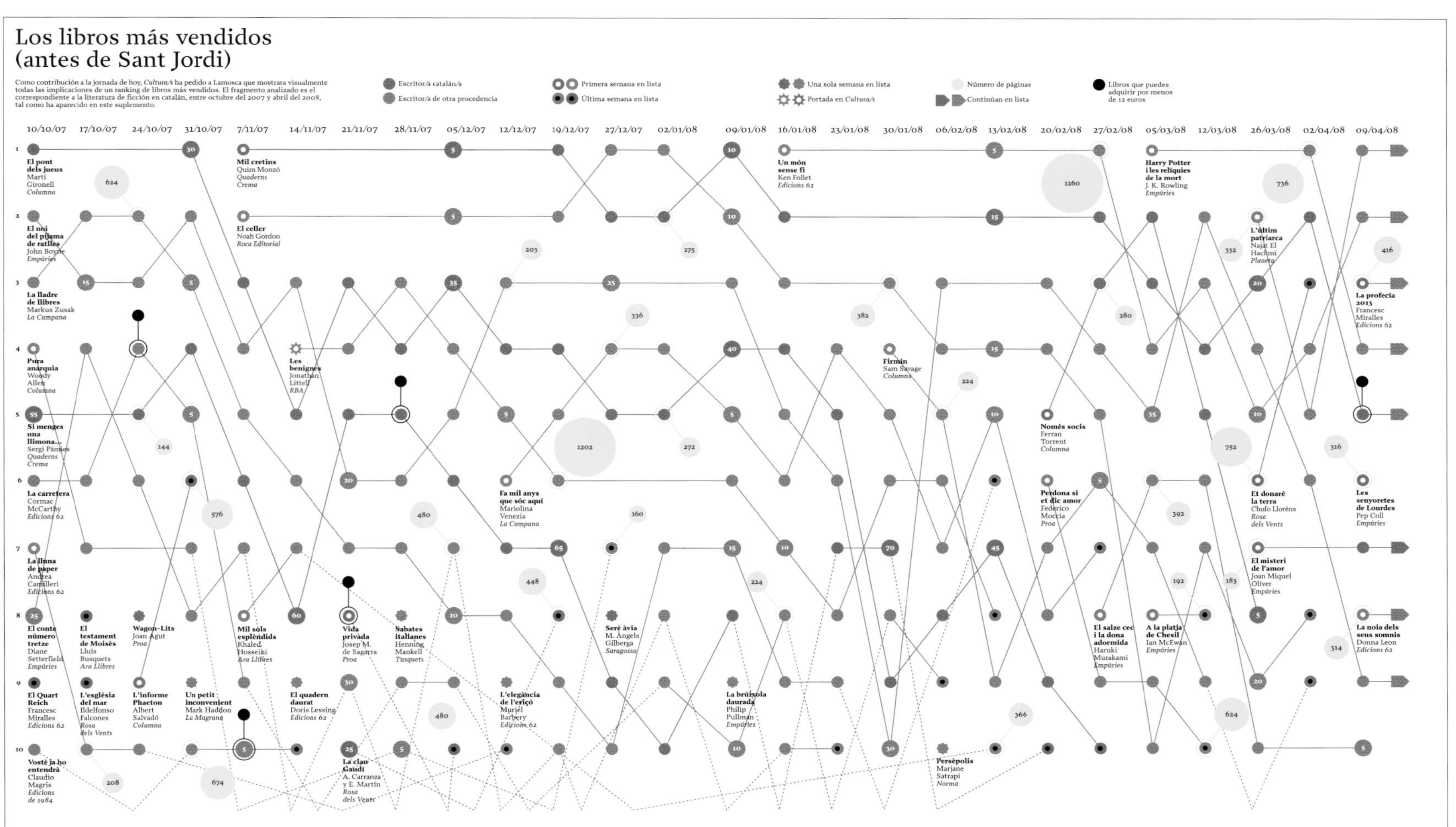

Project Info: *La Vanguardia*, newspaper article, 2008, Spain
Design: Lamosca

Biofuel

This process diagram depicts the cycle of production and usage of biofuels. Icons represent each step in the cycle, from the growing and harvesting of plants for the biomass, via the various conversion steps to the canister of biofuel which allows the car to run.

The connecting step at the top refers to the carbon balance of biofuels – upon combustion, they release only the amount of CO_2 which had previously been bound by the original plant from the atmosphere. However, the effects and the actual carbon balance are the subject of much discussion, with biofuels being a very recent technology.

Dieses Prozessdiagramm zeigt den Zyklus der Herstellung und der Verwendung von Biokraftstoffen. Icons repräsentieren die einzelnen Schritte dieses Kreislaufs, von Anbau und Ernte der Pflanzen für die Biomasse über die verschiedenen Schritte der Umwandlung bis zum Kanister mit Biotreibstoff, mit dem das Auto fährt.

Das verbindende Icon in der Mitte oben verweist auf die Kohlendioxidbilanz von Biokraftstoffen – bei der Verbrennung setzen sie lediglich die CO_2-Menge frei, die die Pflanzen ursprünglich aus der Atmosphäre gebunden hatten. Allerdings sind Wirkung und tatsächliche Kohlendioxidbilanz noch recht umstritten, da es Biokraftstoffe noch nicht so lange gibt.

Ce diagramme de processus illustre le cycle de production et d'utilisation des biocombustibles. Chaque étape du cycle est représentée par une icône, de la culture et la récolte des plantes pour la biomasse, en passant par les différentes étapes de la conversion, jusqu'au jerrycan de biocombustible qui fait fonctionner la voiture.

La connexion entre la fin et le début de ce processus, en haut, se réfère à l'équilibre des échanges de CO_2 des biocombustibles : leur combustion émet la même quantité de CO_2 que celle qui avait été extraite de l'atmosphère par la plante d'origine. Les effets et la réalité de l'équilibre des échanges de CO_2 sont cependant très discutés, car les biocombustibles sont une technologie très récente.

Project Info: *Science News*, magazine article, 2009, USA
Design: Michael Newhouse (Newhouse Design)

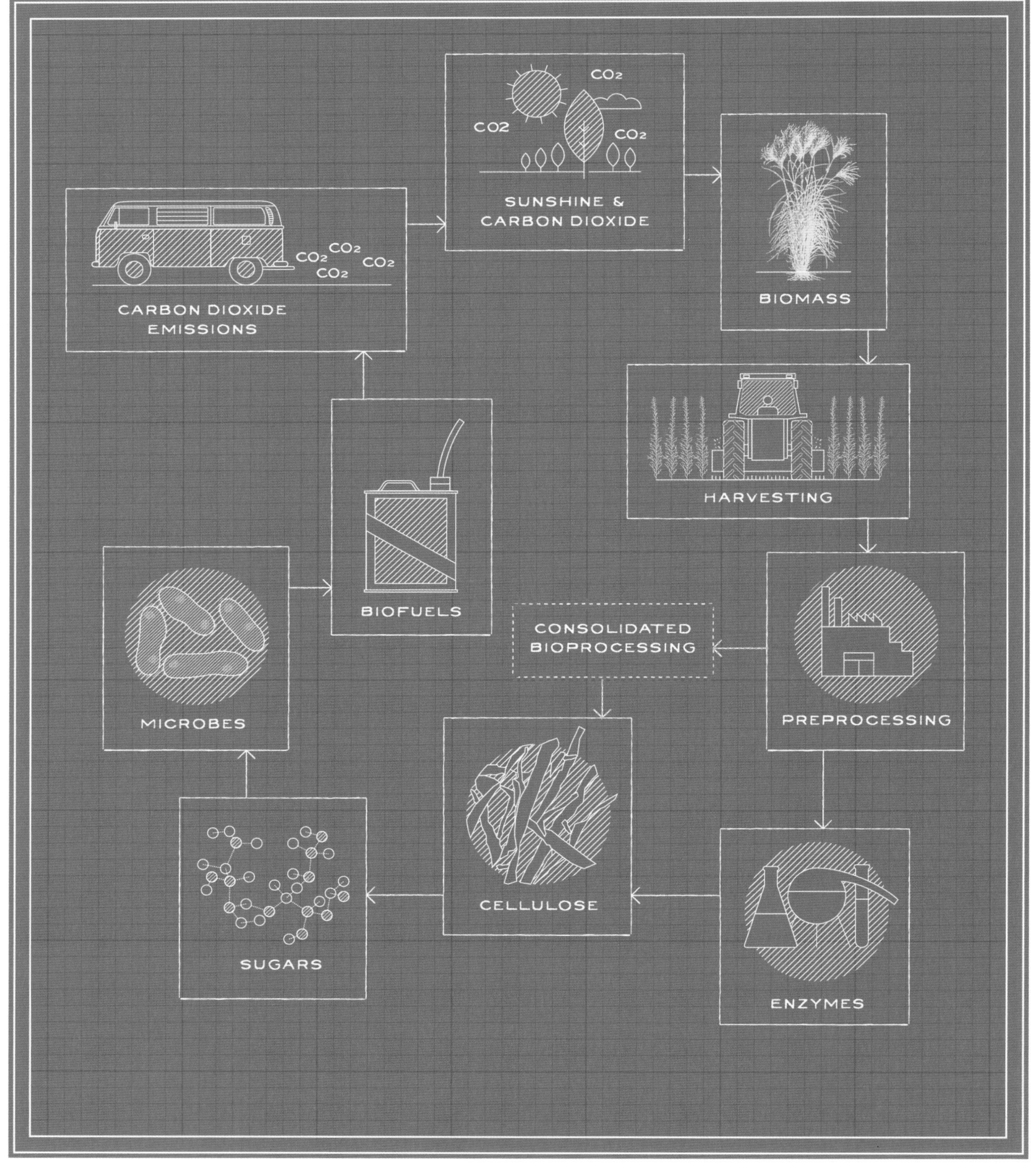

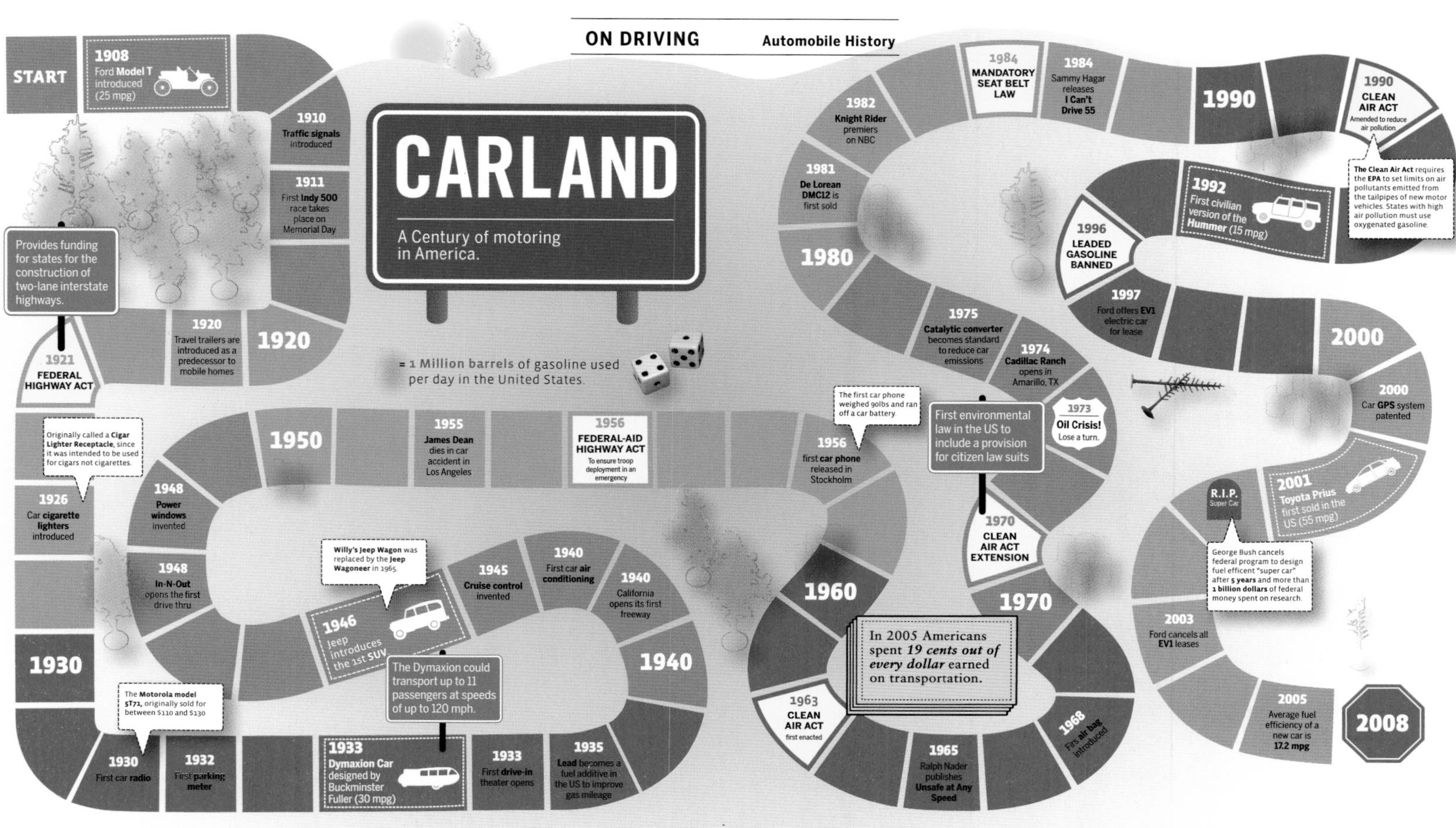

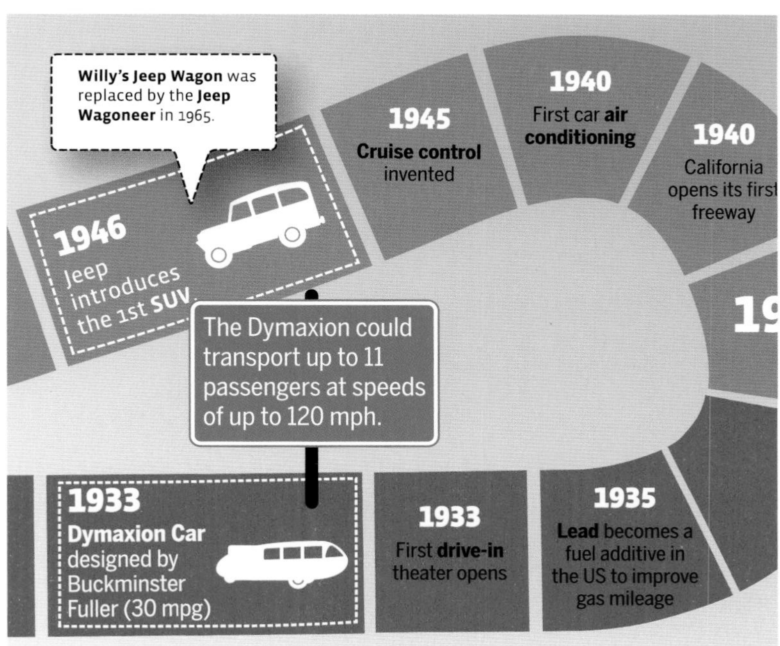

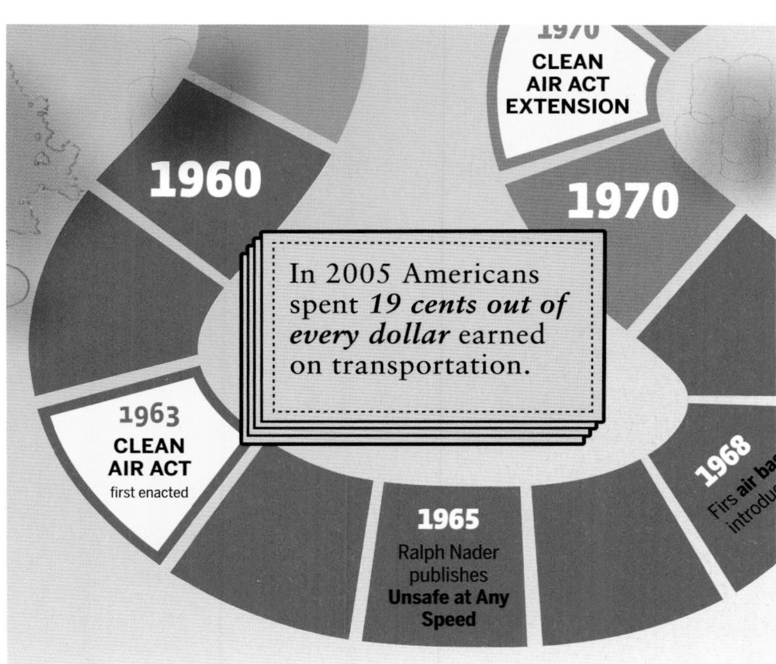

Carland: A Century of Motoring in America

Driving in the United States: this is a history of the automobile in one image. Using the metaphor of a board game, the graphic follows the most important events and milestones in the first 100 years of cars.

It shows some of the most prominent car models and the invention of such things as the car radio in 1930. History is thus conceived of as a path through a landscape, a timeline drawn into a fictional map.

Über das Autofahren in den Vereinigten Staaten: Dies ist die Geschichte des Automobils in einem einzigen Bild. Wie auf einem Brettspiel führt die Grafik durch die wichtigsten Ereignisse und Meilensteine der ersten 100 Jahre des Autos.

Einige der markantesten Modelle werden erwähnt sowie Erfindungen wie etwa das Autoradio im Jahr 1930. Geschichte wird hier als Pfad durch eine Landschaft konzipiert: eine Zeitleiste, die in eine fiktive Landkarte eingezeichnet ist.

Conduire aux États-Unis: ceci est l'histoire de l'automobile en une image. À l'aide de la métaphore d'un jeu de société, le lecteur suit le déroulement des principaux événements des 100 premières années d'existence des voitures.

L'image montre quelques-uns des modèles de voiture les plus marquants, ainsi que des inventions, comme l'autoradio en 1930. L'histoire est donc conçue ici comme un chemin qui serpente dans un paysage, une chronologie dessinée sous forme de carte fictive.

Project Info: *GOOD*, magazine article, 2008, USA
Design: Colleen Corcoran, Joseph Prichard
Art Direction: Casey Caplowe

Collision Course

The road to the future – this cover image sketches the course of the 2007 College Football Season for the two L.A. teams, USC Trojans and UCLA Bruins. Along the road, matches are lined up with dates and team names. Teams are represented by their animal mascots (e.g. BYU Cougars, Washington Huskies). Others are shown by symbols (sunshine for Arizona) or a football-playing corn cob for Nebraska.

The team of the Catholic University of Notre Dame, Indiana is represented by an enraged little Irish mascot. Both roads end at the final game in the lower centre. The design is based solely on fixtures, but the visual arrangement plays with the notion that the two L.A. teams might be successful enough to be playing each other for the championship.

Der Weg in die Zukunft – dieses Cover skizziert den Verlauf der College Football Season 2007 für die beiden Mannschaften aus Los Angeles, die USC Trojans und die UCLA Bruins. Auf dem Weg liegen verschiedene Spiele, die mit Datum und Namen der gegnerischen Mannschaft aufgeführt sind. Einige Teams werden durch ihr Maskottchen repräsentiert (z.B. die BYU Cougars oder die Washington Huskies), andere durch Symbole (Sonnenschein für Arizona); Nebraska etwa wird als ein Football spielender Maiskolben gezeigt.

Ein wütendes irisches Maskottchen steht für die Mannschaft der Catholic University of Notre Dame, Indiana. Beide Wege enden in der unteren Mitte beim Finale. Die Grafik beruht ausschließlich auf vorab festgesetzten Spielpaarungen, doch die visuelle Anordnung spielt mit der Vorstellung, dass beide Teams aus L.A. sehr erfolgreich sind und möglicherweise gegeneinander um die Meisterschaft spielen könnten.

La route vers le futur – cette illustration de couverture trace le parcours des deux équipes de football américain universitaire de Los Angeles, les USC Trojans et les UCLA Bruins, pour la saison 2007. Les matchs sont plantés le long de la route, avec les dates et les noms des équipes. Certaines équipes sont représentées par leur animal mascotte (par ex. le cougar pour BYU ou le husky pour Washington), d'autres par des symboles (le soleil pour l'Arizona) ou encore un épi de maïs footballeur pour le Nebraska.

L'équipe de l'Université catholique de Notre-Dame, dans l'Indiana, est représentée par une petite mascotte irlandaise enragée. Les deux routes mènent jusqu'au match final, au centre, vers le bas. Ce graphisme se base uniquement sur les matchs prévus, mais l'arrangement visuel joue sur l'idée selon laquelle les deux équipes de Los Angeles pourraient arriver à se rencontrer en finale.

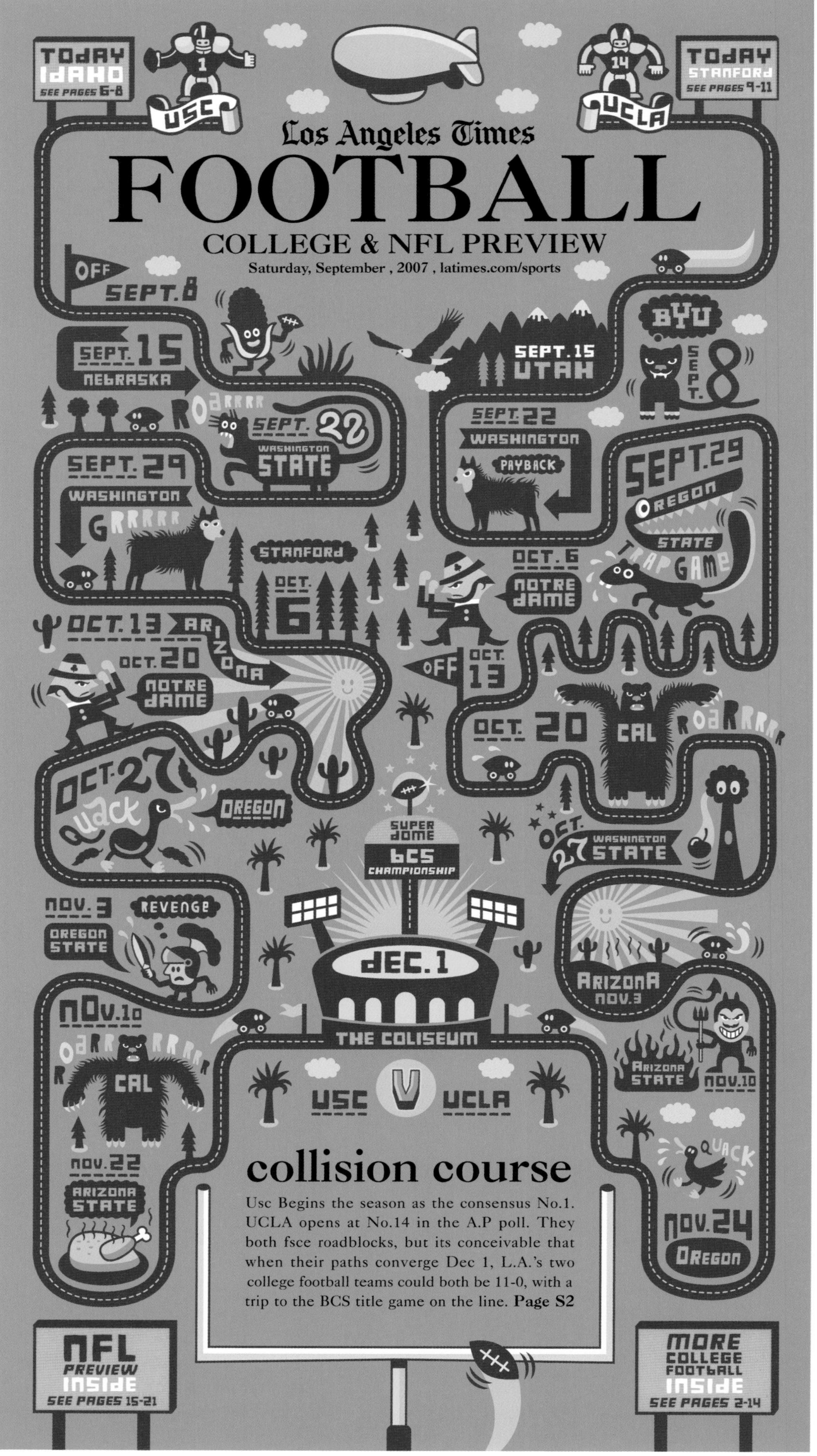
Los Angeles Times
FOOTBALL
COLLEGE & NFL PREVIEW
Saturday, September , 2007 , latimes.com/sports

collision course

Usc Begins the season as the consensus No.1. UCLA opens at No.14 in the A.P poll. They both fsce roadblocks, but its conceivable that when their paths converge Dec 1, L.A.'s two college football teams could both be 11-0, with a trip to the BCS title game on the line. **Page S2**

Project Info: Football College and NFL preview, *The Los Angeles Times*, newspaper article, 2007, USA
Design: Serge Seidlitz
Art Direction: Derek Simmons

Project Info: Poster, 2010, Japan / Switzerland
Data Source: Information Architects' Web Trend Engine; Max Planck Institute for Software Systems; Twitter Research Team
Research: Chris Luescher
Design: Oliver Reichenstein, Takeshi Tanka (Information Architects)
Additional Info: Original size A0

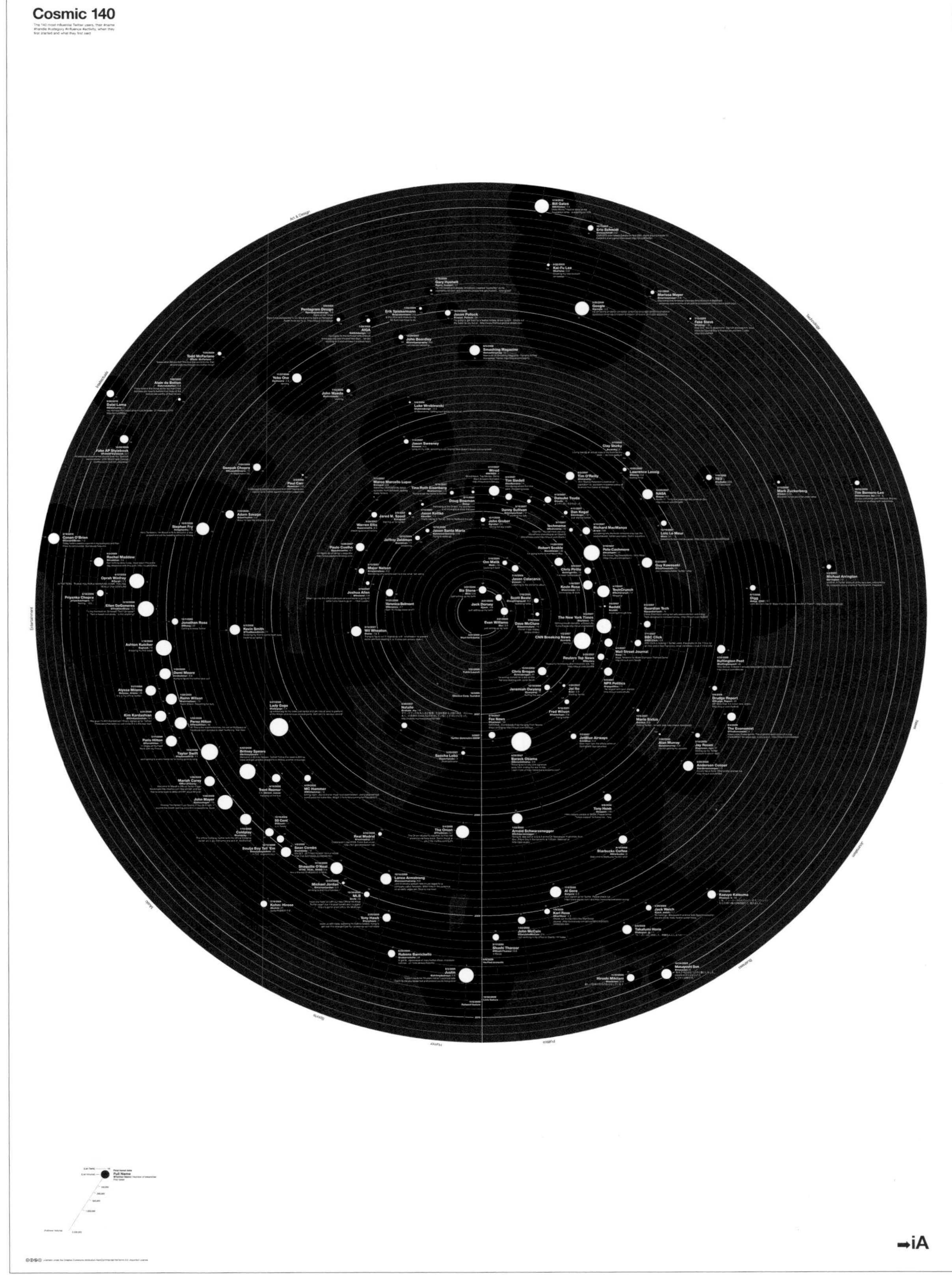

Cosmic 140 – Art for Geeks

Using the layout of star charts, this piece plots the 140 most influential Twitter users. Time runs from the centre outwards, with topics denominated around the outside, like directions on a map. Each of the selected users is marked with a dot, their distance from the centre indicating the time they began tweeting.

Along with name and user name, the average number of daily tweets and the text of the first tweet are given. Black circles around each user indicate the number of their followers, while the full circle represents the total number of Twitter users. The piece thus locates the top Twitter users according to time and category (topics) and demonstrates their hierarchy by circle sizes.

In Anlehnung an das Layout von Sternenkarten verzeichnet dieses Diagramm die 140 einflussreichsten Twitterer. Die Zeit verläuft von der Mitte nach außen. Am äußeren Rand sind verschiedene Themen angeführt, wie Himmelsrichtungen auf einer Landkarte. Jeder der erfolgreichen User ist durch einen Punkt gekennzeichnet, die jeweilige Entfernung zum Mittelpunkt markiert den Zeitpunkt, an dem er zu twittern begann.

Neben Namen und Benutzernamen sind die durchschnittliche Anzahl von Tweets pro Tag sowie der Text des ersten Tweets aufgeführt. Schwarze Schatten um jeden Benutzer verweisen auf die Zahl seiner Follower, während der ganze Kreis für die Gesamtzahl von Twitter-Benutzern steht. Die Grafik sortiert die führenden Twitterer also sowohl nach Zeit wie auch nach Kategorien (Themen), und sie zeigt durch die Kreisgröße ihre Hierarchie.

Cette œuvre présente les 140 utilisateurs de Twitter les plus influents à l'aide d'un format calqué sur les cartes des étoiles. La dimension du temps va du centre vers l'extérieur, et les sujets sont inscrits à l'extérieur du cercle, comme les directions sur une carte. Chacun des utilisateurs sélectionnés est marqué par un point, dont la distance par rapport au centre indique depuis combien de temps il utilise Twitter.

À côté du nom et du nom d'utilisateur sont mentionnés le nombre moyen de tweets quotidiens et le texte du premier tweet. Le cercle noir autour de chaque utilisateur indique son nombre d'abonnés, tandis que le grand cercle représente le nombre total d'utilisateurs de Twitter. Cette œuvre situe donc les utilisateurs clés de Twitter en fonction du temps et des catégories (sujets) et met en évidence leur hiérarchie grâce à la taille des cercles.

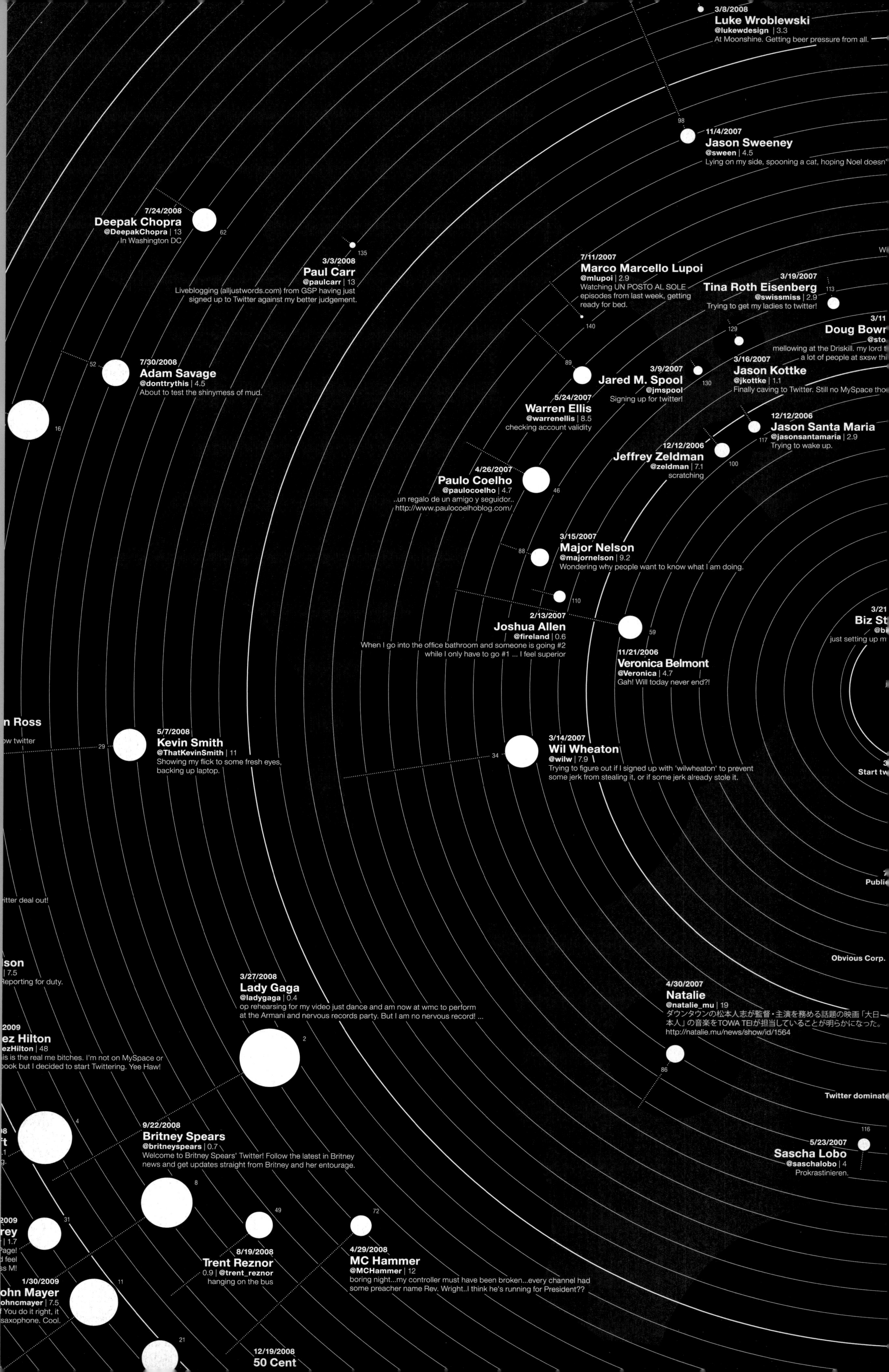

3/8/2008
Luke Wroblewski
@lukewdesign | 3.3
At Moonshine. Getting beer pressure from all.
98
11/4/2007
Jason Sweeney
@sween | 4.5
Lying on my side, spooning a cat, hoping Noel doesn'
7/24/2008
Deepak Chopra
@DeepakChopra | 13
In Washington DC
62
135
3/3/2008
Paul Carr
@paulcarr | 13
Liveblogging (alljustwords.com) from GSP having just signed up to Twitter against my better judgement.
7/11/2007
Marco Marcello Lupoi
@mlupoi | 2.9
Watching UN POSTO AL SOLE episodes from last week, getting ready for bed.
140
3/19/2007
Tina Roth Eisenberg
@swissmiss | 2.9
Trying to get my ladies to twitter!
113
129
3/11
Doug Bowr
mellowing at the Driskill. my lord t
a lot of people at sxsw thi
52
7/30/2008
Adam Savage
@donttrythis | 4.5
About to test the shinymess of mud.
89
3/9/2007
Jared M. Spool
@jmspool
Signing up for twitter!
130
3/16/2007
Jason Kottke
@jkottke | 1.1
Finally caving to Twitter. Still no MySpace tho
16
5/24/2007
Warren Ellis
@warrenellis | 8.5
checking account validity
12/12/2006
Jason Santa Maria
@jasonsantamaria | 2.9
Trying to wake up.
117
12/12/2006
Jeffrey Zeldman
@zeldman | 7.1
scratching
100
4/26/2007
Paulo Coelho
@paulocoelho | 4.7
..un regalo de un amigo y seguidor..
http://www.paulocoelhoblog.com/
46
3/15/2007
Major Nelson
@majornelson | 9.2
Wondering why people want to know what I am doing.
88
110
2/13/2007
Joshua Allen
@fireland | 0.6
When I go into the office bathroom and someone is going #2 while I only have to go #1 ... I feel superior
59
11/21/2006
Veronica Belmont
@Veronica | 4.7
Gah! Will today never end?!
3/21
Biz St
just setting up m
n Ross
ow twitter
29
5/7/2008
Kevin Smith
@ThatKevinSmith | 11
Showing my flick to some fresh eyes, backing up laptop.
34
3/14/2007
Wil Wheaton
@wilw | 7.9
Trying to figure out if I signed up with 'wilwheaton' to prevent some jerk from stealing it, or if some jerk already stole it.
Start tw
Publi
witter deal out!
Obvious Corp.
son
| 7.5
Reporting for duty.
3/27/2008
Lady Gaga
@ladygaga | 0.4
op rehearsing for my video just dance and am now at wmc to perform at the Armani and nervous records party. But I am no nervous record! ...
4/30/2007
Natalie
@natalie_mu | 19
ダウンタウンの松本人志が監督・主演を務める話題の映画「大日
本人」の音楽をTOWA TEIが担当していることが明らかになった。
http://natalie.mu/news/show/id/1564
2009
ez Hilton
ezHilton | 48
is is the real me bitches. I'm not on MySpace or
book but I decided to start Twittering. Yee Haw!
2
86
Twitter dominate
4
9/22/2008
Britney Spears
@britneyspears | 0.7
Welcome to Britney Spears' Twitter! Follow the latest in Britney news and get updates straight from Britney and her entourage.
116
5/23/2007
Sascha Lobo
@saschalobo | 4
Prokrastinieren.
8
49
72
2009
rey
| 1.7
Page!
l feel
ss M!
31
8/19/2008
Trent Reznor
0.9 | @trent_reznor
hanging on the bus
4/29/2008
MC Hammer
@MCHammer | 12
boring night...my controller must have been broken...every channel had some preacher name Rev. Wright..I think he's running for President??
1/30/2009
ohn Mayer
ohncmayer | 7.5
f You do it right, it
saxophone. Cool.
11
21
12/19/2008
50 Cent

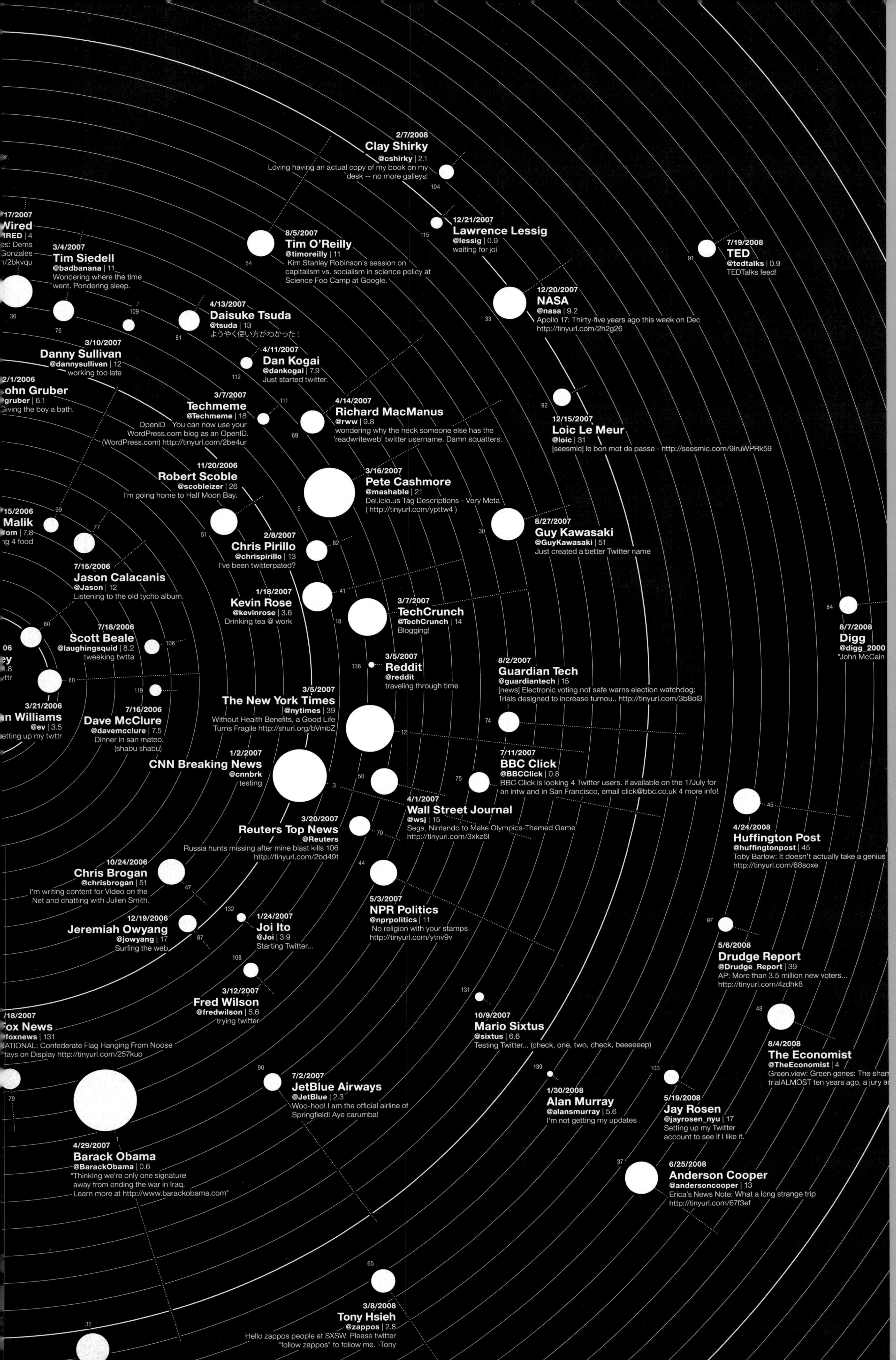
2/7/2008
Clay Shirky
@cshirky | 2.1
Loving having an actual copy of my book on my desk -- no more galleys!
104
12/21/2007
Lawrence Lessig
@lessig | 0.9
waiting for joi
115
7/19/2008
TED
@tedtalks | 0.9
TEDTalks feed!
91
8/5/2007
Tim O'Reilly
@timoreilly | 11
Kim Stanley Robinson's session on capitalism vs. socialism in science policy at Science Foo Camp at Google.
54
3/4/2007
Tim Siedell
@badbanana | 11
Wondering where the time went. Pondering sleep.
36
76
109
4/13/2007
Daisuke Tsuda
@tsuda | 13
ようやく使い方がわかった！
81
12/20/2007
NASA
@nasa | 9.2
Apollo 17: Thirty-five years ago this week on Dec
http://tinyurl.com/2h2g26
33
3/10/2007
Danny Sullivan
@dannysullivan | 12
working too late
4/11/2007
Dan Kogai
@dankogai | 7.9
Just started twitter.
112
ohn Gruber
gruber | 6.1
Giving the boy a bath.
3/7/2007
Techmeme
@Techmeme | 18
OpenID - You can now use your WordPress.com blog as an OpenID. (WordPress.com) http://tinyurl.com/2be4ur
111
4/14/2007
Richard MacManus
@rww | 9.8
wondering why the heck someone else has the 'readwriteweb' twitter username. Damn squatters.
69
92
12/15/2007
Loic Le Meur
@loic | 31
[seesmic] le bon mot de passe - http://seesmic.com/9iruWPRk59
11/20/2006
Robert Scoble
@scobleizer | 26
I'm going home to Half Moon Bay.
3/16/2007
Pete Cashmore
@mashable | 21
Del.icio.us Tag Descriptions - Very Meta (http://tinyurl.com/ypttw4)
5
8/27/2007
Guy Kawasaki
@GuyKawasaki | 51
Just created a better Twitter name
30
99
77
51
2/8/2007
Chris Pirillo
@chrispirillo | 13
I've been twitterpated?
82
7/15/2006
Jason Calacanis
@Jason | 12
Listening to the old tycho album.
1/18/2007
Kevin Rose
@kevinrose | 3.6
Drinking tea @ work
41
3/7/2007
TechCrunch
@TechCrunch | 14
Blogging!
18
84
8/7/2008
Digg
@digg_2000
"John McCain
80
7/18/2006
Scott Beale
@laughingsquid | 8.2
tweeking twtta
106
3/5/2007
Reddit
@reddit
traveling through time
136
8/2/2007
Guardian Tech
@guardiantech | 15
[news] Electronic voting not safe warns election watchdog: Trials designed to increase turnou.. http://tinyurl.com/3b8ol3
60
119
3/21/2006
7/16/2006
Dave McClure
@davemcclure | 7.5
Dinner in san mateo. (shabu shabu)
3/5/2007
The New York Times
@nytimes | 39
Without Health Benefits, a Good Life Turns Fragile http://shurl.org/bVmbZ
12
74
@ev | 3.5
1/2/2007
CNN Breaking News
@cnnbrk
testing
3
50
7/11/2007
BBC Click
@BBCClick | 0.8
BBC Click is looking 4 Twitter users. if available on the 17July for an intw and in San Francisco, email click@bbc.co.uk 4 more info!
75
4/1/2007
Wall Street Journal
@wsj | 15
Sega, Nintendo to Make Olympics-Themed Game
http://tinyurl.com/3xkz6l
45
4/24/2008
Huffington Post
@huffingtonpost | 45
Toby Barlow: It doesn't actually take a genius
http://tinyurl.com/68soxe
3/20/2007
Reuters Top News
@Reuters
Russia hunts missing after mine blast kills 106
http://tinyurl.com/2bd49t
70
10/24/2006
Chris Brogan
@chrisbrogan | 51
I'm writing content for Video on the Net and chatting with Julien Smith.
47
44
5/3/2007
NPR Politics
@nprpolitics | 11
No religion with your stamps
http://tinyurl.com/ytnv9v
12/19/2006
Jeremiah Owyang
@jowyang | 17
Surfing the web.
87
132
1/24/2007
Joi Ito
@Joi | 3.9
Starting Twitter...
97
5/6/2008
Drudge Report
@Drudge_Report | 39
AP: More than 3.5 million new voters...
http://tinyurl.com/4zdhk8
108
3/12/2007
Fred Wilson
@fredwilson | 5.6
trying twitter
131
10/9/2007
Mario Sixtus
@sixtus | 6.6
Testing Twitter... (check, one, two, check, beeeeeep)
48
8/4/2008
The Economist
@TheEconomist | 4
Green.view: Green genes: The sham trialALMOST ten years ago, a jury a
ox News
foxnews | 131
ATIONAL: Confederate Flag Hanging From Noose Stays on Display http://tinyurl.com/257kuo
90
7/2/2007
JetBlue Airways
@JetBlue | 2.3
Woo-hoo! I am the official airline of Springfield! Aye carumba!
139
1/30/2008
Alan Murray
@alansmurray | 5.6
I'm not getting my updates
103
5/19/2008
Jay Rosen
@jayrosen_nyu | 17
Setting up my Twitter account to see if I like it.
79
1
4/29/2007
Barack Obama
@BarackObama | 0.6
"Thinking we're only one signature away from ending the war in Iraq. Learn more at http://www.barackobama.com"
37
6/25/2008
Anderson Cooper
@andersoncooper | 13
Erica's News Note: What a long strange trip
http://tinyurl.com/67f3ef
65
3/8/2008
Tony Hsieh
@zappos | 2.8
Hello zappos people at SXSW. Please twitter "follow zappos" to follow me. -Tony
32

Daily Waterfall

This toppled double-spread covers the subject of water consumption. The main diagram lists the various things we use water for during the course of the day. It presents a comparison between typical and more conscious consumption habits. The quantity of water used per product unit is shown as a blue stream, while the light green to the right shows the amount of water saved by conscious behaviour.

The world map above the diagram lists certain countries with their annual water consumption per capita. The small scheme below explains the concept of virtual water, which was developed to measure the water used in the production of food and consumer products.

Diese hochformatig gedruckte Doppelseite behandelt das Thema Wasserverbrauch. Das Hauptdiagramm nennt unterschiedliche Produkte und Tätigkeiten, für die wir im Verlauf des Tages Wasser verwenden. Es vergleicht zudem ein konventionelles mit einem bewussteren Konsumverhalten. Für jedes Produkt zeigt ein blauer Wasserstrahl die verwendete Wassermenge, während die hellgrünen Linien rechts demonstrieren, wie viel Wasser durch einen bewussten Verbrauch eingespart werden könnte.

Die Weltkarte über dem Diagramm nennt ausgewählte Länder und deren jährlichen Pro-Kopf-Wasserverbrauch. Auf der kleinen Zeichnung wird das Konzept des virtuellen Wassers erklärt. Es wurde entwickelt, um abschätzen zu können, wie viel Wasser bei der Erzeugung von Nahrungsmitteln und Konsumgütern tatsächlich verbraucht wird.

Cette double page renversée traite le sujet de la consommation de l'eau. Le diagramme principal répertorie les différentes utilisations de l'eau au cours d'une journée. Il compare des habitudes de consommation type à une version plus respectueuse de l'environnement. La quantité d'eau utilisée par unité de produit est montrée sous la forme d'un flot bleu, tandis que les flots vert clair de droite montrent la quantité d'eau économisée grâce à une attitude vigilante.

Au-dessus du diagramme, la carte du monde indique la consommation annuelle d'eau par habitant dans certains pays. Juste en dessous, un petit schéma explique le concept d'eau virtuelle, élaboré pour mesurer la quantité d'eau utilisée dans la production des aliments et des produits de consommation.

Project Info: *Intelligence in Lifestyle*, magazine article, 2009, Italy
Data Source: Waterfootprint.org; Worldometers.info/water
Research: Alessandro Giberti
Design: Francesco Franchi, Pietro Buffa

Deprocess

This image visualises how commands are executed while a piece of software is running. The sequence of code, written in the programming language Processing, is visible in the background. Processing was developed by Ben Fry and Casey Reas as a tool for design-oriented programming. The sequence of code shown here is from Casey Reas' artwork *Articulate*, which lets forms emerge and react according to a set of rules.

The blue lines connect individual commands in the code as it is run over time. Immediate patterns can be seen: series of loops are produced in succession as the software is executed. Some lines of code are less interconnected - these define the rules for the way individual commands must be executed and thus "orchestrate" what is happening in the program.

Dieses Bild visualisiert, wie Befehle ausgeführt werden, während eine Software läuft. Im Hintergrund ist der fortlaufende Code zu sehen, geschrieben in der Programmiersprache „Processing". „Processing" wurde von Ben Fry und Casey Reas als Tool für designorientiertes Programmieren entwickelt. Der hier gezeigte Code stammt aus Casey Reas' Projekt *Articulate*, das grafische Formen nach bestimmten Vorgaben entstehen und interagieren lässt.

Die blauen Linien verbinden einzelne Befehle des Programms, die nacheinander ablaufen. Sofort bilden sich Muster heraus: Bestimmte Befehle werden in Schleifen immer wieder nacheinander ausgeführt. Andere Zeilen im Code sind weniger in die Abfolge eingebunden – sie definieren die Regeln für die Ausführung der Befehle und „orchestrieren" damit das, was das Programm erzeugt.

Cette image illustre l'exécution des commandes d'un programme. La séquence de code, écrite dans le langage de programmation Processing, est visible à l'arrière-plan. Processing a été développé par Ben Fry et Casey Reas pour la programmation dans le secteur du design. La séquence de code montrée ici est tirée de l'œuvre *Articulate* de Casey Reas, qui laisse des formes émerger et réagir en fonction d'un ensemble de règles.

Les lignes bleues relient les différentes commandes du code au fur et à mesure qu'elles se lancent. Des schémas apparaissent tout de suite : une série de boucles se crée au cours de l'exécution du programme. Certaines lignes de code participent moins aux interactions : elles définissent les règles de l'exécution des commandes et « orchestrent » donc le déroulement du programme.

Project Info: Print, 2006, USA
Design: Ben Fry, Casey Reas

LIFE ONLINE

With the launch of Sputnik in 1957, the Soviets had increased the tension of the Cold War by demonstrating their advances in missile technology. In response, the United States created ARPA - the Advanced Research Project Agency. ARPA was tasked with creating a new computer network to accelerate the transfer of research information and close the technology gap between America and the Soviet Union. Computer networks at that time relied on a central server which if destroyed in a nuclear attack would shut down the entire network. ARPA's new network would be decentralised so if one node was lost, data could find an alternate route via the other systems on the network.

The early Internet was mainly used as a digital transportation system for files and emails. The World Wide Web was created as way to easily publish information that would be accessible to anyone else connected to the Internet. In the 1990s, the removal of commercial restrictions caused the Web to explode in size as businesses discovered the global reach it could offer. Similarly users found it to be a huge resource of information and anyone could add their own pages. The Web became so large that search engines were essential to find the pages you wanted. Software pirates exploited the Internet as a distribution network in a battle over copyrighted materials that continues to this day.

Towards the end of the 20th Century, a large amount of online businesses were created on a surge of venture capital with stocks being traded for huge amounts, way above the companies' actual values. In 2000 the bubble burst and many of these optimistic start-ups went out of business without ever turning a profit.

The Internet has vastly increased the avenues of communication available to people. Sites such as Youtube are based around user-generated content and allow people to express their ideas and creativity to an international audience. Whilst the online world does have some dark corners, this development of technology has created a global information and communication resource that has been of huge importance to humankind.

UNIQUE VISITORS PER MONTH
GOOGLE
YAHOO
FACEBOOK
MSN
EBAY
YOUTUBE
WIKIPEDIA
AMAZON
MICROSOFT
MYSPACE
BLOGGER
FLICKR
APPLE
TWITTER
BBC

1,596m

LAUNCH DATE

ICQ
DANCING BABY VIRAL
ONLINE PIZZAS
GARRY KASPAROV VS. DEEP BLUE
EMOTICONS
COFFEECAM
JENNICAM
ESTONIAN GENERAL ELECTION
'YOU' ARE TIME PERSON OF THE YEAR
WARCRAFT HAS 11M USERS
FIRST FLASH MOB
IPOD RELEASED
NAPSTER SHUT DOWN
APPLE LEADS MUSIC RETAILERS
BITTORRENT RELEASED
NAPSTER LAUNCHED
DOWNLOADED MUSIC OVERTAKES
NEUROMANCER (BOOK)
MP3 FORMAT RELEASED
UK OFFICIAL DOWNLOAD CHART
WARGAMES (FILM)
HACKERS (FILM)
THE BLAIR WITCH PROJECT (FILM)
US STATES CYBERATTACK POLICY
CYBERCRIME DEFINED
COMPUTER FRAUD AND ABUSE ACT PASSED
KEVIN MITNICK ARRESTED
DOMAIN NAME SYSTEM ATTACKED
FIRST SPAM
8% OF ALL EMAIL IS SPAM
94% OF ALL EMAIL IS SPAM
ELK CLONER VIRUS
CREEPER VIRUS
ARPANET CRASHES
FIRST WORM VIRUS
ILOVEYOU VIRUS
BROWSER WARS
INTRODUCTION OF SSL
MOSAIC
WORLD WIDE WEB RELEASED
FLASH RELEASED
WORLD WIDE WEB
TELENET
802.11 WIFI PROTOCOL CREATED
UK HOME FIBRE OPTIC
FIRST MESSAGE SENT
FIRST INTERNATIONAL CONNECTION
ARPANET IS SPLIT UP
ARPANET DECOMISSIONED
INTERNET DEFINED
BROADBAND INTRODUCED TO THE UK
UK BROADBAND OVERTAKES DIAL-UP
ARPANET
TCP/IP
NSFNET
MILNET
INTERNET

CULTURE: SOCIAL, MEDIA
ABUSE: HACKING, SPAM, VIRUSES
TECHNOLOGY: WORLD WIDE WEB, CONNECTIONS

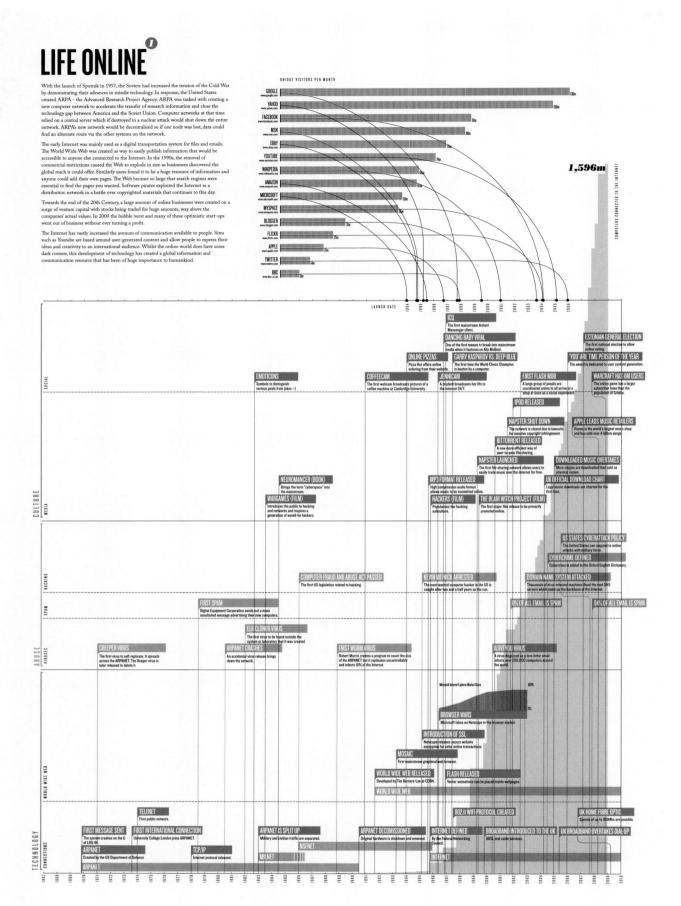

Digital Nostalgia

In this series, Paul Butt looks back at the rise of digital technologies in recent decades. The idea was not just to show the raw numbers but also the social ripples it has caused. Also, by demonstrating how quickly technological devices and data carriers have been developing, the posters indicate the emergence of nostalgic feelings for old and obsolete digital technology.

Four posters use timelines to show the technological progress in the development of the Internet, audio & video formats, computer storage and mobile telephony.

In dieser Serie blickt Paul Butt zurück auf die Einführung digitaler Technologien in den vergangenen Jahrzehnten. Ihr lag die Idee zugrunde, nicht nur Zahlen aufzulisten, sondern auch soziale Veränderungen aufzuzeigen, die mit der Digitalisierung einhergingen. Indem sie die Geschwindigkeit vor Augen führen, mit der Geräte und Speichermedien weiterentwickelt wurden, lassen die Plakate auch nostalgische Gefühle für alte und überholte digitale Techniken aufleben.

Zeitleisten auf vier Motiven veranschaulichen den technologischen Fortschritt im Hinblick auf die Entwicklung des Internets, bei Audio- und Videoformaten, bei der Speicherkapazität von Rechnern und bei der mobilen Telefonie.

Dans cette série, Paul Butt revient sur l'avènement des technologies numériques ces dernières décennies. L'idée n'était pas seulement de montrer les chiffres bruts, mais également les répercussions sociales. En montrant la vitesse à laquelle les appareils technologiques et les supports de données ont évolué, ces affiches indiquent également l'émergence d'une nostalgie pour les technologies obsolètes.

Quatre affiches emploient le format de la chronologie pour montrer l'évolution d'Internet, des formats audio et vidéo, de la mémoire des ordinateurs et de la téléphonie mobile.

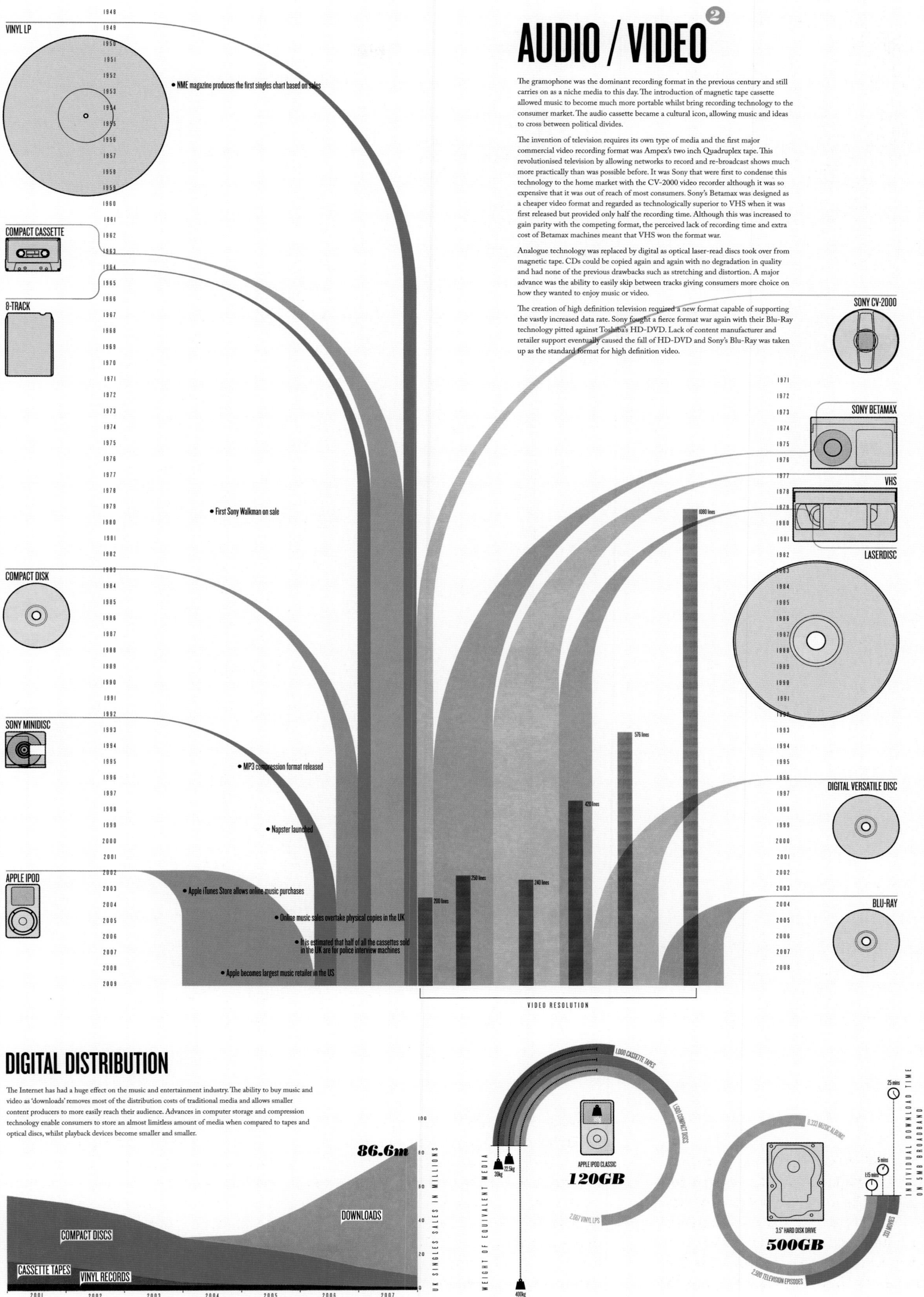

AUDIO / VIDEO
2
The gramophone was the dominant recording format in the previous century and still carries on as a niche media to this day. The introduction of magnetic tape cassette allowed music to become much more portable whilst bring recording technology to the consumer market. The audio cassette became a cultural icon, allowing music and ideas to cross between political divides.
The invention of television requires its own type of media and the first major commercial video recording format was Ampex's two inch Quadruplex tape. This revolutionised television by allowing networks to record and re-broadcast shows much more practically than was possible before. It was Sony that were first to condense this technology to the home market with the CV-2000 video recorder although it was so expensive that it was out of reach of most consumers. Sony's Betamax was designed as a cheaper video format and regarded as technologically superior to VHS when it was first released but provided only half the recording time. Although this was increased to gain parity with the competing format, the perceived lack of recording time and extra cost of Betamax machines meant that VHS won the format war.
Analogue technology was replaced by digital as optical laser-read discs took over from magnetic tape. CDs could be copied again and again with no degradation in quality and had none of the previous drawbacks such as stretching and distortion. A major advance was the ability to easily skip between tracks giving consumers more choice on how they wanted to enjoy music or video.
The creation of high definition television required a new format capable of supporting the vastly increased data rate. Sony fought a fierce format war again with their Blu-Ray technology pitted against Toshiba's HD-DVD. Lack of content manufacturer and retailer support eventually caused the fall of HD-DVD and Sony's Blu-Ray was taken up as the standard format for high definition video.
VINYL LP
COMPACT CASSETTE
8-TRACK
COMPACT DISK
SONY MINIDISC
APPLE IPOD
SONY CV-2000
SONY BETAMAX
VHS
LASERDISC
DIGITAL VERSATILE DISC
BLU-RAY
• NME magazine produces the first singles chart based on sales
• First Sony Walkman on sale
• MP3 compression format released
• Napster launched
• Apple iTunes Store allows online music purchases
• Online music sales overtake physical copies in the UK
• It is estimated that half of all the cassettes sold in the UK are for police interview machines
• Apple becomes largest music retailer in the US
VIDEO RESOLUTION
DIGITAL DISTRIBUTION
The Internet has had a huge effect on the music and entertainment industry. The ability to buy music and video as 'downloads' removes most of the distribution costs of traditional media and allows smaller content producers to more easily reach their audience. Advances in computer storage and compression technology enable consumers to store an almost limitless amount of media when compared to tapes and optical discs, whilst playback devices become smaller and smaller.
86.6m
DOWNLOADS
COMPACT DISCS
CASSETTE TAPES
VINYL RECORDS
2001
2002
2003
2004
2005
2006
2007
UK SINGLES SALES IN MILLIONS
WEIGHT OF EQUIVALENT MEDIA
1,000 CASSETTE TAPES
1,500 COMPACT DISCS
APPLE IPOD CLASSIC
120GB
500GB
INDIVIDUAL DOWNLOAD TIME ON 5MB BROADBAND

Project Info: Series of posters, 2009, UK
Design: Paul Butt (Section Design)

DISK SPACE 3

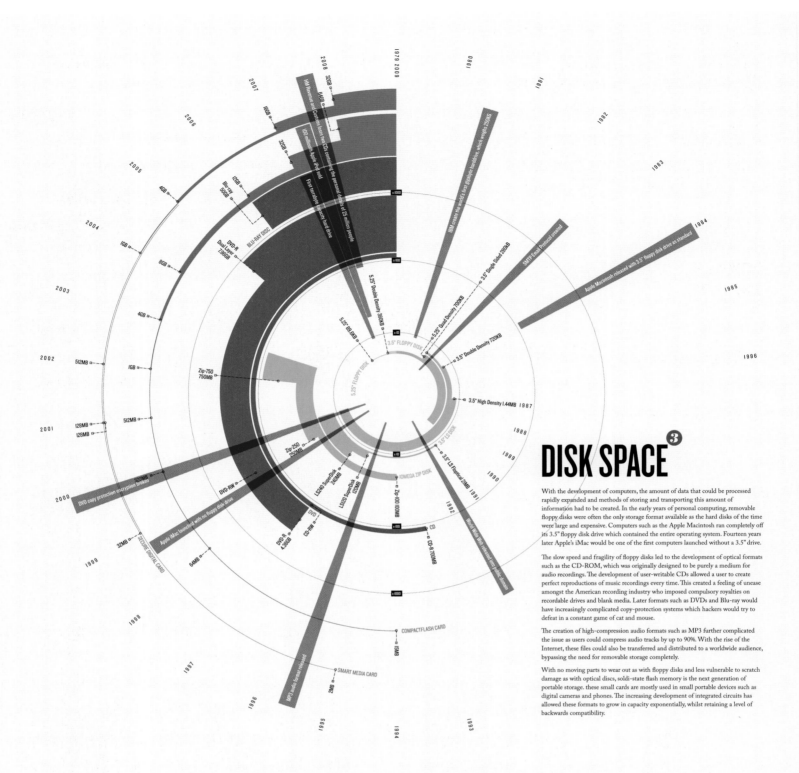

With the development of computers, the amount of data that could be processed rapidly expanded and methods of storing and transporting this amount of information had to be created. In the early years of personal computing, removable floppy disks were often the only storage format available as the hard disks of the time were large and expensive. Computers such as the Apple Macintosh ran completely off its 3.5" floppy disk drive which contained the entire operating system. Fourteen years later Apple's iMac would be one of the first computers launched without a 3.5" drive.

The slow speed and fragility of floppy disks led to the development of optical formats such as the CD-ROM, which was originally designed to be purely a medium for audio recordings. The development of user-writable CDs allowed a user to create perfect reproductions of music recordings every time. This created a feeling of unease amongst the American recording industry who imposed compulsory royalties on recordable drives and blank media. Later formats such as DVDs and Blu-ray would have increasingly complicated copy-protection systems which hackers would try to defeat in a constant game of cat and mouse.

The creation of high-compression audio formats such as MP3 further complicated the issue as users could compress audio tracks by up to 90%. With the rise of the Internet, these files could also be transferred and distributed to a worldwide audience, bypassing the need for removable storage completely.

With no moving parts to wear out as with floppy disks and less vulnerable to scratch damage as with optical discs, soldi-state flash memory is the next generation of portable storage. these small cards are mostly used in small portable devices such as digital cameras and phones. The increasing development of integrated circuits has allowed these formats to grow in capacity exponentially, whilst retaining a level of backwards compatibility.

TRANSFER SPEEDS

Theoretical maximum read speed | Time to transfer 3mb digital music file | Time to transfer 1000mb digital video file

*Theoretical time due to capacity limitations.

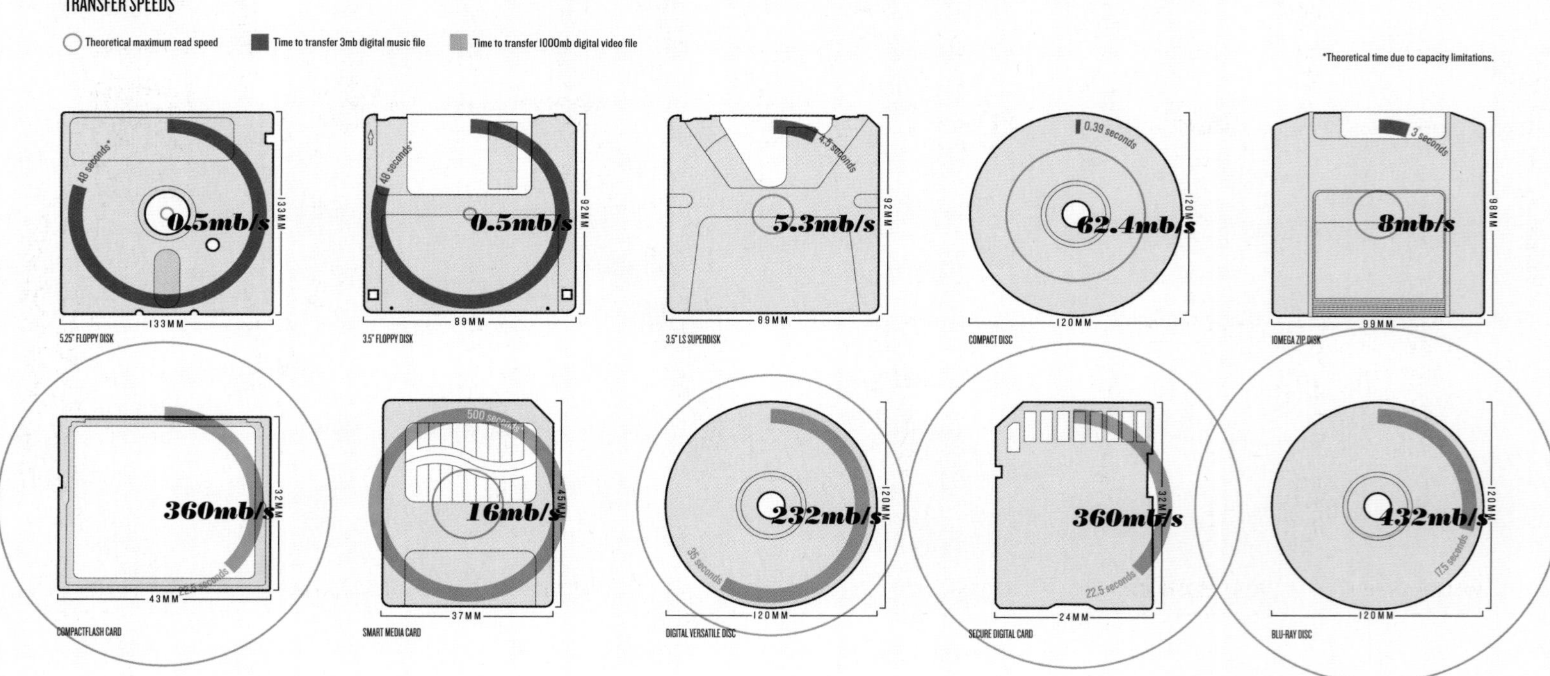

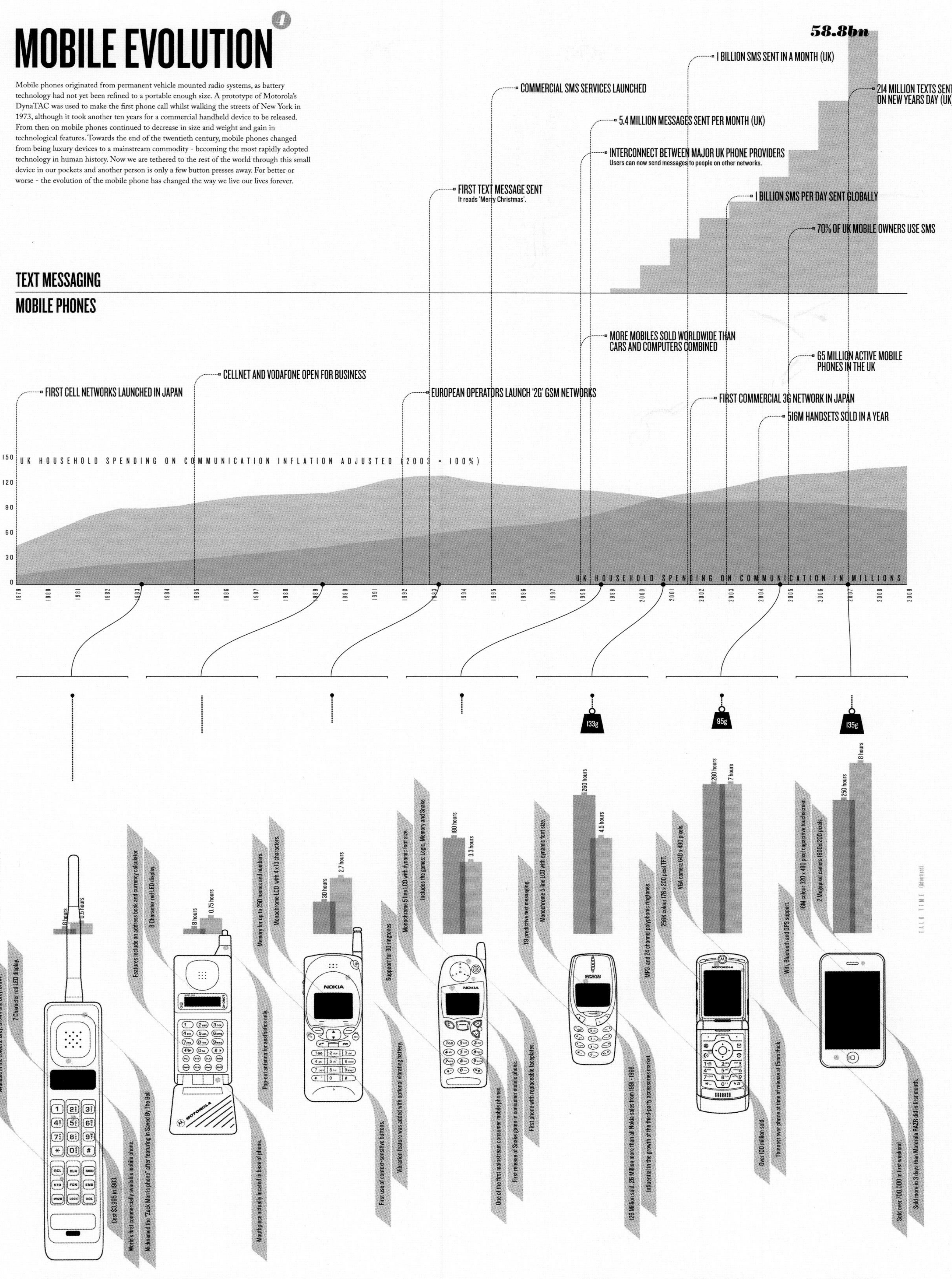
MOBILE EVOLUTION
4
Mobile phones originated from permanent vehicle mounted radio systems, as battery technology had not yet been refined to a portable enough size. A prototype of Motorola's DynaTAC was used to make the first phone call whilst walking the streets of New York in 1973, although it took another ten years for a commercial handheld device to be released. From then on mobile phones continued to decrease in size and weight and gain in technological features. Towards the end of the twentieth century, mobile phones changed from being luxury devices to a mainstream commodity - becoming the most rapidly adopted technology in human history. Now we are tethered to the rest of the world through this small device in our pockets and another person is only a few button presses away. For better or worse - the evolution of the mobile phone has changed the way we live our lives forever.
58.8bn
COMMERCIAL SMS SERVICES LAUNCHED
1 BILLION SMS SENT IN A MONTH (UK)
214 MILLION TEXTS SENT ON NEW YEARS DAY (UK)
5.4 MILLION MESSAGES SENT PER MONTH (UK)
INTERCONNECT BETWEEN MAJOR UK PHONE PROVIDERS
Users can now send messages to people on other networks.
FIRST TEXT MESSAGE SENT
It reads 'Merry Christmas'.
1 BILLION SMS PER DAY SENT GLOBALLY
70% OF UK MOBILE OWNERS USE SMS
TEXT MESSAGING
MOBILE PHONES
MORE MOBILES SOLD WORLDWIDE THAN CARS AND COMPUTERS COMBINED
65 MILLION ACTIVE MOBILE PHONES IN THE UK
CELLNET AND VODAFONE OPEN FOR BUSINESS
FIRST CELL NETWORKS LAUNCHED IN JAPAN
EUROPEAN OPERATORS LAUNCH '2G' GSM NETWORKS
FIRST COMMERCIAL 3G NETWORK IN JAPAN
516M HANDSETS SOLD IN A YEAR
UK HOUSEHOLD SPENDING ON COMMUNICATION INFLATION ADJUSTED (2003 = 100%)
150
120
90
60
30
0
UK HOUSEHOLD SPENDING ON COMMUNICATION IN MILLIONS
1979 1980 1981 1982 1983 1984 1985 1986 1987 1988 1989 1990 1991 1992 1993 1994 1995 1996 1997 1998 1999 2000 2001 2002 2003 2004 2005 2006 2007 2008 2009
133g
95g
135g
STANDBY TIME (Advertised)
TALK TIME (Advertised)
8 hours
0.5 hours
Available in the colours: Grey, Brown and Grey/Brown.
7 Character red LED display.
Cost $3,995 in 1983.
World's first commercially available mobile phone.
Nicknamed the "Zack Morris phone" after featuring in Saved By The Bell
MOTOROLA DYNATAC 8000X
8 hours
0.75 hours
Features include an address book and currency calculator.
8 Character red LED display.
Pop-out antenna for aesthetics only.
Mouthpiece actually located in base of phone.
MOTOROLA MICROTAC 9800X
30 hours
2.7 hours
Memory for up to 250 names and numbers.
Monochrome LCD with 4 x 13 characters.
Support for 30 ringtones
First use of context-sensitive buttons.
Vibration feature was added with optional vibrating battery.
NOKIA 2110
180 hours
3.3 hours
Monochrome 5 line LCD with dynamic font size.
Includes the games: Logic, Memory and Snake
One of the first mainstream consumer mobile phones.
First release of Snake game in consumer mobile phone.
First phone with replaceable faceplates.
NOKIA 5110
260 hours
4.5 hours
T9 predictive text messaging.
Monochrome 5 line LCD with dynamic font size.
126 Million sold. 26 Million more than all Nokia sales from 1991 - 1998.
Influential in the growth of the third-party accessories market.
NOKIA 3310
280 hours
7 hours
MP3 and 24 channel polyphonic ringtones
256K colour 176 x 200 pixel TFT.
VGA camera 640 x 480 pixels.
Over 100 million sold.
Thinnest ever phone at time of release at 15mm thick.
MOTOROLA RAZR V3
250 hours
8 hours
Wifi, Bluetooth and GPS support.
16M colour 320 x 480 pixel capacitive touchscreen.
2 Megapixel camera 1600x1200 pixels.
Sold over 700,000 in first weekend.
Sold more in 3 days than Motorola RAZR did in first month.
APPLE IPHONE

ACUMEN

The Tipsy Turvy Republic of Alcohol

ALCOHOL has triggered extreme cultural mood swings in American history, with periods of binge consumption alternating with periods of enforced abstinence. Enthusiastic tippling was the norm in the colonies and early republic, but in the 1840s a nation of hearty drinkers became zealous abstainers. A similar cycle occurred several decades later as a rise in consumption of alcohol at the turn of the century culminated in Prohibition.

DATAGRAPHIC BY NIGEL HOLMES
RESEARCH BY LORRAINE MOFFA

1770–2000
HOW MUCH WE DRANK

Americans in the late 1700s and early 1800s were awash in beer, wine and spirits—consuming 30-plus gallons a year per capita. On average, the amount of pure alcohol in those libations was 20 percent, a figure that has remained consistent until the modern day. Per capita consumption dropped by more than half in the mid-1800s and in recent years has hovered above 10 gallons a year.

Gallons of alcohol annually, per person (age 15+)

33 gallons (5 bottles to a gallon)

1770	1785	1790	1800	1810	1820	1830	1840	1850	1860	1870	1880	1890	1900
33	30.5	29	33	35.5	34	35.5	15.5	9	10.5	9.5	9.5	10.5	10.5

1787 Two days before completing their work, the 55 members of the Constitutional Convention adjourn to a Philadelphia tavern for a break. They consume:

54 bottles of Madeira
60 bottles of claret
8 bottles of whiskey
22 bottles of port
8 bottles of hard cider
7 bowls of punch so large that people say ducks could swim in them.

We the People HIC!

1794 U.S. navy ration includes "half-pint of distilled spirits."

1794 Near-tripling of excise tax on whiskey results in the Whiskey Rebellion. (The tax is repealed in 1802.)

1799 George Washington's stills, built at Mount Vernon after his presidency, produce 11,000 gallons of whiskey.

1809 James Madison tries to create a new Cabinet position: Secretary of Beer. He fails.

1849 Bartender in Martinez, Calif., invents the martini.

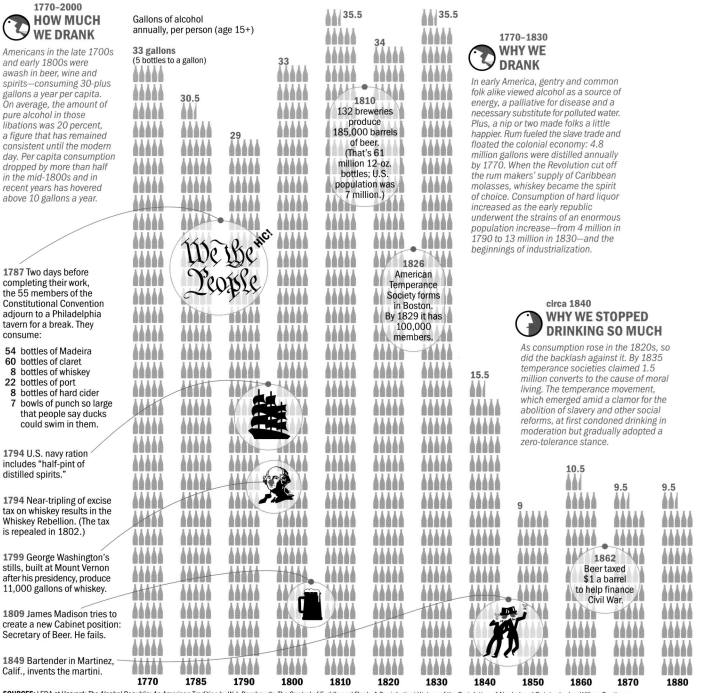

1810 132 breweries produce 185,000 barrels of beer. (That's 61 million 12-oz. bottles; U.S. population was 7 million.)

1826 American Temperance Society forms in Boston. By 1829 it has 100,000 members.

1770–1830
WHY WE DRANK

In early America, gentry and common folk alike viewed alcohol as a source of energy, a palliative for disease and a necessary substitute for polluted water. Plus, a nip or two made folks a little happier. Rum fueled the slave trade and floated the colonial economy: 4.8 million gallons were distilled annually by 1770. When the Revolution cut off the rum makers' supply of Caribbean molasses, whiskey became the spirit of choice. Consumption of hard liquor increased as the early republic underwent the strains of an enormous population increase—from 4 million in 1790 to 13 million in 1830—and the beginnings of industrialization.

circa 1840
WHY WE STOPPED DRINKING SO MUCH

As consumption rose in the 1820s, so did the backlash against it. By 1835 temperance societies claimed 1.5 million converts to the cause of moral living. The temperance movement, which emerged amid a clamor for the abolition of slavery and other social reforms, at first condoned drinking in moderation but gradually adopted a zero-tolerance stance.

1862 Beer taxed $1 a barrel to help finance Civil War.

1898 Beer tax raised to $2 a barrel during Spanish-American War.

1900–1910 Woman's Christian Temperance Union member Carry Nation active in Kansas.

SOURCES: LEDA at Harvard; *The Alcohol Republic: An American Tradition* by W.J. Rorabaugh; *The Control of Fuddle and Flash: A Sociological History of the Regulation of Alcohol and Opiates* by Jan-Willem Gerritsen; OECD 1989; U.S. Office of Management and Budget

1920–1933
PROHIBITION: WE KEPT ON DRINKING

1920 Volstead Act, which ined how Prohibition was ried out under the 18th endment, outlawed the nufacture, sale or nsportation of toxicating liquor"and ved the way for organized me to make a killing in the gal booze trade during the xt 13 years.

Volstead Act was riddled h loopholes, including a k of criminal penalties for ssession and consumption alcohol, so orders for cramental wine spiked arply, and doctors scribed 1.8 million gallons medicinal whiskey in 1927 ne. Another exception owed households to duce 200 gallons of me-brewed cider or fruit ce a year that contained to 0.5 percent alcohol.

1930, 70 percent of the blic—fed up with corrupt orcement officials, courts gged with liquor cases and rocketing homicide es—wanted to change the stead Act. Prohibition hit federal pocketbook ecially hard: The ernment lost $11 billion iquor excise taxes.

21st Amendment ealed Prohibition December 1933.

1792–2008
EXCISE TAX: WHAT THE GOVERNMENT COLLECTS
The percentage of federal revenue that is collected from taxes on alcohol

Alcohol excise taxes were an on-again-off-again source of federal revenue until Uncle Sam began to depend heavily on them during the Civil War. Personal income taxes became the main source of U.S. revenue after passage of the 16th Amendment in 1913 and now account for 45% of the federal budget while only about 3% comes from alcohol.

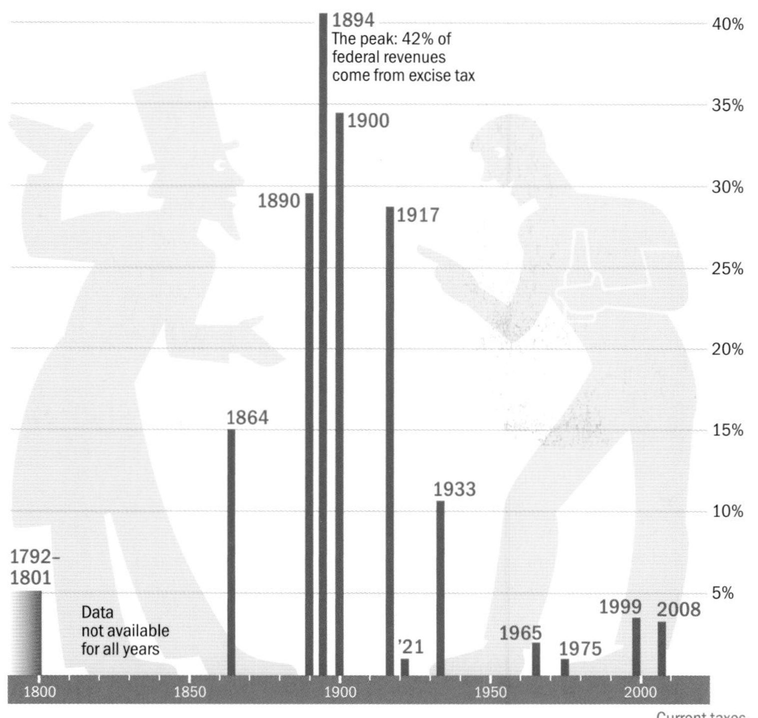

Current taxes
Beer **$18** barrel
Liquor **$13.50** gallon
Wine **$1.07** gallon

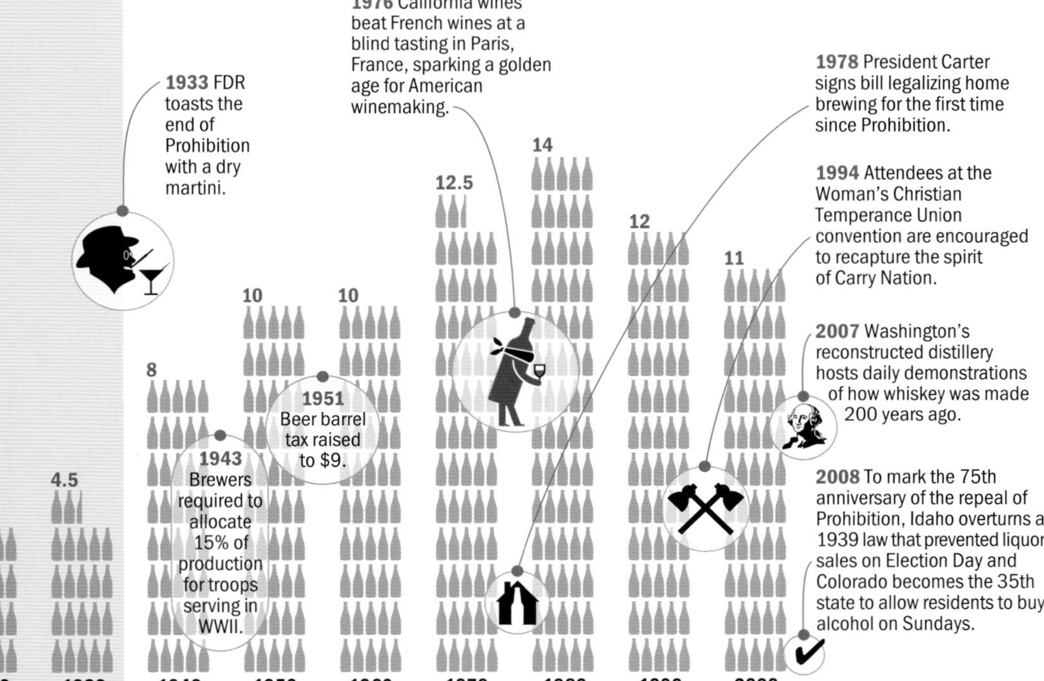

1933 FDR toasts the end of Prohibition with a dry martini.
1976 California wines beat French wines at a blind tasting in Paris, France, sparking a golden age for American winemaking.
1978 President Carter signs bill legalizing home brewing for the first time since Prohibition.
1994 Attendees at the Woman's Christian Temperance Union convention are encouraged to recapture the spirit of Carry Nation.
2007 Washington's reconstructed distillery hosts daily demonstrations of how whiskey was made 200 years ago.
2008 To mark the 75th anniversary of the repeal of Prohibition, Idaho overturns a 1939 law that prevented liquor sales on Election Day and Colorado becomes the 35th state to allow residents to buy alcohol on Sundays.
1943 Brewers required to allocate 15% of production for troops serving in WWII.
1951 Beer barrel tax raised to $9.
4.5
8
10
10
12.5
14
12
11
920
1930
1940
1950
1960
1970
1980
1990
2000

Drinking in the US

Casting a look into cultural history, this graphic demonstrates how drinking habits have changed in the US from 1770 to the present. This is shown as a bar chart, with the bars made up of rows of 5 bottles (there are 5 standard bottles to a gallon). The number of rows then indicates how many gallons of alcohol per capita were consumed annually.

Text blocks address why the US drank so much, and why there was a backlash against drinking around 1840. The prohibition years are specially marked and are given an extended explanation. The bar chart at the top right shows the federal revenue the government collects from taxes on alcohol.

Diese Grafik wirft einen Blick in die Kulturgeschichte und zeigt, wie sich die Trinkgewohnheiten in den USA zwischen 1770 und heute verändert haben. Veranschaulicht wird das durch ein Balkendiagramm. Die Balken bestehen aus Zeilen von je fünf Flaschen (fünf Standardflaschen ergeben eine amerikanische Gallone, rund 3,8 Liter). Die Anzahl der Zeilen (und damit die Höhe der Balken) zeigt, wie viel Gallonen Alkohol pro Kopf jährlich konsumiert wurden.

Die Texte erläutern, weshalb in den USA so viel getrunken wurde und warum es um 1840 einen Einbruch im Alkoholkonsum gab. Die Jahre der Prohibition sind gesondert gekennzeichnet und ausführlich erläutert. Das Balkendiagramm oben rechts verdeutlicht, wie viel Geld durch die Alkoholsteuer insgesamt in die Staatskasse floss.

Ce graphique explore un pan de l'histoire culturelle en montrant comment les habitudes relatives à la boisson ont changé aux États-Unis de 1770 à aujourd'hui. Ces changements sont révélés par un histogramme dont les barres sont constituées de rangées de 5 bouteilles (il y a 5 bouteilles standard dans un gallon). Le nombre de rangées indique donc le nombre de gallons consommés chaque année par habitant.

Les blocs de texte expliquent pourquoi les Américains buvaient autant, ainsi que les raisons du renversement de situation vers 1840. Les années de prohibition sont soulignées et assorties d'une explication approfondie. L'histogramme situé en haut à droite montre les revenus que le gouvernement fédéral collecte grâce aux taxes sur l'alcool.

Project Info: "The Tipsy Turvy Republic of Alcohol", *American History*, magazine article, 2008, USA
Data Source: LEDA at Harvard; W. J. Rorabaugh: *The Alcohol Republic: An American Tradition*; Jan-Willem Gerritsen: *The Control of Fuddle and Flash: A social History of Alcohol and Opiates*; OECD 1989; US Office of Management and Budget
Research: Lorraine Moffa
Design: Nigel Holmes

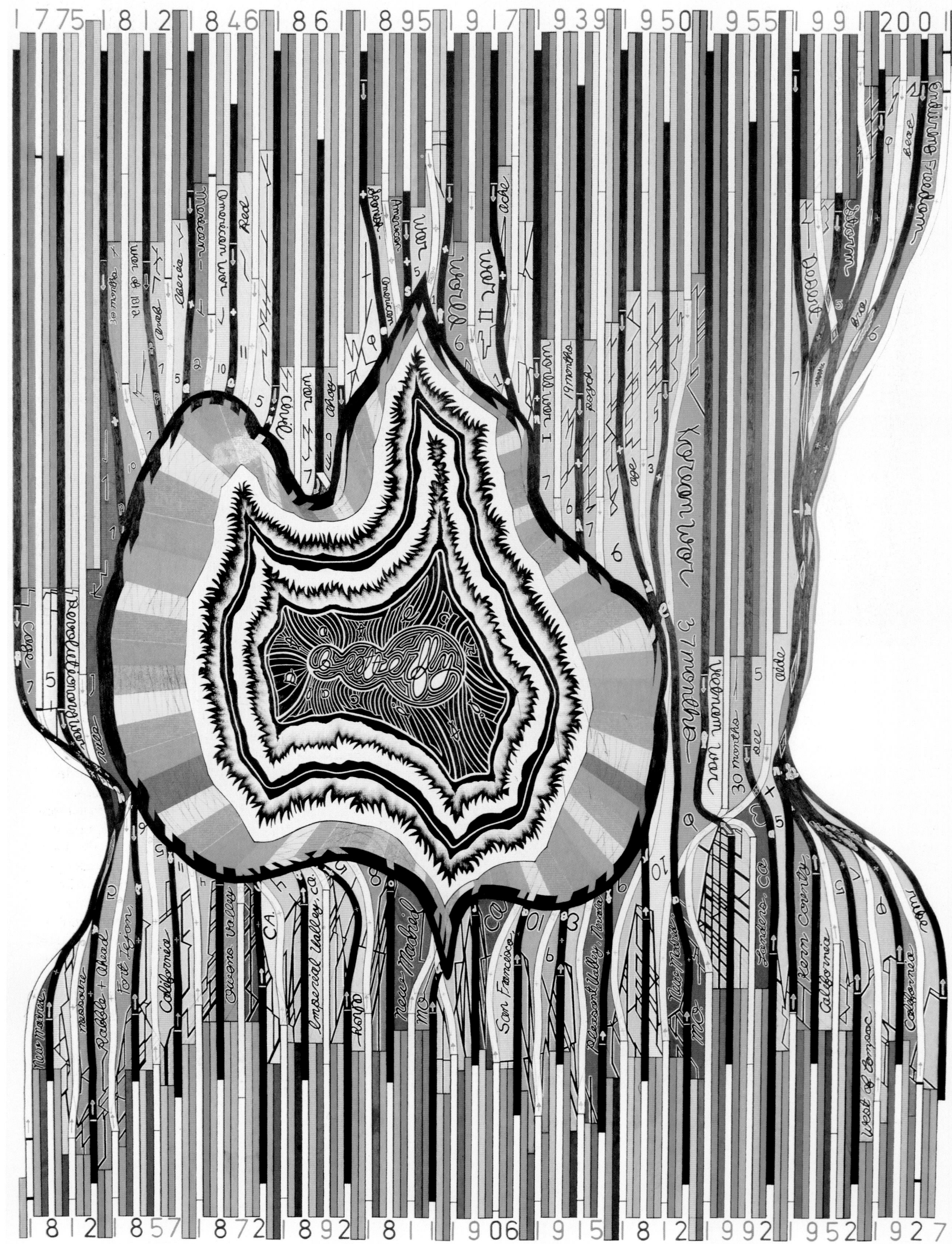
MAJOR AMERICAN WARS
MAJOR EARTHQUAKES IN CONTIGUOUS UNITED STATES

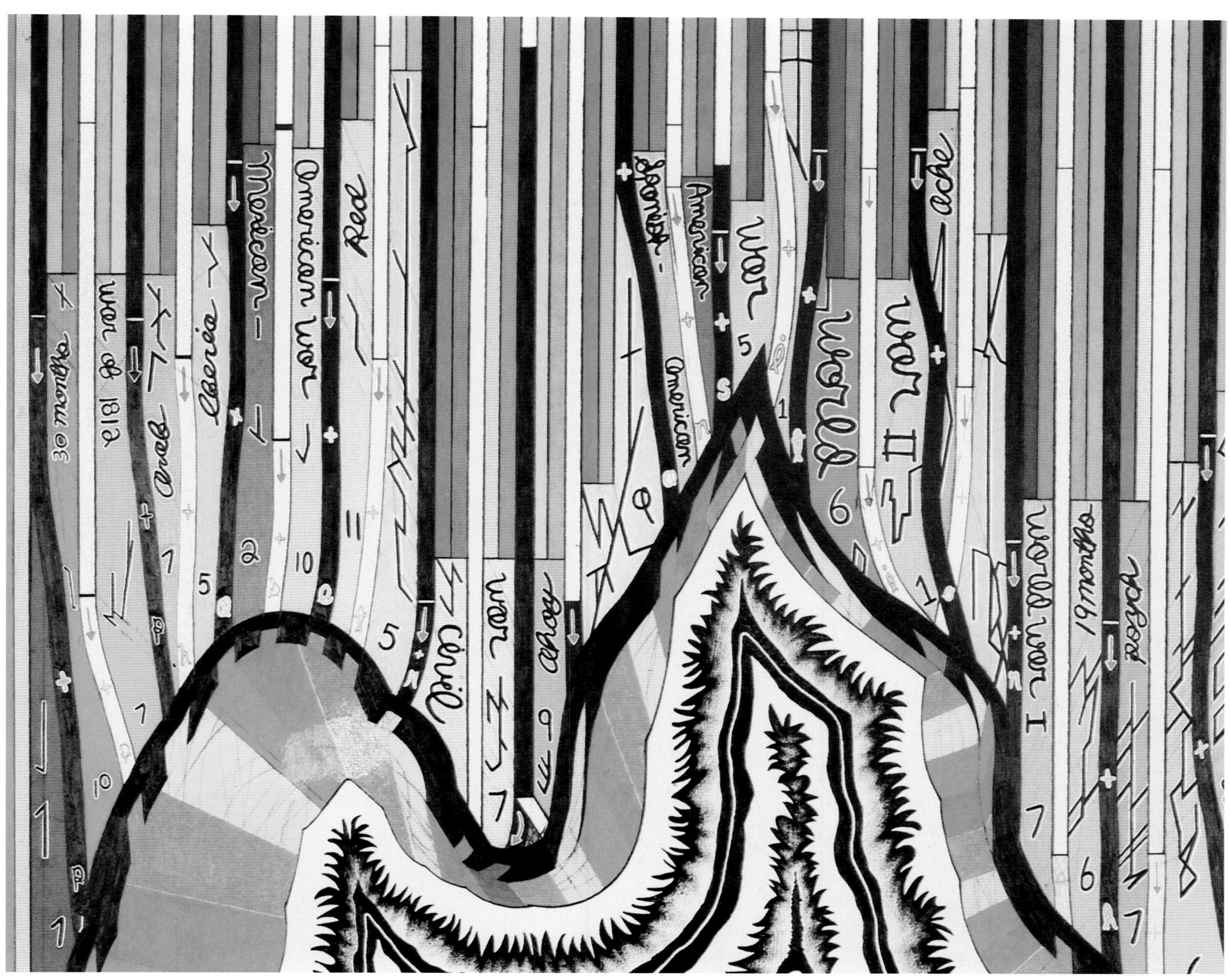

Earthquakes and Wars

This drawing maps posited similarities between wars and earthquakes in the US, including data concerning their duration, location etc. It was created starting from both the top and bottom with thin vertical stripes for each event. The numerics of each particular year determine the length of the thin stripes in inches. From these, more irregularly shaped labels emerge, indicating further data for each event.

Connecting the loose ends of these labels created a butterfly shape in the centre. John J. O'Connor emphasised this shape for its reference to the butterfly effect, a term from chaos theory. The piece is deceptive: instead of actually visualising information, the artist gets lost in the data in order to let it create its own visual shape.

In dieser Zeichnung geht es um postulierte Ähnlichkeiten zwischen Kriegen und Erdbeben in den USA, einschließlich der Daten zu ihrer Dauer, dem Ort usw. Sie wurde von oben und von unten begonnen mit schmalen senkrechten Streifen für jeden Vorfall. Die Ziffern der Jahreszahl bestimmen die Länge der jeweiligen Streifen in Zoll. Daraus wiederum erwachsen unregelmäßig geformte Textfelder, die weitere Informationen zu jedem Ereignis andeuten.

Durch das Verbinden der losen Enden entstand eine schmetterlingsartige Form in der Mitte. John J. O'Connor betonte diese Form wegen ihrer Anspielung auf den Schmetterlingseffekt, ein Begriff aus der Chaostheorie. Die Arbeit ist irreführend: Anstatt tatsächlich Informationen zu visualisieren, verliert sich der Künstler in den Daten und lässt sie ihre eigene visuelle Gestalt annehmen.

Ce dessin examine des similarités postulées entre les guerres et les tremblements de terre aux États-Unis, avec des données sur leur durée, leur emplacement, etc. Il se lit à partir du haut et du bas, et de fines bandes verticales représentent chaque événement. Les chiffres de chaque année déterminent la longueur en pouces de ces bandes. Des étiquettes à la forme plus irrégulière prolongent les bandes et indiquent des données supplémentaires sur chaque événement.

Les étiquettes se rejoignent au centre pour dessiner une forme de papillon. John J. O'Connor a accentué cette forme en référence à l'effet papillon, un terme qui appartient à la théorie du chaos. Ce graphique est trompeur : au lieu de donner une visualisation de l'information, l'artiste se perd dans les données pour les laisser créer une forme visuelle qui leur est propre.

Project Info: Drawing, 2003, USA
Artist: John J. O'Connor
Additional Info: John J. O'Connor is represented by Pierogi Gallery

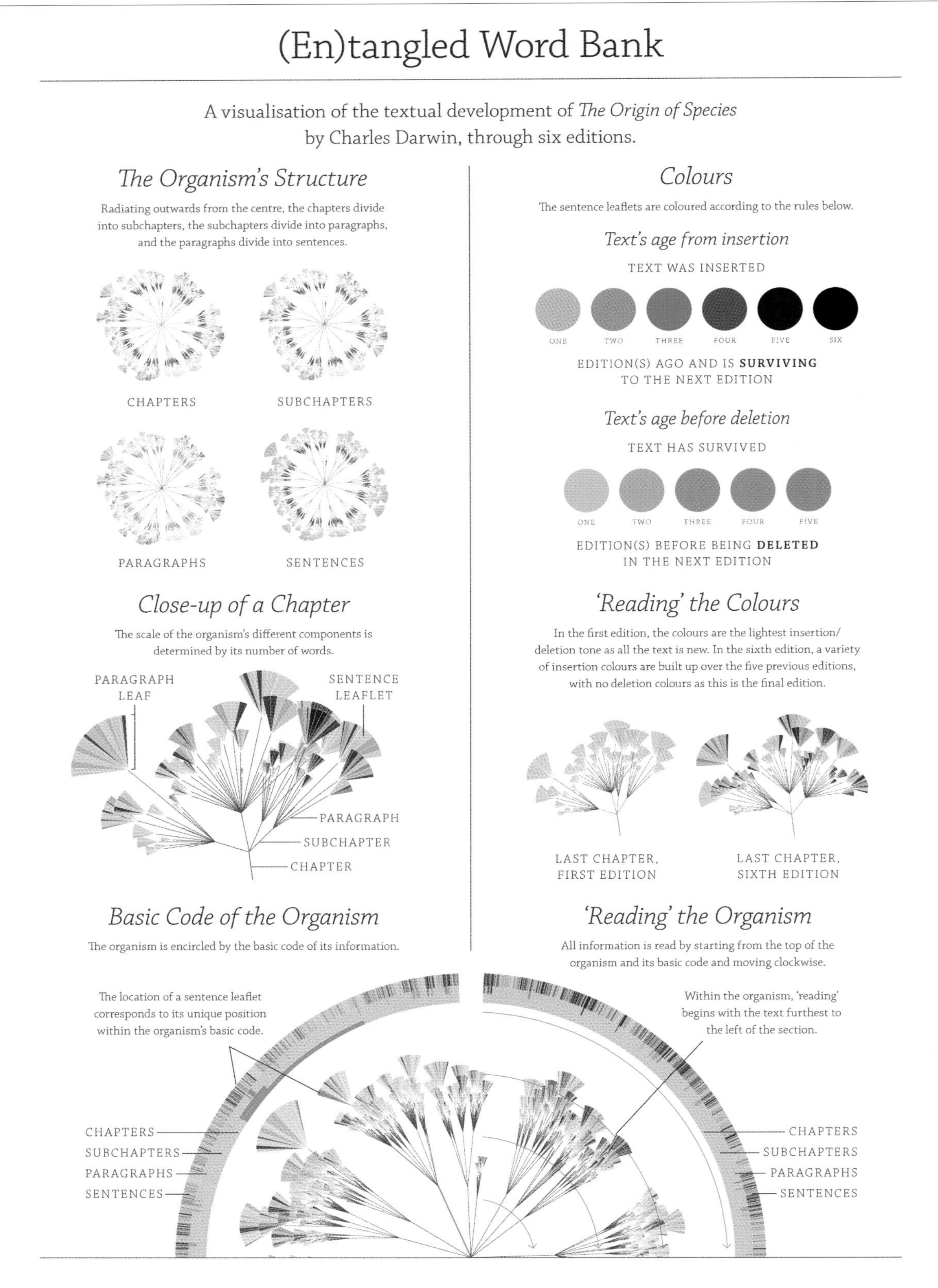

(En)tangled Word Bank
A visualisation of the textual development of The Origin of Species
by Charles Darwin, through six editions.
The Organism's Structure
Radiating outwards from the centre, the chapters divide into subchapters, the subchapters divide into paragraphs, and the paragraphs divide into sentences.
CHAPTERS
SUBCHAPTERS
PARAGRAPHS
SENTENCES
Close-up of a Chapter
The scale of the organism's different components is determined by its number of words.
PARAGRAPH LEAF
SENTENCE LEAFLET
PARAGRAPH
SUBCHAPTER
CHAPTER
Basic Code of the Organism
The organism is encircled by the basic code of its information.
Colours
The sentence leaflets are coloured according to the rules below.
Text's age from insertion
TEXT WAS INSERTED
ONE TWO THREE FOUR FIVE SIX
EDITION(S) AGO AND IS SURVIVING TO THE NEXT EDITION
Text's age before deletion
TEXT HAS SURVIVED
ONE TWO THREE FOUR FIVE
EDITION(S) BEFORE BEING DELETED IN THE NEXT EDITION
'Reading' the Colours
In the first edition, the colours are the lightest insertion/deletion tone as all the text is new. In the sixth edition, a variety of insertion colours are built up over the five previous editions, with no deletion colours as this is the final edition.
LAST CHAPTER, FIRST EDITION
LAST CHAPTER, SIXTH EDITION
'Reading' the Organism
All information is read by starting from the top of the organism and its basic code and moving clockwise.
The location of a sentence leaflet corresponds to its unique position within the organism's basic code.
Within the organism, 'reading' begins with the text furthest to the left of the section.
CHAPTERS
SUBCHAPTERS
PARAGRAPHS
SENTENCES

(En)tangled Word Bank

This project visualises the evolution of Darwin's *Origin of Species* through six editions. Data were gathered from a hierarchical structural analysis of every word in each edition. The resulting 'literary organism' is represented in circular form. From the centre, chapters branch out into sub-chapters, paragraphs and sentences.

The outer circle repeats this structure in four lines. Colour quantifies the life-span of each entity, with saturation indicating how many editions back it was inserted. Orange elements are deleted in the next edition, while blue ones survive. Since the text is arranged clockwise, it can be seen how the final text grew to fill the complete circle in the sixth edition.

Mit diesem Projekt wird die Entwicklung von Darwins Buch *The Origin of Species* über sechs Ausgaben verfolgt und visualisiert. Die Daten wurden gesammelt durch eine hierarchische Strukturanalyse aller Worte in allen Ausgaben. Der daraus entstandene „literarische Organismus" ist als Kreis dargestellt, von dessen Mittelpunkt aus sich Kapitel in Unterkapitel, Absätze und Sätze verzweigen.

Die vier Zeilen des äußeren Kreises wiederholen diese Struktur von innen nach außen und verweisen jeweils auf Kapitel, Unterkapitel, Absätze und Sätze. Der Farbcode gibt die Lebensdauer jeder Einheit an: Die Farbsättigung verdeutlicht, mit welcher Ausgabe ein Element eingefügt wurde. Orangefarbene Elemente werden in der folgenden Ausgabe gestrichen, blaue bleiben bestehen. Da der Text im Uhrzeigersinn angeordnet ist, lässt sich der Textzuwachs ablesen, bis er schließlich mit der sechsten Ausgabe den gesamten Kreis füllt.

Ce projet est une représentation de l'évolution de l'*Origine des espèces*, de Darwin, à travers six éditions successives. Les données ont été recueillies à partir d'une analyse structurelle hiérarchique de chacun des mots de chaque édition. L'« organisme littéraire » qui en résulte est représenté par une forme circulaire. Les chapitres se divisent en sous-chapitres, paragraphes et phrases du centre vers l'extérieur.

Le cercle externe reproduit cette structure sur quatre lignes. La couleur indique la durée de vie de chaque entité, et la saturation indique le nombre d'éditions depuis que l'entité existe. Les éléments orange sont supprimés dans l'édition suivante, tandis que les bleus restent. Comme le texte est disposé dans le sens des aiguilles d'une montre, on peut voir comment le texte final arrive à remplir tout le cercle dans la sixième édition.

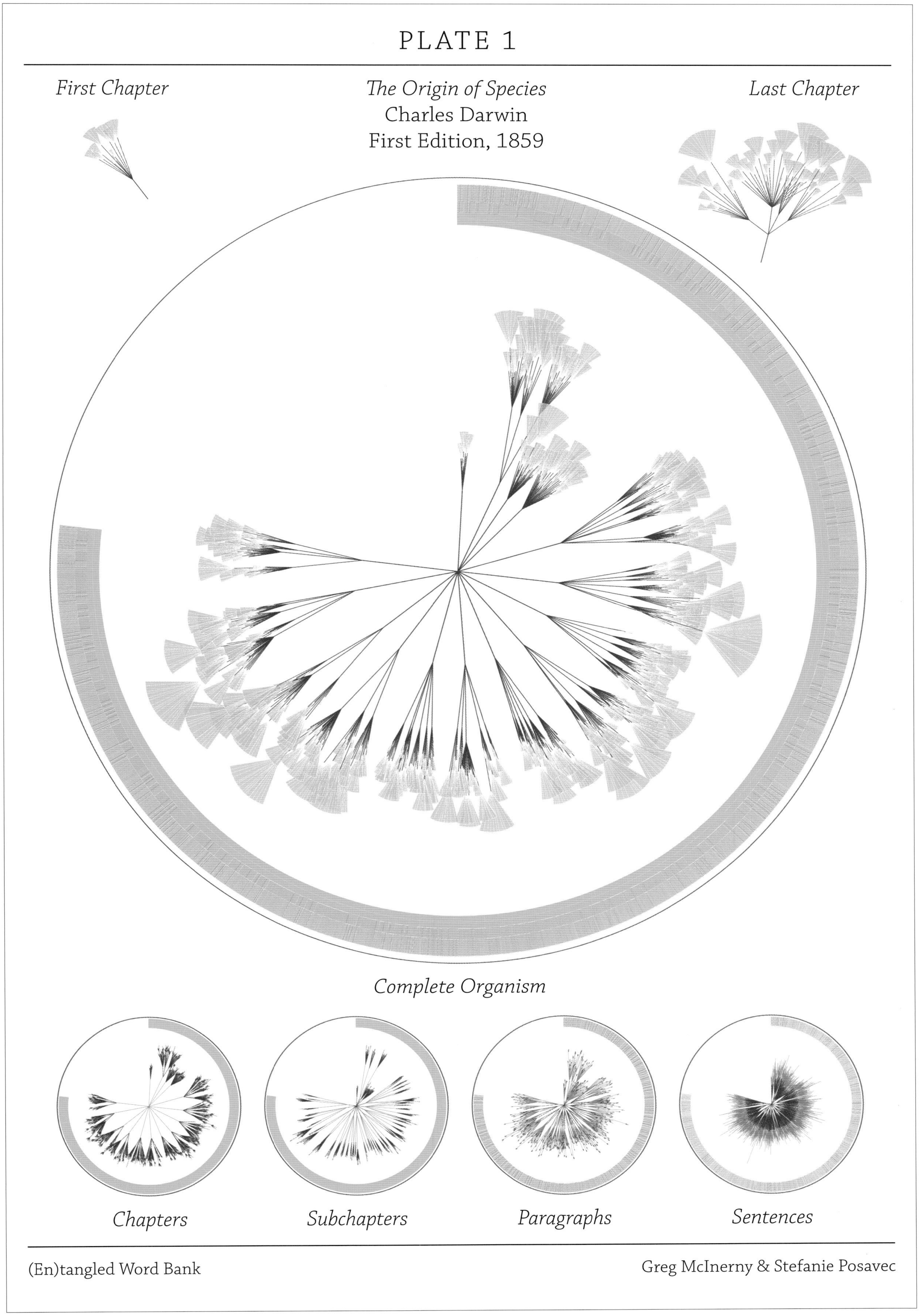

PLATE 1

First Chapter

The Origin of Species
Charles Darwin
First Edition, 1859

Last Chapter

Complete Organism

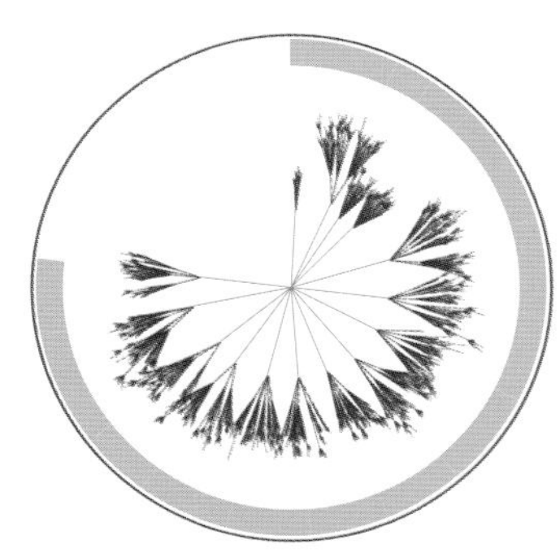

Chapters

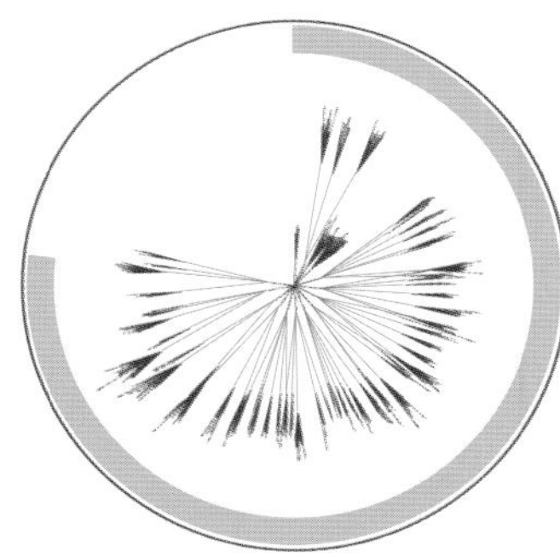

Subchapters

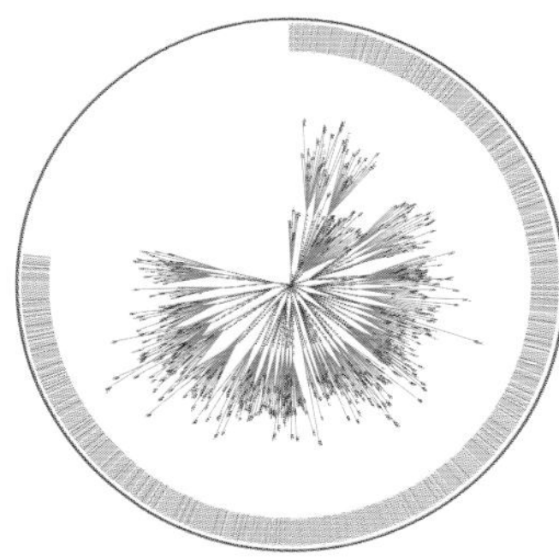

Paragraphs

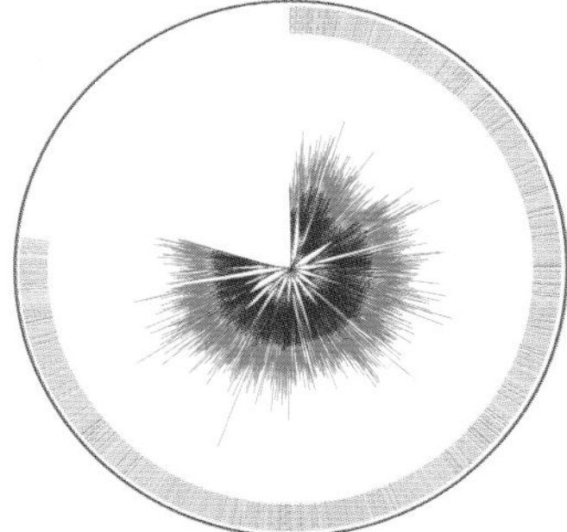

Sentences

(En)tangled Word Bank

Greg McInerny & Stefanie Posavec

Project Info: Microsoft Research, website, 2009, UK
Data Source: The Complete Works of Charles Darwin Online
Design: Stefanie Posavec, Greg McInerny

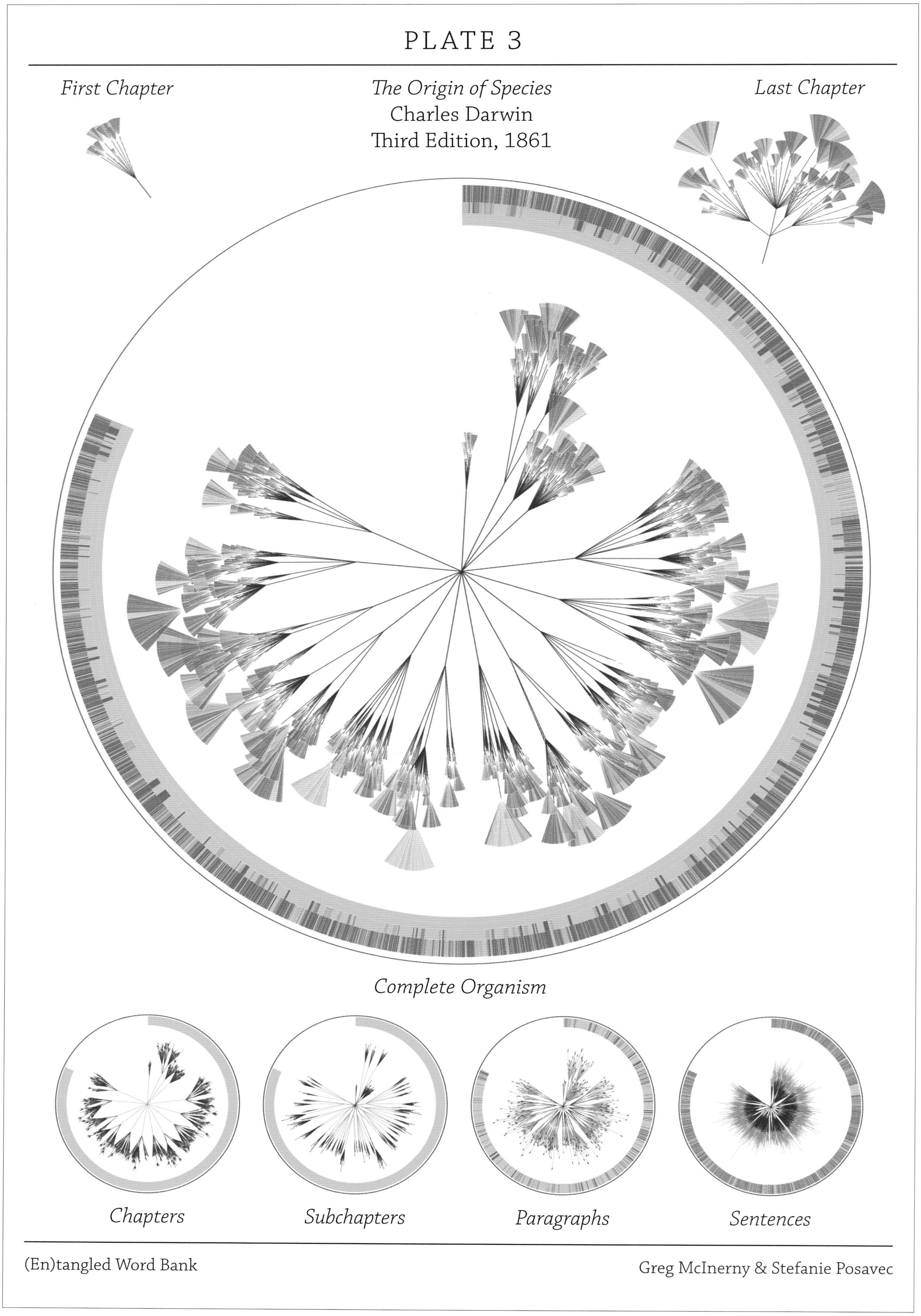

PLATE 3

First Chapter

The Origin of Species
Charles Darwin
Third Edition, 1861

Last Chapter

Complete Organism

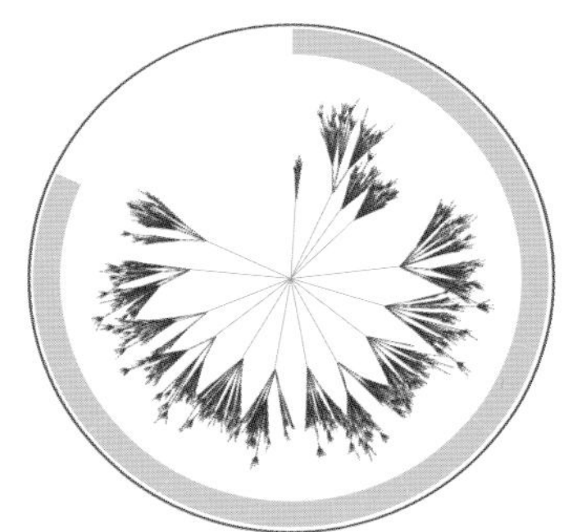

Chapters

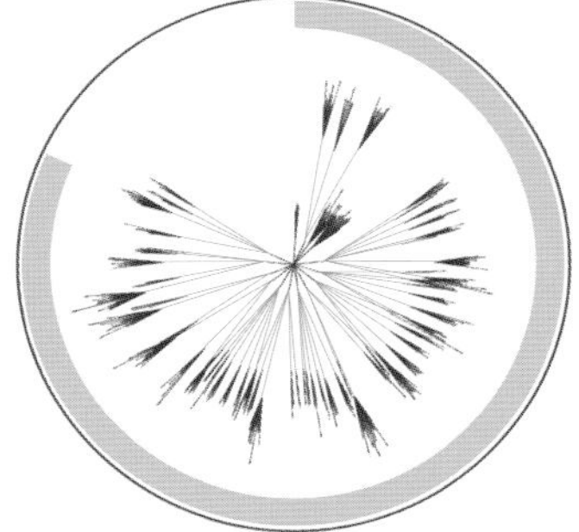

Subchapters

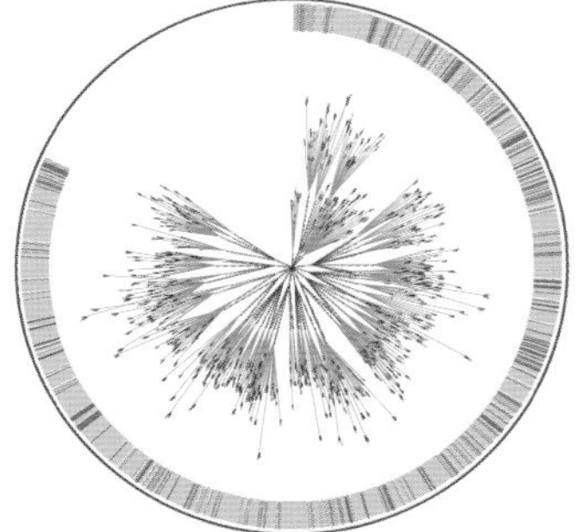

Paragraphs

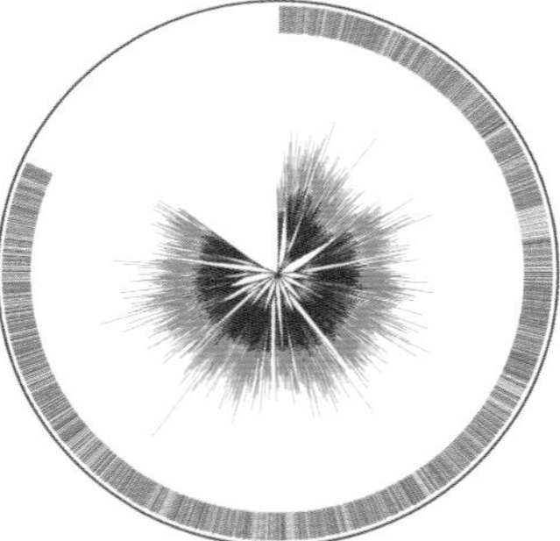

Sentences

(En)tangled Word Bank

Greg McInerny & Stefanie Posavec

PLATE 6

First Chapter

The Origin of Species
Charles Darwin
Sixth Edition, 1872

Last Chapter

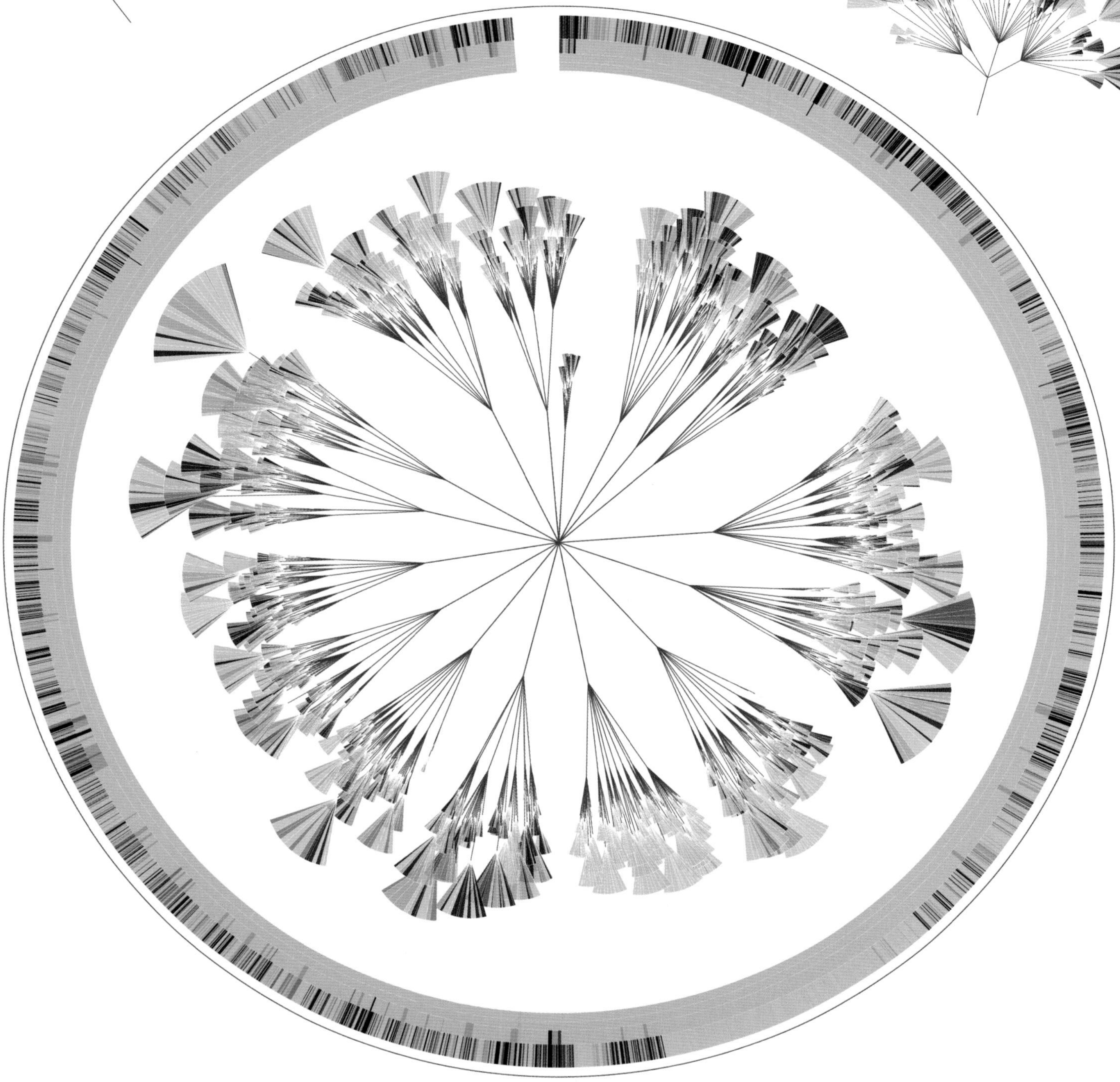

Complete Organism

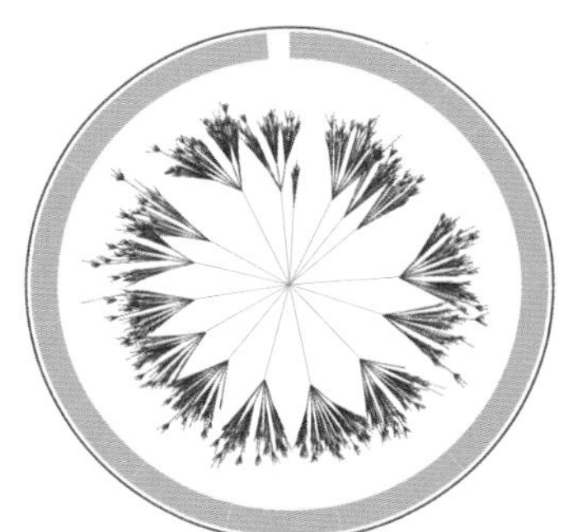

Chapters

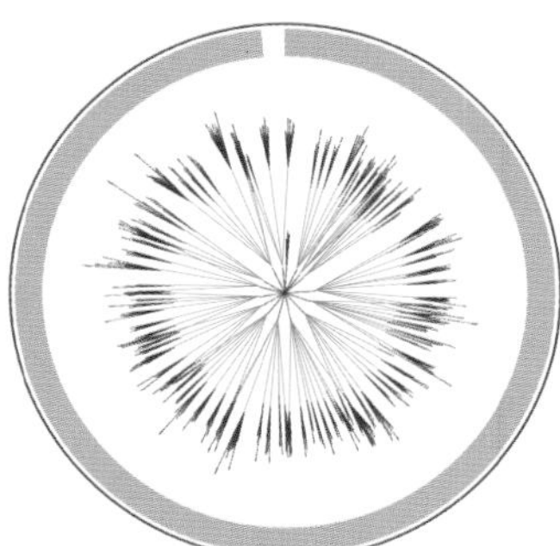

Subchapters

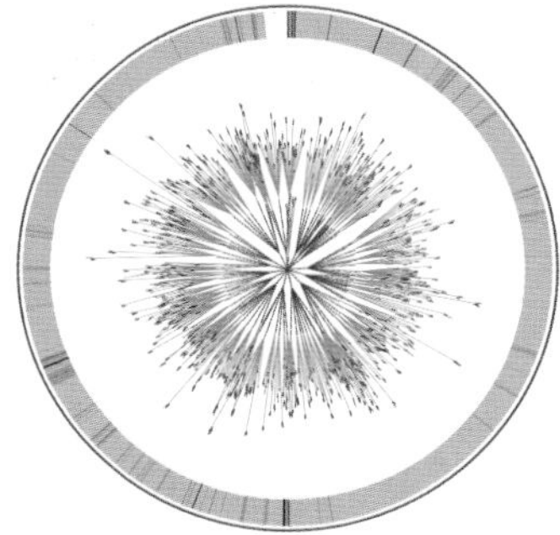

Paragraphs

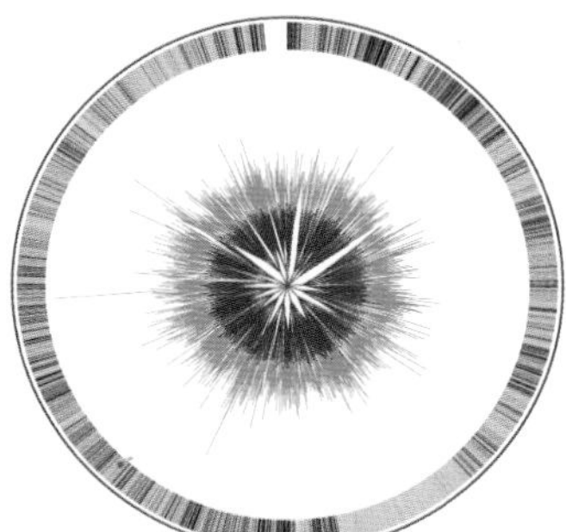

Sentences

(En)tangled Word Bank

Greg McInerny & Stefanie Posavec

Everyone Ever in the World

"Everyone Ever in the World" explores the recorded history of humankind: how many people in total have been born and how many of them were killed in wars? The total number of people ever born is an estimated 77.6 billion and is represented as the total poster area.

The total number of people killed in conflicts is approximately 969 million or ca. 1.25 % of all the people ever to have lived. That number is represented by the die-cut circle in the centre. Around the centre, a time scale lists all recorded conflicts from 3200 BC to 2009 AD. The piece thus represents a rich set of historical data and discusses how militant human history actually is.

„Everyone Ever in the World“ beschäftigt sich mit der dokumentierten Geschichte der Menschheit: Wie viele Menschen wurden insgesamt geboren und wie viele davon in einem Krieg getötet? Die Gesamtzahl der jemals Geborenen wird auf 77,6 Milliarden geschätzt; diese Zahl wird dargestellt als Gesamtfläche des Plakats.

Die Gesamtzahl der Menschen, die in Konflikten zu Tode kamen, beläuft sich auf rund 969 Millionen bzw. etwa 1,25 % aller Menschen, die je gelebt haben. Diese Zahl wird durch den ausgestanzten Kreis in der Mitte dargestellt. Um diesen Mittelpunkt herum sind auf einer Zeitskala alle bekannten Konflikte zwischen 3200 v. Chr. und 2009 n. Chr. angeordnet. Die Grafik versammelt eine Fülle historischer Daten und stellt zur Diskussion, wie stark die Menschheitsgeschichte tatsächlich von Kriegen geprägt ist.

« Everyone Ever in the World » (Tous ceux qui ont existé dans le monde) explore les archives de l'humanité : combien de personnes au total sont nées, et combien ont été tuées par la guerre ? Le nombre total de personnes nées dans le monde est estimé à 77,6 milliards, et est représenté par toute la surface de l'affiche.

Le nombre total de personnes tuées lors de conflits est d'environ 969 millions, soit environ 1,25 % de toutes les personnes qui ont vécu. Ce chiffre est représenté par le cercle découpé au centre. Autour du centre, une échelle temporelle répertorie tous les conflits connus de 3200 av. J.-C. à 2009 de notre ère. Cette image représente donc un corpus de données très riche et examine le poids de la guerre dans l'histoire de l'humanité.

Project Info: Print, 2010, UK
Design: Peter Crnokrak (The Luxury of Protest)
Additional Info: Silkscreen print with transparent ink on matte plastic
Awards: NSF Science Visualization 2011

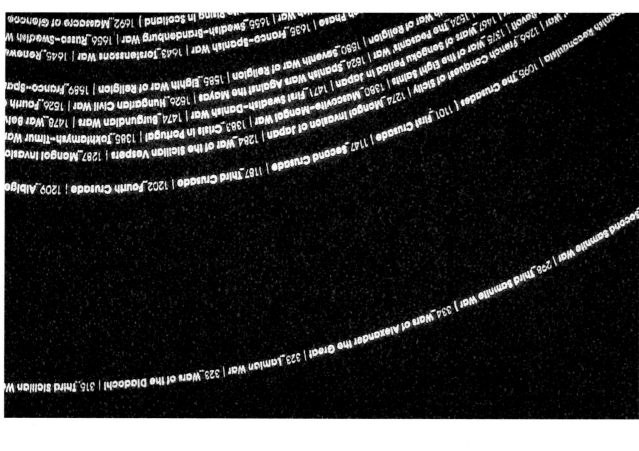

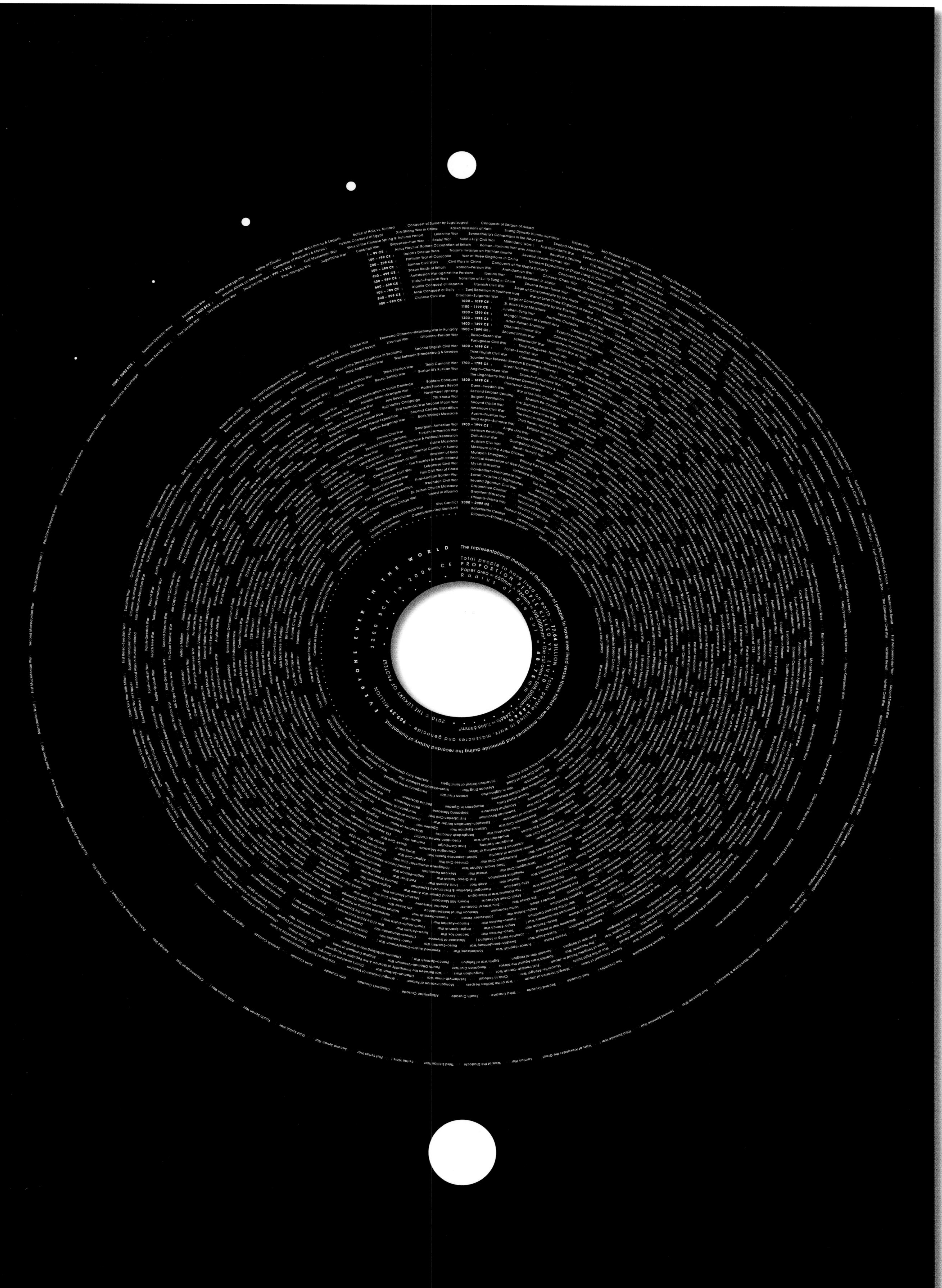
EVERYONE EVER IN THE WORLD
3200 BCE to 2009 CE
The representational measure of the number of people to have ever lived versus those killed in wars, massacres and genocide during the recorded history of humankind

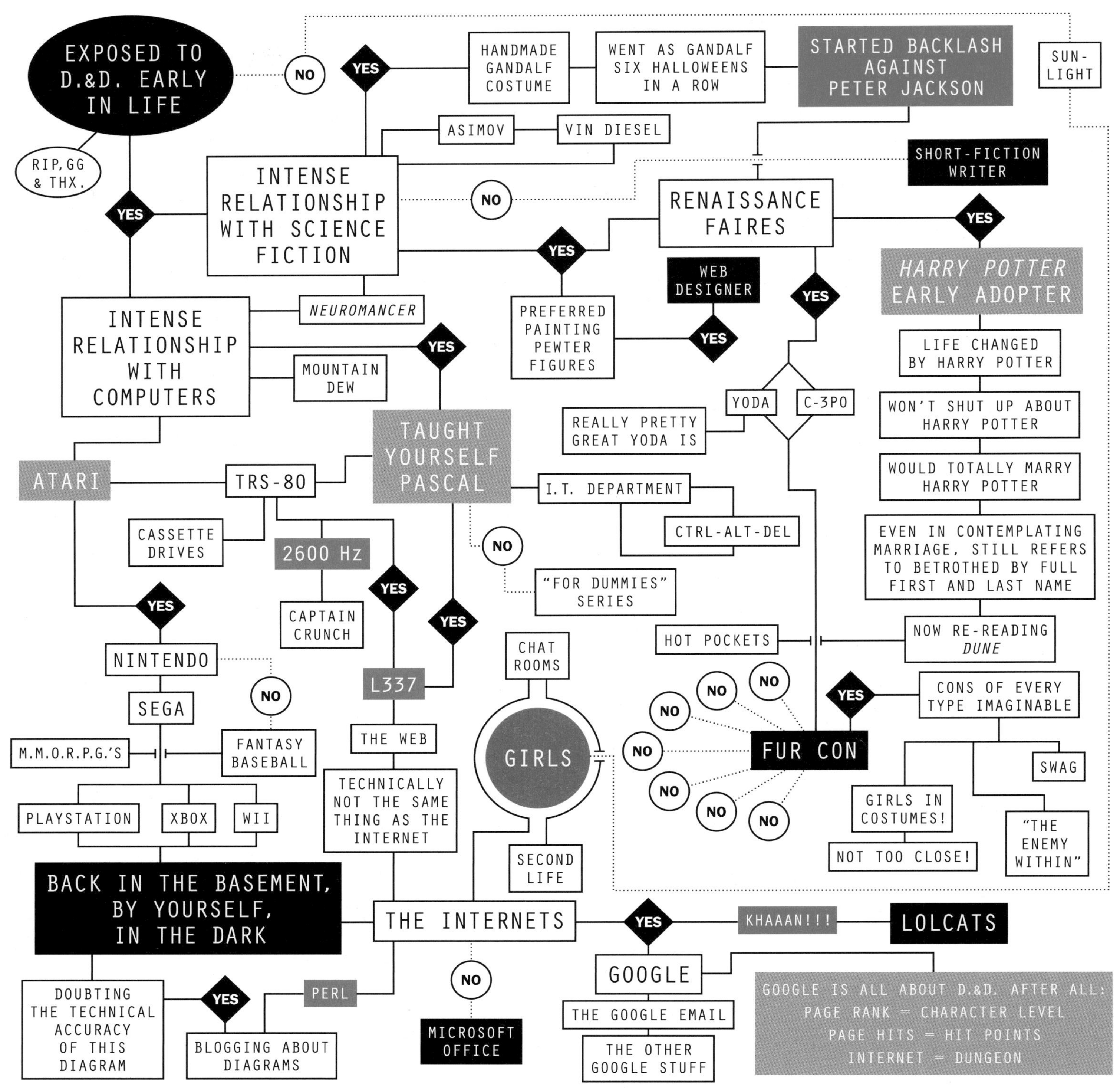

Exposed to Dungeons & Dragons Early in Life

This is a tribute to Gary Gygax, the co-creator of the role-playing game *Dungeons and Dragons* in 1974. With this famous table-top game, a fantasy world was created in which players actually assumed their characters' roles instead of just commanding faceless warriors.

On the occasion of Gygax's death in 2008, Sam Potts created this graphic as a satirical but loving tribute to the world of fantasy-loving, geeky teenagers. Using the model of a flow chart, it plots the possible succession of life experiences following a boy's early exposure to the game. Admittedly, data input for this piece was partly derived from Potts' own life experience.

Dies ist eine Hommage an Gary Gygax, den Miterfinder des Rollenspiels *Dungeons and Dragons* (1974). Mit diesem berühmten Spiel schuf Gygax eine Fantasiewelt, in der die Spieler nicht nur gesichtslose Krieger befehligen, sondern in die Rolle ihrer Figur schlüpfen.

2008 entwarf Sam Potts diese Grafik anlässlich des Todes von Gygax als satirische, aber liebevolle Hommage an die Welt fantasieverliebter Teenager und Geeks. In einem Prozessdiagramm zeichnet sie eine denkbare Abfolge von Lebenserfahrungen für einen Jungen auf, der sehr jung damit begann, *Dungeons and Dragons* zu spielen. Für die dargestellten „Daten" griff Potts, wie er selbst zugab, auch auf eigene Erlebnisse zurück.

Ceci est un hommage à Gary Gygax, l'un des créateurs du jeu de rôle *Donjons et Dragons* apparu en 1974. Ce jeu célèbre a donné vie à un monde imaginaire où les participants jouaient le rôle de leur personnage au lieu de se contenter de commander des guerriers sans visage.

À l'occasion du décès de Gygax en 2008, Sam Potts a créé ce diagramme pour rendre un hommage satirique mais affectueux au monde des adolescents passionnés de *fantasy*. Sur le modèle d'un diagramme de processus, il imagine différents parcours pour un garçon exposé au jeu tôt dans sa vie. Potts reconnaît qu'il s'est inspiré en partie de sa propre vie.

Project Info: "Geek Love", *The New York Times*, newspaper article, 2008, USA
Design: Sam Potts
Art Direction: Brian Rea
Article: Adam Rogers

Food Assistance

The food stamp program is a US federal government program to help low-income people buy food. This graphic looks at the increasing need for food stamps in the period from autumn 2008 to spring 2009.

The consecutive months are shown in lines, with time running top down. Each line works as a bar to show the number of people who are using food stamps, showing the gradual increase towards the bottom. The bars themselves use small food icons to illustrate their subject.

Das Food Stamp Program ist ein staatliches Programm in Amerika, das Einkommensschwache beim Kauf von Lebensmitteln unterstützt. Diese Grafik beleuchtet die steigende Nachfrage nach Lebensmittelmarken in der Zeit von Herbst 2008 bis Frühjahr 2009.

Die einzelnen Monate werden jeweils als Zeile dargestellt, die Zeitleiste verläuft von oben nach unten. Jede Zeile dient zudem als Balken eines Diagramms und zeigt die Anzahl der Menschen, die Lebensmittelmarken verwenden; das Diagramm zeigt nach unten hin einen deutlichen Anstieg. Die Balken selbst bestehen aus kleinen Icons, die das Thema illustrieren.

Le programme de coupons alimentaires est une initiative du gouvernement fédéral américain qui aide les personnes ayant de faibles revenus à acheter de la nourriture. Ce graphique examine la croissance des besoins en coupons alimentaires de l'automne 2008 au printemps 2009.

Chaque mois est une ligne, et l'échelle temporelle va de haut en bas. Chaque ligne est une barre qui représente le nombre de personnes qui ont recours aux coupons alimentaires, et l'ensemble montre une augmentation graduelle vers le bas de la page. Les barres sont constituées de petites icônes représentant des aliments pour illustrer le sujet du graphique.

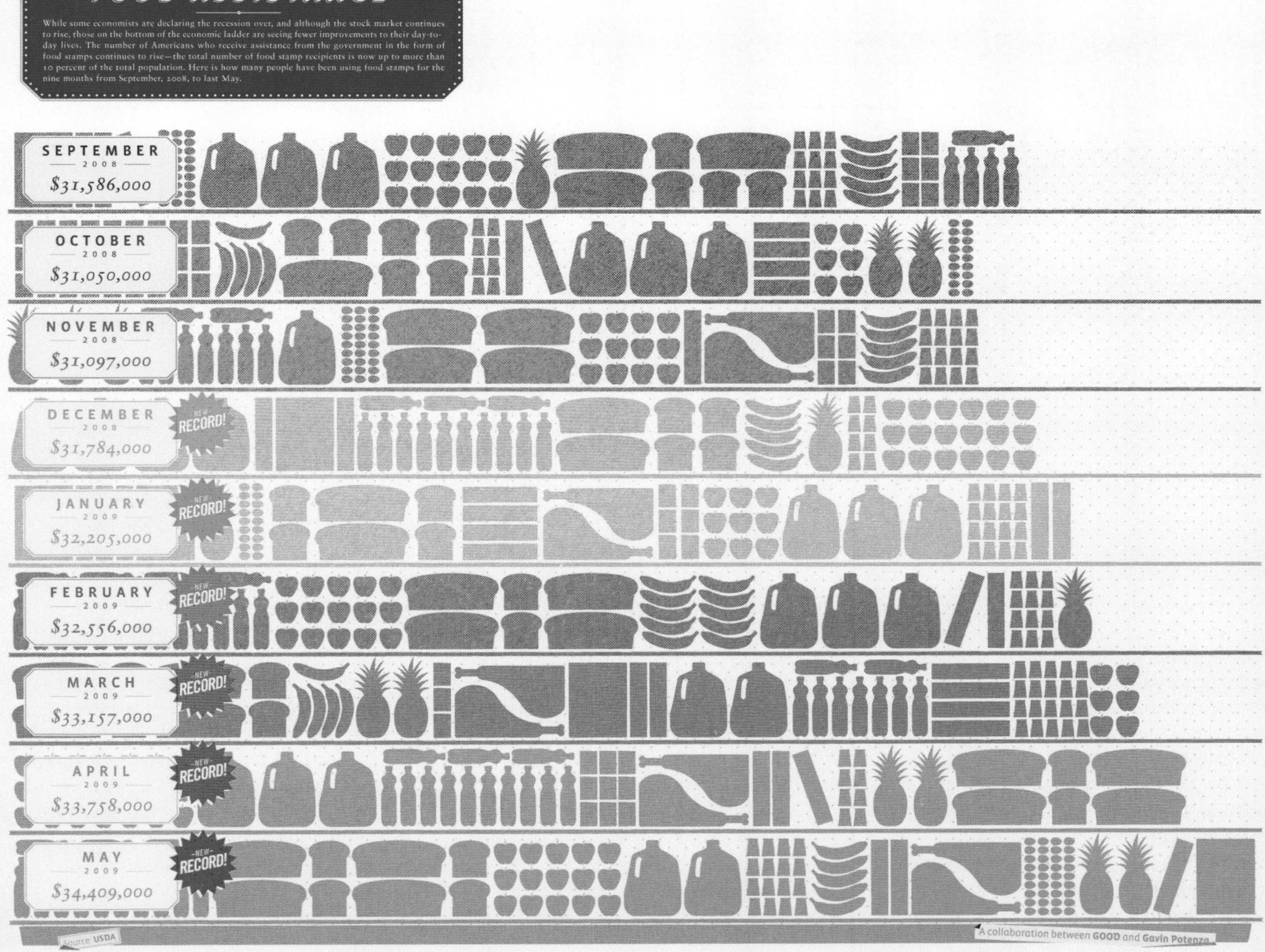

Project Info: "The Growth of Food Stamps", *GOOD*, website, 2009, USA
Data Source: USDA
Design: Gavin Potenza
Art Direction: Morgan Clendaniel

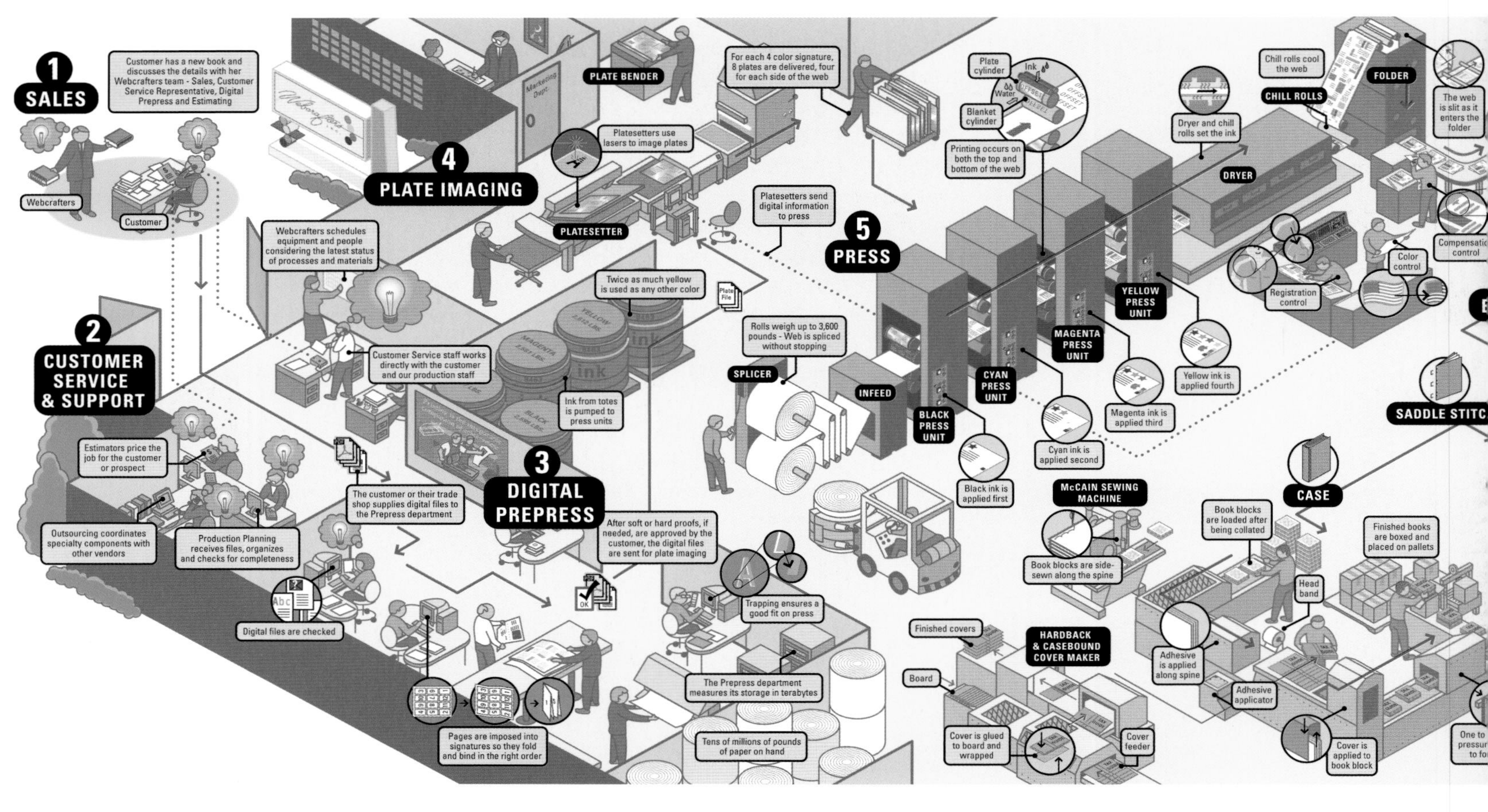

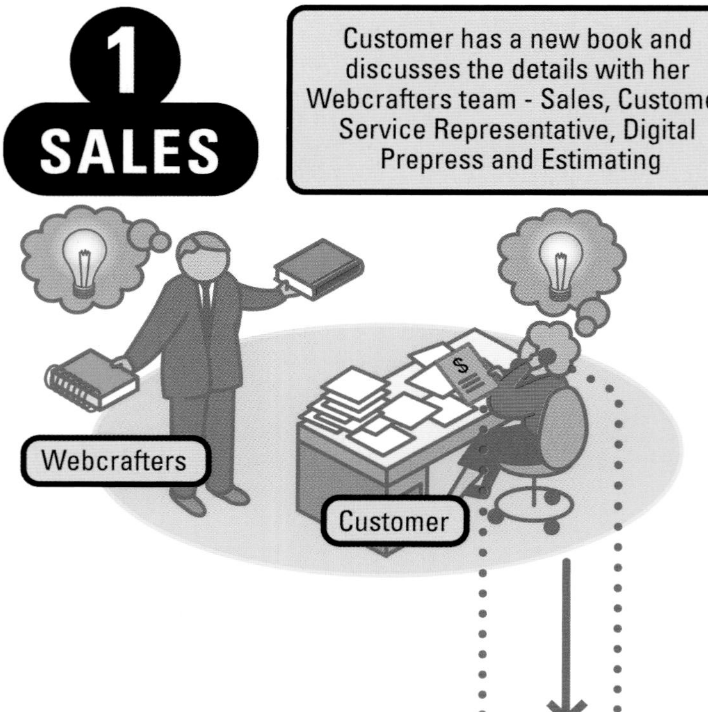

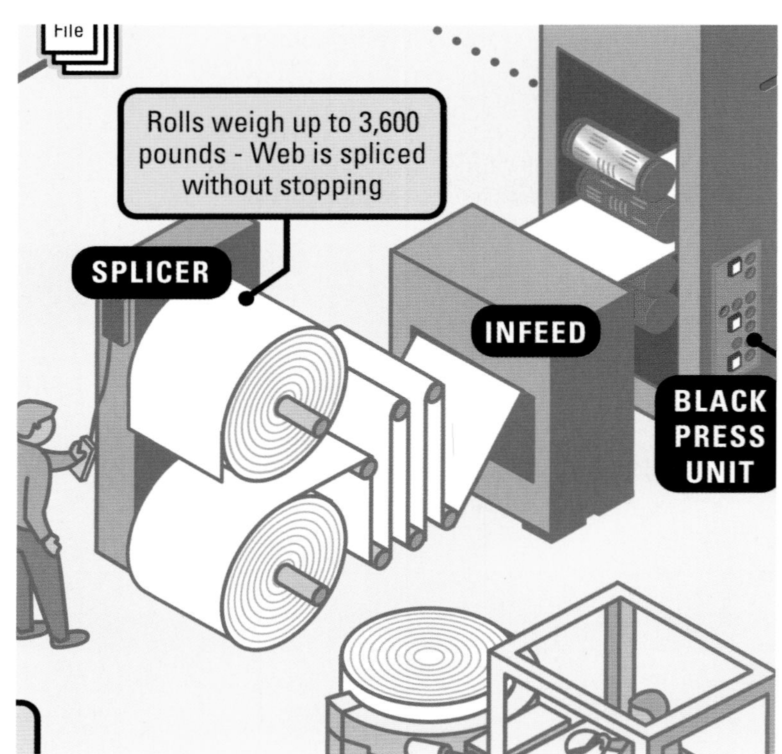

How Books are Made

When tasked to visualise what it takes to produce a book, Funnel Inc. developed a wide panorama that is, at first sight, a model of a printers' factory. Each step in the making of a book is allocated to a specific work-station within the factory, with little tags explaining what is going on.

The starting point is in the top-left corner, and the production process unfolds in a general reading direction towards the lower right. With this piece, designer Lin Wilson employed a somewhat cinematic approach – mapping a developing process on to a physical space which demands to be traversed in order to access the information.

Um zu visualisieren, was alles zur Herstellung eines Buches nötig ist, entwarf Funnel Inc. dieses Panorama, das auf den ersten Blick wie das Modell einer Druckerei aussieht. Jeder Schritt bei der Buchherstellung ist einer bestimmten „Werkstatt" im Unternehmen zugeordnet, kleine Kästen erläutern, was dort vor sich geht.

Angefangen von oben links, folgt der Herstellungsablauf der allgemeinen Leserichtung nach unten rechts. Mit dieser Grafik verfolgte Lin Wilson einen nahezu filmischen Ansatz – nämlich, einen Entwicklungsprozess auf einen geografischen Raum zu übertragen. Dieser Raum muss vom Betrachter durchquert werden, um die Informationen für sich zu erschließen.

Funnel Inc. s'est vu confier la mission de représenter la production d'un livre, et a pour ce faire créé un large panorama qui ressemble à la maquette d'une imprimerie. Chaque étape de la fabrication d'un livre est affectée à une station de travail de l'usine, et des petites étiquettes indiquent l'activité réalisée.

Le point de départ est dans le coin supérieur gauche, et le processus de production suit approximativement le sens habituel de la lecture, vers le coin inférieur droit. La graphiste, Lin Wilson, a adopté une démarche proche du film : le processus est transposé dans un espace physique, que l'on doit parcourir pour accéder à l'information.

Project Info: Webcrafters, poster, 2005, USA
Design: Lin Wilson (Funnel Incorporated)

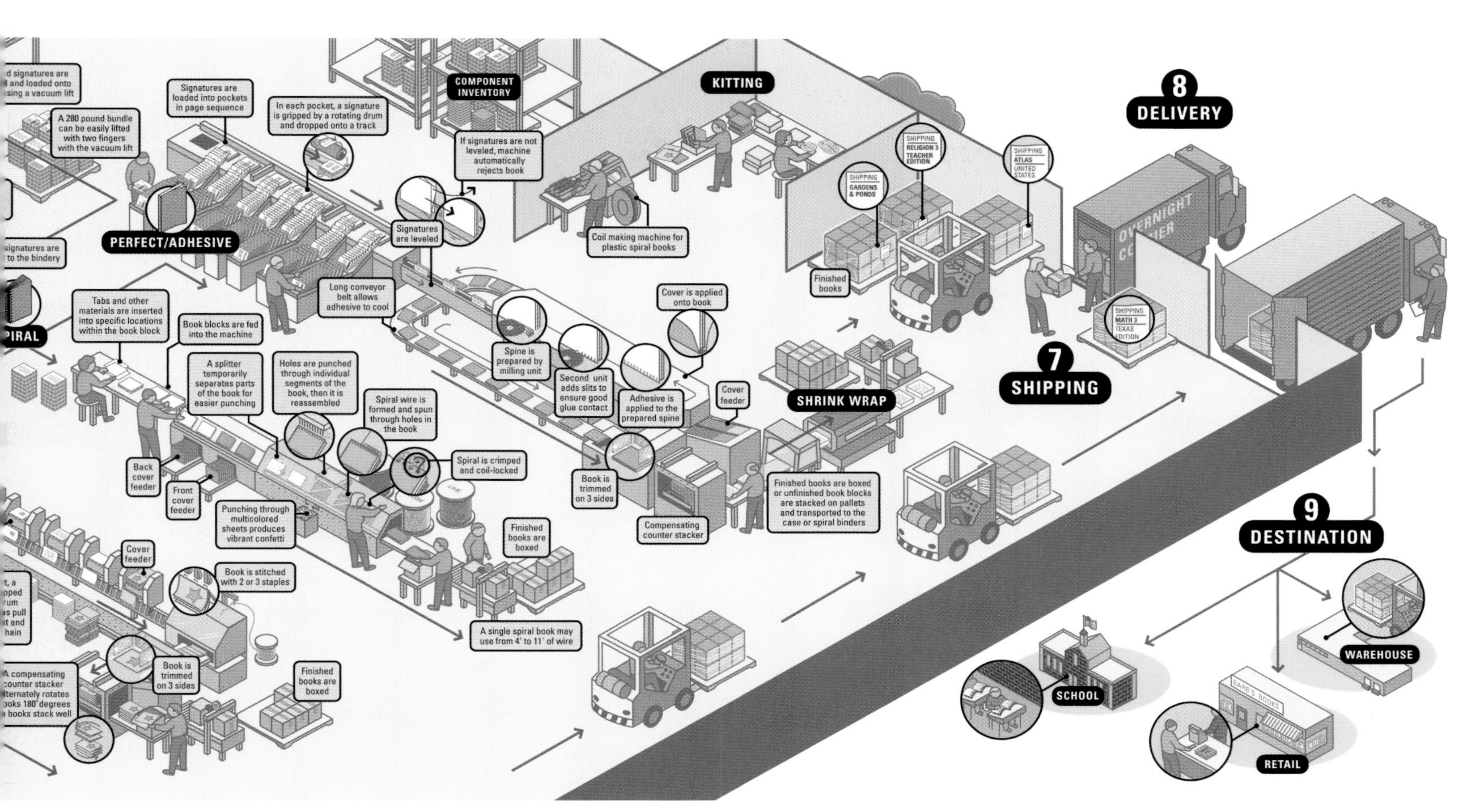
COMPONENT INVENTORY
KITTING
8 DELIVERY
Signatures are loaded into pockets in page sequence
In each pocket, a signature is gripped by a rotating drum and dropped onto a track
A 280 pound bundle can be easily lifted with two fingers with the vacuum lift
If signatures are not leveled, machine automatically rejects book
PERFECT/ADHESIVE
Signatures are leveled
Coil making machine for plastic spiral books
SHIPPING GARDENS & PONDS
SHIPPING RELIGION 3 TEACHER EDITION
SHIPPING ATLAS UNITED STATES
Long conveyor belt allows adhesive to cool
Tabs and other materials are inserted into specific locations within the book block
Book blocks are fed into the machine
Cover is applied onto book
Finished books
SHIPPING MATH 3 TEXAS EDITION
7 SHIPPING
Spine is prepared by milling unit
A splitter temporarily separates parts of the book for easier punching
Holes are punched through individual segments of the book, then it is reassembled
Second unit adds slits to ensure good glue contact
Adhesive is applied to the prepared spine
Cover feeder
SHRINK WRAP
Spiral wire is formed and spun through holes in the book
Spiral is crimped and coil-locked
Back cover feeder
Front cover feeder
Punching through multicolored sheets produces vibrant confetti
Book is trimmed on 3 sides
Finished books are boxed
Compensating counter stacker
Finished books are boxed or unfinished book blocks are stacked on pallets and transported to the case or spiral binders
9 DESTINATION
Cover feeder
Book is stitched with 2 or 3 staples
A single spiral book may use from 4' to 11' of wire
Book is trimmed on 3 sides
Finished books are boxed
WAREHOUSE
SCHOOL
RETAIL

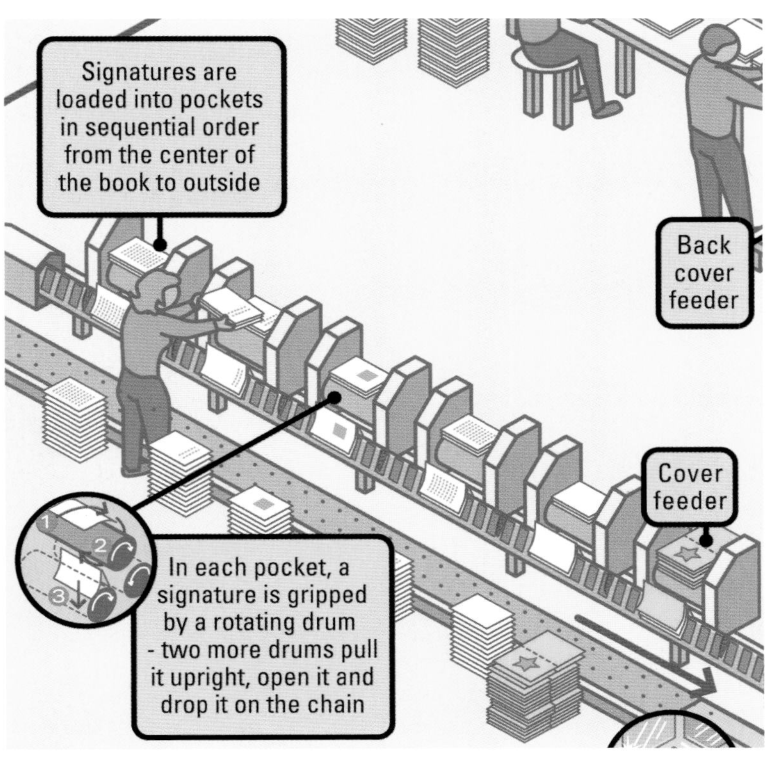
Signatures are loaded into pockets in sequential order from the center of the book to outside
Back cover feeder
Cover feeder
In each pocket, a signature is gripped by a rotating drum - two more drums pull it upright, open it and drop it on the chain

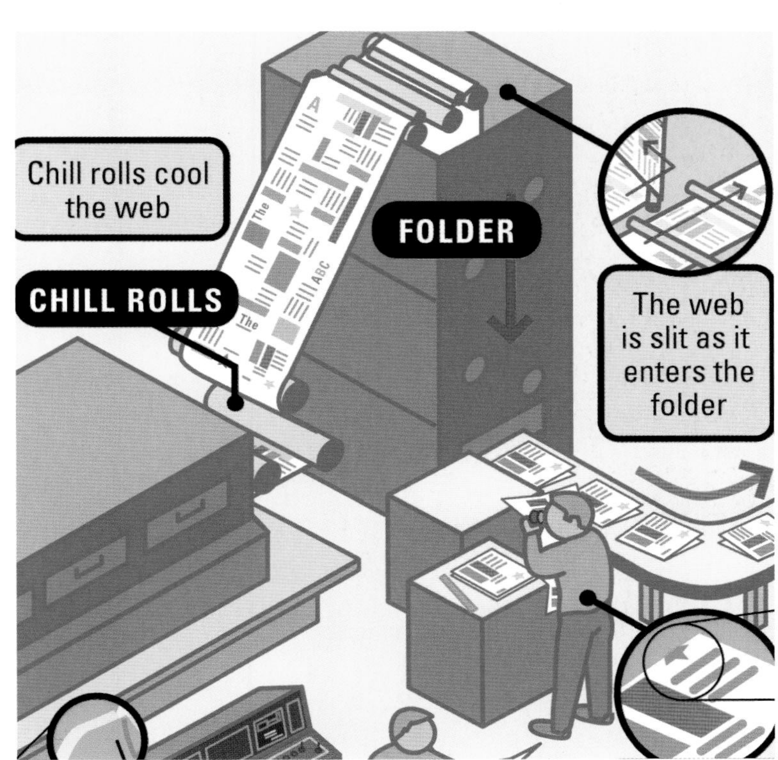
Chill rolls cool the web
FOLDER
CHILL ROLLS
The web is slit as it enters the folder

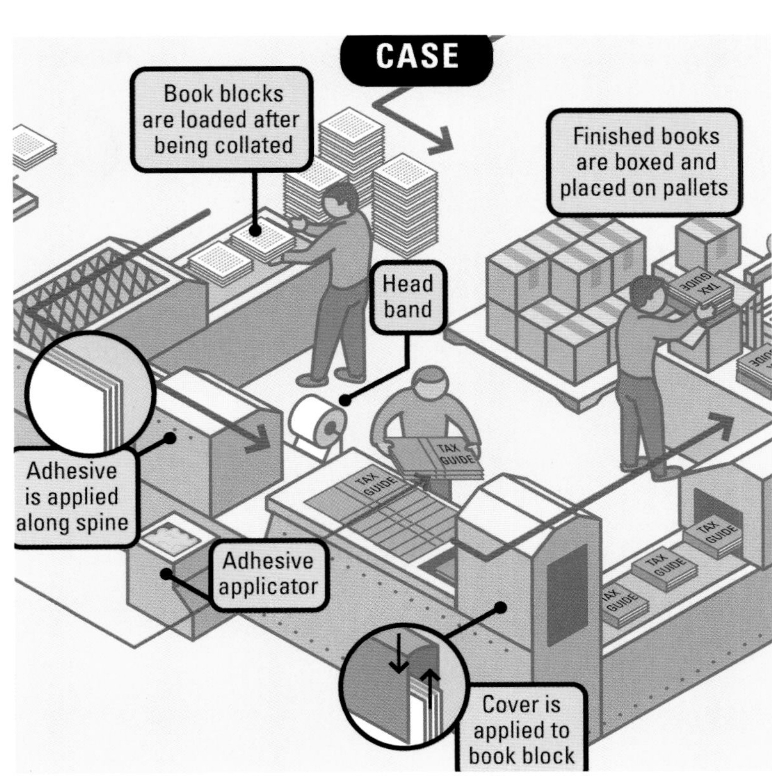
CASE
Book blocks are loaded after being collated
Finished books are boxed and placed on pallets
Head band
Adhesive is applied along spine
Adhesive applicator
Cover is applied to book block

SHIPPING
MATH 3
TEXAS
EDITION
7
SHIPPING

Good Night and Tough Luck

In his blog *Abstract City* for the *New York Times*, German illustrator Christoph Niemann regularly comments on the mysteries of everyday urban life, developing a visual language for each individual series of images. In this series dating from September 2009, he uses hand-painted charts and infographics to explain the complications of a good night's sleep.

The Sleep Agony Chart and its sibling, the Sleep Bliss Chart, mimic the classic format of a diagrammatic time series. The mosquito piece, in contrast, uses a hand-painted process chart to show the annoyance these little suckers are capable of causing on summer nights.

In seinem Blog *Abstract City* für die *New York Times* berichtet der deutsche Illustrator Christoph Niemann regelmäßig über die Rätsel des Großstadtalltags. Dabei entwickelt er für jede Bildserie eine eigene visuelle Sprache. In dieser Ausgabe vom September 2009 verwendete er handgemalte Diagramme und Infografiken, um zu erörtern, was ihn an einem tiefen Nachtschlaf hindert.

Das „Sleep Agony Chart" (dt. etwa „Diagramm eines gequälten Schlafs") und sein Gegenstück, das „Sleep Bliss Chart" (dt. etwa „Diagramm des glückseligen Schlafs") ahmen das klassische Zeitreihen-Diagramm nach. Die Mücken-Grafik hingegen ist ein handgemaltes Prozessdiagramm. Es zeigt, welche Belästigung die kleinen Sauger in Sommernächten sein können.

Dans son blog *Abstract City* pour le *New York Times*, l'illustrateur allemand Christoph Niemann parle souvent des mystères de la vie quotidienne dans les villes, et crée un langage visuel particulier pour chaque série d'images. Dans cette série qui date du septembre 2009, il utilise des graphiques et infographies peints à la main pour expliquer ses difficultés à obtenir une bonne nuit de sommeil.

Le graphique « Sleep Agony » et son pendant « Sleep Bliss » imitent le format d'une série temporelle classique. En revanche, pour le moustique il utilise un diagramme de processus peint à la main afin de montrer l'agacement que ces suceurs de sang peuvent causer pendant les nuits d'été.

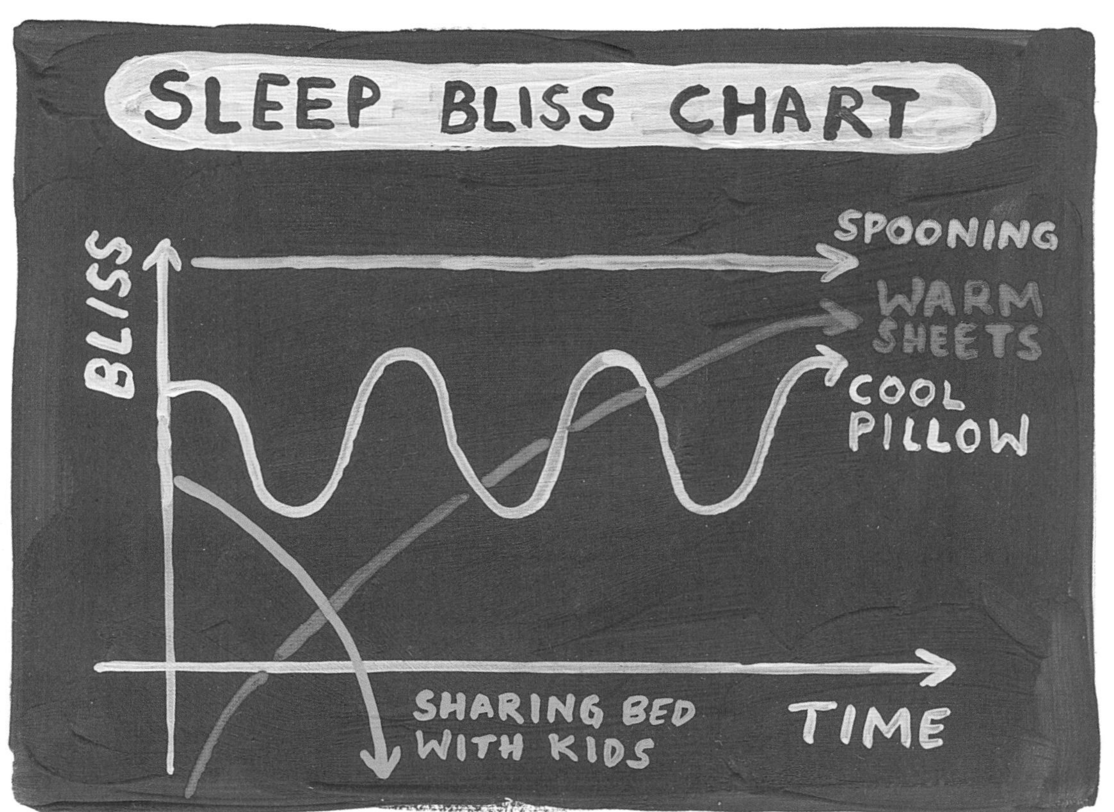

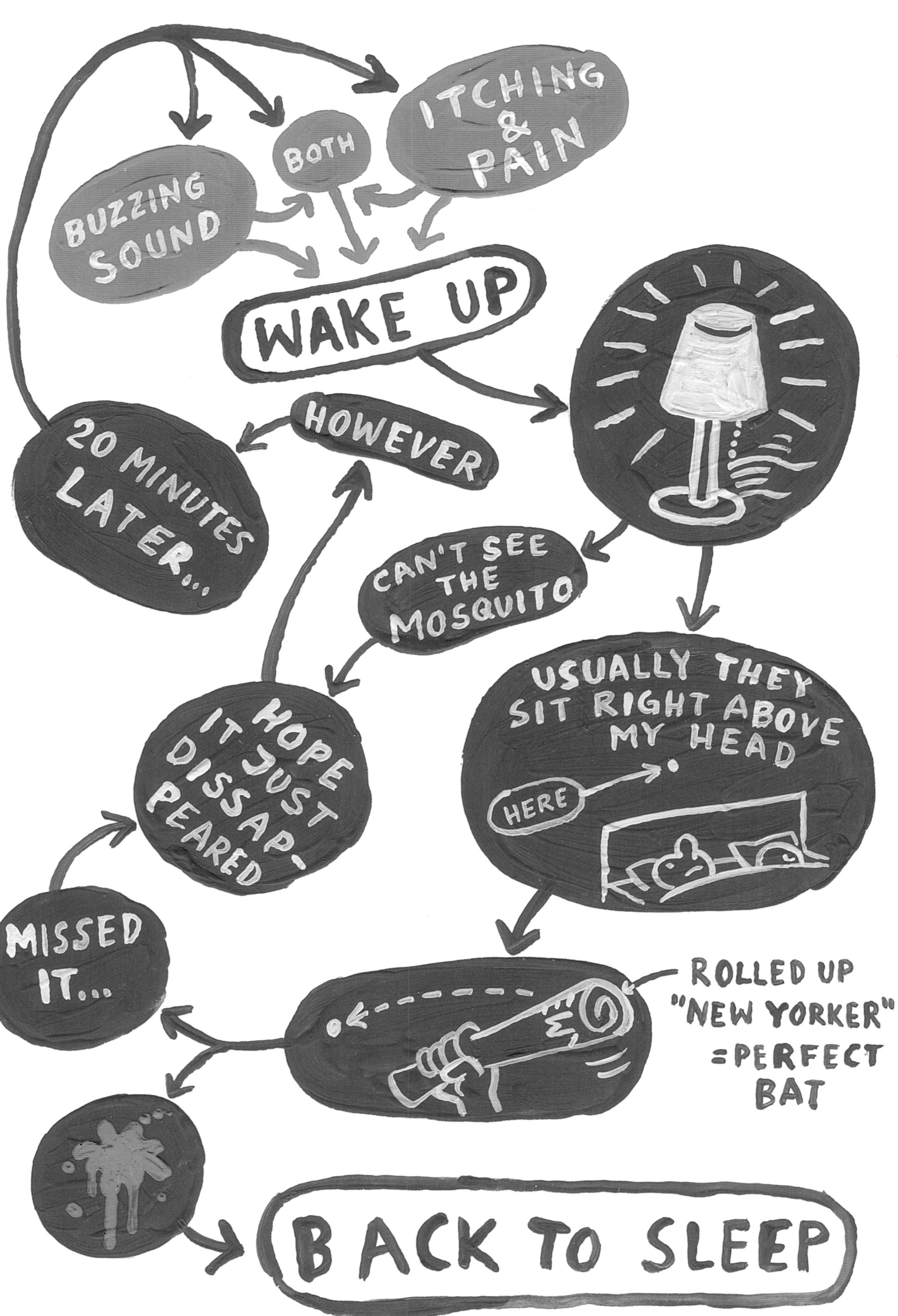

Project Info: *The New York Times*, blog, 2009, USA
Design: Christoph Niemann

Guess Who? Character Identification Chart

This chart was inspired by "Guess Who?", a game for two players common in Great Britain and the United States during the 1980s. The game provided a range of characters, and players had to guess their opponent's current character by asking questions. By a process of elimination, players could eventually make a guess at which character was on their opponent's card.

Beginning in the centre, the chart gives two starting points concerning the character's eyes. Further decisions are then made from there, with the questions leading up to the final character identification. Designed like a flow chart to provide help with complex decision processes, this piece is a happy homage to a childhood game.

Dieses Diagramm ist inspiriert von „Guess Who?", einemSpiel für zwei, das in den 1980er-Jahren in Großbritannien und den Vereinigten Staaten sehr beliebt war. Im Spiel gab es eine Reihe von Figuren, und ein Spieler musste durch geschicktes Fragen die Figur seines Gegners herausfinden. Durch ein Ausschlussverfahren konnte er schließlich erraten, welche Figur auf der Karte seines Gegenspielers abgebildet war.

Der Ausgangspunkt des Diagramms liegt in der Mitte, wo sich zwei erste Anhaltspunkte auf die Augen der Figur beziehen. Von da aus werden weitere Entscheidungen getroffen, bis die Fragen schließlich zur Identifizierung der Figur führen. Die Grafik ist als Ablaufdiagramm gestaltet, das bei komplexen Entscheidungen Hilfe bietet, und ist eine fröhliche Hommage an ein Spiel aus Kindheitstagen.

Ce schéma s'inspire de « Qui est-ce ? », un jeu qui se joue à deux joueurs, populaire aux États-Unis et en Grande-Bretagne dans les années 1980. Les joueurs devaient deviner lequel des personnages était celui de leur adversaire en posant des questions. Par élimination, les joueurs accumulaient des informations pour finalement deviner le personnage qui se trouvait sur la carte de l'adversaire.

Le point de départ du schéma se trouve au centre, et concerne les yeux du personnage. Puis d'autres questions sont posées jusqu'à identifier le personnage. Conçue comme un diagramme d'aide à la prise de décisions complexes, cette œuvre est un hommage souriant à un jeu d'enfance.

Project Info: Poster, 2009, UK
Design: Craig Ward (Words are Pictures)

"Navigating Into A New Night"

Score for Sculptor and Musician

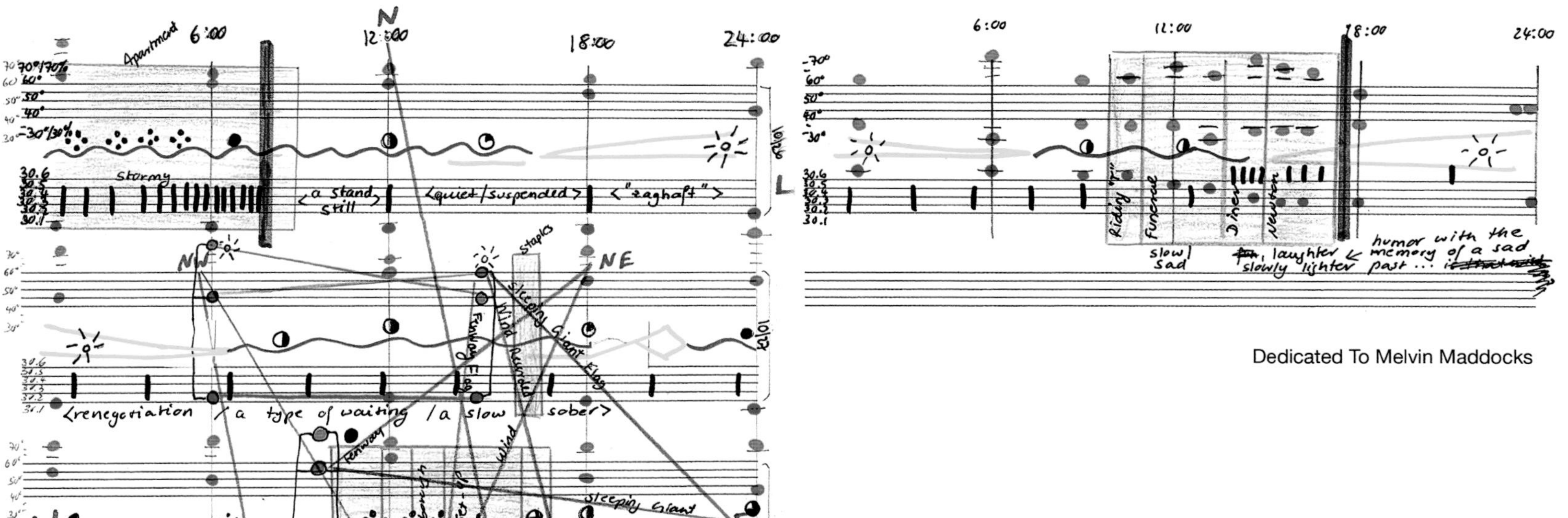

Dedicated To Melvin Maddocks

Gulf of Maine – Sculptural Music Scores

Using a combination of basket-weaving techniques and information graphics, Boston-based artist Nathalie Miebach has transformed scientific data into representational sculptures. "Gulf of Maine" is a large body of work based on detailed weather data about storms, temperatures, winds or barometric pressure in the region. Information relating to marine life, such as whale sightings, was also taken into consideration.

In the series shown here, Miebach introduced an additional dimension: she recorded the data as scores before turning them into sculptures. Besides weather data, these scores also recorded personal memories, which added to the perception of the weather. The results are playable music scores as well as the blueprint for constructing a sculpture.

Mit einer Mischung aus der Korbflechttechnik und Informationsgrafik setzt die Bostoner Künstlerin Nathalie Miebach Forschungsdaten in räumliche Skulpturen um. „Gulf of Maine" ist ein großer Werkkorpus, der auf detaillierten Wetterdaten zu Stürmen, Temperaturen, Winden und Luftdruck in der Region basiert. Sie bezog auch Daten über Meereslebewesen mit ein, wie etwa die Häufung von Fischen oder das Auftauchen von Walen.

Bei dieser Serie baute Miebach eine zusätzliche Dimension ein: Sie zeichnete die Daten als Partituren auf, ehe sie sie zu Skulpturen verwandelte. Neben Wet-terdaten beinhalten diese Partituren auch persönliche Erinnerungen, die die Wahrnehmung des Wetters ergänzen. Das Ergebnis ist sowohl ein spielbares Musikstück als auch ein Entwurf für die Konstruktion einer Skulptur.

À l'aide d'une combinaison de techniques de tressage de panier et d'infographie, Nathalie Miebach, une artiste de Boston, a transformé des données scientifiques en sculptures représentationnelles. « Gulf of Maine » est une grande série basée sur des données météorologiques détaillées sur les orages, la température, le vent et la pression barométrique dans la région. Des informations sur la vie marine, comme le nombre de fois que des baleines ont été aperçues, ont également été prises en compte.

Dans la série présentée ici, Miebach a ajouté une dimension supplémentaire : elle a consigné les données sous forme de partitions avant de les transformer en sculptures. Outre les données météorologiques, ces partitions reprennent également des souvenirs personnels, qui viennent enrichir la perception du climat. Le résultat est une partition musicale qui peut être jouée, mais fait également office de plan de construction pour une sculpture.

Project Info: Series of sculptures and drawings, 2010–2011, USA
Data Source: Gulf of Maine Observation; National Oceanic Atmospheric Administration buoys; US Naval Observatory; Wunderground.com et al.
Artist: Nathalie Miebach
Awards: Visual Arts Sea Grant, Rhode Island

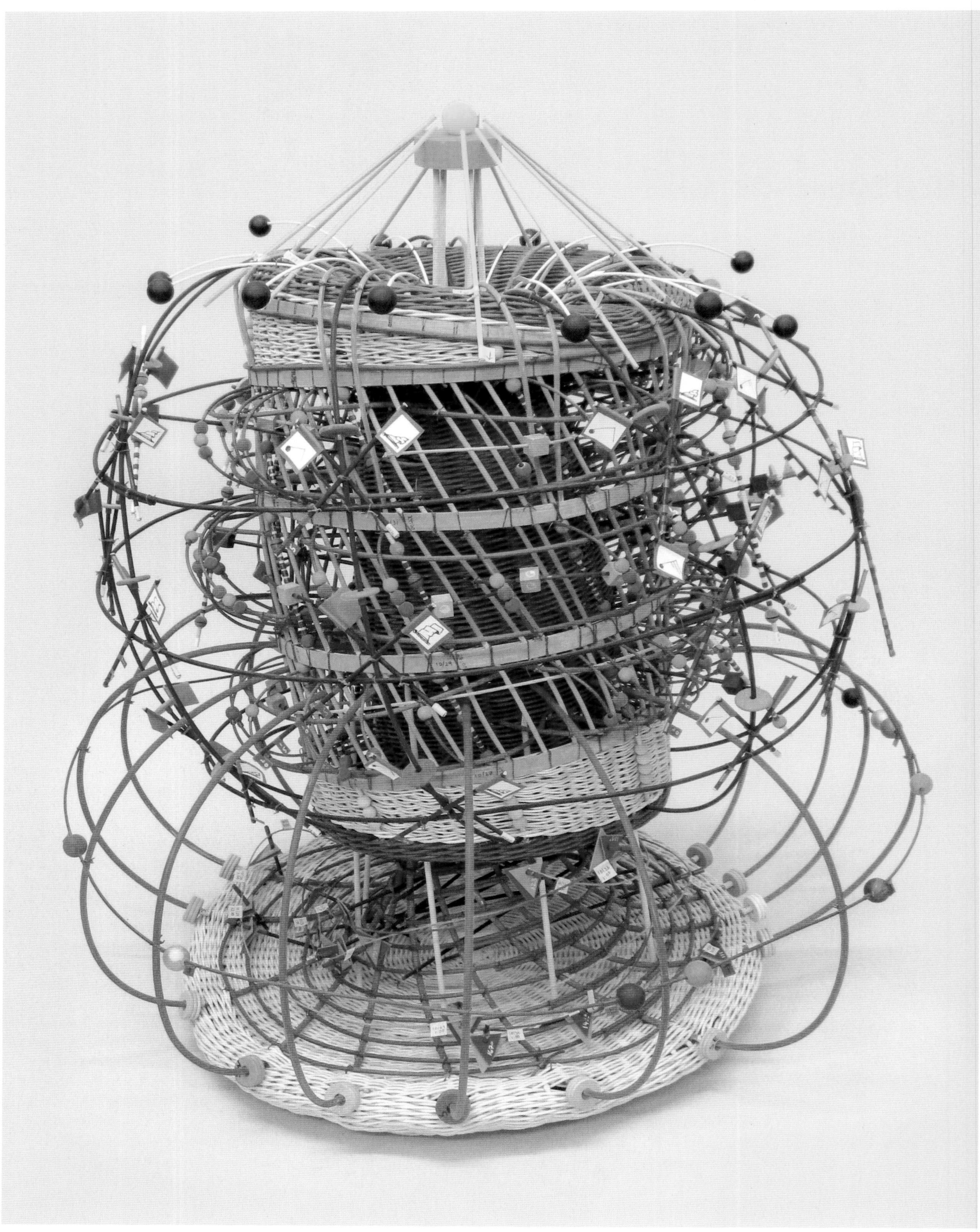

Navigating Into a New Night (above and previous page) translates weather data collected in Boston during autumn 2008. Interwoven with this are events from the artist's life (in pink) that dictate the mood of the musical interpretation. *Hurricane Noel* (right and next spread) presents a time series of the passing of a hurricane through the Gulf of Maine in 2007.

Navigating Into a New Night (oben und vorige Seite) wandelt Wetterdaten um, die im Herbst 2008 in Boston gesammelt wurden. Sie wurden mit Ereignissen aus dem Leben der Künstlerin verwoben (in Rosa), die eine musikalische Lesart vorgeben. *Hurricane Noel* (rechts und folgende Seite) präsentiert eine Zeitreihe, die den Durchzug eines Wirbelsturms durch den Golf von Maine 2007 wiedergibt.

Navigating Into a New Night (en haut et page précédente) traduit les données météorologiques de Boston au cours de l'automne 2008. Elles sont assorties d'événements de la vie de l'artiste (en rose) qui donnent le ton de l'interprétation musicale. *Hurricane Noel* (à droite et page suivante) présente une chronologie du passage d'un ouragan dans le golfe du Maine en 2007.

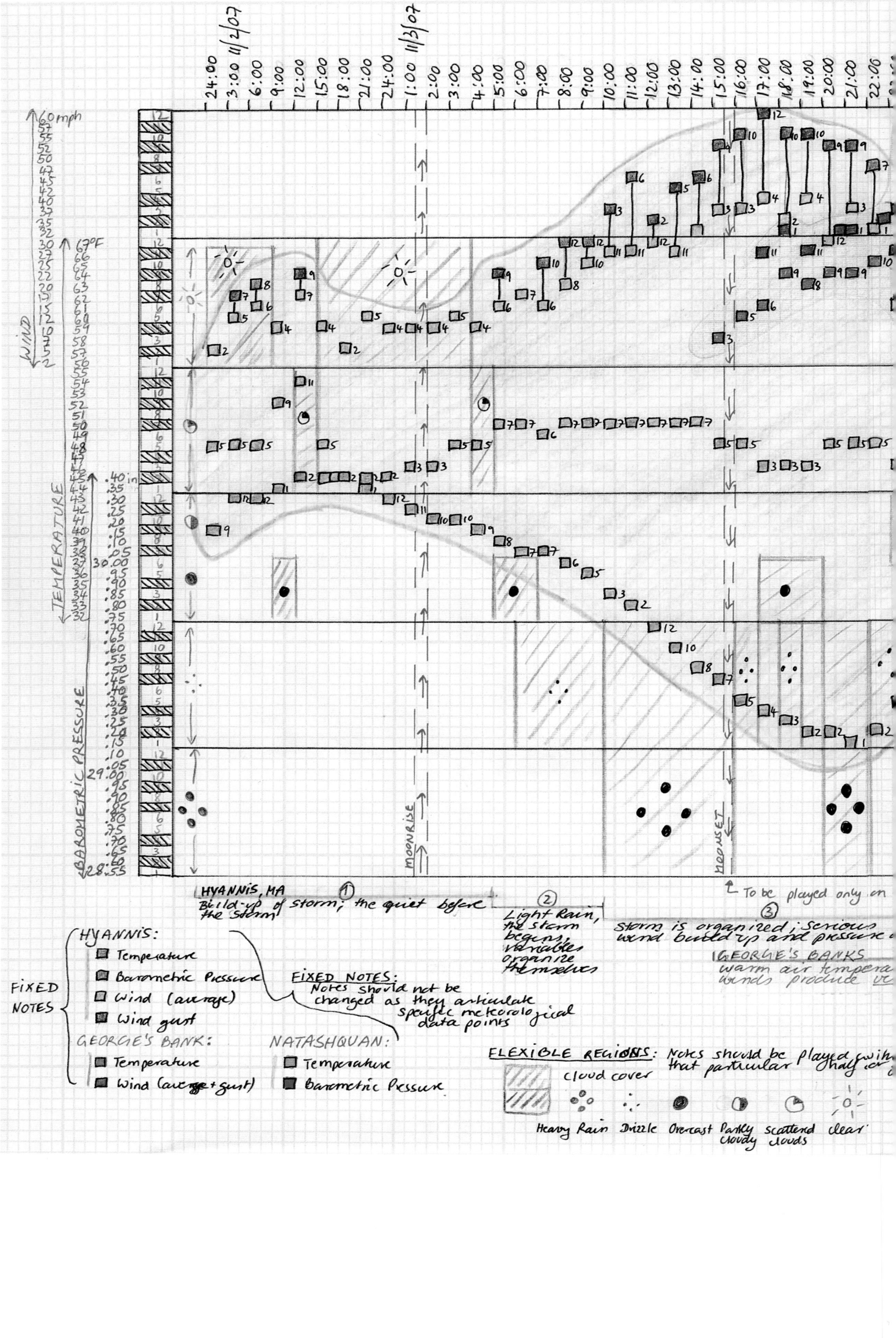

24:00 3:00 11/2/07 6:00 9:00 12:00 15:00 18:00 21:00 24:00 1:00 11/3/07 2:00 3:00 4:00 5:00 6:00 7:00 8:00 9:00 10:00 11:00 12:00 13:00 14:00 15:00 16:00 17:00 18:00 19:00 20:00 21:00 22:00

WIND: 60 mph 57 55 52 50 47 45 42 40 37 35 32 30 27 25 22 20 17 15 12 10 7 5 2

TEMPERATURE: 67°F 66 65 64 63 62 61 60 59 58 57 56 55 54 53 52 51 50 49 48 47 46 45 44 43 42 41 40 39 38 37 36 35 34 33 32

BAROMETRIC PRESSURE: .40 in .35 .30 .25 .20 .15 .10 .05 30.00 .95 .90 .85 .80 .75 .70 .65 .60 .55 .50 .45 .40 .35 .30 .25 .20 .15 .10 .05 29.00 .95 .90 .85 .80 .75 .70 .65 .60 28.55

MOONRISE

MOONSET

HYANNIS, MA ①
Build-up of storm; the quiet before the storm

② Light Rain, the storm begins, variables organize themselves

③ Storm is organized; serious wind build up and pressure ...

↑ To be played only on ...

GEORGE'S BANKS
warm air tempera...
winds produce ve...

FIXED NOTES

HYANNIS:
Temperature
Barometric Pressure
Wind (average)
Wind gust

GEORGE'S BANK:
Temperature
Wind (average + gust)

NATASHQUAN:
Temperature
Barometric Pressure

FIXED NOTES: Notes should not be changed as they articulate specific meteorological data points

FLEXIBLE REGIONS: Notes should be played within that particular half or ...

cloud cover

Heavy Rain | Drizzle | Overcast | Partly cloudy | scattered clouds | clear

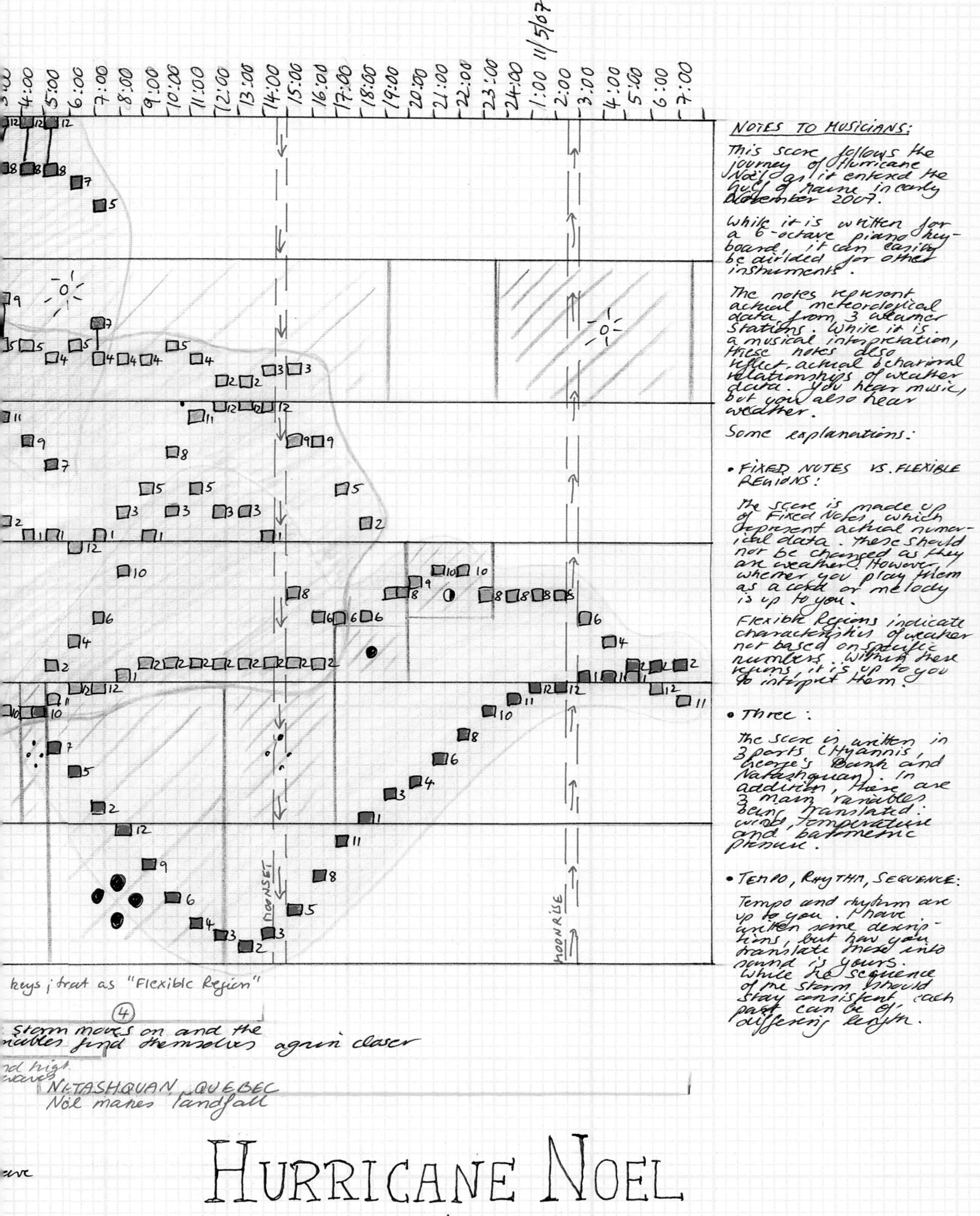

HURRICANE NOEL

SCORE FOR MUSICIANS AND SCULPTOR

History Flow

This project visualises the collaborative writing process of Wikipedia articles. The edit history (which is available for each article via a slider along the top) is turned into a timeline, and the example here shows the article on "Chocolate". Contributions are shown as coloured strips, with colours allotted to individual authors as listed on the left.

The layers of colour reflect the structure of the text, which can be read on the very right in the version from July 27, 2003. The zigzag pattern that occurred during the month of July 2003 reveals an "edit-war": editors disagreed on whether or not to include a note on Surrealist chocolate sculptures. Developed at IBM Research in 2003, "History Flow" helped with understanding Wikipedia when it was very young.

Auf dieser Grafik wird der kollektive Schreibprozess bei Wikipedia-Artikeln visualisiert. Die Versionsgeschichte (die bei jedem Artikel über einen Reiter oben auf der Seite einsehbar ist) wurde als Zeitleiste umgesetzt. Das hier gezeigte Beispiel betrifft den Eintrag zu „Chocolate". Beiträge sind als farbige Streifen zu sehen, die Farben identifizieren die einzelnen Autoren, die links aufgeführt sind.

Die Farbstreifen spiegeln die Struktur des Artikels wider, der ganz rechts in der Fassung vom 27. Juli 2003 zu lesen ist. Das Zickzackmuster im Juli 2003 offenbart einen sogenannten Edit War (dt. etwa „Bearbeitungskrieg"): Die Benutzer stritten, ob ein Hinweis auf surrealistische Schokoladenskulpturen aufgenommen werden sollte oder nicht. „History Flow" wurde 2003 von IBM Research entwickelt und trug zum Verständnis von Wikipedia bei, als der Dienst noch in den Kinderschuhen steckte.

Ce projet donne une visualisation du processus de rédaction collaborative des articles sur Wikipédia. L'historique des versions (disponible pour chaque article en cliquant sur l'onglet correspondant dans l'en-tête) est converti en chronologie, et ici l'exemple montre l'article sur le « Chocolat ». Les contributions apparaissent sous forme de bandes de couleur, et les différentes couleurs correspondent aux différents auteurs répertoriés à gauche.

Les couches de couleur reflètent la structure du texte, reproduit à droite dans sa version du 27 juillet 2003. Les zigzags qui apparaissent en juillet 2003 révèlent une « guerre de modifications » : les auteurs étaient en désaccord sur l'inclusion d'une note sur les sculptures en chocolat surréalistes. Développé par IBM Research en 2003, « History Flow » a aidé à comprendre Wikipédia quand ce concept était encore très récent.

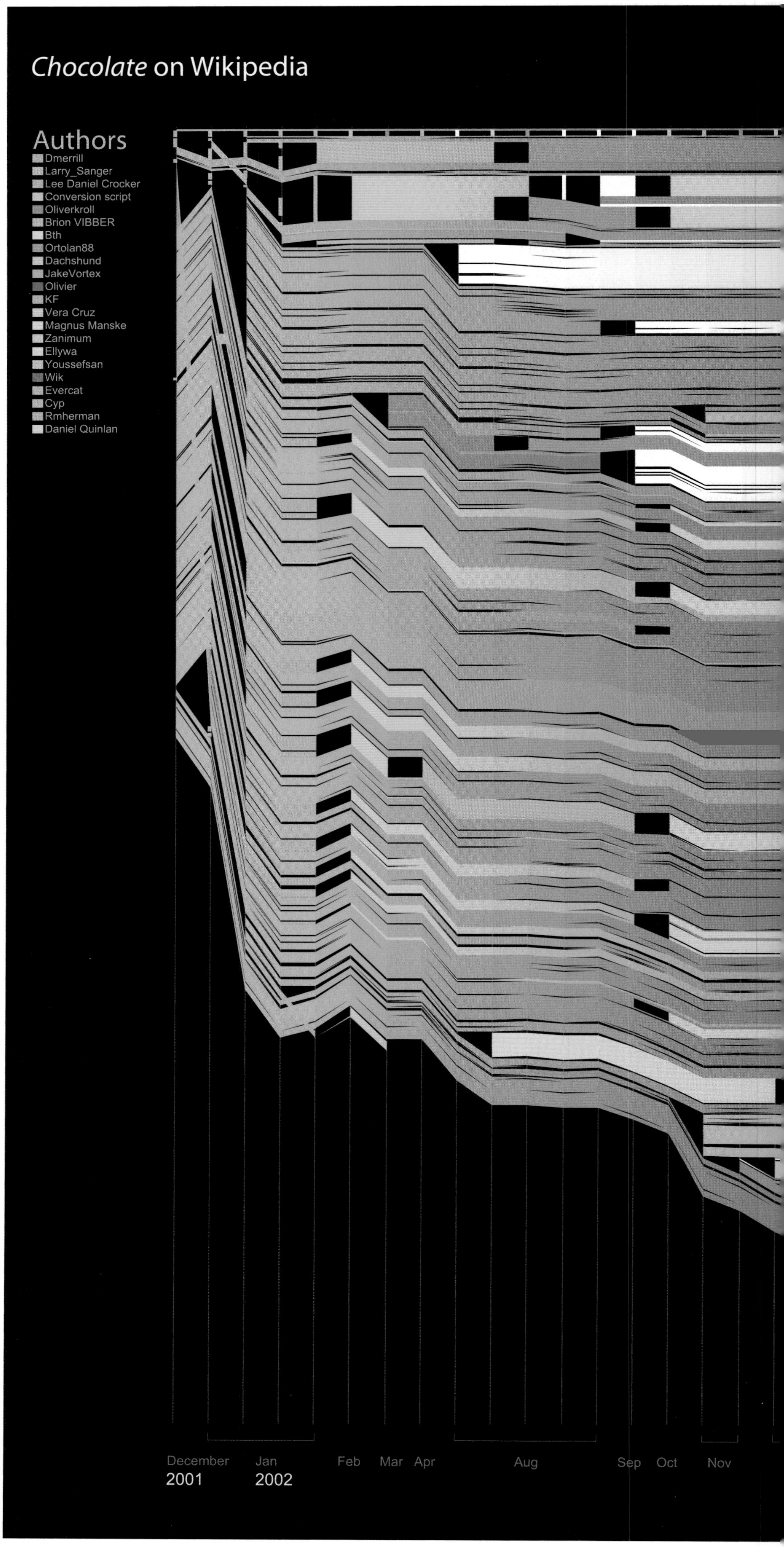

Project Info: IBM Research, website, 2003, USA
Design: Fernanda Viegas, Martin Wattenberg

Chocolate on Wikipedia

Authors
Dmerrill
Larry_Sanger
Lee Daniel Crocker
Conversion script
Oliverkroll
Brion VIBBER
Bth
Ortolan88
Dachshund
JakeVortex
Olivier
KF
Vera Cruz
Magnus Manske
Zanimum
Ellywa
Youssefsan
Wik
Evercat
Cyp
Rmherman
Daniel Quinlan

December 2001
Jan 2002
Feb
Mar
Apr
Aug
Sep
Oct
Nov

Chocolate

Chocolate is a common ingredient in many kinds of sweets -- one of the most popular in the world -- made from the fermented, roasted, and ground seeds of the tropical cacao tree Theobroma cacao. Dictionaries refer to this cacao substance as "chocolate," which is an intensely flavored bitter (not sweet) food, although this is legally defined as cocoa in many countries. This is usually sweetened with sugar and other ingredients and made into chocolate bars (the substance of which is also and commonly referred to as chocolate), or beverages (called cocoa or hot chocolate).

Extremely rarely, melted chocolate has been used to make a kind of surrealist sculpture called coulage.

Contents

Different kinds of chocolate

Chocolate is an extremely popular ingredient, available in many types, and great quantity. Different forms and flavors of chocolate are usually produced by varying the amount of the ingredients used to make the chocolate.

Dark chocolate
Milk chocolate
Semisweet chocolate (used for cooking purposes)

The history of chocolate

The Aztecs associated chocolate with Xochiquetzal, the goddess of fertility. In the New World, chocolate was consumed in a drink called xocoatl, often seasoned with vanilla, chili pepper, and pimento. Xocoatl was believed to fight fatigue, a belief that is probably attributable to the caffeine content. The drink was said to be an acquired taste. Jose de Acosta, a Spanish Jesuit missionary who lived in Peru and then Mexico in the later 16th century, wrote:

Loathsome to such as are not acquainted with it, having a scum or froth that is very unpleasant to taste. Yet it is a drink very much esteemed among the Indians, where with they feast noble men who pass through their country. The Spaniards, both men and women, that are accustomed to the country, are very greedy of this Chocolaté. They say they make diverse sorts of it, some hot, some cold, and some temperate, and put therein much of that "chili"; yea, they make paste thereof, the which they say is good for the stomach and against the catarrh.

Christopher Columbus brought some cocoa beans to show Ferdinand and Isabella of Spain, but it remained for Hernando de Soto to introduce it to Europe more broadly.

The first recorded shipment of chocolate to the Old World for commercial purposes was in a shipment from Veracruz to Seville in 1585. It was still served as a beverage, but the Europeans added sugar to counteract the natural bitterness, and removed the chili pepper. By the 17th century it was a luxury item among the European nobility.

In 1828, Conrad J. van Houten patented a method for extracting the fat from cocoa beans and making powdered cocoa and cocoa butter. This made it possible to form the modern chocolate bar. It is believed that Joseph Fry made the first chocolate for eating in 1847.

Chocolate as a stimulant

Chocolate is very mildly psychoactive since it contains theobromine, small quantities of anandamide, an endogenous cannabinoid found in the brain, as well as caffeine and tryptophan.

Why chocolate tastes so good

Part of the enjoyability of the chocolate eating experience is ascribed to the fact that its melting point is slightly below human body temperature and so it melts in the mouth.

How chocolate is made

Chocolate in the media

Charlie and the Chocolate Factory
Chocolat
The Poisoned Chocolates Case

See also: chocolate milk -- Kinder Egg -- Valentine's Day -- Christmas -- Easter

External Links

http://www.exploratorium.edu/exploring/exploring_chocolate/

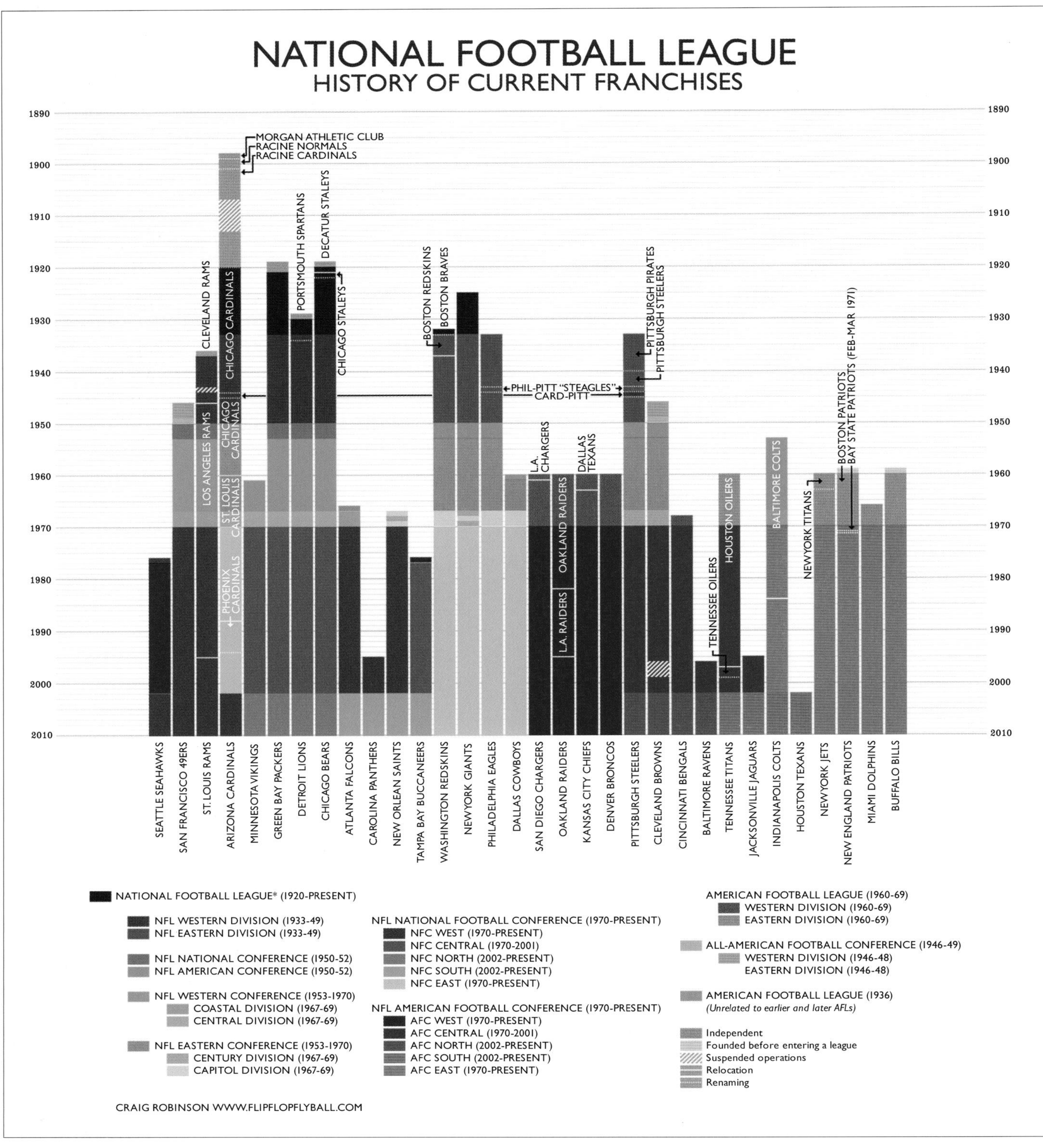

History of Current NFL Franchises

Whilst at first this looks like a bar chart showing the distribution of quantities, it is in fact a somewhat uncommon timeline, with time running top down. It describes the history of the 32 teams ("franchises") which currently form the US National Football League. Each team is represented by a bar, its height showing when the franchise was founded.

Dotted lines through the bars indicate the renaming of a team, solid lines show when a franchise was relocated to another city. Colours show which league each team belonged to throughout its history. There is a clear mark in 1970, when the current structure was introduced with two conferences within the league: the American Football Conference (red) and the National Football Conference (blue).

Auf den ersten Blick wirkt diese Grafik wie ein Balkendiagramm zur Verteilung von Mengen. Stattdessen handelt es sich jedoch um eine ungewöhnliche Zeitleiste, in der die Zeit von oben nach unten verläuft. Sie schildert die Geschichte der 32 Mannschaften („Franchises"), aus denen sich gegenwärtig die amerikanische National Football League zusammensetzt. Jede Mannschaft wird durch einen Balken dargestellt. Seine Höhe zeigt an, wann das Team gegründet wurde.

Punktlinien durch die Balken zeigen an, dass eine Mannschaft umbenannt wurde, durchgezogene Linien bedeuten, dass ein Franchise in eine andere Stadt umzog. Die Farben verweisen darauf, welcher Liga die Mannschaft im Lauf ihrer Geschichte jeweils angehörte. Ein deutlicher Schnitt fand 1970 statt, als die heutige Struktur der National Football League mit zwei Conferences etabliert wurde: der American Football Conference (rot) und der National Football Conference (blau).

À première vue, cela ressemble à un histogramme montrant une répartition de quantités, mais il s'agit en fait d'une chronologie assez originale, dont l'échelle temporelle va de haut en bas. Elle décrit l'histoire des 32 équipes (« franchises ») qui forment actuellement la Ligue nationale de football américain (NFL). Chaque équipe est représentée par une barre, dont la hauteur montre l'ancienneté de la franchise.

Les lignes en pointillés sur les barres indiquent un changement de nom, et les lignes continues montrent un changement de ville. Les couleurs correspondent à la ligue à laquelle l'équipe appartient. 1970 marque un grand changement, l'introduction de la structure actuelle avec deux conférences au sein de la ligue : l'American Football Conference (rouge) et la National Football Conference (bleu).

Project Info: Website, 2009, UK
Design: Craig Robinson

History of the Earth

This graphic covers the unimaginable period of 5 billion years. It is structured along a timeline at the bottom, which also distinguishes periods of development on Earth. The story unfolds in the direction of reading, starting top left and landing in the present on the lower right.

At the same time, the unusual representation of the Earth plays with a fluctuating zoom. On the right, the flora and fauna of the past 300 million years is presented upfront and is the richest and most detailed part of the picture. In contrast, the Big Bang, being the starting point to this story, is lost in the depths of remote space-time.

Diese Grafik umfasst die unvorstellbare Zeitspanne von fünf Milliarden Jahren. Sie ist entlang einer Zeitleiste am unteren Bildrand strukturiert, die verschiedene Entwicklungsperioden der Erde unterscheidet. Die Geschichte entfaltet sich in Leserichtung von oben links bis in die Gegenwart nach unten rechts.

Gleichzeitig spielt diese ungewöhnliche Darstellung der Erde mit einem flexiblen Zoom. Auf der rechten Seite werden im Vordergrund Flora und Fauna der vergangenen 300 Millionen Jahre vorgestellt. Es ist der dichteste und detailfreudigste Teil der Grafik. Der Urknall hingegen, der Ausgangspunkt dieser Geschichte, verliert sich links in den Tiefen der Raumzeit.

Cette affiche couvre une période incommensurable de 5 milliards d'années. Elle est structurée le long d'une chronologie qui indique dans le bas les différentes périodes d'évolution de la Terre. L'histoire se déroule dans la direction de la lecture, d'en haut à gauche jusqu'au présent en bas à droite.

La Terre est représentée de façon inhabituelle, à l'aide d'un zoom fluctuant. À droite, la flore et la faune des 300 millions d'années passées sont présentées au premier plan. C'est la partie la plus détaillée de l'image. Le Big Bang, le point de départ de cette histoire, est par contraste perdu dans les profondeurs de l'espace-temps.

Project Info: *Superinteressante*, poster, 2002, Brazil
Research: Denis Russo Burgierman
Design: Rodrigo Maroja
Art Direction: Alceu Nunes
Illustration: Luiz Iria
Awards: Premio Abril de Jornalismo

How Mariano Rivera Dominates Hitters

In baseball, pitchers employ a variety of techniques to throw the ball, giving it a different velocity and flight-path each time. This is done in order to confuse the batter trying to hit the ball. Mariano Rivera is an outstanding pitcher for the New York Yankees. This animated graphic by the *New York Times* explains his signature throwing technique.

In a three-dimensional reconstruction, the piece shows how his pitches are the most difficult for opposing batters to hit. Rivera is seen on the playing field from the perspective of the batter. The nearly 1,300 pitches that Rivera threw during the 2009 season are mapped according to their trajectory in 3D space, elucidating technical intricacies executed in split seconds.

Beim Baseball setzt der Pitcher unterschiedliche Techniken ein, sodass der Ball mit jedem Wurf eine jeweils andere Geschwindigkeit und Flugbahn hat. Ziel ist es dabei, den gegnerischen Batter zu irritieren, der den Ball zu schlagen versucht. Mariano Rivera ist ein herausragender Pitcher bei den New York Yankees. In dieser animierten Grafik der *New York Times* wird seine charakteristische Wurftechnik erläutert.

In einer dreidimensionalen Rekonstruktion zeigt die Grafik, weshalb Riveras Würfe für den gegnerischen Batter unglaublich schwierig zu schlagen sind. Rivera ist auf dem Spielfeld aus der Perspektive des Batters zu sehen. Die nahezu 1.300 Würfe, die er in der Spielzeit 2009 machte, werden entsprechend ihrer Flugbahn im dreidimensionalen Raum kartiert. Sie zeigen technische Finessen, die in Sekundenbruchteilen ausgeführt werden.

Les lanceurs de baseball emploient tout un arsenal de techniques pour donner à la balle une vitesse et une trajectoire différentes à chaque lancer. Le but est de désarçonner le batteur, qui essaie de frapper la balle. Mariano Rivera est un excellent lanceur, qui joue pour les New York Yankees. Cette animation réalisée par le *New York Times* explique la technique de lancer qui l'a rendu célèbre.

Cette reconstitution tridimensionnelle montre pourquoi ses lancers sont les plus difficiles pour les batteurs. On voit Rivera sur le terrain, du point de vue du batteur. Les quelque 1 300 lancers que Rivera a réalisés pendant la saison 2009 sont analysés selon leur trajectoire dans l'espace tridimensionnel afin de mettre en lumière des subtilités techniques exécutées en une fraction de seconde.

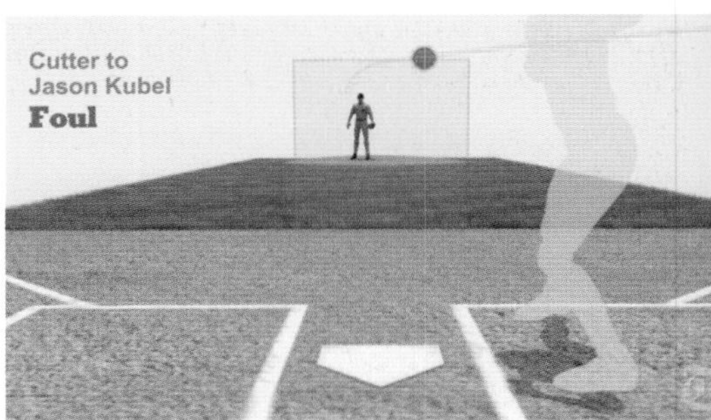

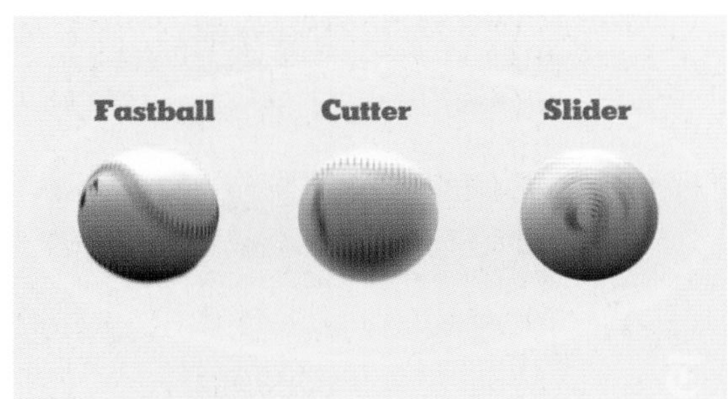

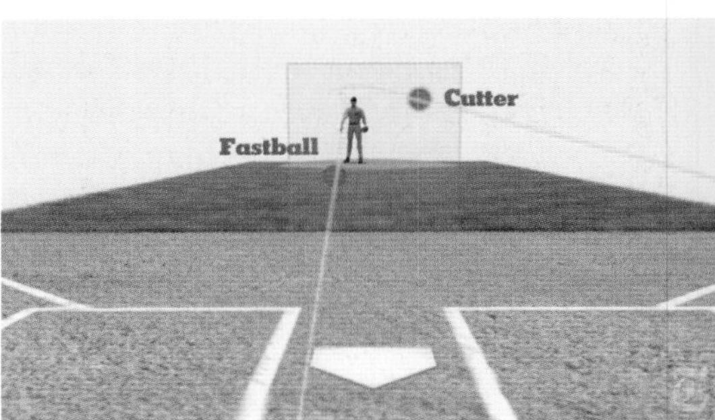

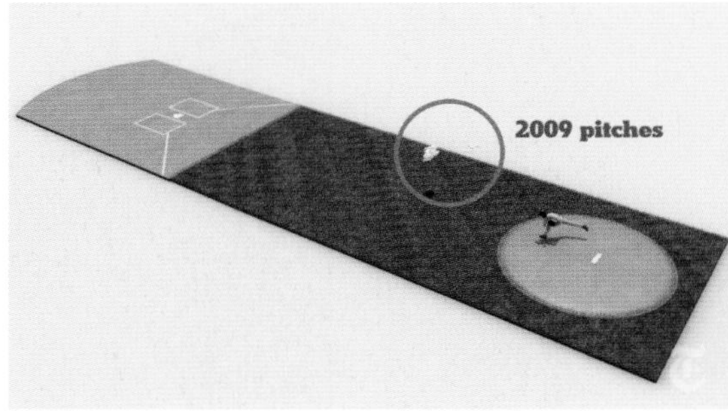

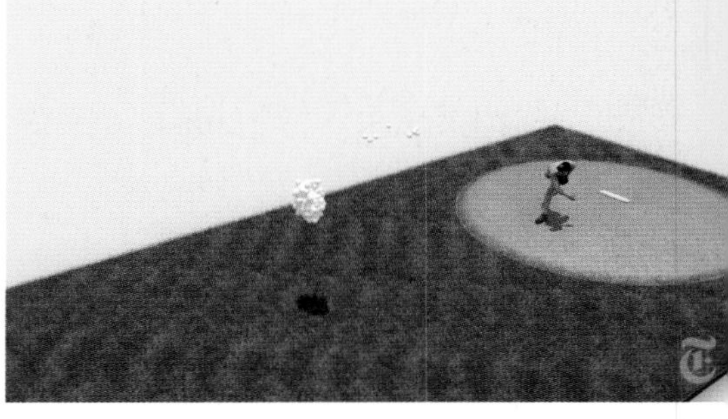

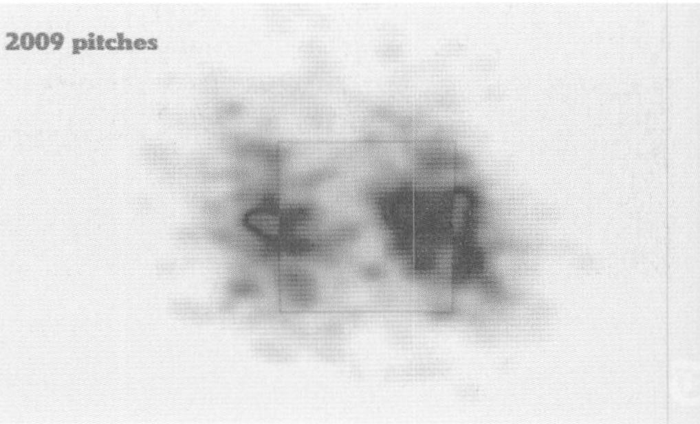

Project Info: *The New York Times,* video, 2010, USA
Data Source: Major League Baseball; New York University Movement Lab
Design: Graham Roberts, Shan Carter, Joe Ward
Graphics Director: Steve Duenes
Deputy Graphics Director: Matt Ericson

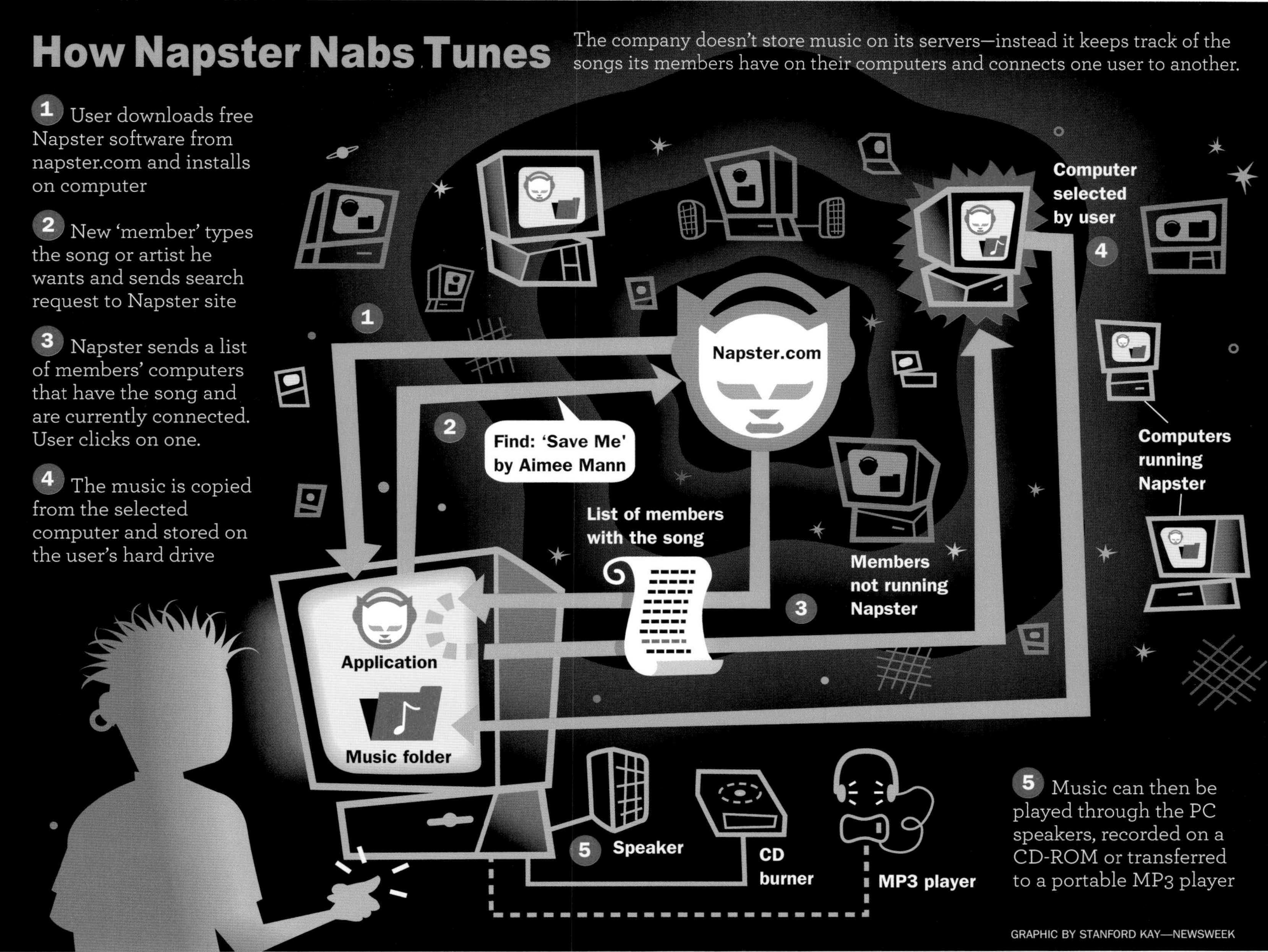

How Napster Nabs Tunes
The company doesn't store music on its servers—instead it keeps track of the songs its members have on their computers and connects one user to another.
1 User downloads free Napster software from napster.com and installs on computer
2 New 'member' types the song or artist he wants and sends search request to Napster site
3 Napster sends a list of members' computers that have the song and are currently connected. User clicks on one.
4 The music is copied from the selected computer and stored on the user's hard drive
Napster.com
Find: 'Save Me' by Aimee Mann
List of members with the song
Computer selected by user
Computers running Napster
Members not running Napster
Application
Music folder
Speaker
CD burner
MP3 player
5 Music can then be played through the PC speakers, recorded on a CD-ROM or transferred to a portable MP3 player
GRAPHIC BY STANFORD KAY—NEWSWEEK

How Napster Nabs Tunes

Designed for *Newsweek* in 2000, this graphic illustrates how the online service Napster facilitated the sharing of music across the Internet. Napster was programmed in 1998 and used a revolutionary peer-to-peer approach. The company didn't have a file archive but allowed users to share files they had on their home computers.

After an incredible growth in user traffic, the community was shut down in 2001 for copyright issues. In a playful style, the graphic visualises the peer-to-peer file-sharing through Napster. With the user in the lower left, the graphic offers the reader an individual look at the network, which is depicted as a dark-blue cosmos of floating computers, with the Napster symbol at the centre.

Diese Grafik entstand im Jahr 2000 für *Newsweek*. Sie veranschaulicht, wie der Onlinedienst Napster den Austausch von Musik über das Internet ermöglichte. Napster wurde 1998 programmiert und arbeitete mit dem damals revolutionären Peer-to-Peer-Ansatz. Das Unternehmen hatte kein eigenes Datenarchiv, sondern ermöglichte den Nutzern, die auf ihrem Computer gespeicherten Dateien mit anderen zu tauschen.

Nach einem unglaublichen Anstieg der Benutzerzahlen wurde die Community 2001 aus Gründen des Urheberrechts abgeschaltet. Die Grafik visualisiert spielerisch den Peer-to-Peer-Datenaustausch mithilfe von Napster. Mit dem Benutzer unten links blickt der Leser auf das Netzwerk. Es ist als dunkelblauer Kosmos mit fliegenden Computern dargestellt, in dessen Zentrum das Napster-Logo prangt.

Réalisée pour *Newsweek* en 2000, cette illustration explique comment le service en ligne Napster a facilité le partage de la musique sur Internet. Napster est un logiciel qui a été programmé en 1998, et qui utilisait une approche pair-à-pair révolutionnaire. L'entreprise ne possédait pas les fichiers, mais permettait aux utilisateurs de partager les fichiers qu'ils avaient chez eux sur leurs ordinateurs.

Après une croissance incroyable du trafic, la communauté a été fermée en 2001 en raison de problèmes liés aux droits d'auteur. Cette illustration adopte un style ludique pour représenter le principe du partage de fichiers en pair-à-pair grâce à Napster. L'utilisateur étant situé en bas à gauche, le lecteur se voit offrir une vision individualisée du réseau, dépeint comme des ordinateurs flottant dans un cosmos bleu nuit, avec le symbole de Napster au centre.

Project Info: "The Noisy War Against Napster", *Newsweek*, magazine article, 2000, USA
Design: Stanford Kay

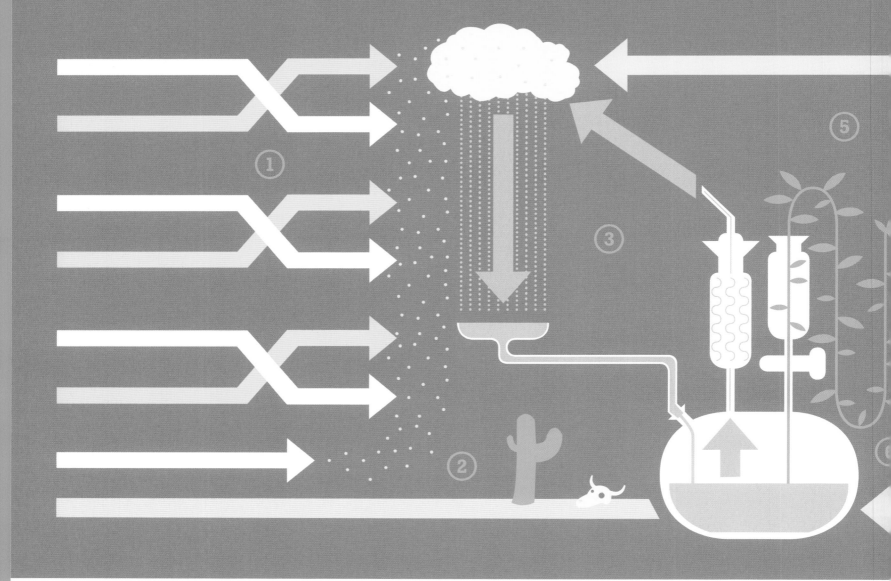

How Plants Grow

This process diagram displays several key stages in plant growth. Simple iconic illustrations differentiate between each step, with the stages explained on the right. Arrows convey how individual elements in the process interact with each other.

The piece shows not only how plants use sunlight, water and CO_2 but also other processes that are more indirect to plant growth, such as where wind comes from and how it forces dust into the atmosphere where water vapour condenses on it and forms clouds and rain.

Dieses Ablaufdiagramm zeigt mehrere Schlüsselstadien beim Wachstum der Pflanzen. Einfache Symbole machen jeden Schritt erkennbar, die Stadien werden rechts erläutert. Pfeile verdeutlichen, wie einzelne Elemente im Prozess zusammenwirken.

Die Grafik zeigt nicht nur, wie Pflanzen Sonnenlicht, Wasser und CO_2 aufnehmen, sondern auch andere Prozesse, die weniger unmittelbar mit dem Pflanzenwachstum zusammenhängen, etwa die Richtung des Windes oder die Tatsache, dass dieser Staubteilchen in die Atmosphäre weht, wo sie gemeinsam mit kondensierendem Wasserdampf Wolken und Regen bilden.

Ce diagramme de processus présente les grandes étapes de la croissance des plantes. Elles sont identifiées par des illustrations simples, proches des icônes, et sont expliquées à droite. Les flèches indiquent les interactions des différents éléments du processus.

Le schéma montre non seulement comment les plantes utilisent la lumière du soleil, l'eau et le CO_2, mais également les autres processus qui interviennent plus indirectement sur la croissance des plantes, comme la formation du vent, qui introduit de la poussière dans l'atmosphère, où la vapeur d'eau se condense et forme les nuages et la pluie.

Project Info: Website, 2010, USA
Data Source: New York City Center for Space Education and Science; US Geological Survey
Design: Zachary Vabolis

Plants are a vital part of human life. They produce the oxygen we breath while taking in harmful carbon dioxide. Numerous plants are suitable for human consumption and they provide useful vitamins and nutrients. Plants are used in medicines to keep us feeling well and they hold the soil together that we build our shelters on. It's a tough life for some plants out there but millions of years of adaptation have provided them with some niffty ways to ensure the survival of the plant kingdom.

1. As the sun warms the earth it also warms the air contained within our atmosphere. We feel wind as the warm air rises and the colder, denser air rushes in to fill its place.

2. Wind blows tiny particles of dust and debris into the atmosphere where they enter clouds and become the nuclei of rain droplets. When these rain droplets become heavy enough they fall back to the earth as rain.

3. When water vapor rises it will condense in the atmosphere to form a cloud. Some of these clouds will go on to produce rain which provides nourishing water for plants back on earth.

4. Humans expel carbon dioxide, a gas that is essential to plant life.

5. Plants use sunlight to power the process of photosynthesis. this is the process by which plants make their energy. The warmth of the sun also prevents water particles in clouds from freezing thus allowing rain to fall.

6. Sunlight heats liquid water on the earths surface which will then turn to water vapor.

Hunting Whales

This maritime panorama explains how whales are hunted. Developed as two double-spreads, it forms one continuous image. The left spread shows two harpoon boats in the process of killing a whale. Snippets of text explain each step, magnifying bubbles show details (like the tiny grenade at the tip of the harpoon, designed to kill the whale quickly with an explosion).

The second spread takes the viewer aboard the accompanying factory ship. Here the whale is cut up, the meat and other parts are prepared for further processing. The box to the right adds information on the hunting of dolphins. The piece is striking in the way it uses an image to explain a process step by step.

Dieses maritime Panorama erläutert, wie Wale gejagt werden. Angelegt auf zwei Doppelseiten, ergeben die Teile ein zusammenhängendes Bild. Der linke Teil zeigt zwei Harpunenboote, deren Besatzung gerade einen Wal erlegt. Kurze Texte erklären jeden Schritt, in Kreisen werden Bilddetails vergrößert dargestellt (etwa die winzige Granate an der Harpunenspitze, die den Wal bei der Explosion rasch töten soll).

Die zweite Doppelseite zeigt eine Ansicht des begleitenden Fabrikschiffs. Hier wird der Wal zerlegt, das Fleisch und andere Teile werden zur Weiterverarbeitung vorbereitet. Im Kasten rechts stehen Zusatzinformationen zur Jagd von Delfinen. Das Besondere an dieser Grafik ist die Art und Weise, wie anhand eines einzigen Bildes ein ganzer Prozess schrittweise erläutert wird.

Ce panorama maritime explique comment les baleines sont chassées. Il forme une image continue qui s'étend sur deux doubles pages. La double page de gauche montre deux baleiniers en train de tuer une baleine. De courts textes expliquent chaque étape et des bulles montrent des détails agrandis (comme la petite grenade au bout du harpon, conçue pour tuer la baleine rapidement).

La deuxième double page emmène le lecteur à bord du navire-usine qui accompagne les baleiniers. C'est ici que la baleine est dépecée, et que la viande et les autres morceaux sont préparés pour leur traitement ultérieur. Le cadre de droite ajoute des informations sur la chasse aux dauphins. Cette œuvre est frappante dans sa façon d'utiliser une image pour expliquer un processus étape par étape.

Project Info: *Mundo Estranho*, magazine article, 2009, Brazil
Data Source: John Frizell, Greenpeace International Ocean Campaigner; Whale and Dolphin Conservation Society; American Cetacean Society
Research: Yuri Vasconscelos
Art Direction: Fabricio Miranda
Illustration: Sattu, Luiz Iria
Awards: Malofiej 2010

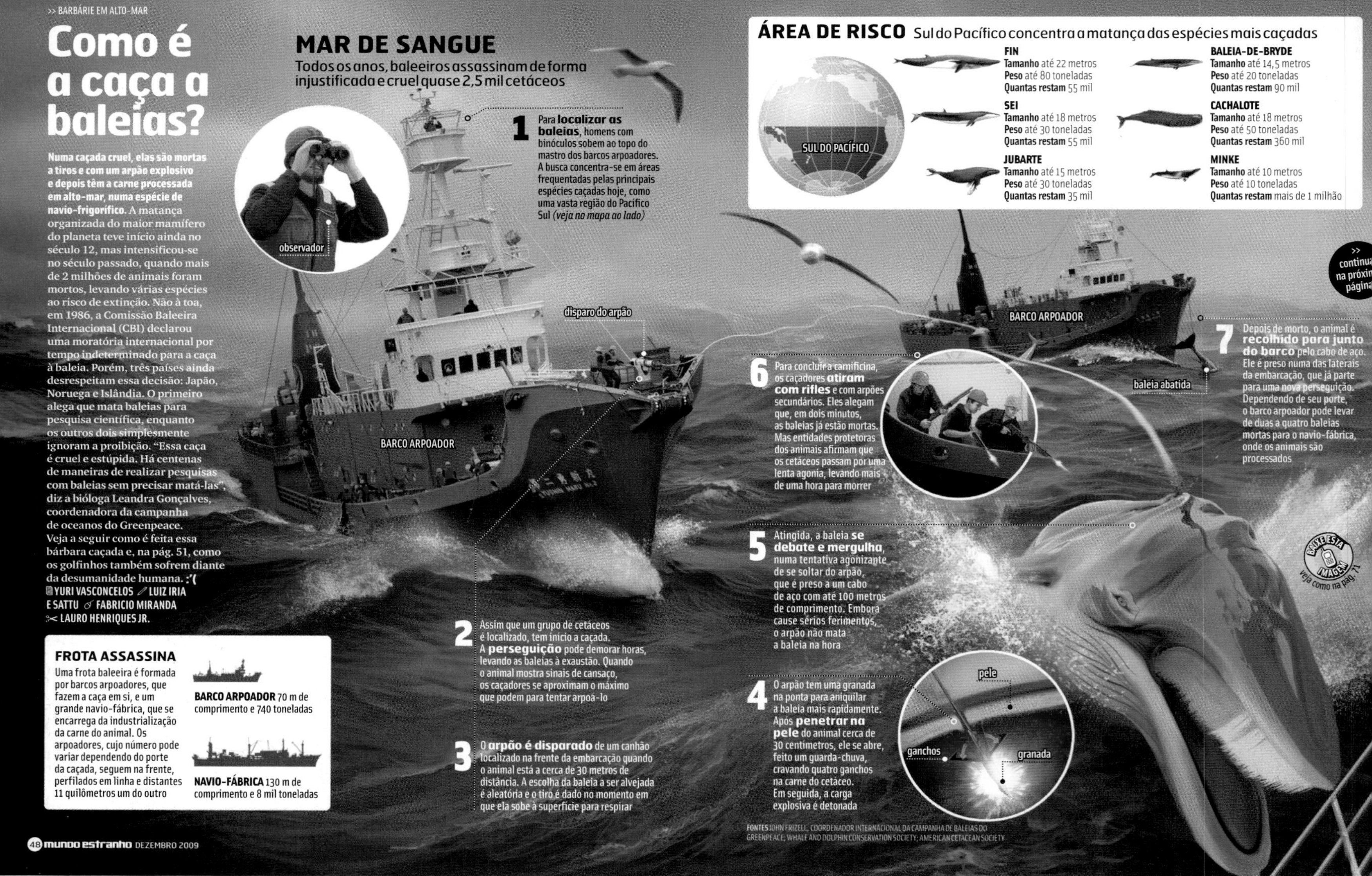

>> BARBÁRIE EM ALTO-MAR

Como é a caça a baleias?

Numa caçada cruel, elas são mortas a tiros e com um arpão explosivo e depois têm a carne processada em alto-mar, numa espécie de navio-frigorífico. A matança organizada do maior mamífero do planeta teve início ainda no século 12, mas intensificou-se no século passado, quando mais de 2 milhões de animais foram mortos, levando várias espécies ao risco de extinção. Não à toa, em 1986, a Comissão Baleeira Internacional (CBI) declarou uma moratória internacional por tempo indeterminado para a caça à baleia. Porém, três países ainda desrespeitam essa decisão: Japão, Noruega e Islândia. O primeiro alega que mata baleias para pesquisa científica, enquanto os outros dois simplesmente ignoram a proibição. "Essa caça é cruel e estúpida. Há centenas de maneiras de realizar pesquisas com baleias sem precisar matá-las", diz a bióloga Leandra Gonçalves, coordenadora da campanha de oceanos do Greenpeace. Veja a seguir como é feita essa bárbara caçada e, na pág. 51, como os golfinhos também sofrem diante da desumanidade humana. :'(

YURI VASCONCELOS LUIZ IRIA E SATTU FABRICIO MIRANDA LAURO HENRIQUES JR.

FROTA ASSASSINA

Uma frota baleeira é formada por barcos arpoadores, que fazem a caça em si, e um grande navio-fábrica, que se encarrega da industrialização da carne do animal. Os arpoadores, cujo número pode variar dependendo do porte da caçada, seguem na frente, perfilados em linha e distantes 11 quilômetros um do outro

BARCO ARPOADOR 70 m de comprimento e 740 toneladas

NAVIO-FÁBRICA 130 m de comprimento e 8 mil toneladas

MAR DE SANGUE

Todos os anos, baleeiros assassinam de forma injustificada e cruel quase 2,5 mil cetáceos

1 Para **localizar as baleias**, homens com binóculos sobem ao topo do mastro dos barcos arpoadores. A busca concentra-se em áreas frequentadas pelas principais espécies caçadas hoje, como uma vasta região do Pacífico Sul *(veja no mapa ao lado)*

2 Assim que um grupo de cetáceos é localizado, tem início a caçada. A **perseguição** pode demorar horas, levando as baleias à exaustão. Quando o animal mostra sinais de cansaço, os caçadores se aproximam o máximo que podem para tentar arpoá-lo

3 O **arpão é disparado** de um canhão localizado na frente da embarcação quando o animal está a cerca de 30 metros de distância. A escolha da baleia a ser alvejada é aleatória e o tiro é dado no momento em que ela sobe à superfície para respirar

4 O arpão tem uma granada na ponta para aniquilar a baleia mais rapidamente. Após **penetrar na pele** do animal cerca de 30 centímetros, ele se abre, feito um guarda-chuva, cravando quatro ganchos na carne do cetáceo. Em seguida, a carga explosiva é detonada

5 Atingida, a baleia **se debate e mergulha**, numa tentativa agonizante de se soltar do arpão, que é preso a um cabo de aço com até 100 metros de comprimento. Embora cause sérios ferimentos, o arpão não mata a baleia na hora

6 Para concluir a carnificina, os caçadores **atiram com rifles** e com arpões secundários. Eles alegam que, em dois minutos, as baleias já estão mortas. Mas entidades protetoras dos animais afirmam que os cetáceos passam por uma lenta agonia, levando mais de uma hora para morrer

7 Depois de morto, o animal é **recolhido para junto do barco** pelo cabo de aço. Ele é preso numa das laterais da embarcação, que já parte para uma nova perseguição. Dependendo de seu porte, o barco arpoador pode levar de duas a quatro baleias mortas para o navio-fábrica, onde os animais são processados

ÁREA DE RISCO

Sul do Pacífico concentra a matança das espécies mais caçadas

SUL DO PACÍFICO

FIN
Tamanho até 22 metros
Peso até 80 toneladas
Quantas restam 55 mil

SEI
Tamanho até 18 metros
Peso até 30 toneladas
Quantas restam 55 mil

JUBARTE
Tamanho até 15 metros
Peso até 30 toneladas
Quantas restam 35 mil

BALEIA-DE-BRYDE
Tamanho até 14,5 metros
Peso até 20 toneladas
Quantas restam 90 mil

CACHALOTE
Tamanho até 18 metros
Peso até 50 toneladas
Quantas restam 360 mil

MINKE
Tamanho até 10 metros
Peso até 10 toneladas
Quantas restam mais de 1 milhão

>> continua na próxima página

FONTES JOHN FRIZELL, COORDENADOR INTERNACIONAL DA CAMPANHA DE BALEIAS DO GREENPEACE; WHALE AND DOLPHIN CONSERVATION SOCIETY; AMERICAN CETACEAN SOCIETY

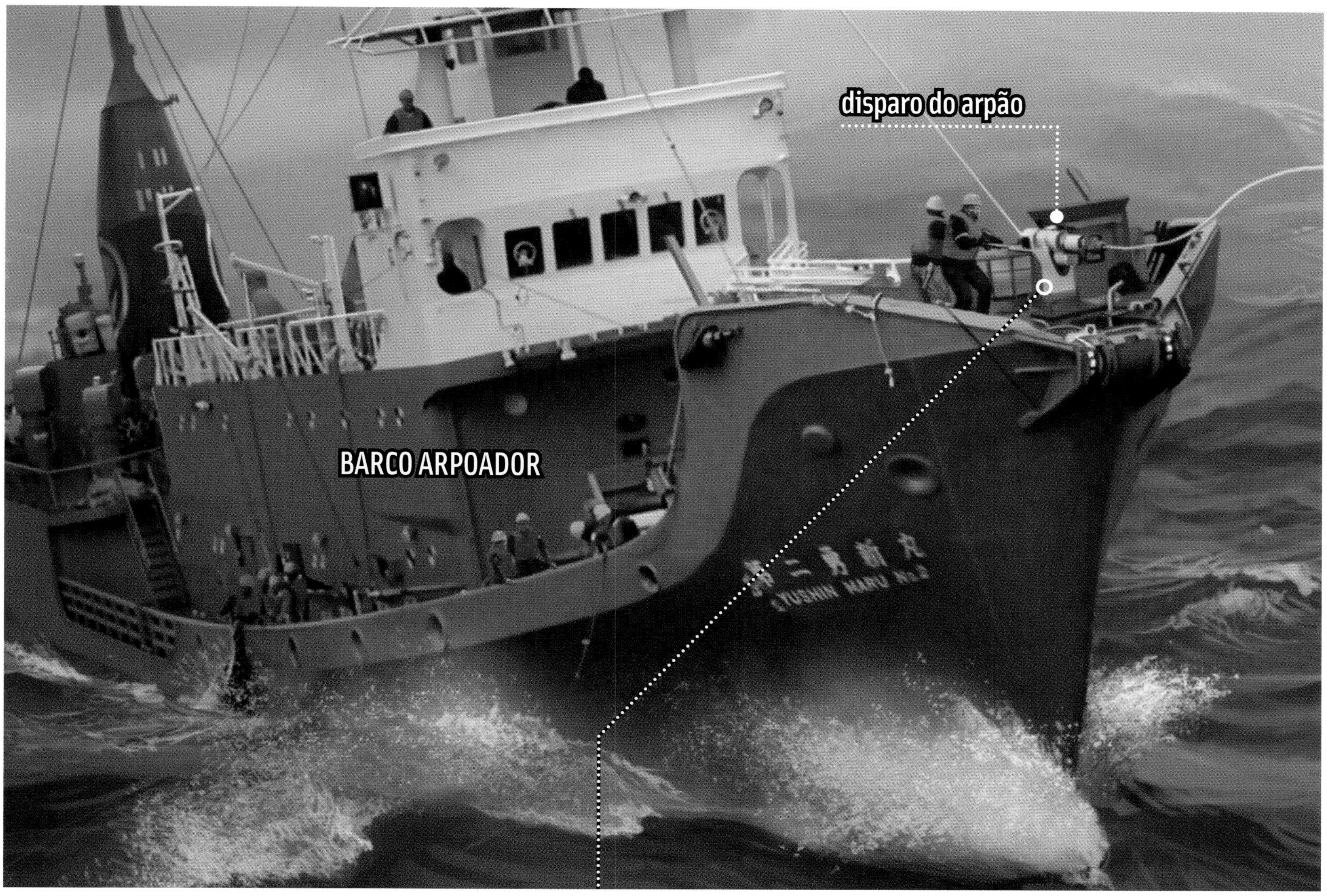

disparo do arpão

BARCO ARPOADOR

8 Enquanto o sangue é derramado no mar, o **navio-fábrica**, líder da expedição, navega pelas redondezas, aguardando a chegada dos animais abatidos. No caso dos japoneses, esse navio é o Nishin-maru, uma traineira de pesca que leva 112 tripulantes

9 A **transferência das vítimas** para o navio-fábrica rola por uma rampa na traseira do barco. O animal é preso a um cabo de aço e içado por um guincho. Quando chega ao convés, começa o trabalho dos açougueiros ou, como alegam os japoneses, dos pesquisadores

10 Como a caça japonesa tem, alegadamente, fins científicos, os animais são **medidos e pesados** antes de serem retalhados. A comida encontrada no estômago seria catalogada para estudos sobre os hábitos alimentares desses grandes cetáceos

guincho

NAVIO-FÁBRICA

Uma das "pesquisas" feitas pelos japoneses com os animais mortos foi a inseminação de vacas com o sêmen de baleias machos. Até hoje, não se sabe para quê...

11 Em seguida, o animal começa a ser descarnado e desossado. A **camada de gordura é separada** do corpo, fatiada e processada em máquinas que a transformam em óleo. Depois de pronto, o líquido é armazenado em tonéis

rampa

gordura

açougueiro

carne

12 Com auxílio de facas afiadas, a carne, a língua e as nadadeiras são **cortadas por açougueiros** profissionais. Em seguida, seguem para a casa de carnes, onde são industrializadas, empacotadas ou enlatadas para venda aos consumidores

ossos

medição

13 Até os **ossos são aproveitados**. Eles são moídos para fabricação de farelo para ração e fertilizante. Os japoneses alegam que só fazem isso porque, após coletar os dados científicos, não teria sentido jogar o bicho fora. Para as entidades de proteção animal, tudo é só um artifício para reiniciar a caça comercial

YES, NÓS TEMOS BALEIA

De perseguidor, o Brasil hoje é um grande defensor do cetáceo

No passado, o litoral brasileiro também foi cenário para a cruenta caça a baleias. O porto de Cabedelo, na Paraíba, era um dos mais ativos e servia de sede para a empresa Copesbra, que, em seus 75 anos de atuação, matou milhares de baleias de várias espécies – o óleo retirado da gordura do bicho era usado para iluminação e preparo de tinta, entre outras coisas. Um decreto do governo proibiu a caça no país em 1986 e, hoje, o Brasil é uma das nações mais ativas na luta contra a caça aos cetáceos. Em 2007, por exemplo, o Brasil aderiu ao grande protesto diplomático em conjunto com outros 30 países contra a carnificina promovida pelo Japão.

BRUTALIDADE SEM FIM

Assim como suas "primas" baleias, os golfinhos também são barbaramente caçados

TRADIÇÃO MACABRA

Estima-se que mais de mil golfinhos-pilotos *(Globicephala melaena)* sejam barbaramente assassinados todos os anos apenas nas ilhas Faroe *(veja no mapa)*. A caçada é feita pelos moradores da própria comunidade, numa espécie de rito de passagem dos jovens para a idade adulta

Ilhas Faroe

EUROPA

A matança de golfinhos rola em três áreas: nas ilhas Faroe, território dinamarquês no Atlântico Norte; em Taiji, na costa do Japão; e nas ilhas Salomão, no oceano Pacífico

ENCURRALADOS

Logo que os golfinhos são avistados, os pescadores rumam em botes na direção dos animais, que são dóceis e pacíficos. Os caras então fazem um semicírculo com os botes para encurralar o bando, conduzindo os bichos para uma baía, de forma que não escapem

ATAQUE BRUTAL

Os jovens trucidam os animais com facas e arpões. Os animais se contorcem de dor e podem levar um tempão para morrer. Enquanto isso, os sobreviventes ficam juntos aos outros, sem esboçar qualquer reação agressiva nem tentar fugir

ÁGUA ESCARLATE

Enquanto os animais mortos são levados para praia ou colocados dentro dos barcos, a sangueira vai tingindo o mar de vermelho. Infelizmente, a Comissão Baleeira Internacional não controla a matança de golfinhos, pois ela rola na costa dos países e não em águas internacionais, como no caso das baleias

IT'S THE ECONOMY, STUPID!

The dollar is weak. Food and oil prices are high. Our nation is spending well beyond its means and owes trillions of dollars in debt to foreign governments. What most of the gloom-and-doom reports don't provide, however, is perspective—a historical survey of an economy that's been through more than a few ups and downs in its day. Here's a farsighted view of how our temperamental economic machine works, and a close-up of how it stands today. KEY DEFINITIONS

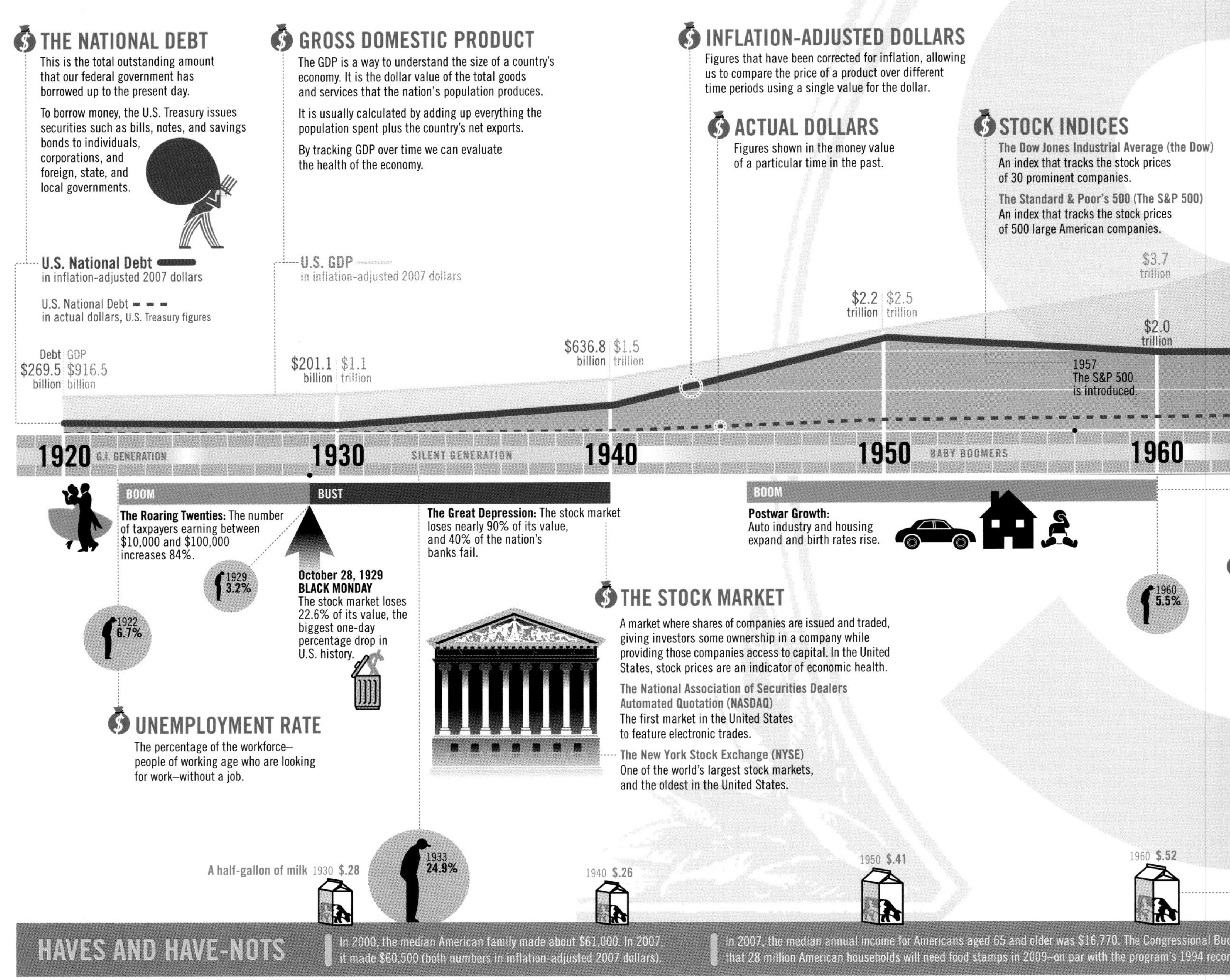

THE NATIONAL DEBT
This is the total outstanding amount that our federal government has borrowed up to the present day.
To borrow money, the U.S. Treasury issues securities such as bills, notes, and savings bonds to individuals, corporations, and foreign, state, and local governments.
GROSS DOMESTIC PRODUCT
The GDP is a way to understand the size of a country's economy. It is the dollar value of the total goods and services that the nation's population produces.
It is usually calculated by adding up everything the population spent plus the country's net exports.
By tracking GDP over time we can evaluate the health of the economy.
INFLATION-ADJUSTED DOLLARS
Figures that have been corrected for inflation, allowing us to compare the price of a product over different time periods using a single value for the dollar.
ACTUAL DOLLARS
Figures shown in the money value of a particular time in the past.
STOCK INDICES
The Dow Jones Industrial Average (the Dow)
An index that tracks the stock prices of 30 prominent companies.
The Standard & Poor's 500 (The S&P 500)
An index that tracks the stock prices of 500 large American companies.
U.S. National Debt
in inflation-adjusted 2007 dollars
U.S. National Debt
in actual dollars, U.S. Treasury figures
U.S. GDP
in inflation-adjusted 2007 dollars
Debt GDP
$269.5 billion $916.5 billion
$201.1 billion $1.1 trillion
$636.8 billion $1.5 trillion
$2.2 trillion $2.5 trillion
$3.7 trillion
$2.0 trillion
1957 The S&P 500 is introduced.
1920 G.I. GENERATION
1930 SILENT GENERATION
1940
1950 BABY BOOMERS
1960
BOOM
The Roaring Twenties: The number of taxpayers earning between $10,000 and $100,000 increases 84%.
BUST
October 28, 1929 BLACK MONDAY
The stock market loses 22.6% of its value, the biggest one-day percentage drop in U.S. history.
The Great Depression: The stock market loses nearly 90% of its value, and 40% of the nation's banks fail.
BOOM
Postwar Growth:
Auto industry and housing expand and birth rates rise.
1922 6.7%
1929 3.2%
1933 24.9%
1960 5.5%
UNEMPLOYMENT RATE
The percentage of the workforce–people of working age who are looking for work–without a job.
THE STOCK MARKET
A market where shares of companies are issued and traded, giving investors some ownership in a company while providing those companies access to capital. In the United States, stock prices are an indicator of economic health.
The National Association of Securities Dealers Automated Quotation (NASDAQ)
The first market in the United States to feature electronic trades.
The New York Stock Exchange (NYSE)
One of the world's largest stock markets, and the oldest in the United States.
A half-gallon of milk 1930 $.28
1940 $.26
1950 $.41
1960 $.52
HAVES AND HAVE-NOTS
In 2000, the median American family made about $61,000. In 2007, it made $60,500 (both numbers in inflation-adjusted 2007 dollars).
In 2007, the median annual income for Americans aged 65 and older was $16,770. The Congressional Budg
that 28 million American households will need food stamps in 2009–on par with the program's 1994 record

It's the Economy, Stupid!

This timeline presents a history of the US economy, starting in 1920. Small red money-bags mark explanations of economic key concepts. Along the bottom, inflation is demonstrated by the changing price of a half-gallon of milk. Above the timeline, both the GDP and the national deficit increase massively. The measuring scale is given in trillions (white lines on red).

Below the timeline, a red line starting in the Sixties indicates how the government started spending more than they earned and thus constantly increased the national debt. This deficit is shown to the same scale as the national debt above, and reaches 357 billion at the end of the line. The magnifying-glass shows this bigger, as it seems such a small amount when shown in the trillions scale.

Diese Zeitleiste präsentiert die Geschichte der US-amerikanischen Wirtschaft seit 1920. Kleine rote Geldsäckchen verweisen auf ökonomische Schlüsselbegriffe. Am unteren Bildrand wird die Inflation anhand des Preisanstiegs für eine halbe Gallone Milch verdeutlicht. Oberhalb der Zeitleiste steigen sowohl das Bruttoinlandsprodukt als auch die Staatsverschuldung massiv an. Die Skalierung ist in Billionen Dollar unterteilt (weiße Linien auf rotem Hintergrund).

Direkt unterhalb der Zeitleiste zeigt eine rote Linie, die in den 1960er-Jahren einsetzt, dass der Staat begann, mehr Geld auszugeben, als er einnahm; dadurch stieg die Verschuldung noch weiter an. Dieses Defizit wird in derselben Skala angegeben wie die Staatsverschuldung oben und erreichte 357 Milliarden Dollar im Jahr 2008. Die Lupe vergrößert diese Angabe, weil sich der Betrag innerhalb der Billionenskala so gering ausnimmt.

Cette chronologie présente une histoire de l'économie des États-Unis à partir de 1920. De petits sacs d'argent rouges indiquent les explications de concepts clés. Dans le bas, l'inflation est illustrée par l'évolution du prix d'un demi-gallon de lait. Au-dessus de la ligne de temps, le PIB et le déficit national suivent une croissance spectaculaire. L'échelle de mesure est donnée en trillions (lignes blanches sur fond rouge).

Sous l'axe du temps, une ligne rouge qui commence dans les années 1960 indique que le gouvernement a commencé à dépenser plus qu'il ne gagnait, augmentant ainsi constamment la dette nationale. Ce déficit est montré à la même échelle que la dette nationale au-dessus, et atteint les 357 milliards à la fin de la ligne. La loupe montre un agrandissement de ce détail, car la quantité semble minuscule à l'échelle des trillions.

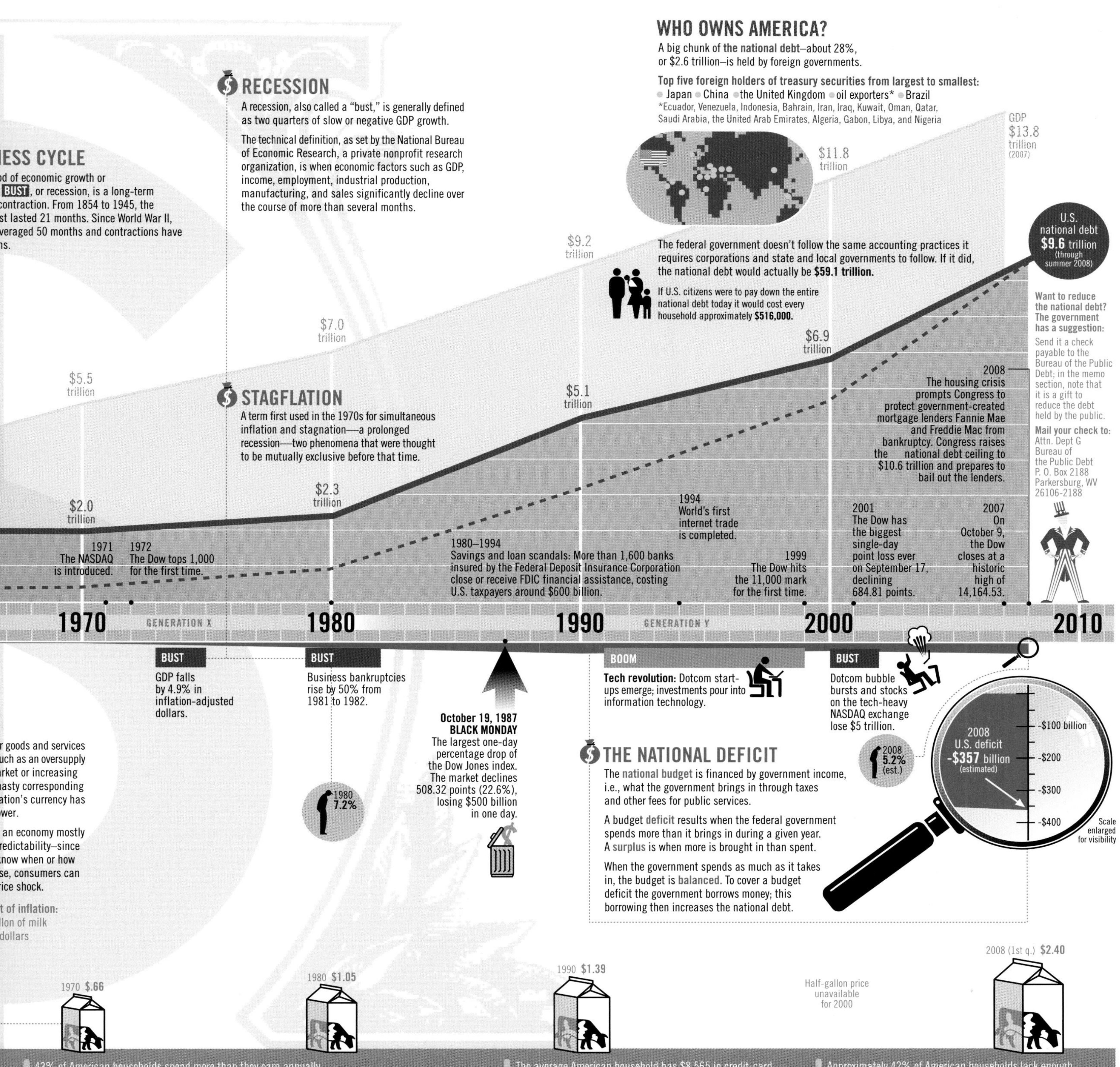

WHO OWNS AMERICA?
A big chunk of the national debt–about 28%, or $2.6 trillion–is held by foreign governments.
Top five foreign holders of treasury securities from largest to smallest:
Japan China the United Kingdom oil exporters* Brazil
*Ecuador, Venezuela, Indonesia, Bahrain, Iran, Iraq, Kuwait, Oman, Qatar, Saudi Arabia, the United Arab Emirates, Algeria, Gabon, Libya, and Nigeria
RECESSION
A recession, also called a "bust," is generally defined as two quarters of slow or negative GDP growth.
The technical definition, as set by the National Bureau of Economic Research, a private nonprofit research organization, is when economic factors such as GDP, income, employment, industrial production, manufacturing, and sales significantly decline over the course of more than several months.
GDP $13.8 trillion (2007)
$11.8 trillion
$9.2 trillion
$7.0 trillion
$5.5 trillion
The federal government doesn't follow the same accounting practices it requires corporations and state and local governments to follow. If it did, the national debt would actually be $59.1 trillion.
If U.S. citizens were to pay down the entire national debt today it would cost every household approximately $516,000.
U.S. national debt $9.6 trillion (through summer 2008)
Want to reduce the national debt? The government has a suggestion: Send it a check payable to the Bureau of the Public Debt; in the memo section, note that it is a gift to reduce the debt held by the public.
Mail your check to: Attn. Dept G Bureau of the Public Debt P. O. Box 2188 Parkersburg, WV 26106-2188
STAGFLATION
A term first used in the 1970s for simultaneous inflation and stagnation—a prolonged recession—two phenomena that were thought to be mutually exclusive before that time.
$6.9 trillion
$5.1 trillion
$2.3 trillion
$2.0 trillion
2008 The housing crisis prompts Congress to protect government-created mortgage lenders Fannie Mae and Freddie Mac from bankruptcy. Congress raises the national debt ceiling to $10.6 trillion and prepares to bail out the lenders.
1994 World's first internet trade is completed.
2001 The Dow has the biggest single-day point loss ever on September 17, declining 684.81 points.
2007 On October 9, the Dow closes at a historic high of 14,164.53.
1971 The NASDAQ is introduced.
1972 The Dow tops 1,000 for the first time.
1980–1994 Savings and loan scandals: More than 1,600 banks insured by the Federal Deposit Insurance Corporation close or receive FDIC financial assistance, costing U.S. taxpayers around $600 billion.
1999 The Dow hits the 11,000 mark for the first time.
1970 GENERATION X 1980 1990 GENERATION Y 2000 2010
BUST GDP falls by 4.9% in inflation-adjusted dollars.
BUST Business bankruptcies rise by 50% from 1981 to 1982.
October 19, 1987 BLACK MONDAY The largest one-day percentage drop of the Dow Jones index. The market declines 508.32 points (22.6%), losing $500 billion in one day.
BOOM Tech revolution: Dotcom start-ups emerge; investments pour into information technology.
BUST Dotcom bubble bursts and stocks on the tech-heavy NASDAQ exchange lose $5 trillion.
1980 7.2%
2008 5.2% (est.)
THE NATIONAL DEFICIT
The national budget is financed by government income, i.e., what the government brings in through taxes and other fees for public services.
A budget deficit results when the federal government spends more than it brings in during a given year. A surplus is when more is brought in than spent.
When the government spends as much as it takes in, the budget is balanced. To cover a budget deficit the government borrows money; this borrowing then increases the national debt.
2008 U.S. deficit -$357 billion (estimated)
-$100 billion -$200 -$300 -$400
Scale enlarged for visibility
1970 $.66
1980 $1.05
1990 $1.39
Half-gallon price unavailable for 2000
2008 (1st q.) $2.40
43% of American households spend more than they earn annually.
44% of American employees said they live "paycheck to paycheck" in 2007, up from 37% in 2006.
The average American household has $8,565 in credit-card debt, which is 15% higher than it was in 2000.
Approximately 42% of American households lack enough liquid savings to support themselves for three months.

Project Info: *GOOD*, poster, 2008, USA
Data Source: American Farm Bureau Federation; Congressional Budget Office; *The Economist*; FDIC; Investopedia; PBS; US Bureau of Labor Statistics; US Census Bureau
Design: Nigel Holmes
Art Direction: Casey Caplowe (*GOOD*)

Jacko: Success in Black, Failure in White

The day after Michael Jackson's death, Spanish newspaper *Público* published this timeline with important personal and professional landmarks in Jackson's life. With time running top down, the graphic shows his career on the left, and details of his personal life on the right. The strong contrast of black and white symbolises Jackson's ongoing quest for 'white' facial features and a lighter skin colour.

The "white period" begins in the late 1980s, when his increasingly pale skin gained widespread media attention. The pink graph towards the left shows numbers of records sold, the bars to the very left indicate his affiliation with the Jackson Five vs. his solo career, and the labels on which he released his records.

Einen Tag nach dem Tod Michael Jacksons veröffentlichte die spanische Zeitung *Público* diese Zeitleiste mit wichtigen persönli-chen und beruflichen Stationen seines Lebens. Die Zeit verläuft darin von oben nach unten. Auf der Grafik ist links Jacksons Karriere dargestellt, rechts sind Ereignisse aus seinem Privatleben zu sehen. Der starke Schwarz-Weiß-Kontrast symbolisiert Jacksons immerwährendes Streben nach „weißen" Gesichtszügen und einem helleren Teint.

Die „weiße Periode" begann Ende der 1980er-Jahre, als sein zunehmend heller Teint großes Medieninteresse hervorrief. Der rosafarbene Graph links zeigt die Anzahl der verkauften Platten, die Balken ganz links verdeutlichen die Dauer seiner Zugehörigkeit zu den Jackson Five und seiner Solokarriere bzw. machen Angaben zu den Labels, bei denen seine Schallplatten erschienen.

Le jour suivant le décès de Michael Jackson, le journal espagnol *Público* a publié cette chronologie qui reprend les événements marquants de sa vie professionnelle et personnelle. Le temps s'écoule de haut en bas, avec sa carrière à gauche, et les détails de sa vie personnelle à droite. Le contraste entre fond noir et blanc symbolise sa quête d'un visage aux traits « blancs » et d'une couleur de peau plus claire.

La « période blanche » commence à la fin des années 1980, lorsque sa peau éclaircie a attiré l'attention des médias. Le graphique en rose sur la gauche montre les chiffres des ventes de ses albums, et les barres à l'extrême gauche indiquent la période des Jackson Five et sa carrière en solo, ainsi que les maisons de disques avec lesquelles il a travaillé.

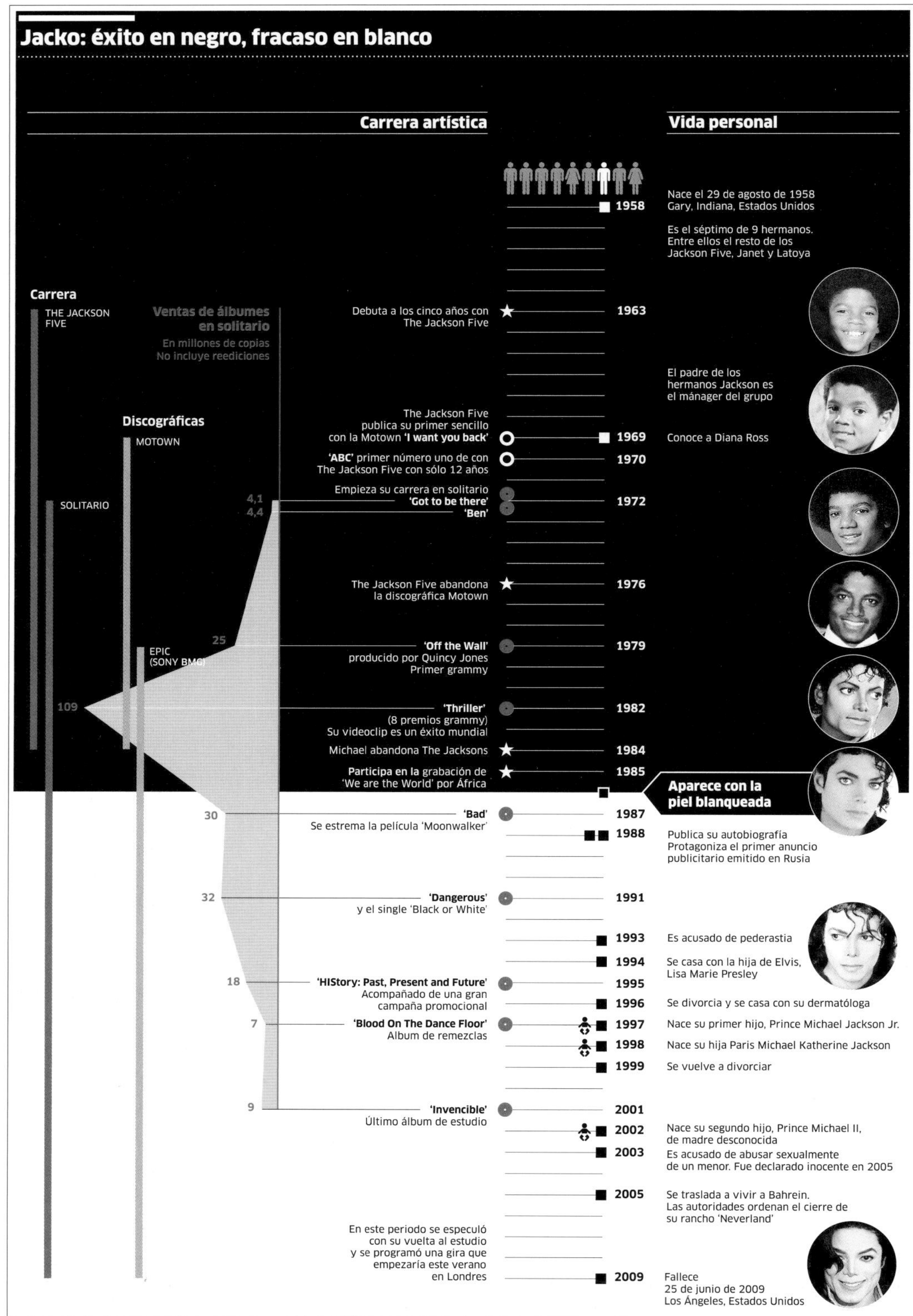

Project Info: "Goodbye to the King of Pop", *Público*, newspaper article, 2009, Spain
Data Source: Billboard; IFPI; Sony Music; MichaelJackson.com
Design: Álvaro Valiño
Awards: Malofiej 2010, Silver

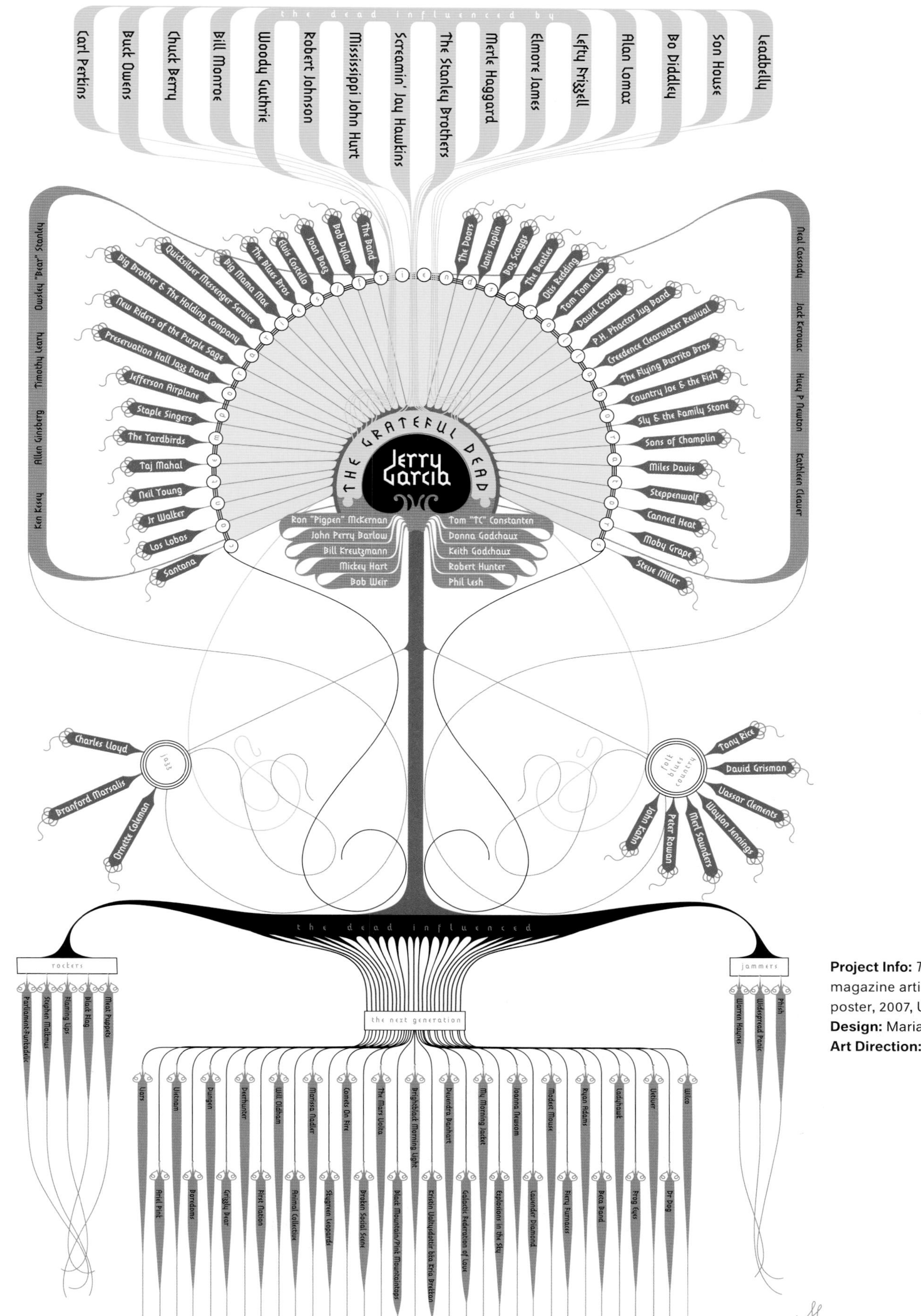

Project Info: *The Fader*, magazine article and poster, 2007, USA
Design: Marian Bantjes
Art Direction: Phil Bicker

Jerry Garcia

Marian Bantjes designed this intriguing diagram for *Fader* magazine in 2007. It depicts the musical cosmos of Jerry Garcia and his legendary American rock band, The Grateful Dead. The history of music evolves top down in this diagram, starting with Garcia's roots in the American blues and rock'n'roll scene of the Fifties and Sixties.

The central flower lists band members of The Grateful Dead, as well as many friends, contemporaries and collaborators Jerry Garcia was in touch with. At the bottom, influences are passed on to the next generations of younger musicians.

Marian Bantjes gestaltete dieses außergewöhnliche Diagramm 2007 für die Zeitschrift *Fader*. Es zeigt das musikalische Universum von Jerry Garcia und seiner legendären amerikanischen Rockband The Grateful Dead. Die Geschichte der Musik entfaltet sich hier von oben nach unten und setzt bei Garcias Wurzeln im amerikanischen Blues und Rock 'n' Roll der Fünfziger- und Sechzigerjahre an.

In der Bildmitte zählt eine „Blüte“ die Bandmitglieder von Grateful Dead auf sowie viele Freunde, Zeitgenossen und Kollegen, mit denen Jerry Garcia in Kontakt stand. Darunter werden Musiker der nächsten Generationen genannt, auf die Jerry Garcia großen Einfluss ausübte.

C'est Marian Bantjes qui a conçu ce diagramme fascinant pour le magazine *Fader* en 2007. Il représente le cosmos musical de Jerry Garcia et de son groupe de rock américain légendaire, les Grateful Dead. L'histoire de la musique évolue de haut en bas dans ce diagramme, en commençant avec les racines de Garcia dans le blues et le rock'n'roll américains des années 1950 et 1960.

Au centre, la fleur est une liste des membres des Grateful Dead, ainsi que de nombreux amis, contemporains et collaborateurs avec lesquels Jerry Garcia était en contact. Dans le bas, les influences sont transmises à la génération suivante de musiciens.

RUI, MINH ANH, VICTOR & "SYLVIA" (THE CAR)

LA×NYC ROAD TRIP 14 DAYS

4129 MI / 6645 KM / 7x LENGTH OF FRANCE / 11 H ON THE ROAD PER DAY / 295 MI 475 KM PER DAY / WE DROVE ACROSS 17 STATES / 94 POSTCARDS.

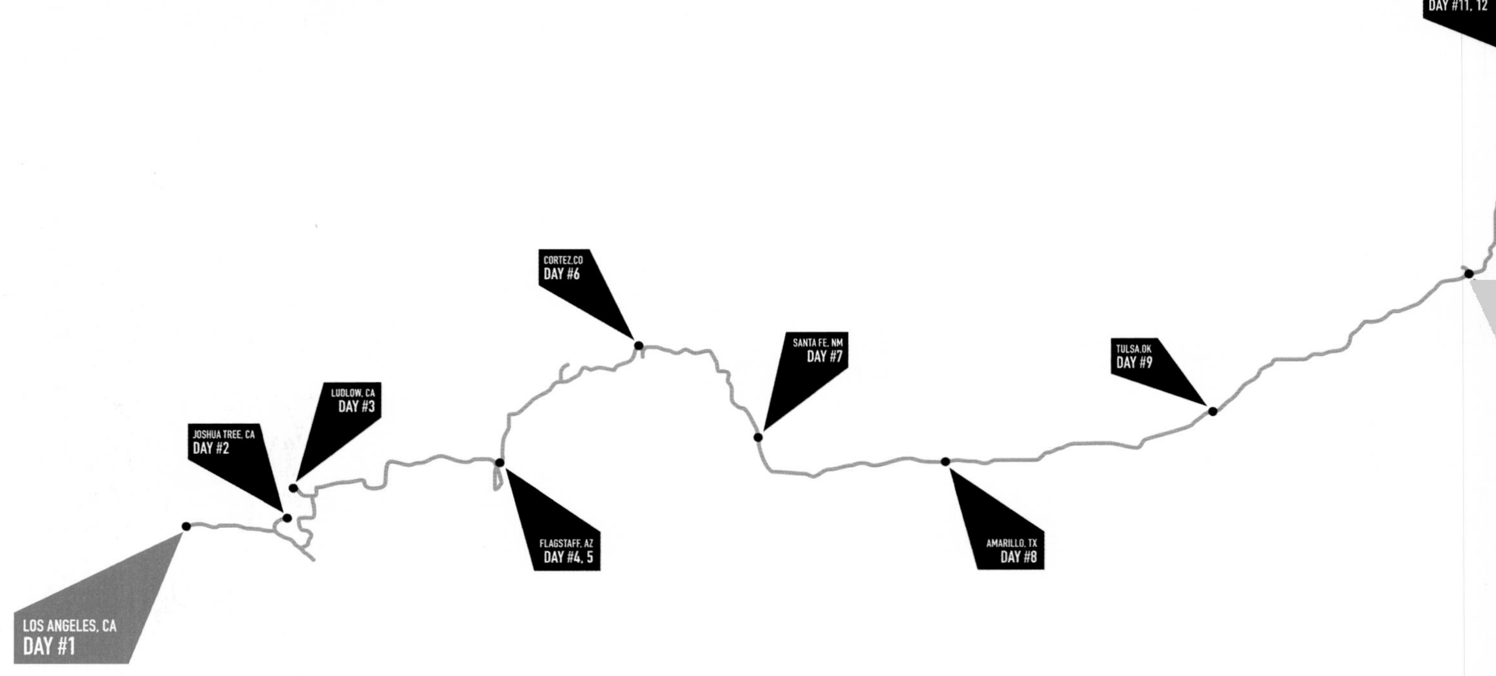

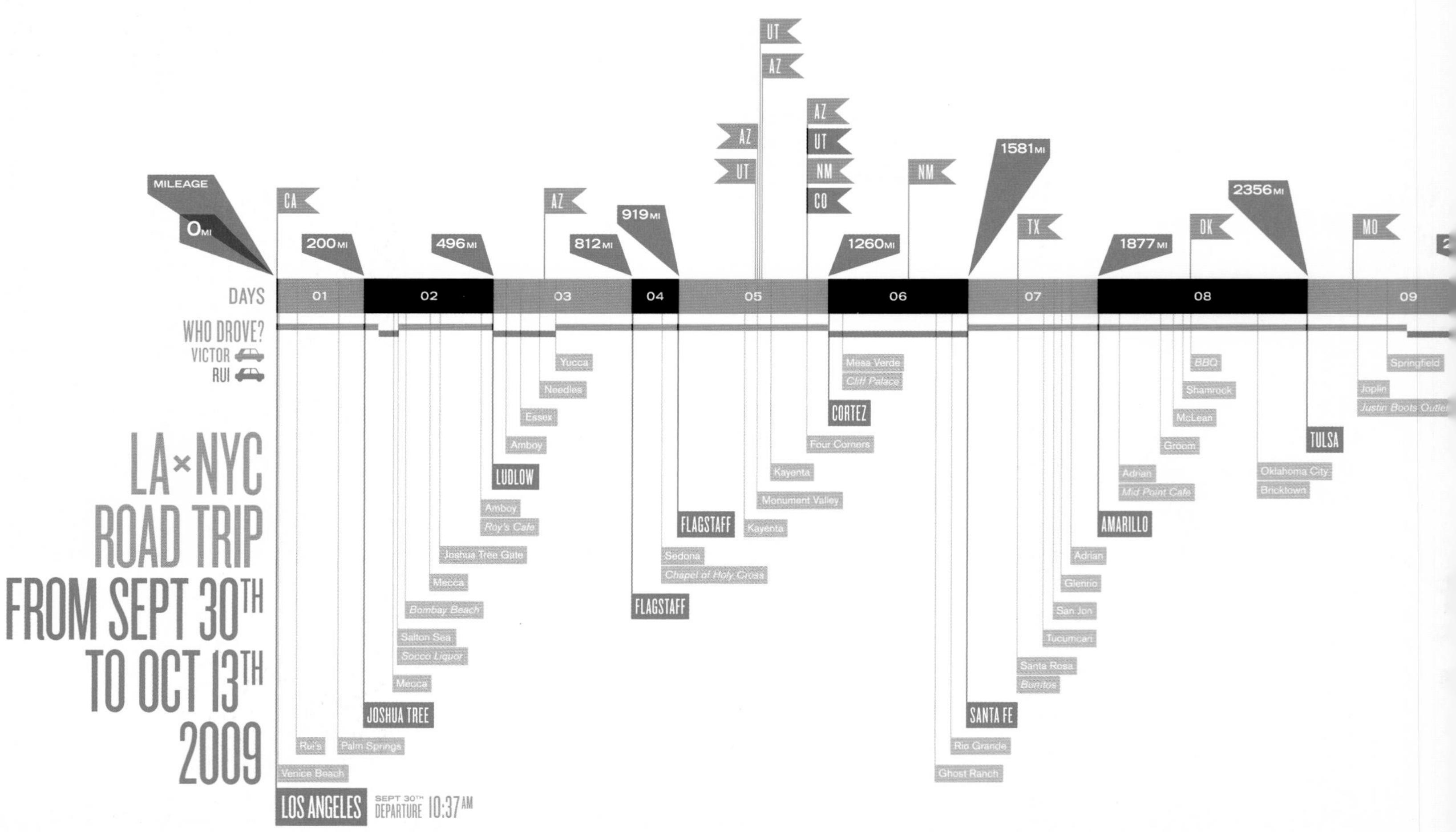

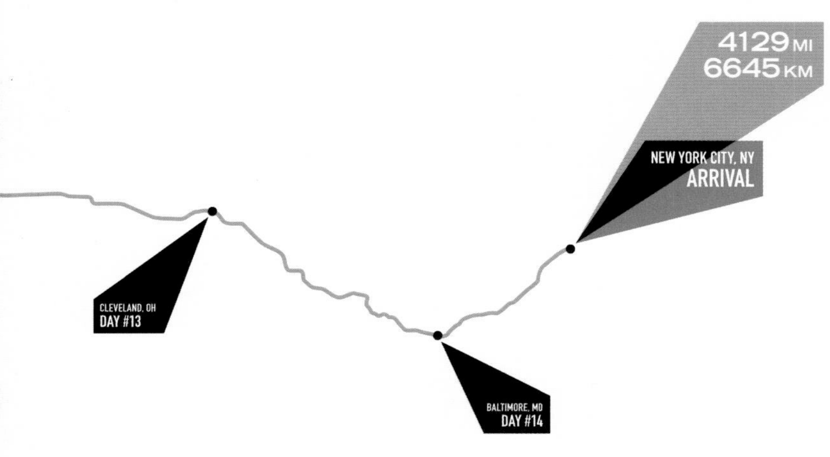

LA–NYC

For the visualisation of their road-trip through the United States in 2009, French designers Minh Anh Vo and Victor Schuft made the timeline their guiding principle. The days of their trip are marked alternately in black and red.

Little flags above mark the states that were crossed, while blue flashes show the mileage. Below the timeline appear individual places travelled through. In the upper part of the image, the red line follows their route on an invisible map of the US, with black tags indicating the succession of days.

Für die Visualisierung ihrer Reise mit dem Auto durch die USA im Jahr 2009 stellten die französischen Grafiker Minh Anh Vo und Victor Schuft eine Zeitleiste in den Mittelpunkt. Die Tage sind darauf abwechselnd in Schwarz und in Rot vermerkt.

Kleine Flaggen am oberen Bildrand verweisen auf die durchquerten Bundesstaaten, blaue Pfeile geben die zurückgelegte Strecke in Meilen an. Unter der Zeitleiste sind einzelne Orte vermerkt, die die beiden passiert haben. Die rote Linie im oberen Teil der Grafik zeichnet die Route auf eine unsichtbare Landkarte der USA ein, wobei schwarze Schildchen die Abfolge der Tage angeben.

Les graphistes français Minh Anh Vo et Victor Schuft ont adopté la chronologie comme principe de référence pour créer une visualisation de leur traversée des États-Unis en voiture en 2009. Les journées de voyage sont colorées tour à tour en rouge et en noir.

Au-dessus, de petits drapeaux indiquent les États traversés, et les miles parcourus sont signalés en bleu. Les différents endroits traversés apparaissent sous la chronologie. Dans la partie supérieure de l'image, la ligne rouge trace leur route sur une carte invisible des États-Unis, avec des étiquettes noires indiquant la succession des jours.

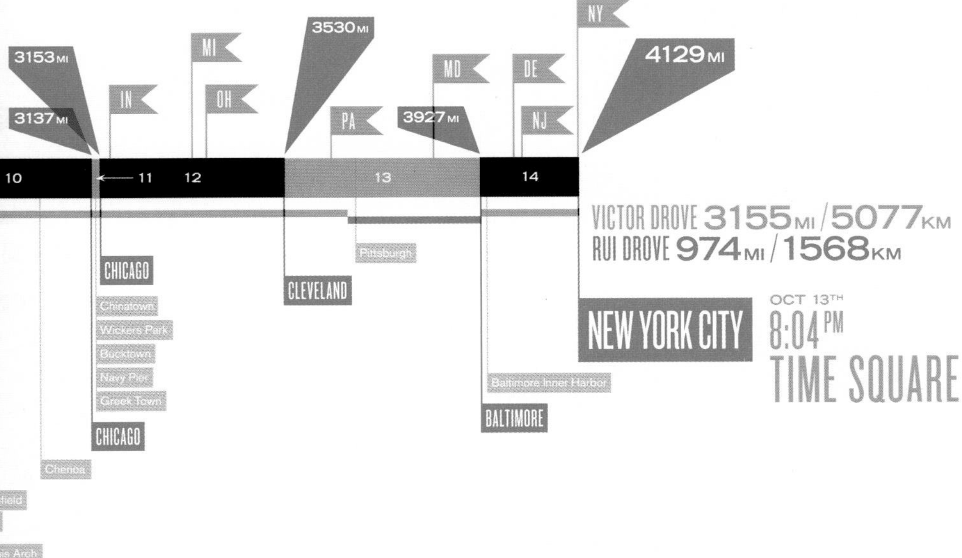

200 MI 400 KM

Project Info: Poster, 2010, USA
Design: Minh Anh Vo, Victor Schuft (Papercut)

Life Map to Quarter-Life Crisis

Whilst diagrams have been constructed to chart statistical data or technical processes, and thus retain a reputation for belonging to the more boring and non-human things on Earth, designers are increasingly "using" them for charting emotional troubles or personal experiences.

Corcoran's "Life Map to Quarter-Life Crisis" is a guide to the life experiences of an average youth in the US. Trying to make the step from adolescence to adulthood seems to entail the inevitable hardship of having to traverse a serious quarter-age crisis.

Während Diagramme erfunden wurden, um Statistiken und technische Abläufe abzubilden, und noch immer in dem Ruf stehen, zu den eher langweiligen und nicht-menschlichen Dingen auf Erden zu gehören, „verwenden" Designer sie zunehmend auch, um emotionale Verwirrungen und persönliche Erfahrungen zu kartieren.

Corcorans „Life Map to Quarter-Life Crisis" ist ein Leitfaden, der die Lebenserfahrungen eines durchschnittlichen Jugendlichen in den USA spiegelt. Der Schritt von der Jugend zum Erwachsenendasein ist offenbar unweigerlich mit einer schwerwiegenden Sinnkrise am Ende des ersten Lebensviertels verbunden.

Les diagrammes ont été inventés pour présenter des données statistiques ou des processus techniques, c'est pourquoi ils ont la réputation tenace d'appartenir à des domaines plutôt ennuyeux et non humains. Pourtant les graphistes les utilisent de plus en plus pour représenter les problèmes émotionnels et les expériences personnelles.

La « Carte vitale de la crise des 25 ans » est un guide de la vie d'un jeune américain type. Le passage de l'adolescence à l'âge adulte semble aller de pair avec une épreuve inévitable : la très sérieuse crise du premier quart de la vie.

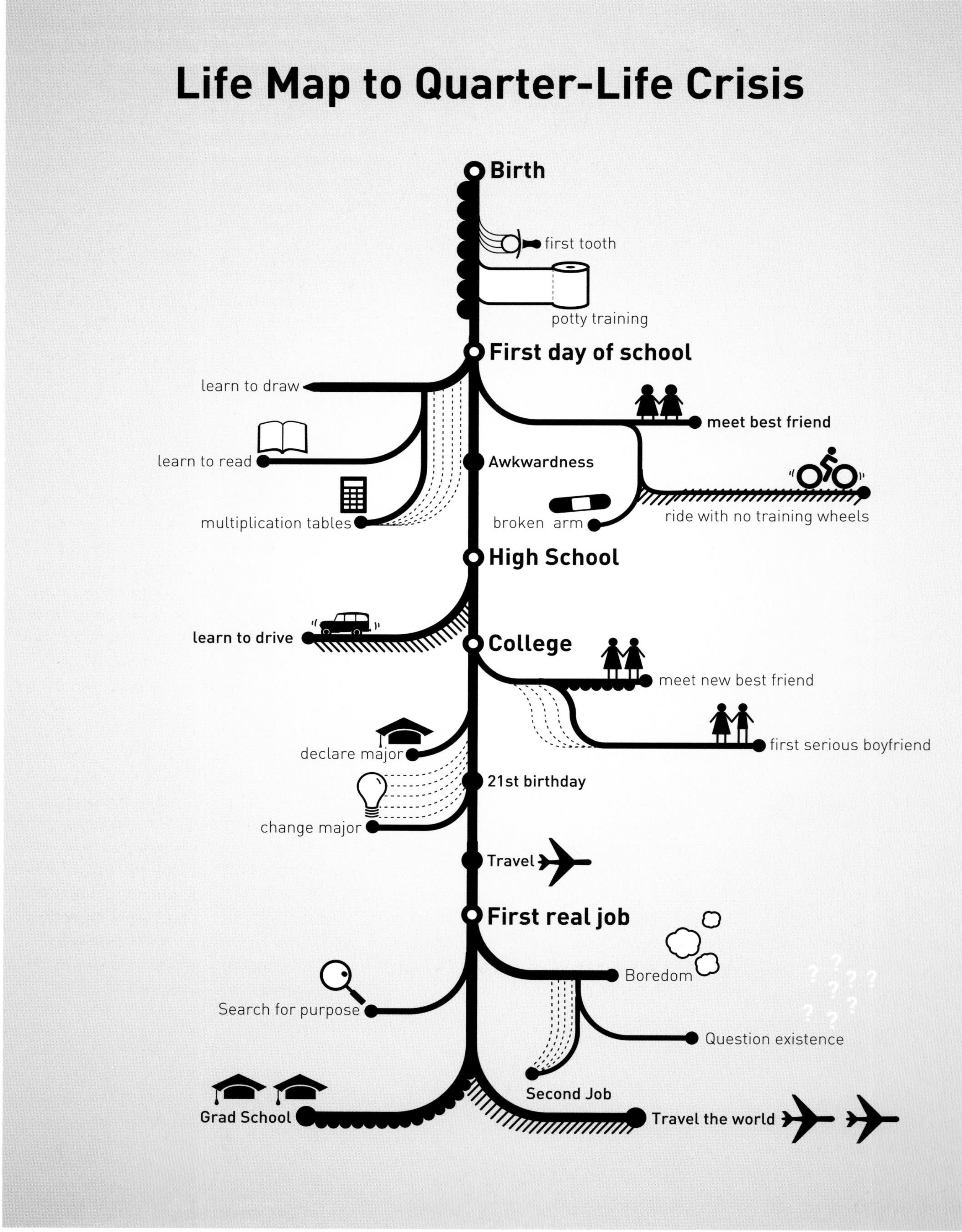

Project Info:
Metro Design Studio, book, 2009, USA
Design:
Colleen Corcoran

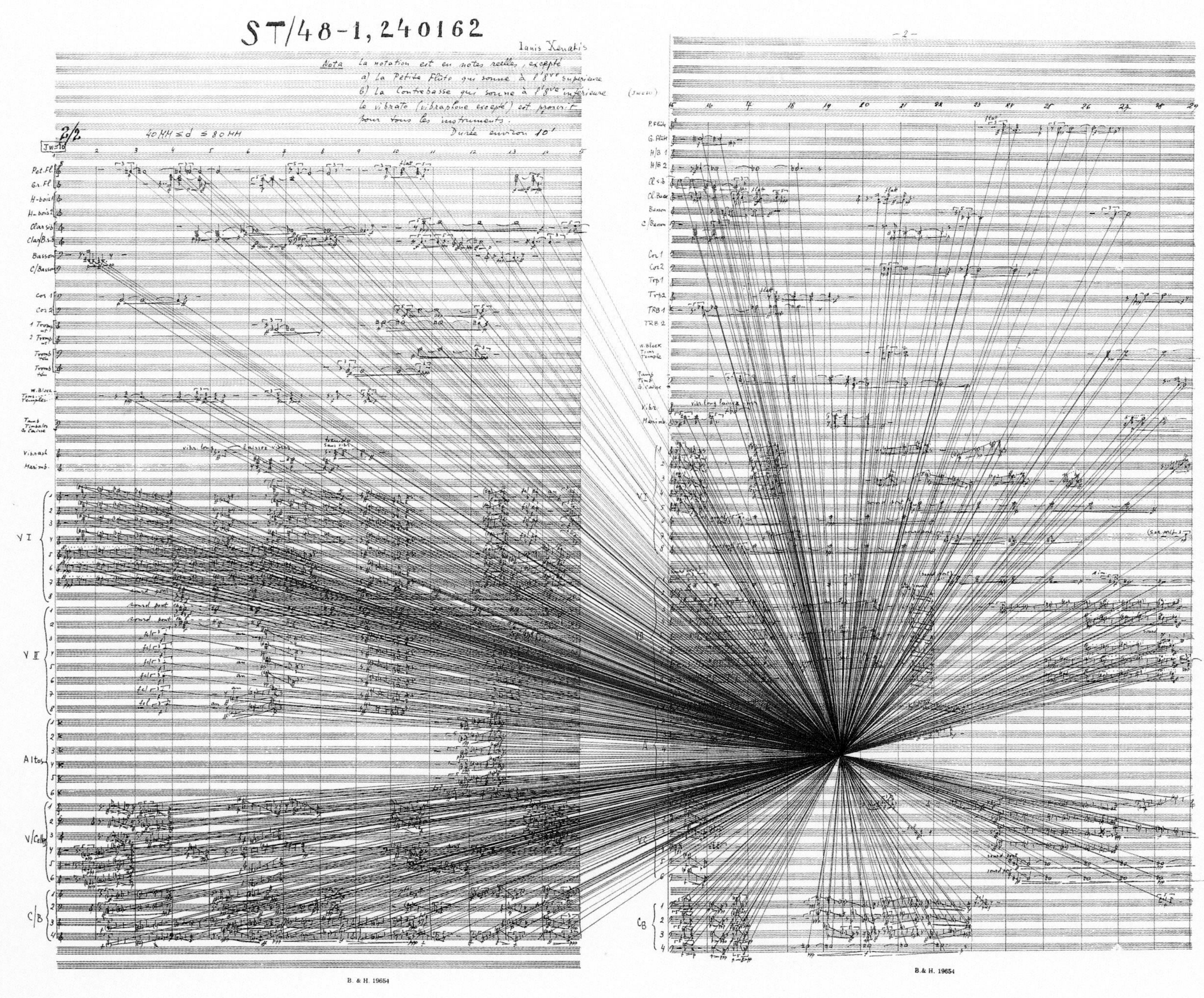

Mass Black Implosion

Australian visual and sound artist Marco Fusinato combines graphics and music in his "Mass Black Implosion" series. The drawings are based on the scores of post-war avant-garde or contemporary composers and on the only composition by painter Yves Klein. Fusinato connects all the notes of the individual pieces with fine lines to a freely chosen focal point – ignoring all other graphic notations in the scores.

The many notes of a fast or polyphonic work result in density and blackness, scores with fewer notes in more spread-out, calmer line drawings. By expanding the music notation, he creates a scheme to picture the style of each piece, and thus "makes visible the sound", or as the title suggests, the point where the music implodes.

Der australische Bild- und Tonkünstler Marco Fusinato verbindet in seiner Serie „Mass Black Implosion" Grafik und Musik. Die Zeichnungen beruhen auf den Partituren von modernen und zeitgenössischen Komponisten sowie auf der einzigen Komposition des Malers Yves Klein. Fusinato verbindet alle Noten einer Partitur durch feine Striche, die sich an einem frei gewählten Fluchtpunkt treffen; alle anderen grafischen Notationen der Partitur werden nicht berücksichtigt.

Die zahlreichen Noten eines schnellen oder polyphonen Werks lassen Dichte und Schwärze entstehen, Partituren mit weniger Noten ergeben weiträumigere, ruhigere Zeichnungen. Indem er die musikalische Notation erweitert, entwickelte Fusinato ein System, um den Stil eines Stücks abzubilden. Damit macht er „den Klang sichtbar" und zeigt, wie der Titel besagt, den Punkt, an dem die Musik implodiert.

Dans sa série « Mass Black Implosion », l'artiste visuel et sonore Marco Fusinato combine le graphisme et la musique. Les dessins sont basés sur les partitions de compositeurs de l'avant-garde de l'après-guerre ou contemporains, et sur la seule et unique composition du peintre Yves Klein. Fusinato connecte toutes les notes de chaque morceau à un point focal arbitraire à l'aide de fines lignes – en ignorant toutes les notations graphiques des partitions.

Les nombreuses notes d'un morceau rapide ou polyphonique créent de la densité et de la noirceur, alors que les partitions qui comportent moins de notes créent des dessins plus calmes, aux lignes plus espacées. En travaillant sur la notation de la musique, il crée un moyen de représenter le style de chaque morceau, et ainsi de « rendre le son visible » ou, comme le suggère le titre, le moment où la musique implose.

Project Info: Series of drawings, 2007–2009, Australia
Artist: Marco Fusinato
Additional Info: Ink on archival facsimile of score; Marco Fusinato is represented by Anna Schwartz Gallery, Melbourne

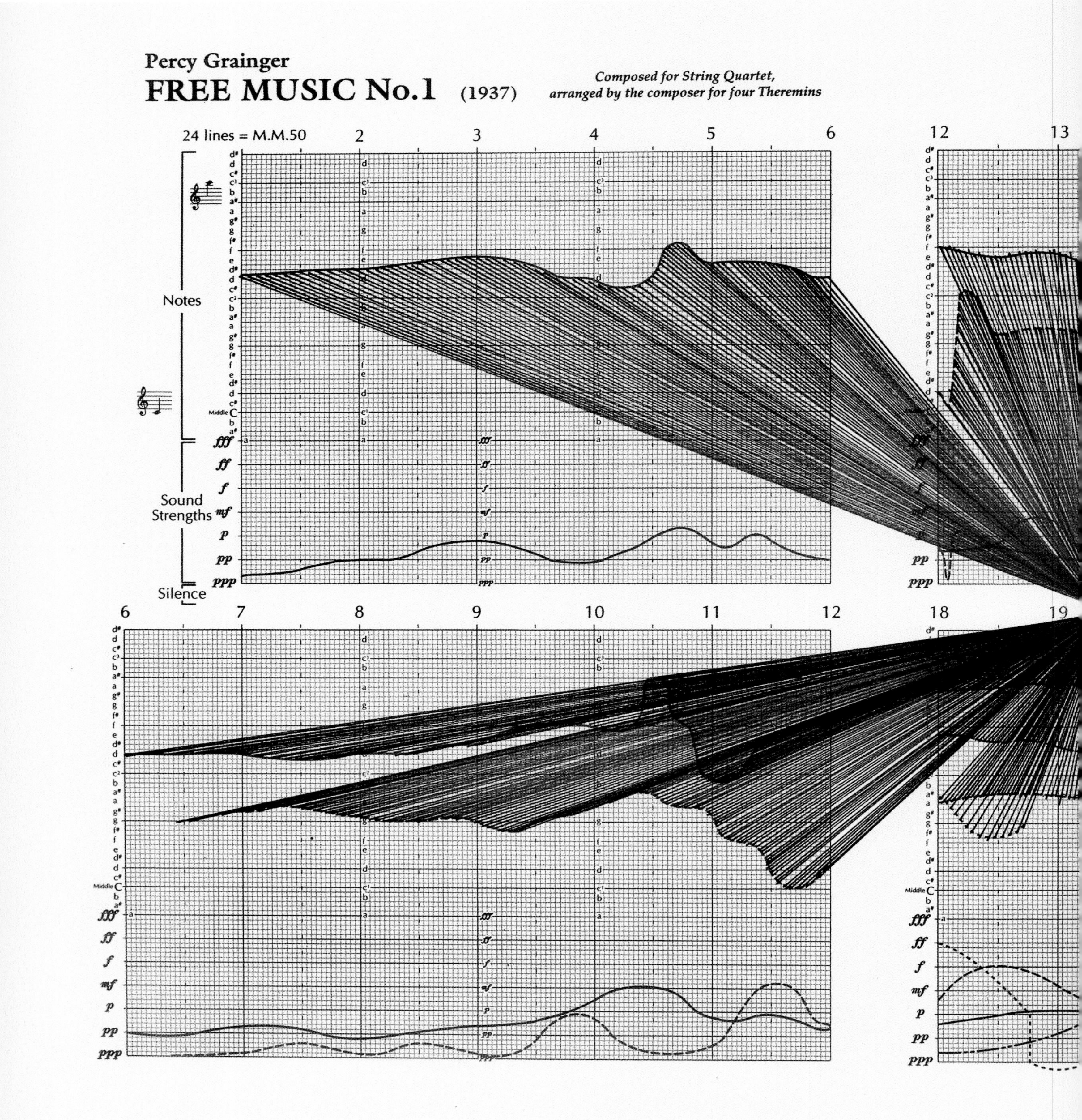

Percy Grainger

FREE MUSIC No.1 (1937)

Composed for String Quartet, arranged by the composer for four Theremins

24 lines = M.M.50

Notes

Sound Strengths

Silence

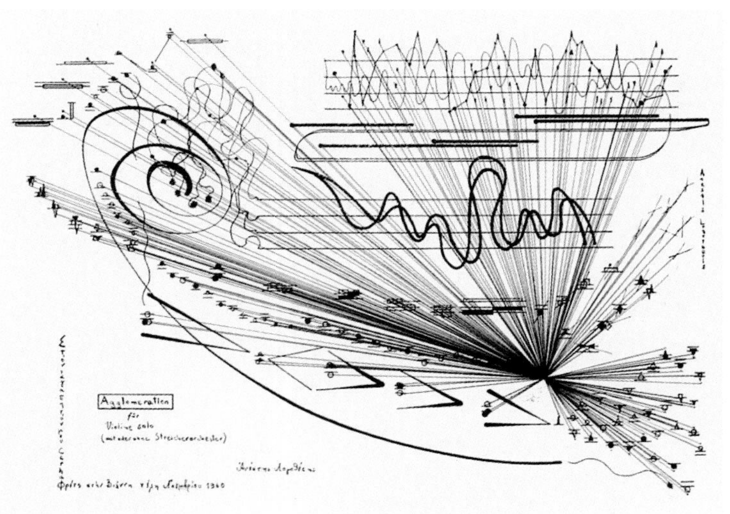

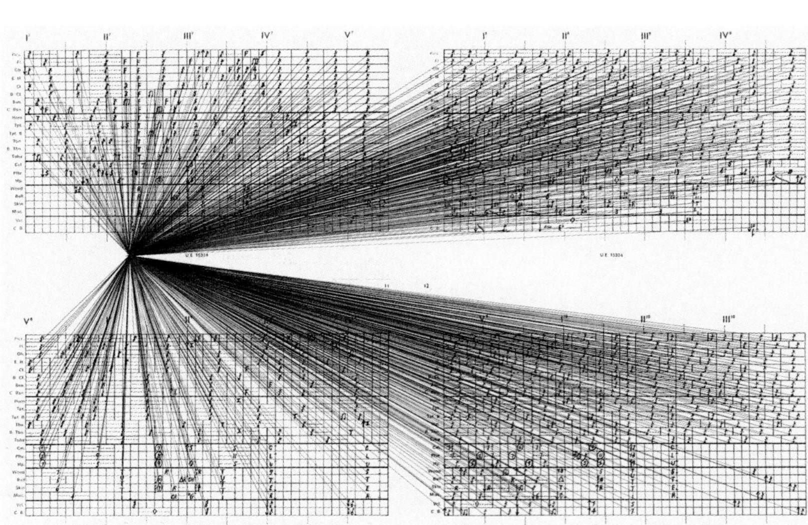

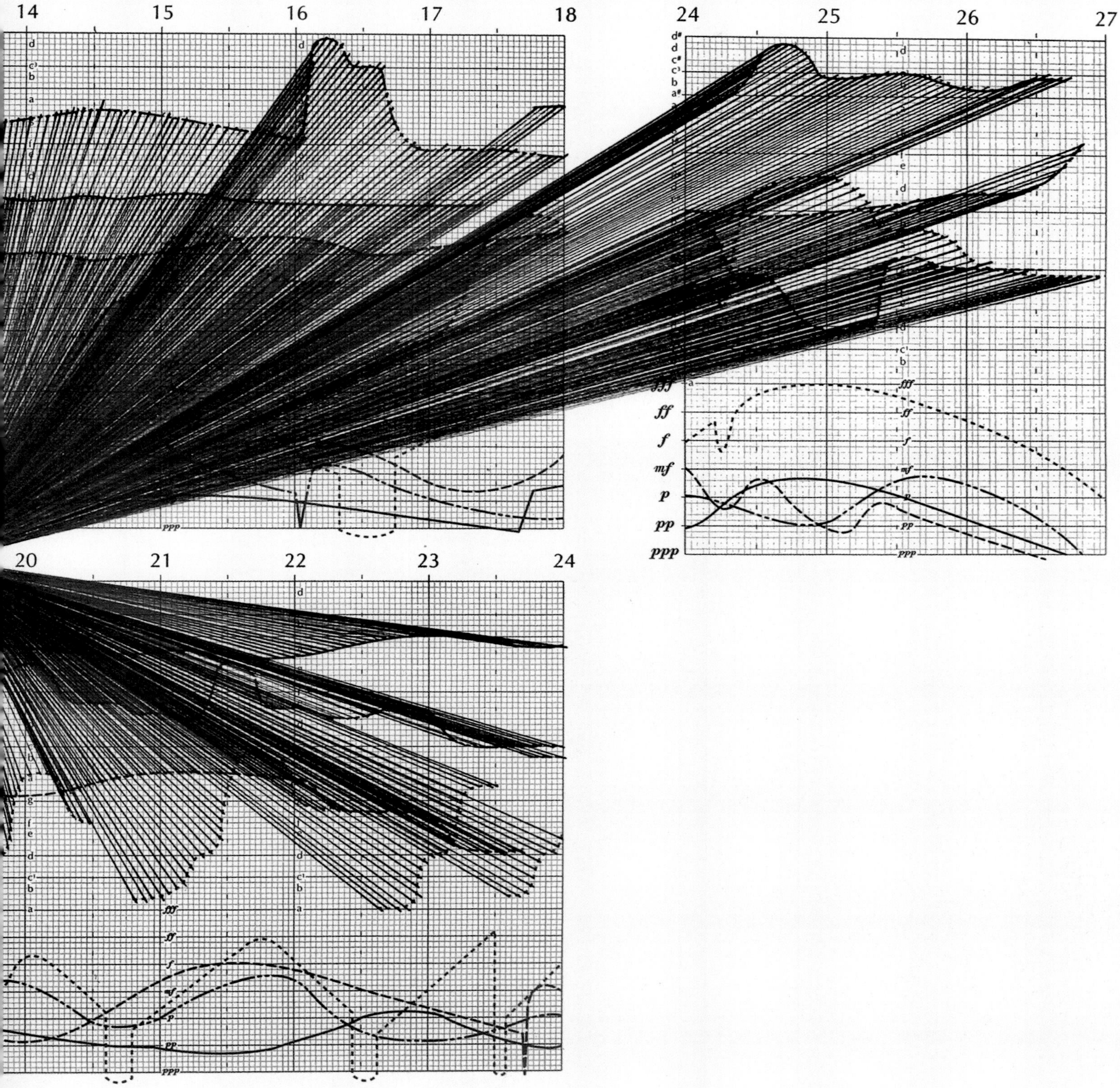

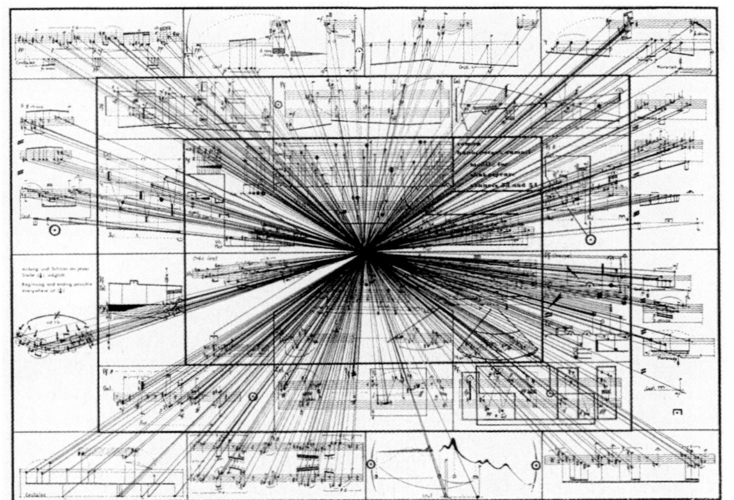

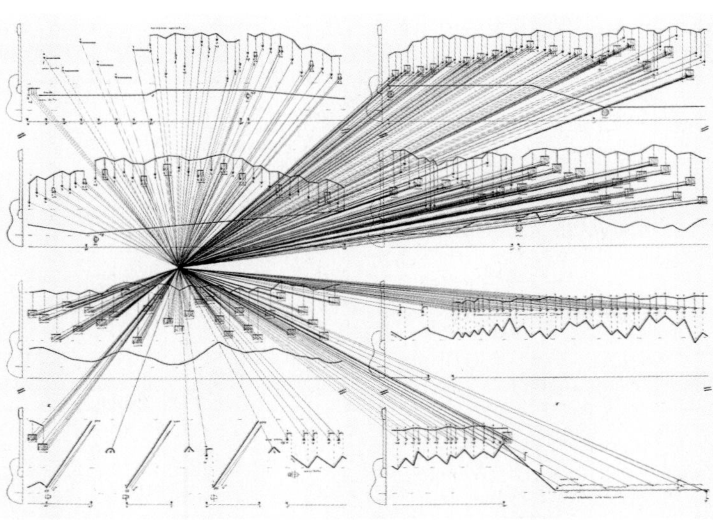

Mission(s) to Mars

Our neighbouring planet Mars has been the destination of numerous space missions, with varying success. Bryan Christie Design developed this graphic for technology magazine *IEEE Spectrum* to show all the attempted missions to Mars, successful and unsuccessful. Traditionally this kind of information is often presented as a table, a simple list of entries, with additional information for each entry.

Here, the designers developed an image of Mars as the target destination for the various missions. The length of the bars shows the level of success and what type of mission it was, i.e. fly-by, orbiter, landing or rover. Colours represent the different countries that sent the missions; the missions themselves were then grouped by year.

Unser Nachbarplanet Mars ist schon länger das Ziel von Weltraummissionen, die von unterschiedlichem Erfolg gekrönt waren. Bryan Christie Design entwickelte diese Grafik für das Technikmagazin *IEEE Spectrum.* Sie listet alle Missionen zum Mars unabhängig von ihrem Erfolg auf. Gemeinhin werden solche Informationen in Form einer Tabelle dargestellt, einer einfachen Liste mit ergänzenden Daten zu jedem Eintrag.

Hier entwarfen die Grafiker ein Bild vom Planeten Mars als Ziel zahlreicher Missionen. Die Länge der Balken veranschaulicht den Erfolg und die Art der Mission, d. h., ob es sich um einen Vorbeiflug, eine Umkreisung, eine Landung oder um eine Erkundung mit einem Rover handelte. Die Farben stehen für die jeweiligen Länder, die die Mission starteten, die Flüge selbst wurden nach Jahren geordnet.

Mars, notre planète voisine, a été la destination de nombreuses missions spatiales, qui ont eu différents degrés de succès. Bryan Christie Design a conçu ce visuel pour le magazine technologique *IEEE Spectrum* afin de montrer toutes les missions vers Mars qui ont été tentées, qu'elles aient été couronnées de succès ou non. Ce type d'information est habituellement présenté sous forme de tableau, une simple liste récapitulant les données de chaque mission.

Ici, les graphistes ont utilisé une image où Mars est mise en scène comme destination des missions. La longueur des barres indique le degré de succès et le type de mission, par ex. survol, mise en orbite, atterrissage ou exploration. Les couleurs représentent les différents pays qui ont envoyé ces missions; les missions ont ensuite été groupées par année.

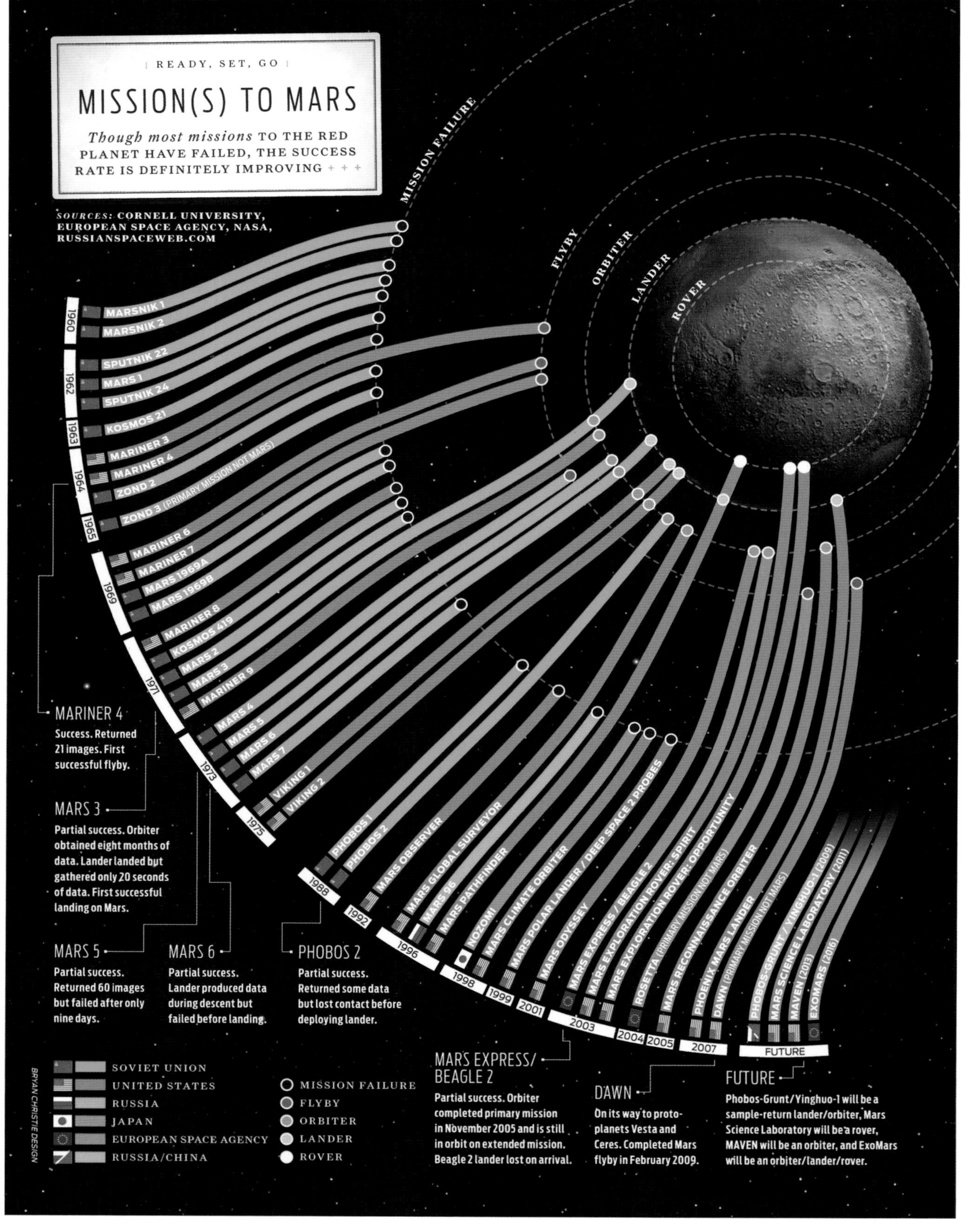

Project Info:
IEEE Spectrum, magazine article, 2009, USA
Data Source:
Cornell University; European Space Agency; NASA; RussianSpaceWeb.com
Design:
Bryan Christie, Joe Lertola
Art Direction:
Mark Montgomery, Michael Solita

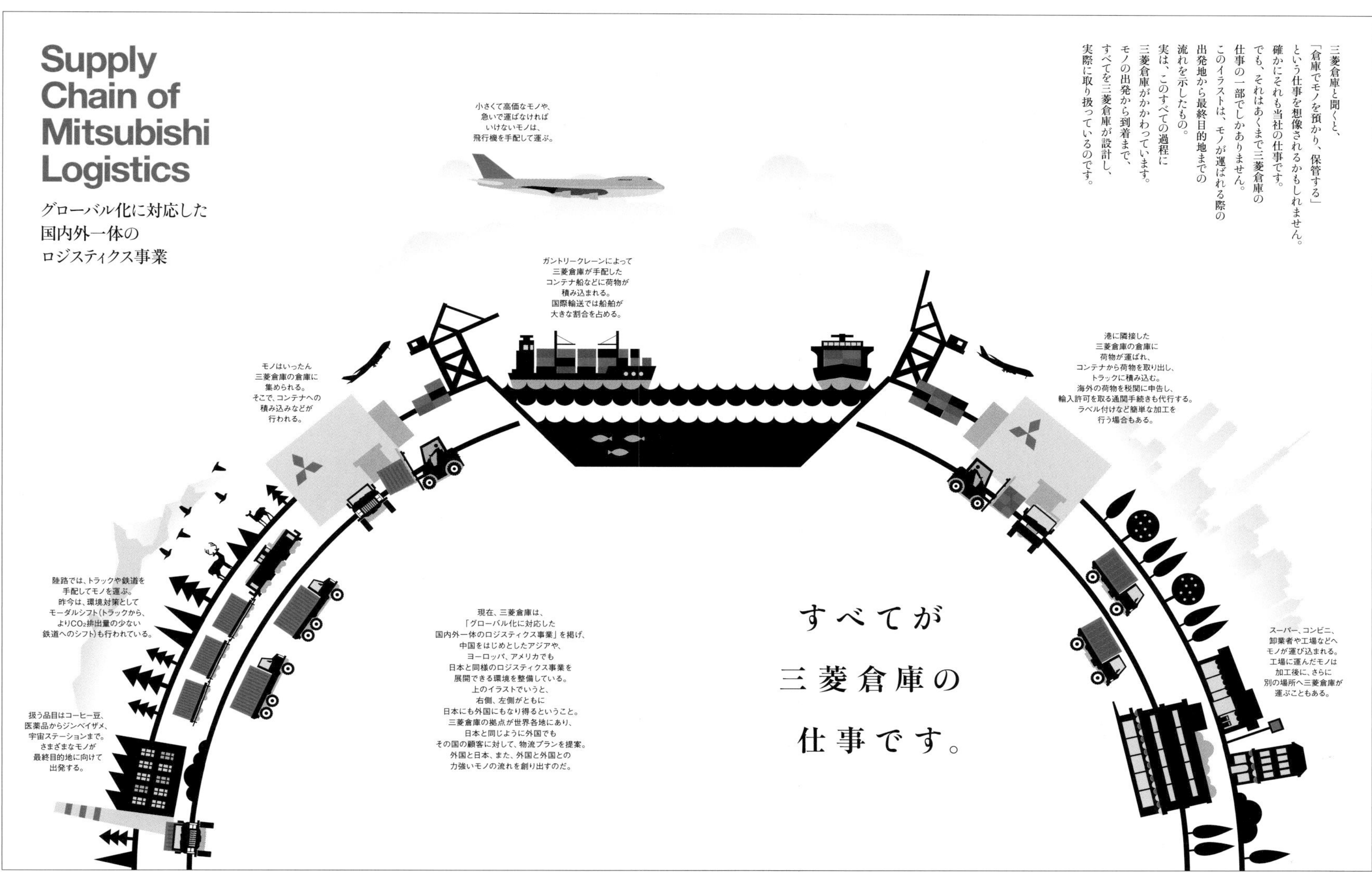

Mitsubishi Logistics Supply Chain

In this graphic developed for a Japanese logistics supplier, the company's portfolio is represented in a flow chart. Whilst the company focused on warehouse services after its founding in the late 19th century, it later branched out into transportation handling to and from Japan.

This is reflected here in representing the full logistics chain in a process chart, from the production of goods through various transportation facilities down to storage and distribution to retailers. From the bottom left around the arc, motion is indicated by the direction in which vehicles move, while layers indicate the variety of services. The monochrome background recalls traditional ink drawings.

Diese Grafik wurde für ein japanisches Logistikunternehmen entwickelt und stellt die Angebotspalette der Firma als Ablaufdiagramm dar. Während sich das Unternehmen nach der Gründung Ende des 19. Jahrhunderts zunächst auf Lagerhaltung spezialisiert hatte, verlegte es sich später auf den Transport und den Warenumschlag von und nach Japan.

Das wird hier verdeutlicht, indem die gesamte Logistikkette als Prozess dargestellt wird, von der Gütererzeugung über verschiedene Transportdienstleistungen bis hin zu Lagerung und Auslieferung an den Einzelhändler. Diese Bewegung wird angezeigt durch die Richtung, in der die Fahrzeuge fahren, von unten links über den gesamten Bogen hinweg. Ebenen veranschaulichen die Vielfalt der Dienstleistungen. Der einfarbige Hintergrund erinnert an traditionelle Tuschzeichnungen.

Dans ce visuel réalisé pour une entreprise de logistique japonaise, le portefeuille d'activités est représenté par un diagramme de processus. À sa création à la fin du XIXe siècle, l'entreprise s'était spécialisée dans les services d'entreposage, mais s'est depuis diversifiée dans le transport international à partir du Japon.

Cela se traduit par la représentation de toute la chaîne logistique sous forme d'un diagramme de processus, depuis la production des marchandises, en passant par les différents modes de transport, jusqu'à l'entreposage et la distribution aux revendeurs. En suivant l'arc à partir de la gauche, le mouvement est indiqué par la direction dans laquelle les véhicules se déplacent, tandis que les strates superposées expriment la diversité des services. Le fond monochrome évoque les dessins à l'encre traditionnels.

Project Info: Mitsubishi Logistics, booklet, 2011, Japan
Design: Kunihiko Nishiue (Dynamite Brothers Syndicate)
Illustration: Tokuma (Bowlgraphics)
Agency: Mainichi Communications Inc.

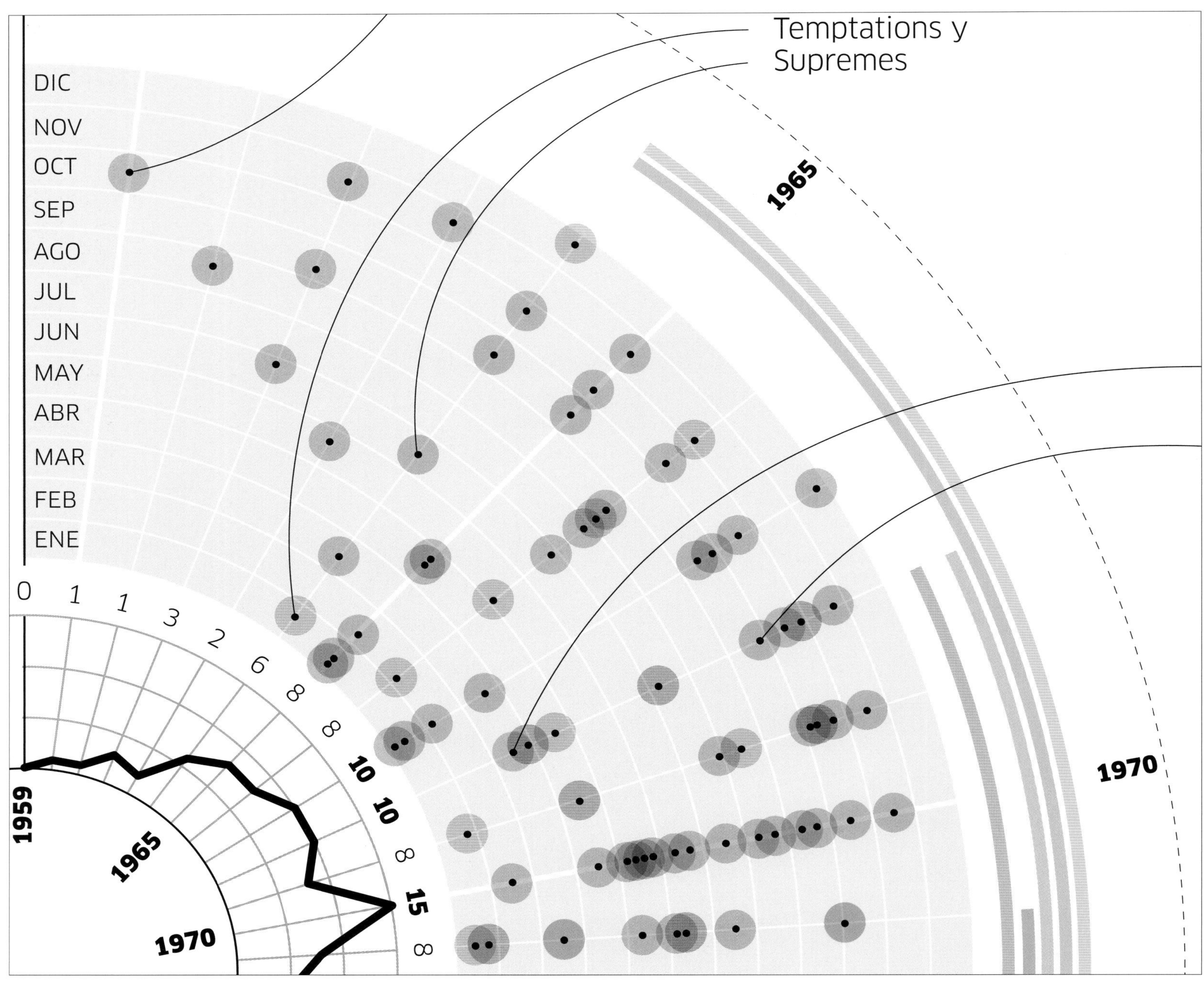

Motown's 191 Number One Hits

This circle timeline shows the history of legendary US record label Motown through its number one hits. With time running clockwise, the years are marked around the outside of the circle, while inner circle lines indicate the months. All 191 number ones in the history of the label are placed on the time-spot when they were released.

Colour coding refers to the most successful artists and is explained by the legend down the right side. The timeline gives an impression at one glance of the label's history and when it had its most successful years. Text and icons along the bottom explain some of the principles label boss Berry Gordy followed in "creating" his musicians and their style.

Die kreisförmige Zeitleiste veranschaulicht die Geschichte des legendären amerikanischen Plattenlabels Motown anhand der Songs, die die Charts anführten. Die Zeit verläuft im Uhrzeigersinn, die Jahreszahlen sind am Außenrand des Kreises angegeben, die inneren Kreise zeigen die Monate an. Alle 191 Nummer-eins-Hits in der Geschichte des Labels wurden nach ihrem Erscheinungsdatum eingetragen.

Die Farbcodierung verweist auf die erfolgreichsten Musiker und wird in der Legende rechts erläutert. Die Zeitleiste ermöglicht einen raschen Überblick über die Geschichte des Labels und seine erfolgreichsten Jahre. Der Text und die Symbole am unteren Bildrand erklären einige Prinzipien, aufgrund deren Labelchef Berry Gordy seine Musiker und ihren Stil „kreierte".

Cette chronologie circulaire montre l'histoire de la légendaire maison de disques américaine Motown, à travers ses succès arrivés en première place des classements. Le temps s'écoule dans le sens des aiguilles d'une montre, et les années sont indiquées sur l'extérieur du cercle, tandis que les mois sont marqués par les lignes blanches à l'intérieur du cercle. Les 191 numéros un de l'histoire du label sont placés à la date de leur sortie.

Le code couleur met en valeur les artistes qui ont rencontré le plus de succès, il est expliqué par la légende verticale sur la droite. Cette chronologie donne un aperçu de l'histoire de la maison de disques en un coup d'œil, ainsi que de ses plus grandes années. En bas, les textes et les icônes expliquent quelques-uns des principes que le patron du label, Berry Gordy, a suivis dans la « création » de ses musiciens et de leur style.

Project Info: "Motown, Half a Century of Churning Out Hits", *Público*, newspaper article, 2008, Spain
Data Source: Universal Music; Discogs.com; Rockhall.com; Top40-charts.com et al.
Design: Álvaro Valiño
Awards: Malofiej 2009, Silver

Los 191 números uno de la Motown

Cincuenta años de la historia del sello negro a través de sus éxitos

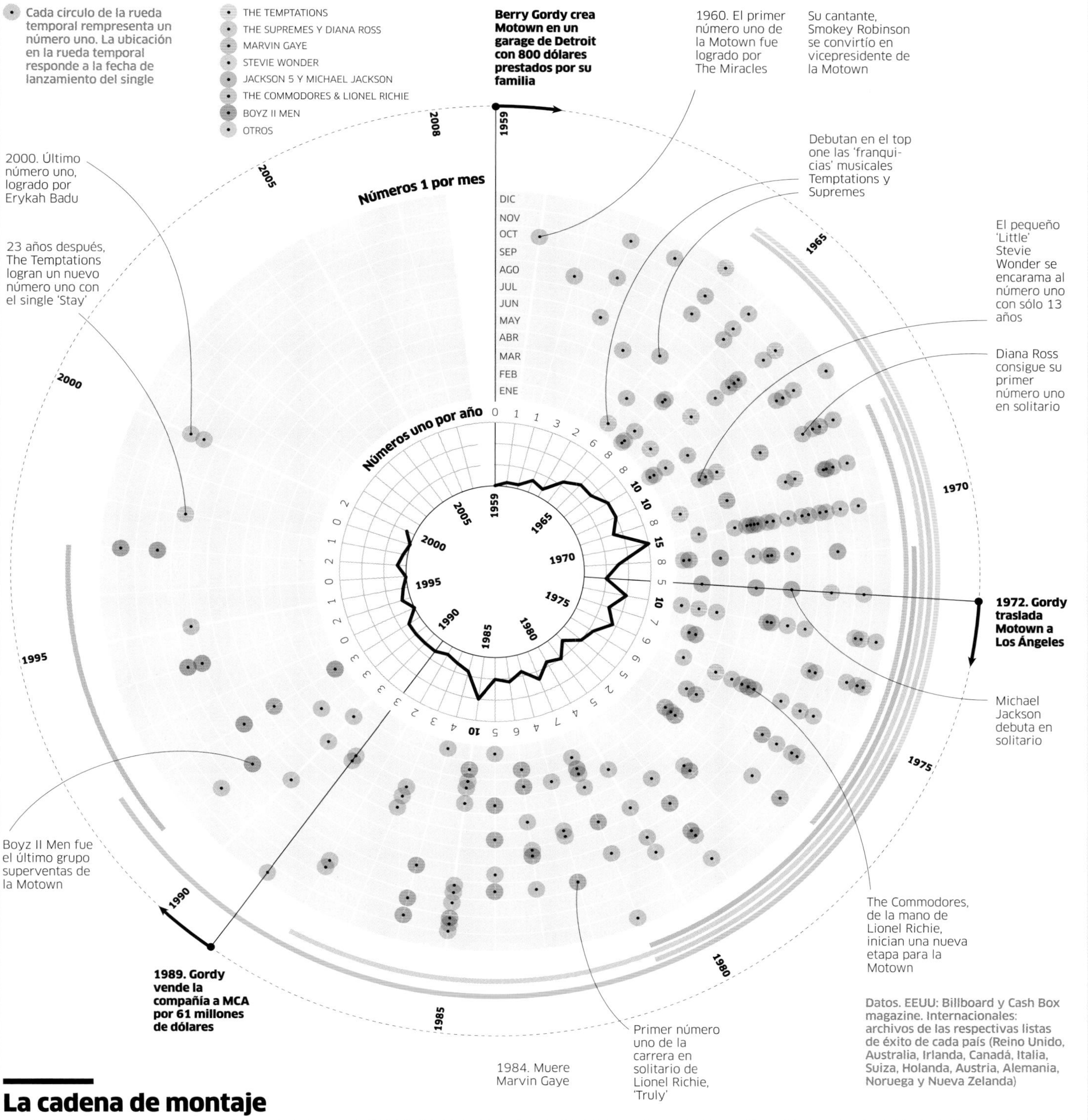

Cada circulo de la rueda temporal rempresenta un número uno. La ubicación en la rueda temporal responde a la fecha de lanzamiento del single

THE TEMPTATIONS
THE SUPREMES Y DIANA ROSS
MARVIN GAYE
STEVIE WONDER
JACKSON 5 Y MICHAEL JACKSON
THE COMMODORES & LIONEL RICHIE
BOYZ II MEN
OTROS

Berry Gordy crea Motown en un garage de Detroit con 800 dólares prestados por su familia

1960. El primer número uno de la Motown fue logrado por The Miracles

Su cantante, Smokey Robinson se convirtío en vicepresidente de la Motown

Debutan en el top one las 'franquicias' musicales Temptations y Supremes

El pequeño 'Little' Stevie Wonder se encarama al número uno con sólo 13 años

Diana Ross consigue su primer número uno en solitario

1972. Gordy traslada Motown a Los Ángeles

Michael Jackson debuta en solitario

The Commodores, de la mano de Lionel Richie, inician una nueva etapa para la Motown

Primer número uno de la carrera en solitario de Lionel Richie, 'Truly'

1984. Muere Marvin Gaye

1989. Gordy vende la compañía a MCA por 61 millones de dólares

Boyz II Men fue el último grupo superventas de la Motown

23 años después, The Temptations logran un nuevo número uno con el single 'Stay'

2000. Último número uno, logrado por Erykah Badu

Números 1 por mes: DIC, NOV, OCT, SEP, AGO, JUL, JUN, MAY, ABR, MAR, FEB, ENE

Números uno por año

1959, 1965, 1970, 1975, 1980, 1985, 1990, 1995, 2000, 2005, 2008

Datos. EEUU: Billboard y Cash Box magazine. Internacionales: archivos de las respectivas listas de éxito de cada país (Reino Unido, Australia, Irlanda, Canadá, Italia, Suiza, Holanda, Austria, Alemania, Noruega y Nueva Zelanda)

Los artistas que lograron más números uno

The Temptations
16

The Supremes y Diana Ross
22

Marvin Gaye
10

Stevie Wonder
20

Jackson 5 y Michael Jackson
8

The Commodores y Lionel Richie
21

Boyz II Men
7

La cadena de montaje

BANDAS DE CHICAS — SOLISTAS — BANDAS DE CHICOS

SUPREMES

STEVIE WONDER

TEMPTATIONS

1 Chico de la calle
Basándose en su experiencia como trabajador en una cadena de montaje de automóviles de Detroit, Gordy, estableció un ciclo de creación de estrellas musicales.

Un chico de la calle con talento salía de la factoría Motown convertido en una estrella rutilante

2 Creación de temas
Hasta que artistas como Stevie Wonder o Lionel Richie escribieron sus propios temas, grupos de profesionales se encargaba de componer los temas que cantaban las estrellas de la Motown.

Por ejemplo, el trío Holland-Dozier-Holland escribió la mayoría de los temas de las Supremes o Marvin Gaye

3 Música
Los músicos de sesión que tocaban en la grabaciones de la Motown raramente aparecían en los créditos de los discos.

Ejecutores de primera fila como los Funk Brothers grabaron temas como 'My Girl', 'I Heard It Through the Grapevine', 'Baby Love' o 'Papa Was a Rollin' Stone'

4 A brillar
Las nuevas estrellas de la Motown eran aleccionadas en todos los aspectos. Como una versión visionario de OT, bandas como The Tempations o The Supremes recibían clases de baile para que sus miembros coordinasen perfectamente los pasos de sus bailes

Music Evolution

This graphic uses an unusual metaphor for an evolution. Stéphane Massa-Bidal based it on an image of a Saturn V rocket, as used for space exploration from the late Sixties. It consists of three stages, two of which burn up and are disposed of in succession when carrying the vessel into space.

Alongside the image of the rocket famous composers are listed, with time running bottom up. Composers are grouped into major periods of European classical music, shown on either side of the rocket, from the Middle Ages up to contemporary spectral music at the top of the spacecraft.

Dies ist eine ungewöhnliche Metapher für einen Entwicklungsprozess. Stéphane Massa-Bidal legte die Abbildung einer Saturn-V-Rakete zugrunde, wie sie ab Ende der 1960er-Jahre in der Raumfahrt eingesetzt wurde. Sie besteht aus drei Stufen, von denen zwei verbrannt und abgeworfen wurden, um das eigentliche Raumschiff in den Weltraum zu befördern.

Entlang der Rakete sind berühmte Komponisten chronologisch aufgelistet. Sie wurden nach den wichtigsten Stilen der europäischen klassischen Musik gruppiert, vom Mittelalter bis hoch zur zeitgenössischen Spektralmusik an der Spitze des Raumschiffs.

Ce graphique utilise une métaphore inhabituelle pour représenter une évolution. Stéphane Massa-Bidal s'est basé sur l'image d'une fusée Saturn V, utilisée pour l'exploration spatiale à la fin des années 1960. Elle est composée de trois étages, dont deux se désintègrent en transportant le vaisseau dans l'espace.

Des noms de compositeurs célèbres sont listés à côté de l'image de la fusée, et la chronologie se déroule de bas en haut. Les compositeurs sont regroupés par grandes périodes de la musique classique européenne, de chaque côté de la fusée, du Moyen-âge jusqu'à la musique spectrale contemporaine tout en haut du vaisseau spatial.

Project Info: *D'ici là* magazine, website, 2010, France
Design: Stéphane Massa-Bidal (Rétrofuturs)

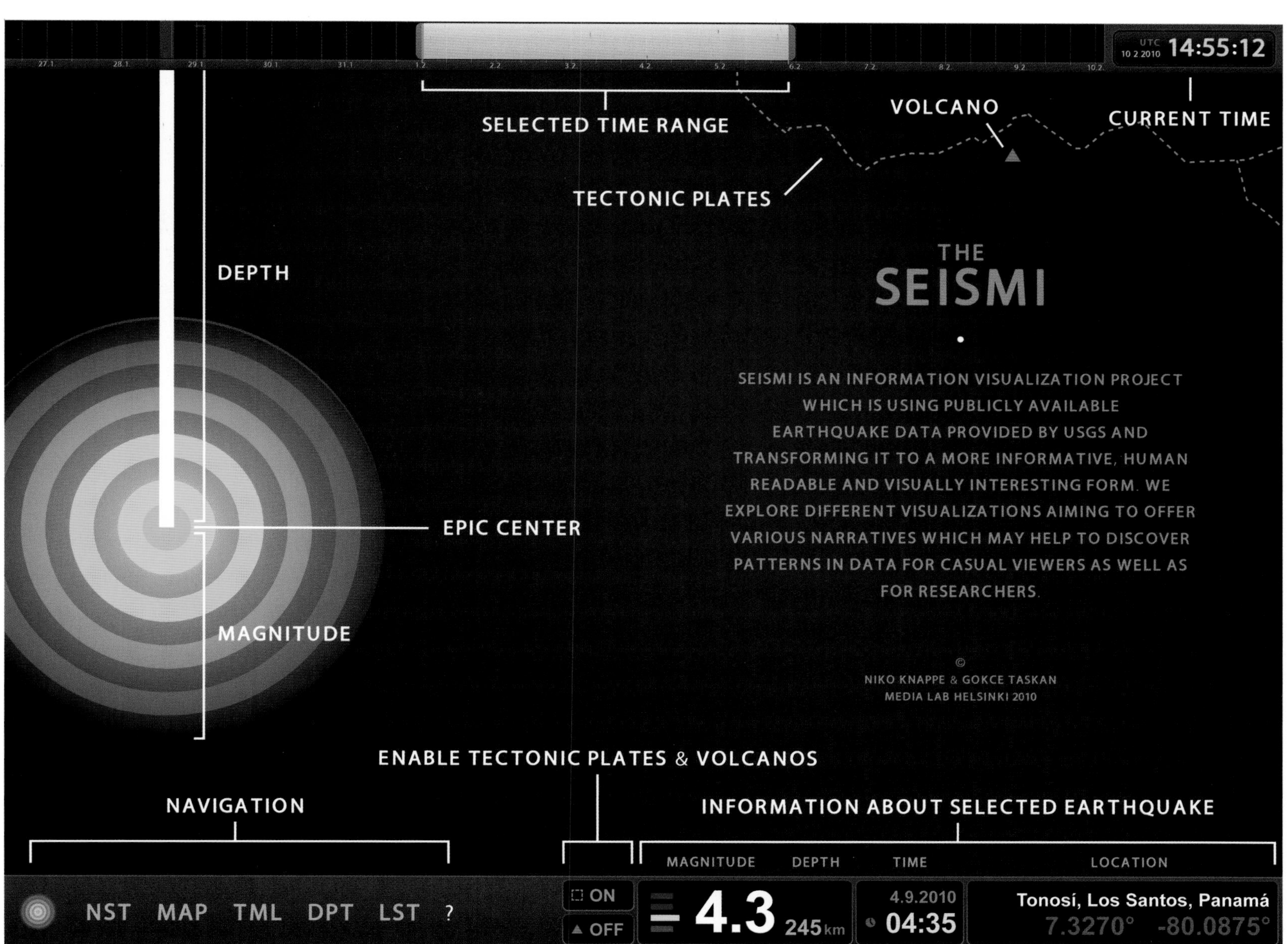

Seismi

Seismi is an interactive visualisation for earthquakes. The data is plotted in five individual schemes, which are accessed through the navigation below left. NST shows the most recent events. MAP locates all earthquakes on a world map. DPT visualises at what depth activity occurred. LST subsumes all quakes as dots in a "list", with colour indicating the magnitude of each one.

In the timeline (TML), all events are sorted chronologically. In all schemes, single events can be selected. The data band at the lower right then discloses information about this particular earthquake: time, depth, magnitude and location. By presenting the information in distinct schemes, the project allows people to draw various narratives from the dataset, both researchers and the general public.

Seismi ist eine interaktive Visualisierung von Erdbeben. Die Daten werden in fünf verschiedenen Modi dargestellt, die über die Navigationsleiste unten links aufgerufen werden können. „NST" zeigt die neuesten Vorfälle. „MAP" verortet alle Erdbeben auf einer Weltkarte. „DPT" zeigt die Tiefe, in der ein bestimmtes Beben stattfand. „LST" fasst alle Beben als Punkte auf einer „Liste" zusammen, wobei die Farbe die Intensität jedes Bebens angibt.

In der Zeitleiste („TML") sind alle Erdbeben chronologisch angeordnet. In allen Modi können einzelne Beben angewählt werden, deren individuelle Daten dann unten rechts angezeigt werden: Zeit, Tiefe des Bebens, Intensität und Ort. Die verschiedenen Modi sortieren die Daten nach unterschiedlichen Kriterien. Das erlaubt es den Benutzern – ob Forschern oder der interessierten Öffentlichkeit –, die Datensammlung jeweils selbst zu interpretieren.

Seismi est une visualisation interactive des tremblements de terre. Les données sont exploitées sous cinq formes différentes, accessibles grâce à la barre de navigation en bas à gauche. NST montre les événements les plus récents. MAP situe tous les tremblements de terre sur une carte du monde. DPT est une visualisation de la profondeur à laquelle l'activité a été enregistrée. LST regroupe tous les tremblements sous forme de points dans une « liste », le code couleur indiquant la magnitude de chaque cas.

Dans la ligne de temps (TML), tous les événements sont triés par ordre chronologique. Chaque modalité permet de sélectionner des événements individuels. La bande de données en bas à droite donne alors des informations sur ce tremblement de terre : l'heure et la date, la profondeur, la magnitude et l'endroit. En présentant l'information selon plusieurs modalités, ce projet permet aux utilisateurs, chercheurs et grand public, d'obtenir différentes perspectives à partir d'un vaste ensemble de données.

Project Info: Website, 2010, Finland
Data Source: US Geological Survey;
National Geophysical Data Center;
The University of Texas Institute for Geophysics
Design: Niko Knappe, Gokce Taskan
(Media Lab Helsinki)

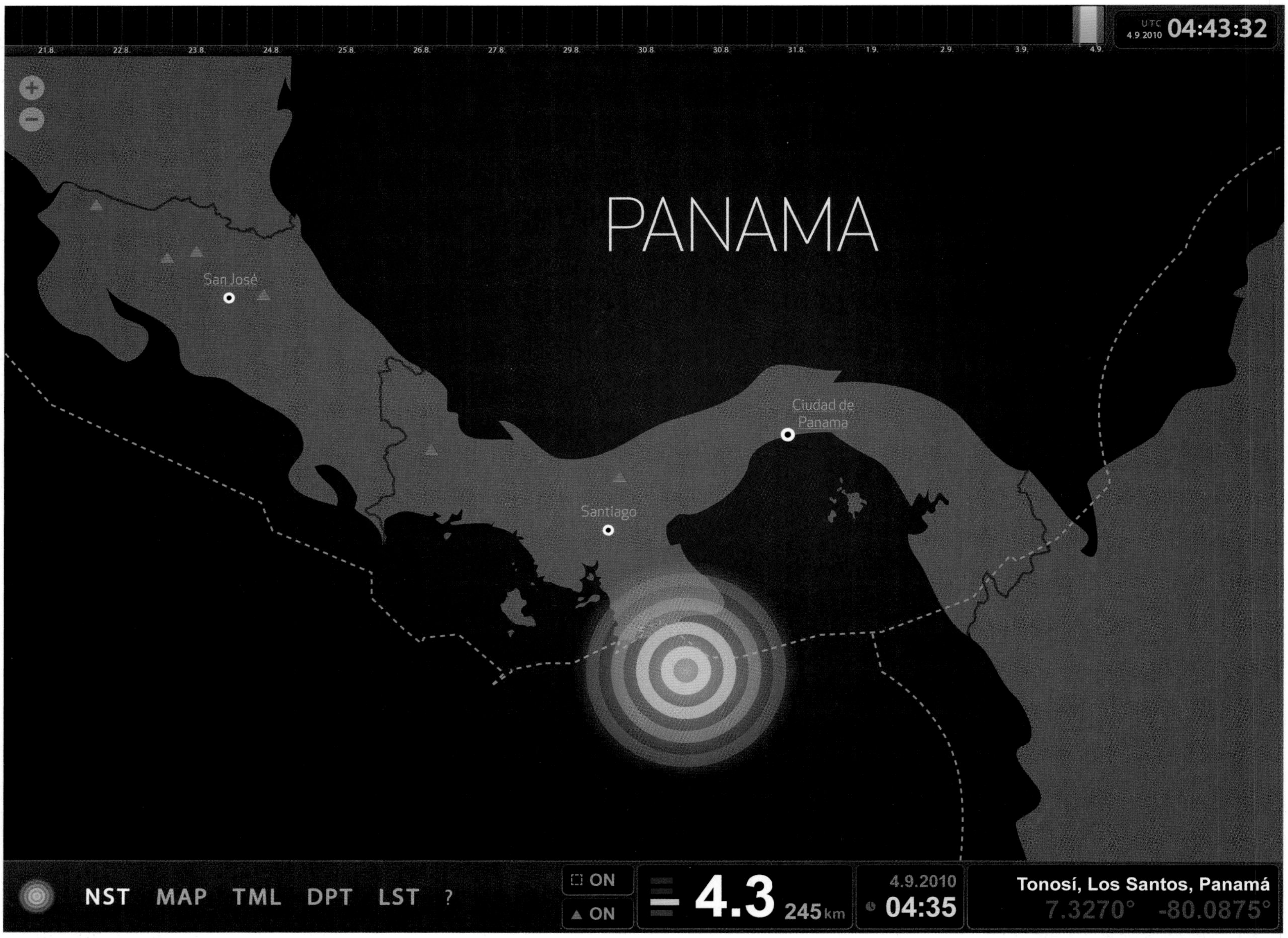

UTC 4.9.2010 04:43:32
PANAMA
San José
Ciudad de Panama
Santiago
NST MAP TML DPT LST ?
ON
ON
4.3 245km
4.9.2010 04:35
Tonosí, Los Santos, Panamá
7.3270° -80.0875°

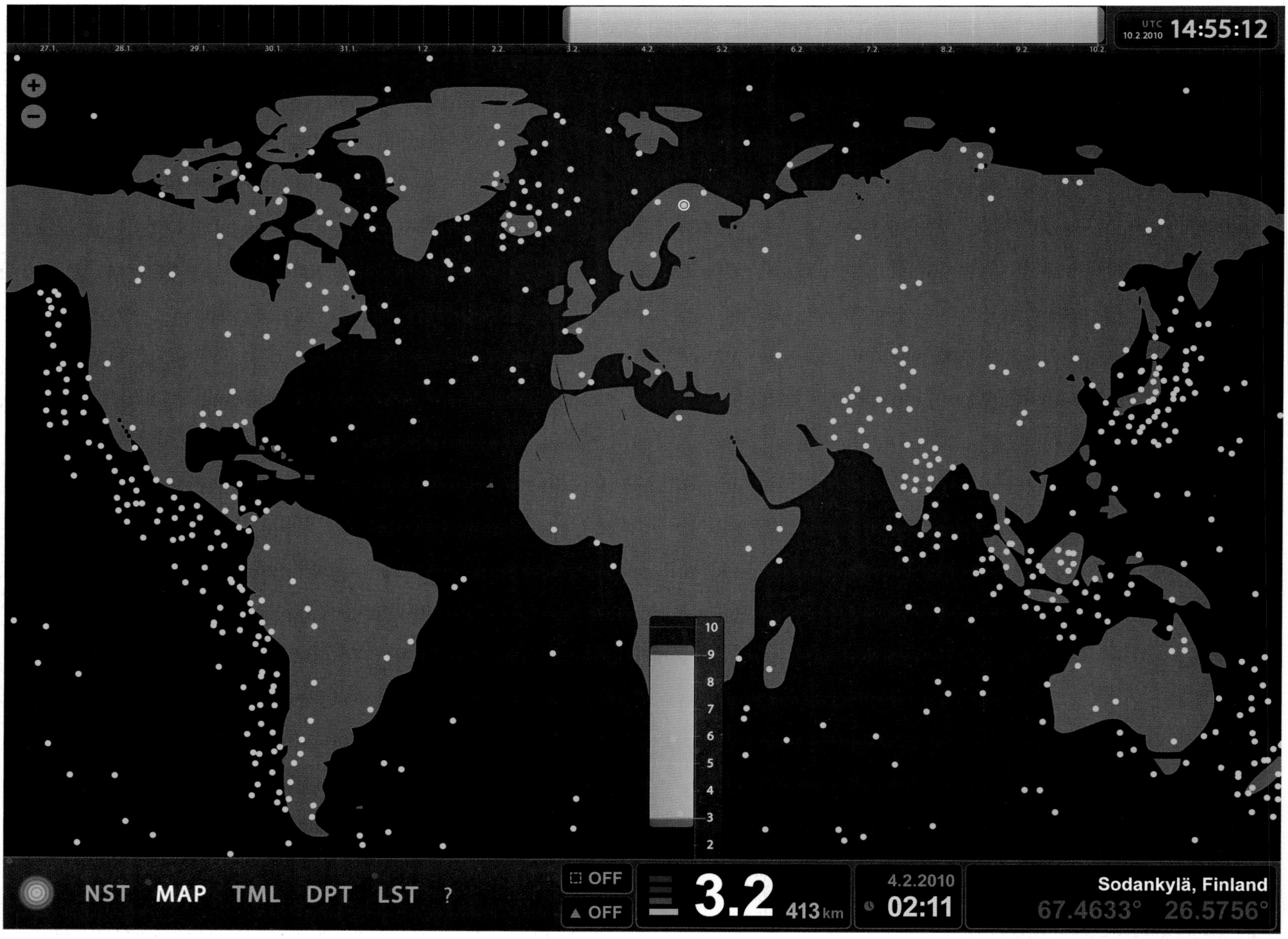

UTC 10.2.2010 14:55:12
10
9
8
7
6
5
4
3
2
NST MAP TML DPT LST ?
OFF
OFF
3.2 413km
4.2.2010 02:11
Sodankylä, Finland
67.4633° 26.5756°

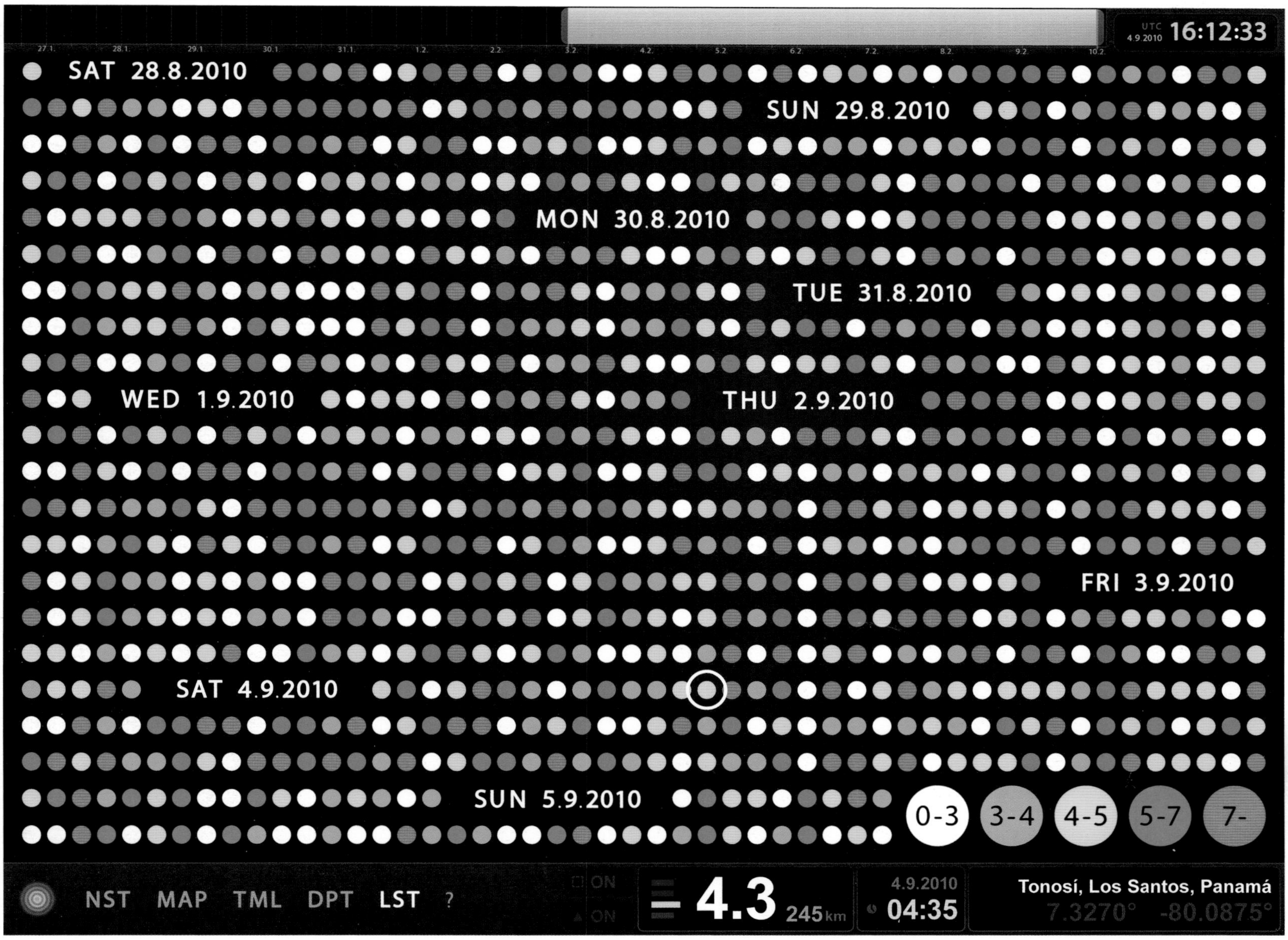

UTC 4.9.2010 16:12:33

SAT 28.8.2010

SUN 29.8.2010

MON 30.8.2010

TUE 31.8.2010

WED 1.9.2010

THU 2.9.2010

FRI 3.9.2010

SAT 4.9.2010

SUN 5.9.2010

0-3 3-4 4-5 5-7 7-

NST MAP TML DPT LST ?

ON

ON

4.3 245km

4.9.2010 04:35

Tonosí, Los Santos, Panamá

7.3270° -80.0875°

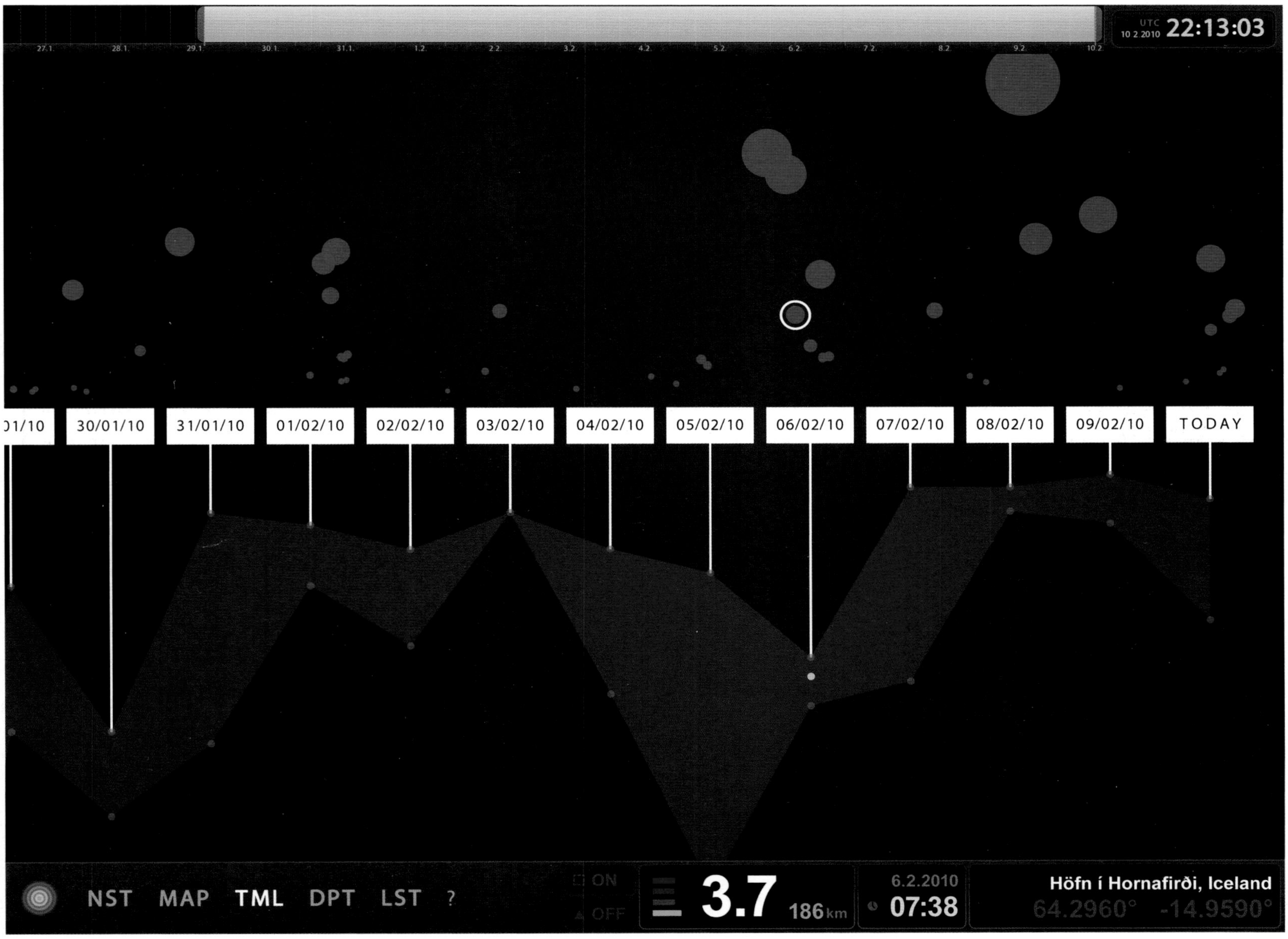

UTC 10.2.2010 22:13:03

01/10 30/01/10 31/01/10 01/02/10 02/02/10 03/02/10 04/02/10 05/02/10 06/02/10 07/02/10 08/02/10 09/02/10 TODAY

NST MAP TML DPT LST ?

ON

OFF

3.7 186km

6.2.2010 07:38

Höfn í Hornafirði, Iceland

64.2960° -14.9590°

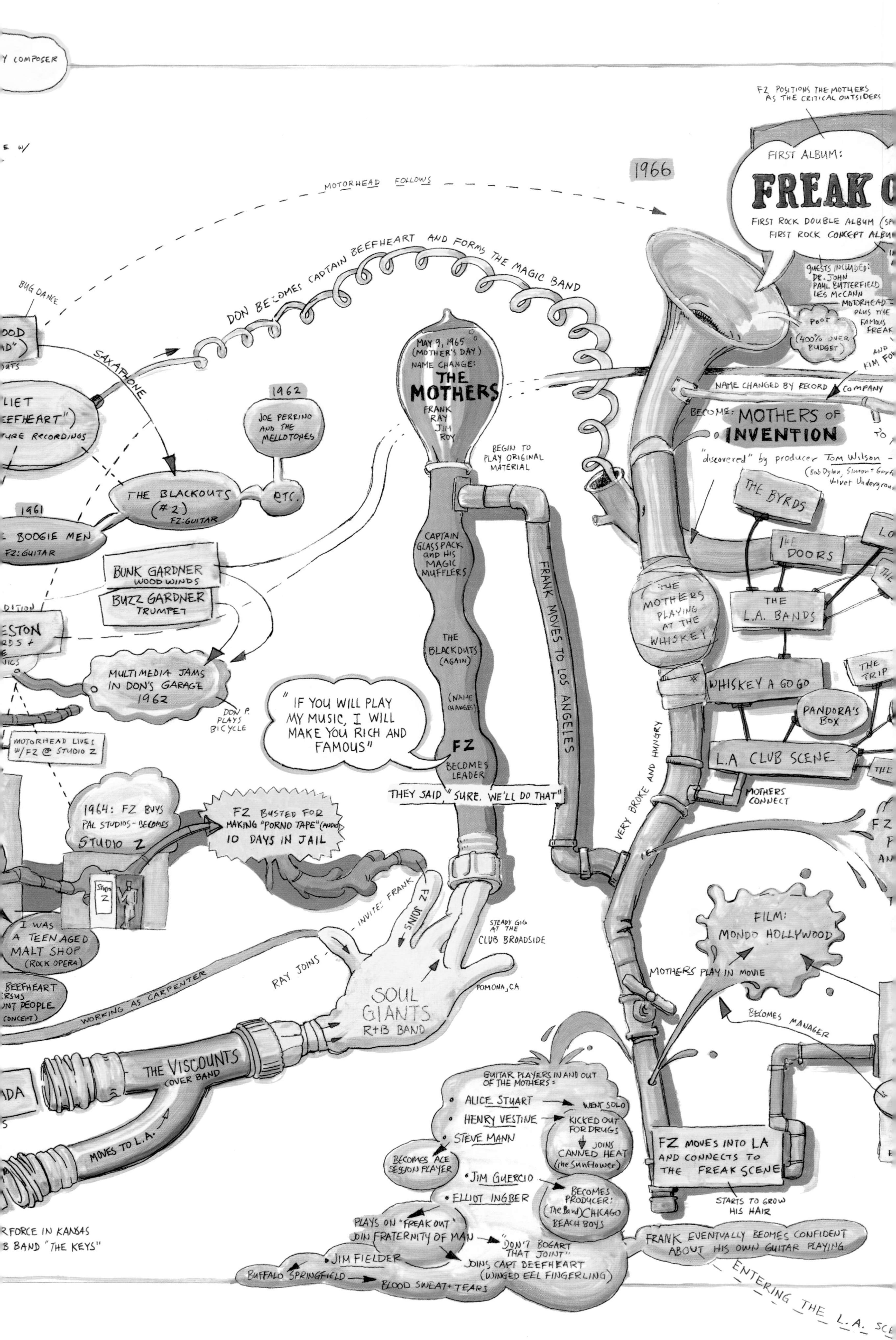

Y COMPOSER
FZ POSITIONS THE MOTHERS AS THE CRITICAL OUTSIDERS
1966
FIRST ALBUM:
FREAK O
FIRST ROCK DOUBLE ALBUM
FIRST ROCK CONCEPT ALBU
GUESTS INCLUDED: DR. JOHN PAUL BUTTERFIELD LES McCANN MOTORHEAD PLUS THE FAMOUS FREAK
POOT (400% OVER BUDGET)
MOTORHEAD FOLLOWS
DON BECOMES CAPTAIN BEEFHEART AND FORMS THE MAGIC BAND
BUG DANCE
SAXAPHONE
MAY 9, 1965 (MOTHER'S DAY) NAME CHANGE: THE MOTHERS FRANK RAY JIM ROY
1962
JOE PERRINO AND THE MELLOTONES
ETC.
THE BLACKOUTS (#2) FZ: GUITAR
1961
BOOGIE MEN FZ: GUITAR
BEGIN TO PLAY ORIGINAL MATERIAL
NAME CHANGED BY RECORD COMPANY
BECOME: MOTHERS OF INVENTION
"discovered" by producer Tom Wilson
THE BYRDS
THE DOORS
THE L.A. BANDS
THE MOTHERS PLAYING AT THE WHISKEY
WHISKEY A GO GO
THE TRIP
PANDORA'S BOX
L.A CLUB SCENE
MOTHERS CONNECT
BUNK GARDNER WOOD WINDS
BUZZ GARDNER TRUMPET
CAPTAIN GLASS PACK AND HIS MAGIC MUFFLERS
THE BLACKOUTS (AGAIN)
(NAME CHANGES)
FZ BECOMES LEADER
FRANK MOVES TO LOS ANGELES
MULTIMEDIA JAMS IN DON'S GARAGE 1962
DON P. PLAYS BICYCLE
"IF YOU WILL PLAY MY MUSIC, I WILL MAKE YOU RICH AND FAMOUS"
THEY SAID, "SURE, WE'LL DO THAT"
VERY BROKE AND HUNGRY
MOTORHEAD LIVES W/FZ @ STUDIO Z
1964: FZ BUYS PAL STUDIOS - BECOMES STUDIO Z
FZ BUSTED FOR MAKING "PORNO TAPE" (AUDIO) 10 DAYS IN JAIL
I WAS A TEENAGED MALT SHOP (ROCK OPERA)
FZ JOINS
INVITES FRANK
STEADY GIG AT THE CLUB BROADSIDE
RAY JOINS
WORKING AS CARPENTER
SOUL GIANTS R+B BAND
POMONA, CA
FILM: MONDO HOLLYWOOD
MOTHERS PLAY IN MOVIE
BECOMES MANAGER
THE VISCOUNTS COVER BAND
MOVES TO L.A.
GUITAR PLAYERS IN AND OUT OF THE MOTHERS:
ALICE STUART
WENT SOLO
HENRY VESTINE
KICKED OUT FOR DRUGS
JOINS CANNED HEAT (the Sunflower)
STEVE MANN
BECOMES ACE SESSION PLAYER
JIM GUERCIO
BECOMES PRODUCER: (The Band) CHICAGO BEACH BOYS
ELLIOT INGBER
PLAYS ON "FREAK OUT"
JOIN FRATERNITY OF MAN
"DON'T BOGART THAT JOINT"
JOINS CAPT BEEFHEART (WINGED EEL FINGERLING)
JIM FIELDER
BUFFALO SPRINGFIELD
BLOOD SWEAT + TEARS
FZ MOVES INTO LA AND CONNECTS TO THE FREAK SCENE
STARTS TO GROW HIS HAIR
FRANK EVENTUALLY BECOMES CONFIDENT ABOUT HIS OWN GUITAR PLAYING
ENTERING THE L.A. SCE
R FORCE IN KANSAS
B BAND "THE KEYS"

Frank Zappa Chart

This is a graphic chronology, showing the life of musician and composer Frank Zappa. Data were drawn from a number of published biographies as well as fan websites. The visual look of the chart is a homage to the artist who created the artwork for many of Zappa's recordings, Cal Schenkel.

The chart lists major events in Zappa's personal and artistic life, bands he was in, information about certain band members and a listing of major recorded works he made or produced. Rather than creating a conventional timeline, Ward Shelley devised a maze-like structure to capture the spirit of Zappa's non-conformity.

Diese grafische Chronologie veranschaulicht das Leben des Musikers und Komponisten Frank Zappa. Die Daten stammen aus biografischen Publikationen sowie von Fanseiten im Internet. Die Optik des Schaubilds ist eine Hommage an den Künstler, der für viele von Zappas Platten das Design entwarf: Cal Schenkel.

Das Bild nennt wichtige Stationen in Zappas persönlichem und künstlerischem Leben, die Bands, denen er angehörte, Informationen zu bestimmten Band-Mitgliedern sowie eine Auflistung der wichtigsten Alben, die er selbst aufnahm oder produzierte. Anstatt eine herkömmliche Zeitleiste zu entwickeln, entwarf Ward Shelley eine Art Irrgarten, um Zappas unkonventionelle Persönlichkeit wiederzugeben.

Cette chronologie graphique montre la vie du musicien et compositeur Frank Zappa. Les données ont été tirées de plusieurs biographies publiées, ainsi que de sites web tenus par des fans. Le style visuel est un hommage à l'artiste qui a créé les couvertures de nombreux disques de Zappa, Cal Schenkel.

Les grands événements de la vie personnelle et artistique de Zappa sont mentionnés, ainsi que les groupes auxquels il a appartenu, des informations sur certains membres de groupe et une liste des principales œuvres qu'il a enregistrées ou produites. Plutôt que de créer une chronologie conventionnelle, Ward Shelley a imaginé une structure labyrinthique pour représenter l'esprit anticonformiste de Zappa.

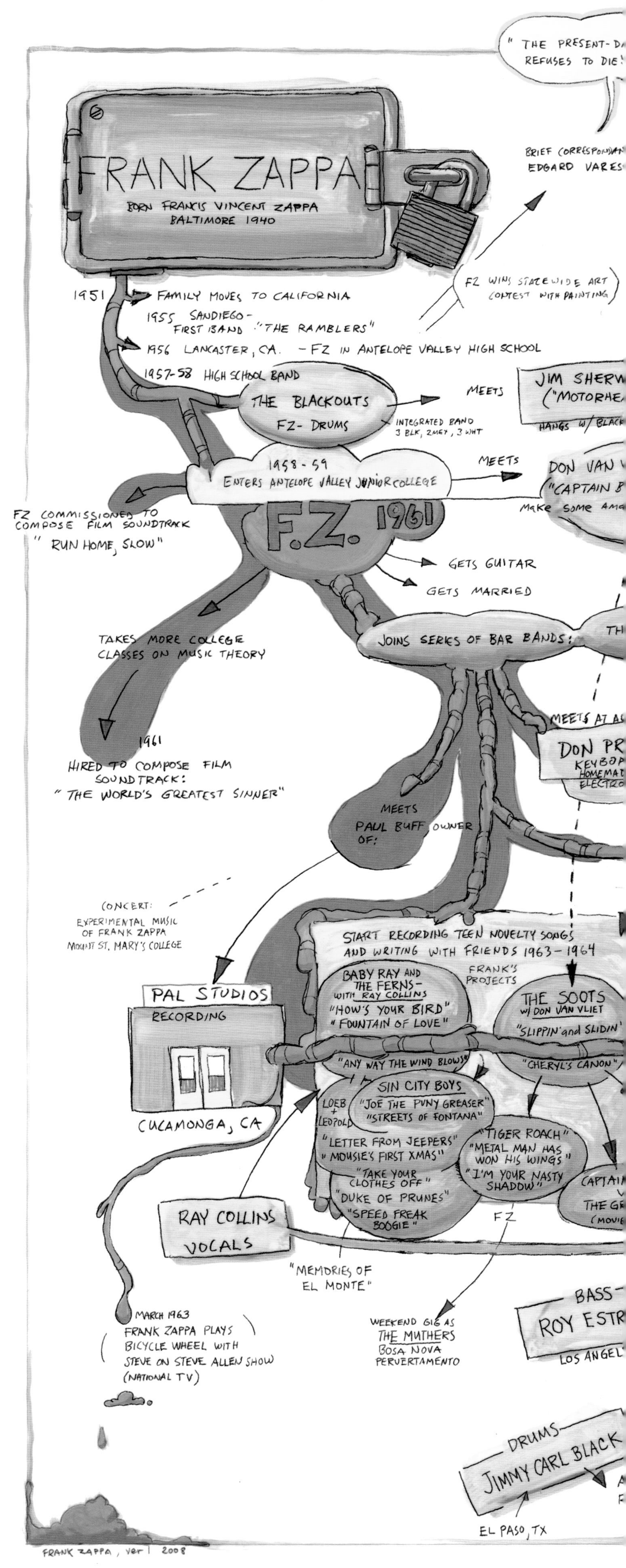

Project Info: Painting, 2008, USA
Artist: Ward Shelley
Additional Info: Original size 164 cm x 81 cm; Ward Shelley is represented by Pierogi Gallery

Overview

Gerhard Richter is one of the most important of contemporary artists. In this editioned print, he has created a survey of Western cultural history which contains the names and dates of early works and important artists and thinkers from the Stone Age and Antiquity up to 2000. Time runs from left to right, with each vertical line marking a decade – except for the period before 1300 AD which is treated as one single unit.

In the coloured sections, professional groups are categorised from top to bottom: painters, architects, composers, philosophers and authors. On simple white tags, only the family names are written, without any further comment. The checked background and bare typography recall administrative timeplans or clinical measurement diagrams.

Gerhard Richter gehört zu den bedeutendsten Künstlern unserer Zeit. Für diesen limitierten Druck entwarf er einen Überblick über die westliche Kulturgeschichte. Er enthält Namen und Daten früher Kunstwerke sowie einflussreicher Künstler und Denker von der Steinzeit über die Antike bis zum Jahr 2000. Die Zeit verläuft von links nach rechts, jeder senkrechte Strich steht für ein Jahrzehnt – mit Ausnahme des Zeitraums vor 1300 n. Chr., der als eine Einheit behandelt wird.

Die farbigen Segmente unterscheiden einzelne Berufsgruppen voneinander. Von oben nach unten sind das Maler, Architekten, Komponisten, Philosophen und Schriftsteller. Schlicht und unkommentiert werden deren Familiennamen auf einfachen weißen Etiketten festgehalten. Der karierte Hintergrund und die nüchterne Typografie lassen an Zeitpläne einer Verwaltungsbehörde oder an klinische Diagramme denken.

Gerhard Richter est l'un des plus grands artistes contemporains. Dans ce tirage limité, il passe en revue l'histoire culturelle de l'Occident avec les noms et les dates des œuvres et des principaux artistes et penseurs de l'Âge de la pierre et de l'Antiquité jusqu'à l'an 2000. La chronologie va de gauche à droite, et chaque ligne verticale indique une décennie - sauf pour la période précédant 1300, qui est traitée comme un bloc unique.

Dans les sections colorées, les groupes professionnels sont classés de haut en bas : peintres, architectes, compositeurs, philosophes et auteurs. De simples étiquettes blanches mentionnent leurs noms de famille, sans autre commentaire. Le fond quadrillé et la typographie dépouillée évoquent les plannings administratifs ou les feuilles de température des hôpitaux.

Project Info: Print, 1998, Germany
Artist: Gerhard Richter
Additional Info: Original size 82.8 cm x 68.2 cm; published as Editions CR 93

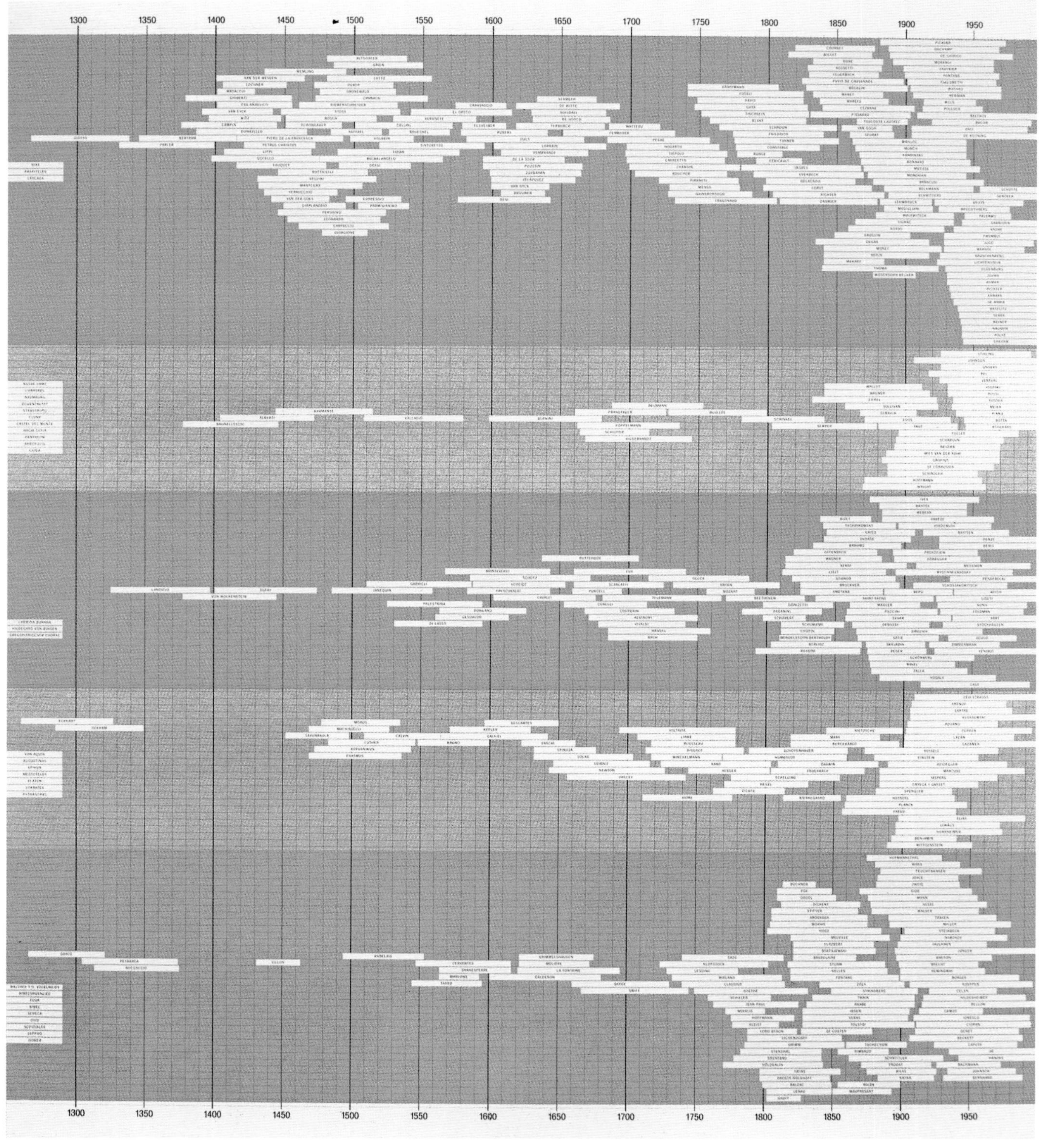

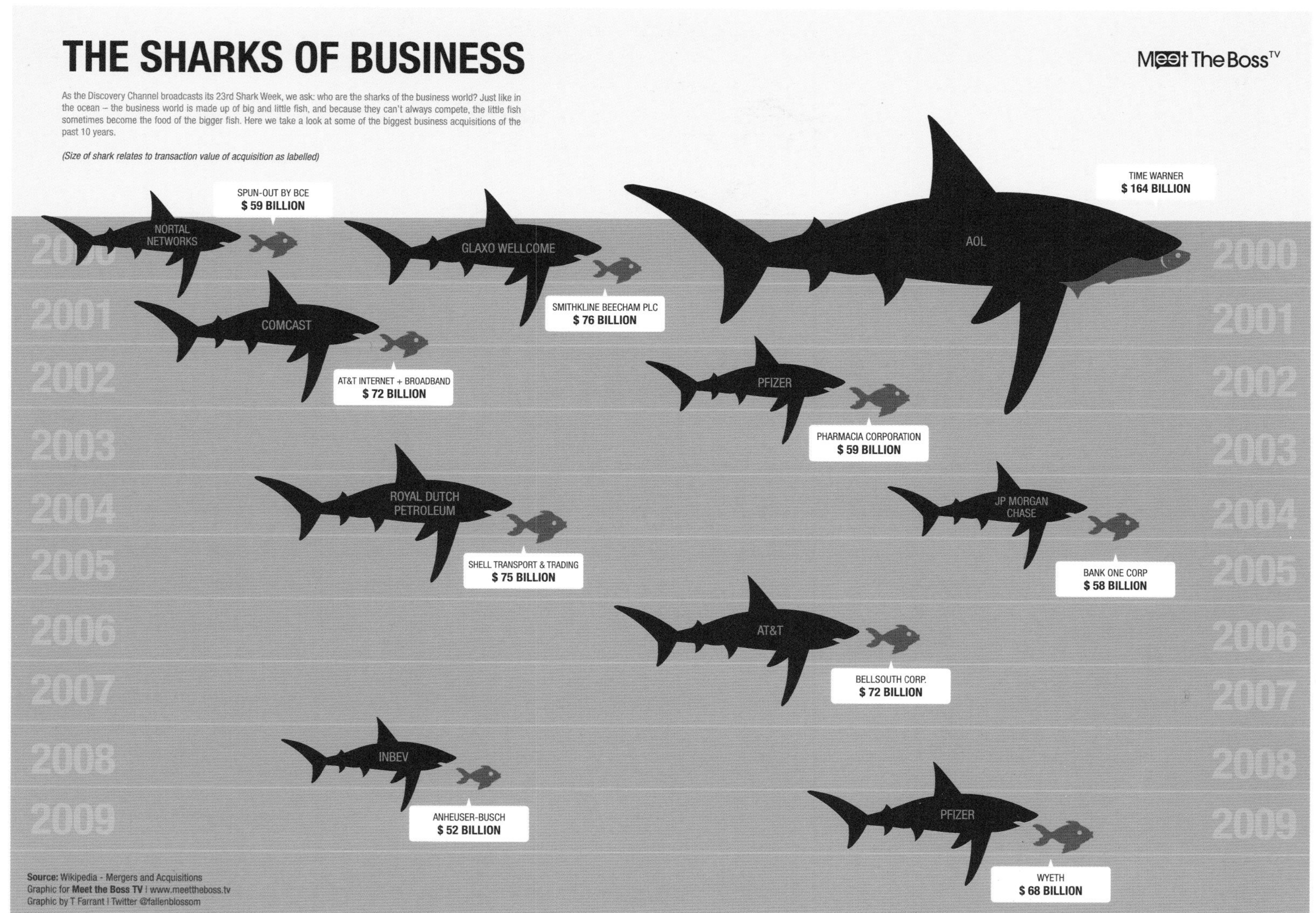
THE SHARKS OF BUSINESS
Meet The Boss TV
As the Discovery Channel broadcasts its 23rd Shark Week, we ask: who are the sharks of the business world? Just like in the ocean – the business world is made up of big and little fish, and because they can't always compete, the little fish sometimes become the food of the bigger fish. Here we take a look at some of the biggest business acquisitions of the past 10 years.
(Size of shark relates to transaction value of acquisition as labelled)
NORTAL NETWORKS
SPUN-OUT BY BCE $ 59 BILLION
GLAXO WELLCOME
SMITHKLINE BEECHAM PLC $ 76 BILLION
AOL
TIME WARNER $ 164 BILLION
COMCAST
AT&T INTERNET + BROADBAND $ 72 BILLION
PFIZER
PHARMACIA CORPORATION $ 59 BILLION
ROYAL DUTCH PETROLEUM
SHELL TRANSPORT & TRADING $ 75 BILLION
JP MORGAN CHASE
BANK ONE CORP $ 58 BILLION
AT&T
BELLSOUTH CORP. $ 72 BILLION
INBEV
ANHEUSER-BUSCH $ 52 BILLION
PFIZER
WYETH $ 68 BILLION
2000
2001
2002
2003
2004
2005
2006
2007
2008
2009
Source: Wikipedia - Mergers and Acquisitions
Graphic for Meet the Boss TV | www.meettheboss.tv
Graphic by T Farrant | Twitter @fallenblossom

Sharks of Business

This graphic takes a look at the biggest business acquisitions of the past 10 years. Each shark represents a company carrying out the acquiring, with the fish in front representing the company being acquired.

The size of each shark indicates the transaction value of the acquisition. The depth of the water relates to a timeline, with the acquisition of Wyeth by Pfizer at the bottom being the most recent.

Diese Grafik untersucht die größten Geschäftsübernahmen der vergangenen zehn Jahre. Jeder Hai stellt ein Unternehmen dar, das ein anderes übernimmt, die Fische symbolisieren die erworbenen Unternehmen.

Die Größe der Haie veranschaulicht den Wert der Übernahme. Die Wassertiefe wird mit einer Zeitleiste gleichgesetzt, die Übernahme von Wyeth durch Pfizer unten ist die jüngste verzeichnete Fusion.

Cette image examine les plus grandes acquisitions d'entreprises au cours des 10 dernières années. Chaque requin représente une entreprise acquéreuse, et le poisson qui se trouve devant est l'entreprise acquise.

La taille des requins indique la valeur de la transaction. La profondeur de l'eau correspond à la dimension temporelle, l'acquisition de Wyeth par Pfizer, tout en bas, étant la plus récente.

Project Info: Meet the Boss, for GDS International, website, 2010, UK
Data Source: Wikipedia, "Merges and Acquisitions"
Research and Design: Tiffany Farrant-Gonzalez

2nd EURO TOUR FZ TO GERMANY: "YOU MUST ENJOY THIS CONCERT"
FZ
FZ
TO AUDIENCE: EVERYBODY IN THIS ROOM IS WEARING A UNIFORM
FIGHTS WITH MGM OVER "MOTHERMANIA" GREATEST HITS
1969
CENSORSHIP BY MGM RECORDS
ZAPPA WRITES ARTICLE IN LIFE MAGAZINE
RUBEN AND THE JETS
UNCLE MEAT
BACK TO LA
FZ BUYS TOM MIX LOG CABIN IN LAUREL CANYON
BECOMES FREAK SCENE
IS THIS PART 2.?
FZ STARTS BIZARRE RECORDS FOR TOTAL ARTISTIC CONTROL
RAY QUITS
SUZY LEAVES
GTOs, SUZY MOVE IN
BORN
DWEEZIL ZAPPA
AUGUST 1969
LAST PERFORMANCE OF THE ORIGINAL MOTHERS OF INVENTION
JIMMY + BUNK FORM BAND "GERONIMO BLACK" LATER "THE GRANDMOTHERS"
MOTORHEAD TOO ↗ — ALSO DID SCIENTOLOGY
ROY PLAYED SOME WITH FZ ALSO WITH BEEFHEART
DON WORKED WITH MEREDITH MONK ALSO BAND CALLED ANT BEE
IAN CONTINUES W/ FZ — MARRIES RUTH, WHO ALSO PLAYS WITH FZ
RAY GOES BACK TO BEING CARPENTER
200 MOTELS
RECORD SOUNDTRACK FOR FILM W/ RINGO STARR KIETH MOON
PENIS DIMENSION
1971
PLAYS WITH JOHN LENNO + YOKO 'SOMETIME IN NEW YORK'
FZ PUBLISHES ARTICLE: "EDGARD VARESE, IDOL OF MY YOUTH"
2 DISASTERS —
FIRE DURING CONCERT IN MONTREAUX ALL MOTHER'S EQUIPMENT DESTROYED
IMMORTALIZED IN DEEP PURPLE'S "SMOKE ON THE WATER"
FZ PUSHED OFF STAGE IN LONDON. FALLS 12 FEET. SERIOUSLY INJURED — CRUSHED LARNYX, BROKEN LEG —
END OF "VAUDEVILLE" MOTHERS
MOTHERS LIVE AT FILLMORE EAST JUNE 1971 ALBUM
MUDSHARK
FZ MOVES TO LONDON → TO WORK ON 200 MOTELS FILM
1972 CAPTAIN BEEFHEART THE SPOTLIGHT KID
1972 CLEAR SPOT
FZ SPENDS NEXT 10 MONTHS IN A WHEELCHAIR

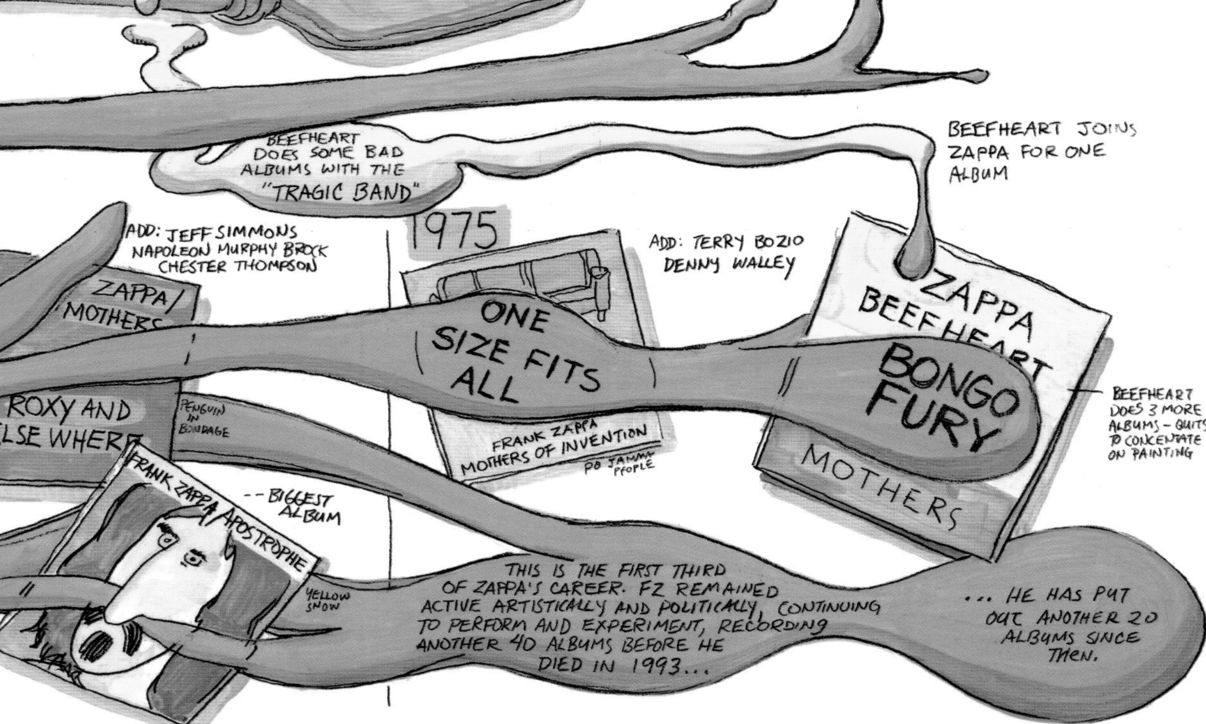

AS AN ARTIST, FRANK ZAPPA WAS MY FIRST SERIOUS ROLE MODEL
WARD SHELLEY, 2008

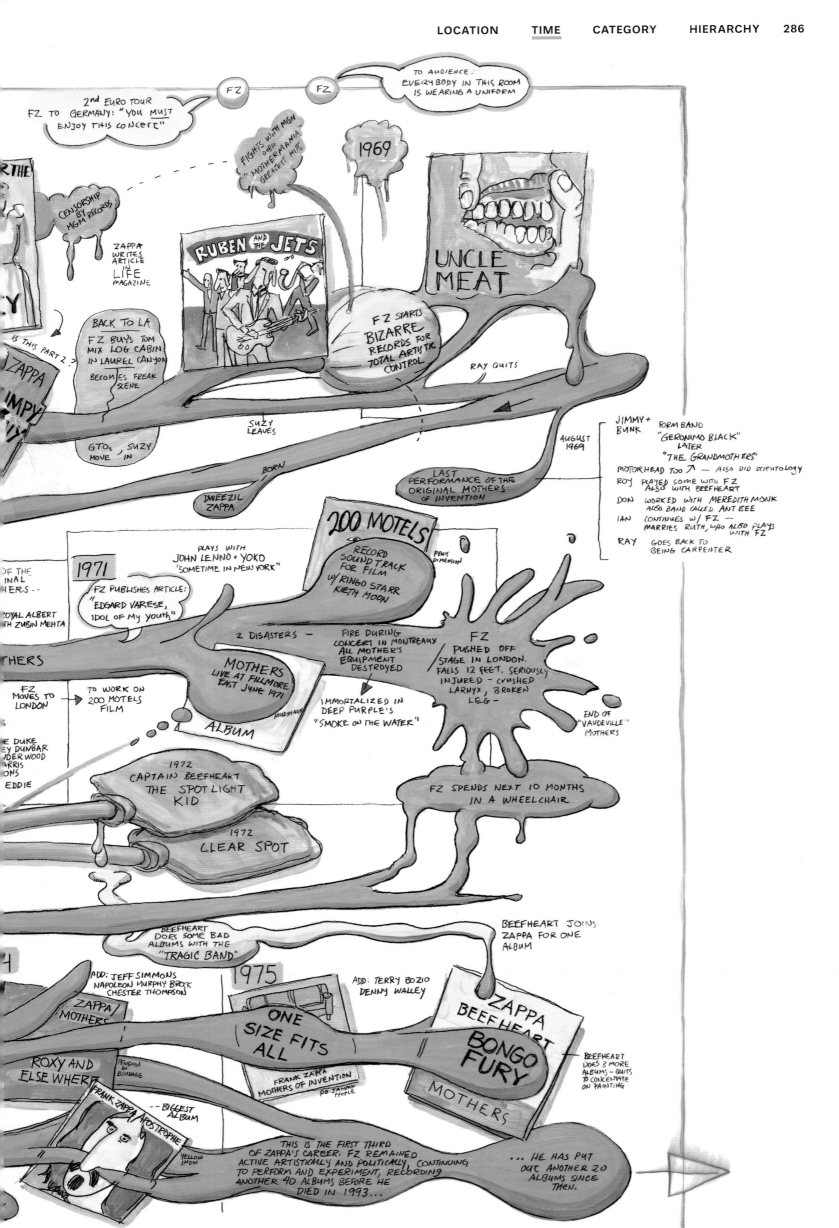

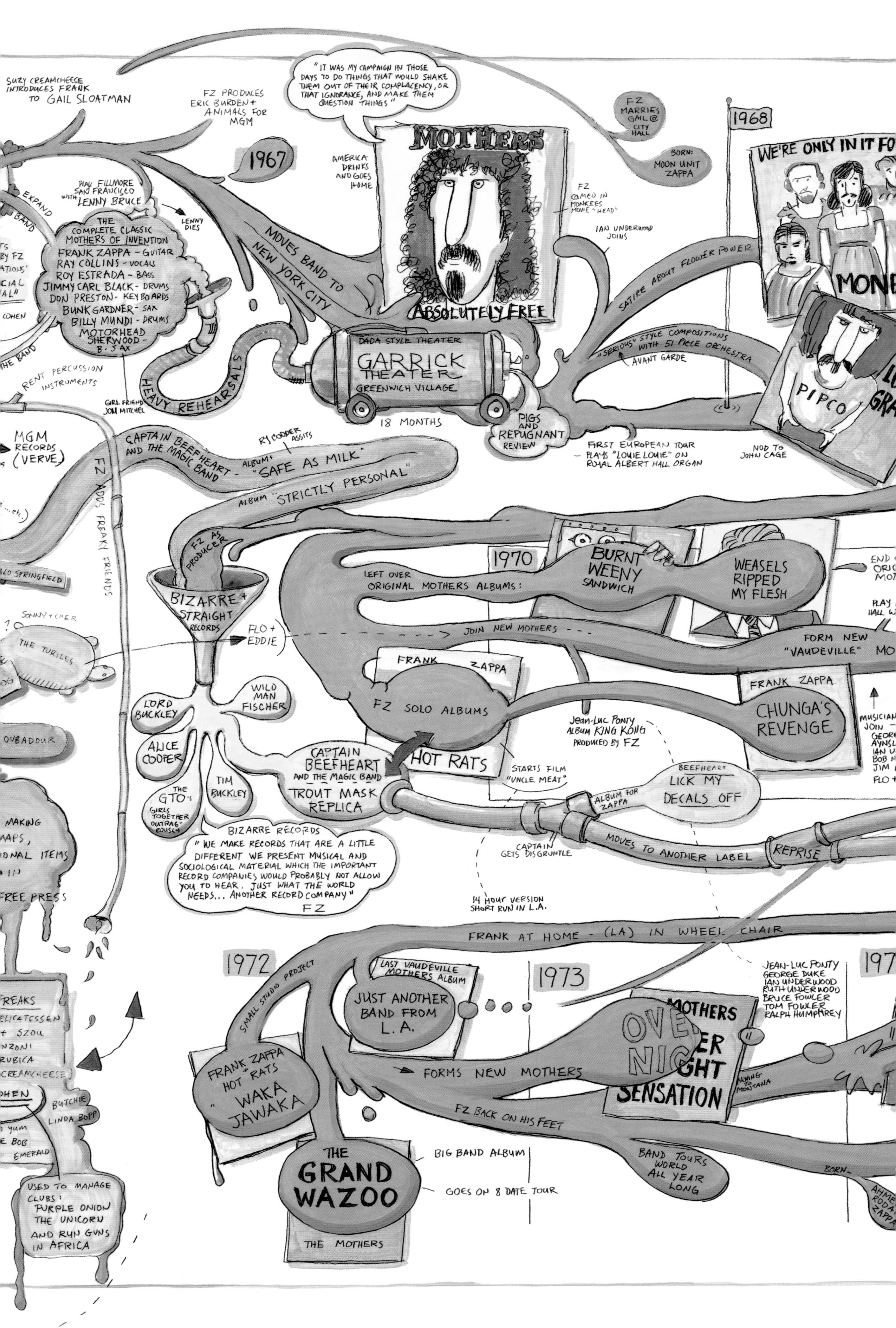
SUZY CREAMCHEESE INTRODUCES FRANK TO GAIL SLOATMAN
FZ PRODUCES ERIC BURDEN + ANIMALS FOR MGM
"IT WAS MY CAMPAIGN IN THOSE DAYS TO DO THINGS THAT WOULD SHAKE THEM OUT OF THEIR COMPLACENCY, OR THAT IGNORANCE, AND MAKE THEM QUESTION THINGS"
FZ MARRIES GAIL @ CITY HALL
1968
1967
BORN: MOON UNIT ZAPPA
AMERICA DRINKS AND GOES HOME
MOTHERS
ABSOLUTELY FREE
WE'RE ONLY IN IT FO
MONE
PLAY FILLMORE SAN FRANCISCO WITH LENNY BRUCE
LENNY DIES
FZ CAMEO IN MONKEES MOVIE "HEAD"
EXPAND BAND
THE COMPLETE CLASSIC MOTHERS OF INVENTION
FRANK ZAPPA - GUITAR
RAY COLLINS - VOCALS
ROY ESTRADA - BASS
JIMMY CARL BLACK - DRUMS
DON PRESTON - KEYBOARDS
BUNK GARDNER - SAX
BILLY MUNDI - DRUMS
MOTHERHEAD SHERWOOD - B. SAX
IAN UNDERWOOD JOINS
MOVES BAND TO NEW YORK CITY
SATIRE ABOUT FLOWER POWER
COHEN
THE BAND
DADA STYLE THEATER
GARRICK THEATER
GREENWICH VILLAGE
"SERIOUS" STYLE COMPOSITIONS WITH 51 PIECE ORCHESTRA
AVANT GARDE
PIPCO
RENT PERCUSSION INSTRUMENTS
HEAVY REHEARSALS
GIRL FRIEND JONI MITCHEL
18 MONTHS
PIGS AND REPUGNANT REVIEW
MGM RECORDS (VERVE)
CAPTAIN BEEFHEART AND THE MAGIC BAND - ALBUM: "SAFE AS MILK"
RY COODER ASSITS
ALBUM "STRICTLY PERSONAL"
FIRST EUROPEAN TOUR - PLAYS "LOUIE LOUIE" ON ROYAL ALBERT HALL ORGAN
NOD TO JOHN CAGE
FZ ADDS FREAKY FRIENDS
FZ AS PRODUCER
1970
BURNT WEENY SANDWICH
WEASELS RIPPED MY FLESH
LEFT OVER ORIGINAL MOTHERS ALBUMS:
BUFFALO SPRINGFIELD
BIZARRE + STRAIGHT RECORDS
SONNY + CHER
THE TURTLES
FLO + EDDIE
JOIN NEW MOTHERS
FORM NEW "VAUDEVILLE" MO
FRANK ZAPPA
FZ SOLO ALBUMS
FRANK ZAPPA
CHUNGA'S REVENGE
WILD MAN FISCHER
LORD BUCKLEY
ALICE COOPER
TROUBADOUR
Jean-Luc Ponty Album KING KONG Produced by FZ
THE GTO's GIRLS TOGETHER OUTRAGEOUSLY
TIM BUCKLEY
CAPTAIN BEEFHEART AND THE MAGIC BAND
TROUT MASK REPLICA
HOT RATS
STARTS FILM "UNCLE MEAT"
BEEFHEART
LICK MY DECALS OFF
ALBUM FOR ZAPPA
MAKING MAPS,
PERSONAL ITEMS
FREE PRESS
BIZARRE RECORDS
"WE MAKE RECORDS THAT ARE A LITTLE DIFFERENT. WE PRESENT MUSICAL AND SOCIOLOGICAL MATERIAL WHICH THE IMPORTANT RECORD COMPANIES WOULD PROBABLY NOT ALLOW YOU TO HEAR. JUST WHAT THE WORLD NEEDS... ANOTHER RECORD COMPANY" FZ
CAPTAIN GETS DISGRUNTLE
MOVES TO ANOTHER LABEL
REPRISE
14 HOUR VERSION SHORT RUN IN L.A.
FRANK AT HOME - (LA) IN WHEEL CHAIR
1972
SMALL STUDIO PROJECT
LAST VAUDEVILLE MOTHERS ALBUM
JUST ANOTHER BAND FROM L.A.
1973
JEAN-LUC PONTY
GEORGE DUKE
IAN UNDERWOOD
RUTH UNDERWOOD
BRUCE FOWLER
TOM FOWLER
RALPH HUMPHREY
FREAKS
CREAMCHEESE
COHEN
BUTCHIE
LINDA BOPP
EMERALD
FRANK ZAPPA HOT RATS
WAKA JAWAKA
FORMS NEW MOTHERS
MOTHERS
OVER NIGHT SENSATION
FZ BACK ON HIS FEET
THE GRAND WAZOO
BIG BAND ALBUM
GOES ON 8 DATE TOUR
BAND TOURS WORLD ALL YEAR LONG
BORN
USED TO MANAGE CLUBS: PURPLE ONION THE UNICORN AND RUN GUNS IN AFRICA
THE MOTHERS

So You Need a Typeface?

This flow chart depicts a complex decision-making process with 40 possible results: choosing the right typeface for a design project. Starting in the middle, the first step in navigating the chart is to choose which kind of project you're working on. Then a carefully created sequence of questions directs you towards a typeface that will fit your practical and style requirements.

While Julian Hansen originally aimed at developing a "serious" model for choosing a typeface, he soon realised most of the decisions that were to be made were closely related to personal taste. He therefore took things one step further and came up with a humorous piece on different typefaces and what people associate with them.

Dieses Ablaufdiagramm zeigt einen komplexen Entscheidungsprozess mit vierzig möglichen Ergebnissen: die Wahl des richtigen Schrifttyps für ein grafisches Projekt. Beginnend in der Mitte, muss man zuerst auswählen, an welcher Art Projekt man arbeitet. Eine ausgetüftelte Abfolge von Fragen führt den Leser schließlich zum geeigneten Schrifttyp, der den praktischen und den gestalterischen Anforderungen des Projekts entspricht.

Ursprünglich wollte Julian Hansen ein „ernsthaftes" Modell entwickeln, um eine passende Schrift auszuwählen. Allerdings stellte er bald fest, dass die meisten dazu notwendigen Entscheidungen reine Geschmacksfragen waren. Deshalb ging er einen Schritt weiter und entwickelte schließlich diese scherzhafte Grafik über verschiedene Schriften und die Assoziationen, die sie auslösen.

Ce diagramme illustre un processus de décision complexe, avec 40 résultats possibles: le choix d'une police de caractères pour un projet de graphisme. En partant du centre, la première étape est de choisir le type de projet sur lequel on travaille. Puis une séquence de questions élaborée avec soin vous guide vers une police qui conviendra à vos critères pratiques et esthétiques.

Au départ, Julian Hansen voulait mettre au point un modèle « sérieux » pour l'aide au choix d'une police, mais il a vite réalisé que la plupart des décisions à prendre dépendaient étroitement des goûts personnels. Il a donc poussé son concept encore plus loin et a créé une œuvre humoristique sur les différentes polices et sur les associations qu'elles évoquent.

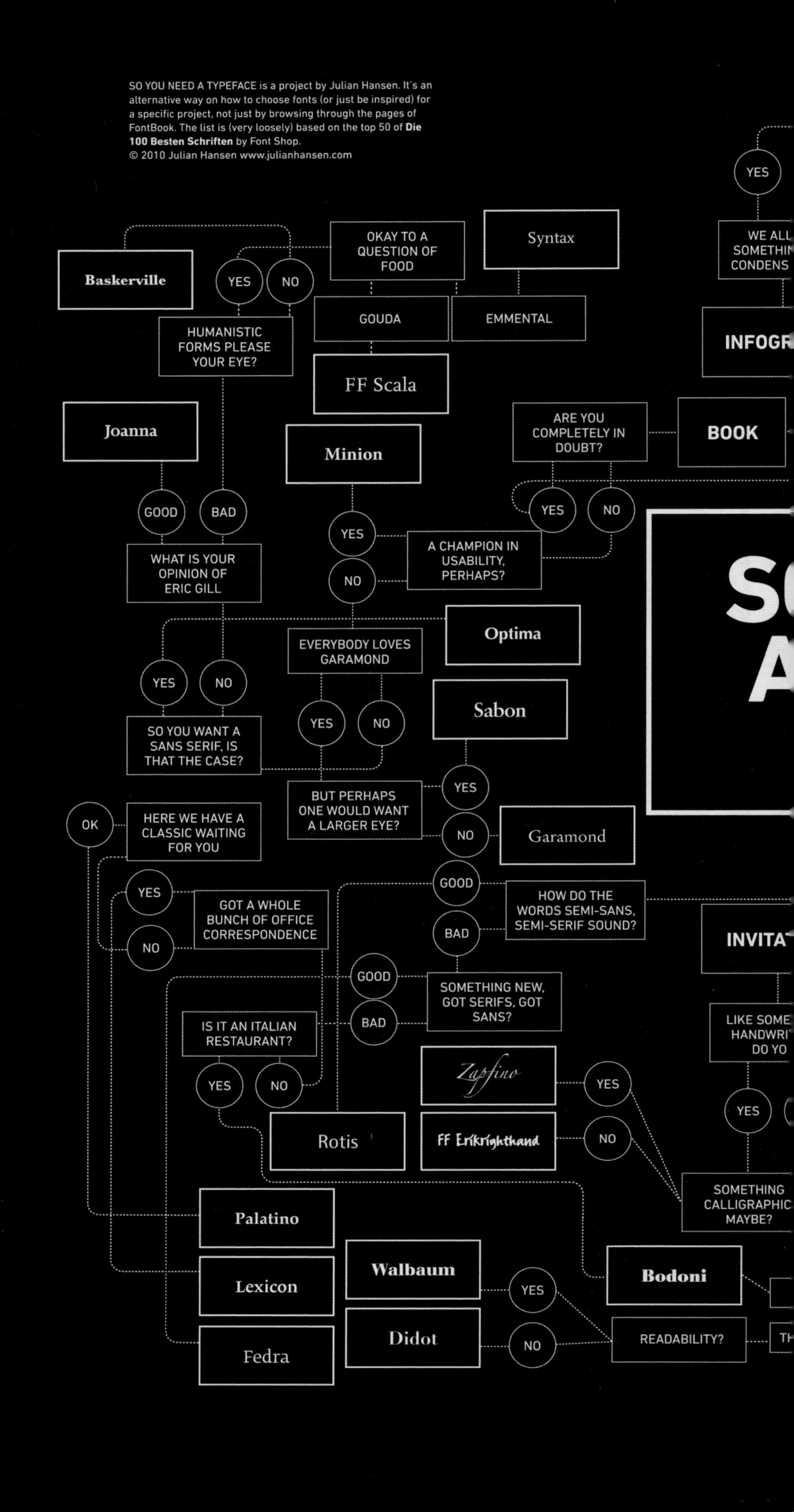

Project Info: Poster, 2010, Denmark
Data Source: FontShop ranking "Die 100 Besten Schriften"
Design: Julian Hansen

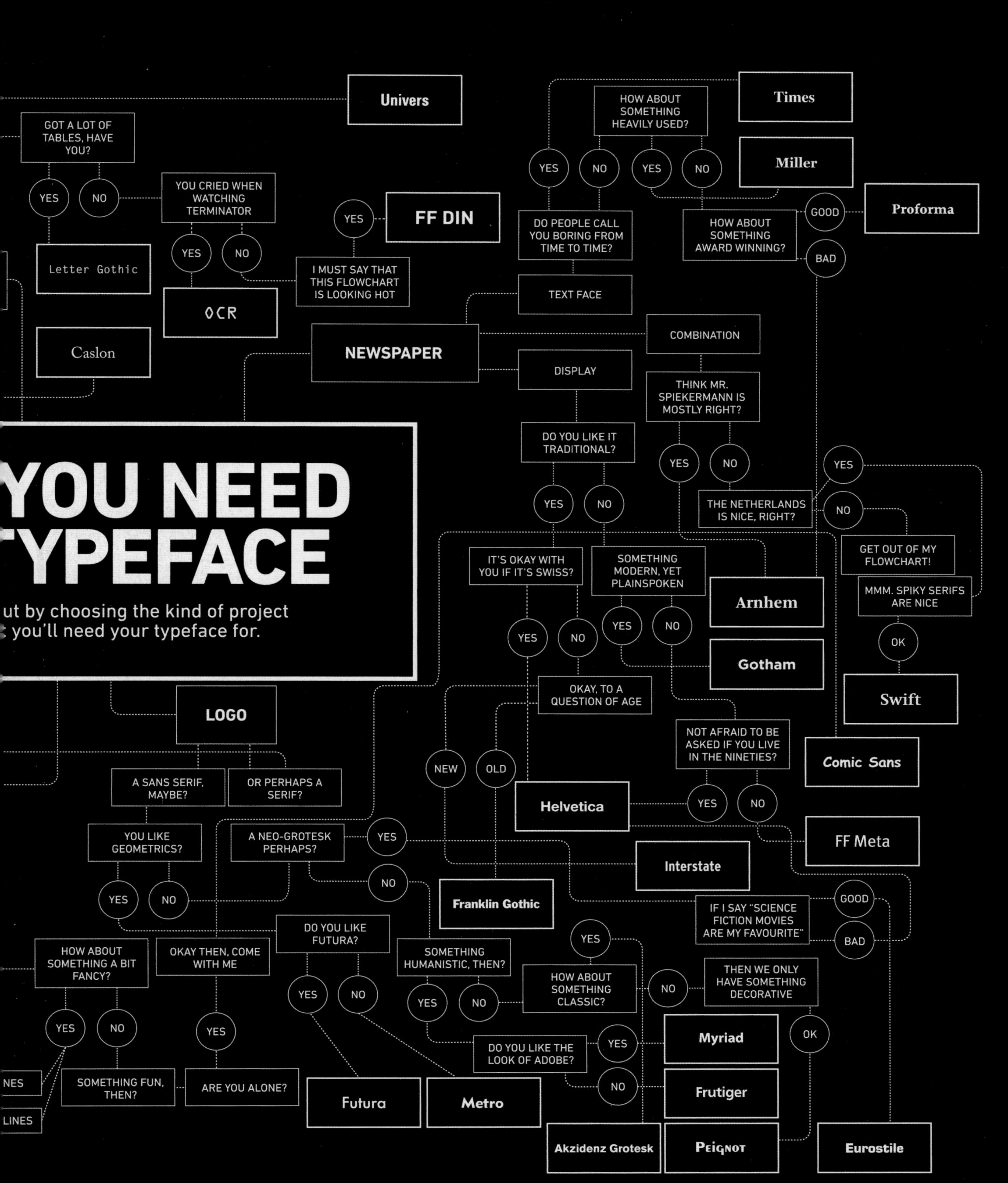

YOU NEED
TYPEFACE
ut by choosing the kind of project
you'll need your typeface for.
Univers
GOT A LOT OF TABLES, HAVE YOU?
YES
NO
YOU CRIED WHEN WATCHING TERMINATOR
Letter Gothic
OCR
Caslon
YES
FF DIN
I MUST SAY THAT THIS FLOWCHART IS LOOKING HOT
NEWSPAPER
HOW ABOUT SOMETHING HEAVILY USED?
Times
Miller
Proforma
DO PEOPLE CALL YOU BORING FROM TIME TO TIME?
HOW ABOUT SOMETHING AWARD WINNING?
GOOD
BAD
TEXT FACE
COMBINATION
DISPLAY
THINK MR. SPIEKERMANN IS MOSTLY RIGHT?
DO YOU LIKE IT TRADITIONAL?
THE NETHERLANDS IS NICE, RIGHT?
GET OUT OF MY FLOWCHART!
MMM. SPIKY SERIFS ARE NICE
OK
IT'S OKAY WITH YOU IF IT'S SWISS?
SOMETHING MODERN, YET PLAINSPOKEN
Arnhem
Gotham
Swift
OKAY, TO A QUESTION OF AGE
NOT AFRAID TO BE ASKED IF YOU LIVE IN THE NINETIES?
Comic Sans
LOGO
A SANS SERIF, MAYBE?
OR PERHAPS A SERIF?
NEW
OLD
Helvetica
FF Meta
YOU LIKE GEOMETRICS?
A NEO-GROTESK PERHAPS?
Interstate
Franklin Gothic
IF I SAY "SCIENCE FICTION MOVIES ARE MY FAVOURITE"
HOW ABOUT SOMETHING A BIT FANCY?
OKAY THEN, COME WITH ME
DO YOU LIKE FUTURA?
SOMETHING HUMANISTIC, THEN?
HOW ABOUT SOMETHING CLASSIC?
THEN WE ONLY HAVE SOMETHING DECORATIVE
DO YOU LIKE THE LOOK OF ADOBE?
Myriad
Frutiger
NES
LINES
SOMETHING FUN, THEN?
ARE YOU ALONE?
Futura
Metro
Akzidenz Grotesk
Peignot
Eurostile

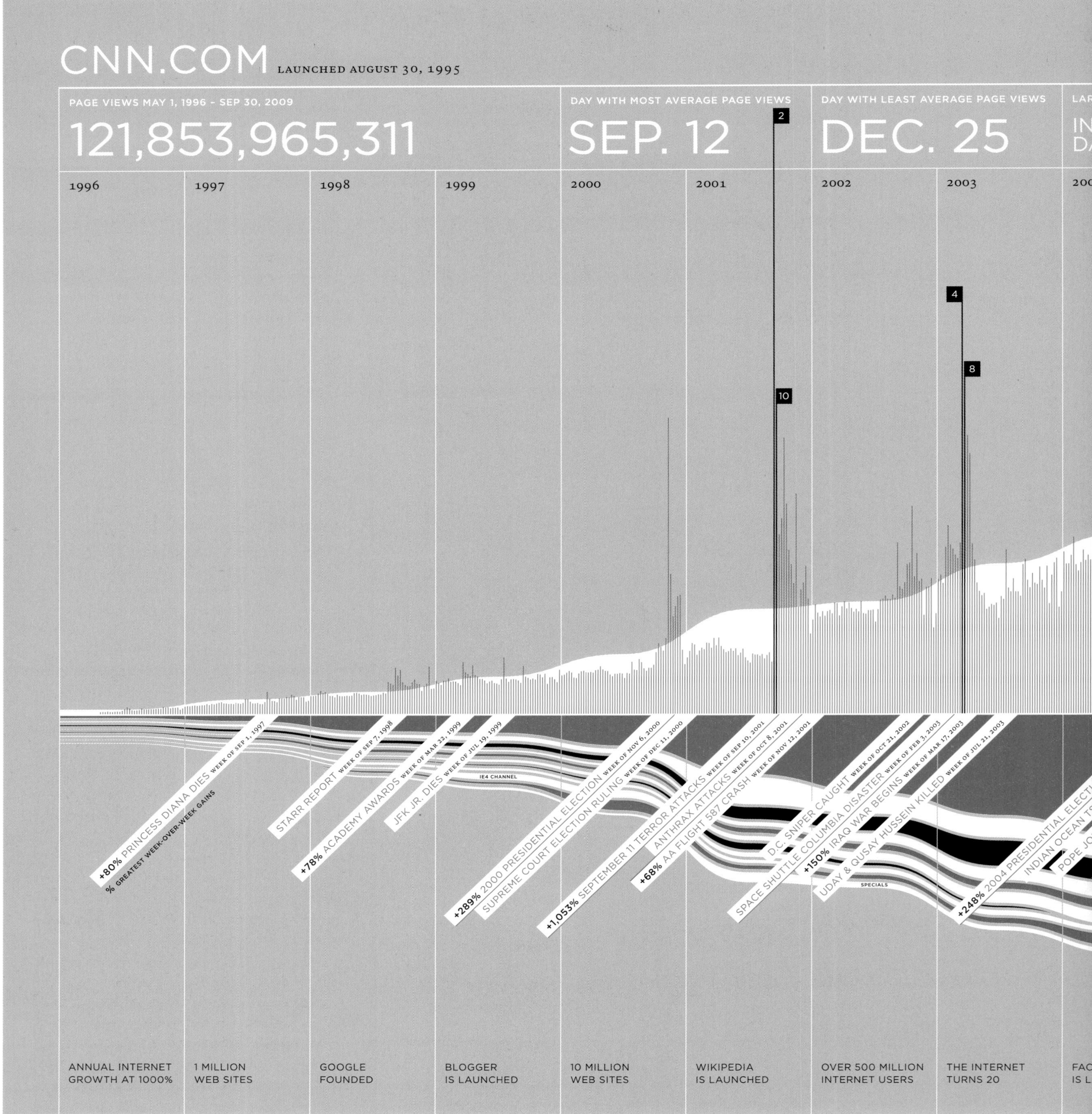

Project Info: CNN, website, 2009, USA
Data Source: Webstats Internal Server Logs; Omniture SiteCatalyst; International Telecommunications Union; United Nations Population Division; AT&T Labs Research; Nielsen Online; Gartner Research
Design: Nicholas Felton

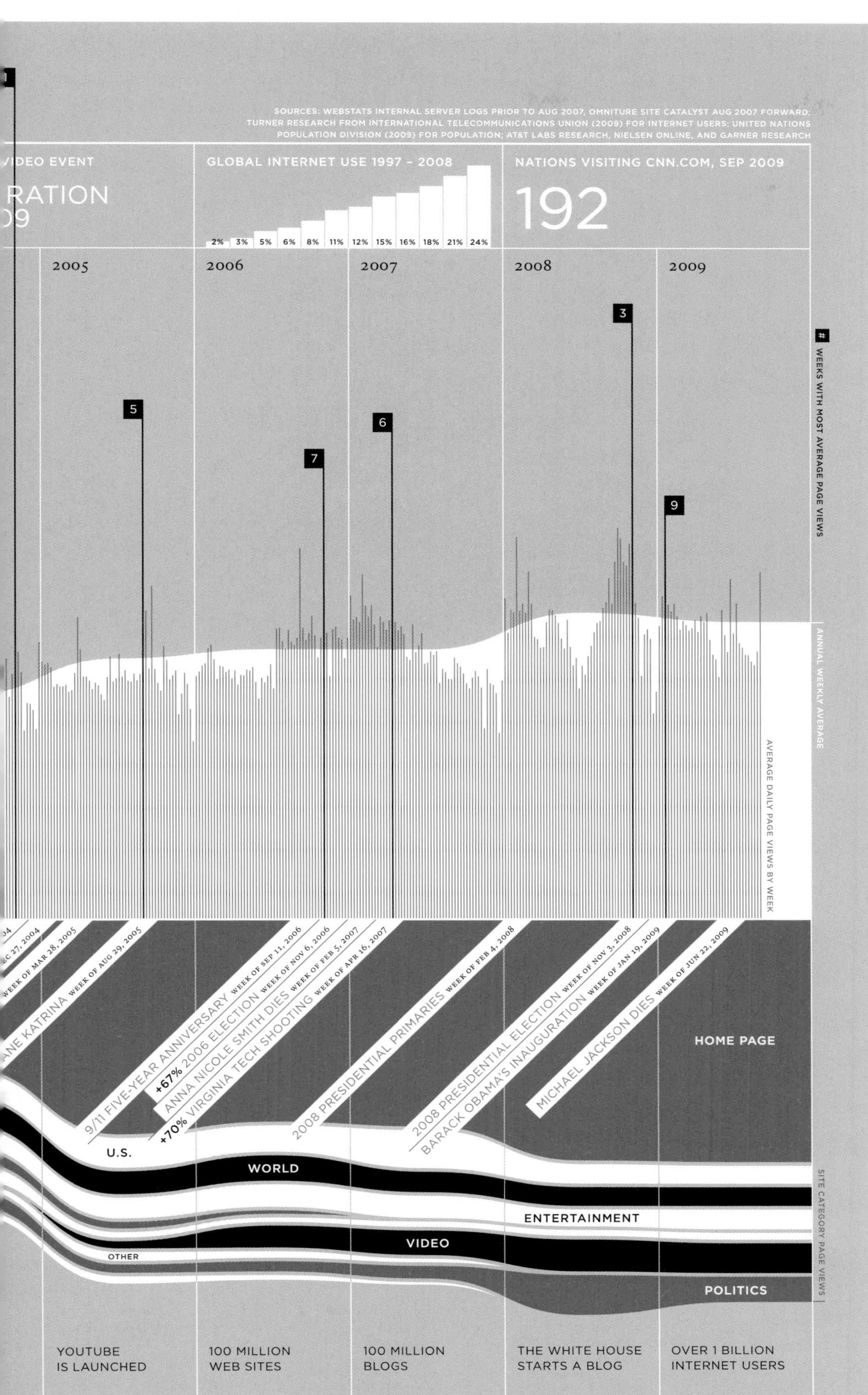

CNN.com Traffic Analysis

In 2009, CNN cooperated with Nicholas Felton to create a visual history of its website since it was launched in 1996. The central spike chart demonstrates weekly page-views over time. Black tags mark the ten busiest weeks, with specific events highlighted with white tags below the central axis. In the lower part, the growth of site categories is tracked.

At the top of the chart, several unique metrics from the site's history are highlighted. To create a larger narrative, milestones in the history of the Internet were placed along the bottom. The piece is strong evidence of how CNN.com became accepted as a timely news source and more generally, how media habits have changed during this period.

2009 kooperierte CNN mit Nicholas Felton, um eine visuelle Geschichte der CNN-Website seit deren Start 1996 zu entwickeln. Das Diagramm in der Mitte zeigt die Zahl der wöchentlichen Seitenabrufe während dieses Zeitraums. Schwarze Markierungen kennzeichnen die zehn Wochen mit den meisten Abrufen, besondere Ereignisse werden in weißen Balken erläutert. Die untere Hälfte des Diagramms zeigt das Wachstum in den einzelnen Rubriken der Seite.

In der obersten Zeile sind verschiedene Rekordwerte in der Geschichte der Website verzeichnet. Um auch den größeren Zusammenhang herzustellen, sind ganz unten Meilensteine in der Entwicklung des Internets aufgeführt. Die Grafik veranschaulicht, wie sich CNN.com im Lauf der Zeit als Bezugsquelle für aktuelle Nachrichten etabliert hat und sich die allgemeinen Mediengewohnheiten in diesem Zeitraum verändert haben.

En 2009, CNN a travaillé en collaboration avec Nicholas Felton pour créer une histoire visuelle de son site web depuis son lancement en 1996. L'histogramme du centre montre le nombre de pages vues par semaine. Les étiquettes noires indiquent les dix semaines les plus actives, et les événements correspondants sont expliqués sur fond blanc sous l'axe central. La partie inférieure rend compte de la croissance des différentes catégories du site.

Au-dessus du graphique, plusieurs chiffres relatifs à l'histoire du site sont mis en valeur. Les grands événements de l'histoire de l'Internet sont mentionnés dans le bas pour élargir le cadre. Ce graphique montre bien que CNN.com est considéré comme une source d'informations en direct et, plus généralement, illustre le changement qui a eu lieu dans les habitudes de consommation des médias.

STAAT / Random I–XI

Using in-depth studies of natural phenomena as her starting point, Jorinde Voigt draws freely conceived motion sequences, visualising partly invisible occurrences. In large-format drawings, this series visualises the evolution of various phenomena, e.g. the flight of an eagle, temperature profiles, kissing, explosions, record charts etc., transferring them into rich graphic structures.

There is no beginning or end to the series, since each phenomenon appears in all the drawings but each begins on a different sheet. The visualisation rules for each phenomenon vary from simple – "plus one" - to more complex patterns as with the Fibonacci numbers, changing too in the course of the series. In contrast to scientific data visualisations, Voigt's works remain open to interpretation.

Ausgehend von ausführlichen Studien über natürliche Phänomene, zeichnet Jorinde Voigt beliebig erdachte Bewegungsfolgen, wobei sie teils unsichtbare Ereignisse visualisiert. Diese Serie veranschaulicht in großformatigen Zeichnungen die Evolution bestimmter Phänomene, etwa den Flug eines Adlers, Temperaturprofile, Küsse, Explosionen, Plattencharts usw., und verwandelt sie in komplexe grafische Strukturen.

Die Serie hat weder Anfang noch Ende, da jedes Phänomen in allen Zeichnungen erscheint, aber jedes auf einem anderen Blatt beginnt. Die Regeln der Visualisierung variieren bei jedem Phänomen von sehr einfachen Mustern („plus eins") bis hin zu komplexen Mustern wie etwa der Fibonacci-Reihe. Zudem verändern sich die Regeln bisweilen im Lauf der Serie. Anders als wissenschaftliche Datenvisualisierungen lassen Jorinde Voigts Arbeiten verschiedene Interpretationen zu.

Jorinde Voigt a utilisé des études détaillées de phénomènes naturels comme point de départ pour dessiner des séquences de mouvement libres et visualiser des événements partiellement invisibles. Les dessins grand format de cette série représentent l'évolution de différents phénomènes, par ex. le vol d'un aigle, des courbes de température, des baisers, des explosions, des classements de disques, etc., en les traduisant en structures graphiques denses et détaillées.

La série n'a ni début ni fin, car chaque phénomène apparaît dans tous les dessins, mais chacun commence sur une feuille différente. Les règles de visualisation des phénomènes peuvent être très simples (« plus un ») ou plus complexes, comme avec la suite de Fibonacci, et peuvent aussi changer au fil de la série. Contrairement aux travaux de visualisation scientifique, les œuvres de Voigt sont ouvertes à l'interprétation.

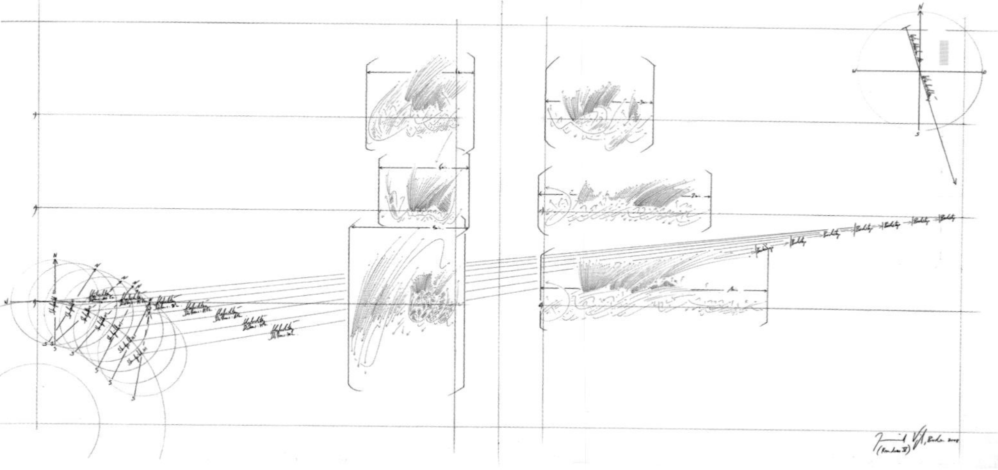

Project Info: Series of drawings, 2008, Germany
Artist: Jorinde Voigt

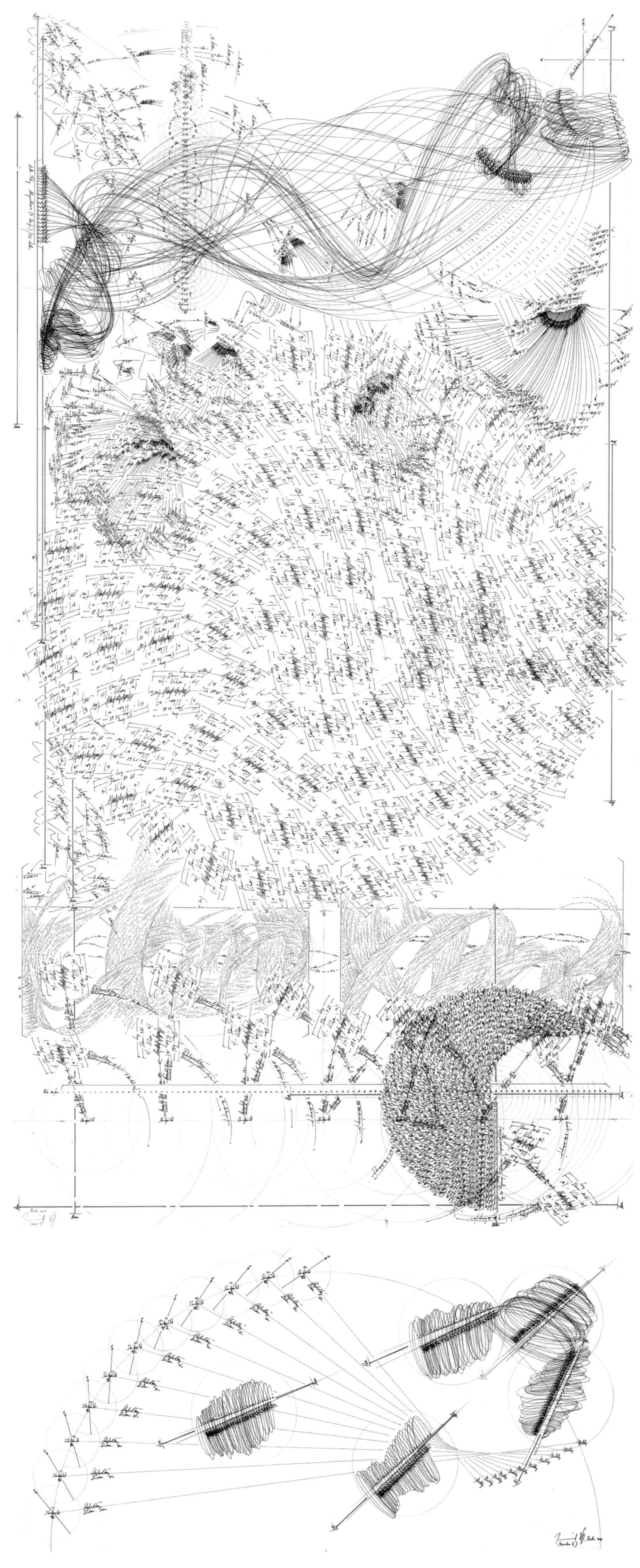

Swine Flu Life Cycle

In 2009 a new sub-type of the H1N1 virus, the so-called Swine Flu, appeared firstly in Mexico and caused the WHO to fear a major global influenza pandemic, similar to the Spanish Flu in 1918–1920. In the subsequent media frenzy, all coverage of the virus became rather sensational.

In contrast, this graphic describes factually the process of how the virus proliferates by attacking human cells. The map beneath shows the number of reported deaths throughout the world by nation, which, compared with deaths caused by typical flu each year, are relatively insignificant.

2009 tauchte eine neue Unterart des H1N1-Virus auf, das sogenannte Schweinegrippenvirus. Die Schweinegrippe trat zunächst in Mexiko auf und rief bei der WHO die Befürchtung einer weltweiten Grippepandemie hervor, ähnlich der Spanischen Grippe von 1918–1920. Im anschließenden Medienspektakel wurde die Berichterstattung über das Virus zunehmend reißerisch.

Im Gegensatz dazu erläutert diese Grafik sachlich, wie das Virus sich vermehrt, indem es menschliche Zellen angreift. Die Weltkarte unten zeigt die Zahl der offiziell bekannten Todesfälle nach Nationen. Sie ist im Vergleich zur jährlichen Todesrate durch eine herkömmliche Grippe relativ bedeutungslos.

En 2009, un nouveau sous-type du virus H1N1, également baptisé grippe porcine, est apparu au Mexique et a fait craindre à l'OMS une pandémie de grippe similaire à l'épidémie de grippe espagnole de 1918–1920. Les médias se sont déchaînés et le virus a fait l'objet d'une couverture médiatique sensationnaliste.

Ici au contraire, cette infographie décrit très factuellement comment le virus prolifère en attaquant les cellules humaines. En dessous, la carte montre le nombre de cas de décès signalés dans le monde par pays. Comparés au nombre de morts causés par la grippe saisonnière classique, ces chiffres sont relativement insignifiants.

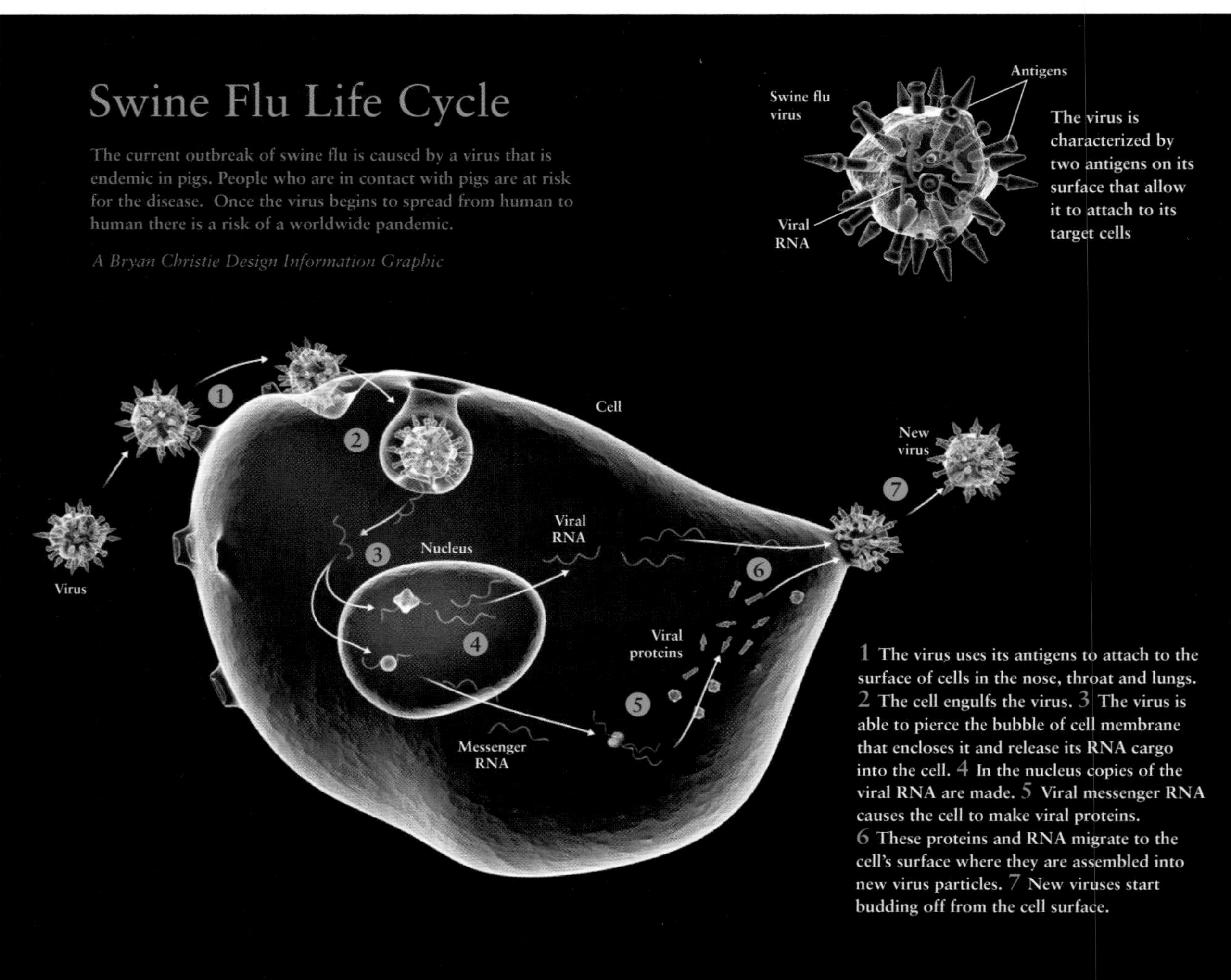

Swine Flu Life Cycle
The current outbreak of swine flu is caused by a virus that is endemic in pigs. People who are in contact with pigs are at risk for the disease. Once the virus begins to spread from human to human there is a risk of a worldwide pandemic.
A Bryan Christie Design Information Graphic
Swine flu virus
Antigens
Viral RNA
The virus is characterized by two antigens on its surface that allow it to attach to its target cells
Cell
New virus
Virus
Nucleus
Viral RNA
Viral proteins
Messenger RNA
1 The virus uses its antigens to attach to the surface of cells in the nose, throat and lungs. 2 The cell engulfs the virus. 3 The virus is able to pierce the bubble of cell membrane that encloses it and release its RNA cargo into the cell. 4 In the nucleus copies of the viral RNA are made. 5 Viral messenger RNA causes the cell to make viral proteins. 6 These proteins and RNA migrate to the cell's surface where they are assembled into new virus particles. 7 New viruses start budding off from the cell surface.

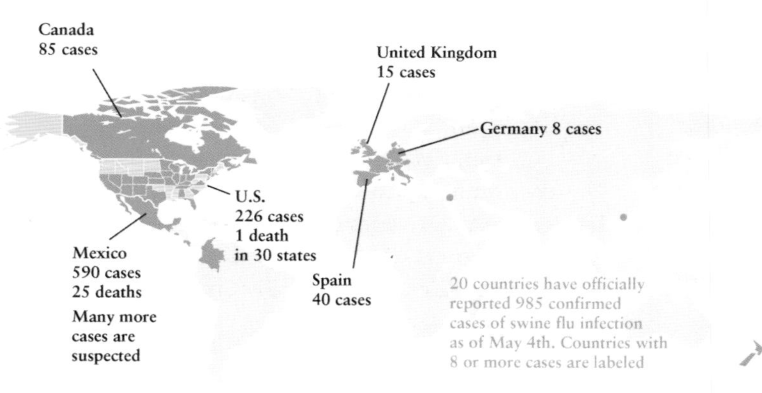

Swine Flu Around The World
The human swine flu outbreak began in Mexico. Authorities in Mexico closed schools, museums, libraries and theaters in the capital on May 24th to try to contain an outbreak.
The disease has been detected in the U.S. and other countries. The World Health Organization has raised the level of influenza pandemic alert from the phase 4 to phase 5, indicating that human-to-human transmission of the virus is taking place in at least two countries.
Sources: WHO, CDC, Scientific American
© 2009 Bryan Christie Design
Canada 85 cases
United Kingdom 15 cases
Germany 8 cases
U.S. 226 cases 1 death in 30 states
Mexico 590 cases 25 deaths
Many more cases are suspected
Spain 40 cases
20 countries have officially reported 985 confirmed cases of swine flu infection as of May 4th. Countries with 8 or more cases are labeled

Project Info: Blog, 2009, USA
Data Source: WHO; CDC; *Scientific American*
Research: Molly Frances
Design: Bryan Christie, Joe Lertola

Synchronous Objects for *One Flat Thing, reproduced*

William Forsythe is one of the most celebrated contemporary choreographers. His stage play *One Flat Thing, reproduced* is an arrangement for 17 dancers under and above a set of tables. The dance is generated from a set of motion themes, cues that dancers give each other and various instants when the movements of individual dancers are aligned.

Forsythe worked with Ohio State University to develop a visualisation for this play. The research team collected two sets of data: spatial data indicating the position of each dancer at any given time, and qualitative data regarding the internal structure of the dance. These data were transformed into various visualisations of the play.

Form Flow (top) shows how the movements of several dancers are aligned in one specific moment, while *3D Alignment* (bottom) traces the dancers' movements in space. *Cues and Themes* (following spread) is a graphic score of themes, cues and alignments over time.

William Forsythe ist ein gefeierter zeitgenössischer Choreograf. Sein Bühnenwerk *One Flat Thing, reproduced* ist ein Arrangement für 17 Tänzer unter und über einer Reihe von Tischen. Der Tanz entsteht aus verschiedenen Bewegungsmotiven, Einsätzen, die die Tänzer einander vorgeben, sowie aus Momenten, in denen sie ihre Bewegungen synchronisieren.

Forsythe kooperierte mit der Ohio State University, um dieses Bühnenstück zu visualisieren. Das Forschungsteam sammelte zwei Arten von Daten: räumliche Daten, die die Position aller Tänzer zu jeder Zeit notierten, sowie qualitative Daten, die sich auf die innere Organisationsstruktur des Tanzes bezogen. Diese Daten wurden in mehreren Visualisierungen dargestellt.

Form Flow (oben) zeigt den synchronen Bewegungsablauf mehrerer Tänzer in bestimmten Momenten, während *3D Alignment* (unten) die Bewegungen der Tänzer im Raum nachzeichnet. *Cues and Themes* (folgende Seite) wertet die Abfolge von Themen, Einsätzen und Synchronisierungen grafisch aus.

William Forsythe est l'un des chorégraphes modernes les plus célèbres. Son œuvre *One Flat Thing, reproduced* a été créée pour 17 danseurs sous et sur des tables. La danse est générée par un ensemble de thèmes de mouvement, des indications que les danseurs se donnent les uns aux autres, et différents instants où les mouvements de plusieurs danseurs s'alignent.

Forsythe a travaillé avec l'Université de l'État de l'Ohio pour mettre au point une visualisation de cette œuvre. L'équipe de recherche a recueilli deux types de données: des données spatiales indiquant la position de chaque danseur à tout moment, et des données qualitatives sur la structure interne de la danse. Ces données ont été transformées en plusieurs visualisations de l'œuvre.

Form Flow (en haut) montre l'alignement des mouvements de plusieurs danseurs à un moment précis, alors que *3D Alignment* (en bas) représente leurs mouvements dans l'espace. *Cues and Themes* (page suivante) offre une représentation graphique de thèmes, de repères et d'alignements.

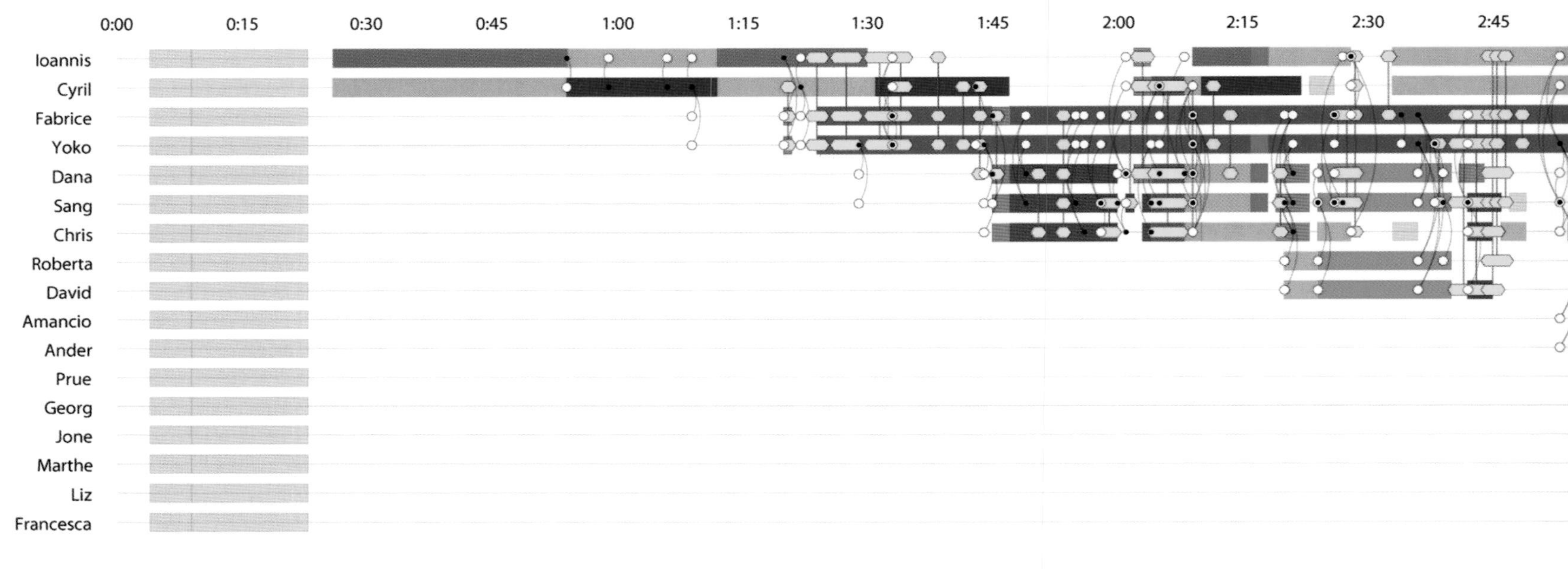

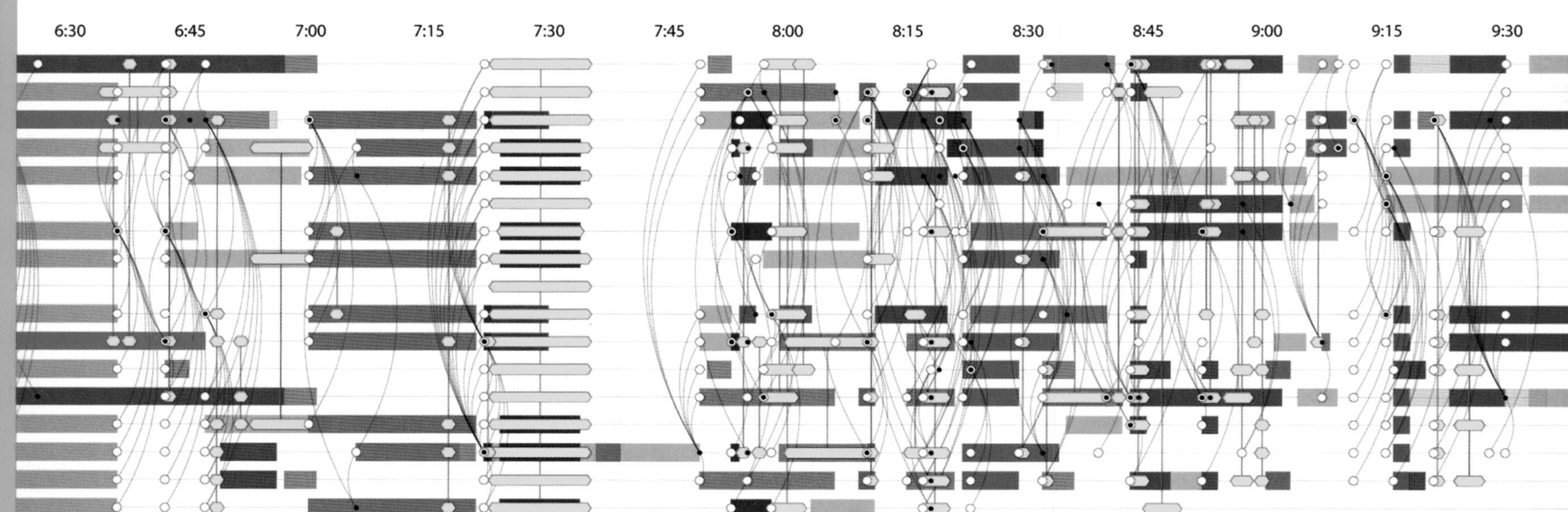

An information graphic from Synchronous Objects for *One Flat Thing, reproduced*
http://synchronousobjects.osu.edu

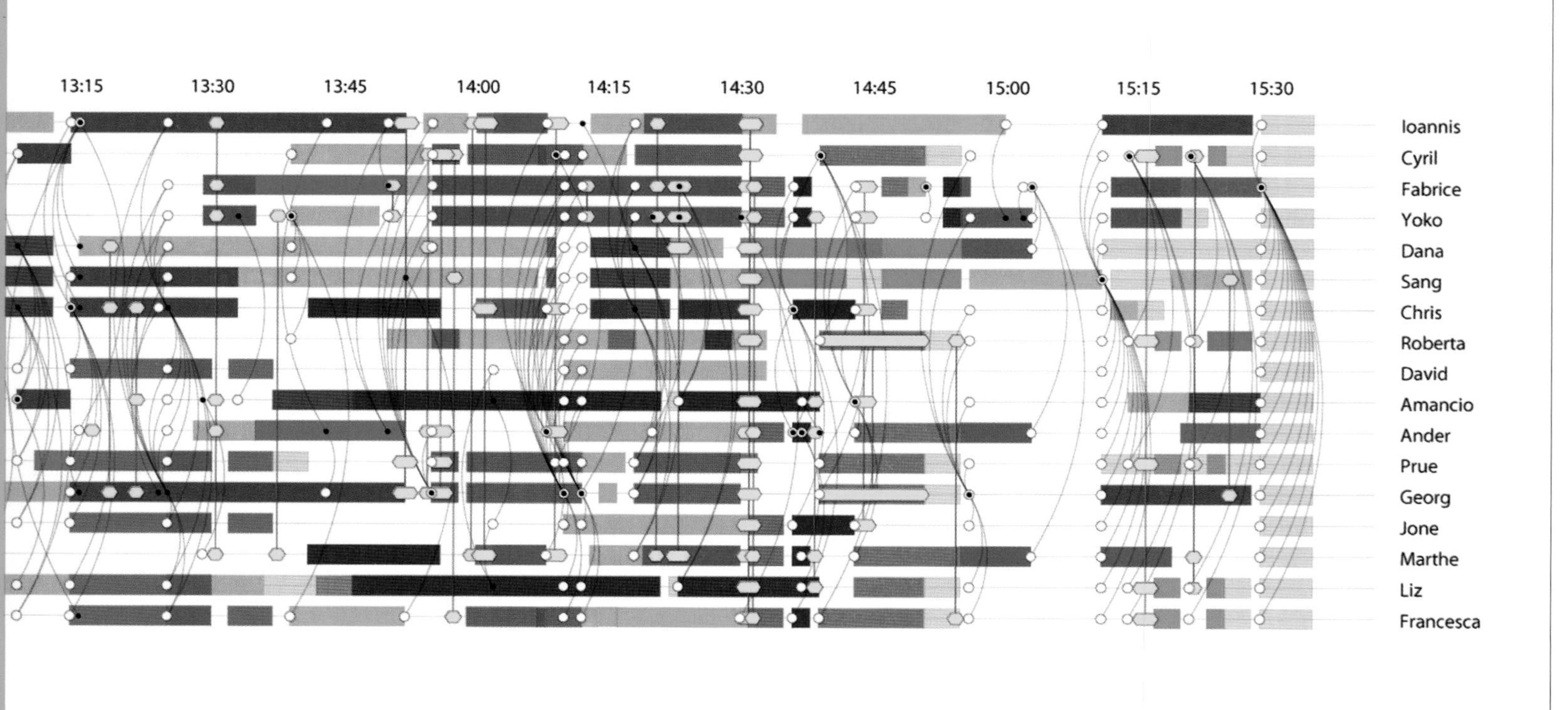

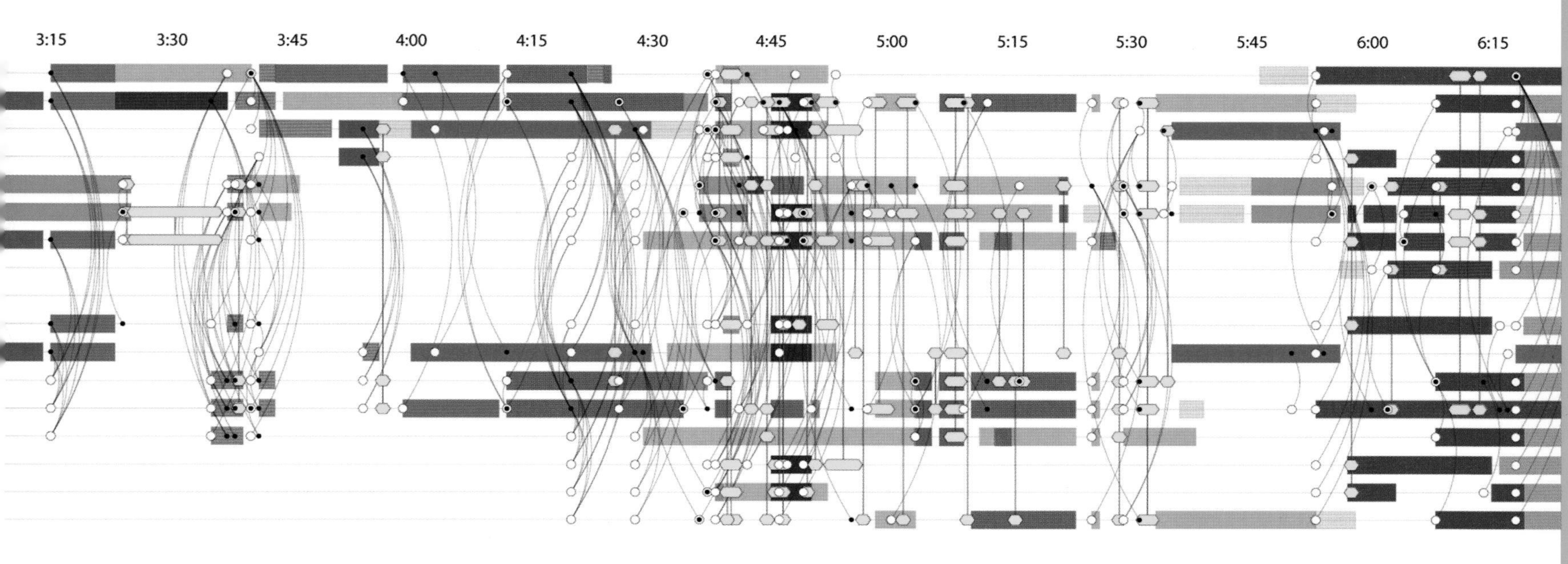

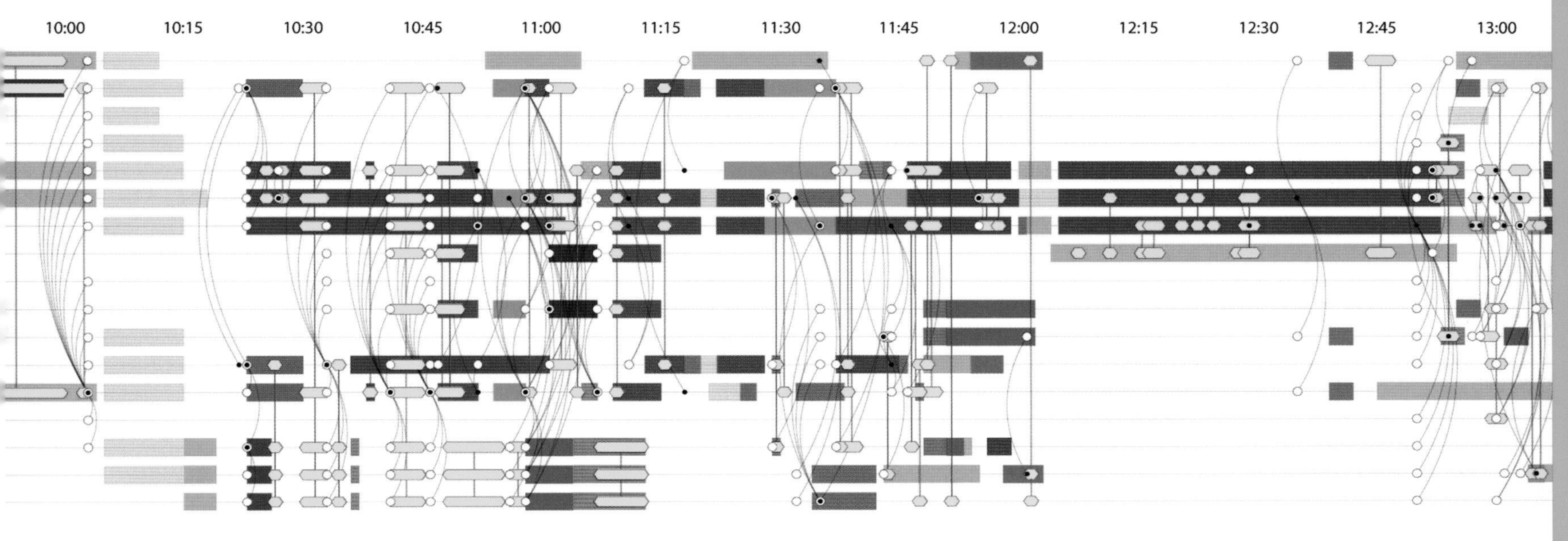

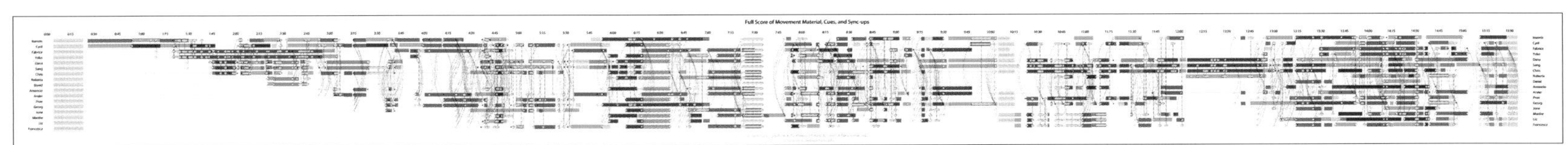

Project Info: The Forsythe Company, interactive visualisation, 2009, Germany/USA
Research: Ohio State University; Forsythe Company; Amsterdam School of the Arts; University of California; University College London
Design: Matthew Lewis (ACCAD, Ohio State University)
Creative Direction: William Forsythe, Maria Palazzi, Norah Zuniga Shaw

cupboard
afterwards
Wonderland
dream
verses
paper
brightened
RETURNED
unimportant
fashion
suppressed
teacup
jury
officers
court
tarts
simple
write
slates
knife
marked
bats
Lizard
blasts persisted
trumpet
jurors
guinea-pigs
book
important
fall
witness
pale
sister
whatever
deep
decided
knee
written
shrill
assembled
shoes
learnt
man
sadly
passage
stupid
frowning
letter
recovered
King
White
gave
trembling
regular
upset
sharply
relief
bread-and-butter
unfortunate
ashamed
explain
Rabbit
rule
eager
Majesty
belongs
toes
beautiful
porpoise
Quadrille
nonsense
French
hastily
begun
distance
picked
Gryphon
taught
cards
beasts
eagerly
unless
fish
week
friend
Mock
Turtle
sea
pack
throw
words
hand
clear
finished
voice
nothing
sentence
Knave
Soup
care
course
consider
feel
school
exclaimed
different
surprised
way
repeated
curious
continued
Drawling
executed
interrupted
ordered
anxious
great
began
Tortoise
crumbs
glad
forgetting
wash
added
slowly
laughed
mine
faster
creatures
alive
sulkily
beginning
wildly
checked
rather
yet
round
quite
concert
meekly
sing
Hearts
custody
choice
talking
large
sighed
savage
garden
Alice
fly
walked
tone
Queen
game
tea
day
right
agree
moral
argument
please
music
wide
whispered
sitting
players
rest
lady
shouted
moved
direction
Hatter
child
arches
fun
otherwise
executioner
instantly
Dormouse
angrily
minute
Miss
flamingo
introduce
Duchess
exactly
work
Cat
play
pinched
soldiers
ground
attending
politely
ear
taken

TextArc: Alice's Adventures in Wonderland

Bradford Paley created TextArc as a text-analysing tool. In this example, all the text lines of *Alice in Wonderland* are arranged in sequence clockwise around a central area which is a map of all the words, placed near the lines in which they are used. Frequently used words thus appear towards the centre. Each word has a small distribution sign next to it, with tiny rays pointing towards all lines in which the word is used.

As an example, the Hatter, Dormouse and March Hare have similarly shaped distribution glyphs, indicating that they always appear together. In this enhanced version, Paley also employed spectral colouring. Chapters are coded in successive colours; key words are brighter, while peripheral words are darker and fade into the background.

Bradford Paley entwickelte TextArc als Tool zur Textanalyse. In diesem Beispiel sind alle Textzeilen von *Alice im Wunderland* im Uhrzeigersinn angeordnet. Im Zentrum steht eine Karte aller im Text verwendeten Wörter, wobei die Wörter jeweils in der Nähe der Zeilen stehen, in denen sie vorkommen. Das führt dazu, dass häufig verwendete Wörter eher in der Mitte stehen. Neben jedem Wort ist ein kleines Verteilungszeichen zu sehen, mit winzigen Pfeilen, die auf alle Zeilen deuten, in denen das Wort vorkommt.

Der Hutmacher (Hatter), die Haselmaus (Dormouse) und der Märzhase (March Hare) haben ähnliche Verteilungszeichen, was darauf verweist, dass sie stets zusammen auftreten. In der vorliegenden erweiterten Version setzte Paley zudem Spektralfarben ein. Die Kapitel sind in chronologischer Folge farblich codiert. Schlüsselwörter sind kräftiger gefärbt, während weniger präsente Wörter blasser sind und im Hintergrund fast verschwimmen.

TextArc est un outil d'analyse de texte créé par Bradford Paley. Dans cet exemple, toutes les lignes de texte d'*Alice au pays des merveilles* sont disposées les unes à la suite des autres dans le sens des aiguilles d'une montre autour d'un espace central qui dresse une carte de tous les mots, placés près des lignes dans lesquelles ils sont utilisés. Les mots les plus fréquents apparaissent donc vers le centre. Chaque mot est accompagné d'un petit signe de distribution à partir duquel de minuscules traits pointent vers toutes les lignes qui le contiennent.

Par exemple, le Chapelier (Hatter), le Loir (Dormouse) et le Lièvre de mars (March Hare) ont des glyphes de distribution similaires, ce qui indique qu'ils apparaissent toujours ensemble. Dans cette version améliorée, Paley a également employé la coloration spectrale. Les chapitres sont codés par couleur en suivant l'ordre du spectre; les mots clés sont plus clairs, tandis que les mots secondaires sont plus foncés et sont relégués à l'arrière-plan.

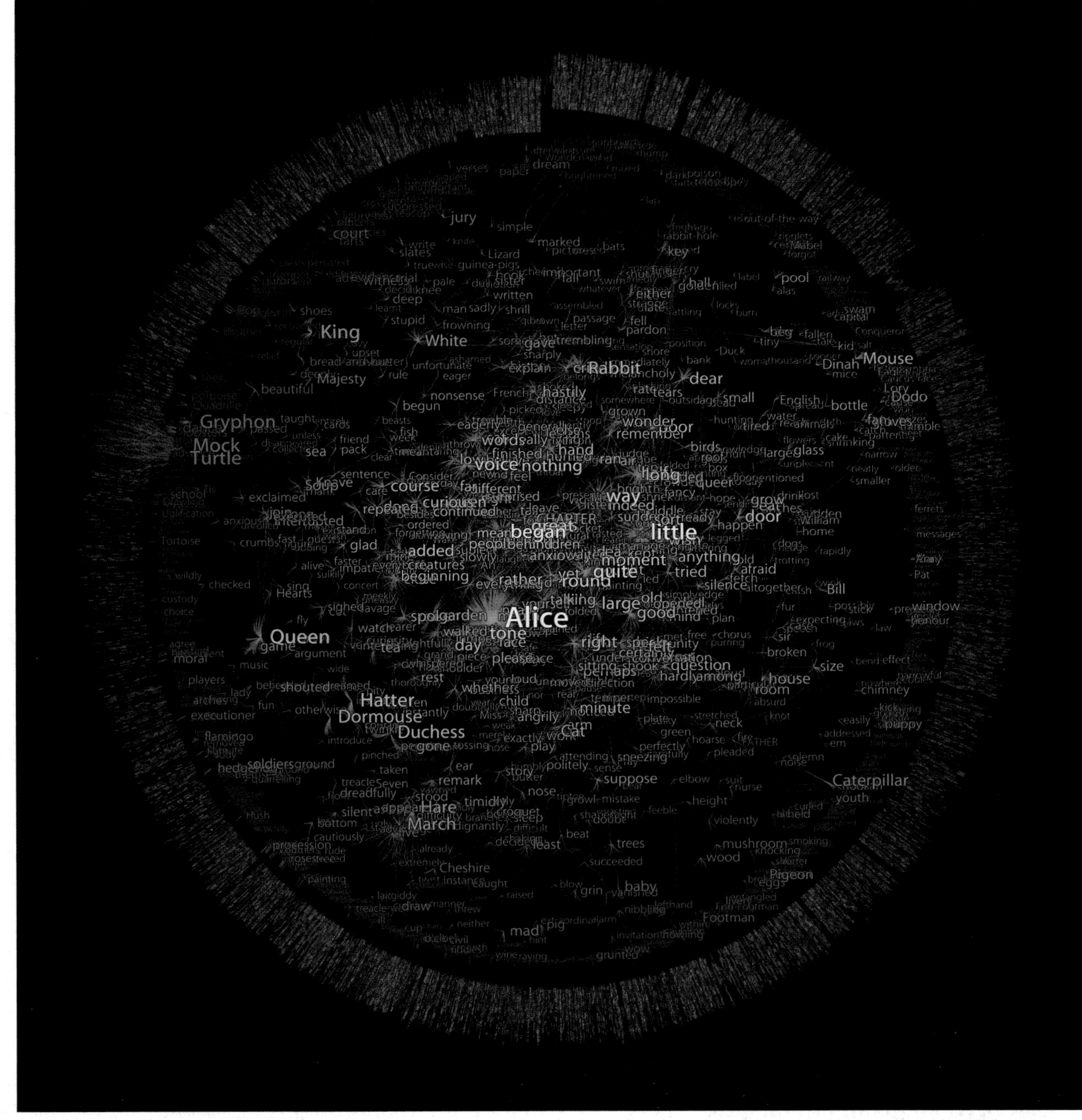

Project Info: Print, 2009, USA
Data Source: Project Gutenberg
Design: W. Bradford Paley (Digital Image Design)

TextArc: Williams' History of Science

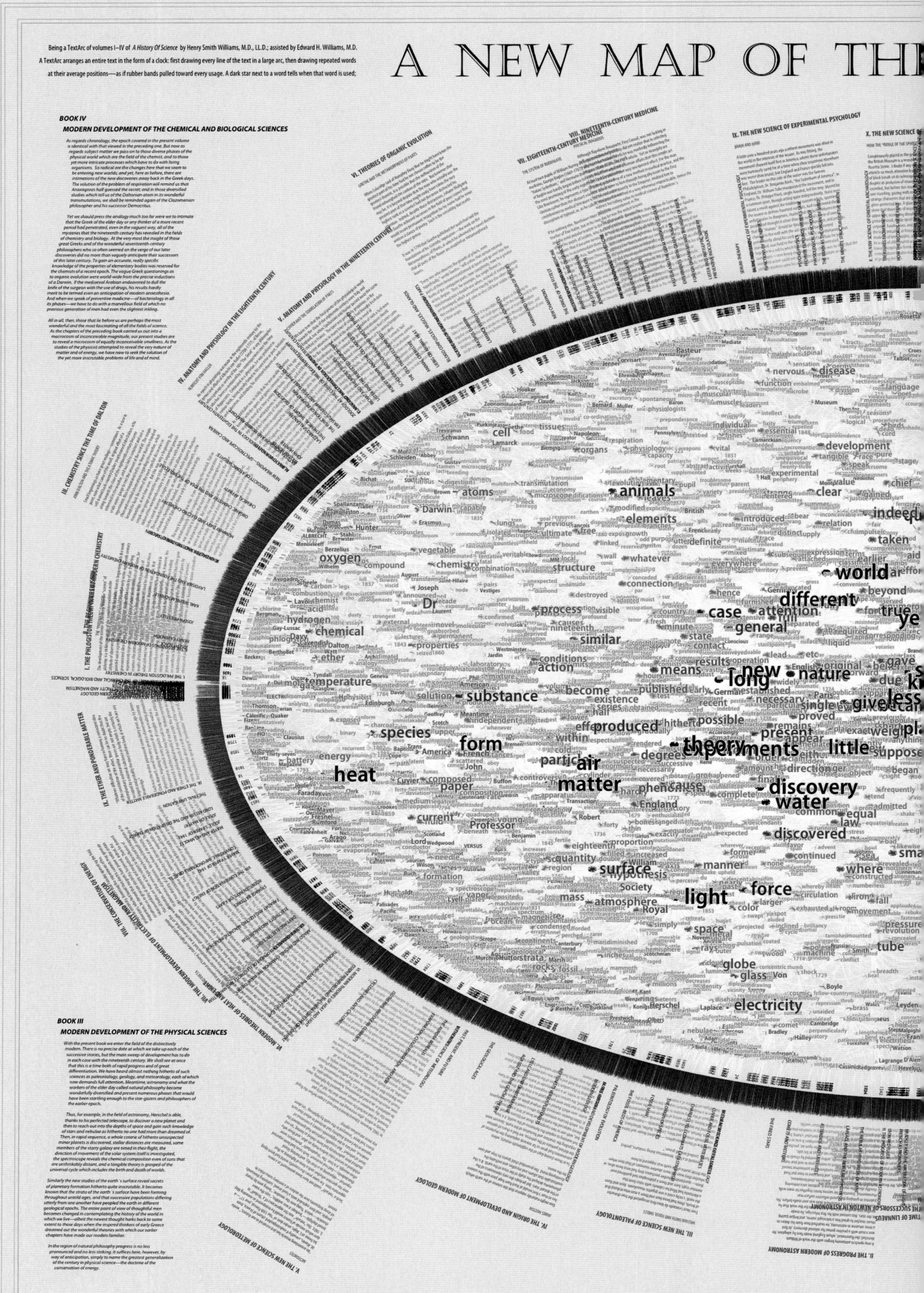

Being a TextArc of volumes I–IV of A History Of Science by Henry Smith Williams, M.D., LL.D.; assisted by Edward H. Williams, M.D.
A TextArc arranges an entire text in the form of a clock: first drawing every line of the text in a large arc, then drawing repeated words at their average positions—as if rubber bands pulled toward every usage. A dark star next to a word tells when that word is used;
A NEW MAP OF TH
BOOK IV
MODERN DEVELOPMENT OF THE CHEMICAL AND BIOLOGICAL SCIENCES

As regards chronology, the epoch covered in the present volume is identical with that viewed in the preceding one. But now as regards subject matter we pass on to those diverse phases of the physical world which are the field of the chemist, and to those yet more intricate processes which have to do with living organisms. So radical are the changes here that we seem to be entering new worlds; and yet, here as before, there are intimations of the new discoveries away back in the Greek days. The solution of the problem of respiration will remind us that Anaxagoras half guessed the secret; and in those diversified studies which tell us of the Oxtonian atom in its wonderful transmutations, we shall be reminded again of the Clazomenian philosopher and his successor Democritus.

Yet we should press the analogy much too far were we to intimate that the Greek of the elder day or any thinker of a more recent period had penetrated, even in the vaguest way, all of the mysteries that the nineteenth century has revealed in the fields of chemistry and biology. At the very least the insight of those great Greeks and of the wonderful seventeenth-century philosophers who so often seemed on the verge of our later discoveries did no more than vaguely anticipate their successors of this later century. To gain an accurate, really specific knowledge of the properties of elementary bodies was reserved for the chemists of a recent epoch. The vague Greek questionings as to organic evolution were world-wide from the precise inductions of a Darwin. If the mediaeval Arabian endeavored to dull the knife of the surgeon with the use of drugs, his results hardly merit to be termed even an anticipation of modern anaesthesia. And when we speak of preventive medicine—of bacteriology in all its phases—we have to do with a marvellous field of which no previous generation of man had even the slightest inkling.

All in all, then, these that lie before us are perhaps the most wonderful and the most fascinating of all the fields of science. As the chapters of the preceding book carried our eye into a macrocosm of inconceivable magnitude, our present studies are to reveal a microcosm of equally inconceivable smallness. As the studies of the physicist attempted to reveal the very nature of matter and of energy, we have now to seek the solution of the yet more inscrutable problems of life and of mind.

BOOK III
MODERN DEVELOPMENT OF THE PHYSICAL SCIENCES

With the present book we enter the field of the distinctively modern. There is no precise date at which we take up each of the successive stories, but the main sweep of development has to do in each case with the nineteenth century. We shall see at once that this is a time both of rapid progress and of great differentiation. We have heard almost nothing hitherto of such sciences as paleontology, geology, and meteorology, each of which now demands full attention. Meantime, astronomy and what the workers of the elder day called natural philosophy become numerously diversified and present numerous phases that would have been startling enough to the star-gazers and philosophers of the earlier epoch.

Thus, for example, in the field of astronomy, Herschel is able, thanks to his perfected telescope, to discover a new planet and then to reach out into the depths of space and gain such knowledge of stars and nebulae as hitherto no one had more than dreamed of. Then, in rapid sequence, a whole coterie of hitherto unsuspected minor planets is discovered, stellar distances are measured, some members of the starry galaxy are timed in their flight, the direction of movement of the solar system itself is investigated, the spectroscope reveals the chemical composition even of suns that are unthinkably distant, and a tangible theory is grasped of the universal cycle which includes the birth and death of worlds.

Similarly the new studies of the earth's surface reveal secrets of planetary formation hitherto quite inscrutable. It becomes known that the strata of the earth's surface have been forming throughout untold ages, and that successive populations differing utterly from one another have peopled the earth in different geological epochs. The entire point of view of thoughtful men becomes changed in contemplating the history of the world in which we live—albeit the newest thought harks back to some extent to those days when the inspired thinkers of early Greece dreamed out the wonderful theories with which our earlier chapters have made our readers familiar.

In the region of natural philosophy progress is no less pronounced and no less striking. It suffices here, however, by way of anticipation, simply to name the greatest generalization of the century in physical science—the doctrine of the conservation of energy.

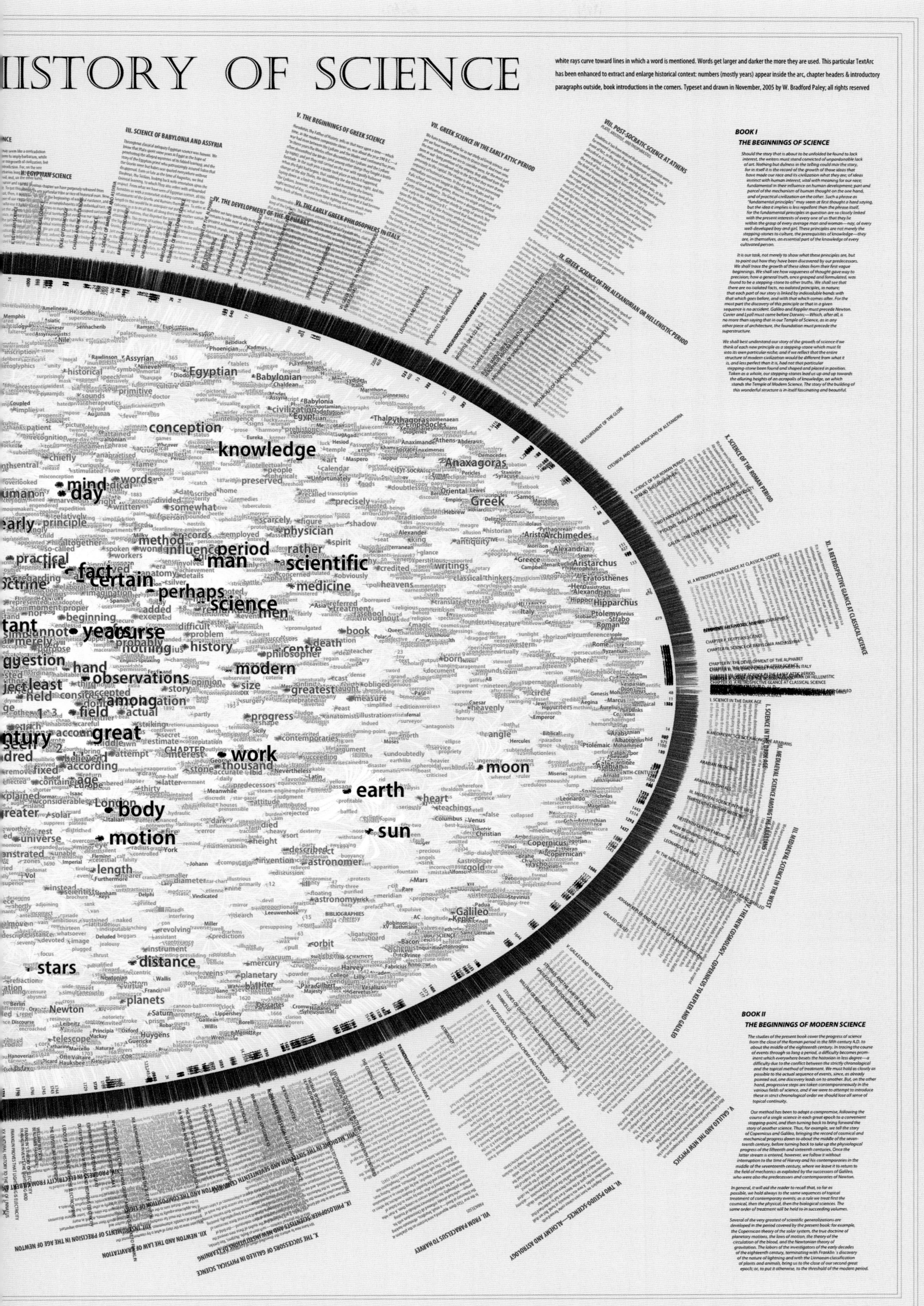
IISTORY OF SCIENCE
white rays curve toward lines in which a word is mentioned. Words get larger and darker the more they are used. This particular TextArc has been enhanced to extract and enlarge historical context: numbers (mostly years) appear inside the arc, chapter headers & introductory paragraphs outside, book introductions in the corners. Typeset and drawn in November, 2005 by W. Bradford Paley; all rights reserved
BOOK I
THE BEGINNINGS OF SCIENCE
Should the story that is about to be unfolded be found to lack interest, the writers must stand convicted of unpardonable lack of art. Nothing but dulness in the telling could mar the story, for in itself it is the record of the growth of those ideas that have made our race and its civilization what they are; of ideas instinct with human interest, vital with meaning for our race; fundamental in their influence on human development; part and parcel of the mechanism of human thought on the one hand, and of practical civilization on the other. Such a phrase as "fundamental principles" may seem at first thought a hard saying, but the idea it implies is less repellent than the phrase itself, for the fundamental principles in question are so closely linked with the present interests of every one of us that they lie within the grasp of every average man and woman—nay, of every well-developed boy and girl. These principles are not merely the stepping-stones to culture, the prerequisites of knowledge—they are, in themselves, an essential part of the knowledge of every cultivated person.
It is our task, not merely to show what these principles are, but to point out how they have been discovered by our predecessors. We shall trace the growth of these ideas from their first vague beginnings. We shall see how vagueness of thought gave way to precision; how a general truth, once grasped and formulated, was found to be a stepping-stone to other truths. We shall see that there are no isolated facts, no isolated principles, in nature; that each part of our story is linked by indissoluble bands with that which goes before, and with that which comes after. For the most part the discovery of this principle or that in a given sequence is no accident. Galileo and Keppler must precede Newton. Cuvier and Lyell must come before Darwin;—Which, after all, is no more than saying that in our Temple of Science, as in any other piece of architecture, the foundation must precede the superstructure.
We shall best understand our story of the growth of science if we think of each new principle as a stepping-stone which must fit into its own particular niche; and if we reflect that the entire structure of modern civilization would be different from what it is, and less perfect than it is, had not that particular stepping-stone been found and shaped and placed in position. Taken as a whole, our stepping-stones lead us up and up towards the alluring heights of an acropolis of knowledge, on which stands the Temple of Modern Science. The story of the building of this wonderful structure is in itself fascinating and beautiful.
BOOK II
THE BEGINNINGS OF MODERN SCIENCE
The studies of the present book cover the progress of science from the close of the Roman period in the fifth century A.D. to about the middle of the eighteenth century. In tracing the course of events through so long a period, a difficulty becomes prominent which everywhere besets the historian in less degree—a difficulty due to the conflict between the strictly chronological and the topical method of treatment. We must hold as closely as possible to the actual sequence of events, since, as already pointed out, one discovery leads on to another. But, on the other hand, progressive steps are taken contemporaneously in the various fields of science, and if we were to attempt to introduce these in strict chronological order we should lose all sense of topical continuity.
Our method has been to adopt a compromise, following the course of a single science in each great epoch to a convenient stopping-point, and then turning back to bring forward the story of another science. Thus, for example, we tell the story of Copernicus and Galileo, bringing the record of cosmical and mechanical progress down to about the middle of the seventeenth century, before turning back to take up the physiological progress of the fifteenth and sixteenth centuries. Once the latter stream is entered, however, we follow it without interruption to the time of Harvey and his contemporaries in the middle of the seventeenth century, where we leave it to return to the field of mechanics as exploited by the successors of Galileo, who were also the predecessors and contemporaries of Newton.
In general, it will aid the reader to recall that, so far as possible, we hold always to the same sequences of topical treatment of contemporary events; as a rule we treat first the cosmical, then the physical, then the biological sciences. The same order of treatment will be held to in succeeding volumes.
Several of the very greatest of scientific generalizations are developed in the period covered by the present book: for example, the Copernican theory of the solar system, the true doctrine of planetary motions, the laws of motion, the theory of the circulation of the blood, and the Newtonian theory of gravitation. The labors of the investigators of the early decades of the eighteenth century, terminating with Franklin's discovery of the nature of lightning and with the Linnaean classification of plants and animals, bring us to the close of our second great epoch; or, to put it otherwise, to the threshold of the modern period.

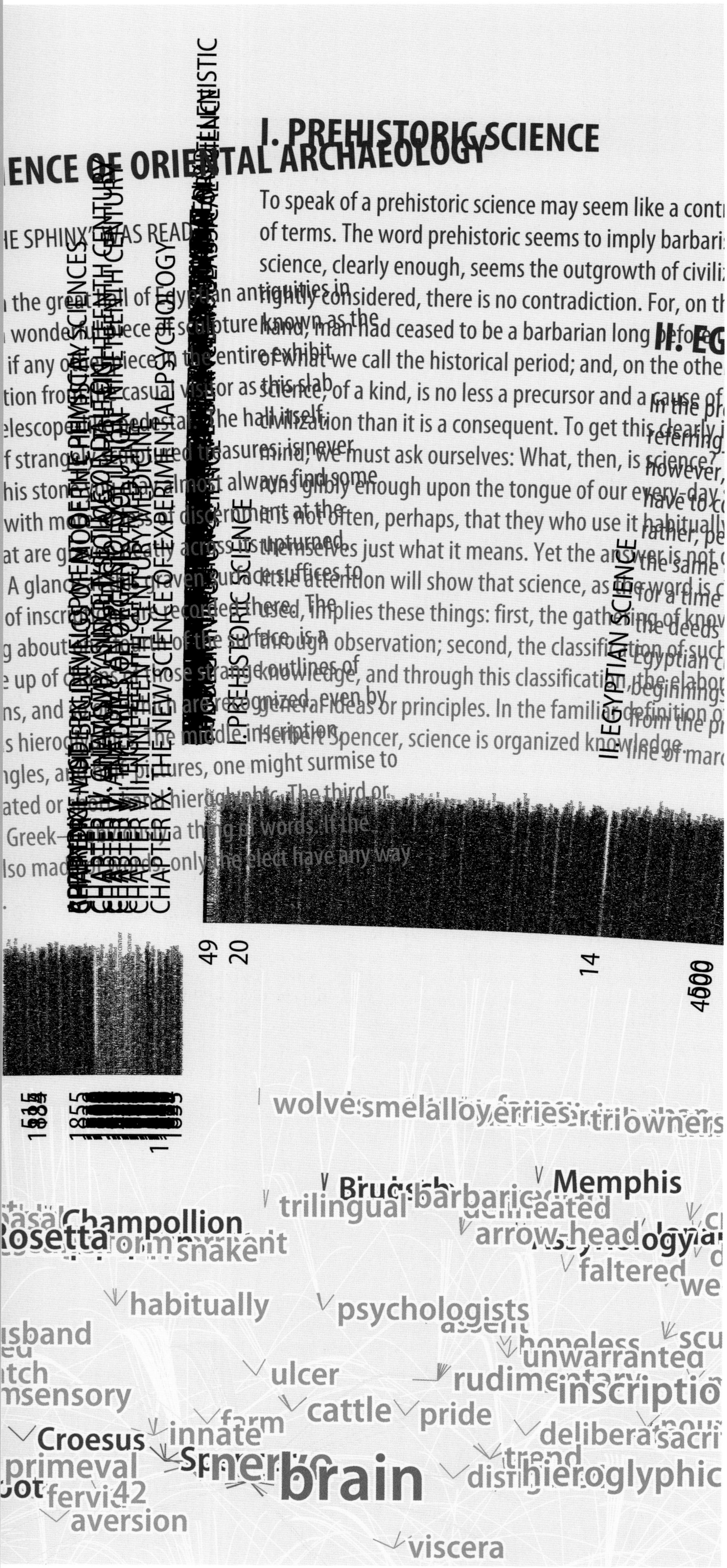

TextArc arranges a body of text clockwise, creating a visual index. Along the outer rim, text-lines are recorded in their order of appearance. Inside this, words are placed in their average position, in proximity to the individual lines around the circle in which they appear. This example covers four volumes of H. S. Williams' *History of Science*. The arc is formed by chapter titles and introductions.

The first two volumes chronicle history until around 1800 (centre bottom). The third and fourth volumes cover the modern sciences. Concepts that are common to the sciences of all eras (like system, theory etc.) are drawn towards the centre, since they occur throughout the whole text. Others, being in use only in certain eras, float nearer specific edges.

TextArc ordnet einen Textkorpus im Uhrzeigersinn an und schafft damit einen visuellen Index. Am äußeren Rand stehen die Textzeilen in der Reihenfolge ihres Erscheinens. Im Inneren sind im Text vorkommende Wörter platziert, je nachdem in welchen Zeilen des äußeren Kreises sie vorkommen. Dieses Beispiel behandelt vier Bände der *History of Science* von H. S. Williams. Um die Ellipse herum stehen alle Kapitelüberschriften und -einleitungen des Werkes.

Die ersten beiden Bände bilden einen historischen Abriss bis etwa 1800 (untere Mitte). Band 3 und 4 befassen sich mit den modernen Naturwissenschaften. Begriffe, die zu allen Zeiten in der Wissenschaft vorkommen (wie System, Theorie etc.), sind eher in der Mitte positioniert, da sie durchgängig im gesamten Text auftauchen. Andere, die nur in einzelnen Epochen in Gebrauch waren, gleiten in das betreffende Feld der Ellipse.

TextArc réorganise les textes dans le sens des aiguilles d'une montre pour créer un index visuel. Les lignes de texte sont rangées le long du bord extérieur dans leur ordre d'apparition. À l'intérieur, les mots apparaissent à leur position moyenne, près des lignes qui les contiennent autour du cercle. Cet exemple couvre quatre tomes de *A History of Science*, de H. S. Williams. L'arc est formé par les titres et introductions des différents chapitres.

Les deux premiers tomes font la chronique des sciences jusqu'à 1800 (au milieu, en bas). Le troisième et le quatrième tome couvrent les sciences modernes. Les concepts communs aux sciences de toutes les époques (comme système, théorie, etc.) se trouvent vers le centre, car ils apparaissent dans tout le texte. D'autres termes qui ne sont utilisés qu'à certaines époques sont plus proches du bord.

Project Info: Print, 2005, USA
Data Source: Project Gutenberg: "A History Of Science" by Henry Smith Williams
Design: W. Bradford Paley (Digital Image Design)

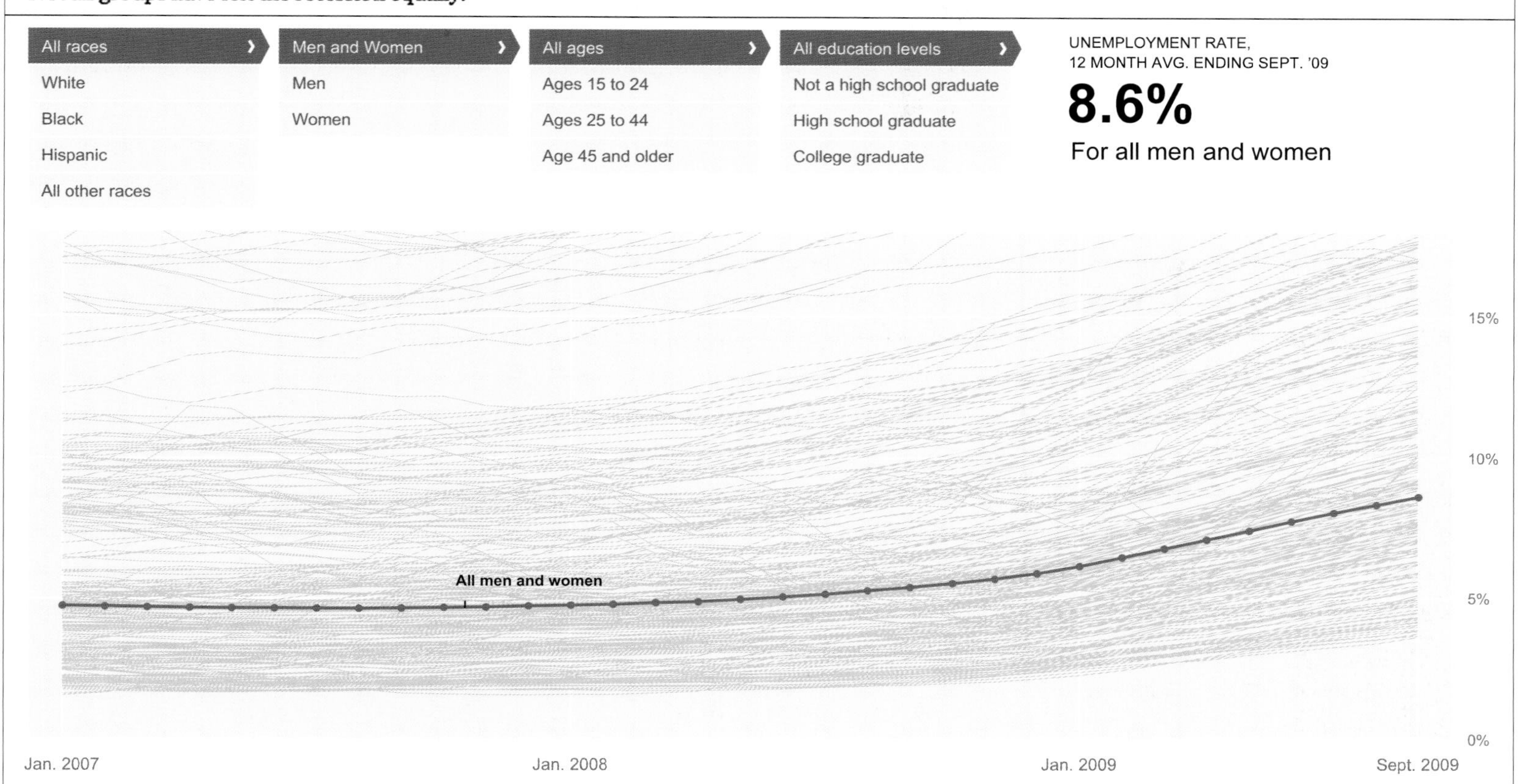

The Jobless Rate for People Like You

This is an interactive time series covering US unemployment rates for the period from January 2007 to September 2009. It takes the general unemployment rate and breaks it down into specific population groups by gender, race, education and age.

While most of the time unemployment rates in the western world are communicated in national average figures, this piece reveals the major social gaps behind these figures. Where the jobless rate is around 4% for white females with a college degree, it climbs to more than 30% for black males who have never received further education.

Diese interaktive Zeitreihe zeigt die Arbeitslosenquoten in den USA zwischen Januar 2007 und September 2009. Darin werden die allgemeinen Arbeitslosenzahlen nach bestimmten Bevölkerungsgruppen aufgeschlüsselt, etwa nach Geschlecht, ethnischer Herkunft, Bildung und Alter.

In westlichen Ländern wird die Arbeitslosenquote üblicherweise als nationaler Durchschnitt angegeben. Im Gegensatz dazu wird hier die soziale Kluft innerhalb dieser Zahlen deutlich: Während die Arbeitslosigkeit bei weißen Frauen mit Collegeabschluss rund vier Prozent beträgt, steigt sie auf über dreißig Prozent bei männlichen Schwarzen ohne Schulabschluss.

Cette série temporelle interactive examine les taux de chômage aux États-Unis de janvier 2007 à septembre 2009. Elle décompose le taux de chômage total pour différents groupes de population par sexe, appartenance ethnique, niveau d'éducation et âge.

La plupart du temps, les taux de chômage des pays occidentaux sont publiés sous forme de chiffres pour l'ensemble du pays, mais ce graphique révèle les profonds fossés sociaux qui se cachent derrière ces chiffres. Le taux de chômage est d'environ 4 % pour les femmes blanches titulaires d'un diplôme universitaire, mais grimpe à plus de 30 % pour les hommes noirs qui n'ont aucun diplôme.

Project Info: *The New York Times*, interactive visualisation, 2009, USA
Data Source: Bureau of Labor Statistics
Design: Shan Carter, Amanda Cox, Kevin Quealy
Art Direction: Steve Duenes

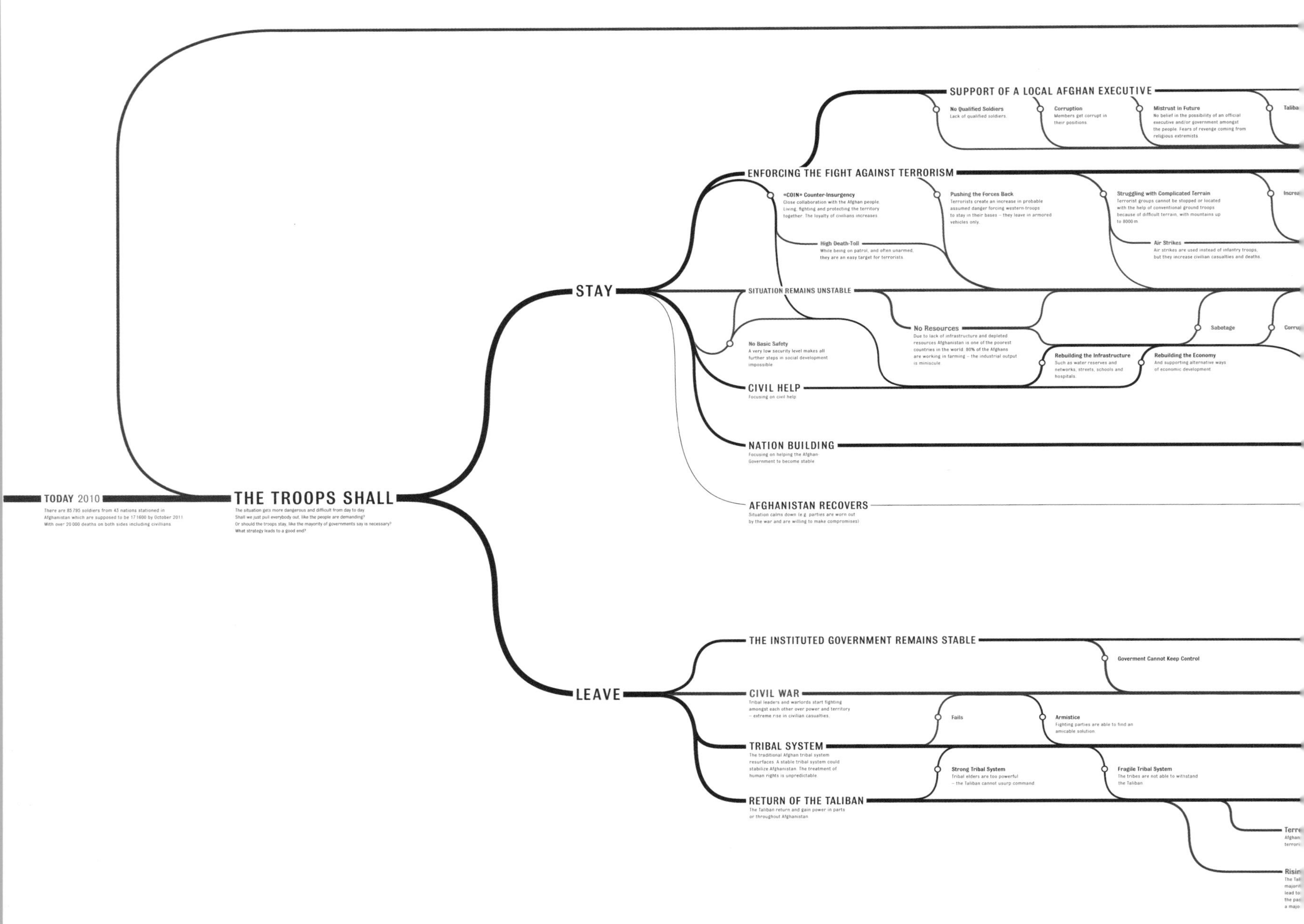

The Afghan Conflict –A Map of Possible Scenarios

This is one of the rare examples where a timeline for the future is driven in order to compare and evaluate future options. In a synchronoptic timeline, the graphic displays various scenarios for the future in Afghanistan. The flow chart starts with a single point in the present and follows two major options: the troops stay or leave.

The scenarios developed consequently are based on wide media research and informed interviews with journalists, research think-tanks and political advisers. The synchronoptic format permits an overview of what political observers expect to happen, and thus makes it easier to evaluate differing political options.

Dies ist eines der wenigen Beispiele, bei denen eine in die Zukunft weisende Zeitleiste entwickelt wurde, um künftige Optionen zu vergleichen und zu bewerten. In einer synchronoptischen Zeitleiste zeigt die Grafik mehrere Szenarien für die Zukunft in Afghanistan. Das Ablaufdiagramm hat einen einzigen Ausgangspunkt in der Gegenwart und folgt zwei grundsätzlichen Möglichkeiten: Die alliierten Soldaten bleiben stationiert, oder sie werden abgezogen.

Die Szenarien, die sich daraus entwickeln, beruhen auf einer breiten Medienrecherche und Interviews mit Journalisten, Wissenschaftlern und politischen Beratern. Die synchronoptische Darstellung ermöglicht einen Überblick darüber, was politische Beobachter für die Zukunft erwarten. Diese Übersicht erleichtert die Bewertung unterschiedlicher politischer Optionen.

Voici l'un des rares exemples de chronologie dont le but est de comparer et évaluer les options futures. Cette ligne de temps synchronoptique présente différents scénarios pour le futur en Afghanistan. Le diagramme commence avec un point unique, le présent, suivi de deux grandes options : les troupes restent ou partent.

Les scénarios qui en découlent sont basés sur une recherche approfondie dans les médias, et sur des entretiens avec des journalistes, des laboratoires d'idées et des conseillers politiques. Le format synchronoptique permet d'avoir une vue d'ensemble de ce que les observateurs politiques prévoient, et facilite donc l'évaluation des différentes options politiques.

Project Info: Poster, 2010, Germany
Data Source: Afghan Conflict Monitor; ZEIT-Stiftung; Heinrich Böll Foundation; Stiftung Wissenschaft und Politik; *The Guardian*; *The New York Times*
Research: Susanne Köbl (*Der Spiegel*); Can Merey (dpa); Hauke Friederichs (*Die Zeit*)
Design: Marc Tiedemann, Pierre la Baume, Karen Hentschel
Additional Info: Original size 164 cm x 70 cm; student project at University of Applied Sciences Potsdam, Germany

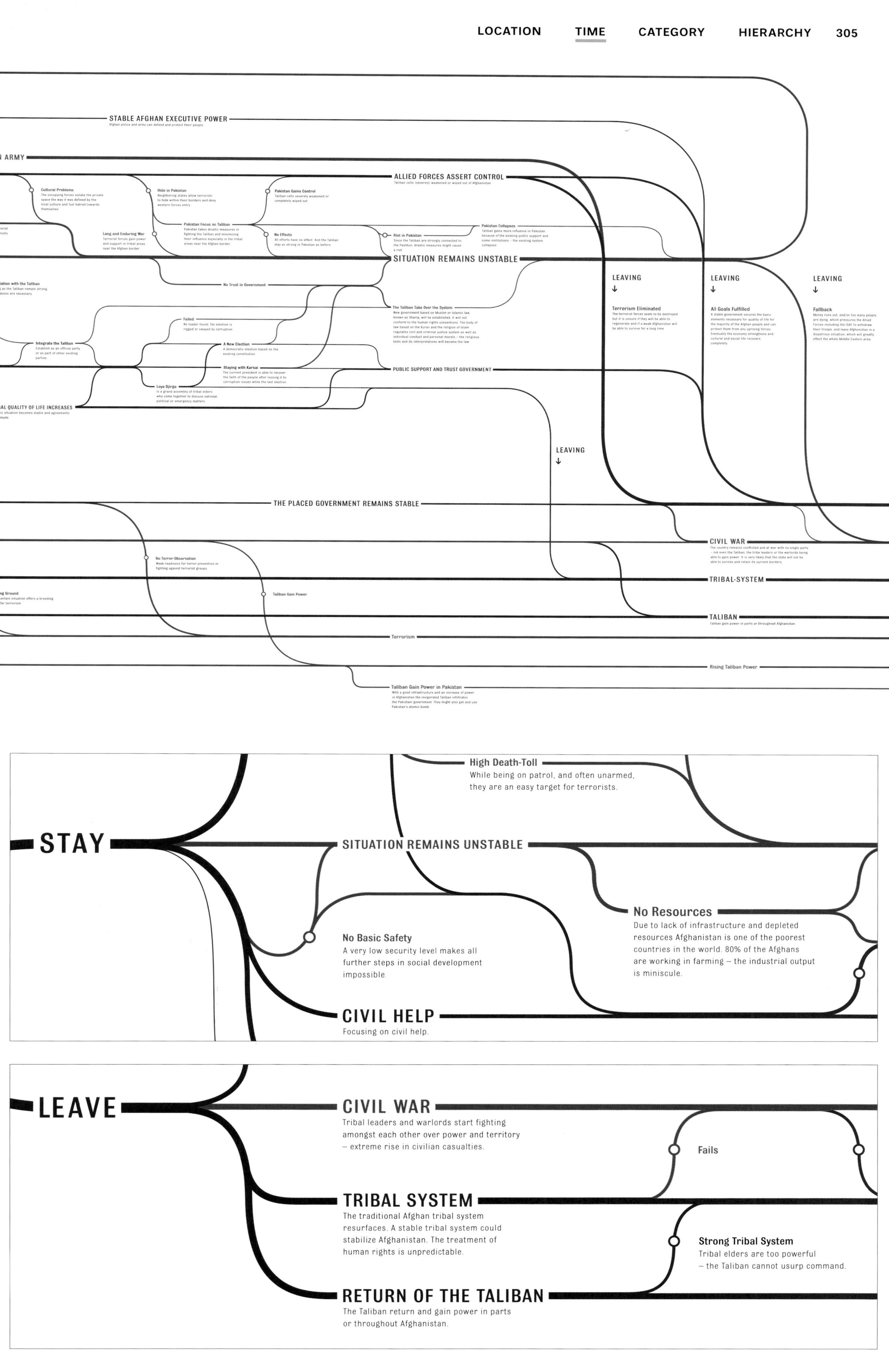
STABLE AFGHAN EXECUTIVE POWER
ALLIED FORCES ASSERT CONTROL
SITUATION REMAINS UNSTABLE
PUBLIC SUPPORT AND TRUST GOVERNMENT
LEAVING
LEAVING
LEAVING
LEAVING
Terrorism Eliminated
All Goals Fulfilled
Fallback
THE PLACED GOVERNMENT REMAINS STABLE
CIVIL WAR
TRIBAL-SYSTEM
TALIBAN
Terrorism
Rising Taliban Power
Taliban Gain Power in Pakistan
STAY
High Death-Toll
While being on patrol, and often unarmed, they are an easy target for terrorists.
SITUATION REMAINS UNSTABLE
No Resources
Due to lack of infrastructure and depleted resources Afghanistan is one of the poorest countries in the world. 80% of the Afghans are working in farming – the industrial output is miniscule.
No Basic Safety
A very low security level makes all further steps in social development impossible.
CIVIL HELP
Focusing on civil help.
LEAVE
CIVIL WAR
Tribal leaders and warlords start fighting amongst each other over power and territory – extreme rise in civilian casualties.
Fails
TRIBAL SYSTEM
The traditional Afghan tribal system resurfaces. A stable tribal system could stabilize Afghanistan. The treatment of human rights is unpredictable.
Strong Tribal System
Tribal elders are too powerful – the Taliban cannot usurp command.
RETURN OF THE TALIBAN
The Taliban return and gain power in parts or throughout Afghanistan.

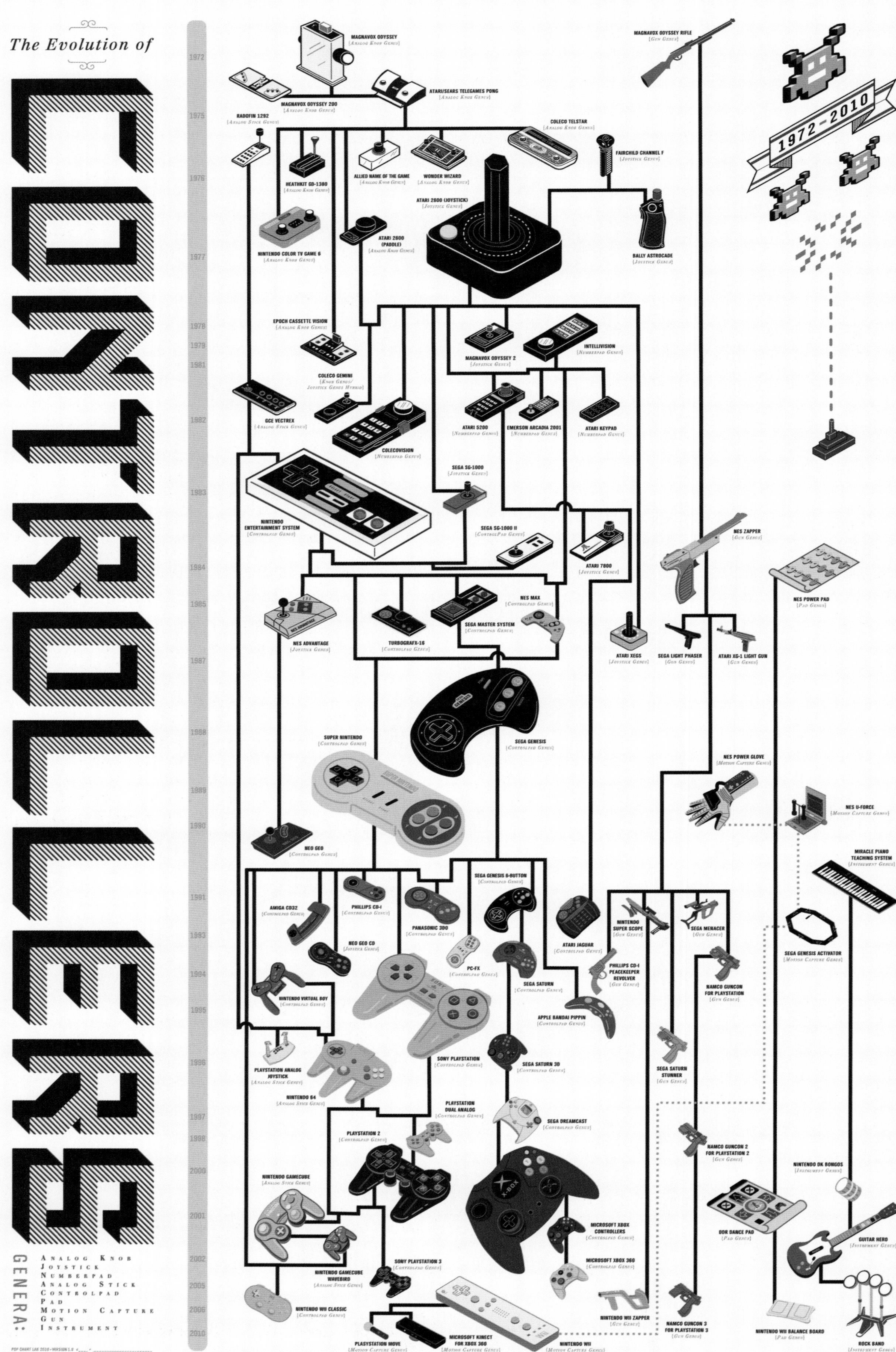

The Evolution of
CONTROLLERS
1972–2010
GENERA:
Analog Knob
Joystick
Numberpad
Analog Stick
Controlpad
Pad
Motion Capture
Gun
Instrument
1972
1975
1976
1977
1978
1979
1981
1982
1983
1984
1985
1987
1988
1989
1990
1991
1993
1994
1995
1996
1997
1998
2000
2001
2002
2005
2006
2010
MAGNAVOX ODYSSEY
MAGNAVOX ODYSSEY 200
ATARI/SEARS TELEGAMES PONG
RADOFIN 1292
COLECO TELSTAR
HEATHKIT GD-1380
ALLIED NAME OF THE GAME
WONDER WIZARD
FAIRCHILD CHANNEL F
ATARI 2600 (JOYSTICK)
NINTENDO COLOR TV GAME 6
ATARI 2600 (PADDLE)
BALLY ASTROCADE
MAGNAVOX ODYSSEY RIFLE
EPOCH CASSETTE VISION
MAGNAVOX ODYSSEY 2
INTELLIVISION
COLECO GEMINI
GCE VECTREX
ATARI 5200
EMERSON ARCADIA 2001
ATARI KEYPAD
COLECOVISION
SEGA SG-1000
NINTENDO ENTERTAINMENT SYSTEM
SEGA SG-1000 II
ATARI 7800
NES ZAPPER
NES POWER PAD
NES MAX
NES ADVANTAGE
TURBOGRAFX-16
SEGA MASTER SYSTEM
ATARI XEGS
SEGA LIGHT PHASER
ATARI XG-1 LIGHT GUN
SUPER NINTENDO
SEGA GENESIS
NES POWER GLOVE
NES U-FORCE
NEO GEO
MIRACLE PIANO TEACHING SYSTEM
SEGA GENESIS 6-BUTTON
AMIGA CD32
PHILLIPS CD-I
PANASONIC 3DO
ATARI JAGUAR
NINTENDO SUPER SCOPE
SEGA MENACER
SEGA GENESIS ACTIVATOR
NEO GEO CD
PC-FX
PHILLIPS CD-I PEACEKEEPER REVOLVER
SEGA SATURN
NAMCO GUNCON FOR PLAYSTATION
NINTENDO VIRTUAL BOY
APPLE BANDAI PIPPIN
PLAYSTATION ANALOG JOYSTICK
SONY PLAYSTATION
SEGA SATURN 3D
SEGA SATURN STUNNER
NINTENDO 64
PLAYSTATION DUAL ANALOG
SEGA DREAMCAST
PLAYSTATION 2
NAMCO GUNCON 2 FOR PLAYSTATION 2
NINTENDO DK BONGOS
NINTENDO GAMECUBE
MICROSOFT XBOX CONTROLLERS
DDR DANCE PAD
GUITAR HERO
NINTENDO GAMECUBE WAVEBIRD
SONY PLAYSTATION 3
MICROSOFT XBOX 360
NINTENDO WII CLASSIC
NINTENDO WII ZAPPER
NAMCO GUNCON 3 FOR PLAYSTATION 3
NINTENDO WII BALANCE BOARD
PLAYSTATION MOVE
MICROSOFT KINECT FOR XBOX 360
NINTENDO WII
ROCK BAND

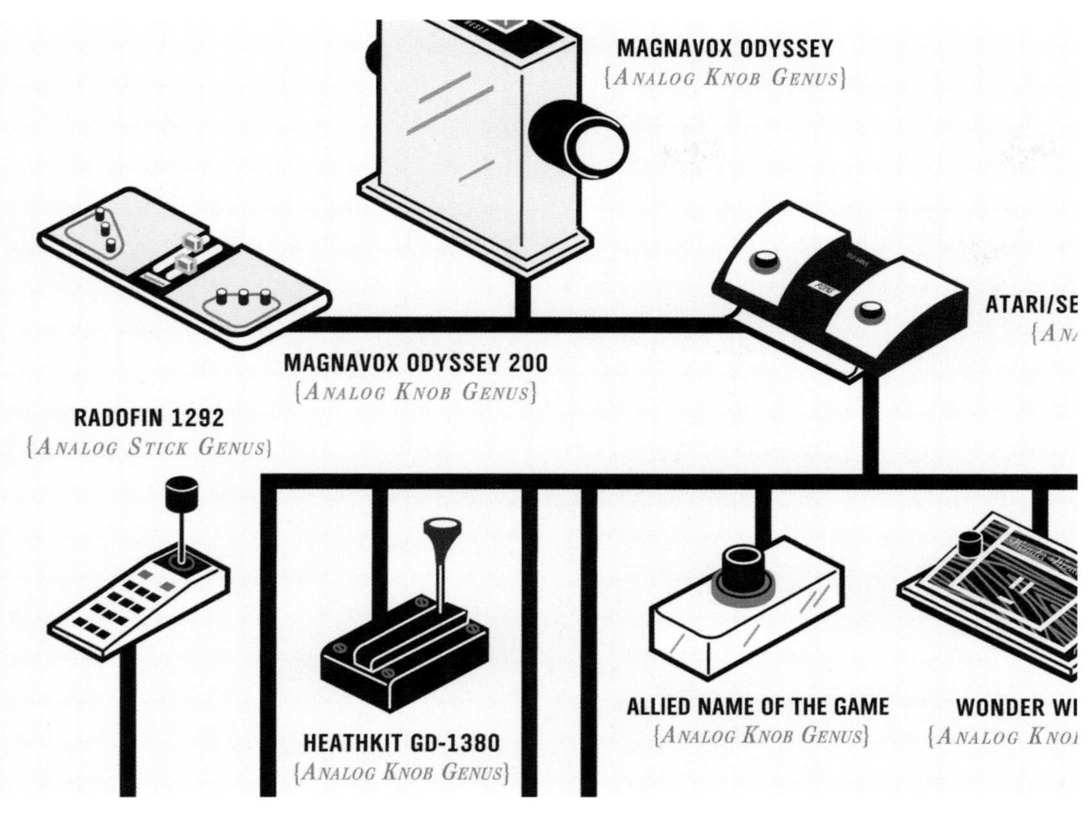

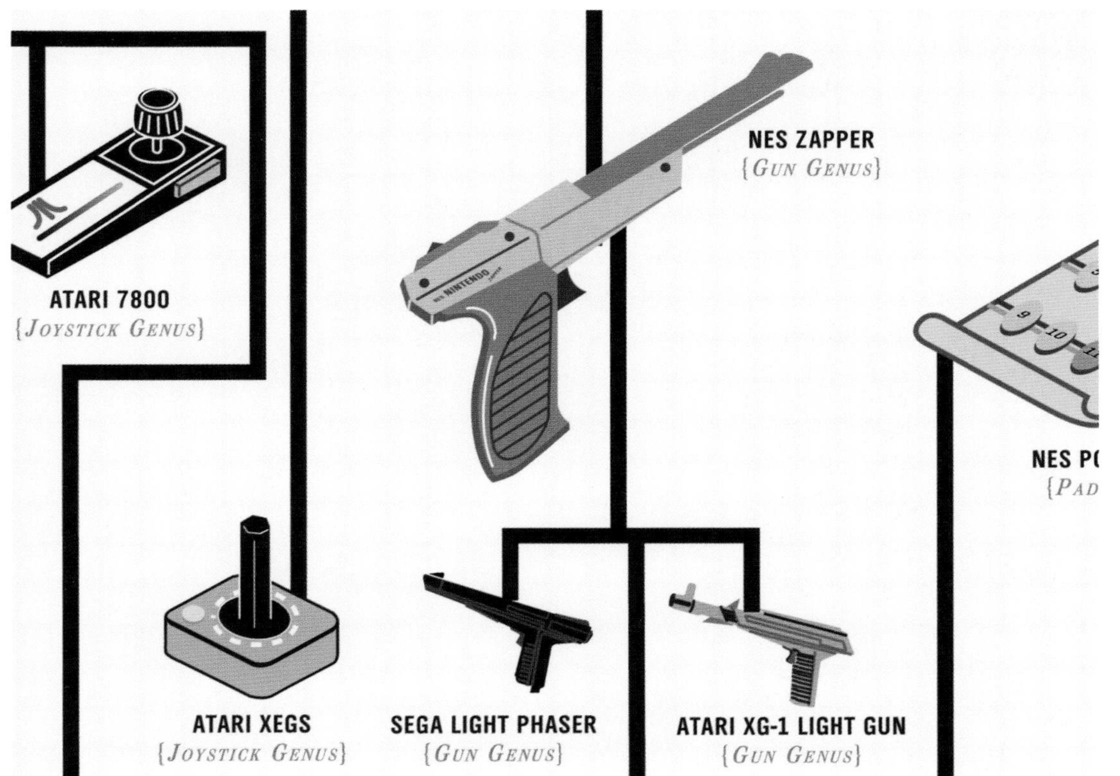

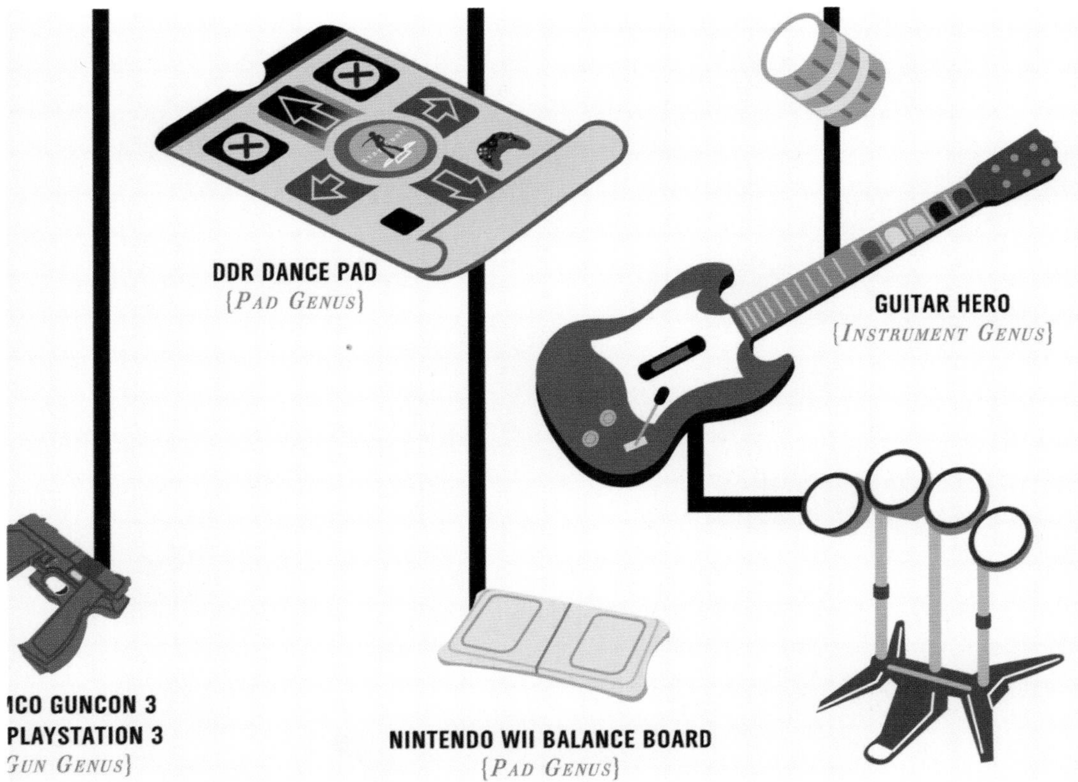

The Evolution of Video-Game Controllers

Much like a biological taxonomy, this piece presents the development of game controllers from the early days of 1972 up until 2010. The grey timeline next to the title works as the guide through the decades.

Evolving top down, the graphic classifies 82 different "species" and 9 "genera", thus referring to two of the major ranks in biological classification. In the main chart, lines show family connections between devices, and along with the title of each one, its "genus" is named.

Ähnlich einer biologischen Klassifizierung stellt diese Grafik die Entwicklung von Gamecontrollern seit ihren Anfängen 1972 bis 2010 dar. Die graue Zeitleiste neben dem Titel dient als Leitfaden durch die Jahrzehnte.

Von oben nach unten gruppiert die Grafik 82 verschiedene „Arten" und neun „Gattungen", verwendet mithin zwei zentrale Begriffe der biologischen Klassifizierung. Linien zeigen familiäre Verbindungen zwischen bestimmten Gamecontrollern auf, neben den Namen sind zudem jeweils die „Gattungen" vermerkt.

À la manière de la taxonomie biologique, cette image présente l'évolution des manettes des consoles de jeu de 1972 à 2010. La ligne temporelle verte près du titre guide le lecteur à travers les décennies.

L'évolution se déroule de haut en bas, et l'on distingue 82 « espèces » et 9 « genres », termes appartenant à la classification biologique. Les lignes qui relient les appareils indiquent leurs ancêtres et descendants, et leur nom est accompagné de leur « genre ».

Project Info: Poster, 2010, USA
Design: Ben Gibson, Patrick Mulligan (Pop Chart Lab)

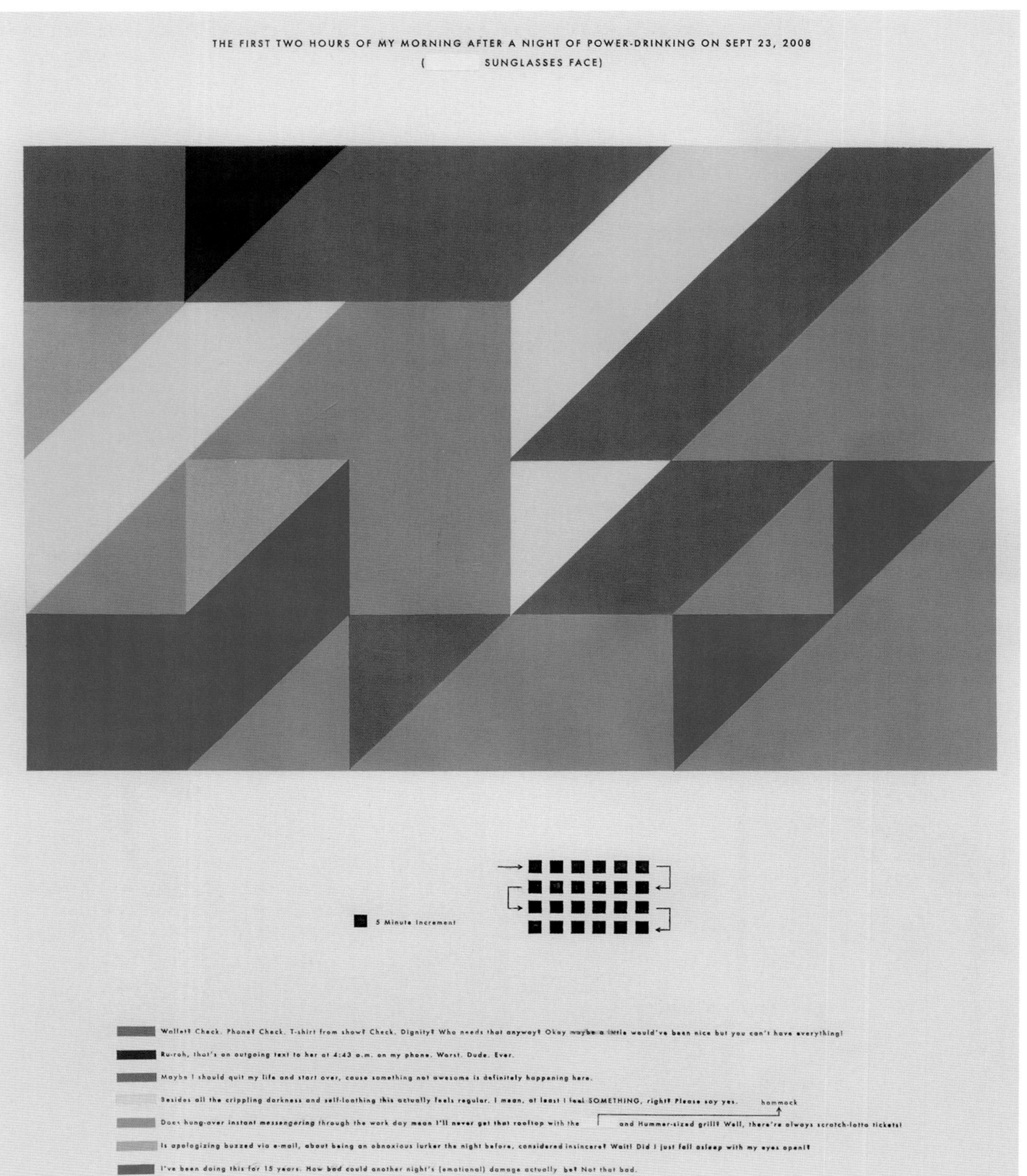

Project Info:
Painting,
2008, USA
Artist:
Andrew Kuo
Additional Info:
Original size
61 cm x 46 cm;
Andrew Kuo
is represented
by Taxter &
Spengemann,
New York

The First Two Hours of My Morning After

Andrew Kuo uses charts as a humorous medium for recording personal experiences and everyday confusion. His charts are single pieces, painted with acrylic on paper. Because of both this handmade look and the fact that his diagrams deal mostly with what's going on in Kuo's head, they mock the notion of the serious, fact-based communication that is associated with diagrams.

This is a timeline of a morning after partying, charting the shame, loss of memory and the attempt to regain balance that typically occur with a major hangover. Each colour refers to one thought. Reading starts at the top left and goes back and forth along the lines. Each square equals five minutes, so that one line makes up half an hour.

Andrew Kuo verwendet Diagramme als humorvolles Medium, um persönliche Erlebnisse und alltägliche Verwirrungen aufzuzeichnen. Dabei handelt es sich jeweils um Einzelstücke, die er mit Acryl auf Papier malt. Durch die handwerkliche Ästhetik und weil sich die Diagramme vorwiegend damit beschäftigen, was in Kuos Kopf vor sich geht, parodieren sie die ernste und sachliche Kommunikationsweise, die man normalerweise mit Diagrammen assoziiert.

Dies ist die Zeitleiste eines Vormittags nach durchfeierter Nacht. Sie zeigt die Scham, den Gedächtnisverlust und das Bemühen um Balance, die meistens zusammen mit einem schweren Kater auftreten. Jede Farbe steht für einen Gedanken. Oben links beginnend, liest man das Diagramm entlang der Zeilen hin und her. Jedes Quadrat entspricht fünf Minuten, eine Zeile folglich einer halben Stunde.

Andrew Kuo utilise les graphiques comme support humoristique pour enregistrer ses expériences personnelles et la confusion de sa vie quotidienne. Ses graphiques sont des œuvres uniques peintes à l'acrylique sur papier. Leur style « fait main » et le fait que ces diagrammes représentent en général ce qui se passe dans l'esprit de Kuo en font une parodie de la communication sérieuse et factuelle normalement associée aux graphiques.

Ceci est la chronologie d'un matin suivant une nuit de fête. Elle rend compte de la honte, de la perte de mémoire et de la tentative de récupération d'équilibre qui suivent souvent une gueule de bois carabinée. Chaque couleur correspond à une pensée. La lecture commence en haut à gauche et serpente le long des lignes. Chaque carré équivaut à cinq minutes, une ligne valant donc une demi-heure.

The Soviet Union Olympic Medals Tally

Against a bright Communist-red background, this time series looks at how many medals were won by the Soviet Union and its successor states at Olympic Games in years after World War II. Along the bottom, the individual Games are labelled with their year. Purely yellow bars show the total number of medals won each year by the Soviet team.

With the US boycott of the Moscow Olympics in 1980, this value peaked at almost 200 medals. The later bars show that, counted together, the individual teams of the successor states weren't doing any worse than in Soviet times. The white line shows the US medal count in comparison.

Vor einem Hintergrund in leuchtendem kommunistischen Rot untersucht diese Zeitreihe, wie viele Medaillen die Sowjetunion und ihre Nachfolgestaaten seit dem Zweiten Weltkrieg bei den Olympischen Spielen gewannen. Am unteren Rand des Diagramms sind die jeweiligen Spiele mittels Jahreszahl ausgewiesen. Die gelben Balken zeigen die Gesamtzahl der Medaillen, die die sowjetische Mannschaft jeweils gewann.

Beim US-amerikanischen Boykott der Olympischen Spiele in Moskau 1980 erreichte die Zahl mit knapp 200 Medaillen einen Höchstwert. Die Balken späterer Jahre zeigen, dass die Mannschaften der Nachfolgestaaten zusammengenommen nicht schlechter abschnitten als zu Sowjetzeiten. Die weiße Linie zeigt im Vergleich dazu die Medaillengewinne der USA.

Sur un fond rouge communiste, cette série temporelle analyse le nombre de médailles remportées par l'Union soviétique et les États qui lui ont succédé lors des Jeux olympiques qui ont suivi la Deuxième Guerre mondiale. Les différents Jeux sont indiqués par leur année le long de l'axe horizontal. Les barres jaune uni montrent le nombre total de médailles remportées chaque année par l'équipe soviétique.

Les États-Unis ayant boycotté les Jeux olympiques de Moscou en 1980, cette valeur a atteint un record de presque 200 médailles cette année-là. Les barres les plus récentes montrent que les résultats cumulés des équipes des États qui ont succédé à l'URSS ne sont pas plus mauvais qu'à l'époque soviétique. La ligne blanche montre le nombre de médailles remportées par les États-Unis, à titre de comparaison.

Project Info: Website, 2008, UK
Data Source: Olympic.org
Design: Craig Robinson

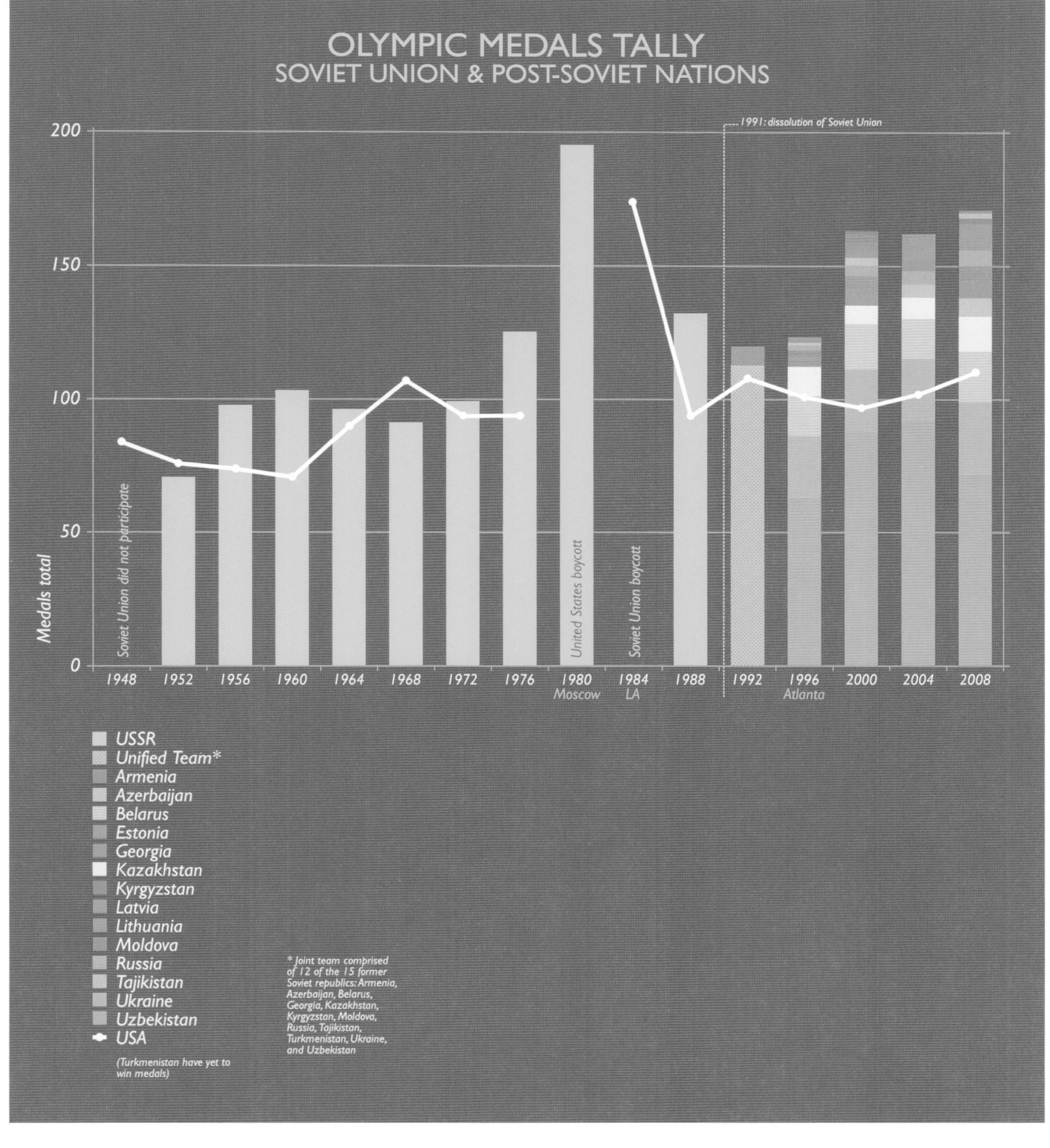

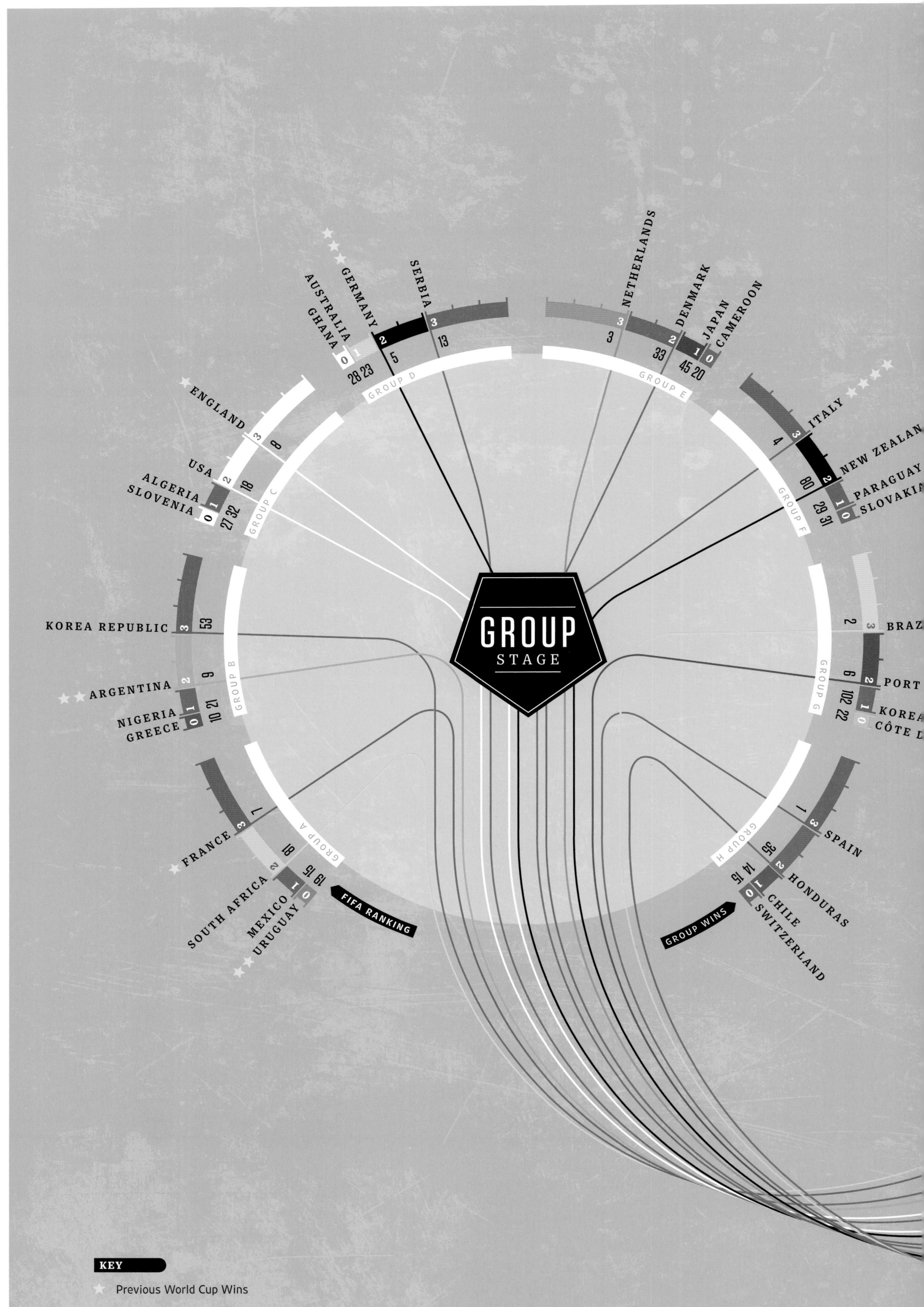
GROUP STAGE
GROUP A
FRANCE
SOUTH AFRICA
MEXICO
URUGUAY
GROUP B
KOREA REPUBLIC
ARGENTINA
NIGERIA
GREECE
GROUP C
ENGLAND
USA
ALGERIA
SLOVENIA
GROUP D
GERMANY
AUSTRALIA
GHANA
SERBIA
GROUP E
NETHERLANDS
DENMARK
JAPAN
CAMEROON
GROUP F
ITALY
PARAGUAY
GROUP G
GROUP H
SPAIN
HONDURAS
CHILE
SWITZERLAND
FIFA RANKING
GROUP WINS
KEY
Previous World Cup Wins

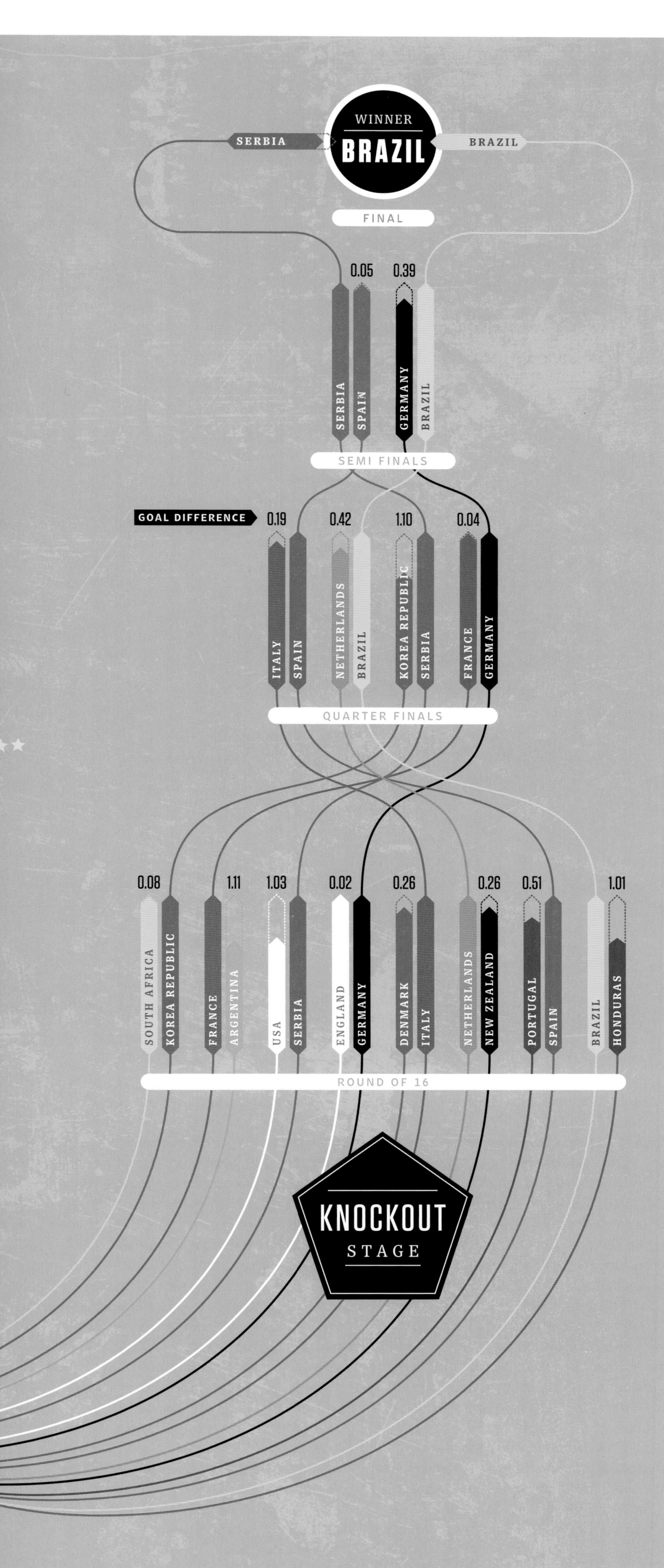

The World Cup Predicted

The intricate economics of football: this graphic draws on a formula developed by Simon Kuper and Stefan Szymanski to forecast international football results based on economic data. According to the model, a team's results are influenced by its country's GDP per capita, population size and experience in football. Here the model was used to forecast the results of the 2010 World Cup in South Africa, with, as it shows, somewhat deficient results.

The left side illustrates the group stage with the teams that qualify then feeding into the knockout stage on the right, leading eventually to the final winner. Each team is represented by its national kit colour, the lines showing each team's progression through the tournament.

Die wirtschaftlichen Hintergründe des Fußballs sind komplex: Diese Grafik beruht auf einer von Simon Kuper und Stefan Szymanski entwickelten Formel, um internationale Fußballergebnisse anhand von Wirtschaftsdaten vorherzusagen. Dem Modell zufolge werden die Ergebnisse, die eine Mannschaft erzielt, vom Bruttoinlandsprodukt pro Kopf, von der Bevölkerungszahl und der Fußballerfahrung des jeweiligen Landes beeinflusst. Hier diente die Formel dazu, die Ergebnisse der Fußball-Weltmeisterschaft 2010 in Südafrika vorherzusagen – Irrtümer vorbehalten, wie man sieht.

Die linke Seite illustriert die Gruppenphase, während der sich die Mannschaften für die Phase des K.-o.-Systems rechts weiterqualifizieren, aus dessen Spielen schließlich der Sieger ermittelt wird. Jede Mannschaft ist durch die Farbe ihres Nationaltrikots dargestellt, die Linien zeigen die Verluste und das Weiterkommen der einzelnen Mannschaften bei der WM.

L'économie complexe du football : ce schéma est inspiré d'une formule mise au point par Simon Kuper et Stefan Szymanski pour prédire les résultats des matchs de football internationaux en fonction de données économiques. D'après ce modèle, les résultats d'une équipe sont influencés par le PIB par habitant et le nombre d'habitants du pays de l'équipe, ainsi que par l'expérience que ce pays a dans le football. Ici, le modèle a été utilisé pour prédire les résultats de la Coupe du monde de 2010 en Afrique du Sud, avec, comme on peut le voir, assez peu de succès.

Le côté gauche illustre le premier tour, avec les équipes qui se qualifient et participent à la phase d'élimination directe sur la droite, qui mène jusqu'au grand gagnant. Chaque équipe est représentée par la couleur de son maillot, et les lignes montrent la progression des équipes au fur et à mesure de la compétition.

Project Info: *Wired*, magazine article, 2010, UK
Data Source: Simon Kuper, Stefan Szymanski: "Why England Lose", 2009
Design: Paul Butt (Section Design)

Two People Kissing / Fibonacci / Re-Write

"Two People Kissing" is based on the Fibonacci numbers. This is an infinite sequence where each subsequent number is the sum of the previous two: 0, 1, 1, 2, 3, 5, 8 etc. Jorinde Voigt applied this concept to kissing: in this piece, more and more couples are made to kiss for longer and longer time. The process begins at various points and moves in different directions.

A couple kisses for one minute. After one minute, two couples kiss for two minutes. After another three minutes, three couples kiss each other for five minutes, after eight minutes, four couples kiss for thirteen minutes and so forth. This is notated with lines, arrows and text. Sometimes Voigt randomly stopped the evolution or restarted with a number out of sequence. Elsewhere, it is the margins of the paper which limited the infinite process.

„Two People Kissing" beruht auf den Fibonacci-Zahlen. Das ist eine unendliche Zahlenfolge, bei der sich die jeweils folgende Zahl aus der Summe der beiden vorherigen Zahlen ergibt: 0, 1, 1, 2, 3, 5, 8 etc. Jorinde Voigt wandte dieses Konzept auf das Küssen an: In diesem Projekt küssen sich immer mehr Paare für eine immer längere Zeitdauer. Der Ablauf beginnt an unterschiedlichen Punkten und bewegt sich in unterschiedliche Richtungen.

Ein Paar küsste sich eine Minute. Nach einer Minute Pause küssten sich zwei Paare zwei Minuten. Nach weiteren drei Minuten Pause küssten sich drei Paare fünf Minuten, nach acht Minuten küssten sich vier Paare 13 Minuten, und so weiter. Das wird mit Linien, Pfeilen und Text notiert. Manchmal brach Voigt die Anordnung unvermittelt ab oder begann sie erneut mit einer Zahl, die nicht der Reihe entsprach. An anderen Stellen fand der unendliche Prozess erst durch den Blattrand ein Ende.

« Two People Kissing » se base sur la suite de Fibonacci. Il s'agit d'une séquence infinie dans laquelle chaque chiffre est la somme des deux précédents : 0, 1, 1, 2, 3, 5, 8, etc. Jorinde Voigt a appliqué ce concept au baiser : dans cette œuvre, de plus en plus de couples s'embrassent de plus en plus longtemps. Le processus commence en différents points, et évolue en différentes directions.

Un couple s'embrasse pendant une minute. Après deux minutes, deux couples s'embrassent pendant deux minutes. Après trois autres minutes, trois couples s'embrassent pendant cinq minutes, après huit minutes, quatre couples s'embrassent pendant treize minutes, et ainsi de suite. Cela est noté par des lignes, des flèches et du texte. Parfois, Voigt a arrêté une évolution arbitrairement, ou l'a fait redémarrer à partir d'un chiffre qui n'appartient pas à la suite logique. Ailleurs, ce sont les marges du papier qui ont limité ce processus infini.

Project Info: Series of drawings, 2007, Germany
Artist: Jorinde Voigt

Understanding Shakespeare

Computer-based language-processing facilitates the analysis of large bodies of literary text to an unprecedented level of detail. The WordHoard database, provided by Northwestern University in Illinois, offers full text versions of Shakespeare's plays, with detailed meta-data on how often each word is used, by which character and what type of word it is.

This allows the texts to be looked at in a somewhat mathematical manner. Stephan Thiel has developed a series of visualisation patterns for these data. Each of his approaches is governed by a different question about what happens in each play. The visualisations were originally realised as large-scale prints, featuring a large variety of sizes – from large visual structures to very fine text details.

Computergestützte Sprachverarbeitung erlaubt es, umfangreiche literarische Werke mit bislang unvorstellbarer Genauigkeit zu analysieren. Die Datenbank WordHoard, aufgebaut von der Northwestern University in Illinois, stellt den gesamten Text von Shakespeares Dramen mit detaillierten Metadaten zur Verfügung, etwa wie häufig jedes Wort verwendet wird, welche Figur es verwendet und um welche Wortart es sich handelt.

Auf diese Weise kann man sich den Texten auch von einer eher mathematischen Warte aus nähern. Stephan Thiel entwickelte eine Reihe von Visualisierungsmethoden für diese Daten. Jeder seiner Ansätze folgt einer anderen Fragestellung dazu, was in den Dramen passiert. Ursprünglich wurden die Visualisierungen als großformatige Drucke angefertigt, auf denen von sehr großen visuellen Strukturen bis hin zu kleinsten Textdetails sehr unterschiedliche Darstellungsgrößen vorkommen.

Le traitement informatique du langage facilite l'analyse de vastes corpus littéraires et permet d'atteindre un niveau de détail sans précédent. La base de données WordHoard, fournie par l'Université de Northwestern, dans l'Illinois, offre des versions intégrales des pièces de Shakespeare, avec des métadonnées détaillées sur le nombre d'occurrences de chaque mot, sur le personnage qui utilise ce mot, et sur le type de mot dont il s'agit.

Cela permet de porter un regard mathématique sur les textes. Stephan Thiel a mis au point une série de modes de visualisation de ces données. Chacune de ses approches est gouvernée par une question différente sur ce qui arrive dans la pièce concernée. À l'origine, ces visualisations ont été réalisées sous forme d'impressions grand format, avec des éléments de tailles très variées, de grandes structures visuelles côtoyant des mots composés en très petits caractères.

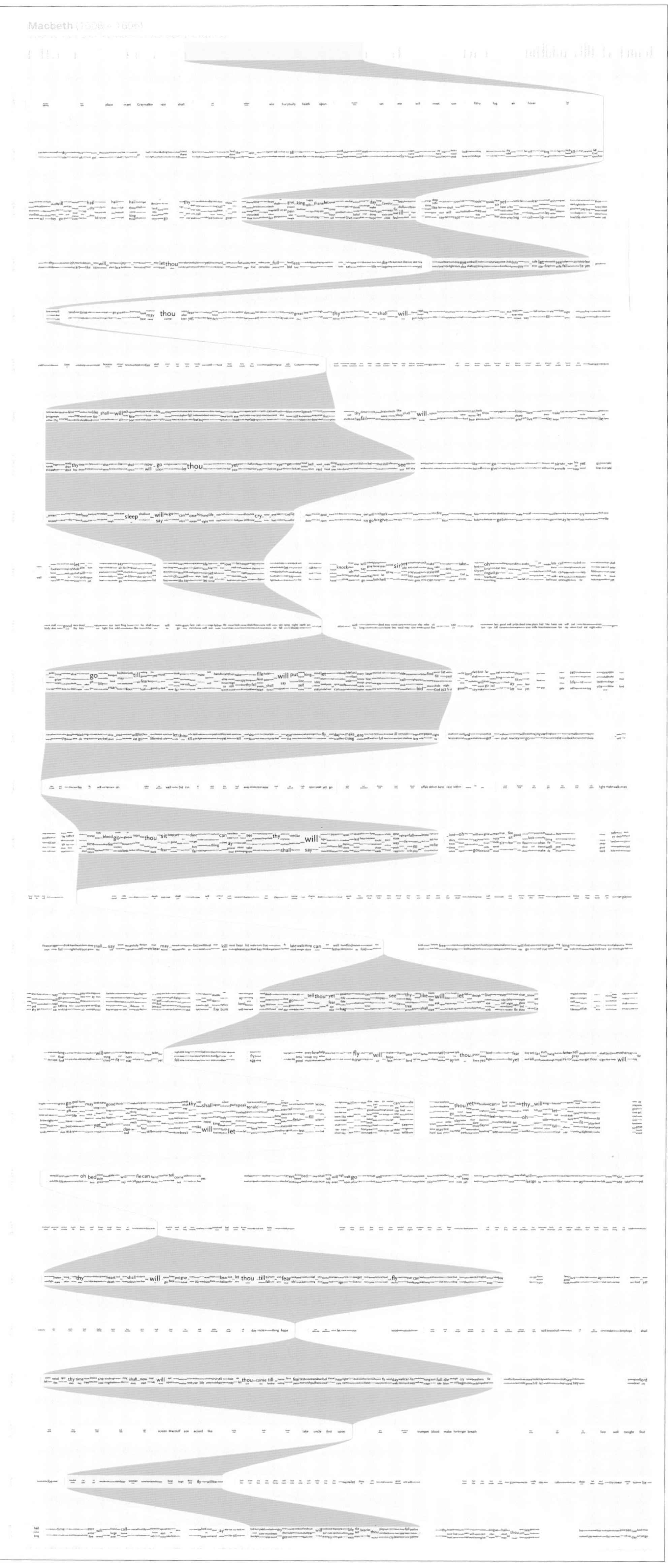

Project Info: Website, poster, 2010, Germany
Data Source: WordHoard (Northwestern University)
Design: Stephan Thiel
Additional Info: Student project at University of Applied Sciences Potsdam, Germany

Act 3, Scene 1

Scene 2

Scene 3

Scene 4

Scene 5

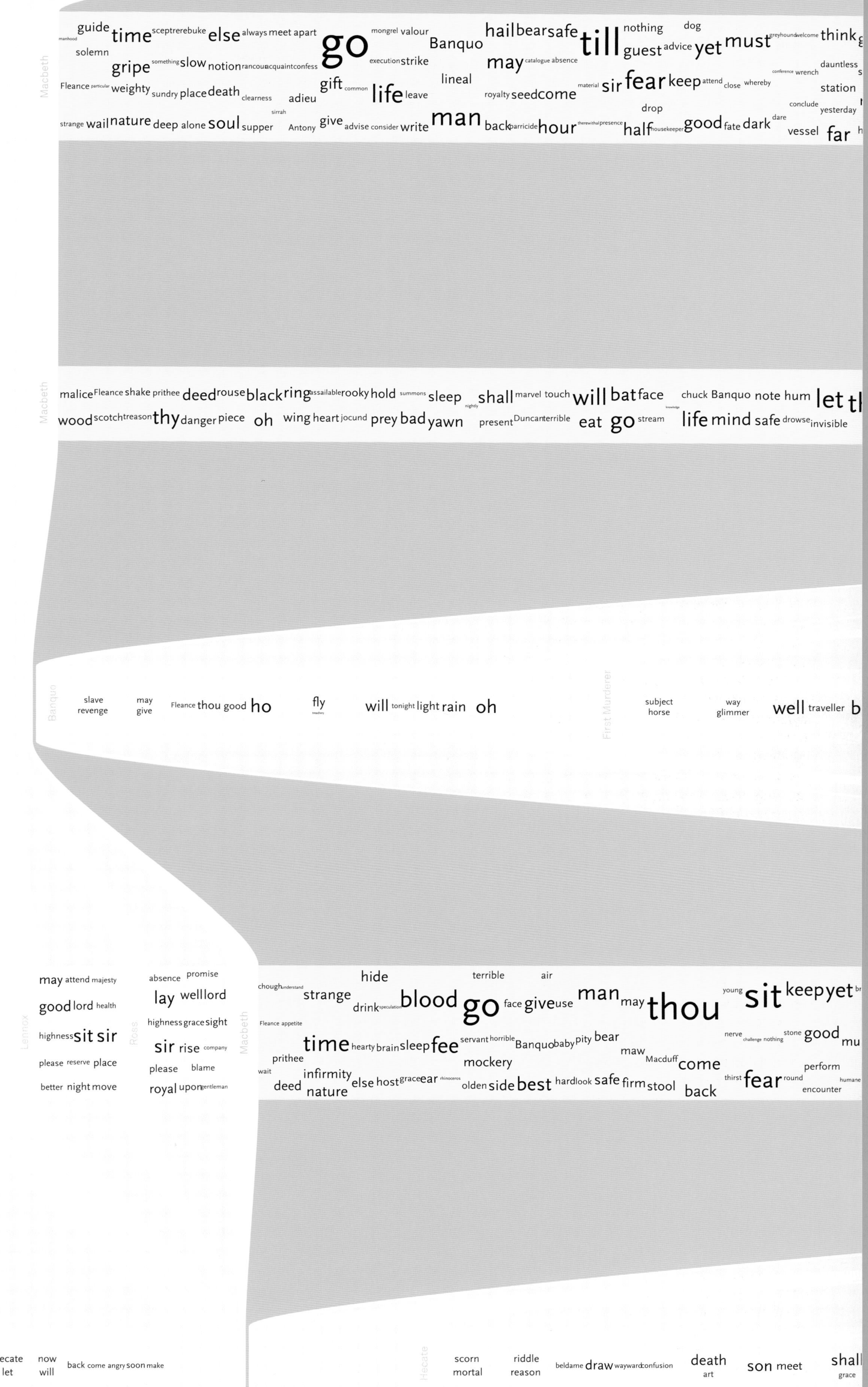

What's the Game, Tusk?

Made in 2009 for Poland's *Newsweek*, this infographic tackles the politics of Polish Prime Minister Donald Tusk. He has been in office since 2007, after unsuccessfully campaigning in the 2005 presidential elections. The piece starts with Tusk's portrait at the lower left. The reader plays Donald Tusk, jumping from field to field.

Red fields represent political events during his mandate, such as the liquidation of the Polish Military Secret Service WSI (in nos. 3 and 15) or the Georgia Conflict in 2008 (in no. 20). No. 28 looks towards the 2010 presidential elections, suggesting a second chance for Tusk to run for president. However, in January 2010 Tusk decided not to campaign and remained as Prime Minister.

Diese Infografik, die im Jahr 2009 für die polnische Ausgabe der *Newsweek* entstand, befasst sich mit der Politik des polnischen Ministerpräsidenten Donald Tusk. Nachdem er 2005 bei der Präsidentschaftswahl erfolglos geblieben war, ist er seit 2007 Premierminister. Das Spiel beginnt mit Tusks Porträt unten links. Der Leser spielt Donald Tusk und springt von Feld zu Feld.

Rote Felder zeigen politische Ereignisse während seiner Amtszeit, etwa die Auflösung der militärischen Informationsdienste Polens WSI (in Nr. 3 und 15) und den Georgien-Konflikt 2008 (in Nr. 20). Nr. 28 widmet sich den Präsidentschaftswahlen 2010 und damit der zweiten Gelegenheit, sich für dieses Amt zu bewerben. Im Januar 2010 beschloss Tusk allerdings, nicht als Präsident zu kandidieren und Ministerpräsident zu bleiben.

Réalisée en 2009 pour le magazine *Newsweek* polonais, cette infographie analyse la politique du premier ministre polonais Donald Tusk. Il est à ce poste depuis 2007, après avoir échoué aux élections présidentielles de 2005. Le départ se situe en bas à gauche, au portrait de Tusk. Le lecteur joue à être Donald Tusk en passant de case en case.

Les cases rouges représentent les événements politiques de son mandat, comme la liquidation du service secret militaire polonais WSI (numéros 3 et 15) ou le conflit de la Géorgie en 2008 (numéro 20). La case 28 concerne les élections présidentielles de 2010, et fait allusion à une deuxième chance pour Tusk. Mais en janvier 2010, Tusk a décidé de ne pas faire campagne, et il est resté premier ministre.

Project Info: *Newsweek*, magazine article, 2009, Poland
Research: Andrzej Stankiewicz, Piotr Śmiłowicz, Joanna Kowalska-Iszkowska
Design: Jan Kallwejt

W co gra Tusk?

Niewinna z pozoru zabawa w kontrolera lotów może się skończyć dla Donalda tuska i PO katastrofą.

Andrzej Stankiewicz, Piotr Śmiłowicz, Joanna Kowalska-Iszkowska

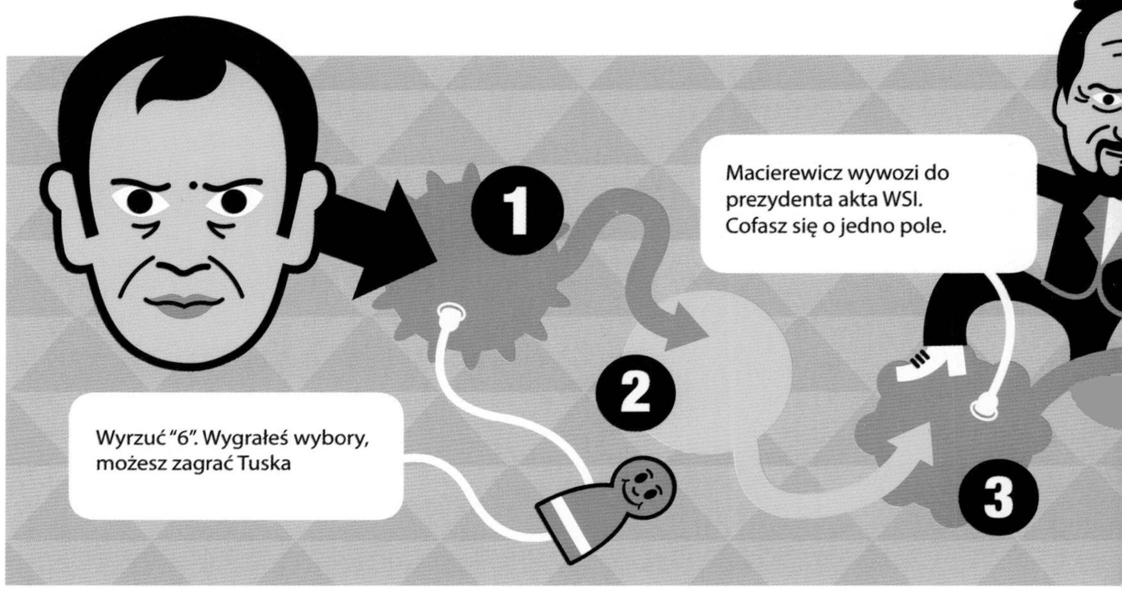

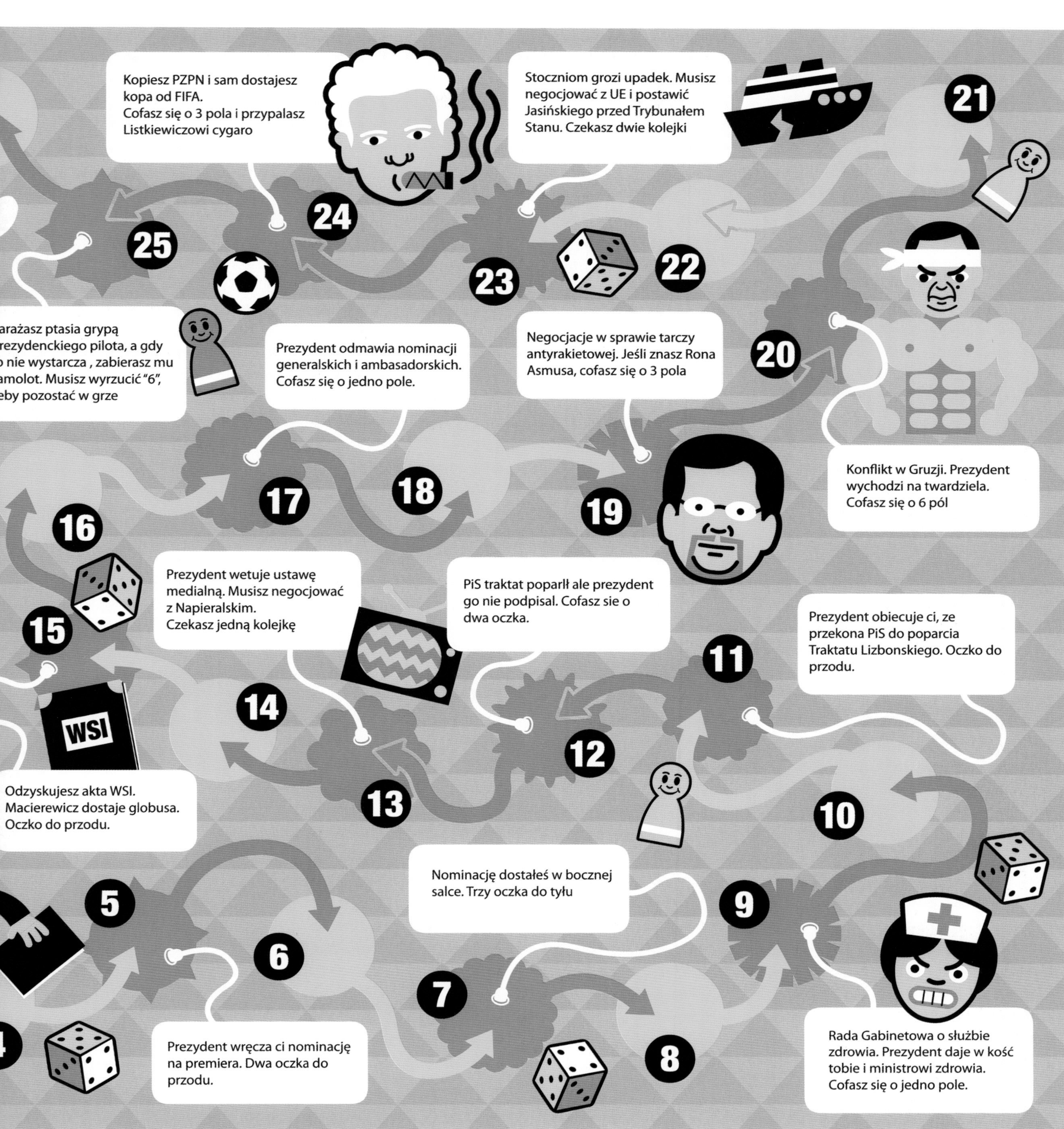
Kopiesz PZPN i sam dostajesz kopa od FIFA. Cofasz się o 3 pola i przypalasz Listkiewiczowi cygaro
Stoczniom grozi upadek. Musisz negocjować z UE i postawić Jasińskiego przed Trybunałem Stanu. Czekasz dwie kolejki
21
24
25
22
23
arażasz ptasia grypą rezydenckiego pilota, a gdy o nie wystarcza , zabierasz mu amolot. Musisz wyrzucić "6", eby pozostać w grze
Prezydent odmawia nominacji generalskich i ambasadorskich. Cofasz się o jedno pole.
Negocjacje w sprawie tarczy antyrakietowej. Jeśli znasz Rona Asmusa, cofasz się o 3 pola
20
17
18
19
Konflikt w Gruzji. Prezydent wychodzi na twardziela. Cofasz się o 6 pól
16
Prezydent wetuje ustawę medialną. Musisz negocjować z Napieralskim. Czekasz jedną kolejkę
PiS traktat poparłł ale prezydent go nie podpisal. Cofasz sie o dwa oczka.
Prezydent obiecuje ci, ze przekona PiS do poparcia Traktatu Lizbonskiego. Oczko do przodu.
15
11
14
WSI
12
13
10
Odzyskujesz akta WSI. Macierewicz dostaje globusa. Oczko do przodu.
Nominację dostałeś w bocznej salce. Trzy oczka do tyłu
5
9
6
7
8
Prezydent wręcza ci nominację na premiera. Dwa oczka do przodu.
Rada Gabinetowa o służbie zdrowia. Prezydent daje w kość tobie i ministrowi zdrowia. Cofasz się o jedno pole.

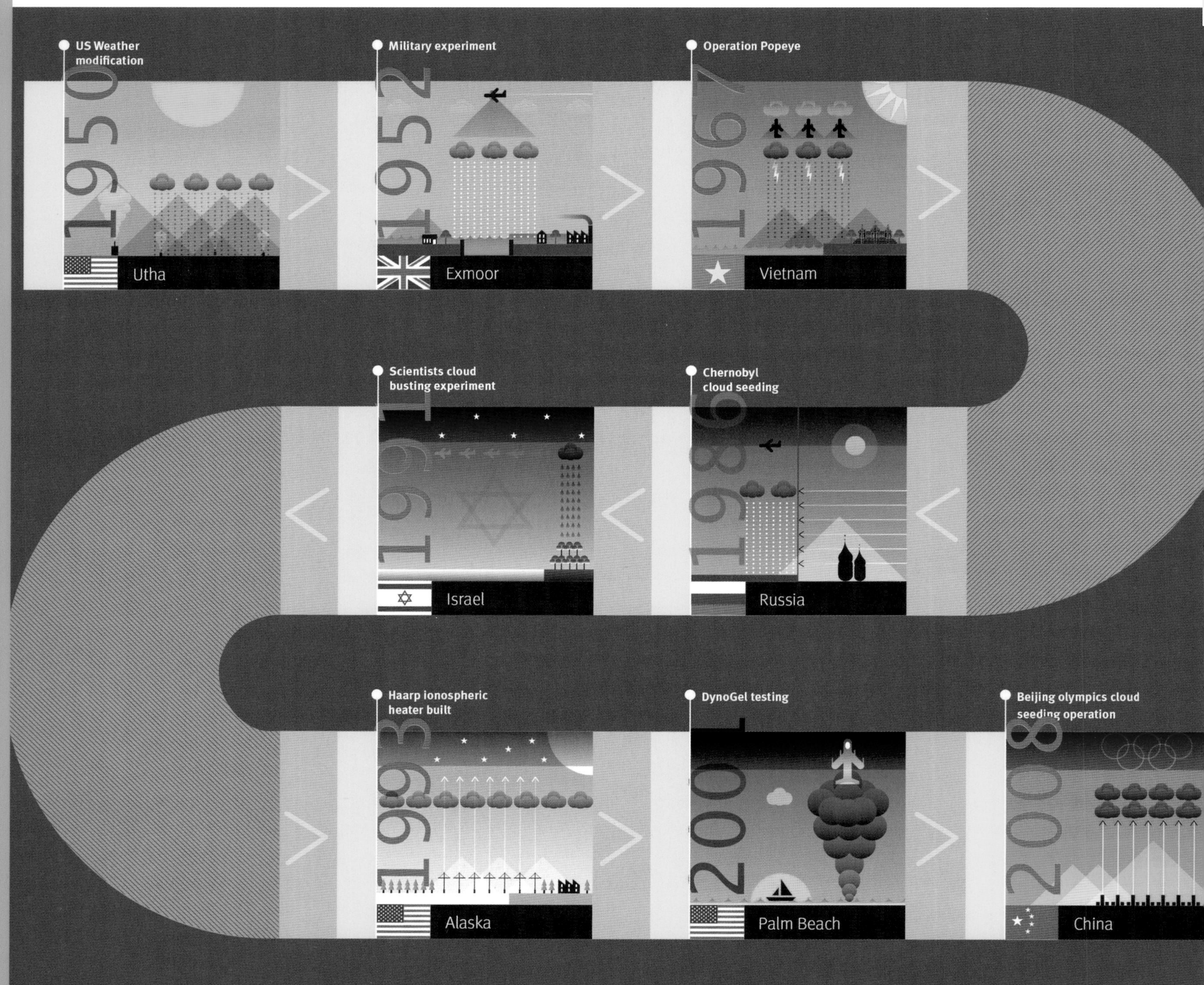
US Weather modification
1950
Utha
Military experiment
1952
Exmoor
Operation Popeye
1967
Vietnam
Scientists cloud busting experiment
1991
Israel
Chernobyl cloud seeding
1986
Russia
Haarp ionospheric heater built
1993
Alaska
DynoGel testing
2001
Palm Beach
Beijing olympics cloud seeding operation
2008
China

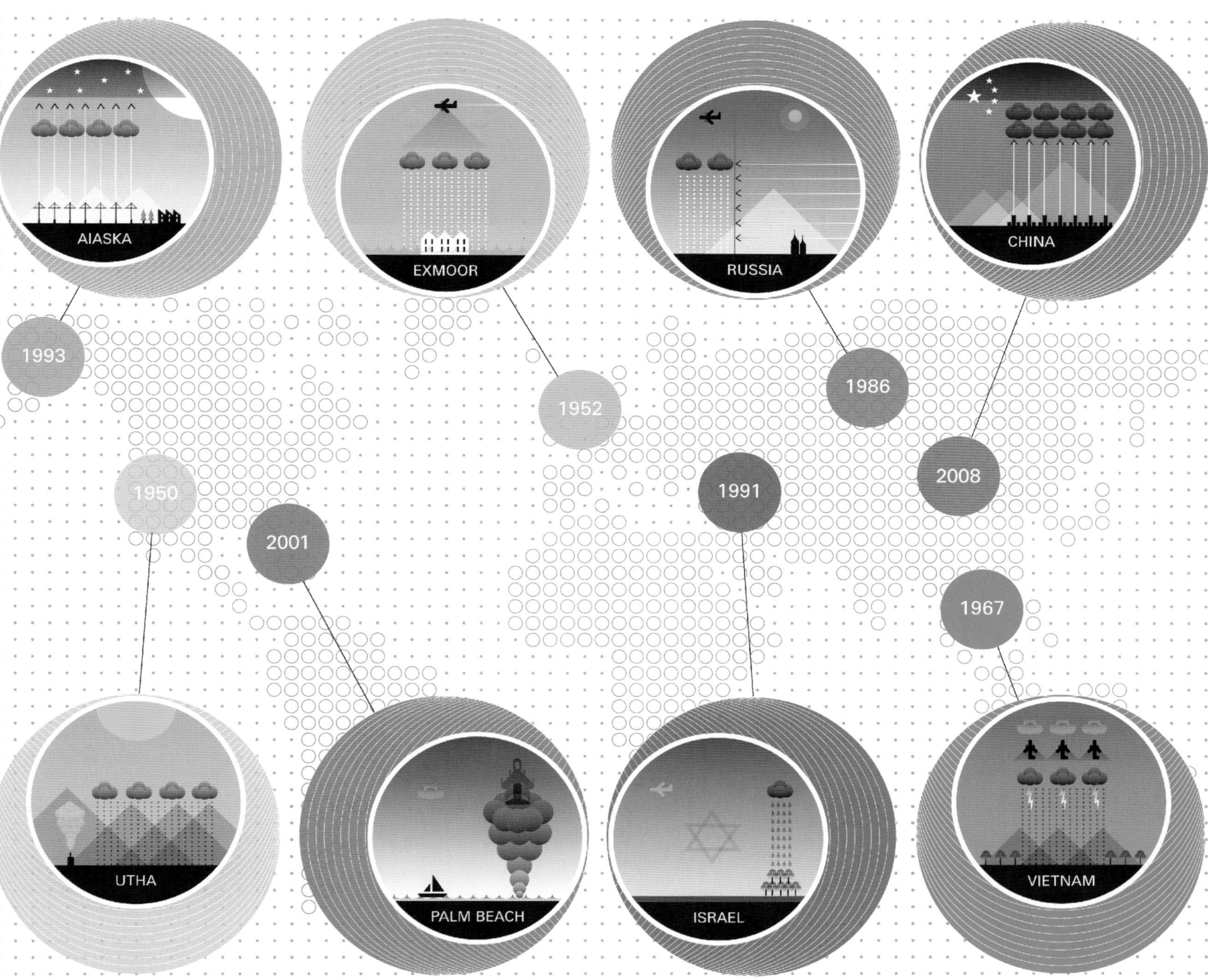

Wicked World Weather

Man has always been exposed to unpredictable weather conditions and always dreamed of controlling it. This double piece presents selected projects from around the world for influencing the weather. The blue timeline shows each event as a small vignette, indicating both the country as well as the occasion of each weather modification project. The second graphic (above) locates all projects on a light grey world map.

Operation Popeye, for example, was a military operation during the Vietnam war – using cloud-seeding, the monsoon was intensified over the years in order to hinder the Vietnamese forces and their trucks from using the muddy roads. Other projects were launched in civil contexts, in the quest to control storms or to relieve drought.

Die Menschen waren immer dem unberechenbaren Wetter ausgesetzt und haben immer auch davon geträumt, es zu beherrschen. Diese Grafik zeigt die wichtigsten Versuchsprojekte zur Beeinflussung des Wetters. Auf der blauen Zeitleiste ist jedes Projekt als Vignette dargestellt, auf der sowohl das Land als auch der jeweilige Anlass für die Wettermodifikation vermerkt sind. Auf der zweiten Grafik (oben) werden alle Projekte auf einer hellgrauen Weltkarte verortet.

Operation Popeye etwa war eine Militäroperation während des Vietnamkriegs: Durch die „Impfung" von Wolken wurde der Monsun über Jahre hinweg verstärkt, um die schlammigen Straßen für vietnamesische Truppen und ihre Fahrzeuge unbenutzbar zu machen. Andere Projekte dienten zivilen Zwecken, etwa um Unwetter zu kontrollieren oder Dürreperioden zu lindern.

L'homme a toujours été exposé à des conditions météorologiques imprévisibles, et a toujours rêvé de les maîtriser. Cette œuvre en deux volets présente des projets du monde entier conçus pour influencer la météo. La chronologie bleue montre chaque événement sous forme de vignette, indiquant le pays ainsi que le contexte de chaque projet de modification du climat. La deuxième partie (ci-dessus) situe tous les projets sur une carte du monde en gris clair.

Par exemple, l'opération militaire Popeye, menée pendant la guerre du Vietnam, a utilisé la technique de l'ensemencement des nuages pour intensifier la mousson sur plusieurs années afin de gêner les forces vietnamiennes et de les empêcher d'utiliser leurs camions sur les routes boueuses. D'autres projets ont été lancés dans le civil, pour essayer de maîtriser les orages ou de remédier à la sécheresse.

Project Info: *Audi* magazine, 2008, UK
Design: Infonauts

Wired Anniversary

For the anniversary of *Wired* in 2008, Fernanda Viégas and Martin Wattenberg created a visual history of the magazine, referring to the noted bold use of colour in its layout. The circles depict every issue before June 2008 in chronological order, with each circle displaying the colours used on the issue's cover. This was done by an algorithm which extracts the "peak" colours from an image.

Circles are arranged in rows, each row being one year. As the magazine began as a bi-monthly, the first row is sparser. Overall circle sizes refer to the magazine's circulation. *Wired* also created a two-sided poster from this piece, showing the circles on one side and the actual covers on the other.

Zum Geburtstag von *Wired* im Jahr 2008 gestalteten Fernanda Viégas und Martin Wattenberg eine visuelle Geschichte der Zeitschrift und bezogen sich dabei auf das überaus bunte Layout des Magazins. Die Kreise stellen jede Ausgabe bis Juni 2008 in chronologischer Reihenfolge dar, jeder Kreis zeigt die jeweils auf dem Cover der Ausgabe verwendeten Farben. Dazu diente ein Algorithmus, der die vorherrschenden Farben eines Bildes herausfiltern kann.

Die Kreise sind in Reihen angeordnet, jede Reihe stellt ein Jahr dar. Da die Zeitschrift zunächst zweimonatlich erschien, mutet die erste Reihe etwas dürftig an. Die Kreisgröße verweist auf die Auflagenstärke. Aus dieser Grafik entwickelte *Wired* ein doppelseitiges Plakat, bei dem auf der einen Seite die Kreise und auf der anderen die real umgesetzten Cover zu sehen waren.

Pour l'anniversaire de *Wired* en 2008, Fernanda Viégas et Martin Wattenberg ont créé une histoire visuelle du magazine en faisant référence à l'utilisation audacieuse des couleurs dans sa mise en page. Les cercles représentent chaque numéro antérieur à juin 2008 en ordre chronologique, et chaque cercle reprend les couleurs utilisées sur la couverture du numéro correspondant. Ils ont pour ce faire employé un algorithme qui extrait les « pics de couleur » des images.

Les cercles sont disposés en rangs, et chaque rang forme une année. Au début le magazine paraissait tous les deux mois, c'est pourquoi la première rangée est plus clairsemée. La taille des cercles correspond au tirage du magazine. *Wired* a également créé une affiche recto-verso à partir de ce visuel, elle montre les cercles d'un côté, et les couvertures de l'autre.

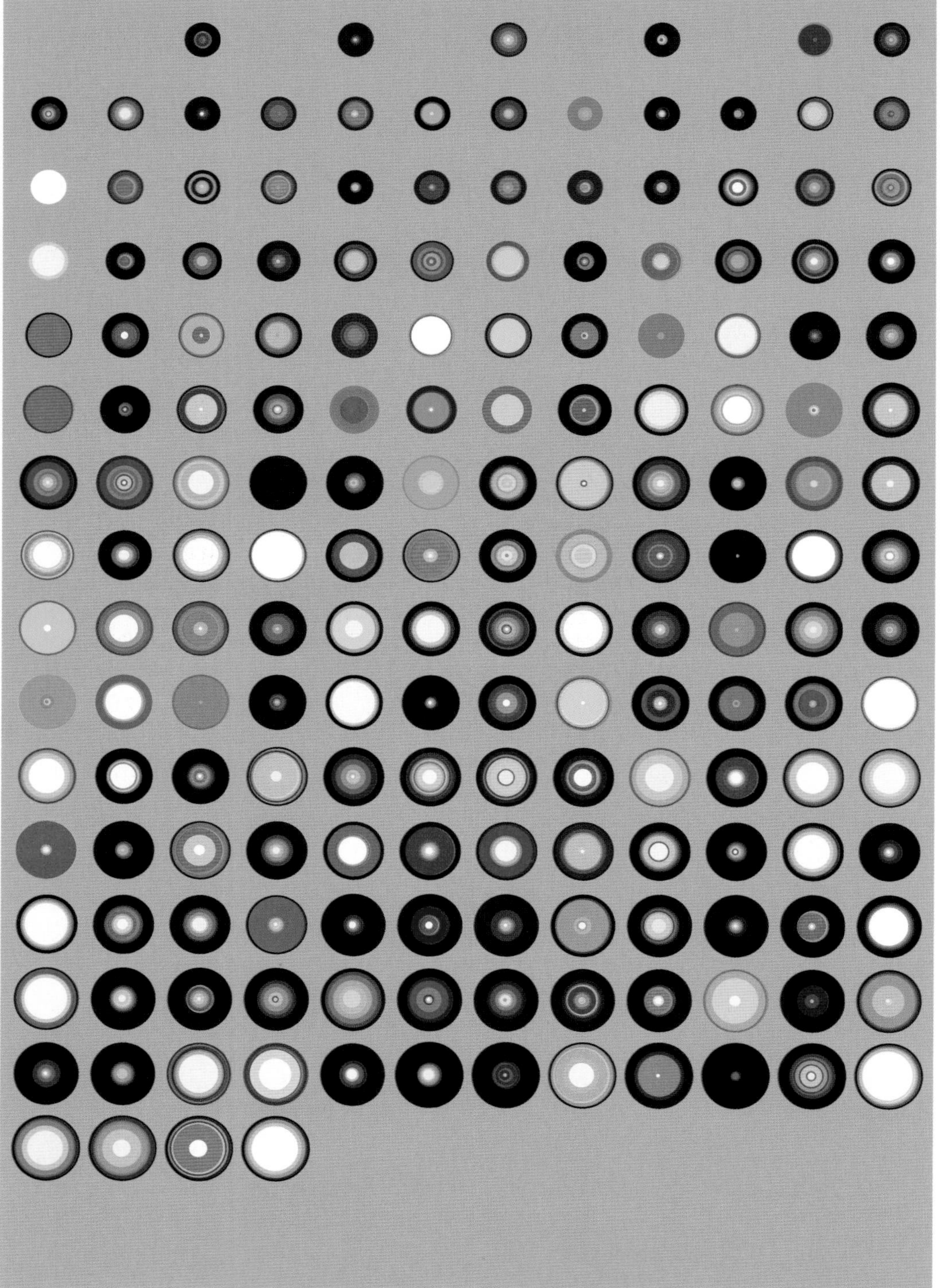

Project Info: *Wired*, magazine article and poster, 2008, USA
Design: Fernanda Viégas, Martin Wattenberg

Category 321–400

"In information visualisation it is often helpful to see data from a different angle and compare it with other information, update it, network it."

„In der Informationsvisualisierung ist es oft hilfreich, Daten aus einem neuen Blickwinkel zu sehen, mit anderen Informationen zu vergleichen, zu aktualisieren und zu vernetzen."

« Dans la visualisation d'informations, il est souvent utile de considérer les données sous un angle différent et de les comparer avec d'autres informations, les mettre à jour, et les mettre en réseau. »

Joachim Sauter

Category

Elements are divided into classes

Category

Elemente werden nach Typ unterschieden

Catégorie

Les éléments sont divisés en classes

Categories create order. A confusing volume of information is easily structured by differentiating by type and by looking for shared characteristics. Key economic figures can be arranged by business sector or demographic group (*Economy Map*, p.334 and *2009: A Job Odyssey*, p.325). War may result in a large number of fatalities and the military powers involved need to know the groups to which the victims belonged (*Function*, p.341).

Distinguishing between types is a theoretical classification and often arbitrary. For instance, the immense number of books in a library could be categorised by size or colour, although it is customary to classify books by their subject matter. However, even sub-division by subject turns out to be so fuzzy that a range of different classification systems exist side by side (*Your Friend, The Library*, p.400).

In *Writing Without Words* (p.396) Stefanie Posavec works on the basis of subject matter when she analyses a novel by Jack Kerouac by dividing the entire text into central themes. *Influences of Edgar Allan Poe* (p.358) is concerned with a topic of a historical nature, namely Poe's place in the history of literature. However, the account's structure is only partially chronological; mostly it is arranged by the literary aspects of his work. On the other hand, what makes Jessica Hagy's blog *This is Indexed* (p.380) so appealing is the fact that she invents abstract categories for everyday problems and depicts them in simple diagrams.

This chapter also gathers together works that combine different aspects of a subject. Many infographics place several data records on an equal footing side by side, linked by a shared framework or central symbol (*Digital Dump*, p.333 and *Hamburgers: The Economy of America's Favorite Food*, p.346). The chapter also considers those series which unite a range of approaches. *Flocking Diplomats NYC* (p.336) creates a visual image of a comprehensive study of parking violations by diplomats in New York by combining a range of different layouts, from timelines and maps to individual graphs.

Mental maps have already been mentioned under Location. This chapter contains examples that no longer bear any reference to real places or images. For instance, when representing scientific disciplines, the position on the paper of mathematics or biology is less important than the relationships between the disciplines (*Relationships Among Scientific Paradigms*, p.368). The situation is similar with regard to modified subway maps where each line stands for a category (*Web Trend Map*, p.388).

Interactive visualisations make it possible to sort large data records into specific categories. Jonathan Harris, for example, collects personal statements from online dating sites (*I Want You To Want Me*, p.352). On-screen visualisation permits users to filter huge volumes of data by age, gender or other categories.

Kategorien schaffen Ordnung. Eine unübersichtliche Menge strukturiert man leicht, indem man Typen unterscheidet und nach gemeinsamen Merkmalen sucht. Wirtschaftliche Kennzahlen lassen sich nach Wirtschaftszweigen oder Bevölkerungsgruppen gliedern (*Economy Map*, S. 334, und *2009: A Job Odyssey*, S. 325). In einem Krieg mag es eine große Anzahl Todesopfer geben. Für die beteiligten Militärmächte ist es wichtig, zu welcher Gruppe die Opfer gehören (*Function*, S. 341).

Die Unterscheidung von Typen ist eine theoretische Einteilung und oft willkürlich. Die unübersehbare Anzahl von Büchern in einer Bibliothek etwa ließe sich nach Größe oder Farbe ordnen, üblich ist jedoch die Klassifizierung nach dem Thema des Buches. Doch auch eine thematische Unterteilung hat so viele Unschärfen, dass verschiedene Klassifikationssysteme nebeneinander existieren (*Your Friend, The Library*, S. 400).

Thematisch geht auch Stefanie Posavec in *Writing Without Words* (S. 396) vor. Sie analysiert einen Roman von Jack Kerouac, indem sie den gesamten Text nach zentralen Themen unterteilt. *Influences of Edgar Allan Poe* (S. 358) behandelt ein historisches Thema, nämlich die Einordnung Poes in die Literaturgeschichte. Die Darstellung jedoch gliedert sich nur teilweise chronologisch, hauptsächlich aber nach literarischen Aspekten seines Werks. Der Reiz von Jessica Hagy's Blog *This is Indexed* (S. 380) wiederum besteht darin, dass sie abstrakte Kategorien für Alltagsprobleme erfindet und in einfachen Diagrammen darstellt.

Dieses Kapitel versammelt auch Arbeiten, die verschiedene Aspekte eines Themas zusammenführen. Viele Infografiken stellen mehrere Datensätze und Maßeinheiten gleichberechtigt nebeneinander, verbunden durch den gemeinsamen Rahmen oder ein zentrales Symbol (*Digital Dump*, S. 333, und *Hamburgers: The Economy of America's Favorite Food*, S. 346). Ebenso werden hier Serien berücksichtigt, die verschiedene Ansätze vereinen. *Flocking Diplomats NYC* (S. 336) visualisiert eine umfangreiche Studie zu falsch parkenden Diplomaten in New York – und verbindet dabei von Zeitreihen über Karten bis hin zu Einzelgraphen verschiedene Varianten.

Mentale Karten wurden bereits unter Location erwähnt. In diesem Kapitel finden sich Beispiele, die keinen Bezug mehr zu realen Orten oder Bildern haben. In der Darstellung wissenschaftlicher Disziplinen etwa ist die Position der Mathematik oder Biologie auf dem Papier nicht entscheidend, wichtiger sind vielmehr die Beziehungen zwischen den Disziplinen (*Relationships Among Scientific Paradigms*, S. 368). Ähnlich verhält es sich bei abgewandelten U-Bahn-Plänen, auf denen die einzelnen Linien jeweils für eine eigene Kategorie stehen (*Web Trend Map*, S. 388).

Interaktive Visualisierungen bieten die Möglichkeit, große Datensätze nach bestimmten Kategorien zu sortieren. Jonathan Harris beispielsweise sammelt persönliche Aussagen aus Online-Kontaktanzeigen (*I Want You To Want Me*, S. 352). Die Visualisierung auf dem Bildschirm erlaubt es dem Nutzer, die riesige Datenmenge nach Alter, Geschlecht oder anderen Kategorien zu filtern.

Les catégories marquent un ordre. Un volume important d'informations est facilement structuré en faisant une distinction par type et en recherchant les caractéristiques communes. Les chiffres économiques clés peuvent être organisés par secteur d'activité ou par groupe démographique (*Economy Map*, p. 334 et *2009: A Job Odyssey*, p. 325). Une guerre peut se solder par de nombreux décès et les forces militaires impliquées doivent connaître les groupes auxquels appartenaient les victimes (*Function*, p. 341).

La distinction entre plusieurs types est une classification théorique et souvent arbitraire. Par exemple, l'énorme quantité de livres dans une bibliothèque peut être catégorisée par taille ou couleur, même s'il est plus habituel d'opter pour un classement thématique. Cependant, même une sous-division par sujet s'avère tellement confuse que plusieurs systèmes de classification coexistent (*Your Friend, The Library*, p. 400).

Dans *Writing Without Words* (p. 396), Stefanie Posavec analyse un roman de Jack Kerouac en divisant le texte en thèmes principaux. *Influences of Edgar Allan Poe* (p. 358) traite d'un sujet de nature historique, à savoir la place de Poe dans l'histoire de la littérature. Toutefois, la structure n'est qu'en partie chronologique ; elle obéit surtout aux aspects littéraires de son œuvre. Par ailleurs, tout l'attrait du blog *This is Indexed* (p. 380) de Jessica Hagy tient au fait qu'elle invente des catégories abstraites pour des problèmes quotidiens et les représente sous forme de diagrammes.

Ce chapitre rassemble également des œuvres combinant différents aspects d'un même sujet. De nombreuses infographies mettent plusieurs informations sur un pied d'égalité en les connectant par une structure partagée ou un symbole central (*Digital Dump*, p. 333 et *Hamburgers: The Economy of America's Favorite Food*, p. 346). Le chapitre retient aussi les créations qui marient plusieurs approches différentes. *Flocking Diplomats NYC* (p. 336) illustre une étude complète sur les infractions de stationnement des diplomates à New York en conjugant plusieurs types de présentation, telles que des chronologies, des cartes et des graphiques.

Les cartes heuristiques ont déjà été mentionnées dans la section Lieu. Ce chapitre contient des exemples sans référence à des images ou endroits réels. Par exemple, pour la représentation des disciplines scientifiques, la position sur le papier des mathématiques ou de la biologie est moins importante que les relations entre ces disciplines (*Relationships Among Scientific Paradigms*, p. 368). La situation est similaire pour les plans de métro modifiés, où chaque ligne correspond à une catégorie (*Web Trend Map*, p. 388).

Les visualisations interactives permettent de catégoriser de grandes quantités de données. Jonathan Harris rassemble par exemple des déclarations faites sur des sites de rencontre en ligne (*I Want You To Want Me*, p. 352). La visualisation à l'écran permet aux utilisateurs de filtrer d'énormes volumes de données par âge, genre ou d'autres catégories.

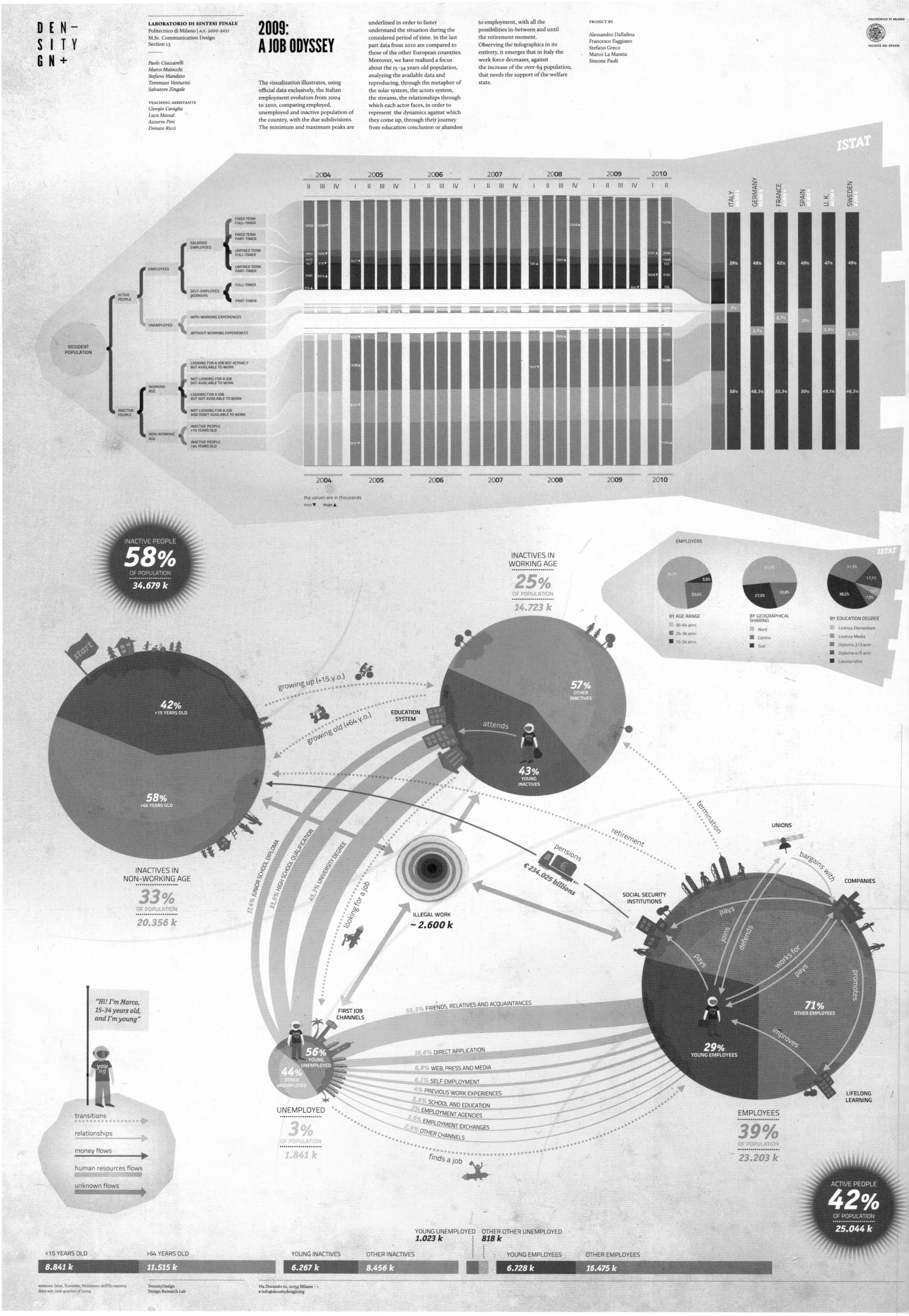

DEN–
SITY
GN+

LABORATORIO DI SINTESI FINALE
Politecnico di Milano | A.Y. 2010-2011
M.Sc. Communication Design
Section c3

Paolo Ciuccarelli
Marco Maiocchi
Stefano Mandato
Tommaso Venturini
Salvatore Zingale

TEACHING ASSISTANTS
Giorgio Caviglia
Luca Masud
Azzurra Pini
Donato Ricci

2009: A JOB ODYSSEY

The visualization illustrates, using official data exclusively, the Italian employment evolution from 2004 to 2010, comparing employed, unemployed and inactive population of the country, with the due subdivisions. The minimum and maximum peaks are underlined in order to faster understand the situation during the considered period of time. In the last part data from 2010 are compared to those of the other European countries. Moreover, we have realized a focus about the 15–34 years old population, analyzing the available data and reproducing, through the metaphor of the solar system, the actors system, the streams, the relationships through which each actor faces, in order to represent the dynamics against which they come up, through their journey from education conclusion or abandon to employment, with all the possibilities in-between and until the retirement moment. Observing the infographics in its entirety, it emerges that in Italy the work force decreases, against the increase of the over-64 population, that needs the support of the welfare state.

PROJECT BY
Alessandro Dallafina
Francesco Faggiano
Stefano Greco
Marco La Mantia
Simone Paoli

POLITECNICO DI MILANO
FACOLTÀ DEL DESIGN

ISTAT

2004 2005 2006 2007 2008 2009 2010

RESIDENT POPULATION
ACTIVE PEOPLE
EMPLOYEES
SALARIED EMPLOYEES
FIXED TERM FULL-TIMER
FIXED TERM PART-TIMER
UNFIXED TERM FULL-TIMER
UNFIXED TERM PART-TIMER
SELF-EMPLOYED WORKERS
FULL-TIMER
PART-TIMER
UNEMPLOYED
WITH WORKING EXPERIENCES
WITHOUT WORKING EXPERIENCES
INACTIVE PEOPLE
WORKING AGE
LOOKING FOR A JOB NOT ACTIVELY BUT AVAILABLE TO WORK
NOT LOOKING FOR A JOB BUT AVAILABLE TO WORK
LOOKING FOR A JOB BUT NOT AVAILABLE TO WORK
NOT LOOKING FOR A JOB AND DON'T AVAILABLE TO WORK
NON-WORKING AGE
INACTIVE PEOPLE <15 YEARS OLD
INACTIVE PEOPLE >64 YEARS OLD

ITALY GERMANY FRANCE SPAIN U.K. SWEDEN

39% 48% 42% 40% 47% 49%
3% 3,7% 4,7% 10% 3,9% 4,5%
58% 48,3% 53,3% 50% 49,1% 46,5%

the values are in thousands
min ▼ max ▲

INACTIVE PEOPLE **58%** OF POPULATION **34.679 k**

INACTIVES IN WORKING AGE **25%** OF POPULATION **14.723 k**

EMPLOYERS
BY AGE RANGE: 35-64 anni, 25-34 anni, 15-24 anni
BY GEOGRAPHICAL SHARING: Nord, Centro, Sud
BY EDUCATION DEGREE: Licenza Elementare, Licenza Media, Diploma 2/3 anni, Diploma 4/5 anni, Laurea/oltre

start
42% <15 YEARS OLD
58% >64 YEARS OLD
growing up (+15 y.o.)
growing old (+64 y.o.)
EDUCATION SYSTEM
attends
57% OTHER INACTIVES
43% YOUNG INACTIVES

INACTIVES IN NON-WORKING AGE **33%** OF POPULATION **20.356 k**

17,4% JUNIOR SCHOOL DIPLOMA
33,5% HIGH SCHOOL QUALIFICATION
45,3% UNIVERSITY DEGREE
looking for a job
ILLEGAL WORK **~ 2.600 k**
pensions **€ 234.025 billions**
retirement
termination
UNIONS
bargains with
COMPANIES
SOCIAL SECURITY INSTITUTIONS
pays, joins, defends, pays, works for, pays, promotes, improves
LIFELONG LEARNING
71% OTHER EMPLOYEES
29% YOUNG EMPLOYEES

FIRST JOB CHANNELS
55,3% FRIENDS, RELATIVES AND ACQUAINTANCES
16,6% DIRECT APPLICATION
6,8% WEB, PRESS AND MEDIA
6,1% SELF EMPLOYMENT
4% PREVIOUS WORK EXPERIENCES
3,8% SCHOOL AND EDUCATION
3% EMPLOYMENT AGENCIES
1,5% EMPLOYMENT EXCHANGES
2,9% OTHER CHANNELS
finds a job

56% YOUNG UNEMPLOYED
44% OTHER UNEMPLOYED

UNEMPLOYED **3%** OF POPULATION **1.841 k**

EMPLOYEES **39%** OF POPULATION **23.203 k**

ACTIVE PEOPLE **42%** OF POPULATION **25.044 k**

"Hi! I'm Marco, 15-34 years old, and I'm young"

transitions
relationships
money flows
human resources flows
unknown flows

<15 YEARS OLD	>64 YEARS OLD	YOUNG INACTIVES	OTHER INACTIVES	YOUNG UNEMPLOYED	OTHER OTHER UNEMPLOYED	YOUNG EMPLOYEES	OTHER EMPLOYEES
8.841 k	11.515 k	6.267 k	8.456 k	1.023 k	818 k	6.728 k	16.475 k

sources: Istat, Eurostat, Ministero dell'Economia
data set: 2nd quarter of 2009

DensityDesign
Design Research Lab

Via Durando 10, 20159 Milano – I
E info@densitydesign.org

2009: A Job Odyssey

This is an overview of unemployment figures in Italy over a period of seven years. The population is categorised using colour coding, with orange representing people who are employed, yellow unemployed people and blue for people who are not in the workforce. The taller bars on the very right show comparative 2010 figures for selected European countries.

In the lower part, developments in people's employment over the course of their lifetime is described, using the symbolism of a planetary system. The colour-coding compares with the upper part: blue represents people too young or too old to be in the workforce, the orange are the employed. Connecting lines between the planets indicate how people make the shift from one professional situation to another.

Dies ist ein Überblick über die Arbeitslosenzahlen in Italien über einen Zeitraum von sieben Jahren. Die Bevölkerung wird mittels Farbcodierung in Kategorien unterteilt: Orange steht für Erwerbstätige, Gelb für Arbeitslose und Blau für Nichterwerbstätige. Die höheren Balken ganz rechts zeigen die Vergleichszahlen ausgewählter europäischer Länder aus dem Jahr 2010.

Symbolisiert durch ein Planetensystem, werden im unteren Teil Entwicklungen dargestellt, die sich im Laufe eines Arbeitslebens vollziehen. Die Farbcodierung entspricht der im oberen Teil: Blau steht für Menschen, die zu jung oder zu alt sind, um erwerbstätig zu sein, Orange für Erwerbstätige. Verbindungslinien zwischen den Planeten zeigen, wie Menschen von einer beruflichen Phase in die andere hinüberwechseln.

Cette illustration présente les chiffres du chômage en Italie sur une période de sept ans. La population est classée grâce à un code de couleurs, les barres orange représentant les personnes qui ont un emploi, les jaunes les personnes au chômage et les bleues celles n'appartenant pas à la population active. Les barres les plus hautes à l'extrême droite montrent les chiffres de 2010 pour certains pays européens.

Dans la partie inférieure, l'évolution de la situation professionnelle des personnes au cours de leur vie est représentée par un système planétaire. Le code de couleur rappelle celui de la partie supérieure : le bleu pour les personnes trop jeunes ou trop âgées pour appartenir à la population active, l'orange pour celles qui ont un emploi. Les lignes connectant les planètes indiquent comment les gens passent d'une situation professionnelle à une autre.

Project Info: Poster, 2010, Italy
Data Source: Institute for the Future, Palo Alto
Design: Alessandro Dallafina, Francesco Faggiano, Stefano Greco, Marco La Mantia, Simone Paoli (DensityDesign)

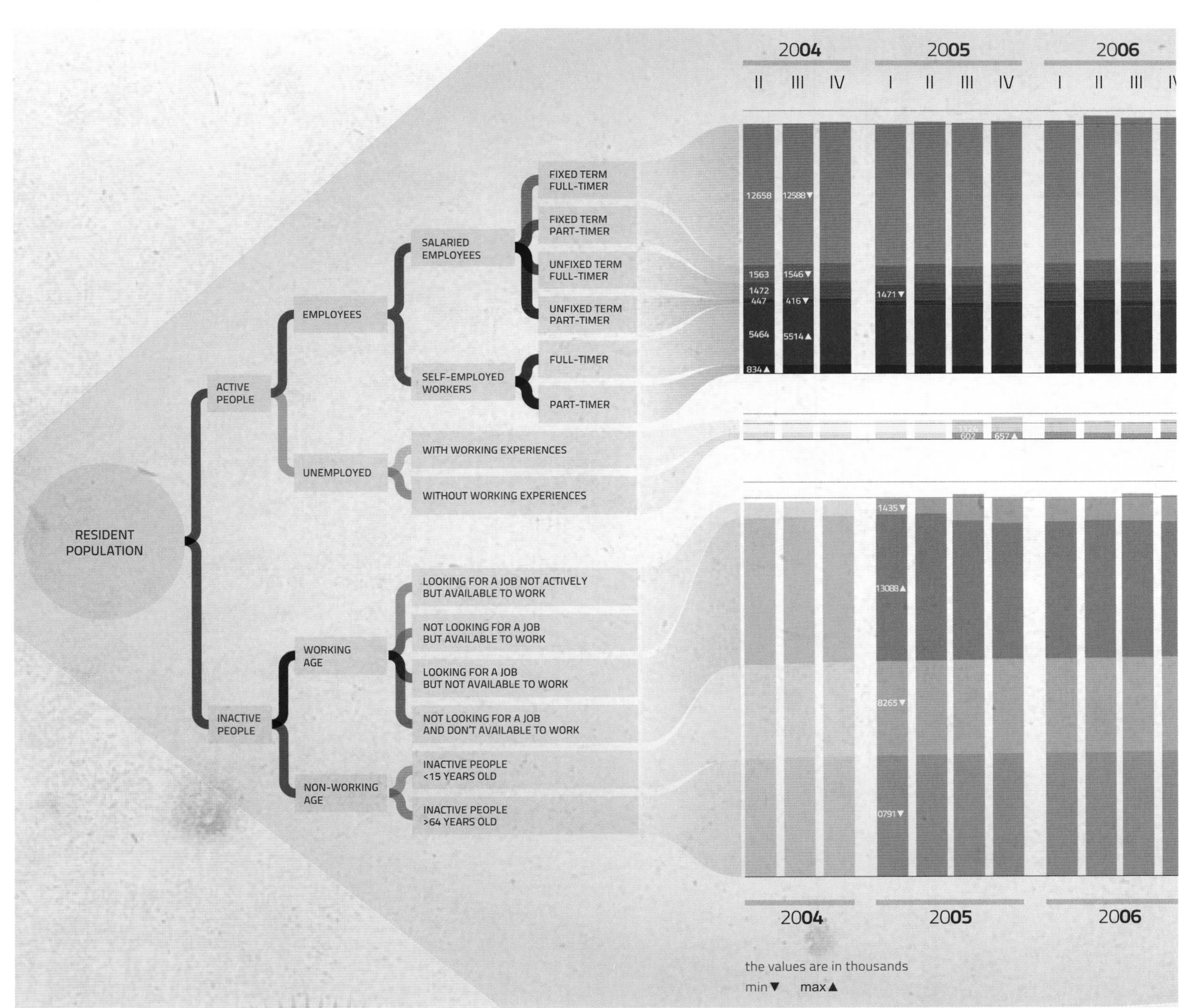

Annual Report Fira de Barcelona

Barcelona-based design studio Lamosca developed this series of infographics for the Barcelona Trade Fair, which has a great history in that city. In its annual report, the fair recounts activities during the last year and the economic impact the fair has had upon the city.

In a series of individual graphics, significant figures derived from the report are shown either as single facts or in relation to each other. The clear and reduced design helps people grasp the facts and thus allows quick access to data covered in the report.

Das Design-Studio Lamosca aus Barcelona entwickelte diese Serie von Infografiken für die dortige Messe, die auf eine lange Geschichte zurückblickt. Im jährlichen Geschäftsbericht werden die Aktivitäten des vergangenen Jahres erläutert sowie die wirtschaftliche Bedeutung, die die Messe für die Stadt hatte.

In mehreren Grafiken werden aussagekräftige Zahlen des Geschäftsberichts entweder als Einzelfakten dargestellt oder in Beziehung zueinander gesetzt. Das klare, reduzierte Design hilft dem Betrachter, die Fakten rasch zu erfassen, und ermöglicht so einen raschen Zugang zu den im Bericht erwähnten Zahlen.

Lamosca, studio de design barcelonais, a créé cette série d'infographies pour le Parc des Expositions de Barcelone, qui a une forte présence dans la ville. Dans son rapport annuel, le Parc détaille les activités de la dernière année et son impact économique sur la ville.

Dans une série de graphiques individuels, des chiffres particulièrement significatifs extraits du rapport sont présentés comme des faits isolés ou liés entre eux. Le design clair et minimaliste permet de comprendre ces aspects et d'accéder rapidement aux données mentionnées dans le rapport.

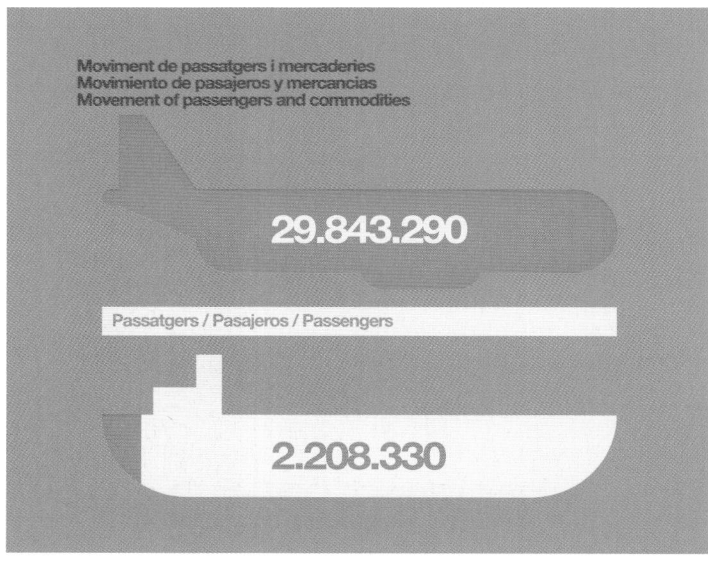

Project Info: Fira Barcelona, video, 2007, Spain
Design: Lamosca

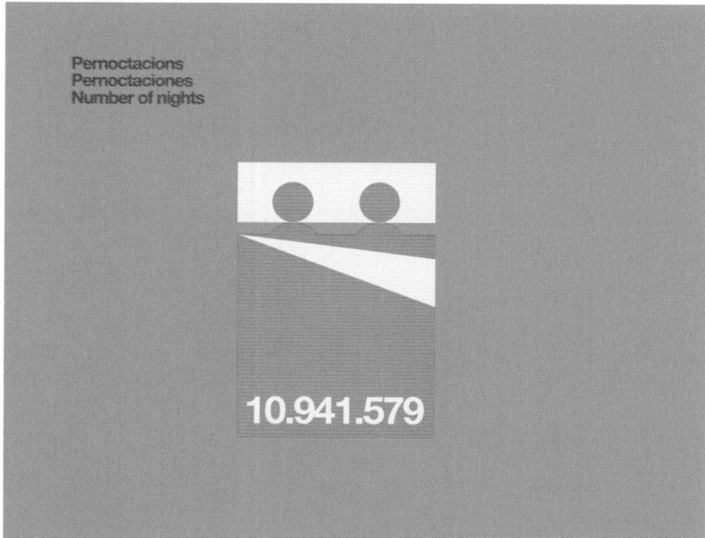

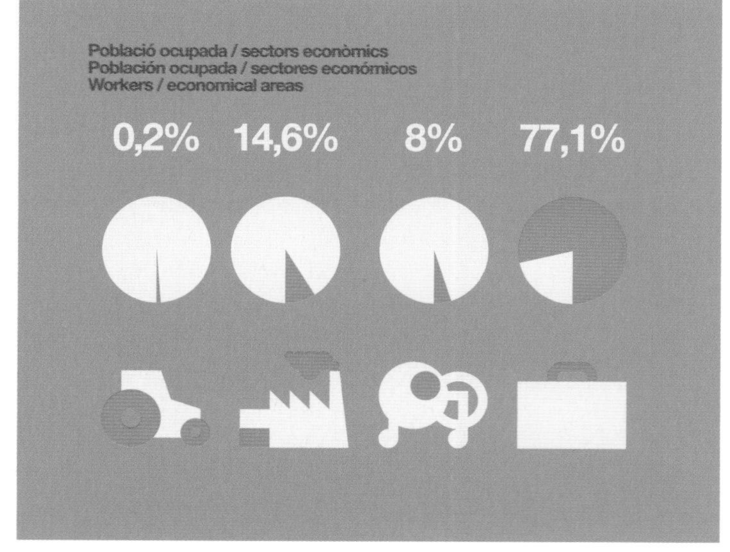

Project Info: *Information is Beautiful*, book, 2009, UK
Design: David McCandless (Information is Beautiful); Always with Honor

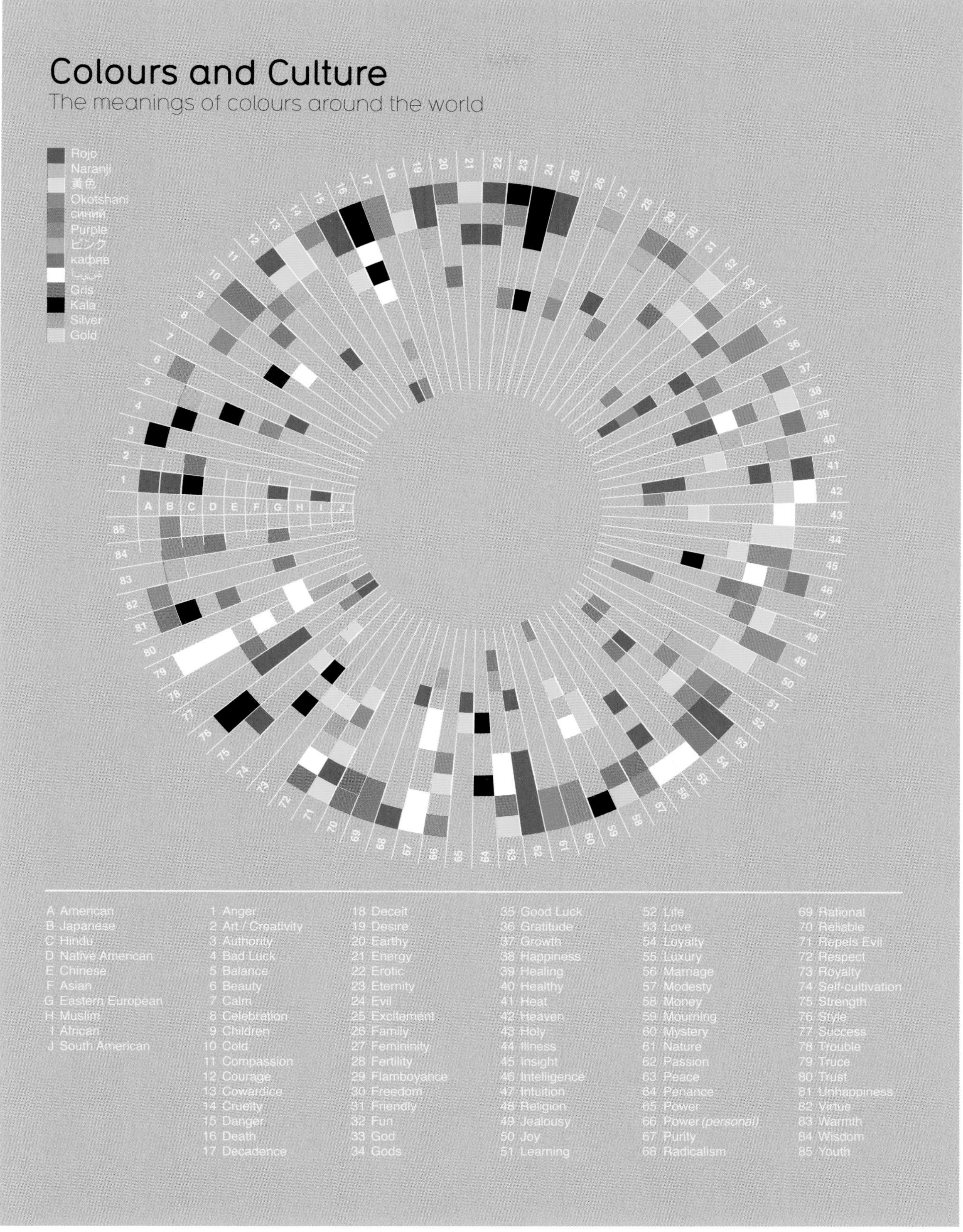

Colours and Culture

In what looks like a wheel of fortune, David McCandless presents an overview of colour symbols among major cultures worldwide. The circle is chequered like a coordinate system: radial lines represent the categories of feelings or qualities numbered 1–84, such as anger or intelligence. Concentric lines around the circle represent international cultures labelled A–J, like Japanese or South American.

In each of the coordinate squares, a colour field shows which colour represents the specific feeling or quality in that respective culture. Line 1 thus shows that red symbolises anger not only in American culture, but also in Japan, Eastern Europe and Africa, while Hindus use black to symbolise anger.

Mit dieser Grafik, die an ein Glücksrad erinnert, gibt David McCandless einen Überblick über die Bedeutung verschiedener Farben in den bedeutenden Kulturen der Welt. Der Kreis ist wie ein Koordinatensystem aufgebaut: Nummeriert von 1 bis 84, repräsentieren strahlenförmige Linien Kategorien bestimmter Gefühle oder Eigenschaften, wie beispielsweise Wut oder Intelligenz. Konzentrische Linien innerhalb des Kreises, von A bis J bezeichnet, stehen für internationale Kulturräume wie den japanischen oder den südamerikanischen.

In jedem Koordinatenquadrat zeigt ein Farbfeld, welche Farbe das jeweilige Gefühl oder die Eigenschaft in der jeweiligen Kultur repräsentiert. So wird aus Zeile 1 ersichtlich, dass Rot nicht nur in der amerikanischen Kultur Wut symbolisiert, sondern auch in Japan, Osteuropa und Afrika, während Hindus Wut durch Schwarz zum Ausdruck bringen.

Dans ce qui ressemble à une roue de la fortune, David McCandless présente un aperçu de la symbolique des couleurs dans les principales cultures du monde. Le cercle divisé en secteurs s'apparente à un système de coordonnées : les lignes radiales signalent les catégories de sentiments ou de qualités numérotées de 1 à 84, comme la colère ou l'intelligence. Les lignes concentriques correspondent aux différentes cultures, désignées par les lettres A à J (comme « Japonaise » ou « Sud-Américaine »).

Chaque carré de coordonnées montre la couleur qui correspond au sentiment ou à la qualité dans cette culture. La ligne 1 indique donc que le rouge symbolise la colère dans la culture américaine, mais aussi au Japon, en Europe de l'Est et en Afrique, alors que les hindous utilisent le noir pour l'exprimer.

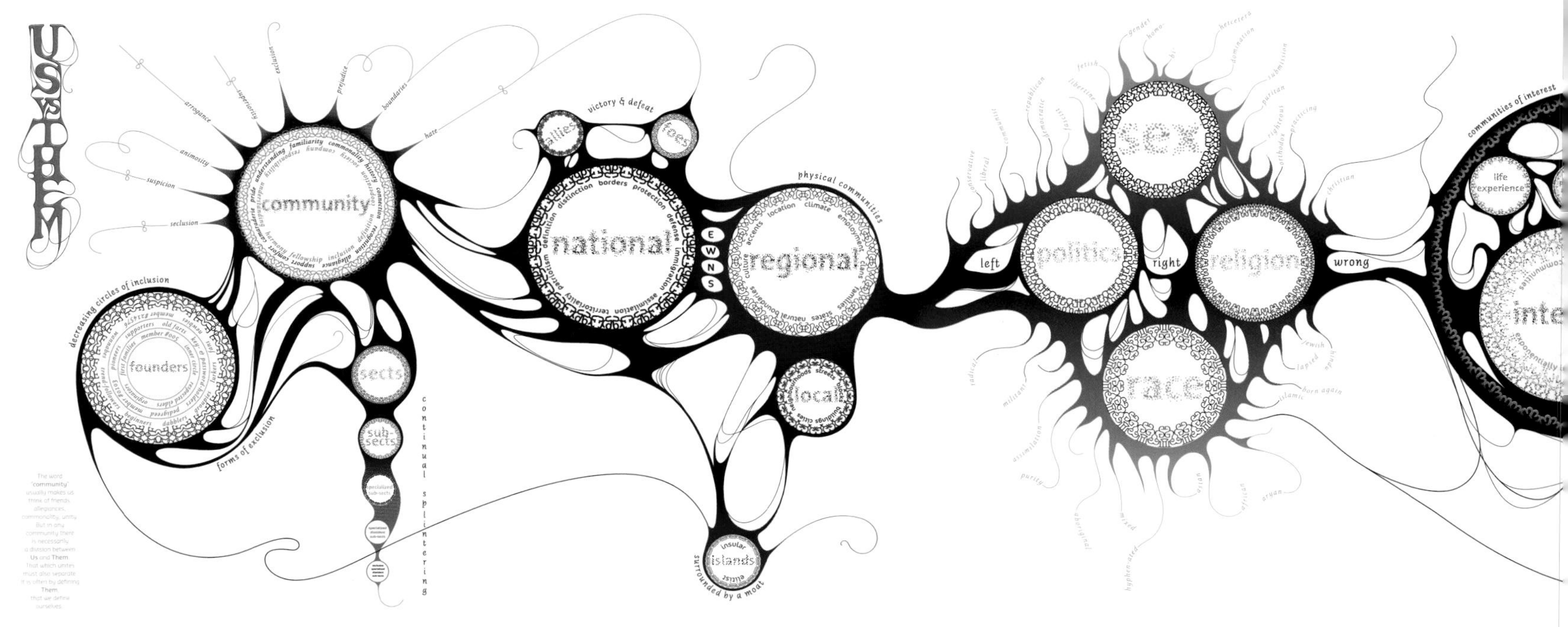
US & THEM
arrogance
animosity
suspicion
seclusion
superiority
prejudice
boundaries
hate
community
decreasing circles of inclusion
founders
forms of exclusion
sects
sub-sects
continual splintering
victory & defeat
allies
foes
national
borders protection
physical communities
regional
local
insular islands
surrounded by a moat
left
politics
right
sex
religion
race
wrong
communities of interest
life experience
The word "community" usually makes us think of friends, allegiances, commonality, unity. But in any community there is necessarily a division between Us and Them. That which unites must also separate. It is often by defining Them, that we define ourselves.

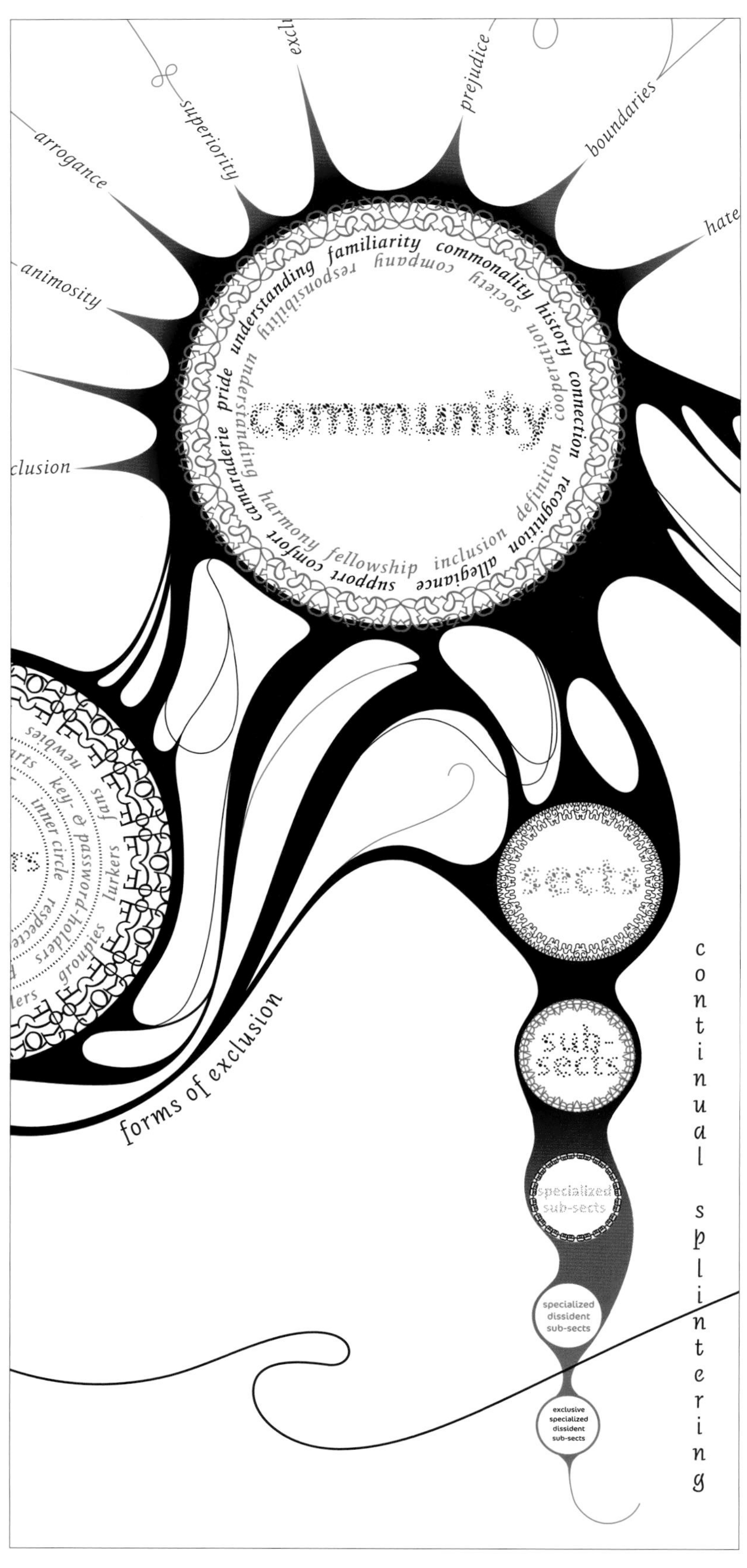
superiority
prejudice
arrogance
boundaries
animosity
hate
community
understanding
familiarity
commonality
history
connection
recognition
allegiance
support
comfort
camaraderie
pride
harmony
fellowship
inclusion
definition
cooperation
society
company
responsibility
newbies
fans
lurkers
inner circle
key- & password-holders
groupies
sects
sub-sects
specialized sub-sects
specialized dissident sub-sects
exclusive specialized dissident sub-sects
forms of exclusion
continual splintering

gender
homo-
bi-
hetcetera
fetish
domination
libertine
submission
puritan
democratic
fascist
righteous
orthodox
sex
politics
right
religion
race
islam
asian
african
aryan
aboriginal
mixed

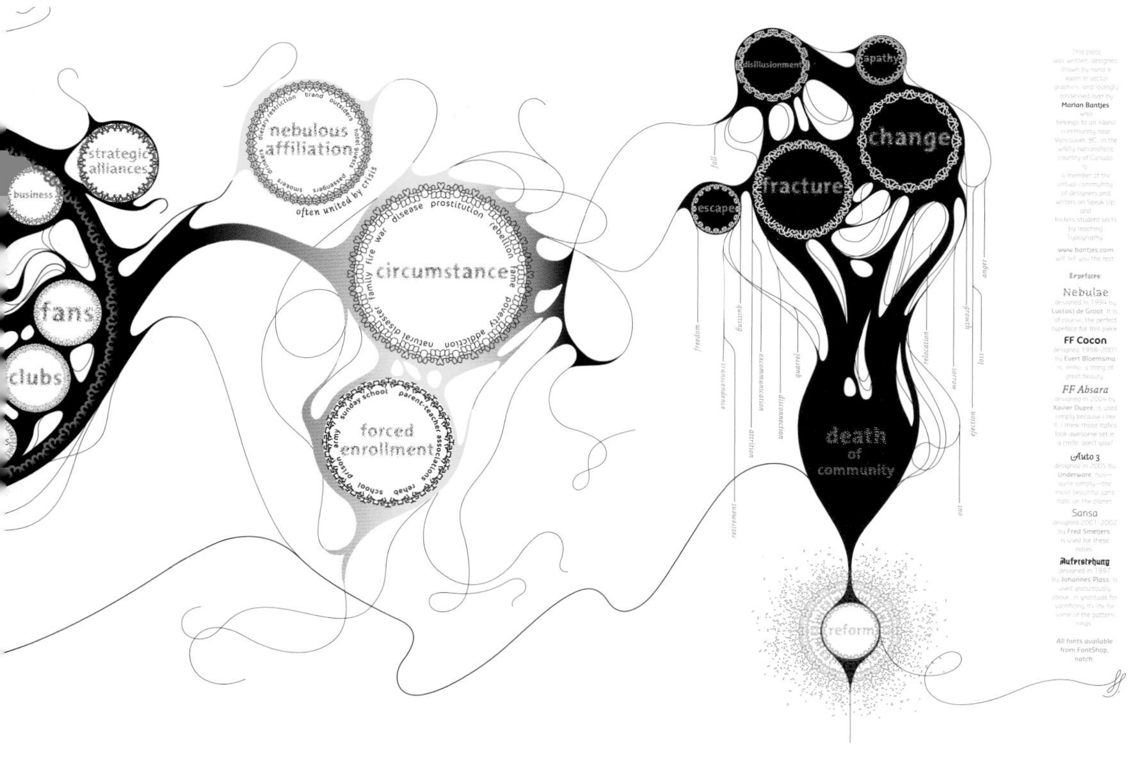

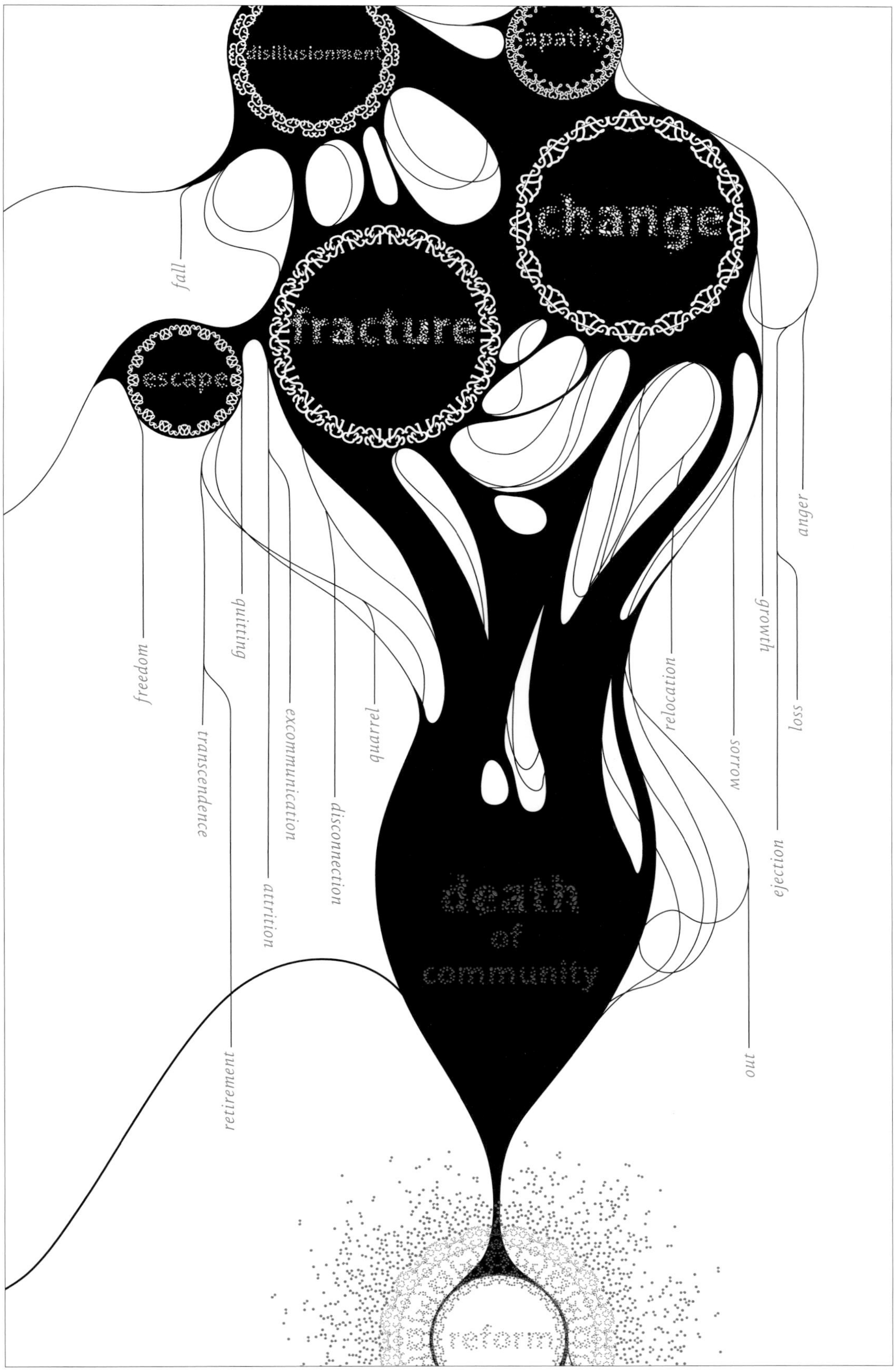

Community

Tasked with developing a piece on the notion of "community" by German font magazine *FontShop*, Marian Bantjes designed this graphic in an extreme horizontal format. Rather than visualising actual statistical data, Bantjes looks into how communities define themselves by defining who does not belong.

Bantjes uses various clusters of circles as the most natural visual metaphor for symbolising a community, and with lines floating and growing from one circle to another she indicates how communities are never fixed phenomena, but keep changing constantly. With this piece, Bantjes delivers a striking example of how topics can be discussed by inscribing concepts into visual structures.

Im Auftrag der deutschen Zeitschrift *FontShop* entwarf Marian Bantjes diese Grafik zum Thema „Gemeinschaft" in einem extremen Querformat. Anstatt konkrete statistische Daten zu visualisieren, richtete sie ihr Augenmerk auf den Umstand, dass sich Gemeinschaften oft dadurch konstituieren dass sie bestimmen, wer nicht zu ihnen gehört.

Als natürlichste visuelle Metapher für Gemeinschaften verwendet Bantjes Kreise in unterschiedlichen Anordnungen; anhand von Linien, die von den einzelnen Kreisen ausgehen, sich vermehren und in anderen Kreisen aufgehen, verdeutlicht sie, dass Gemeinschaften keine starren Phänomene sind, sondern ständiger Veränderung unterliegen. Mit dieser Grafik zeigt Bantjes meisterhaft, wie man Fragestellungen diskutieren kann, indem man Begriffe in visuelle Strukturen einschreibt.

Chargée par le magazine typographique allemand *FontShop* de représenter la notion de « communauté », Marian Bantjes a conçu ce graphique dans un format très horizontal. Au lieu de visualiser les données statistiques réelles, Bantjes étudie comment les communautés se définissent par rapport à l'extérieur.

Bantjes a recours à plusieurs grappes de cercles comme métaphore visuelle la plus naturelle pour symboliser une communauté. Avec des lignes qui flottent et passent d'un cercle à un autre, elle montre que les communautés ne sont jamais des phénomènes statiques et qu'elles changent constamment. Dans cette création, Bantjes offre un remarquable exemple d'illustration en inscrivant des concepts dans des structures visuelles.

Project Info: *Font*, magazine article, FontShop, 2005, Germany
Design: Marian Bantjes

Data

This series appeared in the cultural supplement of Barcelona-based newspaper *La Vanguardia* in an extreme vertical format, as a weekly column lasting 152 weeks. The infographics drew on each supplement's specific theme and represented it in a meaningful dataset, or added extra information to the editorial story.

Various sources, kinds of data and types of visualisations were used throughout the series. The overall design featured a minimalist graphic style.

Diese Serie in einem schmalen Hochformat erschien 152 Wochen in Folge als wöchentliche Kolumne in der Kulturbeilage der in Barcelona erscheinenden Tageszeitung *La Vanguardia*. Die Infografiken bezogen sich auf das jeweilige Hauptthema der Beilage und stellten es in einem aussagekräftigen Datensatz dar oder ergänzten die redaktionellen Artikel um zusätzliche Informationen.

Im Lauf der Serie wurden ganz unterschiedliche Quellen, Datentypen und Visualisierungen verwendet. Das Design der Serie war von einem eher modern-minimalistischen Stil geprägt.

Cette série est parue dans le supplément culturel du journal barcelonais *La Vanguardia* dans un format totalement vertical, une chronique hebdomadaire publiée 152 semaines. Les infographies illustraient chaque semaine un thème particulier avec des données complètes ou en complément de l'édito.

Plusieurs sources, types de données et types de visualisations ont été utilisés dans cette série. Le design d'ensemble repose sur un style graphique minimaliste.

Project Info: *La Vanguardia*, newspaper article, 2007–2010, Spain
Data Source: Recetario de Concepción Atienza; Boeing; POV: "Flagwars". Documentary 2003; Universitat Oberta de Catalunya; Leserglede.com, timesonline.co.uk; Lasker's Chess Primer; Jeffrey Kenworthy: "Traffic: Back to the Future? Urban Transport 2050"; Daylight and Architecture, 2009; otherpower.com; CollectorTimes.com; The Library of Iberian Resources Online; Cinemetrics.lv; metalyou.com; algalita.org; Friends of the Earth
Design: Lamosca

Data19
LAMOSCA
Portabella / Suquet
A. 5 dientes de ajo B. 3 trozos de pan C. 4 gambas
D. 6 almendras E. Perejil F. Pimentón dulce
G. Harina H. Agua I. Caldo de pescado
J. 1/2 Kg. de patatas K. 4 rodajas de rape K. 1 Cabracho
L. Vino blanco seco M. Guisantes N. 4 Mejillones
Receta para 4 personas. Servir con pan tostado con ajo
ACEITE
Fuente: Recetario de Concepción Atienza

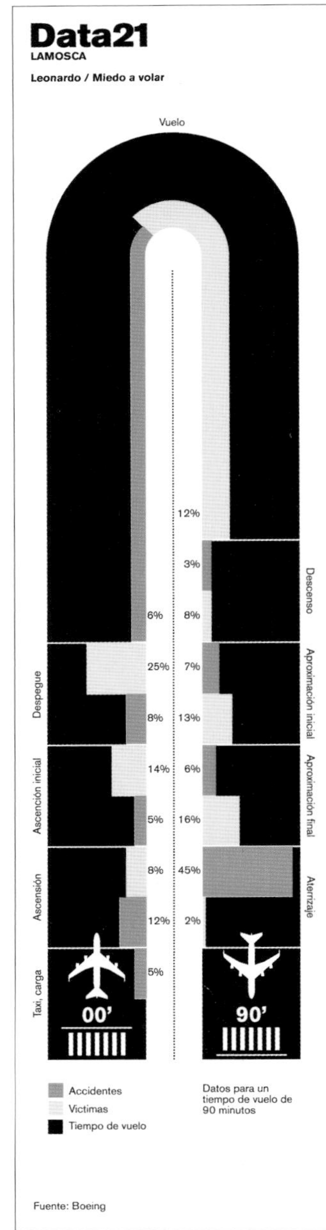

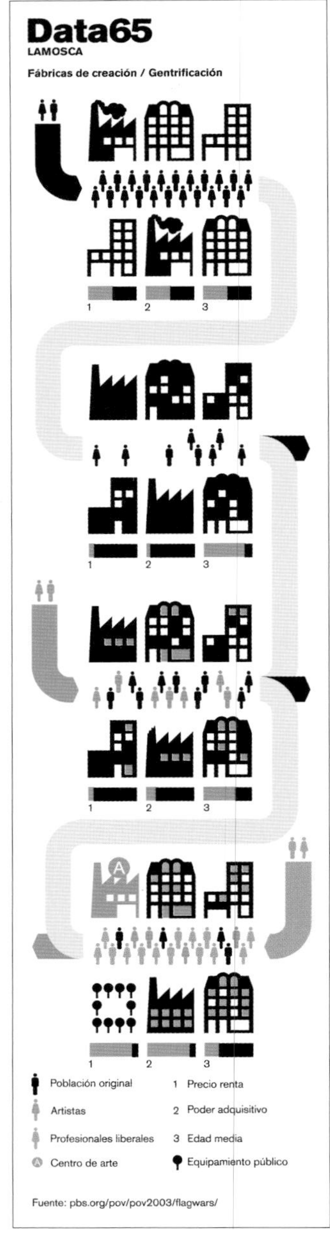

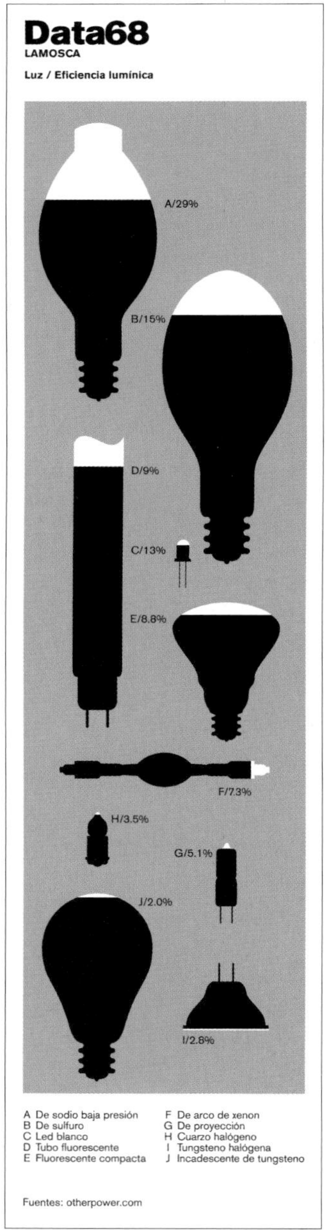

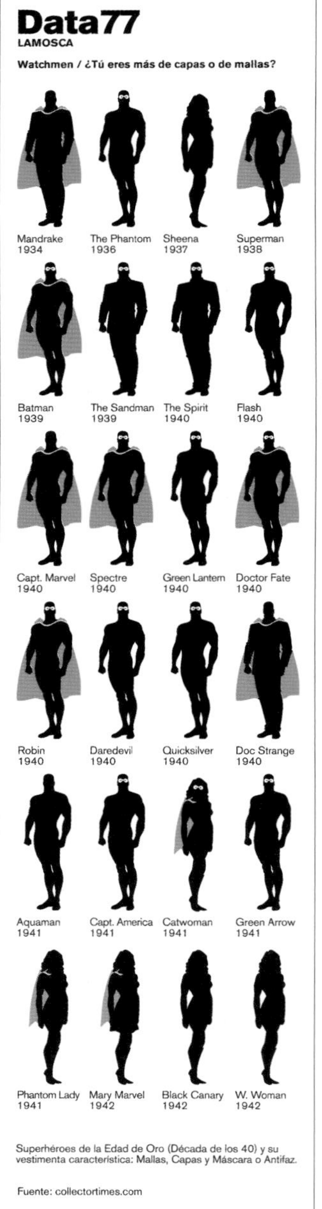

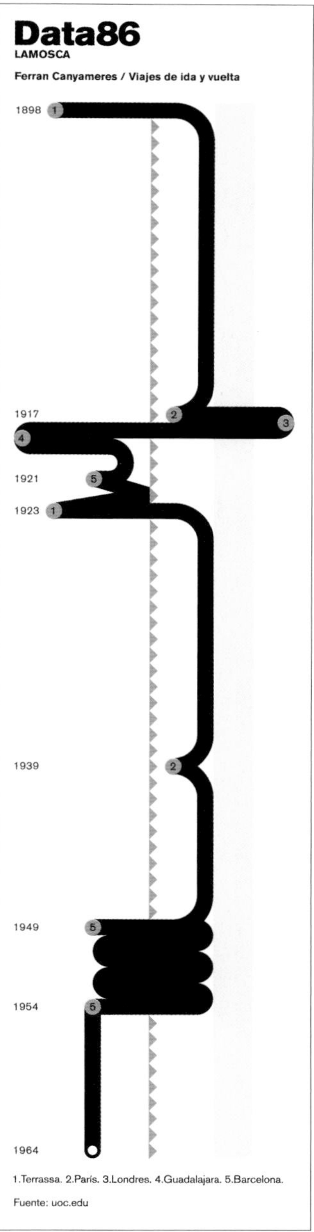
Data86
LAMOSCA
Ferran Canyameres / Viajes de ida y vuelta
1898
1917
1921
1923
1939
1949
1954
1964
1.Terrassa. 2.París. 3.Londres. 4.Guadalajara. 5.Barcelona.
Fuente: uoc.edu

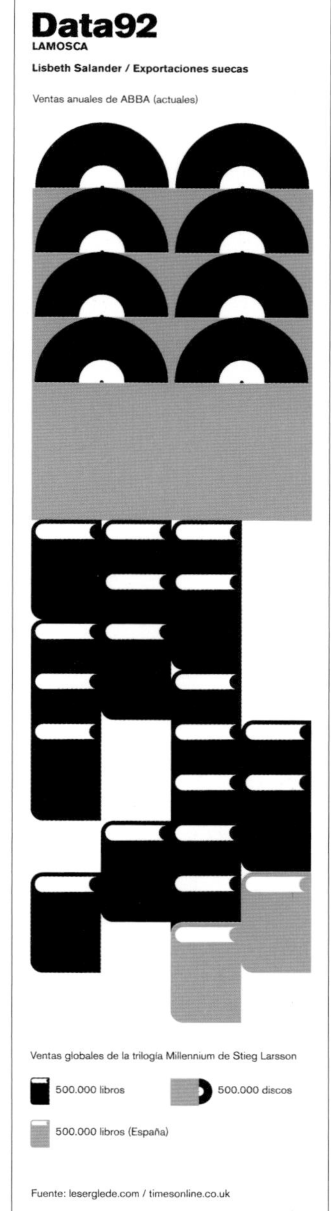
Data92
LAMOSCA
Lisbeth Salander / Exportaciones suecas
Ventas anuales de ABBA (actuales)
Ventas globales de la trilogía Millennium de Stieg Larsson
500.000 libros
500.000 discos
500.000 libros (España)
Fuente: leserglede.com / timesonline.co.uk

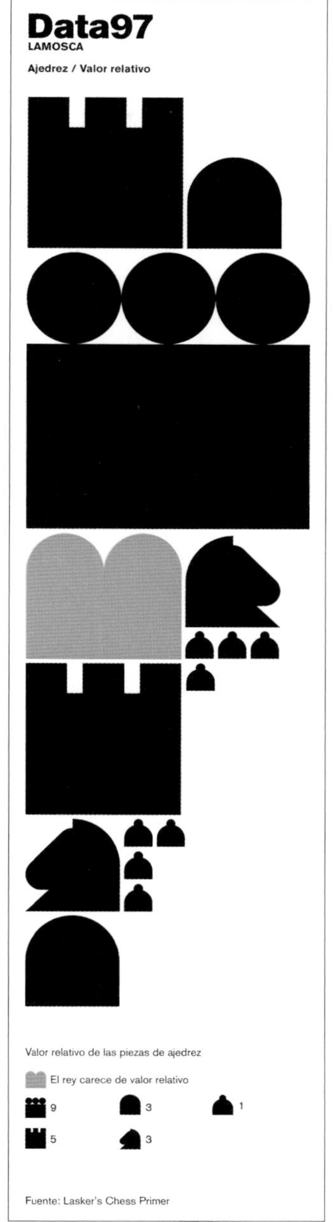
Data97
LAMOSCA
Ajedrez / Valor relativo
Valor relativo de las piezas de ajedrez
El rey carece de valor relativo
9
3
1
5
3
Fuente: Lasker's Chess Primer

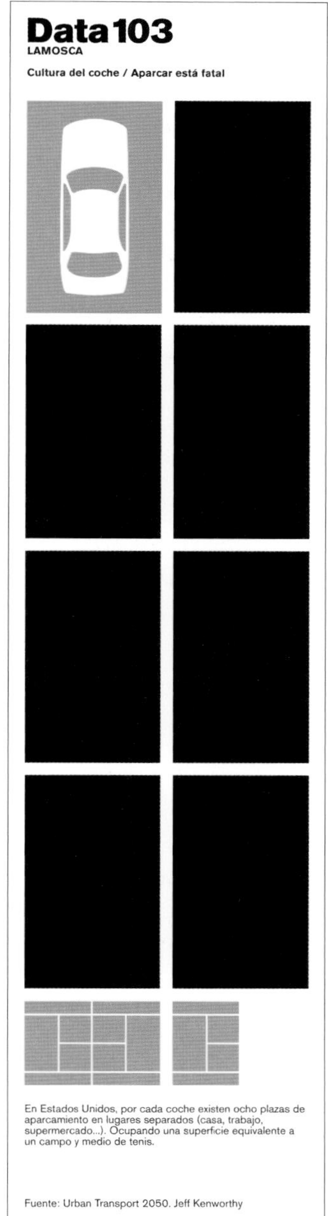
Data 103
LAMOSCA
Cultura del coche / Aparcar está fatal
En Estados Unidos, por cada coche existen ocho plazas de aparcamiento en lugares separados (casa, trabajo, supermercado...). Ocupando una superficie equivalente a un campo y medio de tenis.
Fuente: Urban Transport 2050. Jeff Kenworthy

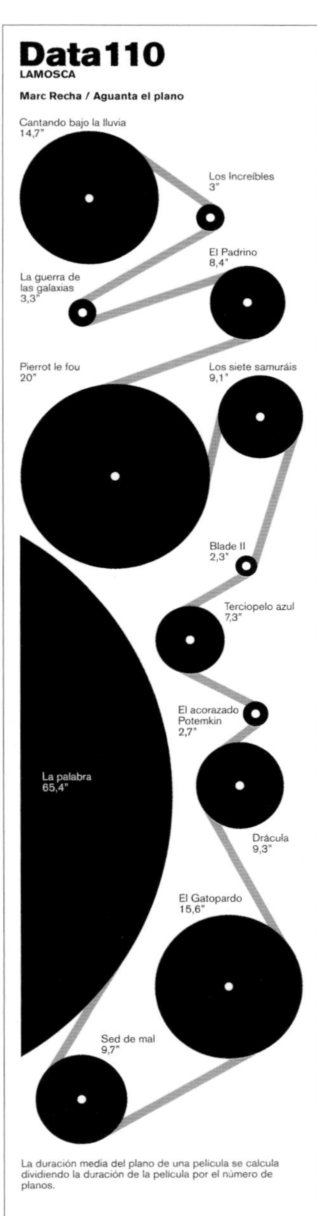
Data110
LAMOSCA
Marc Recha / Aguanta el plano
Cantando bajo la lluvia
14,7"
Los Increíbles
3"
El Padrino
8,4"
La guerra de las galaxias
3,3"
Pierrot le fou
20"
Los siete samuráis
9,1"
Blade II
2,3"
Terciopelo azul
7,3"
El acorazado Potemkin
2,7"
La palabra
65,4"
Drácula
9,3"
El Gatopardo
15,6"
Sed de mal
9,7"
La duración media del plano de una película se calcula dividiendo la duración de la película por el número de planos.
Fuentes: cinemetrics.lv

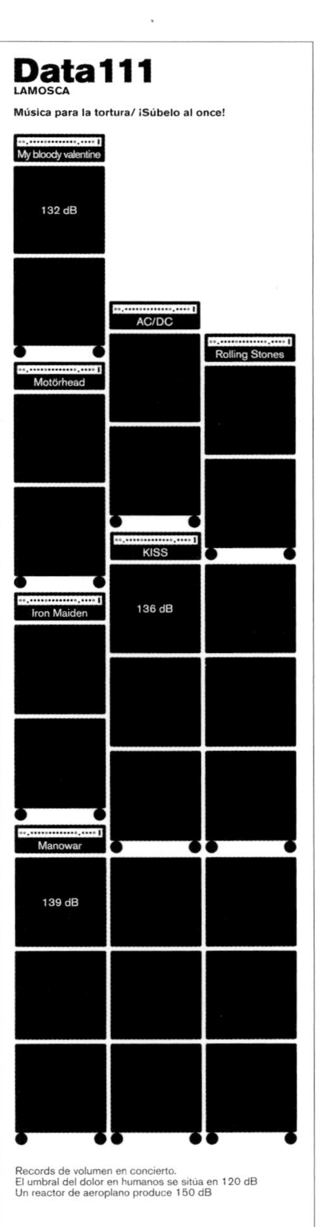
Data111
LAMOSCA
Música para la tortura/ ¡Súbelo al once!
My bloody valentine
132 dB
AC/DC
Rolling Stones
Motörhead
KISS
Iron Maiden
136 dB
Manowar
139 dB
Records de volumen en concierto.
El umbral del dolor en humanos se sitúa en 120 dB
Un reactor de aeroplano produce 150 dB
Fuentes: metalyou.com

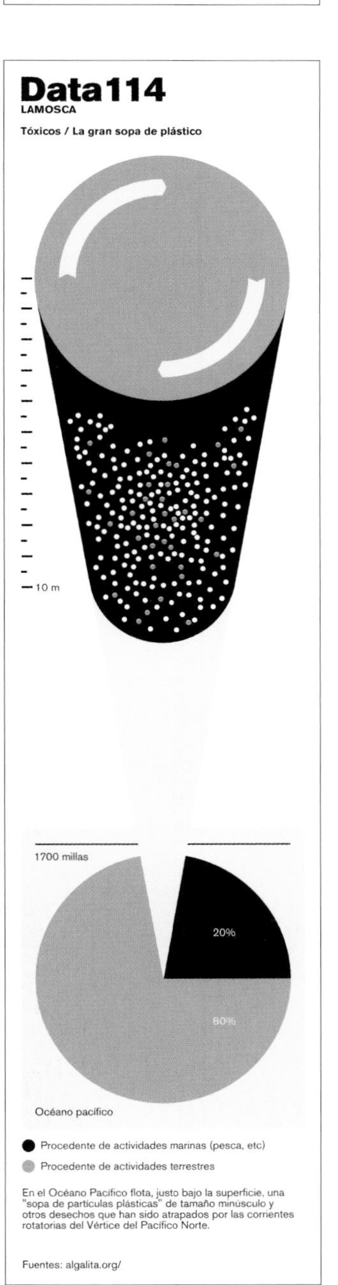
Data114
LAMOSCA
Tóxicos / La gran sopa de plástico
10 m
1700 millas
20%
80%
Océano pacífico
Procedente de actividades marinas (pesca, etc)
Procedente de actividades terrestres
En el Océano Pacífico flota, justo bajo la superficie, una "sopa de partículas plásticas" de tamaño minúsculo y otros desechos que han sido atrapados por las corrientes rotatorias del Vértice del Pacífico Norte.
Fuentes: algalita.org/

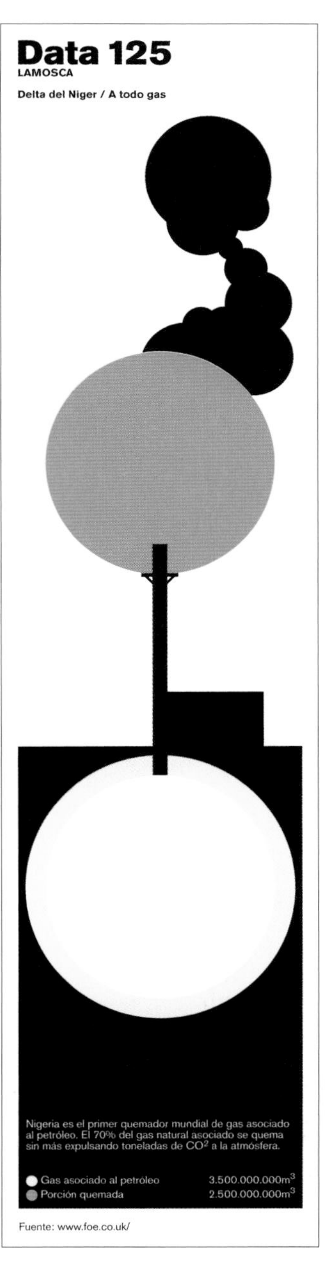
Data 125
LAMOSCA
Delta del Niger / A todo gas
Nigeria es el primer quemador mundial de gas asociado al petróleo. El 70% del gas natural asociado se quema sin más expulsando toneladas de CO2 a la atmósfera.
Gas asociado al petróleo 3.500.000.000m3
Porción quemada 2.500.000.000m3
Fuente: www.foe.co.uk/

THE DIGITAL DUMP

AS TECHNOLOGY ADVANCES AND WE BUILD MORE AND MORE DEVICES, THE NUMBER OF OBSOLETE ELECTRONICS IN NEED OF DISPOSAL IS GROWING AS WELL. THE ISSUE OF GLOBAL E-WASTE IS A MOUNTING CONCERN. AND AS THE PROBLEM PILES UP, MANY COUNTRIES ARE FINDING IT EASIEST TO JUST SHIP THEIR E-WASTE OVERSEAS.

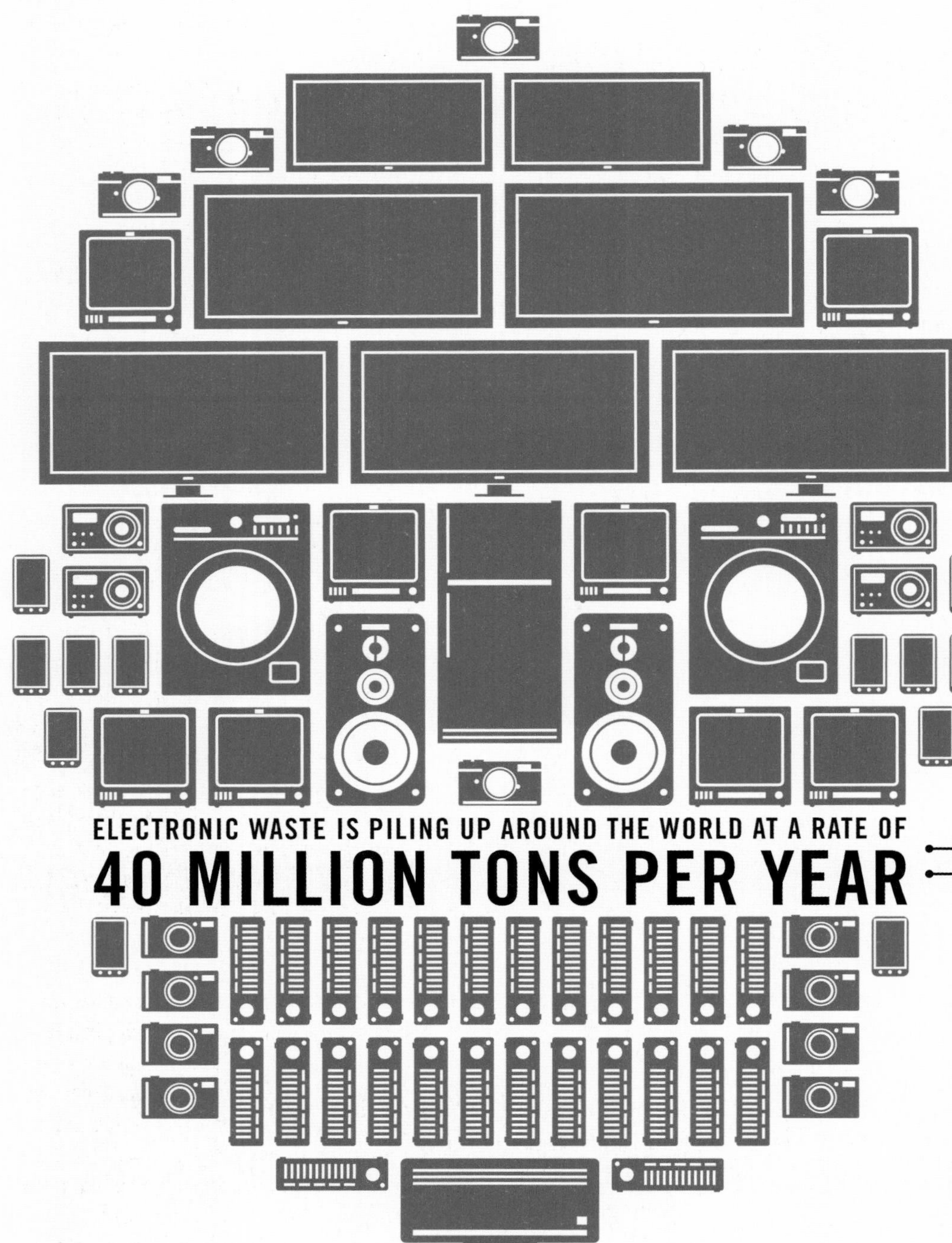

ELECTRONIC WASTE IS PILING UP AROUND THE WORLD AT A RATE OF
40 MILLION TONS PER YEAR

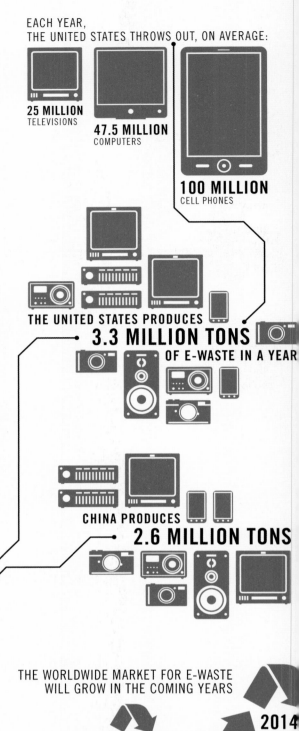

EACH YEAR,
THE UNITED STATES THROWS OUT, ON AVERAGE:

25 MILLION
TELEVISIONS

47.5 MILLION
COMPUTERS

100 MILLION
CELL PHONES

THE UNITED STATES PRODUCES
3.3 MILLION TONS
OF E-WASTE IN A YEAR

CHINA PRODUCES
2.6 MILLION TONS

THE WORLDWIDE MARKET FOR E-WASTE
WILL GROW IN THE COMING YEARS

2001
$5.7 BILLION

2014

A COLLABORATION BETWEEN GOOD AND COLUMN FIVE

Project Info: "The Growing E-Waste Situation", *GOOD*, website, 2010, USA
Data Source: CBS News; ABI Research; US EPA; Basel Action Network; Silicon Valley Toxics Coalition
Research: Brian Wolford
Design: Andrew Effendy (Column Five Media)
Art Direction: Ross Crooks

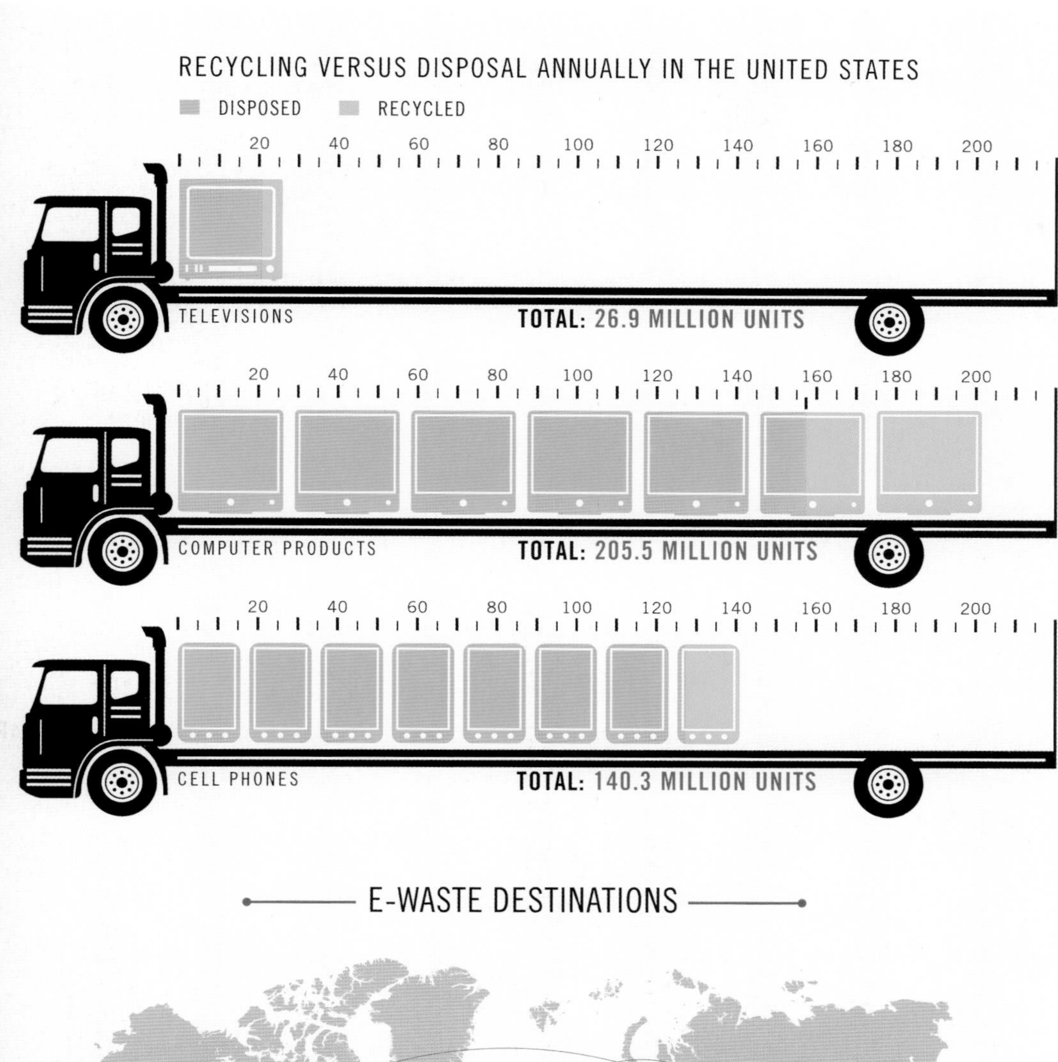

Digital Dump

Technological devices have a rather short life-span these days, but where do they go when they die? This graphic shows the amount of digital waste produced around the globe each year. Being the world's two biggest economies, China and the US are the top producers here.

The graphic combines several elements to show different aspects of the problem. The trucks to the right demonstrate how little of this waste is actually being recycled. But how do people get rid of it then? The map beneath illustrates the alternative option: a lot of waste is being shipped to countries which have more space to dump it somewhere.

Die Lebensdauer technischer Geräte ist mittlerweile recht kurz – aber wohin kommen sie nach ihrem Tod? Dieses Schaubild verdeutlicht die digitale Abfallmenge, die jährlich weltweit anfällt. Da China und die USA die zwei größten Volkswirtschaften sind, nehmen sie die Spitzenstellung ein.

Die Grafik verbindet mehrere Komponenten, um unterschiedliche Aspekte des Problems zu zeigen. Die Lastwagen rechts veranschaulichen, wie gering der Anteil an Müll ist, der tatsächlich recycelt wird. Aber wie entsorgen die Menschen ihn dann? Die Weltkarte unten verdeutlicht die Alternative: Sehr viel technischer Abfall wird in Länder verschafft, in denen ausreichend Platz zur Verfügung steht, um ihn einfach irgendwo abzuladen.

De nos jours, les appareils technologiques ont une durée de vie assez courte, mais où vont-ils après leur mort ? Ce graphique montre la quantité de déchets numériques générés chaque année sur la planète. Les deux premières économies mondiales que sont la Chine et les États-Unis apparaissent ici comme les plus gros producteurs.

Le graphique combine plusieurs éléments pour montrer les différents aspects du problème. Les camions à droite illustrent la faible quantité effectivement recyclée de ces déchets. Où finissent-ils dans ce cas ? La carte en dessous montre l'autre option : un gros volume de déchets est expédié vers les pays qui ont le plus d'espace pour les mettre en décharge.

Economic Activity

in the United States in 1998

Economic activity is calculated based on the exchange of goods and services among the approximately 500 major industrial sectors in the US economy in 1998. Data for these exchanges are collected and published by the Bureau of Economic Analysis (BEA) at the US Department of Commerce in 'make' and 'use' tables. The same tables are used to calculate the annual Gross Domestic Product (GDP).

Industrial inorganic and organic chemicals

BEA Code 270100

SALES	> $1 Bn
Industrial inorganic and or...	$ 24,657 M
Exports of goods and services	$ 19,700 M
Plastics materials and resins	$ 14,554 M
Hospitals	$ 5,495 M
Miscellaneous plastics prod...	$ 4,139 M
State and local government ...	$ 3,207 M
Paints and allied products	$ 3,163 M
Paper and paperboard mills	$ 3,044 M
(other sales > $1 Bn)	$ 25,936 M
Total sales > $1 Bn	$ 103,900 M
(other sales < $1 B)	$ 24,346 M
Total sales	$ 128,247 M
PURCHASES	> $1 Bn
Total value added	$ 41,068 M
Industrial inorganic and or...	$ 24,657 M
Imports of goods and services	$ 19,908 M
Wholesale trade	$ 5,670 M
Crude petroleum and natural...	$ 3,831 M
Electric services (utilities)	$ 2,378 M
Engineering, architectural,...	$ 1,988 M
Natural gas distribution	$ 1,937 M
(other purchases > $1 Bn)	$ 5,561 M
Total purchases > $1 Bn	$ 107,001 M
(other purchases < $1 B)	$ 20,227 M
Total purchases	$ 127,228 M

Economy Map

"Economy Map" is an interactive visualisation of the US economy. The object is to provide an interface for exploring major industrial sectors, both in terms of economic activity and in regard to their ecological impact. Economy Map displays a grid of circles, each representing an industrial sector such as motor vehicles or retail trade. The grey version visualises economic flows between sectors.

Here, circle size represents the sector's financial significance. In further visualisations, the project lists 13 different indicators for ecological impact, such as Land Use or Global Warming Potential. Circle size here represents the sector's ecological impact. Economy Map thus facilitates a synopsis of comprehensive financial and ecological data and allows the evaluation of individual sectors of the economy.

„Economy Map" ist eine interaktive Visualisierung der US-Wirtschaft. Ziel ist es, ein Interface zu entwickeln, um die größten Industriezweige in puncto ökonomischer Tätigkeit und ökologischer Bilanz miteinander vergleichen zu können. Die Grafik baut auf einem Raster von Kreisen auf, die jeweils einen Industriebereich wie etwa Kraftfahrzeuge oder den Einzelhandel repräsentieren. Die graue Version zeigt den ökonomischen Austausch zwischen den einzelnen Branchen. Dabei repräsentiert die Kreisgröße die finanzielle Bedeutung des jeweiligen Industriezweiges.

In weiteren Visualisierungen werden 13 unterschiedliche Indikatoren für Umweltbelastungen aufgeführt, wie etwa Flächenverbrauch oder Treibhauspotenzial. Hier verdeutlicht die Kreisgröße die Umweltbelastungen, die diese Branche verursacht. „Economy Map" ermöglicht somit eine Übersicht über komplexe finanzielle und ökologische Daten und erlaubt auf diese Weise die Bewertung einzelner Wirtschaftssektoren.

« Economy Map » est une représentation interactive de l'économie américaine. L'objectif est d'offrir une interface pour analyser les principaux secteurs industriels, tant en termes d'activité économique que d'impact écologique. « Economy Map » montre une grille de cercles, chacun symbolisant un secteur industriel, comme l'automobile ou le commerce de détail. La version grise montre les flux économiques entre les secteurs.

Ici, la taille des cercles est proportionnelle au poids financier du secteur. Dans les représentations suivantes, le projet relève 13 indicateurs pour l'impact écologique, comme l'utilisation des sols (« Land Use ») ou l'effet de serre (« Global Warming Potential »). La taille des cercles correspond ici à l'impact écologique du secteur. « Economy Map » fournit donc une synopsis des données financières et écologiques complètes, et permet d'évaluer les différents secteurs économiques.

Project Info: Interactive visualisation, 2010, USA
Data Source: US Dept of Commerce;
US EPA: "Sustainable Materials Management: The Road Ahead", 2009
Design: Jason Pearson (TRUTHstudio)

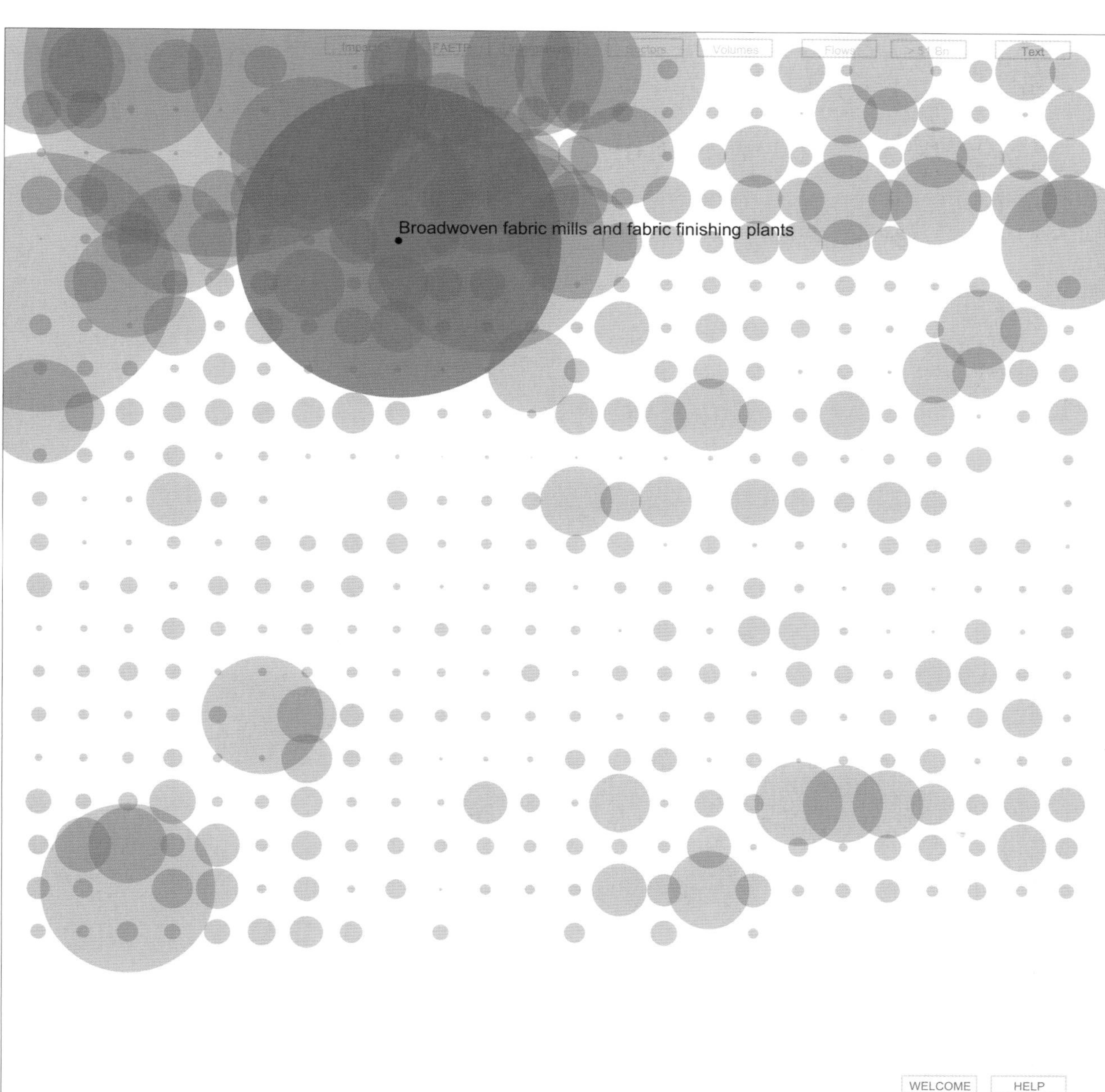

Freshwater Aquatic Ecotoxicity Potential

Fresh water aquatic ecotoxicity refers to the impact of toxic substances emitted to freshwater aquatic ecosystems.

Intermediate Impacts

(kg 1,4-dichlorobenzene eq.)

Intermediate impacts include a sector's direct impacts and the upstream impacts of its purchased goods/services. Sectors with high intermediate impacts offer opportunities for supply chain engagement.

Broadwoven fabric mills and fabric finishing plants

BEA Code 160100

IMPACTS by rank (% of total)	Direct	Intermed	Final
ADP		51 (00%)	199 (00%)
LUC		19 (00%)	77 (00%)
GWP	55 (00%)	43 (00%)	192 (00%)
ODP	234 (00%)	51 (00%)	205 (00%)
HTP	72 (00%)	46 (00%)	190 (00%)
FAETP	67 (00%)	2 (08%)	17 (01%)
MAETP	48 (00%)	44 (00%)	174 (00%)
TETP	68 (00%)	2 (07%)	18 (01%)
FSETP	56 (00%)	46 (00%)	178 (00%)
MSETP	51 (00%)	33 (00%)	168 (00%)
POCP	103 (00%)	62 (00%)	219 (00%)
AP	85 (00%)	47 (00%)	201 (00%)
EP	84 (00%)	6 (02%)	58 (00%)

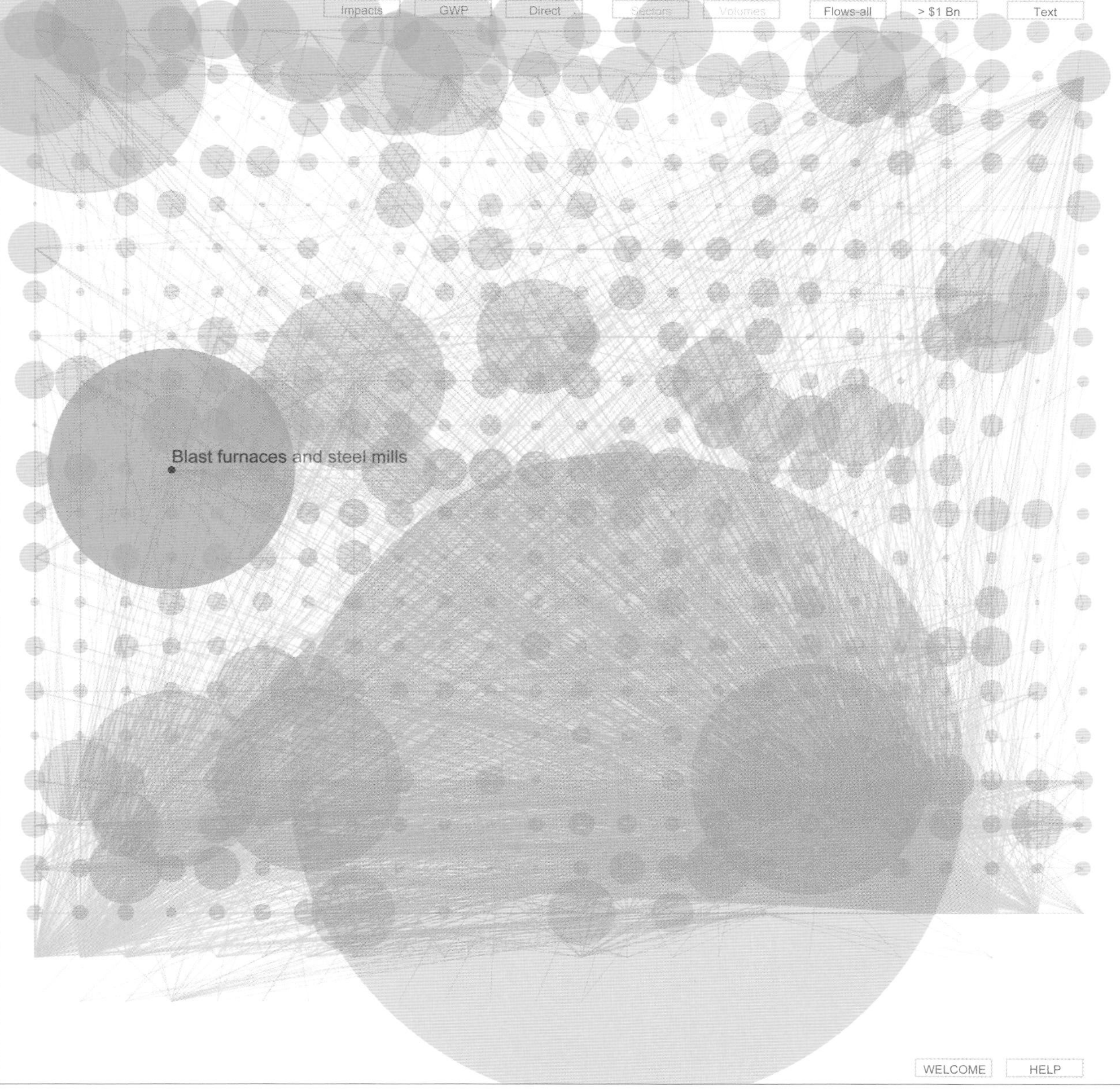

Global Warming Potential

Global Warming Potential ('greenhouse effect') is the impact of human emissions on the heat absorption of the atmosphere, which may have adverse impacts on ecosystem health, human health, and material welfare.

Direct Impacts

(kg CO2 eq.)

Direct impacts are those generated directly by the activities of a sector. Sectors with high direct impacts offer opportunities for direct regulation by government to encourage technology improvement or substitution.

Top 20 Sectors

contributing direct impacts to Global Warming Potential in 1998:

1.	Electric services (utilities)	35.01 %
2.	Crude petroleum and natural...	4.81 %
3.	Blast furnaces and steel mills	4.71 %
4.	Sanitary services, steam su...	4.33 %
5.	Air transportation	2.74 %
6.	Petroleum refining	2.60 %
7.	Trucking and courier servic...	2.55 %
8.	Feed grains	1.78 %
9.	Meat animals	1.77 %
10.	Coal	1.28 %
11.	Land Subdiviers and Develop...	1.25 %
12.	New residential 1 unit stru...	1.25 %
13.	Industrial inorganic and or...	1.10 %
14.	Paper and paperboard mills	1.01 %
15.	Fruits	0.84 %
16.	New office, industrial and ...	0.80 %
17.	Vegetables	0.72 %
18.	Cement, hydraulic	0.70 %
19.	Water transportation	0.69 %
20.	Poultry and eggs	0.67 %

Flocking Diplomats NYC

This project is based on a study which documented parking violations by international diplomats in New York City between 1998 and 2003. In a series of six posters Daniel Gross and Joris Maltha explore different ways to show patterns in the large dataset. Visualisation thus becomes a tool for analysing mass behaviour and showing recurrent trends. FD1 is a time series for every day between 1999 and 2002.

FD6 charts violations on an invisible Manhattan map with the UN headquarters placed at the centre. FD3 is a polar graph which charts addresses, days of the week and time of day, displaying the most frequent combination of these variables. Meanwhile, FD2 traces the frequency of the top 20 diplomats and their accumulated parking violations. Whenever their violation frequency rises or decreases, the graph takes a left or a right turn.

Dieses Projekt geht auf eine Studie über Parkverstöße internationaler Diplomaten in New York zwischen 1998 und 2003 zurück. Auf insgesamt sechs Postern eruieren Daniel Gross und Joris Maltha verschiedene Möglichkeiten, Muster innerhalb der großen Datensammlung zu veranschaulichen. Die Visualisierung wird damit zu einem Instrument, mit dem das Verhalten von Massen und sich wiederholende Trends analysiert werden können. FD1 ist eine Zeitreihe für jeden Tag zwischen 1999 und 2002.

FD6 zeigt Verstöße auf einem unsichtbaren Stadtplan von Manhattan, in dessen Mitte sich das UN-Hauptquartier befindet. FD3 ist ein polarer Graph, der Adressen, Wochentage und Tageszeit dokumentiert und damit die häufigsten Kombinationen dieser Variablen darstellt. FD2 wiederum verfolgt die Häufigkeit der Parkverstöße für die zwanzig auffälligsten Diplomaten. Wann immer deren Frequenz von Parkverstößen steigt oder sinkt, macht die Linie einen Knick nach links bzw. rechts.

Ce projet repose sur une étude montrant les infractions de stationnement commises par des diplomates internationaux à New York entre 1998 et 2003. Dans une série de six affiches, Daniel Gross et Joris Maltha montrent différentes façons d'extraire des schémas de l'ensemble. La visualisation devient ainsi un outil d'analyse des comportements de masse et de présentation des tendances récurrentes. FD1 est une série chronologique pour chaque jour entre 1999 et 2002.

FD6 montre les infractions sur une carte invisible de Manhattan, avec le siège des Nations Unies au centre. FD3 est un graphique polaire regroupant des adresses, des jours de la semaine et des heures du jour et montrant la combinaison la plus courante de ces variables. FD2 illustre la fréquence d'infraction des 20 premiers diplomates et les infractions de stationnement qu'ils ont accumulées. Chaque fois que la fréquence d'infraction augmente ou diminue, le graphique tourne à gauche ou à droite.

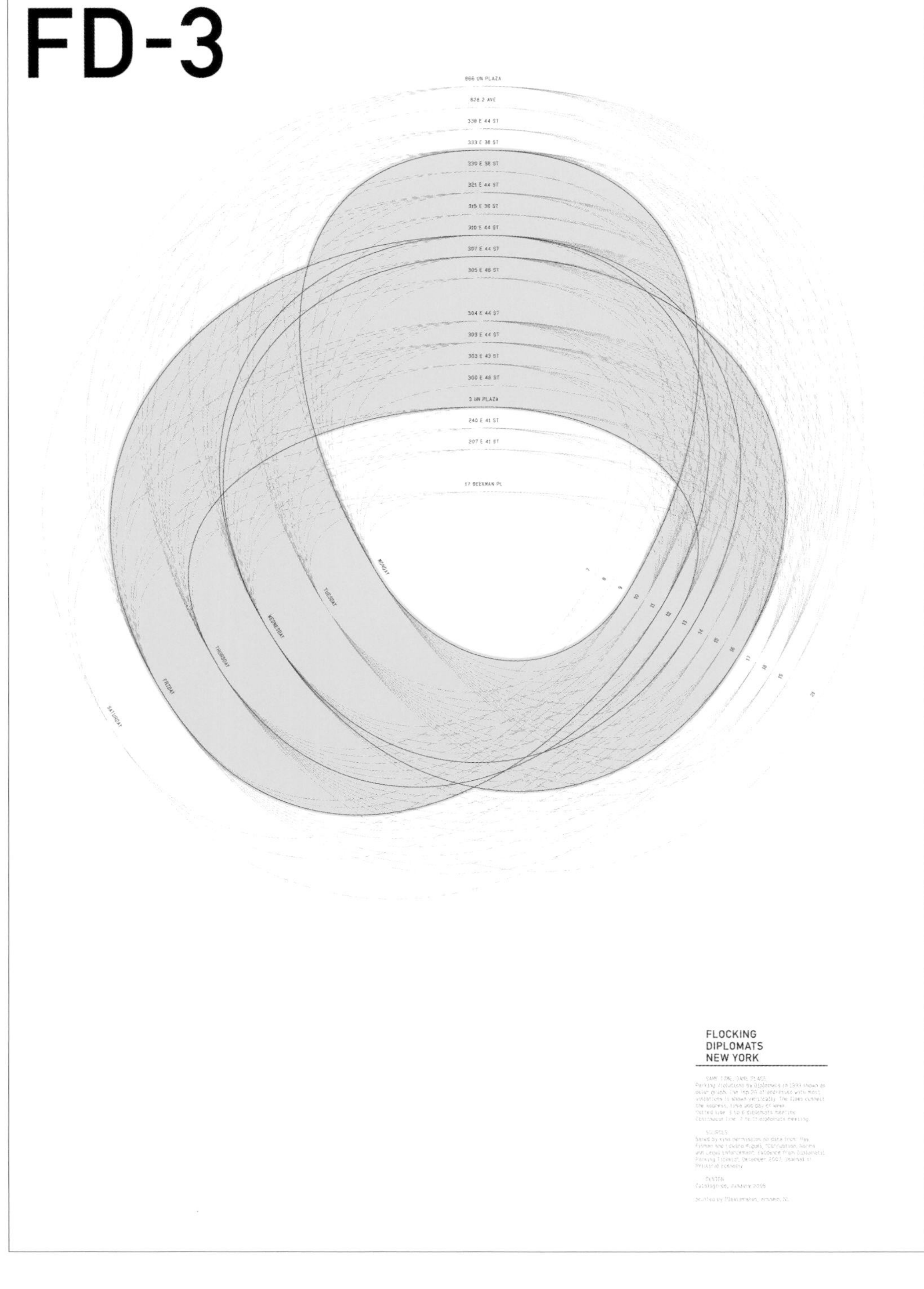

Project Info: Series of posters, 2007/2008, Netherlands
Data Source: Ray Fisman, Edward Miguel: "Corruption, Norms and Legal Enforcement: Evidence from Diplomatic Parking Tickets", Journal of Political Economy, 2007; NYC Department of Finance; NASA; Google Answers (Question-ID 782886); US Naval Observatory/Astronomical Applications Department
Design: Daniel Gross, Joris Maltha (Catalogtree)
Additional Info: Original print size 70 cm x 100 cm, part of the permanent collection of the Cooper-Hewitt Design Museum
Awards: Dutch Design Award 2008

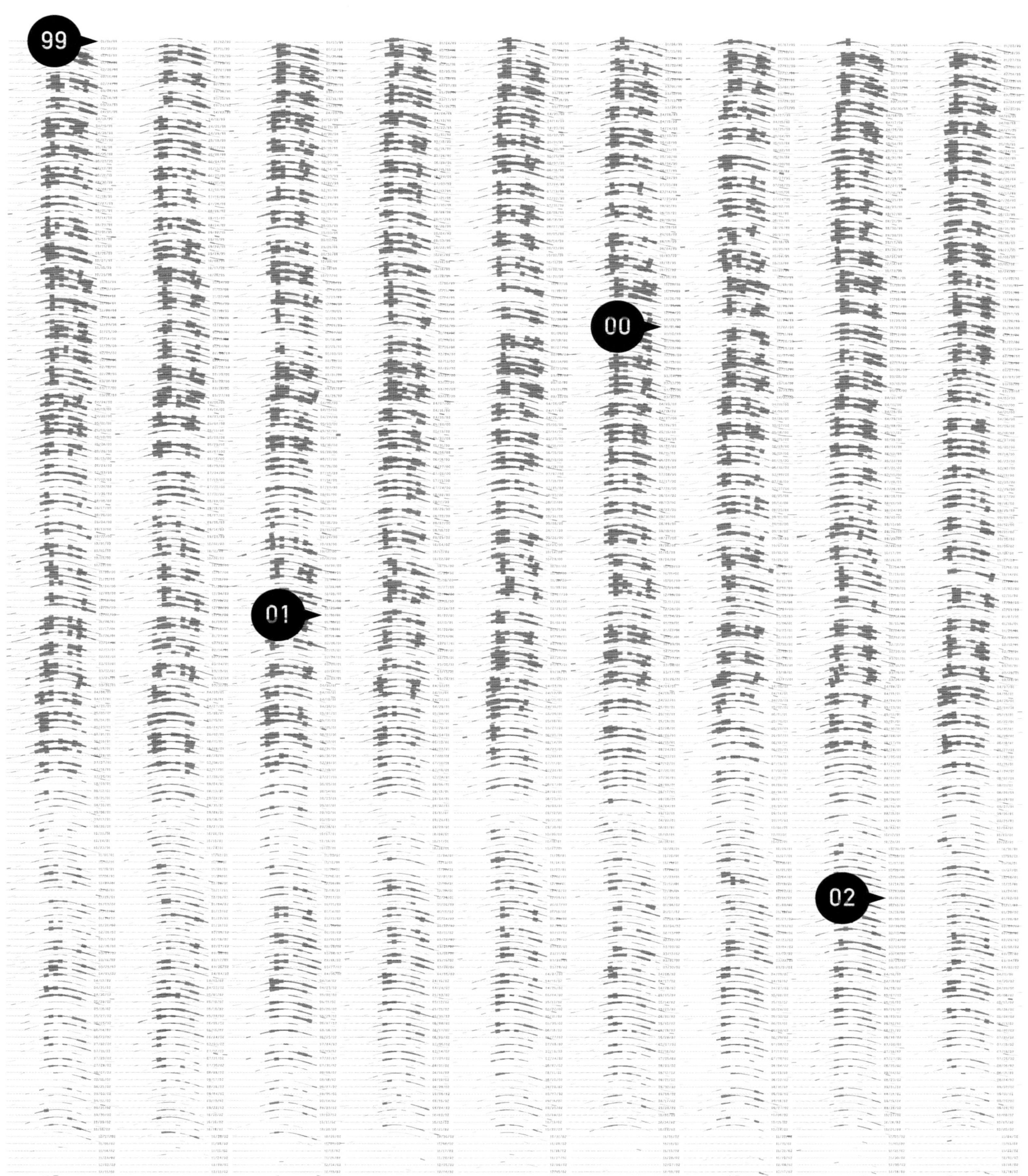

FLOCKING DIPLOMATS NYC 1999 – 2002

// VIOLATIONS/HOUR

Parking Violations by Diplomats / Hour in 1999 to 2002 in New York City. The violations are plotted in relation to the sun-position as seen from Central Park (LATITUDE 40° 47' N / LONGITUDE 73° 58' W).

ANNUAL TOTALS (YEAR: TOTAL (MAX / DATE)

1999: 42.542 (65 / 09-24) -- Security Council / Fifty-fourth Year, 4048th Meeting, Small Arms. Friday, 24 September 1999, 9.30 a.m.

2000: 38.338 (62 / 02-24) -- Security Council / Fifty-fifth Year, 4104th Meeting, The situation concerning the Democratic Republic of the Congo. Thursday, 24 February 2000, 11.30 a.m.

2001: 25.390 (56 / 02-12) -- Security Council / Fifty-sixth Year, 4276th Meeting, The situation along the borders of Guinea, Liberia, Sierra Leone. Monday, 12 February 2001, 3 p.m.

2002: 12.703 (33 / 04-23) -- Security Council / Fifty-seventh year, 4517th Meeting, The situation in Angola. Tuesday, 23 April 2002, 10.30 a.m.

SOURCES

- Based on data from: Ray Fisman and Edward Miguel, "Corruption, Norms and Legal Enforcement: Evidence from Diplomatic Parking Tickets", forthcoming, December 2007, Journal of Political Economy.
- Daylight Saving Time: http://sunearth.gsfc.nasa.gov/eclipse/SEhelp/daylightsaving.html
- Sun-position (method of calculation): http://answers.google.com/answers/threadview?id=782886 (L. Flores)
- Time of sunrise and dawn: http://aa.usno.navy.mil/data/docs/RS_OneYear.php
- New York City Department of Finance

DATA MINING / SCRIPTING / DESIGN

Catalogtree, january 2008

printed at Plaatsmaken, Arnhem

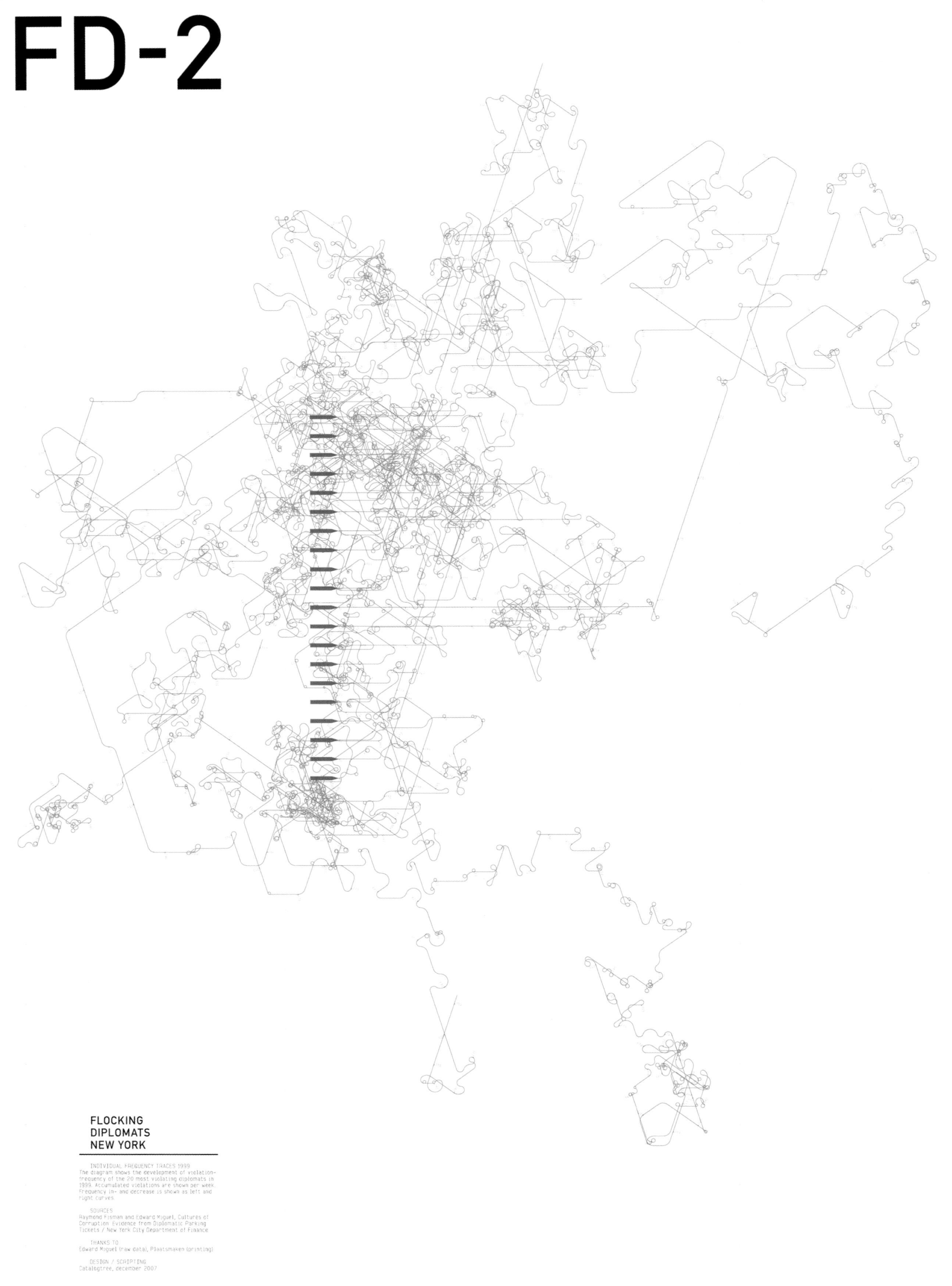
FD-2
FLOCKING
DIPLOMATS
NEW YORK
INDIVIDUAL FREQUENCY TRACES 1999
The diagram shows the development of violation-frequency of the 20 most violating diplomats in 1999. Accumulated violations are shown per week. Frequency in- and decrease is shown as left and right curves.
SOURCES
Raymond Fisman and Edward Miguel, Cultures of Corruption: Evidence from Diplomatic Parking Tickets / New York City Department of Finance
THANKS TO
Edward Miguel (raw data), Plaatsmaken (printing)
DESIGN / SCRIPTING
Catalogtree, december 2007

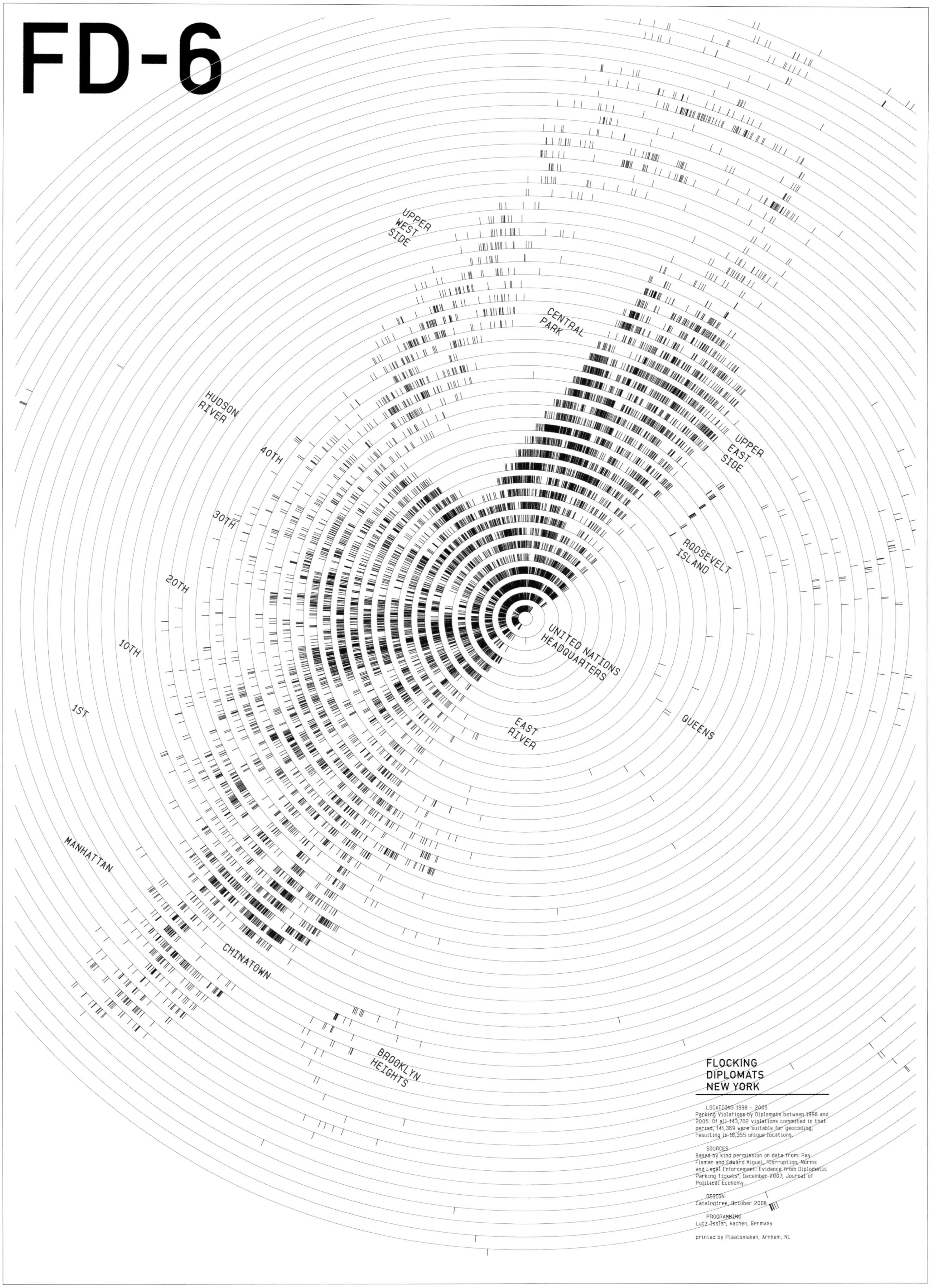
FD-6
UPPER WEST SIDE
CENTRAL PARK
HUDSON RIVER
40TH
30TH
20TH
10TH
1ST
UPPER EAST SIDE
ROOSEVELT ISLAND
UNITED NATIONS HEADQUARTERS
EAST RIVER
QUEENS
MANHATTAN
CHINATOWN
BROOKLYN HEIGHTS
FLOCKING DIPLOMATS NEW YORK
LOCATIONS 1998 - 2005
Parking Violations by Diplomats between 1998 and 2005. Of all 143,702 violations commited in that period, 141,369 were suitable for geocoding, resulting in 16,355 unique locations.
SOURCES
Based by kind permission on data from: Ray Fisman and Edward Miguel, "Corruption, Norms and Legal Enforcement: Evidence from Diplomatic Parking Tickets", December 2007, Journal of Political Economy.
DESIGN
Catalogtree, October 2008
PROGRAMMING
Lutz Issler, Aachen, Germany
printed by Plaatsmaken, Arnhem, NL

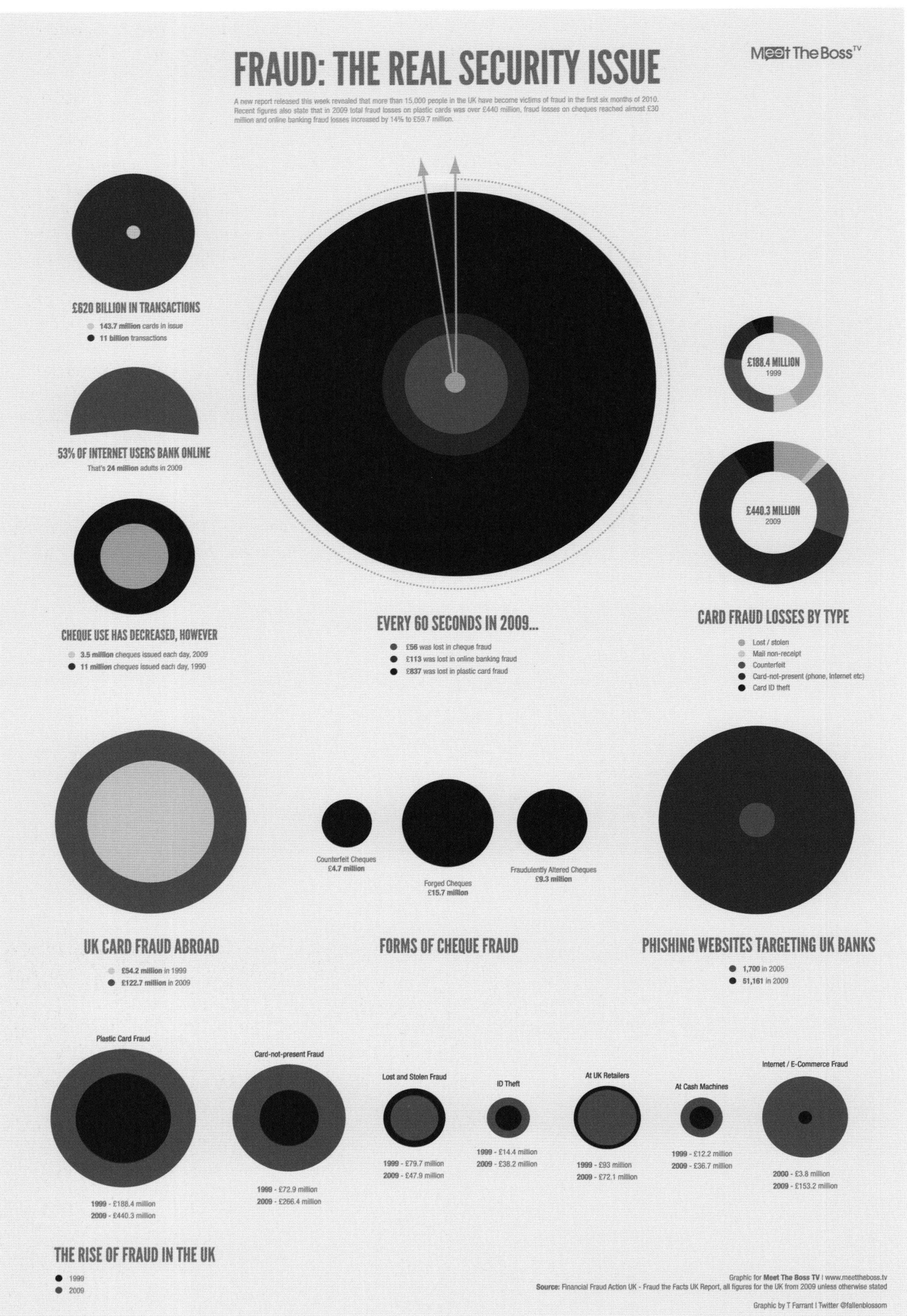

Project Info:
Meet the Boss, website, for GDS International, 2010, UK
Data Source:
Financial Fraud Action UK: "Fraud. The Facts"
Design:
Tiffany Farrant-Gonzalez

Fraud: The Real Security Issue

This infographic takes a look at fraud in the UK and how cases of fraud have substantially increased. The piece lists various types of fraud and compares figures from 1999 and 2009.

The colour coding and sizes vary for the different types of fraud. The graphic gives an overview of how the shift to online banking has facilitated a growth in fraud cases.

Diese Infografik behandelt das Thema Betrug in Großbritannien und den dramatischen Anstieg von Betrugsdelikten. Das Schaubild zeigt verschiedene Betrugsarten und vergleicht die Zahlen von 1999 und 2009.

Farbcodierung und Größenverhältnisse variieren je nach Betrugsart. Die Grafik veranschaulicht, dass mit zunehmendem Online-Banking die Zahl der Betrugsdelikte anstieg.

Cette infographie analyse les fraudes au Royaume-Uni et l'augmentation substantielle du nombre de cas. Elle répertorie les différents types de fraude et compare les chiffres de 1999 et 2009.

Le code de couleur et la taille changent selon le type de fraude. Les graphiques révèlent que l'avènement des transactions bancaires sur Internet a favorisé l'augmentation des cas de fraude.

Function

At first, these images do not appear to be diagrams, but resemble modernist artworks. Only when the four colours are further explained do they reveal their discomforting information and charged subject: they are pixellated representations of deaths in Iraq, as recorded in the WikiLeaks War Logs from 2004 to 2009. Each pixel represents one victim. The colour code refers to how victims have been categorised.

Blue = "friendly" (allied forces) casualties, green = "host nation" (Iraqi government) forces, orange = civilians, grey = enemies (insurgents). The graphic on the left shows all victims by category, the other is a time plot, representing all victims in chronological order. The categories, employed in the US army reports, blur one simple fact: that "host nation" victims, civilians and enemies are all mostly Iraqis.

Auf den ersten Blick wirken diese Darstellungen eher wie moderne Kunstwerke als wie Diagramme. Erst durch die nähere Erklärung der vier Farben offenbart sich der beunruhigende Informationsgehalt: Es sind gepixelte Darstellungen der Todesfälle im Irak, die in den WikiLeaks-Irak-Protokollen von 2004 bis 2009 dokumentiert sind. Jedes Pixel steht für ein Todesopfer, die Farbcodierung verweist auf ihre Einteilung in Kategorien.

Blau = „befreundete" Todesopfer (der Alliierten), Grün = Soldaten der irakischen Regierungskräfte, Orange = Zivilisten, Grau = Feinde (Aufständische). Die Grafik links zeigt alle Opfer nach Kategorie, die andere stellt die Opfer in chronologischer Abfolge während des gesamten Zeitraums dar. Die in den Berichten der US-Armee verwendeten Kategorien verschleiern einen grundlegenden Umstand, nämlich dass die Opfer der irakischen Regierungskräfte, die Zivilisten wie auch die Feinde, allesamt vorwiegend Iraker sind.

À première vue, ces images ressemblent moins à des diagrammes qu'à des œuvres modernistes. C'est seulement quand les quatre couleurs sont expliquées qu'elles dévoilent des informations désagréables et un sujet grave : ce sont des représentations pixélisées des morts en Iraq, telles qu'enregistrées dans les journaux de guerre de WikiLeaks entre 2004 et 2009. Chaque pixel correspond à une victime. Le code de couleur indique la catégorie des victimes.

Bleu = victimes « amies » (forces alliées), vert = forces de la « nation hôte » (gouvernement irakien), orange = civils, gris = ennemis (insurgés). L'image de gauche montre toutes les victimes par catégorie, l'autre est un tracé temporel illustrant l'ensemble des victimes dans l'ordre chronologique. Les catégories employées dans les rapports de l'armée américaine omettent un fait : les victimes de la « nation hôte », les civils et les ennemis sont quasiment tous des Irakiens.

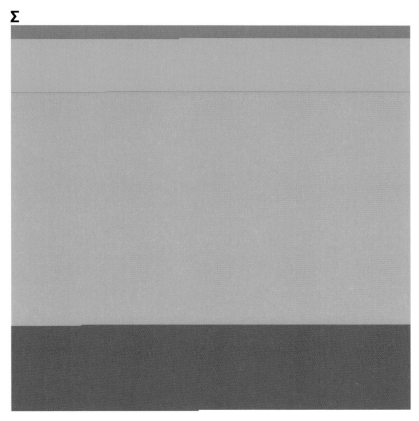

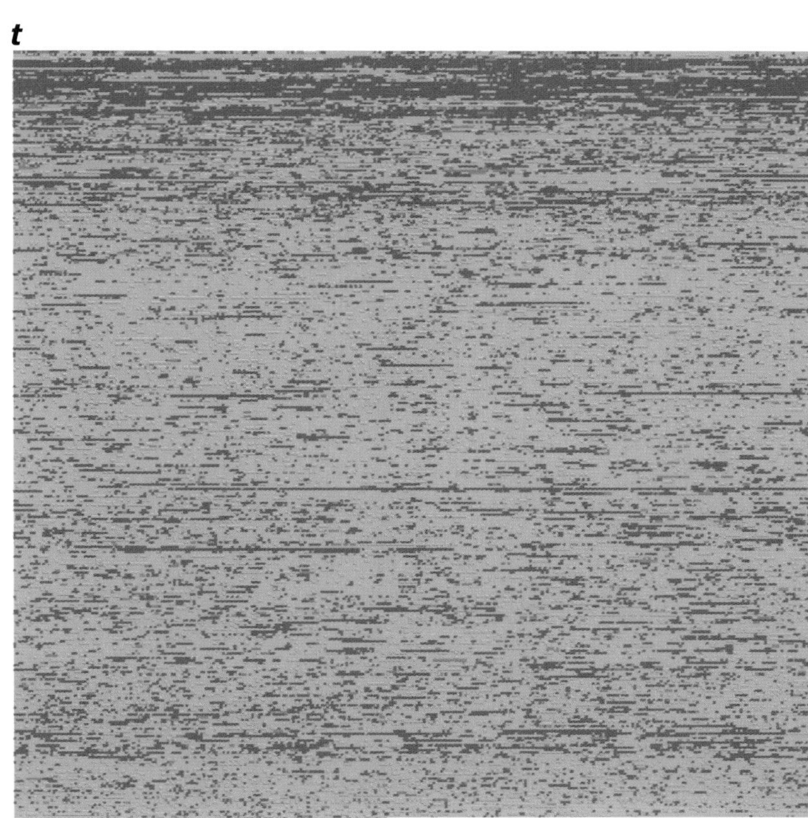

Project Info: Website, 2010, Canada
Data Source: Wikileaks Iraq War Logs (analysed version from *The Guardian* Datastore)
Design: Kamel Makhloufi

G2 Information Spreads

In 2005/2006, Tilly Northedge and Peter Grundy designed a weekly series of rich information spreads for *The Guardian*'s supplement G2. Each week, one topic was chosen and structured into several bite-size parts, each of which was numbered and given a concise question as a heading.

The central image always presented a symbol of the general topic and provided spaces for presenting the individual statistics, using as few words as possible. The briefings were usually confined to the actual words that would be printed, making it a creative challenge to conceptualise each piece.

2005/06 gestalteten Tilly Northedge und Peter Grundy für die G2-Beilage des *Guardian* eine wöchentlich erscheinende Serie opulenter Doppelseiten. Jede Woche ging es um ein Thema, das in leicht verständliche Blöcke untergliedert und jeweils nummeriert mit einer prägnanten Frage überschrieben wurde.

Als Hauptmotiv diente jeweils ein Symbol, das das Thema repräsentierte und genügend Raum bot, um die einzelnen Statistiken darzustellen, wobei mit möglichst wenig Text gearbeitet wurde. Die Briefings beschränkten sich im Allgemeinen auf den spärlichen Text, der später gedruckt wurde. Das machte es zu einer kreativen Herausforderung, eine solche Grafik lediglich aufgrund von Zahlen und Wörtern zu konzipieren.

En 2005/2006, Tilly Northedge et Peter Grundy ont conçu une série hebdomadaire d'information pour le supplément G2 de *The Guardian*. Chaque semaine, un sujet était choisi et structuré en plusieurs parties, chacune numérotée et avec une question concrète en en-tête.

L'image centrale présentait toujours un symbole du sujet général et accueillait des statistiques avec le moins de mots possible. Les instructions relatives aux projets se limitaient en général aux mots qui allaient être imprimés, ce qui supposait un véritable défi créatif pour chaque œuvre.

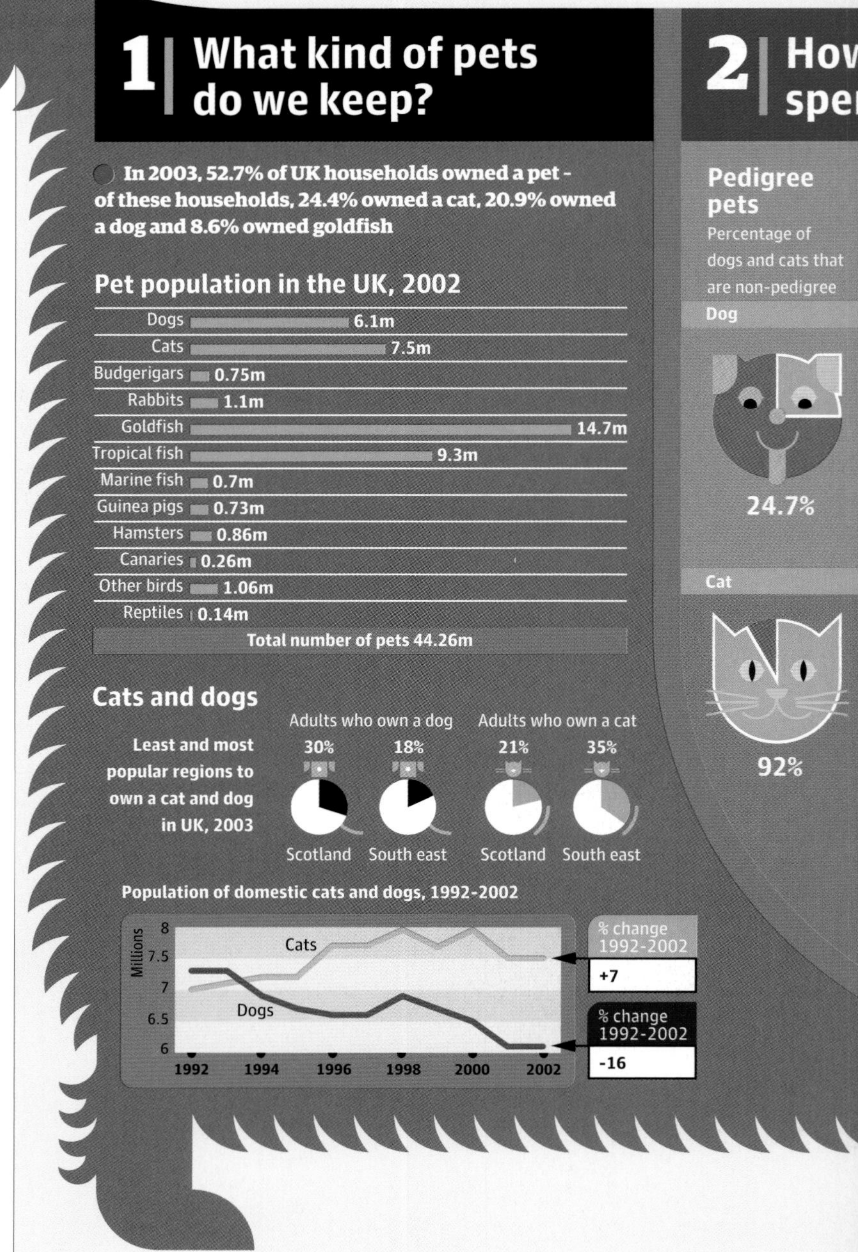

Each week the Guardian's Leo Hickman and award-winning information design agency Grundy Northedge collaborate on a unique in-depth graphic providing an instant briefing on one of the issues of the week

The g2 graphic

Pets

The 103rd Crufts show gets under way on
probably Britain's biggest pet love-in of th
just how many dogs, cats guines pigs and
do we keep? And how much do they reall

1 | What kind of pets do we keep?

In 2003, 52.7% of UK households owned a pet - of these households, 24.4% owned a cat, 20.9% owned a dog and 8.6% owned goldfish

Pet population in the UK, 2002

Dogs	6.1m
Cats	7.5m
Budgerigars	0.75m
Rabbits	1.1m
Goldfish	14.7m
Tropical fish	9.3m
Marine fish	0.7m
Guinea pigs	0.73m
Hamsters	0.86m
Canaries	0.26m
Other birds	1.06m
Reptiles	0.14m
Total number of pets 44.26m	

Cats and dogs

Least and most popular regions to own a cat and dog in UK, 2003

	Adults who own a dog		Adults who own a cat	
	30%	18%	21%	35%
	Scotland	South east	Scotland	South east

Population of domestic cats and dogs, 1992-2002

2 | How ... sper

Pedigree pets

Percentage of dogs and cats that are non-pedigree

Dog

24.7%

Cat

92%

16 The Guardian 07.03.06

Project Info: *The Guardian*, newspaper article, 2005–2006, UK
Data Source: Mintel Report; Royal Society for the Prevention of Cruelty to Animals; Kennel Club; Churchill Insurance; PFMA; RSPCA; IFAW; Guinness World of Records
Research: Lucy Clouting, Saleem Vaillancourt
Design: Peter Grundy, Tilly Northedge (Grundini)

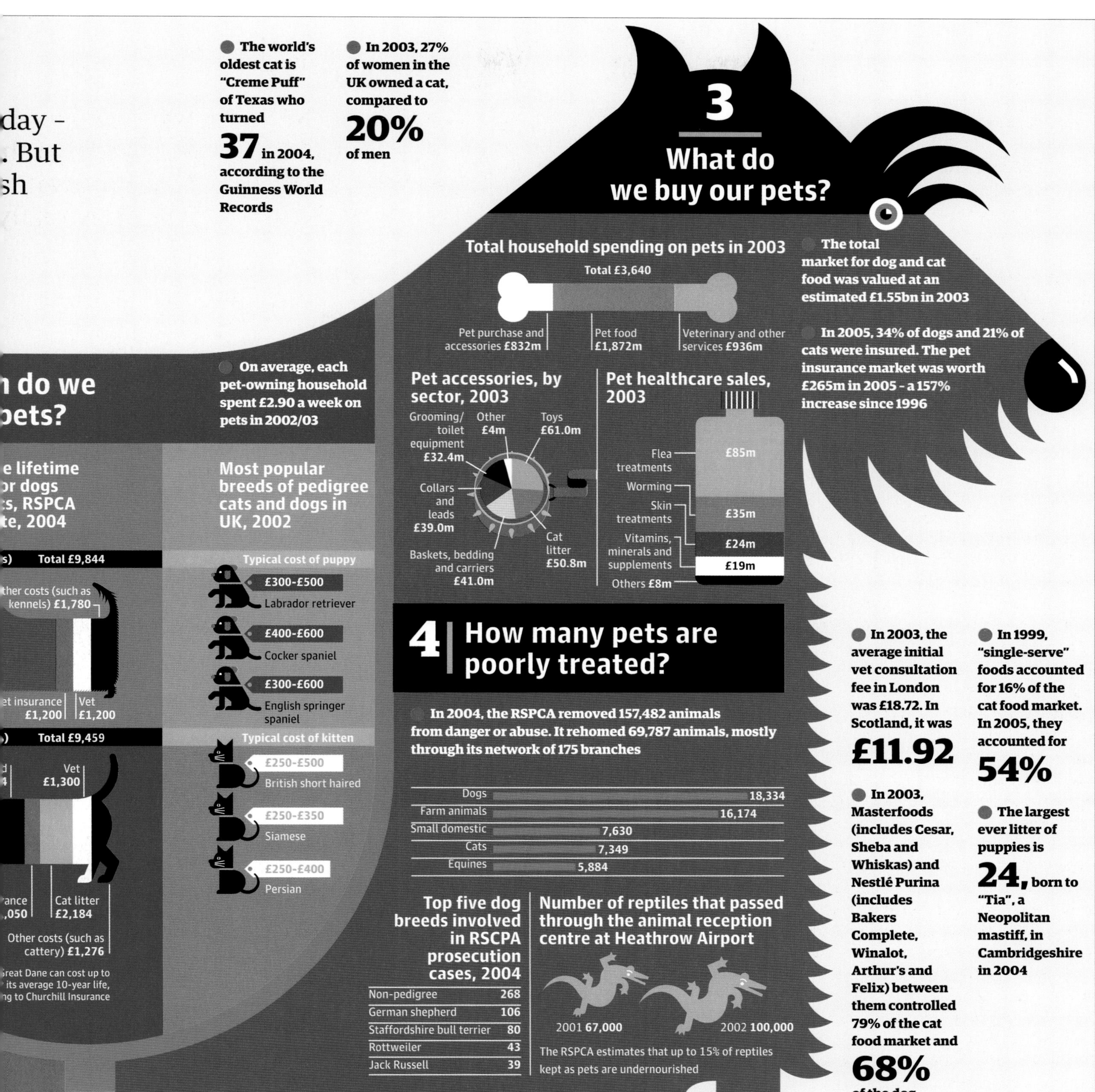

day –
. But
sh
The world's oldest cat is "Creme Puff" of Texas who turned 37 in 2004, according to the Guinness World Records
In 2003, 27% of women in the UK owned a cat, compared to 20% of men
3
What do we buy our pets?
Total household spending on pets in 2003
Total £3,640
Pet purchase and accessories £832m
Pet food £1,872m
Veterinary and other services £936m
The total market for dog and cat food was valued at an estimated £1.55bn in 2003
In 2005, 34% of dogs and 21% of cats were insured. The pet insurance market was worth £265m in 2005 – a 157% increase since 1996
n do we
pets?
On average, each pet-owning household spent £2.90 a week on pets in 2002/03
Pet accessories, by sector, 2003
Grooming/toilet equipment £32.4m
Other £4m
Toys £61.0m
Collars and leads £39.0m
Baskets, bedding and carriers £41.0m
Cat litter £50.8m
Pet healthcare sales, 2003
Flea treatments
Worming
Skin treatments
Vitamins, minerals and supplements
Others £8m
£85m
£35m
£24m
£19m
e lifetime
or dogs
s, RSPCA
te, 2004
Most popular breeds of pedigree cats and dogs in UK, 2002
Typical cost of puppy
£300-£500
Labrador retriever
£400-£600
Cocker spaniel
£300-£600
English springer spaniel
Typical cost of kitten
£250-£500
British short haired
£250-£350
Siamese
£250-£400
Persian
s) Total £9,844
ther costs (such as kennels) £1,780
et insurance £1,200
Vet £1,200
s) Total £9,459
Vet £1,300
rance ,050
Cat litter £2,184
Other costs (such as cattery) £1,276
Great Dane can cost up to its average 10-year life, ng to Churchill Insurance
4 How many pets are poorly treated?
In 2004, the RSPCA removed 157,482 animals from danger or abuse. It rehomed 69,787 animals, mostly through its network of 175 branches
Dogs 18,334
Farm animals 16,174
Small domestic 7,630
Cats 7,349
Equines 5,884
In 2003, the average initial vet consultation fee in London was £18.72. In Scotland, it was £11.92
In 1999, "single-serve" foods accounted for 16% of the cat food market. In 2005, they accounted for 54%
In 2003, Masterfoods (includes Cesar, Sheba and Whiskas) and Nestlé Purina (includes Bakers Complete, Winalot, Arthur's and Felix) between them controlled 79% of the cat food market and 68% of the dog food market
The largest ever litter of puppies is 24, born to "Tia", a Neopolitan mastiff, in Cambridgeshire in 2004
Top five dog breeds involved in RSCPA prosecution cases, 2004
Non-pedigree 268
German shepherd 106
Staffordshire bull terrier 80
Rottweiler 43
Jack Russell 39
Number of reptiles that passed through the animal reception centre at Heathrow Airport
2001 67,000
2002 100,000
The RSPCA estimates that up to 15% of reptiles kept as pets are undernourished

Additional research by Lucy Clouting and Saleem Vaillancourt. Sources: 1) Mintel Report: Cat and Dog Food, May 2004; 2) Royal Society for the Prevention of Cruelty ro Animals, Kennel Club, Churchill Insurance; 3) Mintel, Pet Food Manufacturers' Association; 4) RSPCA, Internaltional Fund for Animal Welfare: also, Guinness World of Records

The Guardian 07.03.06 **17**

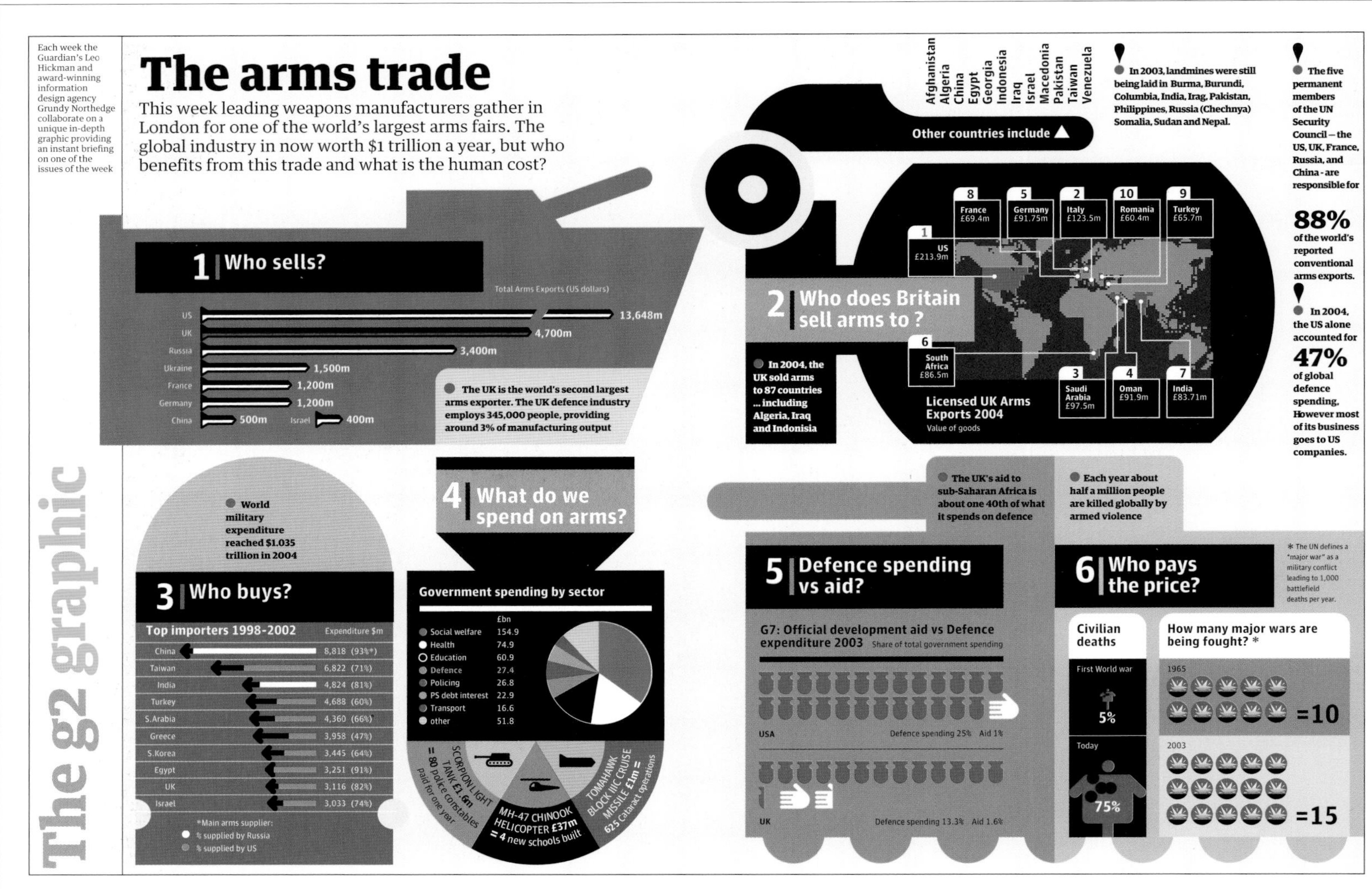

Each week the Guardian's Leo Hickman and award-winning information design agency Grundy Northedge collaborate on a unique in-depth graphic providing an instant briefing on one of the issues of the week
The arms trade
This week leading weapons manufacturers gather in London for one of the world's largest arms fairs. The global industry in now worth $1 trillion a year, but who benefits from this trade and what is the human cost?
1 Who sells?
Total Arms Exports (US dollars)
US 13,648m
UK 4,700m
Russia 3,400m
Ukraine 1,500m
France 1,200m
Germany 1,200m
China 500m
Israel 400m
The UK is the world's second largest arms exporter. The UK defence industry employs 345,000 people, providing around 3% of manufacturing output
Afghanistan Algeria China Egypt Georgia Indonesia Iraq Israel Macedonia Pakistan Taiwan Venezuela
Other countries include
In 2003, landmines were still being laid in Burma, Burundi, Columbia, India, Iraq, Pakistan, Philippines, Russia (Chechnya) Somalia, Sudan and Nepal.
The five permanent members of the UN Security Council – the US, UK, France, Russia, and China - are responsible for
88% of the world's reported conventional arms exports.
In 2004, the US alone accounted for
47% of global defence spending. However most of its business goes to US companies.
2 Who does Britain sell arms to ?
1 US £213.9m
8 France £69.4m
5 Germany £91.75m
2 Italy £123.5m
10 Romania £60.4m
9 Turkey £65.7m
6 South Africa £86.5m
3 Saudi Arabia £97.5m
4 Oman £91.9m
7 India £83.71m
Licensed UK Arms Exports 2004
Value of goods
In 2004, the UK sold arms to 87 countries ... including Algeria, Iraq and Indonisia
The UK's aid to sub-Saharan Africa is about one 40th of what it spends on defence
Each year about half a million people are killed globally by armed violence
World military expenditure reached $1.035 trillion in 2004
3 Who buys?
Top importers 1998-2002
Expenditure $m
China 8,818 (93%*)
Taiwan 6,822 (71%)
India 4,824 (81%)
Turkey 4,688 (60%)
S.Arabia 4,360 (66%)
Greece 3,958 (47%)
S.Korea 3,445 (64%)
Egypt 3,251 (91%)
UK 3,116 (82%)
Israel 3,033 (74%)
*Main arms supplier:
% supplied by Russia
% supplied by US
4 What do we spend on arms?
Government spending by sector
£bn
Social welfare 154.9
Health 74.9
Education 60.9
Defence 27.4
Policing 26.8
PS debt interest 22.9
Transport 16.6
other 51.8
SCORPION LIGHT TANK £1.6m = 80 police constables paid for one year
MH-47 CHINOOK HELICOPTER £37m = 4 new schools built
TOMAHAWK BLOCK IIIC CRUISE MISSILE £1m = 625 Cataract operations
5 Defence spending vs aid?
G7: Official development aid vs Defence expenditure 2003
Share of total government spending
USA Defence spending 25% Aid 1%
UK Defence spending 13.3% Aid 1.6%
6 Who pays the price?
* The UN defines a "major war" as a military conflict leading to 1,000 battlefield deaths per year.
Civilian deaths
First World war 5%
Today 75%
How many major wars are being fought? *
1965 =10
2003 =15
The g2 graphic

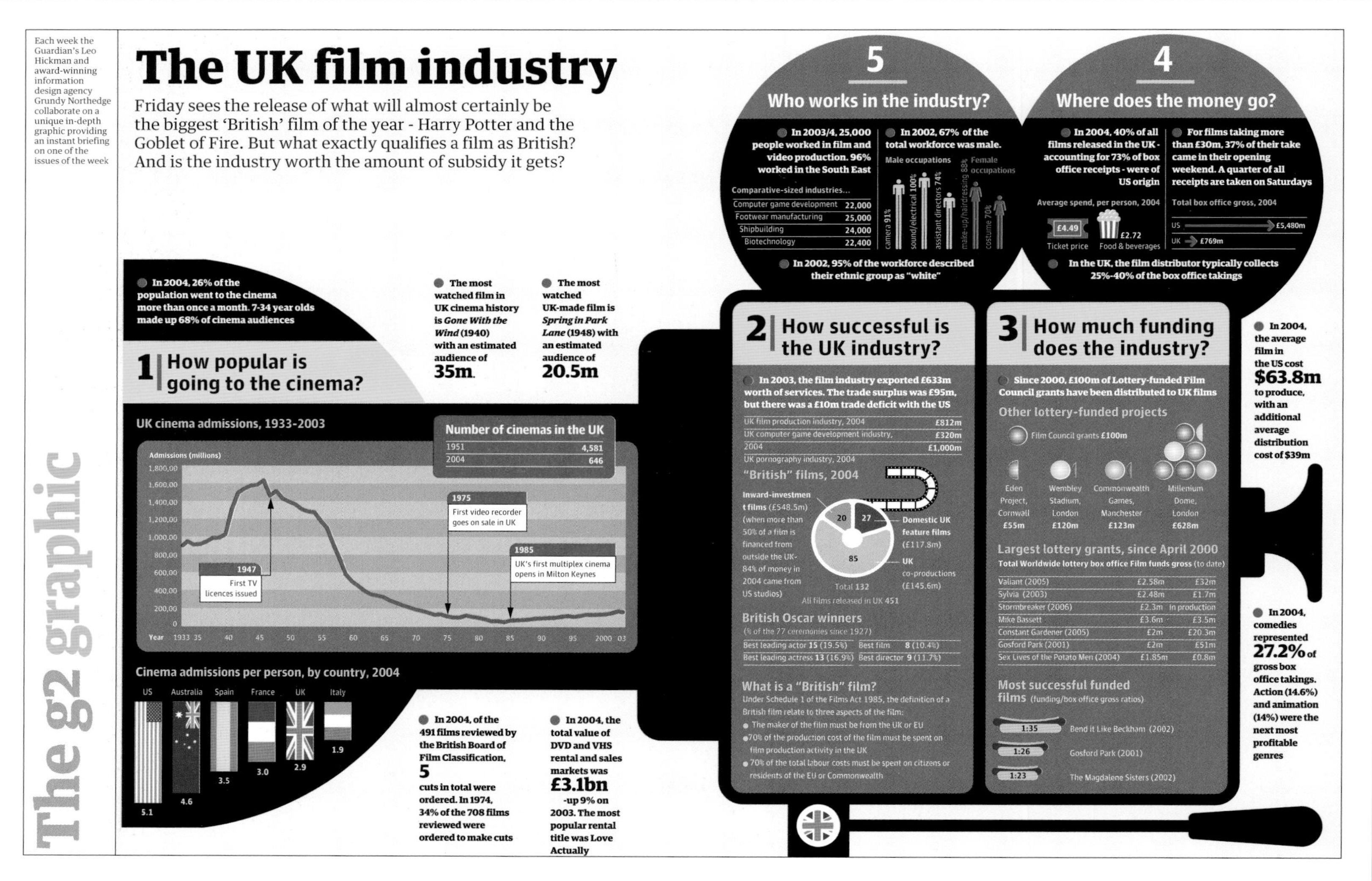

Each week the Guardian's Leo Hickman and award-winning information design agency Grundy Northedge collaborate on a unique in-depth graphic providing an instant briefing on one of the issues of the week
The UK film industry
Friday sees the release of what will almost certainly be the biggest 'British' film of the year - Harry Potter and the Goblet of Fire. But what exactly qualifies a film as British? And is the industry worth the amount of subsidy it gets?
5 Who works in the industry?
In 2003/4, 25,000 people worked in film and video production. 96% worked in the South East
In 2002, 67% of the total workforce was male.
Male occupations
Female occupations
Comparative-sized industries...
Computer game development 22,000
Footwear manufacturing 25,000
Shipbuilding 24,000
Biotechnology 22,400
camera 91%
sound/electrical 100%
assistant directors 74%
make-up/hairdressing 88%
costume 70%
In 2002, 95% of the workforce described their ethnic group as "white"
4 Where does the money go?
In 2004, 40% of all films released in the UK - accounting for 73% of box office receipts - were of US origin
For films taking more than £30m, 37% of their take came in their opening weekend. A quarter of all receipts are taken on Saturdays
Average spend, per person, 2004
£4.49 Ticket price
£2.72 Food & beverages
Total box office gross, 2004
US £5,480m
UK £769m
In the UK, the film distributor typically collects 25%-40% of the box office takings
In 2004, 26% of the population went to the cinema more than once a month. 7-34 year olds made up 68% of cinema audiences
The most watched film in UK cinema history is Gone With the Wind (1940) with an estimated audience of 35m.
The most watched UK-made film is Spring in Park Lane (1948) with an estimated audience of 20.5m
1 How popular is going to the cinema?
UK cinema admissions, 1933-2003
Number of cinemas in the UK
1951 4,581
2004 646
Admissions (millions)
1947 First TV licences issued
1975 First video recorder goes on sale in UK
1985 UK's first multiplex cinema opens in Milton Keynes
Cinema admissions per person, by country, 2004
US 5.1
Australia 4.6
Spain 3.5
France 3.0
UK 2.9
Italy 1.9
In 2004, of the 491 films reviewed by the British Board of Film Classification, 5 cuts in total were ordered. In 1974, 34% of the 708 films reviewed were ordered to make cuts
In 2004, the total value of DVD and VHS rental and sales markets was £3.1bn -up 9% on 2003. The most popular rental title was Love Actually
2 How successful is the UK industry?
In 2003, the film industry exported £633m worth of services. The trade surplus was £95m, but there was a £10m trade deficit with the US
UK film production industry, 2004 £812m
UK computer game development industry, 2004 £320m
UK pornography industry, 2004 £1,000m
"British" films, 2004
Inward-investment films (£548.5m)
Domestic UK feature films (£117.8m)
UK co-productions (£145.6m)
Total 132
All films released in UK 451
British Oscar winners
(% of the 77 ceremonies since 1927)
Best leading actor 15 (19.5%)
Best film 8 (10.4%)
Best leading actress 13 (16.9%)
Best director 9 (11.7%)
What is a "British" film?
Under Schedule 1 of the Films Act 1985, the definition of a British film relate to three aspects of the film:
The maker of the film must be from the UK or EU
70% of the production cost of the film must be spent on film production activity in the UK
70% of the total labour costs must be spent on citizens or residents of the EU or Commonwealth
3 How much funding does the industry?
Since 2000, £100m of Lottery-funded Film Council grants have been distributed to UK films
Other lottery-funded projects
Film Council grants £100m
Eden Project, Cornwall £55m
Wembley Stadium, London £120m
Commonwealth Games, Manchester £123m
Millenium Dome, London £628m
Largest lottery grants, since April 2000
Total Worldwide lottery box office Film funds gross (to date)
Valiant (2005) £2.58m £32m
Sylvia (2003) £2.48m £1.7m
Stormbreaker (2006) £2.3m In production
Mike Bassett £3.6m £3.5m
Constant Gardener (2005) £2m £20.3m
Gosford Park (2001) £2m £51m
Sex Lives of the Potato Men (2004) £1.85m £0.8m
Most successful funded films (funding/box office gross ratios)
1:35 Bend it Like Beckham (2002)
1:26 Gosford Park (2001)
1:23 The Magdalene Sisters (2002)
In 2004, the average film in the US cost $63.8m to produce, with an additional average distribution cost of $39m
In 2004, comedies represented 27.2% of gross box office takings. Action (14.6%) and animation (14%) were the next most profitable genres
The g2 graphic

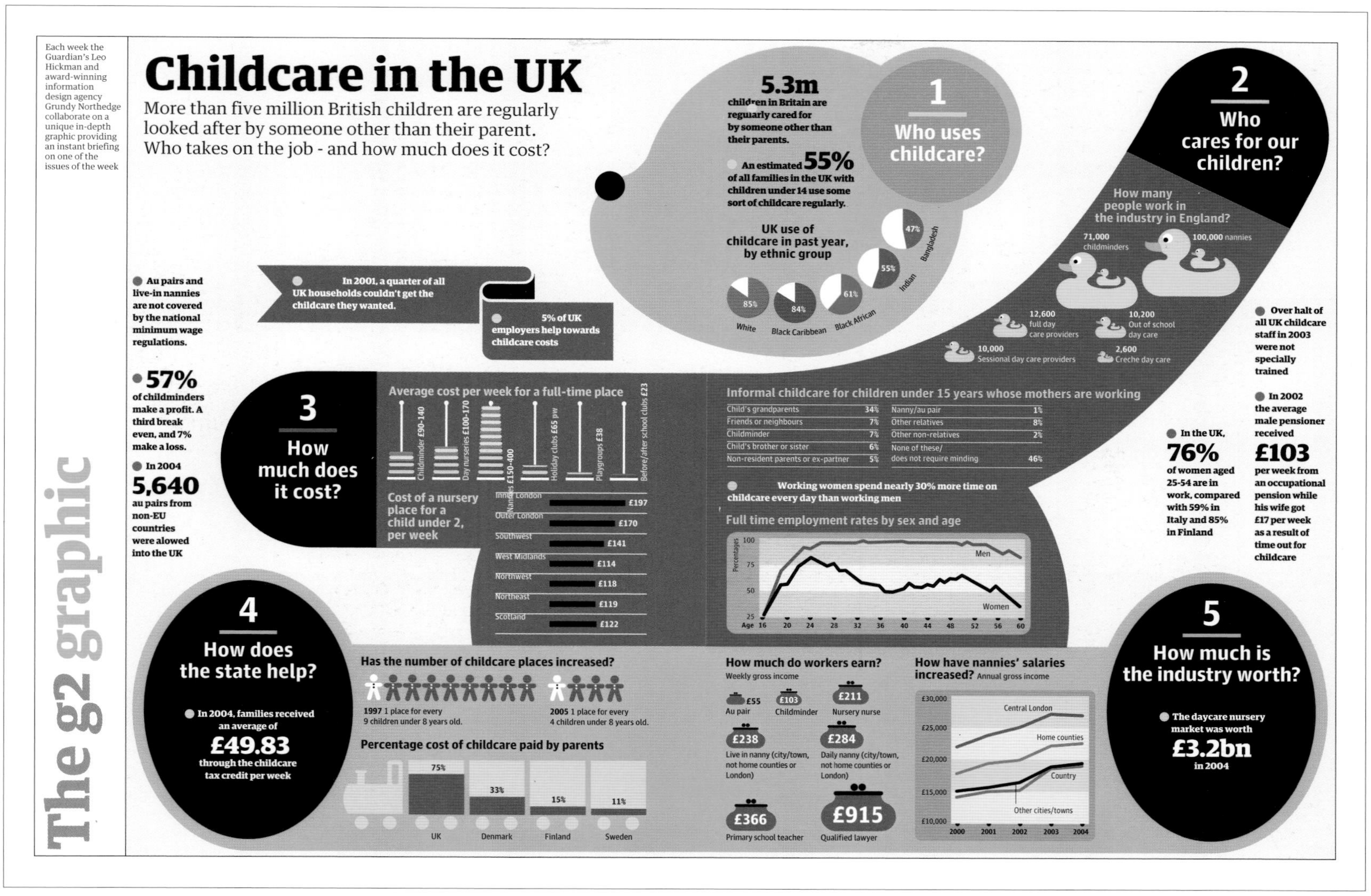

Each week the Guardian's Leo Hickman and award-winning information design agency Grundy Northedge collaborate on a unique in-depth graphic providing an instant briefing on one of the issues of the week

The g2 graphic

Childcare in the UK

More than five million British children are regularly looked after by someone other than their parent. Who takes on the job - and how much does it cost?

1 Who uses childcare?

5.3m children in Britain are regularly cared for by someone other than their parents.

An estimated **55%** of all families in the UK with children under 14 use some sort of childcare regularly.

UK use of childcare in past year, by ethnic group

White 85% · Black Caribbean 84% · Black African 61% · Indian 55% · Bangladeshi 47%

In 2001, a quarter of all UK households couldn't get the childcare they wanted.

5% of UK employers help towards childcare costs

Au pairs and live-in nannies are not covered by the national minimum wage regulations.

57% of childminders make a profit. A third break even, and 7% make a loss.

In 2004 **5,640** au pairs from non-EU countries were alowed into the UK

2 Who cares for our children?

How many people work in the industry in England?

- 71,000 childminders
- 100,000 nannies
- 12,600 full day care providers
- 10,200 Out of school day care
- 10,000 Sessional day care providers
- 2,600 Creche day care

Over halt of all UK childcare staff in 2003 were not specially trained

In 2002 the average male pensioner received **£103** per week from an occupational pension while his wife got £17 per week as a result of time out for childcare

In the UK, **76%** of women aged 25-54 are in work, compared with 59% in Italy and 85% in Finland

Informal childcare for children under 15 years whose mothers are working

Child's grandparents	34%
Friends or neighbours	7%
Childminder	7%
Child's brother or sister	6%
Non-resident parents or ex-partner	5%
Nanny/au pair	1%
Other relatives	8%
Other non-relatives	2%
None of these/ does not require minding	46%

Working women spend nearly 30% more time on childcare every day than working men

Full time employment rates by sex and age

3 How much does it cost?

Average cost per week for a full-time place

Childminder £90-140 · Day nurseries £100-170 · Nannies £150-400 · Holiday clubs £65 pw · Playgroups £38 · Before/after school clubs £23

Cost of a nursery place for a child under 2, per week

Inner London	£197
Outer London	£170
Southwest	£141
West Midlands	£114
Northwest	£118
Northeast	£119
Scotland	£122

4 How does the state help?

In 2004, families received an average of **£49.83** through the childcare tax credit per week

Has the number of childcare places increased?

1997 1 place for every 9 children under 8 years old.

2005 1 place for every 4 children under 8 years old.

Percentage cost of childcare paid by parents

UK 75% · Denmark 33% · Finland 15% · Sweden 11%

How much do workers earn? Weekly gross income

- £55 Au pair
- £103 Childminder
- £211 Nursery nurse
- £238 Live in nanny (city/town, not home counties or London)
- £284 Daily nanny (city/town, not home counties or London)
- £366 Primary school teacher
- £915 Qualified lawyer

How have nannies' salaries increased? Annual gross income

5 How much is the industry worth?

The daycare nursery market was worth **£3.2bn** in 2004

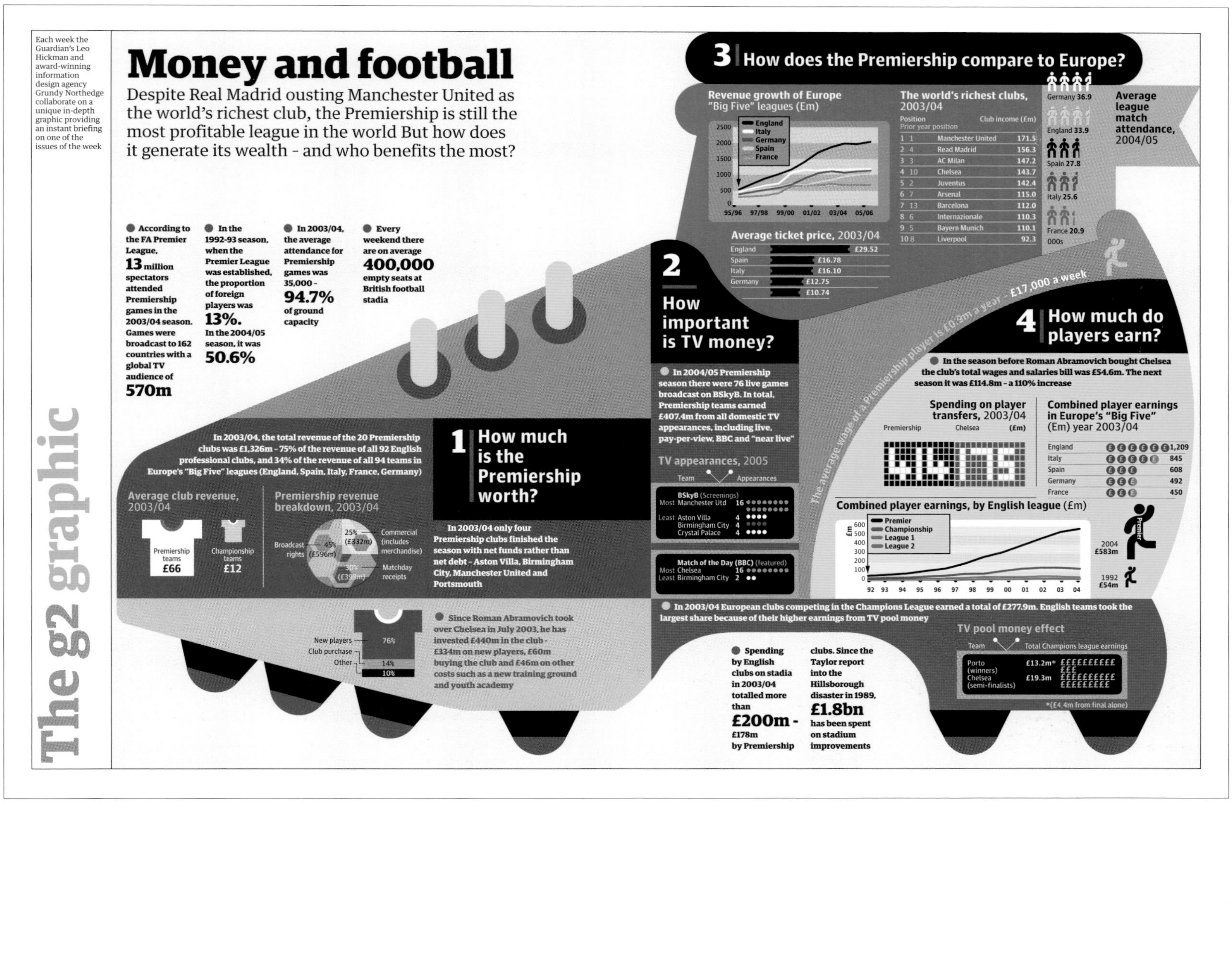

Each week the Guardian's Leo Hickman and award-winning information design agency Grundy Northedge collaborate on a unique in-depth graphic providing an instant briefing on one of the issues of the week

The g2 graphic

Money and football

Despite Real Madrid ousting Manchester United as the world's richest club, the Premiership is still the most profitable league in the world But how does it generate its wealth - and who benefits the most?

According to the FA Premier League, **13 million** spectators attended Premiership games in the 2003/04 season. Games were broadcast to 162 countries with a global TV audience of **570m**

In the 1992-93 season, when the Premier League was established, the proportion of foreign players was **13%.** In the 2004/05 season, it was **50.6%**

In 2003/04, the average attendance for Premiership games was 35,000 - **94.7%** of ground capacity

Every weekend there are on average **400,000** empty seats at British football stadia

In 2003/04, the total revenue of the 20 Premiership clubs was £1,326m - 75% of the revenue of all 92 English professional clubs, and 34% of the revenue of all 94 teams in Europe's "Big Five" leagues (England, Spain, Italy, France, Germany)

1 How much is the Premiership worth?

Average club revenue, 2003/04

Premiership teams £66 · Championship teams £12

Premiership revenue breakdown, 2003/04

Broadcast rights 45% (£596m) · Commercial 25% (£332m) (includes merchandise) · Matchday receipts 30% (£398m)

In 2003/04 only four Premiership clubs finished the season with net funds rather than net debt - Aston Villa, Birmingham City, Manchester United and Portsmouth

Since Roman Abramovich took over Chelsea in July 2003, he has invested £440m in the club - £334m on new players, £60m buying the club and £46m on other costs such as a new training ground and youth academy

New players 76% · Club purchase 14% · Other 10%

2 How important is TV money?

In 2004/05 Premiership season there were 76 live games broadcast on BSkyB. In total, Premiership teams earned £407.4m from all domestic TV appearances, including live, pay-per-view, BBC and "near live"

TV appearances, 2005

Team / Appearances

BSkyB (Screenings)

	Team	Appearances
Most	Manchester Utd	16
Least	Aston Villa	4
	Birmingham City	4
	Crystal Palace	4

Match of the Day (BBC) (featured)

	Team	Appearances
Most	Chelsea	16
Least	Birmingham City	2

In 2003/04 European clubs competing in the Champions League earned a total of £277.9m. English teams took the largest share because of their higher earnings from TV pool money

TV pool money effect

Team	Total Champions league earnings
Porto (winners)	£13.2m*
Chelsea (semi-finalists)	£19.3m

*(£4.4m from final alone)

Spending by English clubs on stadia in 2003/04 totalled more than **£200m** - £178m by Premiership clubs. Since the Taylor report into the Hillsborough disaster in 1989, **£1.8bn** has been spent on stadium improvements

3 How does the Premiership compare to Europe?

Revenue growth of Europe "Big Five" leagues (£m)

Average ticket price, 2003/04

England	£29.52
Spain	£16.78
Italy	£16.10
Germany	£12.75
	£10.74

The world's richest clubs, 2003/04

Position	Prior year position	Club	Club income (£m)
1	1	Manchester United	171.5
2	4	Read Madrid	156.3
3	3	AC Milan	147.2
4	10	Chelsea	143.7
5	2	Juventus	142.4
6	7	Arsenal	115.0
7	13	Barcelona	112.0
8	6	Internazionale	110.3
9	5	Bayern Munich	110.1
10	8	Liverpool	92.3

Average league match attendance, 2004/05

Germany 36.9 · England 33.9 · Spain 27.8 · Italy 25.6 · France 20.9 (000s)

The average wage of a Premiership player is £0.9m a year - £17,000 a week

4 How much do players earn?

In the season before Roman Abramovich bought Chelsea the club's total wages and salaries bill was £54.6m. The next season it was £114.8m - a 110% increase

Spending on player transfers, 2003/04 (£m)

Premiership · Chelsea

Combined player earnings in Europe's "Big Five" (Em) year 2003/04

England	1,209
Italy	845
Spain	608
Germany	492
France	450

Combined player earnings, by English league (£m)

INFRASTRUCTURE
mashability key literacy
self-programming materials
remote e-health
migrant health networks
green = safe
health localism
p2p health man
obile fabrication
urban farming network
NETWORKED GREEN HEALTH
PARTECIPATORY PRODUCTION
household sale waste to energy conversion
eighborhood museums of the future
collective measures for personal health
new global cities
translocal alliances
local & translocal alternative currencies
reverse diasporas
SUSTAINABLE URBANIZATION
TRANSLOCALISM
agricultural waste sequ
rooftop farming
governance = environmental management
disappearing hospitals
people as infrastructure
international scramble for farmland
clean coal renaissance
waste liabilities
REPURPOSED INFRASTRUCTURE
new resource based geo-identities
persisted automated server farms
ver farms as political & economic hubs
Server farms= new nation states
SERVER FARMS

Map of the Future

In this collaborative work, DensityDesign in Milan visualised future scenarios developed by the Institute for the Future, in Palo Alto. Like an elaborate mind map, this piece combines a collage landscape in the background with a map of interrelated ideas. Along the top, five areas of activity are labelled, from politics to society.

Associated with these aspects are ideas about how people will live together in the future and how advances in knowledge will change life on Earth. Each idea is shown in a colour-coded circle: green circles show ideas about how people will create new networks in the future; red relates to future scientific knowledge and understanding; yellow represents changing political and social habits.

Mit diesem Gemeinschaftsprojekt visualisiert DensityDesign in Mailand Zukunftsszenarien, die vom Institute for the Future in Palo Alto entwickelt wurden. Wie eine sorgfältig konstruierte Mindmap verbindet die Grafik eine collagierte Landschaft mit einer Karte zusammenhängender Ideen. Am oberen Rand der Grafik geben fünf Aktionsfelder das Grundgerüst vor, von Politik bis zu Gesellschaft.

Damit verbunden sind verschiedene Ideen, wie Menschen zukünftig miteinander leben werden und wie Wissensfortschritte das Leben auf der Erde verändern werden. Jede Idee wird in einem farbig codierten Kreis dargestellt: Grüne Kreise zeigen Überlegungen zu neuen Netzwerken, Rot bezieht sich auf künftige naturwissenschaftliche Erkenntnisse, Gelb steht für sich verändernde politische und gesellschaftliche Gepflogenheiten.

Dans ce travail collectif, les Milanais de DensityDesign ont illustré des scénarios futurs élaborés par l'Institute for the Future, à Palo Alto. Telle une carte heuristique complexe, cette œuvre est faite d'un collage en arrière-plan pour le paysage et d'un plan d'idées connectées. En haut, cinq domaines d'activités sont indiqués, de la politique à la société.

À ces aspects sont associées des idées sur la façon dont les gens cohabiteront, et sur l'impact que les progrès en matière de savoir auront sur la vie sur Terre. Chaque idée est présentée dans un cercle avec un code de couleur : les cercles verts suggèrent la façon dont les gens créeront des réseaux, les rouges font référence au savoir et à la compréhension scientifiques, et les jaunes représentent les changements d'habitudes dans le domaine politique et social.

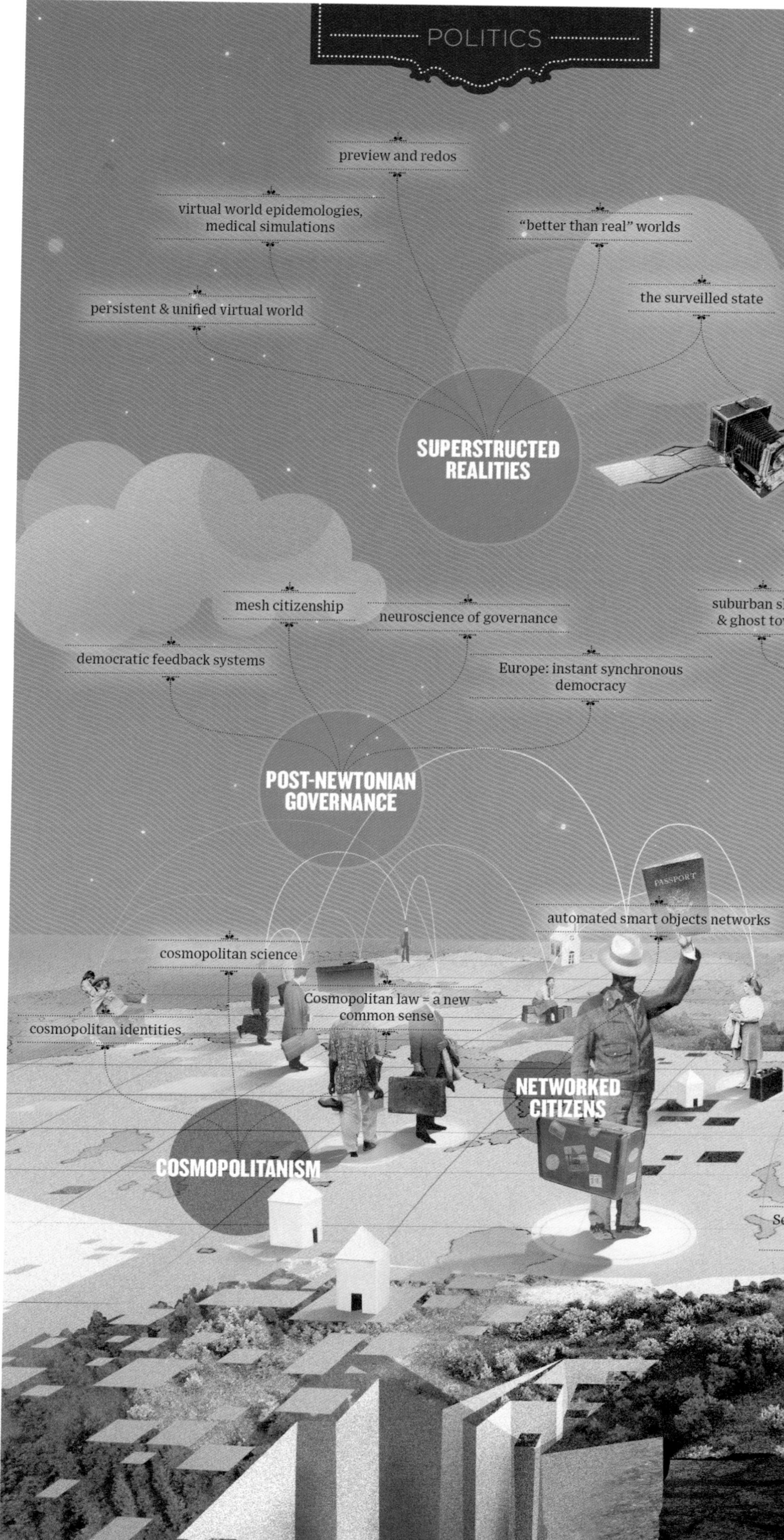

Project Info: *Wired*, magazine article, 2009, Italy
Data Source: Institute for the Future, Palo Alto
Design: Luca Masud, Mario Porpora, Gaia Scagnetti (DensityDesign)
Art Direction: Donato Ricci
Illustration: Michele Graffieti

Hamburgers: The Economics of America's Favorite Food

There is hardly any food that's more American than the hamburger. Many industries capitalise on the burger, including fast-food restaurants, cattle farmers, ketchup and mustard producers. This infographic dissects a typical hamburger, researching into the economics of America's favourite dish.

The graphic is categorised by the ingredients. Attached to the ingredients are three types of data: a few statistics as to which ingredients Americans most prefer; absolute numbers of how much of each ingredient is consumed per capita in the US annually; and lastly, the annual production and value of each ingredient in the US.

Kaum eine Speise ist amerikanischer als der Hamburger. Viele Unternehmen sind involviert, wie zum Beispiel Fast-Food-Restaurants, Viehzüchter, Ketchup- und Senfproduzenten. Auf dieser Infografik wird ein durchschnittlicher Hamburger zerlegt, um die wirtschaftlichen Zusammenhänge des amerikanischen Lieblingsessens darzustellen.

Die Grafik ist anhand der Zutaten aufgebaut. Daneben stehen dreierlei Informationen: einige statistische Angaben hinsichtlich der von den Amerikanern bevorzugten Zutaten, absolute Zahlen zum jährlichen Pro-Kopf-Verbrauch je Zutat in den USA und schließlich Daten zu der Jahresproduktion und den Kosten für jede Zutat in den USA.

Difficile de trouver nourriture plus américaine que le hamburger. De nombreux secteurs tirent parti de ce produit, comme entre autres les fast-foods, les éleveurs et les fabricants de ketchup et de moutarde. Cette infographie décortique un hamburger et analyse les aspects économiques du plat préféré de l'Amérique.

Le graphique est organisé selon les ingrédients, auxquels sont associés trois types de données: des statistiques sur les ingrédients que les Américains préfèrent, les chiffres absolus de consommation annuelle de chaque ingrédient par habitant aux États-Unis, ainsi que la production annuelle et la valeur de chaque ingrédient dans le pays.

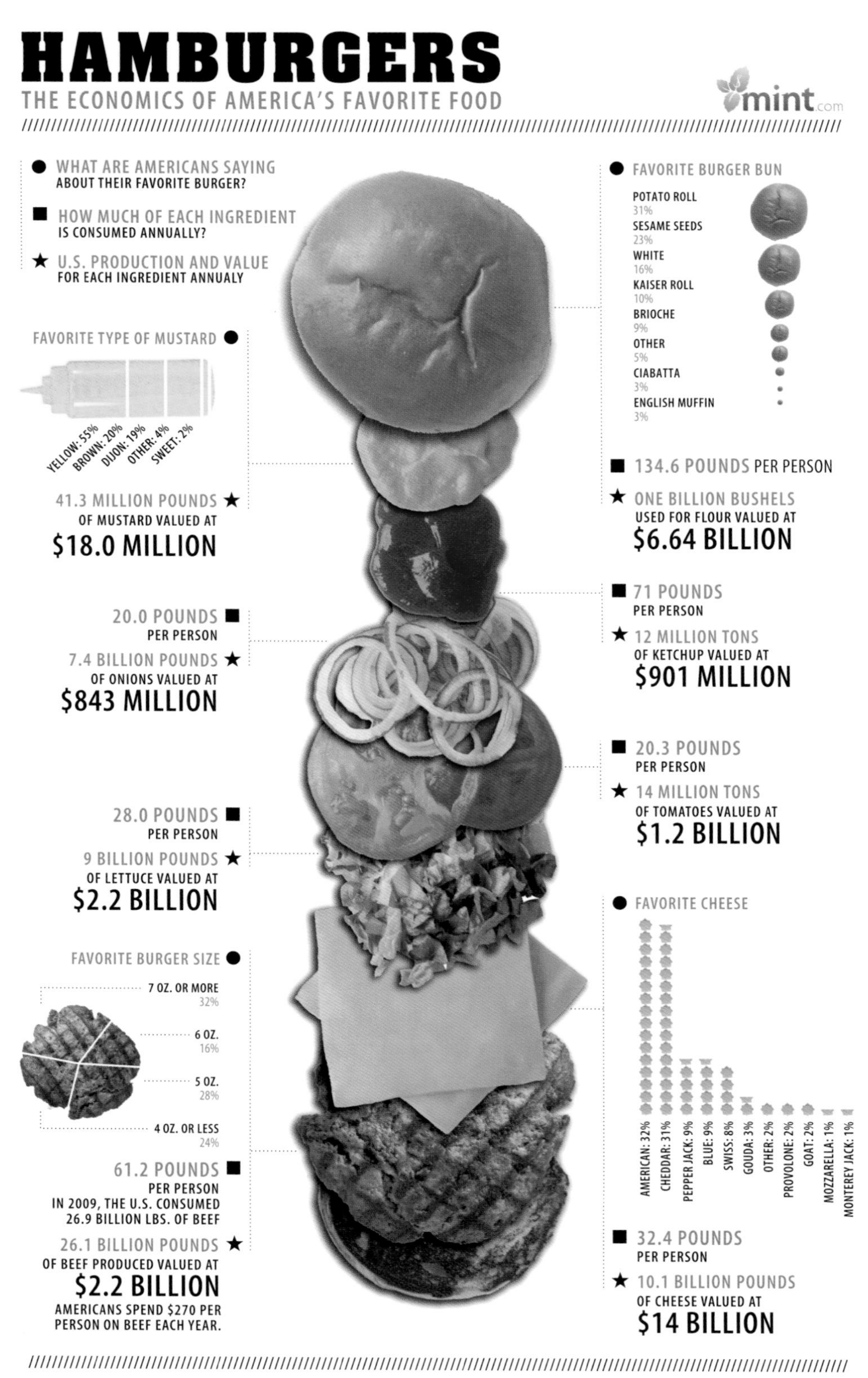

Project Info: Mint.com, website, 2010, USA
Data Source: Agricultural Marketing Resource Center; USDA Economic Research Service; USDA-ESMIS; Blog "A Hamburger Today"
Research: Brian Wolford
Design: Jarred Romley, Andrew Effendy (Column Five Media)
Art Direction: Ross Crooks
Photography: Jimmy Pham

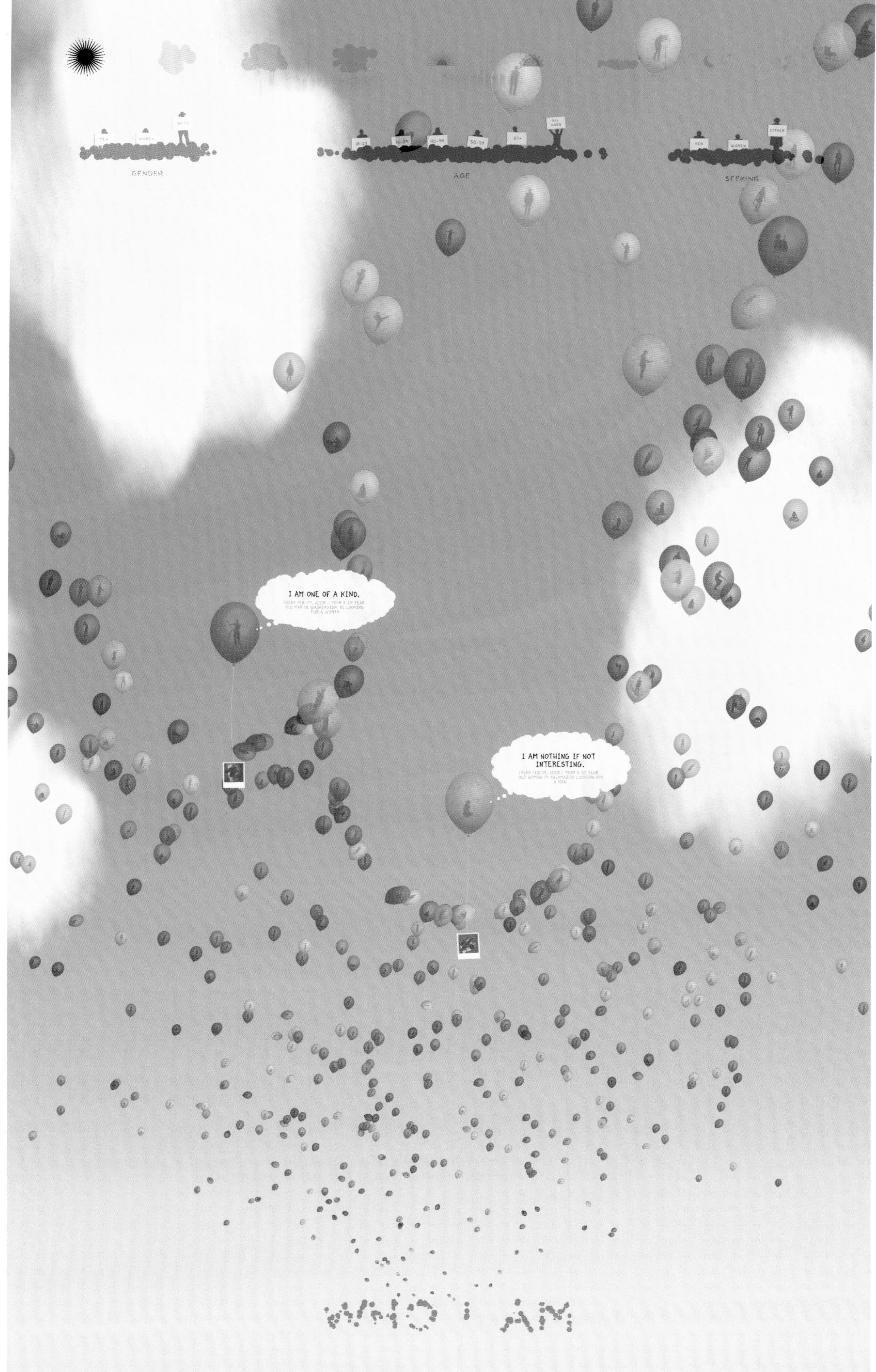
GENDER
AGE
SEEKING
I AM ONE OF A KIND.
FOUND FEB 04, 2008 / FROM A 24 YEAR OLD MAN IN WASHINGTON, DC LOOKING FOR A WOMAN
I AM NOTHING IF NOT INTERESTING.
FOUND FEB 04, 2008 / FROM A 30 YEAR OLD WOMAN IN KALAMAZOO LOOKING FOR A MAN
WHO I AM
WHO I AM
WHAT I WANT
SNIPPETS
MATCHMAKER
BREAKDOWNS

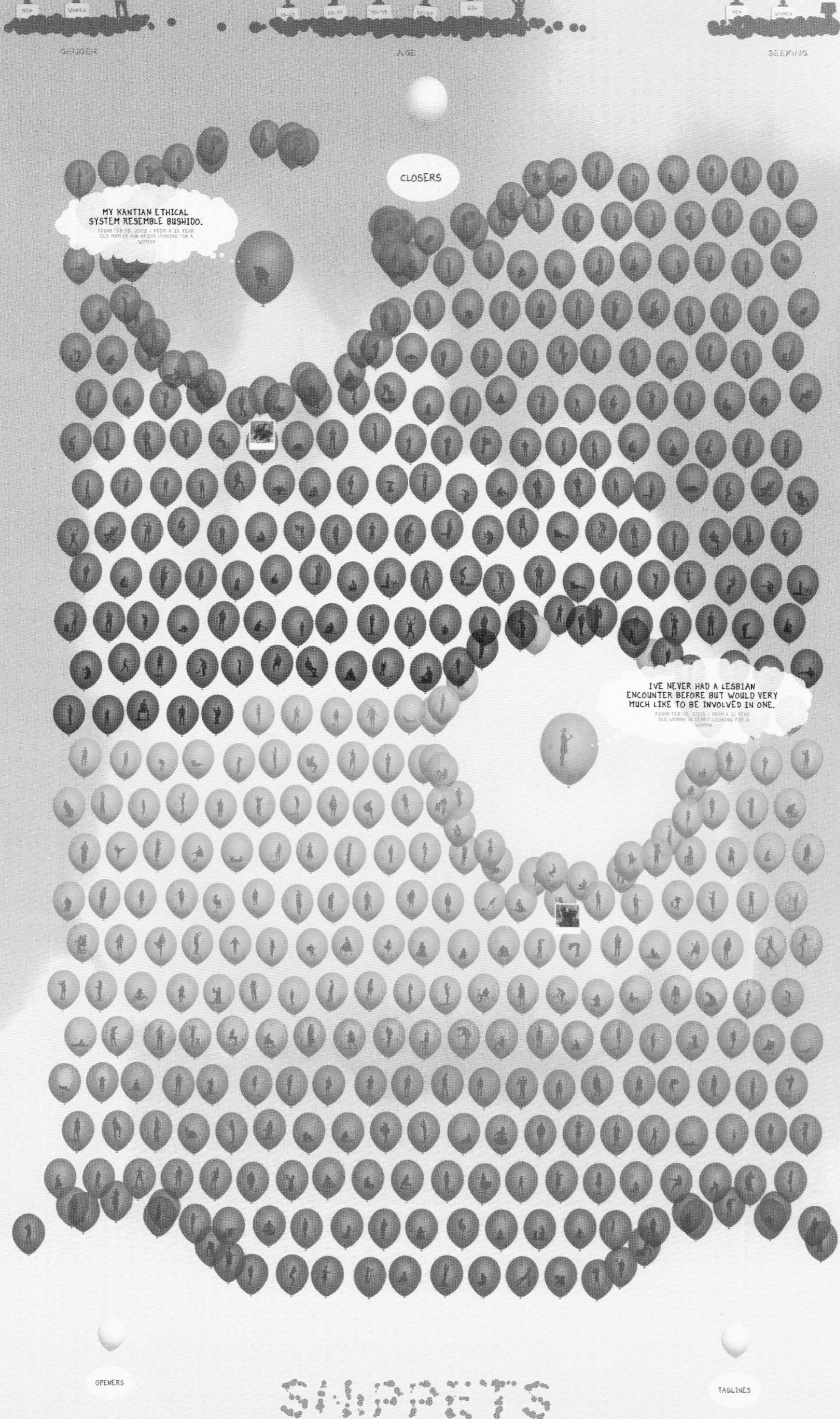

MEN
WOMEN
BOTH
GENDER
18-29
30-39
40-49
50-59
60+
ALL AGES
AGE
MEN
WOMEN
EITHER
SEEKING
CLOSERS
MY KANTIAN ETHICAL SYSTEM RESEMBLE BUSHIDO.
IVE NEVER HAD A LESBIAN ENCOUNTER BEFORE BUT WOULD VERY MUCH LIKE TO BE INVOLVED IN ONE.
OPENERS
SNIPPETS
TAGLINES
WHO I AM
WHAT I WANT
SNIPPETS
MATCHMAKER
BREAKDOWNS

MATCHMAKER
WHO I AM WHAT I WANT SNIPPETS MATCHMAKER BREAKDOWNS

WHAT I WANT
WHO I AM WHAT I WANT SNIPPETS MATCHMAKER BREAKDOWNS

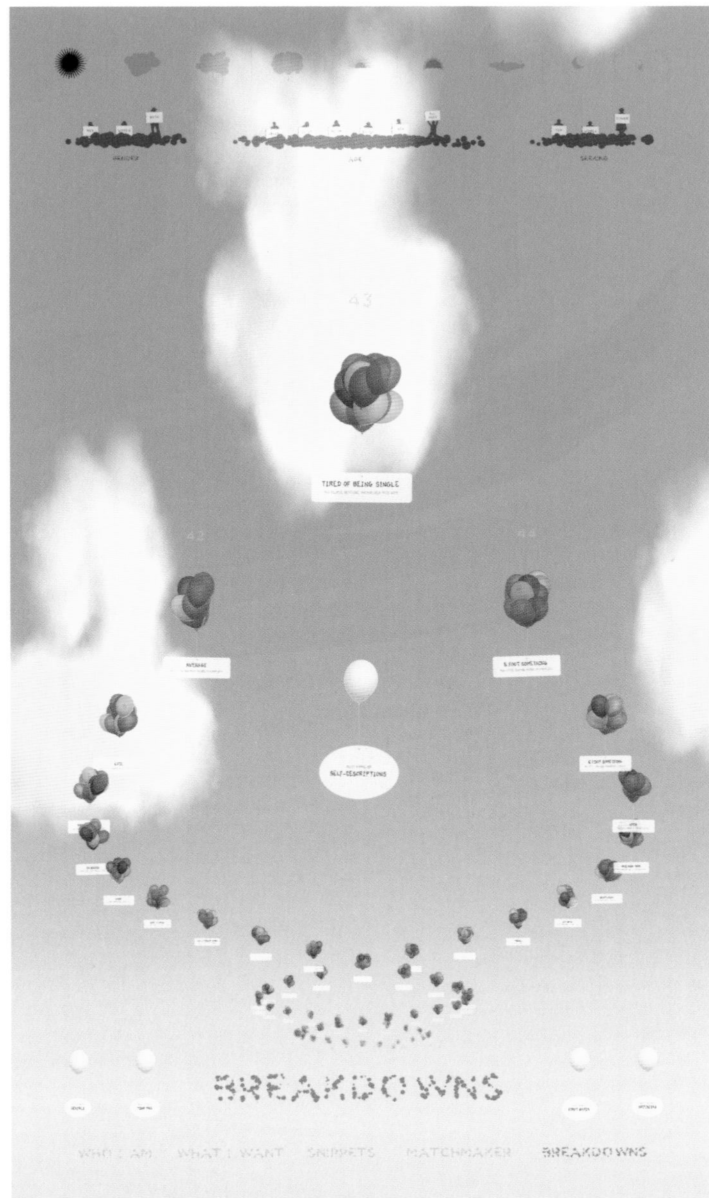
TIRED OF BEING SINGLE
BREAKDOWNS
WHO I AM WHAT I WANT SNIPPETS MATCHMAKER BREAKDOWNS

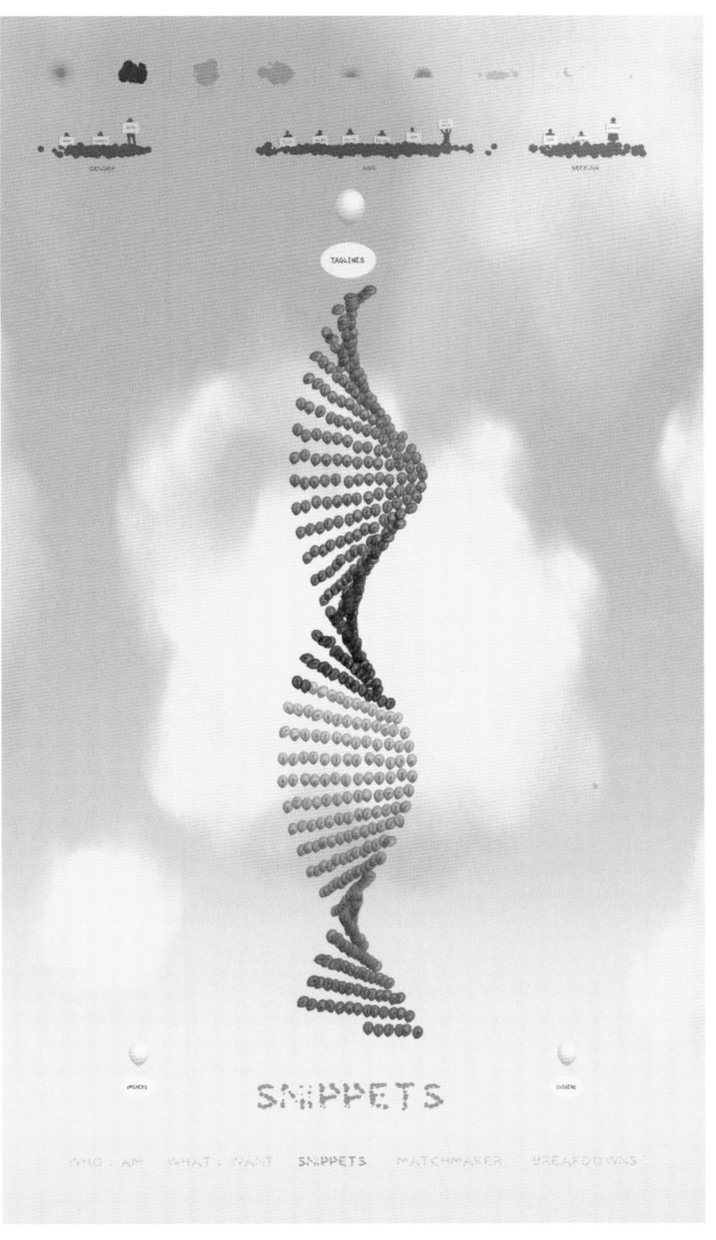
TAGLINES
SNIPPETS
WHO I AM WHAT I WANT SNIPPETS MATCHMAKER BREAKDOWNS

Infinite Jest Diagram

The sheer abundance of characters is a significant feature of the novel *Infinite Jest*. The setting presents a future vision, with Northern America forming one state. The diagram here connects characters and places. Two circles represent locations: the "Enfield Tennis Academy" and the "Ennet House Drug and Alcohol Recovery House". The third represents the "Wheelchair Assassins", a separatist group from Quebec.

The "Great Concavity / Great Convexity" map to the lower left shows a waste dump in the area of the northern US / southern Canada. The map below shows the setting of "Eschaton", a computer-aided war game, which is played every year on November 8 at the Tennis Academy. Students are organised in militaristic groups ("AMNAT" etc.) and are located virtually around the globe.

Die schiere Fülle an Figuren ist ein herausragendes Merkmal des Romans *Infinite Jest* (dt. *Unendlicher Spaß*). Der Roman präsentiert eine Vision der Zukunft, in der ganz Nordamerika eine Nation ist. Das hier gezeigte Diagramm verbindet Figuren und Orte. Zwei Kreise repräsentieren Orte: die „Enfield Tennis Academy" und das „Ennet House Drug and Alcohol Recovery House". Der dritte steht für die „Wheelchair Assassins", eine Separatistengruppe aus Quebec.

Die Karte „Great Concavity / Great Convexity" unten links zeigt eine Müllhalde in der Gegend der nördlichen USA und des südlichen Kanada. Die Karte unten zeigt die Aufstellung von „Eschaton", einem computergestützten Kriegsspiel, das jeweils am 8. November in der Tennis Academy gespielt wird. Studenten sind dabei in militaristische Gruppen (wie etwa „AMNAT" etc.) aufgeteilt und virtuell über die ganze Welt verteilt.

L'abondance de personnages est une caractéristique clé du roman *Infinite Jest*, vision futuriste de l'Amérique du Nord ne formant qu'un seul État. Le diagramme met en relation les personnages et les lieux. Deux cercles symbolisent des lieux : la « Enfield Tennis Academy » et la « Ennet House Drug and Alcohol Recovery House ». Le troisième correspond au groupe séparatiste « Wheelchair Assassins » du Québec.

La carte « Great Concavity / Great Convexity » en bas à gauche montre une décharge au nord des États-Unis / sud du Canada. La carte ci-dessous plante le décor pour « Eschaton », un jeu de guerre sur ordinateur qui est joué tous les 8 novembre à l'Académie de tennis. Les étudiants sont divisés en groupes militaristes (« AMNAT », etc.) et répartis virtuellement à travers la planète.

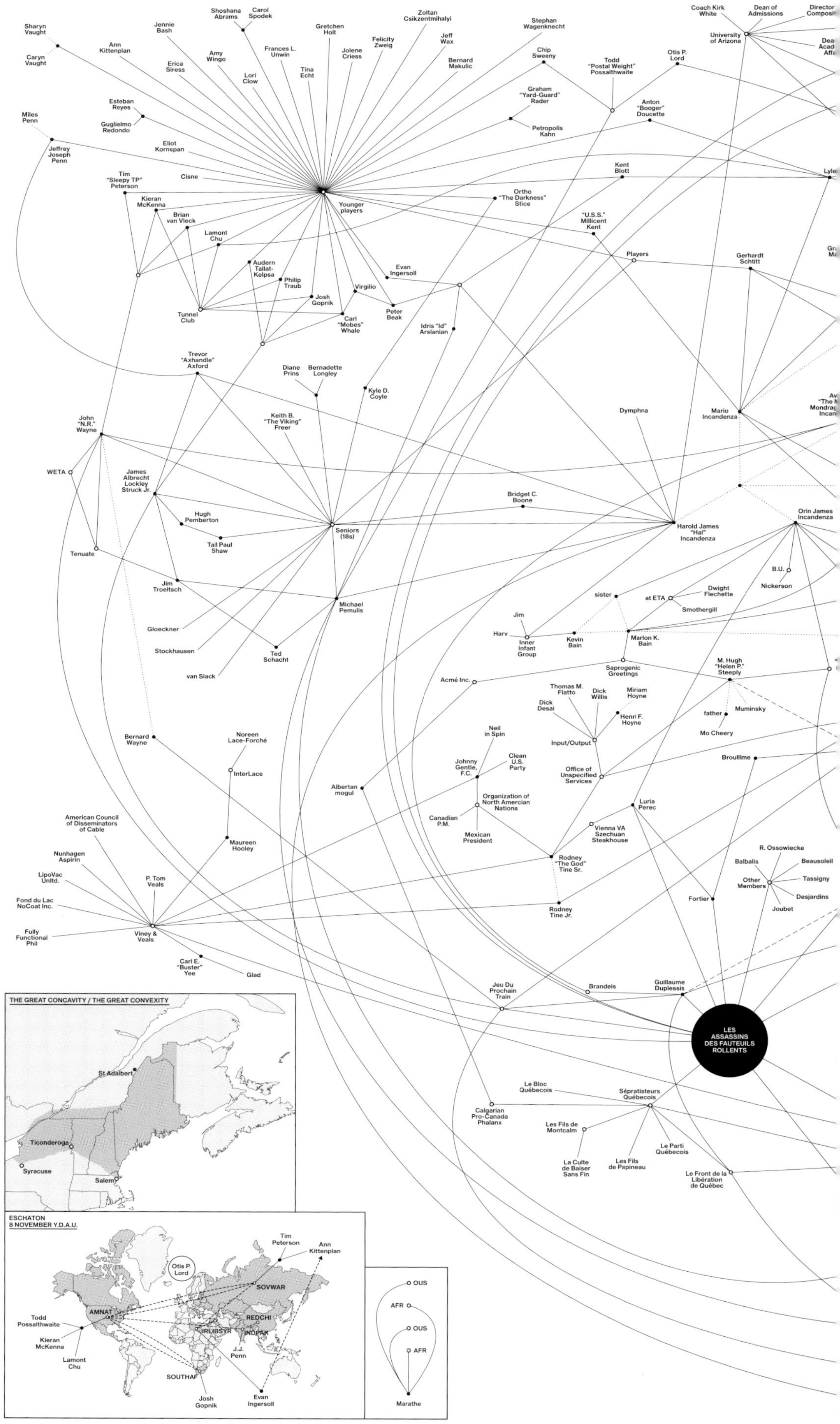

Project Info: Poster, 2010, USA
Data Source: David Foster Wallace: "Infinite Jest", 1996
Design: Sam Potts

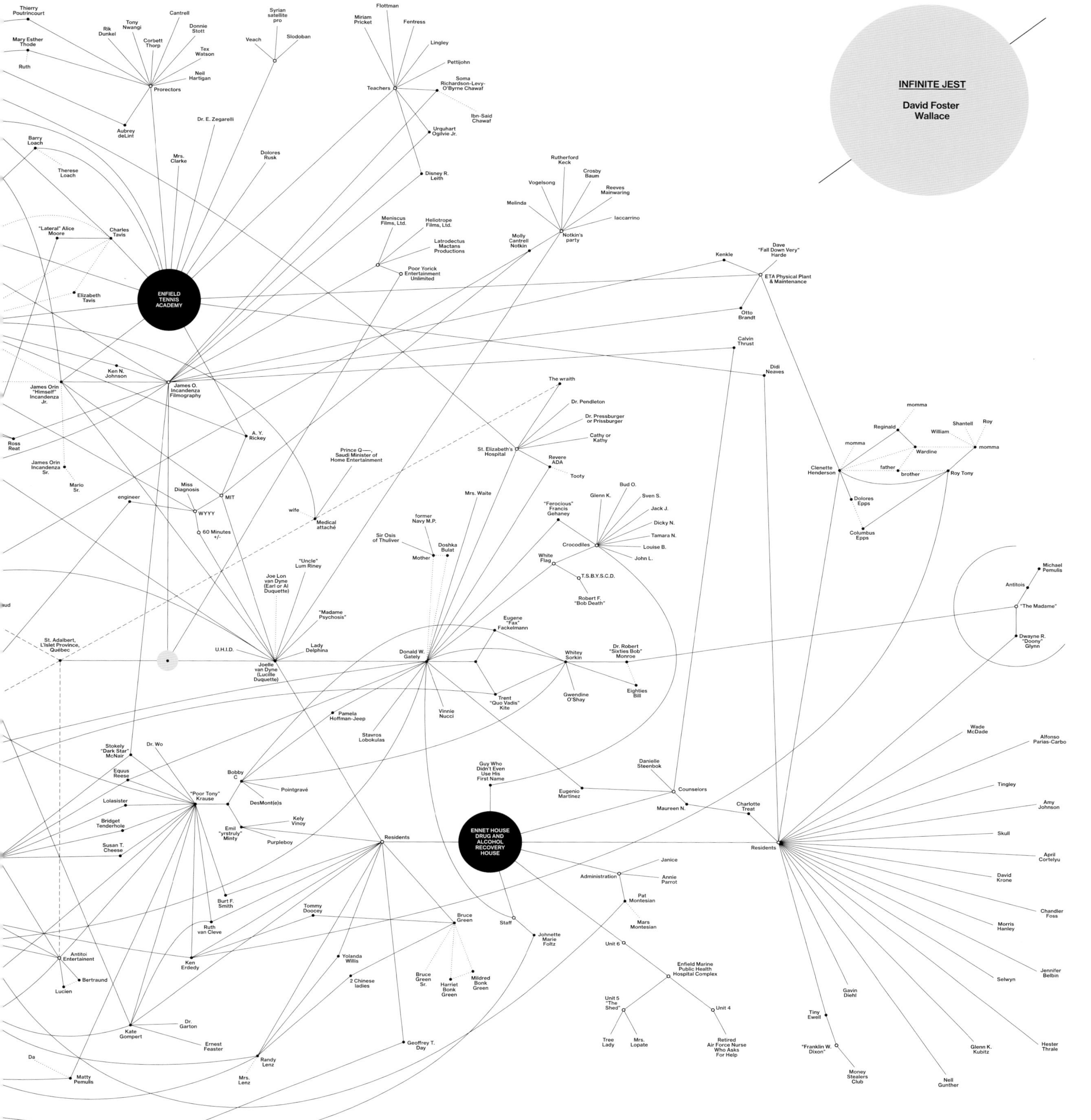

INFINITE JEST

David Foster Wallace

Thierry Poutrincourt
Mary Esther Thode
Ruth
Rik Dunkel
Tony Nwangi
Corbett Thorp
Cantrell
Donnie Stott
Tex Watson
Neil Hartigan
Prorectors
Aubrey deLint
Syrian satellite pro
Veach
Slodoban
Dr. E. Zegarelli
Flottman
Miriam Pricket
Fentress
Lingley
Pettijohn
Teachers
Soma Richardson-Levy-O'Byrne Chawaf
Ibn-Said Chawaf
Urquhart Ogilvie Jr.
Disney R. Leith
Barry Loach
Therese Loach
Mrs. Clarke
Dolores Rusk
Rutherford Keck
Crosby Baum
Vogelsong
Reeves Mainwaring
Melinda
Iaccarrino
Notkin's party
Molly Cantrell Notkin
Meniscus Films, Ltd.
Heliotrope Films, Ltd.
Latrodectus Mactans Productions
Poor Yorick Entertainment Unlimited
"Lateral" Alice Moore
Charles Tavis
Elizabeth Tavis
ENFIELD TENNIS ACADEMY
Kenkle
Dave "Fall Down Very" Harde
ETA Physical Plant & Maintenance
Otto Brandt
Calvin Thrust
Didi Neaves
Ken N. Johnson
James Orin "Himself" Incandenza Jr.
James O. Incandenza Filmography
Ross Reat
James Orin Incandenza Sr.
Mario Sr.
The wraith
Dr. Pendleton
Dr. Pressburger or Prissburger
Cathy or Kathy
St. Elizabeth's Hospital
Revere ADA
Tooty
A. Y. Rickey
Prince Q—, Saudi Minister of Home Entertainment
Miss Diagnosis
engineer
MIT
WYYY
wife
Medical attaché
60 Minutes +/-
momma
Reginald
Shantell
Roy
William
momma
Wardine
momma
Clenette Henderson
father
brother
Roy Tony
Dolores Epps
Columbus Epps
Mrs. Waite
Bud O.
Glenn K.
Sven S.
Jack J.
Dicky N.
Tamara N.
Louise B.
John L.
"Ferocious" Francis Gehaney
Crocodiles
White Flag
T.S.B.Y.S.C.D.
Robert F. "Bob Death"
former Navy M.P.
Sir Osis of Thuliver
Mother
Doshka Bulat
"Uncle" Lum Riney
Joe Lon van Dyne (Earl or Al Duquette)
"Madame Psychosis"
Lady Delphina
U.H.I.D.
Joelle van Dyne (Lucille Duquette)
St. Adalbert, L'Islet Province, Québec
Eugene "Fax" Fackelmann
Donald W. Gately
Whitey Sorkin
Dr. Robert "Sixties Bob" Monroe
Eighties Bill
Gwendine O'Shay
Trent "Quo Vadis" Kite
Vinnie Nucci
Michael Pemulis
Antitois
"The Madame"
Dwayne R. "Doony" Glynn
Pamela Hoffman-Jeep
Stavros Lobokulas
Stokely "Dark Star" McNair
Dr. Wo
Equus Reese
Lolasister
Bridget Tenderhole
Susan T. Cheese
"Poor Tony" Krause
Bobby C
Pointgravé
DesMont(e)s
Emil "yrstruly" Minty
Kely Vinoy
Purpleboy
Residents
Guy Who Didn't Even Use His First Name
ENNET HOUSE DRUG AND ALCOHOL RECOVERY HOUSE
Eugenio Martinez
Danielle Steenbok
Counselors
Maureen N.
Charlotte Treat
Residents
Wade McDade
Alfonso Parias-Carbo
Tingley
Amy Johnson
Skull
April Cortelyu
David Krone
Chandler Foss
Morris Hanley
Selwyn
Jennifer Belbin
Hester Thrale
Glenn K. Kubitz
Nell Gunther
Money Stealers Club
"Franklin W. Dixon"
Tiny Ewell
Gavin Diehl
Administration
Janice
Annie Parrot
Pat Montesian
Mars Montesian
Staff
Johnette Marie Foltz
Unit 6
Enfield Marine Public Health Hospital Complex
Unit 5 "The Shed"
Unit 4
Tree Lady
Mrs. Lopate
Retired Air Force Nurse Who Asks For Help
Burt F. Smith
Ruth van Cleve
Ken Erdedy
Tommy Doocey
Bruce Green
Bruce Green Sr.
Harriet Bonk Green
Mildred Bonk Green
Yolanda Willis
2 Chinese ladies
Antitoi Entertainment
Bertraund
Lucien
Dr. Garton
Kate Gompert
Ernest Feaster
Geoffrey T. Day
Randy Lenz
Mrs. Lenz
Da
Matty Pemulis
"Wild Conceits"

ORGANIZATION OF NORTH AMERICAN NATIONS' REVENUE-ENHANCING SUBSIDIZED TIME™

Whopper → Tucks Medicated Pad → Trial-Size Dove Bar → Perdue Wonderchicken → Whisper-Quiet Maytag Dishmaster → Yushityu 2007 MRCVMETIUFI/ITPSFH,O,OM (s) → Dairy Products from the American Heartland → Depend Adult Undergarment → Glad

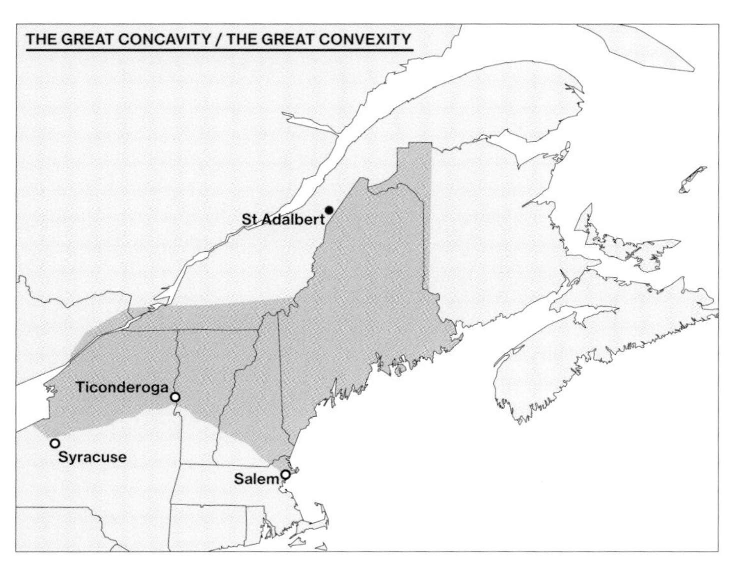

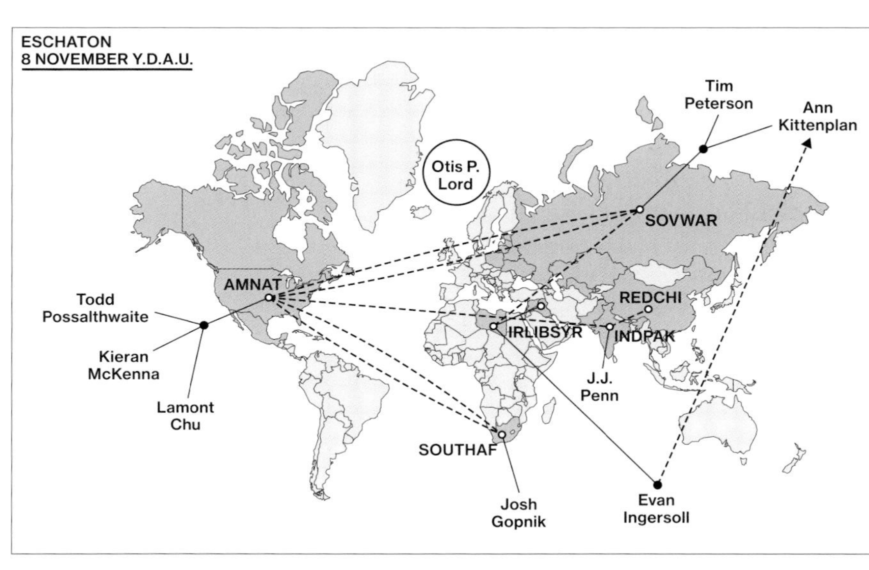

Influences of Edgar Allan Poe

Designed on the occasion of Edgar Allan Poe's 200th birthday, this infographic explains his literary cosmos. The circle diagram places Poe in the centre. Forerunners are shown in blue, while contemporaries with whom he exchanged inspirations are coded in purple. Later writers, who drew upon various aspects of Poe's work, are shown in pink.

Individual aspects of Poe's writing are listed around the inner circles of the diagram, and refer to style, main topics and genres. An axis connects Poe with each author, with dots marking the aspects the author shares with Poe. It is interesting how this piece is mainly structured by the categories of literary writing, whereas the historical succession is elegantly integrated into a closed circle.

Diese Infografik, die anlässlich des 200. Geburtstags von Edgar Allan Poe entstand, veranschaulicht den literarischen Kosmos des Autors. Den Mittelpunkt des Kreisdiagramms bildet Poe selbst. Seine Vorläufer werden in Blau gezeigt, die Zeitgenossen, mit denen er sich austauschte, in Lila. Spätere Schriftsteller, die verschiedene Aspekte seiner Arbeit aufgriffen, sind rosa dargestellt.

Einzelne Aspekte von Poes Werk werden in den inneren Kreisen des Diagramms aufgelistet und beziehen sich auf Stil, Hauptthemen und Genres. Eine Achse verbindet Poe mit den anderen Schriftstellern, wobei Überschneidungen mit dem Poe'schen Werk durch Punkte angezeigt werden. Interessant an dieser Grafik ist, dass sie hauptsächlich nach literarischen Kategorien strukturiert ist, wohingegen die historische Abfolge elegant in den geschlossenen Kreis integriert ist.

Conçue à l'occasion du 200ᵉ anniversaire d'Edgar Allan Poe, cette infographie présente son univers littéraire. Poe se trouve au centre de ce diagramme circulaire. Ses précurseurs apparaissent en bleu, ses contemporains, avec qui il a échangé des inspirations, en violet. Les écrivains postérieurs, qui se sont inspirés de divers aspects du travail de Poe, sont en rose.

Les différents aspects des œuvres de Poe sont représentés par les cercles internes du diagramme ; ils font référence au style et aux principaux sujets et genres. Un axe connecte Poe à chaque auteur, les points marquant ce que les deux ont en commun. L'intérêt est que ce graphique est principalement structuré autour des catégories littéraires, tout en intégrant élégamment la succession historique dans un cercle fermé.

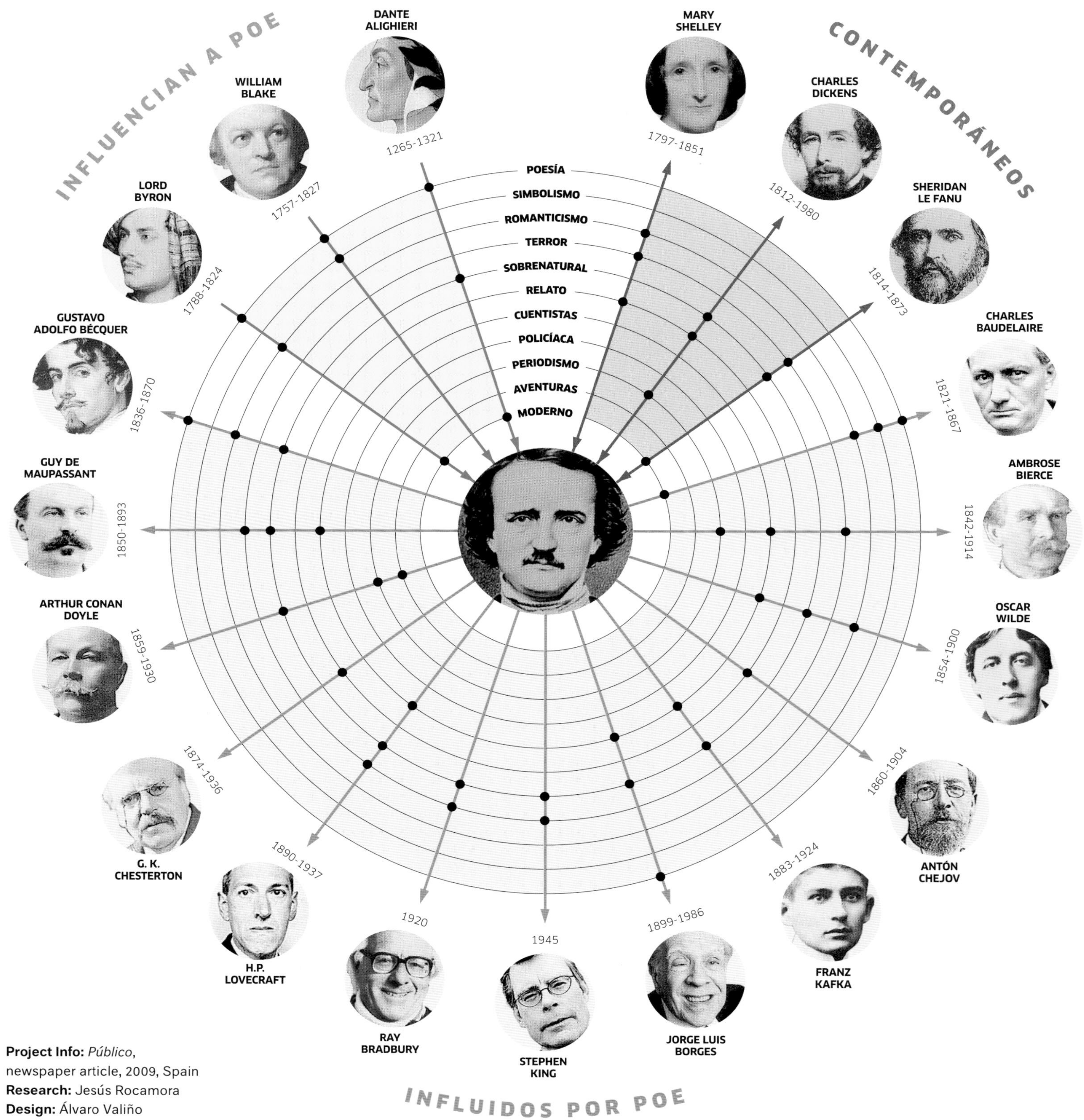

Project Info: *Público*, newspaper article, 2009, Spain
Research: Jesús Rocamora
Design: Álvaro Valiño

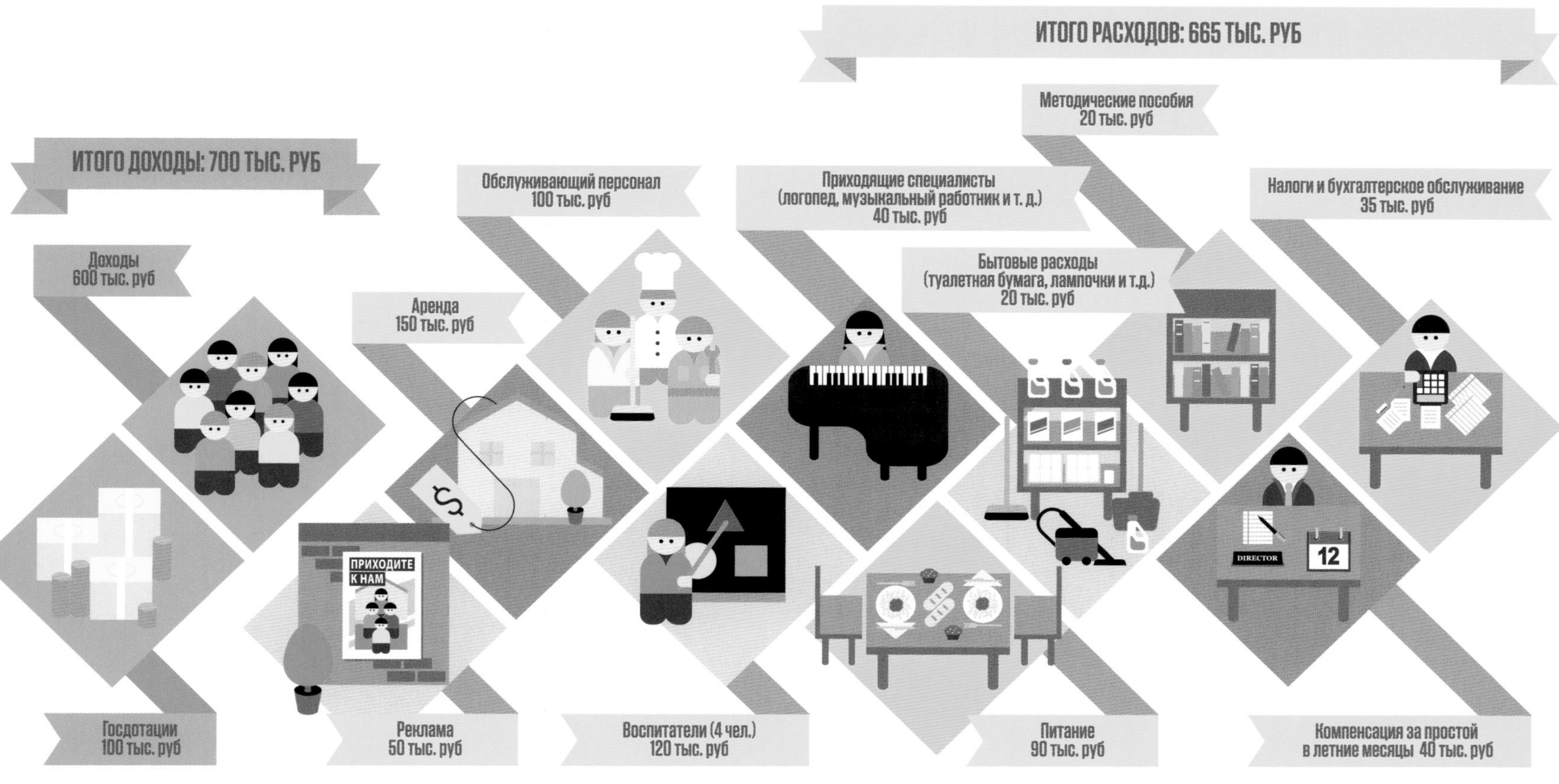

Kindergarten

This infographic, developed for Russian business magazine *Sekret Firmy*, tackles the economic aspects of running a kindergarten. It shows the data for an average kindergarten in Russia, with the budget indicated in the green boxes on the left, differentiated between regular income and state subsidies.

The yellow boxes show the various types of expenses: rent for the premises, teachers' earnings, expenses for service staff, external professionals like music teachers, advertisements or food. Numbers are given in thousands of rubles.

Diese Infografik für das russische Wirtschaftsmagazin *Sekret Firmy* veranschaulicht die wirtschaftlich relevanten Aspekte, um einen durchschnittlichen russischen Kindergarten zu betreiben. Nach regulären Einnahmen und staatlichen Zuwendungen unterteilt, ist der Etat in den grünen Kästchen links zu sehen.

In den gelben Kästchen sind die einzelnen Ausgaben aufgelistet: Raummiete, Gehälter der Pädagogen, Kosten für Dienstleister und externe Mitarbeiter wie Musiklehrer sowie für Werbung und Verpflegung. Die Summen sind in Tausend Rubel angegeben.

Cette infographie, élaborée pour le magazine russe *Sekret Firmy*, aborde les aspects économiques liés à l'activité d'un jardin d'enfants. Elle présente les données pour un jardin d'enfants type en Russie : le budget figure dans les cadres verts sur la gauche, en faisant la différence entre les recettes ordinaires et les subventions publiques.

Les cadres jaunes montrent les différents types de dépenses : loyer du local, salaires des instituteurs, frais du personnel de service, intervenants externes comme des professeurs de musique, publicité et nourriture. Les chiffres sont exprimés en milliers de roubles.

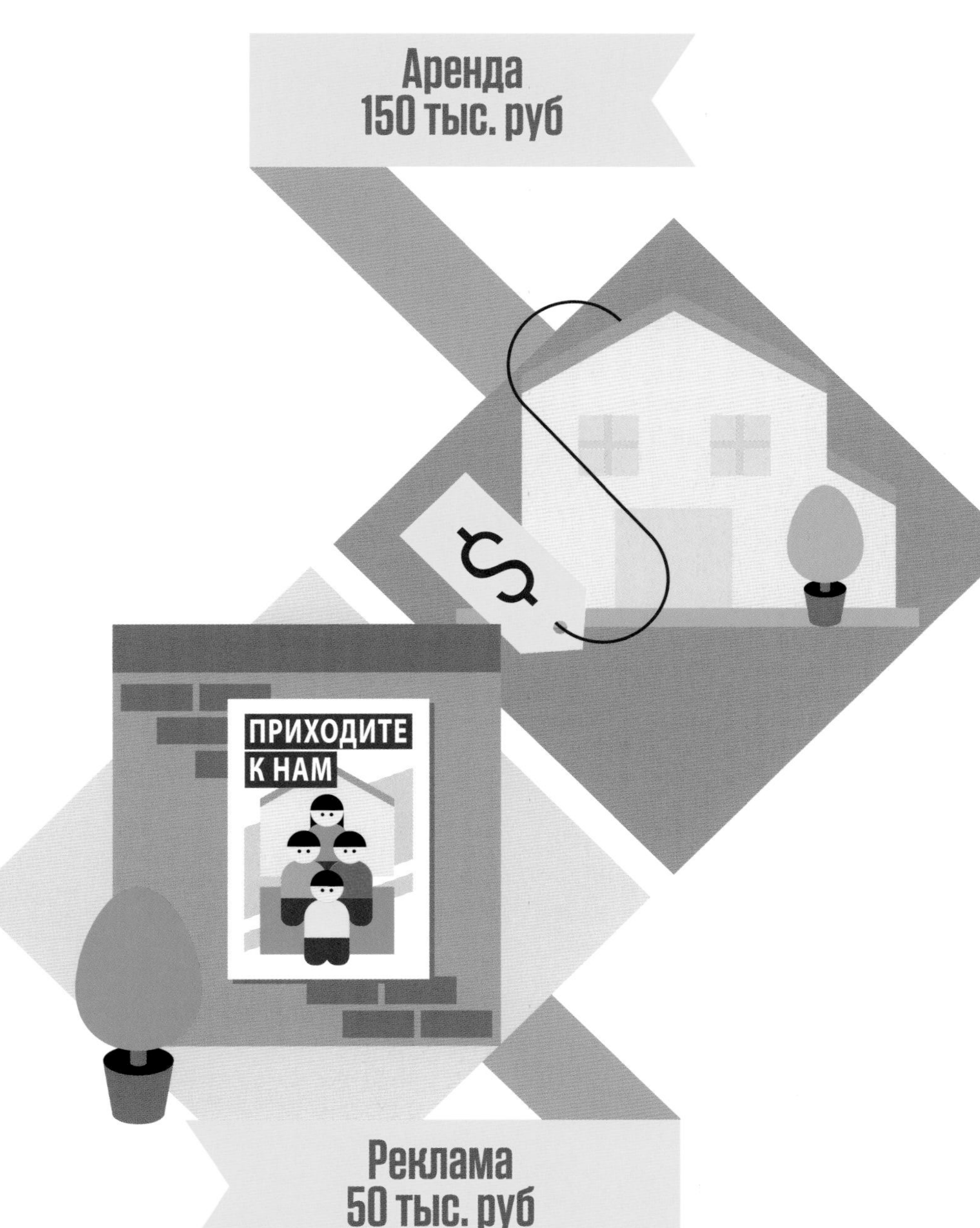

Project Info: *Sekret Firmy*, magazine article, 2010, Russia
Design: Alberto Antoniazzi

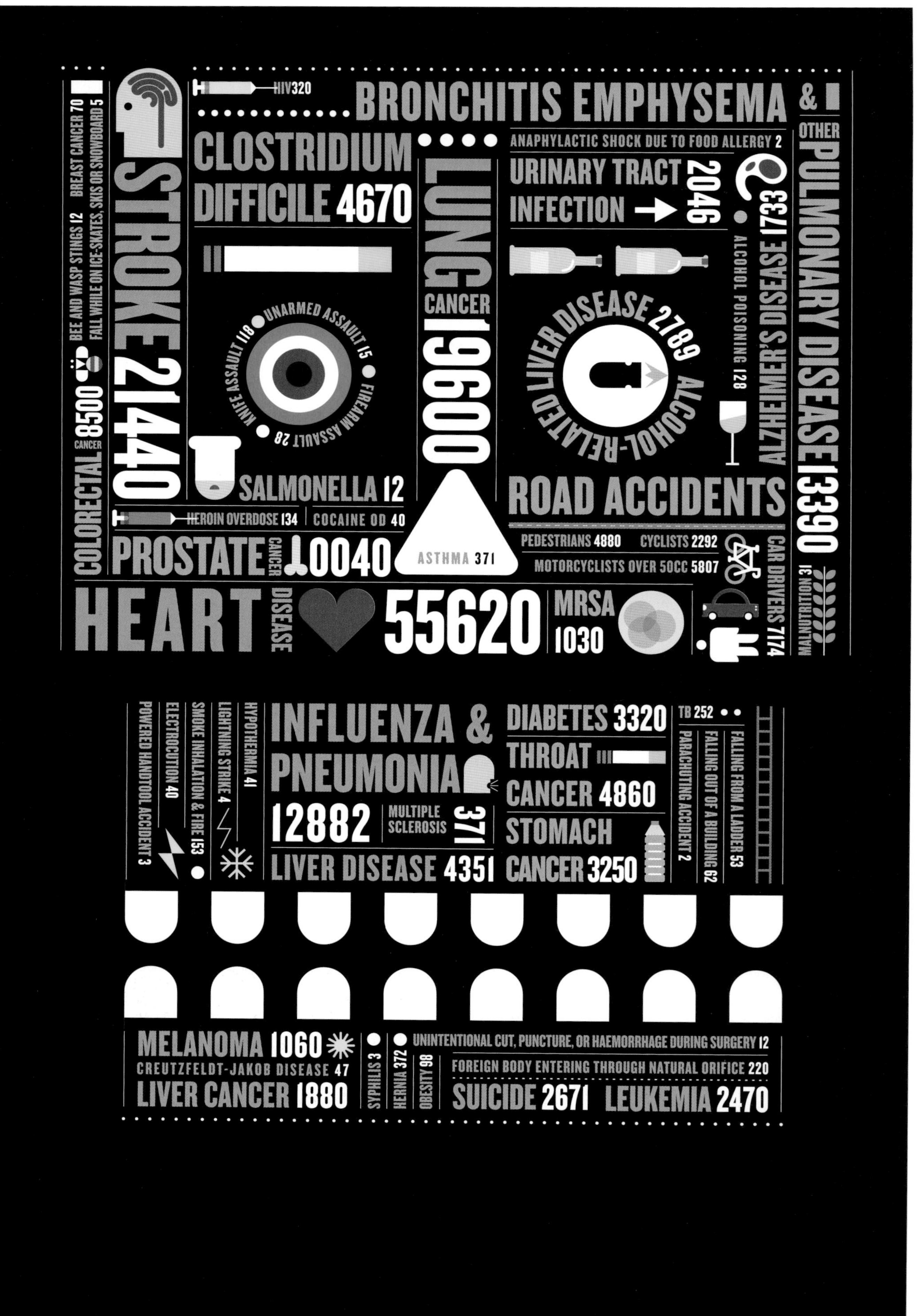

Project Info: *Men's Health*, magazine article, 2008, UK
Design: Peter Grundy (Grundini)
Art Direction: Kerem Shefik
Awards: AOI Images 2009

Life and Death

Peter Grundy designed this piece for the UK edition of *Men's Health*. As he had been tasked to visualise death rates for a health-oriented magazine, he opted for a humorous approach and assembled the letters and figures to create a skull, as a general symbol of death. UK death rates are categorised by cause of death.

Peter Grundy entwarf dieses Schaubild für die britische Ausgabe von *Men's Health*. In Anbetracht des Auftrags, Sterblichkeitsraten für eine Gesundheitszeitschrift zu visualisieren, entschied er sich für einen humorvollen Ansatz und setzte die Buchstaben und Zahlen seiner Grafik zu einem Totenschädel zusammen, der gemeinhin als Symbol des Todes verstanden wird. Die Sterblichkeitsraten in Großbritannien werden nach Todesursache kategorisiert.

Peter Grundy a créé cette œuvre pour l'édition anglaise de *Men's Health*. Chargé d'illustrer des taux de mortalité dans un magazine spécialisé dans la santé, il a opté pour une approche humoristique et a composé des lettres et des chiffres en forme de crâne, symbole universel de la mort. Les taux de mortalité au Royaume-Uni sont classés par cause de décès.

Little Book of Shocking Global Facts: Deforestation

The Little Book of Shocking Global Facts by Jonathan Barnbrook reports political and economic data in a startling variety of designs. In its quest to establish a visual argument, the book challenged widely accepted principles for reporting information, such as that design should be clear and not take a stand of its own. Barnbrook deliberately questioned whether this neutrality was either possible or desirable. The critical reaction the book has given rise to attests to a clash of cultures within graphic design in regard to these basic tenets.

The book is divided into topics, ranging from trade via human rights to drugs. The example below shows how much forest has been gained or lost on each continent. The word "China" is highlighted and linked to other facts elsewhere in the book.

The Little Book of Shocking Global Facts von Jonathan Barnbrook zeigt politische und ökonomische Daten in einer verblüffenden Vielfalt von Designs. In dem Bestreben, „visuelle Argumente" zu schaffen, stellt das Buch allgemein anerkannte Prinzipien der Informationswiedergabe infrage, wie etwa die, dass das Design klar sein muss und keine eigene Meinung andeuten darf. Barnbrook hinterfragte bewusst, ob diese neutrale Haltung möglich oder auch nur wünschenswert sei. Die kritischen Reaktionen, die das Buch hervorrief, verweisen auf eine Art Kulturstreit innerhalb der Grafikerszene hinsichtlich dieser Grundannahmen.

Das Buch ist in verschiedene Kapitel unterteilt, vom Handel über Menschenrechte bis hin zu Drogen. Das Beispiel unten zeigt, welche Waldfläche auf jedem Kontinent vernichtet oder neu angelegt wurde. Das Wort „China" ist markiert und mit anderen Fakten im Buch verknüpft.

L'ouvrage *The Little Book of Shocking Global Facts* de Jonathan Barnbrook présente des données politiques et économiques avec une incroyable variété de designs. Visant à créer un argument visuel, il remet en cause des principes largement acceptés pour diffuser des informations ; par exemple, que le design doit être clair et ne pas prendre position. Barnbrook pose la question de savoir si cette neutralité est possible ou souhaitable. La réaction critique suscitée par l'ouvrage prouve un choc de cultures au sein du design graphique à propos de ces principes de base.

Le livre est divisé en rubriques allant du commerce aux droits de l'homme en passant par les drogues. L'exemple ci-dessous montre combien les forêts ont gagné ou perdu de terrain sur chaque continent. Le mot « Chine » est mis en évidence et associé à d'autres points ailleurs dans le livre.

Project Info: Fiell Publishing, book, 2010, UK
Data Source: UN Food and Agriculture Organization; FAO Global Forest Resources Assessment et al.
Design: Jonathan Abbott, Jonathan Barnbrook (Barnbrook)

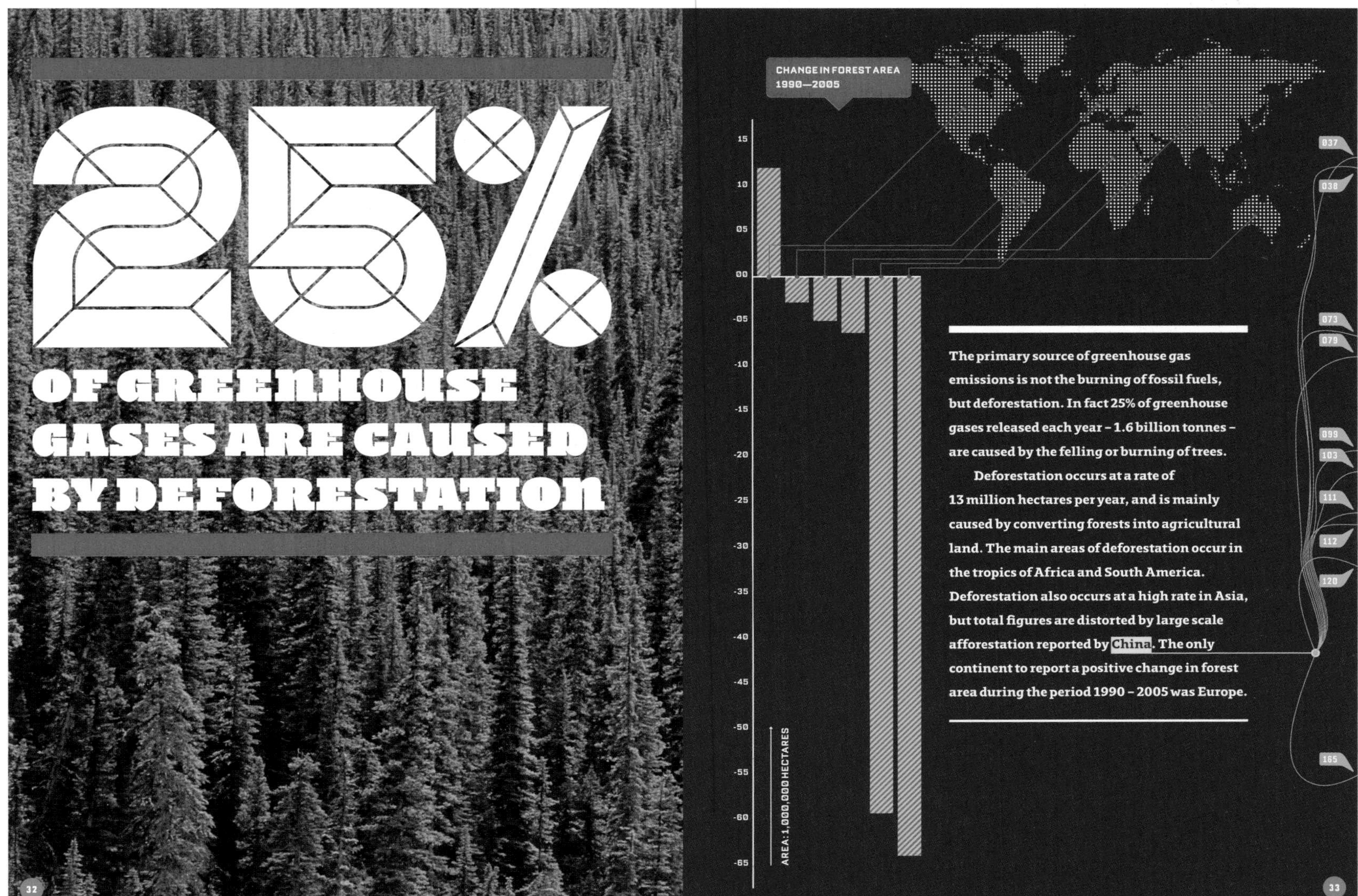

Mini Cooper

This graphic by Fogelson-Lubliner appeared in *Mini Zine*, a miniature issue of *GOOD* magazine. The piece makes clear two major benefits to driving a smaller and more fuel-efficient car like the Mini Cooper.

The road lanes along the bottom demonstrate how small cars take less road space. The billboard display (top right) explains how the fuel-efficient car saves gas costs.

Diese von Fogelson-Lubliner erstellte Grafik erschien in *Mini Zine*, einer Miniaturausgabe der Zeitschrift *GOOD*. Das Schaubild verdeutlicht zwei wesentliche Vorteile, die es mit sich bringt, einen kleineren, verbrauchsarmen Wagen wie den Mini Cooper zu fahren.

Die stilisierten Straßen unten zeigen, wie viel weniger Platz Kleinwagen auf der Straße in Anspruch nehmen, auf der Tafel oben rechts wird erläutert, dass der verbrauchsarme Wagen die Benzinkosten verringert.

Ce visuel de Fogelson-Lubliner est paru dans *Mini Zine*, un tirage miniature du magazine *GOOD*. Il souligne les deux avantages clés de conduire une voiture plus petite et moins gourmande, comme la Mini Cooper.

Les routes du bas montrent que les petites voitures occupent moins de place. Le panneau d'affichage (en haut à droite) explique que les voitures qui consomment moins permettent de réduire les frais d'essence.

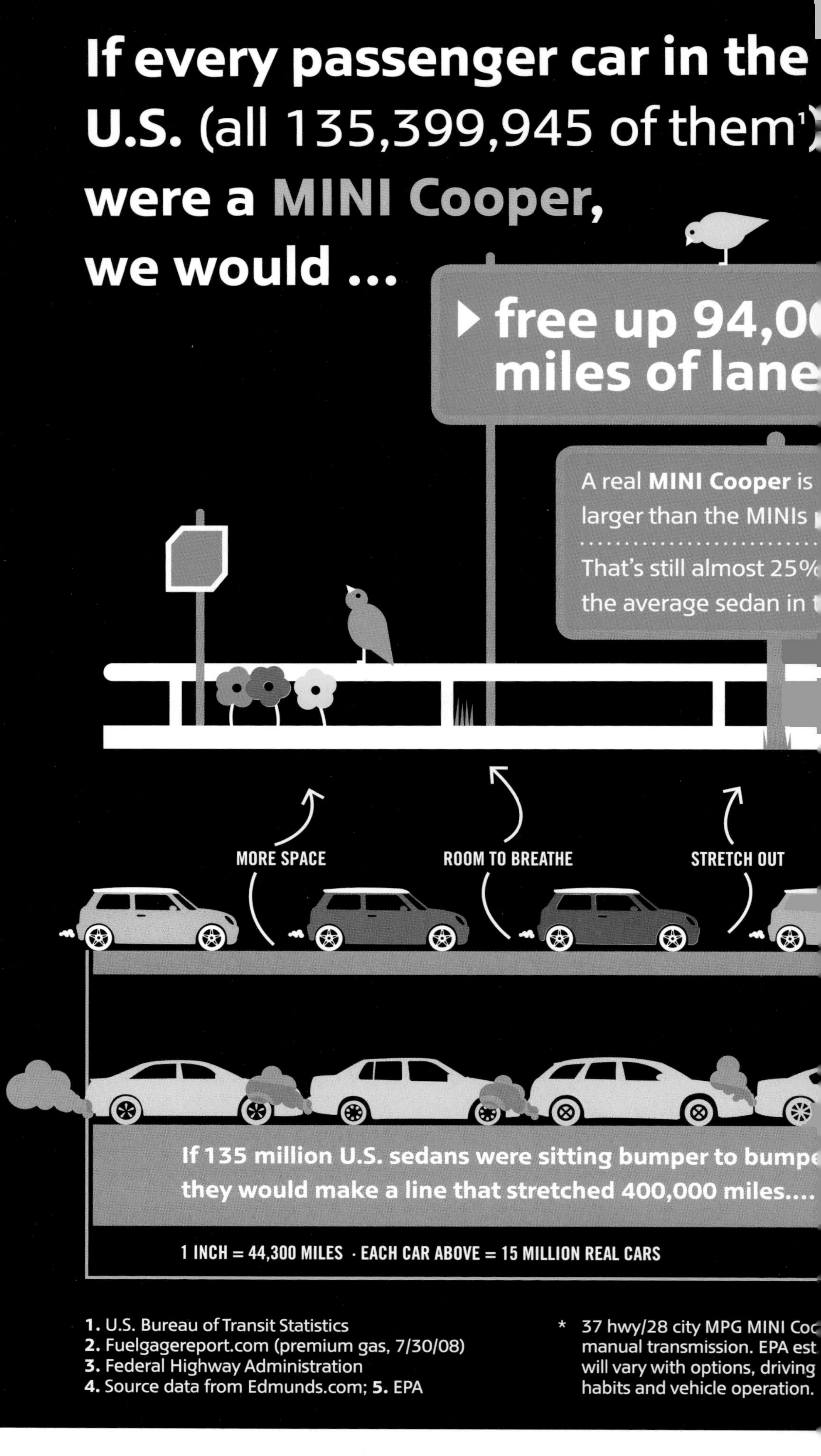

If every passenger car in the U.S. (all 135,399,945 of them[1]
were a MINI Cooper,
we would ...
free up 94,0
miles of lane
A real MINI Cooper is
larger than the MINIs
That's still almost 25%
the average sedan in
MORE SPACE
ROOM TO BREATHE
STRETCH OUT
If 135 million U.S. sedans were sitting bumper to bump
they would make a line that stretched 400,000 miles....
1 INCH = 44,300 MILES · EACH CAR ABOVE = 15 MILLION REAL CARS
1. U.S. Bureau of Transit Statistics
2. Fuelgagereport.com (premium gas, 7/30/08)
3. Federal Highway Administration
4. Source data from Edmunds.com; 5. EPA
* 37 hwy/28 city MPG MINI Coo
manual transmission. EPA est
will vary with options, driving
habits and vehicle operation.

Project Info: *GOOD*, magazine article, 2008, USA
Data Source: US Bureau of Transit Statistics; Daily Fuel Gauge Report; US EPA; Federal Highway Administration; Edmunds Car Buying Guide
Design: Gary Fogelson, Phil Lubliner (Fogelson-Lubliner)

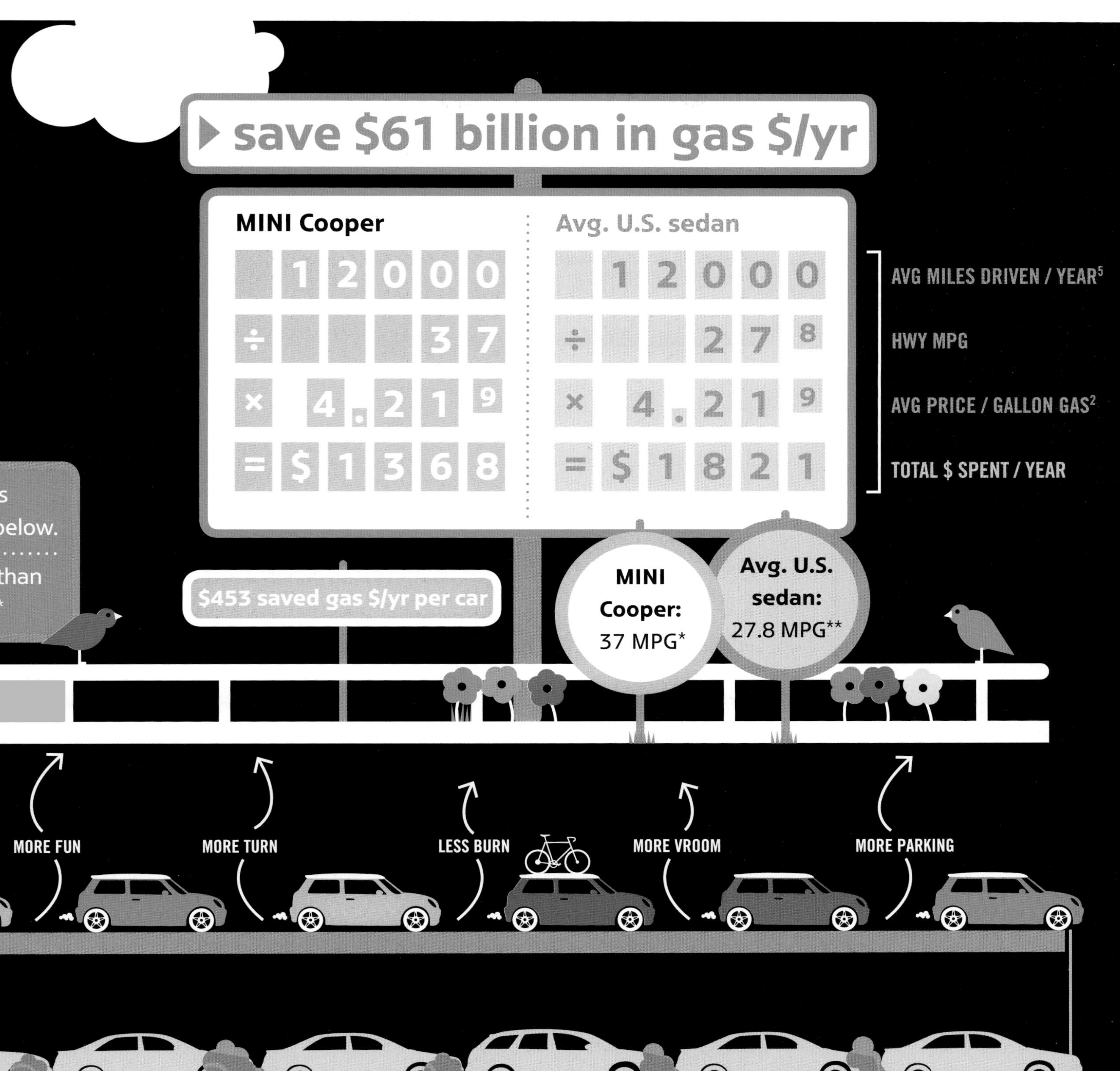

p with
al mileage
driving

** 27.8 highway MPG, is the weighted average of 2007 small, medium, and large-sized cars and wagons according to EPA estimates.

*** Based on the length of the MINI Cooper Hardtop (145.6") and the length of the average U.S. sedan (189.6")[4] and 46,837 total miles of National Higthway System[3]

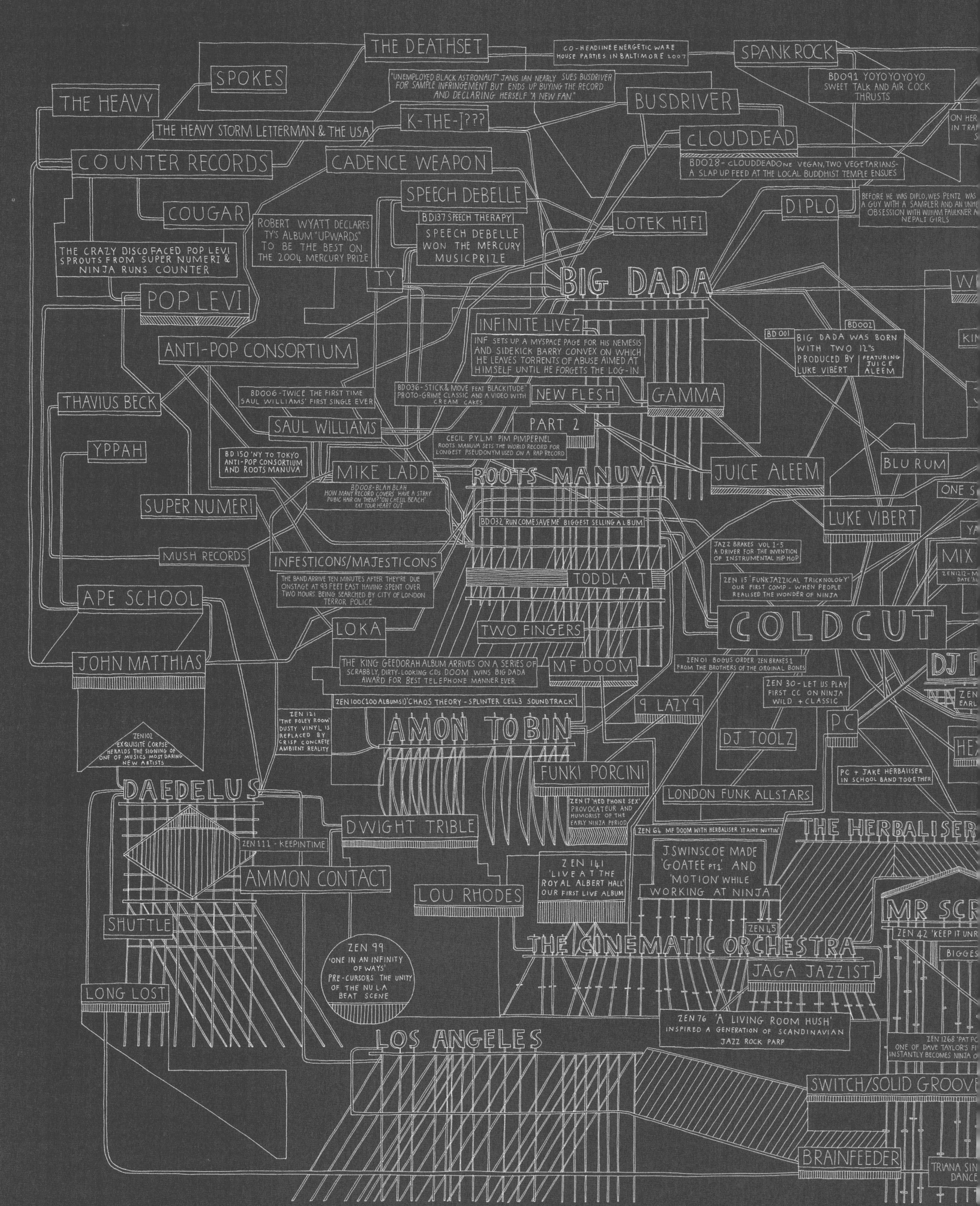

THE DEATHSET
CO-HEADLINE ENERGETIC WAREHOUSE PARTIES IN BALTIMORE 2007
SPANK ROCK
SPOKES
"UNEMPLOYED BLACK ASTRONAUT" JANIS IAN NEARLY SUES BUSDRIVER FOR SAMPLE INFRINGEMENT BUT ENDS UP BUYING THE RECORD AND DECLARING HERSELF "A NEW FAN"
BD091 YOYOYOYOYO SWEET TALK AND AIR COCK THRUSTS
THE HEAVY
BUSDRIVER
THE HEAVY STORM LETTERMAN & THE USA
K-THE-I???
CLOUDDEAD
COUNTER RECORDS
CADENCE WEAPON
BD028-CLOUDDEAD ONE VEGAN, TWO VEGETARIANS-A SLAP UP FEED AT THE LOCAL BUDDHIST TEMPLE ENSUES
SPEECH DEBELLE
COUGAR
ROBERT WYATT DECLARES TY'S ALBUM "UPWARDS" TO BE THE BEST ON THE 2004 MERCURY PRIZE
BD137 SPEECH THERAPY SPEECH DEBELLE WON THE MERCURY MUSIC PRIZE
LOTEK HIFI
DIPLO
THE CRAZY DISCO FACED POP LEVI SPROUTS FROM SUPER NUMERI & NINJA RUNS COUNTER
TY
BIG DADA
POP LEVI
INFINITE LIVEZ
INF SETS UP A MYSPACE PAGE FOR HIS NEMESIS AND SIDEKICK BARRY CONVEX ON WHICH HE LEAVES TORRENTS OF ABUSE AIMED AT HIMSELF UNTIL HE FORGETS THE LOG-IN
ANTI-POP CONSORTIUM
BD001
BD002
BIG DADA WAS BORN WITH TWO 12"s PRODUCED BY LUKE VIBERT FEATURING JUICE ALEEM
THAVIUS BECK
BD006-TWICE THE FIRST TIME SAUL WILLIAMS' FIRST SINGLE EVER
BD036-STICK & MOVE FEAT BLACKITUDE PROTO-GRIME CLASSIC AND A VIDEO WITH CREAM CAKES
NEW FLESH
GAMMA
SAUL WILLIAMS
PART 2
YPPAH
CECIL P.Y.L.M PIM PIMPERNEL ROOTS MANUVA SETS THE WORLD RECORD FOR LONGEST PSEUDONYM USED ON A RAP RECORD
BD 150 'NY TO TOKYO' ANTI-POP CONSORTIUM AND ROOTS MANUVA
MIKE LADD
ROOTS MANUVA
JUICE ALEEM
BLU RUM
BD008-BLAH BLAH HOW MANY RECORD COVERS HAVE A STRAY PUBIC HAIR ON THEM? "ON CHESIL BEACH" EAT YOUR HEART OUT
SUPER NUMERI
LUKE VIBERT
BD032 'RUN COME SAVE ME' BIGGEST SELLING ALBUM
MUSH RECORDS
INFESTICONS/MAJESTICONS
JAZZ BRAKES VOL 1-5 A DRIVER FOR THE INVENTION OF INSTRUMENTAL HIP HOP
THE BAND ARRIVE TEN MINUTES AFTER THEY'RE DUE ONSTAGE AT 93 FEET EAST HAVING SPENT OVER TWO HOURS BEING SEARCHED BY CITY OF LONDON TERROR POLICE
TODDLA T
ZEN 15 'FUNKJAZZICAL TRICKNOLOGY' OUR FIRST COMP - WHEN PEOPLE REALISED THE WONDER OF NINJA
APE SCHOOL
COLDCUT
LOKA
TWO FINGERS
JOHN MATTHIAS
THE KING GEEDORAH ALBUM ARRIVES ON A SERIES OF SCRABBLY, DIRTY-LOOKING CDs DOOM WINS BIG DADA AWARD FOR BEST TELEPHONE MANNER EVER
MF DOOM
ZEN01 BOGUS ORDER ZEN BRAKES 1 FROM THE BROTHERS OF THE ORIGINAL BONES
ZEN 30 - LET US PLAY FIRST CC ON NINJA WILD + CLASSIC
ZEN 100 (100 ALBUMS!) 'CHAOS THEORY - SPLINTER CELL 3 SOUNDTRACK'
9 LAZY 9
ZEN 121 'THE FOLEY ROOM' DUSTY VINYL IS REPLACED BY CRISP CONCRETE AMBIENT REALITY
ZEN102 'EXQUISITE CORPSE' HERALDS THE SIGNING OF ONE OF MUSICS MOST DARING NEW ARTISTS
AMON TOBIN
DJ TOOLZ
PC
FUNKI PORCINI
PC + JAKE HERBALISER IN SCHOOL BAND TOGETHER
DAEDELUS
ZEN 17 'HED PHONE SEX' PROVOCATEUR AND HUMORIST OF THE EARLY NINJA PERIOD
LONDON FUNK ALLSTARS
DWIGHT TRIBLE
ZEN 6L MF DOOM WITH HERBALISER 'IT AINT NUTTIN'
THE HERBALISER
ZEN 111 - KEEPINTIME
ZEN 141 'LIVE AT THE ROYAL ALBERT HALL' OUR FIRST LIVE ALBUM
J.SWINSCOE MADE 'GOATEE PT1' AND 'MOTION' WHILE WORKING AT NINJA
AMMON CONTACT
LOU RHODES
SHUTTLE
ZEN 45
THE CINEMATIC ORCHESTRA
ZEN 42 'KEEP IT UNR
ZEN 99 'ONE IN AN INFINITY OF WAYS' PRE-CURSORS THE UNITY OF THE NU L.A BEAT SCENE
JAGA JAZZIST
LONG LOST
ZEN 76 'A LIVING ROOM HUSH' INSPIRED A GENERATION OF SCANDINAVIAN JAZZ ROCK PARP
LOS ANGELES
SWITCH/SOLID GROOVE
BRAINFEEDER
NINJA TUNE
20 YEARS OF BEATS & PIECES
DRAWN BY NIGEL PEAKE

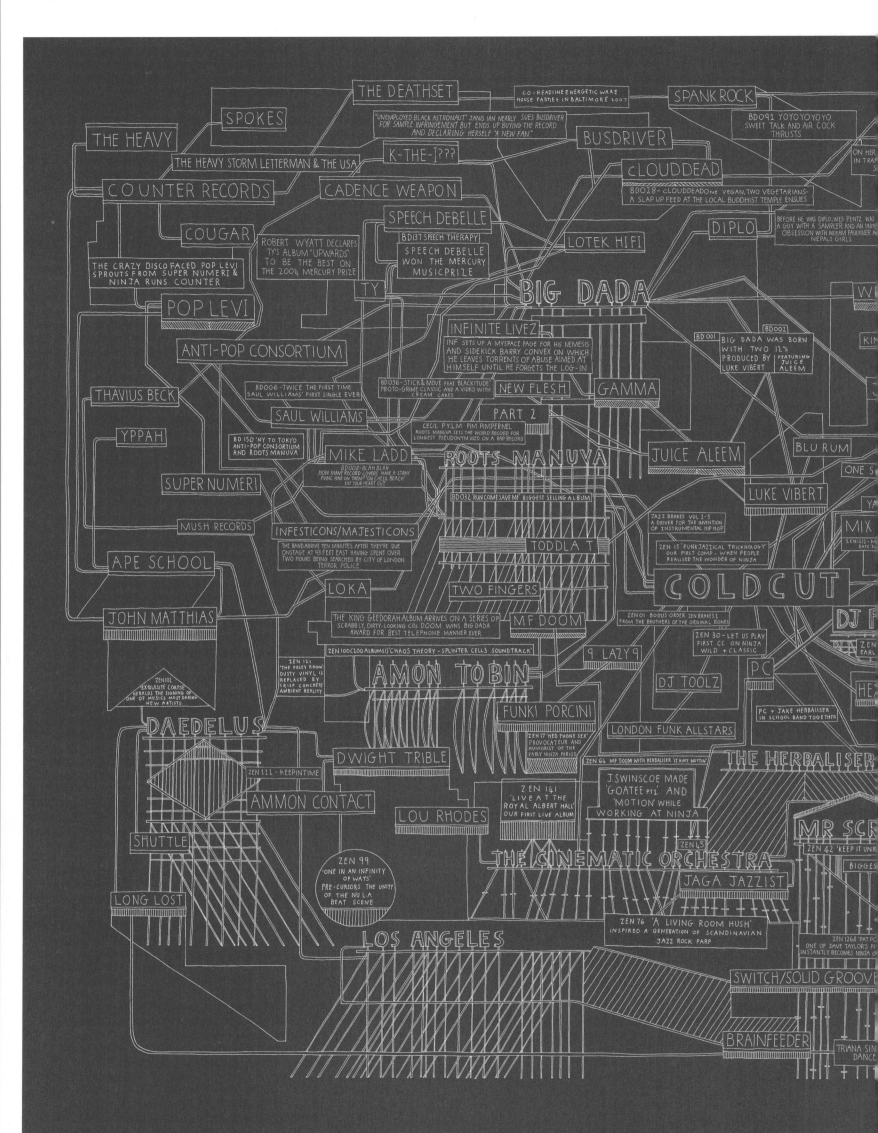

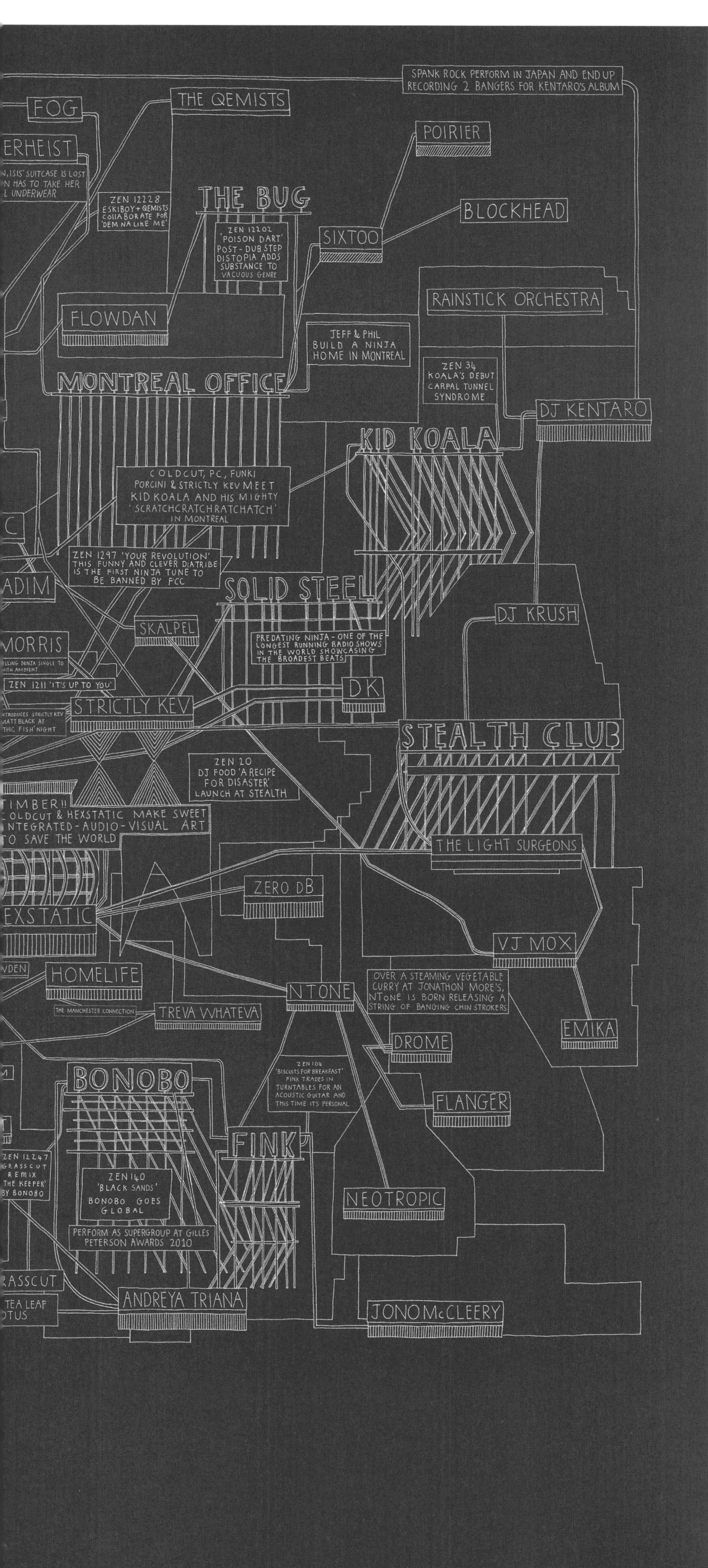

Ninja Tune –Family Tree

This drawing charts the history of London-based record label Ninja Tune, on the occasion of its 20th anniversary in 2010. Despite the title, the piece is not a strict historical genealogy. Rather, the piece unfolds a sort of mental map of the Ninja Tune cosmos, with the founding DJ team Coldcut at the heart.

The individual artists are shown, mentioning their most important projects and collaborations. The piece was originally produced as a poster in two colour versions. As a map, it is a variation on Nigel Peake's distorted maps of real and fictional places.

Auf dieser Grafik wird anlässlich des 20-jährigen Firmenjubiläums 2010 die Geschichte des in London ansässigen Plattenlabels Ninja Tune geschildert. Trotz des Titels handelt es sich dabei nicht um eine strenge historische Genealogie. Vielmehr zeigt das Schaubild eine Art kognitiver Karte, die den Kosmos von Ninja Tune rund um das DJ-Team Coldcut zeigt, das als Labelgründer im Mittelpunkt der Grafik steht.

Die einzelnen Künstler werden mit ihren bedeutendsten Projekten und Kollaborationen gezeigt. Ursprünglich wurde die Grafik als Plakat in zwei Farbvarianten gedruckt. Sie ist eine Spielart von Nigel Peakes verzerrten Landkarten realer und fiktionaler Orte.

Ce dessin illustre l'histoire de la maison de disques londonienne Ninja Tune, à l'occasion de son 20ᵉ anniversaire en 2010. Malgré le titre, l'œuvre n'est pas seulement une étude généalogique. Elle révèle une sorte de carte heuristique de l'univers de Ninja Tune, avec l'équipe fondatrice de DJ Coldcut au centre de tout.

Les artistes sont indiqués en citant leurs principaux projets et collaborations. L'œuvre a initialement été imprimée sous forme d'affiches en deux versions de couleur. C'est une variante des cartes déformées que Nigel Peake fait d'endroits réels et fictifs.

Project Info: Poster, 2010, UK
Design: Nigel Peake
Art Direction: Peter Quicke, Kevin Foakes

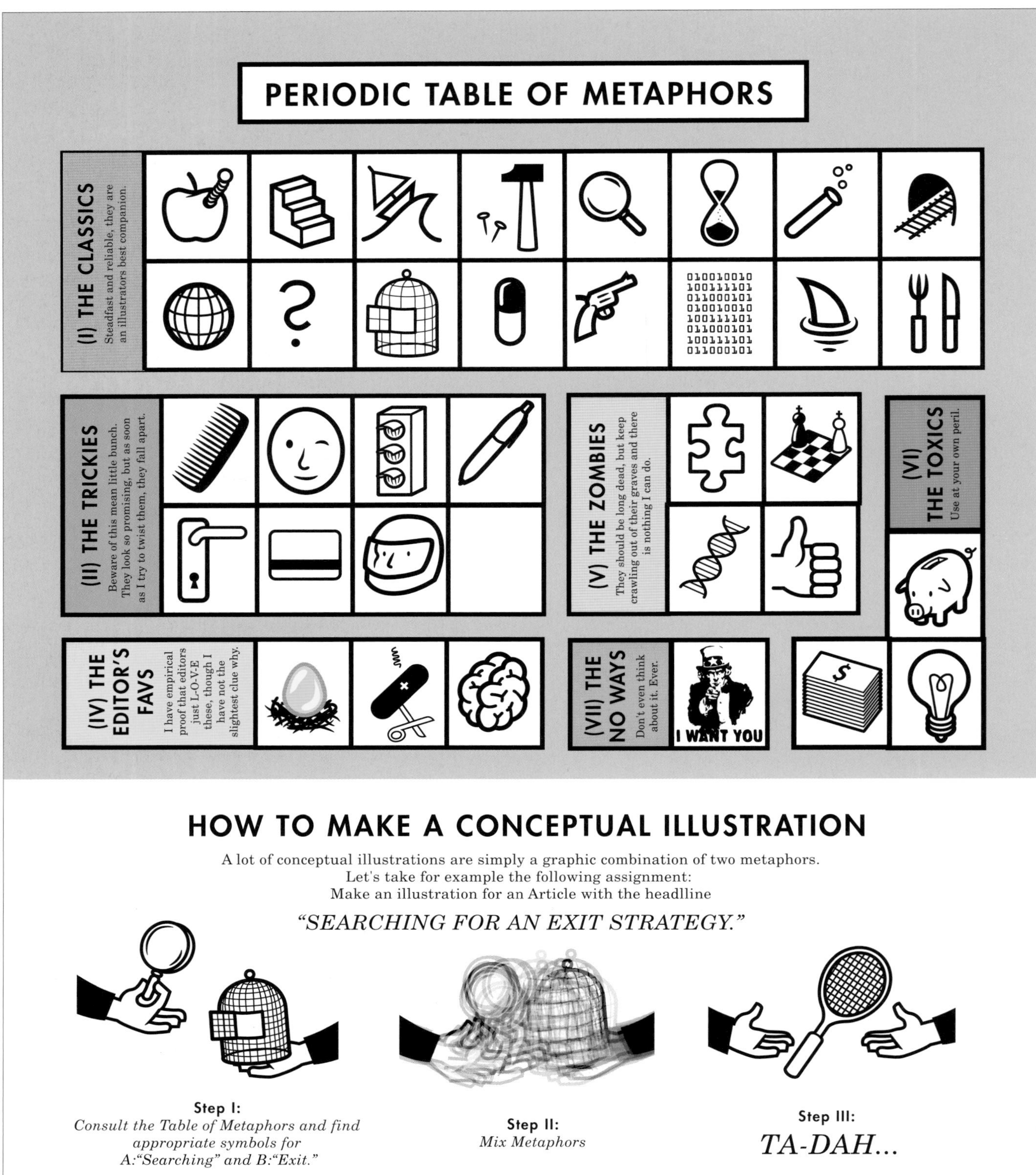

Periodic Table of Metaphors

Christoph Niemann created a series for *Print* magazine in 2004, humorously unveiling the secrets of his life as an illustrator. The series tackled all aspects of an illustrator's working life, including communication troubles with editors, the challenges of working on a chaotic desk or the dilemma posed by the blank piece of paper each job starts with.

In this piece, Niemann drew on one of the most famous scientific visualisation patterns, the periodic table of the elements, in order to display and categorise a tool-kit of metaphors, which illustrators can use to create illustrations on any current topic in a journalistic context. The diagram below explains how to create an illustration by mixing two metaphors together.

2004 entwickelte Christoph Niemann für die Zeitschrift *Print* eine Serie, in der er scherzhaft die Geheimnisse seines Lebens als Illustrator enthüllte. In der Serie ging es um alle Aspekte im Arbeitsalltag eines Illustrators, unter anderem um die Kommunikationsschwierigkeiten mit Redakteuren, um die Herausforderung, an einem chaotischen Schreibtisch zu arbeiten, und um das Dilemma der leeren Seite, mit dem jeder Auftrag beginnt.

Für diese Grafik griff Niemann auf eines der berühmtesten Visualisierungsmuster in der Naturwissenschaft zurück, das Periodensystem der Elemente, um einen Bausatz von Metaphern zu zeigen und zu kategorisieren. Mit dessen Hilfe können Illustratoren jedes beliebige aktuelle Thema in einem journalistischen Kontext bebildern. Das Diagramm unten links zeigt, wie man aus der Verbindung zweier Metaphern eine neue Illustration schafft.

En 2004, Christoph Niemann a créé pour le magazine *Print* une série qui a dévoilé avec humour sa vie d'illustrateur. Elle abordait tous les aspects de la vie professionnelle d'un illustrateur, y compris les problèmes de communication avec les éditeurs, les difficultés de travailler sur un bureau désorganisé ou l'angoisse de la feuille blanche au début de chaque projet.

Dans cette œuvre, Niemann a dessiné l'un des schémas de visualisation scientifique les plus connus, le tableau périodique des éléments, pour montrer et classer l'arsenal de métaphores que les illustrateurs peuvent employer pour n'importe quel sujet dans un contexte journalistique. Le diagramme du bas explique comment créer une illustration en combinant deux métaphores.

Project Info: *Print*, magazine article, 2004, USA
Design: Christoph Niemann

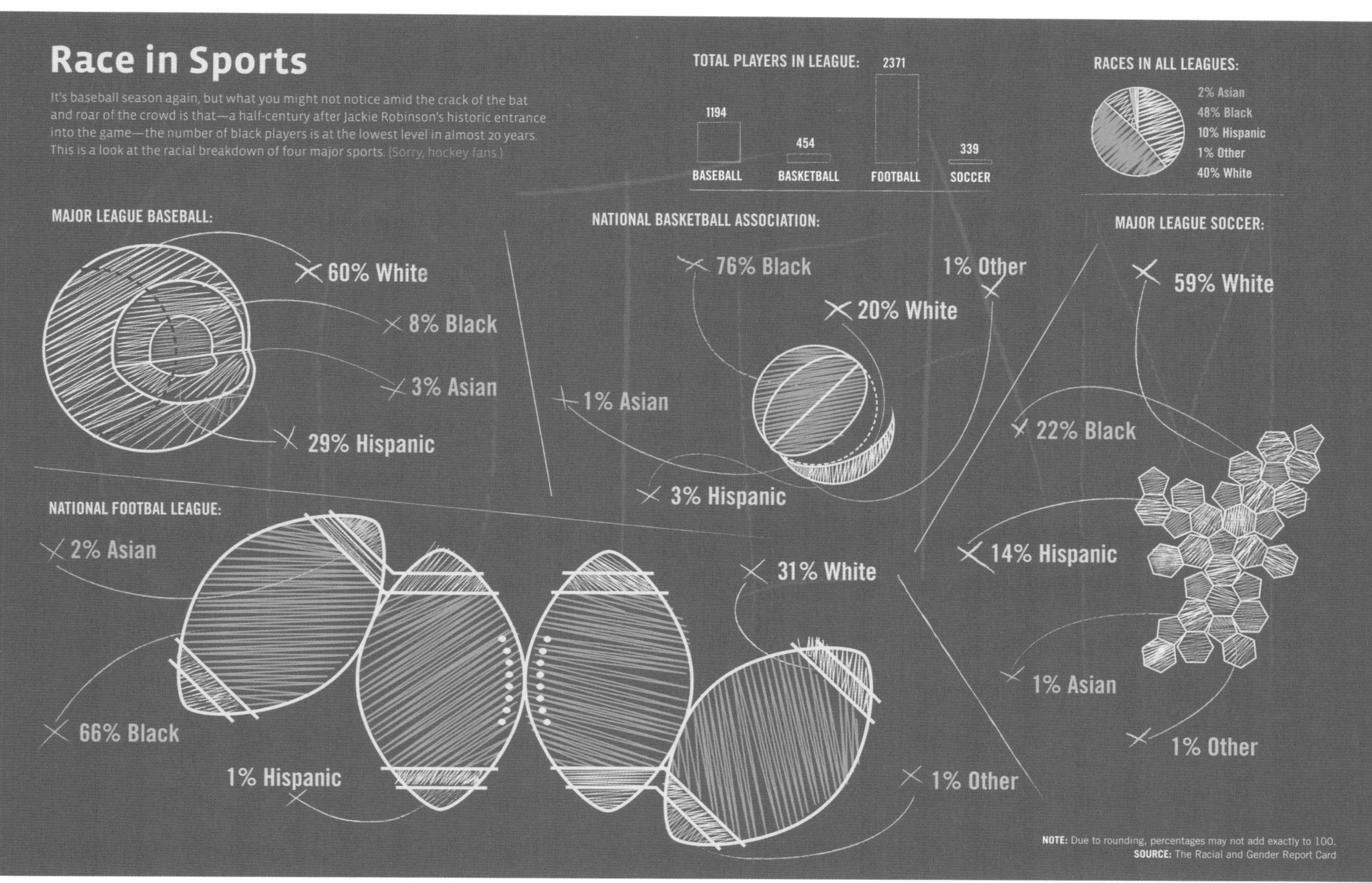

Race in Sports

Developed for *GOOD* magazine, this graphic looks at the racial breakdown in the US's four most popular sports: baseball, football, basketball and soccer. Each sport is represented by its own particular ball. The football and the soccer ball are shown like sewing patterns, with their component parts spread out against a flat background.

The baseball to the left is cut open, showing the composition of the ball in layers. Colours indicate the racial distribution in each sport, indicating that football and basketball are predominantly played by African Americans, while baseball is a mostly "white" sport.

Diese für die Zeitschrift *GOOD* gestaltete Grafik analysiert die ethnische Herkunft von Spielern in den vier beliebtesten amerikanischen Sportarten: Baseball, Football, Basketball und Fußball. Jeder Sport wird durch den Ball, mit dem er gespielt wird, dargestellt. Der Football und der Fußball sind als ausgebreitete Schnittmuster vor dem zweidimensionalen Hintergrund dargestellt.

Der Baseball links ist aufgeschnitten, sodass die einzelnen Schichten sichtbar werden. Die ethnische Verteilung wird bei jeder Sportart durch Farben zum Ausdruck gebracht. So lässt sich erkennen, dass Football und Basketball vorwiegend von Afroamerikanern gespielt werden, während Baseball vor allem eine „weiße" Sportart ist.

Conçu pour le magazine *GOOD*, ce graphique analyse la répartition raciale dans les quatre sports les plus populaires aux États-Unis: baseball, football américain, basket-ball et football. Chaque sport est représenté par sa balle ou son ballon. Les ballons de football américain et de football sont présentés comme des patrons de couture, leurs pièces étalées sur un fond plat.

À gauche, la balle de baseball est coupée et son intérieur révèle la composition par couches. Les couleurs indiquent la distribution raciale dans chaque sport, le football et le basket-ball étant en majorité joués par des Afro-américains, alors que le baseball est un sport principalement « blanc ».

Project Info: "Who Is Playing Sports?", *GOOD*, online article, 2009, USA
Data Source: The Institute for Diversity and Ethics in Sport: "The Racial and Gender Report Card"
Research: Morgan Clendaniel
Design: Joshua Covarrubias (Kiss Me I'm Polish)
Art Direction: Agnieszka Gasparska (Kiss Me I'm Polish)

Relationships Among Scientific Paradigms

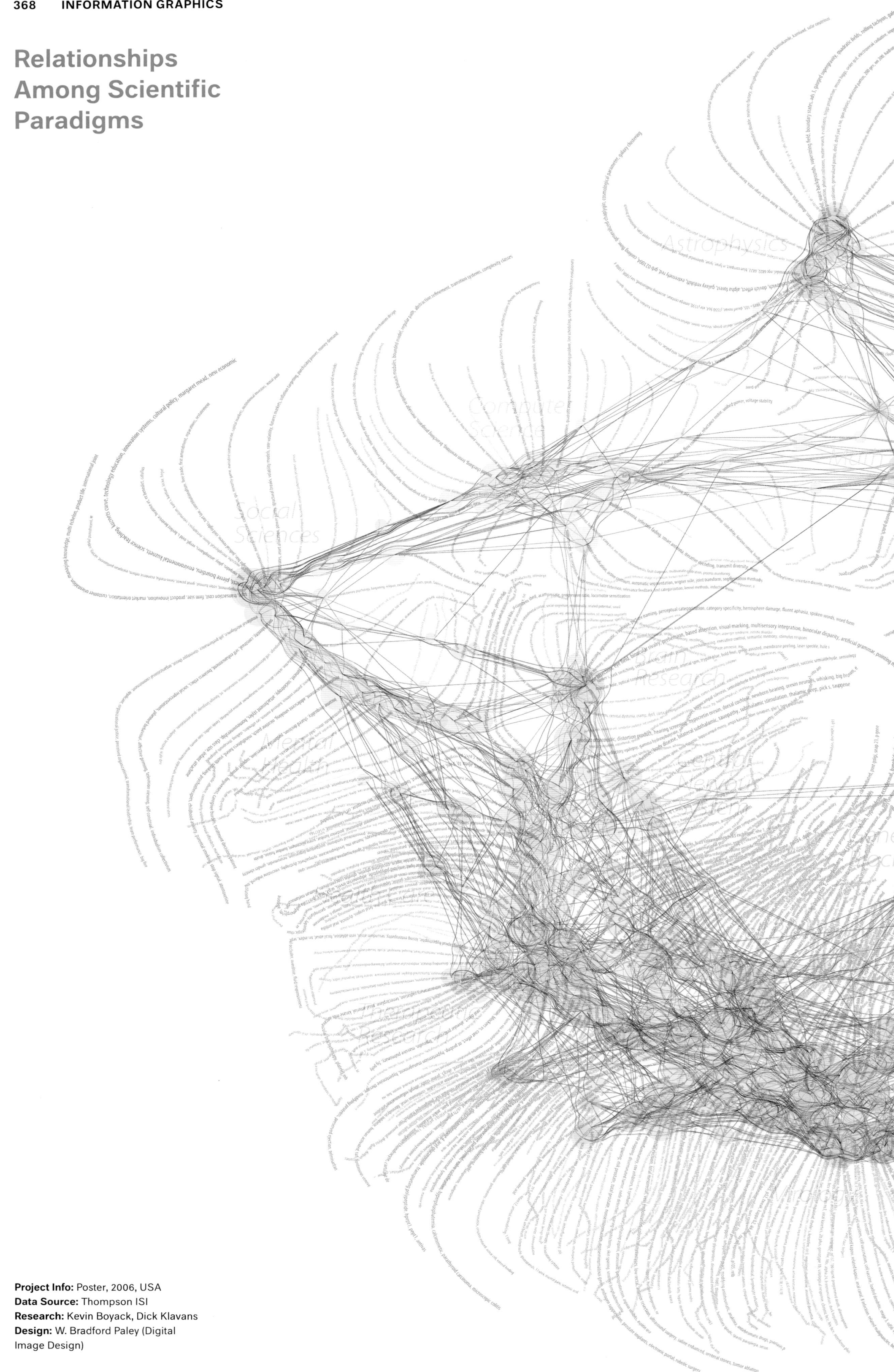

Project Info: Poster, 2006, USA
Data Source: Thompson ISI
Research: Kevin Boyack, Dick Klavans
Design: W. Bradford Paley (Digital Image Design)

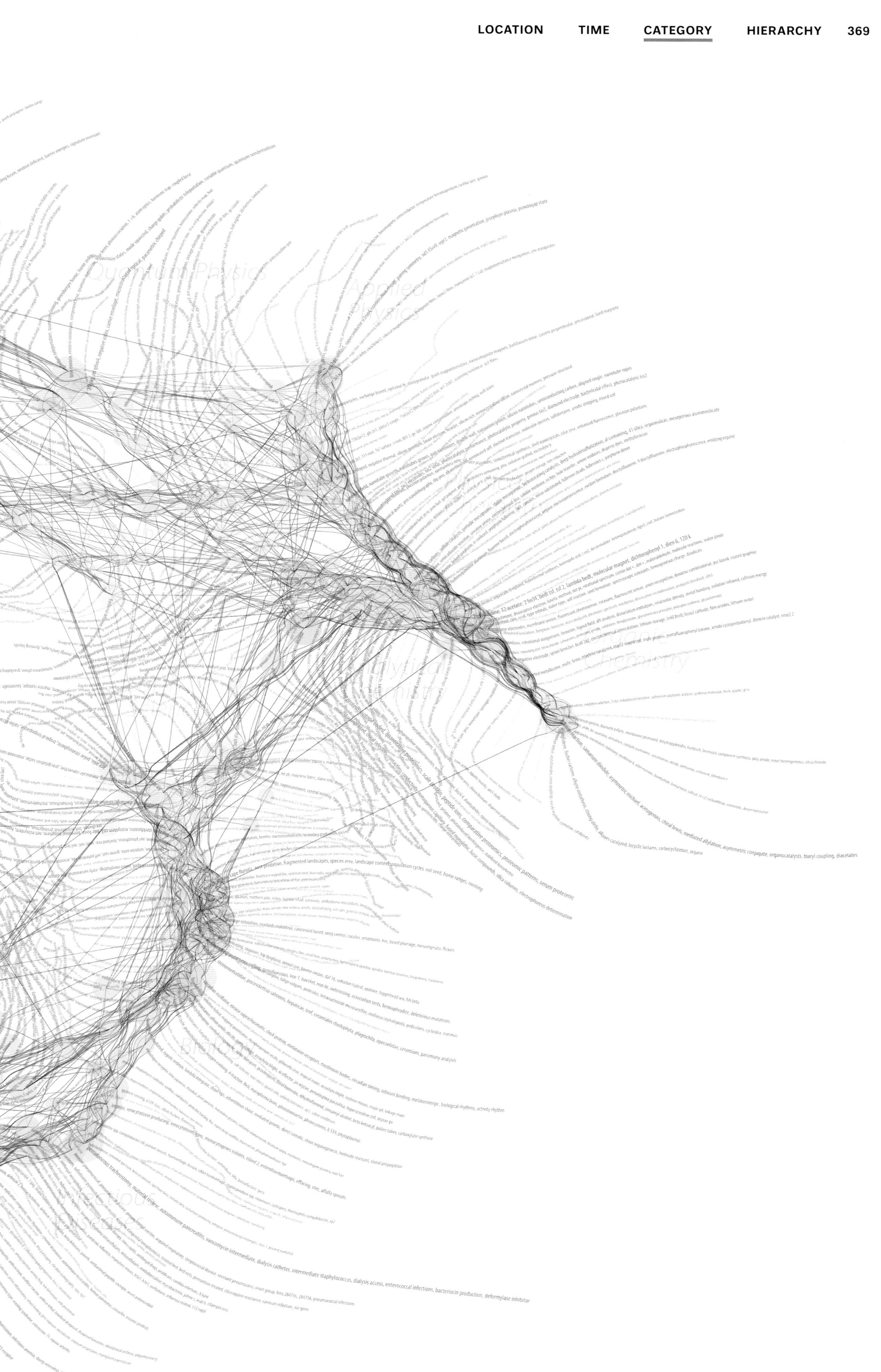

This is a very special "map" – it categorises scientific paradigms. Bradford Paley sorted 800,000 research papers published in 2003 into 776 distinct paradigms based on how often the papers were cited together by authors of other papers. Paradigms are depicted as pale, colour-coded circles: orange for social sciences, pink for medicine, green for biology, etc.

All connections between paradigms, based on quotes in other papers, are visualised by thin hairlines. The spatial layout forces all paradigms to repel each other, while the hairline connections work as rubber-bands keeping similar paradigms connected. The map thus shows relations between paradigms by proximity.

Bei dieser Grafik handelt es sich um eine ungewöhnliche „Karte" – sie kategorisiert wissenschaftliche Disziplinen. Bradford Paley ordnete 800.000 wissenschaftliche Artikel aus dem Jahr 2003 nach 776 verschiedenen Paradigmen, je nachdem, wie oft die Veröffentlichungen von Autoren anderer Schriften zitiert worden waren. Die Disziplinen sind als helle farbcodierte Kreise dargestellt: Orange für Sozialwissenschaften, Rosa für Medizin, Grün für Biologie usw.

Feine Linien visualisieren zusätzliche Verbindungen zwischen verschiedenen Paradigmen – sie beruhen auf Zitaten in anderen wissenschaftlichen Bereichen. Die einzelnen Paradigmen stoßen sich in dieser Visualisierung zunächst gegenseitig ab. Die Verbindungslinien dagegen funktionieren wie Gummibänder, die ähnliche Paradigmen zueinander hinziehen. Die Grafik veranschaulicht damit die Verwandtschaft zwischen zwei wissenschaftlichen Disziplinen durch räumliche Nachbarschaft.

Voici une « carte » très particulière de paradigmes scientifiques. Bradford Paley a trié 800 000 documents de recherche publiés en 2003 et les a classés en 776 paradigmes différents, selon la fréquence des références faites à ces documents par les auteurs d'autres documents. Les paradigmes sont présentés sous forme de cercles de couleur pâle : orange pour les sciences sociales, rose pour la médecine, vert pour la biologie, etc.

Toutes les connexions entre les paradigmes, basées sur leur mention dans d'autres documents, sont illustrées par des filaments. L'agencement spatial oblige les paradigmes à se repousser mutuellement, et les filaments qui les connectent ressemblent à des élastiques reliant les paradigmes similaires. La carte montre donc les relations entre paradigmes par proximité.

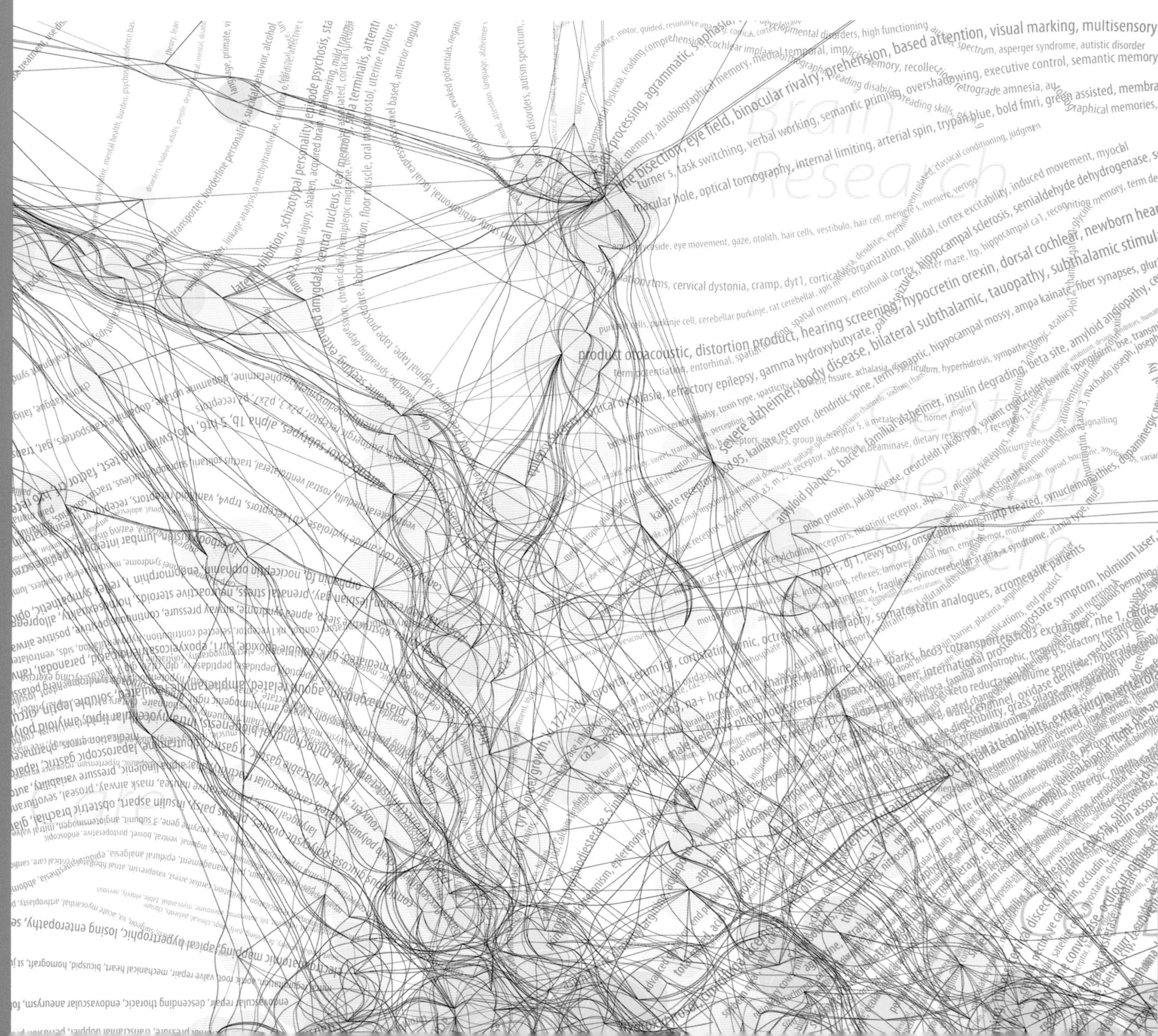

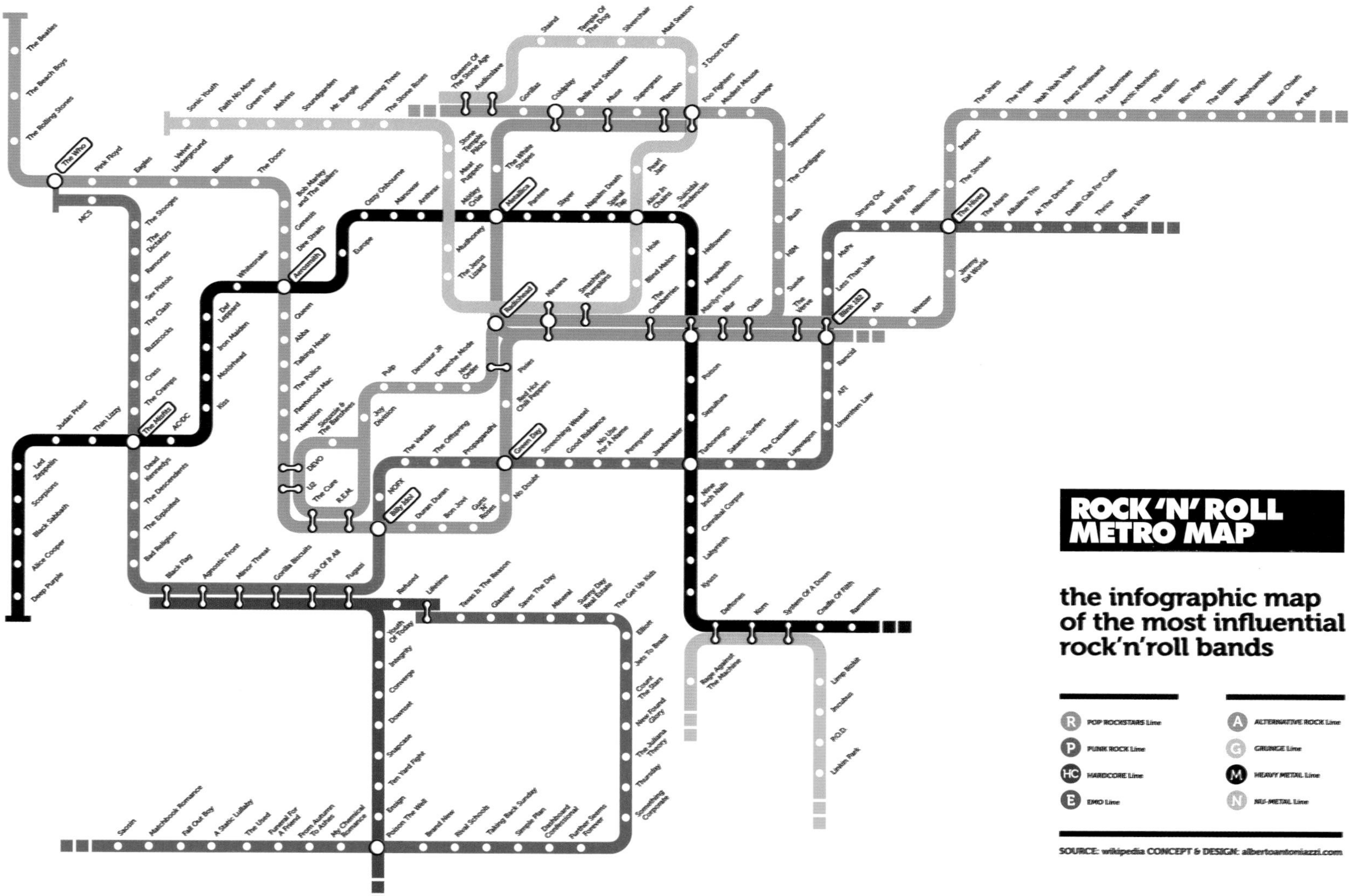

Rock 'n' Roll Metro Map

This graphic is based on the idea of representing the various genres of rock music as separate lines of a subway system. The abstract tube-map here is used to describe categories of rock music: by ascribing a category to each line, the graphic creates a virtual rock-music landscape. Bands are depicted as individual stations, sometimes marking the intersection of two distinct lines.

The graphic considers only bands and not single artists and defines "rock 'n' roll" as music played with drums, bass, guitar(s) and singing voice. Including more than 200 bands, the piece is Alberto Antoniazzi's personal vision of music history since the 1960s.

In dieser Grafik werden die unterschiedlichen Stilrichtungen des Rock 'n' Roll als Linien eines U-Bahn-Netzes visualisiert. Der abstrakte U-Bahn-Plan veranschaulicht Kategorien der Rockmusik: Indem jeder Linie eine Stilrichtung zugeordnet wird, entsteht eine virtuelle Landschaft des Rock 'n' Roll. Die U-Bahn-Stationen stehen für einzelne Bands, bei denen sich bisweilen zwei unterschiedliche Linien kreuzen oder berühren.

Die Grafik berücksichtigt lediglich Bands, nicht einzelne Musiker; als „Rock 'n' Roll" gilt Musik, die mittels Schlagzeug, Bass, Gitarre und Gesang erzeugt wird. Alberto Antoniazzis Grafik umfasst mehr als 200 Bands und stellt seine persönliche Sicht auf die Musikgeschichte seit den 1960er-Jahren dar.

Cette image part de l'idée de représenter différents genres musicaux de rock à l'aide des lignes d'un réseau de métro. Ce plan de métro abstrait sert à décrire les catégories de rock : en attribuant une catégorie à chaque ligne, on obtient un panorama virtuel de la musique rock. Les groupes sont des stations, et certains se trouvent à l'intersection de deux lignes.

Le plan mentionne uniquement des groupes, et non des artistes individuels, et il définit le rock 'n' roll comme une musique jouée avec une batterie, une basse, une ou des guitares et un chanteur. Regroupant plus de 200 groupes, cette création offre la vision personnelle d'Alberto Antoniazzi de l'histoire de la musique depuis les années 1960.

Project Info: Poster, 2010, Italy
Data Source: Wikipedia
Design: Alberto Antoniazzi

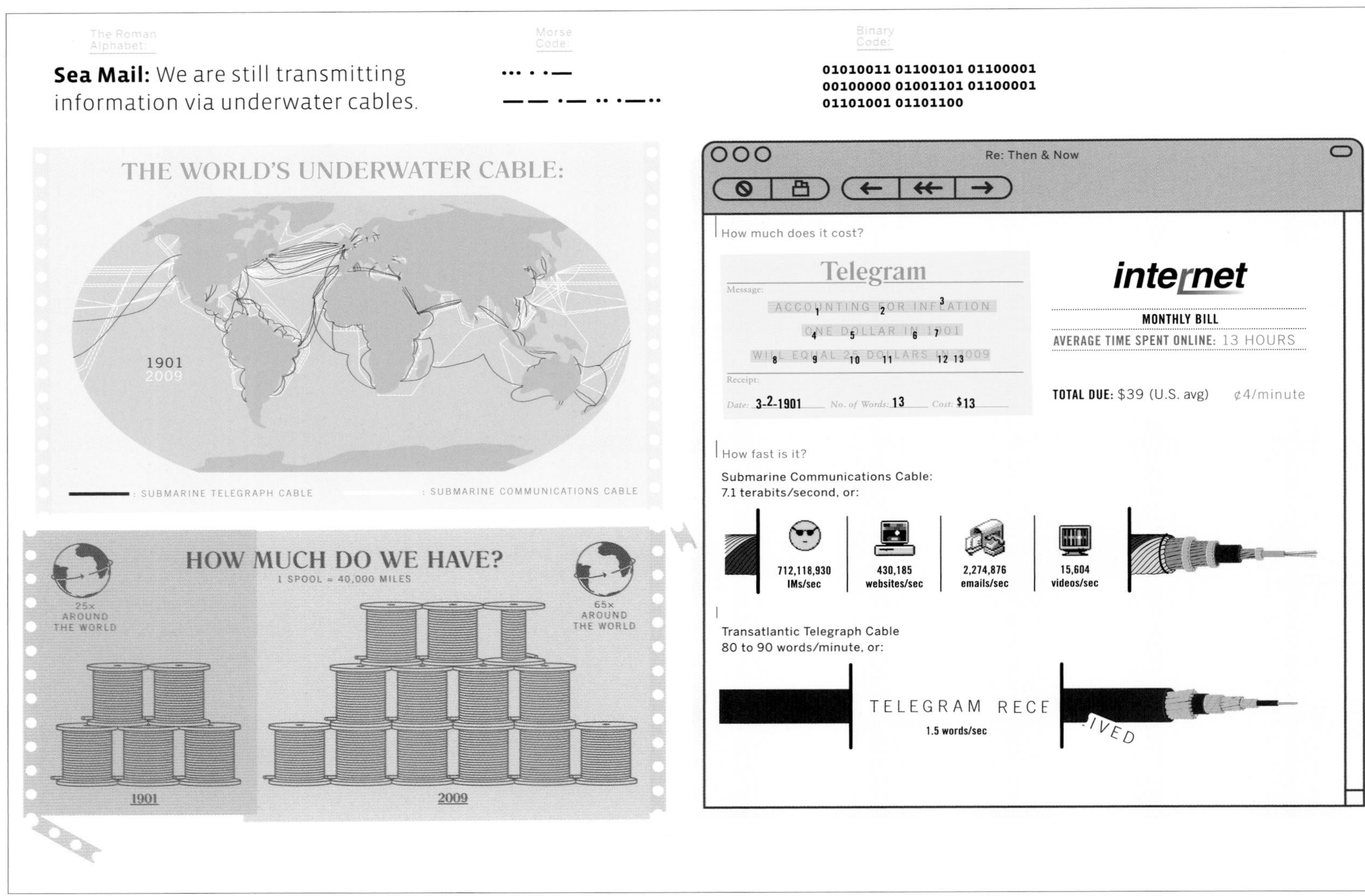

Sea Mail

Already in 1901 telegrams were being transmitted globally through underwater cables. Today, underwater cables transport digital signals and assure access to data available on the Internet.

The graphic compares this submarine data-flow now and in the beginning according to capacities, cable infrastructure and transmission speeds. This has been visualised by using a map chart, cable spools, service receipts and cable cross-sections.

Bereits 1901 wurden Telegramme via Unterseekabel übermittelt. Heutzutage transportieren Unterwasserkabel digitale Signale und sichern so den Zugang zu Daten, die über das Internet verfügbar sind.

Die Grafik vergleicht den heutigen mit dem damaligen unterseeischen Datenfluss hinsichtlich Kapazität, Kabelinfrastruktur und Übertragungsgeschwindigkeit. Zur Visualisierung dienen eine Weltkarte, Kabelrollen, Dienstleistungsabrechnungen und Kabelquerschnitte.

Déjà en 1901, les télégrammes étaient envoyés à travers le monde via des câbles sous-marins. Aujourd'hui, ces câbles véhiculent des signaux numériques et permettent d'accéder aux données disponibles sur Internet.

Ce graphique compare ce trafic sous-marin de données aujourd'hui et à l'origine en termes de capacités, d'infrastructure des câbles et de vitesse de transmission. La représentation a recours à une carte, des bobines de câbles, des reçus et des coupes transversales des câbles.

Project Info: "Where Does the Internet Come From?", *GOOD*, magazine article, 2009, USA
Data Source: Atlantic-cable.com; Da Vinci Institute; Encyclopedia Americana; Naomi S. Baron: "Instant Messaging by American College Students"; Nielsen Company
Design: Gary Fogelson, Phil Lubliner (Fogelson-Lubliner)

The Corporate Vermin that Rules America

With an unusual political emphasis, this piece takes a stand. Produced in 2003, it shows how closely the George W. Bush administration was interwoven with major industries and business. The then president is shown in the centre as a money-driven monkey, while members of his administration are shown as cockroaches, weevils and flies all surrounding him.

For the named politicians, current connections or earlier engagements with major companies are listed, with selected companies explained at the sides. The piece thus strongly suggests how political decisions in the Bush era were driven by corporate interests.

Diese Grafik bezieht mit ihrer dezidierten politischen Haltung deutlich Stellung. Sie stammt aus dem Jahr 2003 und zeigt, wie eng die US-amerikanische Regierung unter George W. Bush tatsächlich mit Schlüsselindustrien und -unternehmen verwoben war. Dargestellt als von Geld getriebener Affe, steht der damalige Präsident im Mittelpunkt der Grafik, während Mitglieder seiner Regierung als Kakerlaken, Rüsselkäfer und Fliegen gezeigt sind, die ihn umschwirren.

Die Politiker werden genannt mit ihren Verbindungen und früheren Engagements für große Konzerne; Erläuterungen zu ausgewählten Unternehmen finden sich links und rechts der Grafik. Sie macht deutlich, wie stark politische Entscheidungen während der Ära Bush an den Interessen der Industrie orientiert waren.

D'un engagement politique inhabituel, cette création prend clairement position. Réalisée en 2003, elle montre la relation étroite entre l'administration de George W. Bush et d'importantes entreprises. Le président est représenté au centre par un singe motivé par l'appât du gain, alors que les membres de l'administration sont symbolisés par des cafards, des charançons et des mouches qui gravitent autour de lui.

Pour les politiciens cités apparaissent les connexions actuelles ou les implications antérieures avec de grandes compagnies, dont certaines sont présentées sur le côté. L'œuvre laisse clairement entendre que les décisions politiques durant l'ère Bush étaient dictées par des intérêts économiques.

Project Info: Poster, 2003, UK
Data Source: AlterNet; Stop Esso campaign; CleanUpGE.org; Disinfopedia.org; Multinational Monitor; World Policy Institutes et al.
Design: Jonathan Barnbrook, Pedro Inoue (Barnbrook)

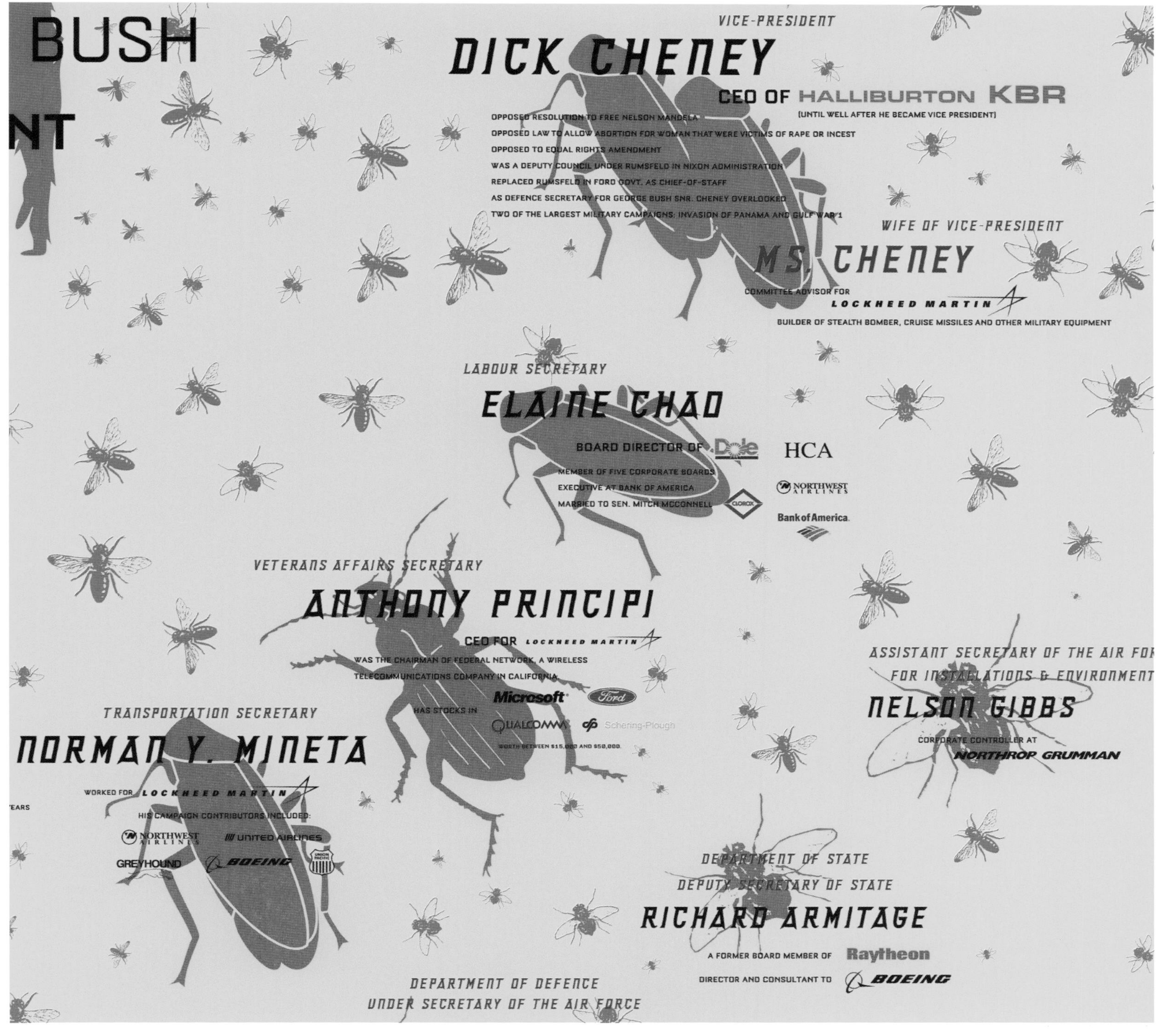

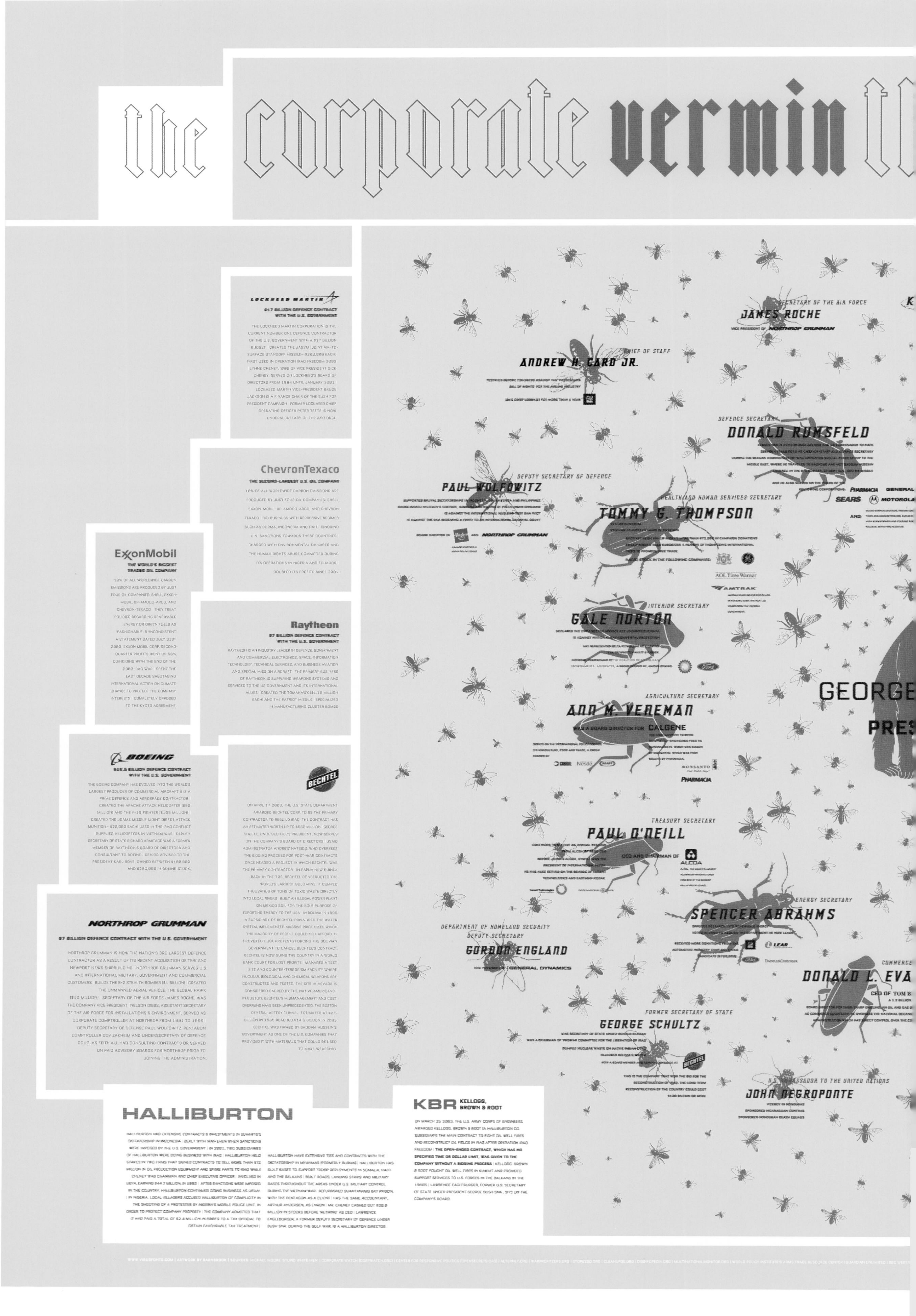

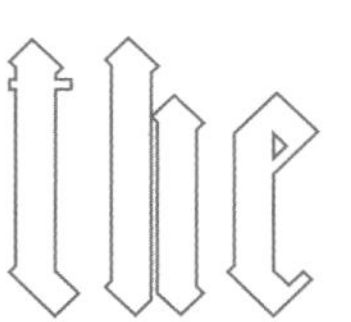

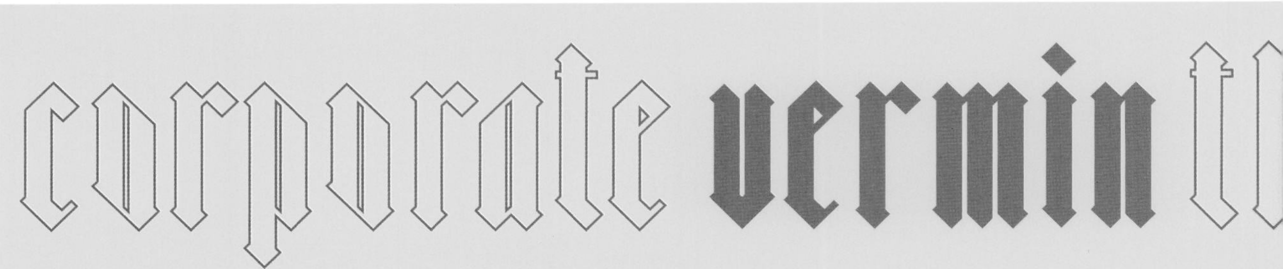

LOCKHEED MARTIN

$17 BILLION DEFENCE CONTRACT WITH THE U.S. GOVERNMENT

THE LOCKHEED MARTIN CORPORATION IS THE CURRENT NUMBER ONE DEFENCE CONTRACTOR OF THE U.S. GOVERNMENT WITH A $17 BILLION BUDGET | CREATED THE JASSM (JOINT AIR-TO-SURFACE STANDOFF MISSILE– $260,000 EACH) FIRST USED IN OPERATION IRAQ FREEDOM 2003 | LYNNE CHENEY, WIFE OF VICE PRESIDENT DICK CHENEY, SERVED ON LOCKHEED'S BOARD OF DIRECTORS FROM 1994 UNTIL JANUARY 2001 | LOCKHEED MARTIN VICE-PRESIDENT BRUCE JACKSON IS A FINANCE CHAIR OF THE BUSH FOR PRESIDENT CAMPAIGN | FORMER LOCKHEED CHIEF OPERATING OFFICER PETER TEETS IS NOW UNDERSECRETARY OF THE AIR FORCE.

ChevronTexaco

THE SECOND-LARGEST U.S. OIL COMPANY

10% OF ALL WORLDWIDE CARBON EMISSIONS ARE PRODUCED BY JUST FOUR OIL COMPANIES: SHELL, EXXON-MOBIL, BP-AMOCO-ARCO, AND CHEVRON-TEXACO | DID BUSINESS WITH REPRESSIVE REGIMES SUCH AS BURMA, INDONESIA AND HAITI, IGNORING U.N. SANCTIONS TOWARDS THESE COUNTRIES | CHARGED WITH ENVIRONMENTAL DAMAGES AND THE HUMAN RIGHTS ABUSE COMMITTED DURING ITS OPERATIONS IN NIGERIA AND ECUADOR | DOUBLED ITS PROFITS SINCE 2001.

ExxonMobil

THE WORLD'S BIGGEST TRADED OIL COMPANY

10% OF ALL WORLDWIDE CARBON EMISSIONS ARE PRODUCED BY JUST FOUR OIL COMPANIES: SHELL, EXXON-MOBIL, BP-AMOCO-ARCO, AND CHEVRON-TEXACO | THEY TREAT POLICIES REGARDING RENEWABLE ENERGY OR GREEN FUELS AS 'FASHIONABLE' & 'INCONSISTENT' A STATEMENT DATED JULY 31ST 2003, EXXON MOBIL CORP. SECOND-QUARTER PROFITS WENT UP 58%, COINCIDING WITH THE END OF THE 2003 IRAQ WAR | SPENT THE LAST DECADE SABOTAGING INTERNATIONAL ACTION ON CLIMATE CHANGE TO PROTECT THE COMPANY INTERESTS | COMPLETELY OPPOSED TO THE KYOTO AGREEMENT.

Raytheon

$7 BILLION DEFENCE CONTRACT WITH THE U.S. GOVERNMENT

RAYTHEON IS AN INDUSTRY LEADER IN DEFENCE, GOVERNMENT AND COMMERCIAL ELECTRONICS, SPACE, INFORMATION TECHNOLOGY, TECHNICAL SERVICES, AND BUSINESS AVIATION AND SPECIAL MISSION AIRCRAFT | THE PRIMARY BUSINESS OF RAYTHEON IS SUPPLYING WEAPONS SYSTEMS AND SERVICES TO THE US GOVERNMENT AND ITS INTERNATIONAL ALLIES | CREATED THE TOMAHAWK ($1.10 MILLION EACH) AND THE PATRIOT MISSILE | SPECIALIZED IN MANUFACTURING CLUSTER BOMBS.

BOEING

$16.5 BILLION DEFENCE CONTRACT WITH THE U.S. GOVERNMENT

THE BOEING COMPANY HAS EVOLVED INTO THE WORLD'S LARGEST PRODUCER OF COMMERCIAL AIRCRAFT & IS A PRIME DEFENCE AND AEROSPACE CONTRACTOR | CREATED THE APACHE ATTACK HELICOPTER ($50 MILLION) AND THE F-15 FIGHTER ($105 MILLION) | CREATED THE JDAMS MISSILE (JOINT DIRECT ATTACK MUNITION - $20,000 EACH) USED IN THE IRAQ CONFLICT | SUPPLIED HELICOPTERS IN VIETNAM WAR | DEPUTY SECRETARY OF STATE RICHARD ARMITAGE WAS A FORMER MEMBER OF RAYTHEON'S BOARD OF DIRECTORS AND CONSULTANT TO BOEING | SENIOR ADVISER TO THE PRESIDENT KARL ROVE, OWNED BETWEEN $100,000 AND $250,000 IN BOEING STOCK.

BECHTEL

ON APRIL 17 2003, THE U.S. STATE DEPARTMENT AWARDED BECHTEL CORP. TO BE THE PRIMARY CONTRACTOR TO REBUILD IRAQ. THE CONTRACT HAS AN ESTIMATED WORTH UP TO $680 MILLION | GEORGE SHULTZ, ONCE BECHTEL'S PRESIDENT, NOW SERVES ON THE COMPANY'S BOARD OF DIRECTORS | USAID ADMINISTRATOR ANDREW NATSIOS, WHO OVERSEES THE BIDDING PROCESS FOR POST-WAR CONTRACTS, ONCE HEADED A PROJECT IN WHICH BECHTEL WAS THE PRIMARY CONTRACTOR | IN PAPUA NEW GUINEA BACK IN THE 70S, BECHTEL CONSTRUCTED THE WORLD'S LARGEST GOLD MINE. IT DUMPED THOUSANDS OF TONS OF TOXIC WASTE DIRECTLY INTO LOCAL RIVERS | BUILT AN ILLEGAL POWER PLANT ON MEXICO SOIL FOR THE SOLE PURPOSE OF EXPORTING ENERGY TO THE USA | IN BOLIVIA IN 1999, A SUBSIDIARY OF BECHTEL PRIVATISED THE WATER SYSTEM, IMPLEMENTED MASSIVE PRICE HIKES WHICH THE MAJORITY OF PEOPLE COULD NOT AFFORD. IT PROVOKED HUGE PROTESTS FORCING THE BOLIVIAN GOVERNMENT TO CANCEL BECHTEL'S CONTRACT. BECHTEL IS NOW SUING THE COUNTRY IN A WORLD BANK COURT FOR LOST PROFITS | MANAGES A TEST SITE AND COUNTER-TERRORISM FACILITY WHERE NUCLEAR, BIOLOGICAL AND CHEMICAL WEAPONS ARE CONSTRUCTED AND TESTED. THE SITE IN NEVADA IS CONSIDERED SACRED BY THE NATIVE AMERICANS | IN BOSTON, BECHTEL'S MISMANAGEMENT AND COST OVERRUNS HAVE BEEN UNPRECEDENTED. THE BOSTON CENTRAL ARTERY TUNNEL, ESTIMATED AT $2.5 BILLION IN 1985 REACHED $14.6 BILLION IN 2003 | BECHTEL WAS NAMED BY SADDAM HUSSEIN'S GOVERNMENT AS ONE OF THE U.S. COMPANIES THAT PROVIDED IT WITH MATERIALS THAT COULD BE USED TO MAKE WEAPONRY.

NORTHROP GRUMMAN

$7 BILLION DEFENCE CONTRACT WITH THE U.S. GOVERNMENT

NORTHROP GRUMMAN IS NOW THE NATION'S 3RD LARGEST DEFENCE CONTRACTOR AS A RESULT OF ITS RECENT ACQUISITION OF TRW AND NEWPORT NEWS SHIPBUILDING | NORTHROP GRUMMAN SERVES U.S. AND INTERNATIONAL MILITARY, GOVERNMENT AND COMMERCIAL CUSTOMERS | BUILDS THE B-2 STEALTH BOMBER ($1 BILLION) | CREATED THE UNMANNED AERIAL VEHICLE, THE GLOBAL HAWK ($10 MILLION) | SECRETARY OF THE AIR FORCE JAMES ROCHE, WAS THE COMPANY VICE PRESIDENT | NELSON GIBBS, ASSISTANT SECRETARY OF THE AIR FORCE FOR INSTALLATIONS & ENVIRONMENT, SERVED AS CORPORATE COMPTROLLER AT NORTHROP FROM 1991 TO 1999 | DEPUTY SECRETARY OF DEFENSE PAUL WOLFOWITZ, PENTAGON COMPTROLLER DOV ZAKHEIM AND UNDERSECRETARY OF DEFENCE DOUGLAS FEITH ALL HAD CONSULTING CONTRACTS OR SERVED ON PAID ADVISORY BOARDS FOR NORTHROP PRIOR TO JOINING THE ADMINISTRATION.

HALLIBURTON

HALLIBURTON HAD EXTENSIVE CONTRACTS & INVESTMENTS IN SUHARTO'S DICTATORSHIP IN INDONESIA | DEALT WITH IRAN EVEN WHEN SANCTIONS WERE IMPOSED BY THE U.S. GOVERNMENT | IN 2001, TWO SUBSIDIARIES OF HALLIBURTON WERE DOING BUSINESS WITH IRAQ | HALLIBURTON HELD STAKES IN TWO FIRMS THAT SIGNED CONTRACTS TO SELL MORE THAN $73 MILLION IN OIL PRODUCTION EQUIPMENT AND SPARE PARTS TO IRAQ WHILE CHENEY WAS CHAIRMAN AND CHIEF EXECUTIVE OFFICER | INVOLVED IN LIBYA, EARNING $44.7 MILLION IN 1993 | AFTER SANCTIONS WERE IMPOSED IN THE COUNTRY, HALLIBURTON CONTINUED DOING BUSINESS AS USUAL | IN NIGERIA, LOCAL VILLAGERS ACCUSED HALLIBURTON OF COMPLICITY IN THE SHOOTING OF A PROTESTER BY NIGERIA'S MOBILE POLICE UNIT, IN ORDER TO PROTECT COMPANY PROPERTY | THE COMPANY ADMITTED THAT IT HAD PAID A TOTAL OF $2.4 MILLION IN BRIBES TO A TAX OFFICIAL TO OBTAIN FAVOURABLE TAX TREATMENT | HALLIBURTON HAVE EXTENSIVE TIES AND CONTRACTS WITH THE DICTATORSHIP IN MYANMAR (FORMERLY BURMA) | HALLIBURTON HAS BUILT BASES TO SUPPORT TROOP DEPLOYMENTS IN SOMALIA, HAITI AND THE BALKANS | BUILT ROADS, LANDING STRIPS AND MILITARY BASES THROUGHOUT THE AREAS UNDER U.S. MILITARY CONTROL DURING THE VIETNAM WAR | REFURBISHED GUANTANAMO BAY PRISON, WITH THE PENTAGON AS A CLIENT | HAS THE SAME ACCOUNTANT, ARTHUR ANDERSEN, AS ENRON | MR. CHENEY CASHED OUT $20.6 MILLION IN STOCKS BEFORE 'RETIRING' AS CEO | LAWRENCE EAGLEBURGER, A FORMER DEPUTY SECRETARY OF DEFENCE UNDER BUSH SNR. DURING THE GULF WAR, IS A HALLIBURTON DIRECTOR.

KBR KELLOGG, BROWN & ROOT

ON MARCH 25 2003, THE U.S. ARMY CORPS OF ENGINEERS AWARDED KELLOGG, BROWN & ROOT (A HALLIBURTON CO. SUBSIDIARY) THE MAIN CONTRACT TO FIGHT OIL WELL FIRES AND RECONSTRUCT OIL FIELDS IN IRAQ AFTER OPERATION IRAQ FREEDOM | **THE OPEN-ENDED CONTRACT, WHICH HAS NO SPECIFIED TIME OR DOLLAR LIMIT, WAS GIVEN TO THE COMPANY WITHOUT A BIDDING PROCESS** | KELLOGG, BROWN & ROOT FOUGHT OIL WELL FIRES IN KUWAIT AND PROVIDED SUPPORT SERVICES TO U.S. FORCES IN THE BALKANS IN THE 1990S | LAWRENCE EAGLEBURGER, FORMER U.S. SECRETARY OF STATE UNDER PRESIDENT GEORGE BUSH SNR., SITS ON THE COMPANY'S BOARD.

SECRETARY OF THE AIR FORCE
JAMES ROCHE
VICE PRESIDENT OF NORTHROP GRUMMAN

CHIEF OF STAFF
ANDREW H. CARD JR.

DEFENCE SECRETARY
DONALD RUMSFELD

DEPUTY SECRETARY OF DEFENCE
PAUL WOLFOWITZ

HEALTH AND HUMAN SERVICES SECRETARY
TOMMY G. THOMPSON

INTERIOR SECRETARY
GALE NORTON

AGRICULTURE SECRETARY
ANN M. VENEMAN
WAS A BOARD DIRECTOR FOR CALGENE

GEORGE
PRES

TREASURY SECRETARY
PAUL O'NEILL
CEO AND CHAIRMAN OF ALCOA

ENERGY SECRETARY
SPENCER ABRAHMS

DEPARTMENT OF HOMELAND SECURITY
DEPUTY SECRETARY
GORDON ENGLAND
VICE PRESIDENT OF GENERAL DYNAMICS

COMMERCE
DONALD L. EVA

FORMER SECRETARY OF STATE
GEORGE SCHULTZ

U.S. AMBASSADOR TO THE UNITED NATIONS
JOHN NEGROPONTE

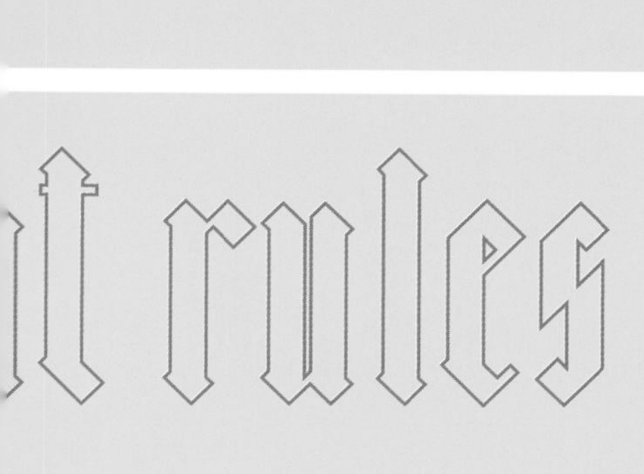

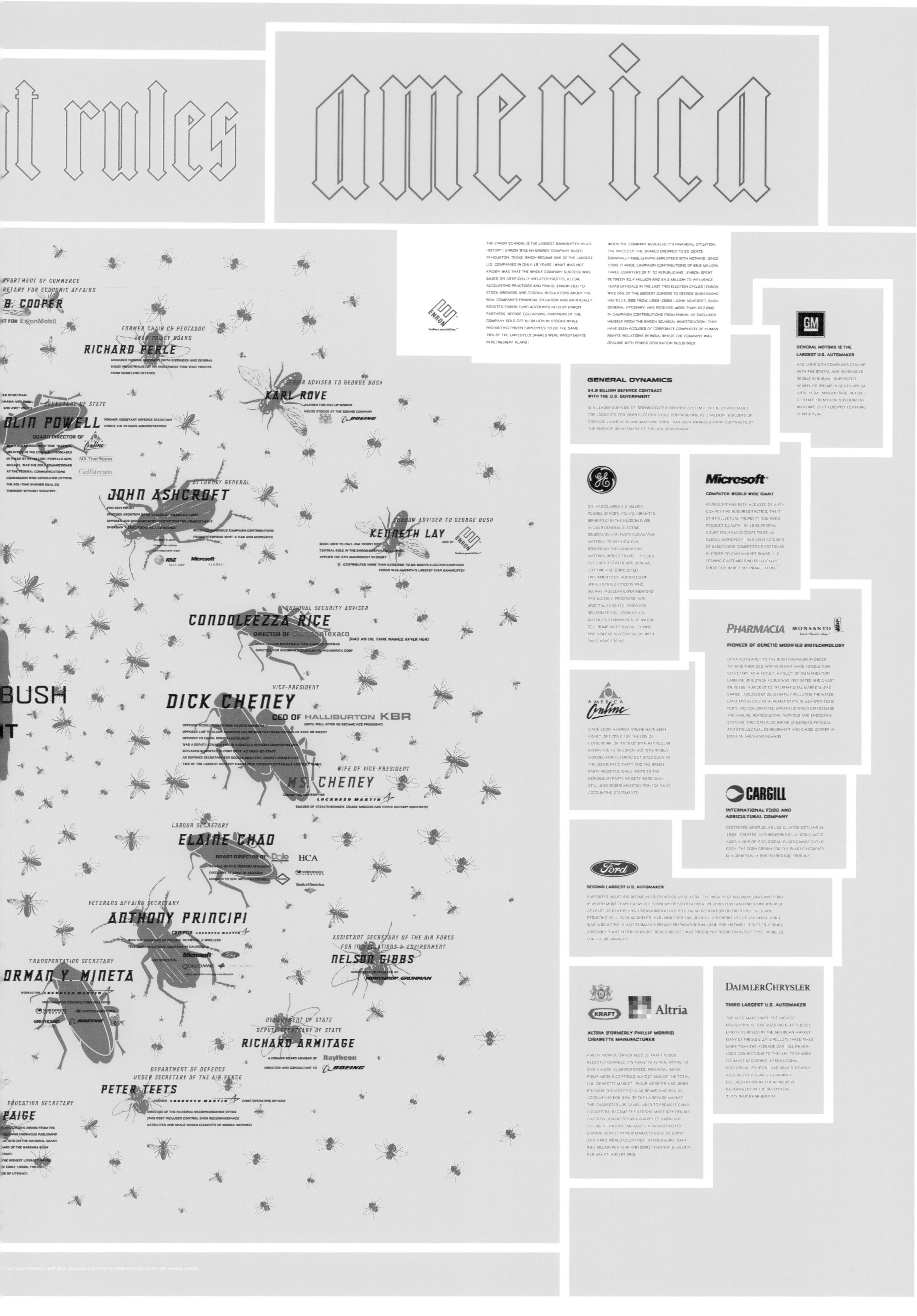

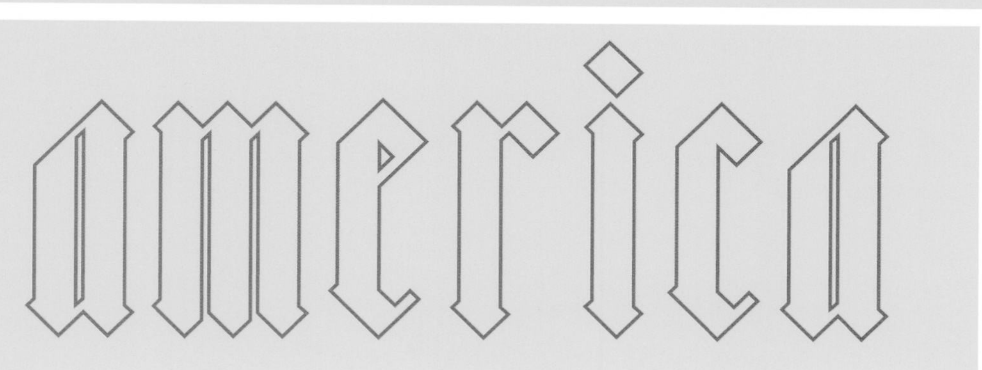

…EPARTMENT OF COMMERCE
…RETARY FOR ECONOMIC AFFAIRS
…B. COOPER
…T FOR ExxonMobil

FORMER CHAIR OF PENTAGON
… POLICY BOARD
RICHARD PERLE
MANAGES TRIREME PARTNERS (WITH KISSINGER AND SEVERAL SAUDI INDUSTRIALISTS): AN INVESTMENT FIRM THAT PROFITS FROM HOMELAND DEFENCE.

SENIOR ADVISER TO GEORGE BUSH
KARL ROVE
ADVISER FOR PHILLIP MORRIS
HOLDS STOCKS AT THE BOEING COMPANY
BOEING

SECRETARY OF STATE
…OLIN POWELL
FORMER ASSISTANT DEFENCE SECRETARY UNDER THE REAGAN ADMINISTRATION
BOARD DIRECTOR OF America Online
WHEN AOL MERGED WITH TIME-WARNER HIS STOCK IN THE COMPANY INCREASED IN VALUE BY $4 MILLION. POWELL'S SON, MICHAEL, WAS THE ONLY COMMISSIONER AT THE FEDERAL COMMUNICATIONS COMMISSION WHO ADVOCATED LETTING THE AOL-TIME WARNER DEAL GO THROUGH WITHOUT SCRUTINY.
AOL Time Warner
Gulfstream

ATTORNEY GENERAL
JOHN ASHCROFT
PRO GUN POLICY
OPPOSES ABORTION (EVEN IN CASE OF INCEST OR RAPE)
OPPOSES JOB DISCRIMINATION PROTECTION FOR HOMOSEXUALS
OVERSAW 7 EXECUTIONS AS A GOVERNOR
RECEIVED GENEROUS CAMPAIGN CONTRIBUTIONS FROM ENTERPRISE RENT-A-CAR AND MONSANTO
AT&T ($25,000) Microsoft ($10,000)

SHADOW ADVISER TO GEORGE BUSH
KENNETH LAY
CEO OF ENRON
BUSH USED TO CALL HIM 'KENNY BOY'
CENTRAL ROLE IN THE ENRON CORPORATE SCANDAL
APPLIED THE 5TH AMENDMENT IN COURT
CONTRIBUTED MORE THAN $290,000 TO MR BUSH'S ELECTION CAMPAIGN
ENRON WAS AMERICA'S LARGEST EVER BANKRUPTCY

NATIONAL SECURITY ADVISER
CONDOLEEZZA RICE
DIRECTOR OF ChevronTexaco (HAS AN OIL TANK NAMED AFTER HER)
DIRECTOR FOR BROKERAGE FIRM CHARLES SCHWAB
DIRECTOR FOR INSURANCE COMPANY TRANSAMERICA CORP

…BUSH
…T

VICE-PRESIDENT
DICK CHENEY
CEO OF HALLIBURTON KBR (UNTIL WELL AFTER HE BECAME VICE PRESIDENT)
OPPOSED RESOLUTION TO FREE NELSON MANDELA
OPPOSED LAW TO ALLOW ABORTION FOR WOMAN THAT WERE VICTIMS OF RAPE OR INCEST
OPPOSED TO EQUAL RIGHTS AMENDMENT
WAS A DEPUTY COUNCIL UNDER RUMSFELD IN NIXON ADMINISTRATION
REPLACED RUMSFELD IN FORD GOVT. AS CHIEF-OF-STAFF
AS DEFENCE SECRETARY FOR GEORGE BUSH SNR, CHENEY OVERLOOKED TWO OF THE LARGEST MILITARY CAMPAIGNS: INVASION OF PANAMA AND GULF WAR

WIFE OF VICE-PRESIDENT
MS. CHENEY
COMMITTEE ADVISOR FOR LOCKHEED MARTIN
BUILDER OF STEALTH BOMBER, CRUISE MISSILES AND OTHER MILITARY EQUIPMENT

LABOUR SECRETARY
ELAINE CHAO
BOARD DIRECTOR OF Dole HCA
MEMBER OF FIVE CORPORATE BOARDS
EXECUTIVE AT BANK OF AMERICA
MARRIED TO SEN. MITCH MCCONNELL
NORTHWEST AIRLINES
Bank of America

VETERANS AFFAIRS SECRETARY
ANTHONY PRINCIPI
CEO FOR LOCKHEED MARTIN
WAS THE CHAIRMAN OF FEDERAL NETWORK, A WIRELESS TELECOMMUNICATIONS COMPANY IN CALIFORNIA
HAS STOCKS IN Microsoft Ford QUALCOMM

ASSISTANT SECRETARY OF THE AIR FORCE
FOR INSTALLATIONS & ENVIRONMENT
NELSON GIBBS
CORPORATE CONTROLLER AT NORTHROP GRUMMAN

TRANSPORTATION SECRETARY
…ORMAN Y. MINETA
WORKED FOR LOCKHEED MARTIN
HIS CAMPAIGN CONTRIBUTORS INCLUDED:
NORTHWEST AIRLINES UNITED AIRLINES
GREYHOUND BOEING

DEPARTMENT OF STATE
DEPUTY SECRETARY OF STATE
RICHARD ARMITAGE
A FORMER BOARD MEMBER OF Raytheon
DIRECTOR AND CONSULTANT TO BOEING

DEPARTMENT OF DEFENCE
UNDER SECRETARY OF THE AIR FORCE
PETER TEETS
FORMER LOCKHEED MARTIN CHIEF OPERATING OFFICER
DIRECTOR OF THE NATIONAL RECONNAISSANCE OFFICE (THIS POST INCLUDES CONTROL OVER RECONNAISSANCE SATELLITES AND SPACE-BASED ELEMENTS OF MISSILE DEFENCE)

EDUCATION SECRETARY
…PAIGE

ENRON Endless possibilities.

THE ENRON SCANDAL IS THE LARGEST BANKRUPTCY IN U.S. HISTORY | ENRON WAS AN ENERGY COMPANY BASED IN HOUSTON, TEXAS, WHICH BECAME ONE OF THE LARGEST U.S. COMPANIES IN ONLY 15 YEARS | WHAT WAS NOT KNOWN WAS THAT THE WHOLE COMPANY SUCCESS WAS BASED ON ARTIFICIALLY INFLATED PROFITS, ILLEGAL ACCOUNTING PRACTICES AND FRAUD. ENRON USED TO STOCK-BROKERS AND FEDERAL REGULATORS ABOUT THE REAL COMPANY'S FINANCIAL SITUATION AND ARTIFICIALLY BOOSTED ENRON FUND ACCOUNTS HELD BY ENRON PARTNERS. BEFORE COLLAPSING, PARTNERS OF THE COMPANY SOLD OFF $1 BILLION IN STOCKS WHILE PROHIBITING ENRON EMPLOYEES TO DO THE SAME. 70% OF THE EMPLOYEES SHARES WERE INVESTMENTS IN RETIREMENT PLANS | WHEN THE COMPANY REVEALED IT'S FINANCIAL SITUATION, THE PRICES OF THE SHARES DROPPED TO 65 CENTS (ORIGINALLY $90), LEAVING EMPLOYEES WITH NOTHING | SINCE 1990, IT MADE CAMPAIGN CONTRIBUTIONS OF $5.8 MILLION, THREE-QUARTERS OF IT TO REPUBLICANS | ENRON SPENT BETWEEN $2.4 MILLION AND $4.8 MILLION TO INFLUENCE TEXAS OFFICIALS IN THE LAST TWO ELECTION CYCLES | ENRON WAS ONE OF THE BIGGEST DONORS TO GEORGE BUSH GIVING HIM $114,000 FROM 1999-2000 | JOHN ASHCROFT, BUSH GENERAL ATTORNEY, HAS RECEIVED MORE THAN $57,000 IN CAMPAIGN CONTRIBUTIONS FROM ENRON. HE EXCLUDED HIMSELF FROM THE ENRON SCANDAL INVESTIGATION | THEY HAVE BEEN ACCUSED OF CORPORATE COMPLICITY OF HUMAN RIGHTS VIOLATIONS IN INDIA, WHERE THE COMPANY WAS DEALING WITH POWER GENERATION INDUSTRIES.

GENERAL MOTORS IS THE LARGEST U.S. AUTOMAKER

HAS LINKS WITH COMPANIES DEALING WITH THE BRUTAL AND REPRESSIVE REGIME IN BURMA. SUPPORTED APARTHEID REGIME IN SOUTH AFRICA UNTIL 1994. ANDRES CARD JR, CHIEF OF STAFF FROM BUSH GOVERNMENT WAS GM'S CHIEF LOBBYIST FOR MORE THAN A YEAR.

GENERAL DYNAMICS

$4.5 BILLION DEFENCE CONTRACT WITH THE U.S. GOVERNMENT

IS A LEADER SUPPLIER OF 'SOPHISTICATED' DEFENCE SYSTEMS TO THE US AND ALLIES. TOP LOBBYISTS FOR 2000 ELECTION CYCLE CONTRIBUTING $1.2 MILLION. BUILDERS OF GRENADE LAUNCHERS AND MACHINE GUNS. HAS BEEN AWARDED MANY CONTRACTS BY THE DEFENCE DEPARTMENT OF THE USA GOVERNMENT.

G.E. HAS DUMPED 1.3 MILLION POUNDS OF PCB'S (POLYCHLORINATED BIPHENYLS) IN THE HUDSON RIVER. IN 1949 GENERAL ELECTRIC DELIBERATELY RELEASED RADIOACTIVE MATERIAL TO SEE HOW FAR DOWNWIND THE RADIOACTIVE MATERIAL WOULD TRAVEL. IN 1986 THE UNITED STATES AND GENERAL ELECTRIC HAD CONDUCTED EXPERIMENTS ON HUNDREDS OF UNITED STATES CITIZENS WHO BECAME 'NUCLEAR EXPERIMENTERS' (THE ELDERLY, PRISONERS AND HOSPITAL PATIENTS). FINED FOR DELIBERATE POLLUTION OF AIR, WATER, CONTAMINATION OF WATER, SOIL, DUMPING OF ILLEGAL TOXINS AND MISLEADING CONSUMERS WITH FALSE ADVERTISING.

Microsoft

COMPUTER WORLD WIDE GIANT

MICROSOFT HAS BEEN ACCUSED OF ANTI-COMPETITIVE BUSINESS TACTICS, THEFT OF INTELLECTUAL PROPERTY AND POOR PRODUCT QUALITY. IN 1998 FEDERAL COURT FOUND MICROSOFT TO BE AN ILLEGAL MONOPOLY. HAS BEEN ACCUSED OF SABOTAGING COMPETITOR'S SOFTWARE IN ORDER TO GAIN MARKET SHARE (I.E. LEAVING CUSTOMERS NO FREEDOM OF CHOICE ON WHICH SOFTWARE TO USE).

PHARMACIA MONSANTO

PIONEER OF GENETIC MODIFIED BIOTECHNOLOGY

DONATED HEAVILY TO THE BUSH CAMPAIGN IN ORDER TO HAVE THEIR CEO ANN VENEMAN MADE AGRICULTURE SECRETARY. AS A RESULT, A POLICY OF NO MANDATORY LABELING OF BIOTECH FOODS WAS INSTIGATED AND A VAST INCREASE IN ACCESS TO INTERNATIONAL MARKETS WAS GAINED. ACCUSED OF DELIBERATELY POLLUTING THE WATER, LAND AND PEOPLE OF ALABAMA STATE IN USA WITH TOXIC PCB'S (POLYCHLORINATED BIPHENYLS) WHICH CAN DAMAGE THE IMMUNE, REPRODUCTIVE, NERVOUS AND ENDOCRINE SYSTEMS. THEY CAN ALSO IMPAIR CHILDREN'S PHYSICAL AND INTELLECTUAL DEVELOPMENT AND CAUSE CANCER IN BOTH ANIMALS AND HUMANS.

SINCE 2000, AMERICA ONLINE HAVE BEEN HIGHLY CRITICISED FOR THE USE OF CENSORSHIP, OR 'FILTERS' WITH PARTICULAR REFERENCE TO CHILDREN. AOL WAS WIDELY EXPOSED FOR FILTERING OUT SITES SUCH AS THE DEMOCRATIC PARTY AND THE GREEN PARTY WEBSITES, WHILE VISITS TO THE REPUBLICAN PARTY WEBSITE WERE OKAY. STILL UNDERGOING INVESTIGATION FOR FALSE ACCOUNTING STATEMENTS.

INTERNATIONAL FOOD AND AGRICULTURAL COMPANY

DESTROYED VENEZUELA'S LOS OLIVITOS WETLAND IN 1999. CREATED 'NATUREWORKS P.L.A.' (POLYLACTIC ACID), A KIND OF 'ECOLOGICAL' PLASTIC MADE OUT OF CORN. THE CORN GROWN FOR THE PLASTIC HOWEVER IS A GENETICALLY ENGINEERED (GE) PRODUCT.

SECOND LARGEST U.S. AUTOMAKER

SUPPORTED APARTHEID REGIME IN SOUTH AFRICA UNTIL 1994. THE WEALTH OF AMERICAN CAR GIANT FORD IS WORTH MORE THAN THE WHOLE ECONOMY OF SOUTH AFRICA. IN 2000, FORD AND FIRESTONE KNEW OF AT LEAST 35 DEATHS AND 130 INJURIES RELATED TO TREAD SEPARATION ON FIRESTONE TIRES AND RESULTING ROLL-OVER ACCIDENTS INVOLVING FORD EXPLORER S.U.V.'S (SPORT UTILITY VEHICLES). FORD WAS ALSO ACTIVE IN NAZI GERMANY'S PREWAR PREPARATIONS IN 1938. FOR INSTANCE, IT OPENED A TRUCK ASSEMBLY PLANT IN BERLIN WHOSE 'REAL PURPOSE'. WAS PRODUCING 'TROOP TRANSPORT-TYPE' VEHICLES FOR THE WEHRMACHT.

ALTRIA (FORMERLY PHILLIP MORRIS) CIGARETTE MANUFACTURER

PHILLIP MORRIS, OWNER ALSO OF KRAFT FOODS, RECENTLY CHANGED IT'S NAME TO ALTRIA, TRYING TO GIVE A MORE 'BUSINESS BASED, FINANCIAL IMAGE'. PHILIP MORRIS CONTROLS ALMOST 50% OF THE TOTAL U.S. CIGARETTE MARKET. PHILIP MORRIS'S MARLBORO BRAND IS THE MOST POPULAR BRAND AMONG KIDS, ACCOUNTING FOR 55% OF THE UNDERAGE MARKET. THE CHARACTER JOE CAMEL, USED TO PROMOTE CAMEL CIGARETTES, BECAME THE SECOND MOST IDENTIFIABLE CARTOON CHARACTER IN A SURVEY OF AMERICAN CHILDREN. HAS AN EMPHASIS ON PROMOTING ITS BRANDS HEAVILY IN NEW MARKETS SUCH AS CHINA AND THIRD WORLD COUNTRIES. SPENDS MORE THAN $9.7 BILLION PER YEAR AND MORE THAN $26.5 MILLION PER DAY ON ADVERTISING.

DAIMLERCHRYSLER

THIRD LARGEST U.S. AUTOMAKER

THE AUTO MAKER WITH THE HIGHEST PROPORTION OF GAS GUZZLING S.U.V.'S (SPORT UTILITY VEHICLES) IN THE AMERICAN MARKET. MANY OF THE BIG S.U.V.'S POLLUTE THREE TIMES MORE THAN THE AVERAGE CAR. BLUEWASH: USED CONNECTIONS TO THE U.N. TO CHANGE ITS IMAGE REGARDING INTERNATIONAL ECOLOGICAL POLICIES. HAS BEEN STRONGLY ACCUSED OF POSSIBLE CORPORATE COLLABORATION WITH A REPRESSIVE GOVERNMENT IN THE SEVEN YEAR 'DIRTY WAR' IN ARGENTINA.

| RAYTHEON WEBSITE | NORTHROP GRUMMAN CORPORATION WEBSITE | RESULTS 2001 | BP ANNUAL REPORT

The French Agro-Food System

French artist group Bureau d'études conducts conceptual research into social and economic systems. The results of their findings are conveyed in complex diagrams. The artists conceive of their diagrams as a compass through a given economico-political system. This piece is a series of four diagrams on economic and political interrelations in French agriculture, with an accompanying legend, the *Pictographic Grammar* (p.378–379).

The diagrams are based on elements that symbolise institutions, groups, laws etc., which are explained in the *Pictographic Grammar*. The allocation of the symbols on a virtual map shows certain invisible relations between different players in the field, whilst interlinking lines further explain these relations.

Die französische Künstlergruppe Bureau d'études unternimmt konzeptionelle Recherchen über gesellschaftliche und ökonomische Systeme. Ihre Ergebnisse veröffentlichen sie in komplexen Diagrammen, die die Künstler als Kompass durch das jeweilige ökonomisch-politische System verstehen. Die vorliegende Arbeit umfasst vier Diagramme zu den wirtschaftlichen und politischen Wechselbeziehungen in der französischen Landwirtschaft sowie eine Legende, die *Piktografische Grammatik* (S. 378–379).

Die Diagramme basieren auf Elementen, die Institutionen, Gruppen oder Gesetze etc. symbolisieren; sie werden in der *Piktografischen Grammatik* erläutert. Die Anordnung der Symbole auf der virtuellen Landkarte verdeutlicht unsichtbare Beziehungen zwischen diversen Akteuren, sie werden durch Verbindungslinien noch näher erläutert.

Le collectif d'artistes français Bureau d'études mène des recherches conceptuelles sur les systèmes socioéconomiques. Les résultats de leur travail sont convertis en diagrammes complexes. Les artistes conçoivent ces diagrammes comme une boussole pour s'orienter dans un système économique et politique donné. Cette œuvre regroupe quatre diagrammes sur les interrelations économiques et politiques en matière d'agriculture et est accompagnée d'une légende, la *Grammaire pictographique* (p.378–379).

Les diagrammes reposent sur des éléments qui symbolisent des institutions, des groupes, des lois, etc., expliqués dans la légende *Grammaire pictographique*. L'agencement des symboles sur une carte virtuelle révèle certaines relations invisibles entre différents acteurs du secteur, et les lignes qui les connectent expliquent ces relations.

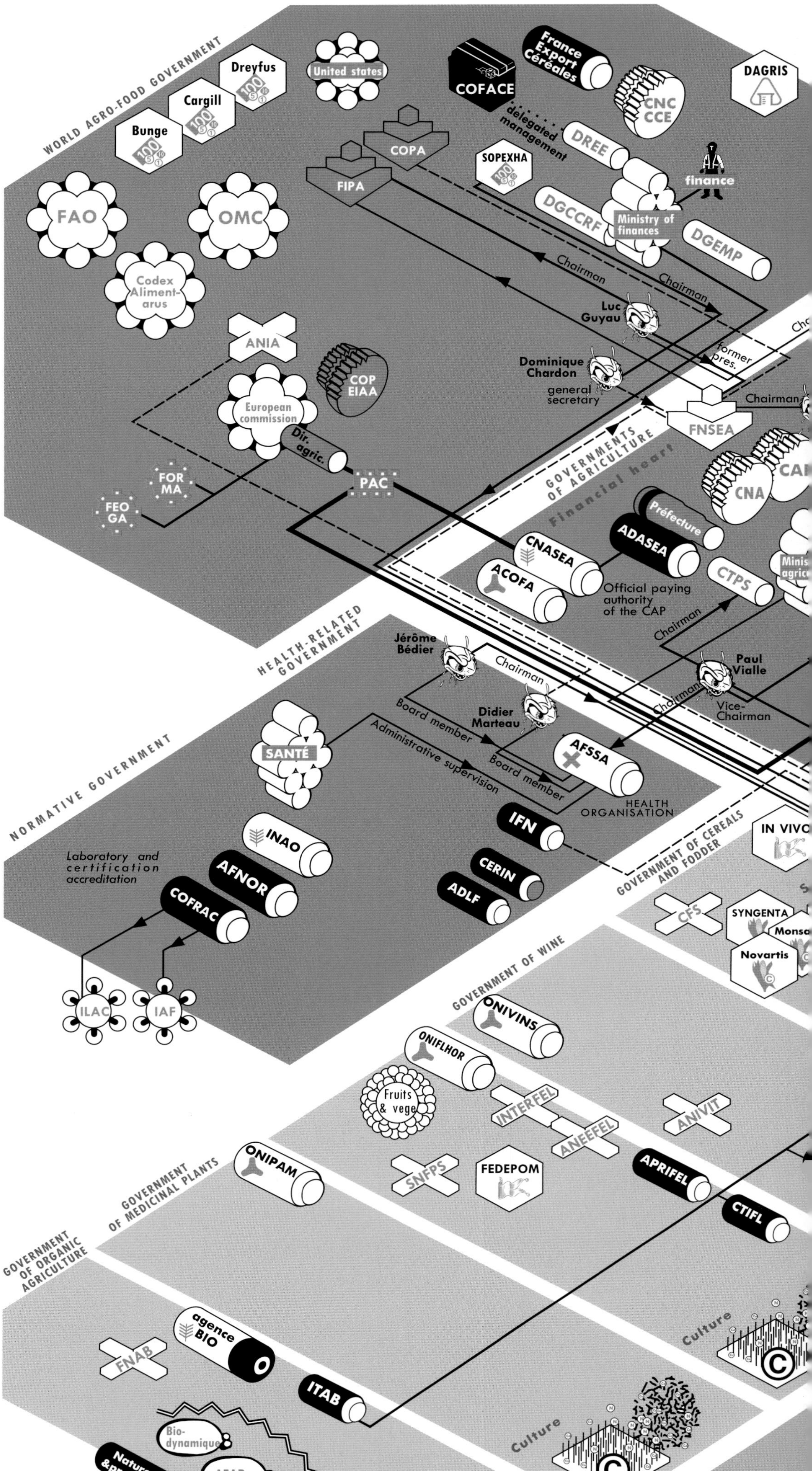

Project Info: Series of diagrams, Le Bon Accueil Contemporary Art Space, 2006, France
Artists: Bureau d'études

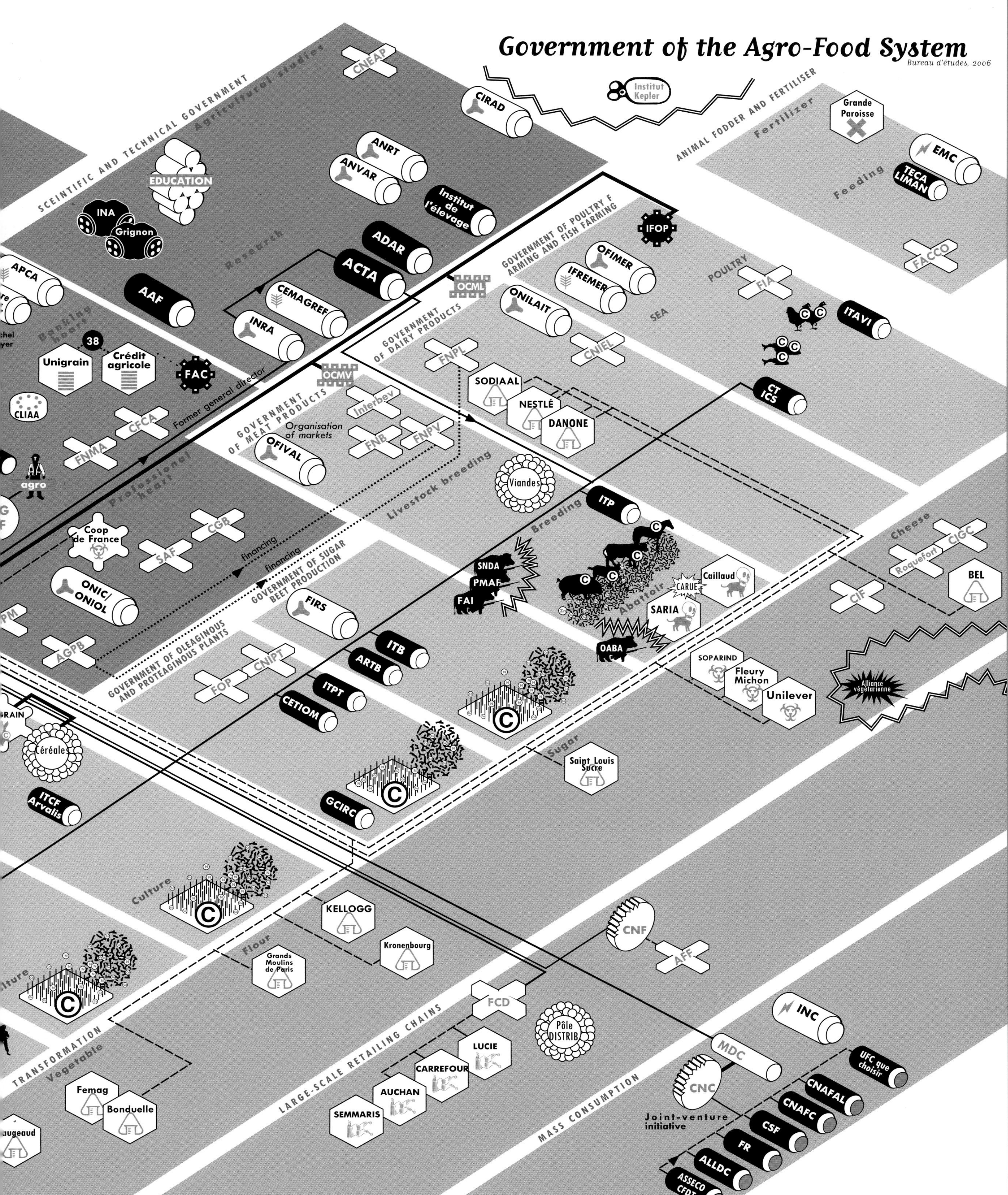
Government of the Agro-Food System
Bureau d'études, 2006
Institut Kepler
SCEINTIFIC AND TECHNICAL GOVERNMENT
Agricultural studies
CNEAP
CIRAD
EDUCATION
ANRT
ANVAR
Institut de l'élevage
INA
Grignon
Research
ADAR
ACTA
AAF
CEMAGREF
INRA
APCA
Banking heart
38
Unigrain
Crédit agricole
FAC
CLIAA
Former general director
CFCA
FNMA
agro
Professional heart
Coop de France
CGB
SAF
ONIC/ONIOL
financing
financing
AGPB
ANIMAL FODDER AND FERTILISER
Fertilizer
Grande Paroisse
EMC
TECA LIMAN
Feeding
IFOP
FACCO
GOVERNMENT OF POULTRY FARMING AND FISH FARMING
OFIMER
IFREMER
SEA
POULTRY
FIA
ITAVI
OCML
GOVERNMENT OF DAIRY PRODUCTS
ONILAIT
CNIEL
FNPL
SODIAAL
NESTLÉ
DANONE
CT ICS
OCMV
GOVERNMENT OF MEAT PRODUCTS
Interbev
Organisation of markets
OFIVAL
FNB
FNPV
Livestock breeding
Viandes
Breeding
ITP
SNDA
PMAF
FAI
Abattoir
CARUE
Caillaud
SARIA
OABA
GOVERNMENT OF SUGAR BEET PRODUCTION
FIRS
ITB
ARTB
GOVERNMENT OF OLEAGINOUS AND PROTEAGINOUS PLANTS
CNIPT
FOP
ITPT
CETIOM
GCIRC
Cheese
CIGC
Roquefort
BEL
CIF
Alliance végétarienne
SOPARIND
Fleury Michon
Unilever
Sugar
Saint Louis Sucre
GRAIN
Céréales
ITCF Arvalis
Culture
KELLOGG
Kronenbourg
Flour
Grands Moulins de Paris
CNF
AFF
FCD
Pôle DISTRIB
INC
MDC
UFC que choisir
CNAFAL
CNAFC
CSF
FR
ALLDC
ASSECO CFDT
CNC
Joint-venture initiative
MASS CONSUMPTION
LARGE-SCALE RETAILING CHAINS
LUCIE
CARREFOUR
AUCHAN
SEMMARIS
TRANSFORMATION
Vegetable
Femag
Bonduelle

Pictographic Grammar

Command

Control

member, subsidiary

1 — dominant human organisations

Inernational organizations

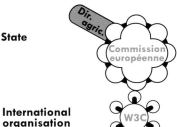

State

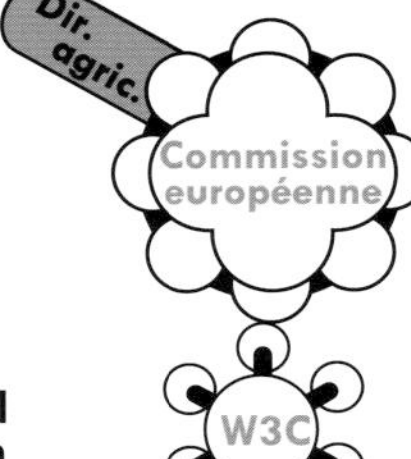

Regional governmental organisation

ITU

International organisation

W3C

International Non Governmental Organisation (NGO)

Central Administration

Outer European Or European — national

MINISTRY *With a nine-branch ministerial structure*

Crisis management group

Ministerial management

Associated service or laboratory

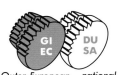

Expert advisory body

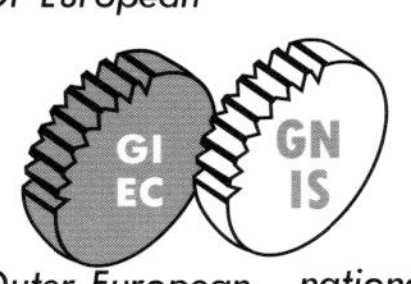

Strategic-control body

Outer European Or European — national

Regulatory or steering body

IA Independent authority

Outer European Or European — national

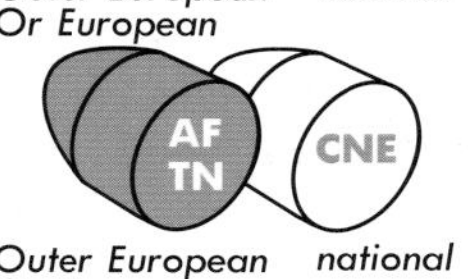

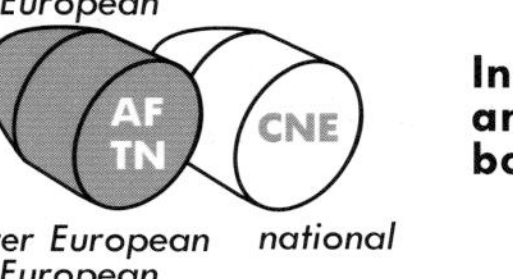

Inspection and accreditation body

Outer European Or European — national

Préfecture

Préfecture

SIB FCE

National domain section

Establishments and organisations

Public commercial, industrial and financial corporation

industrial and commercial

intervention

safety health

health

scientific and technologic

scientific, cultural and professional

administrative

real estate + autonomous ports

AFSSA

SGQA — ***Internal services of a public organisation***

NASA usa

European or outer European public corporation

FNLON — Institut de l'élevage

semi-public association

public service mission — *"avatar" or "sock puppet" of the administration*

Educational and training establishments

SUP *Higher education and research*

Export credit bureaus

ECBs provide loans, guarantees and insurance to export businesses and commercial banks based in their home countries, protecting them against the risks of foreign buyers or debtors failing to respect contracts for political or commercial reasons.

COFACE

CNR ACL

Public social security, pension and health corporation

Public / private group

Consortium

Scientific interest group SIG

Commercial interests group CIG

Public interests group PIG

Outer European Or European

2 — Human organisation in conflict with the state complex or in a minority position

Free seed production network

Biodiversity protection network

Organisation practising organics

Independent research centre

Social and scientific struggles against state health policies

Residents association

Pesticide victims association

NGO fighting pesticide use

Struggles against technology-based social control

Protection of industrial animals / Animal liberation

Protection of farm-raised animals

Protection of wild animals

Vegetarians

3 — Technical and

Social and economic organisations

Social organisations

Interest group / National professional association

International professional federation

Confederation of labour organisations

Production organisation

Business

Co-o

agriculture — food

Farm machinery

Restaurant industry

RFID for an

Central purchasing agency / wholesaler — telecom

Software — transportation — Logistics

Business, venture capital — Information — petroleum — Banks — Chemical, fertiliser — E Con

Breeding promotion unit

Patent use and promotion

Embryonic transfer and artificial insemination

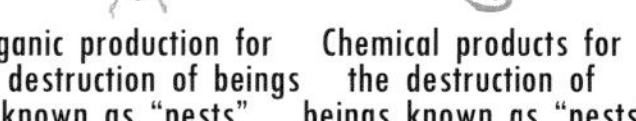

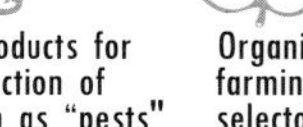

Organic production for the destruction of beings known as "pests" — Chemical products for the destruction of beings known as "pests" — Organic farming selectors

5 — Human beings

High-ranking authority

Senior civil servant in the Defence Department

Haute expertise Grand Corps de l'État

T *Technical body*

A *Administrative body*

Agro-ingeniery body

Telecom-munications body

Mining body

finance

Financial body

Seasonal labourers

Management delegation

Co-operation

Line of struggle between antagonistic forces

Percentage of property: x holds 2,2% of y

…bolic systems

National pressure group (lobby)

International pressure group (lobby)

Think tank

Labour organisation

Large-scale technical systems

Transportation network

Information transportation

S satellite

W internet (network of networks)

European satellite and networks of satellite

American satellite and networks of satellite

RA radar

Physical transportation

R Highways

F Railways

Calculation centre

Operating system used in the information system

Information processing system

Geodesic referencing system

National or european

American

Simulation device

Satellite captor

Electronic identification

Large-scale symbolic systems

Legal-administrative systems

non-european or european

Programme, plan or project

non-european or european

Contract, accord, treaty, law, decree code…

Identity card or certificate

Norm

Financial system

Fund

non european or european

Income tax, other taxes, allocations, lotteries

Research

Laboratory animalery

High security Laboratory (pathogens class 2, 3, 4)

Research network

Competitiveness pole

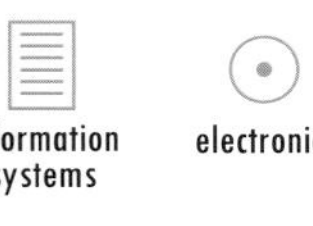
…ormation systems

electronics

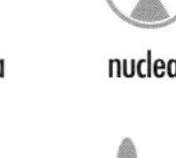
…pharma

nuclear

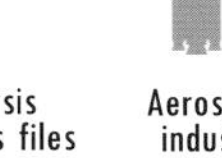
…lysis …cs files

Aerospace industry

…ction / …erm …on

accine producers and animal medicine

…ed …lectors

Meat sector abattoirs

4 — Waste products

Sludge

Manure

Collective sludge
Annually in France: 900.000 tonnes sludge from sewage, 600.000 tonnes from the dredging of ditches, rivers and canals; 300.000 tonnes of animal slurry. Animal waste represents 94 % of all agricultural manuring.

Individual sludge
15 to 20 kg per person per year of sludge (dry matter). 60% of the tonnage of dry matter is used in farm manuring.

Nutriments

Nitrogen
Nitrogen (periodic symbol N) changes its chemical composition very easily, through association with oxygen or hydrogen molecules. Nitrogen and hydrogen form ammonia (NH_4). Nitrogen, by consuming oxygen, forms nitrates (NO_2 or NO_3).

Phosphorus
Nitrogen and phosphorus are the basic ingredients of fertilisers.

Ammonia
95% of ammonia emissions come from agriculture, of which 80% come from livestock farming.

Micro-pollutants

Cadmium
89% of cadmium contamination of French soil is caused by fertilisers.

Zinc
69% of zinc contamination of French soil is caused by pig manure.

Copper
92% of copper contamination of French soil is caused by pesticides.

6 — Non-human beings

Plant life

Plants reproduced by humans for eating

Licensed or certified seeds of plant clones

Unlicensed plant seeds

Cultivated fields with licensed seeds

Freely reproducing plants considered detrimental

Thistles
Plant able to accumulated large quantities of nitrates.

Nettles

Couch grass
Considered one of the most undesirable weeds because of the fact that it has invaded 37 different crops in 65 countries. Certain natural chemical substances extracted from couch grass have shown insecticidal properties against mosquito larvae and molluscs, particularly slugs.

Animals

Animals reproduced by humans for eating

Horses

Cattle
4,15 million dairy cows. 4,3 million suckling calves.

Goats
5,2 million milk ewes. 1,4 million suckling kids. 800 000 goats.

Poultry

Pigs
15 million head

Fish

Insects and micro-organisms reproduced for biological struggle

Bacillus thuringiensis

Beauveria bassiana

Trichogram

Freely reproducing animals considered pests

Mouse

moths

aphids

Fieldmice

moles

slugs

spiders

Genetic capital

Genetic databanks

Breeding databanks

Catalogue of licensed plant clones

Plant databank

Conservatory of plant varieties

Intensification devices

Breeding improvement scheme

Plant selection criteria

Animal selection criteria

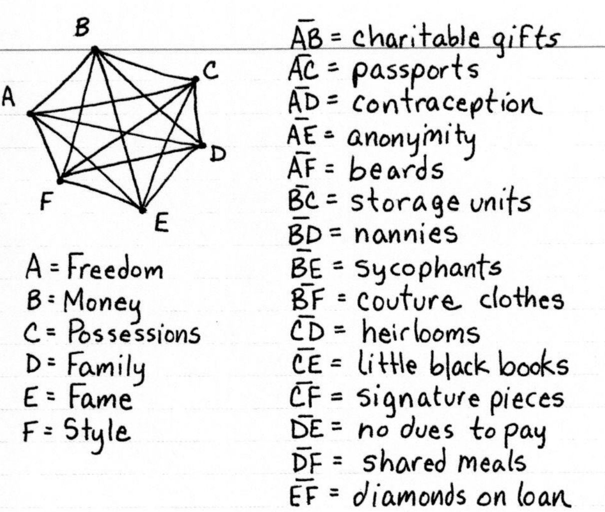

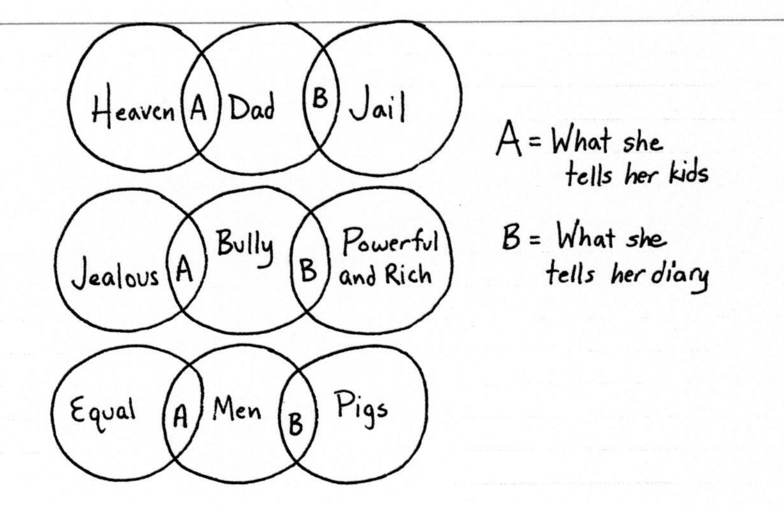

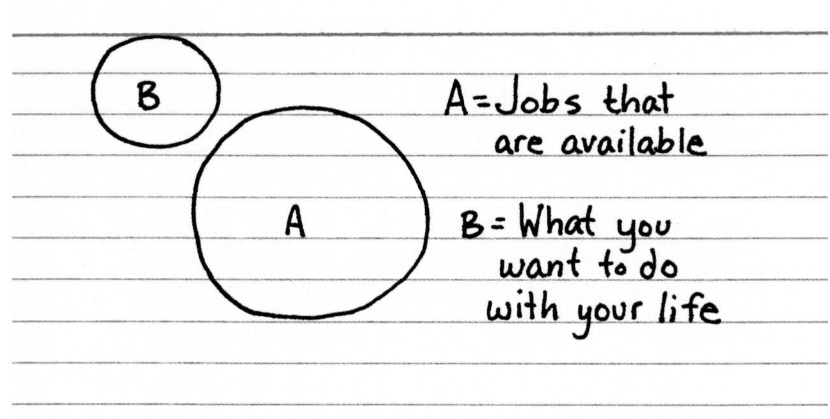

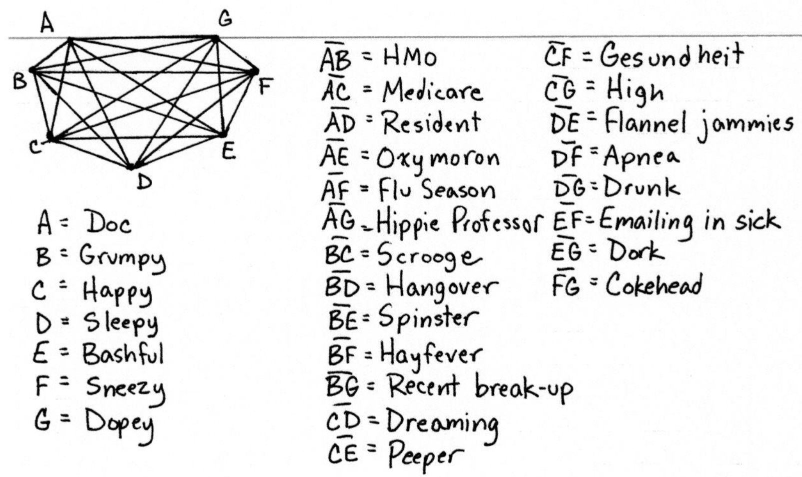

This is Indexed

In her blog, *This is Indexed*, Jessica Hagy uses little hand-drawn infographics "to make fun of some things and sense of others without resorting to doing actual math". Started in August 2006, she has published one piece every week-day. Index cards, the analogue data-carrier for little bits of information, afford the background to her reflecting by charting.

Over time, certain formats have evolved as Hagy's favourites: 1. the set diagram of overlapping circles showing as-yet-undetected intersections between things; 2. the simple two-axis diagram showing an X in relation to a Y; 3. the polygon made of lines, representing multiple connections in a problematic chaos.

Für ihren Blog *This is Indexed* zeichnet Jessica Hagy Infografiken von Hand, mit denen „ich mich über ein paar Sachen lustig mache und andere enträtsele, ohne tatsächlich rechnen zu müssen". Seit August 2006 veröffentlicht sie an jedem Wochentag ein kleines Diagramm. Karteikarten – das analoge Speichermedium für kurze Informationen – bilden den visuellen Hintergrund für ihr „Nachdenken durch Aufzeichnen".

Im Lauf der Zeit haben sich bestimmte Formate als Hagys Lieblingsformate herausgebildet: 1. das Venn-Diagramm mit überlappenden Kreisen, das bislang unbekannte Schnittmengen zwischen Dingen zeigt; 2. das einfache Zweiachsendiagramm, das einen Wert X im Verhältnis zu einem Wert Y zeigt; 3. das aus Linien bestehende Polygon, das vielfältige Verbindungen in einem problematischen Chaos darstellt.

Dans son blog *This is Indexed*, Jessica Hagy a recours à de petites infographies manuscrites pour « rire de certains sujets et en expliquer d'autres sans avoir l'impression de faire des mathématiques ». Depuis août 2006, elle a publié une création chaque jour de la semaine, du lundi au vendredi. Des fiches cartonnées, support de données analogique pour de petits fragments d'informations, servent d'arrière-plan à ses réflexions en forme de graphiques.

Avec le temps, les formats préférés d'Hagy ont changé : 1. diagramme fait de cercles se chevauchant pour montrer des intersections encore inconnues entre les choses ; 2. diagramme simple fait de deux axes pour montrer la relation entre un X et un Y ; 3. polygone fait de lignes pour montrer plusieurs connexions au sein d'un cas complexe.

Project Info: *This is Indexed* blog, since 2006, USA
Design: Jessica Hagy

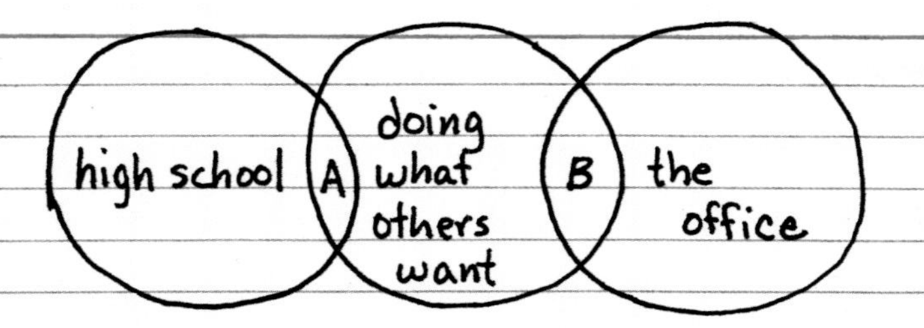

A = Giving in to peer pressure

B = Being a team player

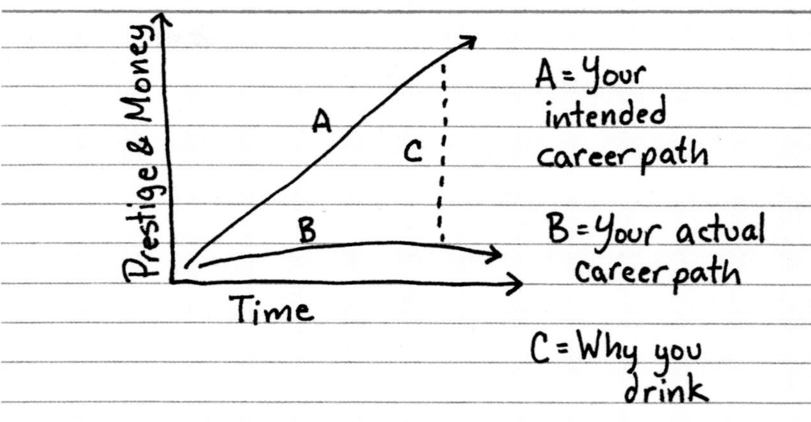

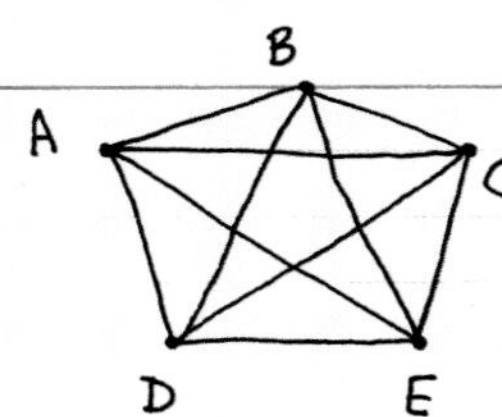

A = Suppliers
B = New Entrants
C = Rivalry
D = Substitutes
E = Customers

$\overline{AB}$ = People smugglers
$\overline{AC}$ = ESPN
$\overline{AD}$ = Asking for wooden toys for Xmas
$\overline{AE}$ = Swap meet
$\overline{BC}$ = Baby brother
$\overline{BD}$ = Trading the convertible for a van
$\overline{BE}$ = Tweens
$\overline{CD}$ = Cola wars
$\overline{CE}$ = Cat fight at the sample sale
$\overline{DE}$ = Winning the lottery

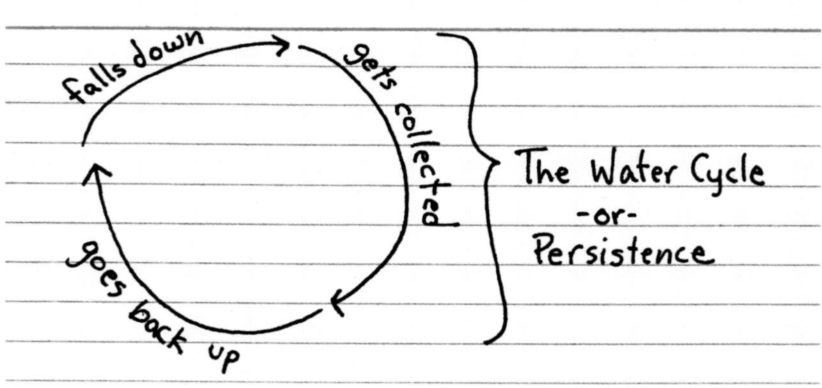

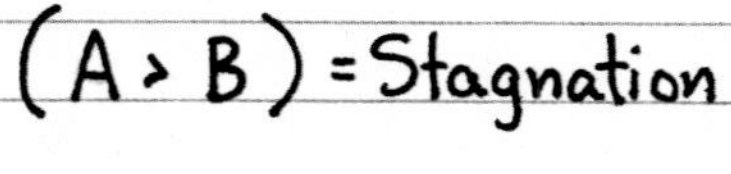

(A > B) = Stagnation

(A = B) = Implementation

(A < B) = Imagination

A = Reality

B = Ideas

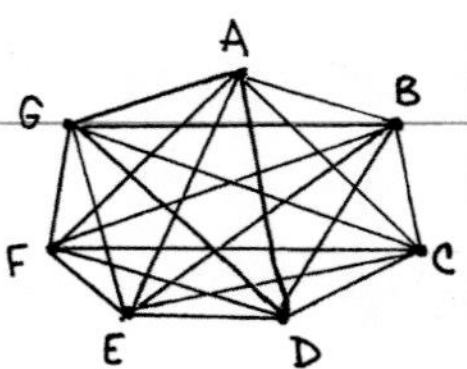
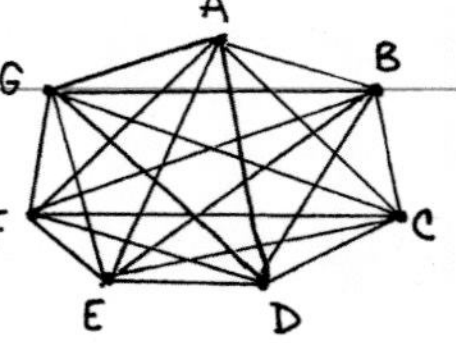

A = Chastity
B = Generosity
C = Moderation
D = Diligence
E = Kindness
F = Patience
G = Modesty

$\overline{AB}$ = Hand job
$\overline{AC}$ = Tease
$\overline{AD}$ = Thinking about baseball
$\overline{AE}$ = Pity date
$\overline{AF}$ = After Prom
$\overline{AG}$ = Granny panties
$\overline{BC}$ = Buying gifts on sale
$\overline{BD}$ = Kissing up to your boss
$\overline{BE}$ = Complimenting bad art
$\overline{BF}$ = Waiting for your rich aunt to die
$\overline{BG}$ = Lending the stripper your coat
$\overline{CD}$ = Procrastination
$\overline{CE}$ = 15% tip
$\overline{CF}$ = Occasional Outbursts
$\overline{CG}$ = Just a little cleavage
$\overline{DE}$ = Forced Smiles
$\overline{DF}$ = Making license plates in prison
$\overline{DG}$ = Always wearing your eye-patch
$\overline{EF}$ = Your friend's Pampered Chef party
$\overline{EG}$ = Keep the door closed, Mom.
$\overline{FG}$ = Holding in a toot

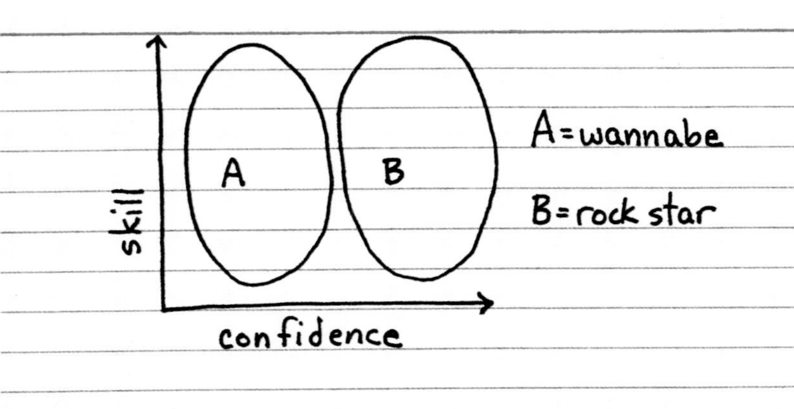

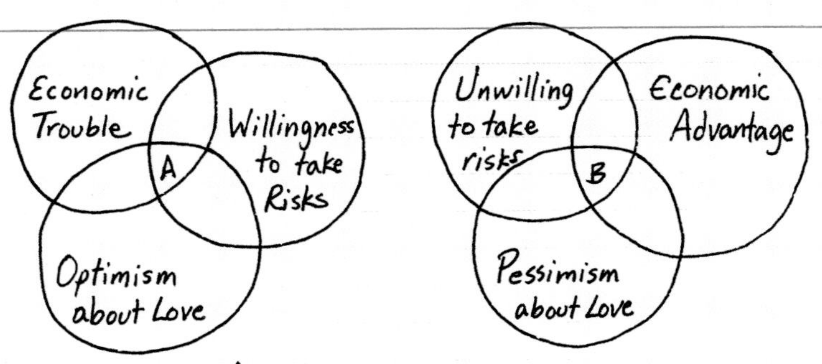

A = Mail Order Bride

B = Who she's going to marry

Tree World

This graphic originally appeared as a sequence of two double-spreads in the Brazilian magazine *Superinteressante*. It explains how a rainforest tree is home to numerous species and an ecosystem of its own. The large tree is imagined and shown from top to bottom, with some animals and plants just named, others accompanied by brief texts.

The bubbles work like magnifying lenses, showing the animals in detail. While each animal is shown in relation to the part of the tree where it lives, the image is not meant to be an accurate map. Rather, the tree is the background for presenting individual animals that live together and sometimes depend on each other in a confined natural space.

Diese Grafik erschien ursprünglich in Form zweier aufeinanderfolgender Doppelseiten in der brasilianischen Zeitschrift *Superinteressante*. Sie erläutert, wie ein Baum im Regenwald zahlreichen Tier- und Pflanzenarten als Lebensraum dient und ein eigenes Ökosystem bildet. Der große fiktive Baum wird in voller Länge dargestellt. Bei einigen Tieren und Pflanzen wird nur der Name genannt, andere werden näher erläutert.

Die Detailabbildungen fungieren wie eine Lupe und zeigen Tiere in Vergrößerung. Auch wenn jedes Lebewesen in dem Baumabschnitt gezeigt wird, in dem es lebt, erhebt die Zeichnung nicht den Anspruch einer exakten Karte. Der Baum dient als Hintergrund für die Darstellung der einzelnen Tiere, die auf engstem Raum zusammenleben und manchmal aufeinander angewiesen sind.

Cette affiche est d'abord parue sur deux doubles pages dans le magazine brésilien *Superinteressante*. Elle explique comment un arbre tropical peut héberger de nombreuses espèces et abriter tout un écosystème. L'arbre est présenté de haut en bas, certains animaux et certaines plantes y étant juste mentionnés, d'autres accompagnés de textes courts.

Les bulles fonctionnent comme des loupes qui montrent les animaux en détail. Chaque animal est présenté dans la partie de l'arbre où il vit, mais l'illustration n'est pas censée être une représentation exacte. L'arbre est plutôt pris comme le décor dans lequel vivent des animaux qui dépendent parfois les uns des autres dans un espace naturel confiné.

Project Info: *Superinteressante*, poster, 2007, Brazil
Research: Yuri Vasconscelos, Sergio Gwercman
Art Direction: Adriano Sambugaro
Illustration: Eber Evangelista, Luiz Iria
Awards: Malofiej 2008; Premio Abril de Jornalismo 2008

Two Mindsets

Dr. Carol Dweck is a psychology professor at Stanford University. According to her there are two major views on where ability comes from – while some people believe their abilities can be improved by working hard, others believe that success comes from innate abilities. Both mindsets can be recognised by how they deal with failures and setbacks.

Nigel Holmes' graphic is a great example of how a visualisation can have the power to allow quick access to a complex theory. Both mindsets are set opposite each other, and in a series of steps the piece explains how someone with a fixed mindset will constantly find his deterministic world-view confirmed by not using opportunities to grow.

Dr. Carol Dweck ist Professorin für Psychologie an der Stanford University. Ihrer Ansicht nach gibt es zwei grundverschiedene Ansichten darüber, worauf persönliche Fähigkeiten zurückzuführen sind. Während manche Menschen glauben, sie könnten ihre Fähigkeiten durch harte Arbeit steigern, vertreten andere die Meinung, Erfolg gehe auf angeborene Fähigkeiten zurück. Wer welchen Ansatz vertritt, lässt sich daran erkennen, wie man mit Versagen und Rückschlägen umgeht.

Nigel Holmes' Grafik führt beispielhaft vor Augen, wie eine komplexe Theorie durch eine Visualisierung schnell und prägnant erläutert werden kann. Die beiden Denkweisen werden einander gegenübergestellt, und in mehreren Schritten wird erklärt, wie ein Mensch mit starrem Denkmuster in seiner deterministischen Weltsicht ständig bestätigt wird, weil er die sich darbietenden Entwicklungsmöglichkeiten nicht nutzt.

Carol Dweck est professeur de psychologie à l'Université de Stanford. Selon elle, il existe deux scénarios possibles pour l'origine des aptitudes : certains pensent qu'ils peuvent améliorer leurs capacités en travaillant dur, d'autres croient que le succès tient à des facultés innées. Les deux mentalités se reconnaissent par leur gestion des échecs et des revers.

Le graphique de Nigel Holmes montre parfaitement qu'une illustration peut permettre de saisir rapidement une théorie complexe. Les deux mentalités sont mises en parallèle et en quelques étapes, l'œuvre explique comment une personne de mentalité fixe verra toujours sa vision déterministe du monde se confirmer en ne saisissant pas les chances de prospérer.

TWO MINDSETS
CAROL S. DWECK, Ph.D.
Graphic by Nigel Holmes
Fixed Mindset
Intelligence is static
Growth Mindset
Intelligence can be developed
Leads to a desire to look smart and therefore a tendency to…
Leads to a desire to learn and therefore a tendency to…
CHALLENGES
…avoid challenges
…embrace challenges
OBSTACLES
…give up easily
…persist in the face of setbacks
EFFORT
…see effort as fruitless or worse
…see effort as the path to mastery
CRITICISM
…ignore useful negative feedback
…learn from criticism
SUCCESS OF OTHERS
…feel threatened by the success of others
…find lessons and inspiration in the success of others
As a result, they may plateau early and achieve less than their full potential.
All this confirms a **deterministic view of the world.**
As a result, they reach ever-higher levels of achievement.
All this gives them a **greater sense of free will.**

Project Info: *Stanford*, magazine article, 2007, USA
Data Source: Carol Dweck: "Mindset: The New Psychology of Success", 2006
Design: Nigel Holmes

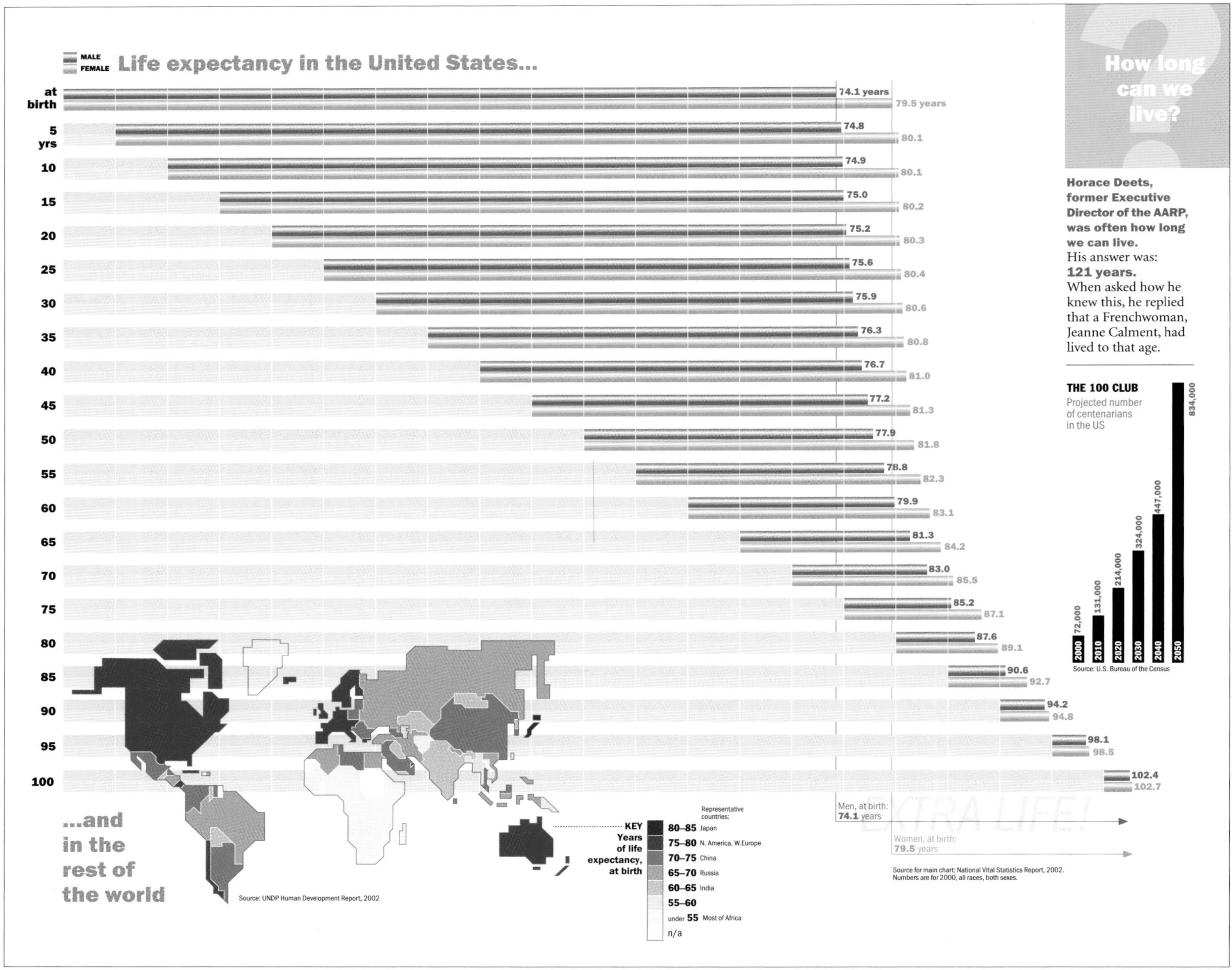

Understanding Healthcare

In *Understanding Healthcare*, Richard Saul Wurman created a visual encyclopedia of healthcare in the US. Like his earlier books, it is driven by the quest to structure all relevant information and statistics in a way that allows the reader to understand the complex topic without any further prerequisites. Every double-spread tackles one specific question.

The book is divided into three chapters. "Understanding Yourself" covers the human body. "Understanding Them" introduces the professionals involved with healthcare. The third chapter is a practical guide to the US healthcare system. All graphics were developed in cooperation between Wurman and a range of graphic designers, creating an individual look for each chapter.

Mit seinem Buch *Understanding Healthcare* entwarf Richard Saul Wurman eine visuelle Enzyklopädie des US-amerikanischen Gesundheitswesens. Wie bei seinen früheren Publikationen bemühte er sich auch hier, alle relevanten Informationen und Statistiken so zu strukturieren, dass der Leser das komplexe Thema ohne weitere Voraussetzungen erfassen kann. Jede Doppelseite ist einem bestimmten Thema gewidmet.

Das Buch besteht aus drei Kapiteln. „Understanding Yourself" befasst sich mit dem menschlichen Körper, „Understanding Them" stellt die einzelnen medizinischen Berufe vor. Das dritte Kapitel bildet einen praktischen Leitfaden zum amerikanischen Gesundheitssystem. Die Schaubilder gestaltete Wurman gemeinsam mit verschiedenen Grafikern, sodass jedes Kapitel ein eigenes Erscheinungsbild hat.

Dans son livre *Understanding Healthcare*, Richard Saul Wurman a créé une encyclopédie visuelle de la santé aux États-Unis. Comme ses ouvrages antérieurs, il obéit à la volonté de structurer toutes les informations et les statistiques pertinentes de façon à permettre au lecteur de comprendre le sujet sans posséder de connaissances particulières. Chaque double page traite une question déterminée.

L'ouvrage est divisé en trois chapitres. « Understanding Yourself » parle du corps humain. « Understanding Them » présente les professionnels impliqués dans le domaine de la santé. Le troisième chapitre est un guide pratique du système de santé américain. Wurman a conçu tous les visuels en collaboration avec une série de plusieurs graphistes pour donner un style différent à chaque chapitre.

Project Info: *Understanding Healthcare*, book, 2004, USA
Data Source: UNDP Human Development Report, 2002; National Vital Statistics Report, 2002; US Bureau of Census; American Cancer Society; Centers for Disease Control an Prevention, 2003; *To Err is Human: Building a Safer Health System*, National Academy Press, 1999; Archives of Family Medicine
Research: Loren Appel
Concept / Art Direction: Richard Saul Wurman
Design: Various designers. Examples shown here by Nigel Holmes, Richard Saul Wurman

Are mammograms important?

average size of breast tumor at diagnosis in early 1980s when only 13% of women were getting regular mammograms

average size of breast tumor at diagnosis in late 1990s when 60% of women were getting regular mammograms

Source: American Cancer Society

What are the leading causes of death?

DEFINITIONS

Accidents are unintentional injuries, including motor vehicle accidents and medical errors. (See below.)

Benign neoplasms are tumors that do not spread throughout the body.

Cancer includes all forms of malignant neoplasms (tumors that grow and spread throughout the body).

Cerebrovascular diseases include stroke (damage to the brain by an interruption of its blood supply), atherosclerosis (narrowing of the arteries) and ruptured brain aneurysm.

Diabetes mellitus is the more common form of diabetes (the other is diabetes insipidus) and has two types. Insulin-dependent Type I is the more severe, and usually first appears in people under 35. Non-insulin-dependent Type II occurs mainly in people over 40.

Lower respiratory diseases include emphysema and asthma.

Nephritis is inflammation of the kidneys.

Septicemia is blood poisoning.

Influenza has surpassed AIDS as a lethal killer and contributes to an average 36,000 annual deaths in the US

Source: Centers for Disease Control and Prevention, 2003.

More people die as a result of **medical errors** than from motor vehicle accidents, breast cancer or AIDS. Reports of the numbers vary widely, but some are as high as **180,000 deaths a year.** It is also possible that some deaths due to hospital errors are never reported as such. **Medication errors** alone, occurring either in or out of the hospital, are estimated to account for over **7,000 deaths** in the US annually.

Source: *To Err is Human: Building a Safer Health System*, National Academy Press, 1999.

Top 10 causes of death in the US, by age

Source: National Vital Statistics Report, 2002. Numbers are for 2000, all races, both sexes.

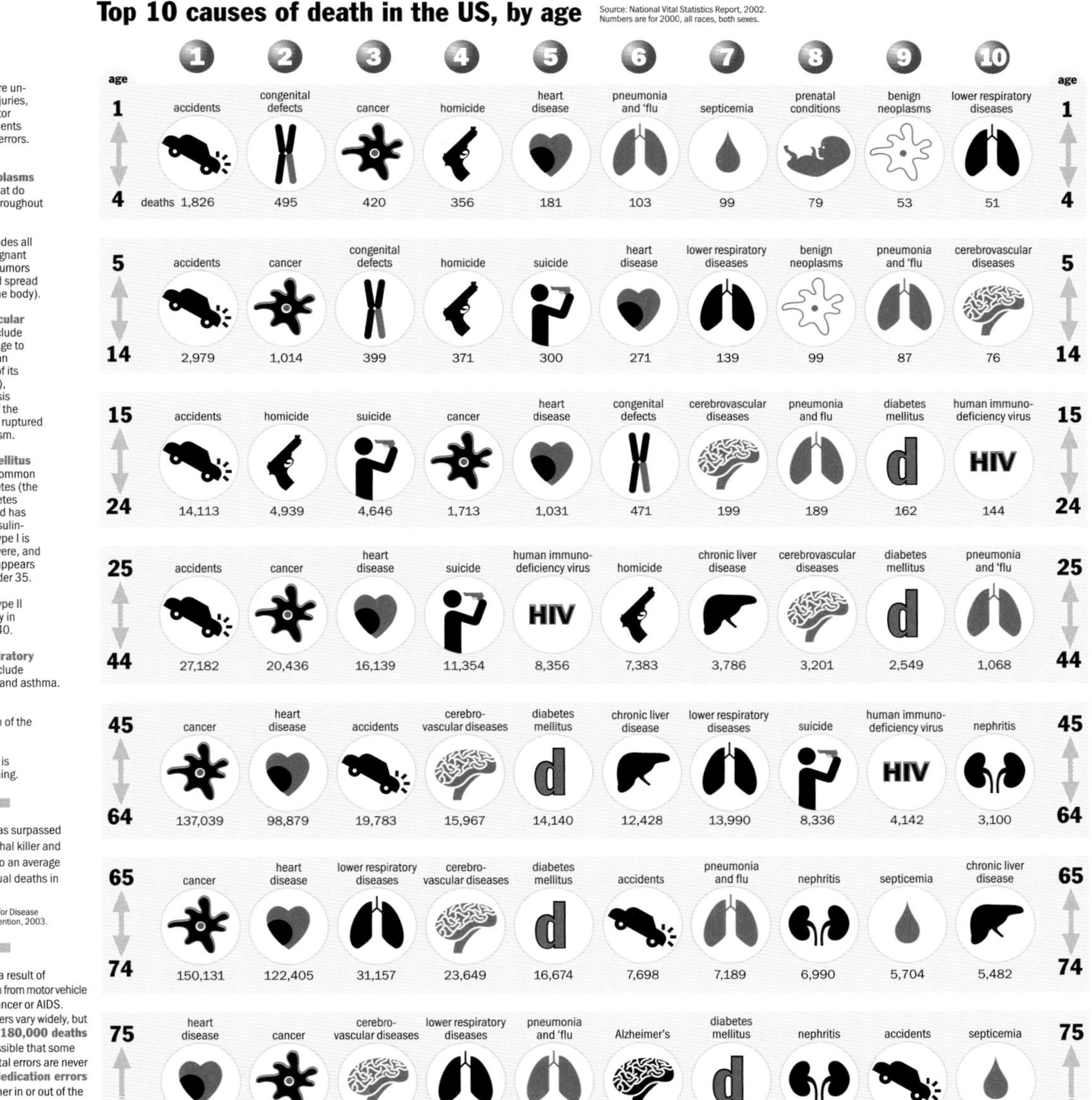

age	1	2	3	4	5	6	7	8	9	10
1–4	accidents (deaths) 1,826	congenital defects 495	cancer 420	homicide 356	heart disease 181	pneumonia and 'flu 103	septicemia 99	prenatal conditions 79	benign neoplasms 53	lower respiratory diseases 51
5–14	accidents 2,979	cancer 1,014	congenital defects 399	homicide 371	suicide 300	heart disease 271	lower respiratory diseases 139	benign neoplasms 99	pneumonia and 'flu 87	cerebrovascular diseases 76
15–24	accidents 14,113	homicide 4,939	suicide 4,646	cancer 1,713	heart disease 1,031	congenital defects 471	cerebrovascular diseases 199	pneumonia and flu 189	diabetes mellitus 162	human immuno-deficiency virus 144
25–44	accidents 27,182	cancer 20,436	heart disease 16,139	suicide 11,354	human immuno-deficiency virus 8,356	homicide 7,383	chronic liver disease 3,786	cerebrovascular diseases 3,201	diabetes mellitus 2,549	pneumonia and 'flu 1,068
45–64	cancer 137,039	heart disease 98,879	accidents 19,783	cerebro-vascular diseases 15,967	diabetes mellitus 14,140	chronic liver disease 12,428	lower respiratory diseases 13,990	suicide 8,336	human immuno-deficiency virus 4,142	nephritis 3,100
65–74	cancer 150,131	heart disease 122,405	lower respiratory diseases 31,157	cerebro-vascular diseases 23,649	diabetes mellitus 16,674	accidents 7,698	pneumonia and flu 7,189	nephritis 6,990	septicemia 5,704	chronic liver disease 5,482
75–	heart disease 471,302	cancer 242,235	cerebro-vascular diseases 124,396	lower respiratory diseases 75,218	pneumonia and 'flu 51,368	Alzheimer's 45,462	diabetes mellitus 35,740	nephritis 24,235	accidents 23,353	septicemia 19,082

Overall, they are:

1. **heart disease** 710,760 deaths; 29.6% of total deaths
2. **cancer** 553,091; 23.0%
3. **cerebro-vascular diseases** 167,661; 7.0%
4. **lower respiratory diseases** 122,009; 5.1%
5. **accidents** 97,900; 4.1%
6. **diabetes mellitus** 69,301; 2.9%
7. **pneumonia and 'flu** 65,313; 2.7%
8. **Alzheimer's** 49,558; 2.1%
9. **nephritis** 37,251; 1.3%
10. **septicemia** 31,224; 1.3%

The diseases people fear most are not necessarily the ones most likely to kill them. For instance, in a survey of women aged 25 or older, these were what they perceived to be their greatest health problems:

BREAST CANCER 34%
STROKE 1%
HEART DISEASE 7%

…but, at the time of the survey, the actual number of deaths from these causes were:

BREAST CANCER 43,000
STROKE 97,500
HEART DISEASE 234,000

Source: *Archives of Family Medicine*.

We Feel Fine

For this interactive project, blogs around the world are searched for the phrases "I feel" and "I am feeling". When these words occur, the full sentence is recorded. Where possible, the age, gender and geographical location of the author are also extracted, as well as the local weather. This rich database is visualised in six modes, available by way of the navigation lower left.

The colour of each dot corresponds to a particular type of feeling, and the diameter indicates the length of the sentence inside. *Madness* shows a swirl of particles, while *Murmurs* simply lists feelings. *Montage* shows entries that include an image. The pink bar at the top opens a panel which allows the feelings on display to be filtered at any time.

Für dieses interaktive Projekt werden Blogs aus aller Welt auf die Ausdrücke „I feel“ und „I am feeling“ durchsucht. Sobald diese Wortfolge erscheint, wird der gesamte Satz aufgezeichnet. Wenn möglich, werden zudem Alter, Geschlecht und Standort des Autors aufgenommen sowie das lokale Wetter. Diese reichhaltige Datensammlung ist in sechs Modi visualisiert, die über die Navigationsleiste unten links aufgerufen werden können.

Die Farbe eines Punktes verweist auf ein bestimmtes Gefühl, das zum Ausdruck gebracht wird, der Durchmesser auf die Länge des Satzes. *Madness* (dt. „Wahnsinn“) zeigt einen Strudel von Partikeln, *Murmurs* (dt. „Gemurmel“) hingegen listet lediglich die Gefühle auf. *Montage* versammelt Einträge mit Bild. Über den pinkfarbenen Balken ganz oben wird ein Eingabefeld geöffnet, über das die visualisierten Gefühle jederzeit gefiltert werden können.

Pour ce projet interactif, les expressions « I feel » et « I am feeling » sont recherchées dans des blogs à travers le monde entier. Quand elles sont trouvées, la phrase complète est enregistrée. Dans la mesure du possible, l'âge, le sexe et l'emplacement géographique de l'auteur sont également extraits, ainsi que la météo locale. Cette base de données riche est représentée dans six modes accessibles depuis la zone de navigation en bas à gauche.

La couleur de chaque point correspond à un type particulier de sentiment, et son diamètre indique la longueur de la phrase. *Madness* montre un tourbillon de particules, alors que *Murmurs* montre simplement une liste de sentiments. *Montage* montre les entrées incluant une image. La barre rose en haut ouvre un panneau permettant de filtrer à tout moment les sentiments à l'écran.

Project Info: Interactive visualisation, 2005, USA
Design: Jonathan Harris, Sep Kamvar

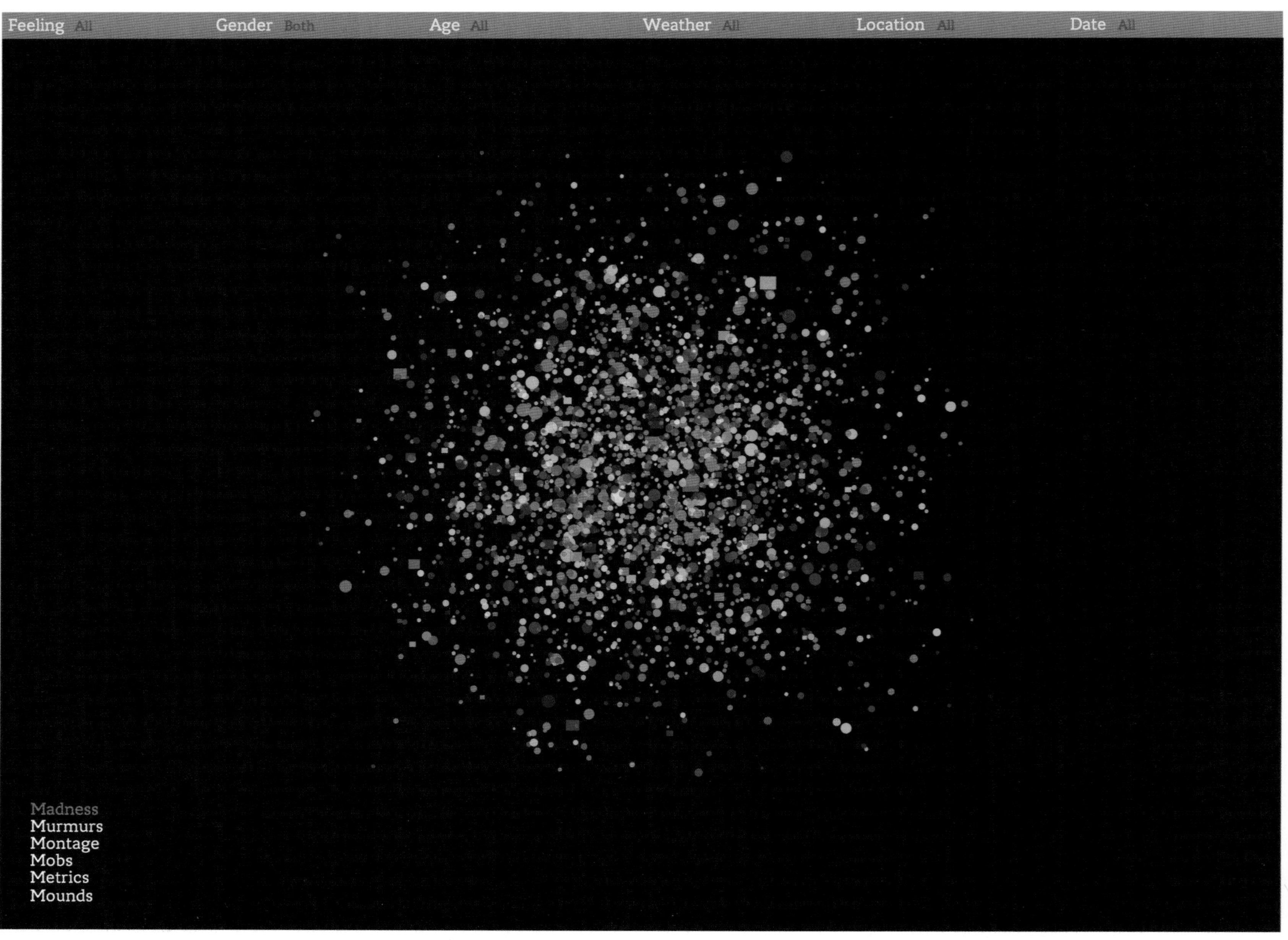

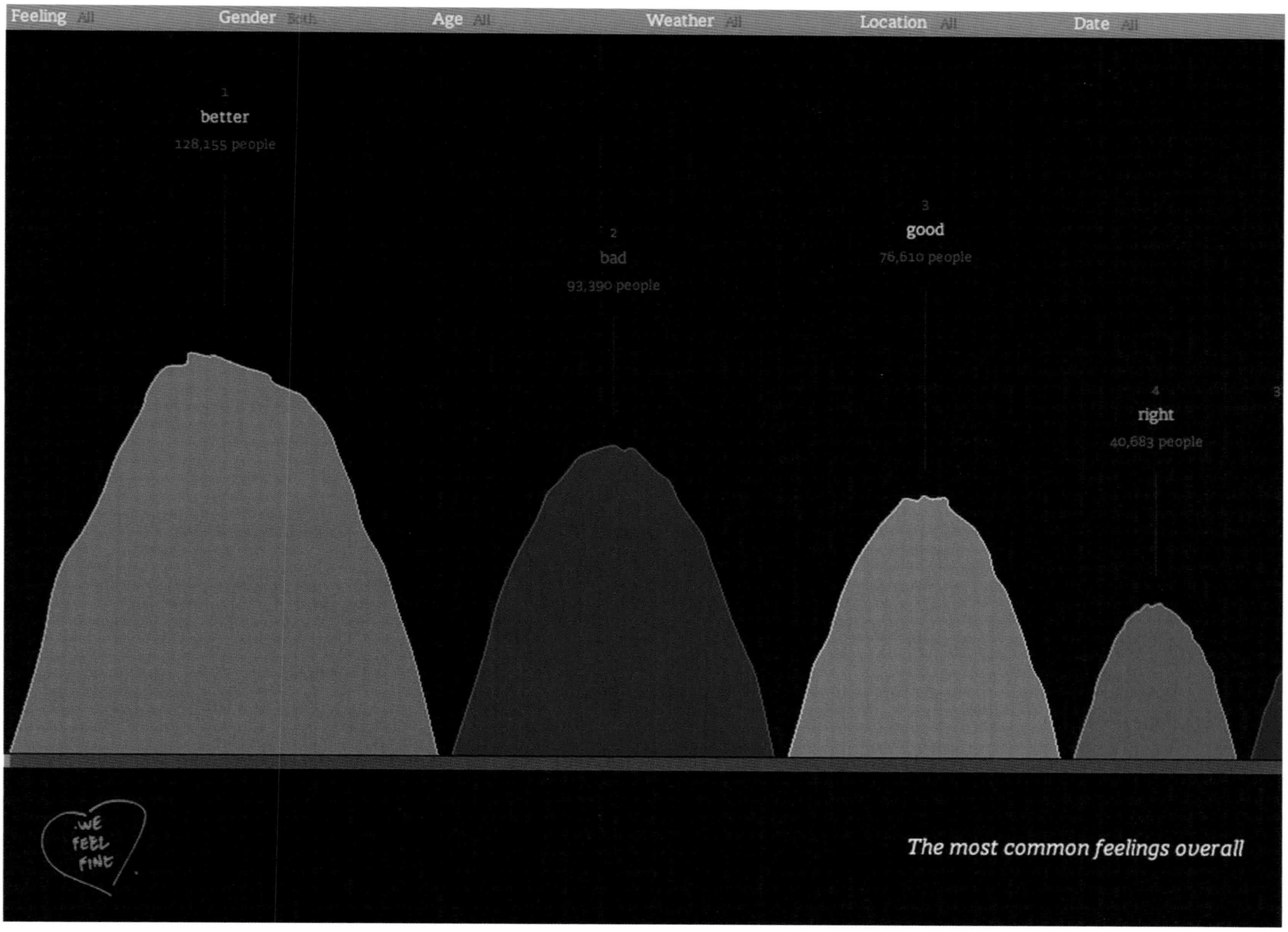

Feeling All | Gender Both | Age All | Weather All | Location All | Date All

1 better 128,155 people

2 bad 93,390 people

3 good 76,610 people

4 right 40,683 people

WE FEEL FINE

The most common feelings overall

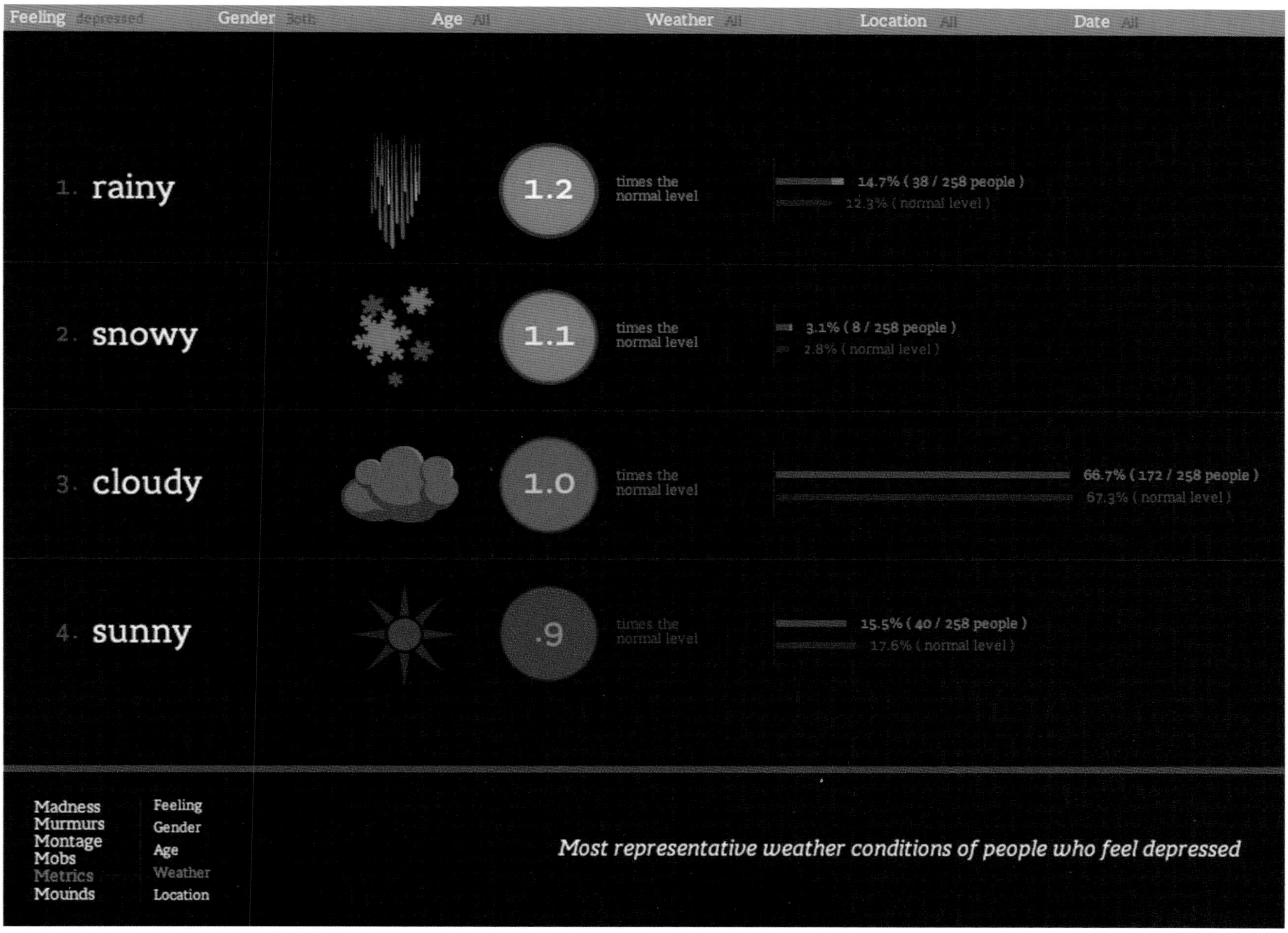

Feeling depressed | Gender Both | Age All | Weather All | Location All | Date All

1. rainy — 1.2 times the normal level — 14.7% (38 / 258 people) — 12.3% (normal level)

2. snowy — 1.1 times the normal level — 3.1% (8 / 258 people) — 2.8% (normal level)

3. cloudy — 1.0 times the normal level — 66.7% (172 / 258 people) — 67.3% (normal level)

4. sunny — .9 times the normal level — 15.5% (40 / 258 people) — 17.6% (normal level)

Madness
Murmurs
Montage
Mobs
Metrics
Mounds

Feeling
Gender
Age
Weather
Location

Most representative weather conditions of people who feel depressed

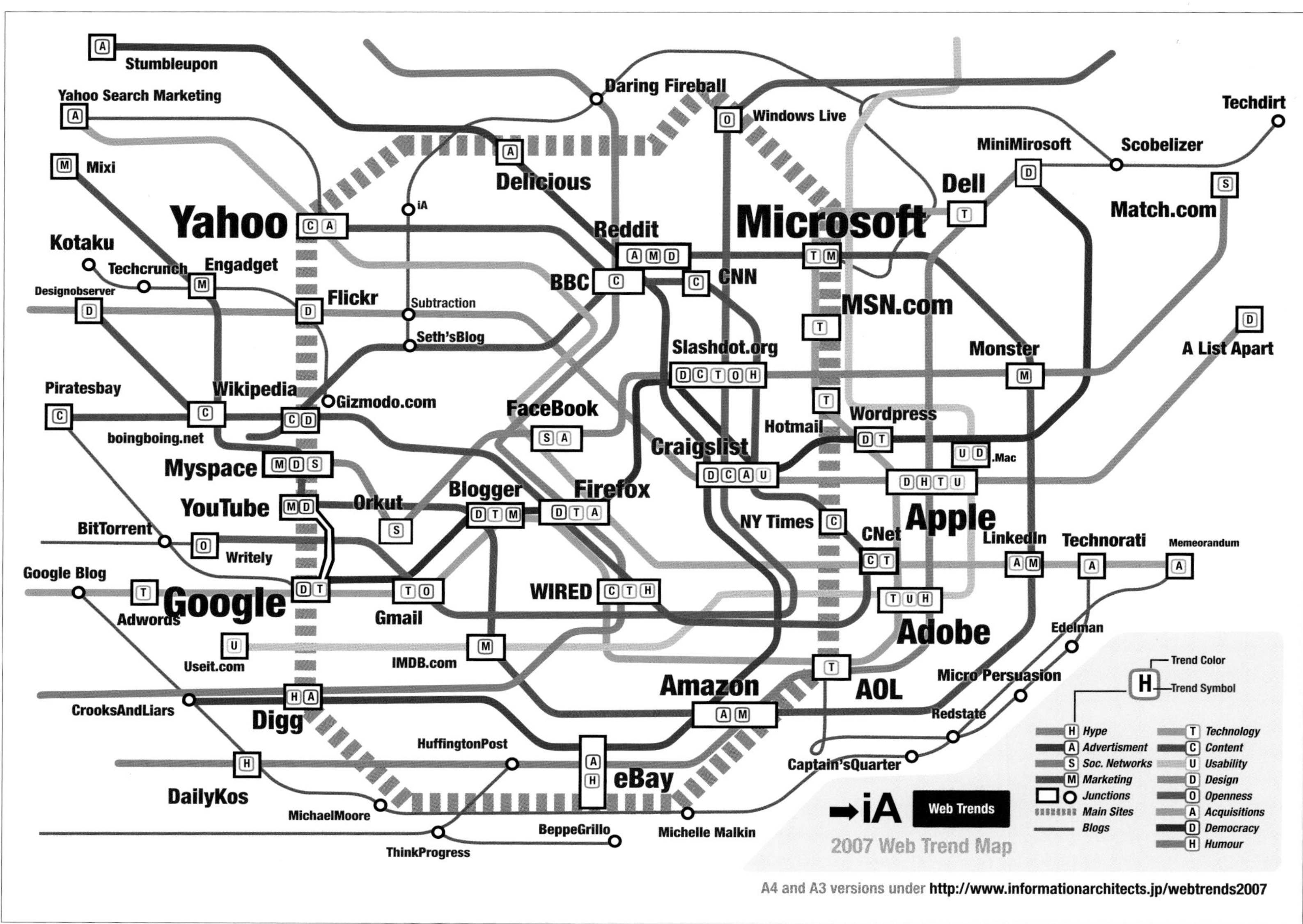

Web Trend Map

Tokyo-based Information Architects developed this piece in 2006 and since then have updated it annually. It categorises online services according to type of business. Categories are shown as subway lines, with each domain being one tube station, with the station symbol showing both the stability (width) and degree of success (height) of each service. Stations are arranged according to popularity (distance from the centre).

While the earlier versions were largely based on the actual Tokyo subway map, the 2010 version employs an individual isometric design. Despite being called a map, it does not allocate information to specific places. Rather, domains are categorised using the metaphor of subway lines. The ranking along the bottom adds a hierarchy for some of the domains above.

Die in Tokio ansässigen Information Architects entwarfen diese Grafik 2006 und aktualisieren sie seitdem jährlich. Onlinedienste werden je nach Art des Unternehmens kategorisiert. Die einzelnen Kategorien sind als U-Bahn-Linien dargestellt, jede Domain ist eine U-Bahn-Station. Das Symbol der Station gibt die Stabilität (Fläche) und den Erfolg (Höhe) des Unternehmens an. Die Stationen sind entsprechend ihrer Beliebtheit angeordnet (Entfernung vom Zentrum).

Während die früheren Versionen größtenteils auf dem tatsächlichen U-Bahn-Plan von Tokio beruhten, basiert die Fassung aus dem Jahr 2010 auf einem individuellen isometrischen Design. Auch wenn die Grafik als „Plan" bezeichnet wird, ordnet sie die Informationen nicht bestimmten Orten zu. Vielmehr werden die Domains anhand der Metapher von U-Bahn-Linien kategorisiert. Das Ranking am unteren Bildrand ordnet zusätzlich einige der oben genannten Domains hierarchisch an.

Le studio tokyoïte Information Architects a conçu cette œuvre en 2006 et l'a depuis lors actualisée chaque année. Elle présente des services en ligne selon le type d'activité. Les catégories apparaissent sous forme de lignes de métro, chaque domaine correspondant à une station dont le symbole indique la stabilité (largeur) et la réussite (hauteur) de chaque service. Les stations sont agencées en fonction de leur popularité (distance par rapport au centre).

Alors que les versions antérieures s'inspiraient surtout du plan réel du métro de Tokyo, la version 2010 fait appel à un design isométrique propre. Même s'il s'agit d'un plan, il ne donne pas d'informations sur des emplacements déterminés. Les domaines sont organisés selon la métaphore des lignes de métro. Le classement au bas ajoute une hiérarchie pour certains des domaines.

Project Info: Series of posters, website, 2006–2010, Japan / Switzerland
Data Source: Alexa; Compete; comScore; Crowdsourcing; Nielsen NetRatings
Research: Chris Luescher
Design: Oliver Reichenstein, Takeshi Tanka, Matt Gerber (Information Architects)

Web Trend Map

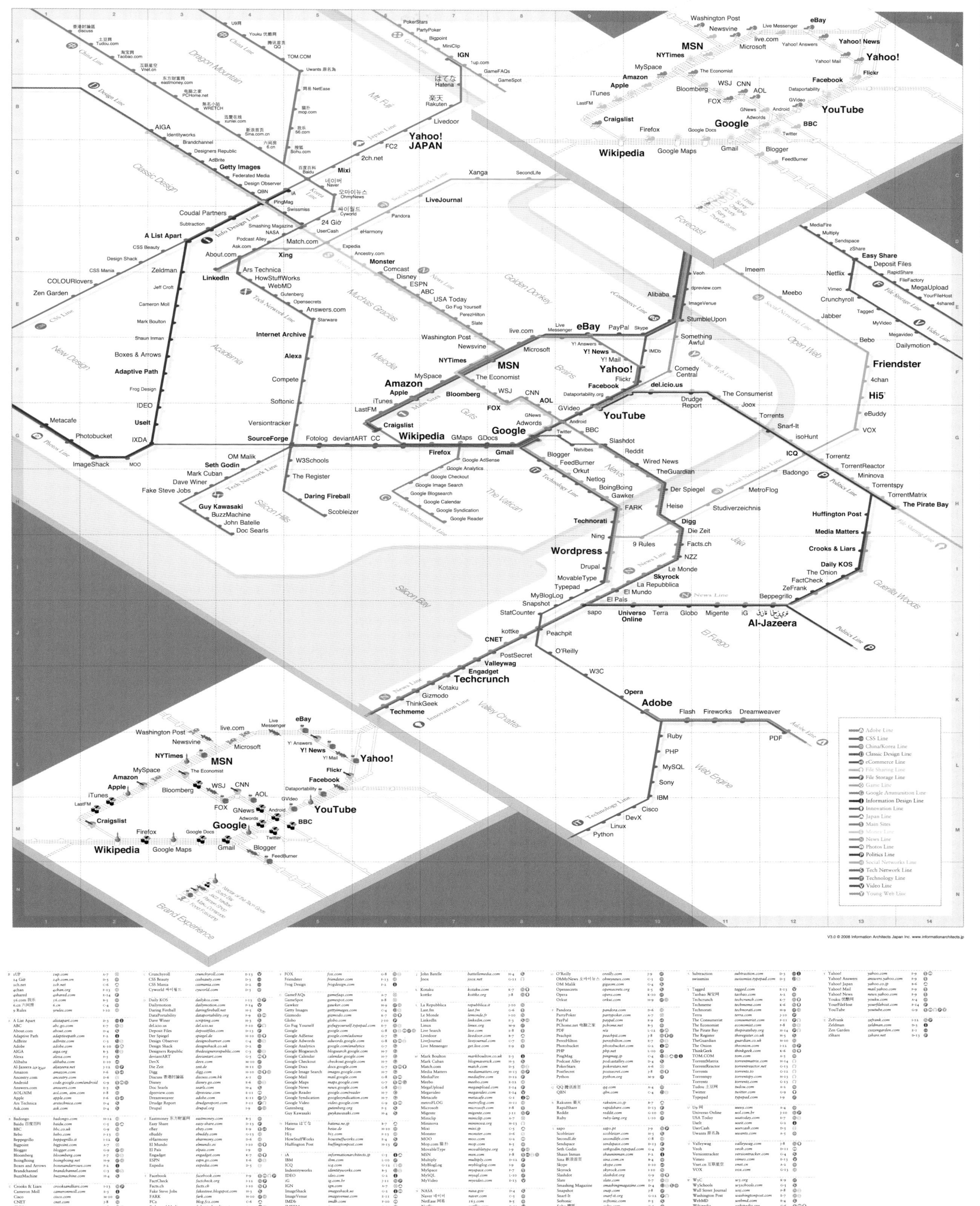

V3.0 © 2008 Information Architects Japan Inc. www.informationarchitects.jp

→iA

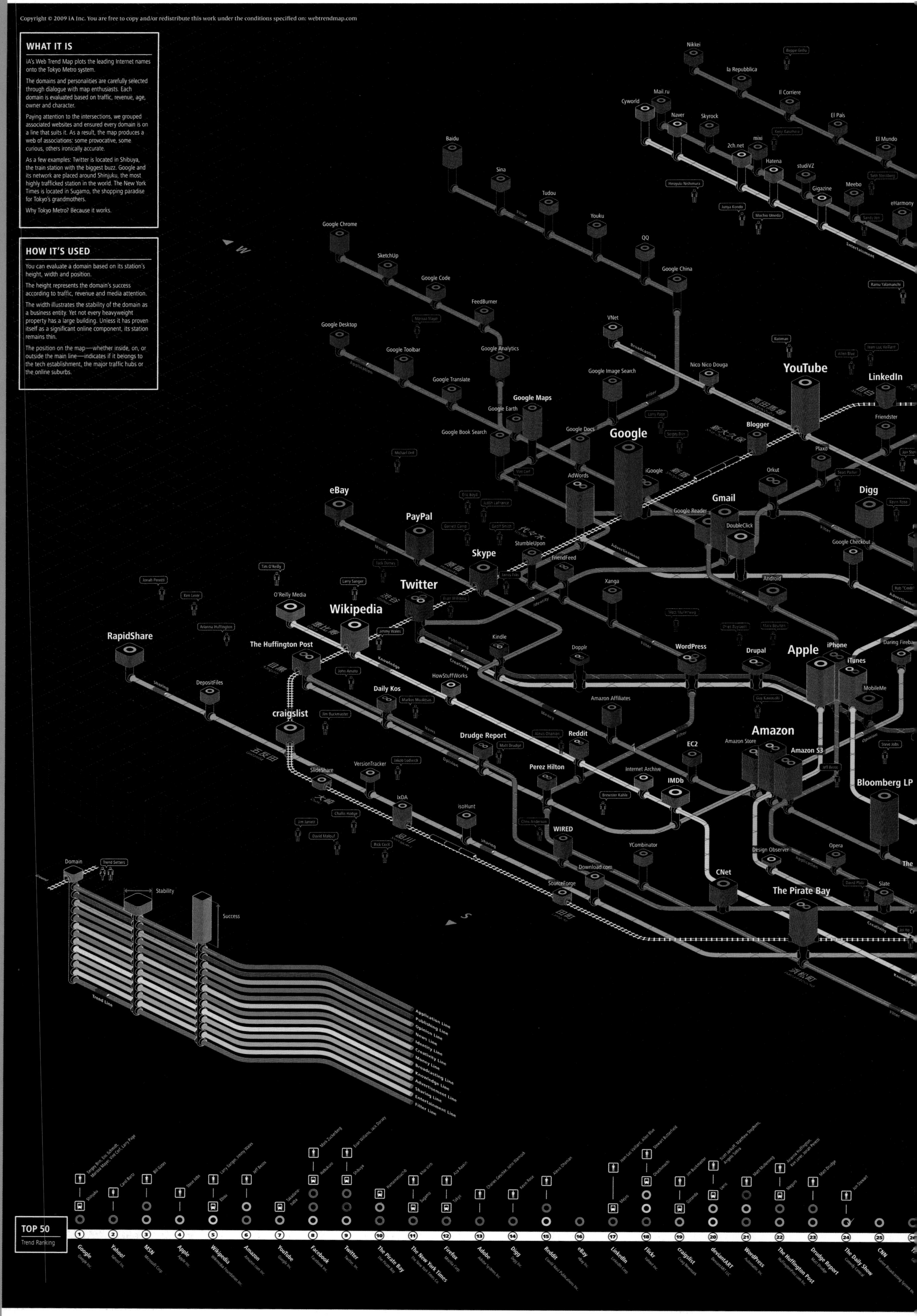

WHAT IT IS

iA's Web Trend Map plots the leading Internet names onto the Tokyo Metro system.

The domains and personalities are carefully selected through dialogue with map enthusiasts. Each domain is evaluated based on traffic, revenue, age, owner and character.

Paying attention to the intersections, we grouped associated websites and ensured every domain is on a line that suits it. As a result, the map produces a web of associations: some provocative, some curious, others ironically accurate.

As a few examples: Twitter is located in Shibuya, the train station with the biggest buzz. Google and its network are placed around Shinjuku, the most highly trafficked station in the world. The New York Times is located in Sugamo, the shopping paradise for Tokyo's grandmothers.

Why Tokyo Metro? Because it works.

HOW IT'S USED

You can evaluate a domain based on its station's height, width and position.

The height represents the domain's success according to traffic, revenue and media attention.

The width illustrates the stability of the domain as a business entity. Yet not every heavyweight property has a large building. Unless it has proven itself as a significant online component, its station remains thin.

The position on the map—whether inside, on, or outside the main line—indicates if it belongs to the tech establishment, the major traffic hubs or the online suburbs.

Domain
Trend Setters
Stability
Success
Trend Line

Application Line
Publishing Line
Opinion Line
News Line
Identity Line
Creativity Line
Money Line
Broadcasting Line
Knowledge Line
Advertisement Line
Sharing Line
Entertainment Line
Filter Line

Nikkei
la Repubblica
Il Corriere
El País
El Mundo
Mail.ru
Cyworld
Naver
Skyrock
mixi
2ch.net
Hatena
studiVZ
Gigazine
Meebo
eHarmony
Baidu
Sina
Tudou
Youku
QQ
Google China
Google Chrome
SketchUp
Google Code
FeedBurner
Google Desktop
Google Toolbar
Google Analytics
Google Translate
VNet
Google Image Search
Nico Nico Douga
YouTube
LinkedIn
Friendster
Google Maps
Google Earth
Google Book Search
Google Docs
Google
Blogger
iGoogle
AdWords
Plaxo
Orkut
Gmail
Google Reader
DoubleClick
Digg
Google Checkout
eBay
PayPal
Skype
StumbleUpon
FriendFeed
Twitter
Xanga
Android
O'Reilly Media
Wikipedia
RapidShare
The Huffington Post
Kindle
Doppler
WordPress
Drupal
Apple
iPhone
iTunes
MobileMe
DepositFiles
HowStuffWorks
Daily Kos
Amazon Affiliates
craigslist
Drudge Report
Reddit
EC2
Amazon
Amazon Store
Amazon S3
Bloomberg LP
VersionTracker
SlideShare
Perez Hilton
Internet Archive
IMDb
IxDA
isoHunt
WIRED
YCombinator
Opera
Design Observer
Download.com
CNet
SourceForge
The Pirate Bay
Slate

TOP 50
Trend Ranking

1 Google
2 Yahoo!
3 MSN
4 Apple
5 Wikipedia
6 Amazon
7 YouTube
8 Facebook
9 Twitter
10 The Pirate Bay
11 The New York Times
12 Firefox
13 Adobe
14 Digg
15 Reddit
16 eBay
17 LinkedIn
18 Flickr
19 craigslist
20 deviantART
21 WordPress
22 The Huffington Post
23 Drudge Report
24 The Daily Show
25 CNN

WEB TREND MAP 4

The State of the Web Mapped onto Tokyo's Metro System

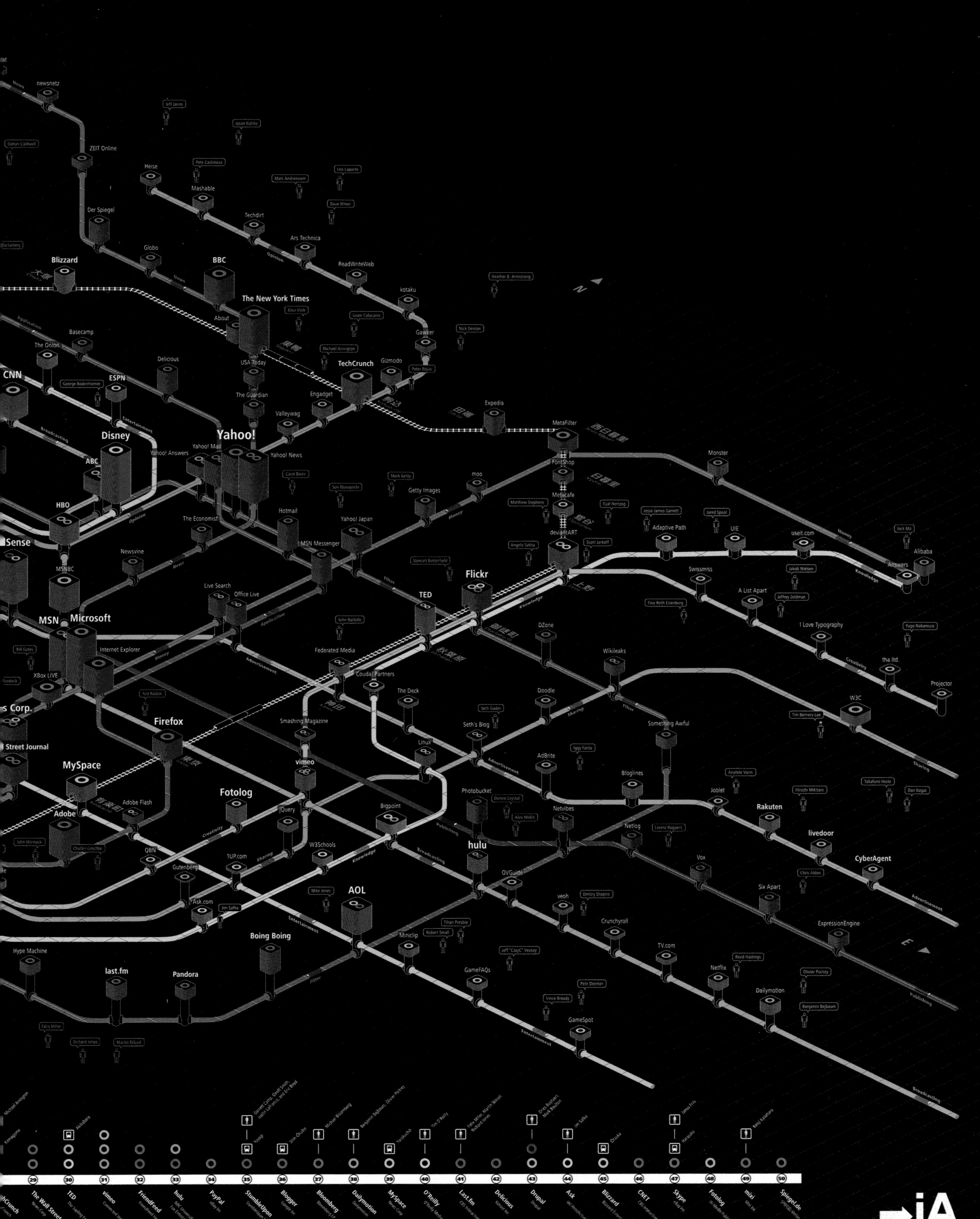

What are Infovis and Datavis About?

Using the metaphor of a tree, the infographic aims to describe the field of Information Visualisation. Roots sketch out the individual skills that are involved in creating complex visualisations. The dark-green strand demonstrates how datasets must be thoroughly analysed. Light blue alludes to visual skills for developing a clear design. The designing of interaction patterns is coded light green.

The dark-blue strand shows how it is necessary to keep up with software development, as this enables ever newer visualisation techniques and broader user interaction. At the top, the tree shows the two main applications: statistical graphics and thematic mapping. The piece illustrates the complexity of the field, and how it is difficult to represent the components as distinct and strict categories.

Diese Infografik beschreibt das Arbeitsgebiet der Informationsvisualisierung und bedient sich dafür der Baum-Metapher. Die Wurzeln veranschaulichen die verschiedenen Fähigkeiten, die zur Gestaltung komplexer Visualisierungen gebraucht werden. Der dunkelgrüne Strang steht für die Voraussetzung aller Visualisierung: die gründliche Analyse der vorliegenden Daten. Der hellblaue Strang verweist auf die visuellen Fertigkeiten, die für ein Design erforderlich sind. Die Gestaltung interaktiver Oberflächen ist hellgrün dargestellt.

Die dunkelblauen Stränge stehen für die Notwendigkeit, mit der Softwareentwicklung Schritt zu halten – sie ermöglicht immer neue Visualisierungstechniken und eine breitere Nutzerinteraktion. Die beiden bedeutendsten Anwendungen, statistische Grafiken und thematische Karten, bilden quasi den Wipfel des Baums. Das Schaubild zeigt die Komplexität des Bereichs und wie schwierig es ist, die Komponenten als streng voneinander getrennte, Kategorien darzustellen.

Avec la métaphore d'un arbre, cette infographie vise à décrire le domaine de la visualisation d'informations. Les racines représentent les compétences intervenant dans la création de visualisations complexes. L'axe vert foncé montre comment les données doivent être analysées. En bleu clair apparaissent les compétences visuelles pour élaborer un design clair. La conception des modèles d'interaction apparaît en vert clair.

Les branches bleu foncé montrent qu'il est nécessaire de se tenir à jour des nouveaux logiciels, afin de profiter de techniques de visualisation toujours plus récentes et d'une plus grande interaction avec l'utilisateur. En haut, l'arbre présente les deux applications principales : les graphiques statistiques et les cartes thématiques. Cette image illustre la complexité du domaine et la difficulté de représenter les éléments sous forme de catégories bien distinctes.

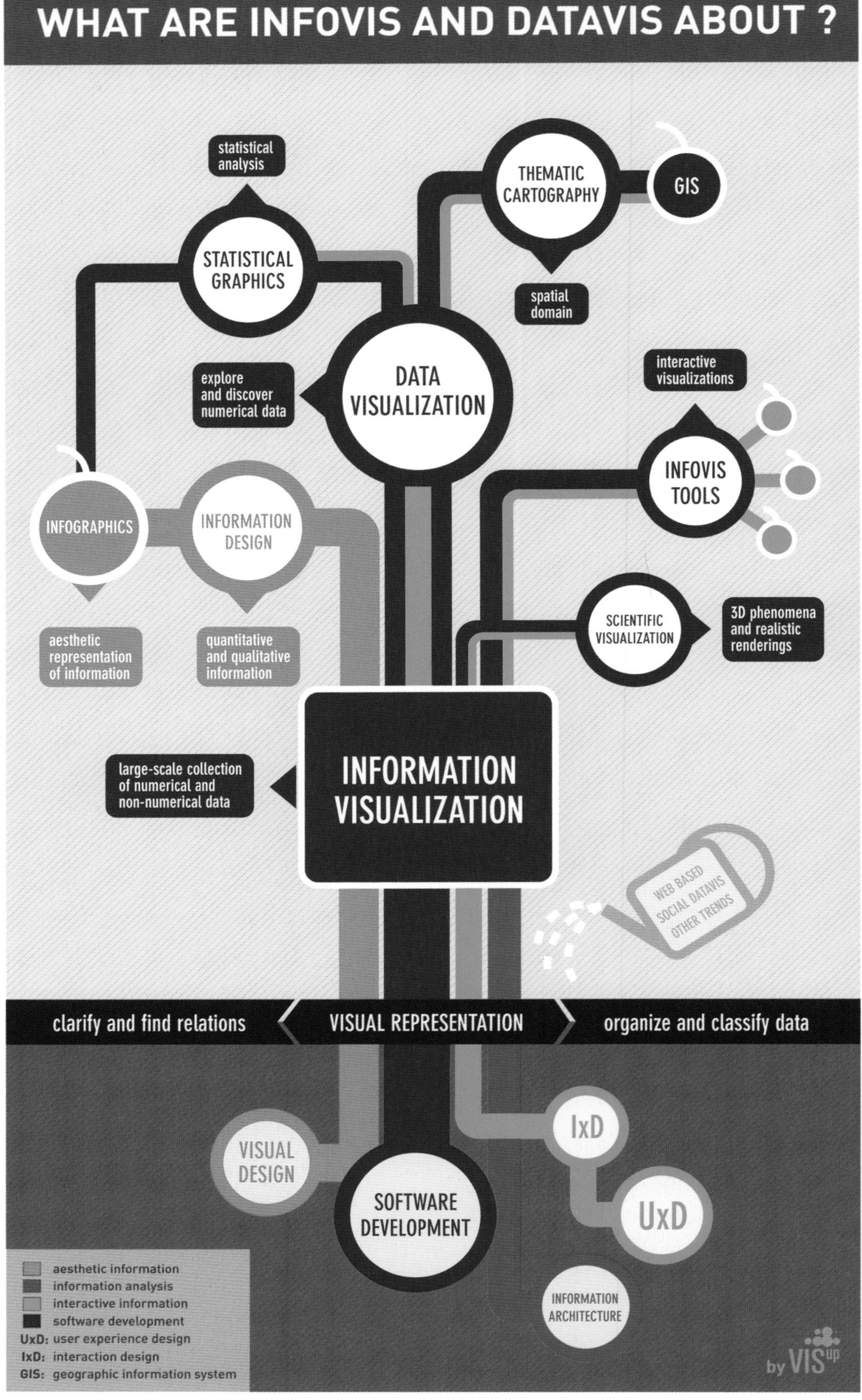

Project Info: Website, 2010, Italy
Design: Eloisa Paola Fontana (VISup)

World Government

Founded in 2000, artist duo Bureau d'études develop research-based diagrams of complex economic or social systems. *World Government* is a piece that analyses the interconnections between political institutions and economic powers, indicating how political decision structures may be distorted by the influence of big money.

The legend in the top-left corner explains the various symbols used. Three major complexes are depicted: the political complex (bottom left), various major business sectors (bottom right) and the financial sector (top right). Some extra space is devoted to the "intelligence complex" (top centre).

Das französische Künstlerduo Bureau d'études, das seine Zusammenarbeit im Jahr 2000 begann, entwickelt Diagramme über komplexe ökonomische und soziale Systeme, basierend auf detaillierten Recherchen. *World Government* analysiert die Wechselbeziehungen zwischen politischen Institutionen und ökonomischen Kräften und veranschaulicht, wie politische Entscheidungsstrukturen durch „das große Geld" beeinflusst werden können.

Die Legende oben links erläutert die Symbole. Drei große Komplexe sind dargestellt: der politische Komplex (unten links), verschiedene große Unternehmenssektoren (unten rechts) und der Finanzsektor (oben rechts). Dem Komplex von Thinktanks, religiösen Organisationen und geheimen Verbindungen wird ein gesondertes Feld eingeräumt (obere Mitte).

Fondé en 2000, le duo d'artistes français Bureau d'études élabore des diagrammes à partir de recherches menées sur des systèmes socioéconomiques complexes. *World Government* analyse les interconnexions entre les institutions politiques et les pouvoirs économiques. Elle montre comment les structures décisionnaires en politique peuvent se laisser influencer par l'argent.

La légende dans l'angle supérieur gauche explique les différents symboles employés. Trois grands ensembles sont illustrés : l'ensemble politique (en bas à gauche), différents grands secteurs économiques (en bas à droite) et le secteur financier (en haut à droite). L'espace restant est consacré au « complexe de l'intelligence » (en haut au milieu).

Project Info: Poster, 2005, France
Artists: Bureau d'études

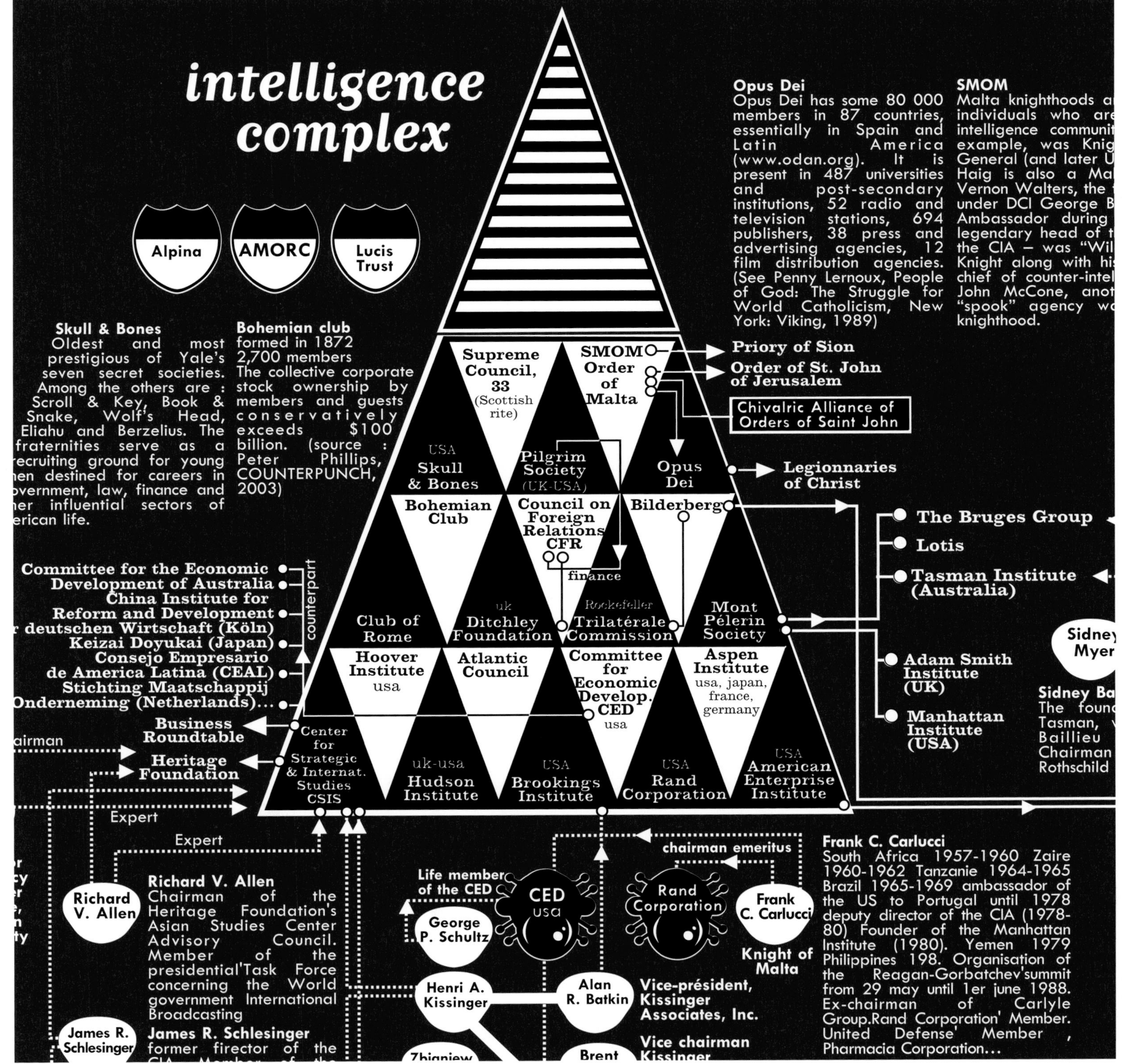

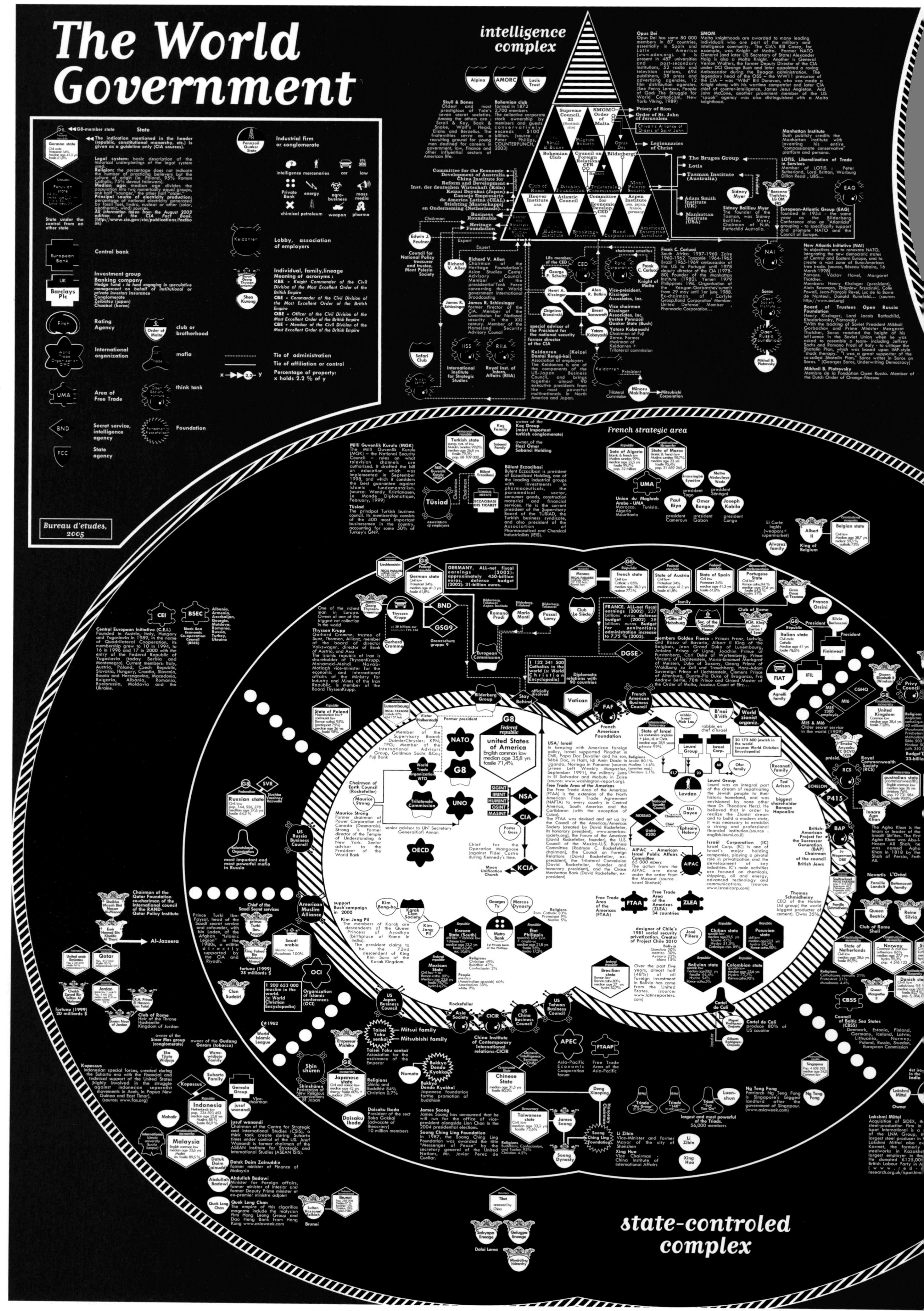
The World Government
intelligence complex
Alpina
AMORC
Lucis Trust
G8-member state
State
Industrial firm or conglomerate
Central bank
Investment group
Banking company
Rating Agency
club or brotherhood
International organization
mafia
Area of Free Trade
think tank
Secret service, intelligence agency
Foundation
State agency
Lobby, association of employers
Individual, family, lineage
Tie of administration
Tie of affiliation or control
Percentage of property: x holds 2.2 % of y
Bureau d'etudes, 2005
Supreme Council 33
SMOM Order of Malta
Bohemian Club
Council on Foreign Relations
Bilderberg
Club of Rome
Hoover Institute
Atlantic Council
Committee for Economic Development
Aspen Institute
Hudson Institute
Brookings Institute
Rand Corporation
Priory of Sion
Order of St. John of Jerusalem
Legionnaires of Christ
The Bruges Group
Lotis
Tasman Institute (Australia)
Adam Smith Institute (UK)
Manhattan Institute (USA)
Business Roundtable
Heritage Foundation
Council for National Policy
French strategic area
UMA
Union du Maghreb Arabe - UMA
GERMANY
BND
GSG9
FRANCE
DGSE
European Commission
Vatican
Bilderberg Group
Stay Behind
FAF
French American Business Council
B'nai B'rith
World zionist organiz.
NATO
G8
UNO
WTO
Trilaterale Commission
NSA
CIA
KCIA
OECD
Mossad
AIPAC
FTAA
ZLEA
Free Trade Area of the Americas (FTAA)
Leumi Group
Israel Corp.
Levdan
OCI
APEC
FTAAP
Asia-Pacific Economic Cooperation forum
CICIR
Mitsui family
Mitsubishi family
Dalai Lama
state-controled complex

financial heart
Mori Clan
Hitotsubashi Clan
Matsushita Clan
Sumitomo Clan
Mitsui Clan
Mitsubishi Clan
Vatican
Bush Clan
Rothschild Clan
Rockefeller Clan
Windsor Clan
Al Saud Clan
Bin Laden Clan
Li family
Soong family
Fitch
Moody's
Standard & Poor's
Carlyle Group
Banco Santander
Rothschild Group
Warburg Dillon Read
Lazard LLC
Rockefeller Group
J. P. Morgan Chase
Fidelity
State Street Corp.
Merrill Lynch
Goldman Sachs
citigroup Inc.
Barclays Plc
HSBC
Lloyds
Société Générale
Crédit Agricole
BNP Paribas
AXA
Allianz
deutsche bank
Federal Reserve
Bank of Japan
European Bank
Bank of England
Bundes Bank
Banque de France
World Bank
CLUB DE PARIS
Citic pacific
Hutchison Whampoa
Mitsubishi Corporation
Bank of Tokyo-Mitsubishi
Mizuho Financial Group
Sumitomo Kichizaemon
Mitsui & co
ITOCHU corp.
Seibu Group
Kikkoman corporation
Keizei Doyukai
Nikkeiren
Samsung
LG Group
TABD
ERT
Davos Economic Forum
psychological complex (medias)
News Corp.
Comcast
Disney Corp.
Viacom
Bertelsman
Reuters
AFP
BBC
VOA
Berlusconi
agro-business cartel
grain cartel
meat cartel
food cartel
Tradax
Cargill
Nestlé
Unilever
Louis Dreyfus
petroleum cartel
Rockefeller
Bush
Queen Beatrix (Netherlands)
Desmarais
Albert Frère
Exxon
Royal Dutch Shell
Chevron Texaco
Total
Rio Tinto
WCC

Writing Without Words

This is an exploration into how to visualise literature. Stefanie Posavec focused her project on Jack Kerouac's *On the Road* and went through the text by hand, marking each word according to a colour code which discerns the themes most prevalent in the book. She developed various visualisations for this body of data.

The *Sentence Drawing* (p.398) follows the course of each sentence. The length of a line indicates the number of words in a sentence. Starting in the top-right corner, the line turns right with the beginning of every new sentence, thus re-writing the whole novel. In *Rhythm Textures* (p.399), Posavec analysed the inner structure of single sentences and visualised them in circle diagrams. Irregular structures indicate variations in the punctuation of a particular sentence.

Dieses Projekt untersucht, wie sich Literatur visualisieren lässt. Stefanie Posavec wählte Jack Kerouacs *On the Road* (dt. *Unterwegs*) als Ausgangspunkt ihres Projekts. Sie ging den Text per Hand durch und markierte jedes Wort farbig nach den häufigsten Themen des Buchs. Für diese Daten entwickelte sie verschiedene Visualisierungsarten.

Sentence Drawing (S. 398) folgt dem Verlauf jedes einzelnen Satzes. Die Länge einer Linie zeigt die Anzahl der Wörter in einem Satz. Oben rechts einsetzend, knickt die Linie bei jedem neuen Satz nach rechts; dadurch wird der ganze Roman ein zweites Mal „nachgeschrieben". Für *Rhythm Textures* (S. 399) analysierte Posavec die innere Struktur einzelner Sätze und visualisierte sie in Kreisdiagrammen. Unregelmäßige Strukturen zeigen Variationen bei der Zeichensetzung in diesem bestimmten Satz.

Ceci est un essai de représentation visuelle de la littérature. Stefanie Posavec a centré son projet sur le roman *Sur la route* de Jack Kerouac et a parcouru le texte en marquant chaque mot d'une couleur correspondant à l'un des thèmes phares de l'ouvrage. Elle a créé plusieurs représentations de ce corps de données.

Sentence Drawing (p.398) suit le parcours de chaque phrase. La longueur d'une ligne indique le nombre de mots dans une phrase. En commençant en haut à droite, la ligne tourne à droite au début de chaque nouvelle phrase, et réécrit ainsi tout le roman. Dans *Rhythm Textures* (p.399), Posavec a analysé la structure interne des phrases et les a illustrées par des diagrammes circulaires. Les structures irrégulières indiquent des variations dans la ponctuation d'une certaine phrase.

Project Info: Series of posters, 2006, UK
Design: Stefanie Posavec
Additional Info: MA project at Central Saint Martins College

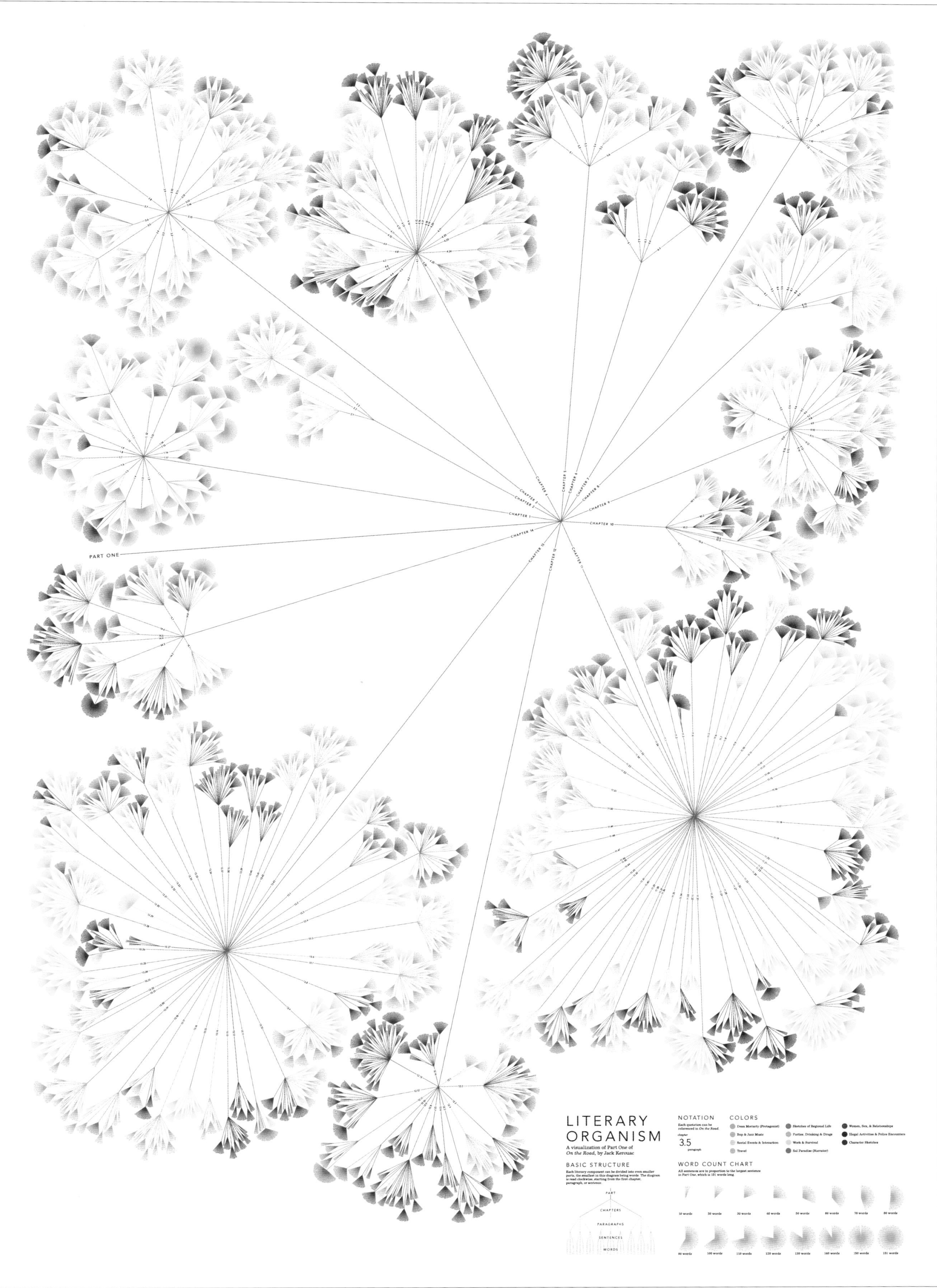
PART ONE
CHAPTER 1
CHAPTER 2
CHAPTER 3
CHAPTER 4
CHAPTER 5
CHAPTER 6
CHAPTER 7
CHAPTER 8
CHAPTER 9
CHAPTER 10
CHAPTER 11
CHAPTER 12
CHAPTER 13
CHAPTER 14
LITERARY ORGANISM
A visualization of Part One of *On the Road*, by Jack Kerouac
BASIC STRUCTURE
Each literary component can be divided into even smaller parts, the smallest in this diagram being words. The diagram is read clockwise, starting from the first chapter, paragraph, or sentence.
PART
CHAPTERS
PARAGRAPHS
SENTENCES
WORDS
NOTATION
Each quotation can be referenced in *On the Road*.
chapter
3.5
paragraph
COLORS
Dean Moriarty (Protagonist)
Bop & Jazz Music
Social Events & Interaction
Travel
Sketches of Regional Life
Parties, Drinking & Drugs
Work & Survival
Sal Paradise (Narrator)
Women, Sex, & Relationships
Illegal Activities & Police Encounters
Character Sketches
WORD COUNT CHART
All sentences are in proportion to the largest sentence in Part One, which is 151 words long.
10 words
20 words
30 words
40 words
50 words
60 words
70 words
80 words
90 words
100 words
110 words
120 words
130 words
140 words
150 words
151 words

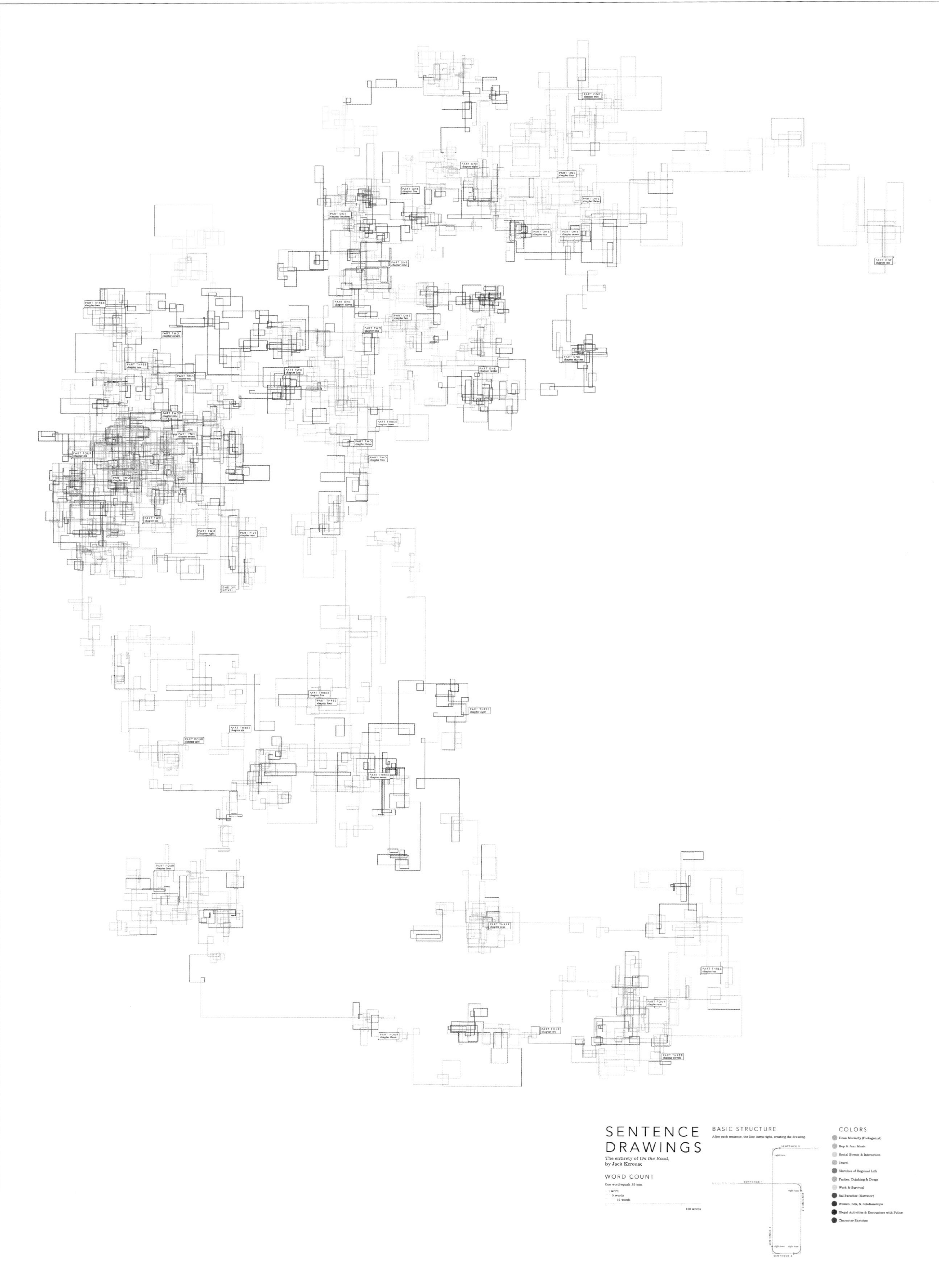
SENTENCE DRAWINGS
The entirety of *On the Road*, by Jack Kerouac
WORD COUNT
One word equals .85 mm.
1 word
5 words
10 words
100 words
BASIC STRUCTURE
After each sentence, the line turns right, creating the drawing.
SENTENCE 1
right turn
SENTENCE 2
right turn
SENTENCE 3
right turn
SENTENCE 4
right turn
SENTENCE 5
COLORS
Dean Moriarty (Protagonist)
Bop & Jazz Music
Social Events & Interaction
Travel
Sketches of Regional Life
Parties, Drinking & Drugs
Work & Survival
Sal Paradise (Narrator)
Women, Sex, & Relationships
Illegal Activities & Encounters with Police
Character Sketches

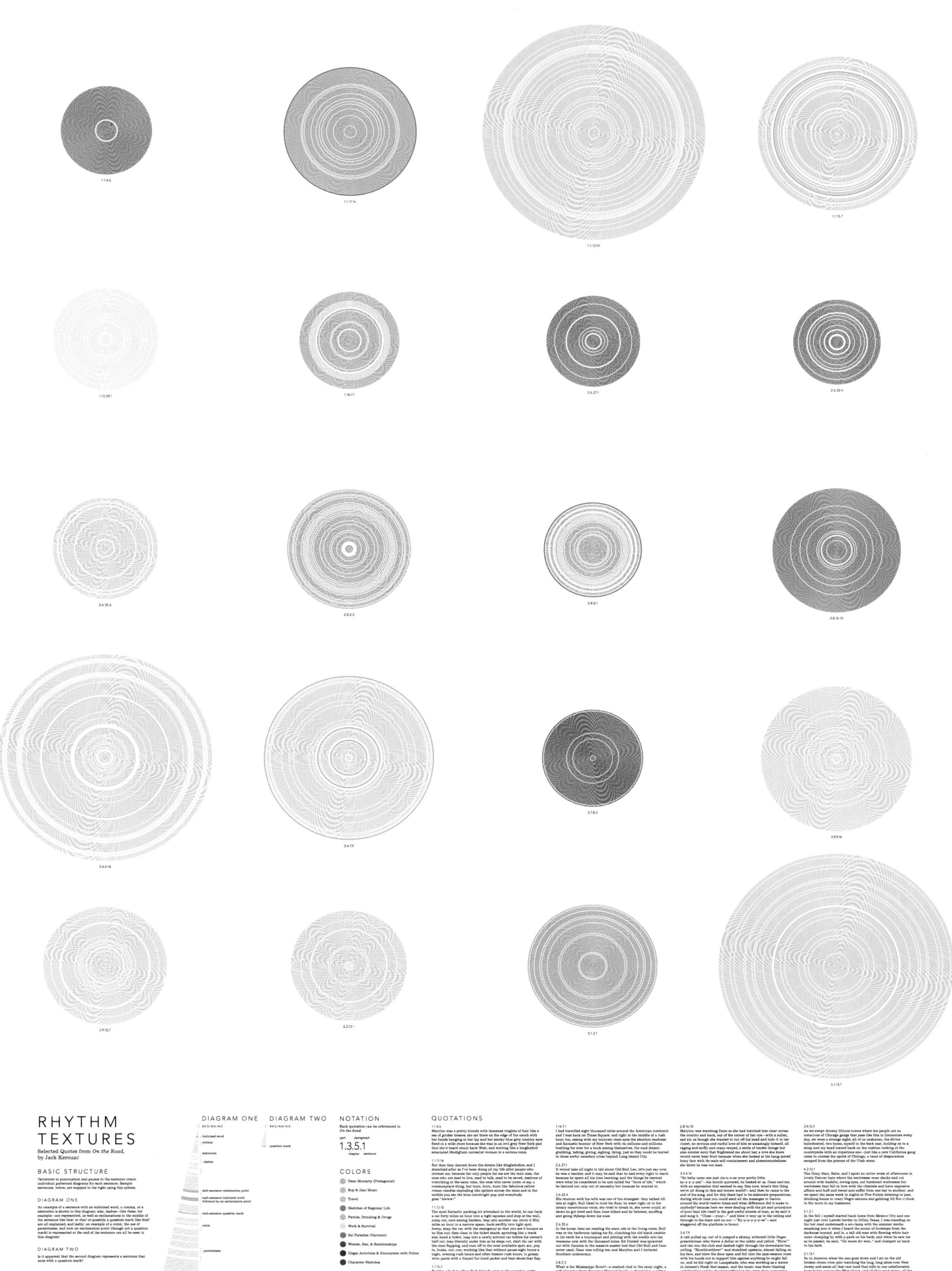

RHYTHM TEXTURES

Selected Quotes from *On the Road,* by Jack Kerouac

BASIC STRUCTURE

Variations in punctuation and pauses in the sentence create individual patterned diagrams for each sentence. Sample sentences, below, are mapped to the right using this system.

DIAGRAM ONE

An example of a sentence with an *italicized* word, a comma, or a semicolon is shown in this diagram; also, dashes—like these, for example—are represented, as well as exclamations in the middle of the sentence like this! or *this!* or possibly a question mark like this? are all explained, and lastly: an example of a colon, the use of parentheses, and how an exclamation point (though not a question mark) is represented at the end of the sentence can all be seen in this diagram!

DIAGRAM TWO

Is it apparent that the second diagram represents a sentence that ends with a question mark?

DIAGRAM ONE

BEGINNING
italicized word
comma
semicolon
dashes
mid-sentence exclamation point
mid-sentence italicized word followed by an exclamation point
mid-sentence question mark
colon
parentheses
exclamation point

DIAGRAM TWO

BEGINNING
question mark

NOTATION

Each quotation can be referenced in *On the Road.*

part, chapter, paragraph, sentence
1.3.5.1

COLORS

- Dean Moriarty (Protagonist)
- Bop & Jazz Music
- Travel
- Sketches of Regional Life
- Parties, Drinking & Drugs
- Work & Survival
- Sal Paradise (Narrator)
- Women, Sex, & Relationships
- Illegal Activities & Encounters with Police
- Character Sketches

QUOTATIONS

1.1.4.6
Marylou was a pretty blonde with immense ringlets of hair like a sea of golden tresses; she sat there on the edge of the couch with her hands hanging in her lap and her smoky blue grey country eyes fixed in a wide stare because she was in an evil grey New York pad that she'd heard about back West, and waiting like a longbodied emaciated Modigliani surrealist woman in a serious room.

1.1.11.14
But then they danced down the streets like dingledodies, and I shambled after as I've been doing all my life after people who interest me, because the only people for me are the mad ones, the ones who are mad to live, mad to talk, mad to be saved, desirous of everything at the same time, the ones who never yawn or say a commonplace thing, but burn, burn, burn like fabulous yellow roman candles exploding like spiders across the stars and in the middle you see the blue centerlight pop and everybody goes "Awww!"

1.1.13.10
The most fantastic parking-lot attendant in the world, he can back a car forty miles an hour into a tight squeeze and stop at the wall, jump out, race among fenders, leap into another car, circle it fifty miles an hour in a narrow space, back swiftly into tight spot, *hump,* snap the car with the emergency so that you see it bounce as he flies out; then clear to the ticket shack, sprinting like a track star, hand a ticket, leap into a newly arrived car before the owner's half out, leap literally under him as he steps out, start the car with the door flapping, and roar off to the next available spot, arc, pop in, brake, out, run; working like that without pause eight hours a night, evening rush hours and after-theatre rush hours, in greasy wino pants with a frayed fur-lined jacket and beat shoes that flap.

1.1.15.7
Besides, all of my New York friends were in the negative, nightmare position of putting down society and giving their tired bookish or political or psychoanalytical reasons, but Dean just raced in society, eager for bread and love; he didn't care one way or the other, "so long's I can get that lil old gal with that lil sumpin down there tween her legs, boy", and "so long's we can eat, son, y'ear me? I'm *hungry,* I'm *starving,* let's *eat right now!*—and off we'd rush to *eat,* whereof, as saith Ecclesiastes, "It is your portion under the sun."

1.13.29.1
In the morning the dew made the tent sag; I got up with my towel and toothbrush and went to the general motel toilet to wash; then I came back, put on my pants, which were all torn from kneeling in the earth and had been sewed by Terry in the evening, put on my rugged straw hat, which had originally served as Johnny's toy hat, and went across the highway with my canvas cotton-bag.

1.14.7.1
I had travelled eight thousand miles around the American continent and I was back on Times Square; and right in the middle of a rush hour, too, seeing with my innocent road-eyes the absolute madness and fantastic hoorair of New York with its millions and millions hustling for ever for a buck among themselves, the mad dream-grabbing, taking, giving, sighing, dying, just so they could be buried in those awful cemetery cities beyond Long Island City.

2.6.27.1
It would take all night to tell about Old Bull Lee; let's just say now, he was a teacher, and it may be said that he had every right to teach because he spent all his time learning; and the things he learned were what he considered to be and called the "facts of life," which he learned not only out of necessity but because he wanted to.

2.6.32.4
His relation with his wife was one of the strangest: they talked till late at night; Bull liked to hold the floor, he went right on in his dreary monotonous voice, she tried to break in, she never could; at dawn he got tired and then Jane talked and he listened, snuffing and going *thfump* down his nose.

2.6.35.6
In the house Jane sat reading the want ads in the living room; Bull was in the bathroom taking his fix, clutching his old black necktie in his teeth for a tourniquet and jabbing with the needle into his woesome arm with the thousand holes; Ed Dunkel was sprawled out with Galatea in the massive master bed that Old Bull and Jane never used; Dean was rolling tea; and Marylou and I imitated Southern aristocracy.

2.8.2.3
What is the Mississippi River?—a washed clod in the rainy night, a soft plopping from drooping Missouri banks, a dissolving, a riding of the tide down the eternal waterbed, a contribution to brown foams, a voyaging past endless vales and trees and levees, down along, down along, by Memphis, Greenville, Eudora, Vicksburg, Natchez, Port Allen, and Port Orleans and Port of the Deltas, by Potash, Venice, and the Night's Great Gulf, and out.

2.8.8.1
In the empty Houston streets of four o'clock in the morning a motorcycle kid suddenly roared through, all bespangled and bedecked with glittering buttons, visor, slick black jacket, a Texas poet of the night, girl gripped on his back like a papoose, hair flying, onward-going, singing, "Houston, Austin, Fort Worth, Dallas—and sometimes Kansas City—and sometimes old Antone, ah-haaaaa!"

2.8.16.10
Marylou was watching Dean as she had watched him clear across the country and back, out of the corner of her eye—with a sullen, sad air, as though she wanted to cut off his head and hide it in her closet, an envious and rueful love of him so amazingly himself, all raging and sniffy and crazy-wayed, a smile of tender dotage but also sinister envy that frightened me about her, a love she knew would never bear fruit because when she looked at his hang-jawed bony face with its male self-containment and absentmindedness she knew he was too mad.

3.4.4.14
"So baby come one just clo-o-o-se your pretty little ey-y-y-y-yes"—his mouth quivered, he looked at us, Dean and me, with an expression that seemed to say, Hey now, what's this thing we're all doing in this sad brown world?—and then he came to the end of his song, and for this there had to be elaborate preparations, during which time you could send all the messages to Garcia around the world twelve times and what difference did it make to anybody? because here we were dealing with the pit and prunejuice of poor beat life itself in the god-awful streets of man, so he said it and sang it, "Close —your—" and blew it way up to the ceiling and through to the stars and on out —"Ey-y-y-y-y-y-es"—and staggered off the platform to brood.

3.4.7.9
A cab pulled up; out of it jumped a skinny, withered little Negro preacherman who threw a dollar at the cabby and yelled, "Blow!" and ran into the club and dashed right through the downstairs bar, yelling, "Blowblowblow!" and stumbled upstairs, almost falling on his face, and blew the door open and fell into the jazz-session room with his hands out to support him against anything he might fall on, and he fell right on Lampshade, who was working as a waiter in Jamson's Nook that season, and the music was there blasting and blasting and he stood transfixed in the open door, screaming, "Blow for me, man, blow!"

3.7.8.2
Everything was collapsing, and to make things inconceivably more frantic there was an ecstatic spastic fellow in the bar who threw his arms around Dean and moaned in his face, and Dean went mad again with sweats and insanity, and to add still more to the unbearable confusion Dean rushed out the next moment and stole a car right from the driveway and took a dash to downtown Denver and came back with a newer, better one.

3.9.9.14
He passed the slow cars, swerved, and almost hit the left rail of the bridge, went head-on into the shadow of the unslowing truck, cut right sharply, just missed the truck's left front wheel, almost hit the slow car, pulled out to pass, and then had to cut back in line when another car came out from behind the truck to look, all in a matter of two seconds, flashing by and leaving nothing more than a cloud of dust instead of a horrible five-way crash with cars lurching in every direction and the great truck humping its back in the fatal red afternoon of Illinois with its dreaming fields.

3.9.10.7
As we swept drowsy Illinois towns where the people are so conscious of Chicago gangs that pass like this in limousines every day, we were a strange sight; all of us unshaven, the driver barechested, two bums, myself in the back seat, holding on to a strap and my head leaned back on the cushion looking at the countryside with an imperious eye—just like a new California gang come to contest the spoils of Chicago, a band of desparadoes escaped from the prisons of the Utah moon.

4.2.12.1
Tim Gray, Stan, Babe, and I spent an entire week of afternoons in lovely Denver bars where the waitresses wear slacks and cut around with bashful, loving eyes, not hardened waitresses but waitresses that fall in love with the clientele and have explosive affairs and huff and sweat and suffer from one bar to another; and we spent the same week in nights at Five Points listening to jazz, drinking booze in crazy Negro saloons and gabbing till five o'clock in the morn in my basement.

5.1.2.1
In the fall I myself started back home from Mexico City and one night just over Laredo border in Dilley, Texas, I was standing on the hot road underneath a arc-lamp with the summer moths smashing into it when I heard the sound of footsteps from the darkness beyond, and lo, a tall old man with flowing white hair came clomping by with a pack on his back, and when he saw me as he passed, he said, *"Go moan for man,"* and clomped on back to his dark.

5.1.13.1
So in America when the sun goes down and I sit on the old broken-down river pier watching the long, long skies over New Jersey and sense all that raw land that rolls in one unbelievable huge bulge over to the West Coast, and all that road going, all the people dreaming in the immensity of it, and in Iowa I know by now the children must be crying in the land where they let the children cry, and tonight the stars'll be out, and don't you know that God is Pooh Bear? the evening star must be drooping and shedding her sparkler dims on the prairie, which is just before the coming of complete night that blesses the earth, darkens all rivers, cups the peaks and folds the final shore in, and nobody, nobody knows what's going to happen to anybody besides the forlorn rags of growing old, I think of Dean Moriarty, I even think of Old Dean Moriarty the father we never found, I think of Dean Moriarty.

Your Friend, the Library

Using the metaphor of a set of bookshelves, this is a comparison of two library classification systems. The Dewey Decimal System, shown in green, is based on ten main classes of themes, like psychology, religion or general arts. They are named on the spines of individual books, starting on the lowest shelf. These main classes are further divided into sub-topics and referred to by three-digit numbers.

The Library of Congress classification, on the other hand, is based on letters to classify the main categories. In order to compare both approaches, books of similar topics are placed on neighbouring shelves. The comparison shows that the classification labels of both systems are not interchangeable just like that.

Mithilfe der Metapher eines Bücherregals werden hier zwei Archivierungssysteme von Bibliotheken verglichen. Das Dewey Decimal System (grün) hat zehn thematische Hauptbereiche wie Psychologie, Religion und Kunst. Sie sind auf dem Rücken der einzelnen Bücher vermerkt, beginnend auf dem untersten Regalboden. Diese Bereiche werden wiederum in Unterbereiche aufgegliedert, die mit einer dreistelligen Zahl versehen sind.

Die Klassifizierung der Library of Congress beruht auf Buchstaben zur Einordnung in Hauptkategorien. Um die Systematiken vergleichen zu können, stehen Bücher zu ähnlichen Themen auf benachbarten Regalböden. Der Vergleich zeigt, dass die Kennzeichnung der beiden Systeme nicht ohne Weiteres austauschbar ist.

Une métaphore d'étagère permet de comparer deux systèmes de classification de bibliothèque. Le système décimal Dewey, en vert, repose sur les dix principales classes thématiques, comme la psychologie, la religion ou les arts. Elles sont écrites sur la tranche des livres, en partant du rayon inférieur. Ces classes sont ensuite divisées en sous-rubriques et désignées par des numéros à trois chiffres.

La classification de la Bibliothèque du Congrès se base pour sa part sur des lettres pour organiser les principales catégories. Pour comparer les deux approches, des livres de sujets similaires sont placés sur des rayons voisins. La comparaison montre que les étiquettes de classification des deux systèmes ne sont pas facilement interchangeables.

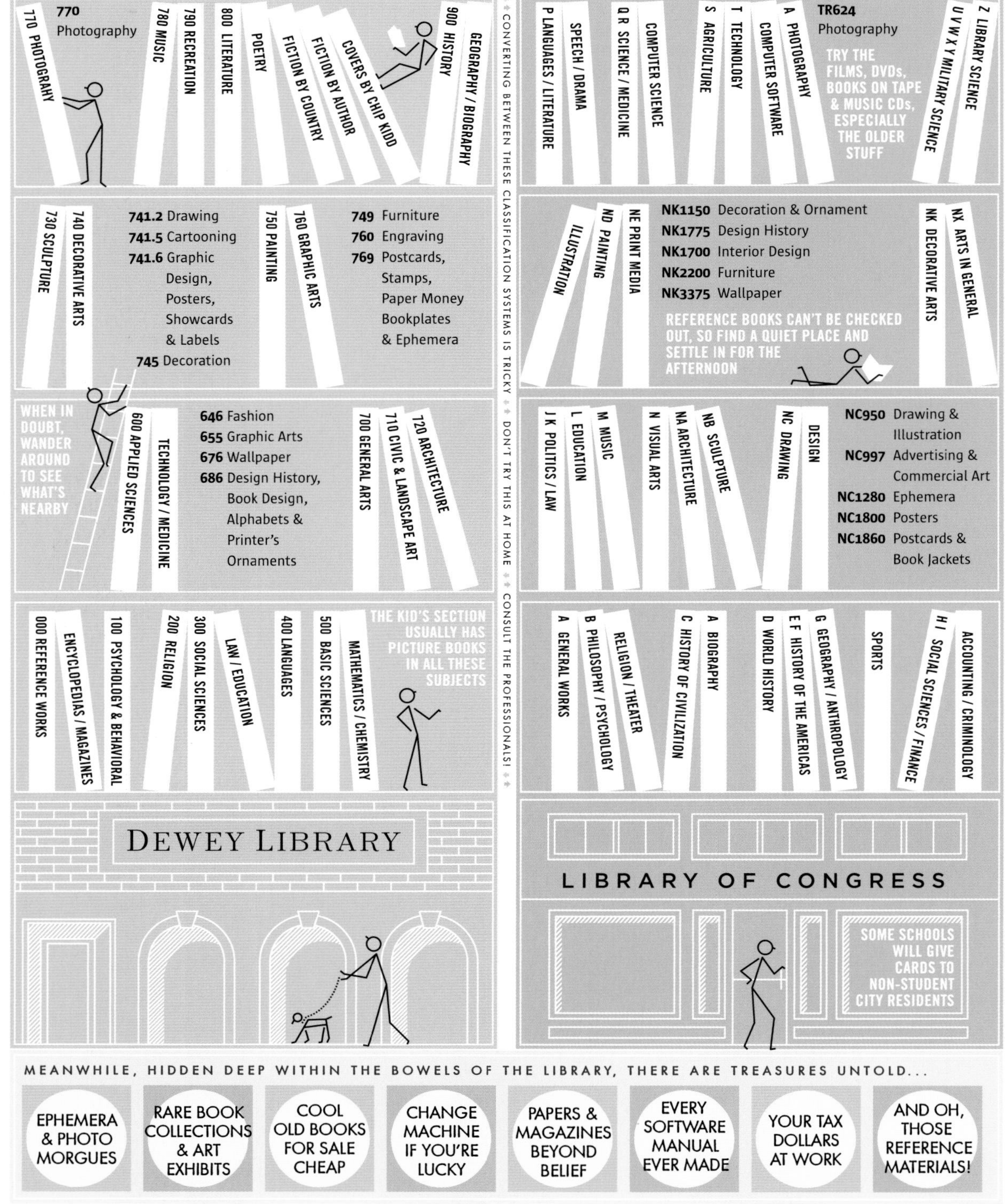

Project Info: *Rough*, Dallas Society of Visual Communications, magazine article, 2007, USA
Design: Michael Newhouse (Newhouse Design)

Hierarchy
401–474

“Excellence in statistical graphics consists of complex ideas communicated with clarity, precision, and efficiency.”

„Herausragende statistische Grafiken zeichnen sich dadurch aus, dass sie komplexe Ideen klar, präzise und effizient vermitteln.“

« L’excellence dans la représentation graphique des statistiques consiste à communiquer des idées complexes avec clarté, précision et efficacité. »

Edward Tufte

Hierarchy

Elements are ranked in order of priority

Hierarchy

Elemente werden in eine Rangfolge gebracht

Hiérarchie

Les éléments sont classés selon leur priorité

Hierarchies are vertical arrangements. Elements are sorted in order of rank, from largest to smallest, highest to lowest, and so on. In a linear hierarchy, e.g. a ranking, there is for each element a superior and a subordinate element, and the rank order results in a continuous sequence. *Fast Faust* (p.424) is a list of all the words in Goethe's *Faust*, arranged according to the frequency with which they appear in the text. *Super Vision Chart* (p.451) paces out at regular mathematical intervals the units of length that occur in the universe, from the smallest subatomic units to the very largest.

Hierarchies are created when ratios are visualised, as in the classic pie chart in which quantities are depicted as a proportion of the area of a circle. The prevalence of these charts in the worlds of business and science has provoked numerous wry comments (*Faces Diagrams*, p.421). Nevertheless, the transmission of data in scaled colour fields remains one of the most effective means by which infographics can clarify proportions. *Billion Dollar Gram* (p.411) shows the international movement of money through various channels as a series of colour fields that provide a visual display of the order of rank between large and small.

Ramified hierarchies split from the highest element into numerous sub-elements – as happens, for example, in large institutions (cf. *Small Industries Development*, p.449). The tree provides a classic way of portraying ramified hierarchies: starting at the root, elements are divided into increasing numbers of sub-groups. This image was frequently used to describe the evolution of species; family trees are another traditional example. In *Natural Selections* (p.435) the tree image is used to group animal and plant logos used by American publishers.

Taxonomies, on the other hand, deal with self-contained fields of knowledge by depicting continuous organisation from largest to smallest in hierarchical diagrams. Hence *A Taxonomy of Complete World Knowledge* (p.408) arranges all of the (imaginary) world knowledge from top to bottom in a tree structure. *Taxonomy of Team Names* (p.453) depicts the shared root at the centre, while the sub-species branch out into a circle around it. In the taxonomy of types of beer, "beer" as the most general category is placed at the centre and forms the starting point from which the various sub-groups of beer are classified (*The Very Many Varieties of Beer*, p.464).

Websites are also organised hierarchically; the site map of an Internet site contains all its individual pages within a tree structure. In the case of a major Internet platform like Facebook this hierarchy of pages is vast and confusing, making it harder to find individual pages. *A Nightmare on Privacy Street* (p.406) illustrates how the website's complicated hierarchic structure conceals privacy settings and makes them very difficult for users to find.

Hierarchien sind vertikale Ordnungen. Elemente werden in eine Rangfolge einsortiert, vom größten zum kleinsten, vom höchsten zum niedrigsten und so weiter. In einer linearen Hierarchie – zum Beispiel einem Ranking – gibt es für jedes Element genau ein über- oder untergeordnetes Element, die Rangfolge ergibt eine kontinuierliche Reihe. *Fast Faust* (S. 424) ist eine Liste aller Wörter in Goethes *Faust*, geordnet nach ihrer Häufigkeit im Text. Das *Super Vision Chart* (S. 451) schreitet in mathematisch regelmäßigen Abständen die Längeneinheiten ab, die im Universum vorkommen, von den subatomaren kleinsten bis zu den größten Einheiten.

Hierarchien entstehen, wenn Größenverhältnisse visualisiert werden, etwa im klassischen Tortendiagramm – Mengen werden als Flächenanteil eines Kreises dargestellt. Der häufige Gebrauch solcher Diagramme im Geschäftsleben oder in der Wissenschaft hat viele ironische Kommentare hervorgerufen (*Faces Diagrams*, S. 421) Die Übertragung von Daten in skalierte Farbflächen bleibt dennoch eines der wirkungsvollsten Mittel, mit denen Infografiken Größenverhältnisse verdeutlichen können. Das *Billion Dollar Gram* (S. 411) zeigt internationale Geldflüsse als skalierte Farbflächen nebeneinander, die visuell die Rangfolge zwischen Groß und Klein anzeigen.

Verzweigte Hierarchien spalten sich vom obersten Element jeweils in mehrere Unterelemente auf. Dies trifft zum Beispiel auf große Institutionen zu (vgl. *Small Industries Development*, S. 449). Das klassische Bild verzweigter Hierarchien ist der Baum – von einer Wurzel aus teilen sich die Elemente in immer weitere Untergruppen. Dieses Bild wurde häufig zur Beschreibung der Evolution der Arten benutzt, Stammbäume sind ein weiteres traditionelles Beispiel. In *Natural Selections* (S. 435) kommt dieses Bild zum Einsatz, um die Tier- und Pflanzenlogos im amerikanischen Verlagswesen zu gruppieren.

Taxonomien wiederum behandeln abgeschlossene Wissensgebiete, in hierarchischen Schaubildern stellen sie die kontinuierliche Ordnung vom Größten zum Kleinsten dar. So ordnet die *A Taxonomy of Complete World Knowledge* (S. 408) das gesamte fiktive Weltwissen in einer Baumstruktur von oben nach unten an. Die *Taxonomy of Team Names* (S. 453) stellt die gemeinsame Wurzel in der Mitte dar, während sich die Unterarten kreisförmig darum verzweigen. In der Taxonomie der Biersorten steht „Bier“ als allgemeinste Klasse ebenfalls im Zentrum. Davon ausgehend, werden die verschiedenen Untergruppen von Bier klassifiziert (*The Very Many Varieties of Beer*, S. 464).

Auch Webseiten sind hierarchisch organisiert, die Sitemap eines Internetauftritts zeigt alle Einzeldokumente in einer Baumstruktur. Bei einer großen Internetplattform wie Facebook ist diese Hierarchie von Einzelseiten umfangreich und unübersichtlich, einzelne Seiten sind schwer zu finden. Die Grafik *A Nightmare on Privacy Street* (S. 406) zeigt, wie im komplizierten hierarchischen Aufbau der Website die Privatsphäre-Einstellungen so versteckt sind, dass die Nutzer sie kaum finden können.

Les hiérarchies sont des organisations verticales. Les éléments sont triés par ordre d'importance, du plus grand au plus petit, du plus haut au plus bas, etc. Dans une hiérarchie linéaire, par exemple un classement, chaque élément possède un parent et un enfant, et le résultat est une séquence continue. *Fast Faust* (p.424) présente la liste de tous les mots employés dans l'œuvre *Faust* de Goethe, en fonction de leur fréquence d'apparition dans le texte. *Super Vision Chart* (p.451) montre à intervalles mathématiques réguliers les unités de longueur présentes dans l'univers, des plus petites unités subatomiques aux plus grandes.

Les hiérarchies illustrent des proportions, comme dans le typique camembert où les quantités apparaissent comme les tranches d'un cercle. L'omniprésence de ces diagrammes dans le monde des affaires et de la science a donné lieu à de nombreux commentaires ironiques (*Faces Diagrams*, p.421). Toutefois, la présentation des données au moyen de champs de différentes tailles et couleurs reste la meilleure façon d'illustrer les proportions dans les infographies. *Billion Dollar Gram* (p.411) représente les flux monétaires internationaux qui passent par divers canaux à l'aide d'une série de surfaces de couleur montrant visuellement l'ordre hiérarchique entre grand et petit.

Les hiérarchies ramifiées partent de l'élément le plus haut et se divisent en nombreux sous-éléments; c'est par exemple le cas pour les grandes institutions (cf. *Small Industries Development*, p.449). L'arborescence est une façon classique d'illustrer des hiérarchies ramifiées: de la racine, les éléments se divisent en un nombre croissant de sous-groupes. Cette image a souvent été employée pour décrire l'évolution des espèces, les arbres généalogiques étant un classique du genre. Dans *Natural Selections* (p. 435), l'arborescence sert à regrouper des logos d'animaux et de plantes utilisés par les éditeurs américains.

Les taxonomies traitent de domaines de connaissances entiers et représentent dans des diagrammes hiérarchiques une organisation continue du plus grand au plus petit. Par exemple, *A Taxonomy of Complete World Knowledge* (p.408) organise toutes les connaissances (imaginaires) sur le monde de haut en bas dans une structure en arborescence. *Taxonomy of Team Names* (p.453) place la racine commune au centre, et les sous-espèces partent d'elle pour former un cercle autour. Dans la taxonomie des types de bière, la catégorie la plus générique, « bière », se trouve au centre et sert de point de départ à tous les sous-groupes de bière classés (*The Very Many Varieties of Beer*, p.464).

Les sites Web sont également organisés de façon hiérarchique. Le plan d'un site Internet contient toutes les pages individuelles dans une structure en arborescence. Dans le cas d'une plateforme Internet importante, comme Facebook, cette hiérarchie de pages est gigantesque et déroutante, et il est difficile d'y retrouver des pages concrètes. *A Nightmare on Privacy Street* (p.406) illustre comment la structure hiérarchique complexe d'un site Web dissimule les paramètres de vie privée et empêche les utilisateurs de les trouver facilement.

1.
Settings

Edit Friends
Manage Pages
Account Settings
Privacy Settings
Application Settings
Help Center
Logout

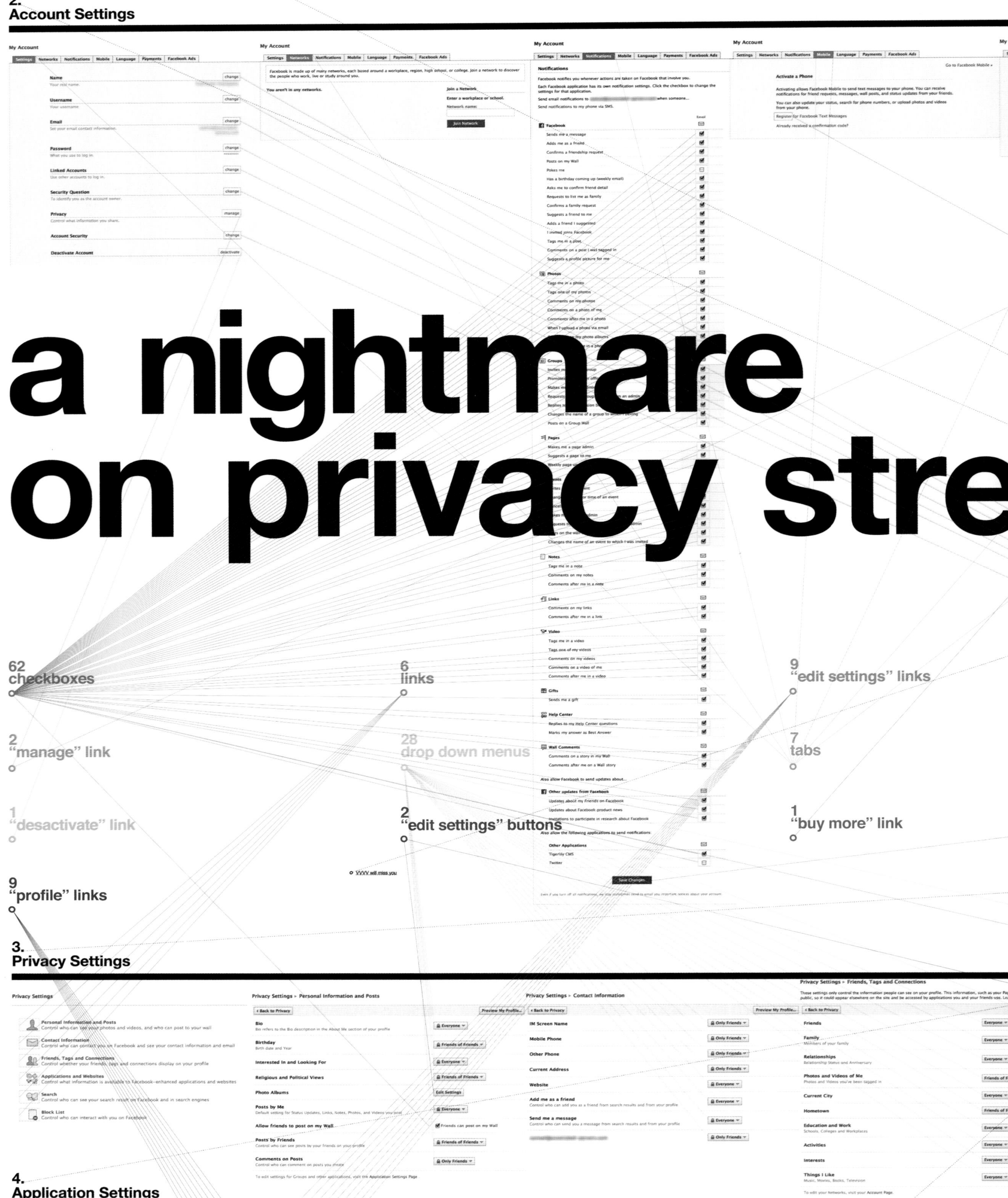

Application Settings – Recently Used

Displaying 9 applications you have used in the past month. Show: Recently Used

Events	Edit Settings	Profile
Gifts	Edit Settings	Profile
Groups	Edit Settings	Profile
Links	Edit Settings	Profile
Notes	Edit Settings	Profile
Photos	Edit Settings	Profile
Tigerlily CMS	Edit Settings	Profile
Twitter	Edit Settings	Profile
Video	Edit Settings	Profile

EEEE will miss you

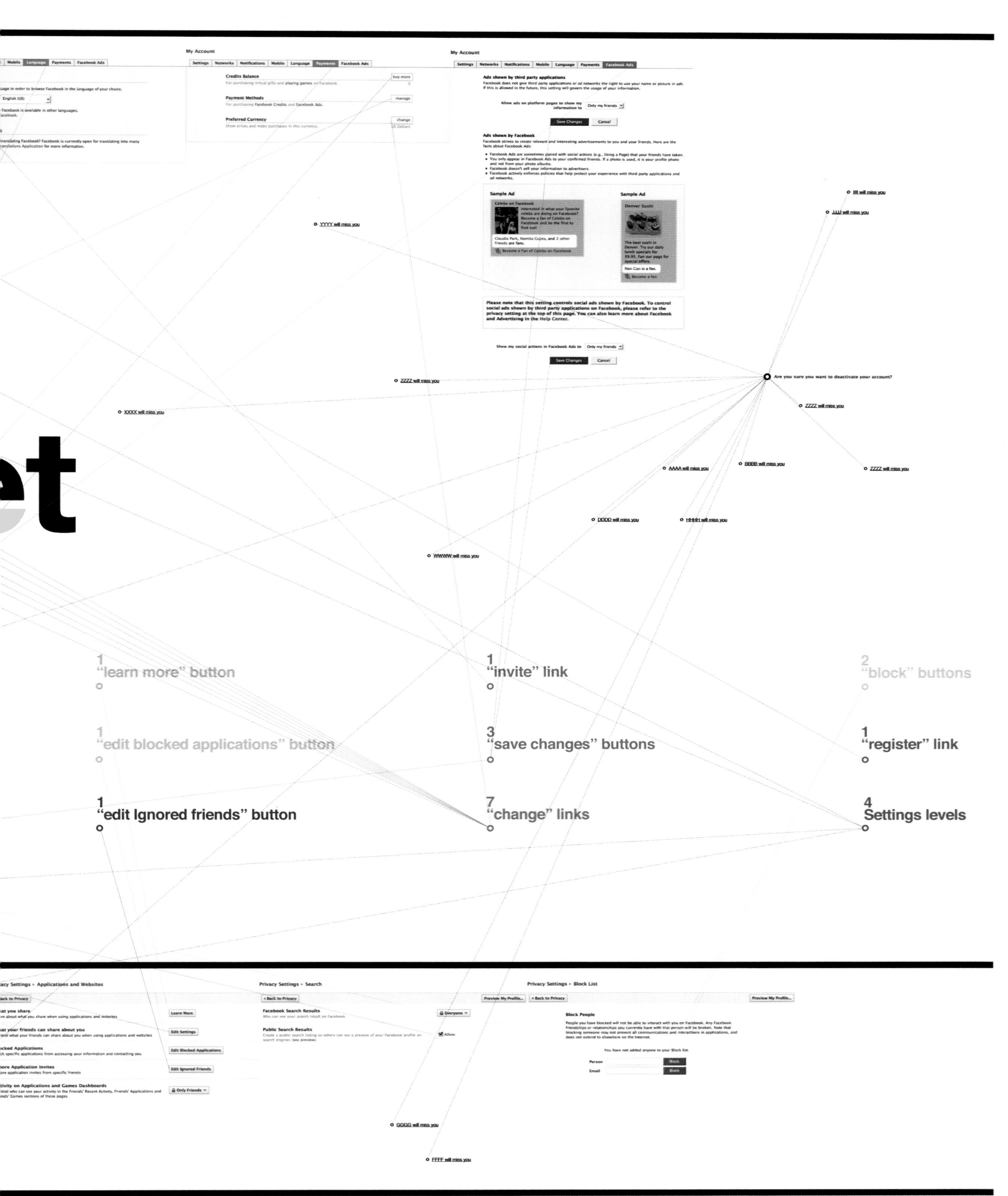

My Account
Credits Balance
Payment Methods
Preferred Currency
Ads shown by third party applications
Save Changes
Cancel
Ads shown by Facebook
Sample Ad
Are you sure you want to deactivate your account?
YYYY will miss you
ZZZZ will miss you
XXXX will miss you
IIII will miss you
JJJJ will miss you
AAAA will miss you
BBBB will miss you
DDDD will miss you
HHHH will miss you
WWWW will miss you
GGGG will miss you
FFFF will miss you
1
"learn more" button
1
"invite" link
2
"block" buttons
1
"edit blocked applications" button
3
"save changes" buttons
1
"register" link
1
"edit Ignored friends" button
7
"change" links
4
Settings levels
Privacy Settings › Search
Privacy Settings › Block List
Block People

A Nightmare on Privacy Street

Since the social network Facebook invites all kinds of personal expressions by its very nature, users have developed an increasing awareness as regards their privacy. In this piece, Florent Guerlain and Samuel Degrémont show the interface structure for users to regulate their individual privacy settings (as of May 2010). Listed from the top down are all four navigation levels in which settings can be regulated.

From left to right, all the interface windows per level are represented. Coloured figures in the middle show the type and absolute numbers of interaction buttons involved. By visually combining all these elements in one graphic, the authors provided strong evidence that the interface for privacy settings is actually counterintuitive.

Es liegt im Wesen des sozialen Netzwerks Facebook, dass es seine Nutzer zu ganz persönlichen Äußerungen im Internet animiert. Viele User bemühen sich daher zunehmend um den Schutz ihrer Privatsphäre. In dieser Grafik visualisieren Florent Guerlain und Samuel Degrémont die Navigationsstruktur, über die die Benutzer ihre Privatsphäre-Einstellungen ändern können (Stand vom Mai 2010). Von oben nach unten sind alle vier Navigationsebenen angegeben, auf denen entsprechende Einstellungen geändert werden können.

Von links nach rechts sind auf jeder Ebene alle Einstellungsmenüs dargestellt. Farbige Ziffern in der Mitte zeigen die Art und Anzahl aller Schaltflächen. Indem Guerlain und Degrémont all diese Elemente in einer Grafik zusammenführen, erhärten sie den Verdacht, dass die Privatsphäre-Einstellungen bei Facebook extrem komplex sind und die Steuerung somit gezielt erschwert wird.

Le réseau social Facebook suscitant par sa nature même toutes sortes d'expressions personnelles, les utilisateurs ont pris conscience de l'importance de la protection de leur vie privée. Ici, Florent Guerlain et Samuel Degrémont montrent la structure de l'interface pour que les utilisateurs choisissent les paramètres qui leur conviennent (mai 2010). Les quatre niveaux de navigation sont indiqués verticalement avec les paramètres qu'il est possible de définir.

De gauche à droite sont présentées toutes les fenêtres de l'interface par niveau. Les chiffres de couleur au milieu indiquent les types de boutons d'interaction concernés et leur nombre absolu. En combinant tous ces éléments dans un même visuel, les auteurs ont prouvé que l'interface des paramètres sur la vie privée est en fait extrêmement complexe, de façon à rendre la navigation plus difficile.

Project Info: Website, 2010, France
Research: Samuel Degrémont
Design: Florent Guerlain

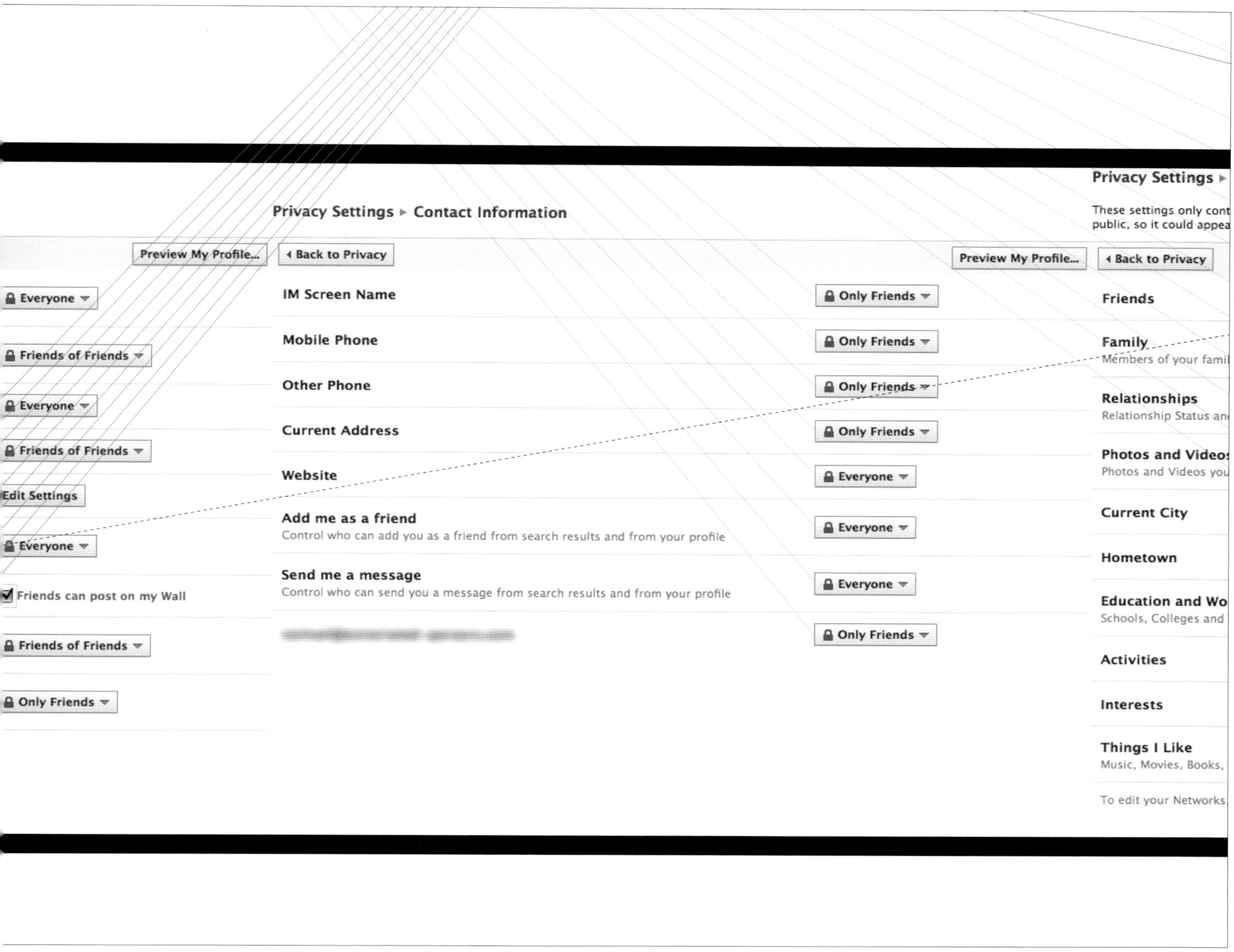

Privacy Settings ▸ Contact Information

Preview My Profile... ◂ Back to Privacy

IM Screen Name	Only Friends
Mobile Phone	Only Friends
Other Phone	Only Friends
Current Address	Only Friends
Website	Everyone
Add me as a friend Control who can add you as a friend from search results and from your profile	Everyone
Send me a message Control who can send you a message from search results and from your profile	Everyone
	Only Friends

Everyone
Friends of Friends
Everyone
Friends of Friends
Edit Settings
Everyone
Friends can post on my Wall
Friends of Friends
Only Friends

Privacy Settings ▸
These settings only cont
public, so it could appea

Preview My Profile... ◂ Back to Privacy

Friends
Family
Members of your famil
Relationships
Relationship Status an
Photos and Videos
Photos and Videos you
Current City
Hometown
Education and Wo
Schools, Colleges and
Activities
Interests
Things I Like
Music, Movies, Books,
To edit your Networks,

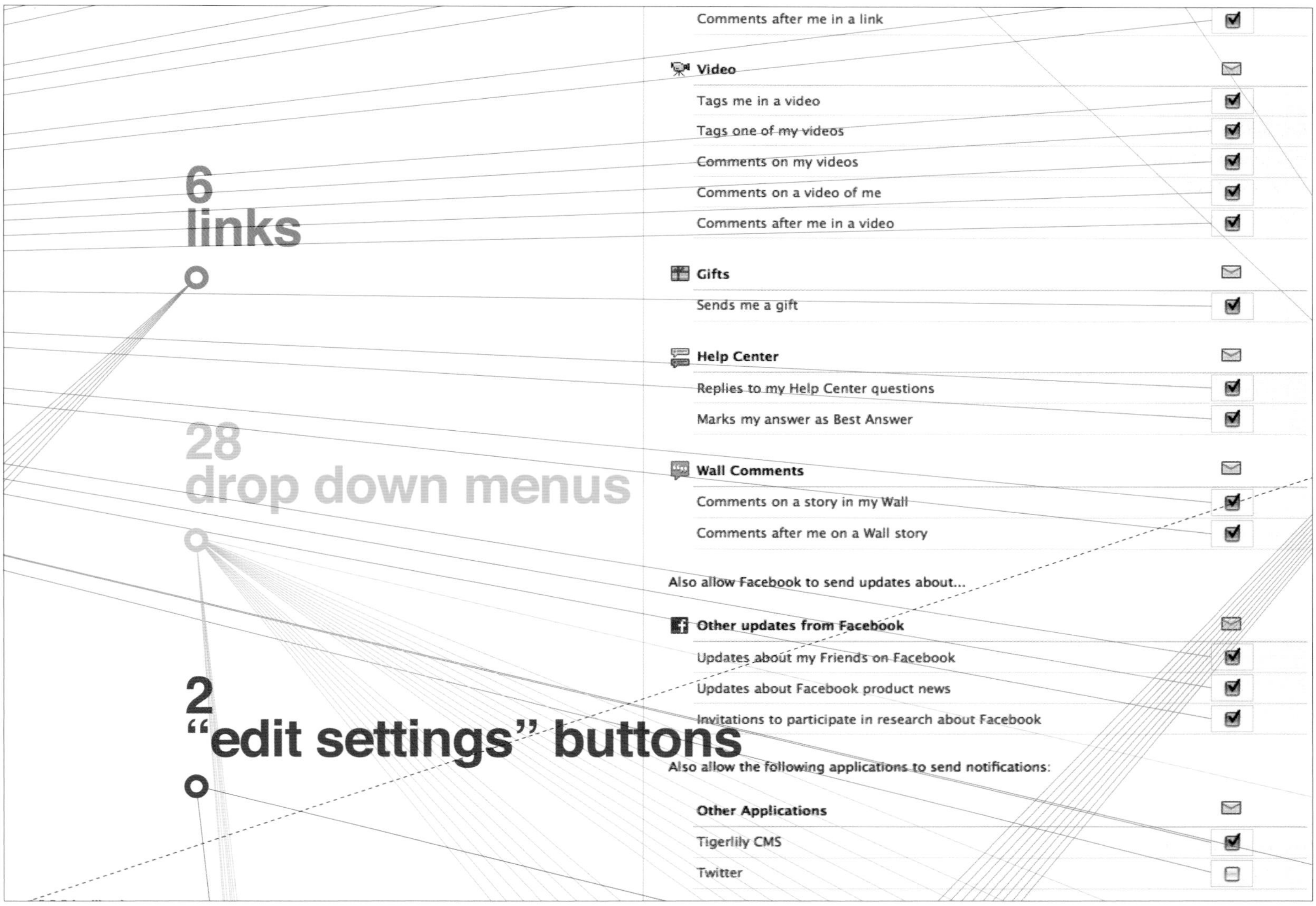

6 links

28 drop down menus

2 "edit settings" buttons

Comments after me in a link

Video
Tags me in a video
Tags one of my videos
Comments on my videos
Comments on a video of me
Comments after me in a video

Gifts
Sends me a gift

Help Center
Replies to my Help Center questions
Marks my answer as Best Answer

Wall Comments
Comments on a story in my Wall
Comments after me on a Wall story

Also allow Facebook to send updates about...

Other updates from Facebook
Updates about my Friends on Facebook
Updates about Facebook product news
Invitations to participate in research about Facebook

Also allow the following applications to send notifications:

Other Applications
Tigerlily CMS
Twitter

A TAXONOMY *of* COMPL

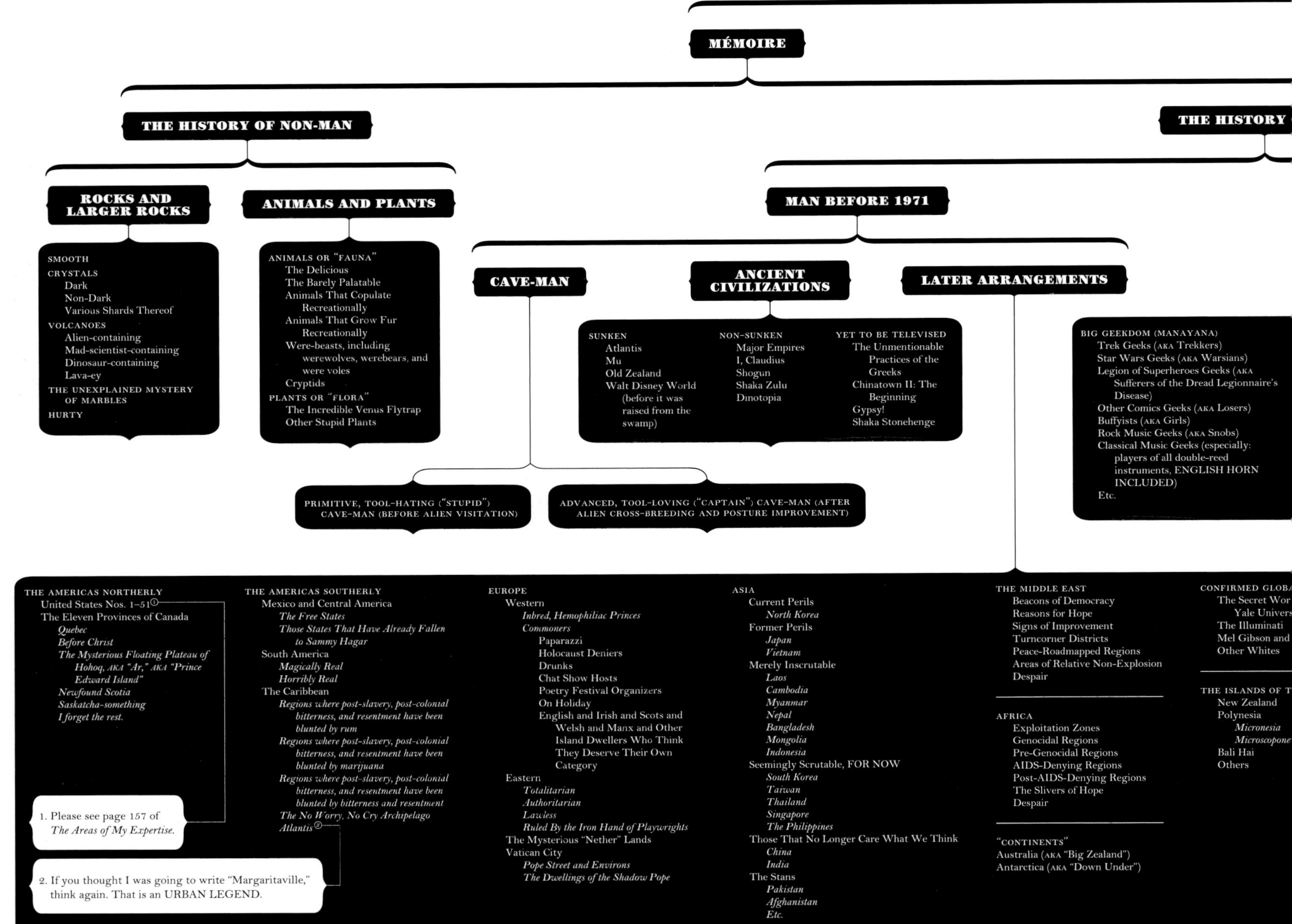

A Taxonomy of Complete World Knowledge

This is a hierarchy of everything, as described by American writer and expert-on-all-things, John Hodgman. The general division into Memory, Reason and Imagination refers to the system of knowledge Denis Diderot created for his *Encyclopedia* in the 18th century. However, with the absurd classification which unfolds beneath, Hodgman creates an ironic account of the world and mocks the traditional scientific taxonomy.

Memory is divided into "The History of Non-Man" and "The History of Man", the latter being divided into "Man before 1971" and "Man since 1971". The complete list of continents, countries and regions of the world is filed under "Later Arrangements" and jolts all the geopolitical knowledge ever taught. The strict black and white design by Sam Potts emphasises the extreme variations in size among the individual categories.

Dies ist eine Hierarchie von allem, so wie es der amerikanische Autor und Allround-Experte John Hodgman sieht. Die grobe Unterteilung in Memory (Gedächtnis), Reason (Vernunft) und Imagination (Fantasie) geht auf die Ordnung des Wissens zurück, die Denis Diderot im 18. Jahrhundert für seine *Encyclopédie* entwickelte. Mit seiner absurden Klassifikation schafft Hodgman jedoch eine ironische Weltsicht und parodiert die naturwissenschaftlichen Taxonomien.

Das Gedächtnis ist unterteilt in „Die Geschichte des Nicht-Menschen" und „Die Geschichte des Menschen", letzterer wird weiter gegliedert in „Der Mensch vor 1971" und „Der Mensch seit 1971". Die vollständige Liste der Kontinente, Länder und Regionen ist unter „Spätere Arrangements" aufgeführt und stellt jegliches geopolitisches Wissen auf den Kopf. Das klare schwarz-weiße Design von Sam Potts unterstreicht die extremen Größenunterschiede zwischen den einzelnen Kategorien.

Ceci est une hiérarchie de tout, comme l'explique John Hodgman, écrivain américain et expert en tout. La division entre la Mémoire, la Raison et l'Imagination renvoie au système de savoir créé par Denis Diderot pour son *Encyclopédie* au XVIIIe siècle. Toutefois, avec la classification absurde qui se déploie en dessous, Hodgman dresse un état des lieux ironique du monde et se moque des taxonomies scientifiques traditionnelles.

La section Mémoire compte les sous-sections « L'Histoire du Non-Homme » et « L'Histoire de l'Homme », cette dernière incluant à son tour « l'Homme avant 1971 » et « L'Homme depuis 1971 ». La liste complète des continents, pays et régions du monde figure sous « Dispositions ultérieures » et bouleverse toutes les connaissances géopolitiques enseignées jusqu'à ce jour. Le graphisme strict en noir et blanc de Sam Potts souligne les écarts extrêmes de taille entre les différentes catégories.

E WORLD KNOWLEDGE

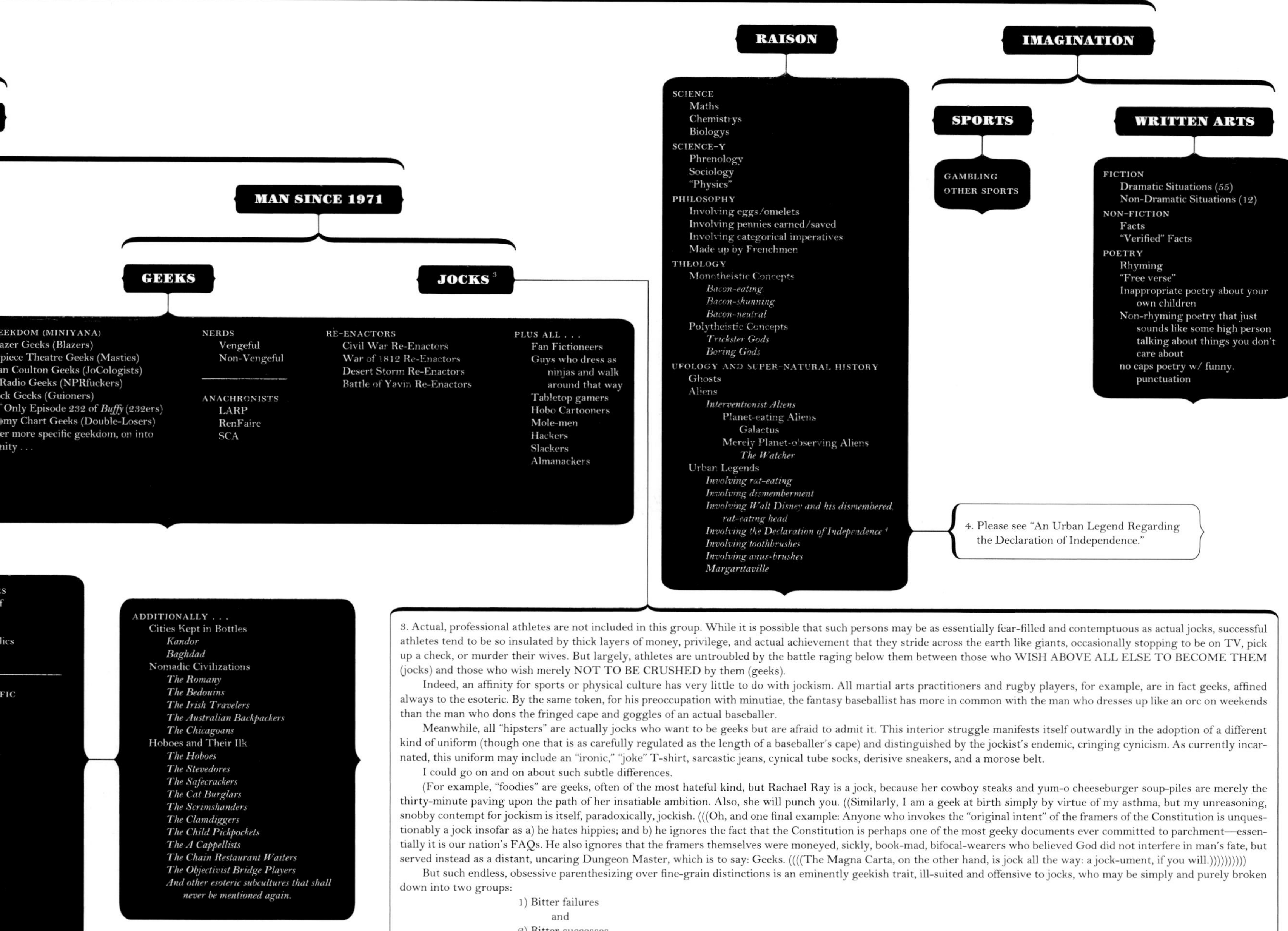

RAISON
IMAGINATION
SCIENCE
Maths
Chemistrys
Biologys
SCIENCE-Y
Phrenology
Sociology
"Physics"
PHILOSOPHY
Involving eggs/omelets
Involving pennies earned/saved
Involving categorical imperatives
Made up by Frenchmen
THEOLOGY
Monotheistic Concepts
Bacon-eating
Bacon-shunning
Bacon-neutral
Polytheistic Concepts
Trickster Gods
Boring Gods
UFOLOGY AND SUPER-NATURAL HISTORY
Ghosts
Aliens
Interventionist Aliens
Planet-eating Aliens
Galactus
Merely Planet-observing Aliens
The Watcher
Urban Legends
Involving rat-eating
Involving dismemberment
Involving Walt Disney and his dismembered, rat-eating head
Involving the Declaration of Independence [4]
Involving toothbrushes
Involving anus-brushes
Margaritaville
4. Please see "An Urban Legend Regarding the Declaration of Independence."
SPORTS
GAMBLING
OTHER SPORTS
WRITTEN ARTS
FICTION
Dramatic Situations (55)
Non-Dramatic Situations (12)
NON-FICTION
Facts
"Verified" Facts
POETRY
Rhyming
"Free verse"
Inappropriate poetry about your own children
Non-rhyming poetry that just sounds like some high person talking about things you don't care about
no caps poetry w/ funny. punctuation
MAN SINCE 1971
GEEKS
JOCKS [3]
EEKDOM (MINIYANA)
azer Geeks (Blazers)
piece Theatre Geeks (Masties)
an Coulton Geeks (JoCologists)
Radio Geeks (NPRfuckers)
ck Geeks (Guioners)
" Only Episode 232 of Buffy (232ers)
my Chart Geeks (Double-Losers)
er more specific geekdom, on into
nity . . .
NERDS
Vengeful
Non-Vengeful
ANACHRONISTS
LARP
RenFaire
SCA
RE-ENACTORS
Civil War Re-Enactors
War of 1812 Re-Enactors
Desert Storm Re-Enactors
Battle of Yavin Re-Enactors
PLUS ALL . . .
Fan Fictioneers
Guys who dress as ninjas and walk around that way
Tabletop gamers
Hobo Cartooners
Mole-men
Hackers
Slackers
Almanackers
ES
of
lics
FIC
ADDITIONALLY . . .
Cities Kept in Bottles
Kandor
Baghdad
Nomadic Civilizations
The Romany
The Bedouins
The Irish Travelers
The Australian Backpackers
The Chicagoans
Hoboes and Their Ilk
The Hoboes
The Stevedores
The Safecrackers
The Cat Burglars
The Scrimshanders
The Clamdiggers
The Child Pickpockets
The A Cappellists
The Chain Restaurant Waiters
The Objectivist Bridge Players
And other esoteric subcultures that shall never be mentioned again.
3. Actual, professional athletes are not included in this group. While it is possible that such persons may be as essentially fear-filled and contemptuous as actual jocks, successful athletes tend to be so insulated by thick layers of money, privilege, and actual achievement that they stride across the earth like giants, occasionally stopping to be on TV, pick up a check, or murder their wives. But largely, athletes are untroubled by the battle raging below them between those who WISH ABOVE ALL ELSE TO BECOME THEM (jocks) and those who wish merely NOT TO BE CRUSHED by them (geeks).
Indeed, an affinity for sports or physical culture has very little to do with jockism. All martial arts practitioners and rugby players, for example, are in fact geeks, affined always to the esoteric. By the same token, for his preoccupation with minutiae, the fantasy baseballist has more in common with the man who dresses up like an orc on weekends than the man who dons the fringed cape and goggles of an actual baseballer.
Meanwhile, all "hipsters" are actually jocks who want to be geeks but are afraid to admit it. This interior struggle manifests itself outwardly in the adoption of a different kind of uniform (though one that is as carefully regulated as the length of a baseballer's cape) and distinguished by the jockist's endemic, cringing cynicism. As currently incarnated, this uniform may include an "ironic," "joke" T-shirt, sarcastic jeans, cynical tube socks, derisive sneakers, and a morose belt.
I could go on and on about such subtle differences.
(For example, "foodies" are geeks, often of the most hateful kind, but Rachael Ray is a jock, because her cowboy steaks and yum-o cheeseburger soup-piles are merely the thirty-minute paving upon the path of her insatiable ambition. Also, she will punch you. ((Similarly, I am a geek at birth simply by virtue of my asthma, but my unreasoning, snobby contempt for jockism is itself, paradoxically, jockish. (((Oh, and one final example: Anyone who invokes the "original intent" of the framers of the Constitution is unquestionably a jock insofar as a) he hates hippies; and b) he ignores the fact that the Constitution is perhaps one of the most geeky documents ever committed to parchment—essentially it is our nation's FAQs. He also ignores that the framers themselves were moneyed, sickly, book-mad, bifocal-wearers who believed God did not interfere in man's fate, but served instead as a distant, uncaring Dungeon Master, which is to say: Geeks. ((((The Magna Carta, on the other hand, is jock all the way: a jock-ument, if you will.))))))))))
But such endless, obsessive parenthesizing over fine-grain distinctions is an eminently geekish trait, ill-suited and offensive to jocks, who may be simply and purely broken down into two groups:
1) Bitter failures
and
2) Bitter successes

Project Info: *More Information Than You Require*, Dutton Books, book jacket, 2008, USA
Design: Sam Potts
Text: John Hodgman

Ballooning CEO Salaries and Mass Layoffs

The Institute for Policy Studies, a think-tank based in Washington, D.C., researched into CEO salaries during the recession of 2008-2010. Results of this study show that those CEOs who have cut the most jobs received 42% more compensation than CEOs on the US average.

The graphic takes a look at the top 10 recession lay-off leaders and how much the CEO received compared to how many people were laid off. The balloon size shows the amount of CEO compensation, the height it floats at indicates the company's revenue, whilst the little silhouettes falling overboard correspond to the number of jobs cut.

Das Institute for Policy Studies, ein Thinktank mit Sitz in Washington, D.C., untersuchte die Gehälter von CEOs während der Rezession der Jahre 2008–2010. Die Studien ergaben, dass diejenigen Vorstandschefs und Geschäftsführer, die die meisten Arbeitsplätze abbauten, 42% mehr Kompensation erhielten als der Durchschnitt ihrer Kollegen in den USA.

Die Grafik beschränkt sich auf die zehn Unternehmen, die die meisten Arbeitskräfte entließen, und setzt das Gehalt ihrer Vorstandschefs ins Verhältnis zum Arbeitsplatzabbau. Die Ballongröße veranschaulicht die Höhe des Gehalts, die Flughöhe den Umsatz des Unternehmens, und die kleinen Silhouetten, die über Bord gehen, spiegeln die Zahl der abgebauten Stellen wieder.

L'Institute for Policy Studies, groupe de réflexion de Washington, D.C., a étudié les salaires des PDG au cours de la récession en 2008-2010. Les résultats de cette étude montrent que les PDG ayant supprimé le plus d'emplois ont reçu 42% de plus de compensation que la moyenne pour les États-Unis.

Le graphique montre les 10 patrons ayant le plus licencié d'employés pendant la récession et combien ils ont touché par rapport au nombre de licenciements effectués. La taille des ballons montre l'ampleur de la compensation reçue par les PDG, et la hauteur à laquelle ils flottent montre les recettes de l'entreprise. Les petites silhouettes tombées par-dessus bord correspondent au nombre d'emplois supprimés.

Project Info: Meet the Boss, for GDS International, website, 2010, UK
Data Source: Institute of Policy Studies: "CEO Pay and the Great Recession, 17th Annual Executive Compensation Survey"
Design: Tiffany Farrant-Gonzalez

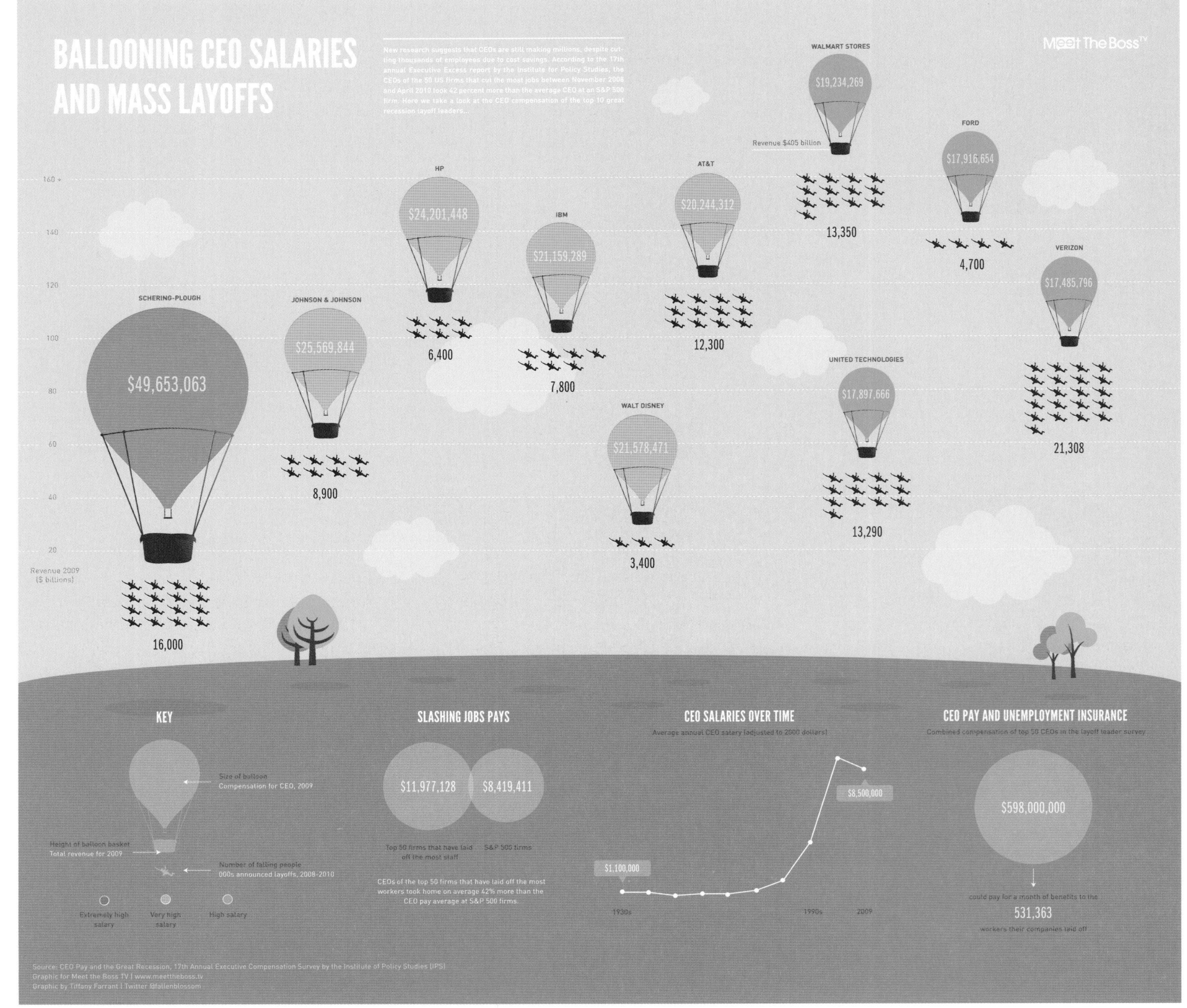

The Billion Dollar Gram

Billions spent on this. Billions spent on that. It's all relative right?

■ spending ■ earning ■ giving ■ fighting ■ losing ■ illin'

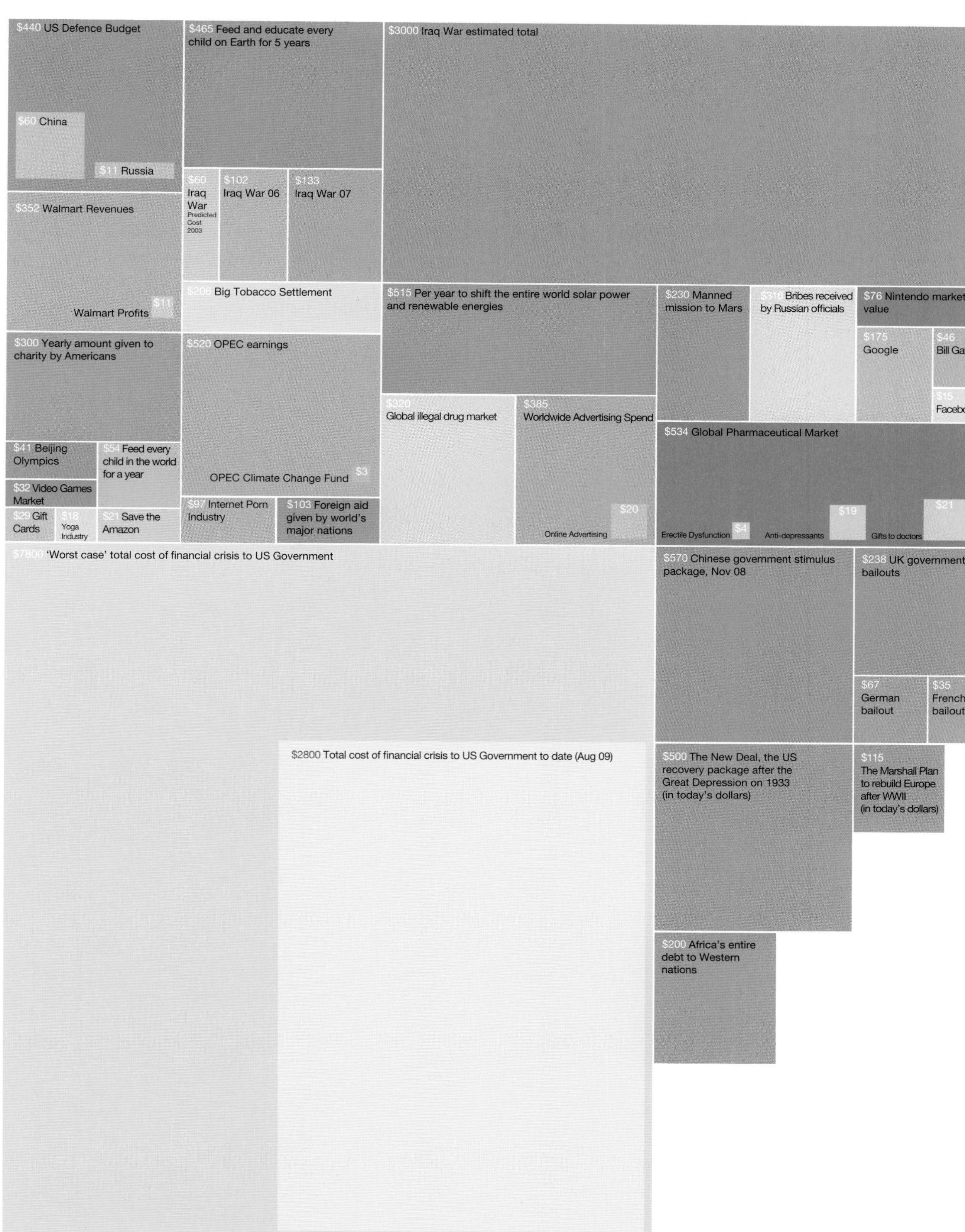

Project Info:
Information is Beautiful, book, 2009, UK
Data Source:
Media Reports from CNN, *The New York Times*, *The Guardian*, BBC et al.
Design:
David McCandless (Information is Beautiful)

Billion Dollar Gram

This piece establishes a direct visual hierarchy. Large sums of money in media reports are hard to comprehend, and remain mostly abstract figures and unrelated to each other. David McCandless works with simple colour fields in order to give an impression of the relative rate of individual money flow in international politics and business.

The colour code refers to what happens with this individual money flow – blue is for business-related revenues, while military spending is coded in purple and illegal money flows are shown in grey.

Diese Grafik stellt eine klare visuelle Hierarchie auf. Große Geldsummen in Medienberichten sind schwer nachzuvollziehen und bleiben meist unzusammenhängende, abstrakte Zahlen. David McCandless nutzt skalierte Farbfelder, um die Größenordnung einzelner Geldbewegungen in der internationalen Politik und Wirtschaft zu zeigen und zueinander in Beziehung zu setzen.

Der Farbcode verweist auf die Herkunft des jeweiligen Geldes – so steht Blau für Unternehmenseinnahmen, Militärausgaben sind lila gefärbt, illegale Geldbewegungen werden in Grau gezeigt.

Cette œuvre crée une hiérarchie visuelle directe. Les grandes sommes d'argent citées dans les médias sont difficiles à assimiler et restent des chiffres très abstraits et sans liens. David McCandless se sert de simples blocs de couleur pour faire comprendre l'importance relative des flux d'argent en politique et commerce dans le monde.

Le code de couleur correspond à ce qui se produit pour chaque flux d'argent : en bleu, les recettes liées au commerce, en violet les dépenses d'ordre militaire, en gris les flux monétaires illégaux.

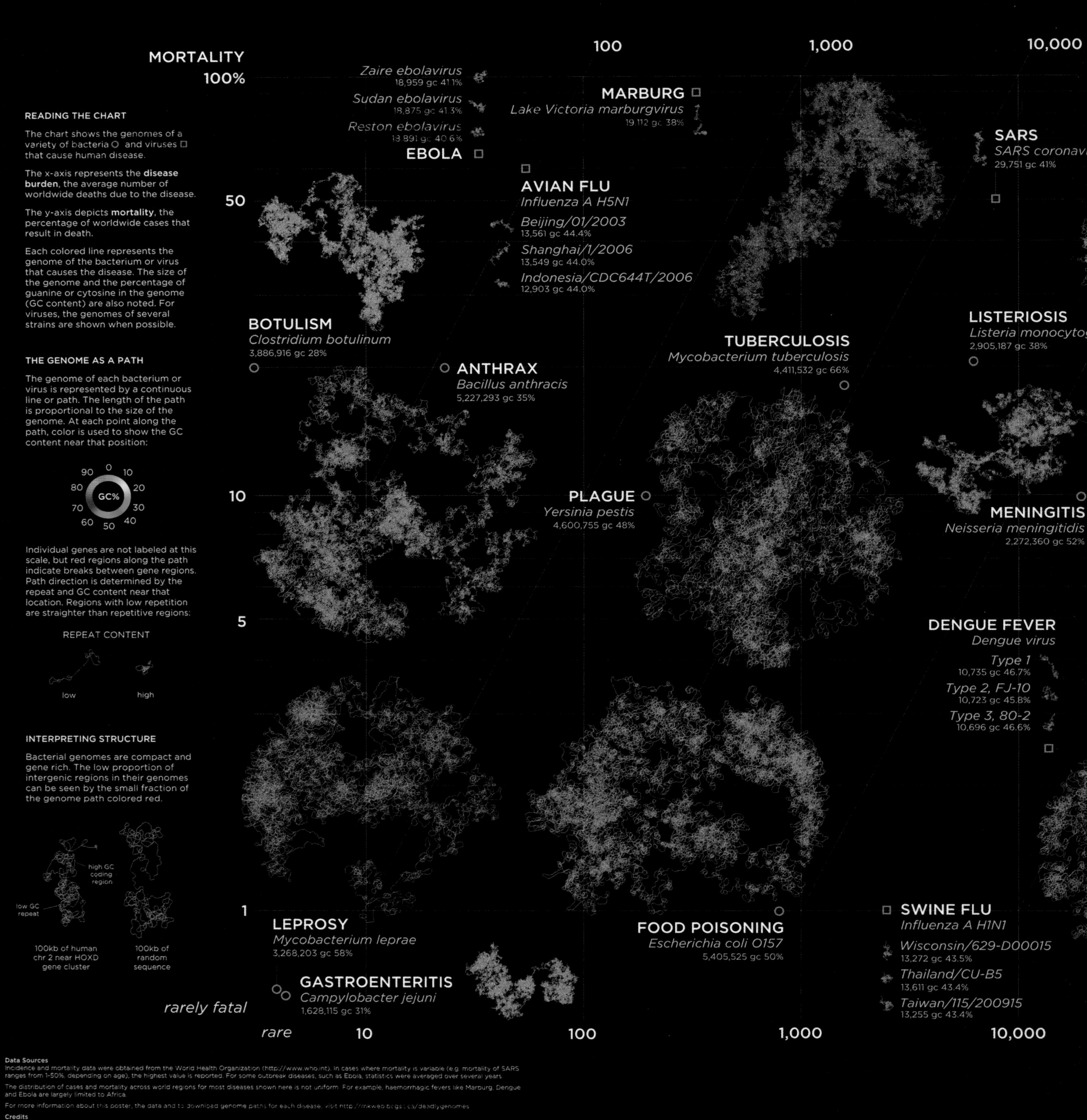

THE DEADLY
GENOME STRUCTURE AND SIZE OF HARMFU
MORTALITY
100%
50
10
5
1
rarely fatal
rare
10
100
1,000
10,000
READING THE CHART
The chart shows the genomes of a variety of bacteria ○ and viruses □ that cause human disease.
The x-axis represents the **disease burden**, the average number of worldwide deaths due to the disease.
The y-axis depicts **mortality**, the percentage of worldwide cases that result in death.
Each colored line represents the genome of the bacterium or virus that causes the disease. The size of the genome and the percentage of guanine or cytosine in the genome (GC content) are also noted. For viruses, the genomes of several strains are shown when possible.
THE GENOME AS A PATH
The genome of each bacterium or virus is represented by a continuous line or path. The length of the path is proportional to the size of the genome. At each point along the path, color is used to show the GC content near that position:
GC%
0 10 20 30 40 50 60 70 80 90
Individual genes are not labeled at this scale, but red regions along the path indicate breaks between gene regions. Path direction is determined by the repeat and GC content near that location. Regions with low repetition are straighter than repetitive regions:
REPEAT CONTENT
low
high
INTERPRETING STRUCTURE
Bacterial genomes are compact and gene rich. The low proportion of intergenic regions in their genomes can be seen by the small fraction of the genome path colored red.
high GC coding region
low GC repeat
100kb of human chr 2 near HOXD gene cluster
100kb of random sequence
Zaire ebolavirus
18,959 gc 41.1%
Sudan ebolavirus
18,875 gc 41.3%
Reston ebolavirus
18,891 gc 40.6%
EBOLA
MARBURG
Lake Victoria marburgvirus
19,112 gc 38%
AVIAN FLU
Influenza A H5N1
Beijing/01/2003
13,561 gc 44.4%
Shanghai/1/2006
13,549 gc 44.0%
Indonesia/CDC644T/2006
12,903 gc 44.0%
SARS
SARS coronav
29,751 gc 41%
BOTULISM
Clostridium botulinum
3,886,916 gc 28%
ANTHRAX
Bacillus anthracis
5,227,293 gc 35%
TUBERCULOSIS
Mycobacterium tuberculosis
4,411,532 gc 66%
LISTERIOSIS
Listeria monocytog
2,905,187 gc 38%
PLAGUE
Yersinia pestis
4,600,755 gc 48%
MENINGITIS
Neisseria meningitidis
2,272,360 gc 52%
DENGUE FEVER
Dengue virus
Type 1
10,735 gc 46.7%
Type 2, FJ-10
10,723 gc 45.8%
Type 3, 80-2
10,696 gc 46.6%
LEPROSY
Mycobacterium leprae
3,268,203 gc 58%
FOOD POISONING
Escherichia coli O157
5,405,525 gc 50%
SWINE FLU
Influenza A H1N1
Wisconsin/629-D00015
13,272 gc 43.5%
Thailand/CU-B5
13,611 gc 43.4%
Taiwan/115/200915
13,255 gc 43.4%
GASTROENTERITIS
Campylobacter jejuni
1,628,115 gc 31%
Data Sources
Incidence and mortality data were obtained from the World Health Organization (http://www.who.int). In cases where mortality is variable (e.g. mortality of SARS ranges from 1-50%, depending on age), the highest value is reported. For some outbreak diseases, such as Ebola, statistics were averaged over several years.
The distribution of cases and mortality across world regions for most diseases shown here is not uniform. For example, haemorrhagic fevers like Marburg, Dengue and Ebola are largely limited to Africa.
For more information about this poster, the data and to download genome paths for each disease, visit http://mkweb.bcgsc.ca/deadlygenomes
Credits
Martin Krzywinski, Cydney Nielsen, Ian Bosdet (Canada's Michael Smith Genome Sciences Center), Jonathan Corum (13pt)

Project Info: Poster, National Science Foundation Visualization Challenge, 2010, Canada
Data Source: World Health Organization; National Center for Biotechnology Information Genbank
Research: Ian Bosdet (BC Cancer Agency), Cydney Nielsen (Genome Sciences Center)
Design: Martin Krzywinski
Illustration: Jonathan Corum

GENOMES

ACTERIA AND VIRUSES

WORLDWIDE ANNUAL CASES
100,000 1,000,000 10,000,000

AIDS
HIV virus
US 1982
9,747 gc 42.5%
Senegal 1995
8,777 gc 41.5%
Spain 2008
8,471 gc 41.3%

MRSA
Staphylococcus aureus 252
2,902,619 gc 33%

LLOW FEVER
ow fever virus
62 gc 49.7%
17DD *17D-213*

100,000,000

SYPHILIS
Treponema pallidum
1,134,371 gc 53%

TYPHOID
Salmonella typhi
4,809,037 gc 52%

CHOLERA
Vibrio cholerae
2,959,609 gc 48%

PNEUMONIA
Streptococcus pneumoniae
2,160,842 gc 40%

C35
3,221 gc 48.9%
GU1214
3,072 gc 48.3%
A1_50115
2,853 gc 49.2%
HEPATITIS B
Hepatitis B virus

MALARIA
Plasmodium falciparum
23,020,762 gc 19%

100,000 1,000,000 10,000,000
WORLDWIDE ANNUAL DEATHS

Deadly Genomes

This diagram charts diseases according to mortality (y-axis) and incident rates (x-axis). While leprosy is both rare and shows a low mortality (below left), AIDS occurs relatively frequently and is still 100% fatal (top right). Although media coverage often focuses on more fatal but rarer diseases such as avian flu, this chart shows how many more people are affected by less relatively fatal diseases like malaria.

Each disease is symbolised by the genome of its agent virus or bacteria. Introducing a new concept, genomic sequence is represented as a continuous line. The genome size is reflected in the line's length, colour refers to guanine-cytosine content in the sequence.

Diese Schautafel verzeichnet Krankheiten nach Mortalitätsrate (y-Achse) und Fallzahlen (x-Achse). Lepra etwa kommt nur selten vor und verläuft selten tödlich (unten links), wohingegen Aids relativ häufig auftritt und noch immer zu 100% tödlich ist (oben rechts). Obwohl die Medien vielfach über tödliche, aber seltene Krankheiten wie die Vogelgrippe berichten, zeigt dieses Diagramm, dass weit mehr Menschen von weniger schwerwiegenden Krankheiten wie Malaria betroffen sind.

Jede Krankheit wird durch das Genom ihres Erregers (entweder ein Virus oder Bakterien) symbolisiert. Die jeweilige DNA wird – ein neues Konzept – als fortlaufende Linie dargestellt. Die Größe eines Linienhaufens entspricht der Größe des Genoms, die Farbcodierung verweist auf den GC-Gehalt (Anteil von Guanin-Cytosin-Paaren) in der DNA.

Ce diagramme présente des maladies en fonction du taux de mortalité (axe y) et du taux d'incidents (axe x). Alors que la lèpre est rare et entraîne une faible mortalité (en bas à gauche), le SIDA est assez fréquent et reste mortel dans 100% des cas (en haut á droite). Les médias insistent souvent sur les maladies les plus mortelles mais aussi les plus rares, comme la grippe aviaire; ce graphique montre quant à lui le nombre de personnes affectées par des maladies moins mortelles comme la malaria.

Chaque maladie est symbolisée par le génome de son virus ou de sa bactérie. Montrant un nouveau concept, la séquence génomique apparaît sous la forme d'une ligne continue. La taille du génome est reflétée par la longueur de la ligne et la couleur correspond au contenu de guanine-cytosine dans la séquence.

Death and Taxes

"Death and Taxes" is a large representational graph of the federal US budget and how it is spent. The total amount of the budget is represented by the central circle, while arranged around it are over 500 programs and federal institutions which receive their funding from this budget. All item circles are proportional in size to the amount of their funding, for visual comparison.

The scaling shows a priority on military- and security-related spending. The exceptionally large circle shown by the dollar bills below the centre visual gives a hint of the enormous size of the US national debt. Jess Bachmann has been producing this piece since 2007 and updates it annually.

„Death and Taxes" ist eine umfangreiche Darstellung des US-Staatshaushalts und zeigt, wie die Gelder verwendet werden. Der große Kreis in der Mitte zeigt den Gesamtetat, um ihn herum sind über 500 Programme und Bundesinstitutionen angeordnet, die aus diesem Etat finanziert werden. Um sie miteinander vergleichen zu können, sind alle Kreise größenproportional zum jeweiligen Etat dargestellt.

Durch diesen Maßstab wird ersichtlich, wie hoch der Anteil militärischer und sicherheitspolitischer Ausgaben ist. Der außerordentlich große, mit Dollarnoten gefüllte Kreis, der unterhalb der Grafik im Anschnitt angedeutet ist, vermittelt einen Eindruck von der enormen Staatsverschuldung. Jess Bachmann gestaltet dieses Schaubild seit 2007 und aktualisiert es jährlich.

« Death and Taxes » est une grande représentation visuelle du budget fédéral américain et des dépenses qu'il couvre. Le montant total du budget se trouve dans le cercle central, et autour gravitent plus de 500 programmes et institutions au niveau fédéral qui tirent leur financement de ce budget. Tous les cercles sont proportionnels à la quantité de financement pour permettre la comparaison visuelle.

On voit tout de suite que la priorité est donnée aux dépenses militaires et liées à la sécurité. L'énorme cercle fait de billets à l'arrière-plan fait comprendre l'ampleur démesurée de la dette nationale des États-Unis. Jess Bachmann a créé ce visuel en 2007 et l'actualise tous les ans depuis lors.

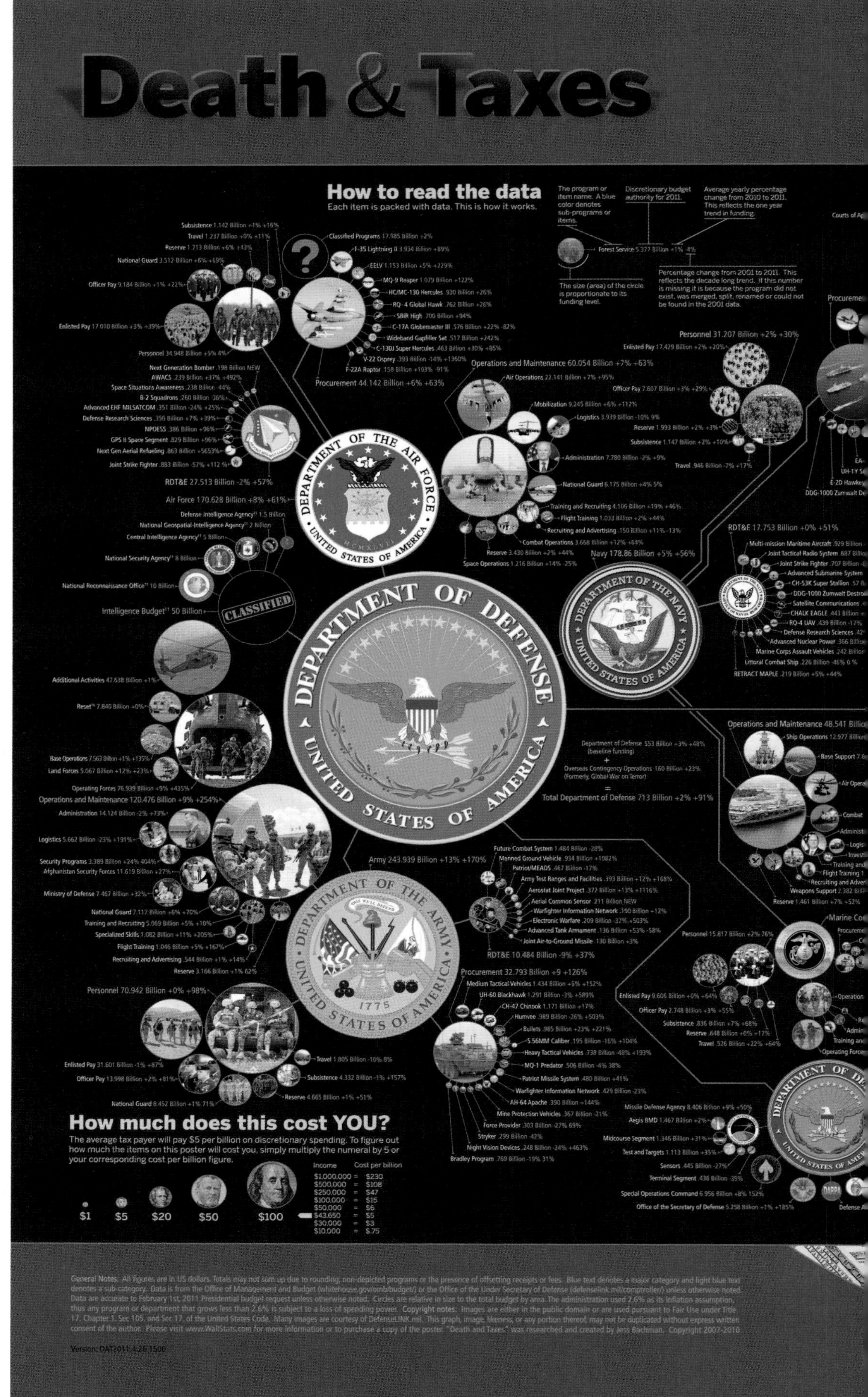

Project Info: Poster, 2010, USA
Data Source: US Office of Management and Budget
Design: Jess Bachmann

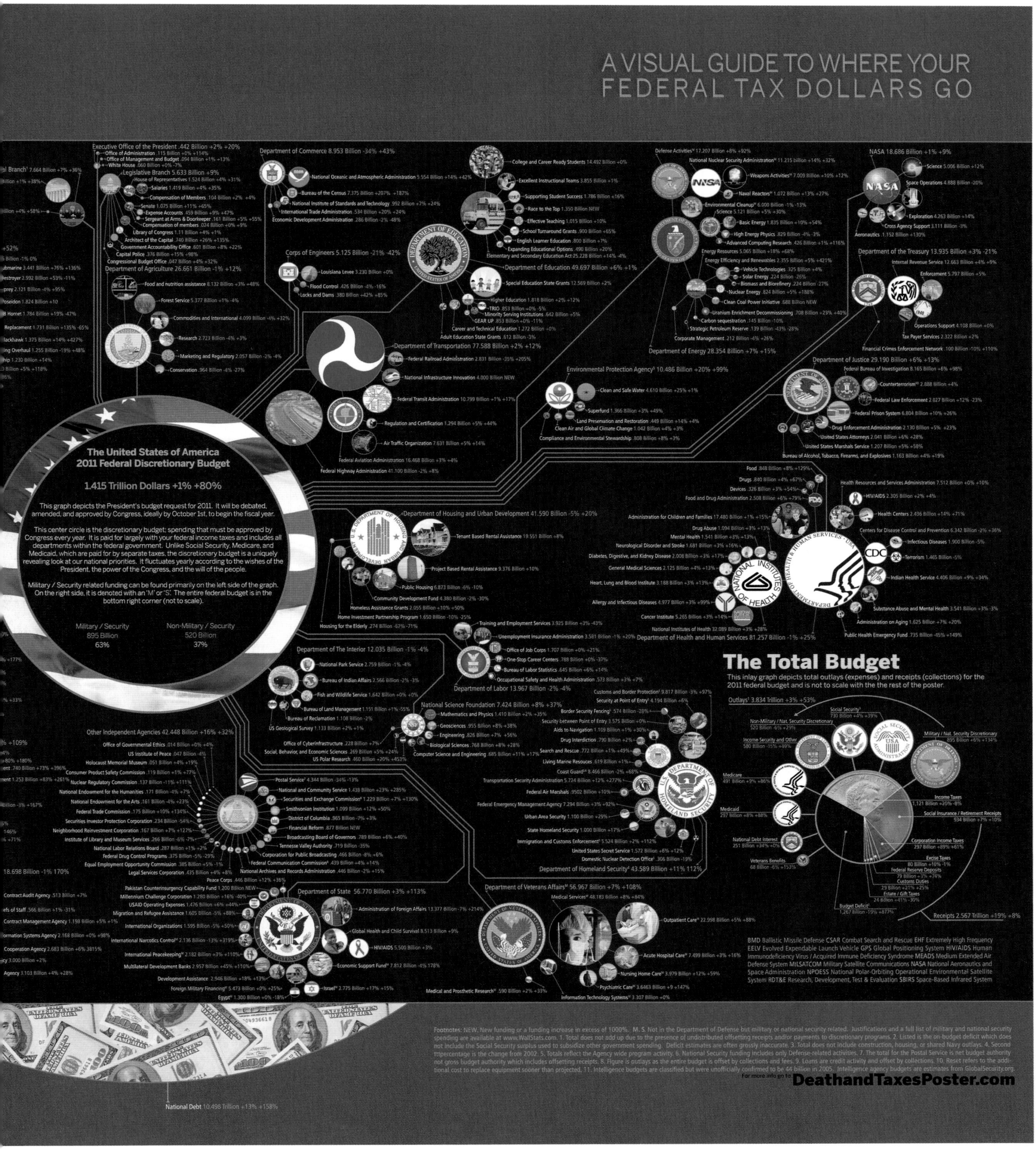

A VISUAL GUIDE TO WHERE YOUR FEDERAL TAX DOLLARS GO

The United States of America 2011 Federal Discretionary Budget

1.415 Trillion Dollars +1% +80%

This graph depicts the President's budget request for 2011. It will be debated, amended, and approved by Congress, ideally by October 1st, to begin the fiscal year.

This center circle is the discretionary budget; spending that must be approved by Congress every year. It is paid for largely with your federal income taxes and includes all departments within the federal government. Unlike Social Security, Medicare, and Medicaid, which are paid for by separate taxes, the discretionary budget is a uniquely revealing look at our national priorities. It fluctuates yearly according to the wishes of the President, the power of the Congress, and the will of the people.

Military / Security related funding can be found primarily on the left side of the graph. On the right side, it is denoted with an "M" or "S". The entire federal budget is in the bottom right corner (not to scale).

Military / Security	Non-Military / Security
895 Billion	520 Billion
63%	37%

Executive Office of the President .442 Billion +2% +20%

Legislative Branch 5.633 Billion +9%

Department of Agriculture 26.661 Billion -1% +12%

Department of Commerce 8.953 Billion -34% +43%

Corps of Engineers 5.125 Billion -21% -42%

Department of Education 49.697 Billion +6% +1%

Department of Transportation 77.588 Billion +2% +12%

Department of Energy 28.354 Billion +7% +15%

NASA 18.686 Billion +1% +9%

Department of the Treasury 13.935 Billion +3% -21%

Environmental Protection Agency 10.486 Billion +20% +99%

Department of Justice 29.190 Billion +6% +13%

Department of Housing and Urban Development 41.590 Billion -5% +20%

Department of Health and Human Services 81.257 Billion -1% +25%

Department of Labor 13.967 Billion -2% -4%

Department of The Interior 12.035 Billion -1% -4%

National Science Foundation 7.424 Billion +8% +37%

Other Independent Agencies 42.448 Billion +16% +32%

Department of Homeland Security 43.509 Billion +11% 112%

Department of State 56.770 Billion +3% +113%

Department of Veterans Affairs 56.967 Billion +7% +108%

The Total Budget

This inlay graph depicts total outlays (expenses) and receipts (collections) for the 2011 federal budget and is not to scale with the rest of the poster.

Outlays 3.834 Trillion +3% +53%

Receipts 2.567 Trillion +19% +8%

BMD Ballistic Missile Defense CSAR Combat Search and Rescue EHF Extremely High Frequency EELV Evolved Expendable Launch Vehicle GPS Global Positioning System HIV/AIDS Human Immunodeficiency Virus / Acquired Immune Deficiency Syndrome MEADS Medium Extended Air Defense System MILSATCOM Military Satellite Communications NASA National Aeronautics and Space Administration NPOESS National Polar-Orbiting Operational Environmental Satellite System RDT&E Research, Development, Test & Evaluation SBIRS Space-Based Infrared System

National Debt 10.498 Trillion +13% +158%

DeathandTaxesPoster.com

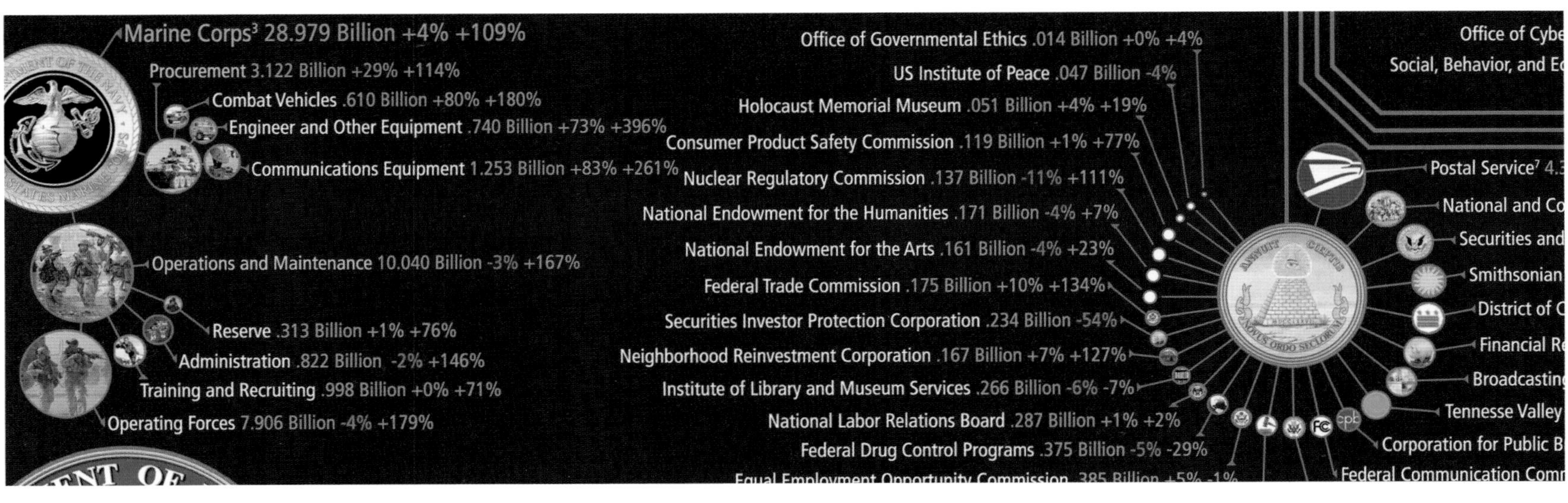

Where your money goes: the definitive atla

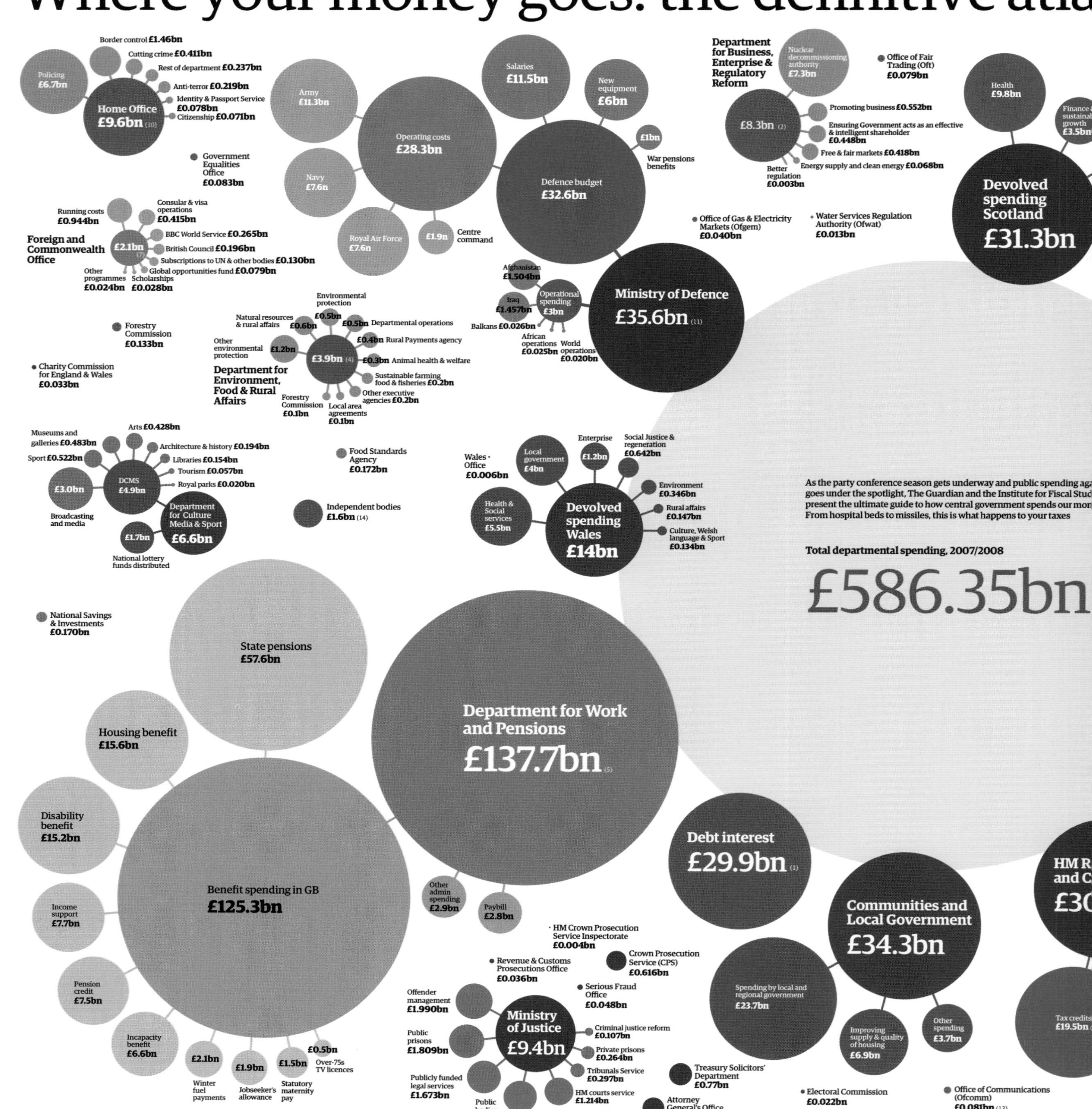

NOTES

The figures give a picture of major expenditure but exclude local government spending not controlled by central government. It also excludes government departments who are predominantly financed by their income, such as the Crown Estate or the Export Credits Guarantee Department. The totals here add up to more than the total budget, because some of the smaller government departments are funded via the larger ones, such as the Parliamentary Counsel Office, funded via the Cabinet Office.

(1) Interest paid on the public debt

(2) Total spending on energy liabilities is actually £6.8bn, less than that spent on the NDA. This is because the department makes money back with efficiency savings

(3) SureStart spending includes childcare and nursery funding

(4) Animal health includes disease prevention, dealing with BSE etc. The Rural Payments Agency is the body that distributes CAP payments - these payments are large but covered by transfers from EU so do not show up as net spending here

(5) Benefit spending excludes child benefit, guardians' allowance; widow's pensions; statutory paternity pay, statutory adoption pay - these paid by HMRC, MoD, DBERR respectively

(6) Hospital and community health services spending is estimated – figures to be published December 2008. Estimate based on previous annual spending. Excludes spending on family health services and GP prescriptions. Wages are also estimated, based on previous year's figures

(7) Running costs includes salaries, hospitalit and overseas accommodation costs. Administ programme amounts combined here

(8) Excludes Northern Rock, 2008-09 spendi £14bn

25

›f UK government spending

Office of rail regulation £0.030bn
Admin £0.2bn
Bus service operators grant £0.4bn
Railways £1.0bn
Other £1.1bn
Net capital expenditure on fixed assets £1.6bn
Department for Transport £17.6bn
Highways Agency £5.4bn
£3.2bn Capital grants to private sector
£2.4bn Capital support to local authorities
£2.4bn GLA transport grants

Wages £30bn
General and acute £27.5bn
NHS £90.7bn
Mental illness £6.6bn
Community health services £5.6bn
£2bn Learning difficulties
Other £2bn
£1.7bn Accident & emergency
£1.6bn Maternity
NHS pensions £14bn
Personal social services £2.1bn

Department of Health £105.7bn (6)

UK trade & investment £0.088bn (15)
Postal services commission (Postcomm) £0.009bn
National School of Government £0.003bn

General schools' spending £31.7bn
Department for Children, Schools and Families £60.9bn (3)
Schools £41.2bn
£4.0bn Investment in school buildings
£2.0bn Sixth form funding (through learning and skills council)
£1.8bn Other schools spending
£0.6bn ICT
£1.1bn Academies & specialist schools
£0.3bn Other
Children & families £2.9bn
Other spending on services for children & families £1.2bn
£1.8bn Sure Start
Young people £5.8bn
Teachers' pension scheme £10.7bn
£4.5bn Learning & Skills Council (excluding sixth form funding)
£0.6bn Education maintenance allowance
£0.8bn Other spending on services for young people

Office for National Statistics (ONS) £0.159bn
Parliamentary Counsel Office £0.012bn (12)
Office for Standards in Education (Ofsted) £0.215bn

Higher education funding council for England £7.0bn
Student loans £4.7bn
Learning & Skills Council £4.5bn
Research councils £3.0bn
Department for Innovation, Universities & Skills £21.5bn
£1.0bn Student grants
£0.553bn Departmental science programmes
£0.479bn Other spending on further education

Northern Ireland Office £1.55bn
£1.27bn Policing & security
Prisons £0.142bn
Compensation agency £0.048bn
Criminal justice £0.047bn
Public Prosecution service £0.037bn
Youth Justice Agency £0.022bn
Bloody Sunday inquiry £0.005bn

Child Trust Fund £0.24bn
Her Majesty's Treasury £0.219bn (8)
Child benefit £10.6bn

Cabinet Office £7.9bn
Security services £1.59bn
Office for the Third Sector £0.172bn
BBC media monitoring £0.025bn
SCOPE programme £0.023bn
E-delivery £0.018bn
Government security programme £0.005bn
Electronic communications assurance programme £0.001bn
Government Actuary's Department £0.424bn

Devolved spending Northern Ireland £8bn
Health, Social Services £3.8bn
£1.7bn Education
Employment & learning £0.7bn
Reg development £0.3bn
Agriculture £0.2bn
Enterprise, trade £0.2bn
Finance £0.2bn
Culture, arts & leisure £0.1bn
Environment £0.1bn

Department for International Development £5.4bn
Eliminating poverty £5.327bn
Conflict prevention £0.051bn
Overseas superannuation £0.058bn

(9) Spending on Child Benefits and Tax Credits etc does not come out of the departmental expenditure pot
(10) Rest of policing funding includes funding of bodies related to policing, such as the Police Complaints Authority and the National Crime Intelligence Service
(11) Includes £3bn extra above budget from Treasury reserves to cover operations. The total amounts may not sum as there are overlapping amounts, ie between salaries and running costs
(12) Now part of the Cabinet Office
(13) The amount of government funding from DBERR and DCMS, rest from licence fees from broadcasters and media organisations
(14) Includes: House of Commons, House of Lords and National Audit Office
(15) Split between Parliament direct, the FCO and DBERR

SOURCES: DEPARTMENTAL REPORTS, INSTITUTE FOR FISCAL STUDIES, PUBLIC EXPENDITURE STATISTICAL ANALYSES (PESA)
RESEARCH: SIMON ROGERS, GEMMA TETLOW, MAX OPRAY
GRAPHIC: JENNY RIDLEY, MICHAEL ROBINSON

Definitive Atlas of UK Government Spending

Large amounts of money are difficult to imagine and therefore difficult to compare. This graphic, developed as a double-spread for *The Guardian*, shows UK spending by each government department, with each circle sized by the amount spent.

The pale circle in the middle represents total governmental spending in 2007/2008, while the coloured circles show the distribution of the budget to various departments. The data is not centrally supplied by the government but gathered from individual departmental reports. Since its first launch in 2008, the piece has been updated regularly.

Große Geldsummen sind schwer vorstellbar und daher auch nur schwer zu vergleichen. Diese Grafik, die als Doppelseite für den *Guardian* gestaltet wurde, zeigt die Ausgaben der britischen Ministerien; der Kreisdurchmesser entspricht proportional der Summe der jeweiligen Ausgaben.

Der helle Kreis in der Mitte steht für die gesamten Staatsausgaben 2007/08, die farbigen Kreise zeigen, wie sich die Haushaltsausgaben auf die einzelnen Behörden verteilen. Die Daten für diese Grafik werden nicht zentral von der Regierung zur Verfügung gestellt, sondern von den Journalisten des *Guardian* anhand der Rechenschaftsberichte der einzelnen Ministerien zusammengestellt. Seit ihrem ersten Erscheinen 2008 wird sie jährlich aktualisiert.

Il est difficile de se représenter de grandes sommes d'argent, et donc de les comparer entre elles. Ce visuel, conçu sur deux pages pour *The Guardian*, montre les dépenses de chaque ministère au Royaume-Uni, la taille de chaque cercle étant proportionnelle à la somme dépensée.

Le cercle clair au centre correspond aux dépenses en 2007/2008, et les cercles de couleur montrent la répartition du budget entre différents ministères. Les données n'ont pas été cédées par le gouvernement, mais ont été extraites de rapports ministériels. Depuis sa création en 2008, cette représentation graphique a été régulièrement mise à jour.

Project Info: "Where Your Money Goes", *The Guardian*, newspaper article, 2008, UK
Research: Simon Rogers, Gemma Tetlow, Max Opray
Design: Jenny Ridley
Art Direction: Michael Robinson

Essentials of Sociology

This series of infographics was developed for a student textbook, *Essentials of Sociology*, published in 2010. As an introduction to the subject, the book is organised around themes of globalisation and everyday life.

The infographics were developed to help make the abstract data more concrete and accessible for students. A selection of sociological surveys is represented in various diagrams, using colour coding and size relations as the main visual tools.

Diese Reihe von Infografiken wurde für das 2010 erschienene Lehrbuch *Essentials of Sociology* entwickelt. Das Buch gibt eine Einführung in die Soziologie und befasst sich mit Themen der Globalisierung und des Alltags.

Ziel der Infografiken war es, die abstrakten Daten greifbarer und damit für die Studenten verständlicher zu machen. Eine Auswahl soziologischer Studien wird in unterschiedlichen Diagrammen präsentiert, die visuell vorwiegend mit Farbcodierungen und Größenverhältnissen arbeiten.

Cette série d'infographies a été conçue pour le manuel scolaire *Essentials of Sociology*, publié en 2010. En guise d'introduction au sujet, l'ouvrage est organisé autour de thèmes liés à la mondialisation et à la vie quotidienne.

Les infographies ont été créées pour rendre les données abstraites plus accessibles aux étudiants. Une sélection d'enquêtes sociologiques sont représentées dans différents diagrammes qui utilisent comme principaux outils visuels le code de couleur et l'échelle de tailles.

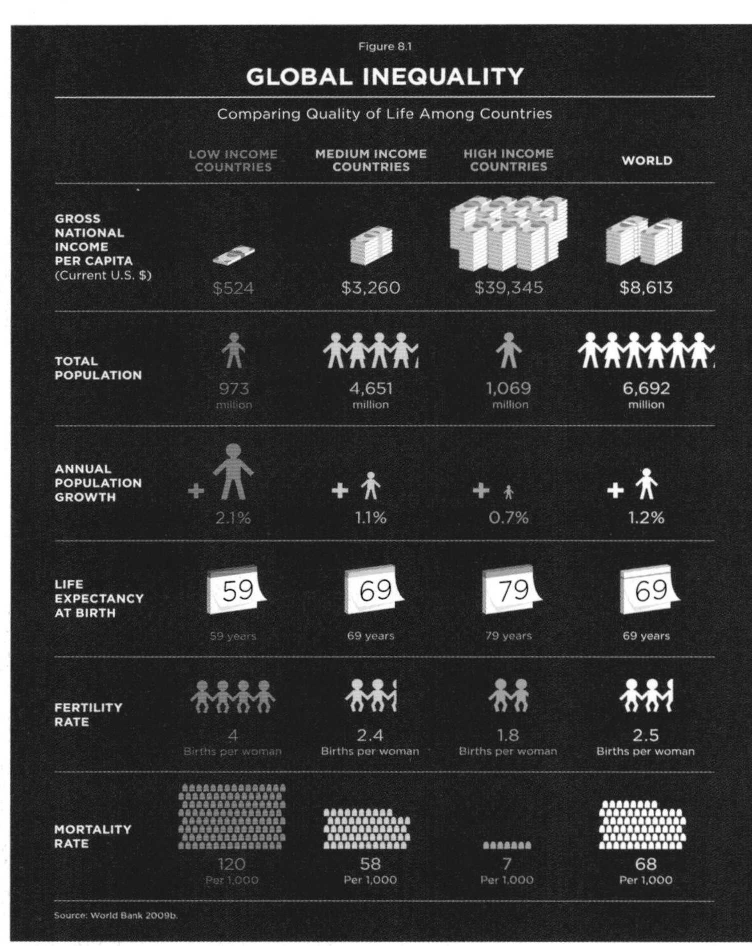

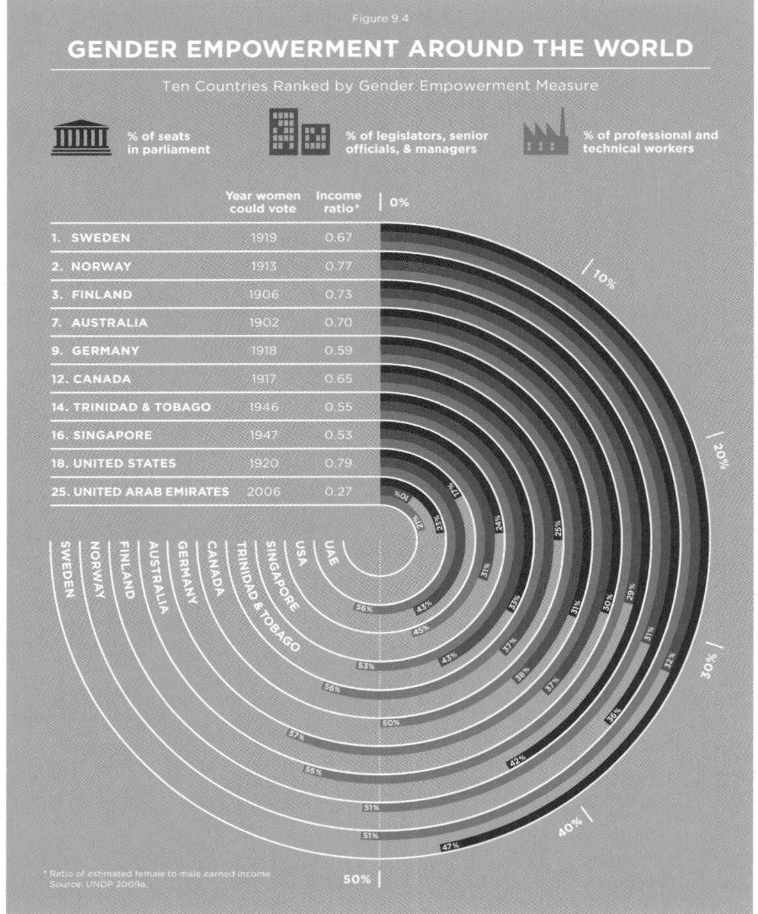

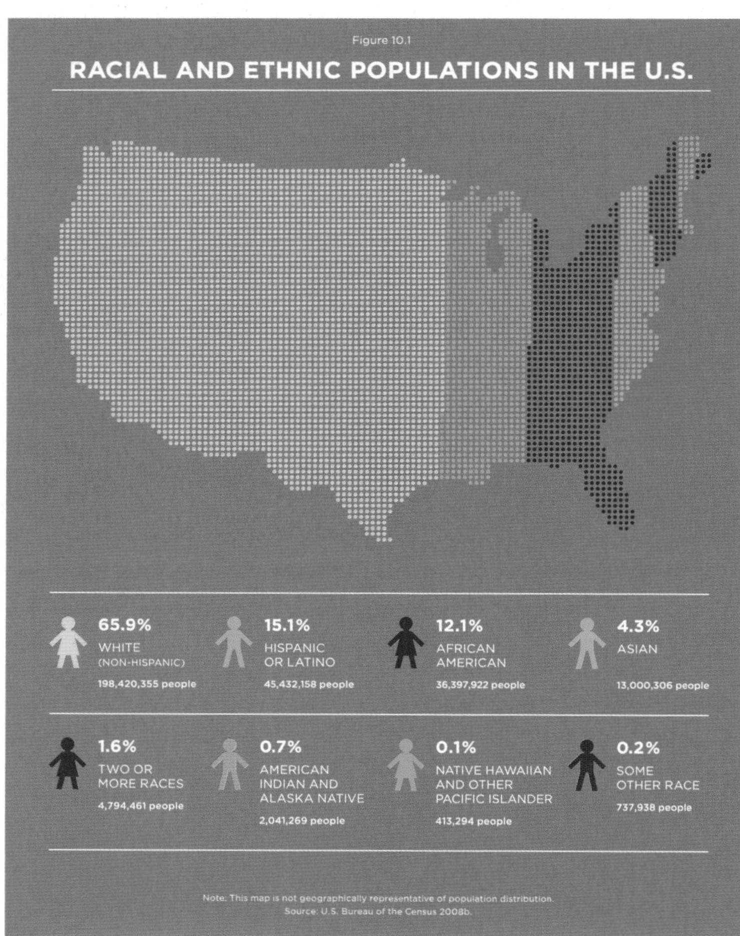

Figure 16.3

THE WIDENING GAP

Between Richer and Poorer Countries, 1800 to 2008

GDP PER CAPITA*	1800	2008
USA	$1,343	$42,922
GERMANY	$1,643	$32,637
JAPAN	$896	$31,824
REPUBLIC OF KOREA	$740	$23,845
BRAZIL	$509	$9,633
SOUTH AFRICA	$759	$9,360
EGYPT	$748	$5,678
CHINA	$992	$5,520
PAKISTAN	$665	$2,671
DEM. REP. OF CONGO	$394	$370

* 2008 U.S. $

Note: GDP for South Africa from 1911; 1900 data not available.

Source: Gapminder.com 2009.

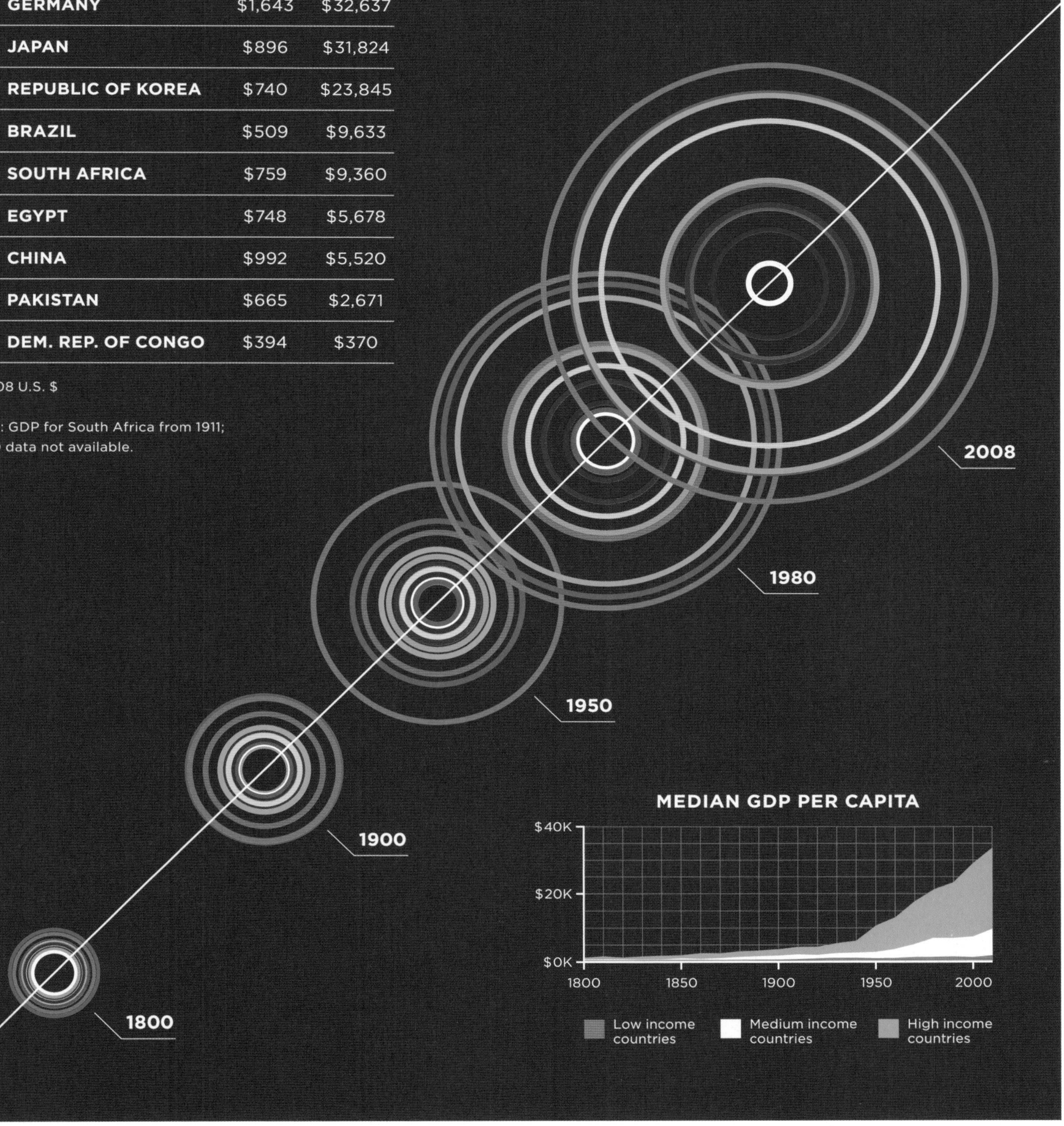

1800

1900

1950

1980

2008

MEDIAN GDP PER CAPITA

$40K
$20K
$0K
1800 1850 1900 1950 2000

Low income countries
Medium income countries
High income countries

Project Info: *Essentials of Sociology*, book, W. W. Norton & Company, 2010, USA
Data Source: The World Bank; UNDP; US Census Bureau; Edward Laumann et al.: *The Social Organization of Sexuality*; Gapminder.com
Design: Louise Ma (Kiss Me I'm Polish)
Art Direction: Agnieszka Gasparska (Kiss Me I'm Polish)

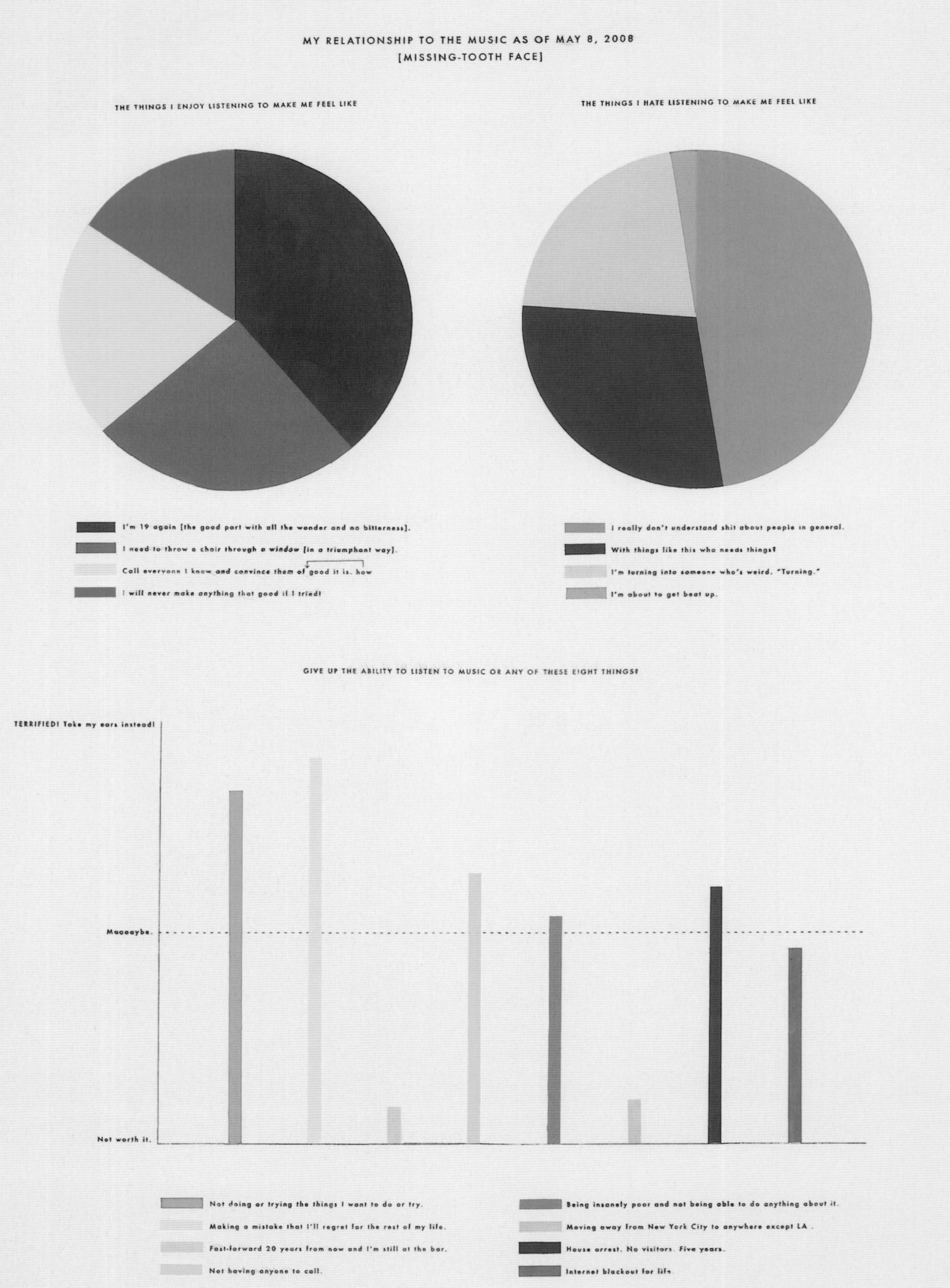
MY RELATIONSHIP TO THE MUSIC AS OF MAY 8, 2008
[MISSING-TOOTH FACE]
THE THINGS I ENJOY LISTENING TO MAKE ME FEEL LIKE
THE THINGS I HATE LISTENING TO MAKE ME FEEL LIKE
I'm 19 again [the good part with all the wonder and no bitterness].
I need to throw a chair through a window [in a triumphant way].
Call everyone I know and convince them of good it is. how
I will never make anything that good if I tried!
I really don't understand shit about people in general.
With things like this who needs things?
I'm turning into someone who's weird. "Turning."
I'm about to get beat up.
GIVE UP THE ABILITY TO LISTEN TO MUSIC OR ANY OF THESE EIGHT THINGS?
TERRIFIED! Take my ears instead!
Maaaaybe.
Not worth it.
Not doing or trying the things I want to do or try.
Making a mistake that I'll regret for the rest of my life.
Fast-forward 20 years from now and I'm still at the bar.
Not having anyone to call.
Being insanely poor and not being able to do anything about it.
Moving away from New York City to anywhere except LA .
House arrest. No visitors. Five years.
Internet blackout for life.

Project Info: Series of paintings, 2008, USA
Artist: Andrew Kuo
Additional Info: Andrew Kuo is represented by Taxter & Spengemann, New York

Faces Diagrams

Andrew Kuo has turned diagrams into his personal means to assess things happening in his life. For some time he has used diagrams to report on his blog how he liked the recent concert of this or that band. In 2008 he developed a series of hand-painted diagrams that portrayed a wider record of what inspired him.

The two examples here chart his relation to fine arts and music, respectively. Both feature two pie-charts at the top and a bar chart along the bottom, mimicking faces. They gain their individual traits depending on which personal feelings and thoughts Kuo decides to evaluate and the subjective order in which he places them.

Diagramme sind Andrew Kuos persönliches Werkzeug, um Erlebnisse aus seinem Alltag zu bewerten. So berichtete er in seinem Blog eine Zeit lang mithilfe von Diagrammen, wie er das jüngste Konzert der einen oder anderen Band bewertete. 2008 schuf er eine Serie handgemalter Diagramme über seine Vorbilder und Inspirationen.

Die beiden hier abgebildeten Beispiele zeigen sein Verhältnis zur bildenden Kunst bzw. zur Musik. Beide enthalten je zwei Tortendiagramme oben und ein Säulendiagramm unten, die zusammen ein Gesicht ergeben. Ihren individuellen Ausdruck erhalten die Gesichter durch Kuos Entscheidung, welche persönlichen Gefühle und Gedanken er abbilden möchte und in welcher subjektiven Abfolge er sie anordnet.

Andrew Kuo a fait des diagrammes un outil personnel pour analyser les événements de sa vie. Pendant un temps, il s'est servi de diagrammes pour évoquer dans son blog les derniers concerts qu'il avait aimés. En 2008, il a conçu une série de diagrammes peints à la main pour illustrer plus largement ce qui l'inspirait.

Les deux exemples montrés ici illustrent sa relation avec l'art et la musique, respectivement. Ils comptent deux camemberts en haut et un diagramme à barres en bas, et font penser à des visages. Leurs traits individuels dépendent des sentiments et des pensées que Kuo analyse et de l'ordre subjectif dans lequel il les place.

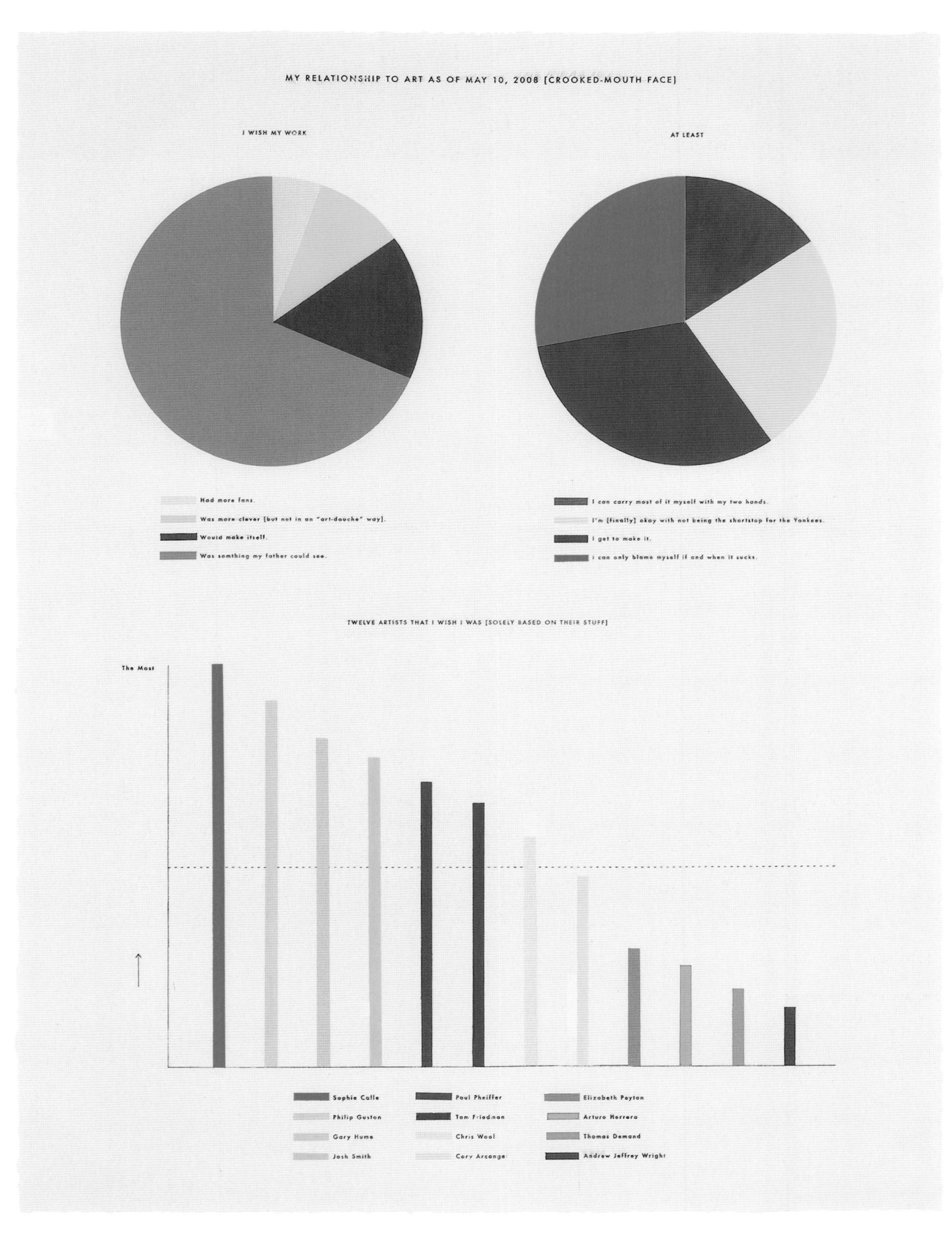

ONE NATION, UNDER GOD

A COLLABORATION BETWEEN GOOD AND CHRIS KORBEY

SOURCE: The 2009 American Religious Identification Survey

GENERIC CHRISTIAN: Born Again, Evangelical, Non-denominational, Unspecified
MAINLINE CHRISTIAN: Episcopalian, Lutheran, Methodist, Presbyterian, United Church of Christ

One Nation, Under God

The US has a wide diversity of religious beliefs, but the number of Americans who consider themselves atheists is rising. This infographic uses a photograph to show the percentage of the population and actual number of people claiming to belong to big Christian, Jewish or Muslim communities.

The image plays with hiding the people's faces, but shows some of them in half profile or in the mirror behind the bar. The female bartender on the other hand, facing the group heavily tattooed and seemingly uninterested, is clearly associated with the atheist figures to the very right of the image by the colour of her shirt.

In den USA gibt es eine große Vielfalt von Glaubensrichtungen, doch immer mehr Amerikaner bezeichnen sich als Atheisten. Diese Infografik bedient sich eines Fotos, um in Prozentangaben und in absoluten Zahlen zu zeigen, wie viele Menschen sich als Angehörige einer christlichen, jüdischen oder muslimischen Gemeinschaft bezeichnen.

Das Bild spielt mit den verdeckten Gesichtern, die zum Teil im Halbprofil oder als Spiegelbild hinter der Theke zu sehen sind. Die Barkeeperin, die der Gruppe mit ihren auffälligen Tätowierungen anscheinend desinteressiert gegenübersteht, ist durch die Farbe ihres Tops mit den Atheisten verknüpft, deren Zahlen oben rechts angegeben sind.

Les États-Unis comptent une grande variété de cultes religieux, mais le nombre d'Américains se déclarant athées est en hausse. Cette infographie se sert d'une photographie pour montrer le pourcentage de la population et le nombre réel de personnes affirmant appartenir aux communautés chrétienne, juive ou musulmane.

Dans l'image, les personnes tournent le dos, mais certaines dévoilent un demi-profil ou leur visage est reflété dans le miroir derrière le comptoir. La barmaid faisant face au groupe arbore de nombreux tatouages et montre un certain manque d'intérêt: elle est clairement associée aux chiffres sur les athées dans l'angle droit grâce à la couleur de son t-shirt.

Project Info: *GOOD*, magazine and online article, 2009, USA
Data Source: The 2009 American Religious Identification Survey
Design: Chris Korbey
Editors: Morgan Clendaniel, Atley Kasky

Gapminder World Map 2010

This diagram shows life expectancy in relation to a country's income. Countries are shown as circles, sized according to their population. The piece originated with the Gapminder Foundation, based in Stockholm, and founded by Hans Rosling, a professor of International Health and an ardent ambassador for educating the public about global population and health trends.

Rosling has campaigned for a more engaging use of statistics in general and higher education. His talks are famous for his humorous way of recounting "deadly serious" global trends. The Gapminder Foundation continues to promote this sophisticated world-view by providing global statistics in animated and interactive presentations. This material is made available for free.

Dieses Diagramm veranschaulicht die Lebenserwartung im Verhältnis zum Einkommen eines Landes. Länder sind als Kreise dargestellt, deren Größe ihrer Bevölkerungszahl entspricht. Die Grafik geht auf die Gapminder-Stiftung mit Sitz in Stockholm zurück. Sie wurde von Hans Rosling gegründet, der Professor für Internationale Gesundheit ist und sich unermüdlich dafür engagiert, die Öffentlichkeit über die Weltbevölkerung und über globale Gesundheitstrends aufzuklären.

Rosling setzt sich für einen intelligenten Einsatz von Statistiken in der allgemeinen und weiterführenden Bildung ein. Seine Vorträge sind bekannt wegen der humorvollen Art, mit der er „todernste" globale Trends referiert. Die Gapminder-Stiftung versucht, diese faktenbasierte Sichtweise zu fördern. Sie entwickelt animierte und interaktive Visualisierungen statistischer Daten und stellt diese der Öffentlichkeit zur Verfügung.

Ce diagramme montre l'espérance de vie par rapport aux revenus du pays. Les pays sont présentés sous forme de cercles, leur taille changeant en fonction de leur population. Ce visuel a été créé par la fondation Gapminder, installée à Stockholm et fondée par Hans Rosling, professeur de santé internationale et fervent ambassadeur de l'éducation du public sur les tendances globales en matière de santé et de population.

Rosling a fait campagne pour un usage plus attrayant des statistiques dans l'enseignement général et supérieur. Ses conférences sont célèbres pour sa façon humoristique d'exposer des tendances globales « mortellement sérieuses ». La fondation Gapminder poursuit la promotion de cette vision sophistiquée du monde en fournissant des statistiques globales dans des présentations animées et interactives. Ces données peuvent être obtenues gratuitement.

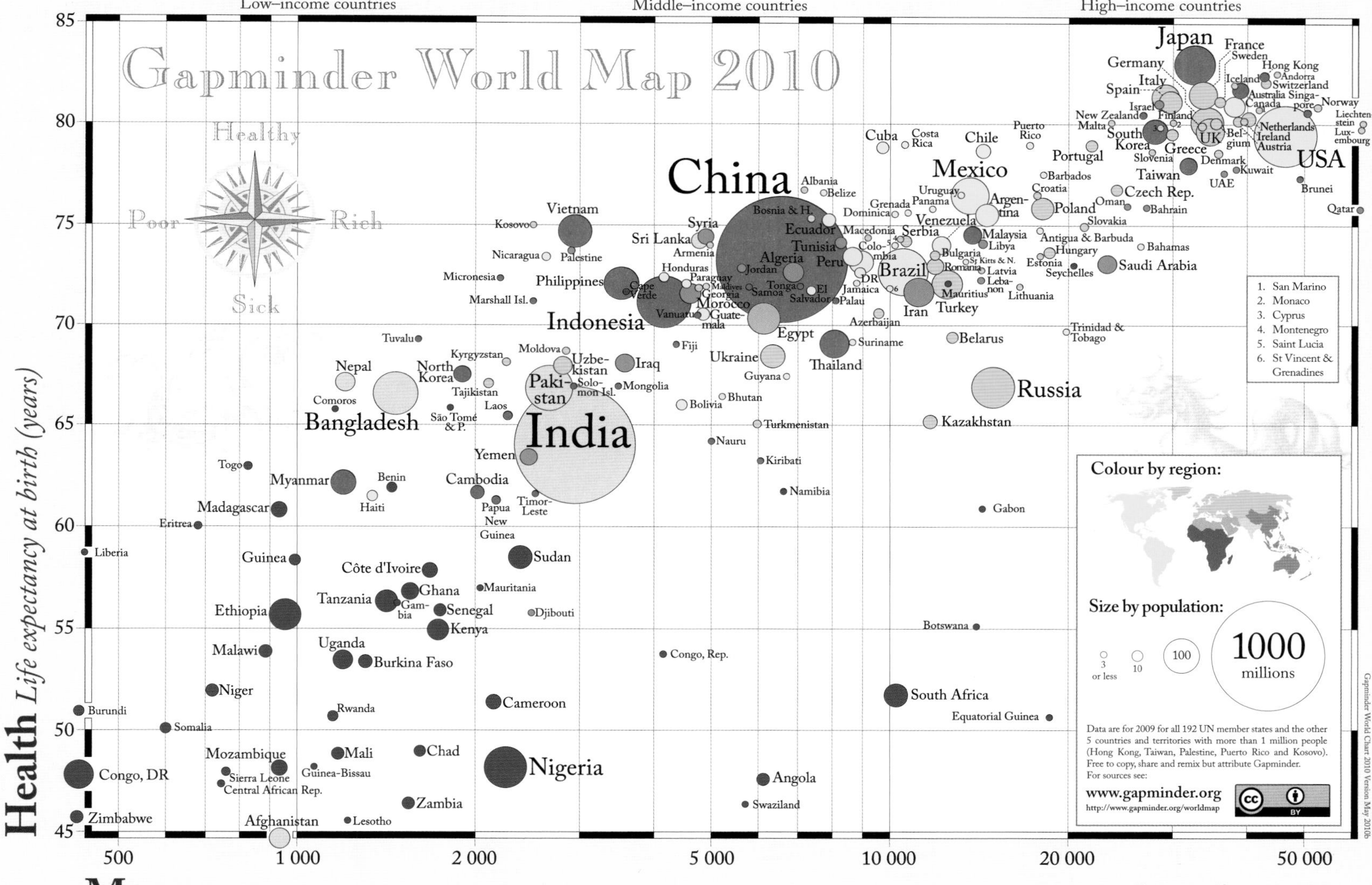

Project Info: Poster, 2010, Sweden
Design: Anna Rosling Rönnlund, Ola Rosling, Daniel Lapidus (Gapminder)

Fast Faust

Fast Faust is a straight hierarchy. It contains all the words Johann Wolfgang von Goethe used in the first part of his famous tragedy *Faust*, sorted and scaled by the frequency of their use throughout the play. The most frequent word "und" (and) occurs 918 times. Since this is classical German literature, the most frequent nouns are "Geist" (mind) and "Welt" (world).

Developed in 2000, the piece anticipated the principle of tag clouds, which later became a prominent feature of web 2.0. As it was hardly possible to translate the frequency of words into exact point sizes for the letters, Boris Müller used logarithmic scaling to show the relative frequency of each word.

Fast Faust zeigt eine unmittelbare Hierarchie. Das Poster enthält alle Wörter, die Goethe im ersten Teil des *Faust* verwendete, sortiert und skaliert nach der Häufigkeit ihres Auftretens. Das häufigste Wort „und" kommt 918-mal vor. Die häufigsten Substantive sind, passend zum Gestus der Klassik, „Geist" und „Welt".

Die Grafik aus dem Jahr 2000 nahm damit das Prinzip der *tag clouds* vorweg, die später zum charakteristischen Element des Web 2.0 wurden. Da es praktisch unmöglich gewesen wäre, die Häufigkeit der Wörter in eine genaue Punktgröße der Buchstaben zu übersetzen, verwendete Boris Müller eine logarithmische Skalierung, um die relative Häufigkeit jedes Wortes abzubilden.

La hiérarchie *Fast Faust* est simple : elle renferme tous les mots employés par Johann Wolfgang von Goethe dans la première partie de sa célèbre tragédie *Faust*, triés et dimensionnés en fonction de leur fréquence d'apparition dans l'œuvre. Le mot le plus courant, « und » (et), apparaît 918 fois. S'agissant d'un classique de la littérature allemande, les autres substantifs les plus fréquents sont « Geist » (esprit) et « Welt » (monde).

Conçu en 2000, ce visuel anticipe le principe des nuages de mots clés, amené à devenir par la suite un élément bien connu du Web 2.0. Comme il était quasiment impossible d'illustrer la fréquence des mots par des tailles de lettres exactes, Boris Müller s'est servi d'une échelle logarithmique.

UND ICH DIE DER
NICHT DAS EIN ZU IST DU
IN SIE ES SO MEPHISTOPHELES
DEN MIT FAUST SICH IHR MIR
MICH ER WAS WIE AUF DEM NUR
VON DOCH AN EUCH WENN IM DICH DA WIR
DASS MAN ALS AUCH MEIN DIR HIER UNS NUN DES
NOCH NACH SCHON MARGARETE AUS WIRD SIND IHN
WOHL HAT VOR FÜR BIN UM KANN EINEN DENN EINE AM SOLL
WAR ZUM SEIN WILL DURCH ACH WER GEIST MUSS WELT GLEICH GAR
ALLE DANN BEI NICHTS O IHM EINEM WO ALLEIN ALLES MARTHE GUT RECHT
JA MEINE MANN SELBST IMMER VOM GEHN HERR LEBEN LASS HAB VIEL WIEDER
MAG MEHR TEUFEL GERN GRETCHEN BIST GOTT HAST ÜBER FORT MEINEM ZUR HERZ INS
TAG NIE NACHT FROSCH ERST GANZ ZEIT KEIN MENSCHEN KOMMT DIESER GEHT SEI IST'S DEIN
STEHT WEISS WEH DEINE MUTTER HABEN HERRN MACHT KOMM BALD SEID AB KIND DIESEM SEH SAGEN
ALLEN ABER HIN LANGE HERZEN EINMAL SEHR WÄR HAUS SCHÜLER SONST FREUND HABT BRUST NEIN MEINER
MEINEN LIEBE SIEBEL DORT EINER WAGNER ALTMAYER HIMMEL BUSEN GEWISS LÄSST BLUT DEINEN DIESEN HEXE
DAVON KRAFT WEIT ERDE DIESE SIEHT ANDERN SEINE DEINEM HAND NATUR GESCHEHN SCHÖNE EBEN SEHN HÖREN
SCHÖNEN LIEB DIES JEDER HER BRANDER JETZT BEIM TRITT FREI EWIG GETAN WARUM KEINE AUGEN DRUM SCHÖN CHOR IHRE
UNTER WEG LIEGT KOPF DARF MUSST GENUG SAGT ENDE SINGT MACHEN LANG ODER GLÜCK SEHT WENIG FRAU TUT GANZE
KEINEN SEELE JEDEM HEREIN FASST GROSS STIMME KÖNNT OFT WEIN LUFT GANZEN SINN WERDEN DAMIT OHNE NIEDER HINAUS HEUTE
MÄDCHEN DRAN SIEH IHREN FREUDE KANNST DRÄNGT HEUT ETWAS SIEHST LUST HABE TAUSEND FEUER SEINEM GEBEN SEINER ALTE HINEIN DEINER
SCHRITT WEIB TAGE LIEBCHEN WELCH GIBT WORT GROSSEN HERREN OBEN MEER ZWAR BLICK LEICHT WOLLEN ANDRE KOMMEN SAG HÖLLE SINNEN
ALTEN SCHWER ALLER WOLLT ZURÜCK KUNST MÜSSEN SCHEINT LIEBT ERSTE HERAN GLAS MENGE FÜHL GEHEN GUTEN TOD NEUEN FÜSSEN RUH WILLST
WELCHE BIS HEISST FÜHREN HÄLT NOT FENSTER HÖRT ZEITEN LIED ERSTEN KREIS TIERE SOLLT VALENTIN LICHT MORGEN TIER HÖR VATER GESCHWIND LOS GEISTER
SEINEN TRANK HALB HÄTT SCHAUEN MIR'S OB ZWEI GEBT ARM LEIB SCHMUCK ZIEHT ACHT BUCH LIEBEN HÄTTE IHREM BESTEN MÖCHTE ARMEN SITZT DAZU LEIBE
GUTE MENSCH DIESES LASSEN SAH ICH'S STEHN LEBT LASST KAUM TOT EINS NAH EI KURZ PUDEL MANCHE JEDES BÖSER PLATZ STEIGT ANDERS GEFÜHL WEIL ZEICHEN FEST
VORBEI HATT ORT KEINER WIRST WERD LEISE HATTE ALLEM KLEIN FLAMME VOLL HINTER SOLLST GIB TRÄGT VIELLEICHT MÖCHT EUREM JUNGE LEBENS WEITER ENGEL BLEIBT JE DOKTOR
DICHTER WIRD'S BESSER HERAUS FÜHRE TUN GEWALT SINNE FASSE BRINGT GESELLSCHAFT GLUT WORTE JENER BEREIT BÖSEN NACH ARME FIND HILFT SCHAFFEN EURE HOHE DABEI
JENEM ELEND TRAGEN WISSEN ART DREI GESELLEN HERUM STERNE GENIESSEN JUCHHE HERRLICH EINES DIESMAL GLAUB LESEN HINAUF WÜRDE SCHAFFT GING GUTER DRINGT FREILICH
FÜHLT TOR JEDEN BESTE SCHÄTZEN HEXEN STETS ALTER JAHR MANCHEN SACHEN HERVOR VOLK GROSSE VORÜBER LAUF SCHMERZ WARD FRISCH NIEMAND BISSCHEN GESANG JAMMER

Project Info: Poster, 2000, Germany
Design: Boris Müller

food poisoning
UNTIL RECENTLY, food-borne illness was most often associated with contaminated meat. But after last year's tomato scare, illness from more innocuous-seeming foods has become more acknowledged. With the exception of meat, which falls under the purview of the U.S. Department of Agriculture, most of America's food sources are overseen by the Food and Drug Administration. Some argue that the FDA isn't empowered to do enough to enforce food-safety regulations, and legislation is currently before Congress to give it more power. Right now, these are the FDA-regulated foods that have made the most people sick since 1990.
CASES of ILLNESS / NUMBER of OUTBREAKS
339.7 25
202.2 31
329.2 31
259.4 74
276.1 83
365.9 108
340.9 132
268
352
362
BERRIES
SPROUTS
TOMATOES
CHEESE
ICE CREAM
POTATOES
OYSTERS
TUNA
EGGS
LEAFY GREENS
A COLLABORATION BETWEEN GOOD AND CHRIS KORBEY
SOURCE: The Center for Science in the Public Interest

Food Poisoning

This piece shows cases of food poisoning in the US since 1990, as caused by foods like vegetables, milk and cheese, seafood or eggs.

In a pleasant dinner-setting, which doesn't fail to suggest images of the Last Supper, each of the foods is shown on a table with a glass of liquid behind it. Quantities on the plates and in the glasses refer to the number of outbreaks and the number of cases.

Diese Visualisierung zeigt die Anzahl von Lebensmittelvergiftungen, die seit 1990 in den USA durch Nahrungsmittel wie Gemüse, Milch und Käse, Meeresfrüchte oder Eier hervorgerufen wurden.

Das Bild zeigt eine sorgsam gedeckte Tafel, die Assoziationen zum Letzten Abendmahl weckt. Jedes Nahrungsmittel liegt auf einem Teller, dahinter steht jeweils ein Glas mit Flüssigkeit. Die Menge des Essens korrespondiert jeweils mit den unten genannten Fallzahlen.

Ce visuel illustre les cas d'intoxication alimentaire survenus aux États-Unis depuis 1990, selon les aliments qui les ont causés : légumes, lait, fromage, fruits de mer et œufs.

Sur une table bien dressée, qui n'est pas sans rappeler la Dernière cène, un verre rempli de liquide est posé derrière chaque aliment. Les quantités dans les assiettes et dans les verres correspondent au nombre d'épidémies et de cas.

Project Info: *GOOD*, website, 2010, USA
Data Source: The Center for Science in the Public Interest
Design: Chris Korbey
Editors: Morgan Clendaniel, Atley Kasky

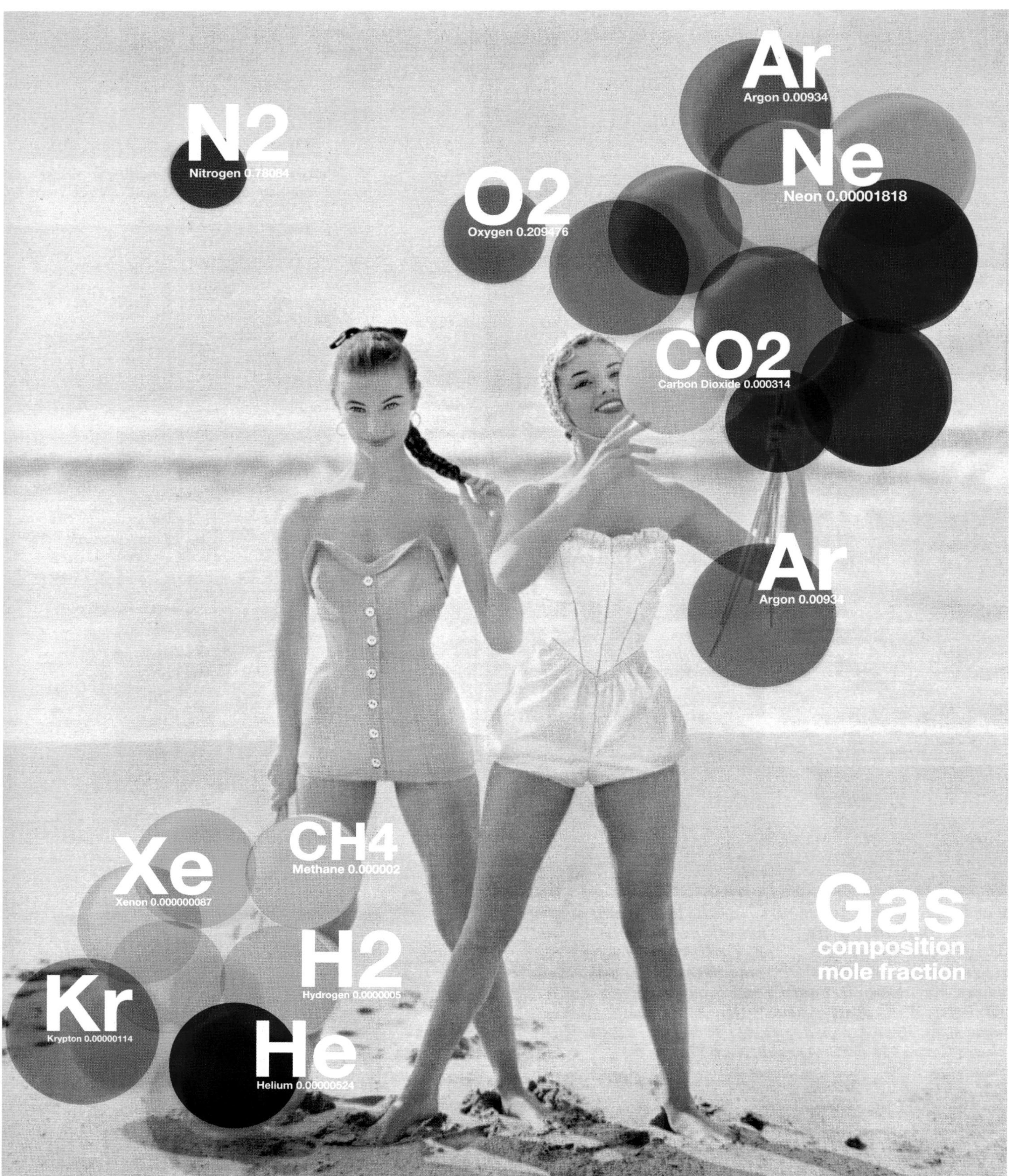

Gas Composition

Like the encounter of a nostalgic postcard with the periodic table of elements: this piece lists the composition of gases in the Earth's atmosphere. The black and white image shows two young ladies holding a bouquet of balloons.

Coloured circles float through the image like bubbles of gas, whilst typographic information provides data about the constituent gases in normal air and the percentage of their concentration. The piece works like a display board to assist with memorising the composition of the atmosphere.

Diese Grafik mutet wie der Wettstreit zwischen einer nostalgischen Postkarte und dem Periodensystem der Elemente an. Sie beschreibt die Zusammensetzung der Erdatmosphäre aus verschiedenen Gasen. Das Schwarz-Weiß-Bild zeigt zwei junge Frauen, von denen jede einen Strauß mit Luftballons in der Hand hält.

Farbige Kreise treiben wie Seifenblasen durch das Bild, während die Typografie über die einzelnen Gase und ihre Konzentration in der Atmosphäre informiert. Die Grafik funktioniert wie eine Schautafel. Sie hilft, sich die Zusammensetzung der Erdatmosphäre einzuprägen.

Telle la rencontre d'une carte postale d'antan et du tableau périodique des éléments, cette image présente la composition des gaz dans l'atmosphère terrestre. L'image en noir et blanc montre deux jeunes femmes tenant des bouquets de ballons.

Les cercles de couleur flottent dans l'image comme des bulles de gaz. Les informations typographiques apportent des données sur les gaz présents dans l'air normal et le pourcentage de leur concentration. L'ensemble rappelle un tableau d'affichage et permet de mémoriser la composition de l'atmosphère.

Project Info: Website, 2009, France
Design: Stéphane Massa-Bidal (Retrofuturs)

How Do We Achieve Harmony?

In their 2009 project "How Do We Achieve Harmony?", *GOOD* magazine looked at a range of global issues pertaining to sustainability and participation. The pieces shown here were contributed by Fogelsen-Lubliner. "The Cell Phone Revolution" looks at how mobile phones became widely available in various countries around the world. The distribution in percentage is compared between 2002 and 2007, with the pattern allowing comparison at a glance.

"War, What Is It Good For?" gives a hierarchy of countries, according to how many armed conflicts they were involved in since the end of World War II, with France leading the list at 25. Each conflict is represented by a drawing of a torn-out headline from a local newspaper.

Mit dem Projekt „How Do We Achieve Harmony?" untersuchte die Zeitschrift *GOOD* im Jahr 2009 eine Reihe globaler Fragen zum Thema Nachhaltigkeit und Partizipation. Die hier gezeigten Grafiken stammen von Fogelsen-Lubliner. „The Cell Phone Revolution" veranschaulicht die Verbreitung von Mobiltelefonen in unterschiedlichen Ländern der Erde. Sie ist für jedes Land in Prozentzahlen angegeben, einmal für 2002 und einmal für 2007. Das Muster erlaubt den unmittelbaren Vergleich.

„War, What Is It Good For?" zeigt eine Hierarchie von Ländern nach Anzahl der bewaffneten Konflikte, in die sie seit Ende des Zweiten Weltkriegs involviert waren. Frankreich führt die Liste mit 25 Konflikten an. Jede militärische Auseinandersetzung wird als Ausriss aus einer örtlichen Zeitung dargestellt.

Dans le cadre de son projet « How Do We Achieve Harmony? » de 2009, le magazine *GOOD* s'est penché sur une série de problèmes mondiaux en matière de développement durable et de participation. Les travaux présentés ici sont de Fogelsen-Lubliner. « The Cell Phone Revolution » montre l'évolution de la disponibilité des téléphones portables dans divers pays. Les pourcentages sont comparés entre 2002 et 2007 et le remplissage des lettres permet de voir les différences en un coup d'œil.

« War, What Is It Good For? » hiérarchise les pays en fonction du nombre de conflits armés auxquels ils ont participé depuis la fin de la Seconde Guerre mondiale; la France arrive en tête avec 25 conflits. Chaque conflit est représenté par le dessin d'un titre extrait d'un journal local.

Project Info: *GOOD*, website, 2009, USA
Data Source: International Telecommunication Union; United Nations Statistics Division; International Peace Research Institute
Design: Gary Fogelson, Phil Lubliner (Fogelson-Lubliner)

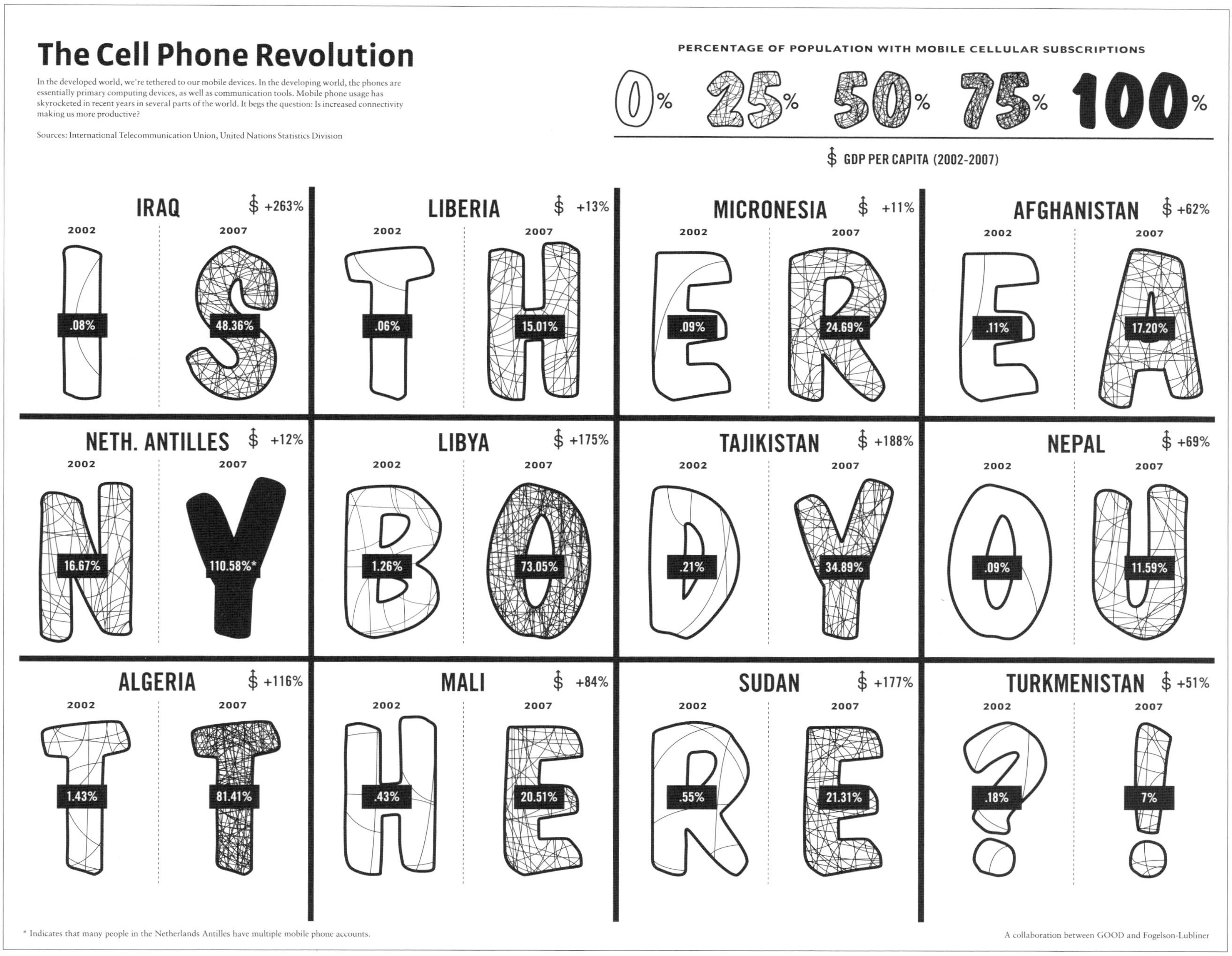

War, What Is It Good For?

Sharing is part of coexisting—and that means fairly distributing land and resources, but also respecting rights and freedoms. Armed conflicts worldwide are down from a peak in the early-1990s, but we're still not enjoying an era of peace. Below are the countries involved in the most skirmishes (both internal and international) since the end of World War II.

FRANCE 25

UNITED KINGDOM 23

RUSSIA 18

UNITED STATES 1

A collaboration between GOOD and Fogelson-Lubliner

INDEX OF MAJOR POST-WWII INTERNAT

A	1946-1949	INDONESIAN NATIONAL REVOLUTION
B	1946-1954	FIRST INDOCHINA WAR
C	1949-1953	KOREAN WAR
D	1956	SUEZ CRISIS
E	1962 & 1967	SINO-INDIAN WAR

AL CONFLICTS

1963-1966	INDONESIA-MALAYSIA CONFRONTATION	K	1991	GULF WAR
1965-1974	VIETNAM WAR	L	1998	KOSOVO WAR
1969	SINO-SOVIET BORDER CONFLICT	M	2001-2008	WAR ON TERROR
1975 -1990	LEBANESE CIVIL WAR	N	2003	IRAQ WAR
1978-2008	WAR IN AFGHANISTAN	O	2004-PRES.	IRAQ OCCUPATION/INSURGENCY

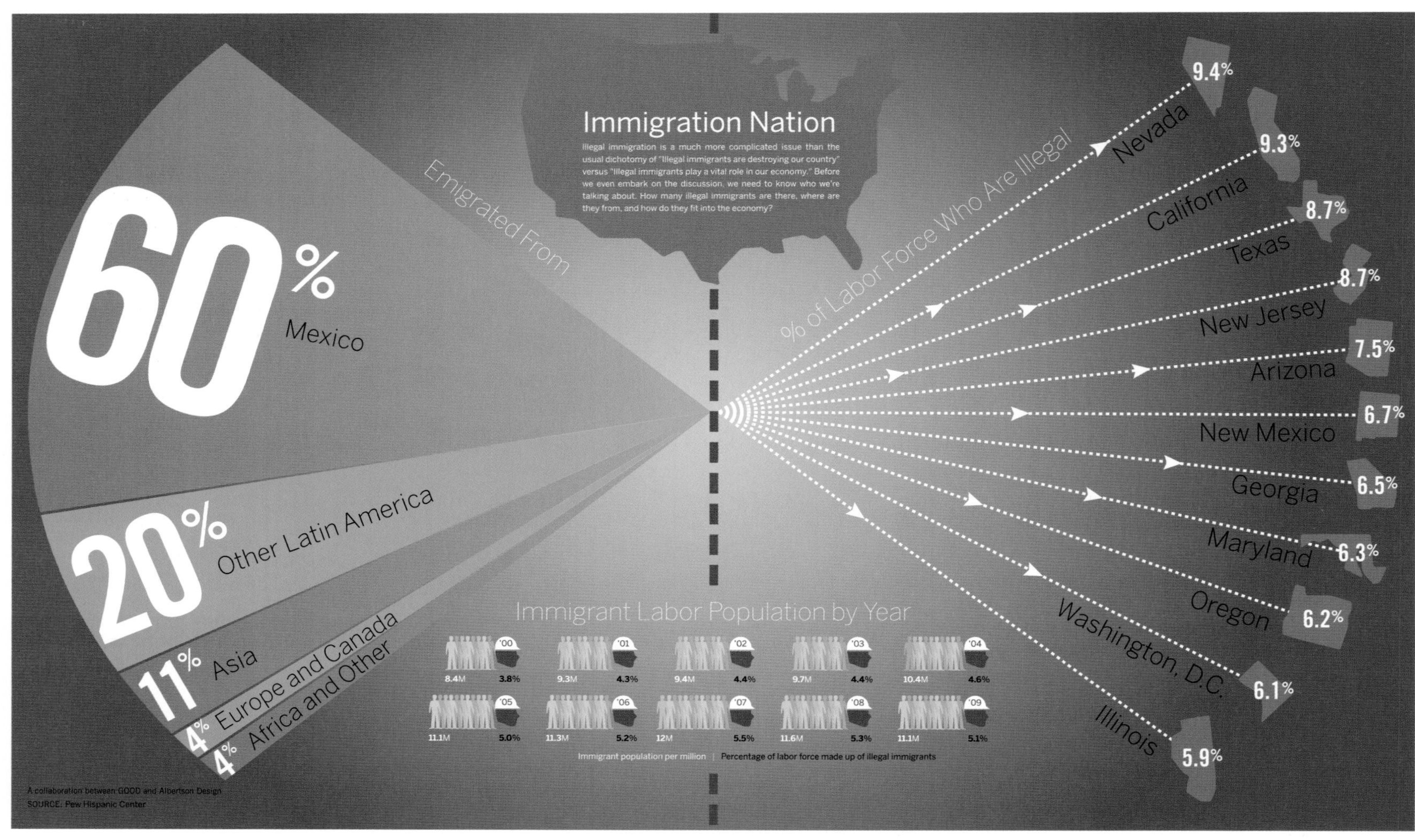

Immigration Nation

With all the talk in the US 2010 mid-term elections about illegal immigrants crossing the borders and threatening the US economy, the editors of *GOOD* magazine wanted to explore what the numbers actually look like.

Albertson Design turned the statistics into a pie chart, showing the breakdown of the countries of origin. On the other side of the central "border", a number of destination states for illegal immigrants in the US are shown. The percentages indicate what proportion of the labour force in these states is made up of illegal immigrants.

Als während der Zwischenwahlen in den USA 2010 häufig von den illegalen Einwanderern die Rede war, die angeblich eine Gefahr für die US-Wirtschaft darstellten, untersuchten die Redakteure der Zeitschrift *GOOD* die tatsächlichen Zahlen.

Albertson Design stellte die statistischen Angaben in einem Tortendiagramm dar, in dem links die Einwanderer nach Herkunftsländern aufgeschlüsselt sind. Auf der anderen Seite der zentralen „Grenze" sind einige US-Bundesstaaten zu sehen, in denen illegale Einwanderer leben. Die Prozentzahlen zeigen, wie hoch ihr Anteil an den Erwerbstätigen in den einzelnen Bundesstaaten ist.

Au vu de la polémique lors des élections américaines de mi-mandat en 2010 sur les immigrants illégaux qui traversent les frontières et menacent l'économie, les éditeurs du magazine *GOOD* ont voulu étudier la réalité des chiffres.

Albertson Design a converti les statistiques en camembert pour montrer la place des pays d'origine. De l'autre côté de la « frontière » centrale figurent plusieurs États de destination des immigrants illégaux. Les pourcentages indiquent la proportion de la main-d'œuvre composée d'immigrants illégaux dans ces États.

Project Info: *GOOD*, website, 2010, USA
Data Source: Pew Hispanic Center
Design: David Albertson, Paul Torres (Albertson Design)

Global Emissions

National CO_2 emissions are a key aspect of climate politics. Created just before the Copenhagen summit in 2009, this graphic looks at how emissions in a selected number of countries have changed in 2006/2007. Each bubble represents a country, placed according to its location on the world map. The bubble size represents how much emissions have changed.

The colour shows whether this was an increase (brown) or decrease (white) of emissions. The figures rank the countries on a global scale, while the gradient of the diameter indicates whether a country climbed or fell in the ranking. This focus on annual development brings countries like Venezuela to the fore because of its significant increase in emissions, while still being only no. 27 in terms of global emissions.

Der CO_2-Ausstoß eines jeden Landes ist eine Schlüsselfrage in der Klimapolitik. Diese Grafik, die kurz vor der Klimakonferenz in Kopenhagen 2009 entstand, zeigt, wie sich der Ausstoß im Zeitraum 2006/07 in ausgewählten Ländern verändert hat. Jeder Kreis steht für ein Land und ist entsprechend auf der Weltkarte angeordnet. Die Kreisgröße zeigt an, wie sehr sich der Ausstoß veränderte.

Die Farbe zeigt, ob es sich um eine Zunahme (braun) oder Abnahme (weiß) von Emissionen handelte. Die Zahlen geben den Rang des Landes auf einem globalen Ranking nach CO_2-Emissionen an, die Neigung des Durchmessers verdeutlicht, ob das Land in diesem Ranking auf- oder abstieg. Der Fokus auf die jährliche Entwicklung wirft ein Schlaglicht auf Länder wie etwa Venezuela, das einen starken Anstieg im CO_2-Ausstoß verzeichnete, obwohl es im weltweiten Vergleich nach wie vor nur den 27. Platz einnimmt.

Les émissions de CO_2 sont une donnée clé dans les politiques sur le climat. Créé juste avant le sommet de Copenhague en 2009, ce graphique analyse l'évolution des émissions dans un certain nombre de pays en 2006/2007. Chaque bulle représente un pays, et est placée selon l'emplacement de ce pays sur la carte du monde. La taille des bulles correspond à l'ampleur de l'évolution des émissions.

La couleur montre s'il s'agit d'une augmentation (marron) ou d'une baisse (blanc) des émissions. Les chiffres classent les pays sur une échelle mondiale, alors que l'inclinaison de la ligne de diamètre révèle si le pays est monté ou descendu dans le classement. Cette étude de l'évolution annuelle fait passer au premier plan des pays comme le Venezuela en raison de ses émissions accrues, même s'il n'occupe que la 27e place en termes d'émissions globales.

Project Info: *GOOD*, website, 2009, USA
Data Source: US Energy Information Administration
Design: Lamosca
Editors: Atley G. Kasky, Morgan Clendaniel

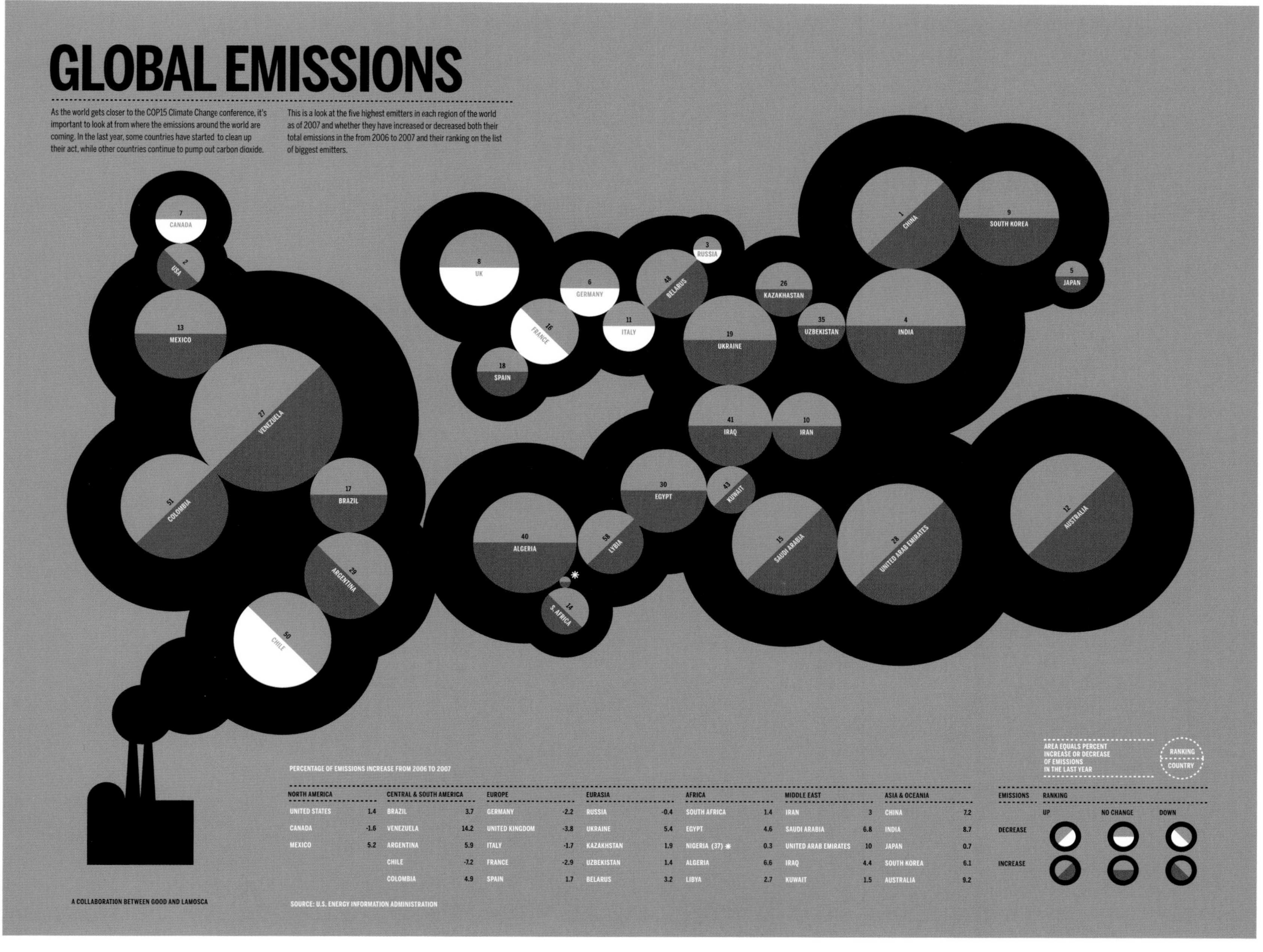

PERCENTAGE OF EMISSIONS INCREASE FROM 2006 TO 2007

NORTH AMERICA		CENTRAL & SOUTH AMERICA		EUROPE		EURASIA		AFRICA		MIDDLE EAST		ASIA & OCEANIA	
UNITED STATES	1.4	BRAZIL	3.7	GERMANY	-2.2	RUSSIA	-0.4	SOUTH AFRICA	1.4	IRAN	3	CHINA	7.2
CANADA	-1.6	VENEZUELA	14.2	UNITED KINGDOM	-3.8	UKRAINE	5.4	EGYPT	4.6	SAUDI ARABIA	6.8	INDIA	8.7
MEXICO	5.2	ARGENTINA	5.9	ITALY	-1.7	KAZAKHSTAN	1.9	NIGERIA (37) *	0.3	UNITED ARAB EMIRATES	10	JAPAN	0.7
		CHILE	-7.2	FRANCE	-2.9	UZBEKISTAN	1.4	ALGERIA	6.6	IRAQ	4.4	SOUTH KOREA	6.1
		COLOMBIA	4.9	SPAIN	1.7	BELARUS	3.2	LIBYA	2.7	KUWAIT	1.5	AUSTRALIA	9.2

Project Info: Website, 2010, UK
Design: Eduardo Salcedo-Albarán
Additional Info: Exhibited during the Map Marathon 2010 at the Serpentine Gallery, London

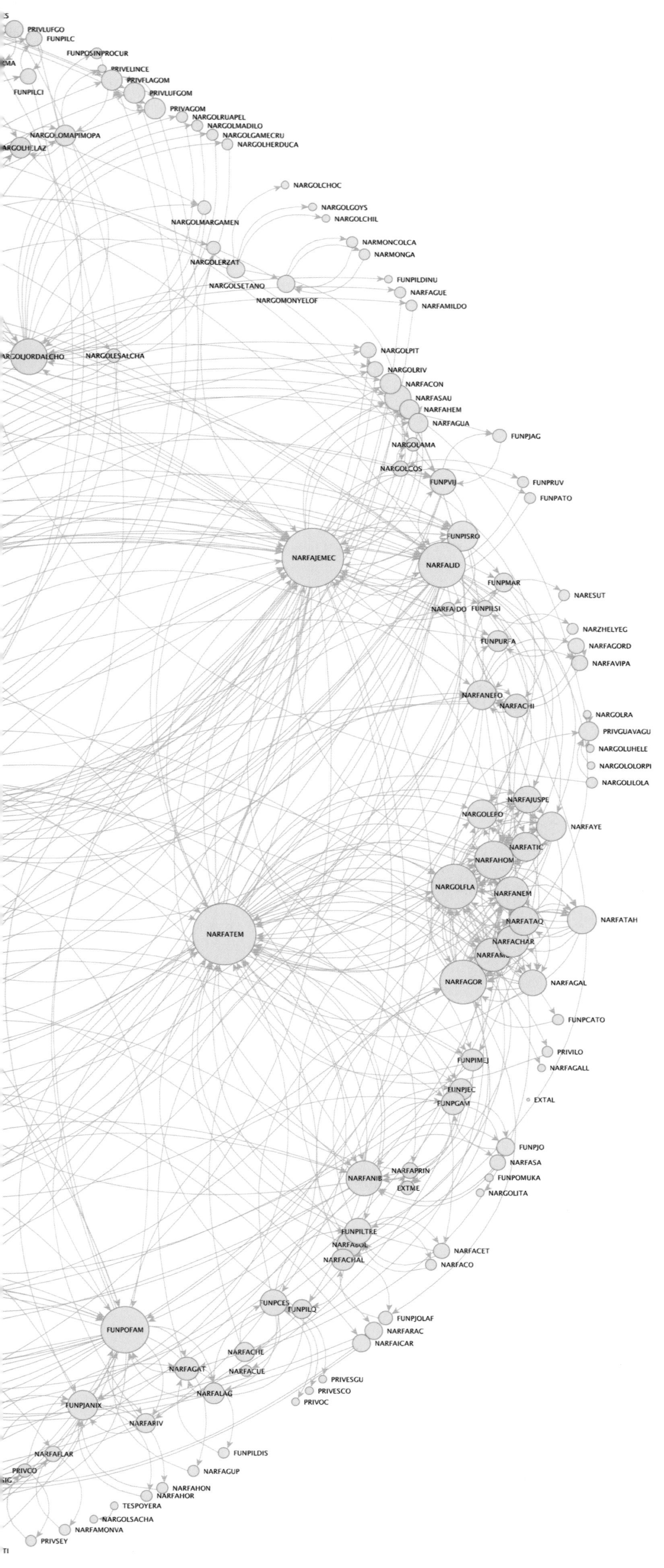

Mexican Drug Cartel "La Familia Michoacana"

"La Familia Michoacana" is a drug cartel based in the Mexican state of Michoacán, controlling the production and distribution of drugs in the area. This network graph reveals relationships within the organisation. A relational matrix of 284 individuals was enriched with qualitative information from judicial files, based on testimonies from members of the organisation. Lines show individual connections.

Nodes represent individuals: drug traffickers ("NAR") and public servants ("FUN"). The graph also shows the hierarchy: the bigger and more central a node, the more influential the person is. The graph is a result of the research project "The Effects of Drug Trafficking and Corruption on Democratic Institutions in Mexico, Colombia and Guatemala", supported by the Foundation Open Society Institute.

„La Familia Michoacana" ist ein Drogenkartell im mexikanischen Bundesstaat Michoacán, das die Herstellung und den Vertrieb von Drogen in der Region kontrolliert. Dieser Netzwerk-Graph zeigt die Verbindungen innerhalb der Organisation. Grundlage ist eine relationale Matrix von 284 Einzelpersonen. Sie wurde um Angaben aus Prozessakten erweitert, die aus den Aussagen einiger Mitglieder stammten. Linien zeigen individuelle Verbindungen an.

Die Knoten stellen einzelne Mitglieder dar, wie etwa Drogenhändler („NAR") und Beamte („FUN"). Auch die Hierarchie wird ersichtlich: je größer und zentraler ein Knoten, desto einflussreicher die dargestellte Person. Die Grafik entstand in Zusammenhang mit dem Forschungsprojekt „The Effects of Drug Trafficking and Corruption on Democratic Institutions in Mexico, Colombia and Guatemala" und wurde von der Stiftung Open Society Institute finanziert.

« La Familia Michoacana » est un cartel de la drogue installé dans l'État mexicain de Michoacán, et qui contrôle la production et la distribution des drogues dans cette région. Ce diagramme en réseau révèle les relations au sein de l'organisation. Une matrice reliant 284 personnes a été assortie d'informations qualitatives extraites de casiers judiciaires, à partir de témoignages des membres de l'organisation. Les lignes montrent toutes les connexions.

Les nœuds correspondent aux individus : trafiquants de drogue (« NAR ») et fonctionnaires (« FUN »). Le diagramme montre aussi la hiérarchie : plus le nœud est grand et au centre, plus la personne a de l'influence. Cette œuvre est le résultat du projet de recherche « The Effects of Drug Trafficking and Corruption on Democratic Institutions in Mexico, Colombia and Guatemala », avec le soutien de l'institut Foundation Open Society.

Monkeys and Typewriters

This is a variation on the so-called "Infinite Monkey Theorem". As a thought experiment, the theorem is used to establish the conceivability of infinity through an image: a monkey randomly hitting keys on a typewriter for an infinite amount of time will – at some point – type any given text, such as the complete works of Shakespeare.

Østring humorously refers to this theorem and makes up events which could also happen, but which are never mentioned: the monkey could be interrupted or he might eat the manuscript. The probability of these events is charted in percentages around the centre. The bar diagram at the very bottom plays with the notion of parallel universes.

Dies ist eine Variation über das sogenannte Infinite-Monkey-Theorem. Dieses Theorem wird als Gedankenexperiment verwendet, um die Unendlichkeit durch ein Bild zu veranschaulichen: Ein Affe, der unendlich lange wahllos auf einer Schreibmaschine herumtippt, wird irgendwann zufällig jeden nur erdenklichen Text tippen, wie etwa die gesamten Werke Shakespeares.

Østring greift dieses Theorem scherzhaft auf und erfindet Ereignisse, die in einer solchen Konstellation ebenfalls eintreten könnten, aber nie erwähnt werden: Der Affe könnte beim Tippen gestört werden, oder er frisst das Manuskript. Die Wahrscheinlichkeit dieser Ereignisse wird im Kreisdiagramm in Prozentzahlen angegeben. Das Balkendiagramm ganz unten spielt mit der Vorstellung von parallel existierenden Universen.

Ceci est une variante du fameux « paradoxe du singe savant ». Il s'agit d'un exercice mental qui permet de concevoir l'infini à travers une image : un singe qui tape au hasard sur le clavier d'une machine à écrire pendant une éternité finira, à un certain point, par taper n'importe quel texte donné, par exemple l'œuvre complète de Shakespeare.

Østring fait référence à ce théorème avec humour et invente d'autres événements qui pourraient aussi se produire, mais qui ne sont jamais mentionnés: le singe pourrait être interrompu, ou il pourrait manger la feuille de papier. La probabilité de ces événements est représentée par des pourcentages autour du centre. Le diagramme à barres tout en bas joue avec la notion d'univers parallèles.

Project Info: Website, 2009, Norway
Design: Ole Østring

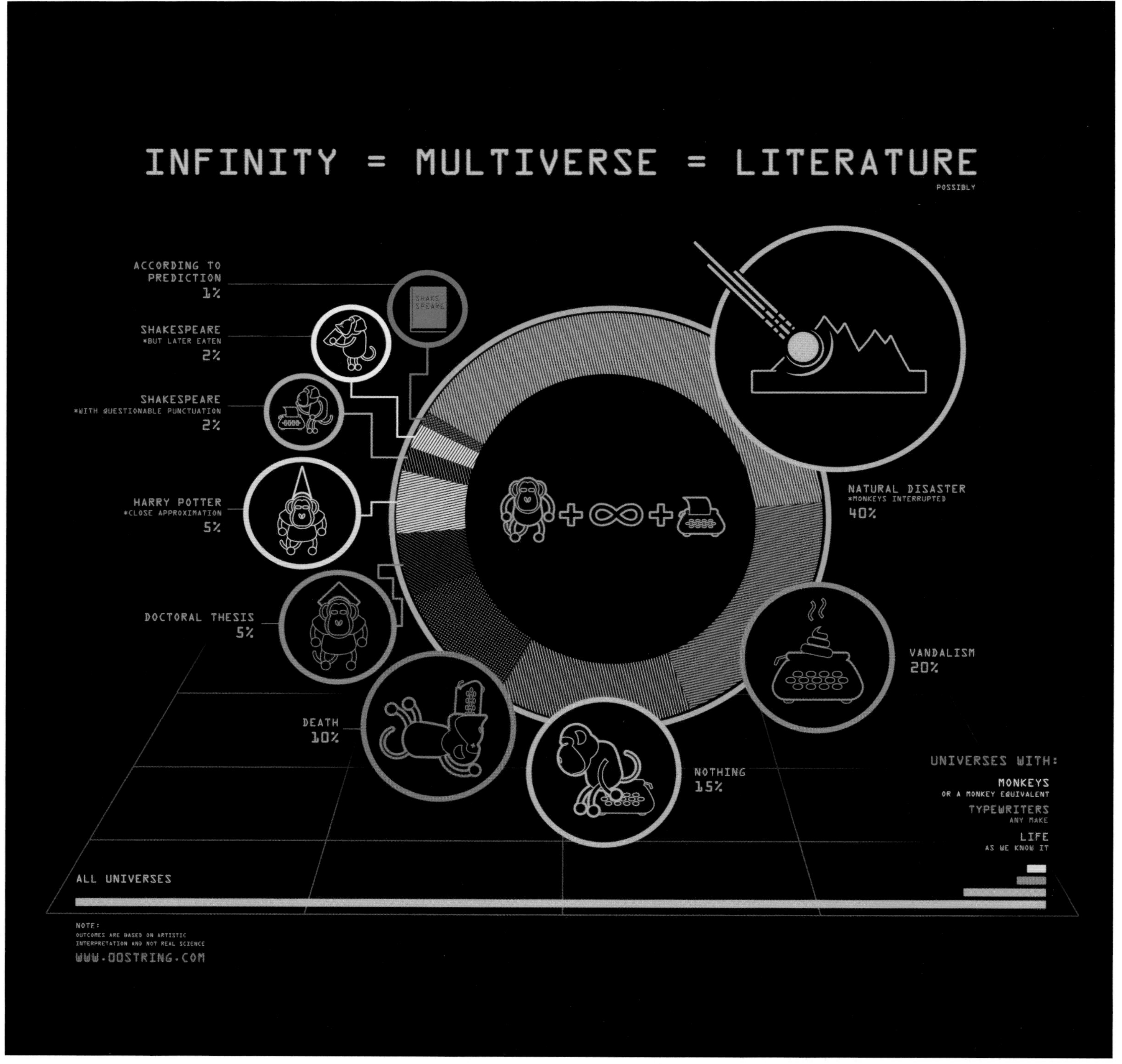

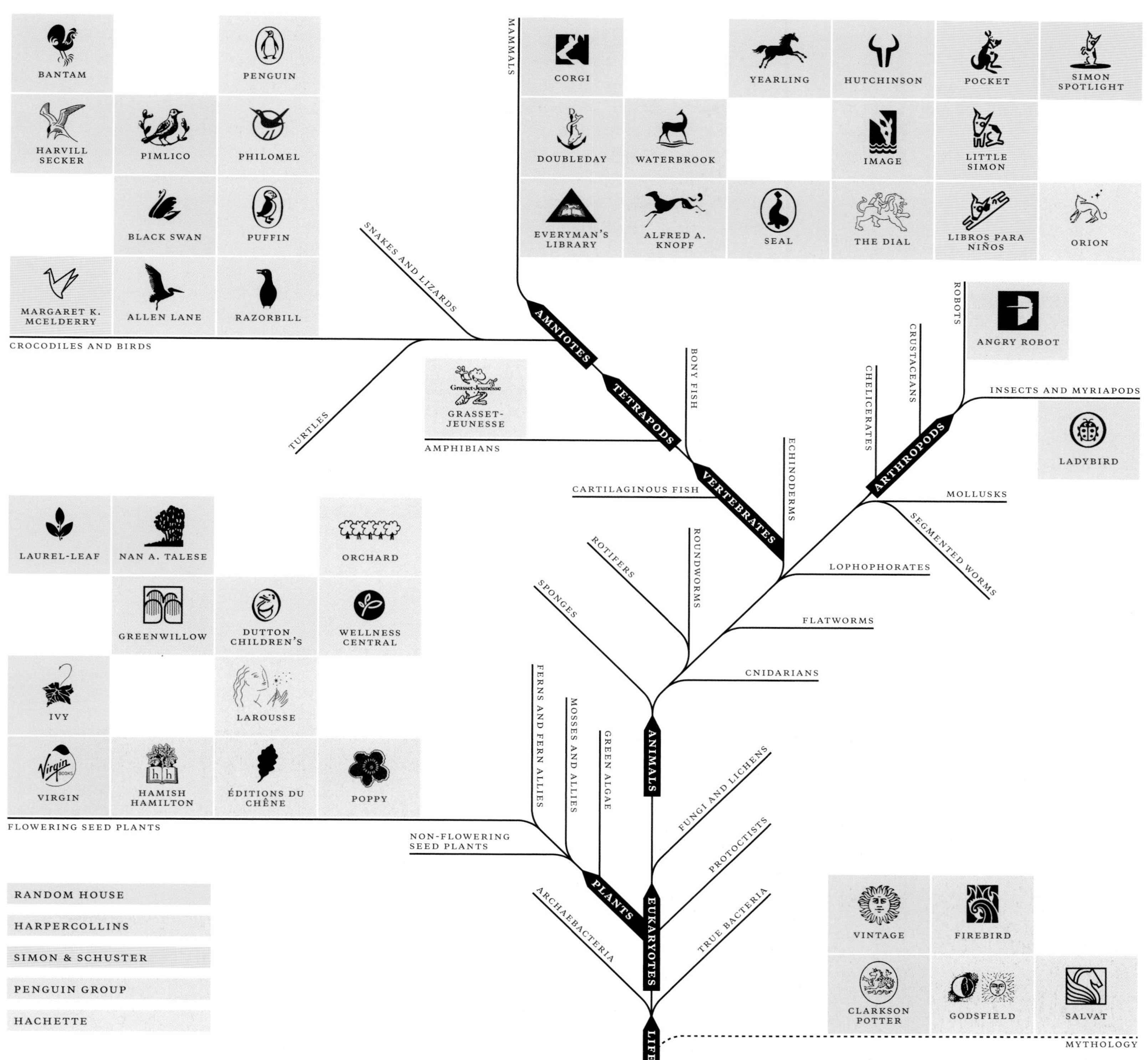

Natural Selections

The tree has been a powerful model for explaining how various species have sprung from a common background in the course of evolution. In this piece for the *New York Times*, Nicholas Felton used this model to explain a different phenomenon: the abundant use of animals and plants in logos of the publishing industry.

Starting from the base and passing by the small "Mythology" family in the lower right, it can be seen that mammals are the most popular of the logo animals, followed closely by flowering seed-plants. Animals like flatworms and sponges, on the other hand, don't seem to make an appropriate mascot for a publishing business. Colour coding indicates to which publishing group the mentioned imprints belong.

Der Baum hat sich als sehr geeignete Metapher erwiesen, um zu erläutern, dass sich im Laufe der Evolution zahlreiche Arten aus einem gemeinsamen Ursprung herausgebildet haben. In dieser Grafik für die *New York Times* verwendete Nicholas Felton das Modell zur Erklärung eines ganz anderen Phänomens: die häufige Verwendung von Tieren und Pflanzen in Verlagslogos.

Beginnt man unten am Stamm, wird deutlich, dass abgesehen von der kleinen mythologischen Familie unten rechts Säugetiere die beliebtesten Lebewesen für Logos sind, dicht gefolgt von blühenden Samenpflanzen. Tiere wie Plattwürmer und Schwämme hingegen scheinen im Verlagsgewerbe weniger als Maskottchen geeignet zu sein. Die Farbcodierung verdeutlicht, welcher Verlagsgruppe die genannten Verlage angehören.

L'arbre a toujours été un modèle pertinent pour expliquer comment différentes espèces sont apparues à partir d'une origine commune au cours de l'évolution. Dans ce visuel créé pour le *New York Times*, Nicholas Felton a pris ce modèle pour expliquer un autre phénomène : le recours fréquent à des animaux et des plantes dans les logos du domaine de l'édition.

En partant de la base et en passant par la petite famille de la mythologie en bas à droite, on constate que les mammifères sont les animaux les plus courants dans les logos, suivis de près par les plantes à fleurs. Les animaux tels que les vers plats et les éponges ne semblent pour leur part pas être la mascotte de prédilection pour une maison d'édition. Le code de couleurs indique à quel groupe d'édition appartiennent les différentes marques.

Project Info: *The New York Times*, newspaper and online article, 2009, USA
Design: Nicholas Felton

Near Earth Objects

Near-Earth objects are asteroids, comets and meteoroids, which come into close proximity to the Earth when orbiting the Sun. These objects are observed by astronomers for the potential danger of a collision with Earth. The unit for measuring the proximity of such an object is an "astronomic unit", which equals the distance between Sun and Earth.

The graphic shows those near-Earth objects which are bigger than 1000 m in diameter and which have, or will approach closest to us. Sorted according to their distance from Earth, asteroid 1999 AN 10 is listed as the closest to approach, set for August 2027. Each object's size is listed by diameter, whilst below, the same objects are listed with the exact date of their closest approach.

„Erdnahe Objekte" sind Asteroiden, Kometen und Meteoroiden, die auf ihrer Umlaufbahn um die Sonne der Erde sehr nahe kommen. Die Objekte werden von Astronomen genau beobachtet, da ein Einschlagsrisiko besteht. Die Maßeinheit für die Entfernung dieser Objekte von der Erde ist die „astronomische Einheit". Sie entspricht dem Abstand zwischen Sonne und Erde.

Die Grafik zeigt alle erdnahen Objekte, deren Durchmesser 1000 Meter übersteigt und die der Erde am nächsten gekommen sind oder noch kommen werden. Angeordnet nach ihrer Entfernung zur Erde, wird die größte Annäherung für den Asteroiden 1999 AN 10 verzeichnet, zu erwarten im August 2027. Für alle Objekte ist der Durchmesser als Größenmaßstab angegeben. Unten sind dieselben Objekte noch einmal mit dem genauen Datum ihrer größten Annäherung aufgeführt.

Les objets géocroiseurs, comme les astéroïdes, les comètes et les météorites, s'approchent de la Terre en orbitant autour du Soleil. Les astronomes observent ces objets afin de connaître le risque potentiel de collision avec la Terre. L'unité de mesure de la proximité de ce type d'objet est une « unité astronomique » équivalant à la distance entre le Soleil et la Terre.

Le diagramme montre les objets géocroiseurs dont le diamètre excède 1000 m et qui se sont approchés ou s'approcheront le plus de nous. Dans ce classement selon la distance à la Terre, l'astéroïde 1999 AN 10 apparaît comme le plus proche, prévu en août 2027. La taille de chaque objet est indiquée par son diamètre et, en bas, ces mêmes objets sont répertoriés avec la date exacte de leur plus grande approche.

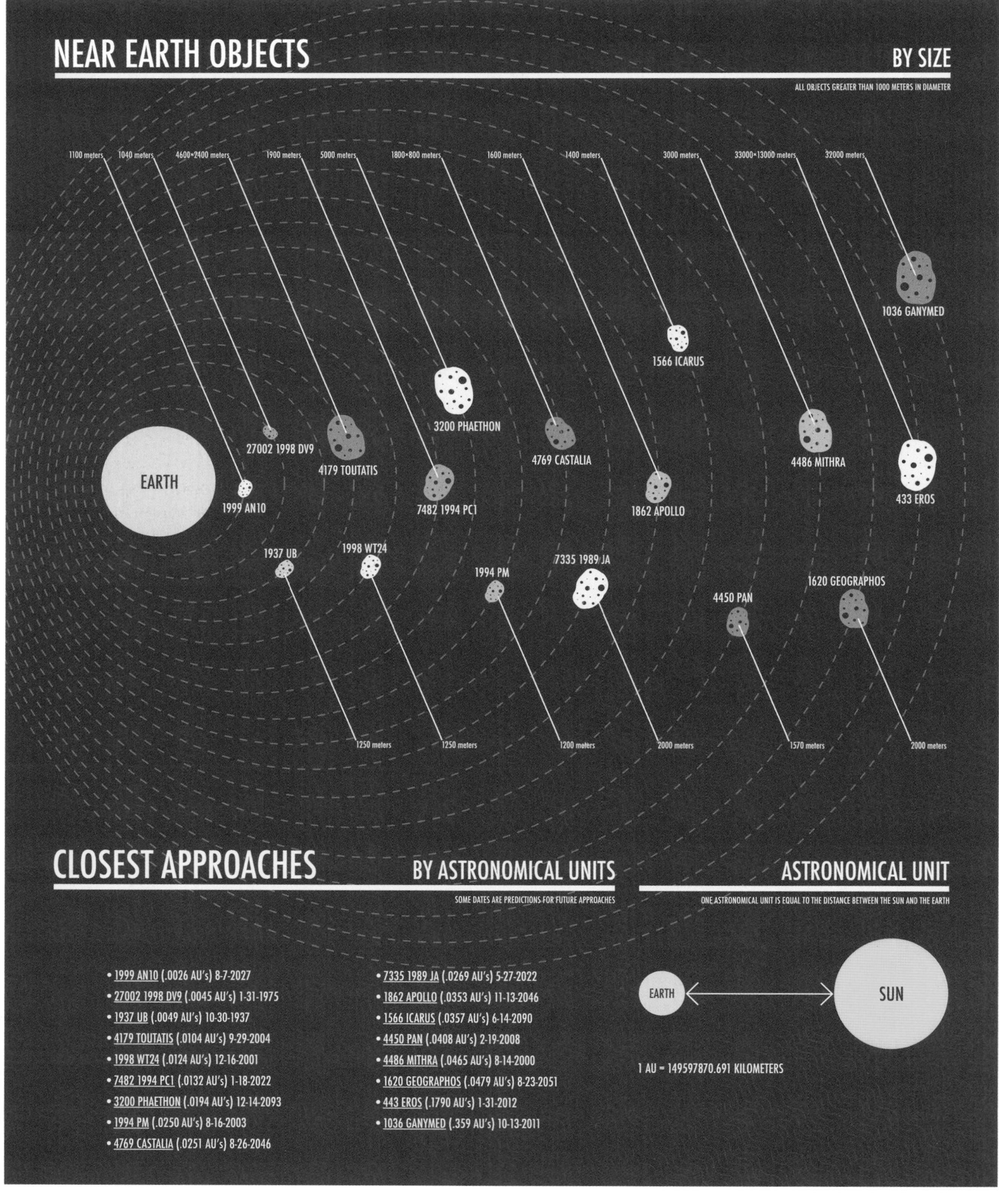

Project Info:
Website, 2010, USA
Data Source:
National Space Science Data Center; National Aeronautics and Space Administration
Design: Zachary Vabolis

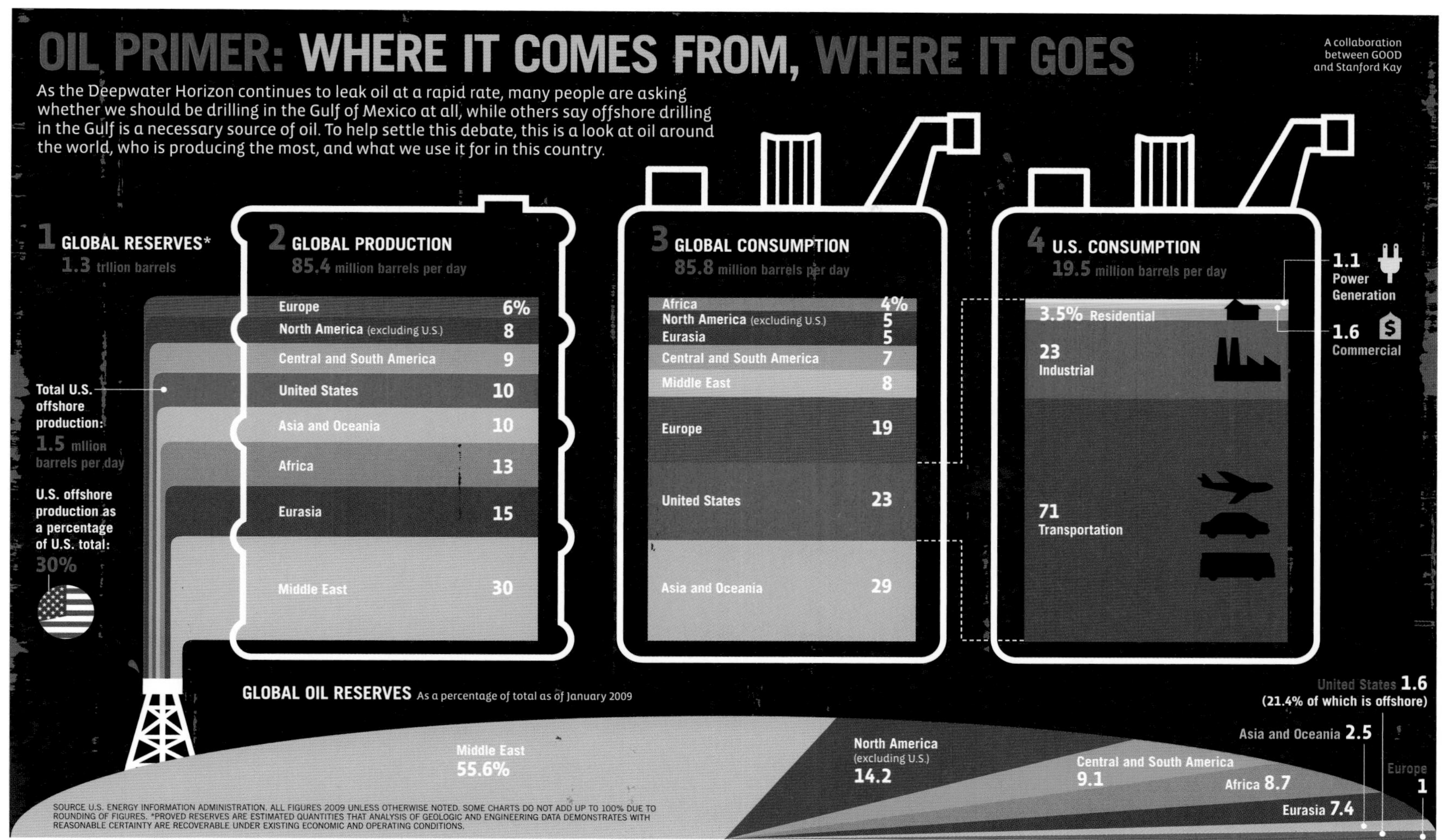

Oil Primer: Where it Comes From, Where it Goes

In a series of four hierarchical sets of statistics, this graphic looks at oil resources and consumption around the world. Statistic number one is a distorted pie chart at the bottom, showing the distribution of global reserves in percentages for individual world regions. The silhouettes of an oil barrel and jerry cans provide the outline for stats number two to four.

Global production and global consumption are shown in percentages for individual world regions. The last part on the right indicates what oil is used for in the US, and how transportation accounts for 71 % of the total US consumption. With its muddy, dark grey colour, the background evokes the consistency of the "black gold".

Mit insgesamt vier hierarchischen Statistiken werden auf dieser Grafik die Ölressourcen der Erde und der weltweite Ölverbrauch erläutert. Die erste Statistik zeigt im unteren Teil ein verzerrtes Tortendiagramm, das die Ölreserven nach einzelnen Weltregionen prozentual aufschlüsselt. Die Statistiken zwei bis vier werden von Silhouetten in Form eines Ölfasses bzw. eines Ölkanisters eingefasst.

Sowohl die globale Produktion als auch der Verbrauch werden für einzelne Weltregionen jeweils in Prozentzahlen angegeben. Das Bild ganz rechts führt auf, wofür Öl in den USA verwendet wird; 71 % des gesamten Verbrauchs entfallen hier auf das Transportwesen. Der schlammig dunkelgraue Hintergrund erinnert an die Konsistenz des „schwarzen Goldes".

Dans une série de quatre groupes hiérarchiques de statistiques, ce visuel analyse les ressources de pétrole et la consommation à travers le monde. Le premier groupe statistique est un camembert déformé en bas qui montre la distribution des réserves mondiales en pourcentages pour les régions de la planète. Des silhouettes de barils et de bidons encadrent les groupes statistiques 2 à 4.

La production et la consommation au niveau mondial sont indiquées sous forme de pourcentages pour chaque région. À l'extrême droite figure le domaine dans lequel est employé le pétrole aux États-Unis, et les transports cumulent 71 % de la consommation totale. L'arrière-plan gris foncé évoque le concept « d'or noir ».

Project Info: "How Much Oil Do We Get From Offshore Drilling?", *GOOD*, website, 2010, USA
Data Source: US Energy Information Administration
Research: Morgan Clendaniel
Design: Stanford Kay

On Hold
Hold On

The relationship between the rise of skyscrapers and economic prosperity is a much-discussed topic in the history of modern architecture. This piece takes a look at skyscraper construction projects around the world which have been put on hold because of the world financial crisis in 2008/2009.

The collage scales the towers according to their projected height, the chart at the bottom listing them all with their names and allocating them to continents. In his text, Theo Deutinger indicates an additional information layer not visualised in the image: an estimate of how many jobs have been lost from putting all these projects on hold.

Die Relation zwischen der Höhe von Wolkenkratzern und wirtschaftlichem Wohlstand wird in der Geschichte der modernen Architektur häufig diskutiert. Diese Grafik beschäftigt sich mit Bauprojekten für Hochhäuser auf der ganzen Welt, die wegen der Weltwirtschaftskrise 2008/09 auf Eis gelegt wurden.

Die Collage zeigt die Türme entsprechend ihrer geplanten Höhe, in der Liste, die sich darunter anschließt, werden deren Namen angegeben sowie der Kontinent, auf dem sie entstehen. In seinem Text fügt Theo Deutinger eine zusätzliche Informationsebene hinzu, die auf dem Bild nicht zu sehen ist: die geschätzte Anzahl von Arbeitsplätzen, die wegen der gestoppten Bauvorhaben verloren gingen.

Le rapport entre la hauteur des gratte-ciel et la prospérité économique est un sujet très discuté dans l'histoire de l'architecture moderne. Cette œuvre analyse les projets de construction de gratte-ciel dans le monde ayant été mis en attente en raison de la crise financière de 2008/2009.

Le collage range les tours selon leur hauteur prévue, alors que le graphique au bas en indique le nom et les situe sur un continent. Dans son texte, Theo Deutinger apporte une autre strate d'informations invisible dans l'illustration: l'estimation du nombre d'emplois perdus suite au report de tous ces projets.

Project Info: *Mark*, magazine article, 2009, Netherlands
Data Source: SkyscraperPage.com; Emporis.com; Oobject.com; BBC News
Design: Theo Deutinger, Barbara Weingartner

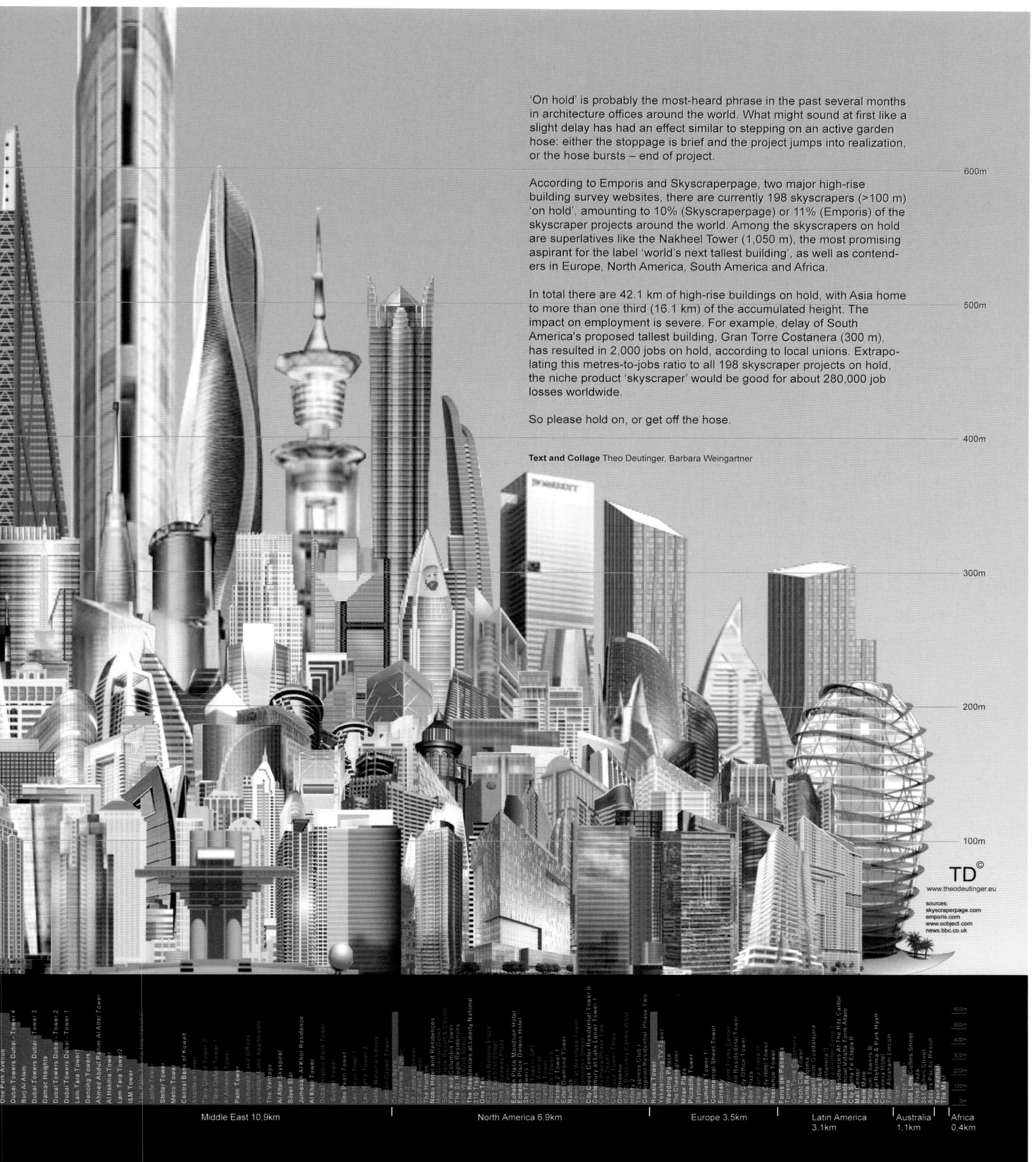

'On hold' is probably the most-heard phrase in the past several months in architecture offices around the world. What might sound at first like a slight delay has had an effect similar to stepping on an active garden hose: either the stoppage is brief and the project jumps into realization, or the hose bursts – end of project.

According to Emporis and Skyscraperpage, two major high-rise building survey websites, there are currently 198 skyscrapers (>100 m) 'on hold', amounting to 10% (Skyscraperpage) or 11% (Emporis) of the skyscraper projects around the world. Among the skyscrapers on hold are superlatives like the Nakheel Tower (1,050 m), the most promising aspirant for the label 'world's next tallest building', as well as contenders in Europe, North America, South America and Africa.

In total there are 42.1 km of high-rise buildings on hold, with Asia home to more than one third (16.1 km) of the accumulated height. The impact on employment is severe. For example, delay of South America's proposed tallest building, Gran Torre Costanera (300 m), has resulted in 2,000 jobs on hold, according to local unions. Extrapolating this metres-to-jobs ratio to all 198 skyscraper projects on hold, the niche product 'skyscraper' would be good for about 280,000 job losses worldwide.

So please hold on, or get off the hose.

Text and Collage Theo Deutinger, Barbara Weingartner

Piemonte: worldwide visits

A barcode infographic about worldwide flows of people moving to Piemonte's provinces in 2008.

This infographic shows the amount of visits to the italian region of Piemonte and their provenance.
The flow has been divided in three main categories:
EU - European states;
EX - Extra-European states;
ITA - Italian regions.

Each category has been respectively divided in the following groups:
EU: Northern, Southern, Eastern, Central Europe, other european states;
EX: North America, South America, Asia, Africa, Oceania, other countries;
ITA: all regions are shown.

The aim of this visualization is to quickly highlight the number and the provenance of each flow of visits towards each specific Piemonte province, and most of all to put these data in proportion, also summing up the top countries. Each flow has been visualized through the metaphore of **barcodes**, for obtaining a "chromatic worldwide barcode" identifying a sort of "Piemonte DNA".

The source of the information is the site http://www.dati.piemonte.it, an Open Data initiative launched by the Region itself.

4.033.122
from Europe

547.154
from the Rest of the World

Top 5
Germania 968.398
Paesi Bassi 526.992
Regno Unito 455.156
Francia 385.412
Svizzera 272.453

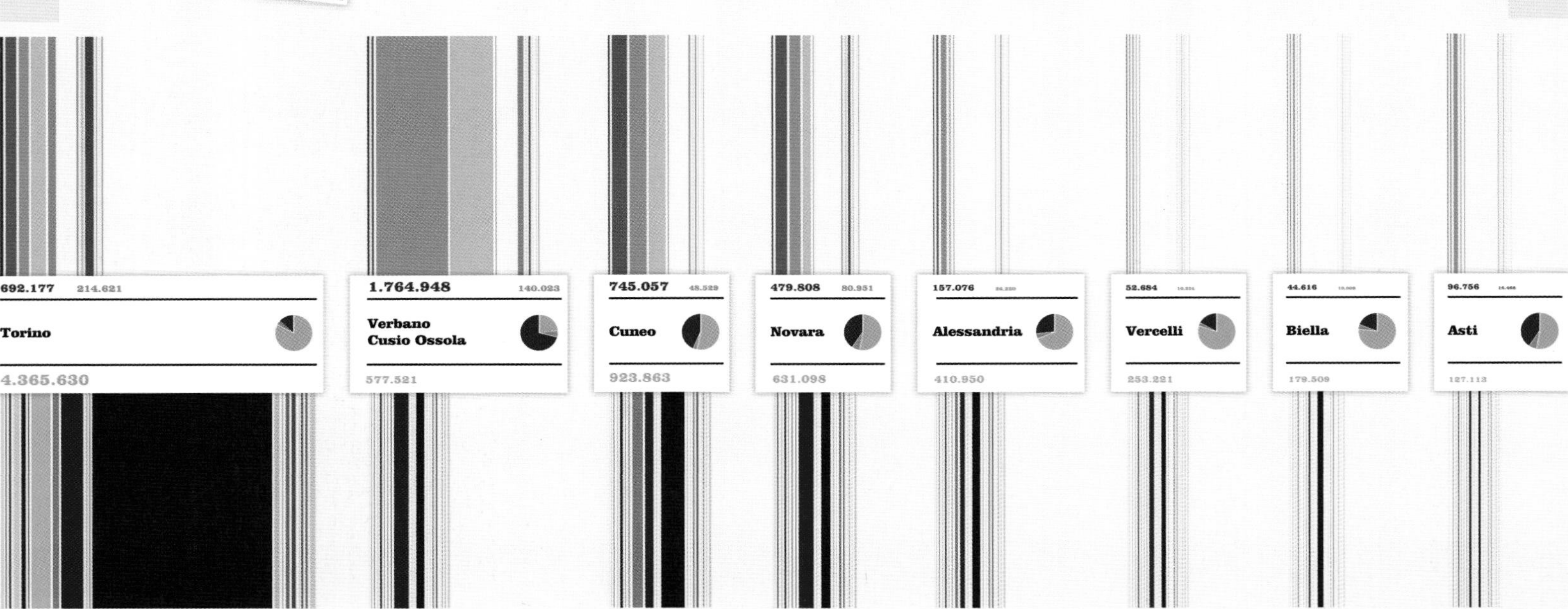

7.473.297
people coming from Italy to Piemonte

How to read this infographic
Barcodes
represent the amount of people moving to each piemonte's province from...
the regions of Italy (on the bottom of the paper)
all european states (on the top-left of the paper)
the rest of the world (on the top-right of the paper)
Pie charts
represent the percentage of people moving to each piemonte's province from...
the regions of Italy
all european states
the rest of the world

Piemonte: Worldwide Visits

This piece shows visitor traffic to the Italian region of Piemonte. Boxes in the centre list all Piemonte provinces. Line diagrams classify visitor groups: line thickness indicates the relative numbers and colour shows the visitors' origin. Above the centre, visitors from outside Italy are shown: blue colours refer to European tourists, while reddish colours are visitors from elsewhere.

Line diagrams below the boxes group visitors from Italy. Separate bars indicate visitor numbers for all of Piemonte. This combined visualisation quickly highlights specific trends. Each flow has been visualised using the metaphor of bar codes, to obtain a "chromatic worldwide bar-code" identifying a sort of "Piemonte Visitor DNA".

Diese Grafik veranschaulicht die Besucherzahlen der italienischen Region Piemont. In den Kästen in der Mitte sind sämtliche Provinzen des Piemonts genannt. Liniendiagramme klassifizieren die Besuchergruppen in der jeweiligen Provinz: Die Breite einer Linie zeigt die relative Anzahl, die Farbe das Ursprungsland der Besucher. Oberhalb der Mitte sind die ausländischen Gäste aufgeschlüsselt: Blaue Farben stehen für europäische Touristen, rötliche Farben für Gäste aus anderen Regionen der Erde.

Die Strichdiagramme unterhalb der Kästen geben die Besucher aus Italien wieder. Gesonderte Balken oben und unten veranschaulichen die Besucherzahlen für das ganze Piemont. Diese komplexe Visualisierung verdeutlicht schnell bestimmte Trends. Jeder Besucherstrom wird mit der Metapher des Strichcodes dargestellt. Der „chromatische weltweite Strichcode", der auf diese Weise entsteht, zeigt eine Art „DNA des Piemont-Besuchers".

Ce visuel montre le nombre de visiteurs dans la région italienne du Piémont. Les cadres du centre indiquent toutes les provinces du Piémont. Les graphiques filaires classent les groupes de visiteurs : l'épaisseur des lignes dépend des nombres relatifs, et la couleur de l'origine des visiteurs. Au-dessus du centre figurent les visiteurs non nationaux : en bleu les touristes européens, en rouge ceux du reste du monde.

Les graphiques filaires sous les cadres regroupent les visiteurs venant d'Italie. Des barres indiquent le nombre de visiteurs pour l'ensemble du Piémont. Cette visualisation combinée souligne rapidement les tendances. Chaque flux a été illustré suivant la métaphore des codes à barres pour donner un « code à barres chromatique mondial », tel un « ADN des visiteurs du Piémont ».

Project Info: Website, 2010, Italy
Data Source: Dati.Piemonte.it
Design: Manuela Ciancilla, Davide Genco (VISup)

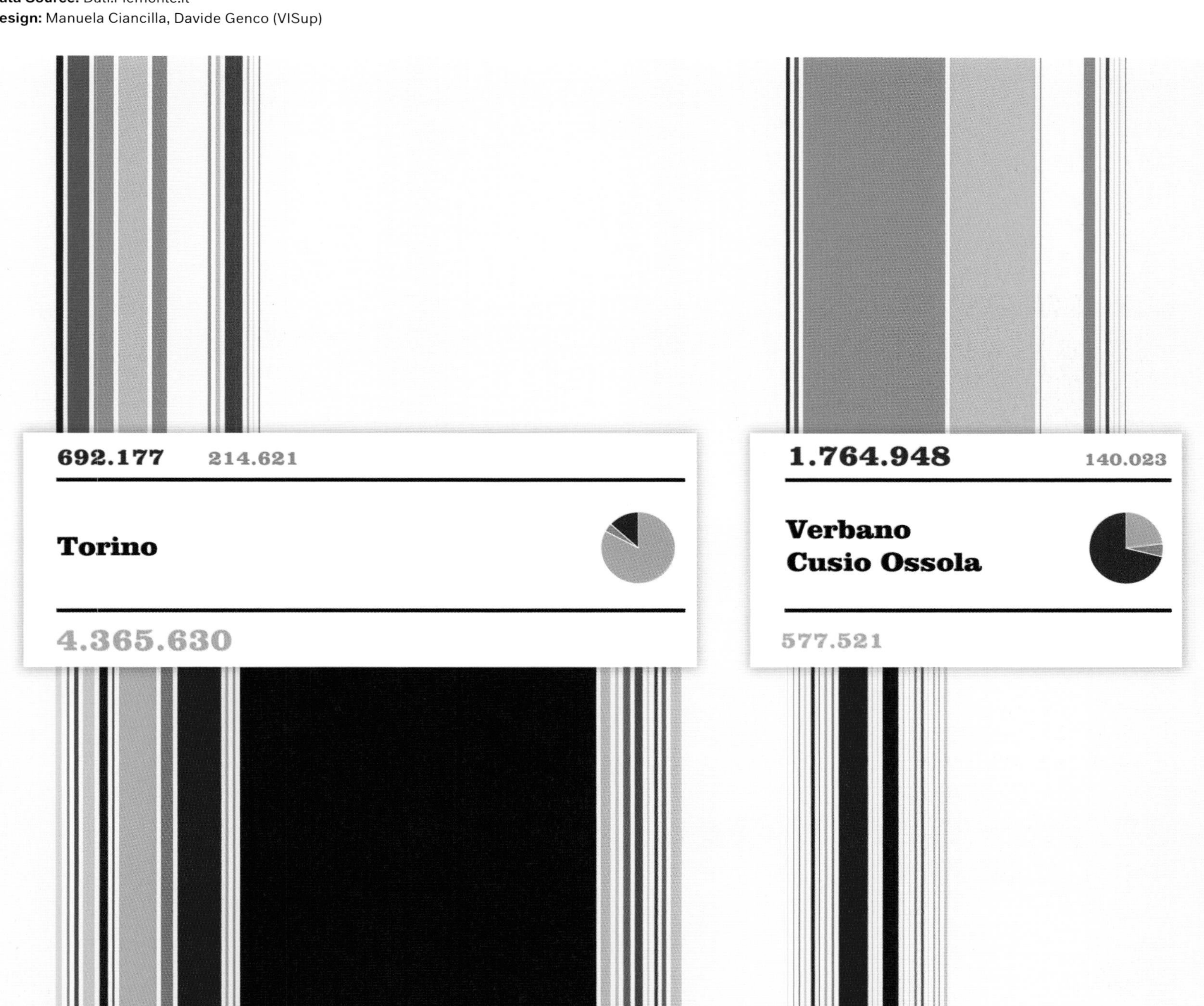

Poetry on the Road

Since 2002, Boris Müller has created the visual theme for an annual German poetry festival. Based on software, he visualises selected poems, using a new set of rules each year. The visual for 2008 lists poems in lines (right page). Words are sorted (left to right) and scaled hierarchically according to their frequency in the poem. Words appearing in several poems are connected by vertical lines.

Seit 2002 gestaltet Boris Müller das Plakat für das Bremer Literaturfestival „poetry on the road". Mithilfe von Software visualisiert er ausgewählte Gedichte, wobei er jedes Jahr andere Regeln der Visualisierung entwickelt. Die Grafik für 2008 gibt die Gedichte in Zeilen wieder (rechte Seite). Wörter werden sortiert (von links nach rechts) und hierarchisch skaliert je nach der Häufigkeit ihres Auftretens im Gedicht. Wörter, die in mehreren Gedichten vorkommen, sind durch Linien in der Vertikalen verbunden.

Depuis 2002, Boris Müller est l'auteur du thème visuel d'un festival annuel de poésie en Allemagne. À partir d'un logiciel, il crée des visualisations des poèmes sélectionnés en suivant chaque année des règles différentes. Le visuel pour l'édition 2008 répertorie les poèmes en lignes (page de droite). Les mots sont triés (de gauche à droite) et organisés de façon hiérarchique selon leur fréquence dans le poème. Les mots qui apparaissent dans plusieurs poèmes sont reliés par des lignes verticales.

Project Info: Poetry on the Road Literature Festival, series of visuals and posters, since 2002, Germany
Design: Boris Müller , Friederike Lambers, Florian Pfeffer, Matthias Woerle (one/one)
Awards: 100 beste Plakate 2002; TDC New York 2002: Certificate of Typographic Excellence

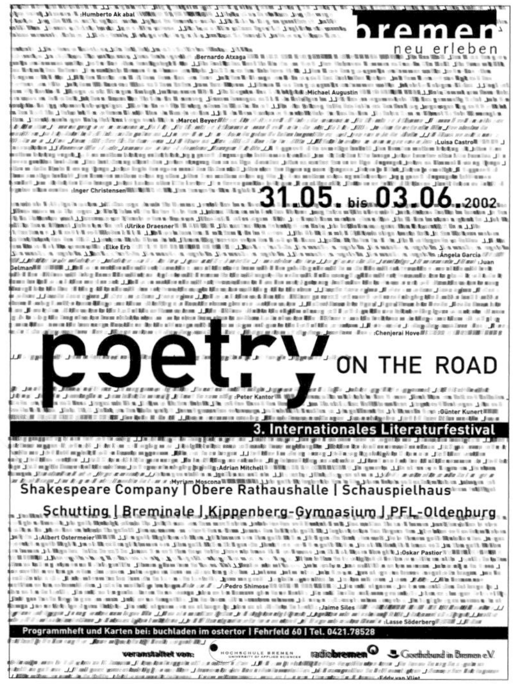

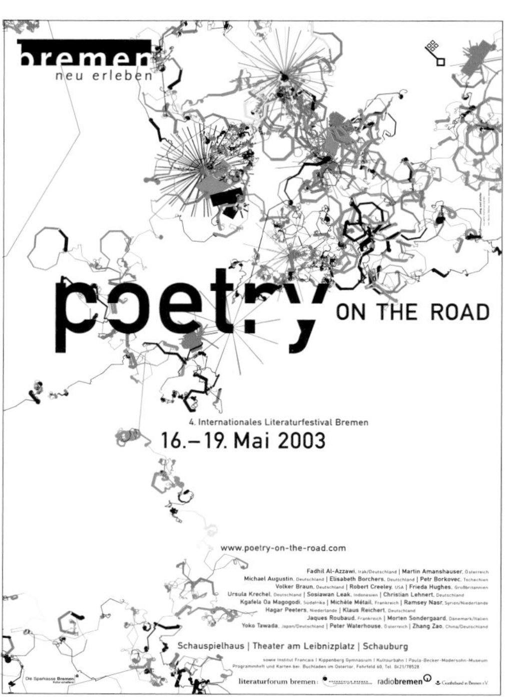

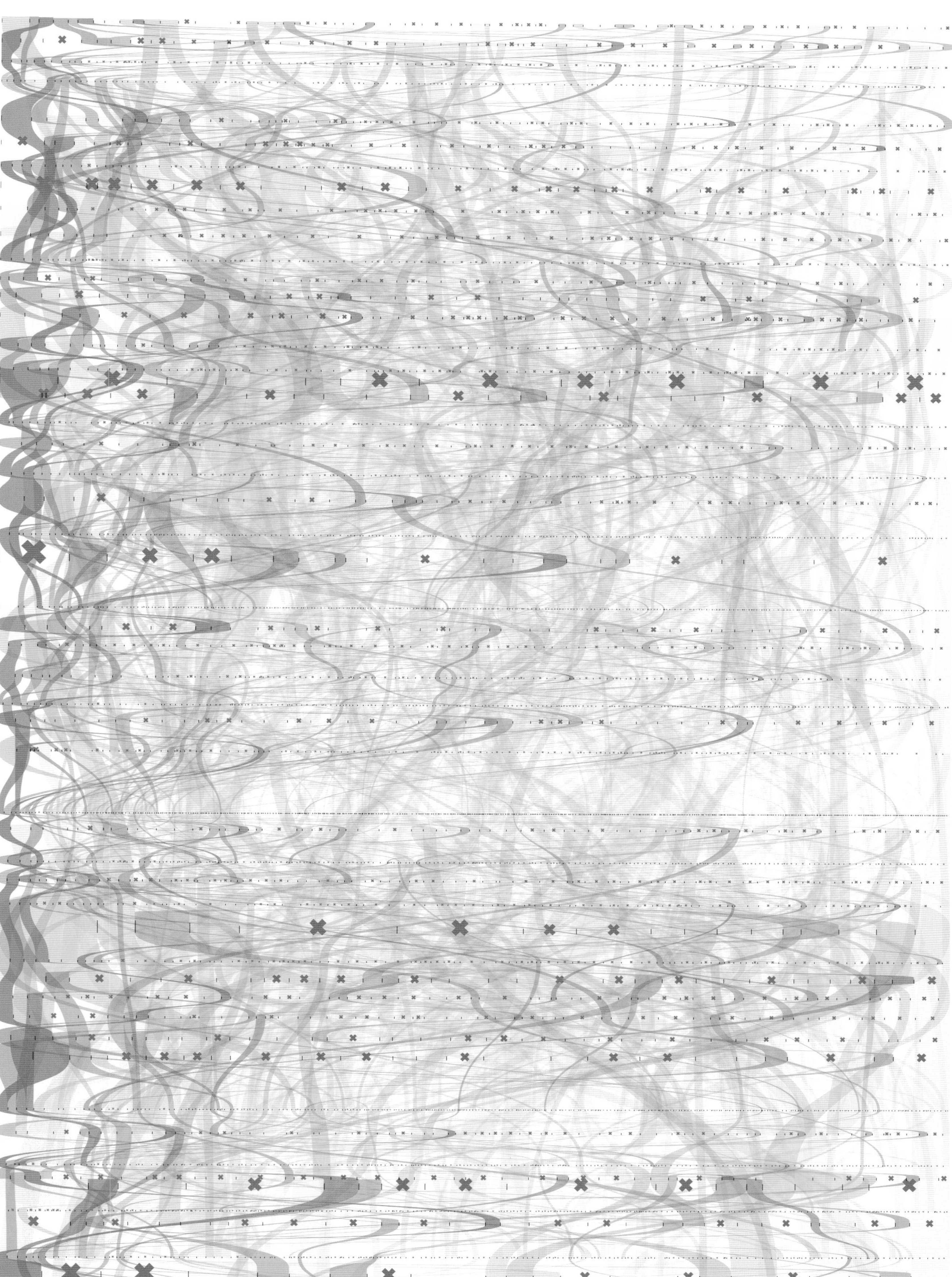

Political Climate

The US mid-term elections of November 2010 resulted in a landslide victory for Republicans. This graphic for *GOOD* magazine visualises which issues were discussed by the parties' candidates in the run-up to the elections. The websites of 29 Democratic and 29 Republican candidates were analysed for the number of times they mentioned the political issues, showing how consistent their messages were.

Political issues dominated by Republicans are shown in red, whereas Democrats' messages are given in blue. Clearly, the Republicans were better at speaking as a party and winning votes by focusing on healthcare and the national debt.

Die Zwischenwahlen in den USA im November 2010 bescherten den Republikanern einen erdrutschartigen Sieg. Diese Grafik für *GOOD* zeigt, welche Themen die Kandidaten der verschiedenen Parteien während des Wahlkampfs ansprachen. Dafür wurden die Websites von je 29 Kandidaten sowohl der Demokraten als auch der Republikaner daraufhin analysiert, wie häufig das entsprechende Thema erwähnt wurde. Die Grafik zeigt, inwieweit die politischen Themen auf beiden Seiten übereinstimmten.

Die politischen Fragen, bei denen die Republikaner dominierten, sind rot dargestellt, die eher demokratischen Themen sind blau. Den Republikanern gelang es deutlich besser, mit einer Stimme zu sprechen. Sie zogen die Wähler auf ihre Seite, indem sie sich auf das Gesundheitswesen und die Staatsverschuldung konzentrierten.

Les élections américaines de mi-mandat en novembre 2010 ont donné une victoire écrasante aux républicains. Ce graphique pour le magazine *GOOD* montre les sujets abordés par les candidats des partis pendant la période préélectorale. Les sites Web des 29 candidats démocrates et des 29 candidats républicains ont été analysés pour voir combien de fois ces sujets avaient été mentionnés et montrer ainsi la cohérence de leurs messages.

Les sujets politiques les plus abordés par les républicains sont montrés en rouge, ceux des démocrates en bleu. Il ressort clairement que les républicains ont su mieux s'exprimer en tant que parti et remporter des votes en donnant la priorité à la santé et à la dette nationale.

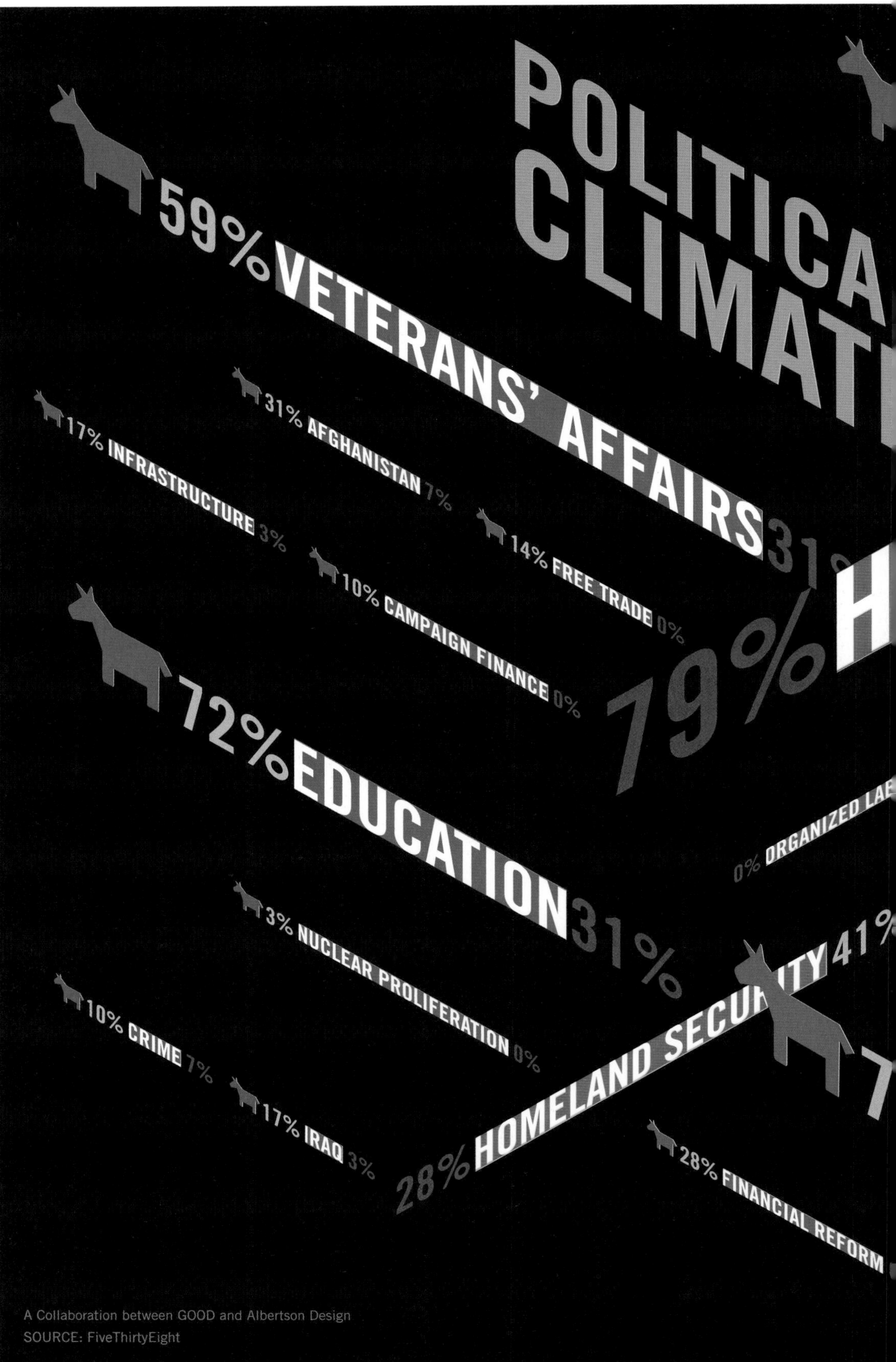

A Collaboration between GOOD and Albertson Design
SOURCE: FiveThirtyEight

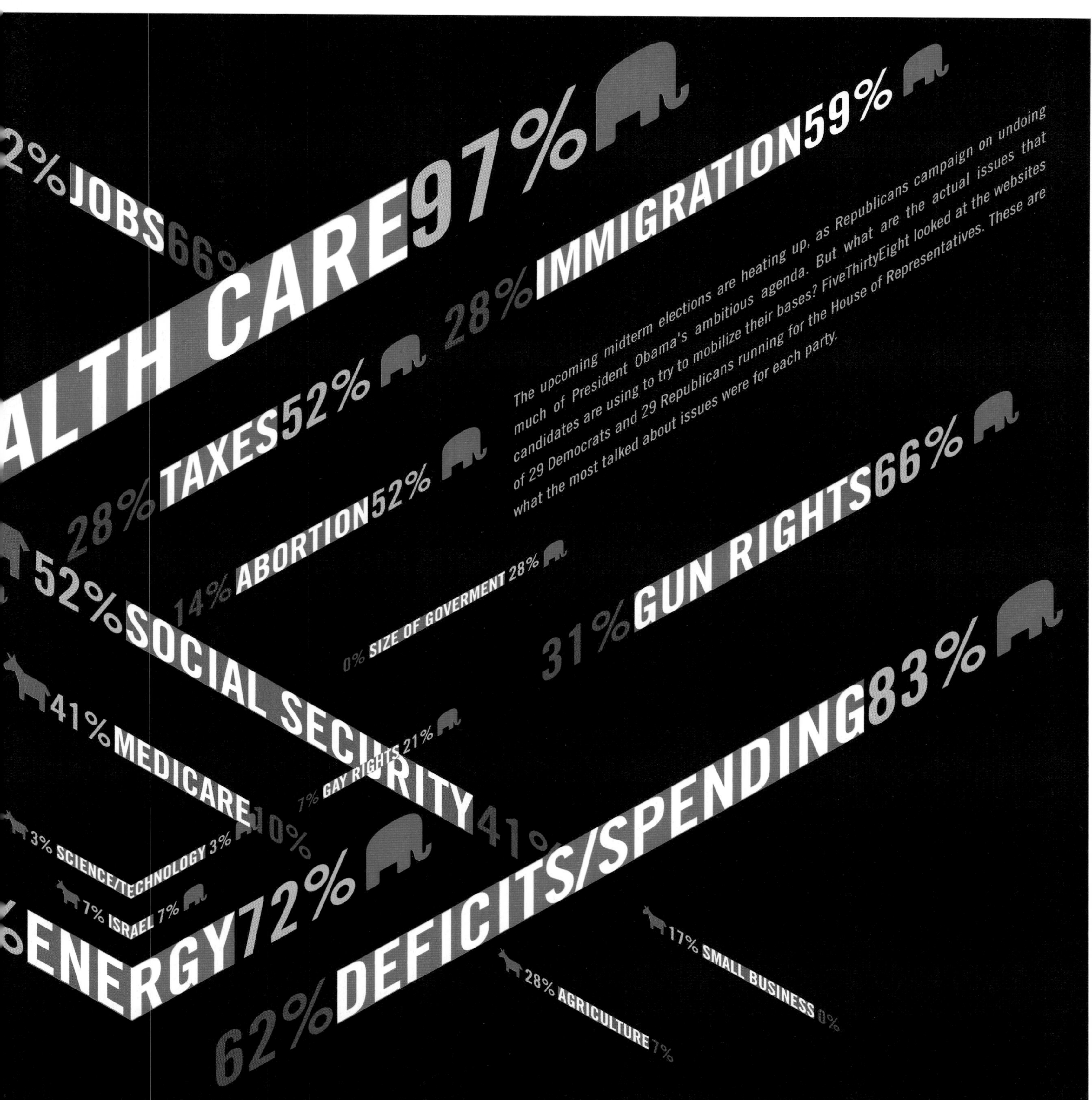
The upcoming midterm elections are heating up, as Republicans campaign on undoing much of President Obama's ambitious agenda. But what are the actual issues that candidates are using to try to mobilize their bases? FiveThirtyEight looked at the websites of 29 Democrats and 29 Republicans running for the House of Representatives. These are what the most talked about issues were for each party.
2% JOBS 66%
ALTH CARE 97%
28% IMMIGRATION 59%
28% TAXES 52%
14% ABORTION 52%
0% SIZE OF GOVERMENT 28%
31% GUN RIGHTS 66%
52% SOCIAL SECURITY 41%
41% MEDICARE 10%
7% GAY RIGHTS 21%
3% SCIENCE/TECHNOLOGY 3%
7% ISRAEL 7%
ENERGY 72%
62% DEFICITS/SPENDING 83%
17% SMALL BUSINESS 0%
28% AGRICULTURE 7%

Project Info: *GOOD*, website, 2010, USA
Data Source: *Five Thirty Eight* blog (*The New York Times*)
Design: David Albertson, Paul Torres (Albertson Design)

Satellites

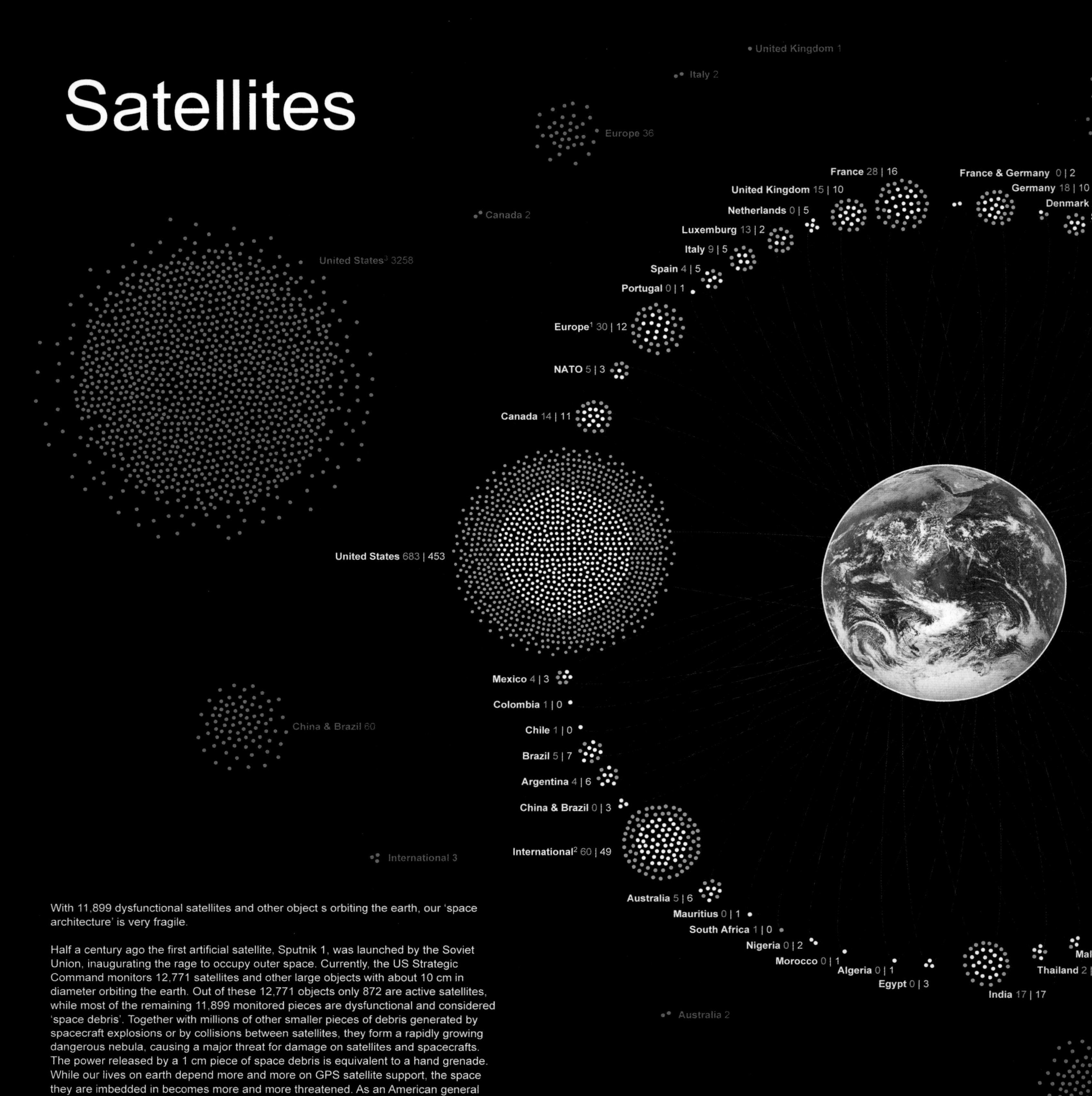

With 11,899 dysfunctional satellites and other object s orbiting the earth, our 'space architecture' is very fragile.

Half a century ago the first artificial satellite, Sputnik 1, was launched by the Soviet Union, inaugurating the rage to occupy outer space. Currently, the US Strategic Command monitors 12,771 satellites and other large objects with about 10 cm in diameter orbiting the earth. Out of these 12,771 objects only 872 are active satellites, while most of the remaining 11,899 monitored pieces are dysfunctional and considered 'space debris'. Together with millions of other smaller pieces of debris generated by spacecraft explosions or by collisions between satellites, they form a rapidly growing dangerous nebula, causing a major threat for damage on satellites and spacecrafts. The power released by a 1 cm piece of space debris is equivalent to a hand grenade. While our lives on earth depend more and more on GPS satellite support, the space they are imbedded in becomes more and more threatened. As an American general put it in The Economist in January this year: 'Our space architecture is very fragile.'

Text and Graphics Theo Deutinger

Project Info: "Space Architecture", *Mark*, magazine article, 2008, Netherlands
Data Source: The Satellite Encyclopedia; Union of Concerned Scientists: Satellite Database
Design: Theo Deutinger

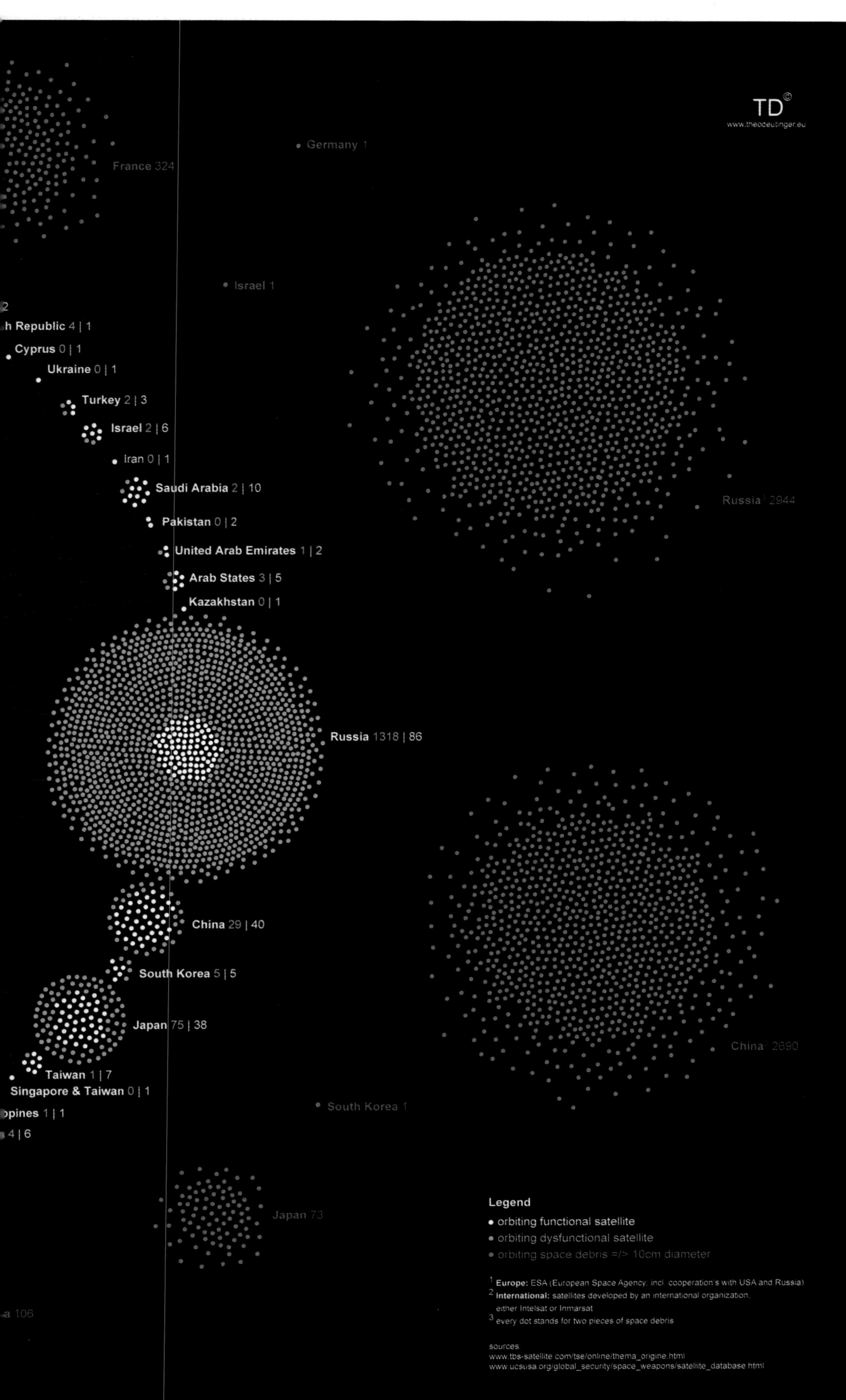

Satellites

Austrian architect Theo Deutinger, based in Rotterdam, uses visualisations as a tool for the analysis of social and environmental phenomena. In this piece, he creates a visual impression of how technological progress in satellite deployment produces increasing amounts of space debris.

Active and obsolete satellites are visualised as clouds of dots and collated to their nation of origin. The US and Russia can be quickly identified as the two major sources of space debris to date. Although the Earth sits at the centre of the graphic, the piece is not a map. Instead, it is a chart showing the distribution of quantities of space debris among different nations.

Der in Rotterdam ansässige österreichische Architekt Theo Deutinger nutzt Visualisierungen als Werkzeug, um soziale und ökologische Phänomene zu analysieren. Auf diesem Schaubild führt er vor Augen, wie der technische Fortschritt beim Einsatz von Satelliten zu mehr und mehr Weltraummüll führt.

Aktive und ausgediente Satelliten sind als Punktwolken dargestellt und nach Herkunftsland gruppiert. Die USA und Russland sind auf den ersten Blick als die zwei größten Verursacher von Weltraummüll zu identifizieren. Auch wenn die Erde im Mittelpunkt der Grafik steht, handelt es sich nicht um eine Karte, sondern um eine Aufstellung, die die Mengenverteilung von Weltraummüll nach einzelnen Staaten erläutert.

L'architecte autrichien Theo Deutinger, installé à Rotterdam, se sert des visualisations pour analyser les phénomènes sociaux et économiques. Dans cette œuvre, il montre comment les avancées technologiques en matière de déploiement de satellites entraînent des quantités accrues de débris spatiaux.

Les satellites en fonctionnement ou obsolètes sont représentés sous forme de nuages de points et regroupés par nation d'origine. Les États-Unis et la Russie apparaissent clairement comme les deux principales sources de débris spatiaux à ce jour. Même si la Terre se trouve au centre du graphique, l'œuvre ne se veut pas une carte. Il s'agit plutôt d'un graphique montrant la répartition des volumes de débris spatiaux entre les différentes nations.

Self Economy

Paris-based conceptual artist group Bureau d'études uses complex diagrams as a tool to conduct and visualise social and economical analyses. This piece is a study on how an individual's identity is formed. The centre is taken up by individual decisions and perceptions in the mind, whilst the second ring lists various perspectives which can be used to define the individual: economical, psychological, biological etc.

The outermost white sphere is occupied by the "Other", beings and forces which don't relate to the concept of the self. Positioning oneself within society thus becomes a complex game of decision-taking and freedom of choice.

Die in Paris ansässigen Konzeptkünstler Bureau d'études visualisieren soziale und ökonomische Analysen mithilfe komplexer Diagramme. Diese Grafik setzt eine Studie zu der Frage um, wie sich die Identität eines Menschen herausbildet. In ihrem Mittelpunkt sind individuelle Entscheidungen und Auffassungen angesiedelt. Der Ring, der dieses Zentrum umgibt, nennt verschiedene Ansätze zur Definition des Individuums: ökonomische, psychologische, biologische etc.

Das weiße Feld, das die Grafik am äußersten Rand umgibt, steht für das „Andere", für Wesen und Kräfte, die nicht mit dem Konzept des Selbst in Beziehung stehen. Welchen Platz man in der Gesellschaft einnimmt, wird demnach zu einem komplexen Zusammenspiel von Entscheidungsfindung und Wahlfreiheit.

Le collectif d'artistes parisien Bureau d'études se sert de diagrammes complexes pour représenter visuellement des analyses sociales et économiques. Cette œuvre étudie la formation de l'identité d'un individu. Au centre se trouvent les décisions et les perceptions individuelles que chacun a en tête, alors que le second anneau indique les différents points de vue pouvant servir à définir l'individu: économique, psychologique, biologique, etc.

La sphère blanche extérieure est occupée par « l'autre », à savoir les êtres et les forces qui ne sont pas liés au concept du soi. Se positionner dans la société est donc un jeu complexe de prise de décisions et de liberté de choix.

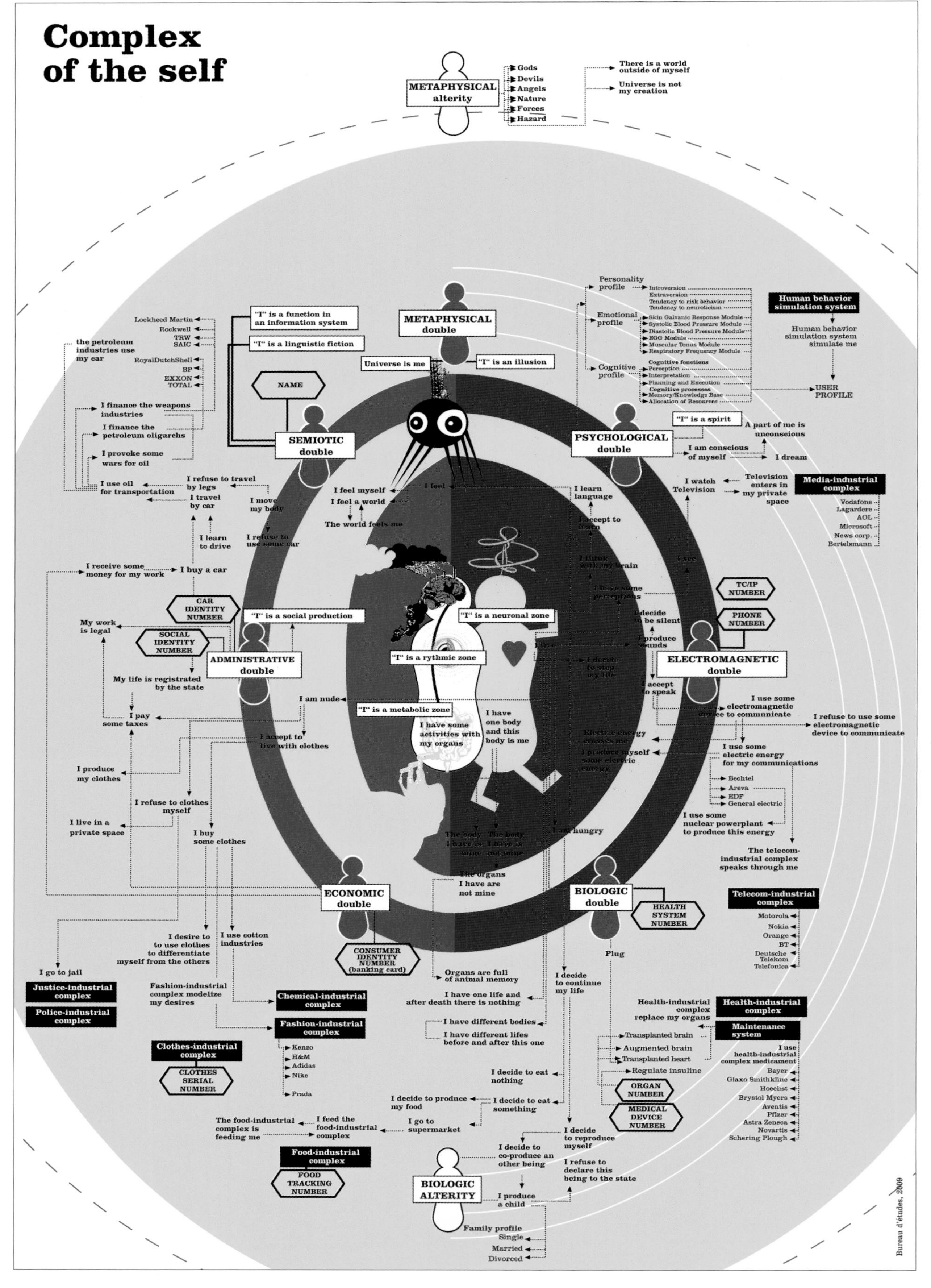

Project Info: Poster, 2009, France
Artists: Bureau d'études

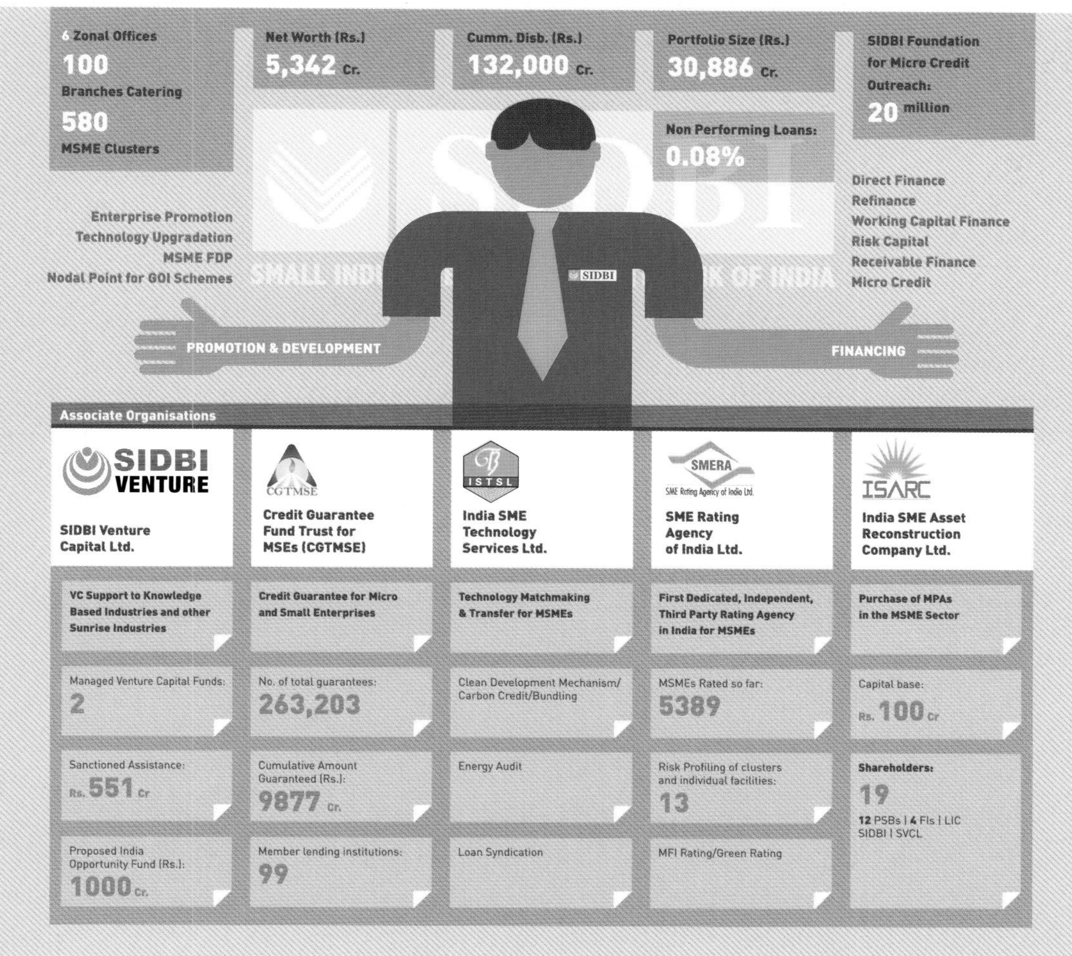

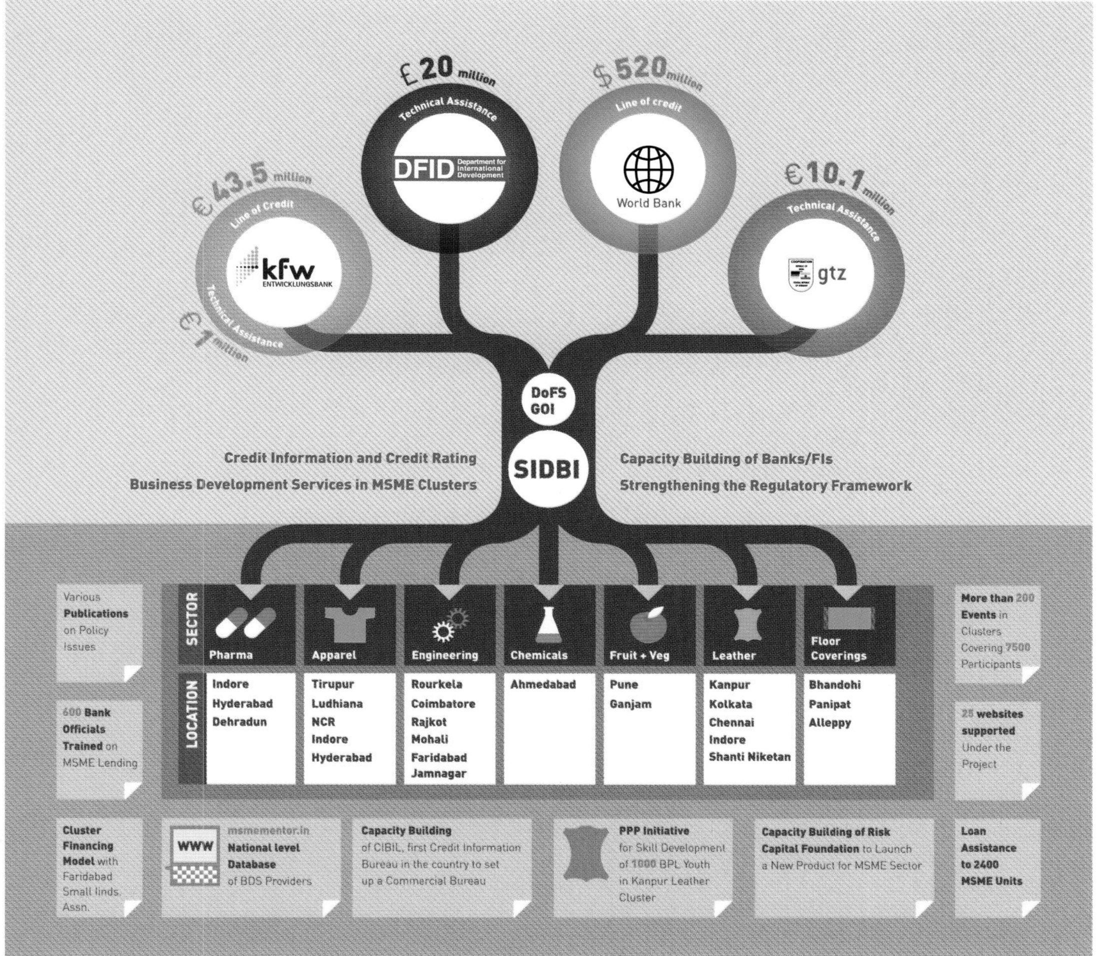

Small Industries Development

In this series of posters, Infonauts studio from New Delhi explains the services and structure of the "Small Industries Development Bank of India" (SIDBI). MSME stands for "micro, small and medium enterprises". The first organisational chart features a welcoming clerk in the middle. Along the top, some key figures about SIDBI are given, while the lower part shows partner institutions with their respective key data.

The second organisational chart explains the services of SIDBI in channelling foreign development funds to receivers in the various branches of the Indian economy.

Mit dieser Serie erklärt das Studio Infonauts aus Neu-Delhi das Dienstleistungsangebot und die Struktur der „Small Industries Development Bank of India" (SIDBI). MSME steht für „micro, small and medium enterprises" (sehr kleine, kleine und mittelgroße Unternehmen). Auf dem ersten Organigramm wird der Betrachter von der zentral positionierten Figur eines Mitarbeiters mit ausgebreiteten Armen willkommen geheißen. Oben stehen einige Eckdaten über die SIDBI, darunter sind die Partnerinstitutionen mit ihren jeweiligen Eckdaten aufgelistet.

Das zweite Organigramm erläutert die Aufgaben der SIDBI bei der Verteilung ausländischer Entwicklungshilfegelder an Empfänger in verschiedenen Branchen der indischen Wirtschaft.

Dans cette série d'affiches, le studio Infonauts de New Delhi présente les services et la structure de la « Small Industries Development Bank of India » (SIDBI). MSME correspond à « micro, small and medium enterprises » (micro, petites et moyennes entreprises). Le premier diagramme structurel montre un employé au centre, avec des chiffres clés sur la SIDBI dans la partie supérieure et les institutions partenaires et leurs données clés au bas.

Le second diagramme montre les services de la SIDBI pour envoyer les fonds de développement étrangers aux destinataires des divers secteurs de l'économie indienne.

Project Info: Series of posters, Small Industries Development Bank of India, 2010, India
Design: Infonauts

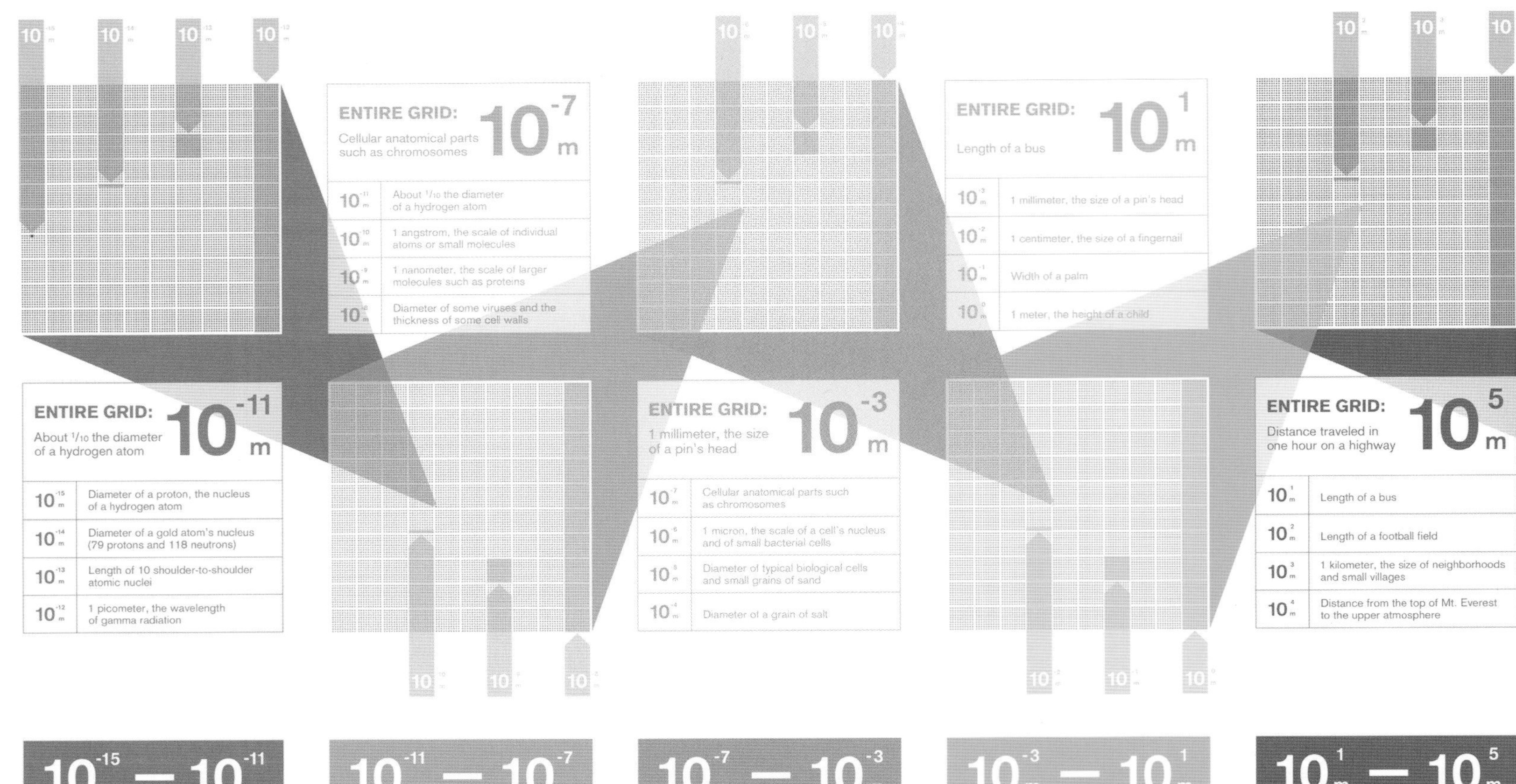

Project Info: *Super Vision: A New View of Nature*, book, Harry N. Abrams, 2003, USA
Design: Agnieszka Gasparska (Kiss Me I'm Polish)
Creative Direction: Michael Walsh, Harry N. Abrams
Book Design: Helene Silverman

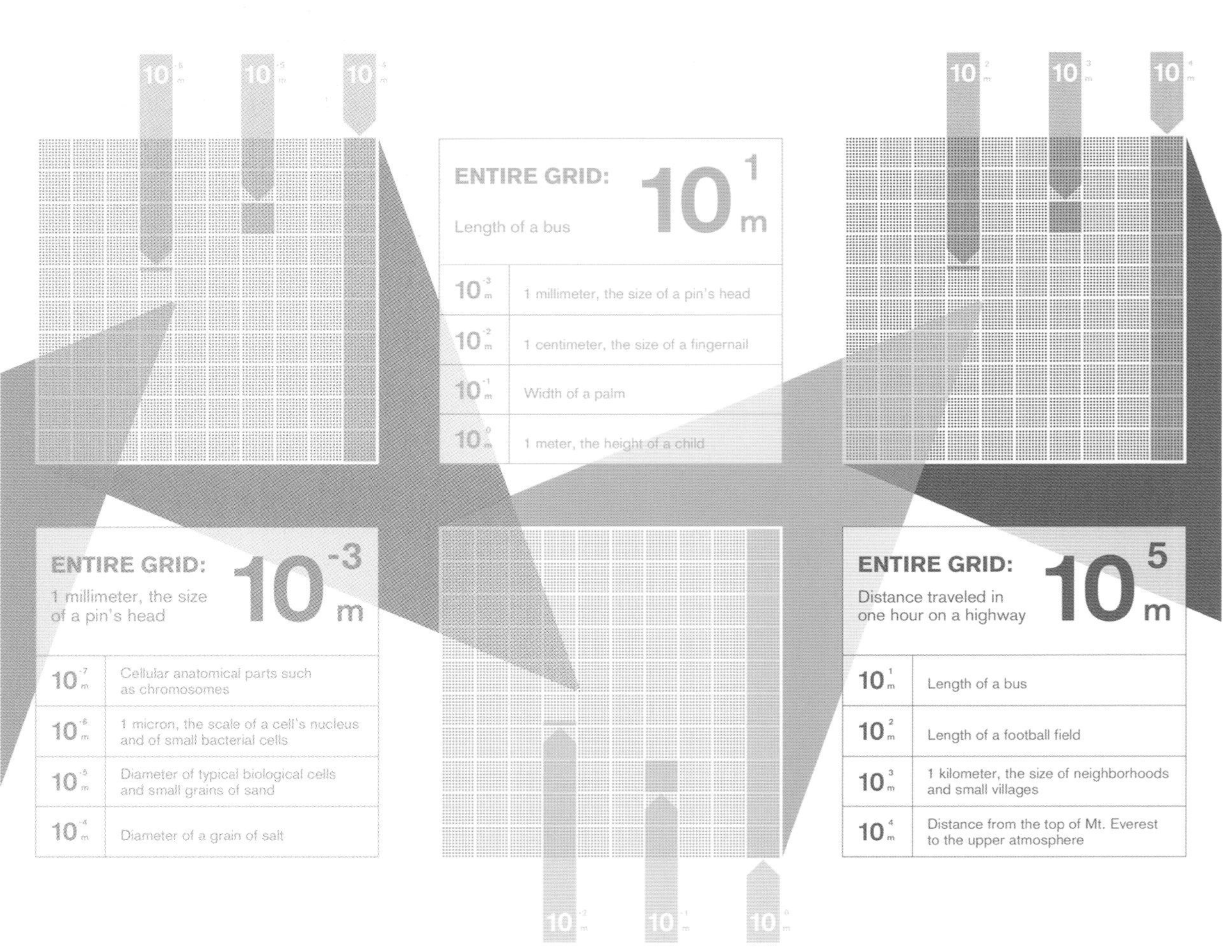

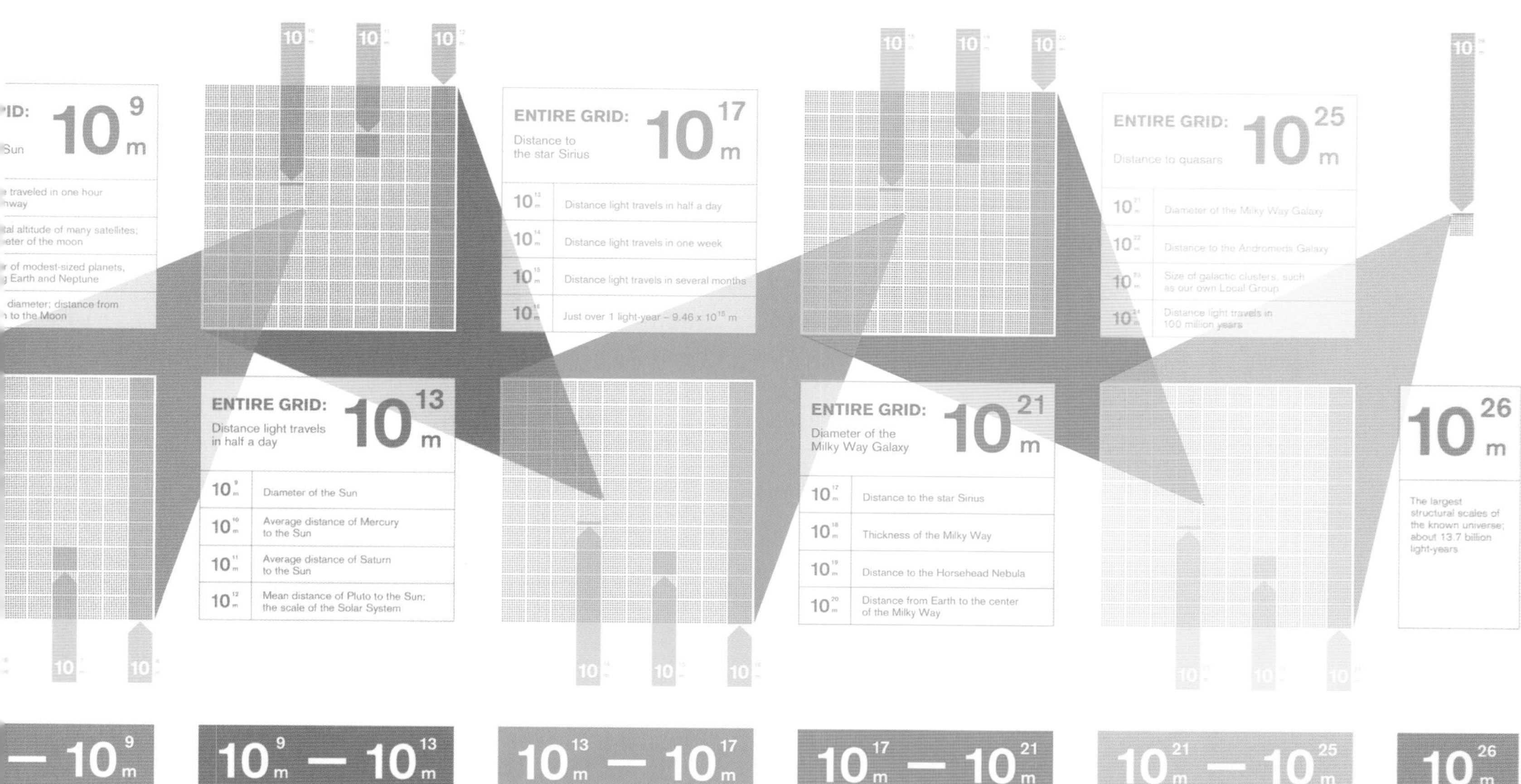

Super Vision Chart

This chart was designed for the book *Super Vision: A New View of Nature* in 2003. The book shows scientific images that span the world of phenomena from subatomic particles to the biggest structures in the universe and explains the technology necessary to perceive and represent these structures.

The chart helps illustrate the relative sizes of the objects documented in the book. Size dimensions are represented as sequential powers of 10 m, shown in order from smallest to largest, broken down into colour-coded groups. For each group of powers, a quadratic grid indicates the full scale of the group's biggest size in order to demonstrate the neighbouring smaller sizes.

Diese Grafik wurde 2003 für das Buch *Super Vision: A New View of Nature* entworfen. Das Buch enthält naturwissenschaftliche Bilder von Phänomenen, die von subatomaren Teilchen bis zu den größten Strukturen im Universum reichen, und erklärt die Technologien, die erforderlich sind, um diese Strukturen sichtbar zu machen und darzustellen.

Das Diagramm soll die relative Größe der im Buch vorgestellten Gebilde veranschaulichen. Längenabmessungen werden auf Basis von Metern in Zehnerpotenzen angegeben, vom Kleinsten bis zum Größten, unterteilt in farbcodierte Gruppen. Bei jeder Gruppe von Potenzen repräsentiert ein quadratisches Gitter die größte Länge, als Vergleichsmaßstab für die benachbarten kleineren Größen innerhalb jeder Gruppe.

Ce diagramme a été conçu pour l'ouvrage *Super Vision: A New View of Nature* en 2003. Le livre rassemble des images scientifiques de phénomènes allant des particules subatomiques aux plus grandes structures de l'univers, et explique la technologie nécessaire pour identifier et représenter ces structures.

Le diagramme permet de comprendre la taille relative des objets présentés dans l'ouvrage. Les dimensions sont montrées sous forme de puissances séquentielles de 10 m, de la plus petite à la plus grande, et divisées en groupes de différentes couleurs. Pour chaque groupe de puissances, une grille quadratique indique l'échelle de la taille la plus grande du groupe afin de comparer avec les tailles plus petites à proximité.

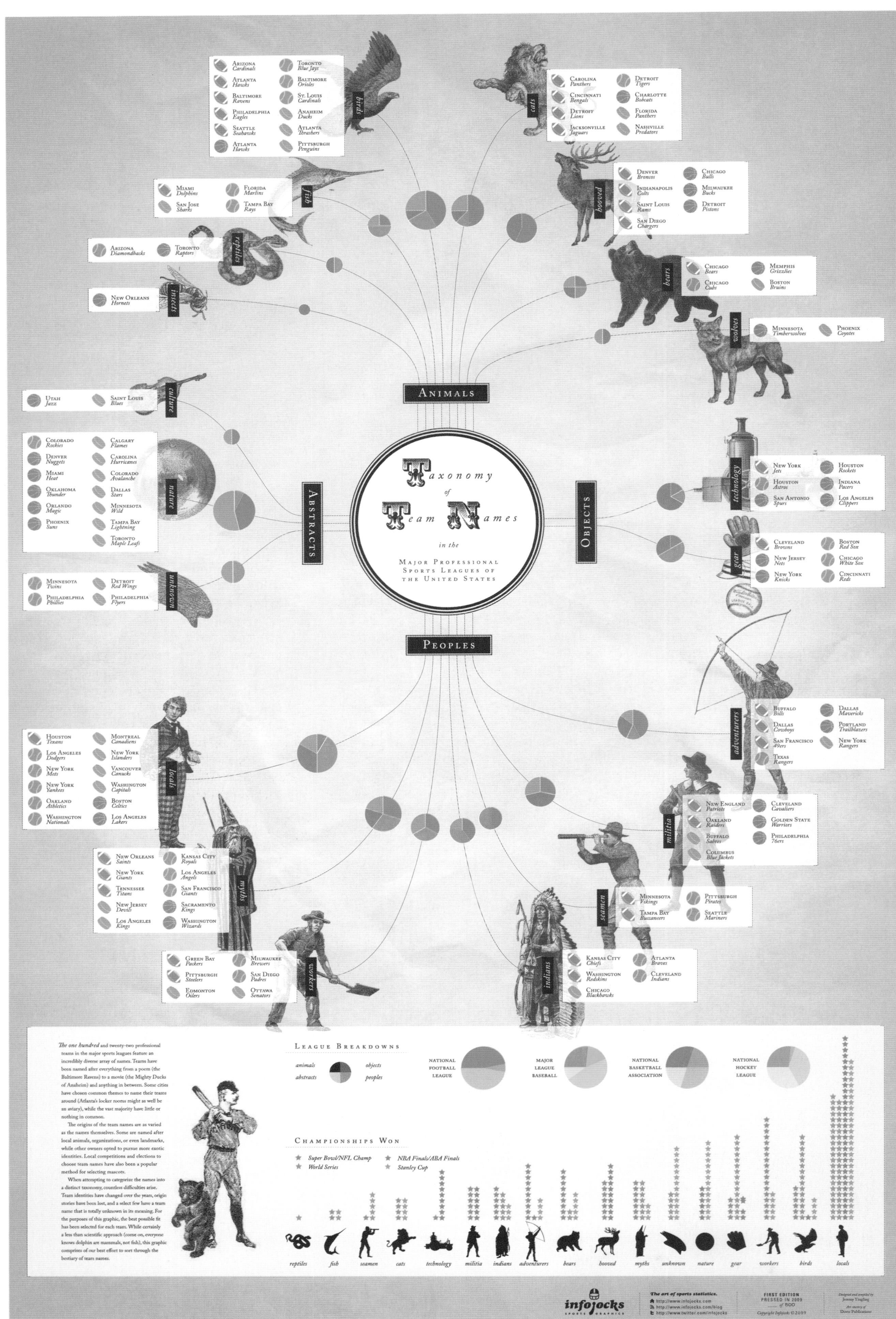
Taxonomy of Team Names
in the
Major Professional Sports Leagues of the United States
Animals
Abstracts
Objects
Peoples
birds
Arizona Cardinals
Atlanta Hawks
Baltimore Ravens
Philadelphia Eagles
Seattle Seahawks
Atlanta Hawks
Toronto Blue Jays
Baltimore Orioles
St. Louis Cardinals
Anaheim Ducks
Atlanta Thrashers
Pittsburgh Penguins
cats
Carolina Panthers
Cincinnati Bengals
Detroit Lions
Jacksonville Jaguars
Detroit Tigers
Charlotte Bobcats
Florida Panthers
Nashville Predators
fish
Miami Dolphins
San Jose Sharks
Florida Marlins
Tampa Bay Rays
hooved
Denver Broncos
Indianapolis Colts
Saint Louis Rams
San Diego Chargers
Chicago Bulls
Milwaukee Bucks
Detroit Pistons
reptiles
Arizona Diamondbacks
Toronto Raptors
bears
Chicago Bears
Chicago Cubs
Memphis Grizzlies
Boston Bruins
insects
New Orleans Hornets
wolves
Minnesota Timberwolves
Phoenix Coyotes
culture
Utah Jazz
Saint Louis Blues
nature
Colorado Rockies
Denver Nuggets
Miami Heat
Oklahoma Thunder
Orlando Magic
Phoenix Suns
Calgary Flames
Carolina Hurricanes
Colorado Avalanche
Dallas Stars
Minnesota Wild
Tampa Bay Lightning
Toronto Maple Leafs
unknown
Minnesota Twins
Philadelphia Phillies
Detroit Red Wings
Philadelphia Flyers
technology
New York Jets
Houston Astros
San Antonio Spurs
Houston Rockets
Indiana Pacers
Los Angeles Clippers
gear
Cleveland Browns
New Jersey Nets
New York Knicks
Boston Red Sox
Chicago White Sox
Cincinnati Reds
adventurers
Buffalo Bills
Dallas Cowboys
San Francisco 49ers
Texas Rangers
Dallas Mavericks
Portland Trailblazers
New York Rangers
locals
Houston Texans
Los Angeles Dodgers
New York Mets
New York Yankees
Oakland Athletics
Washington Nationals
Montreal Canadiens
New York Islanders
Vancouver Canucks
Washington Capitals
Boston Celtics
Los Angeles Lakers
militia
New England Patriots
Oakland Raiders
Buffalo Sabres
Columbus Blue Jackets
Cleveland Cavaliers
Golden State Warriors
Philadelphia 76ers
myths
New Orleans Saints
New York Giants
Tennessee Titans
New Jersey Devils
Los Angeles Kings
Kansas City Royals
Los Angeles Angels
San Francisco Giants
Sacramento Kings
Washington Wizards
seamen
Minnesota Vikings
Tampa Bay Buccaneers
Pittsburgh Pirates
Seattle Mariners
workers
Green Bay Packers
Pittsburgh Steelers
Edmonton Oilers
Milwaukee Brewers
San Diego Padres
Ottawa Senators
indians
Kansas City Chiefs
Washington Redskins
Chicago Blackhawks
Atlanta Braves
Cleveland Indians
The one hundred and twenty-two professional teams in the major sports leagues feature an incredibly diverse array of names. Teams have been named after everything from a poem (the Baltimore Ravens) to a movie (the Mighty Ducks of Anaheim) and anything in between. Some cities have chosen common themes to name their teams around (Atlanta's locker rooms might as well be an aviary), while the vast majority have little or nothing in common.
The origins of the team names are as varied as the names themselves. Some are named after local animals, organizations, or even landmarks, while other owners opted to pursue more exotic identities. Local competitions and elections to choose team names have also been a popular method for selecting mascots.
When attempting to categorize the names into a distinct taxonomy, countless difficulties arise. Team identities have changed over the years, origin stories have been lost, and a select few have a team name that is totally unknown in its meaning. For the purposes of this graphic, the best possible fit has been selected for each team. While certainly a less than scientific approach (come on, everyone knows dolphin are mammals, not fish), this graphic comprises of our best effort to sort through the bestiary of team names.
League Breakdowns
animals
abstracts
objects
peoples
National Football League
Major League Baseball
National Basketball Association
National Hockey League
Championships Won
Super Bowl/NFL Champ
World Series
NBA Finals/ABA Finals
Stanley Cup
reptiles
fish
seamen
cats
technology
militia
indians
adventurers
bears
hooved
myths
unknown
nature
gear
workers
birds
locals
infojocks
sports graphics
The art of sports statistics.
http://www.infojocks.com
http://www.infojocks.com/blog
http://www.twitter.com/infojocks
First Edition
Pressed in 2009
of 500
Copyright Infojocks ©2009

Taxonomy of Team Names

This poster classifies the team names of 122 sports teams in the major US professional leagues. Even though it forms a taxonomy it is not visualised as a tree. Instead, the four types are arranged in four directions, with the sub-types forming a halo around the centre. Each sub-type is represented by a character recalling 19th-century book illustrations. Teams are listed by origin and name.

Colours and icons refer to the sport being illustrated: football, baseball, basketball and hockey. In the lower part, sub-types are broken down by "success". The pie charts show the distribution of types among the team names of each individual league. The bar chart shows how many championships were won according to sub-types.

Dieses Plakat klassifiziert die Namen von 122 Sportmannschaften in den großen professionellen Sportligen der USA. Obwohl es sich um eine Taxonomie handelt, ist sie nicht als Baum dargestellt. Vielmehr sind die vier Arten von Namensgebern nach den vier Himmelsrichtungen angeordnet, sodass die Unterarten eine Gloriole um das Zentrum bilden. Jede Unterart wird durch eine ausgeschmückte Illustration im Stil des 19. Jahrhunderts symbolisiert. Die Mannschaften werden mit ihrem Heimatort und ihrem Namen angeführt.

Farben und Symbole verweisen auf die jeweilige Sportart: Football, Baseball, Basketball und Hockey. Im unteren Teil sind die Namensgeber nach „Erfolg" angeordnet. Die Tortengrafiken zeigen die Verteilung der Arten unter den Mannschaften jeder Liga. Das Säulendiagramm veranschaulicht, wie viele Meisterschaften für jede Unterart gewonnen wurden.

Cette affiche classe les noms de 122 équipes sportives appartenant aux principales ligues professionnelles américaines. Bien que ce classement soit une taxonomie, il ne s'agit pas d'une arborescence. Les quatre types sont en effet organisés dans quatre directions, les sous-types formant un halo autour du centre. Chaque sous-type est symbolisé par un personnage rappelant les illustrations des ouvrages du XIXe siècle. Les équipes sont répertoriées par origine et par nom.

Les couleurs et les icônes renvoient au sport illustré : football, baseball, basketball et hockey. Dans la partie inférieure, les sous-types sont présentés par « victoires ». Les camemberts montrent la répartition des types entre les noms des équipes de chaque ligue. Le diagramme à barres montre le nombre de championnats remportés en fonction des sous-types.

Project Info: Poster, 2009, USA
Design: Jeremy Yingling (Infojocks Sports Graphics)

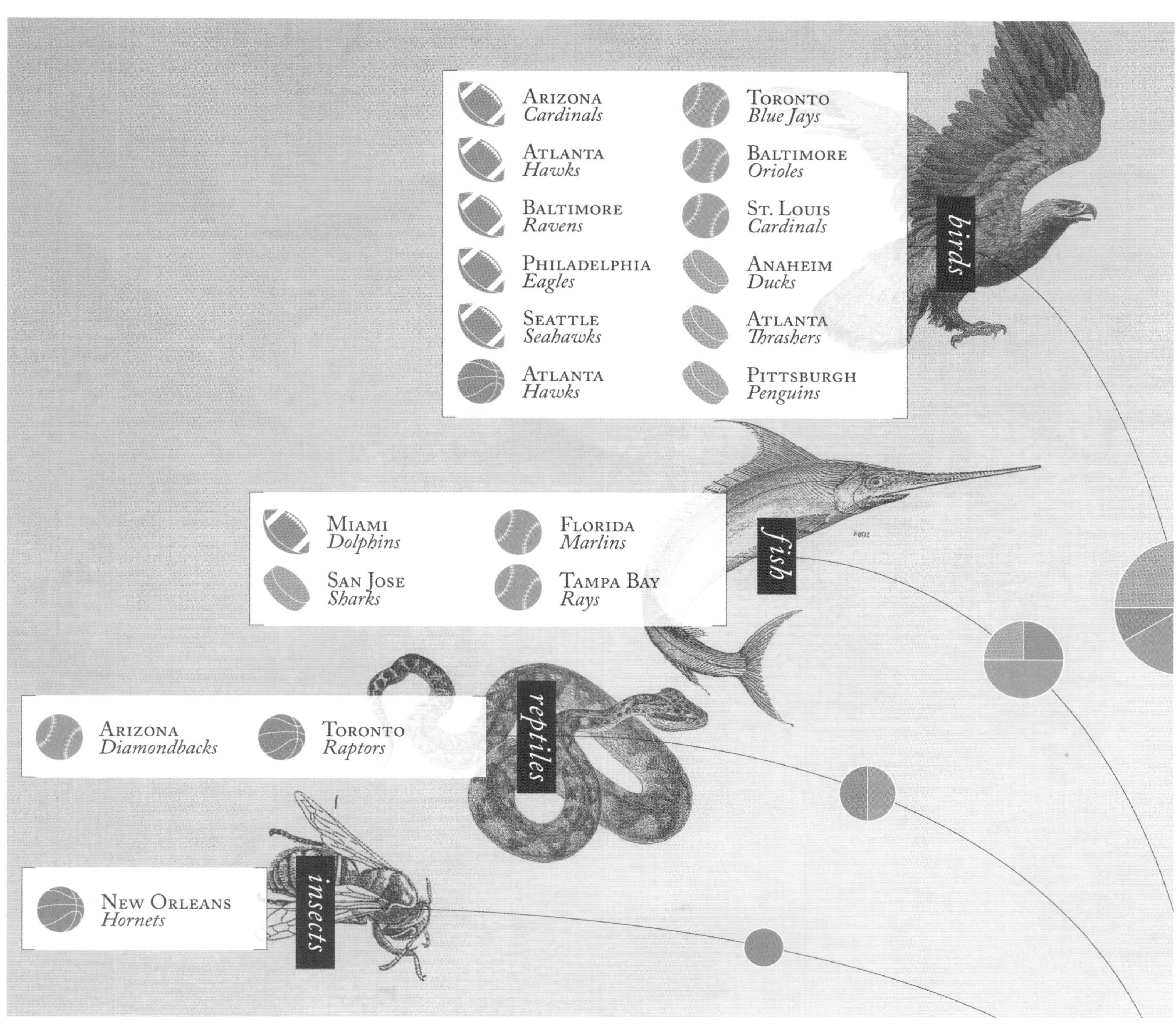

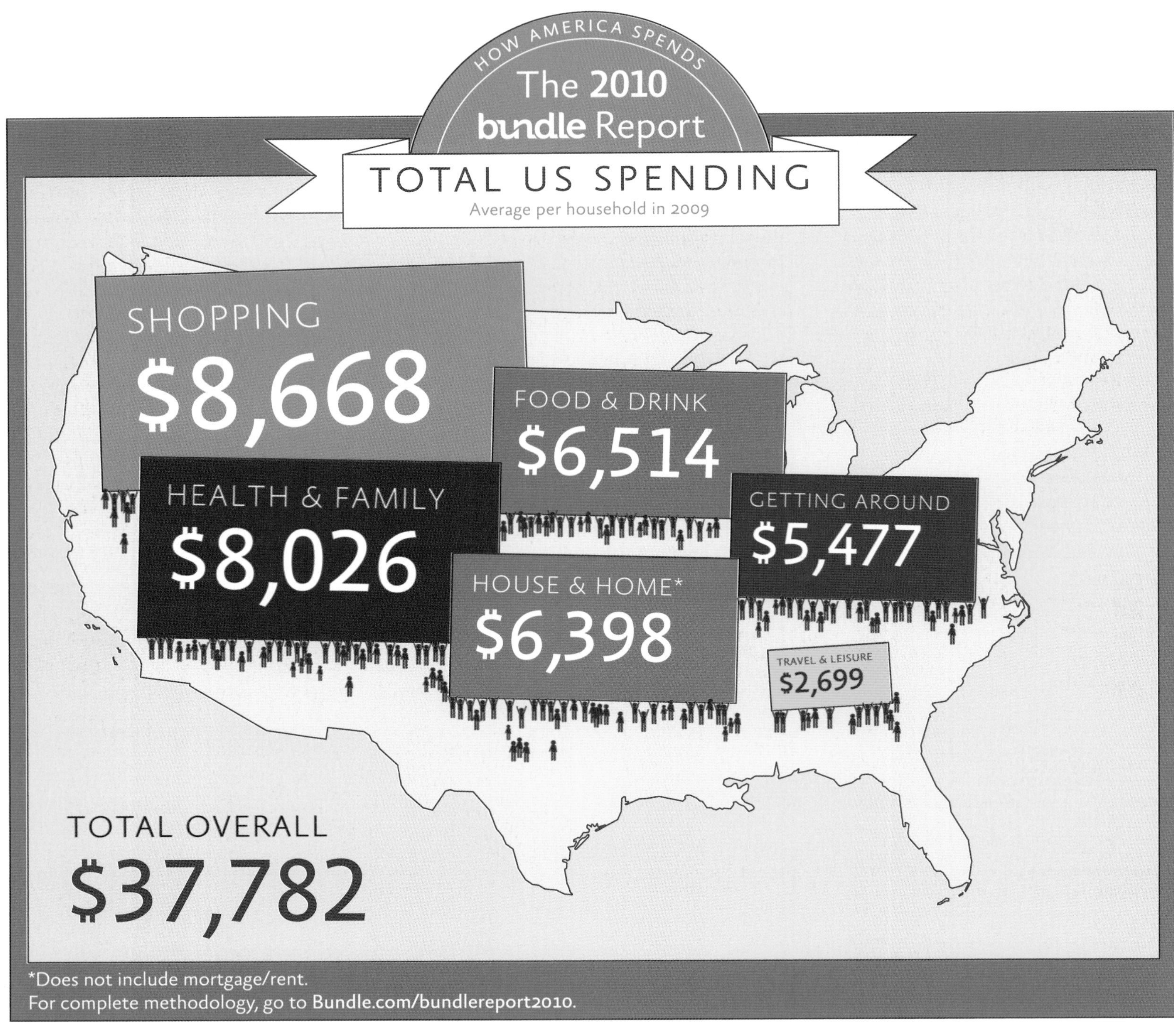

The 2010 Bundle Report

Bundle.com offers an interactive tool which allows people to control their private money flows. The website collaborated with Stefanie Posavec to create a report about private spending in the US in 2009.

Private expenses are broken down into five different graphics to make values comparable: by age, type of household, by US state and by city, whilst a US map lists the major expenses in private spending and gives average national figures.

Bundle.com bietet ein interaktives Tool an, mit dessen Hilfe die Nutzer ihre persönlichen Ausgaben kontrollieren können. In Zusammenarbeit mit Stefanie Posavec gestaltete das Unternehmen einen Bericht über die Ausgaben von Privathaushalten in den USA 2009.

Die privaten Ausgaben sind in fünf Grafiken aufgeschlüsselt, um die Summen vergleichbar zu machen: nach Alter, Haushaltstyp, US-Bundesstaat und Stadt. Die USA-Karte listet Durchschnittswerte für größere Posten bei den Haushaltsausgaben auf.

Bundle.com offre un outil interactif qui permet aux gens de contrôler leurs flux d'argent. Le site Web a collaboré avec Stefanie Posavec pour générer un rapport pour les dépenses privées aux États-Unis en 2009.

Les dépenses privées sont divisées en cinq graphiques pour permettre la comparaison des valeurs : par âge, par type de foyer, par État et par ville des États-Unis, tandis qu'une carte du pays répertorie les principales dépenses privées et donne les moyennes nationales.

Project Info: Website, Bundle, 2010, USA
Design: Stefanie Posavec

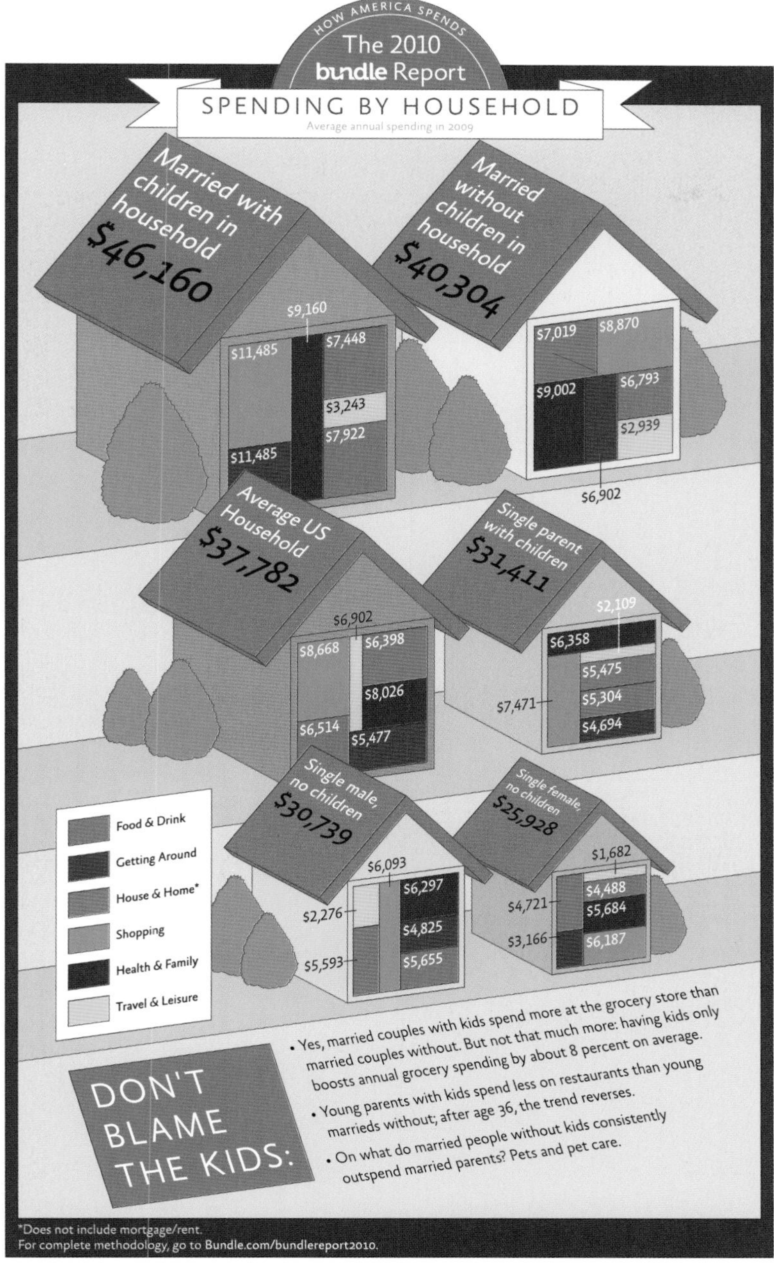

HOW AMERICA SPENDS
The 2010 bundle Report
SPENDING BY HOUSEHOLD
Average annual spending in 2009
Married with children in household $46,160
Married without children in household $40,304
$9,160
$11,485
$7,448
$3,243
$7,922
$11,485
$7,019
$8,870
$9,002
$6,793
$2,939
$6,902
Average US Household $37,782
Single parent with children $31,411
$6,902
$8,668
$6,398
$8,026
$6,514
$5,477
$2,109
$6,358
$5,475
$7,471
$5,304
$4,694
Single male, no children $30,739
Single female, no children $25,928
$6,093
$6,297
$2,276
$4,825
$5,593
$5,655
$1,682
$4,488
$4,721
$5,684
$3,166
$6,187
Food & Drink
Getting Around
House & Home*
Shopping
Health & Family
Travel & Leisure
DON'T BLAME THE KIDS:
• Yes, married couples with kids spend more at the grocery store than married couples without. But not that much more: having kids only boosts annual grocery spending by about 8 percent on average.
• Young parents with kids spend less on restaurants than young marrieds without; after age 36, the trend reverses.
• On what do married people without kids consistently outspend married parents? Pets and pet care.
*Does not include mortgage/rent.
For complete methodology, go to Bundle.com/bundlereport2010.

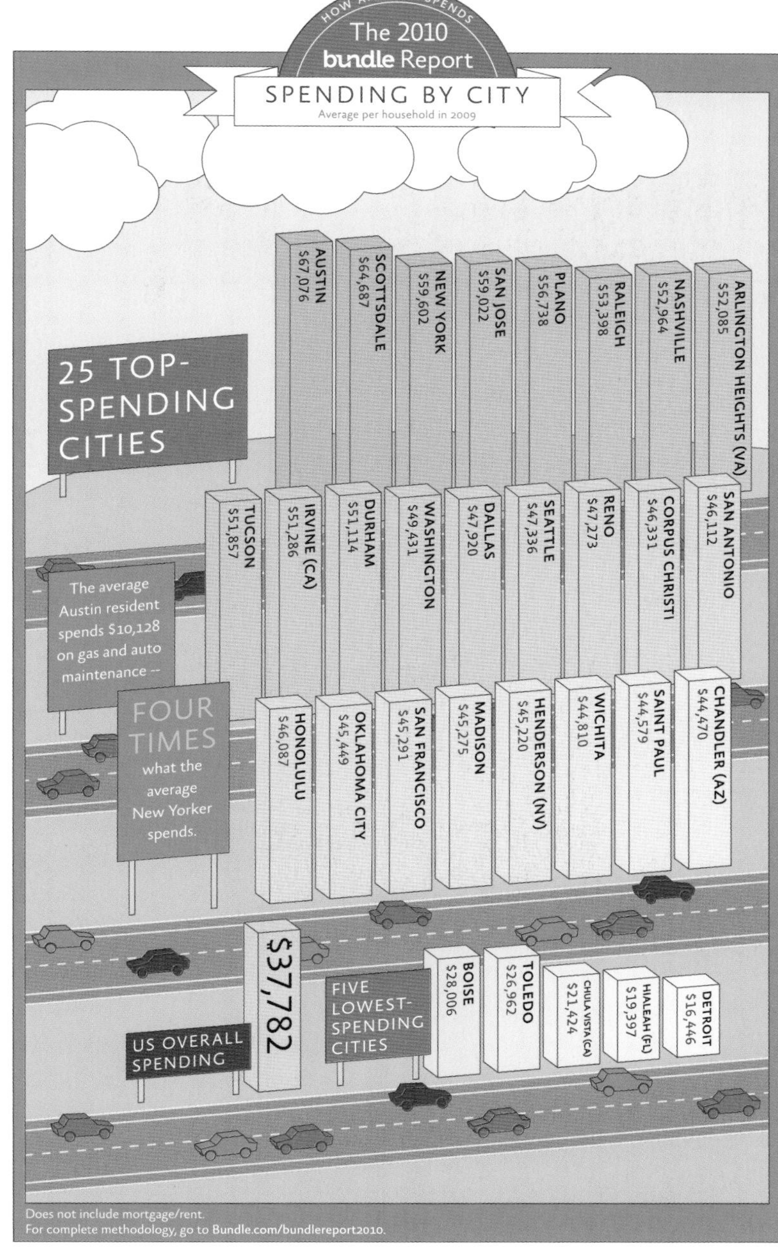

HOW AMERICA SPENDS
The 2010 bundle Report
SPENDING BY CITY
Average per household in 2009
25 TOP-SPENDING CITIES
AUSTIN $67,076
SCOTTSDALE $64,687
NEW YORK $59,602
SAN JOSE $59,022
PLANO $56,738
RALEIGH $53,398
NASHVILLE $52,964
ARLINGTON HEIGHTS (VA) $52,085
TUCSON $51,857
IRVINE (CA) $51,286
DURHAM $51,114
WASHINGTON $49,431
DALLAS $47,920
SEATTLE $47,336
RENO $47,273
CORPUS CHRISTI $46,331
SAN ANTONIO $46,112
HONOLULU $46,087
OKLAHOMA CITY $45,449
SAN FRANCISCO $45,291
MADISON $45,275
HENDERSON (NV) $45,220
WICHITA $44,810
SAINT PAUL $44,579
CHANDLER (AZ) $44,470
The average Austin resident spends $10,128 on gas and auto maintenance --
FOUR TIMES what the average New Yorker spends.
US OVERALL SPENDING
$37,782
FIVE LOWEST-SPENDING CITIES
BOISE $28,006
TOLEDO $26,962
CHULA VISTA (CA) $21,424
HIALEAH (FL) $19,397
DETROIT $16,446
Does not include mortgage/rent.
For complete methodology, go to Bundle.com/bundlereport2010.

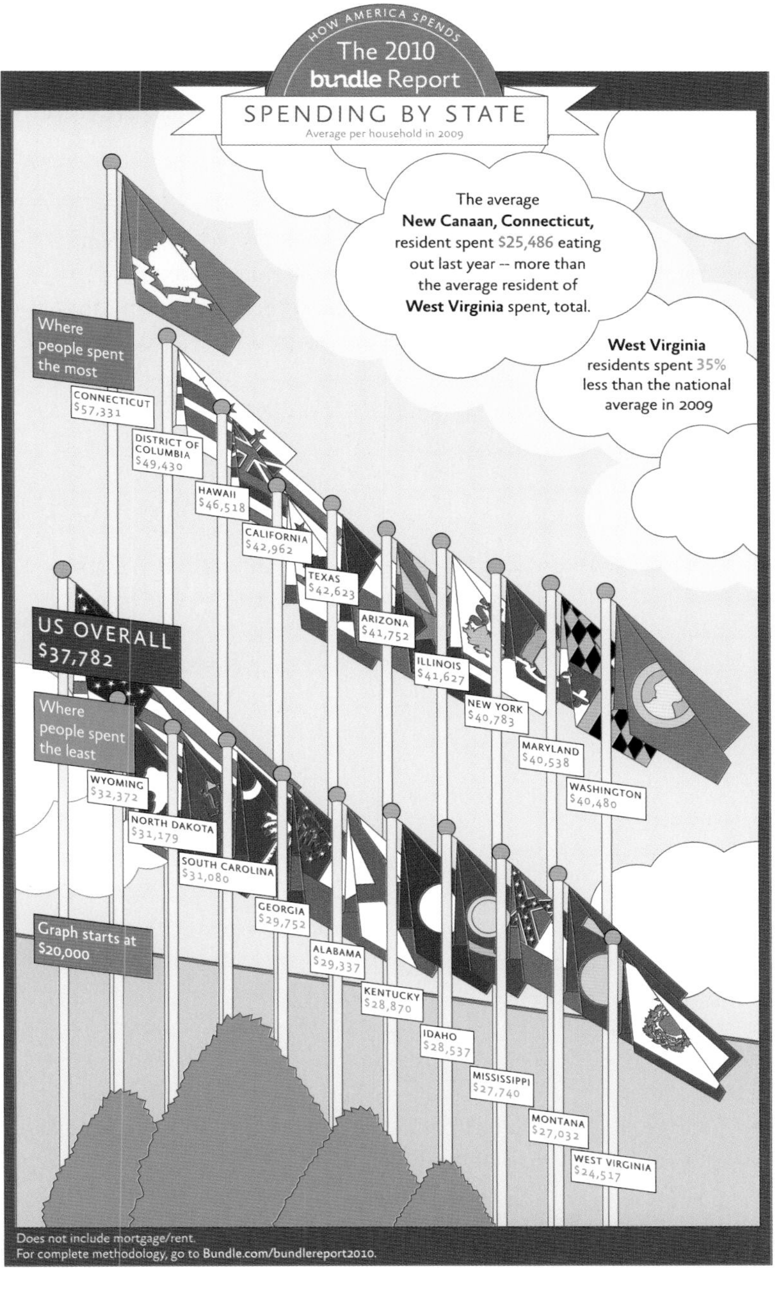

HOW AMERICA SPENDS
The 2010 bundle Report
SPENDING BY STATE
Average per household in 2009
The average New Canaan, Connecticut, resident spent $25,486 eating out last year -- more than the average resident of West Virginia spent, total.
West Virginia residents spent 35% less than the national average in 2009
Where people spent the most
CONNECTICUT $57,331
DISTRICT OF COLUMBIA $49,430
HAWAII $46,518
CALIFORNIA $42,962
TEXAS $42,623
ARIZONA $41,752
ILLINOIS $41,627
NEW YORK $40,783
MARYLAND $40,538
WASHINGTON $40,480
US OVERALL $37,782
Where people spent the least
WYOMING $32,372
NORTH DAKOTA $31,179
SOUTH CAROLINA $31,080
GEORGIA $29,752
ALABAMA $29,337
KENTUCKY $28,870
IDAHO $28,537
MISSISSIPPI $27,740
MONTANA $27,032
WEST VIRGINIA $24,517
Graph starts at $20,000
Does not include mortgage/rent.
For complete methodology, go to Bundle.com/bundlereport2010.

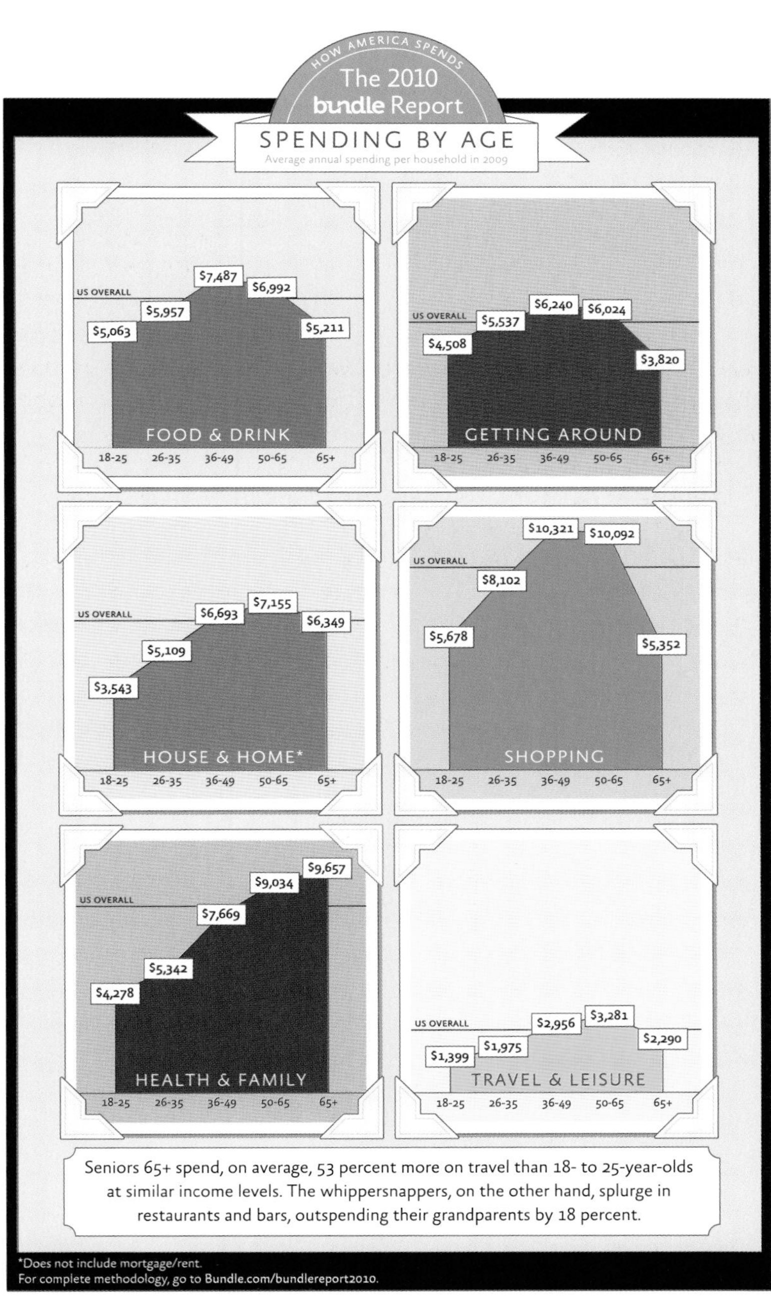

HOW AMERICA SPENDS
The 2010 bundle Report
SPENDING BY AGE
Average annual spending per household in 2009
US OVERALL
$5,063
$5,957
$7,487
$6,992
$5,211
FOOD & DRINK
18-25 26-35 36-49 50-65 65+
US OVERALL
$4,508
$5,537
$6,240
$6,024
$3,820
GETTING AROUND
18-25 26-35 36-49 50-65 65+
US OVERALL
$3,543
$5,109
$6,693
$7,155
$6,349
HOUSE & HOME*
18-25 26-35 36-49 50-65 65+
US OVERALL
$5,678
$8,102
$10,321
$10,092
$5,352
SHOPPING
18-25 26-35 36-49 50-65 65+
US OVERALL
$4,278
$5,342
$7,669
$9,034
$9,657
HEALTH & FAMILY
18-25 26-35 36-49 50-65 65+
US OVERALL
$1,399
$1,975
$2,956
$3,281
$2,290
TRAVEL & LEISURE
18-25 26-35 36-49 50-65 65+
Seniors 65+ spend, on average, 53 percent more on travel than 18- to 25-year-olds at similar income levels. The whippersnappers, on the other hand, splurge in restaurants and bars, outspending their grandparents by 18 percent.
*Does not include mortgage/rent.
For complete methodology, go to Bundle.com/bundlereport2010.

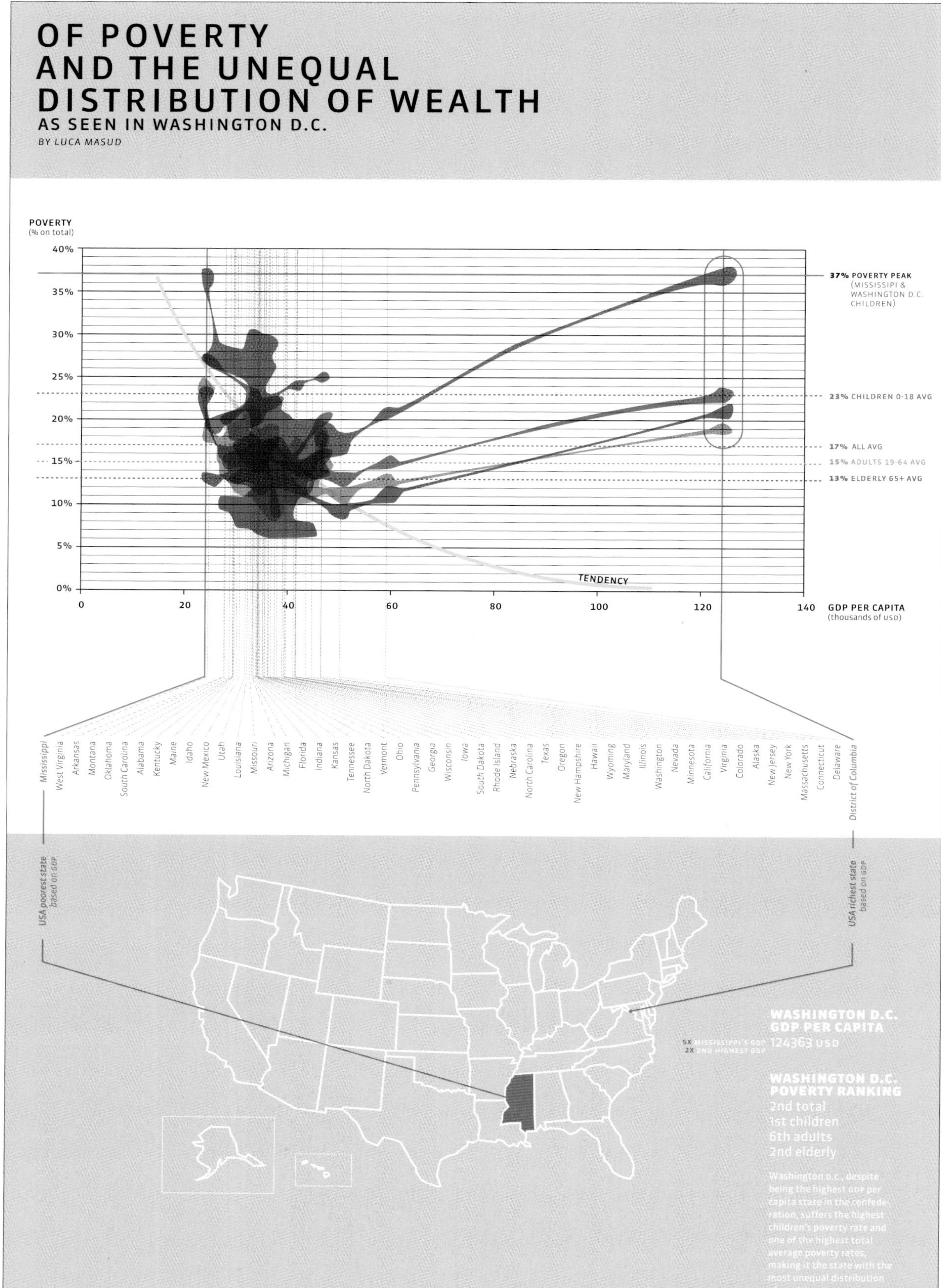

Project Info: Website, 2009, Italy
Data Source: Kaiser State Health Facts
Design: Luca Masud (DensityDesign)

Unequal Distribution of Wealth

This diagram looks at poverty by age in the US. The x-axis shows the GDP per capita, with all states listed below according to their wealth. While many states are rather close to each other, Washington D.C. more than doubles the GDP of the second richest listed, Delaware.

The y-axis represents the percentage of population who live in poverty. Age groups are colour coded: red are children, green are adults etc. The dotted lines show national median values, indicating, for instance, that compared with the national average, 23 % of children are living in poverty. Washington D.C. as the wealthiest state by far exceeds this with 37 % of children living in poverty.

Dieses Diagramm schlüsselt die Armut in den USA nach Altersgruppen auf. Auf der x-Achse ist das Bruttoinlandsprodukt pro Kopf für alle US-Bundesstaaten entsprechend ihrem Wohlstands dargestellt. Bei vielen Staaten sind die Daten relativ ähnlich, in Washington, D.C., hingegen ist das BIP doppelt so hoch wie im zweitreichsten Bundesstaat, Delaware.

Die y-Achse steht für den Prozentsatz der von Armut betroffenen Bevölkerung. Altersgruppen sind farbig codiert: Rot für Kinder, Grün für Erwachsene usw. Punktierte Linien geben landesweite Durchschnittswerte an. Sie offenbaren zum Beispiel, dass im Landesdurchschnitt 23 % der Kinder in Armut leben. In Washington, D.C., dem reichsten Bundesstaat der USA, wird dieser Prozentsatz weit überschritten. Hier sind 37 % der Kinder von Armut betroffen.

Ce diagramme analyse la pauvreté par tranches d'âge aux États-Unis. L'axe X montre le PIB par habitant, et tous les États sont indiqués en dessous en fonction de leur richesse. Beaucoup sont assez proches les uns des autres, mais Washington D.C. affiche plus du double du PIB du deuxième État le plus riche, le Delaware.

L'axe Y représente le pourcentage de la population qui vit dans la pauvreté. Les tranches d'âges ont différentes couleurs : rouge pour les enfants, vert pour les adultes, etc. Les lignes en pointillés montrent les valeurs moyennes au niveau national, avec par exemple 23 % des enfants vivant dans la pauvreté par rapport à la moyenne. L'État le plus riche, Washington D.C., dépasse largement ce chiffre, avec 37 % des enfants vivant dans la pauvreté.

The Real US National Debt

Lorraine Moffa and Nigel Holmes demonstrate the enormous national debt the United States owed to various lenders in 2009. They also explain how the government does not include two major programs, Social Security and Medicare / Medicaid, when publishing figures about the national debt. The graphic is all about making this unimaginable amount of money conceivable.

First, the total 2009 figures are summed up and compared to the figures for 2000. Second, all the big lenders are named. In the next three steps, this enormous debt is compared to an average household to give a relative impression of the amount. A small timeline on the lower left shows how the national debt has grown exponentially over the past 30 years.

Lorraine Moffa und Nigel Holmes zeigen die enormen Staatsschulden, die die USA 2009 bei verschiedenen Kreditgebern angehäuft hatten. Zudem wird ersichtlich, dass der Staat zwei große Programme – Sozialhilfe und Medicare / Medicaid – bei der Veröffentlichung der Staatsverschuldung nicht miteinbezieht. In dieser Grafik geht es insbesondere darum, die unvorstellbaren Geldmengen anschaulich zu machen.

Zunächst werden die Gesamtzahlen von 2009 zusammengefasst und mit den Zahlen von 2000 verglichen. Im zweiten Punkt werden die größten Gläubiger genannt. Die Punkte drei bis fünf vergleichen diese gewaltigen Schulden mit den Ausgaben eines durchschnittlichen Privathaushalts, um die Geldmenge in Relation zu setzen. Die kleine Zeitleiste unten links zeigt, dass die Staatsverschuldung im Lauf der vergangenen dreißig Jahre exponentiell angestiegen ist.

Lorraine Moffa et Nigel Holmes illustrent l'énorme dette nationale des États-Unis envers différents prêteurs en 2009. Ils expliquent aussi que le gouvernement omet deux grands programmes, Social Security et Medicare / Medicaid, dans les chiffres publiés sur la dette nationale. L'objectif de ce visuel est de faire prendre conscience de l'inimaginable quantité d'argent qui est due.

Les totaux pour 2009 sont calculés et comparés à ceux de 2000. Ensuite, tous les grands prêteurs sont mentionnés. Dans les trois étapes suivantes, la gigantesque dette est comparée à une famille moyenne pour donner une impression relative de la quantité. Une petite chronologie en bas à gauche montre la hausse exponentielle de la dette nationale au cours des 30 dernières années.

Project Info: "How Much Do We Really Owe?", *American History*, magazine article, 2009, USA
Data Source: Congressional Budget Office; Jess Bachmann (WallStats.com); Federal Reserve; Patrick Creadon, Christine O'Malley, Addison Wiggin: "I.O.U.S.A."; US Treasury
Research: Lorraine Moffa
Design: Nigel Holmes

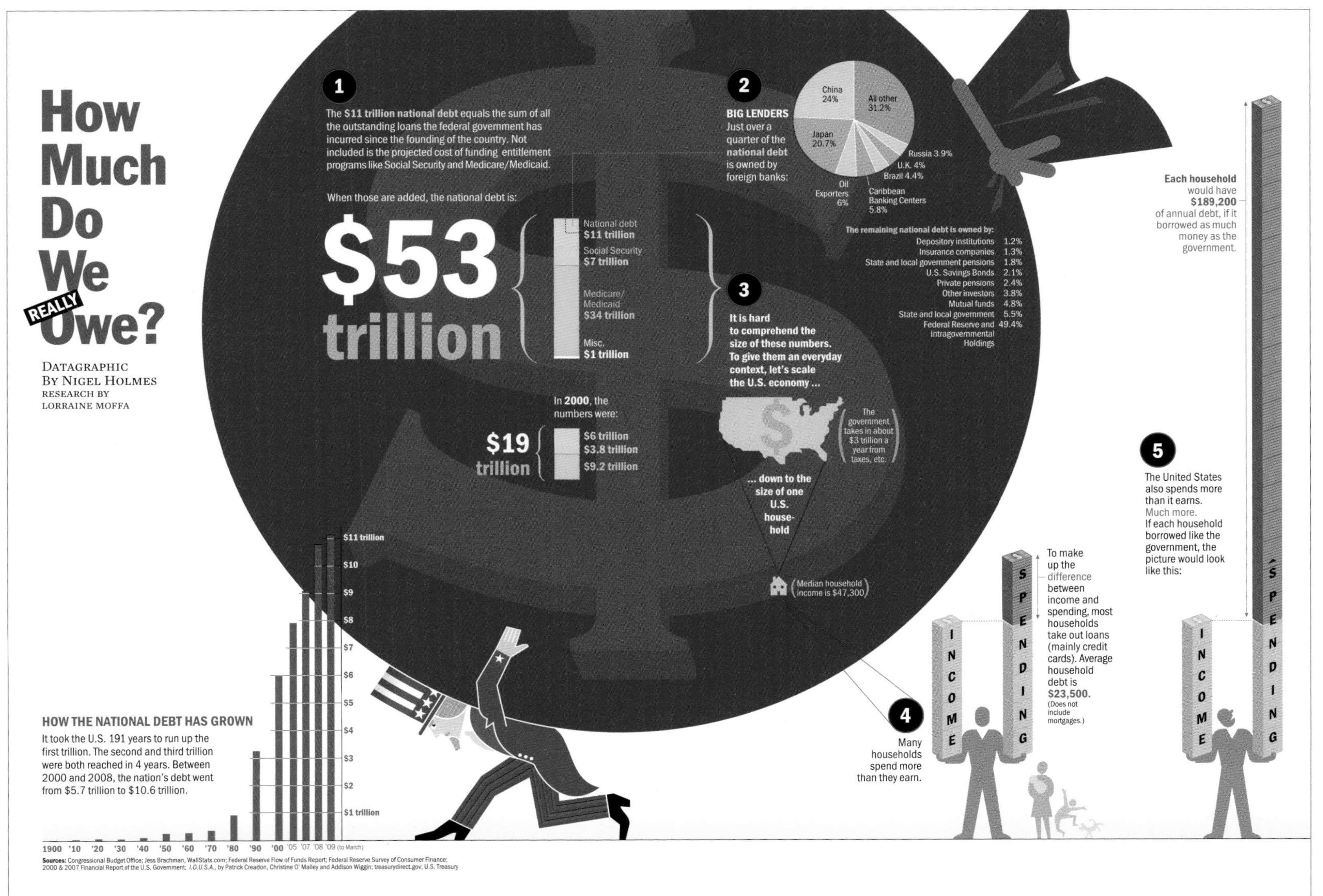

GATTUNGEN DER MASKOTTCHEN

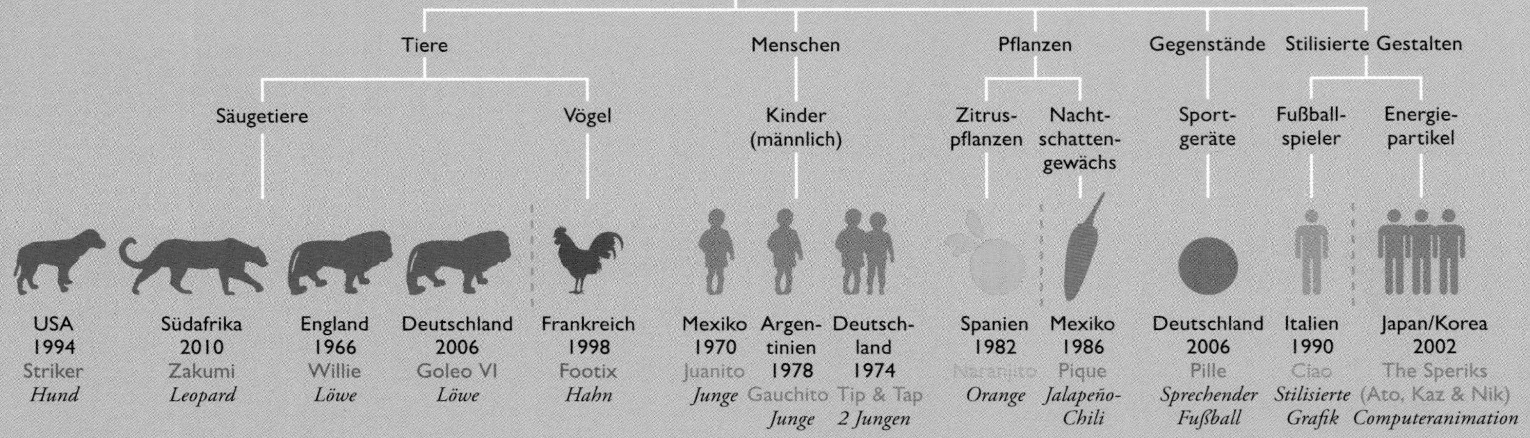
Tiere
Menschen
Pflanzen
Gegenstände
Stilisierte Gestalten
Säugetiere
Vögel
Kinder (männlich)
Zitrus-pflanzen
Nacht-schatten-gewächs
Sport-geräte
Fußball-spieler
Energie-partikel
USA 1994 Striker *Hund*
Südafrika 2010 Zakumi *Leopard*
England 1966 Willie *Löwe*
Deutschland 2006 Goleo VI *Löwe*
Frankreich 1998 Footix *Hahn*
Mexiko 1970 Juanito *Junge*
Argen-tinien 1978 Gauchito *Junge*
Deutsch-land 1974 Tip & Tap *2 Jungen*
Spanien 1982 Naranjito *Orange*
Mexiko 1986 Pique *Jalapeño-Chili*
Deutschland 2006 Pille *Sprechender Fußball*
Italien 1990 Ciao *Stilisierte Grafik*
Japan/Korea 2002 The Speriks (Ato, Kaz & Nik) *Computeranimation*

WM-BABYS

Wie veränderte die WM die Geburtenquote in Deutschland?

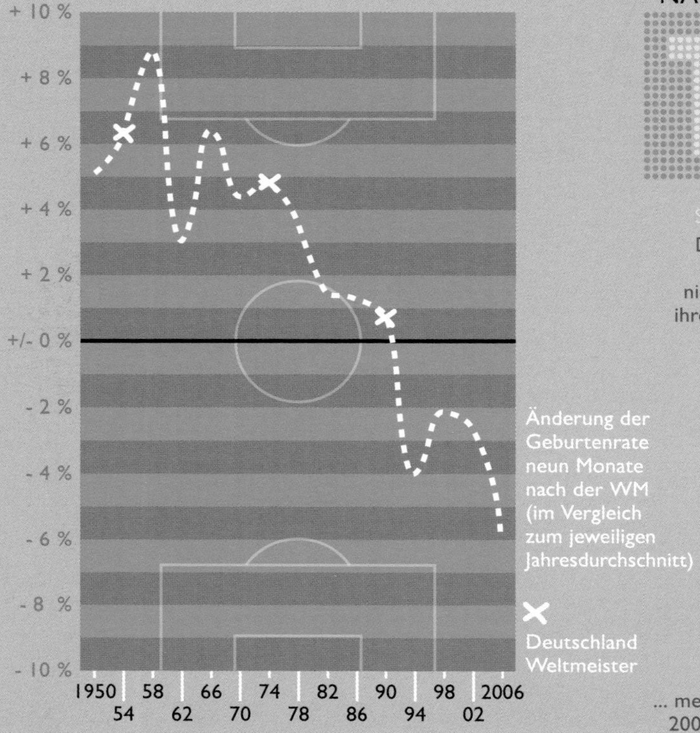
+ 10 %
+ 8 %
+ 6 %
+ 4 %
+ 2 %
+/- 0 %
- 2 %
- 4 %
- 6 %
- 8 %
- 10 %
1950 58 66 74 82 90 98 2006
54 62 70 78 86 94 02
Änderung der Geburtenrate neun Monate nach der WM (im Vergleich zum jeweiligen Jahresdurchschnitt)
Deutschland Weltmeister

BLONDINENQUOTE DER SPIELERFRAUEN DER DEUTSCHEN NATIONALMANNSCHAFT

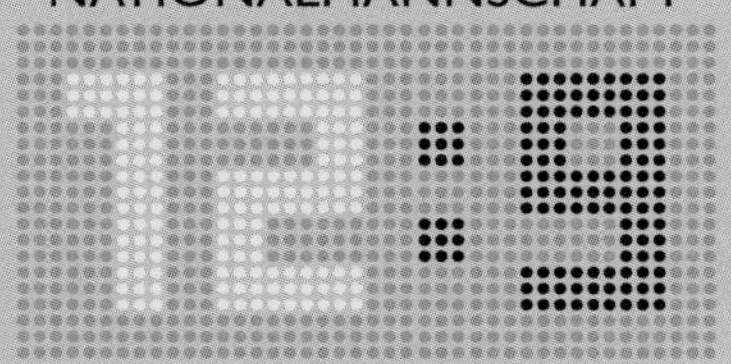
12:9
blonde Spielerfrau
nicht blonde Spielerfrau

Die restlichen sechs Spieler des Kaders sind entweder nicht liiert oder die Haarfarbe ihrer Partnerin ist nicht bekannt
Stand: 18.5.2010

BIERKONSUM

6%

... mehr Bier wurde im WM-Sommer 2006 in Deutschland im Vergleich zum Sommer 2005 getrunken

MICHAEL BALLACKS VERLETZUNGEN

(seit Juni 2006)

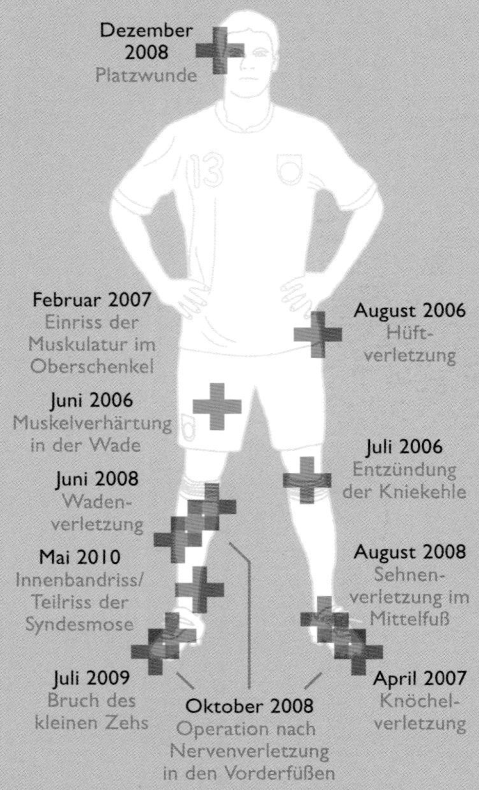
Dezember 2008 Platzwunde
Februar 2007 Einriss der Muskulatur im Oberschenkel
August 2006 Hüft-verletzung
Juni 2006 Muskelverhärtung in der Wade
Juli 2006 Entzündung der Kniekehle
Juni 2008 Waden-verletzung
Mai 2010 Innenbandriss/ Teilriss der Syndesmose
August 2008 Sehnen-verletzung im Mittelfuß
Juli 2009 Bruch des kleinen Zehs
Oktober 2008 Operation nach Nervenverletzung in den Vorderfüßen
April 2007 Knöchel-verletzung

DAS DURCHSCHNITTSALTER DER FIFA-PRÄSIDENTEN bei Amtsantritt im Vergleich

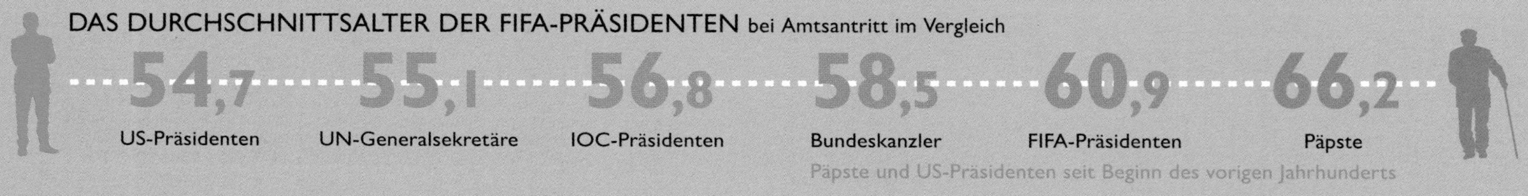
54,7 US-Präsidenten
55,1 UN-Generalsekretäre
56,8 IOC-Präsidenten
58,5 Bundeskanzler
60,9 FIFA-Präsidenten
66,2 Päpste

Päpste und US-Präsidenten seit Beginn des vorigen Jahrhunderts

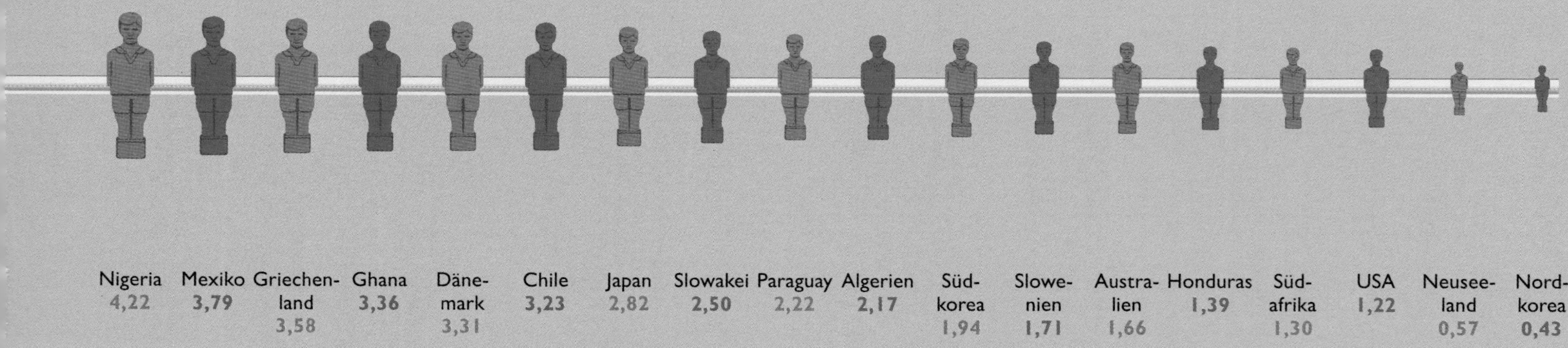
Nigeria 4,22
Mexiko 3,79
Griechen-land 3,58
Ghana 3,36
Däne-mark 3,31
Chile 3,23
Japan 2,82
Slowakei 2,50
Paraguay 2,22
Algerien 2,17
Süd-korea 1,94
Slowe-nien 1,71
Austra-lien 1,66
Honduras 1,39
Süd-afrika 1,30
USA 1,22
Neusee-land 0,57
Nord-korea 0,43

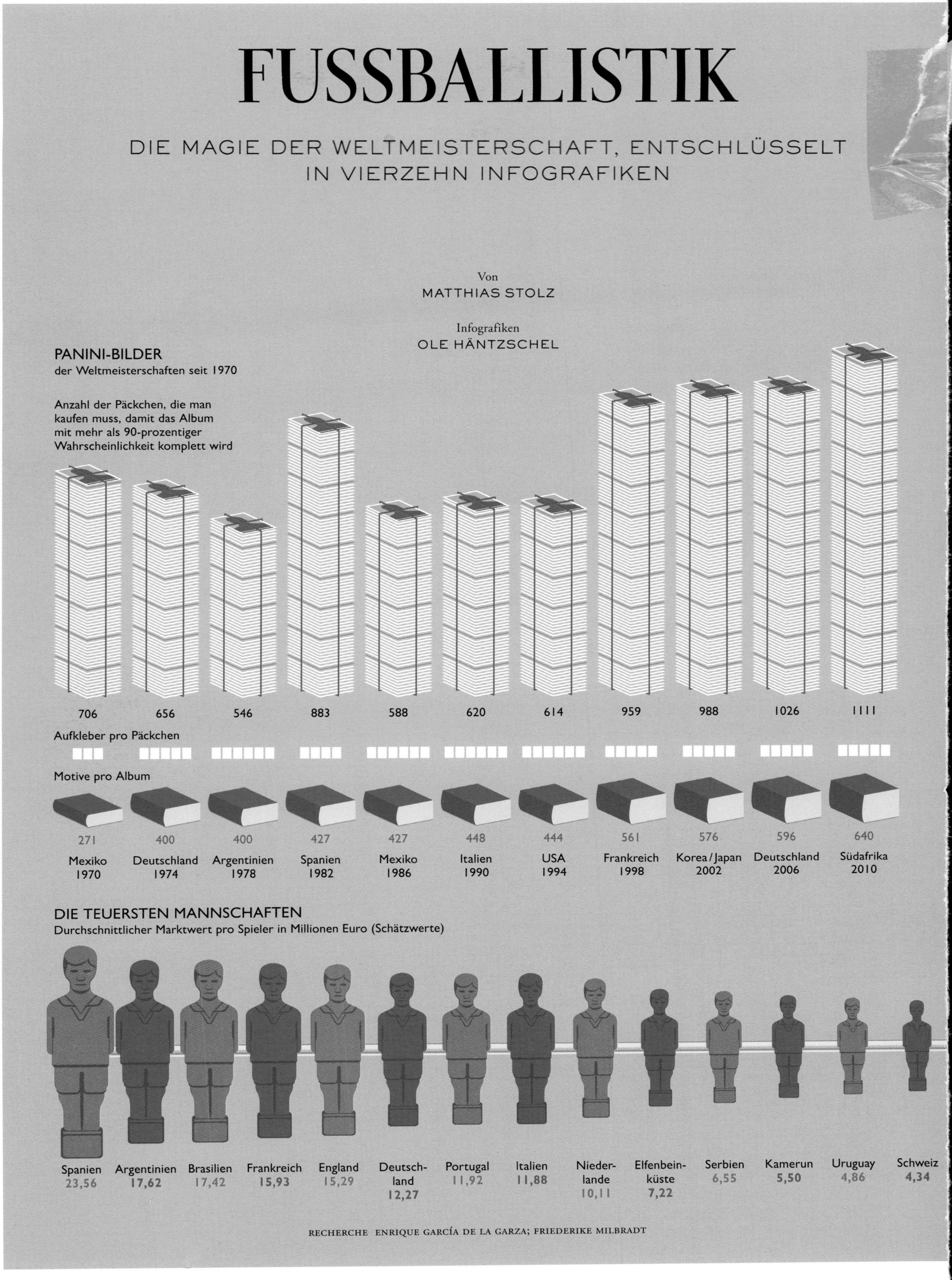

FUSSBALLISTIK

DIE MAGIE DER WELTMEISTERSCHAFT, ENTSCHLÜSSELT IN VIERZEHN INFOGRAFIKEN

Von
MATTHIAS STOLZ

Infografiken
OLE HÄNTZSCHEL

PANINI-BILDER
der Weltmeisterschaften seit 1970

Anzahl der Päckchen, die man kaufen muss, damit das Album mit mehr als 90-prozentiger Wahrscheinlichkeit komplett wird

Aufkleber pro Päckchen

Motive pro Album

	Päckchen	Motive pro Album
Mexiko 1970	706	271
Deutschland 1974	656	400
Argentinien 1978	546	400
Spanien 1982	883	427
Mexiko 1986	588	427
Italien 1990	620	448
USA 1994	614	444
Frankreich 1998	959	561
Korea / Japan 2002	988	576
Deutschland 2006	1026	596
Südafrika 2010	1111	640

DIE TEUERSTEN MANNSCHAFTEN
Durchschnittlicher Marktwert pro Spieler in Millionen Euro (Schätzwerte)

Spanien	23,56
Argentinien	17,62
Brasilien	17,42
Frankreich	15,93
England	15,29
Deutschland	12,27
Portugal	11,92
Italien	11,88
Niederlande	10,11
Elfenbeinküste	7,22
Serbien	6,55
Kamerun	5,50
Uruguay	4,86
Schweiz	4,34

RECHERCHE ENRIQUE GARCÍA DE LA GARZA; FRIEDERIKE MILBRADT

Project Info: *ZEITmagazin*, 2010, Germany
Data Source: Transfermarkt.de; Andreas Binzenhöfer (University of Würzburg); Statistisches Bundesamt Deutschland; Deutscher Fussball-Bund; FIFA
Research: Matthias Stolz (*Die Zeit*), Enrique García de la Garza, Friederike Milbradt
Design: Ole Häntzschel

Footballistics

On the occasion of the FIFA World Cup in 2010, the German magazine *Die Zeit* created two double-spreads to cover the magic with a collection of infographics. Individual topics ranged from how collecting Panini stickers really works through to a timeline with the most significant footballer hair-styles from previous decades.

The hierarchy of little Subbuteo-type figures shows teams ranked from the most expensive according to the market value of individual players. A tree chart divides into groups the mascots of earlier tournaments. The white figure shows German icon Michael Ballack and lists his injuries, which prevented him from joining the tournament. Blue boxes in various sizes indicate selected German players' popularity on Facebook.

Das Magazin der deutschen Wochenzeitung *Die Zeit* entwickelte diese beiden Doppelseiten anlässlich der FIFA-Weltmeisterschaft 2010 und fing die allgemeine Euphorie in einer Sammlung von Infografiken ein. Die einzelnen Themen reichten von der Frage, wie das Sammeln von Panini-Bildern eigentlich funktioniert, bis hin zu einer Zeitleiste mit den auffälligsten Fußballerfrisuren der vergangenen Jahrzehnte.

Beginnend mit der teuersten Mannschaft, führt die Hierarchie kleiner Kicker-Figuren die einzelnen WM-Teams nach dem durchschnittlichen Marktwert ihrer Spieler auf. Ein kleines Baumdiagramm gruppiert die Maskottchen früherer Weltmeisterschaften. Die weiße Figur zeigt den deutschen Star Michael Ballack mit den Verletzungen, die seine Teilnahme an der WM verhinderten. Blaue Kästen in unterschiedlicher Größe demonstrieren die Beliebtheit einiger deutscher Fußballer auf Facebook.

À l'occasion de la Coupe du Monde de la FIFA 2010, le magazine allemand *Die Zeit* a publié deux doubles pages pour couvrir l'événement avec une collection d'infographies. Les rubriques abordaient des thèmes variés : le véritable fonctionnement des collections d'autocollants Panini, ou encore les coiffures des plus grands joueurs au cours des précédentes décennies.

La suite de petits personnages de type Subbuteo montre les équipes, en partant de la plus chère d'après la valeur marchande de chaque joueur qui la compose. Une arborescence divise en groupes les mascottes des précédents tournois. Le personnage blanc symbolise l'icône allemande Michael Ballack et indique les blessures qui l'ont empêché de participer au tournoi. Des rectangles bleus de différentes tailles indiquent la popularité de certains joueurs allemands sur Facebook.

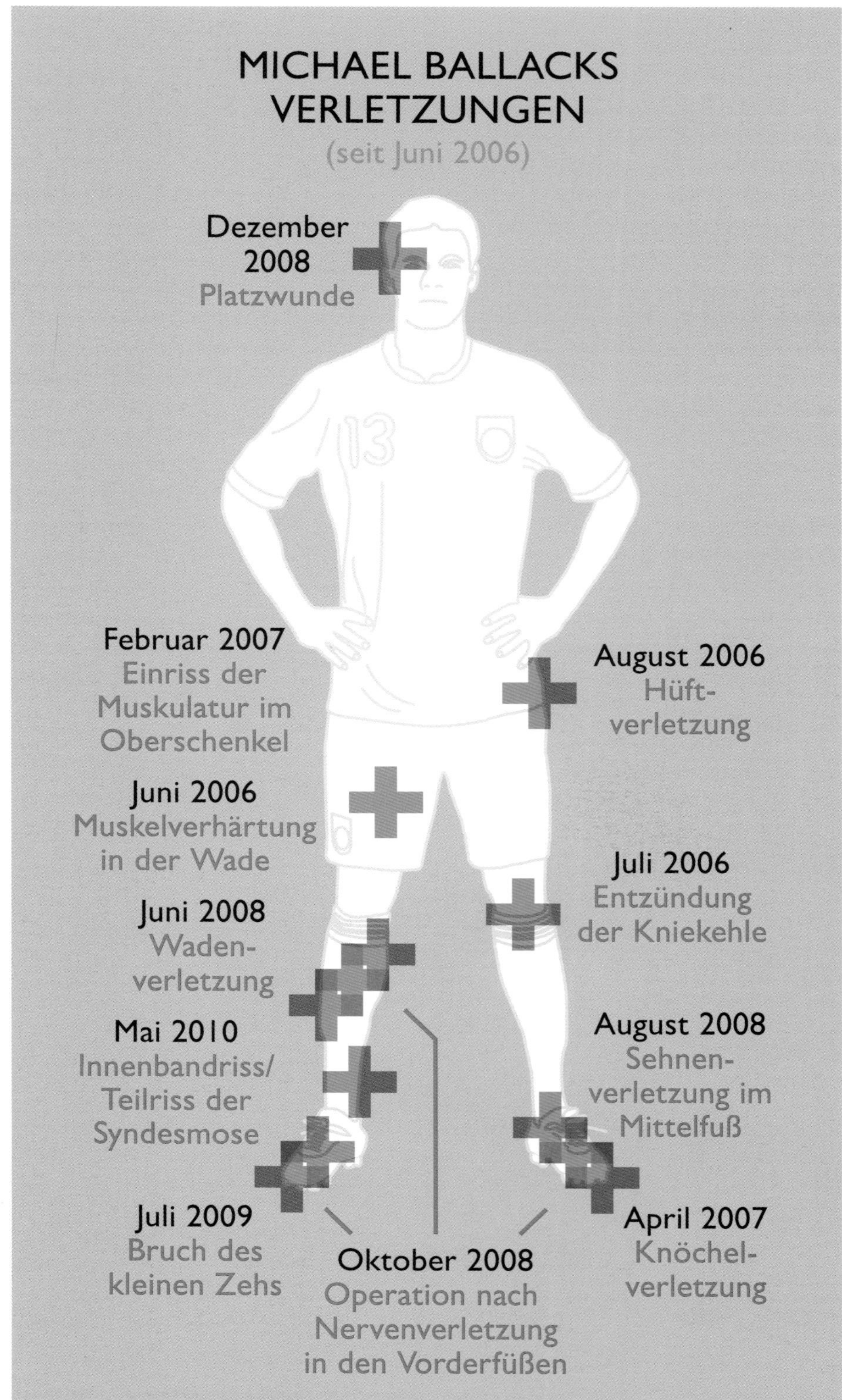

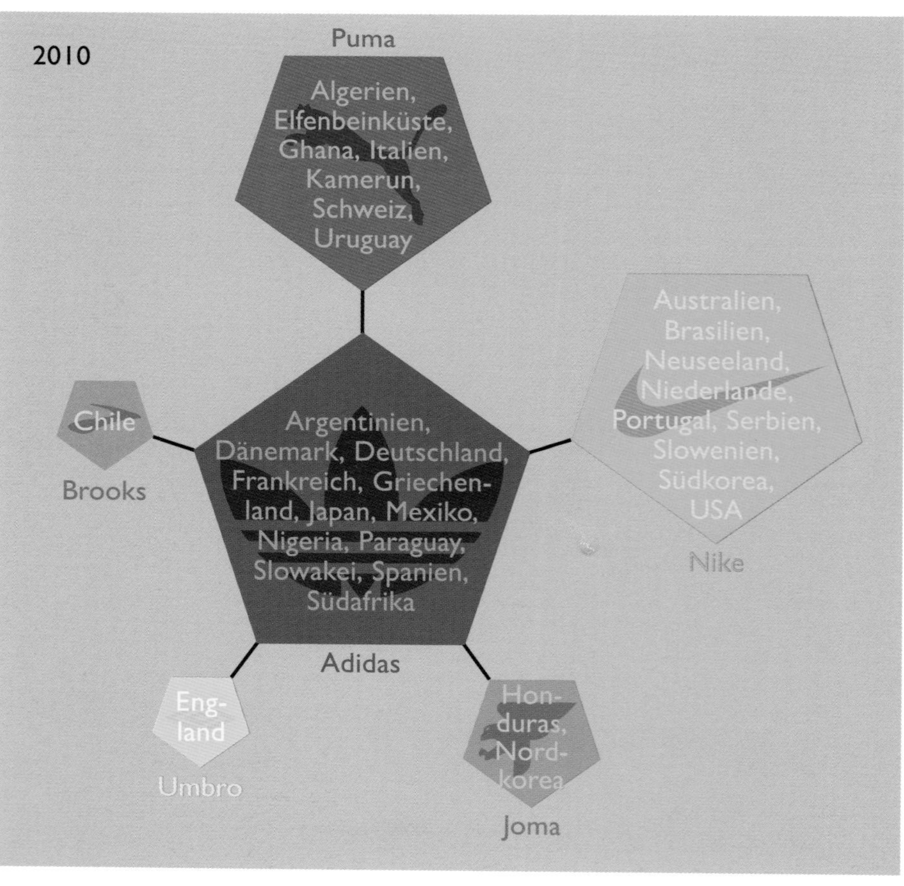

History of the World Series

The World Series is the annual championship in US Major League Baseball, played between the two winning clubs of the American League and the National League since 1903. Despite its title, this isn't a historical timeline. Instead, the circular diagram shows all match-ups between teams and compares victories and defeats.

The bars show how many matches a team played in the World Series and how many of these were won. Teams are arranged by success rate. The not very successful Milwaukee Brewers (MIL, below right) used to belong to the American League but switched to the National League in 1998. This explains the seemingly irregular inner-league match-up with the St. Louis Cardinals (STL, top right), which occurred in 1982.

Die World Series ist die jährliche Meisterschaft im amerikanischen Major-League-Baseball, die seit 1903 zwischen den zwei Siegermannschaften der American League (links) und der National League (rechts) ausgetragen wird. Trotz ihres Titels handelt es sich bei der Grafik nicht um eine historische Zeitleiste, vielmehr zeigt das Kreisdiagramm alle Mannschaftspaarungen und vergleicht Siege und Niederlagen.

Anhand der Balken wird ersichtlich, wie viele World-Series-Spiele eine Mannschaft spielte und wie viele sie gewann. Die Mannschaften sind entsprechend ihrer Erfolgsquote angeordnet. Die weniger erfolgreichen Milwaukee Brewers (MIL, unten rechts) gehörten ursprünglich zur American League, schlossen sich aber 1998 der National League an. Das erklärt die scheinbar ligainterne Paarung mit den St. Louis Cardinals (STL, oben rechts) im Jahr 1982.

La World Series est le championnat annuel de la Ligue majeure de baseball (MLB) nord-américaine, qui se dispute entre les deux clubs vainqueurs de la ligue américaine et de la ligue nationale depuis 1903. Malgré le titre de l'illustration, il ne s'agit pas d'une chronologie historique. Le diagramme circulaire montre toutes les rencontres des équipes et compare les victoires et les défaites.

Les barres montrent le nombre de matchs disputés dans la World Series et combien ont été remportés. Les équipes sont classées par taux de victoire. L'équipe de bas niveau des Milwaukee Brewers (MIL, en bas à droite) appartenait auparavant à la ligue américaine mais est passée à la ligne nationale en 1998, d'où la rencontre de ligue interne apparemment anormale avec l'équipe des St Louis Cardinals (STL, en haut à droite) en 1982.

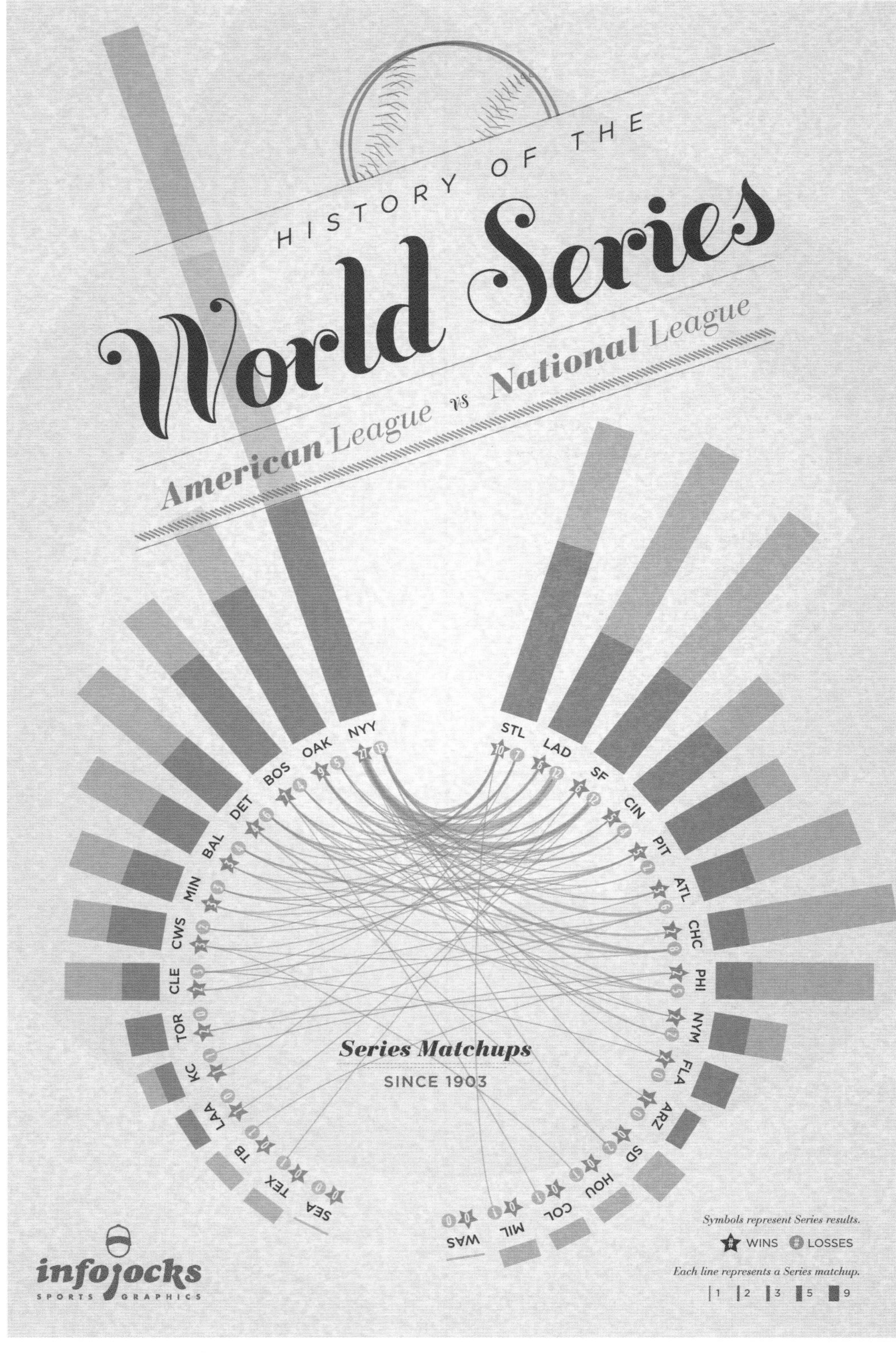

Project Info: Poster, 2009, USA
Data Source: Baseball-reference.com
Design: Jeremy Yingling (Infojocks Sports Graphics)

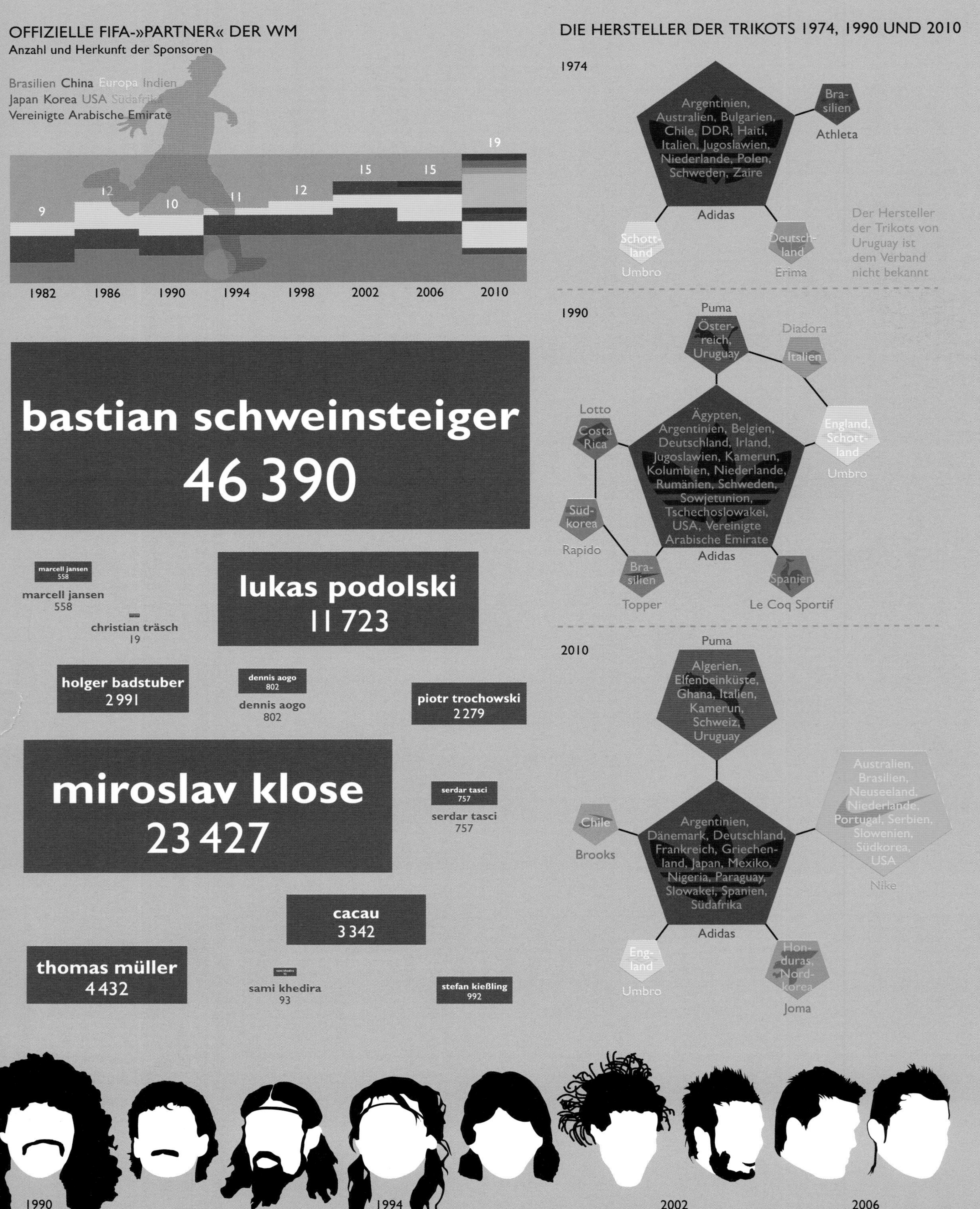
OFFIZIELLE FIFA-»PARTNER« DER WM
Anzahl und Herkunft der Sponsoren
Brasilien China Europa Indien
Japan Korea USA Südafrika
Vereinigte Arabische Emirate
9
12
10
11
12
15
15
19
1982
1986
1990
1994
1998
2002
2006
2010
DIE HERSTELLER DER TRIKOTS 1974, 1990 UND 2010
1974
Argentinien, Australien, Bulgarien, Chile, DDR, Haiti, Italien, Jugoslawien, Niederlande, Polen, Schweden, Zaire
Adidas
Brasilien
Athleta
Schottland
Umbro
Deutschland
Erima
Der Hersteller der Trikots von Uruguay ist dem Verband nicht bekannt
1990
Puma
Österreich, Uruguay
Diadora
Italien
Lotto
Costa Rica
Ägypten, Argentinien, Belgien, Deutschland, Irland, Jugoslawien, Kamerun, Kolumbien, Niederlande, Rumänien, Schweden, Sowjetunion, Tschechoslowakei, USA, Vereinigte Arabische Emirate
Adidas
England, Schottland
Umbro
Südkorea
Rapido
Brasilien
Topper
Spanien
Le Coq Sportif
2010
Puma
Algerien, Elfenbeinküste, Ghana, Italien, Kamerun, Schweiz, Uruguay
Chile
Brooks
Argentinien, Dänemark, Deutschland, Frankreich, Griechenland, Japan, Mexiko, Nigeria, Paraguay, Slowakei, Spanien, Südafrika
Adidas
Australien, Brasilien, Neuseeland, Niederlande, Portugal, Serbien, Slowenien, Südkorea, USA
Nike
England
Umbro
Honduras, Nordkorea
Joma
bastian schweinsteiger
46 390
marcell jansen
558
christian träsch
19
lukas podolski
11 723
holger badstuber
2 991
dennis aogo
802
piotr trochowski
2 279
miroslav klose
23 427
serdar tasci
757
cacau
3 342
thomas müller
4 432
sami khedira
93
stefan kießling
992
1990
René Higuita
Rudi Völler
Alexi Lalas
1994
Claudio Caniggia
Stefan Effenberg
2002
Ronaldinho
David Beckham
2006
Bastian Schweinsteiger
Cristiano Ronaldo

QUELLEN EIGENE RECHERCHEN; TRANSFERMARKT.DE; PANINI UND ANDREAS BINZENHÖFER / UNI WÜRZBURG; STATISTISCHES BUNDESAMT; DFB; FIFA; FACEBOOK

DIE BAYERN-QUOTE

Anteil der FC-Bayern-München-Spieler am Kader der (west-)deutschen Nationalmannschaft

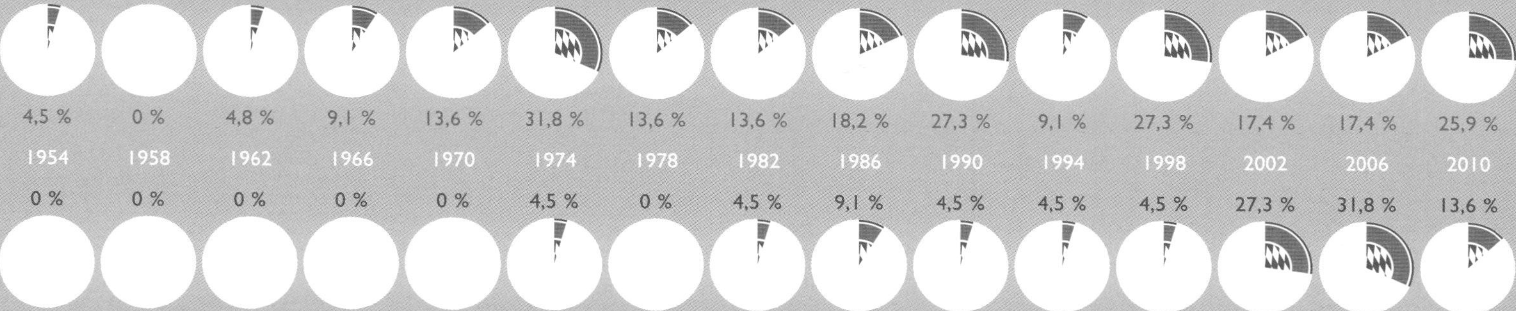

	1954	1958	1962	1966	1970	1974	1978	1982	1986	1990	1994	1998	2002	2006	2010
Anteil am (west-)deutschen Kader	4,5 %	0 %	4,8 %	9,1 %	13,6 %	31,8 %	13,6 %	13,6 %	18,2 %	27,3 %	9,1 %	27,3 %	17,4 %	17,4 %	25,9 %
Anteil für andere Nationen	0 %	0 %	0 %	0 %	0 %	4,5 %	0 %	4,5 %	9,1 %	4,5 %	4,5 %	4,5 %	27,3 %	31,8 %	13,6 %

Anteil der FC-Bayern-München-Spieler, die für andere Nationen an der WM teilnahmen

ZWEITFARBEN

Auf welche Trikots können die 32 WM-Nationen ausweichen, wenn sonst zwei Gegner dieselbe Farbe tragen würden?

ANZAHL DER FACEBOOK-FANS VON SPIELERN DES DEUTSCHEN WM-KADERS

Stand: 18.5.2010

michael ballack
49 458

EINIGE STILPRÄGENDE FRISUREN VON WM-SPIELERN

1954	1966	1974			1986		
Fritz Walter	Bobby Charlton	Günter Netzer	Norbert Nigbur	Paul Breitner	Diego Maradona	Chris Waddle	Carlos Valderrama

The Very Many Varieties of Beer

Beer belongs amongst the most popular drinks on Earth, and there seem to be a million philosophies as to how to brew it. Team Pop Chart Lab employ the rather dull scientific scheme of a taxonomy and turn it into a chart of great use in everyday life: a taxonomy of beer types.

While presenting a hierarchy, the types are not arranged in a tree. Instead, the most general type, "beer", is placed in the middle, and the sub-types branch out from there. All types and sub-types are presented in a circle, whilst specific examples for each type are named in simple lettering.

Bier gehört zu den beliebtesten Getränken weltweit, und offenbar gibt es Millionen Philosophien darüber, wie man es am besten braut. Das Team Pop Chart Lab griff das eher trockene Konzept einer wissenschaftlichen Taxonomie auf und machte daraus ein überaus alltagstaugliches Diagramm: eine Taxonomie der Biersorten.

Diese bilden zwar eine Hierarchie, sind aber nicht als Baum dargestellt. Der allgemeine Oberbegriff „Bier" steht in der Mitte und teilt sich von hier in Gattungen auf. Alle Arten und Unterarten sind als Kreis dargestellt, die dazugehörigen Beispiele sind als einfacher Text angegeben.

La bière fait partie des boissons les plus populaires sur Terre, et il semble exister un million de philosophies sur la façon de la brasser. Team Pop Chart Lab a recours au modèle scientifique plutôt ennuyeux d'une taxonomie et le transforme en un visuel très utile dans la vie de tous les jours : une taxonomie des types de bière.

Même si le résultat est une hiérarchie, les types ne sont pas organisés dans une arborescence. Le type le plus générique, « bière » se trouve en effet au milieu, et les sous-types partent de lui. Tous les types et sous-types sont présentés dans un cercle, alors que des exemples spécifiques pour chacun d'eux sont simplement écrits à côté.

Project Info:
Poster, 2010, USA
Design: Ben Gibson, Patrick Mulligan (Pop Chart Lab)

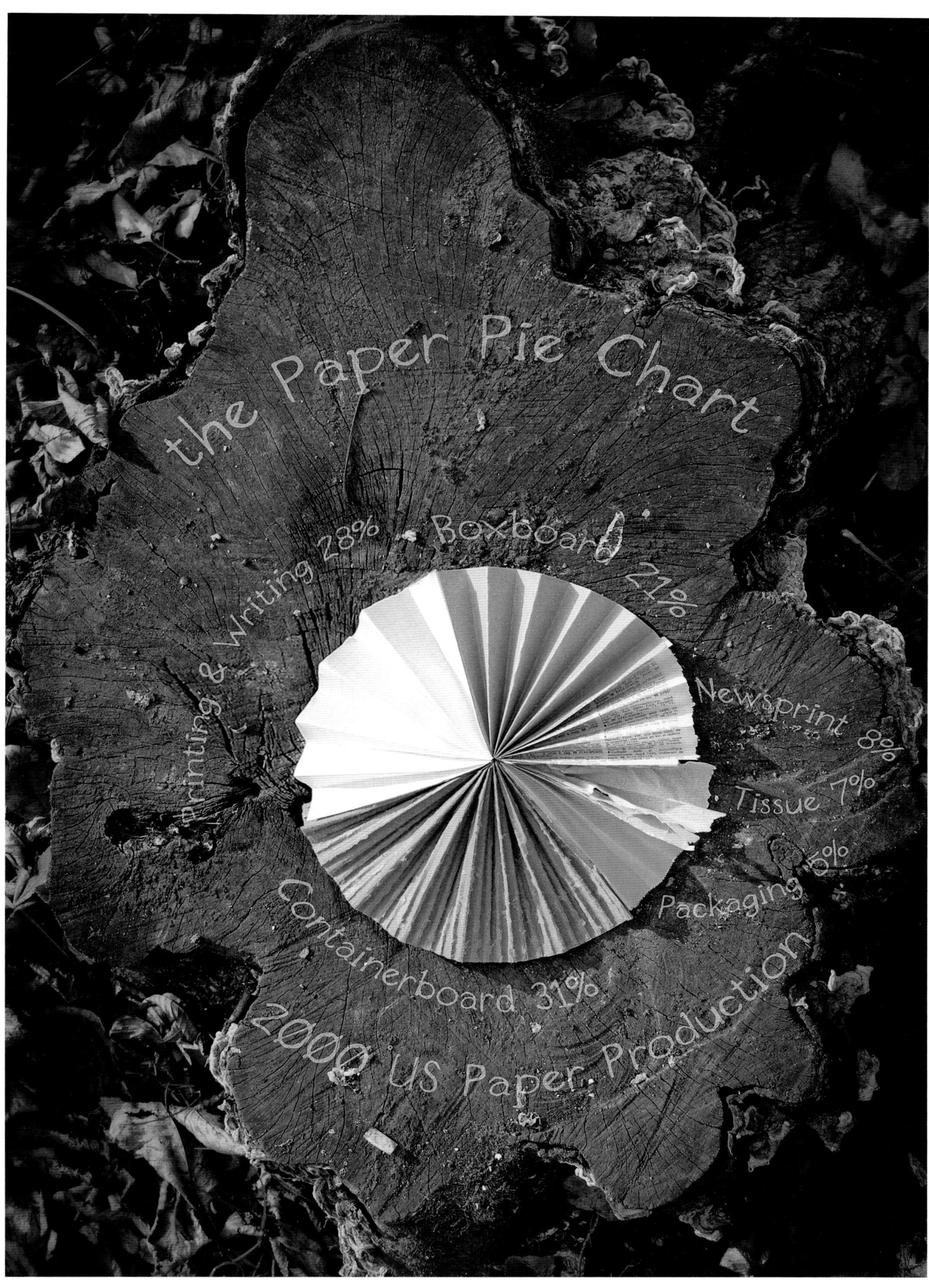

The Paper Pie Chart

The pie chart as physical object: this piece shows annual US paper production in total and the percentage in which various types of paper have been produced, by being literally made from those types of paper.

The graphic thus not only refers to the statistics by means of an abstract diagram, but the elements of the diagram actually show what they are.

Das Tortendiagramm als Realobjekt: Diese Arbeit zeigt die Gesamtmenge des jährlich von der amerikanischen Papierindustrie hergestellten Papiers sowie den Anteil der verschiedenen Papierarten, indem die „Tortenstücke" aus genau jenem Papier gebildet sind.

Die Grafik beschränkt sich nicht darauf, die statistischen Zahlen in ein abstraktes Diagramm zu übertragen. Vielmehr zeigen die Elemente des Diagramms ganz unmittelbar, was sie bezeichnen sollen.

Le camembert comme objet physique : cette œuvre montre la production annuelle totale de papier aux États-Unis et le pourcentage de chaque type de papier produit. Les secteurs du camembert sont littéralement faits avec le type de papier concerné.

Le graphique ne fait donc pas seulement référence aux statistiques à l'aide d'un diagramme abstrait : les éléments du diagramme montrent ce qu'ils représentent réellement.

Project Info: Poster, 2010, Romania
Data Source: American Forest and Paper Association
Design: Alexandra Muresan

Tracking Carbon Emissions

A footprint comparison of total carbon dioxide emissions by nation and per capita shows there's plenty of room for smaller countries to reduce their carbon footprints.

By Stanford Kay

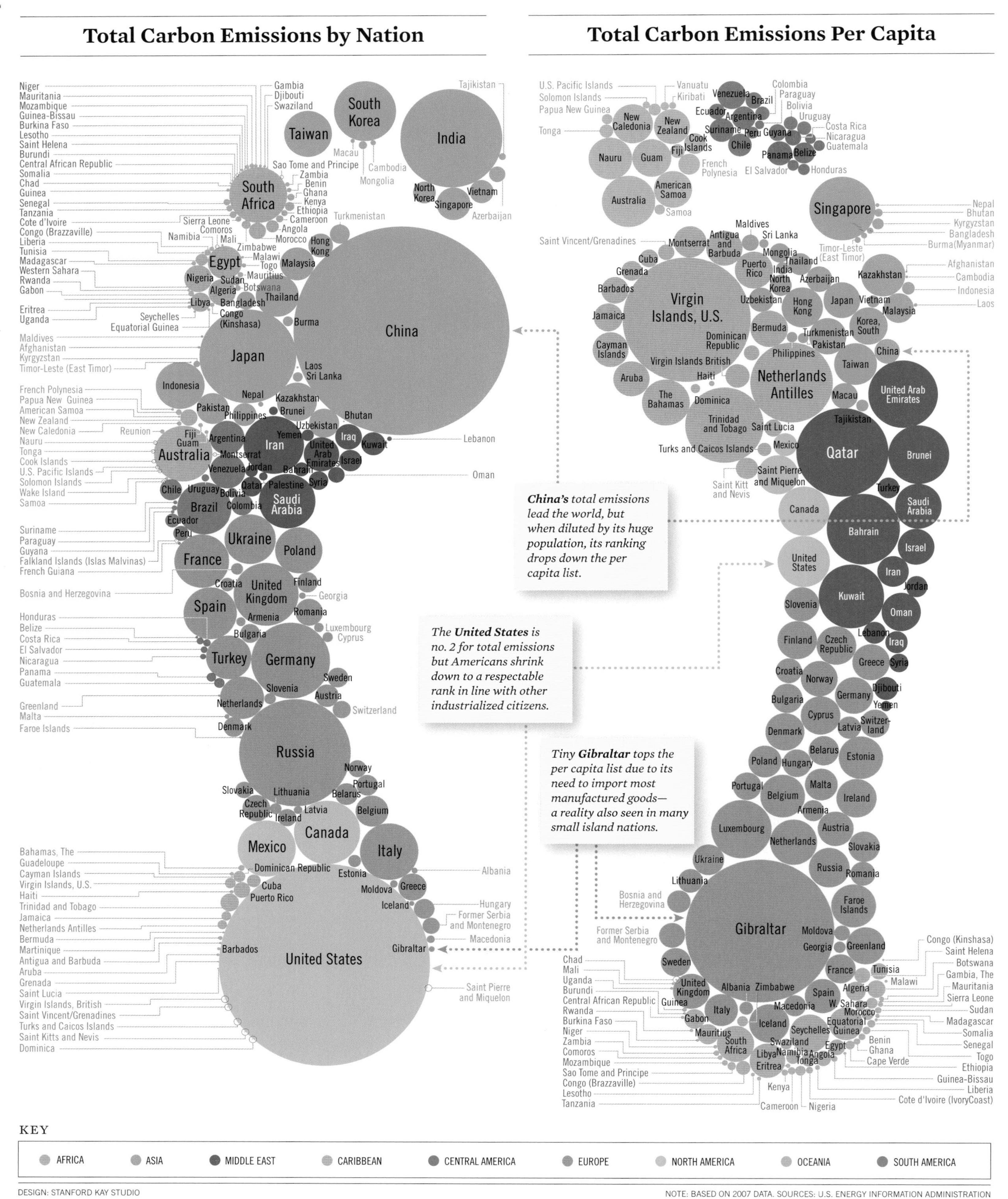

Total Carbon Emissions by Nation
Total Carbon Emissions Per Capita
China's total emissions lead the world, but when diluted by its huge population, its ranking drops down the per capita list.
The United States is no. 2 for total emissions but Americans shrink down to a respectable rank in line with other industrialized citizens.
Tiny Gibraltar tops the per capita list due to its need to import most manufactured goods—a reality also seen in many small island nations.
KEY
AFRICA
ASIA
MIDDLE EAST
CARIBBEAN
CENTRAL AMERICA
EUROPE
NORTH AMERICA
OCEANIA
SOUTH AMERICA
DESIGN: STANFORD KAY STUDIO
NOTE: BASED ON 2007 DATA. SOURCES: U.S. ENERGY INFORMATION ADMINISTRATION

Project Info: Miller-McCune, magazine and online article, 2010, USA
Data Source: US Energy Information Administration
Design: Stanford Kay

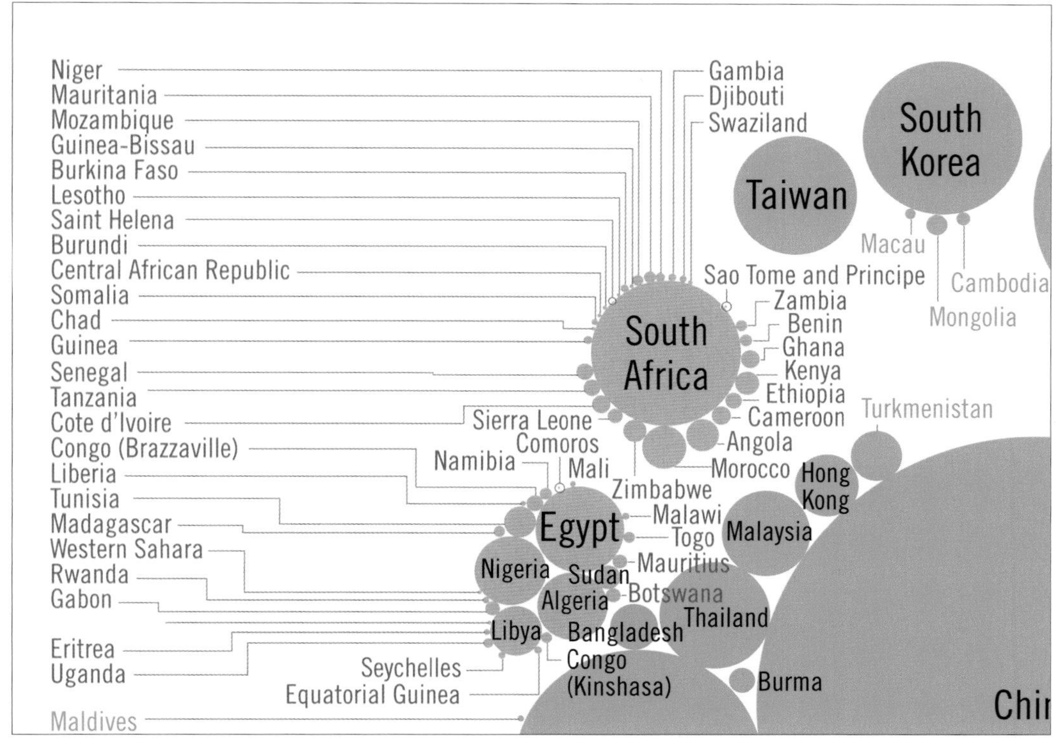

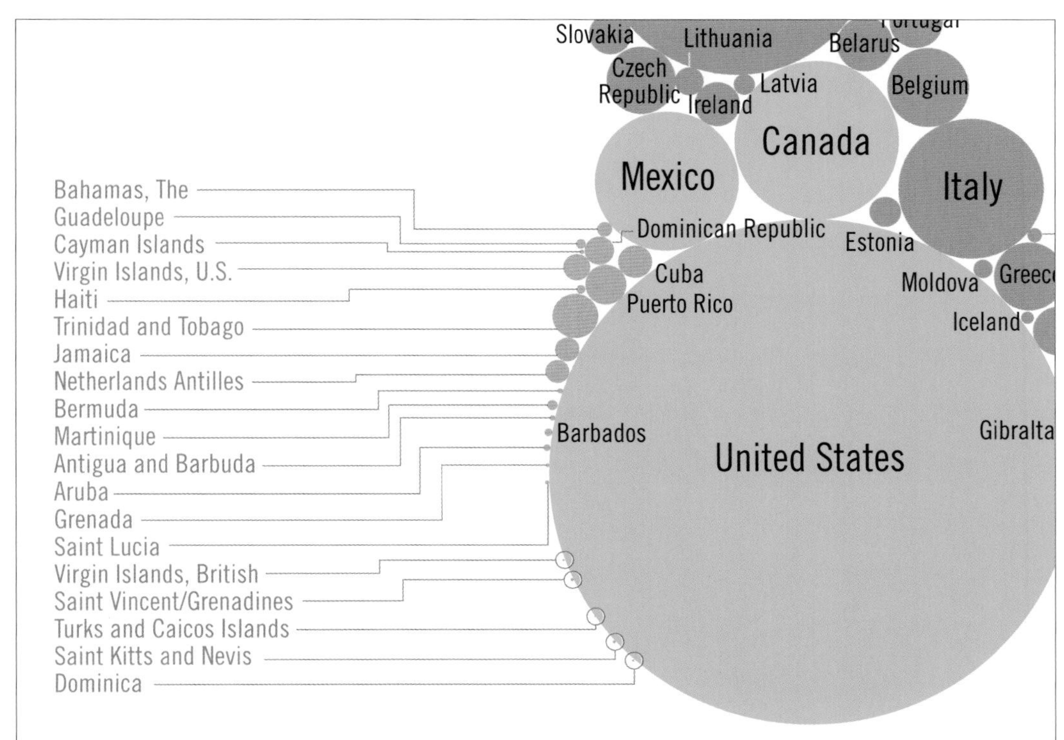

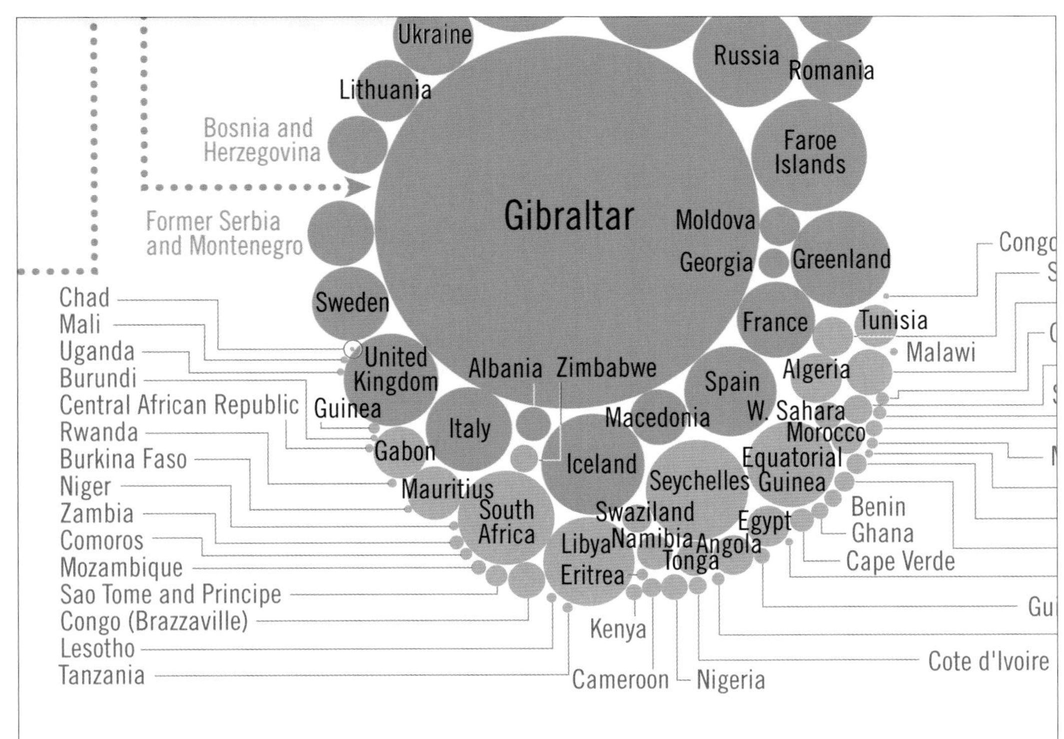

Tracking Carbon Emissions

This graphic shows CO_2 emissions for some 200 nations worldwide. Relative quantities are represented by bubble size. The bubbles on the left show the absolute quantity of emissions per nation, with China and the US being the number one emission sources. The graphic on the right relates emissions to the number of inhabitants, which presents a different picture.

Tiny nations like Gibraltar or the Virgin Islands top this second list as they need to have a lot of goods shipped in, which increases relative emissions per capita. The "footprint" refers to the concept of the ecological footprint, which allows people to quantify the environmental impact of their own lifestyle.

Diese Grafik zeigt den CO_2-Ausstoß von rund 200 Ländern. Die relative Menge ist durch die Kreisgröße wiedergegeben. Die Kreise links zeigen die absoluten Emissionen jeder Nation, wobei China und die USA den größten Ausstoß aufweisen. In der Grafik rechts wird der Gesamtausstoß in Relation zur Bevölkerungszahl gesetzt, was ein anderes Bild ergibt.

In dieser zweiten Grafik sind winzige Staaten wie Gibraltar und die Virgin Islands führend, da sie zahlreiche Erzeugnisse einführen müssen; das steigert den relativen Pro-Kopf-Ausstoß. Der „Fußabdruck" verweist auf das Konzept des ökologischen Fußabdrucks, mit dessen Hilfe sich ermitteln lässt, welche Umweltbelastungen der eigene Lebensstil hervorruft.

Ce visuel montre les émissions de CO_2 d'environ 200 nations dans le monde. Les quantités relatives sont illustrées par la taille des bulles. Les bulles de gauche montrent la quantité absolue d'émissions par pays, la Chine et les États-Unis venant en tête des sources d'émissions. À droite, les émissions sont associées au nombre d'habitants, ce qui donne une tout autre image.

Les petits pays comme Gibraltar ou les Îles Vierges viennent en tête de cette seconde liste car ils ont besoin d'importer de nombreux produits, ce qui augmente les émissions relatives par habitant. L'empreinte de pied évoque l'idée d'empreinte écologique, ce qui permet de quantifier l'impact du mode de vie sur l'environnement.

Upswing with Risks and Side Effects

As a forecast of global and national business developments in 2010, Golden Section Graphics created a series of works in an extreme vertical format for German newspaper *Handelsblatt*. One piece ranks the top world economies according to their contribution to global GDP in 2000 and 2010. Another graphic presents several economic key figures for four countries by way of a toppled diagram. The countries are listed vertically, with the rise and fall of figures shown by right or left movements in the graph.

A third piece ranks Germany's most innovative companies in order. Bubble sizes indicate the business volume of each company, whilst the smaller bubble to the right indicates how much money has been spent on research and development.

Um globale und nationale Wirtschaftsentwicklungen für 2010 prognostizieren zu können, entwarf Golden Section Graphics für das deutsche *Handelsblatt* eine Reihe von Grafiken in extremem Hochformat. Darunter listet eine die führenden Weltwirtschaftsmächte entsprechend ihrem Beitrags zum weltweiten Bruttoinlandsprodukt 2000 und 2010, eine andere stellt einige ökonomische Schlüsseldaten von vier Ländern in einer Art gekipptem Diagramm dar. Die Länder sind vertikal aufgeführt, der Anstieg oder Fall von Werten wird durch eine Kurve nach rechts oder links in den senkrechten Graphen angezeigt.

In einer dritten Grafik werden die innovativsten deutschen Unternehmen nach Größe angeordnet. Die Größe einer Blase gibt das Umsatzvolumen eines Unternehmens wieder, die kleinere Blase jeweils rechts zeigt die Höhe der Ausgaben für Forschung und Entwicklung.

Golden Section Graphics a créé une série de travaux dans un format vertical pour le journal allemand *Handelsblatt* pour illustrer une prévision de la croissance économique au niveau mondial et national en 2010. L'une des illustrations classe les principales économies mondiales selon leur contribution au PIB global en 2000 et 2010. Un autre graphique montre plusieurs chiffres clés de l'économie pour quatre pays à l'aide d'un diagramme renversé. Les pays sont indiqués verticalement, et les mouvements vers la droite ou la gauche indiquent l'augmentation ou la baisse des chiffres.

Une troisième illustration classe les entreprises les plus innovantes d'Allemagne. La taille des bulles correspond au volume d'activité de chaque entreprise, alors qu'une bulle plus petite à droite montre la quantité d'argent dépensé.

Project Info: *Handelsblatt*, newspaper article, 2009, Germany
Data Source: Economist Intelligence Unit; OECD
Research: Susanne Wesch
Design: Paul Blickle, Jan Schwochow (Golden Section Graphics)
Art Direction: Nils Werner

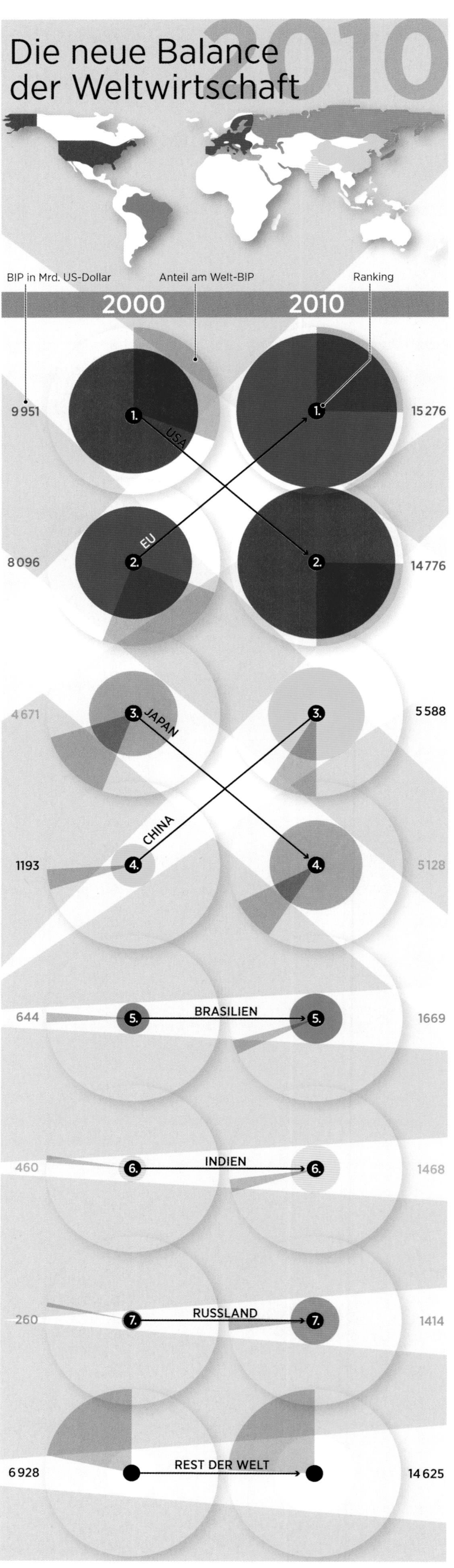

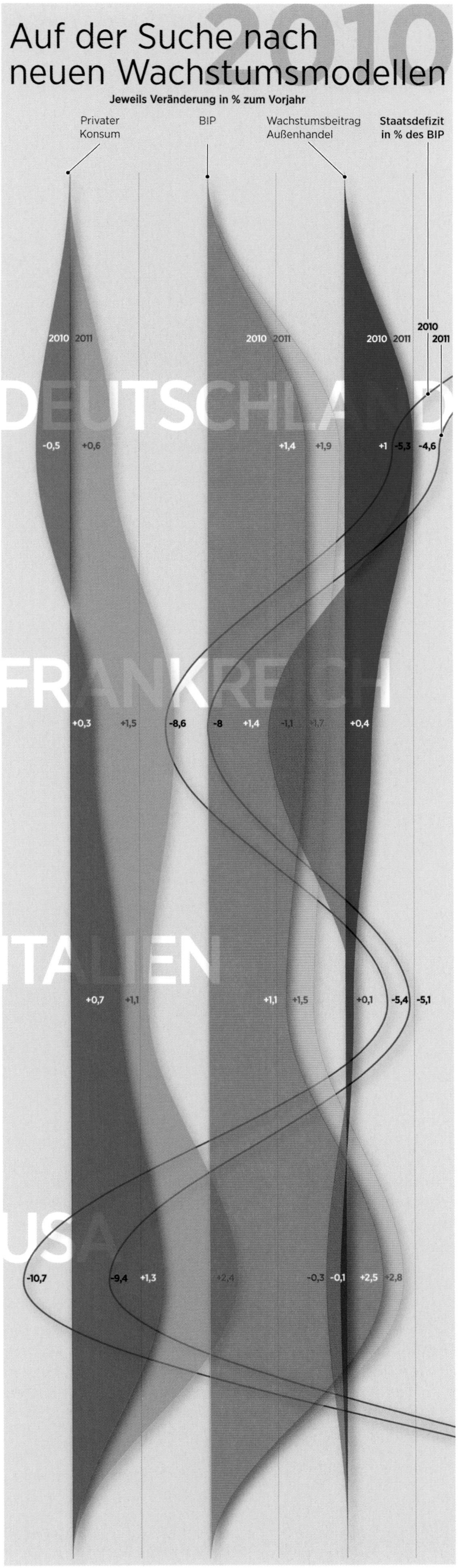

Auf der Suche nach neuen Wachstumsmodellen

2010

Jeweils Veränderung in % zum Vorjahr

Privater Konsum

BIP

Wachstumsbeitrag Außenhandel

Staatsdefizit in % des BIP

2010 2011

2010 2011

2010 2011

2010

2011

DEUTSCHLAND

-0,5 +0,6 +1,4 +1,9 +1 -5,3 -4,6

FRANKREICH

+0,3 +1,5 -8,6 -8 +1,4 -1,1 -1,7 +0,4

ITALIEN

+0,7 +1,1 +1,1 +1,5 +0,1 -5,4 -5,1

USA

-10,7 -9,4 +1,3 +2,4 -0,3 -0,1 +2,5 +2,8

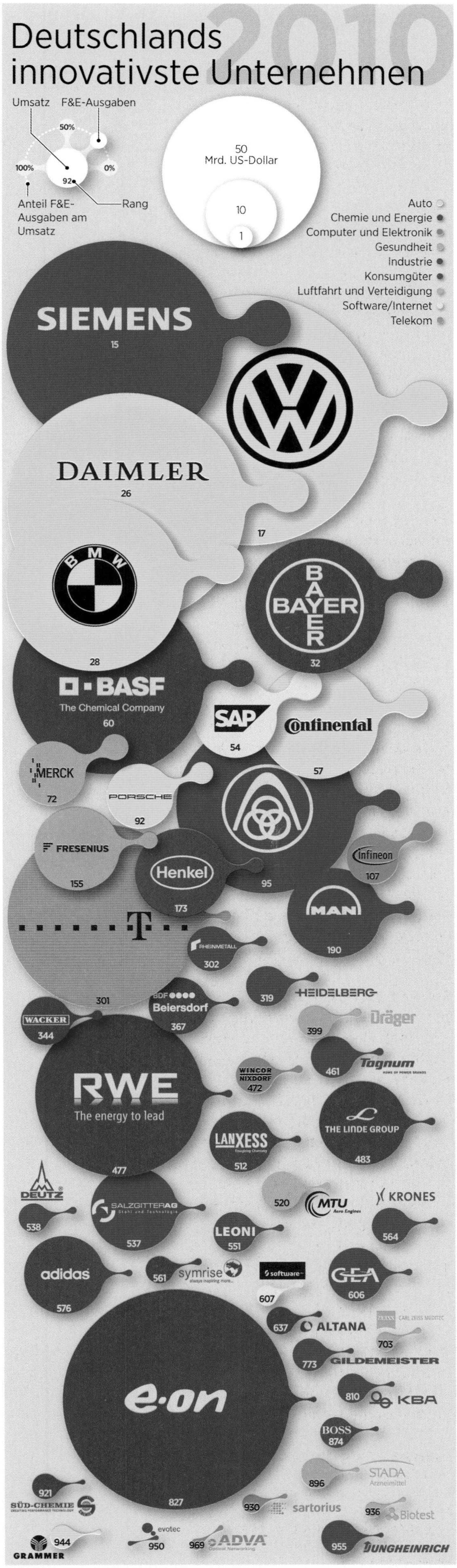

Deutschlands innovativste Unternehmen

2010

Umsatz F&E-Ausgaben

50%

100%

0%

92

Anteil F&E-Ausgaben am Umsatz

Rang

50 Mrd. US-Dollar

10

1

Auto

Chemie und Energie

Computer und Elektronik

Gesundheit

Industrie

Konsumgüter

Luftfahrt und Verteidigung

Software/Internet

Telekom

SIEMENS 15

17

DAIMLER 26

BMW 28

BAYER 32

BASF The Chemical Company 60

SAP 54

Continental 57

MERCK 72

PORSCHE 92

95

FRESENIUS 155

Henkel 173

Infineon 107

MAN 190

T 301

RHEINMETALL 302

319

HEIDELBERG

Beiersdorf 367

WACKER 344

Dräger 399

461

Tognum

WINCOR NIXDORF 472

RWE The energy to lead 477

LANXESS 512

THE LINDE GROUP 483

DEUTZ 538

SALZGITTER AG 537

520

MTU

KRONES

564

LEONI 551

adidas 576

561

symrise

software 607

GEA 606

637

ALTANA

CARL ZEISS MEDITEC 703

773

GILDEMEISTER

810

KBA

e·on 827

BOSS 874

STADA Arzneimittel

896

921

SÜD-CHEMIE

930

sartorius

936

Biotest

GRAMMER 944

evotec 950

969

ADVA Optical Networking

955

JUNGHEINRICH

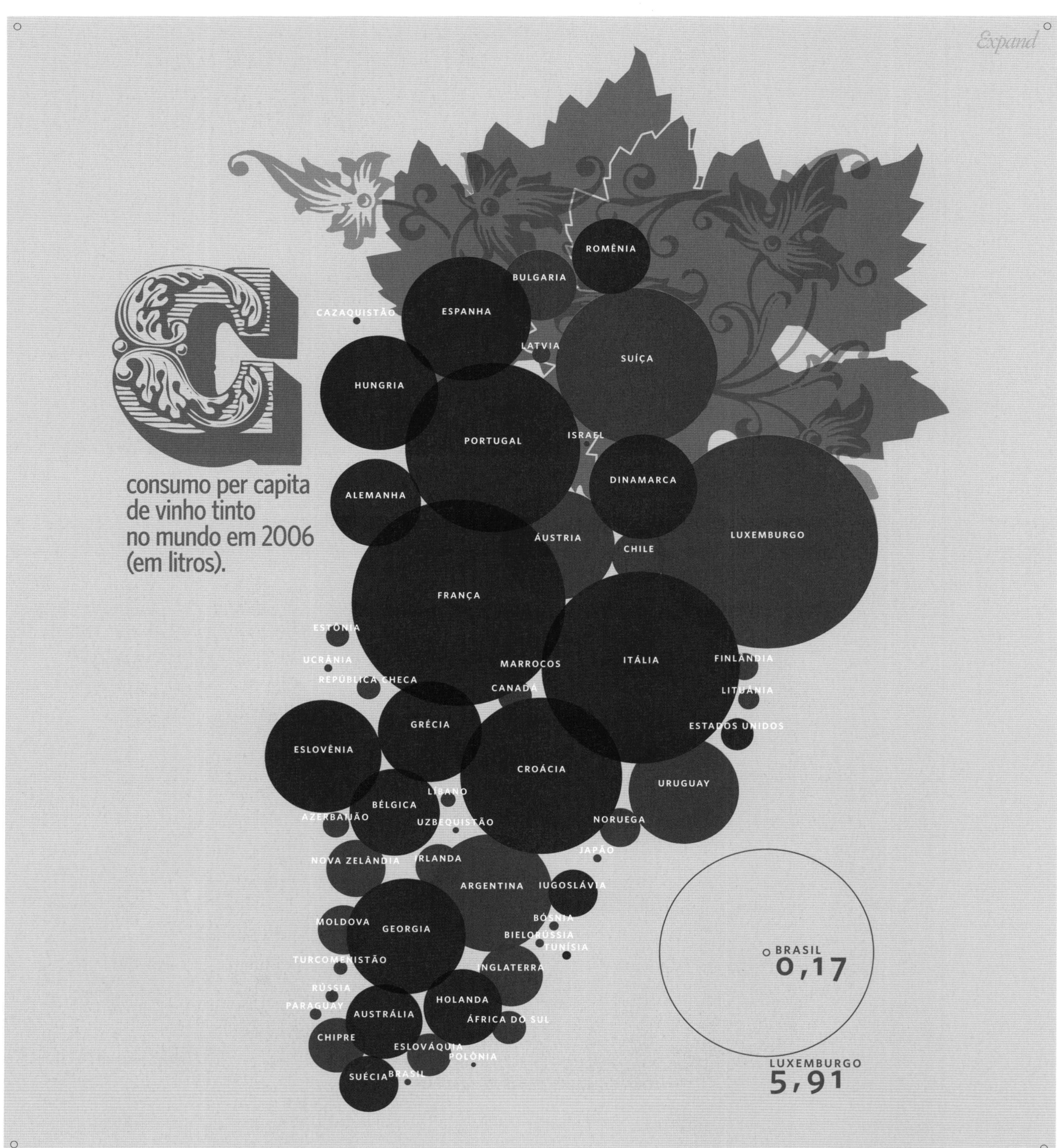

Wine Consumption Chart

Developed for a Brazilian wine exporter, this double piece compares worldwide consumption and the global production of red wine in 2006. Shaped as a bunch of grapes, the countries are represented as circles scaled according to their average total consumption of red wine.

This shows that red wine is very popular in France, Italy and tiny Luxemburg, whereas Brazileiros have yet to introduce red wine as part of their daily habits. The second sheet refers to production quantities, with absolute numbers showing France as the biggest producer worldwide. Quantities in both pieces are structured hierarchically.

Diese Doppelgrafik entstand für einen brasilianischen Weinexporteur und vergleicht den weltweiten Konsum und die globale Produktion von Rotwein im Jahr 2006. Die Länder sind wie Trauben einer Rebe angeordnet, ihre Größe entspricht dem jeweiligen durchschnittlichen Pro-Kopf-Konsum von Rotwein.

Daraus geht hervor, dass Rotwein in Frankreich, Italien und Luxemburg überaus beliebt ist, während er für die Brasilianer noch kein alltägliches Konsumgut ist. Die zweite Grafik befasst sich mit den Produktionsmengen. Die absoluten Zahlen weisen Frankreich als weltweit größten Weinproduzenten aus. Die Mengen sind in beiden Grafiken hierarchisch angeordnet.

Conçu pour un exportateur de vins brésilien, ce diptyque compare la consommation mondiale et la production globale de vin rouge en 2006. Formant une grappe de raisin, les pays sont représentés par des cercles dont la taille varie en fonction de la consommation totale moyenne de vin rouge de chacun d'eux.

L'illustration montre que le vin rouge est très populaire en France, en Italie et au Luxembourg, mais que les Brésiliens ne l'ont pas encore introduit dans leurs habitudes. Le deuxième visuel décrit les volumes de production : les nombres absolus montrent que la France est le plus grand producteur au monde. Les quantités dans les deux œuvres sont structurées de façon hiérarchique.

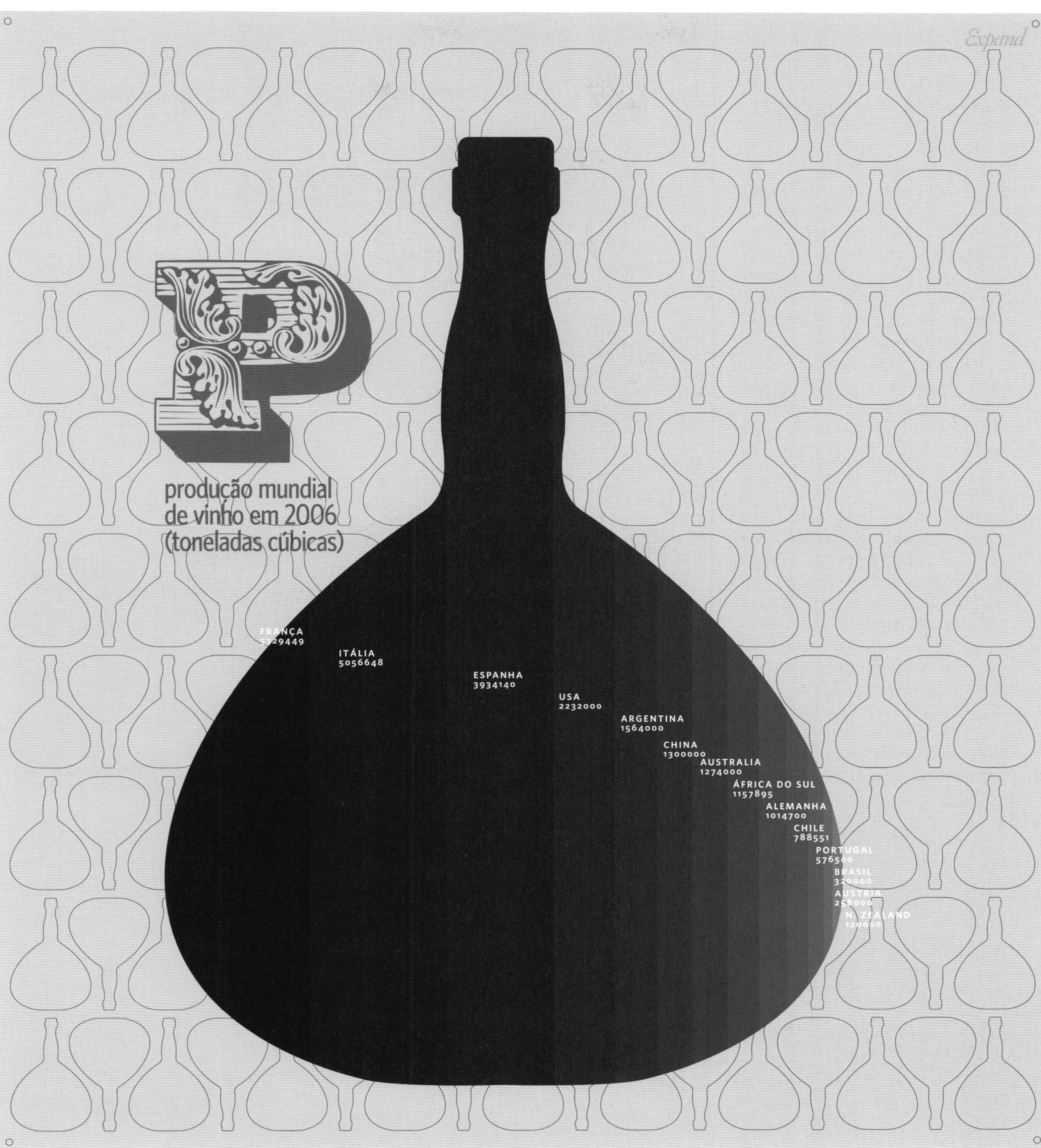

Project Info: Expand Wine Importers, poster and magazine article, 2007, Brazil
Design: Alexandre Suannes

World of 100

This series refers to the popular concept of imagining the world as a village of 100 people. It allows global population statistics to be presented scaled down to a total population of 100 people. The image seems to appeal to people's imagination and breaks unimaginable global figures down to a human scale.

Toby Ng translated the statistical information into a series of posters, each explaining one fact. One major topic is the composition of global population in terms of age or gender or religion. Another strand addresses access to material and non-material goods such as education, clean air, water, computers etc. Each diagram is centred around an icon symbolising the respective topic.

Diese Serie greift die populäre Idee auf, sich die Welt als Dorf mit 100 Einwohnern vorzustellen. Damit kann man weltweite Bevölkerungsstatistiken auf eine Gesamtbevölkerung von 100 Menschen herunterrechnen. Dieses Vorgehen spricht offenbar das menschliche Vorstellungsvermögen an und bringt die unvorstellbaren globalen Zahlen auf ein menschliches Maß.

Toby Ng übersetzte die statistischen Daten in eine Serie von Plakaten, in der jedes Motiv ein bestimmtes Größenverhältnis veranschaulicht. Ein zentrales Thema ist die Zusammensetzung der Weltbevölkerung nach Alter, Geschlecht und Religion. Ein weiterer Aspekt ist der Zugang zu materiellen und ideellen Gütern wie Bildung, saubere Luft, Wasser, Computer usw. Jedes Diagramm ist um ein Icon angeordnet, das das jeweilige Thema symbolisiert.

Cette série renvoie à un concept bien connu, consistant à imaginer que le monde est un village de 100 habitants. Elle permet ainsi de présenter les statistiques de la population mondiale à l'échelle d'une population de 100 personnes. L'image semble convenir à l'imagination et ramène des chiffres impensables à une échelle humaine.

Toby Ng a converti des informations statistiques en une série d'affiches, chacune expliquant un fait concret. L'un des principaux thèmes concerne la composition de la population mondiale en termes d'âge, de genre ou de religion. Un autre thème porte sur l'accès aux biens matériels et non matériels comme l'enseignement, l'air, l'eau, les ordinateurs, etc. Chaque diagramme est centré autour d'une icône symbolisant le sujet correspondant.

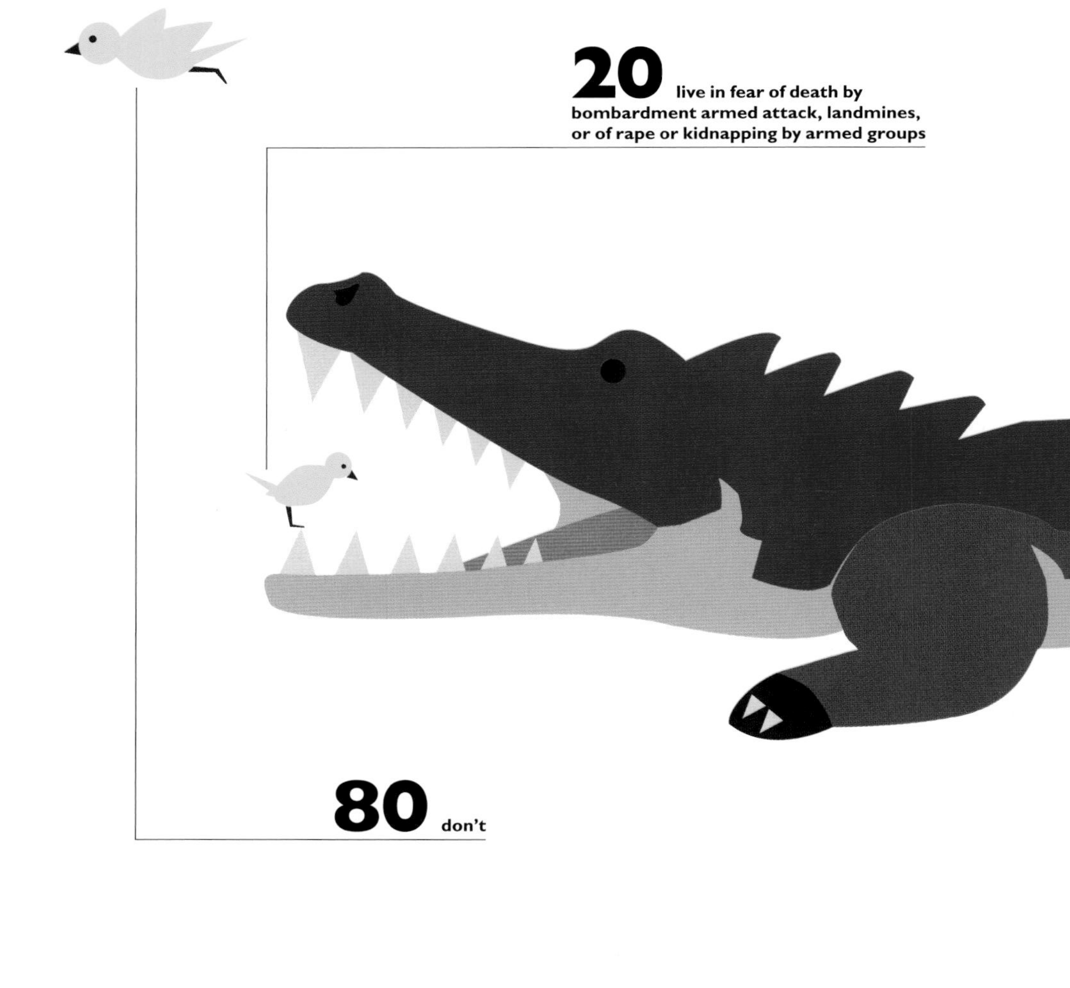

If the world were a village of 100 people
FEAR
20 live in fear of death by bombardment armed attack, landmines, or of rape or kidnapping by armed groups
80 don't

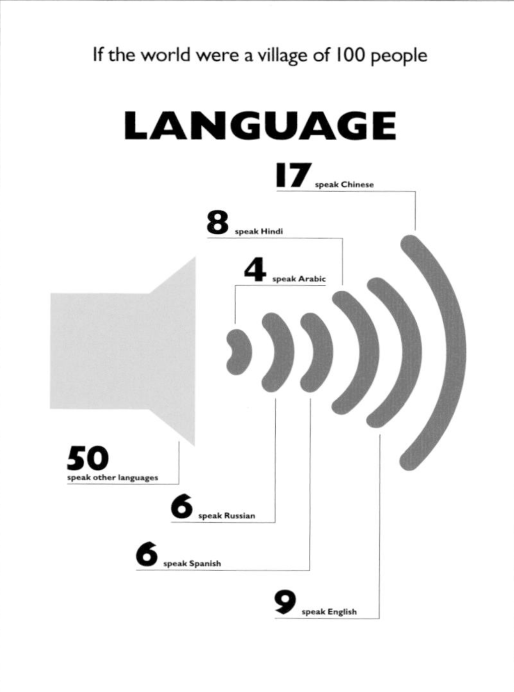

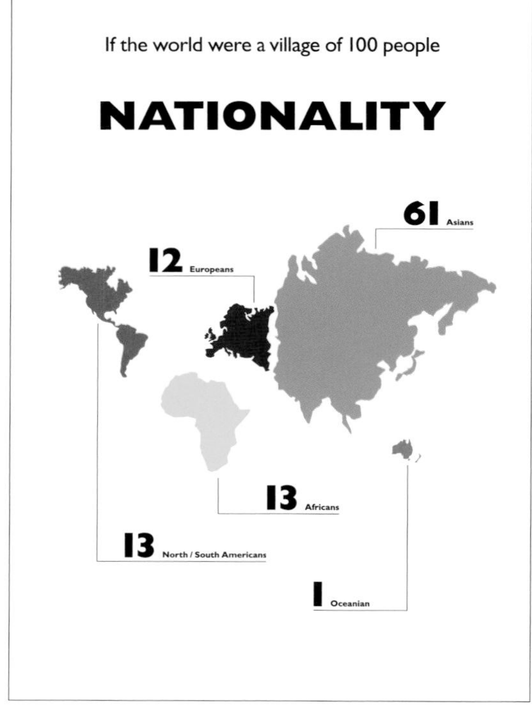

Project Info: Series of posters, 2008, China
Data Source: *If the World Were a Village*, David J. Smith, Kids Can Press
Design: Toby Ng
Awards: Red Dot Award 2009; GDC 09 Awards; International Design Awards 2009; HOW 2010 International Design Awards

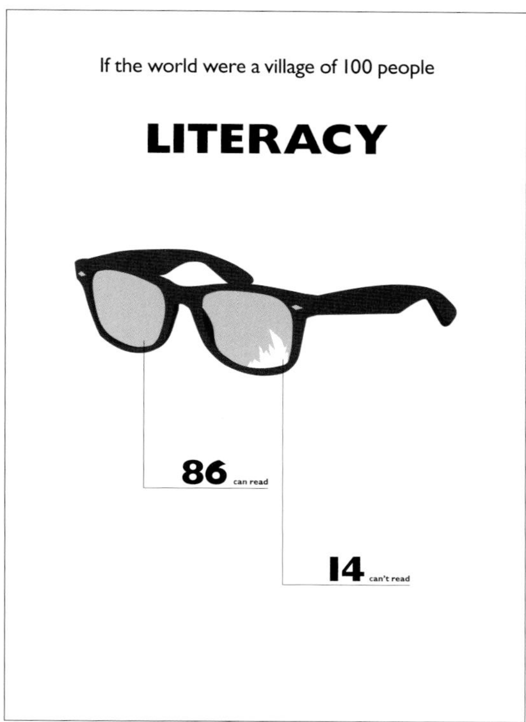
If the world were a village of 100 people
LITERACY
86 can read
14 can't read

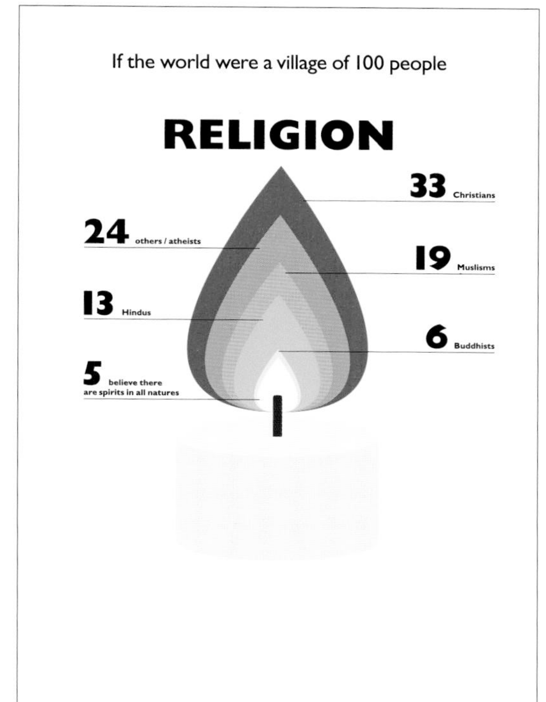
If the world were a village of 100 people
RELIGION
33 Christians
24 others / atheists
19 Muslims
13 Hindus
6 Buddhists
5 believe there are spirits in all natures

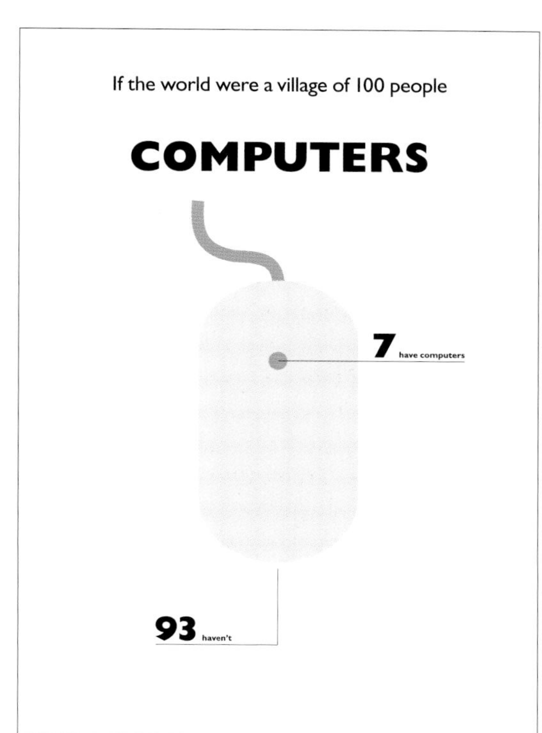
If the world were a village of 100 people
COMPUTERS
7 have computers
93 haven't

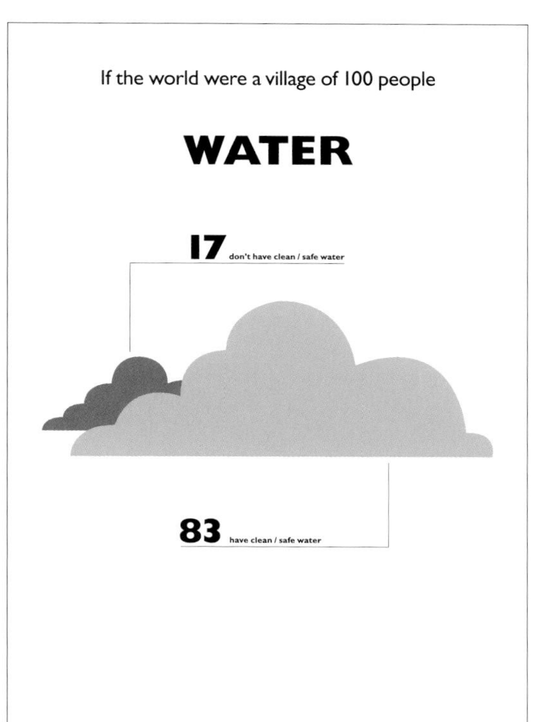
If the world were a village of 100 people
WATER
17 don't have clean / safe water
83 have clean / safe water

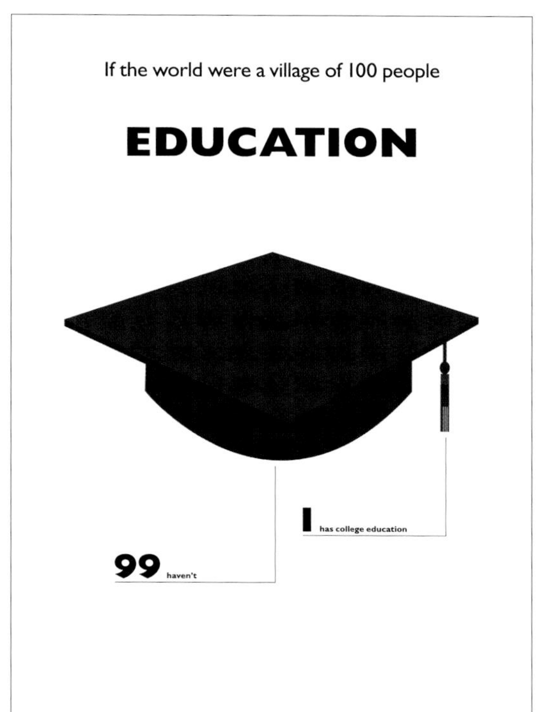
If the world were a village of 100 people
EDUCATION
1 has college education
99 haven't

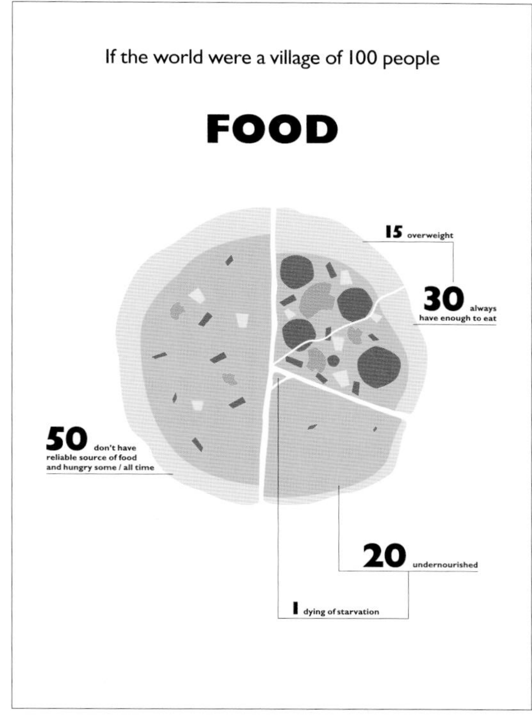
If the world were a village of 100 people
FOOD
15 overweight
30 always have enough to eat
50 don't have reliable source of food and hungry some / all time
20 undernourished
1 dying of starvation

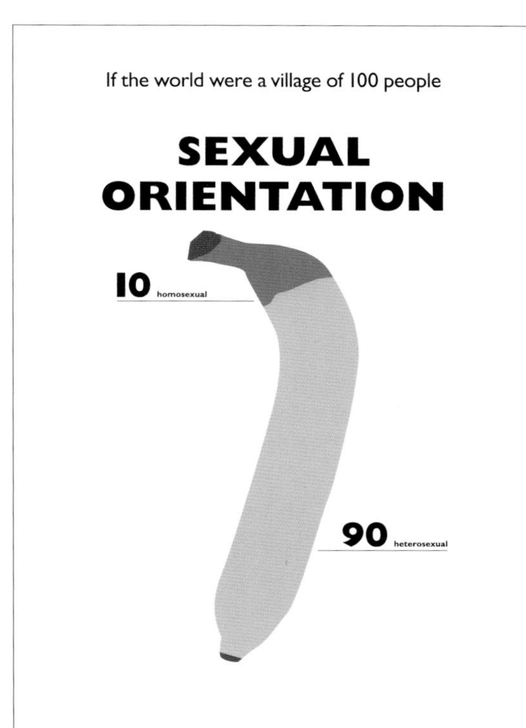
If the world were a village of 100 people
SEXUAL ORIENTATION
10 homosexual
90 heterosexual

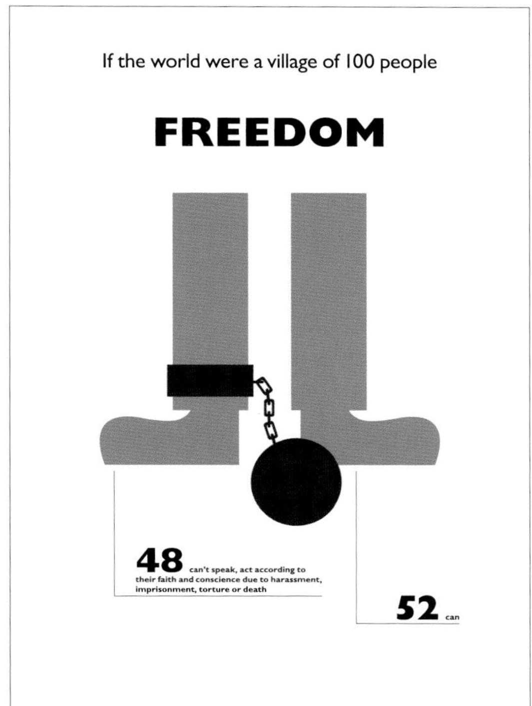
If the world were a village of 100 people
FREEDOM
48 can't speak, act according to their faith and conscience due to harassment, imprisonment, torture or death
52 can

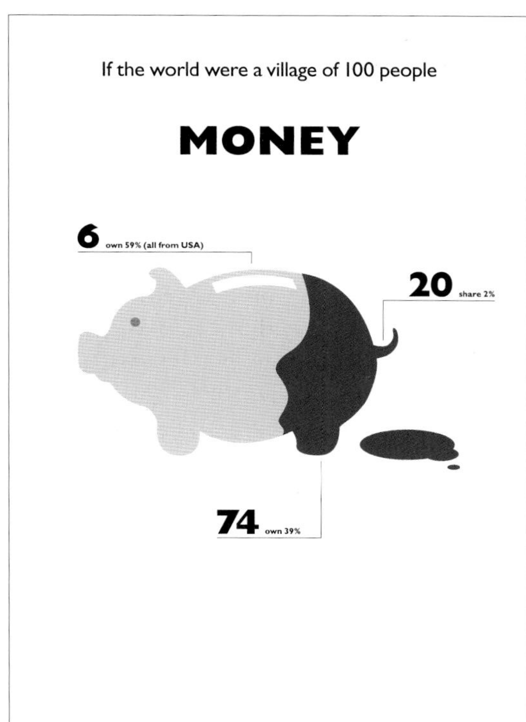
If the world were a village of 100 people
MONEY
6 own 59% (all from USA)
20 share 2%
74 own 39%

The Wheel O' Happiness

The volvelle or wheel chart is a paper construction with rotating parts, used for simple calculations or looking up information before the age of computers. Michael Newhouse uses this type of chart for his guide to career satisfaction. The wheel shows a list of college majors and indicates what percentage of people are satisfied with their job after graduating in each one.

The wheel employs two different ways of structuring this list: from the top down on the right, majors are listed alphabetically, from the top down on the left, majors are listed by satisfaction level, starting with the radically unhappy nutritionists.

Eine Volvelle ist eine Papierkonstruktion mit drehbaren Scheiben. Vor dem Aufkommen des Computers diente sie dazu, einfache Berechnungen anzustellen oder Informationen nachzuschlagen. Michael Newhouse verwendet dieses Motiv für seine Übersicht zu beruflicher Zufriedenheit. Das Rad zeigt eine Liste von College-Abschlüssen und gibt an, wie zufrieden die Absolventen mit ihrem Beruf sind.

Die Liste ist auf zwei Arten strukturiert: Rechts sind die Abschlüsse alphabetisch von oben nach unten angeordnet, links nach Zufriedenheitsgrad, wobei die äußerst unzufriedenen Ernährungsfachleute den Anfang machen.

La volvelle, une règle à calcul circulaire, est un objet en papier avec des éléments mobiles, qui permettait de faire des calculs simples ou de rechercher des informations avant l'ère informatique. Michael Newhouse l'a utilisée pour son analyse de la satisfaction professionnelle. La roue montre une liste de spécialités universitaires et indique le pourcentage de personnes satisfaites de leur emploi après l'obtention de leur diplôme dans chacune d'elles.

La roue structure cette liste de deux façons : de haut en bas sur la droite, les spécialités sont dans l'ordre alphabétique ; de haut en bas sur la gauche, elles sont classées par niveau de satisfaction, en commençant par les nutritionnistes, clairement mécontents.

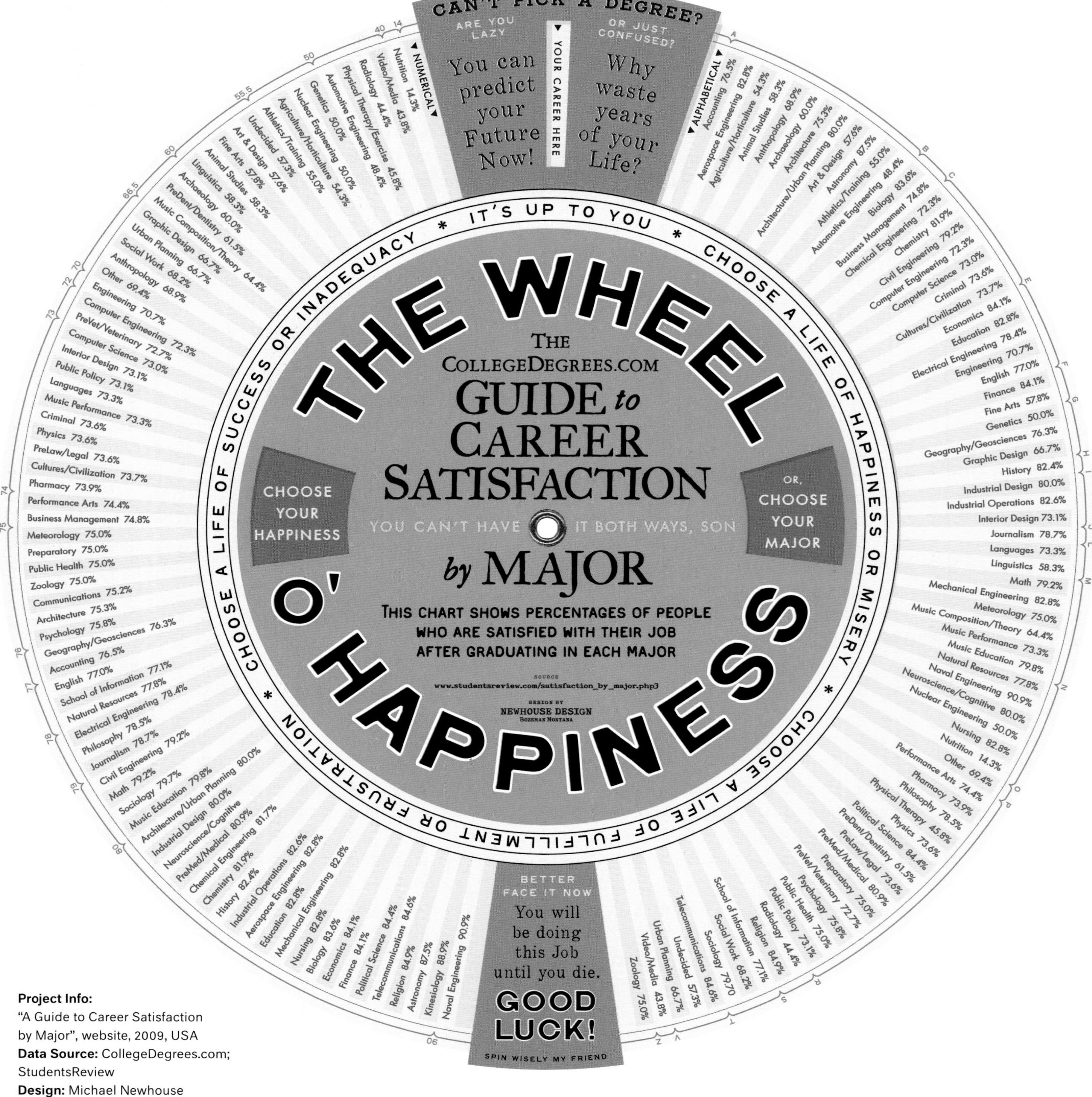

Project Info:
"A Guide to Career Satisfaction by Major", website, 2009, USA
Data Source: CollegeDegrees.com; StudentsReview
Design: Michael Newhouse (Newhouse Design)

Index
475—478

Thanks

I extend my thanks firstly to all the designers, scientists and artists who allowed us to use their brilliant work. Gathering designs from a variety of fields was very inspiring, and I thank everyone who supported this open approach. Paolo Ciuccarelli, Nigel Holmes, Simon Rogers and Richard Saul Wurman contributed their own pieces to this book, and being allowed to work with them was a great privilege.

On the part of the publishing house, Benedikt Taschen and Julius Wiedemann's enthusiastic support for the subject made this publication possible. With his wealth of experience and circumspection, Daniel Siciliano Bretas brought together all the publishing threads, and provided superb project leadership. Jutta Hendricks and Chris Allen edited the book with great feeling and sensitivity. Praline Design have created a fabulous layout for this complex subject. In the print production department, Frank Goehrhardt's execution of the design has been magnificent, and Stefan Klatte in pre-press is the person responsible for the outstanding visual quality.

Technical advice was forthcoming from numerous designers including Joachim Sauter, Jan Schwochow, Boris Müller, Jing He, Monika Hoinkis, Danqing Shi, Axel Pfänder, Anja Lutz, Peter Ruschel and Sven Assmann. Ole Häntzschel has fully supported the project from the beginning. I would also like to thank Julia Guther for all her help, which went beyond creative matters. My deepest thanks go to Ursula Rendgen and Andrej Rendgen and also to Clemens von Lucius for his professional and patient encouragement.

Danke

Mein erster Dank gilt allen Designern, Wissenschaftlern und Künstlern, die ihre großartigen Arbeiten zur Verfügung gestellt haben. Es war sehr inspirierend, Entwürfe aus verschiedenen Bereichen zu versammeln, und ich danke allen, die diesen offenen Ansatz unterstützt haben. Paolo Ciuccarelli, Nigel Holmes, Simon Rogers und Richard Saul Wurman haben persönliche Beiträge für dieses Buch verfasst, die Zusammenarbeit mit ihnen war eine große Bereicherung.

Von Seiten des Verlags haben Benedikt Taschen und Julius Wiedemann das Thema enthusiastisch unterstützt und damit diese Publikation möglich gemacht. Mit großer Erfahrung und Umsicht hat Daniel Siciliano Bretas im Verlag alle Fäden zusammengeführt und das Projekt hervorragend gesteuert. Jutta Hendricks und Chris Allen haben mit feinem Gespür das Lektorat besorgt. Praline Design ist ein fantastisches Layout für das komplexe Thema gelungen. In der Verlagsherstellung hat Frank Goehrhardt Großartiges zur Umsetzung dieses Designs geleistet, während Stefan Klatte in der Druckvorstufe für die ausgezeichnete visuelle Qualität verantwortlich war.

Zahlreiche Gestalter haben fachlichen Rat beigesteuert, so unter anderem Joachim Sauter, Jan Schwochow, Boris Müller, Jing He, Monika Hoinkis, Danqing Shi, Axel Pfänder, Anja Lutz, Peter Ruschel und Sven Assmann. Ole Häntzschel hat das Projekt von Anfang an begeistert unterstützt. Julia Guther danke ich für ihre Hilfe nicht nur in gestalterischen Fragen. Mein tiefster Dank geht an Ursula Rendgen und Andrej Rendgen sowie an Clemens von Lucius für seinen professionellen und geduldigen Zuspruch.

Merci

Je remercie tout d'abord tous les graphistes, scientifiques et artistes qui nous ont autorisés à utiliser leur magnifique travail. La collecte de travaux issus de tant de domaines différents s'est révélée être une activité passionnante, et je remercie tous ceux qui ont apporté leur soutien à cette démarche ouverte. Paolo Ciuccarelli, Nigel Holmes, Simon Rogers et Richard Saul Wurman ont participé à cet ouvrage avec leurs propres créations, et cela a été un grand privilège de pouvoir travailler avec eux.

Du côté de la maison d'édition, l'enthousiasme que Benedikt Taschen et Julius Wiedemann ont manifesté pour le sujet a rendu cette publication possible. Daniel Siciliano Bretas a quant à lui usé de trésors d'expérience et de circonspection pour résoudre tous les aspects de l'édition, et a magnifiquement dirigé le projet. Jutta Hendricks et Chris Allen ont édité ce livre avec beaucoup de flair et de sensibilité. Praline Design a créé une mise en page fabuleuse pour ce sujet complexe. Dans le domaine de l'impression, l'exécution du projet par Frank Goehrhardt a été rien moins que magnifique, et Stefan Klatte en prépresse est la personne responsable de la remarquable qualité visuelle de l'ensemble.

De nombreux graphistes nous ont apporté de précieux conseils techniques, notamment Joachim Sauter, Jan Schwochow, Boris Müller, Jing He, Monika Hoinkis, Danqing Shi, Axel Pfänder, Anja Lutz, Peter Ruschel et Sven Assmann. Ole Häntzschel soutenu le projet inconditionnellement depuis le début. J'aimerais également remercier Julia Guther pour toute son aide, qui est allée au-delà des questions d'ordre créatif. Mes remerciements les plus sincères vont à Ursula Rendgen et Andrej Rendgen ainsi qu'à Clemens von Lucius, pour ses encouragements professionnels et patients.

Essay Image Credits

p.1 Robert Fludd. Oppenheim. 1617–1619 © Getty Images
p.2 Fritz Kahn. Stuttgart 1926 © von Debschitz, www.fritz-kahn.com
p.4 Röyksopp. Music video, Paris 2002. © H5 (L. Houplain & H. de Crécy)
p.6 Cave Paintings, Lascaux © Getty Images
p.8 Tomb of Ramses V, Egypt © Getty Images
p.10 © Bildarchiv Preußischer Kulturbesitz
p.12 Joachim of Fiore. Ca. 1190 © The Bridgeman Art Library
p.13 Roger Bacon. 1280 © AKG Images
p.14 Ebstorf World Map. Ca. 1300. Hartmut Kugler, University of Erlangen
p.16 Mansur ibn Ilyas. Iran, ca. 1390 © AKG Images
p.17 *De Sphaera*. Italy, ca. 1460 © Biblioteca Estense Modena / Courtesy of the Ministero per i Beni e le Attivita Culturali, Italy
p.18 © Bridgeman Art Library
p.20 *Fasciculus Medicinae*. 1491 © Science Photo Library
p.22 Ptolemaic World Map, ca. 1520 © Getty Images
p.23 © Historisches Museum Frankfurt
p.25 Petrus Apianus. Ingolstadt 1533 © Sächsische Landesbibliothek – Staats- und Universitätsbibliothek Dresden
p.26 Luca Pacioli. Toscalano 1523 © The Bridgeman Art Library
p.27 Georg Bartisch. Dresden 1583 © The Bridgeman Art Library
p.28 Christophe de Savigny. Paris 1587 © Herzog August Bibliothek Wolfenbüttel
p.30 Galileo Galilei. Italy 1613 © Getty Images
p.32 Robert Fludd. 1618 © Getty Images
p.33 Christoph Scheiner. Bracciano 1626
p.34 Robert Burton. 1628 © Bridgeman Art Library
p.35 Marin Mersenne. Paris 1636 © Science Photo Library
p.36 John Bulwer. 1644 © Bridgeman Art Library
p.38 Descartes. 1668 © AKG Images
p.40 Jean Francois Niceron. Paris 1638 © Getty Images
p.41 Jan Amos Comenius. 1658 © AKG Images
p.42 Isaac Newton. London 1704 © Getty Images
p.43 Edmund Halley. Ca. 1724 © Royal Astronomical Society / Science Photo Library
p.44 Ephraim Chambers. London 1728
p.47 Gottfried Hensel. Nürnberg 1741 © Bildarchiv Preußischer Kulturbesitz
p.48 J. Mynde after James Ferguson. 1756 © Getty Images
p.50 Benajmin Franklin. 1760 © Getty Images
p.52 William Playfair. London 1786
p.54 Friedrich August Crome. Ca. 1820. © Bildarchiv Preußischer Kulturbesitz
p.55 Thomas Clarkson. 1808 © Getty Images
p.56 Royal Society Journal, David Brewster. Ca. 1834 © Getty Images
p.58 Teaching Card, James Reynolds & Sons. 1850 © Getty Images
p.60 Luke Howard. 1847 © Getty Images
p.63 Eug. Pick, 1858 Paris
p.64 Alvin Jewett Johnson. Washington, D.C. 1862 © Getty Images
p.66 Florence Nightingale. London 1858
p.67 Charles Joseph Minard. Paris 1869 © Bildarchiv Preußischer Kulturbesitz
p.69 Francis A. Walker. 1872 © Getty Images
p.70 Ernst Haeckel. 1879 © The Natural History Museum, London
p.72 Antonio Gabaglio. Italy 1888. Courtesy of Edward Tufte, *The Visual Display of Quantitative Information*. Graphics Press 2001
p.74 *Monthly Notices of the Royal Astronomical Society* Vol. LXIV, 1904 © Getty Images
p.75 *The Sphere* © AKG Images
p.76 Joseph Jules Dejerine. Paris 1914 © The Bridgeman Art Library
p.78 Hinnerk Scheper. 1926 © Nachlass Scheper / Bauhaus-Archiv Berlin
p.80–81 Otto Neurath. Leipzig 1930
p.82 Historic Tube Map, Harry Beck, London 1933 © London Transport Museum
p.83 Tokyo shisei Suhyo. Tokyo, 1935 © The Bridgeman Art Library
p.84 Alfred H. Barr. 1936 © Scala Archives
p.86 Irving Geis, ca. 1940 © Sandy Geis
p.88 Ladislav Sutnar. Ca. 1950. Museum of Decorative Arts, Prague © R.L. Sutnar
p.89 Bayer, Herbert. 1939 © Scala Archives / VG Bild-Kunst
p.90 Ad Reinhardt. 1955. © The Estate of Ad Reinhardt / VG Bild-Kunst. Photograph by Al Mozell, Courtesy The Pace Gallery.
p.92 Jacques Bertin. Paris 1967. La Haye, Mouton, Gauthiers-Villars
p.93 © Science Museum, London / Getty Images
p.94 Mark Lombardi, *World Finance Corporation and Associates, ca. 1970–84: Miami, Ajman, and Bogota-Caracas*. 1999 © Courtesy of Pierogi Gallery
p.95 *Periodic Table of Swearing*. 2010 © Jon Link & Mick Bunnage / moderntoss.com

Hohenzollernring 53, D-50672 Köln
www.taschen.com

To stay informed about upcoming TASCHEN titles, please request our magazine at www.taschen.com/magazine or write to TASCHEN, Hohenzollernring 53, D-50672 Cologne, Germany, contact@taschen.com, Fax: +49-221-254919. We will be happy to send you a free copy of our magazine which is filled with information about all of our books.

Design Praline: Al Rodger, David Tanguy

Cover Design Josh Baker
Cover Illustration Information Architects (see p.388)
Endpapers Illustration Nigel Peake (see p.365)
Poster Design Nigel Holmes

Editor Julius Wiedemann
Editorial Coordination Daniel Siciliano Bretas
Collaboration Jutta Hendricks
Production Stefan Klatte

English Revision Chris Allen
German Translation Ursula Wulfekamp and Karen Waloschek for Grapevine
French Translation Aurélie Daniel for Equipo de Edición

Printed in Italy
ISBN 978-3-8365-2879-5